# INSIDE ADOBE® PHOTOSHOP 6®

**BY**

Gary David Bouton

Barbara Mancuso Bouton

Gary Kubicek

Mara Zebest Nathanson

Jim Rich

Al Ward

New Riders

201 West 103rd Street, Indianapolis, Indiana 46290

# Inside Adobe® Photoshop 6®

## Trademarks

## Warning and Disclaimer

**Publisher**
David Dwyer

**Associate Publisher**
Al Valvano

**Executive Editor**
Steve Weiss

**Product Marketing Manager**
Kathy Malmloff

**Managing Editors**
Jennifer Eberhardt
Sarah Kearns

**Development Editor**
Barbara Terry

**Acquisitions Editor**
Theresa Gheen

**Project Editor**
Linda Seifert

**Copy Editor**
Gail Burlakoff

**Technical Editors**
Ryan Frank
Suzanne Pettypiece
Richard Cordero

**Cover Designer**
Aren Howell

**Compositor**
Kim Scott
www.bumpy.com

**Proofreader**
Debra Neel

**Indexers**
Joy Dean Lee
Chris Morris

**Software Development Specialist**
Jay Payne

# Contents at a Glance

# Table of Contents

## Part III Exploring the Cool Stuff

# Part IV Introducing ImageReady: Moving to the Web

## 23  Optimizing Images for the Web                              815

## About the Authors

*Gary David Bouton* is an author and illustrator who adopted the personal computer after 20 years of traditionally creating artwork. *Inside Adobe Photoshop 6* is Gary's tenth book on Adobe Photoshop. He has written eight other books on computer graphics for New Riders Publishing, in addition to being a contributing author to three books on CorelDRAW.

Gary has won several international awards in desktop publishing and design, and he was a finalist in the 1996 Macromedia People's Choice Awards. A contributing writer to *Corel Magazine* and other publications, Gary is also moderator emeritus of the CorelXARA discussion list on i/us at www.i-us.com/xara.htm.

Gary can be reach at Gary@TheBoutons.com.

*Barbara Mancuso Bouton* has co-authored all editions of *Inside Adobe Photoshop* and was the editor of the *New Riders Official World Wide Web Yellow Pages*. Barbara is a publishing and electronic/Internet document production professional and is a systems consultant for a number of Fortune 500 firms.

Barbara can be reached at Barbara@TheBoutons.com.

Gary and Barbara maintain their own Internet site (www.TheBoutons.com) as a repository of book listings, essays on computer graphics, and as an art gallery of current images.

*Gary Kubicek* has been a contributing author for seven books on Photoshop; he has also been a technical editor for ten books. A professional photographer for more than 20 years, Gary was an early adopter of Photoshop and the "digital darkroom" as an extension of the self-expression he finds in his traditional photographic work.

Gary is also a digital imaging consultant, a Photoshop and Microsoft Office software instructor for a variety of clients, and teaches Photoshop at Manlius Pebble Hill School, DeWitt, New York.

Gary can be reached at gary@kubicek.com. His Web site address is http://home.twcny.rr.com/garykubicek/.

*Mara Zebest Nathanson* is a graphic artist who uses her knowledge and skills in both volunteer work and commercially. Mara donates much of her time to a local school corporation, providing technical support to teachers and administrators, and designing brochures, letterhead, logos, and even T-shirts. Commercially, she designs newspaper and magazine ads, as well as a variety of other graphics.

*Jim Rich* is the president of Rich & Associates, a firm that specializes in publishing, industry pre-press, and computer training. Jim brings a perspective of over 25 years of research, consulting, and training experience with black-and-white and color reproduction methods in the graphics arts and the desktop imaging markets.

Jim enjoys teaching and has developed a variety of training programs that teach the basic-through-advanced fundamentals of black-and-white and color reproduction methods. He is the author of *The Photoshop Grayscale Book* (Rich & Associates, LLC, Chevy Chase, Maryland).

*Al Ward* is a contributing writer, specializing in typography and Photoshop Actions, for the official NAAP magazine *Photoshop User*. Not only is Al a certified Photoshop addict, he's also the Webmaster of Action Fx. In his off time, he enjoys his church, his family, fishing the great Northwest, and scouring the Web for Photoshop-related topics.

*Wil Cruz* is a compositor with New Riders Publishing. Wil holds a BA in Psychology from Oberlin College, Oberlin, Ohio, and a BFA in Photography from the University of Utah in Salt Lake City, Utah.

*Aren Howell* earned degrees in Graphic Design and Photography from Ball State University. She has been a Graphic Designer for 10 years and has spent the last seven of them designing for various imprints within Macmillan USA, including Adobe Press, Hayden, Sams, and Que. She currently works for New Riders Publishing designing book covers and product marketing materials. Aren is a contributing author to *Photoshop Effects Magic* (New Riders Publishing). Aren's work has been recognized in Print's Regional Design Annual, the American Advertising Awards, and the American Graphic Design Awards. If she's not playing golf, she can be reached at aren.howell@pearsonptr.com.

# Acknowledgments

I don't care what anyone says, Photoshop 6 *feels* as though it has twice as many features as its predecessor. And I really like a lot of the enhancements and how things are more easily accomplished than before.

But how does a single writer approach a task—writing this book—that *feels* as though it's twice as big as before? Did I take twice as many Tylenol? Did I kick my computer twice as often? Nope. I was fortunate enough to have about twice as many people *helping me* this year.

And I want to thank them from the bottom of my heart.

- First, I want to thank Development Editor Barbara Terry. She's on the top of this list, and also toward the top of my list of professional workmates who became friends during the course of writing this humble tome. Barb was there when I was pulling all-nighters, insisting that I take a small break (Do you realize I watched all of summer through a window, Barb <g>?); she did everything in her power to help organize a big-time effort here; and most of all, she made it abundantly clear to me that she believes in me as a talent. Thank you, Barb—that's as eloquent as I get.

- Thanks to Gail Burlakoff, for once again (it's been more like twelve times again!) copy editing this book. Gail probably had her hands full with me and my non-sentences, but this time, she ironed out Gary K.'s and Mara Nathanson's chapters, to boot. Not to mention Barbara Bouton and Richard Cordero's doctoral thesis on color management in Chapter 3! Gail, it's that time of year again, and once again, thanks for aiming the arrow straight for me. Ossining was splendorous in the autumn, wasn't it?

- A big thank you to my Publisher, David Dwyer. David and I have had the pleasure of working together for five years now (his title always seems to progress up the totem pole, while I'm still an author. Hmmm… <g>), and during the course of our relationship, David has seen me as more than a writer—he's allowed me to contribute to the book's overall feel. I get to design the color signature and even draw the book cover art. These things mean a lot to me, David, because to call myself an author means I'm defining myself, and self-definition leads to self-limitation. Thank you for letting me be myself in New Riders' books, David.

- Thanks to Gary Kubicek, as always. Gary did not tech edit this book (for the first time in years), but instead became a partner with me. Or more appropriately, he became more of a member of the Bouton Family. Gary wrote all the chapters on photo correction, and even helped me out with some of the typography sections. My only fear is that someday, he will outgrow his need for the *Inside* series, and get his own, much deserved, contract! Thanks, pal, for some fine, fine work in this book.

- Mara Zebest Nathanson is new to the *Inside Photoshop* series. She's been a reader and she became a frequent correspondent of mine over the past two years. She'd send me these to-die-for pieces of art she did in Photoshop. So naturally, I asked this artist if she knew how to write. Before long , she was turning in chapters quicker than I! I hope our readers will appreciate her fresh approach to Photoshop as much as we all do at NRP.

- Thanks to my wife, my friend, and my stand-in on those days when the writing got too thick to handle. Barbara, we have a long history with New Riders, and I know we have a longer one with each other. Thank you, mate.

- Many thanks to Richard Cordero for his technical assistance in writing Chapter 3. Richard was nothing short of a blessing to a lot of us who know art, but get migraines over color profiling, color management, dot gain, and color spaces. Richard's contribution is probably the single most important work that describes how to get the best color out of Photoshop in this book. Richard's expert input to Chapter 3 allowed us to bring you the best information available on how to produce not only excellent color, but consistent color among your hardware. He did a lot of the heavy lifting and left the *fun* stuff to the rest of us. Thank you, Richard.

- Thanks to NRP's own Managing Editor, Jennifer Eberhardt, for getting things done that the Boutons could not possibly accomplish. And she did this paperwork chase sorta stuff in moments, not minutes! I'm glad we can work together, Jennifer! It's been various titles and a few years for us, hasn't it?

- The Weissman cometh. Thank you, thank you, Steve Weiss, Executive Editor at New Riders, for your long-standing confidence, sensitivity, and professionalism throughout this book, and about a dozen other books. Steve and I started work—he as a copy editor, and me as a fledgling author on the same day—back in '92. Steve's done great by me through the years. Thanks, bud.

- Thanks to Ed Guarente, our Photographer of the Airwaves. When Mara and I did not have the setup or the equipment to photograph something we needed for a tutorial, we called Ed. Ed would download a rough sketch from us, get his digital camera and the scene set up, and email us about three different exposures of the image we needed, to size and everything. This shows two things:

    1. Ed is leveraging technology about as well in his craft as is possible technologically at this point.
    2. It doesn't hurt that all of us use Road Runner.

    Can you imagine doing this kind of stuff within ½ hour, going from coast to coast? FedEx has gotta be quaking in their running shoes! Thanks, Ed. I owe you more than a dedication in this book for your spirit of giving.

- Thanks to Marc Pawliger and Chris Cox at Adobe Systems for answering all my questions, and then some during the beta cycle. Also thanks to Chris Conner, and especially to Christie Evans for letting us participate in the creation of this product through suggestions and the beta cycle channels. You folks were incredibly responsive and helpful. We needed that in order to write this book.

- Many, many thanks to Mark Goodall of Xara, Ltd. Mark made it possible at the last moment for Windows users to get a trial edition of Xara X on the Companion CD (no slight here; it's a Windows-only program). See the ad in the back of the book for an incredibly low-priced offer on a program I have been using for five years to get stuff like book covers and annotations, and charts and technical drawings done. And I've done fun stuff, too, that's on the gallery at www.xara.com. Mark, thank you for listening to me, and I realize that you've probably lost huge clumps of hair as a result of reading email from me that started out with the sentence, "Mark, wouldn't it be neat if Xara did…" You and Kate Moir have been the most responsive business contacts I've ever had the privilege to know. Thank you both.

- Thanks to Lois and Sumeet at Andromeda for running a money-saving ad in this book.

- Thanks (always) to John Niestemski and Susan Bird for their money-saving service bureau support in the back of the book. This offer could be your first introduction to the gorgeous, breathtaking, glorious world of 35mm (and up) slides from your digital data. The Boutons have used Graphics Masters for years when we wanted a slide or negative that would blow people away. Thanks, dear friends.

- Thanks to J.B. Popplewell at Alien Skin for extending the money-saving offer on their fantastic Photoshop plug-ins. We sort of have a running gag between us, so look for aliens—some of them wearing T-shirts—in this book.

- Thanks to Technical Editors Suzanne Pettypiece and Ryan Frank for their support of every chapter except Chapter 3, which Richard handled. You people kept it tight, informative, and more than anything, correct for our readers. I'd tip my hat to you, except it's a straw summer hat that has stains on it from mowing the lawn.

- Thanks to Linda Seifert, Project Editor, for making certain the book is a "good read." Sentences have a way of getting jumbled from the mind to the keyboard sometimes! Thank you, sincerely. Thank you for keeping everyone and everything on track! You're a miracle worker.

- Thanks go to Jay Payne, Media Developer, for mastering a CD that is accurate, despite how complex we made it for you!

- Thanks to Steve Mays for emailing me pepperoni. I'd lost the file of a slice of pepperoni—aw, I'm not going to try to explain it, you'll see it in the book. Thanks, friend.

Gary Kubicek thanks his family—Terri, Rachael, and Bethany—for so graciously accepting the fact that our two summer vacations and our (less fun) regular activities, like dental appointments, had to be canceled while I wrote my chapters for this book.

Gary Kubicek also gives a very special thanks to Renee and Ariana (your willingness to model is greatly appreciated and helped make Chapter 16 more successful than I imagined it would be). Thank you, Dr. Marie Sheils-Djouadi (Principal of Wakefield High School, Arlington, VA), for your enthusiasm and willingness to allow me to use my high school's name and photo. Also, thank you Georganna Schell for providing your photos of the school, and Tom Windsor for your assistance.

Gary Kubicek would like to acknowledge all the folks at Manlius Pebble Hill School, especially Baxter Ball, Virginia Satterfield, and Pam Steele for their support of the digital imaging medium. And a special acknowledgment to Tiffany Babiarz, Christian Davies, Nick Jakus, Ryan McCormick, Nick McGraw, Quinn Shamlian, Hilary Small, and Dave Staller for your inspirational and intense dedication to becoming Photoshop power-users!

Mara Zebest Nathanson thanks her husband, Richard, and her children, David and Leah, for their support and understanding that having a wife and mother meant looking at the back of her head in front of a computer monitor for quite some time.

She also sends thanks to Robert Stanley—a friend and fellow author who was always available for brainstorming, support, and constant encouragement.

Mara also gives a special thanks to her Dad, the late Hyman Lee Zebest, for being the best damn Dad a person could ever have. A man that always believed that he would live on through how well he was remembered. You have achieved true immortality in my heart.

# Dedication

For those of you who read the trade papers, have you noticed that magazines about computers, applications, and tips have almost vanished? *Publish* is gone (it has "reinvented" itself, a term I really dislike), as has *PC Computing*. So all I get in the mail are Red Herring clones, all talking about the same two things: What Cisco plans on acquiring today, and what the hottest dot com is in Silicon Valley/Alley.

Where's the "good stuff," like reviews of monitors, DVD players, and processors? You'll have to hunt the net for the news that we computer graphics and DTP people need to know, but I'd like to single out three people for doing their darndest to keep the art of communication alive. They are fellow teachers, and I admire their spirit for continuing through the years to pump it out, usually without satisfactory pay.

- Hats off to Daniel-Will Harris, the most active personality with computer and communications savvy I can think of. Daniel is a font of wisdom, he was instrumental in setting up eFUSE.com to teach users how to make Web sites, and his own home page is at http://www.will-harris.com/.

- Gary Priester was active with *Publish* magazine before it turned dysfunctional. He was a designer spearhead for i/us, a wonderful discussion site for designers before it was sold off, and is on colorize.com, the Tektronix Web site, where he is currently writing monthly articles on color. Gary also hosted the Trompe L'œil Room (http://trompe.i-us.com/), where he delivered monthly lessons in art, mostly using Xara. We hope that the Trompe room will find a new home on the Web. This fellow, and my friend, aims for the fastest method of content dissemination—being an author is one thing—being quicker than a pizza delivery boy with good, solid content has its own place, a valuable place in today's media.

- Fred Showker (http://www.graphic-design.com/) has been faithfully running The Desktop and Publishing Center for years. It's the best online resource I can think of for solid book reviews, tips, tricks—I'll call it what it is: It's about the best magazine of the airwaves on the subject of content creation and presentation. And none of his effort has ever made him a millionaire or made him too important to talk to me <g>.

Dear reader, these gentlemen have, pardon the phrase, *really busted* to bring to the world information, because they love the arts or communication and content creation, and they also love to share. If you care at all about the downward trend in media content, visit these sites, make a contribution, or start out on your own creating *true content*—the stuff all of us *really* like to read.

# A Message from New Riders

As the reader of this book, you are our most important critic and commentator. We value your opinion and want to know what we're doing right, what we could do better, in what areas you'd like to see us publish, and any other words of wisdom you're willing to pass our way.

As Executive Editor at New Riders, I welcome your comments. You can fax, email, or write me directly to let me know what you did or didn't like about this book—as well as what we can do to make our books better. When you write, please be sure to include this book's title, ISBN, and author, as well as your name and phone or fax number. I will carefully review your comments and share them with the authors and editors who worked on the book.

*Please note that I cannot help you with technical problems related to the topic of this book, and that due to the high volume of email I receive, I might not be able to reply to every message. If you run into a technical problem, it's best to contact our Customer Support department, as listed later in this section. Thanks.*

> Email:    steve.weiss@newriders.com
>
> Mail:    Steve Weiss
>
> Executive Editor
>
> New Riders Publishing
>
> 201 West 103rd Street
>
> Indianapolis, IN 46290 USA

## Visit Our Web Site: www.newriders.com

On our Web site, you'll find information about our other books, the authors we partner with, book updates and file downloads, promotions, discussion boards for online interaction with other users and with technology experts, and a calendar of trade shows and other professional events with which we'll be involved. We hope to see you around.

## Email Us from Our Web Site

Go to www.newriders.com and click on the Contact link if you

- Have comments or questions about this book.
- Want to report errors that you have found in this book.
- Have a book proposal or are interested in writing for New Riders.

- Would like us to send you one of our author kits.

- Are an expert in a computer topic or technology and are interested in being a reviewer or technical editor.

- Want to find a distributor for our titles in your area.

- Are an educator/instructor who wants to preview New Riders books for classroom use. In the body/comments area, include your name, school, department, address, phone number, office days/hours, text currently in use, and enrollment in your department, along with your request for either desk/examination copies or additional information.

## Call Us or Fax Us

You can reach us toll-free at (800) 571–5840 + 9+ 3567 (ask for New Riders). If outside the U.S., please call 1–317–581–3500 and ask for New Riders. If you prefer, you can fax us at 1–317–581–4663, Attention: New Riders.

**Note**

**Technical Support and Customer Support for This Book**   Although we encourage entry-level users to get as much as they can out of our books, keep in mind that our books are written assuming a non-beginner level of user-knowledge of the technology. This assumption is reflected in the brevity and shorthand nature of some of the tutorials.

New Riders will continually work to create clearly written, thoroughly tested and reviewed technology books of the highest educational caliber and creative design. We value our customers more than anything—that's why we're in this business—but we cannot guarantee to each of the thousands of you who buy and use our books that we will be able to work individually with you through tutorials or content with which you may have questions. We urge readers who need help in working through exercises or other material in our books—and who need this assistance immediately—to use as many of the resources that our technology and technical communities can provide, especially the many online user groups and list servers available.

- If you have a physical problem with one of our books or accompanying CD-ROMs, please contact our Customer Support department.

- If you have questions about the content of the book—needing clarification about something as it is written or note of a possible error—please contact our Customer Support department.

- If you have comments of a general nature about this or other books by New Riders, please contact the Executive Editor.

To contact our Customer Support department, call 1–317–581–3833, from 10:00 a.m. to 3:00 p.m. U.S. EST (CST from April through October of each year—unlike the majority of the United States, Indiana doesn't change to Daylight Savings Time each April). You can also access our tech support Web site at http://www.mcp.com/support.

# *Introduction*

## What's Twice as Large and a Hundred Times as Deep?

It's Photoshop 6.

So much for an Intro with suspense, huh?

But what's really going to knock your socks off is when you begin to dig into this book and get your hands dirty in the latest edition of the world's favorite imaging application. This is *not* the same Photoshop we've come to know and love. Nope. You'll love it even *more*!

## Photoshop 5.5, Photoshop 6? What's the Diff'?

Um, about a bazillion lines of code went into this new version of Photoshop. You might not see the effort, but you will feel it. A lot of things, such as the color engine (see Chapter 3), the Gradient Editor, the Type tool, and many more things have been rewritten from the ground up to enhance speed and produce the effect you want in no time.

The system requirements for running Photoshop and ImageReady at a comfortable pace are greater than those for earlier versions. But if you want "in," *other* applications—such as Office 2000—are sort of demanding, too. So a G3 or a Pentium II or Pentium III with at least 3GB of hard disk space (we believe that everyone has that—40GB drives cost less than $200 now), at least 128MB of RAM (256MB would be much, much better), and a graphics card with 8MB of RAM (most of them come with 32MB now) will put you in action. Remember, Photoshop is everything *but* a toy—if you want to play big-time, you need to outfit a serious computer with the aforementioned hardware. The rewards are incredible, trust us. You'll be typing in Photoshop as though it were a desktop publishing program, and you'll be creating layers and fills as quickly as you would in a vector drawing application.

Photoshop 6 has an interface that looks like its predecessors, but after you play with it for a while, you'll realize that new and weird and wonderful things will start sprouting. Look at that toolbox carefully. The Slice tool, the Shapes tool, and the other tools lurking behind tool icon flyouts are there to greet you. You aren't exactly sure what they are good for, and that's where we authors are going to help.

The program also features commands and palettes you'll find in other Adobe products, so, for example, a seasoned PageMaker or Illustrator user can quickly get to work in Photoshop 6. Photoshop 6 also hooks almost seamlessly into its sister program, ImageReady 3. Teaching you about ImageReady will not be that much of a chore—you'll already be familiar with palettes and key commands before you open the program. Integration of the Adobe product line has never been so evident as with Photoshop 6. PDF files, PostScript on the Clipboard, and many other features create art that can be exchanged easily between Adobe programs, and somewhat less easily (but still possible) between Photoshop and non-Adobe programs.

## We Interrupt This Introduction for Late-Breaking News

# ★★★★ *NEWS FLASH* ★★★★
# BULLETIN

Guess that got your attention, huh? Seriously, your work on the assignments in this book will be impaired if you do not use the same color space as the authors did when compiling the Companion CD. There's no simple way to put this, but we'll try—Chapter 3 has detailed information on Photoshop color space.

At the last minute, for fairly good reasons, Adobe systems changed the default color space in Photoshop to sRGB, which is a narrow color space best suited for Web work. Now, the authors cover Web design work just fine in this book, but we also understand that designers from *all* occupations need the story on Photoshop 6. And that is why the authors stuck with Adobe's original plans to make Adobe RGB (1998) the default workspace in Photoshop. Adobe RGB (1998) is a very good, wide space (lots of colors), general-purpose imaging environment. But this is not what you'll open Photoshop 6 to the very first time you launch it.

In Figure I.1, you can see the dialog box that pops up the moment you open Photoshop 6 for the first time.

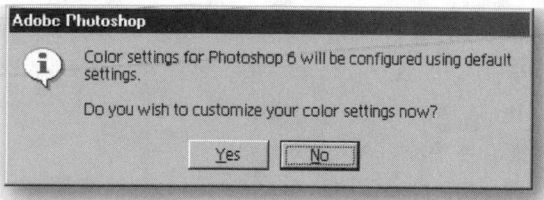

**Figure I.1**    You open Photoshop 6, and immediately it has questions for you <g>!

Okay, you have no idea what customizing color settings means, just as we had no idea until we dug around a lot in this program. If you click No, you will be working in sRGB color space and incessantly get messages when you open image files from this book's Companion CD—cryptic stuff like, "This image's profile doesn't match the default color space in Photoshop. Here are 47 options; what would you like to do?" Okay, we're having a little fun here and exaggerating a tad, but "No" is *not* the choice to make—you should click "Yes" here.

If you click Yes, you'll be taken to a dialog box, as shown in Figure I.2. If you've played with Photoshop before reading this book, and have already clicked No, press Ctrl(⌘)+Shift+K to access the Color Settings dialog box.

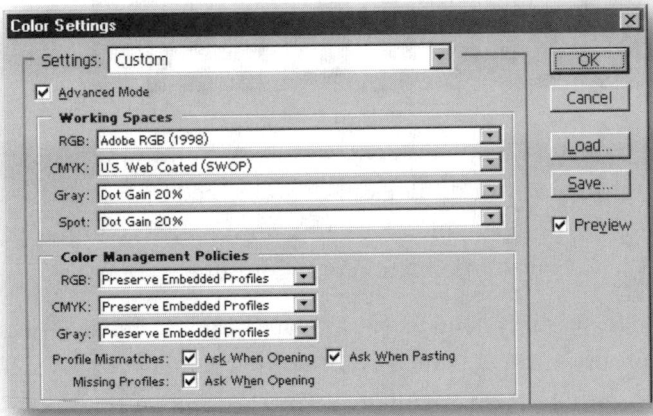

**Figure I.2**    A very serious education in color management begins here.

Let's run down what you should list in these options in Figure I.2, in case the figure is hard to read. You will receive, in Chapter 3, a thorough explanation of *why* these are the recommended settings. But we realize that you might want to get up and running and experimenting with the slew of new features, too.

## Working Spaces

For RGB, choose Adobe RGB (1998) from the drop-down; for CMYK, choose U.S. Web Coated (SWOP) v2, unless you are from a country other than the United States, in which case, you pick your country's standard from the drop-down. Then choose Gray: Dot Gain 20%, and Spot: Dot Gain 20%.

## Color Management Policies

For RGB, CMYK, and Gray, choose the same thing: Preserve Embedded Profiles.

And check the two Ask When Opening options, as well as Ask When Pasting.

That's it. See how easy that was? We take material that could be intimidating and turn it into a cakewalk. We're looking out for you already in the *Introduction*! We want you to have a good time following the steps in this book, so Photoshop's color space needs to be the same as it is in the setups the authors created.

We return you now to our regularly scheduled Introduction...

# Attention *All* Classes of Photoshop Users!

To say that documenting the new version of Photoshop and its pal, ImageReady 3, was a big task is like saying that the water gets deep between Europe and the United States. Photoshop is *huge;* the interface has been somewhat redesigned to accommodate new features and new ways of doing things, and as a result, the authors have developed new techniques we want to share with you.

Where do we begin?

## Engaging Tutorials with Something for Everyone

First, we discovered that teaching Photoshop exactly as we have in the past is not good enough—we'd have a 3,000 page book that would break toes and intimidate teachers as well as students. So we trim away any fat, get right to the heart of this incredible program, and we use tutorial steps to illustrate a concept when using only the printed word is too vague.

We are also aware that beginners don't always want a book that's tailored to beginners. So although we tell the complete story for intermediate to advanced users, this book was written to be accessible to beginners, too. Photoshop 6 is a new experience for the experienced and the novice user alike, and a set of steps is a set of steps, so there's no reason why *everyone* can't get in on the education and the fun.

## Fully Annotated Screen Captures

We also rely on fully annotated screen captures (figures) to illustrate a point. We feel as though there's little point in a screen capture all by itself, so we spent dozens of hours highlighting stuff that will happen on your screen when we tell you to click X to get to Y.

## A Well-Developed Structure

How's a book on Photoshop 6 organized? Well, really good Photoshop books like this one provide information that, in general, will get you up and running fast with no experience other than the authors' guidance. We quickly move on to customizing Photoshop and show you how to create color profiles for all your hardware.

Then, the plot (and this book) thickens. We'll get you going with new layer modes (Layer Effects are called Styles now, and with the Shapes tools you can produce custom layers simply by clicking in the image window). Even an intermediate user can use a refresher course on how to select things, so you might say that once

Photoshop has been tuned, we take you into assignments that focus on the two most important features in Photoshop—selections and layers.

We acknowledge the 1.3 billion email messages we've received that essentially say, "Yo, Bouton. We want more tutorials on retouching." And so we created them. Learn how to create special effects, how to restore a damaged photo—this book has about three times more chapters on photographic manipulation than earlier editions had because, hey, we want our readers to benefit from this book, and you have diverse interests.

Speaking of diverse interests, we gracefully move into the new Type tool capabilities toward the middle of the book because this version of Photoshop has the type of text features you'd expect from PageMaker. Kerning, tracking, all that DTP stuff is now in Photoshop.

And to pay attention to the Web is important, too. So Adobe and the authors are treating ImageReady 3 as its own thing. We have plenty of templates and examples for optimizing images, creating Web effects such as JavaScript rollovers and animation (GIF animation is a blast if you read how we work on a concept first), and we even toss in some tips on manually editing HTML to make a great page look even better.

We feel the book has a pretty good rhythm, pace, and direction. If we were Dick Clark, we'd say, "It's got a good tempo—I can really dance to it. I give it a 99."

## What We Assume about You: The *Least* You Need to Know to Get in the Door

Sort of a smarmy header, eh? But it got your attention, and we want to tell you some important things before you read page 1. The authors have chosen to presume practically *nothing* in teaching you these new programs. Naturally, you need to feel comfortable with your computer's operating system, and you need to know how to save, copy, and move a file. Without a doubt, proficiency with a mouse or a digitizing tablet will get you where you're going more quickly in Photoshop 6 than if you first unpacked your computer from its box moments ago! But the authors have chosen to take a "step back" approach from Photoshop 6, to better include users who might be unfamiliar with such things as anti-aliasing, interpolation, alpha channels, and other computer graphics terms.

## What We Need from You

*Everyone* is new to Photoshop 6; it's an adventure for the pro and the beginner alike, and we didn't want to leave out anything in the steps, the notes, the text, or the discovery process. Do *not* take the attitude of, "Yeah, yeah, I know about the Rubber Stamp tool so I'll skip this section." First of all, it's not called the Rubber Stamp tool anymore; it's the Clone Stamp tool. So, you see, you'll be missing out on valuable information if you gloss over a chapter. The authors didn't presume anything, and as a reader, you shouldn't *either*!

Let us make learning Photoshop 6 an excursion, an adventure. As most adventures go, you must pack a few things first—such intangibles as a positive attitude, a concept, a proficiency with your computer, and an eagerness to learn. And last but not least, you should have a map, so you don't travel too many side roads, as interesting and valuable as they might be. The authors have provided the map (this book), and the following sections describe this map, by way of explaining the *structure* of *Inside Adobe Photoshop 6*.

# A Closer Look at the Insides of this Book

The authors recommend that you use *Inside Adobe Photoshop 6* as a reference guide, but it was also written as a sequential, linear, hands-on tutorial. You might well benefit most from the information in the book by reading a little at a time, from the first chapter to the last. We are aware, however, that this is not the way everyone finds information—particularly in an integrating graphics environment such as Photoshop's, where one piece of information often leads to a seemingly unconnected slice of wisdom. For this reason, most chapters offer complete, self-contained steps for a specific topic or technique, with frequent cross-references to related material in other chapters. If you begin reading Chapter 6, for example, you will learn how to acquire digital images, but you can really get into a niche of image acquisition, such as scanning, if you read Chapter 19. We overlap where it seems necessary—otherwise, we might leave a gap somewhere.

*Inside Adobe Photoshop 6* is divided into five parts, with the appendix and special instructions for installing components of the Companion CD in the back of the book. Here's a breakdown of what's in store:

## Part I: Introducing the Basics of the Powerful New Photoshop

In Chapter 1, "Photoshop 6: A New Imaging Adventure for Novices and Pros Alike," we cover the new "document-centricity" of Photoshop—how, if you know the right moves, you almost never move your cursor far from your work. A discussion of what Photoshop is and isn't is valuable for the beginner who's heard Photoshop mentioned at the supermarket checkout counter. (Let's face it, it's everywhere.) Shortcut key commands are listed for handy reference, and new features are explained for both beginners and advanced users. Photoshop has changed since version 5.5—we wrote this chapter for anyone who doesn't want to take things for granted.

Chapter 2, "Getting your Feet Wet: Your First Masterpiece," is an intricate playground. We felt that all the good stuff should not be crammed into the back of the book, so regardless of how little education you've had in Photoshop, we serve up a series of steps that'll be a blast. Come learn the basics and (gasp!) still have a good time with a very goofy image and the powerful steps you'll learn.

Chapter 3, "Understanding Photoshop's New Color Management System," is about as heavy-duty a chapter as was ever written for a Photoshop book. We provide, in a way you can understand, the very best comprehensive coverage of color management. Although color should be consistent between Photoshop, your monitor, your scanner, your printer, and the equipment used by service bureaus and business partners, it's not. This chapter explains how to get as close as possible to perfect color matching without spending another dime on hardware. Your means to a color correct end is all in Photoshop.

In Chapter 4, "Optimizing your Workspace: Photoshop Preferences," you'll see not only how to work with the Preferences menu, but also how to tweak the workspace so it feels like home. *Your* home, not Adobe's home. Learn some secrets that'll speed up your work and really get this program running like a finely tuned machine.

In Chapter 5, "Introducing Image Formats, Image Modes, and Color Spaces," you'll get a primer on color depth and other characteristics of digital media you should be aware of. "I know about color space. So what's *color depth*?" "Why does this image look crummy?" "What should I save my finished Photoshop work to?" These and other questions are answered when you know what file formats and color organization are all about, and you'll be able to answer things yourself after you read this chapter.

Chapter 6, "Acquiring Photoshop Images," is a series of discussions and some hands-on work with the process of getting a scene from "out there" (outdoors, in the carbon-based world) to "in here" (the Photoshop workspace; silicon-based, climate controlled). Scanning, digital cameras, PhotoCDs, and more are covered. This chapter helps you get the "out-there" images into Photoshop looking their best.

Chapter 7, "Outputting Your Photoshop Work," is *not* about File, Print. No, printing work actually is fairly easy; it's the calculations and considerations involved in moving a digital image to real paper that are covered here. What's resolution? What's a line screen? And how can I squeeze more shades of black out of my laser printer? What's PostScript? We make the math simple, the discussions engaging, and your wisdom about output will blossom in your noggin without your even realizing it.

In Chapter 8, "Enhancing Productivity: Automation and Other Cool Tools," we round out this part of the book with several examples of ways to put Photoshop to work for hours, while you spend only a moment or two writing scripts for Photoshop. This chapter explains how to write an action for the Actions palette, how to move this information into a droplet, how to batch-process folders of image files, and how to neatly arrange multiple copies of images on a single sheet for printing to an inkjet or other printer. Who *doesn't* want to save time?

## Part II: Digging Deeper Into the Treasure Chest

In Chapter 9, "Selecting in Photoshop: Ah, the Many Ways to Select Stuff," you are treated to a comprehensive, fun excursion into one of Photoshop's most powerful facilities. Did you know that there are more than 10 ways to select an image area in Photoshop? By size, by color, and so on? Learn the best way to create Photoshop selections, and create some tasty artwork along the way!

Chapter 10, "Building Images Layer by Layer," gets into creating a photorealistic scrapbook, one layer at a time. Learn to use layers effectively, and get your hands on some secret shortcuts that'll make layers as important a feature to you as selections in Photoshop.

Have you ever wondered how some of the art you see today has an airbrushed look, even though it's a computer graphic? Chapter 11, "Painting with Pen and Path Selection Tools," shows you how to create a beautiful floral design and gets you into using vector paths in Photoshop, yet another valuable feature you can add to your own toolkit.

Chapter 12, "Introducing Shapes: Someplace Between Paths and Selections," is a romp through a new feature in Photoshop. Predesigned vector paths can shave hours off your work, and they are fun to work with. See how to access the custom shapes, and see how you like the author's own custom Shapes palette on the Companion CD (he worked for hours on it; please don't hurt his feelings). Also learn how and when shapes are not Shapes, but instead are rendered to an image window as a work path, a color fill, and, well…read the chapter, and see how weird and wonderful Shapes can be!

Chapter 13, "Creating Special Effects with Type," is another typical *Inside Photoshop* tutorial, where we teach you and also have a mercilessly fun time with the packaging industry. You'll learn how to create special type effects as you help design a label for a can of mystery meat. Just keep telling yourself, "It's only an example. It's only an ex…."

## Part III: Exploring the Cool Stuff

Chapter 14, "Color Correcting and Exposure: Basic Image Improvement," begins our journey into the fine art of image enhancement. Everyone has to begin somewhere, and let's face it—hasn't your aunt or someone been pestering you for two years about retouching family pictures "with that Photoshop computer thing"? Come learn the basics, and see how quickly you'll navigate the chapters that follow.

Chapter 15, "Repairing an Heirloom Photo," is an all-new image with all new problems. We've been featuring the restoration chapter for almost seven years now in the *Inside Photoshop* books and it's been a lot of readers' favorite chapter. So dig in, and see how to bring an image from the past back to life.

In Chapter 16, "Finding (and Fixing) Mistakes in Pictures," we show you what Photoshop is best at: being *invisible*. We have two photos, each of which has an element we want and an element we do not want. See how to blend the pictures so that someone will look at your creation and say, "Nice picture. So what?" Only your models and you will know that the image *never was taken*—it was "choreographed," using Photoshop.

In Chapter 17, "Using the Clone Stamp Tool, Image Selection and Distortion," you'll get the scoop on how the Clone Stamp tool (formerly the Rubber Stamp tool) works now in both its modes. See how to create a finished image from two imperfect images by using only the Clone Stamp tool. Then see how the Extract command works (it first appeared in version 5.5) to select intricate image areas. And finally, have some fun with the Liquify command—bring along a picture of the boss, and be sure he's gone home for the day.

In Chapter 18, "Making the Impossible Look Plausible: Surrealistic Photoshop," you'll learn how to create a boat, complete with water, that is cruising down an interstate highway. Are the cars next to the boat making way? Nah, their drivers are unaware that this is a surrealistic scene. As the title suggests, you make impossible scenes look real by using a little talent, a little magic, and a lot of Photoshop.

Chapter 19, "Saving The Day with Photoshop and a Scanner," shows you how to take direct scans of common, everyday objects, and create a magazine layout that looks (and will print) like the real thing. Learn about resolution, get experience working with Photoshop's new improved Type tool (see how to make wrap-around text in Photoshop!), and get an assignment done without leaving your cube.

Chapter 20, "Mixing 3D Graphics with Photographs," introduces you to the process of combining models with actual photography. This sort of stuff is done in the movies all the time—do you actually believe that George Lucas *built* 35,000 droid soldiers for *The Phantom Menace*? Our presentation in this chapter takes an alien space hunter–type guy, transports him to a Bryce rendered scene, adds a robot, and lights up a laser sword so he can defend the galaxy—or at least upstate New York. C'mon—it's out of this world, and you need a vacation.

Chapter 21, "Using a Boatload of Native Photoshop Filters," takes you on a trip working with some of the fancier of the 100 filters Photoshop ships with. Learn how to make reflections in bubbles, see how to make highlights in images, and experience what a lot of these filters are good for.

Chapter 22, "Working with Type," concentrates on some of the desktop publishing elements of Photoshop, and how you can accommodate clients' type needs without leaving your favorite program. See how to create paragraph control and use hyphenation settings, how to warp text, mix typefaces, and generally have a typographic ball with Photoshop's enhanced text capabilities.

## Part IV: Introducing ImageReady: Moving to the Web

Chapter 23, "Optimizing Images for the Web," departs from the world's most popular imaging program to check out its sidekick, ImageReady 3. This chapter shows you how to make the most beautiful image out of the fewest pixels. If you think that's easy, check out the Web sometime. Learn about optimized image formats, types of dithering, lossy and lossless compression, get the real goods on the PNG file format, and get yourself ready to add the Web to your collection of canvases.

In Chapter 24, "Creating Image Maps and Instant Web Galleries," you learn about two important Web media techniques that don't have anything to do with each other, but the author couldn't think of where else in this book to put Photoshop's automatic Web Gallery feature. Learn how to create a single image that has several hot spots (links to other Web sites), get the scoop on HTML scripting language and how ImageReady generates it. And learn how to hack the finished script so that the image map presentation looks more polished—without springing for an HTML editing program! Also see how simple a Web gallery can be to create by choosing File, Automate, and Web Photo Gallery. You pick the images, and Photoshop writes the HTML.

Chapter 25, "Creating Rollovers and Animations," will get you thinking seriously about creating stuff that's interactive and *moves* on the Web! See how to create buttons on a page that respond to a visitor's cursor movements. Then, see how to become an animation factory with the proper mindset, a whole bunch of ideas on how animation can work, and a step-by-step fiesta of how to finish animations and optimize them in ImageReady.

## Part V: Closing Thoughts

Chapter 25½, "Here's Where the Path Divides," contains practically nothing about Photoshop, and just about everything about *you*, the designer. Where do you go from here? Should you quit the day gig and freelance as a Photoshoppist? What other programs should you buy to stock up on the latest effects and features? These are natural questions, and we wouldn't want you to close this book without some answers from your teachers.

## The Back O' the Book

You've finished the chapters but that does *not* mean you can't benefit from turning a few more of these back pages. You'll find some neat stuff! We're leaving you with:

- An appendix that describes all the goodies included on the CD that accompanies *Inside Adobe Photoshop 6*. More on those goodies later.
- Ads that follow the appendix. Check them out and save money on everything from applications to service bureau work. These offers can save you hundreds of dollars!
- An index that exhaustively cross-references terms and topics in this book. Many people judge a technical book by its index, and New Riders has provided the best one imaginable for *Inside Adobe Photoshop 6*.

*(At this point, a small New Riders stagehand tugs at Gary Bouton's pant leg.)*

**Bouton:** Please don't do that.

**Stagehand:** But Mr. Bouton, you're forgetting to tell the readers about the Companion CD.

**Bouton:** I was just getting to that, small New Riders stagehand. Ahem...

On the Companion CD, you will find a number of important resources for your continuing adventures in Photoshop, long after you've pored through the pages of this book:

- **Resource files for the chapter examples.** We recommend that you work through the steps shown in this book, using files (carefully prepared by the authors) that demonstrate specific procedures and effects. The files, located in the Examples folder on the Companion CD, are platform-independent and can be used on any Macintosh or Windows system with Photoshop 6 installed. Sorry, Photoshop 6 itself is *not* included on the Companion CD! You need to bring *some* ingredients in the recipe for imaging fame and fortune to the party yourself!

- **The *Inside Adobe Photoshop* eGlossary.** This Acrobat PDF file contains color examples, shortcuts, definitions, and other material pertaining to this book, to Photoshop, and to computer graphics in general. We recommend that you install the eGlossary on your system, and then launch Adobe Acrobat Reader 4 when you need a quick explanation of a technique or interface element in your Photoshop work. We've beefed this fellow up to about 300 pages for this version of Photoshop.

- **Fonts, textures, and scenes in Windows and Macintosh formats, a stupendous collection of resource materials, and more.** The authors have produced a fairly extensive collection (in our opinion) of frequently needed items for Web pages, traditional publication, and other types of media construction. Check out the documentation and the license agreement in the BOUTONS folder on the Companion CD; these are completely unique, one-of-a-kind, Photoshop-oriented files and programs.

## Push Down and Twist: The Directions for Accessing This Book

Examples described in the book are documented in a step-by-step format. If you follow along, your screen should look exactly like this book's figures (except that your screen will be in color). Each chapter leads you through at least one set of numbered steps, with frequent asides explaining why we asked you to do something. The figures show the results of an action, and we explain what the effect should look like.

Most of Photoshop 6's tools have different, enhanced functions when you hold down the Shift, Alt, or Ctrl keys (Shift, Opt, ⌘ Command keys, for Macintosh users) while you click with the mouse or press other keyboard keys. These *modifier keys* are shown in the steps as Ctrl(⌘)+click, Alt(Opt)+click, Ctrl(⌘)+D, and so on. We even devote Chapter 1 to getting the most from Photoshop with tips and techniques, so future chapters will come more easily to you. *Inside Adobe Photoshop 6* is a multi-platform documentation of the application; Windows key commands are shown first in the steps, followed by the Macintosh key equivalent (enclosed in parentheses). UNIX users will also find the steps easy to follow; the primary difference in Photoshop 6 across platforms is the "look" each operating system lends to interface elements.

To show you how easy it is to follow along in this book, here's how we tell you how to access the Feather command:

1. Press Ctrl(⌘)+Alt(Opt)+D (Select, Feather), and then type **5** in the pixels field. Click OK to apply the feathering. Alternatively, if you have the Options bar displayed, you can enter **5** in the Feather field.

The translation? You hold down the first key while you press the second and third keys (then release all three keys to produce the intended result). We frequently refer to a more efficient way to perform a step after the first way, so experienced users can change their way of working, after they've become very familiar with the older ways of using Photoshop. The authors are trying to get you comfortable with modifier keys rather than menu commands because this constant reinforcement, highlighted throughout the book, will eventually make you work more efficiently in Photoshop 6. It is entirely possible in this version—through pop-up menus and modifier keys—to go through a set of steps and never use the main menu. And that's good, because this means you can always keep your cursor close to your work. Who wants to get frequent flier miles on the cursor when creating and retouching images is the goal?

If the steps in an application that's available in both Windows and Macintosh formats are significantly different, we fully explain the steps used in this book.

As mentioned earlier, the Photoshop interface itself is practically identical on all operating platforms. The only real differences lie in the system "padding"—the screen elements that the Macintosh OS and different versions of MS-Windows add to windows, palettes, and menus—and the system font used to display text. Most of the screen figures show Photoshop's interface under Windows 2000. There is no difference in the *features* offered in the two versions of Photoshop.

**Note**

Okay, here's a list of the *real* differences in features between the Windows and Macintosh versions of Photoshop 6:

- In the Macintosh version of Photoshop, the Document Sizes field and the Zoom Percentage field are located at the bottom of the current image window. In Windows, the Document Sizes and Zoom Percentage field are on the Status line at the bottom of the screen, where you can also see options displayed for the currently selected tool.

- Windows users right-click to access the Context menu in Photoshop. Macintosh users hold Ctrl and click to get the menu.

## Terms Used in This Book

The term *drag* in this book means to hold down the primary mouse button and move the onscreen cursor. This action is used in Photoshop to create a marquee selection and to access tools on the toolbox flyout. On the Macintosh, dragging is also used to access *pull-down menus;* Windows users do not need to hold the primary mouse button to access flyout menus and main menu commands.

*Hover* means to move your cursor onscreen without holding down a mouse button. Hovering is most commonly used in Photoshop with the Magnetic Pen and Magnetic Lasso tools, and also with the Eyedropper tool when seeking a relative position in an image and the color value beneath the tool (the Info palette, F8, must be displayed to determine the values the Eyedropper reads).

*Click* means to press and release the primary mouse button once.

*Double-click* means to quickly press the primary mouse button twice. Usually you double-click to perform a function without the need to click an OK button in a directory window.

*Shift+click* means that you should hold down the Shift key while you click with the primary mouse button.

*Right-click*, as noted earlier, is a Windows action that the Macintosh input devices cannot perform, so we've put the equivalent command in parentheses (Hold Ctrl+click) whenever this command is necessary.

### Nicknames for Well-Known Products

*Inside Adobe Photoshop 6* would be an even larger book than it already is if every reference to a specific graphics product or manufacturer included the full brand manufacturer, product name, and version number. For this reason, you'll occasionally see Adobe Photoshop 6 referred to as simply "Photoshop" in the text of this book. Similarly, Adobe Illustrator is referred to as "Illustrator," and other products are mentioned by their "street names."

New Riders Publishing and the authors acknowledge that the names mentioned in this book are trademarked or copyrighted by their respective manufacturers; our use of nicknames for various products is in no way meant to infringe on the trademark names for these products. When we refer to an application, it is usually the most current version of the application, unless otherwise noted.

## Folks Just Like You

Chapter 3 is intended to help you prepare Photoshop 6 for your personal use, and we think it's only fair to tell you what *the authors* used to prepare this book and the CD. Nothing out of the ordinary—we used Photoshop 6, a few outside applications, and systems configured to what we believe go from high-end to modest specifications. For the photographic images, we used available lighting most of the time, a 35mm SLR camera, and family and friends as patient subjects. We also used more *people* to author and provide photography for this book, because let's face it—you'll quickly learn that Photoshop is positively *huge,* and the Boutons versus the Adobe Programmers just isn't a fair match <g>!

We wrote this book for a wide range of people, from imaging professionals to people who got Photoshop as their first application. We believe that business professionals will see where the book's examples can lead in their own work, and that the novice won't be intimidated by a super-polished compendium of imaging work. The systems include a Pentium II 266 mHz with 256MB of RAM running Windows 2000; Pentium III 540 mHz with 256MB of RAM, running Windows 2000 and Windows Millennium; and a Macintosh G3 running System 9 with 128MB of RAM. All machines have 200–500MB of empty hard disk space on hard disks of different sizes, from 3GB to 60GB. These are not "tough specs," folks—Photoshop requires a machine with some power, more than a machine that only runs a text editor, you know? And if you check with Dell and other manufacturers, you'll be surprised at what a "muscle machine" goes for these days. *Hint:* It's far less than your kid's orthodontic work.

Electronic imaging is such a wonderful, magical thing that it's impossible to keep the child in us quiet. (Aren't you getting a whiff of it right here?) For that reason, many of the examples in this book are a little whimsical—they stretch reality a tad, in the same way you'll learn to stretch a pixel or two, using Photoshop. We want to show you some of the fun we've had with a very serious product, and hope that perhaps we will kindle or fan the flame of the creative spark in you, as well.

So adventurers and explorers, let's get cracking. Take a deep breath, turn the page, and pretend you're Neil Armstrong back in 1969.

What a rush—

# Part I

# Introducing the Basics of the Powerful New Photoshop

# Chapter 1

## Photoshop 6: A New Imaging Adventure for Novices and Pros Alike

Photoshop has metamorphosed over the

years, and sometimes many of us didn't

notice how we were working differently

to artistically *leverage* the changes in

Photoshop. It has grown, to be sure, and we thought we'd begin this book by devoting quality time not only to what's new in Photoshop 6, but also to how you can get the most out of the program by changing the way you work. Um, beginners obviously don't have to change the way they work in Photoshop.

## Bouton's Version of the History of Photoshop

At the beginning of the 1990s, Photoshop was a sleek image editor renowned for its quality anti-aliasing (smooth edges in a selection or image), the capability to paste behind an image, to float and duplicate an image, and the capability to save paths and alpha channels in a file. And it came on four floppy disks.

By the mid-1990s, Photoshop was almost as popular on Windows as it was on the Macintosh. It no longer fit on four floppy disks, however, because the feature set had exploded, and in addition to it being the el primo image editor, it was adopted by lots of illustration folks. Why? Because the third-party plug-in market was now mature and you could do almost anything with Kai's Power Tools, Alien Skin's Black Box, and other filters. Also, we were handed layers, and along with that, layer masks, so editing became much more intuitive—you hid image areas as though they were erased, and then restored areas to visibility until you wanted to make your edits permanent. Layers are like sheets of clear plastic upon which you can put paint, paste image areas, or add filtering. Photoshop also adopted the Windows right-click convention, offering it to the Macintosh as a Ctrl+click to access a Commands palette. And you could put anything you liked on the menu.

And then Photoshop matured.

This Commands palette stuff, probably more than any other feature, started the trend away from the main menu for commands, and moved palettes closer to where you were working on an image. We also started to discover keyboard shortcuts, another way of staying at our work and not scrolling 50 miles to the main menu for one single command. We believe that there are around 20 keyboard shortcuts in Photoshop 6 that you should commit to memory. We'll list them shortly, and if you memorize them, you will work about 10–30% faster in Photoshop.

And not to forget version 4; it introduced the Actions palette and batch mode processing, which made ho-hum, repetitive tasks run themselves with one or two user clicks.

So we've had Photoshop for the photographer, Photoshop for the artist, and Photoshop for the pre-press folks. Photoshop 5's appeal was to color-critical professionals, and its tiny sidekick ImageReady, in version 5.5, was meant for Web people. So what *is* Photoshop 6?

It's something for everyone, professional and novice alike, and it will embrace you like an octopus.

Being something for everyone is a pretty hard task, unless you're Coca-Cola, Sara Lee, or Scot's bathroom tissue. Look, for a second, at CorelDRAW. Its developers tried to make it be *everything* to everyone a few years ago and it wound up being a disaster of an application. Disgruntled users said the program wasn't enough for *anyone*, instead of the somewhat lofty and unrealistic goal of being *everything* to everyone. But the engineers at Adobe have *almost* pulled the "something for everyone" off, and they should be commended.

Not generally known as a pioneer of features, Photoshop 6 marks the beginning of a fantastic evolution of the program. Without suffocating the user interface, you've got tools for drawing, retouching, painting, typesetting, color correction, batch processing, Web slicing, color reduction, and more. And these are all "class act" tools.

How were the Photoshop people able to pull this off? They appear to want to be second instead of first with a new feature and get it *right* the first time out. There's something to be said about sitting back a little and waiting—beware of chess players who do this to you!

So regardless of your profession, many of the following sections are going to appeal to you because we're going to work from the outside in: How you work your way from the core of Photoshop outward, and then we'll concentrate on the new features.

## The Three Ultimate Truths About Photoshop

If you understand but three things about Photoshop, you will lop off *months* in the learning curve of this program. These nuggets are as follows (and then we'll elaborate on them):

- Photoshop engineers encourage you to use layers.
- Photoshop should be handled as though it's document-centric.
- The best work you will do in Photoshop will go unnoticed.

Admittedly, these observations are a tad cryptic unless they're understood in the context—and in the workspace—of Photoshop. So let's take them one at a time.

## Photoshop Layers: A Blessing in Disguise

There was a time, as in version 3 of Photoshop, when RAM was expensive, and so were hard drives. And although a Photoshop layer didn't add exactly 50% to the overall saved file size—it did add to the file size. So we authors recommended, at regular intervals in your work, that you merge layers and save the file. This strategy helped users to complete sophisticated editing on what's considered—in terms of power today—to be an arcade gaming machine and not a personal computer.

Everything has changed in 2000. RAM is cheaper than a Happy Meal, hard drives that used to come in MB now come in GB for the same price, and Photoshop layers have fundamentally changed. Now, layers are *good!* We *like* layers! Layers no longer drag your computer to a crawl.

In Photoshop, a layer is an actual place within an image file. (Other image-editing programs treat pixels surrounded by transparency as one single object.) Photoshop lets you put a number of Clipboard image snippets (or paint) in various places on a layer. Photoshop can treat all these areas as members of a single layer or let you select individual elements on the layer. If you think of a layer as a sheet of plastic wrap on top of your image, layers will feel very comfortable as you work. Try this simple, "we don't give out grades," example.

### Example 1.1    Goofing with Layers in Photoshop

1. Create a new image by pressing Ctrl(⌘)+N. In the New dialog box, specify that the new image is 7 inches in Width, 5 inches in Height, 72 pixels per inch in Resolution, RGB color mode; click the White button in the Contents field, and then click OK.

**Note**

**Color Profiling on Startup**   If this is your first time opening Photoshop, it might ask whether you want to calibrate your system now or allow Photoshop to operate under its defaults for something called *color profiling*.

As this is being written, the defaults are not what the authors recommend. Adobe's sRGB is the default color space simply because it was this way in version 5.5—not a really good excuse for offering novices a small color space more suited for Web graphics than image retouching. But as long as you do not *save* any images you really like to the sRGB color space, the color space is serviceable for the moment.

*Please* read Chapter 3 before you get too engrossed in Photoshop's features, so that you can profile your monitor, Photoshop, and your output the way it *should* be profiled.

2. Click the Paintbrush tool on the toolbox (or press P), and then Shift+right-click (Macintosh: hold Ctrl and click), and pick the top row, far-right Brush tip. Press Enter (Return) to make the Brush palette disappear.

3. Click on the foreground color selection box on the toolbox (it's a black square when you open Photoshop for the first time). The clicking action displays the Photoshop Color Picker (see Figure 1.1). By dragging on the circle in the color field, you determine the brightness and amount of saturation of a color; and by working the hue slider directly to the right of the color field, you determine the color with which you will paint. Click OK after you've made your color choice and you're back at the untitled document you created.

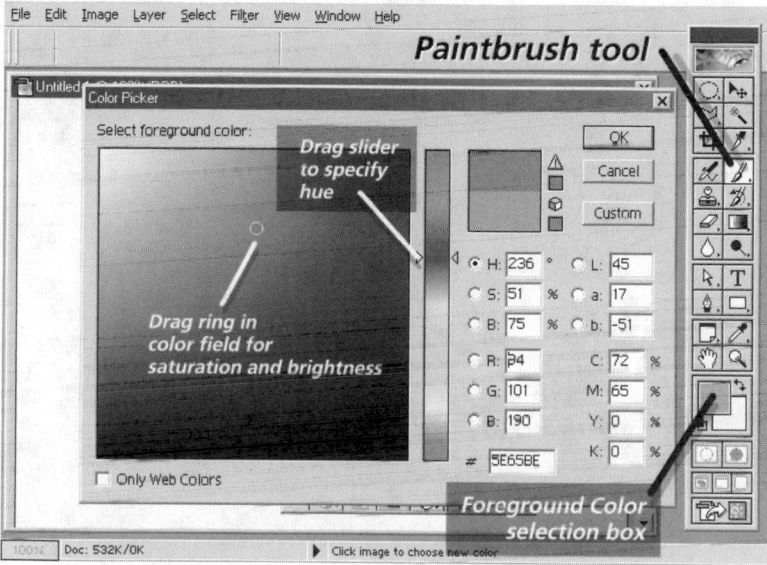

**Figure 1.1**   Photoshop's Color Picker has an easy, intuitive layout for choosing the exact color you want.

4. Paint a doodle—a shapeless blob—on the image window.

5. Click on the foreground color selection box on the toolbox and choose an entirely different color. Click OK to return to the scene.

6. Press F7 to display the Layers grouped palette in the workspace.

   This is the first shortcut you should commit to memory. You will be incessantly using the Layers, Channels, and Paths palette in your Photoshop adventures.

7. Alt(Opt)+click the Create a new layer icon at the bottom of the Layers palette, *called out* (#1) in Figure 1.2. Hold down the Shift key when you Alt(Opt)+click, and you do more than merely create a layer in the image: You get a dialog box that enables you to give the layer a name before it appears in the image window and is displayed on the Layers palette as an

image thumbnail (#2). Name the layer anything you like. (If you're stumped, **More doodles** is a perfect name.) Click OK to create the named layer.

Naming layers is a good Photoshop practice. The thumbnail images on the Layers palette don't always show you what you need to identify the contents of the layer.

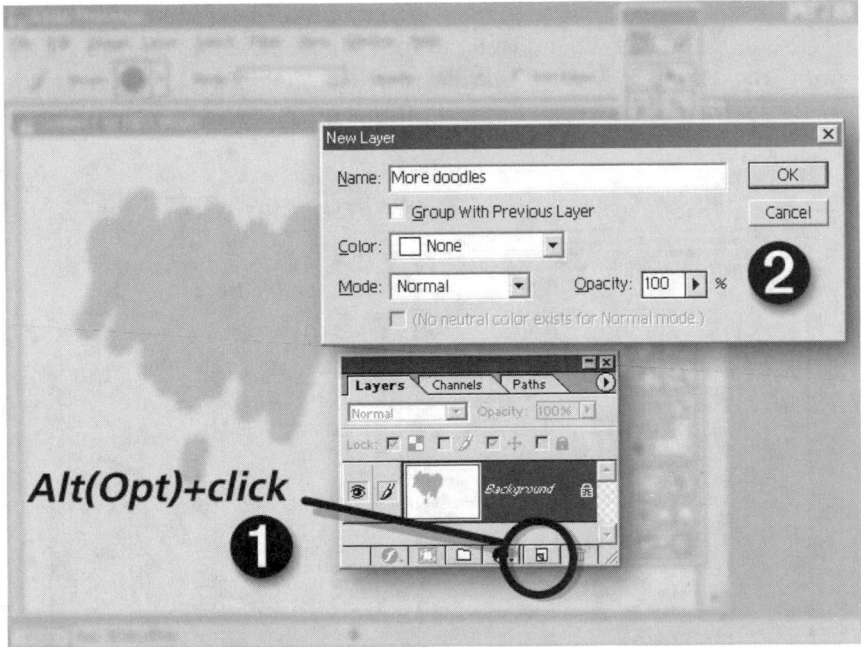

**Figure 1.2**   Name a layer and then add it to the image window.

8. Paint a doodle on the new layer and allow some of the doodle to overlap the doodle you created on the Background of the image.

9. Press V (this is the shortcut for the Move tool, another one to commit to memory because this one tool is the only one you can use to move anything on layers). Drag the doodle around the layer until the amusement fades.

10. Ctrl(⌘)+click on the layer title on the Layers palette. See the funny animated dotted line around the doodle? This is the way Photoshop shows you selections. Now, this selection is based on the geometric shape of your doodle. Although you can move the doodle with or without the selection (by using the Move tool), a creative opportunity is presented here. With a selection tool (press M, for the Rectangular Marquee tool—you'll get a more comprehensive selection education in Chapter 9), drag inside the selection *marquee* (the animated dots). You have not moved the doodle—you've only moved the selection shape of the doodle. See Figure 1.3.

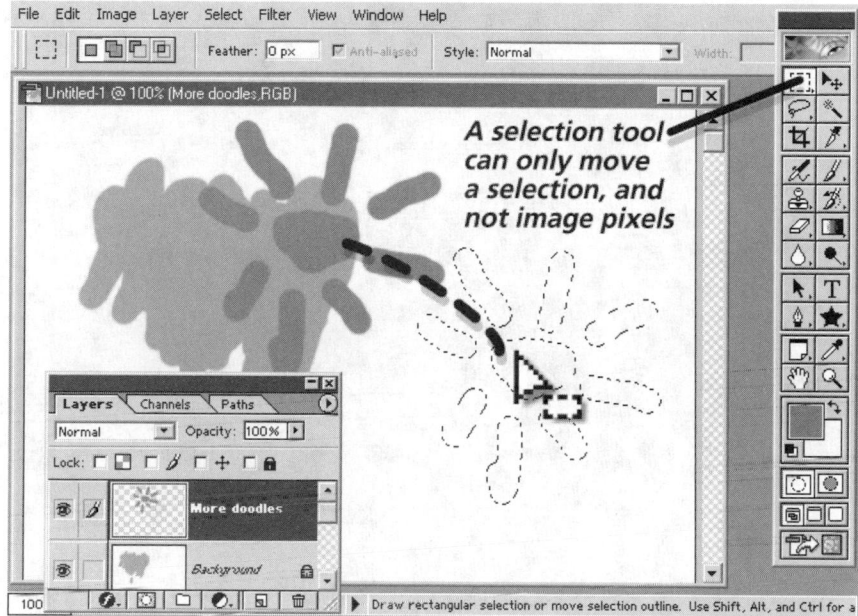

**Figure 1.3** Only the Move tool moves nontransparent areas of a layer. Selection tools are used to move only selection marquees, which are not part of a layer.

11. For kicks, press Alt(Opt)+Delete (Backspace) to fill the selection marquee with foreground color. The marquee's above the layer, but the foreground color is now *part* of the layer. Then press Ctrl(⌘)+D to deselect the marquee. It's gone—there's no chance of accidentally using it to mess up your fine work here.

12. Take a break for a second. Keep the image open.

Rest assured that the tutorials in this book are more sophisticated than this simple layers exploration, but we're trying to prove a point here: There is a *ton* of stuff you can do with layers *beyond* what you'd expect.

Ready for a short, second crack at layers?

## Example 1.2 More Weirdness with Layers

1. Click the *f* icon at the bottom of the Layers palette, as shown in Figure 1.4 (#1) and choose Bevel and Emboss from the drop-down list (#2). A huge dialog box appears (#3). You are going to turn this normal layer into an Effects layer.

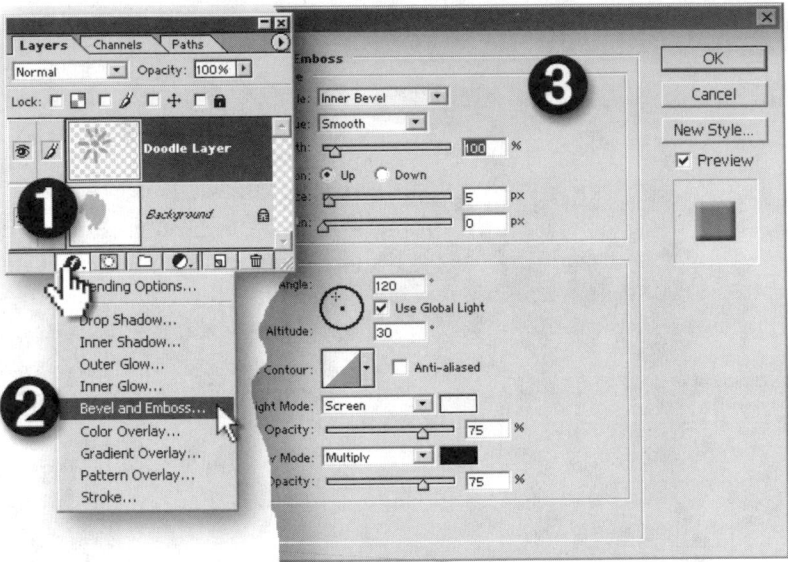

**Figure 1.4**   You have a wide range of effects that you apply to the layer, and then anything that subsequently is added to the layer takes on the same effect.

2. Drag the dialog box out of the way so you can see the doodle on the layer. Play with the Structure area controls, which are circled in Figure 1.5. We thought it was interesting to make the doodle look 3D, but do what you like—we don't grade your papers <g>.

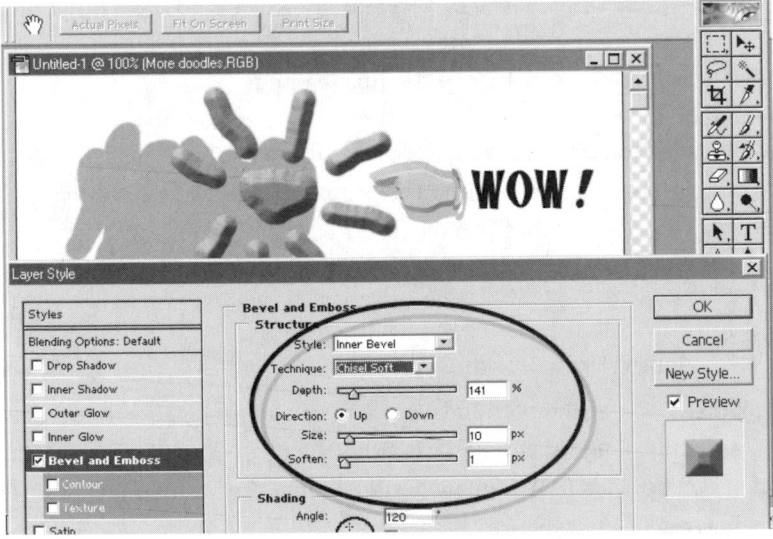

**Figure 1.5**   Add dimension to anything on a layer when you assign the layer one or more effects.

3. Paint away on the layer. As you can see, everything you paint has the same Bevel and Emboss effect.

4. Finally, with the Move tool (V), move the layer over so that your primary doodle eclipses the doodle on the Background. With the Move tool, everything on a layer moves unless you move an area that has a selection marquee active around it. So don't be surprised when everything moves!

5. On the Layers palette, click the drop-down modes blending list (it says Normal by default), and choose Exclusion. You can't see it very well in Figure 1.6, but everywhere the two doodles intersect, the color of the doodle on the layer takes on the color of the doodle on the Background. And where the doodles don't overlap, the doodle on the layer reverses color—green becomes magenta, for example. And this is only one blending mode for layers.

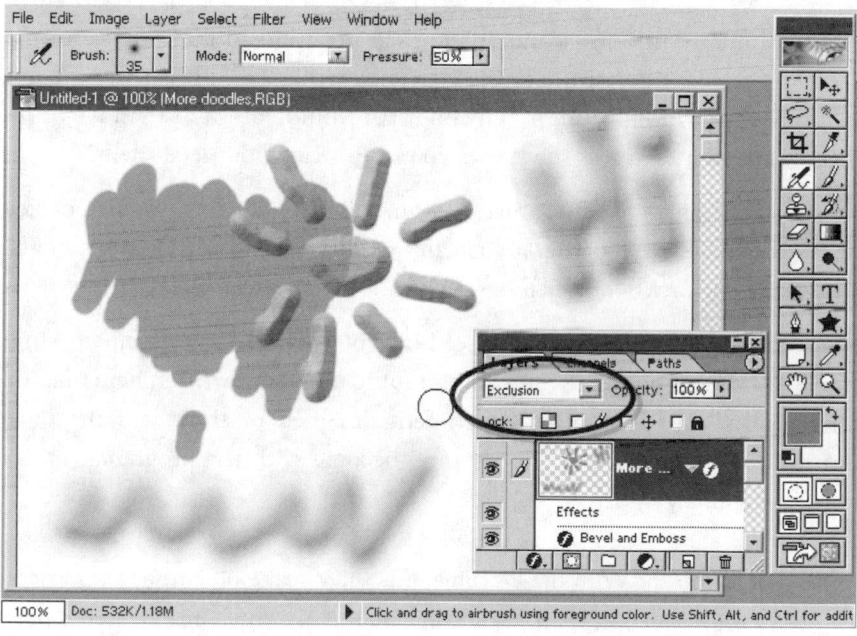

**Figure 1.6**  Layer blending modes enable you to creatively merge designs on different layers.

6. Okay, enough about layers. You can close the image at any time without saving it.

Is that the story with layers? Hardly. The preceding steps covered only about 25% of what you can do with layers. You also have Adjustment layers, clipping groups on layers, clipping paths on layers, Opacity changes on layers...and these are only *features;* we haven't talked *at all* about creative techniques!

Have we justified making the importance of layers the first of the Three Ultimate Truths? <g>

## Everything Revolves Around the Document (Document-Centricity)

We realize that surgeons might send us mail about the following analogy, but here goes:

If you've ever seen a group of surgeons working on a patient, the lead surgeon is constantly being handed the tools s/he calls for, and the current tool is taken away. Now, to an insensitive clod, this might be seen as service you'd only dream of in a restaurant. But let's get serious for a moment—operating room procedures are created to maximize efficiency, and that's why the surgeon doesn't have to leave a patient (who's usually wide open) to go and hunt down some suture and clips.

(Vaguely) similarly, artists, by their nature, do not want to go hunting for the linseed oil, the turpentine, or the brush they need while working on wet canvas. The same thing is true in Photoshop. Why on earth would you want to move the cursor all over the screen to access the things you need when you need them?

Photoshop 6, more than any other version, has adopted this practice of keeping your hands where they belong. If you can memorize some keyboard shortcuts, you can keep the cursor where it belongs—on your work.

Come along on a short excursion to see how you might find yourself working after you've finished this book. It's more important to do what's written here than to realize the results. This is only an experiment designed to show you the power of Photoshop, not how good you'll instantly become with the program. That's what the *rest* of the book is for!

### Example 1.3    Working With the Document as the Visual Hub in the Workspace

1. Press Ctrl(⌘)+N, and then press Enter (Return). You've just created a new document window using whatever the previous settings were.

2. Press F8 to display the Info palette, as shown in Figure 1.7. Click the XY crosshairs, and choose pixels from the flyout list. Everything—the Image Size, Canvas size, rulers, the kitchen sink—will now be displayed in units of pixels instead of inches or other units of measurement.

3. Suppose you change your mind and want inches as the global unit. Press Ctrl(⌘)+R to display the rulers, and then double-click on a ruler. Doing this takes you to the Rulers & Units Preferences dialog box. Choose Inches from the Rulers drop-down box, and then press Enter (Return).

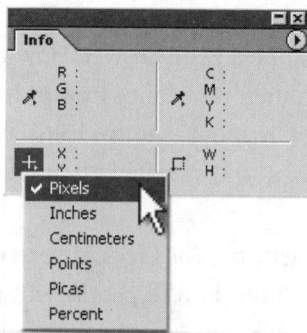

**Figure 1.7**   You pressed a key, you clicked an area, you clicked a preference, and now all of the units displayed for design areas will be read out in units of pixels.

4. Suppose you want to make the canvas (the image window) smaller. Right-click (Macintosh: hold Ctrl and click) on the image window title bar, and then choose Canvas Size from the drop-down menu.

5. Enter any new values you like in the Canvas Size dialog box. The important thing to see here is that the dimensions are offered in Inches, as you specified in step 3. Press Enter (Return) to exit the box.

6. Press M (Marquee tool—the rectangular one will probably be the one chosen if you have not played in Photoshop before reading this). Drag a selection marquee in the image window, and then right-click (Macintosh: hold Ctrl and click).

7. From the context menu, choose Layer via Cut. If the Layers palette is not onscreen at the moment, press F7. You will see that a new layer is in the image, and a hole has been cut out of the Background.

8. Press D. This sets the colors on the toolbox to black foreground and white background. Press B and make a few paint strokes in the window. Press X. This swaps the foreground and background colors, and you can paint over some of your design.

9. Hold down Ctrl(⌘)+spacebar. Surprise! Your new tool (for as long as you hold these keys) is the Zoom in tool. Click a few times in the image window to zoom in.

10. Release the Ctrl(⌘) key. While holding down the spacebar, pan the image window's contents by simply dragging.

11. Press B for the Paintbrush tool again, and then press 5. Yoiks! You are now painting at 50% opacity. Press 0 to return to 100% opacity.

12. Press Ctrl(⌘)+W to close this image window, and answer No when asked whether you want to save this masterpiece.

Do you have any idea by how few pixels your cursor traveled to do all that stuff in steps 1–12? "Very few" would be a good answer. How about the speed with which you could change things? Wouldn't it be nice to work this way on your *own* pieces? That's *another* thing this book is about, and we think we've proven Ultimate Truth Number Two.

## Your Best Work in Photoshop Will Go Unnoticed

Say *what*? You work hard in Photoshop so people will ignore your labors? Em, not exactly. Think of yourself as a special effects department while you work in Photoshop. We aren't surprised at all that John Knoll, the co-creator of Photoshop back in the late 1980s, is presently heading up George Lucas' Industrial Light & Magic (ILM). Do you think he rose to this position because you could "see the wires" in films in which he worked? Absolutely not. Rent a copy of *Mission: Impossible*, and fast forward to the scene where Tom Cruise is fighting with Jon Voight, and Jean Reno is following in a helicopter. All of this takes place while they're riding atop a high-speed underground transit from England to France.

Now, everyone knew that there had to be some special effects during this grip-your-seat scene, but after watching it a few times, this author still cannot tell how it was done. That's the whole point. It's *okay* if people think you created a special effect—but it's *not* okay (IOW, you failed in Photoshop) if people can point to the exact location where you did your retouching. There are many examples in this book of the plausible and the implausible, but photographically, all the images are firmly rooted in visual reality.

Here's a good example. In Figure 1.8, Gary K., our co-author and frequent tech editor, is either standing next to his identical twin, or else someone did some really good make-up work on a stand-in. Or...Photoshop was used to its peak, allowing the artist to carefully graft two separate poses.

Be honest. How many people will immediately assume that this is a picture of twins? This is proof positive of Ultimate Truth Number Three.

Every day, you see advertisements whose products have been retouched using Photoshop, and photographs in the tabloids where people's heads have been inexpertly swapped onto other people's bodies. Practically every 3D-computer graphic in Hollywood has been passed through Photoshop for a clean up, and the corner film store probably offers photo-renewal services for those shoebox pictures you thought could never look good again.

**Figure 1.8**   Reality is what you make it in Photoshop.

In a way, the best Photoshop work *idealizes reality*. Photoshoppers are indeed in the business of reality. We shudder when we hear people talking about the visual lies that digital image editing offers. There's good and bad in every business.

The authors are here to teach you how to be the *best*.

We think that covers our Ultimate Truths. Now, on to explaining some of the finer points of Photoshop—what you can expect from it, what it requires from you, and a small revelation here and there.

## Quick Keys to Get You Going in the Right Direction

As promised, we have some version 6 keyboard shortcuts for you that will keep your cursor closer to your work, and not incessantly trying to pry the lid off the main menu for important but too-well-hidden stuff.

Here goes, in easy chart format. You might want to photocopy Table 1.1 and stick it next to your computer. This is not as comprehensive as Photoshop's Quick Start Guide, but we feel these are the most important commands and the ones you'll want to memorize.

**Table 1.1   Essential Keyboard Shortcuts**

| What You Press | What It Does |
| --- | --- |
| F7 | Toggles Layers/Channels/Paths palette |
| F8 | Toggles Info palette |
| Ctrl(⌘)+Shift+I | Creates the inverse of the current selection marquee |
| Ctrl(⌘)+spacebar | Toggles to Zoom In tool |
| Ctrl(⌘)+Alt(Opt)+spacebar | Toggles to Zoom Out tool |
| Ctrl(⌘)+Plus key | Zooms in |
| Ctrl(⌘)+Minus key | Zooms out |
| Spacebar | Toggles to Hand tool |
| M* | Marquee tool |
| L* | Lasso tool |
| B* | Paintbrush tool |
| Right-click (Macintosh: hold Ctrl and click) | Displays Context menu |
| Ctrl(⌘)+T | Displays Transform box around current selection |
| Ctrl(⌘)+L | Levels command |
| Ctrl(⌘)+U | Hue/Saturation command |
| Ctrl(⌘)+B | Color Balance command |
| Keypad numbers | Increase or decrease opacity by 10% |
| If you press two numbers in quick succession, such as 4,5, you get 45% opacity. | |
| V | Move tool |
| Ctrl(⌘) held with a selection tool | Move tool |
| Ctrl(⌘)+R | Rulers |
| Ctrl(⌘)+H | Hide screen elements, usually the marquee selections |
| Ctrl(⌘)+D | Deselect active selection |
| Ctrl(⌘)+A | Select all |

*By holding Shift, and repeatedly pressing these keys, you toggle through the hidden tools you'd normally have to go fetch by clicking+holding on the face of a tool.

Again, this is not a complete list of shortcuts, but you will find as you edit images, you will tend to memorize these to speed up your work. Use 'em in combination with the Context menu.

By the way, all system keyboard shortcuts work in Photoshop. Ctrl(⌘)+C is Copy, Ctrl(⌘)+V is Paste, Ctrl(⌘)+N is New, and so on.

# At What Does Photoshop Excel?

In addition to Photoshop's features and powers, it also has some character. Let's get real: You don't have 40 engineers working on a product and have it come out faceless! By character, we mean that Photoshop has strengths and preferences that are coded into it—a program that approaches having honest-to-gosh traits.

And by understanding these traits, you will come closer to understanding the Zen of Photoshop.

## Photoshop Is the Great Integrator

Some very talented Photoshoppists never paint or create anything in Photoshop. That is because Photoshop is terrific at being the host to media created in other applications. You can render a 3D model, perform some nozzle work in Painter, render an illustration in Illustrator—and import a digitized photo, and seamlessly sew all of them together in Photoshop.

Photoshop has many, many import and export filters, and this is part of the reason it's the ideal workspace for mixed media. The rest of the reason it's such a good creative host is that no matter what you import to Photoshop, all art is eventually converted to pixels, and there is no difference between a pixel from a photo and a pixel from art designed in a vector program. Where all the pixels came from is of no concern. You learn Photoshop's tools and develop your technique, and very quickly you will find that Photoshop is the only logical place to assemble your fantastic work.

## Photoshop Has Become Everyone's Tool

Photoshop has so many diverse features that regardless of what profession you're in, regardless of what applications you've used in the past, Photoshop will probably fit your specific need(s). As mentioned earlier, Photoshop does not try to accommodate all of everyone's needs, but there are top-notch tools in Photoshop that folks from all types of trades seek.

The photographer couldn't ask for a more sumptuous digital darkroom. For production and prepress people, version 6 has the features for consistent, predictable output to film or paper. For the artist, Photoshop blends the best of the worlds of pixels and vectors into a tightly integrated package that is user friendly.

But you'll learn all of this as you proceed through the book. No matter what you do for a living or hobby, if it has to do with visual expression, chances are Photoshop fits the bill as your core application.

## There's More Than One Way to Do It in Photoshop

Don't you hate it when you're halfway through something in an application, only to discover that the application has limited features? Worse still, don't you lose a little hair out of frustration when you find you must perform 45 steps to arrive at a step that logically should be right out in the open?

One of Photoshop's traditional strengths has always been that it has about a zillion ways to perform a task, so you're never stifled with that "you can't get there from here" feeling. If one method fails, there are almost certainly two or three other ways to accomplish the same thing. For example, there are nine different types of selection tools on the toolbox alone, as shown in Figure 1.9. Add to this the capability to select by shape, by color, by image layer, and by mask, and you have over 15 ways to select part of an image. "Stifling," it *isn't!*

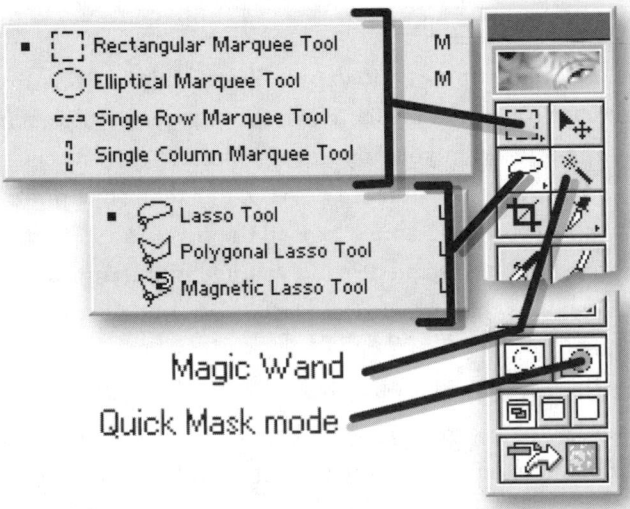

**Figure 1.9**   On Photoshop's toolbox alone, there are nine tools for selecting areas of an image.

As another example, Adobe understands that you need a custom view of an image that changes as you refine a piece. That is why you have not only two different ways of zooming from the keyboard, but also the Zoom tool on the toolbox. Additionally, you can use the keyboard to zoom in and out of an image (most of the time) while you have a dialog box open. This means, for instance, that you can zoom into a small area while you are operating the Levels command, and use the Levels command eyedropper to precisely pick a tone.

So, you don't have to back out of commands because you've forgotten procedures in Photoshop. As you read this book, you'll discover additional methods for making selections, and painting and modifying work, and indeed you can develop your own personal style of working in Photoshop.

## You Made a Good Investment That Will Grow with You

Photoshop will grow with you. In fact, the authors exhaustively research every new version, only to find that a *new* version pops up before we've experimented with all the tools in the current version!

They say that most good applications are used to only about 10% of their capability. If you're new to Photoshop, you will get an *excellent* 10% return on your efforts—even using one or two of the features will pay off with handsome work. As you grow more experienced, you will demand more of yourself and your applications. Guess what? Photoshop's still the one for you. From special effects to system and commercial press color calibration, Photoshop is the professional imaging tool...that *beginners* can get into.

## Photoshop's More Than an Application—It's an Environment

Through its features, Photoshop is trying to be an *environment,* not simply an application for creativity. This is the age-old WordPerfect philosophy—you start your machine, launch into WordPerfect (or Photoshop 6) and you stay there until the 5 o'clock whistle.

You need vector tools? Photoshop has them. You want Acrobat output? You've got it. You need expertly spaced text? Photoshop now has both Character and Paragraph palettes for adjusting text onscreen instead of in a dialog box (as in previous versions). You need special effects but can't afford third-party plug-ins? Photoshop has over 100 creative filters that can be applied to a selection or to a whole layer, continually updating as you add paint or a selection to that layer. You even have optimized Web output!

Quite literally, what more could you ask from a creative application?

You've tried out a few of the tools so we could prove a point, and you've heard our speculations as to why things are the way they are in Photoshop. Now it's time to level the playing field and introduce some new features in version 6 that will amaze both the newcomer and the seasoned pixel pusher.

# Terms and Features New to Photoshop

Photoshop 6 comes with features, some of which have obvious names, while other are quite cryptic. We'll show as many of these new features as possible (and only the really good ones). We want you to be as familiar as possible with them, in case you skip over a chapter that highlights one or two.

### First Class File Formats

It seems as though it's been forever that Photoshop has offered around 19 different import and export options. So chances were that if you had a pixel-based image, Photoshop could read it.

However, different file formats have different capabilities. The most obvious example is the GIF file format, to which you cannot save more than 256 unique colors. At the other end of the spectrum, just about everything you decided to toss into a Photoshop native PSD file would stay there; other applications usually wouldn't open a PSD file; and the "extras" you placed in the file—the special information— would remain intact until you opened the image again in Photoshop.

Adobe has opened the First Class file format to TIFF and Acrobat PDF formats with this version. This means that anything you can save in a PSD format image, you can also save in the PDF and TIFF formats. And this is pretty wonderful, considering that you can now save text as vector text in a PDF file. This author used to use only PageMaker to make PDF files, but now he has a second application that's Acrobat capable.

Some surprises may leap out at you with the TIFF file format. For years, our books have recommended TIFF as

- The most robust image exchange between the Macintosh and Windows.
- The only file format that hangs onto image resolution. Now, PNG does image resolution, but all other file formats that are not proprietary to Photoshop (PICT, BMP, Targa) default to screen resolution.

With version 6, we feel it's necessary to gently inform you that you should flatten a copy of an image before saving it as a TIFF. Adobe is the official keeper of the TIFF standard, and this new TIFF (version 7) was brought out in response to video people who want layers in videos.

By default, Photoshop will not save all the extras to the TIFF file format, but you want to watch that Save As dialog box when you do save. Make certain no

Photoshop extras (except an alpha channel, if you want one) are included by checked boxes in the Save dialog box.

There is a possibility for errors, not in file formats, but in communication with your client now that a Photoshop TIFF need no longer have the limitations it used to have. Not everyone is going out to buy Photoshop 6 when their graphics needs are limited to viewing files.

For example, if your client still owns a Macintosh Classic running MacPaint, or Windows 3.0 featuring PC Paintbrush, it's safe to assume they will not be able to read TIFF version 7.

So flatten that file before you save a copy.

## Options Bar

This element of the screen is where you find options pertaining to the currently chosen tool. It can be undocked from its position at the top of the screen and placed at the bottom of the screen, but that's about it because it cannot be resized. Whenever you select a tool and want to do something special with it, chances are that the option you seek is on the Options bar. Also, many tools have an options drop-down list that is accessed from the Options bar for even more tool customization. For experienced Photoshop users, this bar replaces the Options palette and the Brushes palette. After using the Options bar for several months, the authors give it a big thumbs up because never again do we have to search for the location of the Options palette. Additionally, for new users, we feel this is the right start for having access to as many controls as possible in Photoshop while still keeping a pretty healthy area of the workspace sparse and uncluttered. You can see the Options bar in Figure 1.6.

## Boolean Selection Mode

This is an author-generated name for the four buttons that are frequently on the Options bar when selection and shape (path tools) are chosen. In Figure 1.10, we've called out what each button does. Now, clipping paths aren't as straightforward in their operations as selections are. In Add mode, when you add a path to a path, the intersecting region is *not* eliminated. Nope. But a *fill* you apply via the Paths palette will fill the intersecting region. Also, a selection based on the current path positions will weld the selections, eliminating the overlapping area, so a fill is applied to all the interior of the added selections. If you play with clipping paths on a layer along with these Boolean buttons, you'll create some interesting shapes. Check out Chapter 12 for the full story on the new Shapes tools.

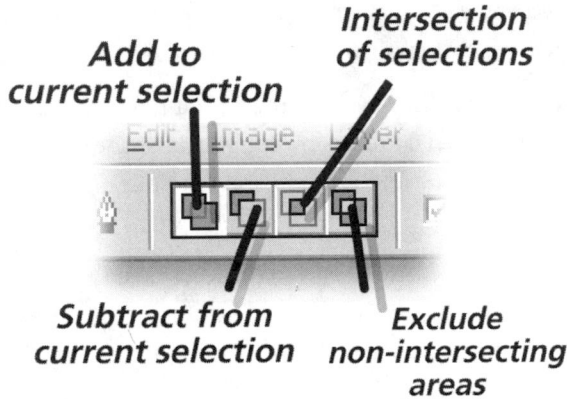

**Figure 1.10**    *Boolean operations* is the math term used to describe the outcome of adding, subtracting, intersecting, and performing other events on two or more areas. Controls for selections and path fills can be found on the Options bar.

## Palette Well

When you are running video resolutions greater than 800×600, you will see a palette well at the far right of the Options bar. What you can do is drop your palettes in the well, and then click on their title tabs to activate them, as shown in Figure 1.11. Nice feature, but we feel it would make more sense to offer a palette well to those who are *not* running high resolutions and don't have a lot of space to spare!

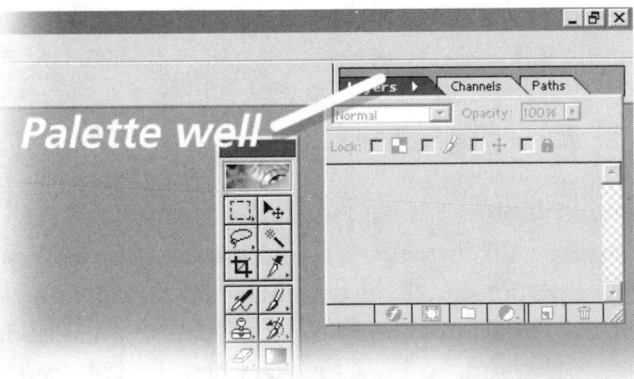

**Figure 1.11**    The palette well is only visible (and usable) at greater than 800×600 pixel video resolution.

## Layer Locking

We used to have only Preserve Transparency on the Layers palette. This was a good feature; it kept you from accidentally painting on an area that was transparent—that you could see through to the underlying layers. Now the palette is designed so that beginners can make their layer work goof-proof—and come to think of it, it'll be a hit with experienced users, too. Use these options and you cannot accidentally move or paint on a layer you specify by clicking on its title.

See Figure 1.12? That's the story.

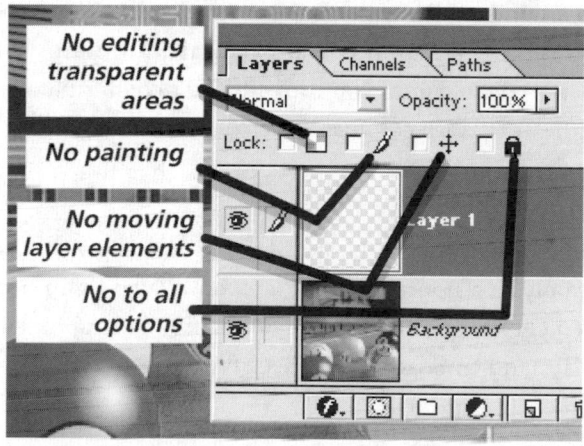

**Figure 1.12**  Layers can be made edit-proof, move-proof, and all protection options can be activated at once.

## Shape Tools

These new tools are grouped on the toolbox: the Rectangular, Ellipse, Polygonal, and Line tools, and most notably the Custom Shape tool. To add some of the core features of Illustrator to Photoshop, this group of tools can be used to create shapes that are crisp when printed (because they are vector in nature, not bitmap). You can also use a shape in combination with an image to make the outside areas transparent, and then import the image to PageMaker, where only the interior of the shape is visible. See Chapter 12 for the story on this fascinating addition to Photoshop.

## Open Recent

This is a new feature for Macintosh users; Windows users are accustomed to finding a similar File command at the bottom of the File menu. Open Recent enables you to quickly load files you've used recently. The Preferences menu (see Chapter 4) enables you to specify the number of recent files you want on the list. The authors prefer 8; the default is 4 under Saving Files.

### Paragraph Palette and Character Palette

You'll welcome these new typesetting features. Basically, anything you can do in a DTP program you can now do in Photoshop, from leading to kerning to mixing typefaces. And the best thing of all—particularly for experienced users—is that text is now directly entered in an image. No more Texas-sized dialog box in which to guess your way around while type of the wrong size is entered in the image! Additionally, you can use a new Text Warp command to warp your text, and the warped text remains editable until you convert it to pixel format. See Chapter 13 to get a handle on the Text Warp command.

### Styles Palette

This feature can be found in both Photoshop and ImageReady. Basically, a style is something you apply to a nontransparent area on a layer in an image by selecting the area, and then clicking on a style icon. Styles are made up of Layer Effects such as gradient overlays and embosses. You'll see styles used and hand-modified in the ImageReady chapters in this book.

Well, we think you can sail through this book now, if you like, instead of running ashore left and right with all this definition stuff. In fact, if you remember half of it, you might be mistaken for a keynote speaker at Comdex instead of an attendee at refreshment hour!

## The Verdict?

Naturally, you expect us to come to an overall observation about this version of the world's most popular image editing software.

Well, to be honest, our heads are still aching, but it's a *good* kind of aching—the sort you feel after encountering all the wisdom in the Universe, and then being told you have half an hour to soak it all up. But we're not going to do this to you—we've done the studying so that we can better distill what you need to know in a well-organized, occasionally entertaining, silly way.

There's a lot of ground to cover. In Photoshop 6, at least 40% of the features are new, modified, or improved. So hang on to your hats as we take a crack at teaching you these features—and how they are used to create something that's artistically compelling.

## Summary

Hopefully, you now understand why most non-artists *don't* understand what Photoshop is. It's an omnibus suite of tools that, armed with some understanding, you can quickly walk away from with exactly what you've envisioned—and it wouldn't hurt if you walked away with an award or two! Don't let this chapter intimidate you—we've got the rest of this book to put new and/or confusing existing features under the microscope and thoroughly investigate them.

The purpose of this chapter, in addition to mentioning new features, is to get you into the "Photoshop head." You'll be amazed at what you can do if you meet this program halfway.

In Chapter 2, we indulge your's, our's, everyone's secret whim—to play with a sophisticated application, having absolutely *no* background, and get some very interesting results. We call it "Getting Your Feet Wet," and it's such an exhilarating experience (somewhat like driving a car for the first time), we may need to toss you a rope before you go wading in Photoshop beyond way above the knees!

# Chapter 2

# Getting Your Feet Wet: Your First Masterpiece

The authors had a hard time deciding

on a name for this chapter. We thought

of "Flying Solo Without Lessons,"

"Working with Power Tools without Reading the Instructions," and the ever-popular, "Running with the Scissors into the Pool, Right After Eating." None of them did much for us, and hopefully not for you, either. Our point is to present you with some "good stuff" right up front in this book. Does an understanding of Photoshop have to come before you experiment with it? We believe the answer is "no"—you can't accidentally break anything in Photoshop. You probably want to see some magic before, say, you reach Chapter 20 in this book, and we want to get you excited ASAP.

Therefore, we settled on "Getting Your Feet Wet" for this chapter's title for two reasons:

- It describes the exciting beginning of an adventure. Who knows? Every champion swimmer had to begin by getting their feet wet.
- The image you'll work with is all about the ocean and the beach, and oddly enough is called WetFeet.psd.

So let's get to it. There are only a few things we need to state up front, and you'll be paddling around in Photoshop's workspace without water wings before you know it.

## Understanding the Bottom of Photoshop: Selections and Layers

To swim to the top in Photoshop (okay, we're knocking off the water metaphors now), you have to understand what Photoshop is all about. Here are a couple of paragraphs that took more time to write than you'd imagine because they not only give you a terse description of what Photoshop can mean to you, they're also a definition of the program.

Photoshop is both an editor and a creator of artistic pieces made up of pixels, the smallest unit of "canvas" in which you can work. Photoshop is not a drawing program such as Illustrator or CorelDRAW; a file in a drawing program is actually made up of a bunch of math applications written to a printer, a file, or to the screen. Illustrator is a vector application and not a pixel application. Pixels can be used to re-create continuous tone photographs, usually called *digitized images*.

What sets Photoshop apart from other image editing programs, such as Paint Shop Pro? The answer is the elegance of the selection tools, and the convenience of layers. Layers and selections make up more than 50% of Photoshop's power—if you understand how to manipulate selections and layers in Photoshop, you will become a better designer than you could by using some other program (and the authors have *tried* just about every program in the past 10 years).

A *selection* (as you'll really understand by working through Chapter 9) is an area you define in an image, using any one of at least 14 selection methods. You can select image areas with Lasso tools (you simply drag around the area you want to select), you can use paths you create and then turn into selections, you can select by color, by where you paint using a special tint called Quick Mask, and you can select something if it's on a layer.

Layers are like sheets of acetate where you can put one or many distinct areas. You can paste Clipboard contents into an image window to create contents on their own layer. You can create a new layer and paint on it, change the opacity of paint on a layer, change how it looks when blended with underlying layers, and you can even reorder and delete layers.

*Whew*. That was the entire book's contents! We're kidding, of course. The preceding paragraphs simply point to what's in store with the tutorials you'll run in this chapter. Yeah, we'll do a little color correction and painting, but basically we will make every effort to explain the way selections and layers work—in a fun and graphical way. Hey, there's enough dry stuff out there to read—art is an organic process, and understanding it is going to get you wet!

## Selections and Layers: A Micro-Tutorial

It's unfair for us to ask you to take the plunge before you've had a chance to orient yourself with this selection and layers stuff. Therefore, we have the world's simplest, least challenging set of steps for you to perform with the world's simplest image to give you a feel for layers and selections.

Once you've worked a little with the tools and features, then it will be time for work on a more challenging piece of art:

### Example 2.1    Introducing Layers and Selections

1. Open the Hamburger.tif image from the Examples/Chap02 folder on the Companion CD.

   As you can see on the toolbox, there's a Lasso tool (See Figure 2.1).

   This is a selection creation tool, but "the pros" use it only on special occasions. It's a freeform tool; your selection can be any shape you like—there are no constraints. Um, it is a good idea to close the selection (by releasing the mouse button) when you return to the beginning of the selection.

> **Warning!**   If an error message appears when you open the CD files, press Ctrl(⌘)+Shift+K and then choose Adobe RGB (1998) from the Working Spaces, RGB drop-down list. See Chapter 3 for more information.

2. Try to define a selection around the edge of the burger, using the Lasso tool. Take your time.

   As you'll probably experience (and as shown in Figure 2.1), even with a point-and-click device as precise as a stylus and digitizing tablet, you cannot make a precise outline selection around the burger. Hey, this is okay; you're not using the right tool to select the burger, but we'll get there. There are more than a dozen different ways to select areas in Photoshop. Let's try a different tool.

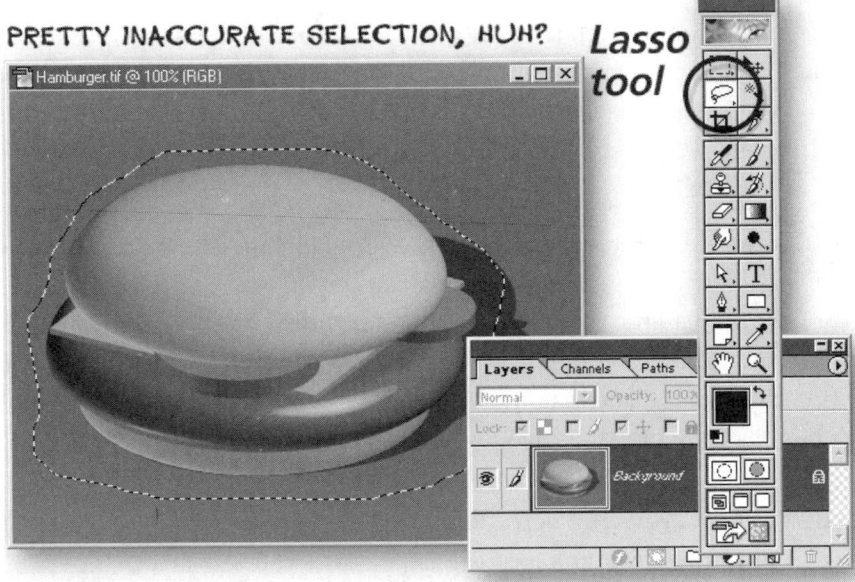

**Figure 2.1**    The Lasso tool is only one of Photoshop's selection tools. Every tool has its strengths—the Lasso tool's is not accuracy.

3. Choose the Paintbrush tool from the toolbox, and then click the down arrow to the right of the Brush icon on the Options bar at the top of the screen. Choose the brush at the far right in the top row. You're going to select the burger by painting a tint overlay on it, an overlay that can then be converted to a selection. This tint overlay is called *Quick Mask*, and to use it, you must be in Quick Mask mode. Look at Figure 2.2, where we have already begun masking with the Paintbrush tool. You want the Quick Mask icon to look like a shaded circle inside a rectangle. If it does not look like this, hold down the Alt key and then click the icon. Then start painting the interior of the burger.

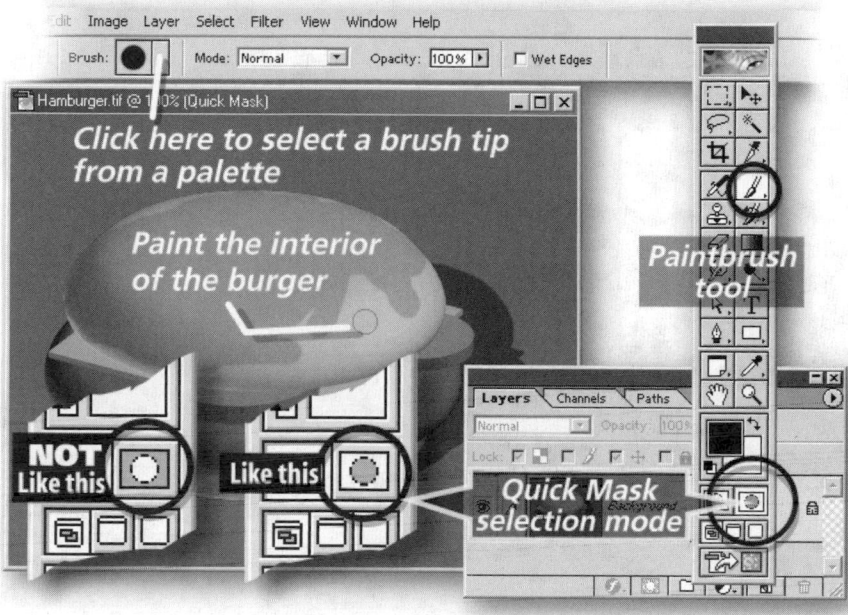

**Figure 2.2** Painting a tint overlay (Quick Mask) is yet another way to select something—and this method is inherently more accurate than the Lasso tool.

**Tip**

**Undoing Mistakes** If you make a mistake, press X to swap foreground and background colors; then, wherever you paint, you will remove Quick Mask.

4. Click the Standard (editing) mode icon toward the bottom of the toolbox.

As you can see in Figure 2.3, we came close to, but did not exactly select the burger. There are gaps in the selection. The silhouette of the burger looks better than the Lasso tool attempt, but we know we can do better. Don't get frustrated here; we are deliberately showing you the "second best" or outright wrong tools to use, so you can better evaluate the *right* tools to use in assignments of your own.

The third time's the charm. Notice that the burger is surrounded by a deep blue color, and the color appears to be pretty uniform. Let us then select the inverse of the burger—the background—using a tool that selects by color similarity: the Magic Wand tool. You can then switch the selection to its inverse, the burger.

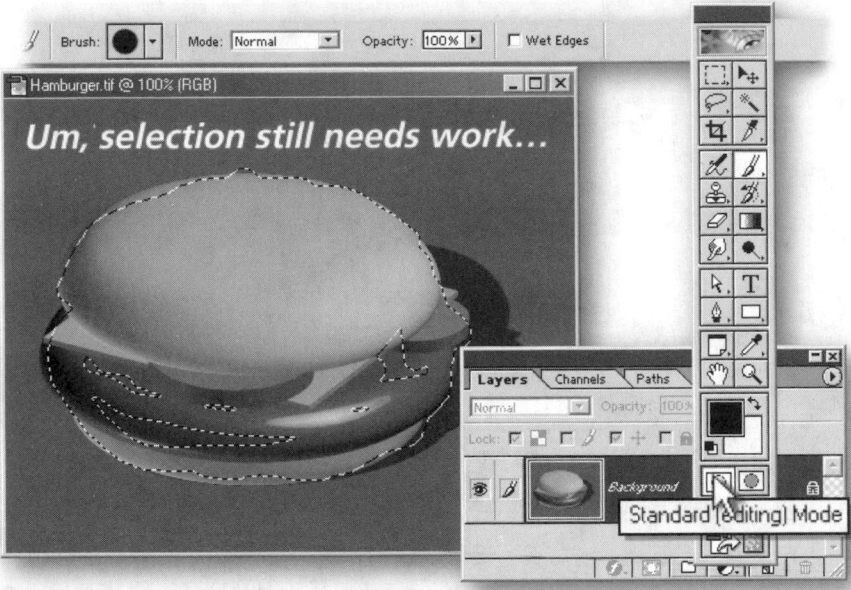

**Figure 2.3**    Quick Mask mode painting is a very good method of selection in Photoshop, but your success depends on the shape of what you are masking.

5. Choose the Magic Wand tool from the toolbox, and on the Options bar, type **32** in the Tolerance field, and check the Anti-aliased and Contiguous options. The burger has a soft edge around it where its edge pixels make a color transition to the background. That's why you need a medium-strength color Tolerance, and to have *anti-aliasing* (smoothing) turned on.

    Click, as shown in Figure 2.4.

6. Hold Shift and click in the shadow area of the burger. This adds the different shade of blue to the overall selection.

7. Press Ctrl(⌘)+Shift+I to choose the inverse of the current selection.

    Surprise! The burger is now chosen, and the selection marquee looks as though the selection fits perfectly around the silhouette of the burger. Okay, we're moving from exploring selections to layers now.

8. Right-click (Macintosh: hold Ctrl and click) and choose Layer via Copy from Photoshop's Context menu, as shown in Figure 2.5.

    You can't really see the result of what you've done because one burger is lying directly on top of the other on a different layer. Let's create some room to play here.

**Figure 2.4** Clicking with the Magic Wand tool selects similar colors within a certain tolerance you define.

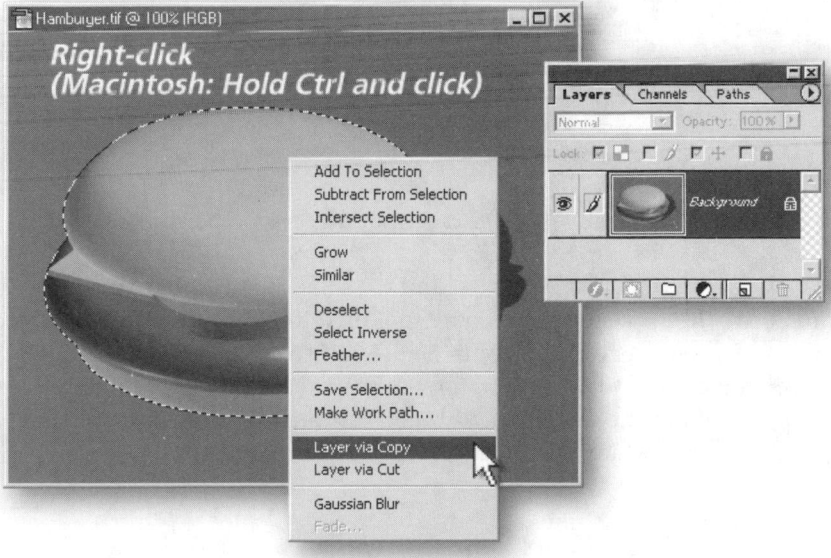

**Figure 2.5** You can send a copy of what the selection marquee is encompassing to a new layer in the image window.

9. Choose the Eyedropper tool from the toolbox. The Eyedropper tool is for applying Visine™ to the eyes of people in digital images. O*nnnnnn*ly kidding—this tool can sample either the foreground or the background color in an image. Now, because you're going to increase the size of the image window, you want the background color—the blue—to fill in where you increase the canvas. Hold Alt(Opt) and click on the background. It doesn't matter which layer is the current layer; whatever is beneath the eyedropper cursor now becomes the background color (Tiny Note: If you don't hold Alt, you determine the foreground color on the toolbox).

10. Choose Image, Canvas Size. In the Canvas Size dialog box, type **500** in the Height field (make sure pixels are the units shown in the drop-down boxes; you do *not* want a 500-inch image). Then click the bottom-center chiclet in the Anchor area—this tells Photoshop from which direction the canvas should grow (see Figure 2.6).

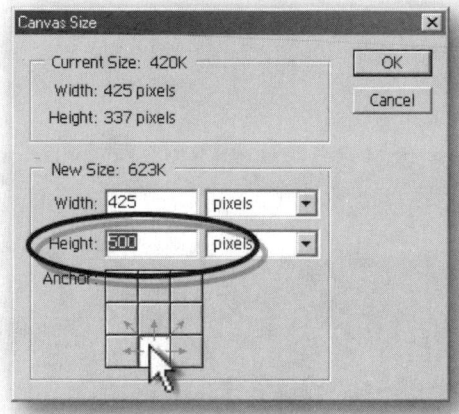

**Figure 2.6**   According to this figure, the canvas for the burger will extend upward.

11. Click OK in the Canvas Size box, and then choose the Move tool from the toolbox. The Move tool is the only tool used in Photoshop to move the contents of a layer. As you can see in Figure 2.7, Layer 1 is the name of the new layer you created when you performed the Layer via Copy command. If you drag upward in the image window, you can turn a simple burger into a double-decker, which will surely cause heartburn.

As a grand finale to our irrelevant experimenting with layers and selection in Photoshop, let's leave the image with a bang. Layers in Photoshop have both *opacity* (the degree to which you can see through objects on layers) and *blending* modes (we tend to call them simply modes in this book). *Modes* are useful for bleaching or multiplying color density in areas of a layer; we'll get to this feature later in the book.

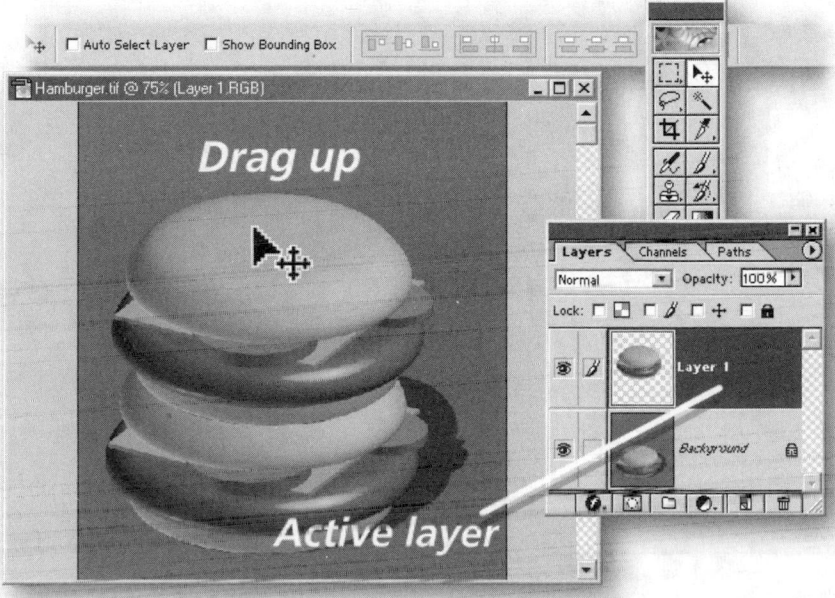

**Figure 2.7**   Drag the duplicate of the burger up so that it appears to rest on top of the original burger on the Background layer.

12. For now, hide the Background layer—you do this by clicking the eye icon to the left of the Background title. Now, all you can see is the duplicate burger on Layer 1. Type **78** in the Opacity field on the Layers palette. As you can see in Figure 2.8, you now have a GhostBurger with cheese. The checkered pattern you see is Photoshop's way of signaling you that transparency exists.

    That's it! You can close the image at any time, and the sooner, the better. Why? Because we now have a comprehensive tutorial image to play with, and there's a lot more experimentation and (gasp!) *fun* up ahead.

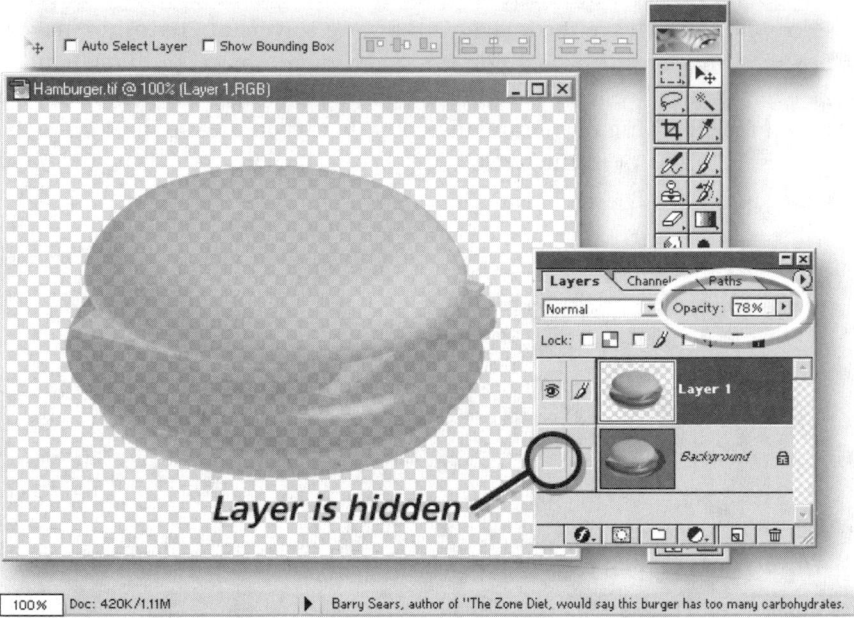

**Figure 2.8**   You can determine the opacity of the contents of any layer in an image window.

**Note**

The authors have received at least three letters in the past few years from readers who are thwarted by the mechanics of the Layers palette. The thwarting happens because they think you can edit the palette's thumbnail images themselves. Don't laugh, folks—there's a *lot* of weird stuff in Photoshop that makes no sense without guidance from experts.

For the record, the Layers palette is a navigation device—you do not change images or the contents of the layers in any way by using the palette. The palette tells you the relative position of layers in the active image window; you can specify opacity and blending modes, and you can create new layers and drag existing layers into the Trash on the Layers palette. You can also create layer masks (as you will in the following example) by using the Layers palette, but that's about it. You cannot make selections on the thumbnail images, nor can you paint on them. An image exists separately from the Layers palette—it's like the difference between the navigation controls in an airplane and the space the airplane is flying through.

## Introducing WetFeet.psd: Part Layer, Part Goof

When you open WetFeet.psd shortly, you'll realize that the authors had a lot of fun putting together the scene. Almost every cliché known to the Western world has been built into this image. But more important than the beach ball, the drowning swimmer, and the litter on the beach is the reality that everything in the image is on its own layer. Here comes a profound one:

> *Creating a scene on layers enables you to edit one element without messing up another element.*

Precision is built *into* layers—even if you have 12 thumbs, you cannot do anything unintentional if you're working on the right layer. This is extremely good news for those of you who are intimidated by the name Photoshop—let's face it, you hear "Photoshop" about as often as you hear "Scotch tape" these days—it's a registered name that people use as a generic term for computer image editing.

So let's work at a pace that lets you can soak up what you're discovering, and let's get into the beach scene. Our first stop (the authors' favorite) is to play with the sand pail in the image. Let's see how to choose it, recolor it, and add a sorely needed shadow to it on the beach. Let's face it; the scene doesn't look realistic if the pail doesn't have a shadow.

### Example 2.2    Selecting and Changing Hues

1. Open the WetFeet.psd image from the Examples/Chap02 folder on the Companion CD. If a dialog box tells you that the profile of the image does not match the current color space, click on Adobe RGB 1998 and check the box to save the image to this working space. You'll learn all about color spaces in Chapter 3. Double-click the Zoom tool (the magnifying glass button) on the toolbox to zoom the image to 100% viewing resolution. Drag the corners away from the center of the image if you have scroll bars on the window edges.

2. Choose the Move tool, the upper-right tool on the toolbox. This tool moves the contents of layers, and it can be used also in lieu of the Layers palette to move to different layers, making them active and editable.

3. Right-click (Macintosh: hold Ctrl and click) on the pail in the image, as shown in Figure 2.9. This image has 10 layers—there are only 2 where you clicked: the pail and the background. Choose Lighter shade of pail from the pop-up list. You're now working on a layer that contains only the pail and shovel.

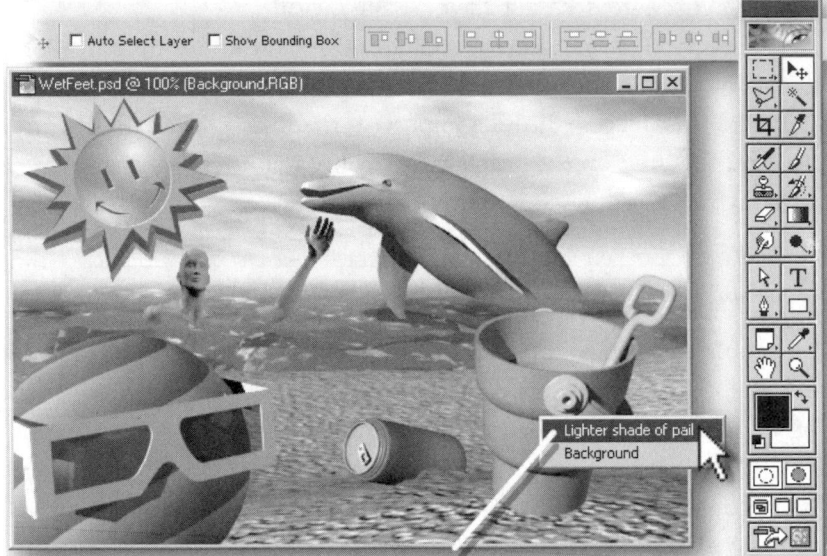

**Right-click (Mac:Hold Ctrl+click) when Move tool is chosen**

**Figure 2.9**   From the layer pop-up list, choose the layer you want to edit. Different areas in the image will have different layers as choices on the pop-up list. It's all determined by where you click and whether there's an opaque area where you click.

4. Press Ctrl(⌘)+U to display the Hue/Saturation dialog box. In the dialog box, drag the Hue slider to +143. Hmmm...the colors are different but a little too intense (saturated). Drag the Saturation slider to –39, as shown in Figure 2.10.

   Okay, this is one of those figures that tells you less than looking at your monitor (hopefully, a color model) tells you. The turquoise pail turns to magenta, the golden handle bolts turn blue, and the pink shovel handle turns lime. Weird, huh? Click OK to apply the changes.

5. Press F7 to display the Layers palette, and then click on the Lighter shade of pail title. Now, Alt(Opt)+click the Create new layer icon, as shown in Figure 2.11. The Alt modifier key causes a dialog box to appear; this is where you get to name the layer instead of allowing a layer with a default name to be added to the image. In the Name field, type **Pail shadow**, and then press Enter (Return).

   Oh, oops. We forgot to tell you that each new layer is created directly *above* the current editing layer, which in this scene is the Lighter shade of pail. However, the shadow needs to go *behind* the Lighter shade of pail layer. Bouton, what *were* you thinking? Okay, calm yourself.

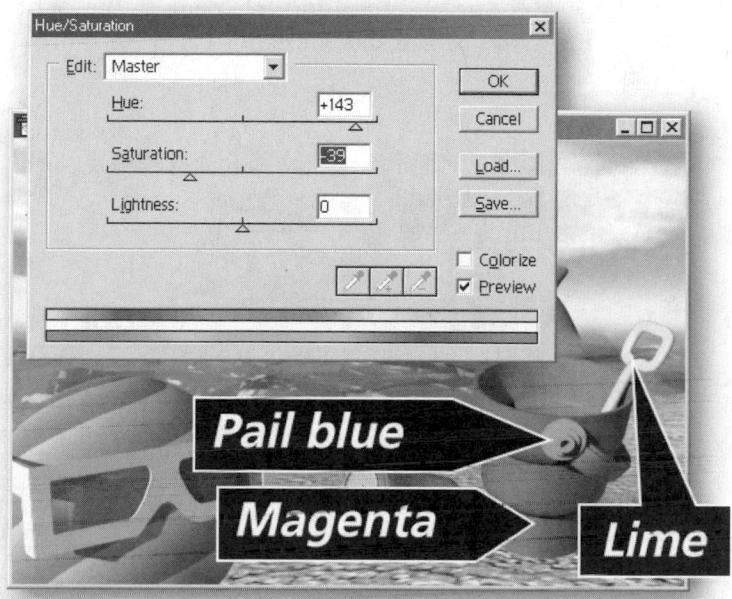

**Figure 2.10**    Shift the hue of everything on the selected layer by manipulating the Hue/Saturation dialog box's controls.

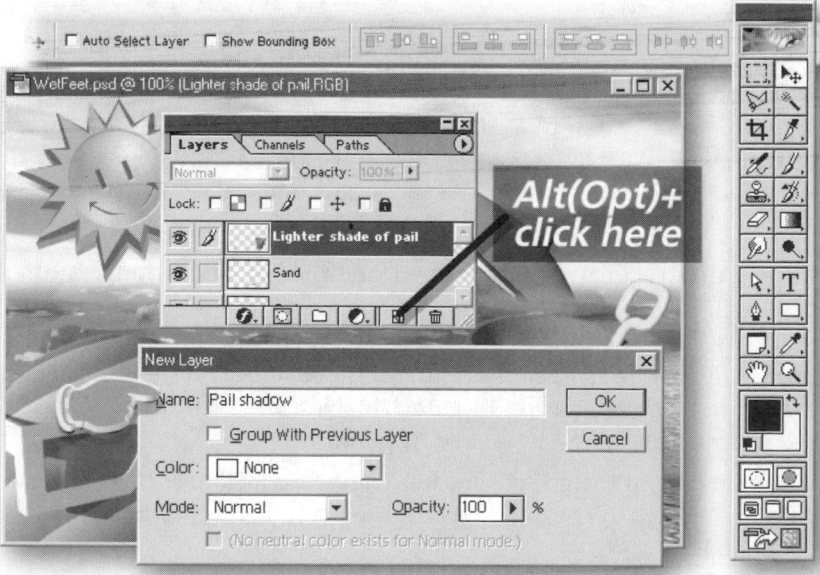

**Figure 2.11**    Alt(Opt)+click the Create new layer icon to name the layer, and then add it to the image.

6. Click on the new layer title, and then drag it to beneath the Lighter shade of pail title on the Layers palette and release the cursor, as shown in Figure 2.12.

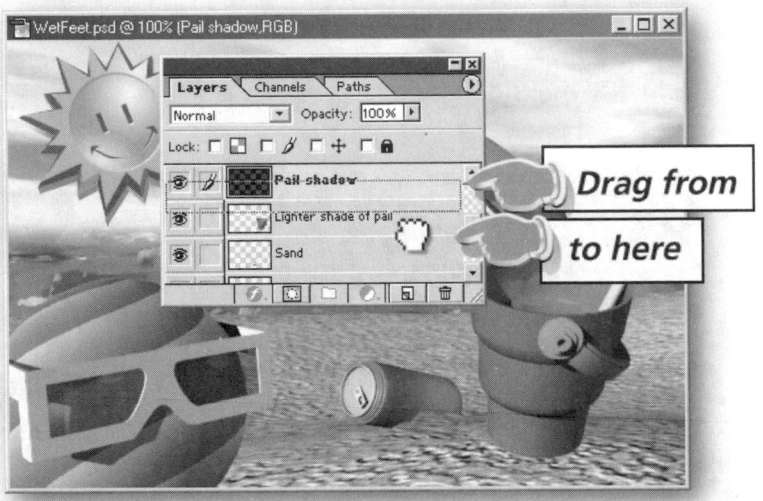

**Figure 2.12**    Reordering layers is a snap using the Layers palette.

**Tip**

**Use Ctrl + Brackets to Change Order of Layers**    You can also send the current editing layer down by one in the stack by pressing Ctrl(⌘)+[ (left bracket), or move it one up by pressing Ctrl(⌘)+] (right bracket).

It's no coincidence that these are the same keyboard shortcuts you use in (Adobe) PageMaker 6.5 and (Adobe) Illustrator 9 to move objects up and down in a stack.

7. Choose the Rectangular Marquee tool, and then draw a rectangle from the base of the pail to the right edge of the image. The sun's on the left, so the shadow has to be on the right of the pail. Press D (default colors), and then press Alt(Opt)+Delete (Backspace) to fill the marquee on the Pail shadow layer with black, as shown in Figure 2.13. Now press Ctrl(⌘)+D to deselect the selection marquee—it's served its purpose.

   Hey, take note of these keyboard shortcuts—it is a Statue of Liberty–sized pain in the neck to constantly search the main menu for frequently used commands.

8. Drag a rectangular marquee around the black on the Pail shadow layer— make it about twice as large as the black color.

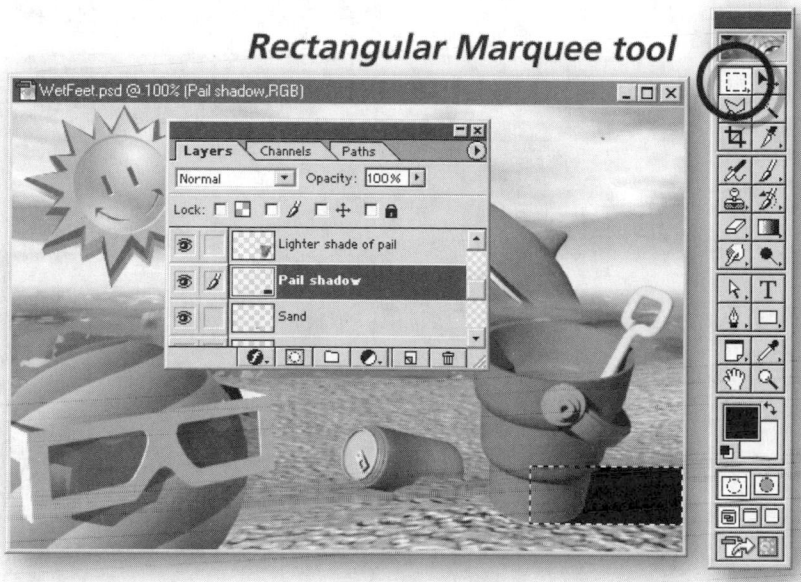

**Figure 2.13**    Fill the active selection marquee by using the popular Alt(Opt)+Delete (Backspace) keyboard combination.

Why are you doing this? So that the next command you make—the Gaussian blur—has to calculate only the area inside the marquee, and not the whole image. Believe us; isolating an area to be filtered speeds up the process.

9. Choose Filter, Blur, and then choose Gaussian Blur. Drag the slider to 8.8 pixels, as shown in Figure 2.14, and then click OK to create a realistic, soft shadow.

   Let's make this shadow a little more subtle.

10. On the Layers palette, drag the Opacity slider (the slider pops out when you click the Opacity field's triangular button) down to about 50%, and change the layer blending mode to Multiply, as shown in Figure 2.15.

    Multiply mode treats any opaque area on a layer as though it were a stain created by a felt tip marker that was left too long on a napkin.

11. Choose File, Save, and then save the image as WetFeet.psd, in Photoshop's native format, to your hard disk. Allow Photoshop to save the image with an embedded Adobe RGB 1998 color profile—this is an option in the Save As box that should be checked by default. Keep the image open. There's more fun in store.

Say, that was a pretty mean feat, totally changing the colors of the pail. And the shadow adds a touch of realism. But you know what?

**Figure 2.14**   The Gaussian blur effect is very popular with designers to create soft shadows. You can't buy an issue of *PC Magazine* without seeing headlines with this type of shadow.

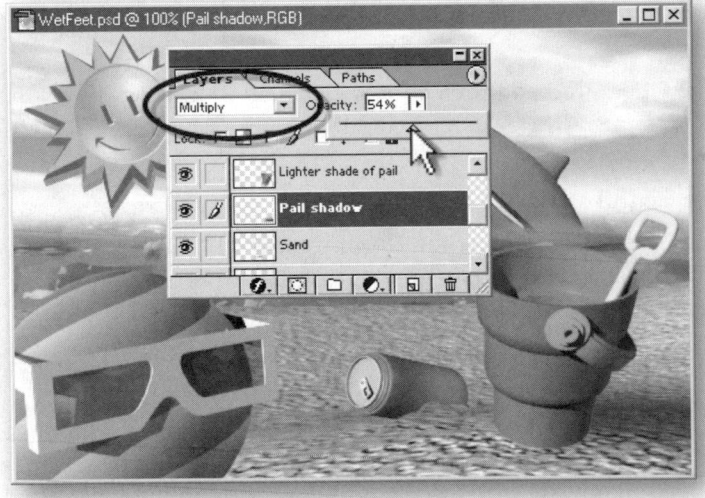

**Figure 2.15**   Choose Multiply (blending) mode and about 50% opacity from the Layers palette.

## Correcting Other Aspects of the Pail

A number of things are still wrong with the pail. First of all, it's floating—it is not partially embedded in the sand. And the midtones in the pail are a little too dense to look realistic on such a sunny day.

Here's how to make the final corrections to the pail:

### Example 2.3 Enhancing the Realism of the Pail

I. Choose the Eraser tool from the toolbox. Although it looks like the eraser you used in high school, the icon image is only a handy at-a-glance representation. In actuality, you have your choice of using an eraser with Pencil, Paintbrush, Airbrush, or plain Block erasing (like an actual eraser) characteristics. Choose the Paintbrush Eraser mode from the drop-down Mode list on the Options bar, and then, from the palette flies out when you click the down arrow directly to the right of the brush tip icon on the Options bar, choose the second from the right brush tip in the top row.

2. Now, click the Lighter shade of pail title on the Layers palette to make it the active editing layer. With the Eraser tool, erase some of the lower-left side of the pail, as shown in Figure 2.16.

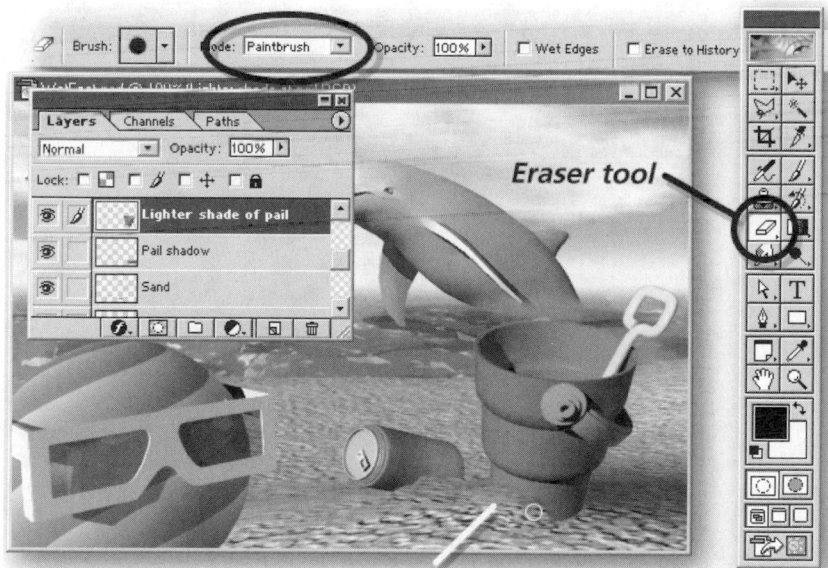

**Figure 2.16** Erase some of the bottom of the pail so that the sand on the Background layer shows through and creates the illusion that the pail is resting in, not on, the sand.

It looks like sand is covering part of the pail, right? You know why you can't do this on the right side of the pail? Because there is a shadow on the layer beneath, and you'd ruin the illusion of the shadow if you erased the pail's bottom-right side.

The fewer eraser strokes you make, the better. In art, adopt the subtle approach, like the authors (yeah, right). Now, you need to leave the highlights and shadow areas alone in the pail image, but open up the midtones so you can better see the color of the pail.

3. Press Ctrl(⌘)+L (Levels command—you'll use this keyboard shortcut a lot in your own work—memorize it) and then, as shown in Figure 2.17, drag the middle slider to the left until the pail's colors look as though they have a better relationship to one another—the tones are predominant and play off one another.

   Hint: Most visual detail in images is in the midtones. Press Enter (Return) to apply the tone correction and return to the beach.

4. Press Ctrl(⌘)+S; keep the file open.

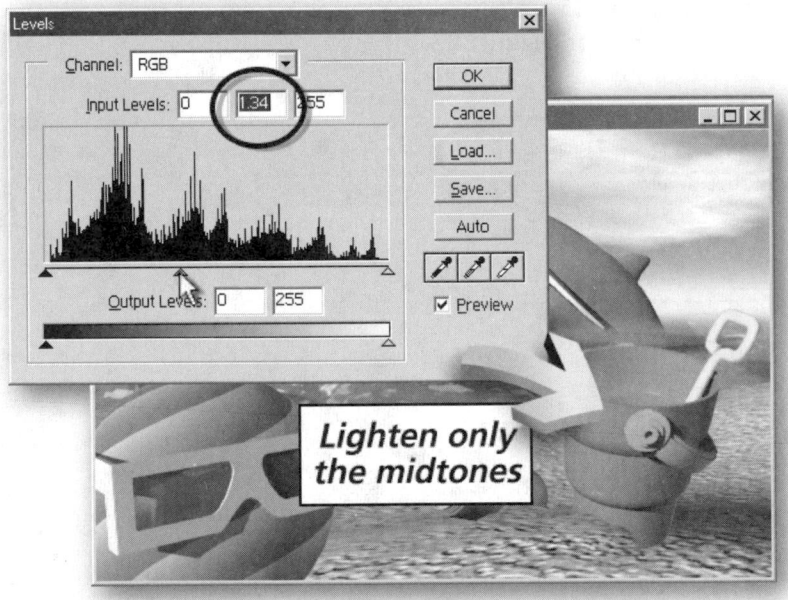

**Figure 2.17**    Drag the midtone slider to the left to decrease contrast and allow more detail to show in the image or image selection.

Not bad! Your editing is getting more elaborate and sophisticated. What do you say in the next section that the sky's the limit?

# Using Photoshop Filters and Free Transform

Photoshop ships with more than 100 filters, many of them special effects filters. Probably the hardest part in Photoshop is deciding which filter suits your artistic needs the best. It depends on the content of the artwork, doesn't it?

You'll be using Photoshop's Clouds filter in the following section because you want to change the clouds in the picture (boy, was that self-explanatory or what?). And you'll also use the Free Transform feature that rotates, skews, scales, and distorts a selected image area as though it was so much Silly Putty.

## Adding a New Sky to the Image

One of Photoshop's lesser-used filters is called Clouds. Clouds produces a certain type of fractal pattern that is puffy and wispy and can resemble clouds. (*Fractal* designs have a near-infinite variety, but their trademark is that they all look like natural, organic stuff—rocks, leaves, etc.

The ability to render the Clouds filter to suggest a sky has to do with the foreground and background colors that are on the toolbox when you make the command. The nice thing about Clouds is that no two applications of this filter look alike—that's fractal math with no terminator in the equation. So you can keep pressing Ctrl(⌘)+F to apply the last-used filter over and over until you get a sky you like.

Enough talk! Let's replace the sky in the image.

### Example 2.4   Creating a Sky Using Photoshop Filters

1. Click on the Background layer on the Layers palette to make it the active editing layer. This is where the sky is, and where you'll replace it.

2. Slowly, carefully drag a rectangular marquee (with the Rectangular Marquee tool) around the sky in the image, from the top to where it gets misty and meets the ocean.

3. Right-click (Macintosh: hold Ctrl and click) and then, from Photoshop's Context menu, choose Feather, as shown in Figure 2.18. What does it mean to feather the sky? Well, you get a lot of mallards, and toss them way up...I'm kidding. *Feathering* is the softening of a selection marquee edge, so that a transition is made between unselected (masked) areas and selected areas. When you apply an effect (as you'll do shortly), feathering helps disguise any possible hard edges in your work. Type 5 in the Feather dialog box and then click OK to soften the edge of your selection.

**Figure 2.18**    Select the sky, and then feather the selection so there will be no hard edge on the bottom where the ocean meets the sky in the mist.

**Note**

**Feathering Has Its Limitations**    Feathering only works on selection edges that are not flush with the image window. In other words, the feathering currently in the image is only on the bottom side of the rectangular marquee. The other three edges that are flush with the image window are not feathered at all.

This is good to remember when you're working on your own assignments.

4. Pick two appropriate colors for the Clouds effect. A background color of white is fine, but chances are you don't have blue as the current foreground color on the toolbox. Click on the foreground color selection box on the toolbox.

5. In the Color Picker, by default, brightness and saturation (two of the three components of color in the HSB color model—more on this in future chapters) are chosen by scooting that little circle around using the cursor. Hue is determined by dragging the arrows up or down on the color strip directly to the right of the color field, as shown in Figure 2.19. Pick a deep blue; we'll change the depth of the color later, but the Clouds effect is fairly punk without two colors that have contrast between them. Press Enter (Return) to return to the beach.

Ahhh! The moment you've been waiting for—drum roll, please.

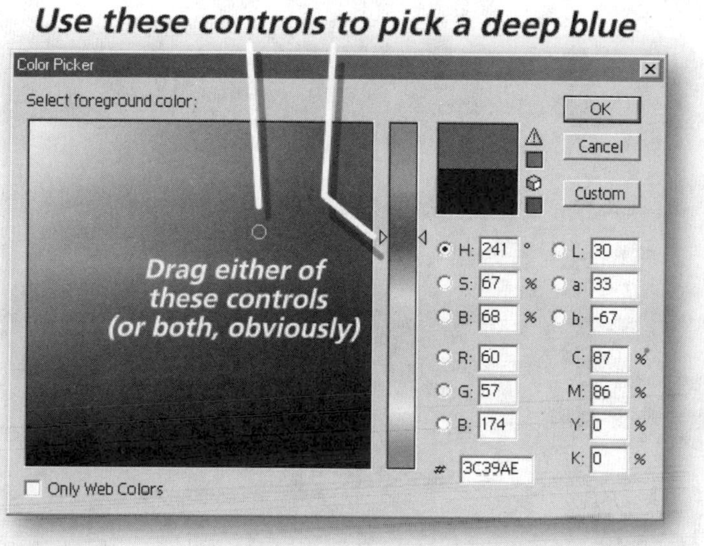

**Use these controls to pick a deep blue**

**Figure 2.19** Pick a rich blue to contrast with the background color of white for the Clouds filter.

6. Choose Filter, Render, and then choose Clouds. As you can (sort of) see in Figure 2.20, the sky is now puffy looking, a combination of white cottonball–like clouds and deep blue sky. So you say your sky doesn't look dramatic enough? Press Ctrl(⌘)+F, and then look at the new fractal sky. If that doesn't do anything for you, slowly (as you'd advance frames in a slide show) press Ctrl(⌘)+F until you find the sky of your dreams. As mentioned earlier, you'll run out of inspiration before you run out of permutations on the Clouds math formula.

   And notice that there's no hard edge at the bottom of the new sky, thanks to feathering.

   Now the beach scene is a sunny day, and the rich blue in the sky makes it look a little like impending storms or something. Now that the fractal Clouds filter has written the sky to the image, let's change the sky's tones. Do *not*, accidentally or otherwise, deselect the marquee selection in the image.

7. Press Ctrl(⌘)+L to display the Levels dialog box. (See? I told you to memorize this shortcut.) Drag the midtone slider to the left, and drag the white point slider also to the left, as shown in Figure 2.21. To peek at the sky to see how it's shaping up, move the Levels dialog box. Not bad—it now looks like a sunny day with a few clouds. Press Enter (Return) to get back to them waves.

8. Press Ctrl(⌘)+S; keep the file open.

**Figure 2.20**    The Clouds filter is designed to provide natural-looking textures, such as this sky.

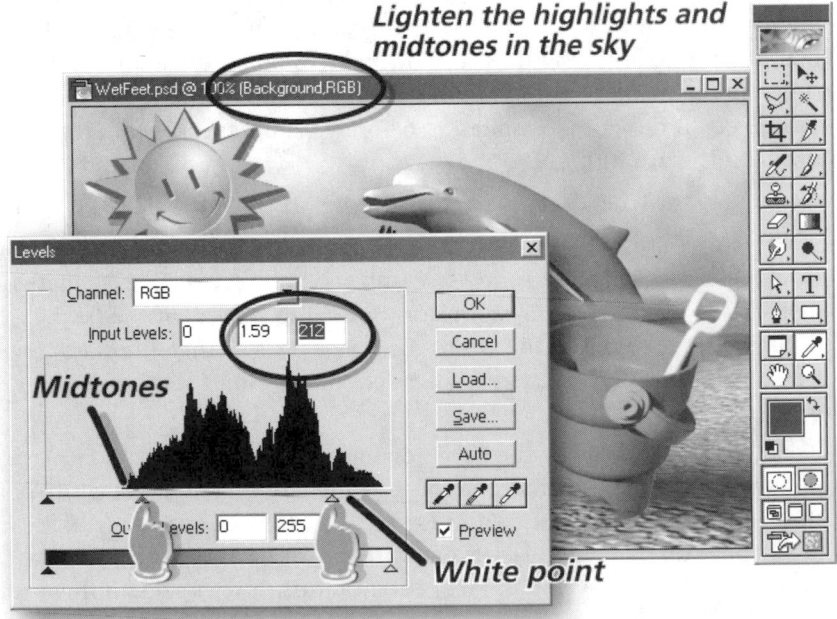

**Figure 2.21**    Increase the amount of highlights (using the white point slider) and broaden the midtones in the sky by dragging both sliders to the left.

Okay, the sky looks terrific, and everyone except the guy out in the deep water looks like they're having fun. One eyesore in this image, however, is that can a thoughtless litterbug casually tossed away. In the section that follows, you'll remove the sand from the can, and do what most litterbugs do—you'll fling the can as far as possible away from you.

## Working In Free Transform Mode

The steps to follow are broken into two discrete editing actions. First, you'll trash the sand that is on a layer that's hiding the bottom of the can. Then, you'll do something that not a lot of folks consider when they do editing work in Photoshop. You see, we all tend to move objects up, down, left, and to the right, because we all know that images are two-dimensional. However, we'd be forgetting perspective if we didn't take the opportunity once in a while to make objects smaller or larger, to create the impression that something is more distant or closer to the camera.

And resizing objects on layers is something Photoshop's Free Transform command excels at. Here's how to play with the can on the beach. Watch out for the rough edges...

### Example 2.5    Uncovering and Tossing a Can in the Image

1. On the Layers palette, scroll down to the Sand layer title, which is right above the Garbage layer.

    As you can see, a lump of sand image was placed on top of the can's bottom.

2. Click the eye icon to the left of the Sand layer's title to hide the sand. Doing this will sort of make the can look as though it's floating, as shown in Figure 2.22. Incidentally, in addition to making something look as though it's been pushed into the sand, shadows also help "ground" an image on a layer. You could, if you wanted to at this point, paint a shadow beneath the can and really make it look like it's floating. Nahhhh.

3. The beach has plenty of sand, so we can afford to drag the Sand layer into the Trash, as shown in Figure 2.23.

    By the way—and you'll see lots of this in later chapters—you could also drag the Sand layer title to the bottom of the stack and then merge the sand with the rest of the sand on the beach.

    Now that you can see the whole can, what say we toss the can toward the ocean? This isn't a real scene, so it's not actual littering.

**Figure 2.22**    Hide the layer that has the sand, and the can's bottom is revealed.

**Figure 2.23**    You can keep the Sand layer invisible indefinitely, even from one Photoshop session to another. But it's probably more productive right now to delete a layer we will not use in the remainder of this chapter.

4. Click on the Garbage layer on the Layers palette to make it the current editing layer, and then press Ctrl(⌘)+T to surround the can—the only object on the layer (you can't transform transparency, sadly <g>) with the Free Transform bounding box.

   Although you can constrain proportions when you shrink this can by using the option on the Options bar, it's more fun and expert-like to use key combinations here.

5. Hold Shift to constrain proportions, and then drag a corner handle of the Free Transform bounding box, as shown in Figure 2.24, toward the center of the can. Stop dragging when the bounding box is about half its original size.

*Hold Shift and drag corner toward center of can*

**Figure 2.24**  Shrink the can by using the Free Transform command.

6. Once the can is pint-sized (sorry), either press Enter (Return), or double-click inside the Free Transform box to finalize your editing work.

7. With the Move tool, drag the can out toward the ocean. As you can see, the can really does look as though it's been moved *deeper* into the image.

   Let's try out the Clone Stamp tool (called the Rubber Stamp tool in previous versions of Photoshop) to remove the can from the scene altogether.

8. Click the Clone Stamp tool on the toolbox.

9. On the Options bar, click the down arrow directly to the right of the Brush tip preview, and then choose the 17-pixel diameter tip. Check the aligned option on the Options bar.

With this option chosen, the sampling point for the Clone Stamp tool will always tag along behind the painting cursor for the tool, always providing the tool with new image areas.

10. Click the Use All Layers option on the Options bar.

   This is an important step; you want to sample sand from the Background layer, but you want the sand *deposited* on the Garbage layer.

11. Alt(Opt)+click on an area of sand that's in the clear of other objects—a good place to do so is the area directly to the right of the can. Now you have set the origin for the traveling sampling point of the Clone Stamp tool. Release Alt(Opt).

12. Drag across the can once or twice. As you can see in Figure 2.25, the can has vanished.

   However, it should be noted that the Garbage layer is getting a can replaced with sand image areas. You have not truly erased the can—you've sort of covered it up.

**Figure 2.25**   Cover up that annoying can with Clone Stamp tool samples from the Background of the image.

13. Why not drag the Garbage layer title into the Trash right now, seeing as we're done with it?

14. Press Ctrl(⌘)+S; keep the file open.

# Digging Deeper into Layers

The Free Transform feature is exceptionally cool, but in the section to follow, we're going to concentrate a little more on layers. Layers rule the world in Photoshop, and there's hardly a sophisticated editing step you can make without the use of a layer.

## Examining Hidden Layers and Linking Layers

The authors deliberately set up some stuff in this image for you to discover and work with. For example, did you know that Mr. Sun actually has a pair of sunglasses? It's not that they're in his breast pocket or something—they're hidden on the beach, and the sunglasses layer is hidden.

In the steps that follow, you'll reunite Mr. Shades (American colloquialism for "sunglasses," for our foreign readers) with Mr. Sun, and then link the two layers to which the objects belong so you can do the impossible—you'll move the sun in the sky. Oh, the power...,

### Example 2.6   Layer Editing and Linking

1. On the Layers palette, scroll to the very top of the list until you can see the Mr. Shades title, as shown in Figure 2.26.

   Notice that the eye icon is not in its slot to the left of the title; that means the shades are hidden.

**Figure 2.26**   No wonder the sun in the image isn't adhering to the cliché that "postcard-style" suns must have glasses. His sunglasses are hidden on a layer.

2. Click in the slot where the eye icon should be, and you will see the sunglasses where the soda can used to be. Click on the title to make Mr. Shades the current editing layer. Choose the Move tool from the toolbox, and then drag Mr. Shades on top of Mr. Sun's eyes, as shown in Mr. Figure 2.27.

Don't you feel a little as though Mr. Rogers is talking to you now?

**Figure 2.27**    Drag the glasses on the Mr. Shades layer on top of the sun on the Mr. Sun layer.

3. Click the Mr. Sun title on the Layers palette to make it the current editing layer. Then, next to the Mr. Shades title on the Layers palette, click the slot closest to the title. A chain will appear; this means that everywhere you drag the sun object, the shades will follow, as shown in Figure 2.28. Try this out—move the sun to the right of the picture, and then move it back. Having the sun at the right of the image makes the lighting in the scene wrong.

Hey, chances are now that Mr. Sun has his shades, there's no reason for him to take them off again. If you think about it, it's *always* bright around him. So we do not need to keep the layers linked.

4. Click on the Mr. Shades title to select it, and then press Ctrl(⌘)+E to merge the glasses into the layer underneath it—the Mr. Sun layer, as shown in Figure 2.29. Note that the name of the layer isn't correct now. If you want to be really tidy, right-click (Macintosh: hold Ctrl and click) on the title, and then choose Layer Properties. In this dialog box, type **Mr. Sun** (or any name you like) and then press Enter (Return) to make the name change.

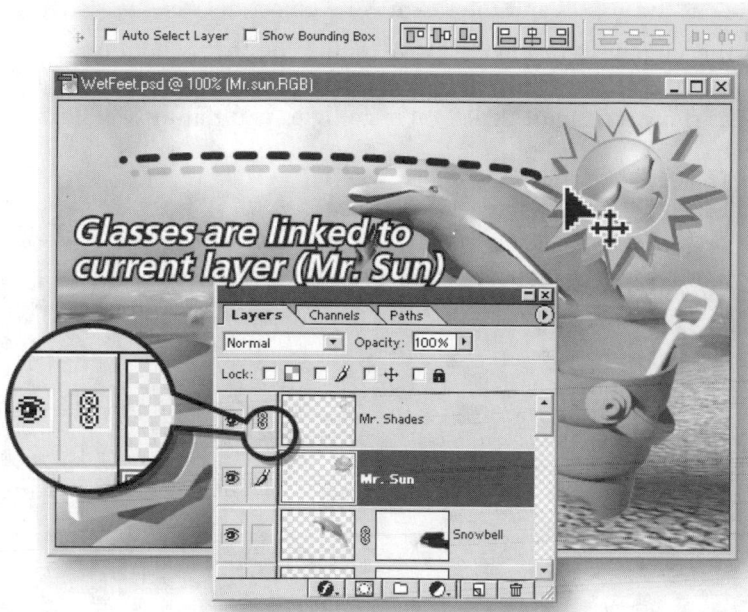

**Figure 2.28**    Linked layers' nontransparent contents move in synch with contents moving on the current editing layer.

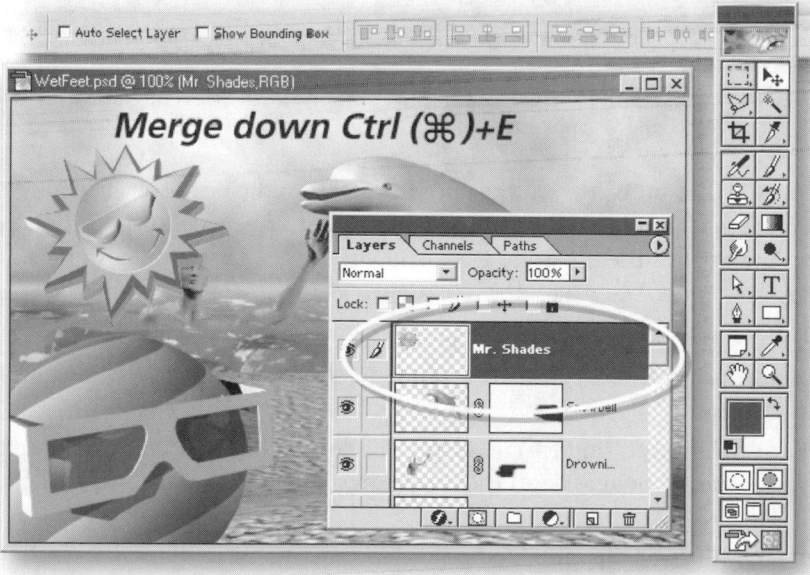

**Figure 2.29**    Merging layers is a permanent method, which unlike layer linking, makes the contents of two or more layers into a single layer.

As long as the glasses and the sun are one object, let's create a setting sun.

5. Drag the sun object (using the Move tool) so he (it) is about one-quarter of the way into the water. Then, on the Layers palette, click the Add a mask icon, as shown in Figure 2.30. You're going to paint away Mr. Sun's bottom quarter.

**Figure 2.30**   Click the Add a mask icon to hide portions of the current editing layer when black color is applied.

6. Press D (default colors) so the current foreground color is black. Choose the Paintbrush tool, and then on the Options bar, click the down arrow directly to the right of the Brush tip icon, and choose the far-right brush tip in the top row. Press Enter (Return) to close the palette.

7. Paint across the bottom of the sun, as shown in Figure 2.31.

8. With the Move tool, drag the sun down a little so it sits in the mist on the horizon.

   Both the masked (hidden) areas and the sun will move when you drag the sun, because the mask and the image on the layer are linked, as you can see in Figure 2.32.

9. Press Ctrl(⌘)+S; keep the file open.

**Figure 2.31**    Black foreground color hides foreground image content on layers when the layer is in mask mode.

**Figure 2.32**    By default, layer masks are linked to their layers. You can unlink them, but the authors are hard pressed to think of a reason you'd want to.

As long as we're having fun with the sun, why don't you create a photorealistic glow around it?

## Creating a Glow Around the Sun

Okay, technically, the sun already has energy emanating from it with that cartoon explosion outline all around it. But we feel we can really polish the piece if you add an element of realism to the sun. This doesn't mean cutting the sun out from its present cartoon glow—you're only going to *enhance* the glow effect.

Here's how to really make the sun shine. Let's get glowing...

### Example 2.7    Using the Screen Effect on a Layer for a Glow

1. Click on the Lighter shade of pail title on the Layers palette. You're nobody's fool—we told you earlier that new layers pop into the image directly on top of the current layer. Therefore, you can Alt(Opt)+click the Create a layer icon now, type **Sunshine** in the Name field, and then press Enter (Return). The new layer is behind the sun, as it should be.

2. With the Eyedropper tool, click on a light part of the sun, as shown in Figure 2.33.

    This will basically be the color of the glow around the sun.

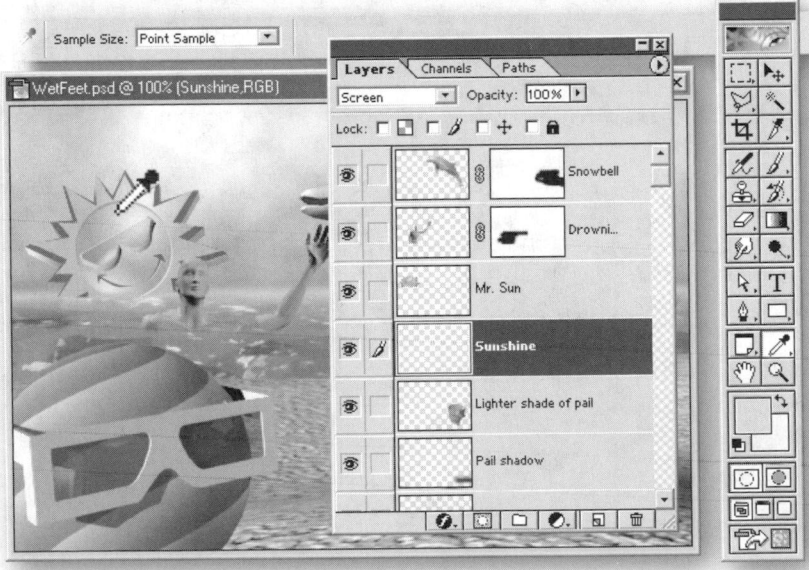

**Figure 2.33**    Set the foreground color to a pale lemon by sampling a highlight on the sun object.

3. Ctrl(⌘)+click on the Mr. Sun title.

   This loads the nontransparent areas on the Mr. Sun layer as a marquee selection. This *does not* choose the Mr. Sun layer—the current layer should be the Sunshine layer.

4. Choose Select, Modify, Expand from the main menu.

   Might we point out that this is the first time in more than 15 pages that you have had to go to the main menu? Photoshop is document-centric!

5. In the Expand By field, type **16**, as shown in Figure 2.34, and then press Enter (Return) to create the expansion.

**Figure 2.34**    The Expand command expands any selection, and it also softens the edge of the selection (you cannot change this feature, but it's okay for our purposes in this assignment).

6. Press Alt(Opt)+Delete (Backspace) to fill the marquee with foreground color. We know—this doesn't look like a glow effect yet. Choose Screen (blending) mode from the drop-down list on the Layers palette, as shown in Figure 2.35.

7. Press Ctrl(⌘)+D (Select, None) because you need to apply a blurring filter next and you can't blur outward if a marquee selection is corralling the color on the layer. Choose Filter, Blur, and then Gaussian Blur.

8. Drag the slider to about 9 pixels, as shown in Figure 2.36, and then click OK.

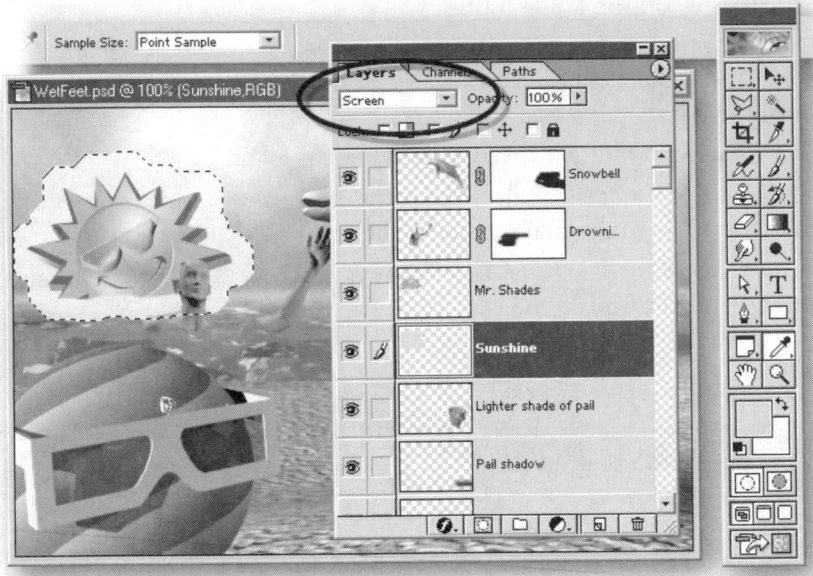

**Figure 2.35**    Screen mode accentuates the light properties in any color on a layer.

**Figure 2.36**    A Gaussian blur applied to the enlarged, filled outline of the sun really makes the sun look as though it's lighting up the sky.

Pretty cool effect, huh? And part of the beauty of this editing technique is that some of the sunshine color spills into the mist above the ocean (it looks as though it was deliberately rendered there).

**9.** Press Ctrl(⌘)+S; keep the file open.

By now, you're probably saying, "These guys are ruthless! First, they have no one named Ruth on staff, and second, how long is that drowning guy going to hang in there?" In all fairness, that is a *model* of a guy we created in Poser. (We are uncertain about who owns Poser this week—we think it's Corel Corp.) That's why he looks so shiny—his skin texture is plastic, and plastic *floats*.

Okay, okay. Let's save him anyway.

## Uncovering a Life Saver and Applying It

It's time to see what other silly stuff the authors have hidden in this image. And the only true way to find out is to scroll the Layer palette list for stuff that is named but not visible. Ahoy! If you hide the Beach Ball layer, you will discover the life saver that's directly behind the ball, as shown in Figure 2.37.

**Figure 2.37** Life savers are only one of many things people bring to the beach and forget.

This next set of steps gets you more into layer masking, which is honestly a good thing, because editing on layers, Photoshop-style, is the easiest way to edit things. Trust us on this one—we've been documenting Photoshop for almost a decade now.

### Example 2.8     Editing Together the Guy and the Life Saver

1. First, drag the life saver (use the Move tool) to where the guy is located.

   Now, surprise, surprise. If you look carefully at the Layers palette (or Figure 2.38), you'll notice that the guy has an active layer mask going around his torso, so there's more room to fit a life saver around him. Also, the Life Saver layer is way underneath the Drowning Guy layer—you need to bring the life saver on top of the Drowning Guy layer.

**Figure 2.38**     Hey, the guy appears to be coming through the front of the life saver! That's because the two layers—guy and lifesaver—are in the wrong order in the image.

First let's get rid of the layer mask on the guy, so we can better move and position the life saver.

2. Drag it into the Trash, as shown in Figure 2.39.

   You will see the guy appear, totally unmasked and opaque, from his head to just below his belly button. Hey, this is a *family* book, okay?

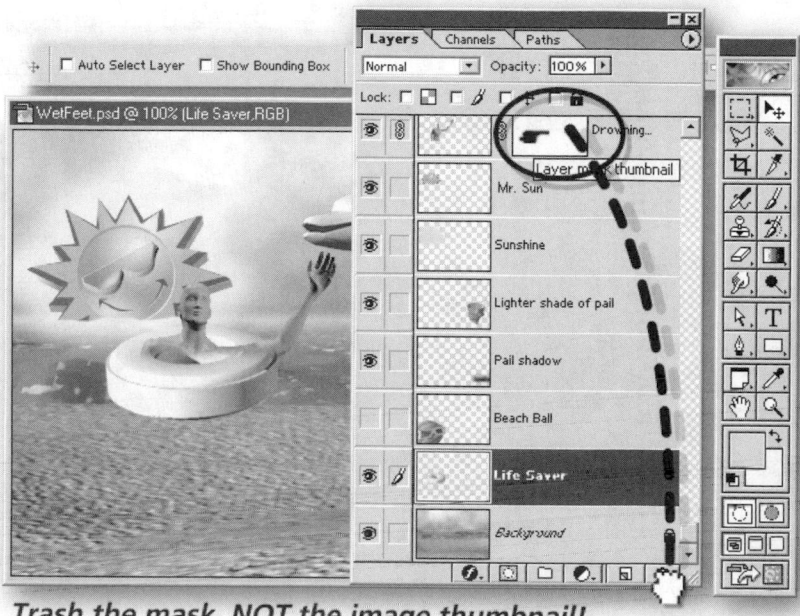

**Trash the mask, NOT the image thumbnail!**

**Figure 2.39** Removing the mask from the guy will make him appear to be drowning less, but more importantly, unmasking the figure enables you to position the life saver properly.

3. You can either click on the Life Saver title on the Layers palette, and then press Ctrl(⌘)+right bracket (]) a lot of times to place the life saver on top of the drowning guy, or you can click the Life Saver layer and *dragggggggg* it all the way to the top of the Layers palette's list. We prefer to use the keyboard because we can't see the entire Layers list at this screen resolution to make such a significant move.

   Now, the life saver has to be masked (hidden) where it apparently goes behind the drowning guy. But here's a problem: How do you know where and how far to mask? A very quick-and-dirty solution to where to hide the life saver is to make it partially transparent. Then you can see both the guy and the parts of the life saver that should be behind him. This technique might not be as "proper" as working back and forth between white and black to reveal and hide your editing work, but it's quick and produces professional results.

4. Choose the Paintbrush tool. With the Life Saver layer chosen as the current editing layer, click the Add a mask icon on the Layers palette. Then decrease the Opacity on the layer to about 60%, and press Ctrl(⌘)++ to zoom into the image. Hold the spacebar to move the image in the window until you can see both guy and life saver, and perform some editing like that shown in Figure 2.40.

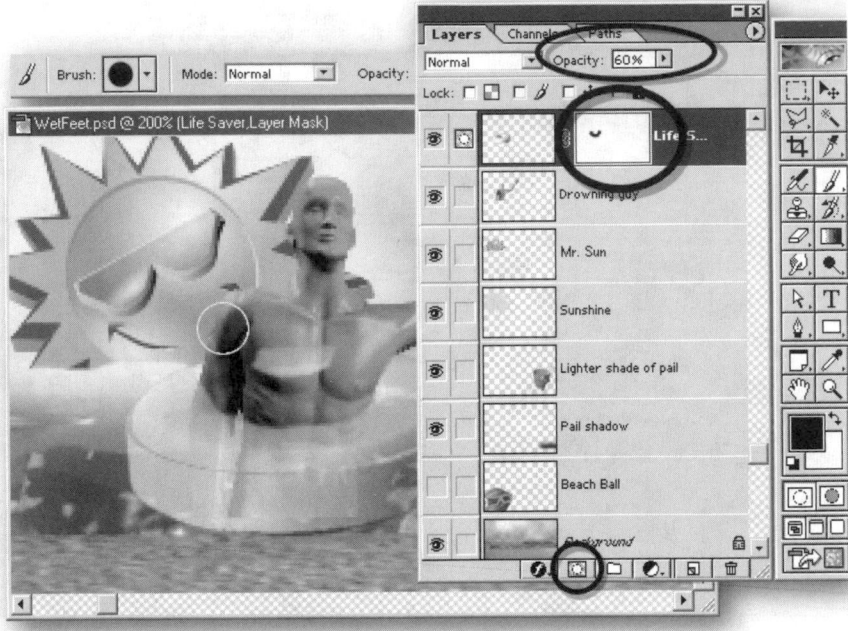

**Figure 2.40**    Decrease the opacity of the layer you are editing in Layer Mask mode to see which areas go and which stay.

As you can see, we're erasing the back portion of the life saver. With the entire life saver in front of the guy, at 100% opacity on the Life Saver layer, you would not be able to tell which portions of the life saver need to be removed.

5. When the life saver is fitted securely about the man, make sure his seat and tray table are in the upright and locked position. Sorry—let me try this again:

   Return the Life Saver layer to 100% opacity when you've finished editing. You might want to use the Move tool on the Drowning Guy layer to push him up or down so his positioning inside the life saver looks natural. You will delete parts of the drowning (now rescued) guy a little later, and positioning him now is key to successful editing later.

6. Click the Life Saver mask thumbnail (the black and white icon to the right of the layer image thumbnail), and then paint away the bottom of the life saver, so it's in (not on top of) the ocean, as shown in Figure 2.41.

   What you must contend with now is that the bottom of the guy is peeking out underneath the life saver.

**7.** Click on the Drowning Guy layer title, click the Add a mask icon on the Layers palette, and then in one deft stroke or two, remove any guy-like material from the bottom of the life saver (see Figure 2.42).

**8.** Press Ctrl(⌘)+S; keep the file open.

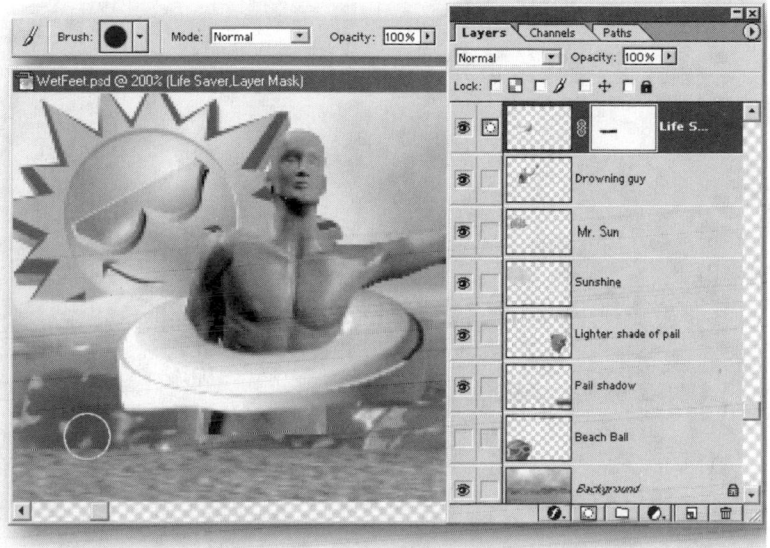

**Figure 2.41**   Hide (mask) part of the bottom of the life saver. Life savers are never 100% buoyant!

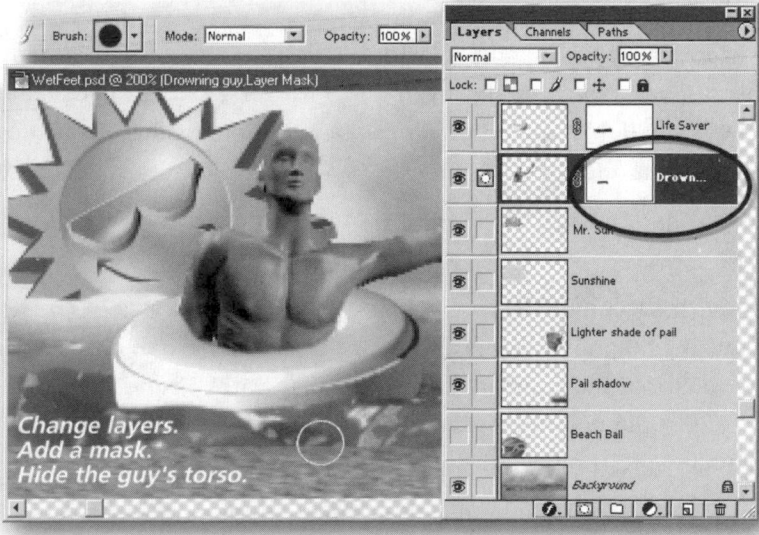

**Figure 2.42**   You should see only one end of the guy sticking out of a life saver in the ocean. Hide (mask) the bottom-of-the-guy object using black foreground color.

My tailbone is beginning to hurt after sitting here and writing the last example. Why don't we all get up and stretch for a moment, and gaze at the monitor and see how far the work has come? In Figure 2.43 (I'm typing this standing now), you can see that you've made lots of professional edits and the scene definitely ain't what it started out to be.

**Figure 2.43**    This is only Chapter 2. Look what you can do already! You'll probably be snapped up in the graphics market by the time you reach the end of this book!

We have been aching to go and play with the dolphin since the beginning of the chapter because this type doesn't get you wet or ask for a lot of dead fish. In the section to follow, you'll finesse our finny friend, and fathom further…you know, I like alliteration about as much as you do.

On with the show!

## Working with Dolphins

Like the guy, the dolphin image is also masked. All you need to do is to delete the mask and you'll have a complete dolphin to play with. In the steps that follow, you'll reposition the dolphin, rotate it using Free Transform mode, and apply a mask of your own to complete the scene.

You're getting a little more comfortable working with Photoshop's features already, aren't you?

### Example 2.9   Using Layer Mask in Combination with Free Transform

1. Double-click the Zoom tool on the toolbox (yet another shortcut to memorize!) to zoom the image window so you're looking at its contents at a 1:1 (100%) viewing resolution.

2. Click the mask thumbnail of Snowbell (the dolphin) and drag it into the Trash, as shown in Figure 2.44.

**Figure 2.44**   Trash the layer mask belonging to the dolphin to see the complete dolphin onscreen.

Let's do one of those numbers with Snowbell that they train dolphins to do at Sea World: Swim straight up and down in the water using only your tail for propulsion.

3. Press Ctrl(⌘)+T to place the dolphin selection in Free Transform mode. Hover around one of the corners of the Free Transform bounding box until your cursor turns into a two-headed bent arrow. Then rotate the selection clockwise by dragging in the direction shown in Figure 2.45.

**Tip**

**Use the Context Menu to Have Goof-Free Transforming**   A goof-proof way of making the cursor manipulate the Free Transform box exactly as you want it to is to right-click (Macintosh: hold Ctrl and click) after pressing Ctrl(⌘)+T. You can then choose the type of transformation you want from the context menu. This way there's no fumbling to get the right cursor at a precise location onscreen.

**Figure 2.45**   Corner handles on a Free Transform box can be used for scaling or rotating. Hover the cursor around a bounding box corner until the cursor changes to a bent double-headed arrow.

You know something? This image isn't large enough to let Snowbell do its thing, so let's simply put Snowbell in the sand pail.

4. Using the Move tool, position Snowbell so that the dolphin is centered over the pail. Snowbell is already on a layer higher than the Lighter shade of pail layer, so click the Add a mask icon.

5. With the top-row, far-right brush tip on the Brushes palette (and black as the foreground color), paint over Snowbell's tail, right up to the lip of the pail. If you goof, press Ctrl(⌘)+Z to undo your last editing move, or press X to switch to white foreground color and then paint to reveal hidden areas that you don't want hidden (see Figure 2.46).

   Okay, once the dolphin's tail has been edited away, it's time to save this image in a format that everyone can see. The PSD format limits most of your audience to Photoshop owners, but the TIFF file format is supported by just about every image browser on earth.

6. Choose File, Save As from the main menu. What you want to do is to save a copy to your hard disk, and leave the masterpiece you've created in Photoshop's workspace right where it is. Therefore, in the Save As dialog box, choose the TIFF format from the format drop-down box. As you can see in Figure 2.47, the ICC profile should be Adobe RGB (1998), the Save As a Copy option is checked for you, the Layers option is dimmed (because TIFF images can't contain layers), and you have this warning that some of the image data cannot be preserved using this file format.

**Figure 2.46**   A dolphin cannot actually fit in a sand pail. At least not comfortably.

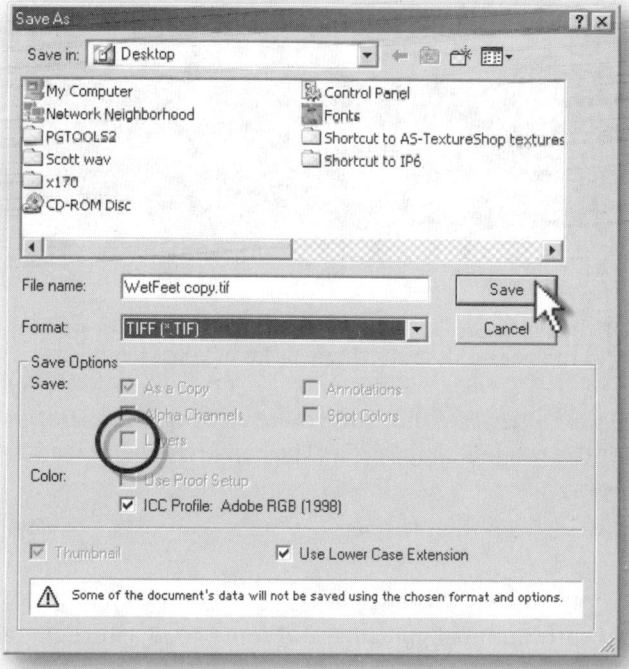

**Figure 2.47**   The Save As a Copy option is now located under File, Save as.

You know what Adobe is talking about? This warning means that all layers and layer masks in this copy of the work will be flattened, and you will not be able to edit the TIFF copy. This is okay, though—you still have the original you worked on.

7. Click Save. You'll see a dialog box like the one shown in Figure 2.48. Save to the type of computer you or the intended recipient of the copy uses, and you can compress the file using LZW compression.

LZW compression compresses a file about the same amount as StuffIt or WinZip, but no decompression utility is necessary here. You essentially save hard disk space, but files take a little longer to open if you have used LZW to compress them. *LZW* stands for Lempel-Zif Welsh, three mathematicians, and knowing this will make you sound most impressive <g>!

**Figure 2.48**    TIFF is a widespread format for digital images. Choose options that are tailored to your needs or the future needs of your clients.

8. Click OK, wait a nanosecond, and you're viewing Photoshop's workspace again with the original image in it. The copy has been saved to hard disk and life's okay.

9. Press Ctrl(⌘)+S; keep the file open.

In Figure 2.49, you can see the result—actually, only one of many possible results—you can achieve with minimal guidance and some good source material. There are lots of other things you could do in this image; remember this if you get stuck with an image of your own that you are composing.

**Figure 2.49**    You probably don't want to hang a print of this over your sofa, but the piece indeed shows your diligence (the quality that will make you a Photoshop Master) and the capability to really dig in there and get some of the power of Photoshop working for you.

Possibilities are what the digital imaging game is all about. This author couldn't be happier that the digital imaging revolution happened in his lifetime. Instead of artwork deteriorating through the years, I can pull a clean new print of work done 10 years ago and it looks as fresh as the day I created it. And you know what? Photoshop images saved in the PSD format can be reworked a day or 10 years from now. In Figure 2.50, some of the existing pieces on layers have been shuffled around a little. Is it a better picture than the one you saved? Who *cares*? The important thing is that you now have this capability to mold a composition as though it were a never-hardening piece of clay.

## Summary

Now, c'mon, admit it—this chapter was fun, right? You had no due dates, no responsibilities to a client or the authors to deliver a piece on time, and you learned many of the keys to Photoshop. Layers and selections both flow through your work in Photoshop, and the little twists and turns in the stream are variations on principles you now know. So when you learn about Adjustment layers later in this book, or about Layer Effects, you'll know exactly where to find the Layers palette. Chances are good some of the controls are on the palette or the Context menu, and off you go, much faster and more wisely than someone who didn't read this. You also learned three different ways to select things.

**Figure 2.50**   Photoshop is not about carving a piece in stone. Your imaging work is always as flexible as your imagination.

All in all, this has not been a bad education, especially since we clearly stated up front that we *weren't* trying to educate you <g>!

In Chapter 3, you will learn about how digital artists bridge the gap between the physical world and the world of computer images. That chapter revolves around the use of profiles—tiny lists of physical characteristics your hardware has so one device can speak more accurately to another. Think of it this way if this lead-in sounds too weird: Wouldn't it be nice if what you saw onscreen looked the same when printed? Wouldn't you love to scan something that looks the same in Photoshop's work-space? Of course you would. And that's what profiling and the following chapter are all about.

# Chapter 3

## Understanding Photoshop's New Color Management System

What you are going to learn in this chapter is the most important thing you can learn about Photoshop—how to get predictable, consistent output and how to get your scanner, monitor, and printer to display approximately the same thing. This is the graphic artist's dream, but it doesn't come without a price, and that price is this is a very serious, very technical chapter.

Our advice up front is that you take two or three days to digest what we teach in this chapter. We also realize that the other chapters in this book are light and occasionally humorous when compared to this chapter. So, keeping in mind that you're human and need a break when involved in anything serious, we present to you Figure 3.0. Now, *this* is a funny picture. Any time you find your attention drifting from this chapter, turn back to this page.

Aren't you glad the authors have a sense of perspective?

**Figure 3.0**    Return to this page and this image any time you're reading this chapter and find you're in over your head.

## Understanding Photoshop's New Color Management System (CMS)

If you followed the advice offered in previous *Inside Photoshop* books, you just didn't bother trying to make color management work for you. It wasn't worth the effort. Establishing a color-managed workflow was something attempted only by large organizations with big, fat budgets for equipment and dedicated color management technicians. And it didn't always work, even for them. Photoshop 5 introduced a color management process for the individual desktop, and Photoshop 5.5 improved upon that beginning. But those efforts fell short of being impressive; and most users, including us, continued to run, screaming, for the exits. Even talking about color management was too horrible to contemplate.

Well, times have changed. Adobe's new color management system (also referred to as CMS) is probably the single most important feature in Photoshop 6, in Illustrator 9, and in every other new Adobe product coming out of the pipeline. Adobe deserves a lot of credit, but so do Apple and Microsoft and a whole bunch of other companies that make up the organization International Color Consortium (ICC). All these companies have made a serious commitment toward making color management work. It is now possible for mere mortals to understand and use color management. And this is great news!

Having a usable system for managing color is a big deal. It is headline news. It is worth writing home about. Why? Because when you have set up your system to use color management and you've learned how to use these new color management tools, you'll never have to play the "What color is it, really?" game again. The colors you see on your monitor will be surprisingly close to what will come streaming out of a high-speed printing press or tumbling out of your desktop inkjet printer.

Adobe has made a splendid CMS that works the same in all of its products. Apple and Microsoft have done their part by providing operating system–level support for color management, so that every program, even non-Adobe programs, can use color management. Equipment manufacturers have made descriptions of the color capabilities of their products available so that the information can be plugged into the CMS. Now you can master the concepts of color management and take up the new tools that have been placed at your disposal.

## Coming to Terms with Color Management

To be frank, color management is still not an easy topic to understand and it can't be mastered by reading a few paragraphs. But we promise you that it is possible to learn, that it is worth the effort, and that if you take your time going through this chapter, you will be able to use Adobe's CMS and still have enough brain cells to do creative, artistic work.

In this section, we take a look at some of the key terms used in talking about color management. Along the way, you'll catch a little of the history of the way this newest CMS evolved.

### Color Spaces and Color Gamut

Throughout this chapter you are going to frequently see the terms "color spaces" and "color gamut." *Color space* is a *model* for representing color in terms of values that can be measured, such as the amount of red, green, and blue in an image. CMS works with standard color spaces, including RGB (Red, Green, Blue), LAB (L for relative lightness, A for relative redness-greenness, and B for related yellowness-blueness), and CMYK (Cyan, Magenta, Yellow, Black). *Color gamut* refers to a contiguous range of colors describing the limitations of a device or image. Color gamut might be called *color capability* when referring to a specific color space. "How many colors can this model represent?" is the question put forth by color gamut.

Life would be very boring and one dimensional if the universe and every manmade device had only one color space. That's not the case, however, and so the issue of color gamut is a big concern for anyone involved in color-critical work. Here's a quick summary of why:

- Every device—monitor, printer, printing press, camera, film, ink and media combination—can produce only a limited number of colors.

- No two devices or processes have the exact same color gamut.

- Even two printers or monitors of the same make and model vary from each other, although new generations of desktop printers with built-in densitometer and automatic self-calibration tend to be reliable from printer to printer.

- A device changes in its color-rendering capability because of age, lighting, or other operating conditions.

Ugh. These varying factors drive digital artists and production people up a virtual wall!

## Color Calibration

Before you explore the Adobe CMS further, you need to calibrate your devices. What do we mean by the term "calibrate?" *Calibration* is the process of bringing a device, such as a printer or monitor, to an absolute standard to ensure consistency over time and across devices of the same make and model. That is, you are attempting to make the color gamut and characteristics of a physical device adhere to some empirical, mathematically perfect standard.

Calibration is critical when you want accurate color output on a monitor. A good place to start is to match the white point and gamma from monitor to monitor, using monitor calibration software such as Adobe Gamma, or third-party software and hardware when available.

## Working Space

Time for a new term: *working space*, which includes RGB and CMYK color spaces. A *working space* is the pool of possible colors available when you edit a file. In the early days of color management, the monitor's color capability (color gamut) was the same as the space in which you worked with your image (the working space). If there were only one monitor in the world, and it never changed, then you could consider the color gamut and the working space to be the same. But such is not the case, and a CMS shouldn't assume it is.

A much better idea is to assign actual numbers to specific color values (sometimes referred to as *data*) and then reference and manipulate the data within the context of an ideal, standard working color space, rather than use the settings of a fallible and limited physical device. How is such an ideal, a standard, established when the world is full of so many different types of monitors, printers, scanners, and other devices?

## Commission Internationale de l'Eclairage (CIE)

CMS creators needed a uniform way to describe the color space of devices and standard color spaces. They also needed to define a standard set of rules that govern the way information about color values is exchanged between color spaces that do not overlap.

In the 1930s, the Commission Internationale de l'Eclairage (CIE), based in France, began the task of establishing color standards by assigning numbers to every color visible to the human eye. The color spaces the CIE defined, such as CIELAB, form the foundation of device-independent color for color management. However, the group's work was only a beginning; it did not resolve the color management issues encountered in electronic publishing. Who had PageMaker in 1930 <g>?

## International Color Consortium (ICC)

In 1993, International Color Consortium (ICC)—a group of companies recognized as leaders in the fields of electronic publishing, software development, and digital prepress—formed a committee to establish standards for *electronic* color publishing. The ICC based its standardized color information on the CIE LAB color space, and developed device profiles that would easily transfer color information from one device to another and from one computing platform to another.

Here is the problem the ICC tackled: Each printing device, scanner, digital camera, and monitor has its own way of *rendering* a color (that is, assigning a meaning to a color). This meaning is called the device's *color space*.

Monitors, for example, specify colors as values of red, green, and blue (RGB). The values R:100, G:20, B:30 specify a certain shade of red on a particular monitor. These values are said to be *device-dependent*; if these values are sent to a second monitor with different colored phosphors, a different color red will be displayed. If they are sent to a printer that describes colors as percentages of cyan, magenta, yellow, and black (CMYK), yet a different red will be printed.

Which is the correct color? The color seen on the first monitor? The color seen on the second monitor? Or the color printed on the printer?

## Photoshop 6 Color Working Spaces

Fast forward to today. To enable Photoshop 6 to provide uniform ways of describing color space, Adobe needed to offer several different standard color working spaces. Thanks to the foundation laid by the CIE and the ICC, Adobe was able to do so. For RGB images Photoshop 6 offers sRGB, Adobe RGB 1998, Apple RGB, and Color-match RGB working spaces. For CMYK working spaces, Photoshop 6 offers US Web Coated SWOP, US Web Uncoated, US Sheetfed Coated, US Sheetfed Uncoated, Japan Standard, Euroscale Uncoated, and Euroscale Coated.

Establishing these color working spaces wasn't enough. How could that information be exchanged between devices?

Enter ICC profiles.

## ICC Profiles

ICC profiles are an essential element of the color management equation. Because no device can be brought into perfect calibration, and because no two devices—monitors, printers, or scanners—perform identically even if they are the same make and model, profiles are created to document the ways a specific device strays from the standard. What kind of documentation is this? Read on.

The Adobe CMS uses ICC standard device profiles to ensure that colors are accurately converted across devices. *Profiles* are data files that record all the relevant information for a particular device, including its color space, capabilities, and limitations. Each profile relates a device's color space to the CIE-referenced color space. By doing so, a profile assigns an absolute meaning to each color that a device can produce.

When you transfer an image between two devices that have ICC profiles, a *Color Management Module* (CMM) compares the ICC profile of the source device (such as the monitor) with the ICC profile of the destination device (such as the printer) to create consistent color results. With the information contained in the ICC profile, the CMM transforms colors in image files to produce consistent color simulation on the monitor and the proofing device. For every RGB value in the monitor color space, for example, the color transformation produces a similar CMYK value in the printer's color space. If a color space specified on one device falls outside the color gamut of another device, the CMS may automatically reassign the actual values put out from the devices to preserve the *relationship* of colors from one device to another. The CMS in effect *remaps* colors that fall outside of the other device's gamut, but it does so in a way the human eye accepts.

**Note**

**In Windows It's ICM**   Because the Windows operating system had already assigned the ICC suffix to another system component, Windows refers to ICC profiles as ICM. The suffixes ICC and ICM are interchangeable in the language of CMS.

How do you get ICC profiles? Adobe and your operating system offer generic profiles for popular brands of monitors. In Photoshop, Adobe also offers Adobe Gamma, which creates a custom ICC profile the Adobe CMS can use to understand how your monitor handles color. (Hang on. We cover Adobe Gamma next.)

Even if one of the generic profiles fits your monitor, we recommend that you create a custom ICC profile. It is *not* recommended (at least, not by the authors) to use preset monitor profiles. They are of little value, due to aging and varied viewing conditions of the devices that the profiles describe. Custom profiles are always better. After all, would you rather have a picture of an ideal family or a picture of *your* family?

> **Note**
>
> **Profiling**    When you create an ICC profile for your monitor, you are making a *system-level* adjustment; *any* program that is color management–capable uses the ICC profile you've created for your monitor.

You can (and you should) have multiple ICC profiles for printing devices—one profile for a specific working condition. But use only one profile at a time. Also, be careful that you are using the correct profile for the current condition. For example, you may have one profile for your inkjet printer that you use with the manufacturer's standard glossy paper, and another that you use with a third party's glossy paper.

In addition to performing regular calibration and profiling of the monitor, an artist should try to maintain consistent lighting conditions. The monitor will need to be calibrated and profiled at least once a month. Of all the devices that require ICC profiles, the monitor is the one that most quickly loses its calibration.

## Translation, Please

The Color Management Module (CMM), mentioned earlier, is a color transformation engine that translates data from one device's color to another via an independent color space. The CMM receives the necessary information from the profiles so that it can accurately transform a color from one device to another. The CMM interprets the data and, in essence, says to the monitor, "The file data says to display a blue that has the RGB values of 66, 66, 150, but I've looked at your profile and you always make things too red. You will display RGB value 60, 66, 150 so that it *looks like* the ideal 66, 66, 150. Photoshop doesn't have to know about our arrangement. When it does something to the color 66, 66, 150, use the color in the file data."

When Photoshop performs an operation that requires it to calculate a new color value, that color must be contained in the current working space. The working space's color mode and the position and size of the color gamut of the working space are determined by the ICC profile. To successfully move color values from one color space to another is a difficult problem because color spaces do not generally share the same color gamut. How is this conversion done?

In order to bring all the possible color spaces into a common space where accurate color translation becomes possible, a very large device-independent color space is needed. For example, to translate monitor colors to printer colors, a space must exist that is large enough to encompass all *device-dependent spaces* (spaces that are different, according to device) as well as standard color spaces. At the heart of Adobe's Color engine is a Profile Connection Space (PCS) that is device-independent and has a large enough color gamut to hold both the source and the target color spaces. That PCS is based on the CIELAB color space.

Figure 3.1 shows a representation of LAB color space. It is tongue-shaped because visible light is broken down into uneven amounts, with green being predominant. Our eyes are more sensitive to greens than to blues or reds; hence the distortion in the shape of a color space. In the color section in this book, there is an image (a color image, natch') of the CIELAB color model in two dimensions and three dimensions. It also shows how Adobe RGB (1998)—our recommendation for working spaces) neatly fits inside of the gamut of the LAB space.

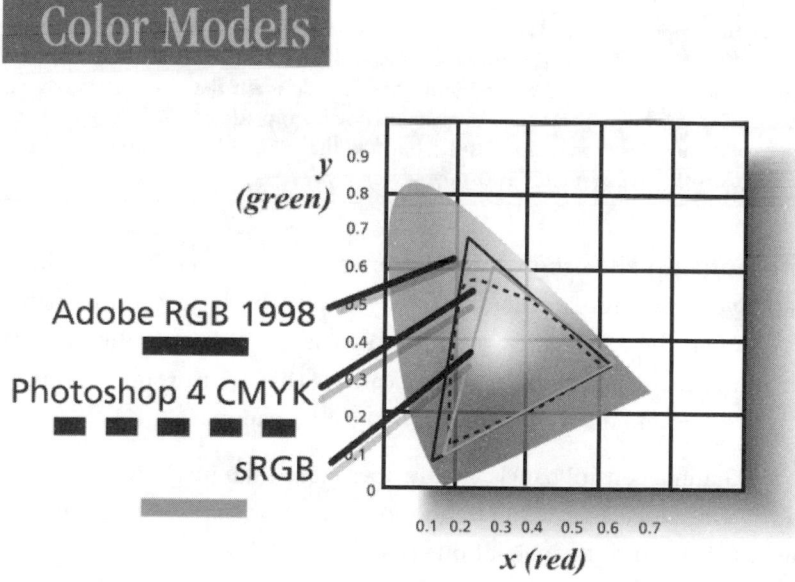

**Figure 3.1**  Different color spaces often fit inside one another, and often overlap.

In the illustration, the working space is Adobe RGB 1998. This color space, larger than anything your monitor can show you, fits within the translation color space making it possible for every point in the space to be mapped—without color loss—

to the translation space (LAB). The colors in printer space, whether it's a commercial press or an inkjet, are CMYK. They represent a smaller space than RGB color and have a few areas that RGB cannot reproduce. Fortunately, the translation layer *can* reproduce those colors. That is why, in the illustration, the printer space eclipses the monitor space slightly, but overall, fits within the working space.

## Adobe Gamma

The term *gamma* is the error measured between a straight, linear mapping of voltage applied to your monitor's circuitry and brightness you see on your monitor. Huh? Okay, example time:

Suppose you were holding a lever that applied voltage to your monitor's blue phosphors. In theory, the screen would be black at zero voltage, medium blue (half blue) at half power, and as bright a blue as possible at full voltage. This is a linear plotting of voltage versus brightness, and it *does not exist*. There is a *sag* in the midrange of the voltage versus brightness graph, which is why we perform gamma correction.

> **Note**
>
> **Gamma Settings Debate Rages On**   You may have heard that Windows gamma is 2.2, or 1.8 for the Macintosh. Do not be confused by the Control Panel's default settings for gamma; don't argue with them. Monitor gamma is different than the gamma of working spaces. Some CMS experts tend to favor 2.2 for both platforms. You very well could have a profile for your monitor that is 2.2, but find that Photoshop's working space displays images with deeper midtones than you'd expect.

When you installed Photoshop, the setup program installed a feature called Adobe Gamma in your Control Panel(s) folder. If you own a Macintosh, the path to the panel is through the Apple menu—Control Panels. In Windows, the Control Panel is under Start, Settings, Control Panel. You can use this Adobe Gamma control panel and your eye to calibrate your monitor or adjust its gamma.

The Adobe Gamma control panel actually does more than just adjust your monitor's gamma. It also builds an ICC profile of your monitor that your operating system CMS can use instead of the default one that was installed when you installed your monitor or operating system. In fact, the Adobe Gamma control panel provides a much better profile, one that is tailored to the way your monitor actually operates and not just what the engineering specification for the monitor said should be happening.

**Note**

> **Use Third-Party Software If Your Work Is Color Critical**   If your work is color critical, you may want to use a more precise, less subjective method to calibrate and profile your monitor. Third-party folks like Monaco, X-Rite, and Gretag Macbeth all offer special color measurement hardware and software that produces a more precise result, but a result that can cost anywhere from $300 to tens of thousands of dollars. For most people, however, the Adobe Gamma software does a good enough job profiling the monitor, and the price certainly can't be argued.

For most computers, Adobe Gamma's control of the monitor's white point and gamma affects your view of everything and every program displayed onscreen, whether it uses color management or not. (The *white point,* or *highlight,* is the lightest part of the picture; it is the point along the range of tones in an image after which light tones appear white.)

There are some situations in which Adobe Gamma doesn't have full control: Windows NT 4 and some Windows 95 machines with video cards do not allow software to manipulate display hardware on a global basis. If you use Windows NT 4 or Windows 95 and have one of the stubborn video cards, you're not totally out of luck—Windows allows programs such as Photoshop and PageMaker that "understand" color management to alter the display and use the information Adobe Gamma provides (along with the info in the ICC profile) to adjust the information sent to the display, even if *every* program and the system itself do not permit that alteration and adjustment. On the Windows NT 4 operating system, the ICM must reside in the Color folder within the System32 folder in order to be available to graphic applications that support system-level profiles.

**Warning**

> **Watch Out for Double Color Management**   If you use Adobe Gamma to calibrate and set the gamma of your monitor, don't use another program's software to do the same thing. Pick one system and use it.

## Color Clipping

You now know that, for physical reasons, every device—monitor, printer, camera—is limited in the number of colors it can use. The group of colors available to a device—its *color space*—differs from that of other kinds of devices (monitors and printers, let's say). When one color space can express 10 shades of green, for example, you will see nice transition or good detail in parts of the image that use green. But what happens when you ask a different device to display the same image, and that device has a smaller color space or one with less variety in the number of greens available to it? What if it can express only two shades of green? All 10 of the greens will have to be expressed as one or the other of the two available greens in the new color space. The result will be a poster effect—areas of flat, saturated color where lots of different colors (green, in this example) were. This posterization of color is called *color clipping*. The way a color that is clipped is mapped into the new gamut is called *rendering intent*. We talk more about rendering intent later.

Color clipping can happen when you move an image between standard color spaces, such as RGB and CMYK, as well as when you move between subsets of each color space (Adobe RGB to sRGB, for example) or between the color gamuts that different inks or dyes can produce. It is the color management engine that uses the ICC profiles for the different devices and color gamuts and determines the best way to resolve the differences in color capability.

If you're striving for a lighter color or a more saturated one, and nothing seems to work, you've reached the greatest possible parameters for such a color when it is output using the media and methods you've chosen. To get the color you want, you'd have to step outside the image's color gamut. In the CMYK print world, that usually means adding an extra ink, a spot color. A *spot color* is a custom ink that is prepared to represent a color that's unavailable in the CMYK color space. It is applied as a separate color plate, in addition to the cyan, magenta, yellow, and black printing plates.

## Preparing to Create a Custom Profile

Before we start building custom profiles and plugging them into the system, let's look at other issues that impact color management. Getting these issues squared away will make your custom profile more accurate.

### Check Out Yourself, Your Environment, and Your Equipment

All the color profiling and monitor calibration on earth won't help you achieve color consistency across devices if you don't get your physical working conditions in order. Here are a few questions you should ask yourself:

- Have you been to the eye doctor lately?
- Are you taking cold medication? If so, it will really affect your color perception.

- Have you cleaned the smudges off your eyeglasses? Your glasses aren't tinted, are they? Did you remember to park your sunglasses at the door?

- Have you wiped the monitor screen clean lately? You aren't using a glare filter or one of those polarizing privacy screens, are you?

- Is the monitor warmed up? Has it been on for at least 30 minutes before you use it for color work or before you create a new profile?

- Do you work in a windowless room or one with heavily draped windows? You should, because the constantly changing qualities of natural light make it impossible to achieve accurate consistent color.

- Is your artificial lighting even? No bare bulbs peeking out from under their shades? No hot spots reflected in the monitor, or shadows cast across it?

- Is your lighting a neutral, subdued white? Or is the light in your work space too blue because it is lit with fluorescent tubes, or too yellow because incandescent lamps provide your lighting. See if you can't get your boss to install professionally color-balanced lighting, or at least try to get the fluorescent tubes that profess to have fuller frequency ranges to mimic daylight. If you are using fluorescent bulbs, the next time they need replacing change them to 5000K bulbs, available at most home improvement stores.

- Are your walls, furniture, curtains, posters, paintings, and plants all a nice neutral, medium gray? Probably not. Be aware that light reflecting off everything in the room can change the color of the light in the room and alter your perception of the colors on your screen and the output from your printer.

- Did you know that even the color of your clothing can make a difference? If your work is color critical, put on a light gray lab coat or artist's smock when you sit down to work. Who knows; your customers might be so impressed with your "technical" uniform that you could charge more. Or more likely, if you pay attention to everything on this list and in this chapter—your color work will be so dead on, your customers will *beg* to pay you more. Wouldn't that be nice (this is a rhetorical question)?

- Have you extended the neutral gray color scheme to your desktop wallpaper, Windows title bars, and other screen elements? Let the color live in your work and not in your immediate surroundings.

We know you're anxious to get to the fun stuff, creating something in Photoshop or ImageReady, and that you'd like to finish all this hardware, techie stuff ASAP. But just as you have to do your exercises if you want to keep fit and trim, you have to put in some time now to get your *system* in shape so you can enjoy the good life of a successful Photoshop user.

## Read Your Monitor Manual

Before you start to calibrate and create a profile for your monitor, using Adobe Gamma or any other calibration device, you need to find out on what color temperature your monitor bases its display. A monitor's temperature, also called its *white point,* is a value, measured in degrees Kelvin that describes the point at which white light is produced from equal amounts of red, green, and blue light. Monitors are designed to operate at a white point that matches one of the standard illuminant temperatures defined by the CIE standards body. Some monitors offer a selection of operating temperatures from which the user can pick, while others offer only one fixed setting.

As you can see in Table 3.1, the default white point setting for Windows monitors is 6500 degrees Kelvin. This may be referred to as 6500K, D65, or daylight. The Macintosh OS default color temperature is 9300K (D93, or Cool White) The color temperature most often used in the publishing (to paper) community is 5000K (D50 or Warm White, Page White, or Paper White), because it produces a view that more closely resembles material printed on white paper. Other common white point settings are 5500K and 7500K. One of the latest trends among the CMS gurus is to use 6500K for both platforms.

### Table 3.1   Default White Point Settings

| Environment | Default White Point | Standard Abbreviation | Commonly Referred To As |
| --- | --- | --- | --- |
| Windows | 6500K | D65 | Daylight |
| Macintosh | 9300K | D93 | Cool White |
| Publishing to Paper | 5000K | D50 | Warm White, Page White, or Paper White |

Check your monitor's manual, its onscreen help, or the manufacturer's Web site to see whether your monitor offers a user-definable color temperature and how to make that selection. If your monitor does offer a choice of color temperature or white point, you should choose based on the work you do most often. If your work centers around print, use the monitor's controls to set the white point at 5000K. If you design mostly for Web or onscreen presentation, you could set your white point to the default temperature of the operating system used by most people who view your work. Or you could split the difference and set your hardware temperature to 7500K, if your monitor offers that choice (the author's monitor doesn't). Or you could set it to match the default setting for your operating system.

Older monitors may not offer user-definable color temperature, but you should still see what the fixed temperature of the monitor is. Whatever type of monitor you have, find out what the current white point setting is, change it if you can and want to, and then write it down. You will need this value handy when you use Adobe Gamma to calibrate and make an ICC profile for your monitor.

If you are unable to find any of this information, don't panic. Adobe Gamma has a measurement feature that will provide an approximate value for your monitor's white point.

Setting the color temperature and gamma when calibrating and profiling the monitor can be referred to as "setting the *target*." In work environments with more than one monitor, it is important to always use the same target when you're trying to achieve consistent color from one workstation to another.

### Install the Latest Drivers for Your Equipment

Before you begin to set up your system and Photoshop to use color management, make sure that you have installed all the latest drivers for your equipment. Monitor, video card, scanner, and printer manufacturers often update their drivers to fix bugs and to add or update the ICC profiles they have created for their products. These default manufacturer profiles are what you'll use if you don't create custom-made profiles for your equipment. In addition, they are often used by products that profile things, including Adobe Gamma, as a basis for the custom profile. So, fire up your Internet browser or give customer service at each place a call, and get the newest drivers your equipment's manufacturers have to offer. Follow their instructions for installing the drivers on your computer.

## Creating an ICC Profile for a Monitor

Okay—gamma, brightness/contrast, and other parameters lie ahead of us. Follow these steps to create an ICC profile for your monitor, using Adobe Gamma:

### Example 3.1    Profiling Your Monitor

1. If you haven't done so already, go to the *monitor* manufacturer's Web site and download, and then follow their instructions to install the most recent drivers for your monitor.

   By installing the latest drivers, you ensure that the Adobe Gamma will base its work on the most accurate information available about your monitor.

2. With Photoshop and other applications closed, open the Control Panel(s) (folder), and double-click the Adobe Gamma icon.

   The Adobe Gamma control panel opens. You can choose to work with a single dialog box that has a number of different tasks, or use a step-by-step method that involves a Windows Wizard or a Macintosh Assistant.

3. Click to set the Control Panel option, and then click Next. We'll show you how the single dialog version (shown in Figure 3.2) of this application works, but you're free to switch to the step-by-step method at any time by clicking the Wizard (Assistant) button.

   In the Description field, you should see one or more profiles listed for your monitor. These profiles are already installed on your system and assigned to your monitor. If there are two, one was probably installed when you installed your operating system and the other is the one you just down-loaded and installed from the monitor manufacturer. Unless you told the install program differently, the last installed profile is the one currently in use.

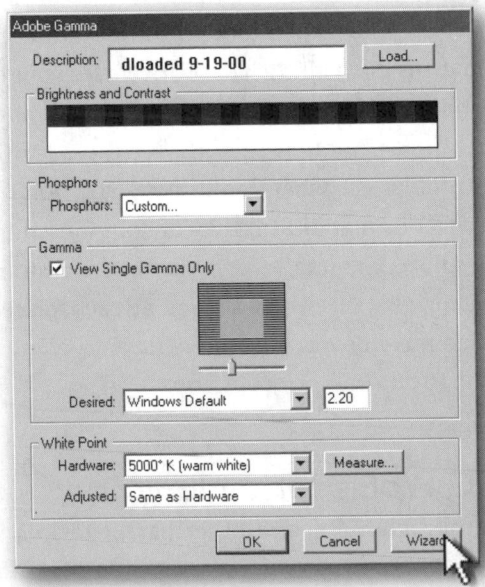

**Figure 3.2**    If you want to walk through the process of using the Adobe Gamma Control Panel screen by screen, click the Wizard or Assistant button.

4. Highlight the profile you just installed in step 1, and type a meaningful name, like **dloaded-9-19-00**, to indicate that you downloaded it on Sept. 19, 2000. This will make it easier to pick the profile from a list, if you choose to use this profile at a later date.

   Adobe Gamma will base the new profile being created on the highlighted profile in the Description field.

5. Click the Load button if you want to base the new profile on a profile other than the one currently in the field.

6. Using the controls on your monitor, increase the Contrast to 100%, or as high as the control will go. With your eye on the Brightness and Contrast section of the Adobe Gamma Panel, use the monitor's brightness control to adjust brightness up or down until the gray squares in the gray-and-black checkerboard strip are almost black (see Figure 3.3). The goal is to end up with an almost black-and-black checkerboard strip above a crisp, bright white strip. If the white gets dirty, be sure to increase the brightness.

**Figure 3.3**   Use your monitor's brightness and contrast knobs or onscreen controls to make the gray squares in the Adobe Gamma Control Panel almost black.

> **Warning**
>
> **Changes to Contrast and Brightness Will Affect Profiles**   If you change the monitor's contrast and brightness settings later in the profile-making process, or at any time in the future, the profile will no longer be accurate and you will have to create a new profile. If your monitor has external knobs that adjust brightness and contrast, you should use duct tape—or stronger—to tape them down so they can't be changed by accident.

7. Change the Phosphors setting only if you are *absolutely certain* that what is shown is wrong. If you are *certain* it is wrong, but you don't know what the right setting is, the best guess would be Trinitron.

   Adobe Gamma sets the Phosphors properties based on information from the manufacturer's profile. If you installed the latest driver and profile from your monitor's manufacturer, you probably won't have to make any changes with the Phosphors drop-down list. For many users, the setting will be Custom; you should leave it alone and move on to the fun control: Gamma.

8. Make sure that the View Single Gamma Only option is checked. Then, lean back and squint, and drag the slider to the left or to the right until the solid tone in the center has the same apparent tone as the stripes outside the box.

   You just defined gamma by using a composite control that applied the same gamma setting to each of the three RGB channels. This "one-gamma-setting-fits-all-channels" method works just fine for most people. However, if you want greater control or if you think that your monitor's RGB channels are a bit out of synch with each other, clear the View Single Gamma Only option and, one by one, drag the slider under each box until the center box fades into the striped frame around it. Then move on to the next step.

   If you are using Windows NT 4 or Windows 95 with certain video cards, you will not have the option of choosing a setting from the Desired drop-down list, as shown in the next step. This is a limitation imposed by the operating system and not by Adobe Gamma. Some Windows 95 users, and all Windows 98 and Windows 2000 users, will have the option available to them and should follow the advice in the next step.

9. Choose Windows Default, Macintosh Default, or Custom from the Desired drop-down list. I chose Windows Default (see Figure 3.4) because I'm working on a Windows computer. If you use a Macintosh, you probably want to choose Macintosh Default from the list. If you choose Custom, you will need to enter a value in the field next to the drop-down. We don't recommend choosing a custom setting unless you are very experienced in color management and have a very compelling reason to do so.

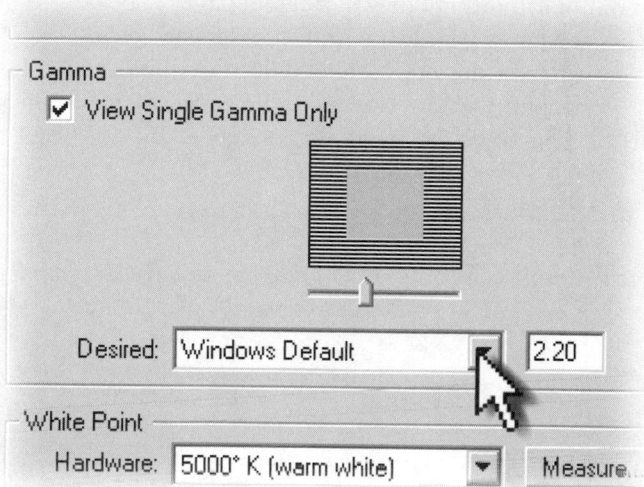

**Figure 3.4**   Choose either Windows Default or Macintosh Default from the (Gamma) Desired drop-down. Your choice should match your operating system.

In the White Point area of the Adobe Gamma Control dialog box are two drop-down lists. The first refers to the actual hardware setting of your monitor.

10. Click on the Hardware drop-down list and choose the color temperature your monitor *actually* uses. Earlier in the chapter, this is the value you set or determined in the "Read Your Monitor Manual" section.

11. If you were unable to determine the hardware setting, or if your monitor is old and you think it might not be operating as well as it used to, click the Measure button next to the Hardware drop-down list. Follow the onscreen instructions carefully. Removing all ambient light means the room should be dark. You may even want to wait until night to do this if your work space has windows. Click on the center square when you are done. The entry in the Hardware drop-down list will now read Custom.

The Adjusted drop-down box offers the same color temperature choices as the Hardware drop-down list did. Adobe Gamma can override the hardware settings and force the monitor to display other standard white points.

The lighting conditions present when you're calibrating and profiling the monitor should be maintained when you use that profile. If you use other lighting conditions you should recalibrate and reprofile. In other words, don't calibrate your new computer in the store and expect the profiles to hold true when you get the machine home.

12. If you ever need to use a nonstandard white point, choose Custom from the list, and enter the values that describe the custom white point.

If your monitor can display the color temperature you want to use, then you should choose Same as Hardware from the Adjusted drop-down list. If your monitor has a fixed color point of 9600K, for example, and you want to use a 5000K white point to more closely mimic paper, then choose 5000K from the Adjusted drop-down list, as shown in Figure 3.5.

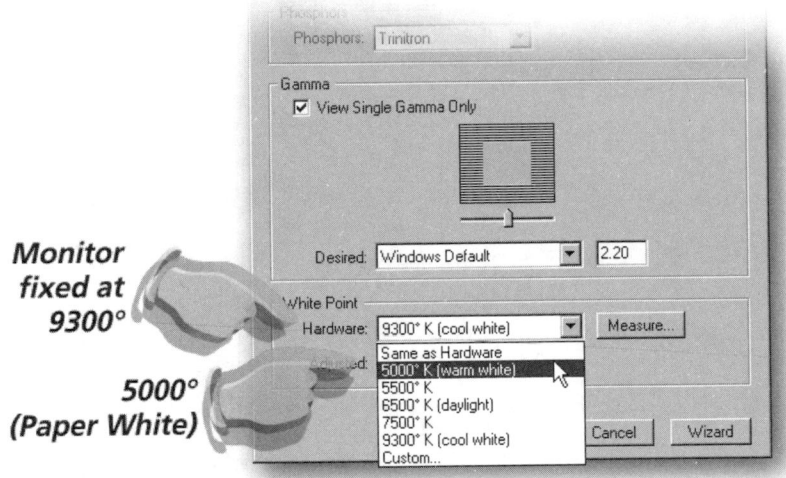

**Figure 3.5**   Choose a color temperature in keeping with the way you view your final output in Photoshop.

13. Click OK, and then in the Save As dialog box, give a descriptive name to your monitor's custom profile. On the Macintosh, the file extension will be .PF; in Windows, it's *.ICM.

    For example, I'm calling the settings for one of my machines **Win98 machine 8-26-00.icm**. In this way, I can tell how recently I profiled the monitor.

14. Click Save, and then click OK in the Gamma Control Panel to finish calibrating and profiling your monitor.

It probably took longer to read how to calibrate and profile your monitor than it took to actually *do* it! Which is a good thing, because if you want to keep your colors consistent you really should recalibrate and reprofile your monitor at least once a month, if nothing noticeable has changed in the environment. Recalibrate and reprofile right away if something *does* change in the environment. Changing a light bulb or repainting the room both qualify as events that should cause you to open up Adobe Gamma and run through it one more time.

Now that every color management–aware piece of software on your system has a target profile for your monitor, it will be easier to establish color consistency when you print or do Web work in Photoshop. The next thing to do is to set up a working color space for Photoshop.

Photoshop and the CMS look in specific folders for profiles. The location of the folder that stores profiles depends on the operating system you use. Table 3.2 shows where you should save profiles you've created or obtained if you want to make them available for use.

**Table 3.2    Required Locations for ICC Profiles**

| Operating System | Installed Location of ICC Profiles |
| --- | --- |
| Windows 98 | Windows\system32\Color |
| Windows NT version 4 | WinNT\system32\Color |
| Windows 2000 | WinNT\system32\spool\drivers\color |
| Macintosh OS using ColorSync, earlier than version 2.5 | System Folder, Preferences, ColorSync Profiles |
| Macintosh OS using ColorSync version 2.5 or later | System Folder, ColorSync Profiles |

To recap: You've profiled your monitor, And the operating system has assigned that profile to your monitor. Now it is time to open Photoshop and start setting up the rules for the way it should do its part in the color management process.

## Setting Photoshop's Color Management Defaults

Setting Photoshop Color Setting defaults doesn't take much time, but it does require a little thought to make them work best with the kind of work you do most. These settings can be changed at any time. These are defaults, which means they are the rules Photoshop will use unless you tell Photoshop to do something else. You can always override default settings on a per-file basis; when you find that you frequently are overriding the default settings, just press Ctrl(⌘)+Shift+K and set new defaults.

To make matters even simpler, Adobe has come up with different collections of settings that suit common needs of different types of work: printing to U.S., European, or Japanese printing presses, creating graphics for the Internet, working in the color spaces of Photoshop 4, or even turning off color management. If one of the default settings is good for your kind of work, your stay in this dialog box will be brief. But if the defaults don't cut it for you, or you just want greater control over things, there are lots of choices you can make. In the next sections you'll discover what all the choices are, and I'll offer some recommendations for what you should choose.

Most of the recommendations are based on the premise that you are looking for a good, general-purpose work space profile; one that enables the monitor's color capability to show through, one that embraces most other color output spaces, and gives a reasonably accurate view of images that come from different color spaces. Some images might be RGB, some might be LAB color, while others might have been saved in CMYK mode. It all depends on where you work!

### A Word on Your "Out Of The Box" Experience

You haven't ruined anything if you ran Photoshop for the first time, and you answered no to Photoshop's offer to help you determine Custom color settings. It only means that you need to press Ctrl(⌘)+Shift+K and change one or two things in the Color Settings box to get a better color space going in Photoshop than the default. More importantly, the authors have saved all images on the Companion CD to Adobe RGB 1998 color space. You will get annoying, confusing dialog boxes when you open every image on the CD if you do not go with our recommendations concerning color space.

In a nutshell, Adobe has chosen sRGB as the default color space in Photoshop, and the authors disagree. We feel you should be working most of the time in Adobe RGB 1998 color space. Read on!

## The Color Settings Dialog Box, or Laying Down the Rules

This section takes you to color management central, the Color Settings dialog box. We won't cover this as an exercise with lots of numbered steps, because we don't know what the best choices for you will be. That's up to you to decide. What we do want to do is explain what all the choices mean, and translate the jargon of color management into more understandable and accessible terms. Here's what we'd like you to do, to make following along easier:

> Open Photoshop (you do not need an image to be open), and then choose Edit, Color Settings, or press Ctrl(⌘)+Shift+K.

> The Color Settings dialog box pops up onscreen, where you can refer to it as you proceed through the following sections.

The Color Settings dialog box on your screen (and in Figure 3.6) has two major functions. It is used to define the default working color space that will be used when you create an image, and to "tag" the image with the ICC profile of the work space. The work space tag is kind of like a short biography that tells what color space the file was born in and where it currently lives. The tag is also used to set the rules or color management policies for what happens when you work with files that don't have work space tags or have tags that don't match the default space you've set.

For most folks, the choices shown in Figure 3.6 should be perfect for getting right down to work in Photoshop. If your screen doesn't look like this figure, manually select the options, so that your screen will match what you're reading here. As mentioned earlier, the authors cannot adopt Adobe's decision to make the default space the teensy, Web-friendly sRGB color space.

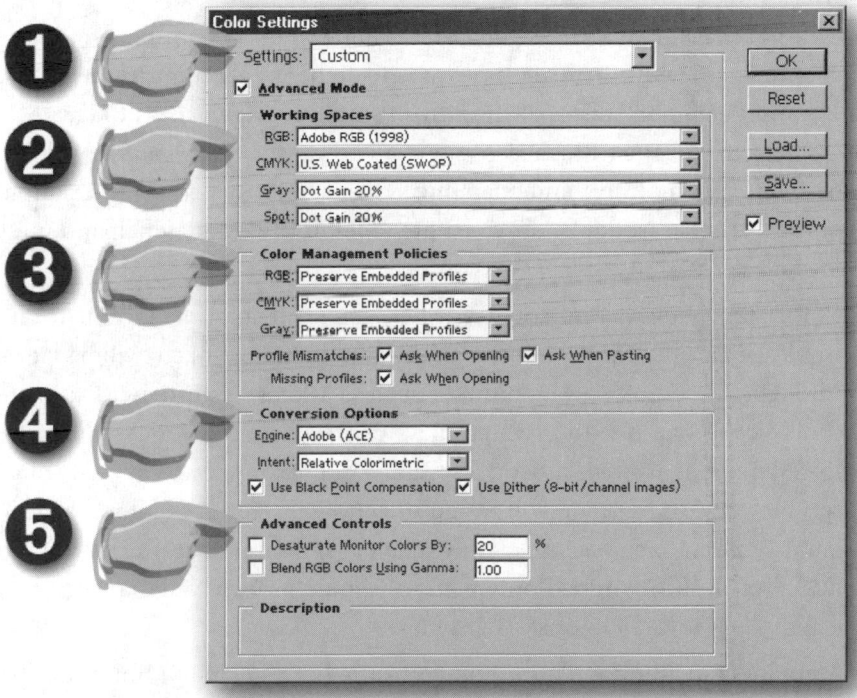

**Figure 3.6** There are five areas you need to set in the Color Settings dialog box to make the work space foolproof and easy to work in.

## The Settings Drop-Down List

The Settings drop-down list is used to choose either a preset collection of settings or to enable you to set the various settings in the dialog box independently. Adobe has provided some very useful presets, and you, of course, can also create your own presets and choose them from this drop-down list. When you choose one of the presets in this drop-down list, the preset specifies and sets all the other fields and options in the dialog box for you. If none of the shipping color setting files meet your needs, go through the dialog box, make your choices, and then save all the changes you've made to a new color setting file. From then on, you can access your custom settings with the convenience and precision of the shipping presets. You can even share these settings with other people by giving them the file that was created.

If you click the arrow for the Settings drop-down list you'll see that Adobe has provided the following presets:

- **Color Management Off.** As good as it is under most circumstances to use color management, there are times when you definitely want to turn it off. The most common reason for turning off color management is to create graphics that in their finished version will be viewed only onscreen, by users with different monitors and operating systems, or for video work. Examples of such material would be onscreen help files, reference material, and multimedia presentations.

- **Color Management On.** Instances when you want color management on would be material for the Web or an intranet that most likely will be viewed through an ICC color-aware browser, such as Microsoft's Internet Explorer should be managed with sRGB profiles. Also, if you know for certain that material will be viewed only on a specific kind of monitor or by users of a specific operating system, you would not choose to turn off color management. For example, Macintosh-only material should probably carry an Apple RGB profile, and Windows-only material should probably be managed by using Adobe RBG 1998 or sRGB profiles.

- **Emulate Photoshop 4.** Photoshop 4 was the last version of Photoshop that did not have any color management features. Internally, both Macintosh and Windows versions of Photoshop 4 (and earlier versions) used a working space based on the characteristics of a Macintosh monitor. Choose this preset if you are working with files created in early versions of Photoshop, files you used successfully in projects of that era that you might need to reproduce. Choose them also when you are working with older graphics and DTP software that does not have color management features.

- **Europe Prepress Defaults, Japan Prepress Defaults, and U.S. Prepress Defaults.** Each of these three separate presets defines conditions suitable for common commercial press conditions of the specific region. These are generic conditions and are good as a starting point for creating a custom definition for the area of the world and the kind of press/ink sets and paper conditions you typically use.

- **Photoshop 5 Default Spaces.** This preset lands your Photoshop working space back in the sRGB mode, which we tell you is only good for screen presentations and Web work. Only make this your preset if you did oodles of work in Photoshop 5, and you have no business that requires photographic realism when going to print.

- **Web Graphics Default.** The settings specified by this preset are optimal for creating graphics that will be viewed on the Web or on an intranet through ICC-aware Web browsers.

- **ColorSync Workflow (Macintosh OS only).** Choose this setting if you are using ColorSync version 3.0 or higher, and you are using the ColorSync Control Panel to choose profiles.

## Working Spaces

The settings in the Working Spaces section of the Color Settings dialog box determine which of the many ICC profiles is the default working space profile assigned to newly created files. It's critical to understand here that when you convert from—say RGB to CMYK—the resulting color space that the CMYK image is saved to is not necessarily the CMYK space you want. The image will default to the current CMYK Working Space in the Color Settings dialog box. Unless you only have one output device, and you've chosen the profile for that device in the Color Settings box, then you will get more accurate results by changing color mode using Image, Mode, Convert to Profile instead of depending on the Image, Mode colors listed in the main menu.

The Working Spaces section of the Color Settings dialog box contains four dropdown lists labeled RGB, CMYK, Gray, and Spot, respectively. The working space for each color mode is defined by the ICC profile you want to attach automatically to new documents that use the same color space: RGB, CMYK, Grayscale, or Multichannel.

When the Advanced Mode option is checked, the ICC profiles available at the system level are displayed. Those are the ones in the ColorSync folder (Macintosh) or Color folder (WIN). If you have loaded profiles in these locations and you need to access them, you should activate the Advanced Mode.

### Choosing from the RGB Work Spaces Drop-Down List

When you click the down arrow to expose the choices offered by the RGB drop-down list, you may find a *huge* list of profiles to choose from. The number of profiles in the RGB drop-down list depends on the number of RGB profiles loaded at the system level, and whether the Advanced Mode is activated. If Advanced Mode is not activated, the list is rather short. The profiles are grouped into the following categories:

- **Custom.** (Available in Advanced Mode only.) At the top of the list is Custom RGB. If you choose this option you can define your own custom RGB space. Unless you are an expert in color management trying to solve a particular problem, we strongly recommend that you avoid the potential masochism in creating your own RGB work space. That said, the only reason ordinary Photoshop users might use this feature would be to create a profile for BruceRGB. (For information on BruceRGB, see the Note at the end of this section.)

- **Load RGB and Save RGB.** (Available in Advanced Mode only.) These two commands are found in the second section of the drop-down list. Load RGB enables you to cruise your hard disks for an ICC profile that's not in the system level Color folder—oddly, this is not an option when Advanced Mode is not checked. Photoshop can convert the monitor setup file (*.AMS) into an ICC profile if you save it by using the Save RGB command after you've loaded it with the Load RGB command. Save RGB will save any currently chosen RGB work space profile to any location on your hard disk, which is handy when you need to share a custom profile with another Photoshop user.

- **Other.** This section contains any profile you've created with the Custom command but have not yet saved with the Save RGB command.

- **Adobe Gamma Created Profiles.** If you are using Windows NT 4, you will use Adobe Gamma to load custom monitor profiles created by third-party hardware and software. This is where your monitor profile designated by Adobe Gamma will show up. In Photoshop 5, the Adobe Gamma created profiles category was displayed in the RGB Color Settings. Although not labeled as such, the next area of the list contains the custom ICC monitor profile(s) that you created with Adobe Gamma.

- **Standard Working Spaces.** This part of the list contains the profiles that are the best as default working spaces. Unless you are working under unusual conditions, you should choose one of the profiles in this section. The profiles are Adobe RGB (1998), Apple RGB, ColorMatch RGB, and sRGB IEC61966-2.1 (commonly referred to as sRGB).

  - **Adobe RGB (1998).** A good all-around RGB working space with a color gamut large enough to produce decent RGB or CMYK printed output. This is our recommendation as a default working space.

  - **Apple RGB.** A good working space if your finished work will be seen only on Macintosh OS monitors, or if you are using older software that is not capable of color management. This is the working space used by the Emulate Photoshop 4 preset.

  - **ColorMatch RGB.** Corresponds to the color space of the Pressview monitor. A small color space, it is sometimes used for images that will be output to a CMYK commercial printing press. Many prepress experts prefer to use a larger space than this for print work.

  - **sRGB IEC61966-2.1.** The working color space of choice for the creation of Web graphics. If you think you will use an image on the Web and also in print, choose Adobe RGB (1998) as your work space instead. sRGB is too narrow for print work, even on RGB inkjet printers.

  On the Macintosh, ColorSync RGB is also available as a standard working space. The actual working space used when Macintosh ColorSync is chosen depends on what you've chosen in the Apple ColorSync control panel.

- **More RGB Profiles.** (Available in Advanced Mode only.) The last section of the list contains all other RGB profiles available in your computer's System level Color folders. You'll see all kinds of default device profiles for monitors, printers, scanners, and cameras, as well as profiles installed by RGB equipment you own. A few standard working spaces are listed here also; they include NTSC (1953) and PAL/SECAM,SMPTE-C, which refer to TV and video color spaces; CIE

RGB and Wide Gamut RGB, both very wide, large color spaces that are *not* recommended unless you are working with files that are 16 bits per channel. Kodak Open Interchange RGB also may be in your list; it is very close to CIELAB and is used with color profile editing software.

Adobe RGB (1998) is the best overall choice for working with or creating images that will output in a variety of ways. Logos, for example, typically are used in print, on the Web, in videos, and on product packaging. If you want to be able to set and forget your work space profile, Adobe RGB (1998) is the one to choose because it is the most flexible work space. If you want to tweak images from the moment the first pixel is laid down, you should choose one of the special-use profiles that will work best for your intended output.

**Note**

**Meet BruceRGB**   One other standard RGB space, BruceRGB, is worth mentioning. Bruce Fraser, a prepress guru and writer, felt that Adobe RGB was too large a color space and that ColorMatch was too small for most prepress work. BruceRGB has become one of the accepted standard work spaces in the pre-press world. Unfortunately, Adobe doesn't install BruceRGB profile along with the other standard RGB working spaces. You can use the Custom RGB feature described earlier, however, to create this profile. To obtain the values you must enter in the Custom RGB dialog box to create the profile, and for other information about the color space, visit Mr. Fraser's Web site. You'll find the address in the resource section at the end of this chapter.

### Choosing from the CMYK Work Spaces Drop-Down List

The profile you choose in the CMYK drop-down list is the profile that will be applied to new CMYK images you create. You should be aware that what you specify as your default working CMYK space is also the default space when you use the View menu's proofing feature. Unless a custom proofing space is specified, the default CMYK working space is used for the soft-proof view, even when the image being proofed is an RGB image or has a different CMYK working space. The structure of the drop-down list parallels that of the RGB list:

- **Custom.** When you click on the CMYK Custom option, you'll see a dialog box that will be familiar if you ever looked at or changed the CMYK settings in Photoshop 5.5. If you need to tweak the settings of an existing profile or create one of your own, this is the place to do it. But if you are trying to re-create a custom setting you created and saved in an earlier version of Photoshop, it's easier to use the Load CMYK and Save CMYK options instead.

- **Load CMYK and Save CMYK.** Use these two commands to load new ICC profiles you may have obtained, or to load CMYK Setup files (*.API) or Separation Setup files (*.ASP) you may have created in previous versions of Photoshop. Use Save CMYK to save a loaded ICC profile to disk or to convert and save a CMYK Setup file or Separation Setup file you've loaded to the now-standard *ICC profile* that Photoshop 6 uses.

- **Other.** This section contains any profile you've created with the Custom command and have not yet saved with the Save CMYK command.

- **Standard CMYK Work Spaces.** This section contains the profiles you'll use most. These standard profiles were designed to describe the colors that can be printed using various kinds of presses and papers under print conditions typical in the U.S., Europe, and Japan. You should choose for your default the profile that matches the CMYK press conditions you most often use. If you are working with files from Photoshop 4 or earlier, or files that will be used in older publishing programs that are not capable of color management, you may prefer to choose a standard profile—the Photoshop 4 Default CMYK or Photoshop 5 Default CMYK profile—from the next section on the list instead. On the Macintosh, ColorSync CMYK is also available as a standard working space. The actual working space used when Macintosh ColorSync is chosen depends on what you've chosen in the Apple ColorSync control panel.

  Generally, the CMYK ICC profile you use for soft-proofing would be the same one you use for conversion from RGB or LAB to CMYK.

### Choosing from the Gray Work Spaces Drop-Down List

By now you've surely (and correctly) guessed that the Gray drop-down is used to specify which profile is used by default with grayscale images. This one has a twist—it has two custom commands:

- **Custom Dot Gain.** (Available in Advanced Mode only.) Choose this command to display the Custom Dot Gain dialog box, where you can enter values or click points and drag on the curve to create a profile that matches the way dot gain occurs at different halftone percentage points when printed. *Dot gain* is the amount by which a printed halftone dot increases or decreases in size when the ink, dye, toner, or other pigment is applied to the printed surface. To determine how to construct the curve, you should use a densitometer to take readings from an gradient bar that actually used the same inks, media, and output device you will ultimately use. For example, if the densitometer produces a reading of 16% when it reads the 10% portion of the gradient tint bar, you would type **16** in the 10% field of the Custom

Dot Gain dialog box. If you do not have access to test prints, ask the folks who run the press which values you should use.

- **Custom Gamma.** (Available in Advanced Mode only.) With this command you can create a profile for grayscale images that mimics their display on a monitor that has a custom gamma setting. Gamma determines the contrast of the midtones in an image. If you want to use a profile that reflects the gamma settings for Macintosh and Windows monitors, use either the Gray Gamma 1.8 or 2.2 settings at the bottom of the list.

- **Load Gray and Save Gray.** (Available in Advanced Mode only.) Use these commands to load custom gray ICC profiles you may have obtained but that are not installed, or to save a custom setting you've created.

- **Other.** This section contains any profile you've created with the Custom command but have not yet saved with the Save Gray command.

- **Standard Gray working spaces.** The balance of the list contains standard profiles that reflect dot gains of 10, 15, 20, 25, and 30 percent. This section also contains standard profiles called Gray Gamma 1.8 and Gray Gamma 2.2. Gray Gamma 1.8 mimics the default gamma of a Macintosh OS monitor and also corresponds to the default grayscale setting used in Photoshop 4 and earlier versions. Gray Gamma 2.2 corresponds to the default gamma of a Windows OS monitor. Choose the default setting that most closely matches the behavior of your most common grayscale output.

### Choosing from the Spot Working Spaces Drop-Down List

The default choice you make in the Spot working spaces drop-down list differs from the others in that it governs the way spot color channels and duotones display. These profiles are the only ones that are not attached to files themselves, as you would embed other types of profiles in saved files. The choices here are identical to those offered in the Gray Working Spaces drop-down, except that Custom Gamma and the two Gray Gamma choices are not available here. You create custom dot gain profiles and choose between standard default profiles based on the same information and concerns you would for dot gain in the Gray Working Spaces. If the system level Color folder holds custom Grayscale ICC profiles, another section (the custom Grayscale set) will appear after the Standard set.

## Color Management Policies

The default working spaces profiles you just went through apply primarily to newly created files. But what happens when you open a file that doesn't have a color management profile attached to it, or that has a different working space profile attached to it than the default profile you've selected? Similarly, what happens when you cut from and paste into images that have different working spaces? The next section in the dialog box takes care of situations in which profiles are mismatched. Adobe calls the actions taken by Photoshop to reconcile color mismatches and missing profiles the *Color Management Policies*.

Each of the three drop-down lists—RGB, CMYK, and Gray—offers the same three Color Management Policy options:

- **Off.** This setting doesn't exactly mean no color management at all. It means that an ICC work space will *not* be assigned to newly created files. This is not to say that the working spaces you have designated are not affecting the soft-proofing capabilities while working on a newly-created file in Photoshop. Very large gamut RGB working spaces usually create printed output that is prone to excessive clipping, so a choice here other than off might be the solution when you aren't happy with the output.

  Off also means that profiles attached to documents that are opened will be ignored, and they will be discarded if they do not match default working space. On the other hand, if the profile of the opened document matches the current default profile, the profile will be preserved.

  And Off means that when part or all of an image is pasted into another image, the colors will be added based on their absolute numeric value.

**Note**

**Perception Versus Numerical Value in Color Conversion**   When the numerical value of a color takes precedence in determining how colors are translated from one color space to another, the perceived color often changes, and many observers would not think it a faithful translation. The reason is that the perceived color of inks and dyes is greatly affected by the surface to which they are applied. For example, when a numerically specified color (RGB 97, 176, 224) is applied to newsprint it appears darker and duller than the same color printed on glossy, coated cover stock.

When the perceived appearance takes precedence over the numerical value of a color, the goal is to create a color that appears to be the same on newsprint as on cover stock, even though the actual ink or combination of inks used is wildly different. Maintaining perceptual color fidelity is very important when you are working with corporate colors or most photographic material.

- **Preserve Embedded Profiles.** This color management policy means that profiles attached to open documents are used and preserved. When material from one file is copied into another and the working space profiles of the two do not match, this policy attempts to maintain perceptual color values when the receiving image is an RGB or grayscale image, and will use absolute numeric color values when the receiving image is a CMYK image.

- **Convert to Working.** When this policy is in effect, the default behavior is to convert all opened images to the current working color space regardless of whether they have a profile attached. Additionally, when image data is copied from one file into another, the appearance of the color always takes precedence, regardless of the color mode of either image.

We recommend that you use the Preserve Embedded Profiles Color Management Policy for all three color modes. You can always change the profile that is attached to an image, but we believe that is a decision you should make consciously and not have happen on a default basis.

### Second Guessing Default Color Management Policies

The default policies are useful but they are not always what you really want to have happen. So, Adobe has provided you with the option of asking Photoshop to notify you whenever there is a mismatch between image profiles when documents are opened or created, and when you open an image that doesn't have a profile. We recommend that you always keep the Profile Mismatches and Missing Profiles options checked so that you get to make these critical color decisions.

Having Photoshop notify you of mismatches or missing profiles when you open a document is a good idea if your workflow has only a few workstations and the artist is trained to make such choices. In a high volume workflow with many workstations, however, such on-the-spot decision making can really slow things down.

## Advanced Color Settings Options

We've now covered all the Color Setting options that Adobe thinks most people need to make. But other options are available in this dialog box. If the Advanced Mode option in the upper-left corner of the dialog box is checked, the dialog box expands to reveal additional important color management settings. Even if you don't want to change these default settings, you should read on because the choices offered in the section on Conversion Intents are those you are asked to make when you convert an image's profile, when you choose a custom soft-proofing profile, and when you assign a print profile.

Check the Advanced Mode option in the Color Settings dialog box if it is not already checked, and then let's move on to the next section.

## Conversion Options: Which Engine to Use

The default color management engine used in new Adobe products is ACE (*Adobe Color Engine*). Windows (excluding NT 4) users can choose to use Microsoft ICM engine instead of Adobe's engine, and Macintosh users can use the ColorSync engine instead, if they prefer. All three engines are similar to each other because all three are based on Linotype AG's LinoColor Color Management System.

At first glance, the Adobe engine provided in all new Adobe products seems like a great choice because having the same engine available on both Macintosh and Windows makes trading files between the two operating systems entirely compatible. But because the Adobe ACE engine can be accessed only by Adobe products, you might *not* want to use Adobe's color management engine. Color management engines really should belong to the operating system so they are available to all programs that use color management.

In the ideal world, we'd all be 125 pounds, blonde, rich, never flame a jerk in a newsgroup, and only one color management engine would be used and it would work exactly the same on any operating system. But we haven't reached—and are not likely ever to find ourselves in—such a world. Unless you count Hollywood as a "world."

So what engine should you use? Use the one that is used by the most people who will handle the file. If you, your colleagues, clients, service bureaus, and printers use only Windows (excluding NT 4), choose the Microsoft ICM system; if everyone in the chain uses Macintosh OS systems, choose the ColorSync engine. If your files move across platforms now, or may in the future, then your best bet is probably to choose the Adobe ACE engine, because Adobe graphics products are the leading products on both platforms and the ACE engine works identically on both platforms. What you want to strive for is *consistency*. For the purposes of this book we will assume that you are using the Adobe ACE engine.

## Conversion Intents

*Intent,* in the context of color management, is not exactly what it sounds like. It does *not* mean what your plans are. Rather, it asks, "What overall rules do you want to use when you're moving an image from one color gamut to another?" Whenever you change the profile an image uses, the color management engine must somehow decide how the numbers that define the colors are changed, or how the interpretation of those numbers changes to fit within the confines of the new profile. Exactly how this conversion takes place is governed by the source and destination profiles. When the source and destination profiles are created they usually are assigned a default rendering intent. This default intent can be overridden by applications capable of designating rendering intent, like Photoshop.

Four intents have been defined by the ICC: *Perceptual* (sometimes called Image), *Saturation* (sometimes called Graphic), *Absolute Colorimetric,* and *Relative Colorimetric.* These four intents are used by all color management engines. Only one of the four intents can be applied during a conversion, but any one of the four could be specified. Which rendering intent you choose as the default intent depends on which qualities of your original image you want to preserve during a color transformation from one gamut to another. As mentioned earlier, it is important to understand what these intents do, because you are asked to choose an intent whenever you convert an image's color space, when you choose a custom soft-proofing profile, and when you assign a print profile. A brief description of each of the four intents follows.

### Perceptual Intent

Perceptual intent is usually the best overall choice for working with photographic images. When Perceptual is chosen, the white points of the source and the destination color spaces are matched to each other. Then all the colors in the source space are shifted to new color values that maintain the original relative difference between colors. This means that the actual color values (the numbers) are changed in a way that preserves the overall look of the image rather than preserving the actual colors.

Because photographic and photorealistic images most often are moved from a large RGB editing working space to a smaller RGB or CMYK printing space, source colors either have to be clipped or the gamut of colors needs to be compressed. The Perceptual intent avoids having to clip colors, which would result in loss of image detail, by desaturating the colors that are in common between both spaces. Desaturating the common colors produces the room needed to assign color slots to colors that would otherwise be clipped. Consequently, using Perceptual rendering sacrifices absolute color fidelity to preserve detail and the overall look of the image. Perceptual's strategy of using desaturation works particularly well for photographic images that are making the large to small color space transition, because the human eye doesn't notice the desaturation of colors as much as it notices color clipping or posterization.

However, when images are being converted the other way around, from a small color gamut to a destination with a larger color gamut, the Perceptual intent would not be the best choice for a photograph or photorealistic image. Because almost all the colors will fit within the new, larger space, desaturation of common colors is no longer necessary to avoid excessive loss of detail due to clipping. Consequently, conversions of photographic and continuous tone images from smaller to larger color spaces usually turn out better if the Relative Colorimetric is chosen for the conversion intent.

It is also important to note, since Perceptual intent maintains the relationships between colors by remapping most, if not all, colors in an image by compressing them to fit into the new gamut, Perceptual would not be the correct choice when the destination gamut is very small—a flexographic newsprint press, for example. In that instance, it would be better to take the clipping hit and try to remap manually the colors that have turned to mud.

### Saturation Intent

Saturation is a good intent to choose for images in which the actual color (hue) is not as important as the purity or distinctiveness of the color. The Saturation intent is most often used for business graphics, such as bar graphs, pie charts, and presentation graphics. These kinds of graphics typically don't require precise color matching; rather, they need non-subtle, easily distinguishable color that makes reading data easy or that doesn't wash out when projected. The rules inherent in the Saturation intent essentially tell the conversion process to focus on producing distinctive colors rather than maintaining an exact color specification. The Saturation intent is also good for re-creating psychedelic posters of the 1960s, and for producing cartoons.

### Absolute Colorimetric Intent

Absolute Colorimetric is the conversion intent most often used when the most important goal is to ensure that as many colors as possible in the source image are matched exactly in the destination image. Colors that cannot be matched exactly in the destination space will be clipped. White points in the source and the destination color gamuts are not matched. *Color clipping* (total saturation of an area in an attempt to render a specific color) will occur during a move from a profile with a large color gamut to a profile with a smaller color gamut, but the colors that do fall within output gamut are faithfully preserved. When a color(s) is clipped it is generally moved to the edge of the new gamut, which generally translates as "muddy." Clipping can also take several dissimilar colors and assign them to the same color in the new gamut. With the power of preview soft-proofing, the artist has the opportunity to manually remap those colors that will be clipped before the change occurs. This intent is the best one to use when you are working with corporate logos, spot colors, or other specific colors that must be used in an image.

### Relative Colorimetric Intent

Relative Colorimetric intent maps the white point (the hottest point in an image— absolute white) of the source profile to that of the destination profile, and then shifts all the colors so that they maintain the same relative position to the white point. Source colors that fall out of gamut in the destination profile's color space are clipped (changed to the nearest color in gamut). Resorting to clipping colors (reducing the number of unique colors) instead of preserving the absolute number of different colors by desaturating some of them is what makes Relative Colorimetric intent different from Perceptual intent. It is a good choice if the destination space is capable of producing almost all the colors, or if you have done a lot of tweaking to bring colors into the destination's gamut. Examples of this would be if you turned on gamut warning and then used color correction techniques to bring the color used in the image into the CMYK gamut, or if you only used Web-safe colors when creating the image. You should base your default rendering intent on the nature of the images you work with and the kind of output to which these images typically are sent.

The Conversion Options section contains two other options, which we'll look at next.

## Black Point Compensation

The tonal range of an image is determined by the number of intermediate grays the image contains between pure white (the white point) and pure black (the black point). ICC profiles have rules that govern how and when white points are matched to each other when conversions take place, but surprisingly, they don't have rules about how black points should be matched. When black points are not considered when an image's color space is converted, the translation between color spaces does not always look as good as it should or would if the black points had been evaluated. Adobe has developed a fudge factor, called *black point compensation,* that evaluates source and destination black points and then makes corrections to help ensure that the blacks in the converted file aren't blocked in or washed out. But like most workarounds, it doesn't suit all situations. The rule of thumb commonly used is that the Use Black Point Compensation option should be enabled when you're converting an image from RGB to CMYK or from one CMYK profile to another, and that it probably should not be enabled when you're converting from one RGB space to another.

**Note**

**Controlling Contrast**    The human eye is more sensitive to tonal changes in the low end of the spectrum than the eye's sensitivity to changes approaching the white point. This is another reason why it's important to control the contrast of darker tones.

It should also be avoided when the conversion from RGB has a destination gamut in which the paper and inks used have a low black density, such as CMYK newsprint, which has a washed-out black.

## Use Dither (8-Bit per Channel Images)

*Dither* refers to a process (dithering) that uses different colored dots, shapes placed close to each other, or patterns made up of different colors to fool the viewer's eye into seeing a color that is not actually there. When small motes of colors are intermingled, the eye blends the colors together and interprets them as the color that would be produced if the colors were actually mixed together. This phenomenon of human vision is what makes both the painting style of Pointillism and CMYK halftone printing work. Activating the Use Dither (8-bit per channel) option enables profile-conversion processes to use dithering to *reduce the perceived amount of banding that is caused by color clipping.* This is a good option to use, but it will increase file size and make file compression techniques less effective.

## Advanced Controls

The last set of options in the Color Settings dialog box is Desaturate Monitor Colors By, and Blend RGB Colors Using Gamma. Adobe recommends that only advanced users use this option, but we're not sure that it's useful even for advanced users.

Desaturating the monitor colors by a user-definable percentage could, if you have a really good imagination, give you a general idea of what colors that cannot be displayed on the monitor might look like when output. The second option, Blend RGB Colors Using Gamma, is more useful than desaturating your monitor, but only if the image will be created and output from Photoshop. The default gamma setting of 1.0 for this option produces slightly better color choices on the edges of sharp color transition in RGB images. You probably shouldn't bother to enable either of these options.

Wow—we've looked at *all* the options in this dialog box. You might want to recalibrate your *eyeballs* now! The only other thing to do is to click the Save button to save a color settings file if you've made changes that aren't the preset color settings files. And that, Fellow Photoshoppist, brings us back to where we were before we started looking at the settings in this dialog box.

## Choosing Between Assigning and Converting to Profile

The default color settings you have specified and the color management policies you've set in the Color Settings dialog box are not the only place where profiles can be assigned to images. The Image, Mode menu is another. It has two very important entries, Assign Profile and Convert to Profile, that perform very different functions. And it is *quite* important that you understand the difference.

When we look at an image we've created and saved, it is irresistible to imagine that an actual image of some sort exists inside the file image; a cyber version of a photographic print. In actuality, the image is just a bunch of numbers that represent the individual flecks (pixels) of color. Photoshop reads these numbers, figures out what to do with them in terms of color, and then puts them onscreen. Our eyes and our brain then take in all the bits of color and decide what they represent, what they look like. Is it a representation of a loved one or just a splash of color?

Some of the rules Photoshop uses to figure out what to do with the numbers it finds in image files are found within Photoshop's own program code. This part of the process of making an image out of numbers is out of Photoshop users' hands. It reflects the logic, decisions, and preferences of the programmers who wrote the Photoshop. If a CMS is used, Photoshop's actions are guided and modified by an additional set of rules: the rules laid out in ICC profiles that are used in concert with the image. You decide which profile rules are associated with an image file.

## Assigned Profile

Photoshop uses ICC profiles in two ways. It looks to an *assigned profile* for instructions on how to interpret or change the numbers in the file. Assigning a profile to an image tells Photoshop how to interpret the numbers in an image file. When you use the Image, Mode, Assign Profile command to assign to an image a profile other than the default one you designated in the Color Settings dialog box, you are telling Photoshop to look at the numbers as though they had been changed to fit the requirements of some other color space. But the numbers, the data in the file, have not really changed.

An assigned profile instructs Photoshop how to *interpret* the numbers. The assigned profile is similar to a statement that might be associated with or assigned to this paragraph, a statement that says, "The groups of letters that form this paragraph are to be thought of as being English words that are arranged in a way that makes sense to English language readers. Additionally, if any modification (editing) takes place, interpret that in the same way you interpret the original paragraph."

But a new profile could be assigned to take the place of the first one; the new one could say to interpret the groups of letters in the paragraph according to the rules and grammar of the German language. This new interpretation might not be very pleasing or be the best way to interpret the current order and grouping of the letters, but it would let you know how much or little of the intended communication would be understood if "output" to a German language speaker. In both cases, the only things that change are the interpretation instructions (assigned profile) and not the actual letters, their grouping, or their sequence.

Changing an assigned profile is a game of "what if...." What would this data, these colors, look like if they were transferred to another color space? The color space could be anything that you have an ICC profile of: another monitor, a television, an Epson inkjet print, an HP inkjet print, a press using newspaper, or a Matchprint.

This is the important thing to remember: Assigned profiles tell Photoshop and other color management–aware programs how to *interpret* the data.

But sometimes you want to change the *data*, not just its interpretation. To use the English-German analogy, sometimes we want to change the letters and their order, translate the data so that it is useful in another context, so that the paragraph makes sense to a German reader. In color management terms, that means that the data within the file, the *numbers themselves*, must be changed. The way that is done is covered in the next section.

**Note**

**Changing Your View**    Dr. Alvy Smith, who founded PIXAR and is partially responsible for inventing the HSB color model, has a profundity that would seem to fit right in here:

Change your *view* of the data before you change the data.

In other words, when you change your view, and you've been shown plenty of examples of how to change image view, you are not disrupting original data. Nor are you making the potentially false presumption that your monitor is calibrated perfectly, and the person who did the artwork's system was off.

When you make physical changes to image data, you can almost never get back to the original's content. It's kinda like a turnstile in a subway station—try exiting from one of the ones that are for entrance. Manipulating the colors in an image, similarly, is a one-way trip. Choose to change your view as a first, second, and third measure for viewing a file accurately.

## Using Profiles to Change the Color Mode of an Image

As stated before, profiles are sets of rules, definitions of color spaces, that programs use to interpret color data. But profiles are also used to provide some of the rules on how to actually *change the data* in the file to make all the colors fit within a particular color space. The intent—Perceptual, Saturation, Absolute Colorimetric, or Relative Colorimetric—that is chosen for the conversion also provides rules to guide the conversion process.

To continue with the English-German language analogy, a bilingual person who acts as the translator (the CMS) would look at the letters (the numerical color data), consult the rules of the German language (the destination profile) and the German language dialect that is desired (the intent), and then change the letters (the data) so that the data would actually be transformed from something that could be translated into German to something already written in German.

If you want to permanently change the data in an image file, use the Convert to Profile command on the Image, Mode menu. Read the previous sentence out loud once or twice; it is an important concept.

This is not the only way to change the data in an image file. Photoshop users have been changing file data for years whenever they changed an image's color mode, from RGB to CMYK, for example. You still can go the traditional route, using the Color commands at the top of the Image, Mode menu, but you will give up the ability to fine-tune the process. When you use the Convert to Profile command you choose which ICC RGB profile or which ICC CMYK profile you want to use. The traditional color mode commands use the default ICC profile settings you set in the Color Settings dialog box.

**Note**

**Precise Conversion**   Internally, Photoshop uses the LAB color model as the heart of the conversion engine when going from one Image, Mode to another. So, the conversions are still fairly good, but not as precise as choosing Convert to Profile.

## Putting Theory into Practice

If your head hurts from trying to assimilate all this data, you're in good company (see Figure 3.0 again). Color management is *not* a topic to digest the first or even the second time around. But when the light bulb goes on in your head and you shout, "Eureka! I really understand how this works!" you will have moved a long way from hoping your print jobs go OK, to *knowing* what they will look like before you see the finished results. So let's put into action the concepts of color management we've discussed. We'll start by creating a custom Color Settings preset file and then practice assigning and converting profiles.

### Example 3.2   Creating a Custom Color Settings File

1. Launch Photoshop, if it is not already open.

2. Press Ctrl(⌘)+Shift+K to display the Color Settings dialog box. Make sure the Advanced Mode and Preview options are checked. Make the changes specified in the following four steps, if the options are not already set that way.

3. Set the RGB working space to Adobe RGB (1998); the CMYK working space to U.S. Web Coated (SWOP); the Gray and Spot working spaces to Dot Gain 20%.

4. Set all three Color Management Policies to Preserve Embedded Profiles. Check both Ask When Opening options and the Ask When Pasting options.

5. In the Conversion Options section, set the Engine to Adobe (ACE). Set the Intent to Relative Colorimetric. Check both the Use Black Point Compensation and the Use Dither options.

6. Make certain that the options in the Advanced Options section are not checked.

7. Click the Save button. In the Save dialog box that appears, use the Save In drop-down and other controls to navigate your way to the folder in which the other color setting files are saved, if you are not already there. Then type **IP6** in the File name field, and click Save.

8. In the Color Settings Comment dialog box that appears, type something that describes these settings, such as **Set used for exercise in Inside Adobe Photoshop 6.** Click OK.

   IP6 now appears as the selected setting in the Settings drop-down list.

9. Click OK to put these settings into use.

You can now choose the IP6 set of custom settings just as you would the ones that Adobe provided.

Now that you have the IP6 defaults set, you will be sure to get the same results as we do in the exercises that follow. As promised, the next set of steps gives you hands-on experience with assigned profiles.

### Example 3.3    Color Management Policies in Action

1. Choose File, Open, and open Vision.tif from the Examples/Chap03 folder on the Companion CD. This file has no profile attached, so a warning box should appear.

2. In the Missing Profile dialog box that appears (see Figure 3.7) choose the Assign Working RGB: Adobe RGB (1998) option. Click OK. Vision.tif opens.

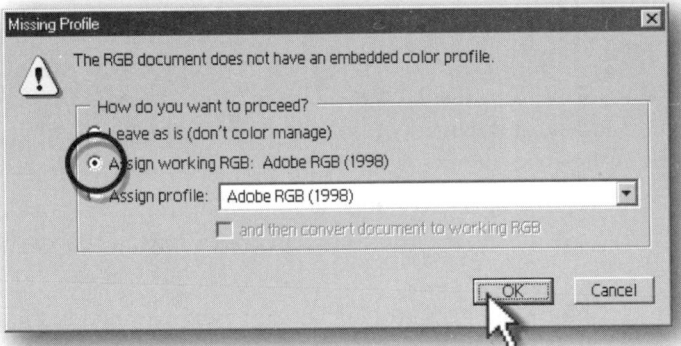

**Figure 3.7**    The Missing Profile dialog box appears when you open files to which a color management profile is not attached. Use its options to assign a profile.

You could choose any working space by selecting one from the drop-down, but because you don't know which working space this file was created in, and you haven't decided on a use for this file, the best choice is to assign Adobe RGB (1998). If you knew this file would be used for Web use only, choosing sRGB would also be okay. Remember—at this point you are only deciding how Photoshop should *interpret* and show the file to you; you have *not changed* any of the numerical *data* in the file.

If you had chosen the third option, Assign Profile, and picked from the pop-up list the same profile as the default working profile *and* checked the "and then convert the document to working RGB" option you would have done two things at once. You would have set the interpretation of the data to Adobe RGB (1998) and *changed* the data (the word *convert* is your clue) to data that fits in Adobe RGB (1998) space. If you chose to assign some other profile you would have made your view of the file that of the assigned profile, but with the option checked the data would have been converted to the working space profile Adobe RGB (1998). It is usually not a good idea to create a mismatch when you open a file; doing so distorts your view and can lead to unexpected color shifts when the assigned profile is eventually matched to the data profile.

3. Press Shift+Ctrl(⌘)+S to open the Save As dialog box. Note that toward the bottom of the dialog box, in the section labeled Color, the option ICC Profile: Adobe RGB (1998) is checked (see Figure 3.8).

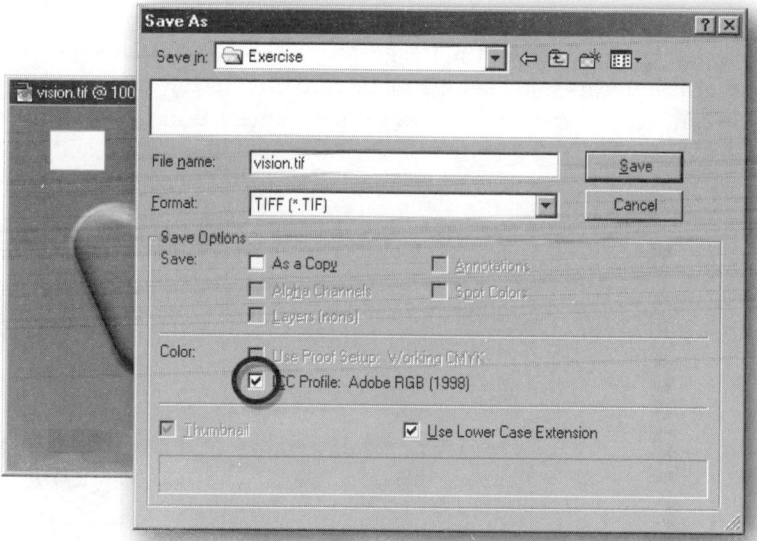

**Figure 3.8**   The Color section of the Save As dialog box has options for embedding profiles in images.

If you leave this option checked, the profile you assigned and noted here will be embedded in the file. This will become the profile that always governs your view of the file until you either assign a new profile or convert to another profile. If you remove the check from the profile the file will not be color managed. Until you close the file, however, your view of the file will be from the perspective of the Adobe RGB (1998) profile.

4. Find a place on your hard disk to save the file, and then click Save. In the TIFF Options dialog box leave LZW Compression unchecked, and choose the Byte order of your choice, and then click OK. Leave the image open.

To recap, you've opened an image that did not have a color management profile attached to it and assigned a working profile to the file. You then embedded the profile in the file by saving the file to disk with the profile option checked. But how do you change the assigned profile for a file that already *has* a profile? In the next section, you'll seek out the rather obviously named Assign Profile command.

### Example 3.4    Changing the Assigned Profile

1. With Vision.tif open in Photoshop's work space, choose Image, Mode from the menu. Note at the top of the Image menu that RGB is checked. From this section of the menu you could change the file to an entirely different color mode, like Grayscale or CMYK, but you can't change to a different RGB color space.

2. Choose Assign Profile from the Image, Mode menu. In the Assign Profile dialog box that appears (see Figure 3.9), be sure the Preview option is checked. As you can see, this dialog box offers three choices: Don't Color Manage This Document, Working RGB: Adobe RGB (1998), and a Profile drop-down list that contains the standard RGB working spaces as well as every other RGB profile that has been made available to the CMS.

**Figure 3.9**    With the Preview option checked, you can see how different assigned profiles would look.

3. Choose sRGB IEC61966-2.1 from the Profile drop-down list. Notice that the colors in Vision.tif become duller. This is what the file would look like in the editing window if you were to click OK now. But remember, you are only changing the interpretation, your *view* of the data, and not the data itself. (But this is what the data would look like if you *did* convert it.) Choose other profiles to see how they affect the view of Vision.tif. Then click Cancel to close the dialog box without changing the Assigned profile. Leave Vision.tif open in the work space.

Okay, let's say a client calls to say they've decided they really want to use the Vision.tif file on the Web, but that they have decided not to use it for their print campaign. So you figure that now's the time to get this image prepped, and one of the first steps toward doing that is to move the file to the preferred color space of the Web, sRGB IEC61966-2.1. To move the file to that color space, you need to do more than just change the assigned profile; you need to change the data in the file to ensure that all the colors in the image are within the smaller color space the Web uses. To change the data, you must convert the profile, and you'll see how to do that in the next set of steps.

## Example 3.5    Converting a Profile Means Changing the Data

1. Press Shift+Ctrl(⌘)+S to open the Save As dialog box. Choose the As a Copy option and then click Save. Because converting profiles involves changing the data, this is the right time to make a backup copy of Vision.tif. You or the client may change your mind about the way you want to use this file at some point.

2. With Vision.tif open in Photoshop's work space, choose Image, Mode, Convert to Profile from the menu. The Convert to Profile dialog box opens (see Figure 3.10). Position the dialog box so that you can still see most, if not all, of Vision.tif, and make sure the Preview option is checked.

   The Convert to Profile dialog box is divided into three sections. The first lists the profile of the Source Space. This corresponds to the working color space profile. The middle section is where you choose a profile that defines which color space and color mode the CMS will change the data to fit inside. The last section, Conversion Options, should look familiar; it involves options, such as Intent and color management engines, that you learned about earlier in the chapter.

3. Click the arrow next to the Profile drop-down list. Notice that in addition to the standard RGB color spaces you saw in the Assign Profile dialog box, this list includes profiles not only for RGB but also for other color modes.

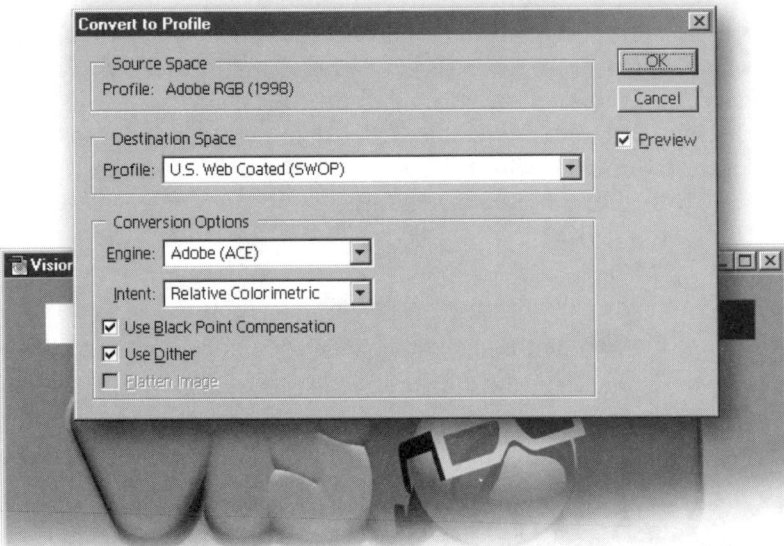

**Figure 3.10**    Use the Convert to Profile dialog box to convert from one color profile to another in the same color mode, or to one in an entirely different color mode. This is the preferred way to change from RGB to CMYK.

4. Choose sRGB IEC61966-2.1 from the Profile drop-down list. Notice that the image got brighter, not duller as it did in the previous exercise, because the dialog box opens with a CMYK profile chosen, instead of the current working profile. And CMYK is always duller than RGB, even sRGB.

5. While watching to see how the image changes or doesn't change, try each of the four rendering intents. You'll notice that for this image, there is little if any change in the image preview when you change the rendering intent. For some images there would be noticeable changes.

   Based on the earlier discussion of Intents, Relative Colorimetric is probably the best choice. This is not a photograph, and with the white-to-gray squares and the full spectrum gradient at the bottom, maintaining the white point, and then using absolute values where possible will most likely produce the best conversion of values.

6. Choose Relative Colorimetric from the Intent drop-down list. To see what will happen if you choose Relative Colorimetric, you can look at the preview if you have that option selected (see Figure 3.11). Leave the Engine option set at Adobe (ACE), leave Use Dither checked and uncheck Use Black Point Compensation. As mentioned in the Color Settings section of the chapter, the rule of thumb is to turn off Black Point Compensation when you're converting from one RGB profile to another.

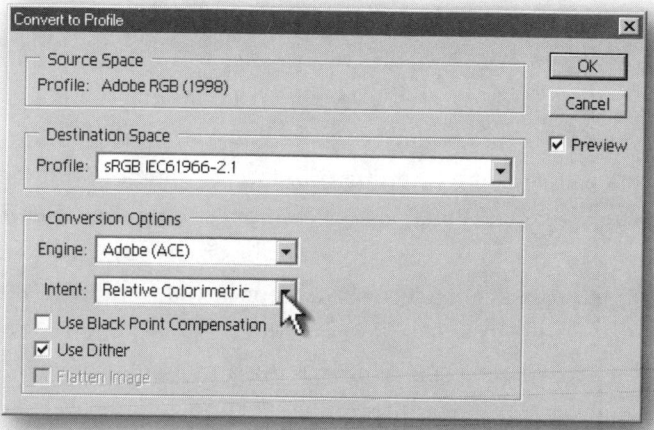

**Figure 3.11**   With the Preview option checked, you can see how different Intent choices change the look of the image.

7. Click OK. Press Ctrl(⌘)+Z three times, pausing between clicks to see what effect the Convert to Profile had on the image colors. The shift in color is particularly noticeable in the greens. This is not surprising because Adobe RGB (1998) has a lot more greens in its color space than does sRGB IEC61966-2.1. By the third Undo/Redo the image should be back in Adobe RGB (1998) mode; leave it there and leave the image open in Photoshop's work space.

**Tip**

**Look in File, Save As for the Current ICC Profile**   If you ever get confused as to which profile is currently the assigned profile, choose File, Save As, and look at the Color section of the dialog box. The profile listed next to ICC Profile is the current assigned profile. You then can cancel out of the save by pressing Esc or clicking Cancel.

Seeing how the image changes depending on which profile you assign or convert to might have given you the idea that whenever you want to see how a particular image will look when it's output to the Web or to print you could or should change the image profile. *Don't!* There is a much easier, safer, and more elegant way to do it. It's called *soft-proofing* an image. Read on, and you'll find that Adobe has tucked this time-, money-, and fingernail-saving feature in the View menu.

## Soft-Proofing, or Seeing Onscreen What an Image Will Look Like When It's Printed

Because Adobe's soft-proofing feature is driven by ICC profiles, it is a very good idea to collect ICC profiles for every device you use in your work and for every output device your work will be sent to. Getting your local commercial printers to give you an ICC profile for their press, let alone for their press using the exact paper and ink you want to use, is next to impossible. What *is* possible is to get ICC profiles for traditional hard-proofing materials, such as Matchprints. Most printers will set up their presses to produce results that match the color of an agreed upon hard-proof. What is also possible is to obtain the ICC profiles of the wonderful new inkjet printers that many folks are using for short-run printing. Additionally, you already may have noticed that Adobe and your operating system have gifted you with generic ICC profiles for many proofing devices and conditions, as well as default ICC profiles for standard press conditions. Generic ICC profiles are never as precise as custom-made ICC profiles, which is why we showed you how to create a custom ICC profile for your monitor instead of using the default one. But using generic profiles with a CMS is better than not using *any* CMS. So hop on the Net, go to the manufacturers of the equipment you and your customers use, and download the profiles for the devices. It is worth your while to collect ICC profiles for some of the more popular inkjet printers made by Epson, HP, and others. If you don't own one of these printers now, you really should put it on your wish list. Install the profiles, and then move on to the next example.

**Note**

**Printer Profiles and Paper Color**   Most ICC printer profiles are based on a specific paper color, generally a neutral bright white.

### Example 3.6    Soft-Proofing and Color-Correcting an Image

1. Vision.tif should still be open in Photoshop's work space. This is the file we've been working with. In the last example, we converted the profile associated with the image from Adobe RGB (1998) to sRGB IEC61966-2.1, and then used the Undo command to cancel the conversion of the data and the assignment of a new working profile.

2. Choose View, New View. A new window opens; it contains an additional view of the original image, not a new copy of the image. Arrange the two image windows so you can see each image.

3. Choose View, Proof Setup, Custom. In the Profile drop-down list, choose the profile for the inkjet printer you have installed. In the Intent drop-down list, leave the entry as Perceptual, and check Simulate: Paper White, as shown in Figure 3.12. Click OK.

If you don't have any inkjet or other desktop color printer profiles installed, use the Euroscale Coated profile.

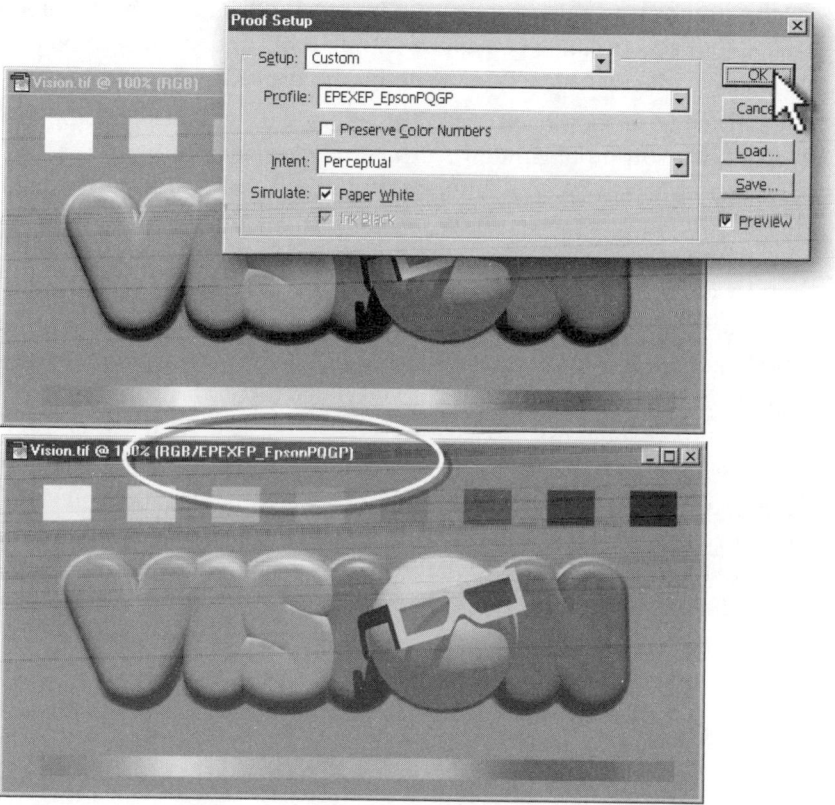

**Figure 3.12**   In the Proof Setup dialog box, choose the output device to which you want to print, and Photoshop will display the document more or less as it will print.

4. Notice that the title bar of the inactive window remains the same but that the active image title bar now reads RGB/EPEXEP_EpsonPQGP. The EPEXEP_EpsonPQGP part corresponds to the Epson printer picked in step 3 and is your soft-proof view. Your title bar will probably say something different because you chose a different output profile. Notice also that the colors in the RGB/EPEXEP_EpsonPQGP window are duller than in the original RGB window. The data hasn't changed, only your view has. Think of it as looking at the RGB/EPEXEP_EpsonPQGP image with Epson glasses on.

Chances are 100% that the image in the soft-proof window is not everything you hoped it would be. The solution? Edit the image. Because these two windows are different views of the same image, any edits you make will be reflected in both windows. It doesn't matter which window is the active window when you make the edits. To improve this image for printing to the inkjet printer, move on to the next step.

5. Click the Create new fill or adjustment layer icon at the bottom of the layers palette (fourth icon from the left). Choose Color Balance from the menu. The Color Balance dialog box appears. Drag it off to one side so you can see the images. Make sure the Preview option is checked.

   The neutral background and the white-to-black boxes across the top of the image in the soft-proof window show an unwanted color cast. Because you've most likely chosen a different printer to soft-proof to than we have, you may not have a color cast or it may be different from ours. Make your adjustments to suit your image. For the purposes of this example, we'll report what works according to our setup and what looks good to us.

   Although you have set up and are using the CMS in Photoshop, you should not abandon the use of the Info palette for color feedback (correcting by the numbers). Your experience with your intended target device, combined with the Photoshop CMS, will yield better results than just using either CMS or experience/Info palette alone.

6. Keep your eyes on the soft-proof window. That is the window you want to look good. The problem appears to be mostly in the midtones. Preserve Luminosity should be checked. Drag the Cyan slider toward Red (right) to a value of +7; drag the Magenta slider toward Green (right) to a value of +14; drag the Yellow slider toward Yellow (left) to a value of –3, as shown in Figure 3.13. Click OK.

   Now the soft-proof window doesn't have a color cast, but the original window does. That is okay. An image often looks terrible onscreen but prints beautifully. That is because the monitor and the printer have different color spaces. If you want good printed output, don't get hung up on how it looks onscreen in the working space. Pay attention to the soft-proof view.

7. Click the Create new fill or adjustment layer icon on the Layers palette. Choose Levels Layer on the menu. The image lacks punch because it doesn't really have a good white or black point. Drag the White point slider to around 226. Drag the Black point slider to around 13, and drag the Midpoint slider left to about 1.14, as shown in Figure 3.14. Click OK.

8. Take a good look at the preview window. If you like what you see, flatten the image by choosing Flatten Image from the Layers palette menu.

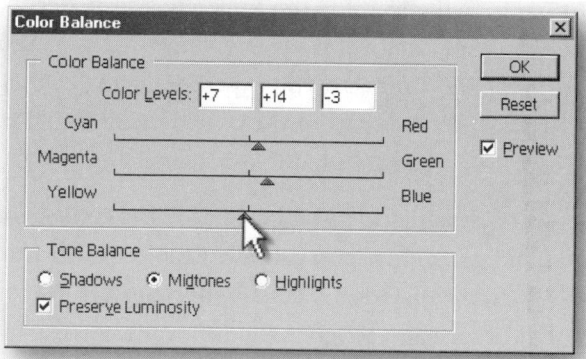

**Figure 3.13**   Use a Color Balance adjustment layer to remove an unwanted color cast that will develop when the image is printed to the inkjet.

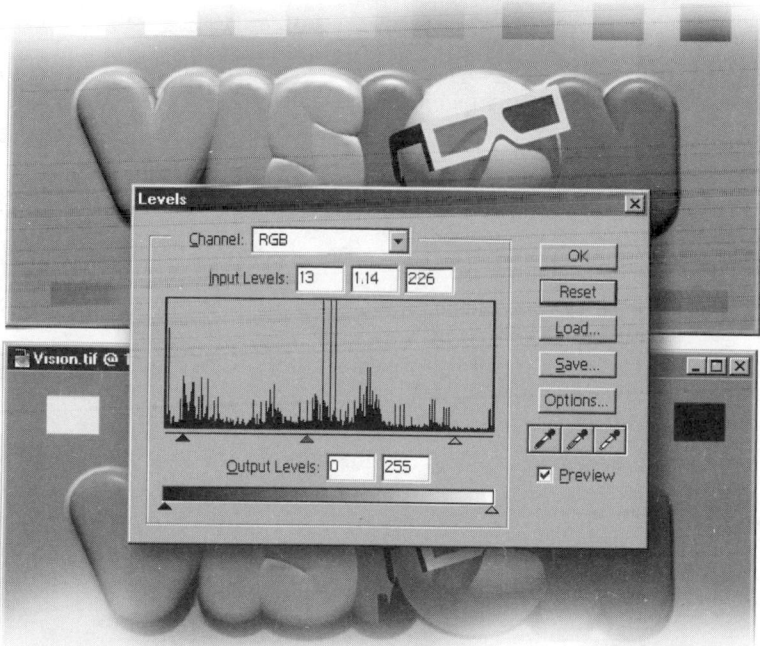

**Figure 3.14**   Use a Levels adjustment layer to create a better tonal range.

9. Choose File, Save As. In the File name field, enter **Vision for Inkjet**. Notice that the image still has the original profile listed in the Color section, and not the inkjet profile you proofed to. That is because the proof view was a *view* and not a *conversion* of the data to a new color space. You *did* change data when you edited, but it was changed in the context of the working space, not the proofing space of the inkjet. Click Save.

When it comes time to actually print the image to the inkjet printer to get the results you saw in the proof, you will want to change the data. You can do that by using the Convert to Profile command you experimented with in a previous example, or you can choose to do it as part of the print process.(We'll take a closer look at this route in Chapter 7, on custom halftone schemes.)

Bear in mind that while it takes fewer steps to specify the conversion from the print dialog boxes, you don't get a chance to preview what different Intent options look like. Consequently, we recommend that you use the Convert to Profile command to change the data in the image and assign the same profile you used for soft-proofing.

## Summary

That's it! If you've followed along, you've just joined the ranks of color management specialists. And you probably need to focus on postcards of Hawaii to rest your eyes for a week or so. We realize that you may hold the title of designer a little closer to your heart than that of color management specialist, but it will look great on your résumé. It will signal to all that you are an artist who can produce work that can be counted on to look fabulous in any and every media.

## Resources

http://www.apple.com/colorsync/
Apple's ColorSync site has a lot of information on its color management engine.

http://www.pixelboyz.com
Bruce Fraser's site, where you can find out more about the BruceRGB color working space.

http://www.cie.co.at/cie/
Commission Internationale de L'Eclairage (CIE)

http://www.linocolor.com
Heidelberg CPS GmbH has some good beginner information on color management. They also have information on very expensive software to create ICC profiles.

http://www.inkjetmall.com/store/index.htm
Inkjetmall.com, a division of the famous Cone Editions Press, is a great place to buy ICC profiles for Epson printers. These profiles not only profile the printer but also specific paper and ink combinations. The site even offers a few free profiles.

http://www.color.org

International Color Consortium (ICC)

http://search.microsoft.com/

Microsoft has lots of information on color management available, but it is not neatly organized in one place. Your best bet is to do a search on its site, using the keywords "color management" or "ICC profiles."

http://www.praxisoft.com

Good information on color management is available on the Praxisoft site. They also sell a reasonably priced (under $100) program called WiziWYG that can create good custom ICC profiles for your scanner and for printers.

http://www.xrite.com/

X-Rite, Inc., makes all kinds of hardware tools for measuring color and calibrating devices. Most of their solutions are rather high-end, very precise, and geared in price toward large, big-budget operations.

# Chapter 4

## Optimizing Your Workspace: Photoshop Preferences

Don't you really hate it when you find the perfect jacket, the jacket that will go with everything, that will make all of last year's stuff look it just walked off a Paris runway, and it doesn't fit? Not only does it not fit, but you find out it doesn't come in your size. It only comes in the default, one-size-fits-all. You *know* that size, for it's the size where the sleeves either cover your fingertips or not so gracefully graze your elbows.

Smart manufacturers make products adapt to fit people, all kinds of people. *Unenlightened* vendors force all people to contort themselves or the way they work to fit a product. Adobe is a smart manufacturer who recognizes one-size-does-*not*-fit-all. Adobe has provided Photoshop and ImageReady users with convenient ways to tailor almost every aspect of its features and user interface.

As mentioned in Chapter 1, Photoshop and ImageReady become more and more alike as time passes, and it will surprise no one if they are merged into one seamless program in the near future. Some steps toward the merging of these programs have already been taken. We need to get used to the reality that these programs are almost identical in interface layout, features, and the way tools work. Most importantly, though, when you set a feature preference in Photoshop, the setting automatically carries over to ImageReady. This is the best two-for-one deal going: you get two customized workspaces but only need to put in the effort of customizing a single program.

In this chapter you'll discover what program settings can be customized, how the program will work differently if you change the settings, when and why you might want to change the settings, and, lastly, what settings we recommend you change and which you should probably leave alone. Photoshop is the primary focus of this chapter. Anything we mention about setting Photoshop preferences or ways to customize the workspace will work the same way in ImageReady, unless we mention otherwise.

There is so much to cover in this chapter that one entire set of preferences—those related to color management—were covered in Chapter 3. Adobe scrapped the color management system used in previous versions and replaced it with a much better one that will be used in all new versions of Adobe's product line.

Enough talk about other chapters, though. Let's take out a virtual pincushion and get some digital tailor's chalk and mark up Photoshop's preferences so they fit you like a one-of-a-kind creation.

## Locating the Preferences Dialog Box

Oops! You won't find this on the File menu anymore; it has moved to the Edit menu. Fortunately for previous Photoshop users, the shortcut key used to display the Preferences dialog box hasn't changed; it is still Ctrl(⌘)+K. If you're a new Photoshop or ImageReady user, commit this one to memory; it will save you lots of time.

Most global preferences are made in the Preferences dialog box. Global preferences affect features or program mechanisms that are related to the entire workings of the program, such as the amount and type of memory and cache that is available to the program or the display properties of the cursor. Some changes you make in this set of dialog boxes take place immediately while others, memory usage settings and file locations for example, only take effect after you've restarted Photoshop. Photoshop tells you when setting changes won't take place in the current Photoshop session so you won't have to guess. The first group of global preferences you'll look at are found on the General page of the Preferences dialog box.

## Setting the General Preferences

Because this chapter is all about personal preferences, there won't be a lot of num-bered lists for you to follow. But you *can* (and should) follow along and customize your copy of Photoshop as you go through this chapter.

To begin the customization process, open Photoshop and then press Ctrl(⌘)+K or choose Edit, Preferences, General from the menu. The Preferences dialog box, with General preferences displayed, is shown in Figure 4.1

**Tip**

**When Your Preferences Dialog Box Looks Different**    If what you see doesn't exactly match what we describe, it means that you or your system administrator have already customized some settings.

The General preferences page is the first of eight pages of settings you can access from the Preferences dialog box. To move to a different page of settings you can either choose from the drop-down box at the top of the page, or you can use the previous and next buttons that are on the right side of the page.

Let's walk through the options you have here, and we'll provide you with explana-tions for some of the more cryptic check boxes.

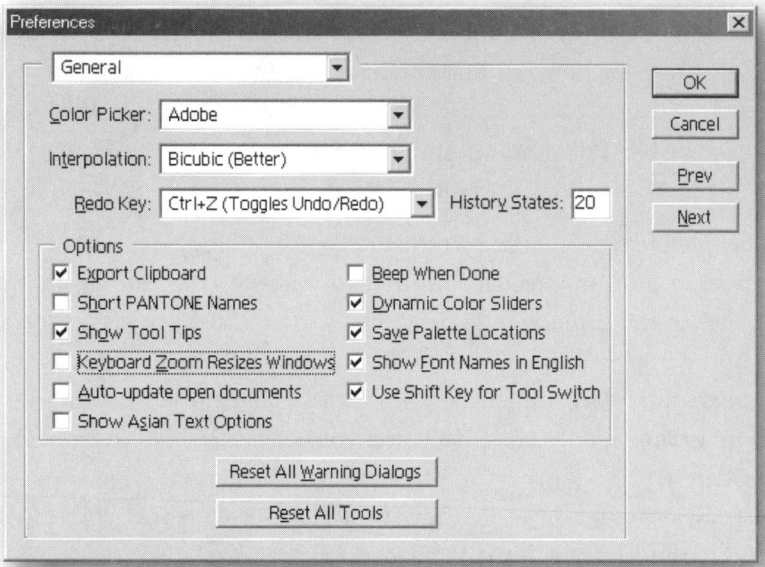

**Figure 4.1**    Make changes to global settings in the Preferences dialog box's General page.

## Picking a Color Picker

The Color Picker drop-down box offers two choices, depending on which operating system you use. The Windows version offers Adobe's Color Picker and Windows system colors. The Macintosh version of Photoshop 6 offers Adobe's Color Picker and the Macintosh system color picker (the color picker is different depending on the OS version number). Photoshop's Color Picker, seen in Figure 4.2, makes it easy to choose color using common color spaces such as RGB, CMYK, or LAB or to work with special ink colors defined by PANTONE, TruMatch, and others. If you choose a color that won't print well using CMYK print processes or that won't display well on the Web, the Photoshop Color Picker warns you and then offers a way to select the nearest color that will print or display well. The authors cannot think of many circumstances under which you'd want to use the system color picker over the Photoshop Color Picker. If you were creating a Macromedia Director show for a specific platform, you'd use the system colors. You'd also probably choose system colors in Photoshop if you needed to write a file for someone on the same operating system whose video card has a limited capacity to show colors.

We recommend that you leave this drop-down set to its default setting, because it offers a lot more than your operating system's Color Picker.

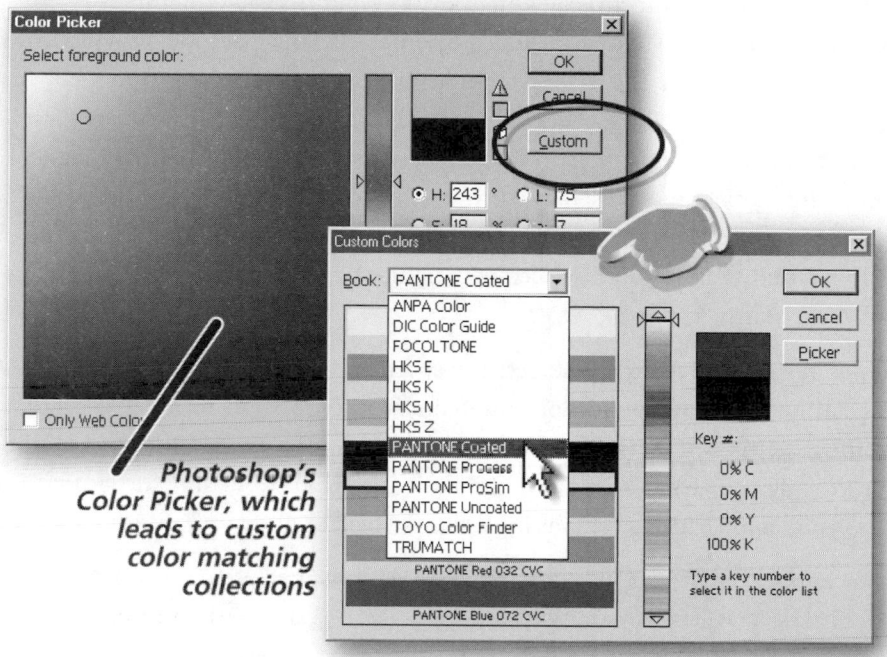

*Photoshop's
Color Picker, which
leads to custom
color matching
collections*

**Figure 4.2**   Photoshop's Color Picker is tailored to the needs of artists and designers. Also, it is the only avenue for choosing from color-matching specifications such as PANTONE.

**Note**

**When Your Color Picker Looks Different from Ours**   You may find more choices in the Color Picker drop-down list if you've installed a third-party filter or application that supplied an additional color picker(s) for your use.

## Choosing a Method of Interpolation

When you change the size of an image by changing the number of pixels in the image, or when you use any of Photoshop's transformation commands on an image, Photoshop must interpolate, or reassign, the remaining pixels different colors. Image resizing is accomplished by invoking a set of predefined rules, an algorithm, which determines the characteristics and placement of pixels that are added to or discarded from an image.

Nearest Neighbor interpolation, bilinear interpolation, and bicubic interpolation are three widely used resampling algorithms. The Interpolation drop-down box is used to choose which one of the three algorithms Photoshop will use by default.

*Nearest Neighbor* is not technically interpolation, but instead a method of duplicating neighboring pixels when an image is enlarged. This method provides lowest image quality but it's the fastest method of resizing. Because it produces hard, jagged, aliased edges, Nearest Neighbor should be used only when working with line art. Line art loses its crispness if sophisticated averaging filters such as bicubic or bilinear interpolation are used on such an image. Nearest Neighbor interpolation should only be used on images that are of Indexed mode—the fewer colors, the better. Program interfaces can be scaled with clarity by using this method—pictures of your Aunt Martha cannot.

*Bilinear interpolation* is a trade-off between speed and quality and sharpness and softness. Although many applications use bilinear interpolation to resize images, it is not the most refined method to use for continuous tone images. Bilinear interpolation provides good but unremarkable results, and probably should be used only when your composition contains both sharp-edged and continuous-tone imagery.

We recommend that you leave interpolation set to its default setting of Bicubic and only change it when working with line art. Figure 4.3 shows an example of each kind of interpolation.

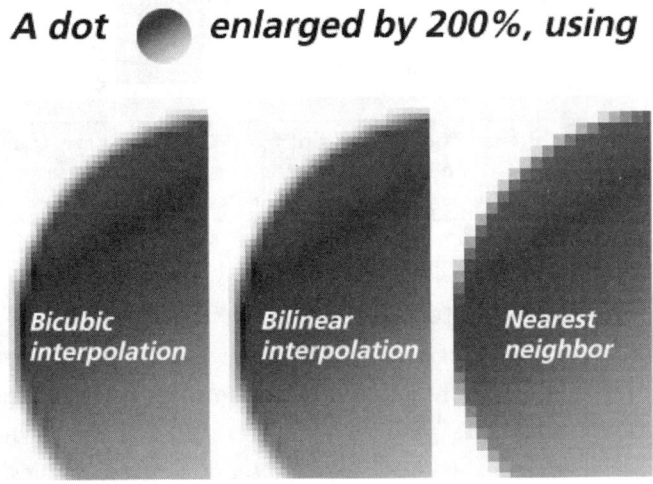

**Figure 4.3**     Select the interpolation to use based on the content of your image.

> **Note**
>
> **Use Bicubic Interpolation for Resizing**    Reality check time. We have been recommending Bicubic interpolation for years now because it's the best method of resizing a photographic image down or up. But we always put a warning tag on it: it's the most processor-intensive interpolation method.
>
> Um, it's the year 2000 now, the average speed of a processor is 500 mHz and up, so you really should not let filters that even Adobe calls "processor-intensive" prevent you from using them in your work. There's no such thing as "processor-intensive" these days— with the exception of tracking a space shuttle—and the difference between intensive and nonintensive work with a muscle machine is the difference between cutting through butter with a hot knife and cutting through it with a white-hot knife.

## Assigning the Redo Key

This drop-down list enables you to assign one out of three possible key combinations to be the one used for the Redo keyboard shortcut. This option is actually mislabeled, because the command that is affected by this option is called Step Forward on the Edit menu, and not Redo. The Step Forward menu item, and its related key combination, is not available for use until you have used the Edit, Step Back command.

The default choice for the key combination is Ctrl(⌘)+Z, which has been the only choice for Redo in Photoshop up to now (as well as in many other programs), which might have reinforced your reflexes by now! To make things as easy as possible for you, Adobe lets you select

- Ctrl(⌘)+Z (Toggles Undo/Redo)
- Ctrl(⌘)+Shift+Z
- Ctrl(⌘)+Y

as keyboard shortcuts that can be used instead of Ctrl(⌘)+Z. Choose the key combination that you feel most comfortable using. But keep in mind that the somewhat popular Ctrl(⌘)+Y in today's programs is used by Photoshop for View, Proof Setup, and then the current Proof Setup configuration. If you choose to use Ctrl(⌘)+Y for Redo, you'll have to use the menus to turn Proof Preview on and off. For the purposes of this book and our assignments, we will assume that you are using the default Ctrl(⌘)+Z as the keyboard shortcut to toggle from Step Forward to Step Backward (Undo/Redo).

## Establishing the Number of History States

The History States option is found to the right of the Redo Key option. In previous versions of Photoshop, this option was called Maximum History Items and was found on the History palette menu under History Options. The number you enter in the History States field determines the number of states (things you did to the image) that are available in the History palette. It also is the maximum number of Steps Back you can go using the Step Back commands.

In other words, History States is how many steps back in a file (how many undo times) that you can tap into. Each History State requires a hunk of RAM to store the undo data; so how many states you enable is a balancing act between how big a safety net you want and the amount of RAM you have installed on your computer. The default number of History States is 20. This means that you can undo up to the previous 20 commands or tool strokes you made. Once you make your twenty-first command or stroke, the undo state for the first command or stroke is deleted to allow room to undo the most current command or tool stroke.

So even though you'd probably like to set this option to a thousand—*don't*. If you have 96MB of RAM installed on your computer (the minimum amount of RAM that Photoshop requires to run), 10 is probably a reasonable setting for History States. If you have 128MB of RAM (the amount you *really* need to run Photoshop so you don't feel as though you're working underwater), 20 History States is a good figure. If you have lots and *lots* of RAM, you can probably bump up the number some. But whatever number you set for this option, if your system acts sluggish or if Photoshop pops you a warning that available memory is low, you probably have too many History States set. Besides, if you plan on making more than 20 mistakes at a clip, you don't belong in Photoshop—you belong in government work.

## Deciding How to Export the Clipboard

When the Export Clipboard option is checked, data copied from Photoshop to the Clipboard can be pasted into other applications. If you turn off this option, you won't be able to paste an image from Photoshop to Microsoft PowerPoint, for example. Clipboard copying can be quicker than saving a file and then importing it using a different program. When Export Clipboard is enabled, remember to *empty* the Clipboard (Edit, Purge, Clipboard) and free up system RAM *before* exiting Photoshop if you won't be pasting anything from Photoshop into another application. When this option is unchecked, Photoshop automatically clears the Clipboard on exit. We recommend that you leave the Export Clipboard option checked.

## Specifying the Length of PANTONE Names

PANTONE brand inks are commonly used in the United States when specific colors, particularly those that can't be created by a mixture of the four-process colors (Cyan, Magenta, Yellow, and Black), are needed in a printed piece. The PANTONE color specification system is used by Photoshop and other graphics and desktop publishing programs to specify which inks are used in a document. Many programs, when referring to a PANTONE ink, use the "short" version of the ink name, while other programs use the full version of the name. When this option is checked, Photoshop uses the short name. Photoshop can use either long or short PANTONE names.

Before saving a file for use in another program, be sure that the PANTONE names are saved in the naming format used by the other program. For example, an image that uses a PANTONE spot color should be saved with Short PANTONE Names when the file will be used in Adobe PageMaker (we're talking version 6.5 at this time). When the image is brought into the PageMaker document, PageMaker recognizes the custom color by its short PANTONE name and makes that color available on PageMaker's Colors palette so you can use the same ink for matching text, rules, or other elements in the layout. Using short PANTONE names also ensures that an extra plate will be produced if you print separations from PageMaker.

## Showing Tool Tips

Tool tips are small pop-up boxes that contain a name or a description of a tool, button or screen element. Tool tips jump out and display their messages whenever you let your cursor hover over a screen element for more than a second or two. Show Tool Tips is a good feature to turn on whenever you're getting acquainted or reacquainted with Photoshop or ImageReady. When you become familiar with Photoshop's layout and the tool tips progressively feel as welcome as mosquitoes, just come back and uncheck the Show Tool Tips option.

## Using Keyboard Zoom to Resize Windows

This is a feature that you will find either very useful or very annoying. The Keyboard Zoom Resizes Windows preference works well with the shortcuts for zooming—Ctrl(⌘)++(plus) to zoom in, or Ctrl(⌘)+− (minus) to zoom out. When this option is enabled, the image window expands or contracts in size to display as much of the image as it can at the new viewing resolution. This behavior reduces the amount of scrolling or image window resizing you need to do. When the option is turned off, the size of the image window remains constant. When zooming in, scrollbars usually appear in the window frame. When you have a lot of windows and palettes open, maintaining window size can be useful, because it prevents one window from covering up another. By default, this feature is turned off although we agree that the preferred setting is on. To be fair, you should try it both ways and decide for yourself.

## Automatically Updating Open Documents

The Auto-Update open documents option works with the Jump To feature found in both Photoshop and ImageReady. Briefly, Jump To enables you to move your editing work to another program without having to:

- Close the file,
- open it in the new program,
- close it there
- and then reopen in the original application.

Auto-Update is sort of like Microsoft OLE, except Microsoft did not create this Adobe feature. The most common use for Auto-Update is to jump from Photoshop to ImageReady, work on the file there, and then move the image back to Photoshop. Alternatively, when you are working in ImageReady, moving your image to an HTML editing application such as Adobe GoLive, NetObjects, Fusion, or even Microsoft FrontPage is easy.

**Jump from ImageReady to Photoshop**

If you want to jump to ImageReady from Photoshop, or vice versa, there's a convenient button at the bottom of the toolbox (see Figure 4.4) that you click (or press Ctrl(⌘)+Shift+M). If you want to jump to other applications, you need to choose File, Jump To, and then mull around in this box for the application to which you want to hop.

**Figure 4.4**   The joint is jumping! Move your work to other applications with the Auto-Update Open Documents option enabled, and when you return to your original program, changes will be made to the active document.

Enabling the Auto-Update Open Documents is a good way to handle the problem of changes you make always being the ones you want to keep. If you don't enable this option, your screen will be peppered with dialog boxes to alert you to file mismatches when you save in the jumped to program and/or when you make the originating program active. You will be asked if you want to update the original file or save the changed file to another name.

Leaving Auto-Update Open Documents option unchecked means your workflow is interrupted more often by dialog boxes demanding decisions, but at least the decisions end up being yours, not a program's default ones. For this reason, we recommend that this option not be enabled.

## Deciding Whether to Show Asian Text Options

If you did a custom installation when you installed Photoshop and ImageReady, you were given the opportunity to install files to support Asian languages. Photoshop and ImageReady can be used to set Chinese, Japanese, and Korean typefaces. When this option is checked, the Paragraph palette offers additional features for working in these languages. For example, you are given choices between the different sets of hyphenation rules you want to use. To work with Asian fonts, you will need to purchase these fonts and make whatever hardware and software changes that your operating system requires for working with double-byte fonts.

## Killing that Beeping When Done Sound

Not that long ago, Beep When Done was a feature that almost everyone found handy. This feature, if you're not familiar with it, beeps whenever Photoshop completes a processor or memory intensive operation such as the application of Gaussian or Motion blur. Even if you had a top-of-the-line computer, the sounding of the system beep was very useful for waking you up from a nap or signaling that break time was over, at least for now. But desktop and even laptop computers have gotten so powerful that unless you are working with billboard-size files, there really aren't any long operations anymore. If you are really into aural feedback—or just want to antagonize the user in the neighboring cube—check this option. Otherwise, give your ears and your co-workers a rest and uncheck it.

## Enabling Dynamic Color Sliders

Checking this option makes mixing colors using the sliders on the Color palette easier. With the Dynamic Color Sliders option enabled, the strip above each of the sliders changes from a gradient composed of a single color to a strip made up of multiple colors. As you move any one slider all the strips change colors to reflect the color that would be achieved if the slider was moved to a position underneath that color. This is a much easier, more visible way to mix color. See how the Dynamic

Color Sliders option works by playing with it, because it's easier than reading about it here! Our advice is to always keep this option checked unless it conflicts with other system components (it's unlikely, but video drivers and other files might not "play nice" with the dynamic sliders).

## Getting Fancy with the Save Palette Locations Option

Be sure this option is checked. Just before you exit Photoshop or ImageReady, the Save Palette Locations option, if it is turned on, keeps a record of the exact location of the Options bar, the toolbox, and all palettes onscreen or in the Docking well. It also takes note of what palettes are not onscreen. The next time you open Photoshop or ImageReady your workspace is just as you left it.

If you ever want to restore the order and onscreen position of the palettes to their shipping default, just choose Window, Reset Palette Location from the menu. The reset feature on the menu is also handy for teachers and technical support folks who need to be able to quickly set up a known palette configuration for teaching or troubleshooting purposes.

## Getting Font Names to Show in English

If you're using non-Roman character fonts such as the double-byte Asian fonts or Cyrillic fonts, the names of the fonts may not appear on the font list in a form that you can read. If the font has an English font name in the file header, enabling the Show Font Names in English option makes the English name show up in the font list. If you are using the English version of Photoshop, this is probably what you want to have happen, so check this option.

## Flipping the Use Shift Key for Tool Switch

Once upon a time all the tools on the toolbox had single-character keyboard short-cuts that could be used to make that tool the active tool. And if a tool belonged to a group of tools, such as the Dodge, Burn, and Sponge tools, you could switch to that group of tools by pressing their common shortcut of O and then press O again...and again if necessary, to get the exact tool you wanted in that group.

Then things changed. Dinosaurs became extinct, gas prices went up, and Adobe added about 50,000 extra shortcut keys to Photoshop, and the single-key tool short-cuts were not enough. You had to use the Shift key *and* the letter key to do what just a letter key did before.

Fortunately, things have changed again, except for gas prices. If you want to return to the happy times when tools could be called pressing a single key, *uncheck* the Use Shift Key for Tool Switch option. If you like pressing lots of keys, or if you don't want to retrain your fingers, *check* this option. For the purposes of this book, we will assume you have turned this option *off* and we have written steps such as, "press Z to switch to the Zoom tool," or "press B and then press it again if necessary to make the Paintbrush tool the active tool."

## Choosing the Reset All Warning Dialogs Button: A Blast to the Past

Photoshop has some warning dialog boxes, mostly to do with color management profiles that can be prevented from displaying ever again by checking an option on the face of the dialog box. But if the dialog box never again shows its face, how are you ever going to get a chance to uncheck the option if you change your mind and want to be warned? Simple: press Ctrl(⌘)+K and click the Reset All Warning Dialogs button at the bottom of the General Preferences dialog box.

## Clicking the Reset All Tools Button: Danger, Will Robinson!

This reset button on the General Preferences dialog box returns *all* the tools to their default settings. You will also find this command on a menu that appears when you click the first icon on the left on the Options bar. After clicking Reset All Tools, you will get a confirmation box asking you if you really mean it. You should pause and think about your answer, because resetting all tools to default can undo a lot of changes you might have made. On the other hand, if someone has messed up all your settings or if you are a teacher or helpline technician, resetting all the tools to default can make your job a lot easier.

**Tip**

**Reset Settings for a Tool**    If you're unhappy with the current settings for a *single* tool, you can reset just that tool. How? Be sure the tool you want to change is the active tool. The first icon on the Options bar should be the same one that the toolbox uses to identify the tool. Click the first icon and choose Reset Tool, the top item on the menu that pops out of the icon.

General Preferences will get you only so far on your way to Bob or Sue's Ultimate Photoshop Workspace. You need to specify default settings for rulers, transparency, what your Photoshop cursors look like, and for access to a whole bunch of personal productivity enhancers. Click the Next button or choose Saving Files from the drop-down list at the top of the dialog box to travel to our next stop.

# Setting Your Preferences for Saving Files

The second page of the Preferences dialog focuses on options that are related to saved files. This is one area in Photoshop where operating system differences between Windows and Macintosh are evident. The biggest difference is that the Macintosh OS supports more types of image previews and that it does not, by default, use file extensions to indicate the kind of file or the program which can be used to open the file. Image previews are miniature pictures of the actual image contained in a file. These miniature versions of the file are also sometimes called *thumbnails*.

Let's take a look at the Windows Saving Files Preferences first.

## Saving File Preferences in Windows

In the Windows version of Photoshop, you can see the Saving Files page of Preferences (see Figure 4.5). Here is where you decide what the default behavior should be for Image Previews and the letter case of file extensions. Here you can also specify if the files should be saved in a backward-compatible format, and how many files should be listed on the recent file list.

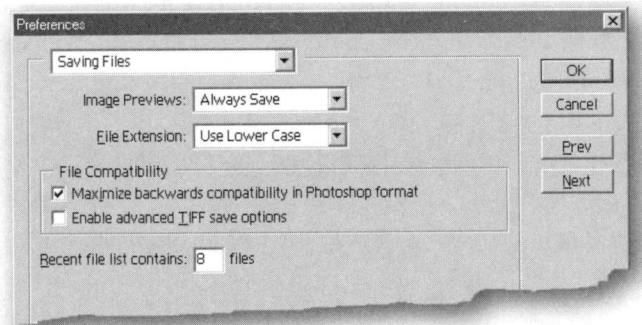

**Figure 4.5**   The Windows version of the Saving Files Preferences dialog box.

### *Saving Image Previews Options*

The default setting for the Image Previews drop-down list, Always Save, is the setting we recommend you use. Your other choices are Never Save and Ask When Saving. These settings are very straightforward; they do exactly what they say. Saving an Image Preview is particularly useful for files saved in the Photoshop's PSD file format.

Photoshop PSD files, when saved with a preview image, will show up as little thumbnails of the file on your desktop and in folders (when large icons are the viewing mode). In Photoshop's Open dialog box, if you choose Thumbnails from the View Menu dropdown, PSD, TIFF, GIF, PNG, and JPG files will display as minia-ture pictures, which makes it very easy to spot the file you want to open.

Also, you can right-click on a PSD image, choose Properties from the shortcut menu, and you will see a larger thumbnail of the image, with relevant data (file size, dimensions, date of birth, and so on).

The Enable Advanced TIFF option was a last minute change in Photoshop. The TIFF file format, version 7 is capable of holding layers, paths, and can be compared to Photoshop's native PSD file format. But, we recommend that both Mac and Windows users keep this feature off. Why? Because the world doesn't own Photoshop, and an "enhanced" TIFF cannot be read by non-Adobe products. TIFF is the *lingua franca* of bitmap images—you make the format proprietary and generally unaccessible by others when you turn on its special properties. This feature was basically designed for digital video editors who have been screaming for this feature for years.

And last, but not least, when images that have been saved with an image preview are selected in Photoshop's and ImageReady's Open dialog box, the preview of the image is displayed at the bottom of the dialog box. Extra file formats can be dis-played on the bottom of the dialog box: EPS, GIF, JPG, PCT, PNG, PSD, Photoshop PDF, SCT, and TIFF.

Saving an Image Preview in a file does add a nominal amount to the size of the file when it is saved to disk. But the convenience of being able to see what a file looks like before opening it far outweighs the teensy extra disk space used.

### Choosing a File Extension Option

You can choose the letter case of file extensions. Use Lower Case is the default. Unless you have an in-house rule that says that all filenames have to be in upper-case, choose Use Lower Case. Who on earth wants a file extension shouting at them from a long list of files?

### Handling the Maximize Backwards Compatibility Option

As you have no doubt noticed, each new version of Photoshop comes with tons of new features. The downside to all the new features is that older versions of Photoshop, as well as other programs that can import Photoshop files, don't *know* about the features. At best, these programs will ignore stuff in the file that it doesn't understand (type layers, effect layers, etc.), and, at worst, these programs may not be able to open the newer version Photoshop files at all. Backward compatibility issues have always focused on Photoshop's native file format, PSD files. But now, because Adobe has enhanced the capability of the TIFF and PDF file formats, you need to watch out for backward compatibility problems with files saved in these formats as well.

For these reasons, the default setting for the Maximize Backwards Compatibility option is enabled. When this option is checked, TIFF, PDF, and PSD images are saved with extra information in them, a flattened version of the file. Doing so allows programs that don't know about the latest version of Photoshop to open those files. Saving this extra version of the file within the saved file increases the file's size noticeably.

You can turn off this feature and save disk space, but it will be at the expense of compatibility. If you are like most Photoshop users, you use a variety of programs and exchange files with colleagues and clients. If the previous sentence describes you, leave this feature enabled and save yourself a lot of headaches.

**Note**

As mentioned in Chapter 5, the TIFF format is up to version 7 now and Adobe is the official keeper of the TIFF standard. By default, a TIFF format image can have alpha channels, but not layers, paths, annotations, or other new features. The TIFF image format is capable of retaining all these extras, but by default, when you save to the TIFF format, the Extra Features options is turned off (and you can turn it on if you want a TIFF image that can only be opened in Photoshop 6). So the Backwards Compatibility option doesn't really apply to the TIFF standard file format.

### Establishing the Length of the Recent File List

The Recent Files List option is accessed by choosing File, Open Recent from the menu. The default number of files that Photoshop displays on the list is 4, but you can specify as many as 30 files on the list by entering a number in the Recent File List Contains field. I use Open Recent command frequently because it saves time— I don't have to scour my hard drives to find the images I've worked on lately. This feature also helps me locate images when I forget where I've saved them. I've set this option to 10 on my copy of Photoshop; you should set the option to the number that works the best for you. This feature requires no additional memory usage.

**Tip**

**Photoshop Tracks 30 Files**   The number of files you set in the Recent File List Contains option is the number of files Photoshop displays on the Open Recent list, but Photoshop *actually keeps track* of the previous 30 files you used. If you are having trouble finding a file you've worked on recently, open up Saving Preferences and change the number of files in the Recent File List Contains option to 30. Click OK and then choose File, Open Recent. You may be pleasantly surprised to find the file you're looking for on the list!

## Saving File Preferences on a Macintosh

You have slightly different choices on the Saving Files page of the Preferences dialog box on the Macintosh, so here's the scoop on the different options:

### Image Previews

As with Windows, you have a choice of Always Save, Never Save, and Ask When Saving the thumbnails, but there's also a sub-choice here. Do you want to save to Icon, Macintosh Thumbnail, Windows Thumbnail, or Full Size?

- **Icon.** Displays the picture at 32×32 pixels on the desktop and in folder windows. This is a very sensible option to check and adds practically nothing to the saved file size.

- **Macintosh or Windows Thumbnail.** This is the image you see in preview boxes. The image is larger than an icon thumbnail and smaller than a Winnebago. Check this option if you want the saved file size to be a little larger than the Icon option but want to have an easier time previewing files before you load them. Your choice of Windows or Macintosh thumbnail has to do with the final destination for the file. Are you a Macintosh user who sends work to a Windows service bureau? Then make your preview choice here (see Figure 4.6).

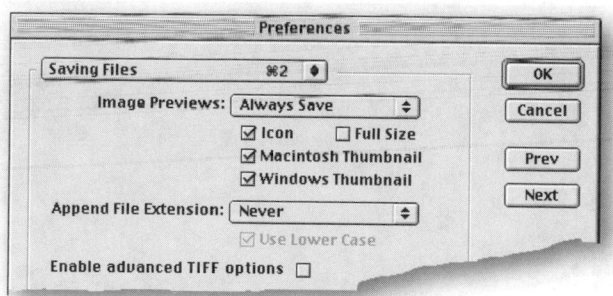

**Figure 4.6**    The Macintosh dialog box for File Saving Preferences has options that are different from those in Windows.

- **Full Size.** Whoa! Isn't a full size image preview redundant? No; what is meant here is that some applications such as Quark can place and link at full-page preview at 72 pixels/inch resolution. The actual picture might be the same size in inches, but its resolution could be something such as 266 pixels/inch. Yes, this option does, indeed, increase the size of your saved file significantly, but you will work more quickly in Quark when the on-page image links out to the 72 pixels/inch preview for display.

### Append File Extension

We have Never, Ask, and Always as choices in the Append File Extension option. If you design for the Web, browsers insist on file extensions. Many, many Web servers use UNIX as the operating system and GIF, JPEG, and HTML files *must always* have the file extensions (*.gif, *.jpg, and *.html, respectively) appended to a document name in order for the server to successfully pass the correct image type to the visitor's browser. And even if there weren't a Web, there are multiplatform companies out there, and it makes it that much more difficult to share your work with Windows users if neither of you know the file format.

It's time to move on to the Display & Cursors page of the Preferences dialog box.

## Specifying How Documents and Cursors Display

This area of preferences determines how you view a document in its window and what Photoshop's cursors look like. See Figure 4.7 for a view of this page in Preferences.

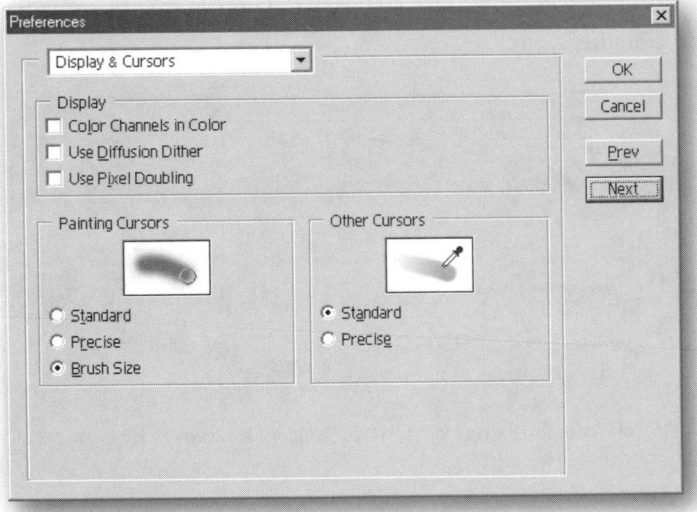

**Figure 4.7**    The Display & Cursors page in Preferences enables you to change cursor shapes and the way you see files that are open in Photoshop.

## Setting Up the Display

This area determines how an image is presented to you in an image window.

- **Color Channels in Color.** Leave this unchecked. All it does is tint the view of channels in a document window to help remind you to what channel you are tuned. Color image channels in reality, contain *grayscale* information that is mixed with all the color component channels to make a color composite view of the image. So, why start your imaging adventures with an unnecessary layer of candy coating?

- **Use Diffusion Dither.** This option only applies to users whose video card has something like 20KB of video memory on board. Seriously, you will almost never work on a system today that doesn't support 24-bit color, so you can leave this box unchecked. This option will dither images that are beyond the video capacity of your system settings for video.

- **Use Pixel Doubling.** Enable this? Not really, unless you want to view your movements on an image at half the image area's resolution. It's disconcerting to see an image area move at low resolution and then go to normal resolution once it's been moved. Today's processors will usually remove any need for this fancy screen mapping while you edit.

## Choosing Your Painting Cursors

Again, because of today's video cards with a typical 32MB of RAM on them, and the sheer processing speed of computers, you can afford to choose Brush size in this area, which used to cause a noticeable dragging effect on slower machines. After making this choice, whenever you choose the Pencil, Paintbrush, Clone Stamp, Eraser, and other paint and paint removal tools, the size of the cursor is clearly drawn out for you onscreen. If you need to quickly switch to a precise, crosshair cursor while you work, press CapsLock. Pressing CapsLock a second time changes the cursor back to Brush size mode.

## Deciding Which Other Cursors to Use

If you are just getting into Photoshop, we recommend the Standard (icon) display of the tools. Why? Because there are around 70 million tools on the toolbox, and their unique cursors will help you to more quickly identify the tool you need (or are using) at any given moment. Like Painting cursors, pressing CapsLock will turn these other cursors into a crosshair for precision work.

Let's tackle the invisible now <g>—Transparency and Gamut preferences. Click Next.

## Understanding How to Choose Transparency & Gamut Settings

It's funny, but the correct choice on the Transparency & Gamut page of Preferences depends entirely upon the color content of the image at hand. For example, if you want Photoshop to display a tinted overlay in areas in your image that cannot be faithfully reproduced in CMYK colors, you'd usually press Ctrl(⌘)+Shift+Y (or choose View, Gamut Warning). The default for this is gray at 100% opacity. So here's the obvious question now: How can you tell something's out of gamut if the original picture contains a lot of grays?

The answer is, "You can't. You need to change the color of Gamut Warning in Photoshop." And Transparency can be hard to spot, too, especially if you're masking around an object whose background is white (which is fairly common). See Figure 4.8 for the display of the Transparency & Gamut preferences page.

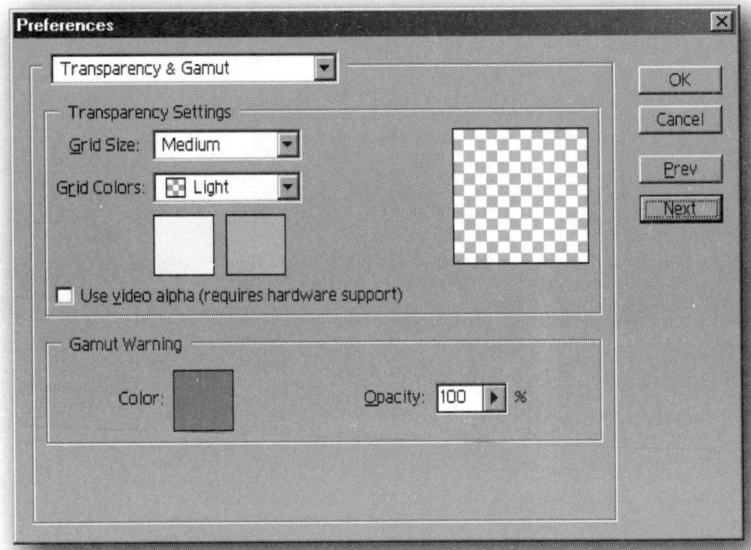

**Figure 4.8**   The Transparency & Gamut box in the Preferences dialog box is shown here.

In the following set of steps, we'll demonstrate a problem to you and then show you how to fix it in about four keystrokes.

### Example 4.1   Changing Transparency Display

1. Open the visible.psd image from the Examples/Chap04 folder of the Companion CD. Viewing Resolution 100% is fine.

2. Click the Add a mask mode button (the button to the right of the *f*; the icon is a circle within a rectangle) on the bottom of the Layers palette. Press F7 if the Layers palette isn't visible.

> **Warning!**   If an error message appears when you open the CD files, press Ctrl(⌘)+Shift+K and then choose Adobe RGB (1998) from the Working Spaces, RGB drop-down list. See Chapter 3 for more information.

3. Choose the Paintbrush tool, choose the top row, far right tip from the palette on the Options bar, press D (default colors). Press X if necessary to make black the foreground color. Make sure Opacity is set to 100% and then start hiding the white background by painting over it. Carefully, work your way to the edge of the "v" in "visible." When you think you've trimmed around the outside edge of the "v," then stop.

As you can see in Figure 4.9, it's very hard to tell where the transparent background ends and the graphic begins.

**Figure 4.9**   How can you accurately edit this image if part of the transparency representation and part of the image are the same color?

4. Press Ctrl(⌘)+K, click the top drop-down list, and choose Transparency & Gamut.

Don't even *try* to remember the shortcut key, as it is displayed next to the name of the Preferences page. There are much more useful shortcut keys to remember—such as Ctrl(⌘)+K.

5. Open the Grid colors drop-down list and choose Dark, as shown in Figure 4.10. Click OK to change the display of Transparency.

6. Press Ctrl(⌘)++ until you are at 300% viewing resolution of visible.psd. Maximize your view by clicking the Maximize/Restore window button (Macintosh: drag the window edges away from the image), hold the spacebar and drag in the window until you see the area where you were editing.

Wow! There were areas you didn't even *see* that are unedited, aren't there? See Figure 4.11. However, now that you've defined a different color transparency grid, you can accurately trim around the lettering.

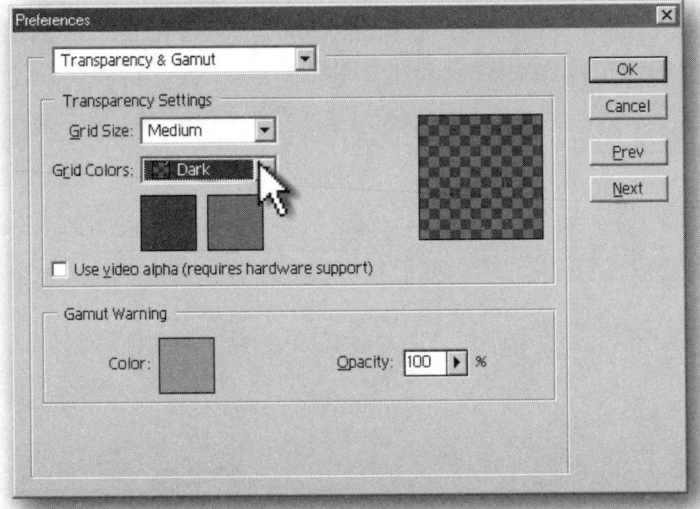

**Figure 4.10**   Choose a transparency representation whose component colors do not exist in the image you are editing.

The point's been made here, so it's really not necessary to completely edit around the lettering. But if you want the experience of working with the Paintbrush tool, choose a tip that is two sizes smaller for going around the lettering. When the white background is completely gone, drag the Layer Mask thumbnail into the Trash icon on the Layers palette, and choose Apply in the attention box that follows this action.

7. You can save visible.psd to your hard drive, or simply close it without saving. Keep Photoshop open.

Our next stop in the Preferences dialog box is Units & Rulers.

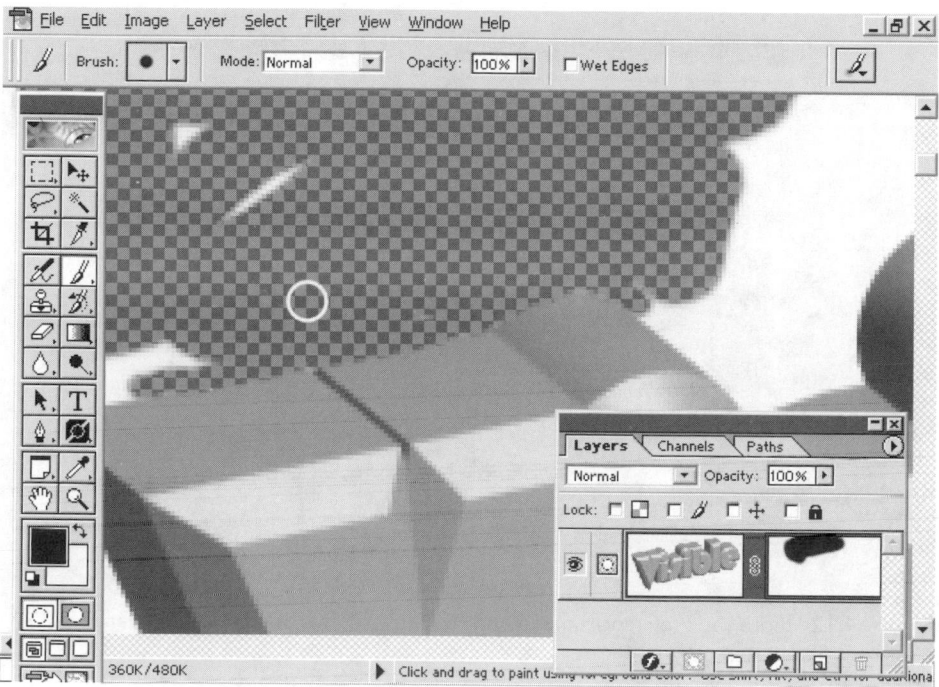

**Figure 4.11**    A different transparency representation onscreen can help bring to light areas you've missed editing.

## Determining Which Units and Rulers to Use

There are two different ways to specify units for rulers in Photoshop. Whenever you press Ctrl(⌘)+R, rulers will pop up to the left and top of the document window. Besides being able to measure things, the rulers are the only interface element that enable you to drag guides from them (so if you need to place a guide, you need the rulers visible).

**Tip**

To go directly to the Rulers & Units Preferences page, press Ctrl(⌘)+R to display the rulers, and then double-click on a ruler.

In the Rulers drop-down list, we suggest that you specify inches (unless you work somewhere that uses centimeters or picas), and for Type, points (and every once in a while picas) is the choice, as shown in Figure 4.12.

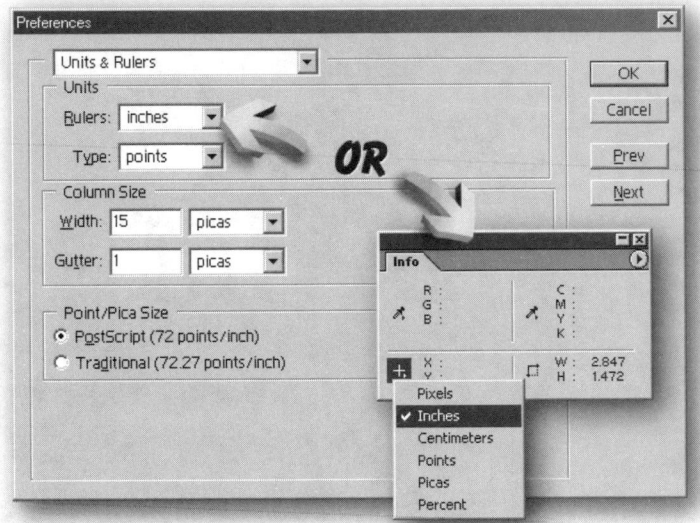

**Figure 4.12**   Both the Preferences menu and the Info palette can be used to change units of measurement.

Now, when you begin editing images for the Web, pixels prevail and inches and most of the other units become irrelevant. There are three ways to do this:

- Press Ctrl(⌘)+K, choose Rulers & Units from the top drop-down list, and then choose pixels.
- Press Ctrl(⌘)+R to make the rulers visible, right-click (Macintosh: hold Ctrl and click) over a ruler, and choose pixels. Next press Ctrl(⌘)+R once more to hide the rulers.
- Press F8, click the crosshairs on the bottom left of the Info palette, and choose pixels.

If you try this all three ways, you will see that displaying the Info palette is a quicker way to change units. And as we travel through this book, you'll see that it's not just the rulers that change units: Image Size and Canvas Size units are both changed by either device here.

The Column Size and Gutter preferences in Units & Rulers are used when you want to measure an image that will cross a gutter (the space between columns) when the image is printed in a publication. You'll probably never need to use these preferences, but If you're suddenly drafted for the composing room(s) at *The New York Times*, this is a welcome feature to know about.

# Specifying Guides and Grids Measurements and Colors

The Guides & Grid preferences should be chosen, like the transparency colors, with a specific piece of art in mind. Chances are much less than 50/50 that your art will feature the default light blue guide color in many areas, so you might not need to change this. Additionally, you can choose from solid lines or dashed lines. When you *really* need to see your work underneath guides, choose dashed lines, because they cover 50% less of the design.

My spouse and I frequently tell ambitious novice Web designers that creating Web graphics is actually two arts: the art of good design and the art of making every pixel count—because you have so few of them compared to press work.

Measuring is definitely part of Web art, so let's run through a set of steps in which you create a Web button using the Grid feature to precisely define the area you want as a button.

### Example 4.2    Creating a Button of Precise Measurement

1. Press F8 and choose pixels from the drop-down list on the Info palette. Press F8 again to close the Info palette.

2. Press Ctrl(⌘)+N and specify that the new image is 400 pixels wide by 300 pixels high, RGB color mode, Background is white, and Resolution is 72 pixels/inch. Press Enter (Return).

3. Press Ctrl(⌘)+K, choose Guides & Grid from the top drop-down box in General Preferences.

4. In the Gridline Every field, type **50** and make pixels the unit of measurement. In the Subdivisions field, type **10**, as shown in Figure 4.13.

    Now when you display the Grid in the image window there will be a marker every 50 pixels, and between markers will be increments marked off every 10 pixels.

5. Press Ctrl(⌘)++ until the new document window is at 200% viewing resolution. Maximize the window in the workspace.

6. Press F7 if the Layers palette is not currently onscreen. Click the Create a new layer icon on the bottom of the palette (the page icon with one corner folded over, next to the Trash icon). You can close the palette now.

    You're working on a layer, so you can apply a style to the button you will create.

7. Choose Window, Show Styles (or commit to memory F6 as the keyboard shortcut).

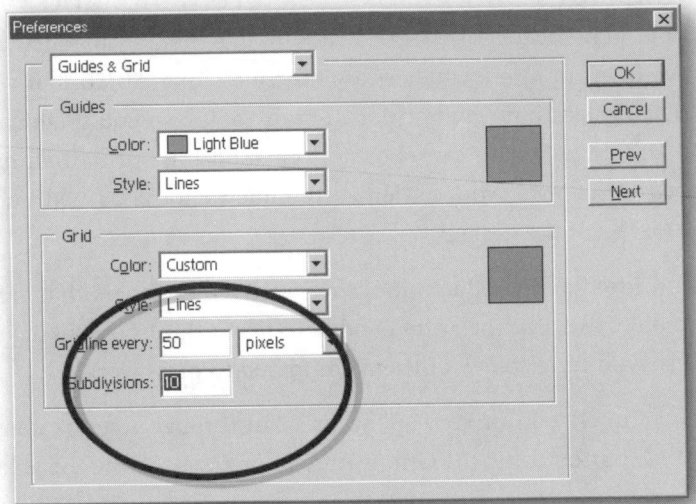

**Figure 4.13**    Web work, such as making buttons, is always measured in screen units—pixels. Choose an amount and pixels in the Guides & Grid preferences that enables you to precisely mark off an area you need filled.

8. Choose View, Show, and click Grid.

9. Drag the zero point (box) to a division point both horizontally and vertically, as shown in Figure 4.14.

10. With the Rectangular Marquee tool, drag a rectangle that is 100 pixels wide by 60 pixels high. Click the Foreground Color selection box, and in the Color Picker, drag the circle in the color field and drag on the color strip until you have a nice, pastel color—any color—and press Enter (Return). Press Alt(Opt)+Delete to fill the marquee selection with foreground color. Press Ctrl(⌘)+D to deselect the marquee.

11. Click a Style icon whose bevel goes inward, not outward (because then the button will be larger than 100 by 60 pixels), as shown in Figure 4.14.

12. Press Ctrl(⌘)+H. This hides the grid and all other "extras" unless you change this option; see the following Note. Now press Ctrl(⌘)+R. If you do not put away rulers, grids and such from an image, all subsequent images you bring into the workspace will have (unwanted) rulers and grids.

    See Figure 4.15 for the handsome Web button you designed without screen clutter.

13. You can close your work now at any time without saving. Keep Photoshop open.

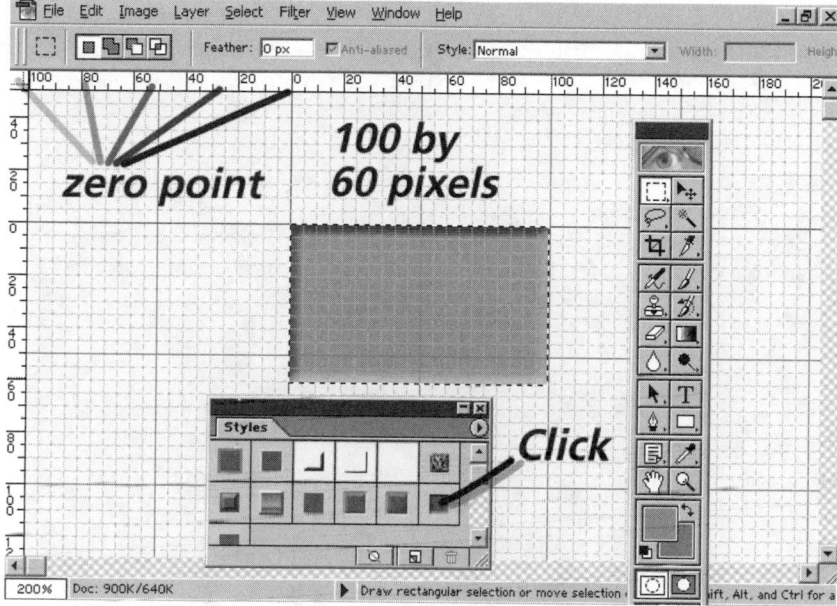

**Figure 4.14**    When you have the workspace set up to measure in pixels using the grid, button-making takes only two steps!

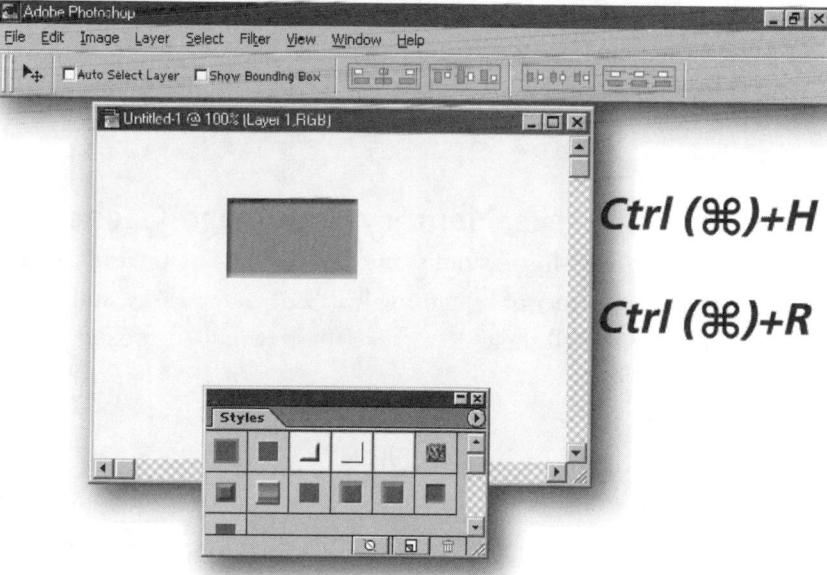

**Figure 4.15**    You can remove all measuring tools from the screen using two key commands.

> **Note**
>
> **Hide One But Not the Other**   There are a lot of nonprinting screen elements, such as selection, guides, paths, and so on in Photoshop. You might want to hide one without hiding the other. For example, what if you want to see a marquee selection, but not the guide to which it is aligned?
>
> Once you get a feel for your guideline needs, choose View, Show, and then Show Options. Check the element that you want to persist onscreen, and then all elements (except the ones you checked) will vanish when you press Ctrl(⌘)+H (see Figure 4.16). You can manually deselect and hide these extras when the time comes in your assignment.

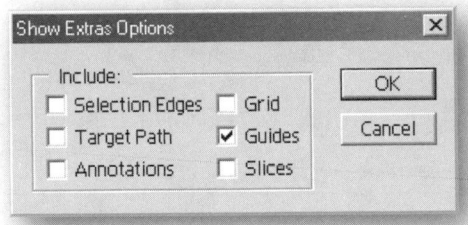

**Figure 4.16**   The Show Extras Options box makes the Ctrl(⌘)+H command customizable.

We didn't have time on our tour here to show guides, but they act and have snap-to properties like guides in any other program, such as InDesign or Illustrator. Snap-to properties can be found under the View menu. Between guides and the grid feature, you can have a ball *and* design *accurate* Web media in Photoshop.

# Plug-Ins, Scratch Disks, Memory, and Image Cache

With the exception of Plug-Ins locations, the next two dialog boxes in Photoshop really should be sewn together or something because Scratch Disks, and Memory & Image Cache are very related topics. Let's take these two dialog boxes' preferences one at a time here.

## Ranking the Importance of Scratch Disks

The Scratch Disk is probably as important a preference in Photoshop as color settings are for the workspace. Photoshop needs hard-disk space in which it saves History pieces, Clipboard pieces, multiple copies of an active file for Undo purposes, and more. If you do not give it enough hard-disk space, your work will come to a grinding halt even with gigabytes of RAM on your system.

Let's get the trivial preference here out of the way, so we can talk memory management with you.

## Specifying the Directory for Plug-Ins

Plug-ins, those third-party enhancers from Alien Skin, Andromeda software, and others, can be installed to Photoshop's Plug-Ins directory. Now, here's the catch: What if you also own, say Painter and want to use the same plug-ins in Painter? No problem. You create a folder on one of your drives, plunk your third-party plug-ins in the folder, and then point Photoshop toward this folder as an additional place to look for plug-ins. BTW, you need to check the option so Photoshop will go looking the next time you start it. Changes to plug-ins folder location(s) don't take place until you restart Photoshop.

Okay, memory management...

## Doling Out System Resources to Photoshop

It might come as a surprise to new users that Photoshop doesn't use that nice hunk of temp space you set away for applications to use. Nope, Photoshop wants its *own* space that no other application's going to touch while it is running—and it wants it to be as large as possible. Adobe, like virtually no other company, knows how to handle memory in an elegant way. This means where other applications might gag and crash over handling a 40MB image file, Photoshop can do it—*if* you set up memory and scratch disk allocation the way it wants.

As a rule of thumb, Photoshop wants three to five times the size of a saved image file to work with. That means that if you are working on a 5MB file, you need to have 15MB to 25MB free of both scratch disk space and physical RAM. If you have less scratch disk space than RAM, Photoshop will not use any more RAM than it has access to scratch disk space. Therefore, if you have 1GB of RAM and have assigned Photoshop 200MB of scratch disk space, Photoshop will only use 200MB of that huge RAM amount you have installed.

Now, the Windows and Mac OS handle memory differently, so we need to break out the following sections on smart memory handling for each operating system. Let's start with Windows first.

### The Windows Scratch Disk Assignment and RAM Requirements

The fundamental difference between Windows and Macintosh OS memory handling is that Macintosh users define how much memory is allocated to an application. On the other hand, Microsoft Windows dynamically resizes the memory pool to allow applications to extend their use of RAM while you work.

Still, it's a good idea to devote hard-disk space to as many drives as you can afford in the Plug-Ins & Scratch Disks page of Preferences. Good candidates to which you assign a scratch disk location are these:

- **A drive that has a lot of free space.** 1GB is not unreasonable, and naturally, you get this space back after you close Photoshop.

- **A drive that does not use a compression scheme.** Microsoft DriveSpace is not cool on the drive to which you assign the Primary scratch disk.

- **A drive that has been defragmented.** Use the Disk Defragmenter utility to optimize any drive to which you assign scratch disk status.

As you will notice in Figure 4.17, drive H is the first scratch disk drive on this particular machine. This drive happens to have the most free, uncompressed space on its system. If there were any other drives that have a lot of free space, you can assign them as Second, Third, and Fourth drives. Photoshop *honestly needs* this kind of hard-drive space to enable you to work quickly and flawlessly in it. You might even want to re-think running other applications while Photoshop is loaded to give maximum memory support to Photoshop.

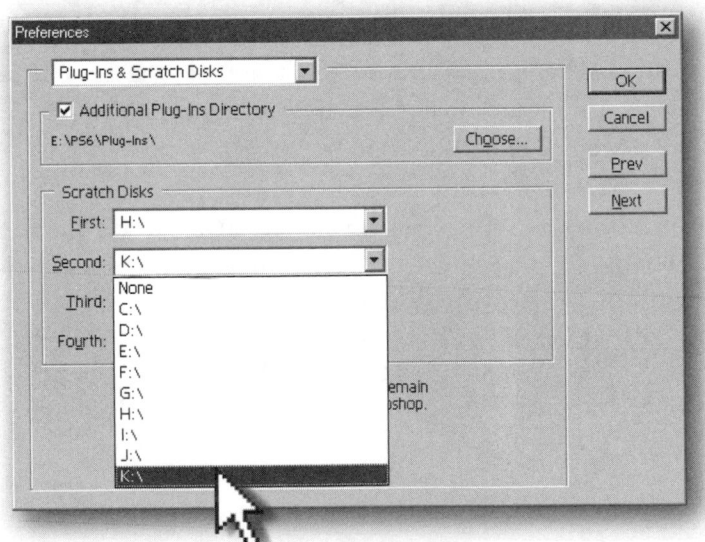

**Windows users: do *NOT* choose the startup drive.**

**Figure 4.17**    Specify which drives have the most free space on your system for Photoshop to set up a scratch disk.

**Warning**

**Don't Put a Scratch Disk on Your C Drive**    It is not a good idea to put a scratch disk on your C drive. Not only is this usually the drive where your operating system is located, but it's also where temp folders for other applications are placed. If you attempt to dynamically resize a space on a drive on Windows that's been assigned as a scratch disk, you *will* have system problems.

If you click Next now, you see the Memory & Image Cache settings.

Cache setting for images helps speed up their display in the same way that caching on your system helps speed up display of frequently-used screen areas. The default level is 4, and we see no need to change this, because it is a good trade-off between snappy display and overall system performance.

The Use Cache for Histograms is not really a preference you want. We recommend that you leave this unchecked. Even if you have the system resources to dedicate to caching histogram information, caching is performed on a *sampling* of pixels in the image, instead of *all* the pixels in the image.

The Available RAM you dedicate to Photoshop depends on which operating system you use. Windows 2000 achieves optimal performance running Photoshop at anywhere between 50% and 60% of total system resources. Windows 98 can use anywhere from 60% to 75% of your system resource, as shown in Figure 4.18.

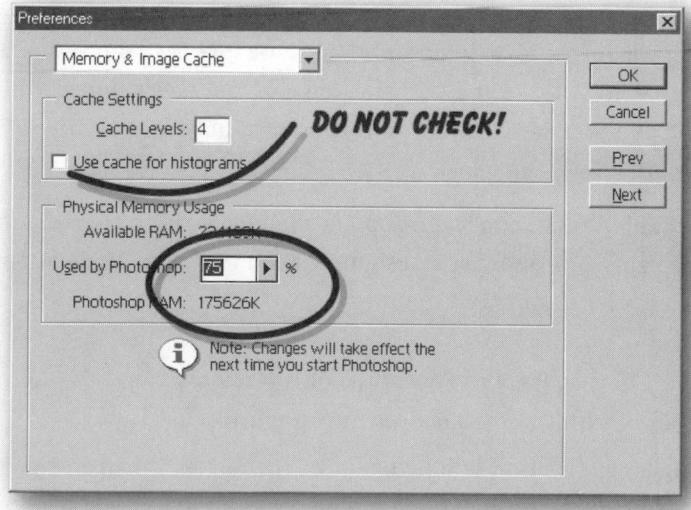

**Figure 4.18**    Use the Memory & Image Cache preferences to determine how much RAM is allocated to each purpose.

It is not necessarily a good idea to dedicate all resources (100%) to Photoshop for two reasons:

- You actually decrease efficiency of Photoshop as the RAM dedicated approaches 100%. This is because the Windows system itself can use software caching, and Photoshop and Windows will enter a fight over how much RAM is actually available.

- Windows will never allow an application to take as many resources as it likes; it will always protect the amount of memory it needs to keep running—even if this means shutting down an application to conserve resources. So even if you typed 100% in the Available RAM field in Memory & Image Caching, Windows would only allow about 85% of all RAM resources to go to Photoshop.

We are trying to give you reasons behind these recommendations because some day you may need to change your preferences.

### The Macintosh Scratch Disk Assignment and RAM Requirements

As far as allocating Photoshop a scratch disk space on a Macintosh system, use the same guidelines as mentioned for Windows. Pick a large drive with nothing on it, use a utility such as Norton Utilities to defrag the drive regularly, and use no drive compression on the target drive. Pick as many as four locations for scratch disk space.

The first thing you ought to do to optimize RAM use is check your system to see how much RAM is on it. A lot of the G3s and some of the G4s shipped with 64MB of physical RAM, and you need 128MB to work comfortably in Photoshop. So call and order some more RAM.

Even with 128MB of RAM, applications other than Photoshop are memory hogs (*all* of today's programs are), and if you absolutely need to run an application alongside Photoshop, here's what you need to do:

#### Example 4.3    Allocating RAM to Photoshop on a Macintosh

1. Start your machine and do *not* run any applications.

   Running an application or logging on to check your email will potentially fragment your system's memory and give you an inaccurate reading in step 3.

2. Start any other application you think you will want to use while Photoshop is running. Ideally, you should have no other program running, but doing this is a productivity dampener.

3. Go to Finder, and choose About This Computer from the Apple menu. This box will tell you the largest unused block of RAM that is available. Let's suppose the number is 120MB.

4. In Finder, choose the Adobe Photoshop program icon and choose File, Get Info.

5. Regardless of what values are in the box, in the Info window, set the Preferred Size to no more than 90% of the Largest Unused Block value you saw earlier, such as 90% of 120MB.

6. Close out of the Info box and launch Photoshop.

## Analyzing Your Computer's Performance

Now, there's memory handling and there's memory handling. By this somewhat cryptic phrase, we mean that you can indeed run Photoshop on less than 128MB of RAM, but you probably won't like the performance. What happens when there is not enough RAM that Photoshop can tap into? Photoshop starts writing image fragments to the scratch disk(s). This is bad. Why? Because the fastest drives today are still measured in milliseconds, while RAM is measured in nanoseconds. Do you want to use the family junker or a sports car to get to the market quickly?

You can tell when Photoshop's performance is not what it should be by clicking on the Document Sizes area on the lower-left of the status bar. (Macintosh does not have a status bar. You find document sizes at the bottom left of the current window.) Click and select scratch sizes by holding on the triangle to reveal the flyout. The left side of the fraction tells how much scratch disk space you are using, and the right side tells you how much scratch disk space you currently have allocated. If the left number reaches 75% of the right number, save, increase the size of your scratch disk in Preferences, and start again.

Also Efficiency is an interesting option to study, and it, too, is on the document Sizes flyout. When the Efficiency setting reads 100%, all of Photoshop's calculations are taking place in physical RAM. When the number dips, Photoshop is writing out to hard disk, and when the Efficiency drops to say, 50%, this means that half the time in Photoshop, Photoshop is writing to disk, and you really need to go out and buy more RAM.

## All This Is Important Stuff!

Guess what? We have covered all the preferences in the Preferences dialog boxes, and you are a much richer person for this small investment of time. Your copy of Photoshop will run better and things will be more obvious than Photoshop copies belonging to the uneducated. We strongly advise you that if something in this chapter does not make sense at first, read it a second time. This is not "kiddy stuff" and the difference between tuning and not tuning Photoshop can cost you that extra 15 minutes you need to get an assignment in on time. We've been writing chapters in our books on Photoshop optimization since 1994, so please do trust us on our calls.

# Summary

From naggley things, like the shape of the cursor, to critical things, like memory handling, you've learned it all now and can refer to this chapter whenever you feel like performing some more customizing.

Our adventures in customizing aren't over by a country mile, though (which we believe to be equivalent to a "city mile"). There are ways to customize interface palettes, brushes, image layers while you work, and more. But we felt that scattering the "really fun stuff" about the other areas of the book would keep both you and the authors entertained. Chapter 5 takes you into what *really* happens when you change colors or color modes onscreen. Photoshop has provided you with visual controls that are easy to handle, but eventually, you'll need to know what *out-of-gamut* colors are (and naturally, what a "gamut" is!), why a GIF image can only hold 256 colors, why you can do special things with certain file types (such as transparency), and a color trick or two.

Just turn the page. It won't spring into glorious color, but your *education* on color will!

# Chapter 5

## Introducing Image Formats, Image Modes, and Color Spaces

Although this author adopted Photoshop

early on, vector graphics was the first

thing he learned as he taught himself

electronic art. CorelDRAW version 2 was simple to understand, and you could change your mind about almost every aspect of what you were creating in the program.

Perhaps you, too, grew up on, say, Illustrator, but like the author, you wanted more. You wanted photorealism, you wanted your work to include things that just plain looked phony when rendered to vectors and fills. And if you're like most of us, the concept of bitmap artwork and the notion of a pixel were mysterious, to say the least!

This chapter is for the vector designer, and also for a lot of us who bootstrapped our way into Photoshop and didn't find the answers to some basic questions. Our goal in this chapter is to leave you with lots more information than you'll want, and fewer questions about color capability (also called *color depth*), image modes in Photoshop (sometimes interchangeable with the term *color spaces*), and image formats. What makes a GIF image a GIF image, and why do the authors keep going on about saving to the TIFF format?

We are going to explore the roots of computer imaging, if you will, in this chapter, and shake a little dirt off the roots so you have a better understanding of what's happening on the other side of that monitor screen!

## Learning About Color Capability

We use descriptions of Photoshop Image mode items in concert with descriptions of color capability, because many aspects of the two areas overlap. To spare you a potential headache here, we can loosely interpret the modes on the Image menu to be color spaces—the RGB color mode, for example, reaches out farther than Indexed mode images do, in the visible spectrum of color. A *color space* is a finite boundary within the space of all visible colors. Color spaces aren't always located in the center of all visible colors, either—the CMYK color space has a preference for certain hues in the spectrum of visible color. This means that color spaces occupy areas of certain hues and fall short of embracing other hues. *Color capability*, on the other hand, tells us how many bits of color information can be stored in any given pixel of an image. Color capability is more commonly called *color depth*.

So color space and color depth are characteristics found in any given image file. And, often, understanding one aspect of an image's color helps  solve a question about a different aspect. The third player in this chapter, file formats, can be considered to be the vessel that holds color space and color depth. And if you've ever shopped at the Pottery Barn, you know that vessels come in different sizes.

We begin with color capability, run through the modes in Photoshop, tell you about their color depth, and the way the file's color information is organized. At the end of this chapter, we tell you which file format is the best for storing these various collections of color.

## In the Beginning, There Was One Bit Per Pixel

Everyone in the computer graphics field has used the term *bitmap* at one time or another to describe an image whose structure is made up of a mesh of pixels. It's not an accurate description of pixel-based images, but we put up with the misuse of the term. But if we're going to play in Photoshop with different spaces and modes and stuff, we should make it clear the term bitmap, used in Photoshop, means, "a *map* (mesh, grid) of color placeholders whose color capability is limited to one *bit* of information." One bit of computer information has two states, and only one of them can be active at a time—it's on or off. It's not hard to see how this one bit of information can be used to turn on a pixel and make it white, or turn off a pixel and make it black. It's that simple: An image in Photoshop's Bitmap mode can be made of pixels that are either black or white.

What good is Bitmap mode? Well, because there are no intermediate colors—*blends* of black and white—Bitmap mode presents the artist with a clean, unambiguous rendering of something. On scanners, the color mode Bitmap often is called Line Art. Although the image is not refined-looking (bitmaps, upon close inspection, tend to look a lot like bad Etch-A-Sketch art), a bitmap can be a good resource to trace over in other programs. In contrast, images with higher color capabilities do not make good tracing fodder. Why? Because all the colors tend to meld together and it's hard to determine where lines start and end. *Anti-aliasing* (the smoothing of curved and diagonal lines in pixel art) is not possible with only one bit of information per pixel, so the harsh appearance of bitmap art is unavoidable.

## Two Examples of Bitmap Art

It's not fair to go on about a Photoshop color mode without showing you what it looks like! Now, here's the deal—an image in Bitmap mode can appear one way or another:

- If you are painting in Bitmap mode, you are creating black lines and dots on a white canvas, or vice versa.

- If you have converted a more color-capable image to Bitmap mode, the image will sort of look like a high-contrast image made out of dust.

Figure 5.1 shows what we're talking about here. The drawing on the left was done in Bitmap mode. The photograph on the right was color-reduced to one bit per pixel, using a type of dithering. We'll get to a working definition of dithering later in this chapter. It's an important feature any time you go from a high color capability to a lower one.

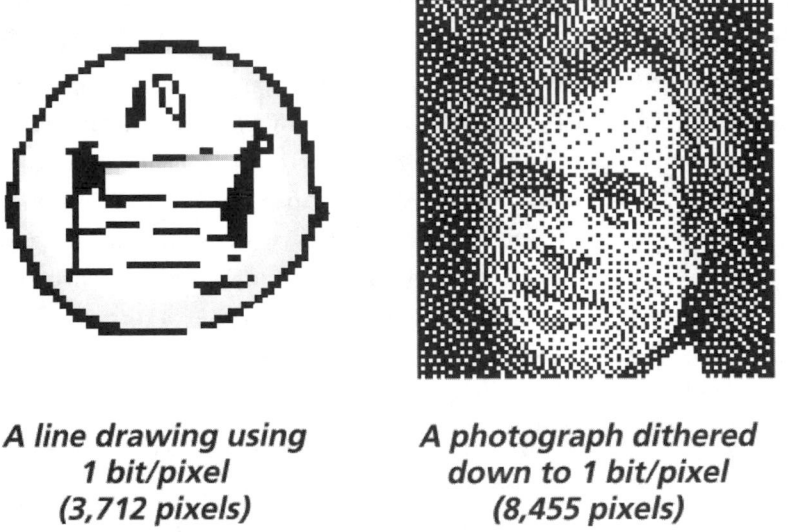

**A line drawing using
1 bit/pixel
(3,712 pixels)**

**A photograph dithered
down to 1 bit/pixel
(8,455 pixels)**

**Figure 5.1**   A drawing done in one-bit-per-pixel mode, and a photograph reduced to a color depth of one bit per pixel.

One bit per pixel spells lousy artwork—it's that simple. But to be completely fair, there are three things you can do to minimize the harsh look of one-bit-per-pixel artwork:

- You can use lots of pixels in the image, and force the audience to look at the artwork from a distance. A little later in this chapter you'll learn that as image dimensions decrease, resolution increases. So without touching a pixel in the image, if you increase the apparent distance from the audience, the resolution of the image makes it look a little better. Figure 5.2 uses 480,000 pixels, whereas each image in Figure 5.1 uses only a few thousand pixels. If you hold the image of the fruit in Figure 5.2 at arm's length, it comes together visually better than the art in Figure 5.1 because the fruit image contains more data—more pixels.

**Figure 5.2**   This image is one bit per pixel, the same as Figure 5.1, but because the image resolution is higher, the image looks better.

- You could also change the white in the image to a color, but that's sort of cheating because, technically, a bitmap is full of colors turned on (white) or full of colors turned off (black). Photoshop would consider such an image to be an Indexed mode image consisting of two colors. We know this sounds odd, but this chapter has a lot to do with the way Photoshop works with color.

- You could make a supergraphic out of a very small piece of one-bit-per-pixel artwork. (*Supergraphic,* a term from the early 1970s, means "a very simple design, blown up a thousand times or so.") In Figure 5.3, we have sort of Minimalist art on a T-shirt. It's simply a Wait cursor rendered on a T-shirt. But your mind is taken away from its low color depth because many people are familiar with the cursor; and at its enormous size, you look at the shape and size first, and don't think about color mode at all. So if you have an inkjet and a favorite tool or cursor (all of Photoshop's cursors are one bit per pixel), you can make an odd but eye-catching T-shirt. We hope it goes without saying that to *sell* such a T-shirt might break a few laws unless you are the person who created the icon.

**Figure 5.3**    You can create an enlargement of a simple graphic, and folks won't really notice that the graphic is only one bit per pixel.

We left out the definitions of two terms that are relevant to working with different color modes: resolution and anti-aliasing. These are "helpers" to color modes to improve the apparent quality of images of all color modes.

So here goes, without further fanfare.

## Resolution

Image *resolution* is defined as an amount, expressed as a fraction (a ratio). For example, viewing resolution is the apparent closeness of an image. When you zoom into an image in Photoshop, and you've zoomed 200%, your viewing resolution is 2:1. The resolution of scanners is expressed in samples/inch, that of screen images in pixels/inch, and that of printers in dots/inch. Image dimensions are directly affected by resolution, as is image quality.

When an image is resolution dependent, as are pixel-based images, the size of the pixels, the height, and the width of a bitmap image are fixed. You can't change any of these parameters of an image without degrading the image's quality or otherwise distorting it.

In Figure 5.4, the image at left is 72 pixels per inch, and you can see the image fairly well. But what happens if the image is resized to 8 pixels per inch? As you can see, you can barely make out the visual content of the image because the resolution is much, much lower than the original. And it's smaller in resolution.

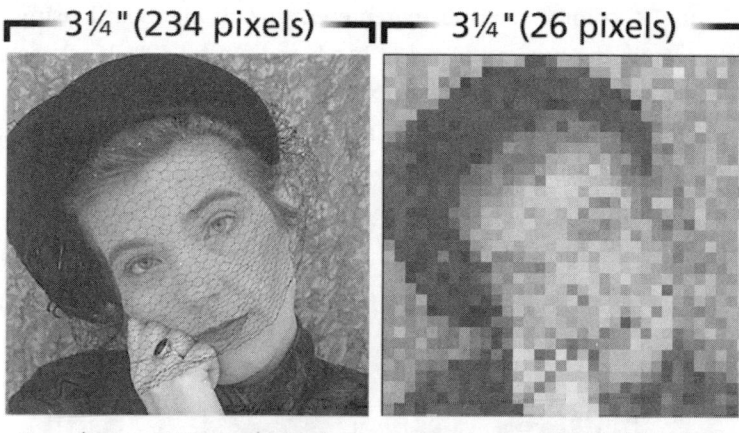

**Figure 5.4**   The higher the resolution of the image, the more samples were taken. This means there's more visual data to present, and the picture becomes of higher quality.

> **Note**
>
> **Changing the Resolution of an Image**   The only way to make a resolution-dependent bitmap image larger or smaller (as expressed in inches) is to change the resolution. There's a law here:
>
> *Image resolution is inversely proportional to image size (expressed in real-world units).*
>
> For example, an image that is 1" by 1" by 300 pixels/inch can also be expressed as an image that's 2" by 2" by 150 pixels/inch. If you increase the dimensions, you must decrease the resolution. By doing this, you ensure that not one pixel of information is changed. And no resizing of the image has happened.
>
> If you change size or resolution while holding the other value constant, you change the content of the image, and the change usually is visible. And ugly.

## Anti-Aliasing

We cannot provide the full technical explanation of anti-aliasing. To do this would take 20 pages and really isn't relevant to Photoshop use. But a very good example of *anti-aliasing* goes something like this:

Suppose, using white and black, you drew a two pixel–wide by two pixel–high checkerboard in Photoshop. Now, you want to make the image 50% its original size so that the entire checkerboard is one pixel. Would the pixel be black or white?

The answer: neither color. To artistically represent the checkerboard, using only one pixel, would require the use of a blend of black and white: 50% black, to be exact. To use either white or black in the one pixel would be to use a color as an *alias* for the correct color. Therefore, *anti-aliasing* attempts to reconcile colors in locations around bitmap shapes that are difficult because the area is either rounded or at a diagonal.

In Figure 5.5, you can see a close-up of a diagonal line, with and without anti-aliasing. Squint a little at this figure and then ask which diagonal line looks better.

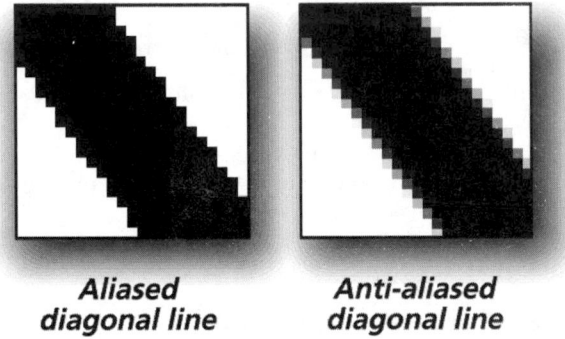

**Aliased
diagonal line**          **Anti-aliased
diagonal line**

**Figure 5.5**    Anti-aliasing makes diagonal and curved (aliased) bitmap lines look smooth.

Let's simplify this explanation of anti-aliasing even further. Anti-aliasing is the placement, at the edge of a shape, of pixels whose color(s) is/are a combination of the shape's pixel color and the background pixel color.

In Photoshop, brush tips are anti-aliased; feathering is a type of anti-aliasing; and when you resize images by using the default resizing interpolation, the new pixel colors, especially around the edges, are anti-aliased. *Interpolation* is the mathematical averaging of new pixel colors in an image that has been resized to include extra pixels, or has had pixels deleted.

## Moving Up the Color-Capability Ladder

If you look at the Mode menu, you'll see that Grayscale and Duotone should be our next stop—hey, they're right beneath Bitmap, right? Yes, but no—these two *special* image types need to be discussed after we present two other modes.

Indexed Color, and then RGB Color, are the next two highest rungs in color capability, but their internal organization is entirely different. We know this sounds geek-like, but please follow along, because all you digital artists and photographers do need to know this stuff to ensure that your artwork is written to disk (saved) correctly.

## Indexed and Color Channel Images

When computers started displaying images in addition to text, engineers and color experts needed to find a way to organize colors in an image format. It was decided that red, green, and blue values could be expressed implicitly (indirectly) for a given color by measuring the color's component values, and then giving that color a value that would go in the header of the computer image file. This is called the *indexed color file type,* and about the only image formats that use indexed color today are GIF and PNG.

In Figure 5.6, you can get an idea of the way indexed color works. When an indexed color image is opened in Photoshop, Photoshop looks at the header in the file, sees that, for example, a shade of purple used in the image is in the number 7 register of the header and the color values that should be displayed are Red: 193, Green: 34, and Blue: 222. This indexing stuff can produce smaller files than color channel images (definition coming up) produce, because the header values are small and the color definitions are used many times in the image. Indexed color is limited, however: All of Photoshop's tools aren't available to indexed color images. Also, the header of the file becomes ungainly if the image contains more than 256 unique colors, so GIFs and one type of PNG files contain only 256 (or fewer) unique colors.

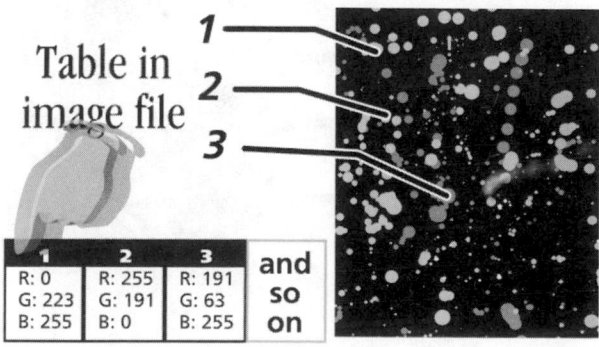

**Figure 5.6**   Indexed color images tell an application indirectly what the recipe is for any given color.

**Note**

**The Tables That Files Use to Keep Track of Color Formulas**    The header of a file that tells programs the formula for colors is called:

- A lookup table
- A color table
- A color lookup table (CLUT)
- A lookup or color palette

All these terms mean approximately the same thing.

When computer hardware became more affordable and capable, it was decided that a good way to build images was through component channels, with each channel containing brightness values. In Photoshop (and other fine pixel editors), an RGB image is called that because it has red, green, and blue channels, and each channel is capable of showing any of 256 brightness levels under any given pixel. If you cheat at math as I do and ask an expert, 256 colors can be expressed as 2 to the 8th power, and three color channels as 2 to the 24th power (3×8). If you play with your computer's calculator for a moment, you'll see that an RGB image can therefore have 16.7 million unique colors. In Figure 5.7, you can see a sort of stylized representation of an "RGB sandwich." This interpretation looks very much like your view of the Channels palette when you are viewing an RGB image.

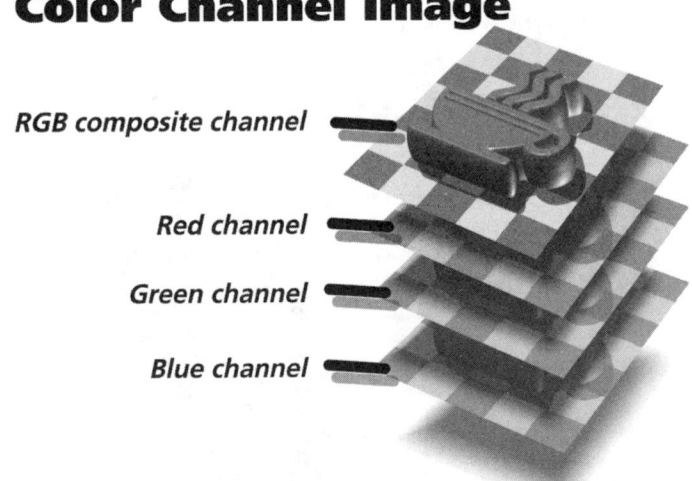

**Figure 5.7**    A color channel image contains many more colors than an indexed image, and most of Photoshop's tools are available when a color channel image is the target image in the workspace.

The reason we're bothering to make the distinction between indexed images and color channel images is that Photoshop makes that distinction. Although there is not a precise match between color modes and color depth (discussed next), you will lose less time trying to make a square peg fit in a round hole if you understand the organization of color files. Here's an example right now. If you bring a GIF image into Photoshop, you cannot paint on it using the soft brush tips, and feathering will not work. You need to convert the image to RGB color, LAB color, or some other mode.

## Color Depth in Detail

As you've learned by now, color depth has nothing to do with how deep a color is, such as navy blue being deeper than sky blue. *Color depth* is the gauge by which images are evaluated for the number of colors they can hold.

Let's take a look at the different, common color depths; and along the way, we'll provide you with the street names for the image types, and tell you whether an image with a specific color depth is indexed or color channel in style. First, toward the bottom of the ladder are 1 bit/pixel and 4 bits/pixel images, shown in Figure 5.8. Both of these depths are indexed, but Photoshop calls the single 1 bit/pixel channel a Bitmap channel, as defined earlier. And there is no special mode in Photoshop for a 4 bits/pixel image—it would be saved to Indexed color mode, which can contain up to 256 colors.

# Color Depth

•*1 bit/pixel ($2^1$)*
•*2 possible colors*
•*AKA Line Art, bitmap*

•*4 bits/pixel ($2^4$)*
•*16 possible colors*
•*AKA VGA color*

 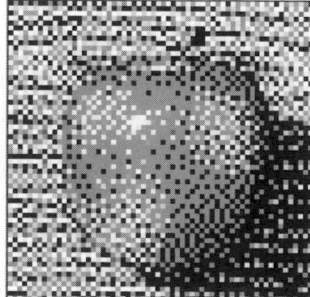

**Figure 5.8** 1 bit/pixel equals a total color depth of 2 colors and 4 bits/pixel is 2 to the fourth power, or 16 total colors.

## Grayscale: Sometimes a Mode, Sometimes Indexed Color

Up a rung on the color depth ladder are Indexed color (2 to the 8th power, or 256 maximum colors—also a mode in Photoshop), and Grayscale. Grayscale mode and the construction of the file format don't really fit color depth or channel color rules. On one hand, some programs other than Photoshop consider grayscale to be the same as an indexed color image, because Indexed color has 256 possible colors and grayscale images have 256 possible tones. The reason grayscale has its own mode is that it is a single-channel image and that channel has 256 possible brightness values (see Figure 5.9—yeah, yeah...we know the book is in black and white). This construction of file format is the same as, for example, an RGB (color channel) image, except grayscale has one 8-bit/pixel channel instead of RGB's three.

# Color Depth

•*8 bits/pixel ($2^8$)*
•*256 possible colors*
•*AKA Indexed color*

•*8 bits/pixel ($2^8$)*
•*256 possible tones*
•*AKA grayscale*

**Figure 5.9**    Indexed color is both a color depth and a Photoshop mode. It can hold 256 colors. Grayscale images can hold 256 unique tones (brightness values).

In Figure 5.10, we've departed from the image of the apple because we need to show you something about color—in a black and white book—that is too subtle to be shown on an apple. HiColor, a color mode invented a few years ago by scanner manufacturers and video card people, is almost extinct today because technology has become affordable. HiColor is not a mode in Photoshop—a 15-bit (32,000 colors) and 16-bit (64,000 colors) HiColor image is considered to be an RGB color channel image.

Although it brought down the price of equipment, HiColor has a fatal flaw: It cannot display gradients without banding. There are simply too many transitional colors. On the other hand (on the right of Figure 5.10), the RGB image, with 16.7 million possible colors, can indeed display a gradient without visible banding.

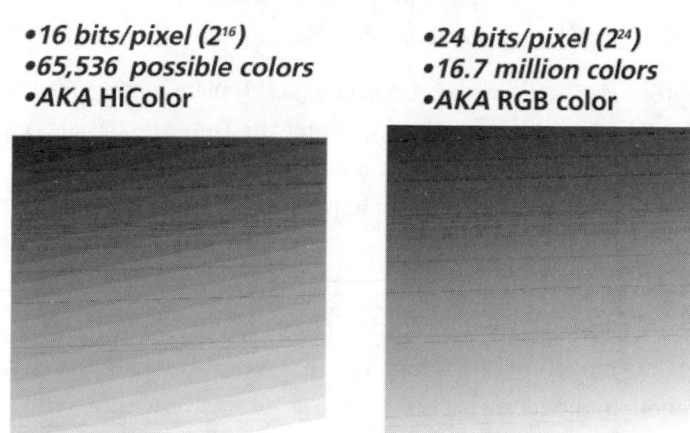

# Color Depth

- •16 bits/pixel ($2^{16}$)
- •65,536  possible colors
- •AKA HiColor

- •24 bits/pixel ($2^{24}$)
- •16.7 million colors
- •AKA RGB color

**Figure 5.10**   HiColor and 24 bits/pixel color depths are the ones that most users work with today.

## LAB, Duotone, and CMYK

There is an option in the Image Mode menu to use channel color images that are 16 bits/channel. This would make an RGB image 48 bits/pixel, and have the color capacity of 28 billion unique colors, give or take a few. But most of us will not use this setting, because:

- We don't have a video card or any other equipment that supports 48 bits/pixel color.

- This setting is only for some very high-end scanners and medical imaging equipment.

Now, we've left LAB color, Duotones, and CMYK color off this color depth list, even though they are modes under Photoshop's Image list. LAB color is a larger color space (definition coming up) than RGB color, but our monitors are designed around displaying RGB color (red, green, and blue phosphors), so LAB color and RGB color are typically assigned the same color depth, 24 bits/pixel. In fact, LAB is the only color mode you can switch in and out of from other color modes and color depths without losing any color information. CMYK color mode is a printing color mode that is simulated on your monitor (your monitor does not have cyan, magenta, yellow, and black phosphors, so Photoshop fakes CMYK display accuracy), and because it has four channels of 8 bits/pixel color, it has a color depth of 32 bits/pixel. Because the color space of CMYK is narrower than that of RGB color, the depth is greater than RGB color, but you will not find as many unique colors in CMYK mode.

Finally, a Duotone is actually two plates of color, each plate having a color capability of 8 bits/pixel. We are not going to tell you that the Duotone has any color depth, because it is a printing process, and not a depth you can work in with Photoshop. Photoshop and your monitor display an approximation of the colors in a Duotone image.

## Moving from Color Depth to Color Space

We frequently use models to describe things that we cannot easily envision. In fact, if you think about it, modeling programs such as Adobe Dimensions show us a more complete view of something in 3D space than if we were looking at the same visual data on a flat, 2D page. Models enable us to work with the intangible, sometimes.

Color is this way—we need a model to better understand color space. *Color space* is the area within all emitted or reflected light that serves a specific purpose for the computer user. For example, RGB color space is the space in which we usually work in Photoshop, but LAB color space embraces RGB color space. LAB color is larger than RGB color, in fact, it's the largest color space we've come up with to date. The space within which an image can be edited is called the *color gamut*.

For visual examples of these different spaces, let's turn to Figure 5.11. On the left is the LAB color space. On the right is Adobe RGB (1998) color space inside the LAB color space. If you look at this figure in color (it's in the color plate section), you'll see that there are a lot more greens in LAB color than RGB color can express. There are also some golds that LAB color can express that RGB color cannot.

Photoshop's Help file has a very good piece on CIELAB color (or more simply, LAB color), and we'll contribute our own two cents shortly in this section.

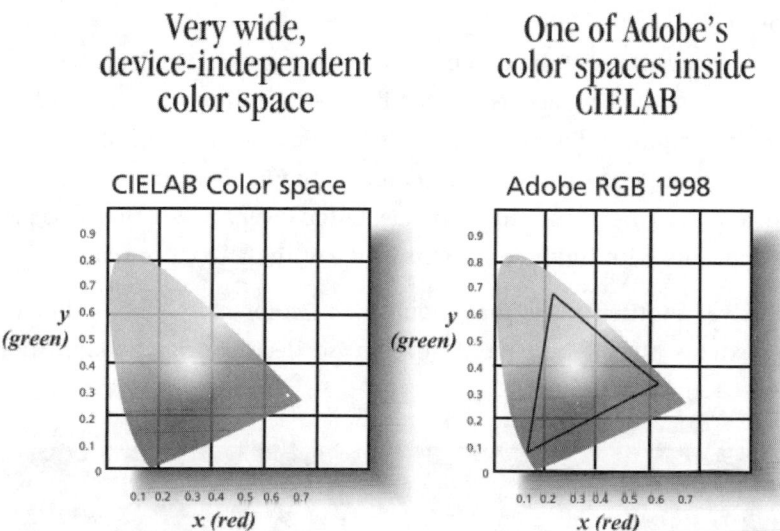

**Figure 5.11**    Color spaces are unique to specific color modes and devices. Some spaces fit inside others, while some overlap others.

## CMYK

CMYK is an image mode in Photoshop and a color space used in commercial printing. Because RGB color is additive in nature (you add 100% of all channels together, and you get white), it is useful for displaying Web work, but is not useful for showing what subtractive inks or pigments look like when color channels of cyan, magenta, yellow, and black are combined. You can make color plates from color channels of an image in CMYK mode in Photoshop as easily as choosing Image, Mode, and then CMYK.

The most current information from color commercial presses today is that they'd prefer that you send them RGB images, and allow the commercial press places to perform the RGB to CMYK color conversions. This is easy to understand; commercial pressmen understand better than most of us what the specifics and characteristics of their print presses are. This is an example of, "simply because you *can* make your own CMYK separations doesn't mean that you *should* make your own CMYK separations." Once you go from the RGB color space to the smaller CMYK color space, you've lost original colors forever, and going back to RGB color mode does not restore the discarded colors.

## LAB Color

LAB color was an invention of the Commission Internationale de l'Eclairage (CIE) as a device-independent color space (color that is consistent from monitor to printer, to someone else's monitor, for example). CIELAB color, or more simply LAB color, exists as a Luminance channel, with two chromacity channels, one running from red to green, and the other from yellow to blue. LAB is a very wide color space; every color space you work with in Photoshop fits inside of the LAB color space.

Figure 5.12 is yet another image that should be in color in this book, but we've marked the extents of color in the illustration, so deciphering it should not be too difficult.

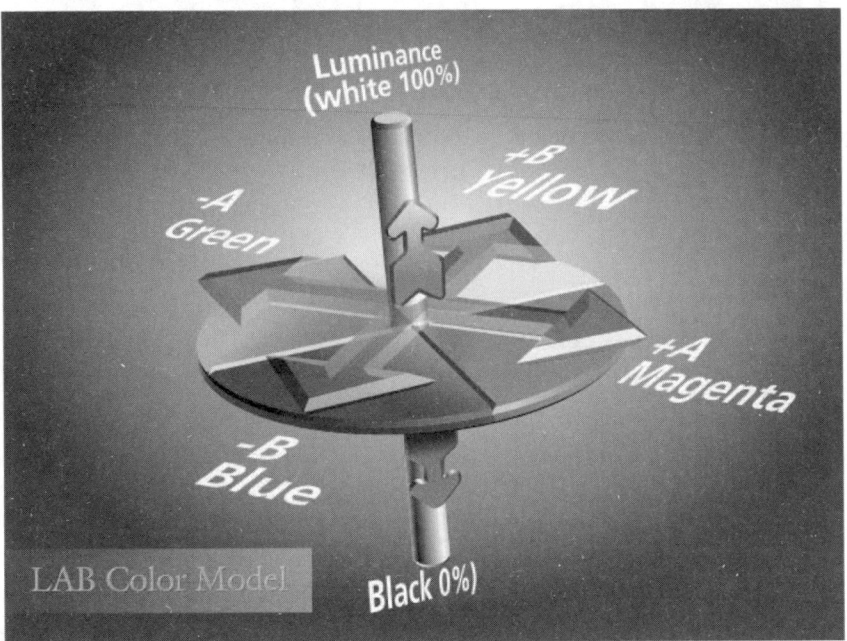

**Figure 5.12**   The LAB color space consists of one brightness channel and two channels of chromacity.

## Multichannel Mode

If you're new to Photoshop, or you're only interested in creating Web media, you might never need to switch an image to Multichannel mode, the bottom entry on the Modes menu. A multichannel image consists of color channels that can contain up to 8 bits/pixel of brightness information (256 possible tones). Its only real uses are for converting a Duotone mode image to an imagesetting image such as Scitex. Additionally, by converting most other images to multichannel, you are converting them to channels consisting of printing information—cyan, magenta, yellow, and black spot color channels are the result.

## All About Dithering (See Chapter 23!)

It would not be fair of the authors to leave color spaces and color modes to work on file formats without giving you the answer to an inevitable question:

"I can understand that when going from a lower color capability to a higher one should make no visual difference, but what happens when you go from a high color capability image to that of a lower color depth?"

What happens is Photoshop asks you whether you want the image dithered, and if so, what type of dithering should be applied. Dithering is covered quite thoroughly in Chapter 23, in the section "Dithering Options." You should read this chapter before you go off and create your first GIF image, because the image will look real ugly if you specify unsuitable options for the conversion from lotsa colors to only a few.

Okay, it's time now for a section in this book that serves two purposes, both of them having to do with file format saving.

# Getting the Authors' File Format Recommendations

Quite simply, Photoshop has too many file formats from which you can export designs and photos! This statement was meant as a catchy lead-in, and not as a criticism of what Adobe has accomplished. In a nutshell, Photoshop has a collection of very good export (Save As) filters, and as a typical users, you will use no more than five of them in 95% of your work. The catchword above is "typical," and that sort of has us authors caught by our authorly suspenders on the proverbial picket fence. There is no "typical" Photoshop user. There are all sorts of vertical implementations of Photoshop—medical imaging, Hollywood films, photo restoration, and so on. So, this author got the bright idea of explaining first what image formats are best for mainstream creative work. A little later, we feature a reference guide for all the other formats that most people will not use daily.

We hope this sounds good and equitable, and here goes with the recommendation part of this chapter...

### There's TIFF—and Then There's TIFF

Here is Big-Time Truth #716:

> *Most file formats were created by someone (or many individuals), and a company out there is probably the keeper of the specifications.*

What does this mean? It means that if someone other than the Joint Photographers Experts Group created a new JPEG format, it would mess up everyone's work because the new format would probably mean nothing to most browsers and image editing programs. That's why there's a tacit agreement in the graphics community that only the keeper of a file format can make changes.

The Tagged Image File Format (TIFF) has been around for almost a decade; it was originally developed by Aldus, Altsys, and Adobe Systems. What these firms were looking for was a file format that's *extensible*—that can be enhanced in the future without much recoding. Aldus was purchased by Adobe in years past, and Altsys was bought by Macromedia. Which sort of leaves Adobe as the keeper of the TIFF standard.

The authors endorse the TIFF file format for saving high-quality images for these reasons:

- TIFF is the only nonproprietary file format around (besides PNG, and we don't see a lot of support for PNG as of this writing) that can save resolution information. Almost all other file formats default to 72 pixels/inch. But not TIFF. If you save a TIFF image at 2" by 2" by 157 pixels/inch, you can place it in PageMaker and the image will be exactly 2" on each side. Think about this for a moment—intrinsic accurate sizing from one application to another is probably the single most important image quality a desktop publishing firm could ask for.

- The TIFF image file format is easily exchanged between Macintosh and Windows machines.

- TIFF images can hold an alpha channel. In several programs, the alpha channel can act as a mask, separating the foreground design from the background. The image on the left in Figure 5.13 has an alpha channel. On the right is a vector drawing program, XARA, with the alpha channel masking outside the cup so the cup can rest on top of another bitmap image. And XARA isn't even a product of Adobe Systems. Yet because of the consistency and extensibility of the TIFF standard, many applications can be used to tap into a single file written out of Photoshop 6.

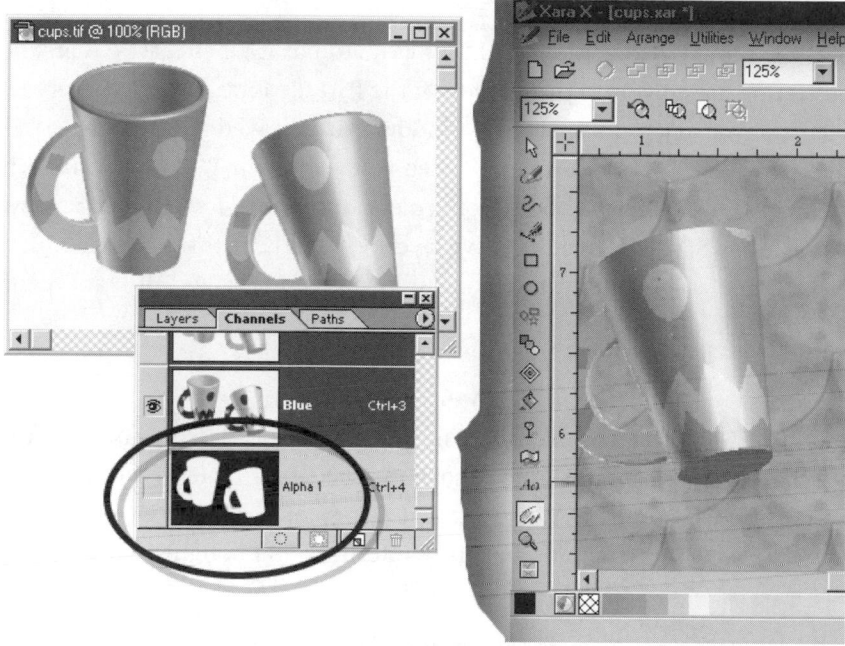

**Figure 5.13**    The standard TIFF file format is a good exchange configuration for high-quality files.

We've been talking about the garden variety TIFF. Now it's time to discuss what Adobe Systems calls the enhanced TIFF.

If you press Ctrl(⌘)+K and then go to the File Saving page, you will notice that there is an option you can check to enable the saving of an enhanced TIFF. Terrific. What *is* an enhanced TIFF? For years, Adobe Systems has taken it on the chin from digital video professionals (and After Effects and Premiere sort of qualify as digital video products) unhappy with the lack of TIFF layer support. And if Adobe Systems didn't enhance the TIFF format, some other company would.

So if you check this option in Preferences, you can save everything in a TIFF file that you can save in a Photoshop native PSD file.

And that's precisely why we recommend that you do *not* check the enhanced box. You can always use the PSD format for saving layers, and keep using the older version of TIFF to stay in touch with business contacts, who might not own Photoshop 6.

### Photoshop's PSD Format

The PSD file format is so complicated...it's easy. To put it a better way, a great deal of engineering has gone into this version of the PSD file format, so that every effect and element you put into an image window can be saved exactly the way you intend. There is no loss of information when you save to the PSD file format, which makes saving to this format both convenient and worry-free. If you're new to Photoshop, the PSD file format can save layers, channels, paths, adjustment layers, layer styles, text as editable text, document credits (under File, Info), and perhaps the kitchen sink.

### The Photoshop PDF Format

The Acrobat PDF file has been around since the first 486-class machine, but only recently have Photoshop and other Adobe products been able to write a PDF file with no assistance from the Adobe Acrobat trilogy of products (Distiller, Acrobat (Editor), and Reader). When you bought Photoshop, you bought into the PDF file format.

Actually, the PDF format is good for a number of reasons:

- You can share your work with anyone who owns Reader, the free reading utility from Adobe. When the PDF file generated by Photoshop is opened later, you can edit layers, paths, and text as though you'd saved the file to PSD format.

- Press houses like the PDF format because it is a variety of PostScript that will almost never cause a problem rendering. PostScript is notorious for failing to print on the first try, but a PDF file is gloriously stable.

- It's not 100% there yet, but watch out. PDF files generated by programs as disparate as PageMaker and Photoshop might very well use PDFs as an exchange medium in the future. This author tried to open a Photoshop PDF in Illustrator 9. The results were not professional in appearance, but indicated promise.

### The JPEG File Format

We recommend that you export a *copy* of a high-fidelity image to JPEG format by using ImageReady, and not Photoshop. Photoshop has made progress with their JPEG export options, but there's nothing like seeing what the optimized (and shrunk) image will look like before you process it. ImageReady's workspace has a much better design for converting RGB mode images to JPEG. In addition to the full-size preview, the Optimize palette in ImageReady has every option you could imagine for making a quality conversion.

JPEG images are not your first choice to save to—use TIFF or PSD on your original artwork, and use a copy for JPEGging. JPEG is the only file format we recommend that uses lossy compression to decrease the size of a file. The JPEG process discards unique hues that the eye might not see, and averages the hues while maintaining the original brightness values. The human eye is much more sensitive to changes in tones than it is to changes in colors. See Chapter 23 for more details.

### The Compuserve GIF Format

Also known around town as the GIF89a file format, GIF is a lossless file format—you discard colors during the process of making a GIF image, and the loss of color decisions are made by you, not by the export filter. This format enables you to choose a single color out of the maximum of 256 in this format, and make that color drop out of the image when the image is viewed in a Web browser. The drop-out enabled GIF is called a Transparent GIF.

GIFs, in general, can look good or crummy depending entirely on your subject matter. The more monochromatic (having similar hues, with brightness values making the difference in colors) an image is, the more suited for GIF89a format. Also, text in Photoshop that is anti-aliased can look terrific as a GIF and produce a very small saved text file, because one text color anti-aliased against a solid background typically generates no more than about 11 unique colors. So the text GIF image can have a very small color palette.

We also recommend that you prepare GIF images in ImageReady, and not Photoshop. Why? Because you will have to perform dithering on the image to reduce the number of overall colors to fit the maximum capability of GIF's 256 colors. And ImageReady gives you lots of options (dithering type, what sort of palette needs to be created, ability to define exactly how many colors you want, and so on). Also, in ImageReady, you can animate several GIF images, and Photoshop does not have a feature for animation.

To an artist the GIF file format might seem a little feeble, but when you're building a Web site, GIF is an indispensable file format. Read Chapter 23 for the details of the GIF, JPEG, and PNG file formats.

That's about it! These five file formats should suit almost every occasion, except when your work is not purely design work. This is where our handy-dandy resource section comes into play.

## A Reference of Photoshop File Formats

When you choose File, Save, you reveal a long drop-down list of file formats, and many of them are as clear as listening to a harp recital while wearing earmuffs.

We decided that if Adobe can dish it out, we can define it for you. The following are explanations of the file formats not covered so far.

### Photoshop 2.0

This file format is from an older version of Photoshop and is available on the Macintosh, making it possible for you to open an image in version 2.0 or to export an image to an application that supports only Photoshop 2.0 files. Because Photoshop 2.0 was not available for the Windows operating system, this is a Macintosh-only option. Saving in Photoshop 2.0 format flattens an image and discards layer information. The main reason to use this option is to creating images that will have to be opened in Photoshop 2.

### BMP

Also known as the Microsoft Windows Bitmap (BMP) file format, the BMP file format was originally created for images to be saved and shared on Windows 3.0, and DOS (Disk Operating System) computers. The BMP file format supports Bitmap, Grayscale, RGB, Indexed Color modes, 4-bit and 8-bit images, and alpha channels, although Macromedia X-Res (a now defunct product) was the only program that could successfully save an alpha channel to BMP format. BMP does not support the CMYK color space. This is sort of a "toy" file format, designed by Microsoft to keep budding artists happy (and brand-loyal) a decade ago. Programmers who want to make certain that a Windows user can open a file default to the BMP format.

### PCX

The PCX format, originally an invention of Z-Soft, the folks who first engineered Photo-Paint for Corel Corporation, is seldom used today. But when it was used—about 10 years ago—it was used by Windows-based computers. You can also exchange the PCX file format between Windows and the Macintosh—but today there are better formats, such as TIFF. This file format supports all image modes that include all image modes, including Bitmap, Grayscale, Indexed Color, RGB, Lab, guides, and 4-bit, 8-bit, 24-bit images.

## Photoshop EPS

The Encapsulated PostScript (EPS) file format is related to PostScript, the page description language. An EPS file can be written to include

- Printing information only
- Bitmap and vector information together
- Vector information that can be interpreted by Illustrator and other drawing programs

Photoshop only saves to encapsulated printer commands, with a low-resolution header in the file that's used for placement in programs such as PageMaker and InDesign.

Ironically, the only type of EPS file that Photoshop can import is the vector data file. Most applications make it clear whether Photoshop can import an EPS file. If the file is called an EPS *placeable* file, it contains no information that Photoshop can parse (read) into image data. If an EPS file is an *interpreted* EPS file, it contains only vector information that Photoshop can render to pixel format. For Windows users, the terms interpreted EPS and Adobe Illustrator file format are interchangeable. All Illustrator files are EPS, but not all EPS files are compatible with Illustrator.

Photoshop offers more than one type of EPS file for export. The reason for this to handle different types of EPS options for EPS, DCS 1.0 and 2.0 files.

### Opening EPS Files

You will see one of two behaviors when you open an EPS file. When the EPS file contains only raster image data, the low-res header, and not the printer code appears in an image window. When the EPS file contains vector graphics, Photoshop always offers a dialog box option to rasterize the image. Rasterizing the file data converts the vector graphic to pixel data. The EPS open dialog box also provides choices to change the image resolution and convert the image data to Grayscale, RGB, CMYK, or LAB.

The EPS file format supports Bitmap, Grayscale, Duotone, RGB, Index Color, CMYK, and LAB color modes, 8-bit images as well as guides, Annotations, ICC profiles, Halftone Screens, Transfer Functions, PostScript Color Management, Vector Data, and Clipping Paths.

### Photoshop DCS 1.0

The Photoshop DCS 1.0 format is part of the EPS format that enables you to generate five files for a CMYK color separation image. These are individual high-resolution files for each color channel in the CMYK image file. The fifth file is a low-resolution 72 ppi grayscale or color version that represents the composite of all of the channels. This fifth separation is used for placing the EPS file in a publication, such as InDesign creates.

In the beginning years of desktop publishing, using the five-file Desktop Color Separation (DCS) system was an interesting way to work. The idea was to create a low-resolution master file for the designer so this low-rez image could be placed in a page. This created a link to the four high-resolution CMYK files. Typically, a service bureau would hold on to the four high-resolution CMYK files. When the page was returned from the designer with the low-resolution master, the page was processed and the other four CMYK linked files were swapped into the place of the low-resolution waster. While this seems like a good scheme, it creates a file management problem. There were just too many files of one image to keep track of.

### Photoshop DCS 2.0

The Photoshop DCS 2.0 format is also a part of the EPS format that allows you to save and export images containing CMYK data, spot color channels, or multichannel files. Its main purpose is to support spot colors.

Spot colors are used to print one, two, or three special colors using special color inks that typically fall outside the color space of CMYK. Fluorescent pink, for example, is a wonderful spot color to use on detergent boxes, but fluorescent pink is not found in the printing color space. Although you can use more than three colors, it's easier to create a CMYK file and add spot colors as necessary, instead of building a stack of (expensive) spot colors for reproduction. Another common use of spot colors is in four-color process printing when you need a fifth or sixth color. This is also referred to as a *bump plate* to bump up the color or create a varnish plate in a certain area of an image.

The Photoshop DCS 2.0 file format supports Grayscale, RGB, CMYK, and color modes, 8-bit images as well as guides, Annotations, ICC Profiles, Halftone Screens, Transfer Functions, PostScript Color Management, Vector Data, and Clipping Paths.

The DCS 2.0 format option also enables you to create different types of single and multiple files with various previewing options. Using this feature will depend on how large or small you want to program your DCS files for your workflow. Options include:

- **Single File DCS or Multiple Files DCS, with No Composite.** Although this option produces a smaller file size, it does not have a preview, so there goes pinpoint placement in a DTP program's page.

- **Single File or Multiple Files Grayscale Composite.** This option creates a grayscale preview. It makes the preview file smaller and is therefore more efficient when placed in a page layout program and printed.

- **Single File or Multiple Files Color Composite.** This creates a color preview file.

### Reasons to Use the EPS Format

Now that you've learned a bit more about the EPS file format, here is when you would want to use it:

- To save Duotones for print-oriented projects.

- To compensate for image setter calibration problems using Transfer Functions.

- To save Line Screen and Screen Angle data to override the data in a page layout program.

- The Photoshop DCS 1.0 format enables you to generate five files for a CMYK color separation image or a low-resolution preview file for one CMYK color image.

- The Photoshop DCS 2.0 format supports images containing CMYK data, spot color channels, or multichannel files. Its main purpose is to support spot colors.

### Compressing EPS (DCS 1.0, DCS 2.0) Files

All the EPS formats offer four quality levels of JPEG compression (encoding):

- JPEG (low quality)
- JPEG (medium quality)
- JPEG (high quality)
- JPEG (maximum quality)

The best way to determine which quality level is best for your images is to run some tests.

### EPS Preview and Encoding (for Photoshop EPS, DCS 1.0, and DCS 2.0)

Photoshop EPS previews enables you create low-resolution preview files. For example, these previews are used with page layout programs. Here are the preview options for Macintosh and Windows operating systems:

- Preview options for Windows files are TIFF and None. To share EPS files between Windows and Macintosh systems, use the TIFF preview.

- Preview options for Macintosh files are Macintosh 1-bit and 8-bit-per-pixel.

## PICT File

The PICT format is commonly used by Macintosh computers for presentation graphics. It is also used sometimes as an intermediate file format for transferring images between applications.

The PICT file format supports Bitmap, Grayscale, Indexed Color, and (16-bit) RGB with a single alpha channel. The PICT format offers resolution and compression options for Grayscale and RGB images. For a grayscale image, there are 2-bit, 4-bit, or 8-bits/pixel options. For RGB, 16-bits and 32-bits/pixel. The 32-bit option supports the single alpha channeled. In ImageReady, the PICT format is supported in Macintosh OS only. The PICT file format uses RLE (run-length encoded) compression (similar to the Windows BMP file) when you select the 16-bit or None options. 32-bit options support RLE and JPEG compression.

**Warning**

**Don't Mix PICT and PostScript**   Never use the PICT format for the PostScript imaging process. PICT has proven to cause errors (such as halting an imagesetter) when it is sent to a PostScript output device.

## PICT Resource

The PICT Resource is another Macintosh computer system feature. A *PICT resource* is a PICT file that contains a Macintosh operating system's file's resource fork that allows you to save an image and place it into a startup screen. To do this the image should be exactly 72 dpi. Use the File, Save As, PICT Resource. Name the image StartupScreen, and then save the image in your System Folder. In the PICT Resource dialog box, use the Name SCRN. Use None for compression.

An example of a file with a PICT Resource is the contents of the Macintosh Scrapbook. The PICT Resource file format supports Bitmap, Grayscale, RGB with a single alpha channel, and Indexed Color.

Either the Open command or the Import command is used to open a PICT resource. When saving a file as a PICT Resource, you have the option to define the resource ID and resource name. The PICT resource includes other PICT files save options such as depth and compression options.

The use of a PICT Resource file is primarily one of personal computer cosmetics, like Windows support programs, such as Microangelo, that can produce 8-bit or 24-bit desktop icons. If you want a more interesting-looking desktop, PICT resource files fit the bill. But PICT resource files are not used on the Web, nor are they something you'd send to an inkjet printer.

## PIXAR

PIXAR format is designed specifically for exchanging files with PIXAR imaging workstations that are slated for high-end graphics applications and for three-dimensional imaging and animation. PIXAR format supports Grayscale and RGB images with a single alpha channel.

## PNG

PNG (pronounced *ping*) stands for Portable Network Graphics. PNG offers the best of GIF and JPEG. It uses lossless compression, supports gamma settings, alpha channel transparency, image resolution, and supports 8-bit, 24-bit, and 32-bit images. PNG can maintain the original image details with little or no loss of quality. The good news is that this file format has lots going for it (except animation). The bad news is, it is not yet widely supported by Web browsers. Stay tuned. For more about the PNG format, see Chapter 23.

## RAW

RAW is a flexible file format that enables you to transfer images between applications and computer platforms. This format supports Grayscale, RGB, and CMYK images with alpha channels, and LAB and multichannel images without alpha channels.

To work with the RAW file format you need to know key information about the image you are opening. This information includes the file dimensions, number of channels, bit depth, and any header information.

## Scitex CT

Scitex CT stands for the Scitex Continuous Tone. This file format is used in Scitex computers for high-end image processing. The Scitex CT format supports Grayscale, RGB, CMYK, and image clipping paths; it does not support alpha channels.

## Targa

The Targa (TGA) format, designed for systems using the TrueVision video board, is commonly used today in modeling applications in Windows. The Targa format supports Grayscale images without alpha channels, RGB 16-bit, 24-bit with alpha channel, 32-bit, and Indexed Color.

# Summary

To put color space, color depth, and file format into very pedestrian parlance, we had a good chat in this chapter concerning these questions:

- Where in the visible spectrum is a color space located, and what is its shape and size?

- How deeply can an image file dig to produce the greatest number of colors within that color space?

- What's the best container for your finished work?

Working with pixels is not simple. Illustrator is a hayride compared to all the considerations that go into a finished bitmap image. We only covered three aspects of pixel images; there are still gamma settings, contrast, color cast, and on and on. But once you understand the structure of a pixel-based image, the rest will come easily to you. And the rewards are far greater than a masterpiece you'd create in Illustrator. The rewards are photorealism, realism, and every expression of painting you can think of. And it doesn't stop there. There are many pixel-based pieces of artwork that we've yet to put in *any* category! The medium is that fresh.

In Chapter 6, you'll be escorted through all the possible ways the authors could think of to capture a real-world scene and digitize it. It's not only about scanners, but what to do so that your images look as good inside that monitor as they do outside—in the park, the ocean, and underneath the coffee table. The more you know about capturing a digital image, the less correction work you'll need to do in Photoshop. Save your time for the fun and the important stuff!

# Chapter 6

# Acquiring Photoshop Images

Photoshop is most often used to enhance

or combine existing images. The most

obvious way to get the images you work

with into Photoshop is to open an existing file or to buy some artwork in digital form from a stock agency, another artist, or a photographer. But what if the source materials you want to work with are not already in a digital format? How would you go about *converting* a physical thing, such as a photographic print, into the collection of pixels that make up a Photoshop document? We can think of five ways to move imagery taken from the real world into Photoshop:

- If you are an accomplished painter, you could use Photoshop's tools to paint a likeness of a physical object. This is perhaps the most basic method of getting an image into Photoshop, but it requires a great deal of time and skill to produce results that are both artistically pleasing and photorealistically accurate. (Just ask Bert Monroy, author of the book *Bert Monroy: Photorealistic Techniques* (New Riders Publishing, Indianapolis, IN).

- You can have photographs you've taken or commissioned put on a Kodak PhotoCD. This is the most common procedure for getting high-quality color or black-and-white images digitized at a low price, and PhotoCDs get our attention first in this chapter.

- You can use a common flatbed scanner to digitize artwork, a photograph, or even small objects. This option is discussed at length in this chapter.

- You can use a transparency scanner to digitize a slide or a negative of a photograph. This method yields perhaps the best quality image to work with in Photoshop, but you cannot digitize artwork by using a transparency scanner.

- You can use a digital camera to acquire a digital image. We'll discuss this comparatively new piece of technology in this chapter.

This chapter covers only the four mechanical digitizing methods for bringing an image into Photoshop. These mechanical methods level the playing field; you don't have to be Bert Monroy to get images into Photoshop (which is good, because your spouse might be shocked if you came home as Bert Monroy). Almost anyone, even with a modest budget, can afford PhotoCDs or the hardware (a scanner or even a digital camera) required to "hook up Photoshop to the real world."

## Working with Kodak PhotoCDs

One of the easiest ways to get a digitized version of an image these days is to take your film or negatives to a photo-finisher and ask that the media be transferred to a Kodak PhotoCD. The processing lab will then use Eastman Kodak's proprietary PCD writer to scan your negatives and write the images to a CD-ROM that can be read by your computer's CD-ROM drive. So with only a camera, a CD-ROM drive, and a willingness to write a check for PhotoCD processing, you can get good-quality digital image files of your photographs. In 2001, you'll be hard pressed to find a photo-finisher who *doesn't* offer PhotoCD writing as a service.

**Note**

**How a PCD Writer Works**   PCD writers are a combination negative scanner and file writer. After each negative is scanned, the PCD writer (a very expensive piece of hardware) writes a single PhotoCD file for that image. The PhotoCD file format is a proprietary compressed format that Photoshop and many other graphic applications can read.

A photo-finisher might or might not actually have a PhotoCD (PCD) writer on its premises. As mentioned earlier, the PCD hardware is about $750,000, so don't expect a "mom and pop" photo-finisher or even a big retailer such as Target or Wal-Mart to have this machine at its store. Usually when a local photofinisher offers PhotoCD service, the film you give them is shipped to a large custom processing plant that has a PCD writer. Because the processing probably won't be done locally, you might have to wait a few days to get your finished PhotoCD back from your local photo-finisher.

On your end, ordering a PhotoCD is simple. You bring either undeveloped film or negatives to the photo-finisher (slides will cost extra because of the extra time required to handle each slide), and tell the clerk you want a Kodak PhotoCD made of the images. You have the option to have your images written to the PhotoCD in a specific sequence, either on a frame-by-frame basis or roll by roll. You will be charged an additional fee for PhotoCD developing. On the average, the price for dig-itizing a single image to PhotoCD is less than a dollar and dropping even as we write this. PhotoCD technology is mature, high-quality, accessible, and affordable.

A single PhotoCD can contain about 100 images, so be sure to take several rolls or several strips of negatives to the photo-finisher. You can also have images added to a partially filled PhotoCD you already have, but this decreases the overall space on the PhotoCD.

When you get the PhotoCD from the photo-finisher, all you need to do is plop the CD into your CD-ROM drive and launch Photoshop. There is nothing special about a PhotoCD; physically, it is the same as any other CD you might load. What makes a PhotoCD special is the file format the images are stored in, and the com-pression format, which is part of the file format.

## Understanding the Kodak PhotoCD Format

Each image on a Kodak PhotoCD is stored in a single file called an *image pac*. The following five sizes (resolutions) of the image can be opened from a single image pac:

- 72KB (128 by 192 pixels)
- 288KB (256 by 384 pixels)
- 1.13MB (512 by 768 pixels)
- 4.5MB (1024 by 1536 pixels)
- 18MB (2048 by 3072 pixels)

The image pac file itself actually contains the file at 4.5MB. An application's PhotoCD import filter uses a proprietary method of interpolation (resizing), along with special hinting information found in the image pac, to produce the other sizes from the 4.5MB file. *Interpolation*, sometimes called resampling, is a method of changing the dimensions of digital images by adding pixels to make an image larger or subtracting pixels to make it smaller.

Because the five different sizes of the image are not actually stored in a PCD file, a combination of compression/decompression and interpolation must take place when you choose to open the image in Photoshop at the 72KB, 2.88KB, 1.13MB, or 18MB size. The author recommends that you choose to work with the 4.5MB size image whenever practical. The 4.5MB image will have the sharpest focus. The reason? Even the best interpolation degrades the focus of an image as pixels are added or removed to create a new image size.

The PCD writer prints an index print to go along with every PhotoCD. The *index print*, (tiny, numbered thumbnails of all the images stored on the PhotoCD), is something you *don't* want to lose because, from the outside, every PhotoCD looks identical. The numbers next to the thumbnails on the index print correspond to each image file on the PhotoCD—the first image on a PhotoCD is Img0001.pcd, the second is Img0002.pcd, and so on. Because the thumbnails are so tiny (and as added insurance in case you lose the index print), you might want to take advantage of Photoshop's Contact Sheet feature to create your own, more legible digital contact sheet. You can find the Contact Sheet Feature under File, Automate, Contact Sheet II.

**Note**

**Keep Your Index Prints for Backup**    Keep your index print(s) when sending the CD in for more transfers. The lab doesn't need the print and they are trashed after the new index print is printed to update the contents of the CD. At least you'll have a backup of the CD contents before the latest transfer when you keep the index print, and pack off the PhotoCD and new images.

Again, there is nothing special about the physical PhotoCD itself; PhotoCD image files can be copied from the PhotoCD and stored on hard disk, removable media like Zip or Jaz cartridges, or even written to another CD-ROM. In fact, the Examples/Chap06 folder on the Companion CD contains PCD images that you'll work with in the rest of this section. In the following two examples, you load two different-sized images and use the PhotoCD import filter's Destination controls to specify what color space and resolution the images will be brought into. The first example shows you how to load and view a PhotoCD image.

Example 6.1    Loading a PhotoCD Image

1. In Photoshop, choose File, Open, and then choose Img0006.pcd from the Examples/Chap06 folder on the Companion CD.

> **Warning!**    If an error message appears when you open the CD files, press Ctrl(⌘)+Shift+K and then choose Adobe RGB (1998) from the Working Spaces, RGB drop-down list. See Chapter 3 for more information.

2. In the Kodak PCD Format dialog box, the Image Info box tells you that the medium of the original picture is a color negative. You'll use this important news for defining a source for opening the PhotoCD image.

3. In the Source Image box, you will see the name of the original image. You can choose the pixel size that you want to use for the image, and you can also choose the Profile of the original source, as seen in Figure 6.1.

4. Choose a pixel size for the PhotoCD image. As mentioned earlier, the 4.5MB file on PhotoCDs has the best focus because all other sizes are interpolated versions of the 4.5MB file. Choose 1024×1536 from the drop-down list, as shown in Figure 6.2.

5. In the Destination Image box, choose the resolution that you want the final image to be and also choose the color space that you want the image in, as shown in Figure 6.3. Again, in the Resolution box, you can see that the image, by default, will open at 72 ppi in RGB 8 Bits/Channel mode, which is a smaller color space than Kodak's YCC color space. (One channel of brightness (AKA luminance) and two channels of color make up the YCC model of color.) To ensure that you lose no color when you import the image, click on the LAB 8 bits/channel selection in the Color space drop-down list. LAB color space, as you'll learn in Chapter 3, is the color space Photoshop uses

internally for converting between color spaces. So regardless of whether this image will wind up in RGB mode, or even in Grayscale, image fidelity is preserved when you import a PhotoCD using the LAB color space. Click OK to open the image.

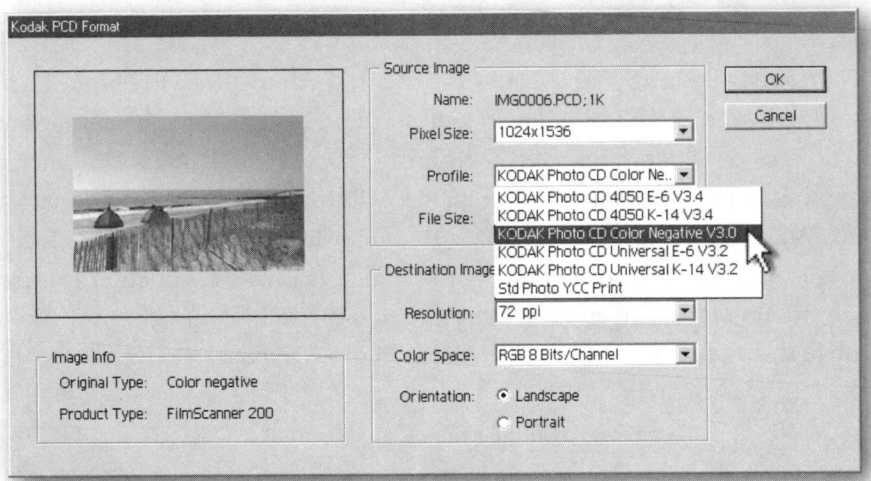

**Figure 6.1**    Choose a source profile that matches the medium that was originally used to capture the image.

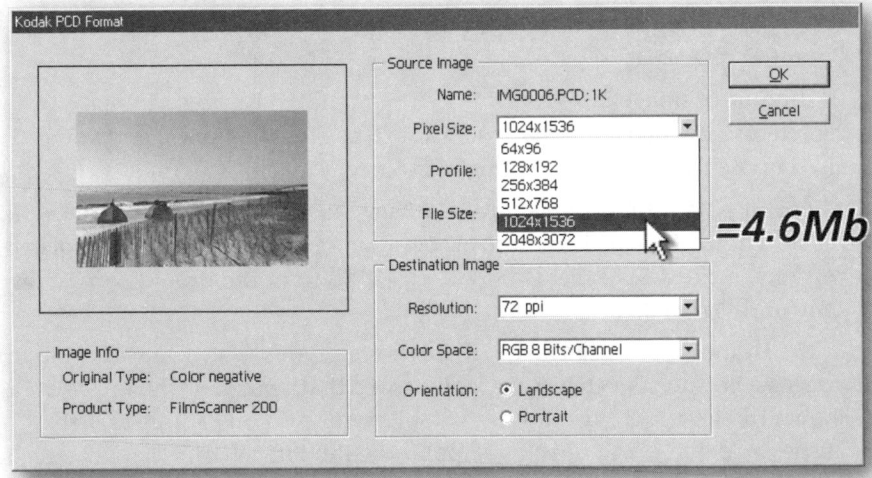

**Figure 6.2**    Although you can choose from any of the available sizes for a PhotoCD image, it is recommended that you choose the 1024×1536 version for the best focus.

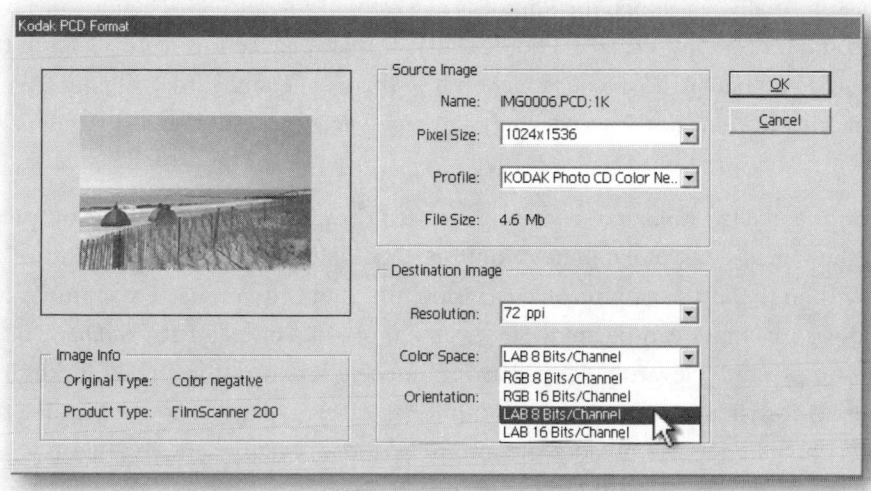

**Figure 6.3**   Choose a wide color space as the destination—such as the LAB color space—to preserve the colors of the image as they were written to PhotoCD.

 **Tip**

**16 Bits Versus 32 Bits**   The 16 bits/channel option in the PhotoCD dialog box, under the Image, Mode menu is designed for acquiring (usually scanning) at 32 bits/channel, and outputting to a commercial press that handles 32 bits/channel. Unless you are a professional state-of-the-art pressman, there is little use in acquiring an image at 32 bits/channel. Your video card probably doesn't support it, your monitor circuitry probably doesn't support it, and the use of a wider color space is something most of us will gradually grow into.

But not right now.

6. That's it! You now have the highest-quality and sharpest focus image from this PCD file. The file is currently in LAB mode, so keep the image open and you'll see shortly how to perform minor tonal changes while the image is in this color space (Photoshop calls it a *mode*) while you never touch the colors in the image. Tone changes *without* color changes—pretty neat, eh?

## Correcting the Gamma of a PCD Image

Although Kodak has improved in recent years by offering the folks who operate the PCD writer additional color balance data (*profiles,* again, check out Chapter 3) they can use to tweak the scans they create, a little bit of history can shed some light on why many PhotoCD images are brighter and more washed out than you would expect them to be.

Kodak originally developed the PhotoCD as a *consumer technology*. The idea was that you could rent or buy a special PhotoCD player that plugged into your TV, plop the PhotoCD you had made of your vacation into the player, and gather all your friends and family around the TV to watch a high-tech version of the dreaded family slide show.

Unfortunately, the *gamma* of television sets—the brightness versus voltage output—isn't the same as that of computer monitors. Originally, the gamma of all PhotoCDs was written to 2.2, the gamma of a television tube, but the gamma of Macintosh and Windows machines can be anywhere from 2.0 to 1.8. For us artists, *gamma* can be more simply and relevantly defined as the amount of contrast in the midtones in a picture. Most image detail is in the midtones of everyday photographs, and the higher the gamma, the broader the midtones and the higher the highlights. Now the gamma of a newly written PhotoCD depends on what settings the operator of the PCD writer chooses. Most still choose a gamma of 2.2, even when you ask them to use a computer-friendly gamma profile.

Fortunately, Photoshop has a very simple way to gamma-correct PhotoCD images that you want to save as TIFFs or PSD images. As mentioned earlier, PhotoCD images are written to a unique color space known as *YCC*. We call the extent to which a color space (color model) can express color the *gamut* of a color space. The LAB color space that Photoshop uses embraces the YCC color space, and the two color spaces are virtually interchangeable. To decrease the gamma (lower the midtones) of a PhotoCD image without shifting the colors in the image, you open the PCD image in LAB color mode.

**Tip**

**LAB Color Versus RGB**    You will notice no difference in the color quality of the LAB mode image when you compare it to RGB color, because LAB is a *superset*—it is larger than and encompasses the RGB color mode.

Here's a quick and easy set of steps you can perform to bring a PhotoCD image back into the acceptable range of color expression that computer monitors display.

### Example 6.2    Adjusting Gamma Through LAB Color Mode

Hmmm. The picture you've just opened from the PhotoCD in the previous set of steps lacks visual snap (contrast), and the midtones seem a little blocked-in.

1. On the Layers palette (press F7 if it's not onscreen), click the Channels tab, and then click the Lightness channel, (the channel that needs work), as shown in Figure 6.4.

**Figure 6.4**   Click on the channel that contains only lightness information about the photograph.

2. Press Ctrl(⌘)+L to open the Levels command dialog box. Drag the black point slider up to about 35, and drag the midtone slider to the left so that the middle Input Levels box reads about 1.15, as shown in Figure 6.5.

   Increasing the Black point makes the shaded areas of the picture a little more dense and increasing the gamma (lowering the midtones) makes areas of visual importance a little lighter so that you can see more visual detail.

3. Click OK to apply the changes, and then press Ctrl(⌘)+~(tilde) to move your view back to the color composite of this image.

4. Choose Image, Mode, and then choose RGB Color. You will not notice a color change because the image is going to a *subset* of the LAB color space. Our reason for switching modes is because many other applications cannot read a file saved in LAB mode.

5. If you want to keep the image, save it to your hard disk in the TIFF file format, as shore.tif. Close the image.

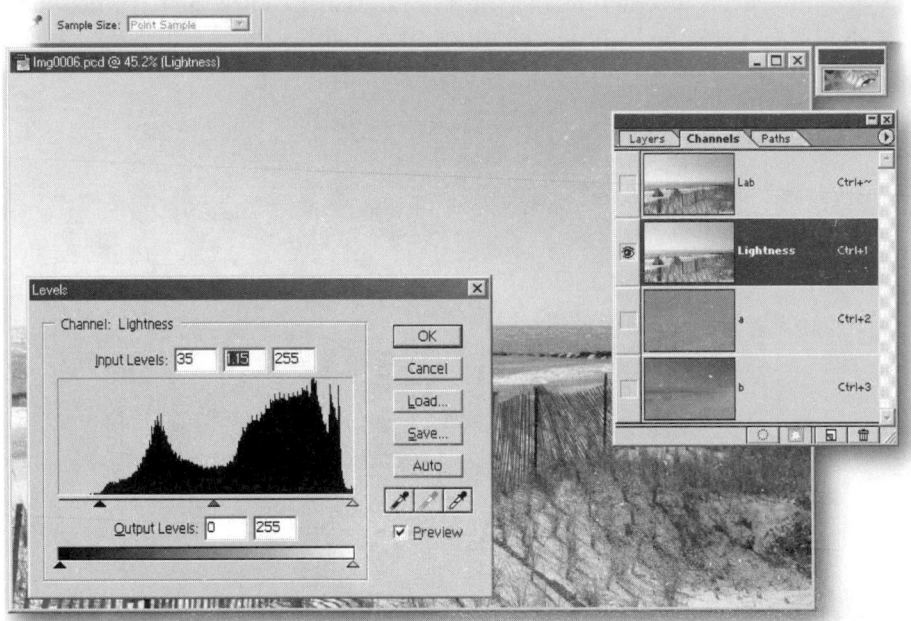

**Figure 6.5**    Treat the Lightness channel in a LAB mode image as you would treat a grayscale image. If it looks good in black and white, it'll look superb in color.

That's the story on PhotoCDs. They're cheap and quick to get, they can hold more than 100 high-resolution images (so they're not taking up space on your hard disk), and you can open PCD images in different sizes and modes for editing work. Now let's move on to other ways to digitize an image.

## Using a Scanner to Acquire an Image

Whether you use a scanner, a digital camera, or a transparency scanner, you should keep in mind this common guideline for acquiring an image before you click the Scan button or the shutter:

*Your input should approximately equal your output.*

What do these words of wisdom mean? They mean there is no point in "overscanning"—sampling more pixels than can possibly be rendered to your output devices, such as a laser or inkjet printer, film, or the Web, to mention a few. If you don't know the dimensions and resolution of your output, ask the service that is outputting your file for guidance or check the documentation that came with your laser or inkjet printer for recommendations on the sampling resolution you need to use.

You can also check out Chapter 7 for additional information on the resolution requirements of common output devices.

The following table gives a general idea of the settings you would use to get good printed results from printers of various capabilities. Higher dpi values in the first column correspond to more refined and better-looking output from common laser printers to expensive printers and printing presses. The table also assumes that you are working with something that is approximately 4" by 6" in physical dimensions and that you want to output the image at a 1:1 size ratio. (A 1:1 ratio means that the dimensions of the printed image are the same as the object you scan.)

### Various Output and Input Resolutions

| Resolution of Printed Work | Lines per Inch Output Device Uses | Recommended Scanning Resolution | File Size |
| --- | --- | --- | --- |
| 300 dpi | 45 lpi | 90–100 samples/inch | 570KB |
| 600 dpi | 95 lpi | 170 samples/inch | 1.99MB |
| 1200 dpi | 125 lpi | 225 samples/inch | 3.48MB |
| 2450 dpi | 133 lpi | 266 samples/inch | 4.86MB |

As you can see, the sampling rate for input needs to be far less than the resolution of the output. The most common mistake users make when scanning images is to equate a pixel to a dot of toner or ink. As the chart indicates, the scanning resolution should be more or less two times the frequency of the *line screen* used to create commercial printed work. *Line screen* (AKA line frequency) refers to the grid of halftone dots used to print, and lines per inch (lpi) is the number of dots of ink that are side by side within an inch. The only exception to this "times 2" rule is when your output is to a film recorder.

Unlike printers and presses that use line screens to print half-tone images created from dots of ink, film recorders produce *continuous tone images* by exposing film to light. Consequently, the total amount of information captured by the scanner is measured in saved file size, and saved file size determines the quality of film recorder output. The authors have found that you can get a very decent 35mm slide from an image file that is at least 4MB in size; the higher the saved file size, the better the image you receive. With larger-format film recorders that render, for example, a 4"-by-5" transparency, you should consider scanning an image to yield at least a 14MB file.

Acquiring images destined for the Web or other onscreen presentations requires far fewer of your computer's resources. This is because the resolution of the image file created needs to match only that of a monitor, which is typically 72 pixels/inch. A full-screen, RGB color mode graphic that measures 640 pixels by 480 pixels and is 72 pixels/inch is only 900KB when saved to disk. The same image saved as a grayscale mode image would only be a third that size—300KB.

When scanning, always scan to meet the requirements of your intended output device. For example, if you want to output the image to a printer or a film recorder, and use the image on a Web page, scan the material three times—once for each device. One size *never* fits all! As the saying goes in the imaging trade, "Get it right in the camera," which means "Photograph only what you need through the lens." Similarly, you should get it right when you scan. You should not depend on Photoshop to resize images; resized bitmap images always suffer some loss of focus that can never truly be restored, even with Photoshop's magical sharpening filters.

Let's take a look first at the best piece of hardware used for getting an image photo into Photoshop: the transparency scanner.

## Transparency Scanning

The transparency scanner uses the same first step that goes into making a PhotoCD image: negative scanning. Light is passed through a negative or a slide and captured by photo-sensitive cells that record the color with all the life and brilliance seen by the human eye.

In Figure 6.6, you can see a Nikon CoolScan-like device. You put the strip of film in the holder, and place it in the opening in the front (many of these models are designed to mount inside the computer). The basic principle behind transparency scanning is that a light behind the source passes the colors of the source, through a lens system, to an array of sensing devices that produces the digital information needed to write a computer file.

Because a transparency scanner, such as a Nikon CoolScan, is not a standard computer item, we didn't include a formal tutorial in this section. We will walk through the process by which you scan a negative, however. The results of the scan made with the Nikon CoolScan are on the Companion CD, which gives you the opportunity to compare, with your own eyes, the results you can expect from using a desktop transparency scanner versus the image produced by CoolScan.

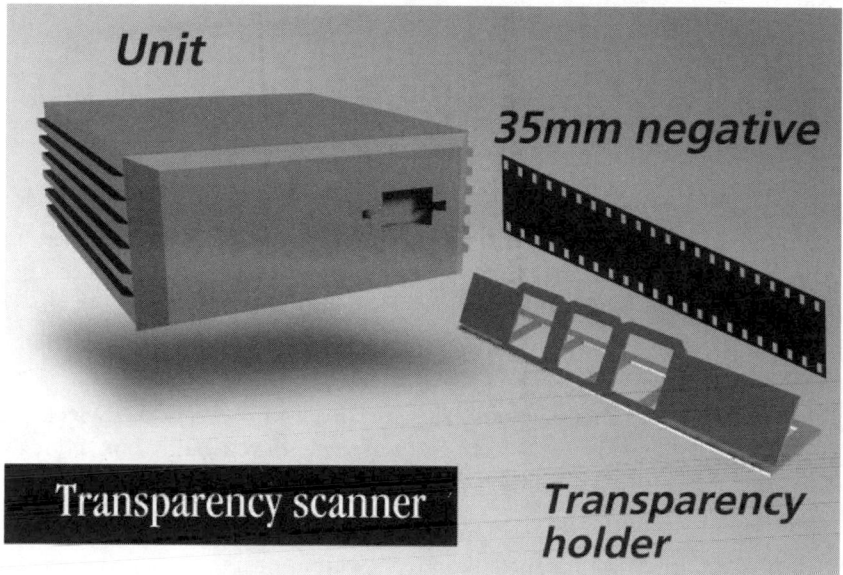

**Figure 6.6**   Transparency scanning used to be a service you'd shop for. Now, depending on your profession, transparency scanners are within the reach of most budgets.

The following example shows you how the Nikon CoolScan works. If you don't own a transparency scanner (or you don't feel like going through the hassle of using your negative scanner, open image Dock2.pcd at 512×768 pixel resolution from the Examples/Chap06 folder on the Companion CD, and then open Dock3.tif in Photoshop. Compare the quality side by side. The color is far more accurate with the transparency scan, the focus is a teensy bit sharper in the transparency scan, and there appears to be less of an overall "haze" to the transparency scan image. (Also, you don't see any lint on Dock3.tif because the authors took the time to clean the negative before scanning it. Cleanliness goes a long way in acquiring a great image when using transparency scanning!)

### Warning

**Handle with Care!**   An *extremely* important part of scanning film is to make sure that your negatives are dust, hair, and fingerprint free! If there is *any* foreign substance on either side of the negative, the scanner will see it and add it to your image. This is definitely not a case where more is better.

It is highly recommended that you invest in a pair of cloth film-handling gloves to wear before you even think about taking your negatives out of their sleeves and that you blow the dust off both sides of the film with a compressed-gas duster such as Dust-Off by Falcon. The gloves and the compressed gas can be found in most photo stores.

### Example 6.3    Transparency Scanning

1. Power on the transparency scanner and restart your computer. Most computers need to see devices attached to the computer on startup to make use of them. Additionally, scanning can tax your system's resources, and it's a good idea to start with maximum resources available.

2. Start Photoshop.

3. Place the strip of negatives that contains the image you want scanned into the scanner's transparency holder, and close the holder firmly. Insert the transparency holder into the scanner, following the instructions in the scanner's owner's manual. (Figure 6.6 illustrates the components of the transparency scanner.)

4. From Photoshop's menu, choose File, Import, and then choose Select TWAIN_32 Source (Twain Select). In the Select Source dialog box, choose Nikon CoolScan (32), and then click Select. The Select Source box closes.

5. Choose File, Import, and then choose TWAIN_32 (Twain Acquire).

   The TWAIN interface for the Nikon CoolScan appears.

6. Choose 512×768 pixels as the size of the scan. This is the exact size of the "base 1" PhotoCD image. Choose Color Neg from the drop-down list, and then click Preview.

7. Click Scan in the TWAIN interface, and then close the TWAIN interface.

   The unnamed image is now in Photoshop's workspace, and it's sideways because the images on a strip of negatives are scanned in portrait mode. (If you scan 35mm slides, you can decide on the orientation.)

8. Choose File, Save As, and then save the image to your hard disk in the TIFF file format.

If you're a professional photographer who develops your own film, you might want to search around in that checkbook for the price of a transparency scanner or a flatbed scanner that also has the capability to scan transparencies. Demanding photographic work necessitates a hands-on, personal approach. Next, we look at the most common way of acquiring images—the flatbed scanner.

## Examining the Flatbed Scanner

A few years ago, flatbed scanners were only for the richest of users, with scanner prices starting at about $1,200. These scanners were slow and noisy because three passes were required to sample an RGB image, one pass for each individual RGB component color—red, green, and blue. They were also extremely delicate. Bump the scanner and the scanning heads could come out of alignment, and your RGB scans would look as sharp as a comic book graphic.

Times have changed; you can now buy a single-element color scanner for around $200 (or less). And the quality of these scanners is terrific because they contain the same type of electronics the more expensive scanners of a generation ago had. The economics of all computer hardware is that the "early adopters" pay for the research and development of technology, and if you wait, you pay a significantly lower price for identical or even superior technology. (We don't know whether the "things" in Mom's adage "Good things come to those who wait" are always good, but usually they're cheaper!)

As remarkable as flatbed scanners are, the advice we are about to give may seem startling. The advice? *Don't* scan photographic prints. You should use a flatbed scanner only as a last resort, such as when the client does not have the negative of an image.

The problem with flatbed scanners is that they use a reflective scanning method to sample images. In short, flatbed scanners use a two-step process to gather samples. First, they direct a light source toward the opaque artwork, and then the scanner's "camera"—its array of photo-sensing sampling elements—records the pattern and characteristics of the light that has bounced (been reflected) back from the artwork. Figure 6.7 illustrates how light travels with reflective, flatbed scanning.

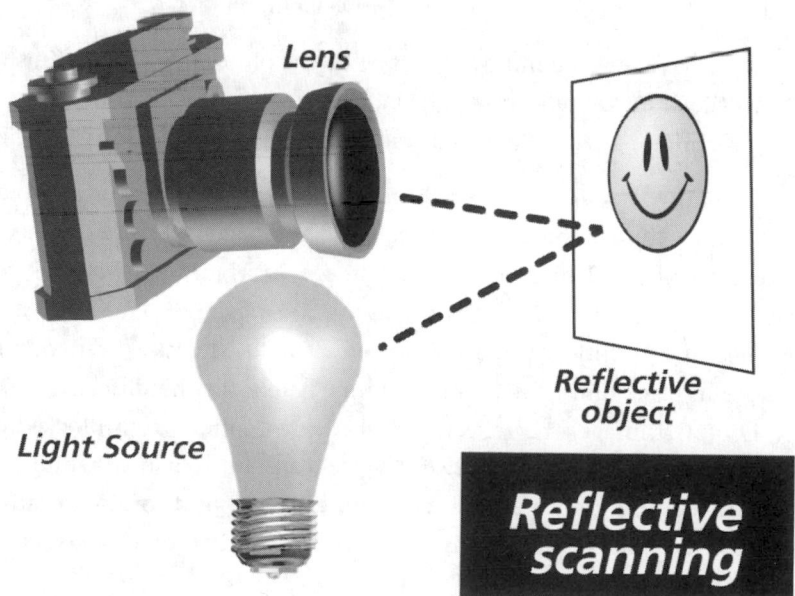

**Figure 6.7**   Reflective scanning technology bounces light off the target image, and the light is then passed along to the digitizing element in the scanner.

It's not immediately obvious that reflective, flatbed scanning presents a degraded version of the original image. This is because the print that you scan isn't the original source—the *film negative* that was used to create the printed photograph is the true source. If you compare the digital image created by the flatbed scanner to one created by a transparency scanner that scans the actual negative, you'll find that scanning the negative produces superior results.

> **Note**
>
> **Reflective Is Dull**   Monitors are the counterpart to transparency scanners, in a way, because they emit light. In contrast, when we look at a magazine, our eyes are performing reflective scanning, and the magazine appears duller than if we were looking at a file of the same magazine cover on our monitors.

*Brilliance* is the name of the game. A scan of a photo of a brilliant flower cannot hope to look as bright onscreen as the same photo looked at as a 35mm slide. Why? Because reflective scanning loses color in the process, as light needs to travel twice as far to the digitizing element in the scanner. Additionally, you're a generation away from the original film when you scan a print. If you allow light to pass through the target image, brilliance is retained—you're actually directing light, colored light to be precise, at a photosensitive element.

This process becomes even more difficult when the photo has a matte finish because the matte finish makes reflecting light much more difficult. If you know you must scan from a photo, always have your prints developed with a glossy finish.

You can see for yourself in Figures 6.8 and 6.9 how the flatbed scan stands up to the image produced by scanning a film negative. The image in Figure 6.8 was carefully scanned from a good photograph. The image in Figure 6.9 was taken from a PhotoCD. (A PhotoCD is made by scanning film negatives and then storing the image files in a proprietary file format on a CD-ROM disk.) Even though these images are in black and white, you can immediately see the difference. Compared to the PhotoCD image, the reflective flatbed scan suffers from blocked-in darker tones, and the whites are overpowering—delicate areas of near-white have been wiped out. You might say that the scan, and even the print of the negative of this image, has exaggerated the contrast of the photo. And when contrast is increased, image content and detail are lost.

If you'd like to witness the qualitative difference between a reflective scan and a transparency scan, open (in Photoshop) both the Dock1.tif and Dock2.pcd images from the Examples/Chap06 folder on the Companion CD. Dock1 is from a flatbed scanner, and Dock2 is from a PhotoCD.

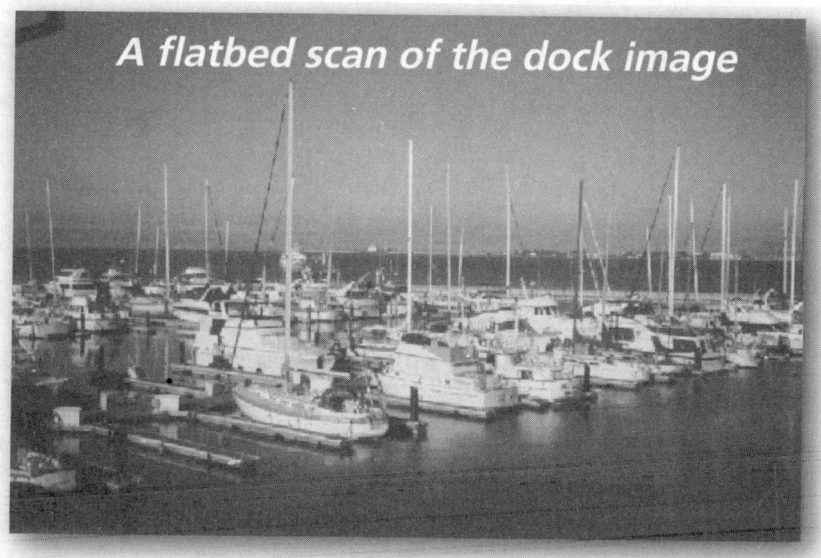

**Figure 6.8**   Reflective scanning emphasizes the extremes in tonal distribution within a photograph.

**Figure 6.9**   Transparency scanned PhotoCD images retain clarity in the tonal extremes, good focus, as well as a good tonal balance in the midtones.

Now, let's say that your client does not have the negative to Dock1.tif. You are forced to work with this image in Photoshop. Don't despair; with a few cosmetic touch-ups you can bring some life to the image, as you'll learn in the following example.

### Example 6.4    Adjusting Tone, Balance, and Focus from a Scanned Image

1. Open the Dock1.tif image from the Examples/Chap06 folder on the Companion CD. You might also want to open Dock2.pcd as a reference for your work; open it at 512×768 pixel size.

2. With Dock1.tif in the foreground, press Ctrl(⌘)+L to display the Levels command.

3. Drag the midtone slider until the middle Input Levels field reads about 1.19, as shown in Figure 6.10. Doing this expands (opens up) the range of the midtones in the image. Most of the image's visual content is located in the midtones. In essence, you're allowing more of the midtone detail to show through in the picture and also allowing for more color to be added to the overall picture later.

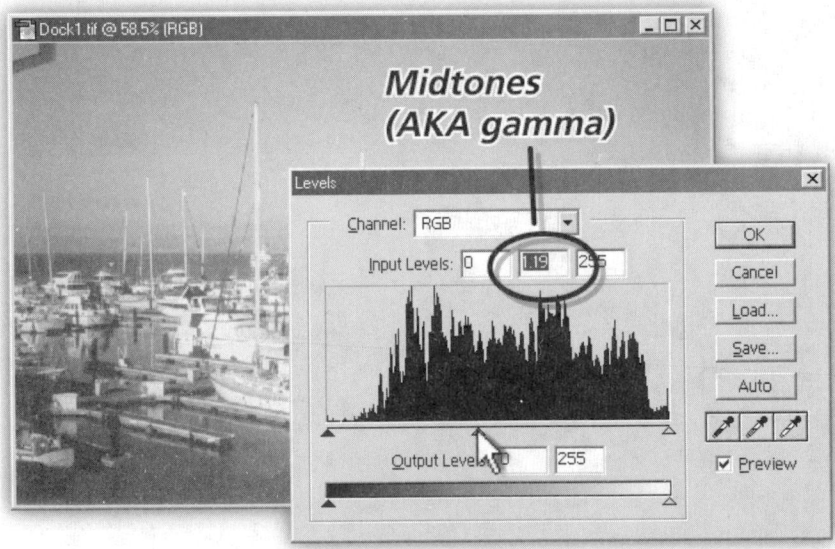

**Figure 6.10**    The midtones in a scanned photograph are often blocked in, hiding image detail. The Levels command helps redistribute pixels in this zone to allow less contrast and thus, greater detail.

4. Click OK, and then press Ctrl(⌘)+B to display the Color Balance command. The Dock1 image has an unwanted bluish cast that needs to be eliminated.

5. With the Midtones button clicked, drag the Yellow/Blue slider until the far-right Color Levels box reads –33 or so.

6. Because you also don't want the cyan in the image, drag the Cyan/Red slider until the first Color Levels field reads +18, as shown in Figure 6.11. You've created a dramatic change in the overall feeling of the scanned photo; it's much more realistic now. Click OK to apply the change.

## Warming up the image also reveals more colors

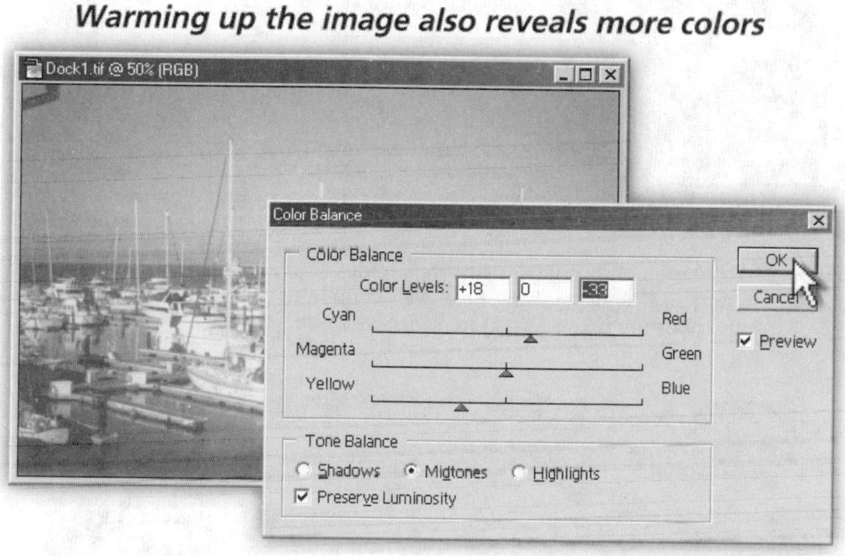

**Figure 6.11**    Color shifts in the midtones can dramatically change the warmth and overall feeling of a color picture. Use the sliders in the Color Balance command to remove unwanted, predominant color casts.

7. Press Ctrl(⌘)+U to display the Hue/Saturation command.

8. Drag the Saturation slider to about +23, and then drag the Lightness slider to about +3, as shown in Figure 6.12. There is plenty of denseness in this scanned print, and lightening the image, overall, helps bring out a little additional detail in the shadow areas. Notice that you can now see the reflections of some of the masts. Click OK to apply the changes.

The focus of this image is pretty pathetic because the photo-finisher didn't focus the negative properly on the photographic paper, and because the picture wasn't perfectly flat against the scanner's platen (glass imaging surface).

9. Choose Filter, Sharpen, and then choose Unsharp Mask.

10. Drag the Amount slider to 39%, type **0.9** in the pixels field, and then type **1** in the Threshold field. (These settings are the author's secret recipe for gently sharpening images that are 1.5MB and lower in file size.) In Figure 6.13, you can see the correct settings. Click OK to apply the sharpening.

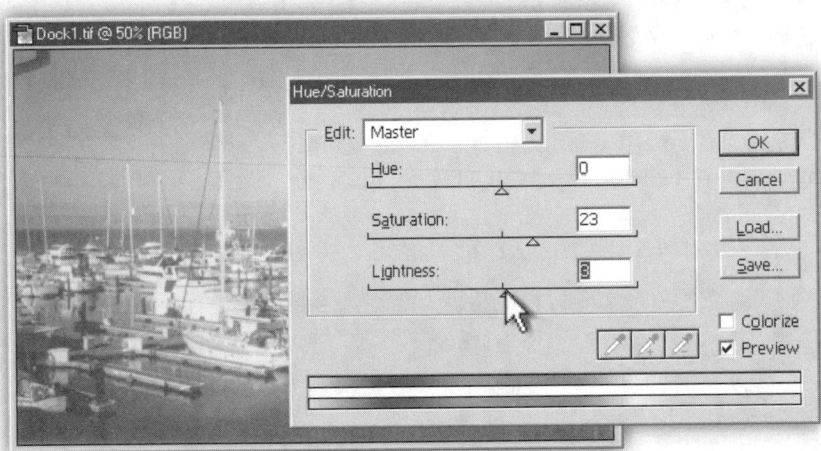

**Figure 6.12**    Saturation and tonal density are a trade-off. Because you lightened the midtones in the image using the Levels command, there is now more "space" in the midtone pixels to add (to saturate) color.

**Figure 6.13**    The Unsharp Mask filter provides a small but necessary amount of sharpening to the image with little change in image content.

You're nearly finished! The scan looks much better now, but not as good as the PhotoCD version of the scene. Look at both images onscreen. You've done all that you can to improve the scanned image, short of finding the negative and scanning it.

11. You can save the image, or discard it now by closing it without saving.

Unfortunately, visual information that is not in a photo will definitely not be acquired through scanning, and if you compare Dock1 to Dock2, you'll see that the whites in Dock1 are so blown-out, there's no visual information beyond a pure white. The names and numbers on the boats can be seen in the PhotoCD version, but not in the scan.

In spite of all the bad things said about reflective scanning up to this point, it is important to keep in mind that there are some things you'll want to do that only a flatbed scanner can do for you. For example, Chapter 19 absolutely depends on flatbed scanning real world objects. The scanner in this chapter spells the difference between having a finished layout in the morning, and having a poor excuse for the boss.

What are we saying here? Check out the following section for some completely inspired, fantastic, guaranteed-to-void-your-warranty uses for flatbed scanners.

## Scanning Three-Dimensional Objects

You can use your flatbed to scan *three-dimensional* objects. Direct scanning of physical objects is fun, innovative, and can provide you with better results than you'd expect. In the next section, you'll see how your flatbed scanner can be used as a digital camera.

### Direct Scanning Do's and Don'ts

*Direct scanning*, as the name implies, is the scanning of objects placed on the scanner's imaging surface. You're essentially treating the scanner like an expensive color photocopier, except that the results are in far better focus, and the objects scanned can be of different resolutions (different sampling rates).

### Cover Your Imaging Surface: A Warning Before You Scan

If you dislike white spots in photographs (a result of not properly cleaning the negative) you've received from a photo-finisher, then you will *detest* getting scans that contain dust, lint, hair, and other particles that show up in your beautiful image. Guess who would be to blame for these goodies in your work? That's right; it would be you.

Flatbed scanners usually have a plastic gasket that holds the glass imaging plate in place as the scanning head passes across the underside of the glass. This gasket is meant to hold the glass and to buffer the glass against the vibration caused by the machine's components, but the gasket *is not* airtight. Therefore, if you were to scan, say, a bunch of flowers, the pollen and dirt left on the scanning surface might well remain lodged in the edges of the gasket, even though you wiped off the particles after you scanned the flowers. And with time, these particles will eventually get under the gasket, and then you'll have particles *inside* your scanner, placing dots all over your future work. There's really nothing you can do at that point except send the scanner in for repair.

To alleviate this pollution problem and still allow you to scan freely whatever comes to mind, the author recommends taping a sheet of acetate over the entire imaging surface of the scanner. The acetate will also protect the glass from scratches and nicks.

The authors have scanned practically everything in the office and the fridge in recent years, even a sloppy tomato slice as you'll see in Chapter 19, by keeping the acetate over the scanner's platen. The scan is good, the acetate is disposable, and the scanner remains in perfect condition optically.

Take reasonable care of your scanner, and protect the glass and scanner with an acetate sheet when you're scanning sooty, dusty, or pollen-bearing objects, or any object that might scratch the glass. If you always remember to use the acetate, your scanner will thank you and you'll be able to look forward to many years of creating fun and innovative designs using direct-scanned images.

### Choose Your Object Carefully

Naturally, there is a practical limit to the overall size, weight, and depth of the objects you can scan on a flatbed scanner. Generally, the objects you place on the scanner's platen should not be any deeper than ½" or so. Here's a brief list of things you can scan:

- Crayons (as long as identifying trademarks on the paper don't show. Better still, remove the paper).
- Flowers, artificial grass, moss, or leaves (which are used in the following examples).
- Floor tiling made from natural materials such as slate, marble, granite. Don't use synthetic tiles that have a pattern applied to them. That pattern belongs to the company that makes the tile!
- Buttons.
- Generic candy. This would include candy corn, but not something like a Tootsie Roll, which has trademarked graphics on the wrapper.

- Generic cereal, such as puffed wheat or rice. You cannot, however, acquire distinctive, trademarked cereal shapes such as Lucky Charms.

- Sponges. Sponges produce really interesting textures when scanned at high resolutions.

- Feathers. Craft stores carry a wide variety of dyed feathers.

- Clip art from royalty-free clip art books, such as those that Dover produces. In these physical books, which can be picked up at any art supply store, you can find ornamental type initials, borders, and other artwork. The only thing you cannot do with these clip art images is scan them and then sell the electronic versions under your own name. However, the clip art is okay to use as an element in a page layout.

- Pasta. This includes those spiral shapes, shells, spaghetti, elbow macaroni, and so on.

Here's a list of objects for which you would need permission from the manufacturer, or that you should not scan at all:

- American currency.

- Trademarked food items and drugs, such as aspirins.

- Textiles, wallpaper, gift wrap that have patterns. You should not, for example, scan a Hawaiian shirt, because the design most certainly is protected by either a trademark or a copyright.

- Trademarked art supplies such as scissors, pencils, rulers, and drafting paraphernalia. You can, however, scan these items and then carefully clone over identifying trademarks, but only if the *shapes* of such objects don't have trademark, patent, or copyright protection. For example, a Bic pen has a trademarked design, and you can't scan and use an image of the pen commercially without the manufacturer's consent, even if the name "Bic" doesn't appear in the scan.

The best guideline for acquiring images directly is to stay away from items that you think have a trademarked shape, or that carry a prominently displayed logo.

## Let a Layout Dictate a Scan

Let's suppose that you're an art director for a publication, and you need to come up with an image to accompany an article on the colors of fall leaves, "Catch Me, I'm

Falling." To feature an image of leaves on the page is a natural decision, but before you design the page you must ask yourself:

- What's the best design idea I can come up with?
- How much RAM and scratch disk space do I need, and do I really need to cover an 8½" by 11" page with leaves?

Image size, as measured in megabytes, truly is a consideration when you create a page design. You'll notice very few full-page ads or articles with photos or scans because an 8½" by 11" area, at commercial printing quality, which is 266 pixels per inch, weighs in at 18.9MB! But wait, the news gets worse. Bleed pages—pages with images that run right up to the corner of the printed page—usually need to be trimmed from a larger size paper. This is because bleed pages need space for the printing press gripper to hold onto the page as it passes through the printing plates. This also means that the photo or scan *must* occupy the full size of the printed page before it's trimmed down (to *trim size*, 8½" by 11" in this example). If the pressman tells you, for example, that bleed runs ¼" outside the trim size, then the image you must scan will be 9" by 11½", or 21MB in file size. And to top it off, these are the RGB sizes; when you finish editing your work and convert the images to CMYK for printing, the files sizes will increase by another 25%.

Hey, *we* had to go through this stuff to bring you the color signature in this book, and we have additional information on page layout in Chapter 19, where the flatbed scanner is the only acquisition device we document.

Photoshop needs three to five times the image size in system RAM and hard disk space to run at a comfortable clip and not swap data out to scratch disk. So to create the bleed-size buttons page, your system needs at least 64MB of RAM and an equal if not larger amount of free scratch disk space. (For information about memory settings and specifying scratch disk space, see Chapter 4. This RAM is *in addition to* the RAM required by Photoshop 6, which *realistically* (*not* the wording on the box) is 96MB. If you don't have sufficient RAM for the task, you have three options:

- Buy more RAM. A good suggestion in today's technology market, because one MB of RAM is now about as expensive as a Quarter Pounder with cheese.
- Define as much uncompressed space on your hard disk(s) as possible for Photoshop to use as scratch disk space. Again, see Chapter 4 for configuring scratch disk and memory allocation. This is not an optimal solution for working with large files; swapping to disk space takes an order of magnitude more time than swapping in and out of RAM.

- Rethink your design. Can you accomplish the same goal—to make a stunning page layout with text and graphics—by using more "white space" on the page, and less image? Can a smaller image be used more effectively than a large one? The answer is yes.

## A Brief, Extremely Important Discussion of EPS

Very shortly in this section, and at later points in this book, we recommend that you use Illustrator or another vector drawing application to accomplish an effect or to design a rough layout. Our reason for encouraging you to do this is because a lot of designers feel right at home in a vector drawing program, while they feel that Photoshop is only for image editing. Regardless of how true these notions actually are, when you work in Illustrator (or another program capable of generating Illustrator-format designs), caution should be taken when choosing options for saving or exporting the design.

An EPS file is short for *Encapsulated PostScript*. What this means is that Illustrator and other EPS-capable programs have created a PostScript-language file that can be inserted into a document. When the document is sent to a PostScript printer, and the printer hits the "nugget" of PostScript, it simply follows the instructions in the EPS implant. Then, the printer proceeds along its merry way rendering the remainder of the document.

Now, Adobe (naturally) would like every designer to find all their solutions in Adobe brand products—this is why you find all the integration between ImageReady and Photoshop, for example. For our purpose—which is to design a "rough" for Photoshop into which you will place measured scans of leaves—it makes absolutely no difference what choices you make when exporting from Illustrator 5.5 or later (we used Illustrator 9 in this chapter's files) to the EPS format. Both Photoshop and Illustrator can read an EPS file whether it has a thumbnail header placed in it or not. The problem users might have, however, in generating an EPS layout in say CorelDRAW, FreeHand, or Xara lies in the header thumbnail, because the header thumbnail determines the type of EPS file that is exported. There are actually *two* different kinds of EPS files for users who do not use Adobe products to create EPS files.

Outside of AdobeLand, there are the *placeable* EPS file and the *interpreted* EPS file. The placeable EPS file contains printer language that describes to the printer what to render, and it also can contain a low resolution image file that the user places and positions on a page in, for example, PageMaker or InDesign. This placeable EPS file is of no concern to us in the layout example to follow because Photoshop cannot rasterize the information in a placeable EPS file—IOW, Photoshop cannot convert the design information into pixel format.

Enter the *interpreted* EPS file format. This file format has no header image, and contains code that can be opened in most vector drawing programs for editing. This is the type of EPS file you'll find on the Companion CD because an interpreted EPS file can be rendered to bitmap format by Photoshop, to any size you like, with sharpness and detail of the original vector design. In fact, as you will see, an EPS file contains information about the dimensions of the design, so one less step is required—sizing—when an interpreted EPS file is imported to Photoshop.

By the way, all this interpreted and placeable stuff is a moot point if you save your work in Illustrator format (in Windows, an Illustrator file has the file extension .ai). Photoshop and other vector programs can read Illustrator files because all Illustrator files are EPS, but not all EPS files are generated by Illustrator. Illustrator files are more complicated, and at the same time more digestible than what Adobe calls a "generic EPS file" (an EPS file created using a non-Adobe product).

So, if the following section inspires you to create roughs on your own for ads or page layouts, and you do not own Illustrator, not to worry. Photoshop will import and convert to pixel format Illustrator files, EPS files created using Illustrator, and interpreted EPS files created using a non-Adobe vector drawing program.

Now, let's get on with sizing up your need for direct scanning of artwork for the layout.

### Scanning the Object

Let's examine the most ambitious layout design first, keeping the scanning requirements within reason so that any user with 24MB of system RAM or more can play along in this layout game. In Figure 6.14 you can see the full-page layout of "wall-to-wall" leaves; the dotted line in the image represents the trim size for the page. This layout is also in the Examples/Chap06 folder of the Companion CD, as Leaves1.eps, in case you'd like to view or edit it as an editable vector page layout in Illustrator, CorelDRAW, FreeHand, or Xara.

There are some general rules for creating an EPS file to use as a template in Photoshop, into which you place the scanned material. In Figure 6.14 (not that we have three callouts here), these are the three rules you should use when preparing a template to use in Photoshop:

- If you're working with others on an assignment, be kind and either tell them what font is used for the headline, or convert the text in your layout to curves. If you do this, the headline is no longer editable (so make a backup copy), but other users (and Photoshop) will have no problem opening the document without the need to install extra fonts.

  Conversely, if your layout was created in Illustrator 9, there's an option to embed the fonts used so you can keep the text as text in your EPS export file, and you don't have to convert text to curves.

- Do not create a color layout, if it is for the purposes of placing scanned elements. Do the layout in grayscale, and then import it to Photoshop in grayscale mode. Then, when you want to add the direct scans to the image, convert the image to RGB color mode or CYMK. You're asking a lot less of Photoshop and your processor when you import to grayscale instead of in color. It takes one-third the processing "umph," in fact.

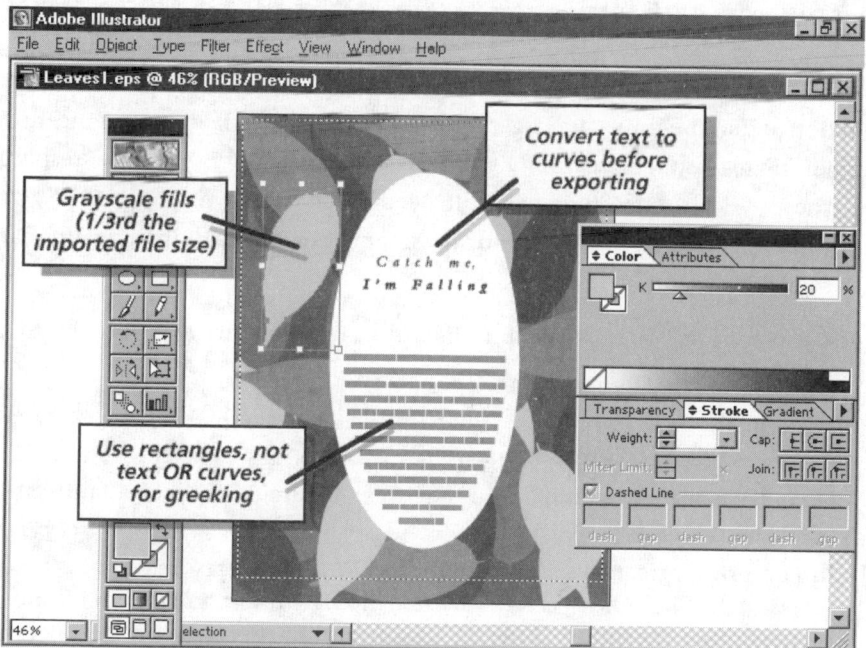

**Figure 6.14**   For this ambitious page layout, you must scan 9" by 11½" of leaves. The Illustrator document was exported to (interpreted) EPS file format for Photoshop.

- Do not use text for greeking in your layout. Instead, use lines of gray color that are broken up at irregular intervals. Why? Because Photoshop will need to interpret a whole lot of text for nothing if you feed it text as greeking. If you send Photoshop gray rectangles, you're only sending it 4 points in space as coordinates on the page and a color fill. In contrast, even the shortest line of text can have more than 1,000 anchor points in its construction. Do yourself a favor and keep it simple.

The EPS files you'll work with were created in Illustrator 9, and Illustrator 9 enables you to attach a low resolution header to an EPS file. Not only can the file can be placed in a DTP program such as InDesign or PageMaker, but it can also be edited in a vector drawing program. As mentioned in the previous section, you must choose to export an EPS file as an interpreted EPS file if you want to edit it in the future, and if you want Photoshop to be able to read the file. You'll import the layout to Photoshop shortly, to give you a guide for the finished layout.

**Note**

**When You Don't Have a Scanner**   If you'd like to participate in this direct scanning layout adventure but don't have a scanner, use Leaves1.tif in the Examples/Chap06 folder on the Companion CD.

You'll notice that the leaves are larger than 1:1 in the design layout. This means that the *physical* area you'll be scanning will be less than 9" by 11½", but the resolution times the physical dimensions will still need to come out to 9" by 11½", which means that we'll need to show you how to set up your scanner's interface to scan at larger than 1:1 resolution.

This example shows you how to fulfill the layout requirement for a page, bleed size, of leaves.

### Example 6.5   Creating a Direct Scan Layout

1. Go outside and gather a handful of leaves that are different sizes and various colors and shapes.
2. In Photoshop, create a new image that is 9"×11½" at a resolution of 200 pixels/inch. Click OK to create the new file. The resolution was determined by the output capability of the device the author used to print the layout.
3. Choose Image, Image Size, and then drop down the Width and Height measurement boxes, and choose pixels.
4. Write down the measurements (Width should be 1800, and Height 2300, in case your scanner measures in pixels instead of inches).

5. Cover the scanner's imaging surface with leaves. You don't need to cover the full width and height of the scanner's imaging surface because you are cropping the image at a larger than 1:1 resolution.

6. Choose File, Import. If you are using a Macintosh, choose File, Import, Twain Acquire. Choose TWAIN_32 if you are using Windows 95, or Windows NT 4 or later.

   The scanner interface will load on top of Photoshop's workspace. By the way, the "32" in TWAIN_32 has nothing to do with the bit depth of your scan. Your scan will be (for 99% of our readers) 8 bits per channel. The 32 here means that Photoshop is taking advantage of Windows' 32-bit architecture.

7. Set the scanner to RGB color, Reflective type scanning, and 266 pixels/inch scanning resolution.

8. Drag a crop box in the image, watching the pixel measurements until the Width reads 1800 and the Height reads 2300. Now, all scanner interfaces are different and they have different features. On the AGFA scanner the ppi has to be adjusted to 260 to allow a scan that is bigger than the maximum imaging width of the scanner bed. On some scanners, you can type the width, height, and resolution of the scan directly into fields. Figure 6.15 gives you a view of our scanner's interface as well as an idea of the way the leaves were arranged and what the scanner settings look like for this assignment. Due to the amount of overlapping in the leaves, they were attached to a piece of paper and arranged before being placed on the scanner.

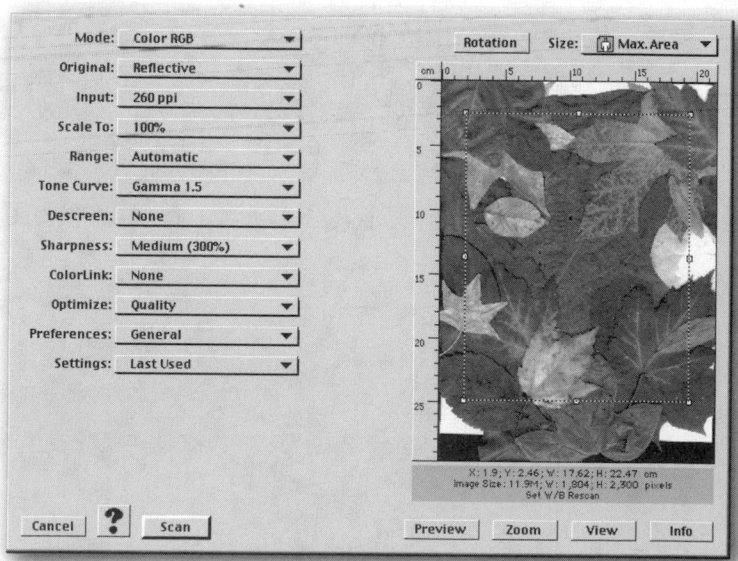

**Figure 6.15**   Adjust the Width and Height in inches or in pixels, and specify the resolution you want for the scan.

9. Click Scan (or OK, or whatever launches the scan on your model of scanner). In a moment, the scanned image will appear in Photoshop and the scanner interface will disappear.

10. Because the scan was done at 260 ppi, go into Image, image size, and with the Resample Image button turned off, change the Resolution to 200. Save the file as Leaves1.tif to your hard disk. Keep the file open.

### Editing a Scanned Image

According to the EPS layout shown in Figure 6.14, an oval needs to be knocked out of the center of the page to create a space for the headline and body copy. This example overlays the layout on the image and finishes the graphics part of the page layout.

#### Example 6.6    Editing the Leaf Image

1. Choose File, Open, and then choose the Leaves1.eps file from the Examples/Chap06 folder on the Companion CD.

2. In the Rasterize Generic EPS Format dialog box, choose inches from the Height and Width drop-down boxes. The values in these boxes will say 8.5" in Width and 11" in Height because Photoshop reads the page size information from the file. Type **200** in the Resolution field, choose Grayscale (Grayscale takes less time to interpret than RGB color), and then click OK (see Figure 6.16).

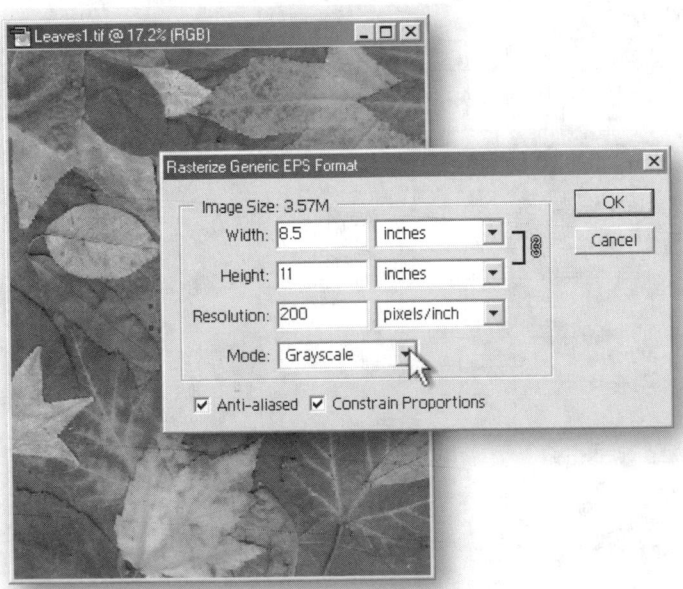

**Figure 6.16**    Create a bitmap copy of the vector layout to place on top of the image.

We're using 200 pixels/inch as the resolution because the author's intended output is to an inkjet printer that can output approximately 600 dots per inch. The author took the time (as you should in your own Photoshop work) to call Epson-Seiko and ask what the recommended sampling rate should be for optimal output, and the fellow said, "About one-third the printer resolution."

3.  With the Layers palette visible and the Leaves.eps image as the active foreground image, hold Shift and drag the Layer 1 title on the Layers palette into the Leaves1.tif window. Holding Shift centers the copied layer as shown in Figure 6.17.

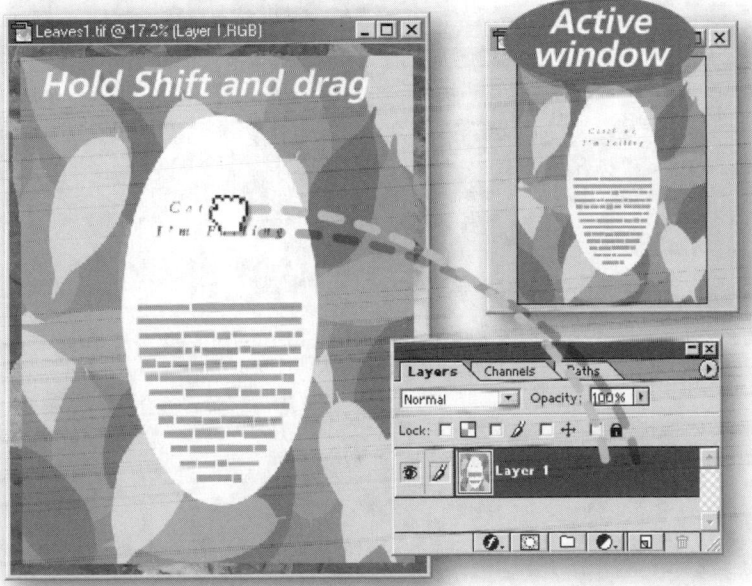

**Figure 6.17**   Center the copied layer by holding Shift.

You will be able to see that the two layers differ in size by ¼" all around the layout. This is the area that will be used as the bleed in the final layout that goes to the printer, as shown in Figure 6.18.

4.  Press Ctrl(⌘)+R to display rulers in the image window.

You won't be measuring anything, but you need the rulers visible to drag guides out of them.

5.  Zoom out to a viewing resolution so you can see the whole image. Drag a vertical guide out of the vertical ruler, placing it so that it touches the left of the circle in the image, and then drag a horizontal guide out of the horizontal ruler so that it touches the top of the circle, as shown in Figure 6.19. If

you need to adjust the placement of the guides, press V to switch to the Move tool. The Move tool is the only tool that can adjust guides that have already been placed.

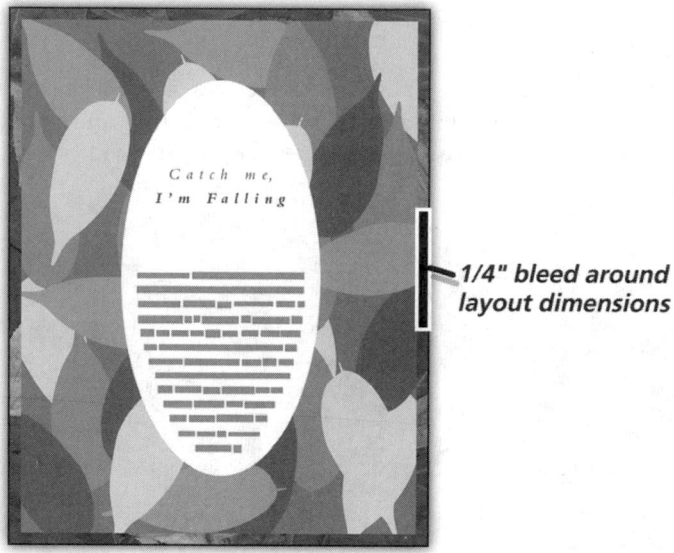

1/4" bleed around layout dimensions

**Figure 6.18**    Copy the layout to a new layer in the Buttons1 image. You can see that there is a ¼" area around the layout that will be your bleed area.

**Figure 6.19**    Mark the top and left edges of the circle so that you can create a selection marquee.

6.  Choose the Ellipse Shape tool from the toolbox, and click the Creates work path icon (the middle of the three icons) on the left of the Options bar. Drag starting from the intersection of the guides to the bottom right of the ellipse.

7.  Press D (default colors), then press X to make the foreground color white.

8.  Click the Create new layer icon on the bottom of the Layers palette, and then click on the Path palette tab. Click on the Fills path with foreground color icon.

    You've created a white area in the image that is the same size and in the same location as the circle in the layout, as shown in Figure 6.20.

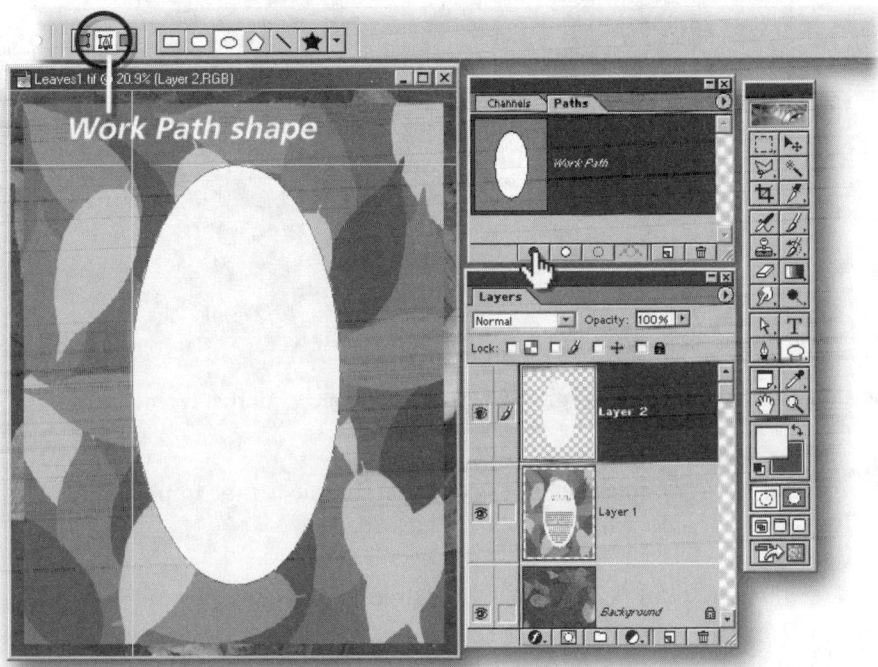

**Figure 6.20**   Create a hole of 100% white by filling the Work Path shape.

9.  Put the guides back into the rulers using the Move tool. Press Ctrl(⌘)+R to lose the rulers. Drag the Layer 1 title on the Layers palette into the Trash icon. Press Ctrl(⌘)+E to Merge Down and make the image a single layer image (This is another good shortcut to remember.) Press Ctrl(⌘)+S to save the changes you made to the Leaves1.tif. See Figure 6.21 for your finished layout.

**Figure 6.21**    The background to this layout is now complete. All that is required now is some text.

You can close the image at any time now. The file can be imported to PageMaker or InDesign to have the text added.

Whew! Working with an 8.5MB image in addition to the 2MB layout in Photoshop is quite a strain on systems with a modest amount of RAM and hard disk space. And it's not exactly a picnic for users with plenty of RAM. In the next section, you'll take a look at a layout that conveys the same message as the preceding one but requires less RAM and hard disk space to execute.

### Varying the Layout: The Vertical Strip

In Figure 6.22 you can see an alternative layout "Catch me..." This layout is different than the first in two significant ways:

- The page is white, and therefore the images of the leaves against white can be floated on the page.
- The page is not a bleed page, so you, the designer, do not have to whip up a huge 9"×11½" file.

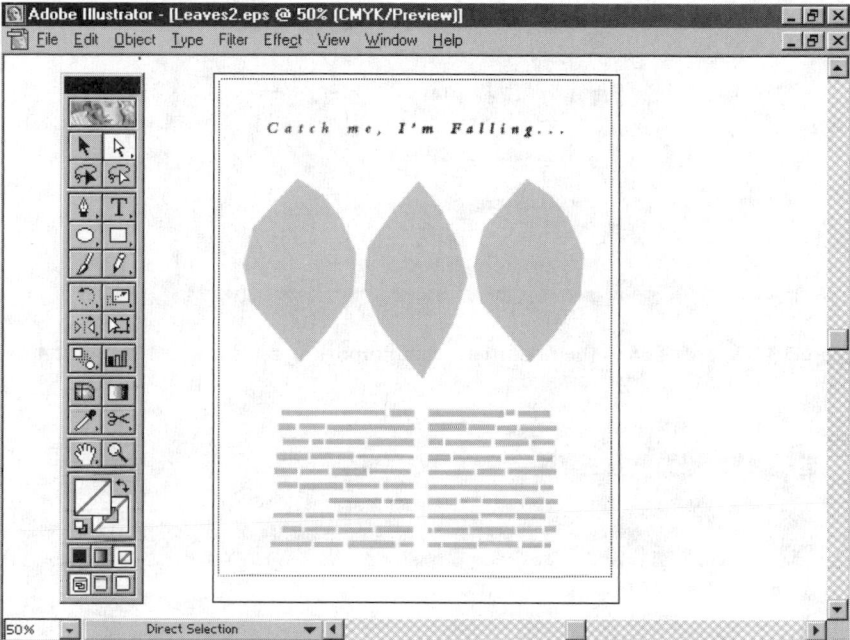

**Figure 6.22**   This layout demands fewer system resources because it uses a smaller graphic than the first layout.

Because this layout was deliberately designed to require less of your scanning input, let's pretend, in the next set of steps, that this layout is destined for a magazine printed on a commercial press instead of a personal inkjet. Magazines are usually printed on presses that have a resolution of 2540 dpi and use a line screen of 133 lines/inch, which means that your artwork needs to have a resolution of at least 266 pixels/inch.

This example sizes up the resolution requirements for the direct scan.

### Example 6.7    Importing a Layout

1. Choose File, Open, and then choose the Leaves2.eps file from the Examples/Chap06 folder on the Companion CD.

2. In the Rasterize Generic EPS Format box, shown in Figure 6.23, set the increments to inches, choose Grayscale mode, and type **266** in the Resolution field. Click OK to render the file to bitmap format.

3. With the Crop tool, drag a rectangular selection around just the leaves in the layout, as shown in Figure 6.24; leave only a little white space outside the leaves.

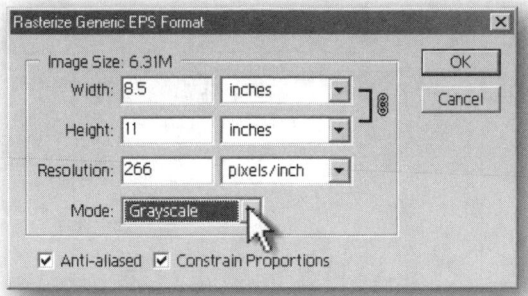

**Figure 6.23**    Specify 266 as the resolution when importing a file that will be printed on a high-quality commercial press.

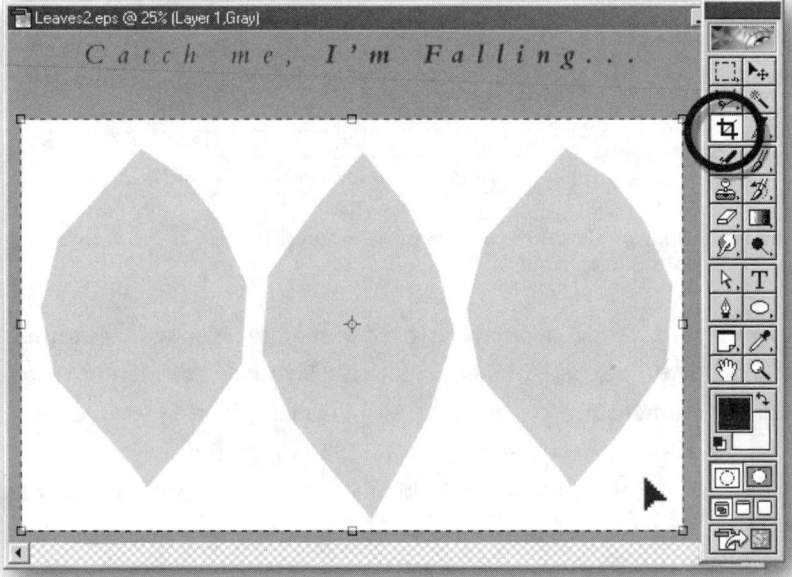

**Figure 6.24**    Crop around only the area you'll need to measure for your scanning work.

4. Press Enter (Return), and then save the file as Leaves2.psd in Photoshop's native file format.

   The Crop tool has characteristics very similar to the Free Transform bounding box. Pressing Enter (Return) commits the crop you defined, while pressing Esc cancels the crop. You can also double-click inside the crop to commit to it, or right-click (Macintosh: hold Ctrl and click) to choose either Crop or Cancel.

5. Zoom in to a 100% view of the leaf drawings, and then choose the Measure tool. Press F8 to open the Info Palette, if it is not already open.

**6.** Hold down Shift and drag a line across the widest part of the leaves, leaving a little white space to the left and right sides, as shown in Figure 6.25. As you can see on the Info palette, the leaves need to be scanned at a width of about 1917 pixels.

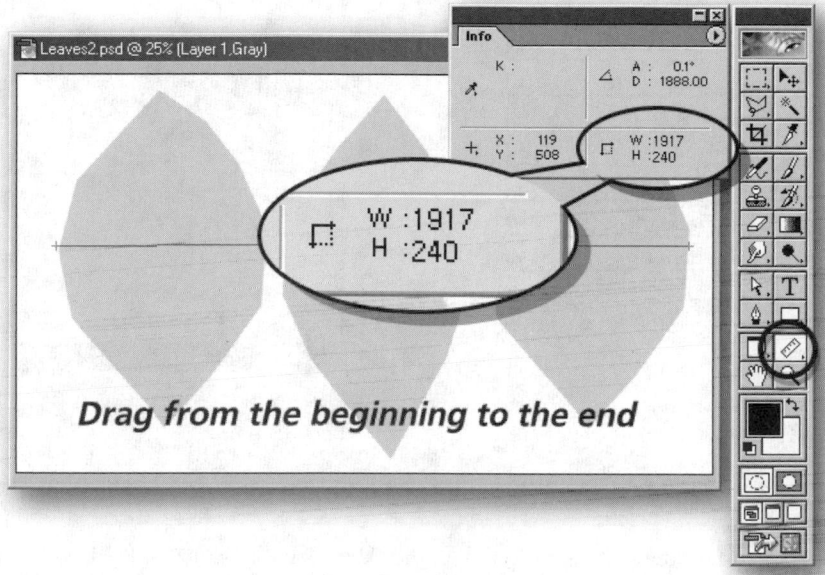

**Figure 6.25**   Measure the width of the image in pixels.

**7.** Because this is about a 1:1 ratio of the leaves that I collected, I will attach them to a piece of white paper in a layout reflecting my original EPS file. You can always adjust the leaves in Photoshop if you need to make the spaces between the leaves larger or smaller; however, if you have a scan that is close to what you want your final layout to look like, it will save you time in Photoshop.

**8.** Choose File, Import, and then choose TWAIN_32 (Mac: Twain Acquire). The scanner's interface opens.

**9.** Drag the crop box around the leaves and then adjust the scaling and resolution so the leaves are being scanned at 100% at 266 ppi and they are approximately 1920 pixels, as shown in Figure 6.26. Click Scan (or OK, or whatever launches the scanner).

Chances are that the background of the leaves is not 100% white because leaves have depth and allow some ambient coloration to seep between the lid of the scanner and the imaging surface. This is easily corrected.

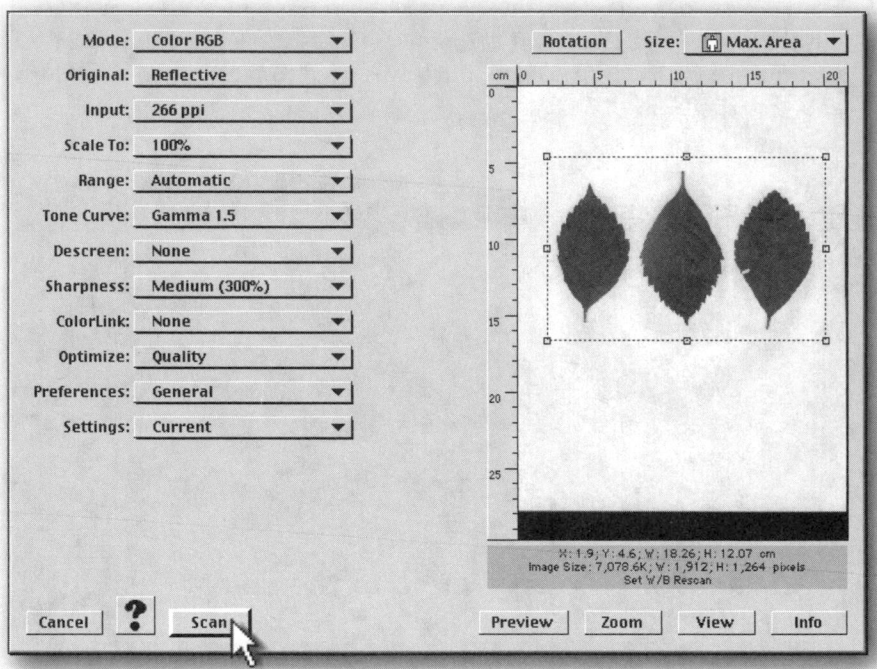

**Figure 6.26**   Make the marquee selection of the leaves equal in width to the layout you
measured.

10. Save the file as Leaves2.tif. Press Ctrl(⌘)+L to display the Levels command.

11. Choose the White Point eyedropper and then click in the image toward the
image edge where the tone should be white. As you can see in Figure 6.27,
doing this brings the white point up to paper white and brightens the
leaves. Click OK to apply the change.

12. Click on the title bar of Leaves2.psd, choose Image, Mode, and then choose
RGB color.

13. With the Rectangular Marquee tool, drag a selection around the leaves in
Leaves2.tif, and then while holding down Ctrl(⌘), drag inside the selection
marquee and drag the selection into the Leaves2.psd window, as shown in
Figure 6.28.

14. The Leaves2.psd image is the active image in the workspace, and the image
of the leaves is the top and active layer. Press 5 on the keypad to reduce the
opacity of the layer to 50%. Then, with the Move tool, drag the layer to
align the button image with its underlying layout counterpart. After the
image of the leaves is aligned with the underlying layout, press 0 (zero) on
your keypad to restore the leaves image to 100% opacity.

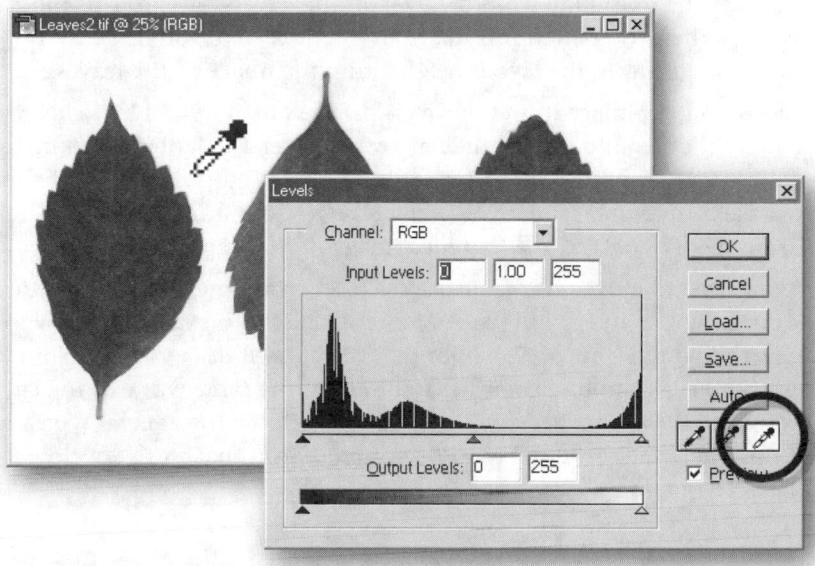

**Figure 6.27**   Set a new white point in the image by using the White Point Eyedropper tool.

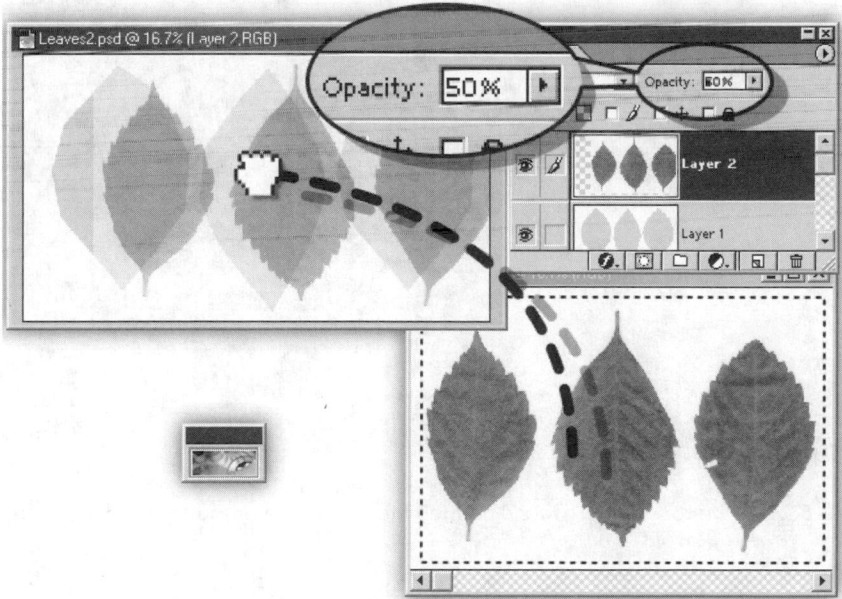

**Figure 6.28**   Hold down Ctrl(⌘) and drag the selection into the Leaves2.psd window to copy the selection. Set the opacity of the new layer to 50%.

15. Click Layer 1's visibility icon (the eye) on the Layers palette. This hides the layout. When you flatten this image in the next step, you do not want shards of gray from the layout neighboring the image of the leaves.

16. Choose Flatten Image from the Layers palette's menu flight and click OK in the attention box to discard hidden layers (Layer 1). Flattening an image reduces file size on hard disk, but it also makes it possible to save the image to a file format that can be viewed by others without owning Photoshop. TIFF is a good format for a flattened image, for example.

17. If you need to move one of the leaves closer to another, draw a selection around the leaf and use the Move tool to adjust it to exactly where you want it, as shown in Figure 6.29. Notice that the current background color is white—the background color has to be about the same white as the background of the photo. Because I knew ahead of time the general type and size of the leaves that I wanted to use, I created a scan that was very close to the actual layout.

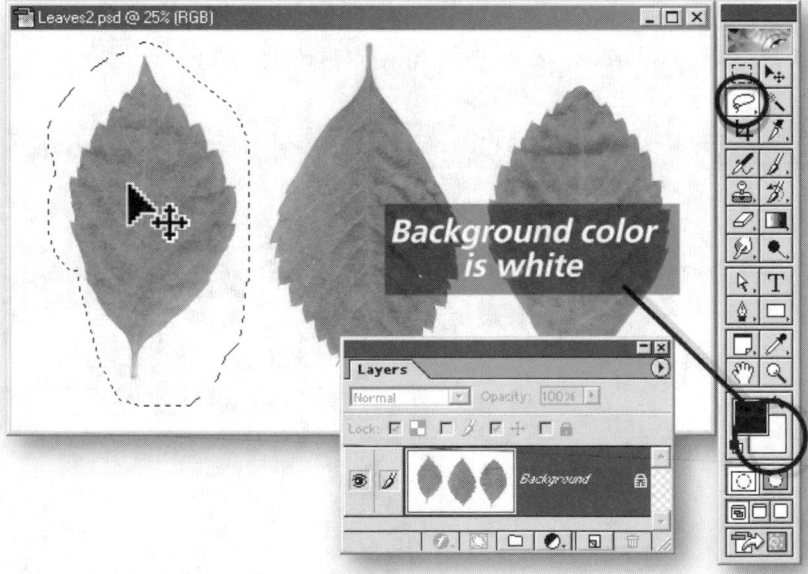

**Figure 6.29**    Draw a selection around an individual leaf if you need to move it to match the layout.

18. Choose File, Save As, and save the image as Leaves2Finished.tif, in the TIF file format. You can close both images now. You can also turn Leaves2Finished.tif over to the Production department—or a service bureau or whomever is going to finish the design—along with the layout so that they can add the text and make the finishing touches.

## Using Simplicity and Economy to Improve a Design

In Figure 6.30, you can see a third layout for the article on leaves. You'll notice that only one leaf is used against white, and that the text wraps around the outside of the leaf.

This stark but imaginative design is an eye-catcher. Best of all, you need to scan only one leaf at larger-than-life size.

In case you don't own a scanner, Leaves3.tif is in the Examples/Chap06 folder on the Companion CD and can be used with the following steps.

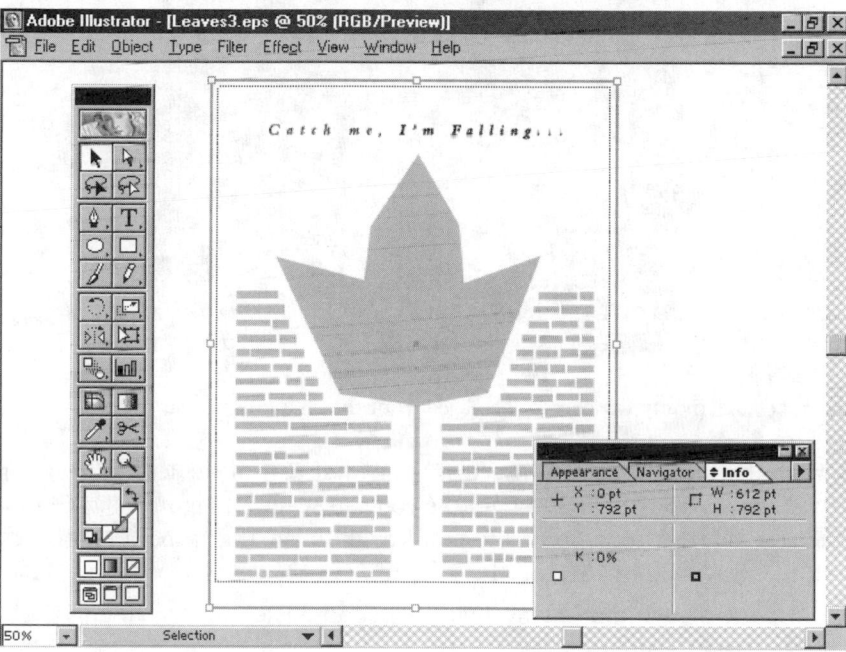

**Figure 6.30**   Good use of white space and a powerful graphic can sometimes drive the point home better than a wall-to-wall graphic.

This next example measures and scans the artwork for the third layout.

### Example 6.8   Measuring and Scanning a Single Design Element

1. Open the Leaves3.eps file from the Examples/Chap06 folder on the Companion CD. In the Rasterize Generic EPS Format dialog box, change the units to inches, type **266** in the Resolution field, specify Grayscale mode from the drop-down list, and then click OK.

2. When the EPS image appears in Photoshop, use the Crop tool to draw a selection that encompasses the leaf in the design, as shown in Figure 6.31, and press Enter (Return).

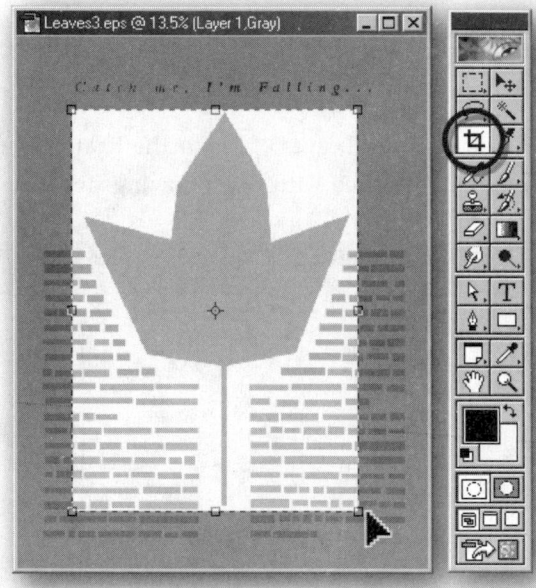

**Figure 6.31**   Keep only the part of the page layout that requires measuring.

3. With the Measure tool, drag across the widest part of the leaf, leaving some white space to the left and right. As you can see from Figure 6.32, you need to scan a leaf (with a border) to produce an image that's about 5.5" wide at 266 pixels/inch, or 1463 pixels.

4. Close the file without saving, and then choose File, Import, TWAIN_32 (Mac: Twain Acquire).

5. Place the leaf on the scanner's imaging surface, close the lid, and then use the scanner's interface features to create a marquee selection around the leaf at 450 pixels/inch to make the final size of the leaf about 1463 pixels wide, as shown in Figure 6.33. Click Scan.

6. After the scan is complete, close the scanning interface, choose Image, Image Size and adjust the ppi to 266 with the Resample Image button *off*. Save the image as Leaves3.tif, in the TIFF file format.

7. Use the same technique you used with the Leaves2 image and the Levels command to make the background of the button 100% white.

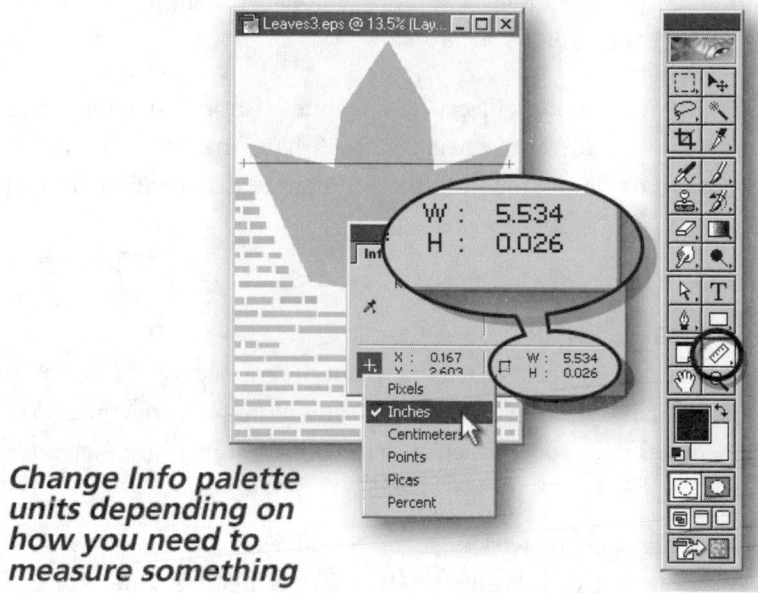

**Change Info palette units depending on how you need to measure something**

**Figure 6.32**   Your target image size for the scan of the single leaf is a little larger in width than 1463 pixels (about 5.5" at 266 ppi).

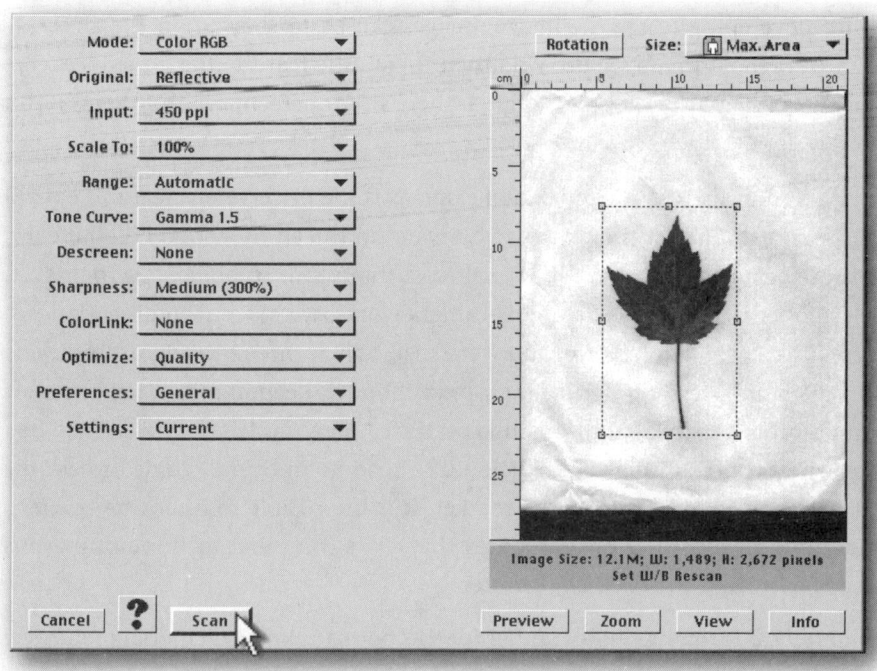

**Figure 6.33**   Leave a little white space around the leaf you scan.

**8.** Close the file, and proudly pack it off to whomever Is adding the typesetting and/or footing the bill for your work!

So you see, dumping common objects on a scanner is not a frivolous pastime. A flatbed scanner can be a lifesaver when you don't have the time for conventional photography, and most of the time you'll capture more detail with a scanner than with a camera.

## Using a Digital Camera

The filmless digital camera is not exactly new, but the number of manufacturers'has increased exponentially in the past few years. And along with new manufacturers come different makes and models, each with different features, and each with a different price tag.

There are advantages and drawbacks to be found with all digital cameras. The biggest advantage is that of immediacy; a newspaper photographer, for example, can use a digital camera to capture the moment, upload the images through a cellular modem, and the pictures are ready to be placed and printed before the photographer even gets back to the newsroom. And the photographer doesn't need to wait for developing to see the image; images can be previewed on the LCD screen that most digital camera's sport. And then there's the feature that benefits everyone on earth—because the process is digital, there's zero percent environmental impact from developing chemicals and silver.

The largest drawback to today's digital cameras is the price-versus-features equation. It is difficult to find all the features you want and need in a single digital camera, and those cameras that "have it all" can cost thousands of dollars. In the next section, we briefly explain how a digital camera works, we make recommendations on features you'd want to look for, and we take a look at three models: an inexpensive one, a medium-priced one, and a high-priced model. Keep in mind that because the information on pricing, features, and specific camera models very well may be different when you read this book, it should be read as an overall guide or baseline to what you may actually find in the market. It is impossible to offer timeless recommendations for digital cameras, an area that—like computer technology—seems to change faster than the click of a shutter.

Incidentally, our roving photographer for this book took several digital pictures with his top-of-the-line digital camera. Ed made it possible for the authors, who are spread from New York to California, to get images within the hour usually, to fit specific needs for the book. And guess what? We'll bet you that you cannot tell which images were taken conventionally and which were taken digitally. Hint: At least one of the images in the color section is a digital image.

## Understanding the Process Behind Digital Photography

You will see many odd-shaped digital cameras at stores and in mail-order catalogs. Some look like the classic "Brownie" camera, others look like a paperback book, and still others look like a science-fiction weapon of sorts. There are a couple of reasons for all the different shapes:

- The manufacturer is trying to come up with the least intrusive viewfinding system. Some digital cameras use the typical rangefinder method, some use a liquid crystal display (LCD) that's actually a tiny monitor, and the most expensive cameras offer single-lens reflex (SLR) viewing through the camera lens *and* LCD display.

- Film doesn't pass through the camera, so the notion of winding and needing spools to wind a physical medium are obsolete. Therefore, engineers can concentrate more on the cosmetic look and the ergonomic feel and balance of the digital camera.

For the most part, all digital cameras operate as the illustration in Figure 6.34 shows. There is a pipeline from images captured by the lens to images you can work with in Photoshop. The process goes like this:

1. The electronic shutter opens for a brief amount of time, and light passes through the lens system.

2. The lens focuses and organizes light to be passed onto an imaging surface consisting of hundreds of thousands (and more with expensive cameras, millions) of photo-receptors.

3. The visual information gathered passes to and is stored on some kind of fixed or removable storage media within the camera. Removable media is the most flexible and is often referred to generically as a "flash card." A clear standard for removable storage has not yet been adopted. Today's digital camera is usually designed to use only one of three current "flash card" formats. Flash cards in any of the three formats can usually be found, with capacities ranging from 4MB to 128MB. The type of flash card and capacity that can be used in any particular camera depends on the camera's design.

4. The images stored on the camera's storage media are downloaded to your computer in one of two ways:

- The quickest way to transfer the files to your computer's hard disk is to attach an internal or external card reader to your computer. The card reader and the flash card itself must, of course, be compatible with one another, and card readers normally read only one kind of card.

- The second, more conventional method is through an "umbilical cord," a cable that connects the camera to a serial, USB, or parallel port on the PC, and through which information is transferred from the flash card to the system's hard drive. This method is slower than a direct "dump" from a flash card.

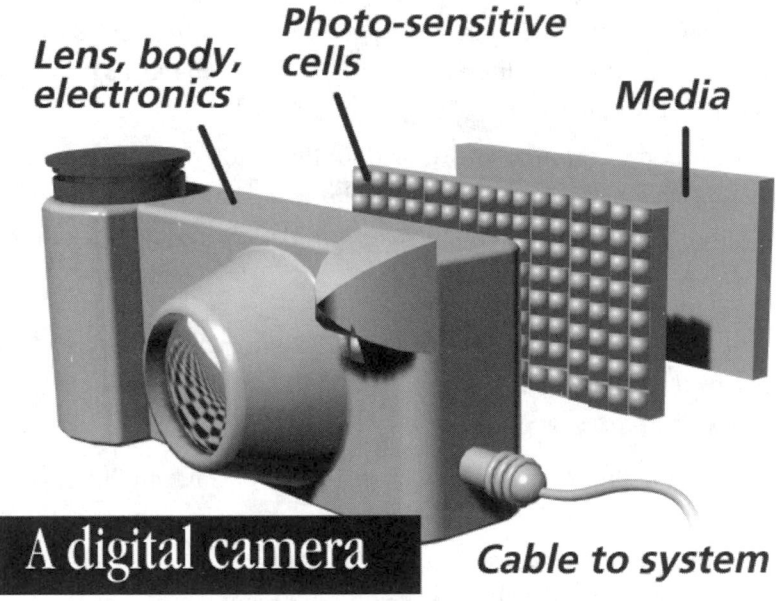

**Figure 6.34**    From lens to imaging surface to storage, the digital camera takes and saves pictures without using chemicals.

Camera manufacturers are working on a variety of other transfer methods to make the process faster and easier to use. Some methods being worked on are infrared transfer and transfer via the floppy disk controller.

Several factors will influence your decision to invest in a digital camera, and the following sections take a look at the details.

## Choosing a Digital Camera

Today's digital camera is both like and unlike a traditional film camera. If you're a professional photographer, you should know in advance that you'll be handling a digital camera a little differently, unless you spring for the top-of-the-line model. Here are the features you should consider before you plunk down serious cash for a digital camera.

### Film Speed

Traditionally, the speed of film—its ISO number—determines the depth of field (f-stop) you can use, and the amount of light necessary to take a picture. Surprise; the digital camera doesn't use film, so ISO *equivalencies* have to be built into the camera itself. In other words, the success with which you take an indoor picture depends a great deal on the camera's ISO capability and whether you need a flash to take the picture.

On the inexpensive end of digital cameras, the authors have seen an ISO as low as 100, equivalent to ISO 100 film in a traditional camera. This 100 ISO means that your best pictures can be taken outdoors on a very sunny day, without the need for a flash. On the high end of the digital camera market, some cameras offer a flexible ISO that can be specified from 200 to 1,600.

In general, if you can find a camera whose ISO is at least 400, then you can take pictures indoors without a flash.

### The Lens System

The optics of almost all digital cameras provide good, sharp images, but the real difference in the price you pay among models lies in the flexibility of the lens system.

In the early models of digital cameras, most models under $1,000 offered a fixed lens system with automatic exposure control. A fixed lens system means that the camera is essentially "point and shoot"; you cannot zoom in, you cannot change the focus of the lens from foreground to midground, and your creative adventures with the camera are artistically hampered due to the fixed lens. Not all Photoshop users are professional photographers, however, and if you simply want to get a waist-up image of a person, a landscape, or a picture with loose framing of the gang, a fixed lens system is an adequate solution. Fixed lens systems essentially have an f-stop of about 1.5 feet to infinity, and you must be a minimum distance from your subject to get a focused image.

Even with the low-priced digital camera today, you will find auto-focus, auto-exposure cameras that provide more flexibility in your work. These lens systems are more akin to the $300+ priced 35mm film cameras that are popular with travelers today, and provide good focus and acceptable distances from your subject.

More expensive are the 3x and 10x zoom lenses on digital cameras. These offer greater creative control because you can set the framing (the distance) through the lens. On the high end of digital cameras (you'll read of one later in this chapter), the lens system is identical to that of an SLR film camera. You can focus automatically or manually, you have zoom and macro options, you can exchange lenses, and you can set the f-stop.

### Types of Compression and the Storage Card

If you're planning an all-day outing, it is wise to invest in several cards that fit your model of digital camera. Like film, it's a bummer to run out of memory in your camera just when that once-in-a-lifetime sunset comes by.

Memory capacity has two trade-offs: the size of the picture you're storing, and what sort of compression, if any, the camera system uses. JPEG is a popular compression format for photographic images, and many digital cameras, both cheap and expensive, sometimes offer on-the-fly JPEG compression of your work to enable you to store either larger images or more images. The author does not recommend JPEG compression, especially with your one-and-only image because JPEG is *lossy* compression—some visual information is averaged (discarded) during the compression process.

The authors recommend that you buy a camera that *doesn't* offer a JPEG subsystem (or one whose JPEG capability can be turned off), and to find a model with the features you want plus the capability to take storage cards with large storage capacity.

### Amount of Samples

Because a digital camera operates with memory as storage, there is another trade-off to be made when you are purchasing a camera. Some less expensive cameras take 640×480 pixel images. And the card can hold a lot of them. But a 640×480 image is only 900KB; you do get a full-screen image on a monitor running 640×480, but consider the size when printed. An Epson Stylus color inkjet printer, for example, can write about 700 dots per inch, and can optimally take an image that is about 150 pixels per inch. The author's done the math for you here: A 640×480 pixel image can be optimally printed from an Epson at 4" by 3"—a little small for framing on the wall!

The next step up in expense as well as image quality are cameras that can take 1024×768 pixel images, which is equivalent to a 2.2MB file, or approximately a 5" by 7" image when printed to a 700 dpi printer. This resolution would be good for a postcard-sized image to mail to friends, but you'd need a camera that can capture at least a 4.5MB file to fill an inkjet printer page with adequate resolution, and that will cost a lot more.

The authors advise you to choose the highest-resolution camera you can afford. What with the way digital camera technology has advanced, you can buy a camera that has the capability to capture images that are 2048×1536, but be sure to invest in several storage cards to pack along on your trips. Using multiple storage cards is much easier and safer than lugging a laptop around with you on a photographic session.

## Summary

What digital acquisition means to the Photoshop user is the capability to bring the real world into the computer for manipulation. As with anything, the trade-off we as designers must all face is quality versus price. If you have no negatives to work with in your profession, a flatbed scanner is a must. You've also seen in this chapter how you can do creative things by direct-scanning with a reflective scanner. If your budget is tight and you have a little wait time, PhotoCD technology offers crisp, small to large images at a pittance of a price per image, and PhotoCDs keep the large number of images you'll take in your career out of precious hard disk space. For the demanding traditional photographer, a transparency scanner fits the bill. You can scan transparencies to any resolution you like, and you get better quality pictures than PhotoCDs, and in less time. If you need real-world photography at a moment's notice for Web work or personal reasons, you can easily afford one of the less expensive models of digital cameras. On the opposite end of the spectrum, the high-end digital cameras provide absolute photographic quality compared to conventional film cameras, and we strongly suspect that if your profession demands a megacamera, hopefully you work for a large company, and *they* will buy one for you to use!

# Chapter 7

# Outputting Your Photoshop Work

What I've written here is a lecture cleverly disguised as a reference guide, which is cleverly disguised as a chapter—specifically, as a chapter on output.

We tend to use the term "output" these days because hard copy isn't necessarily rendered to paper. You can print to film, to glossy paper, T-shirt transfers—there are oodles of ways you can get an image off your monitor and onto something in the physical world.

Throughout this chapter I'm going to hand you tools in the guise of math formulas and nuggets of information that will

- Give you the confidence that your printing skills are top-notch.
- Give you the straight story on many of the parameters surrounding the action of output, rather than some of the myths that give you headaches and cause your work to look crummy.

Let's begin with a simple term that you will hear more and more often as you gain experience not only with personal printing, but also with commercial printing. The term is "interpolation."

## Interpolation Means "Interpretation"

"Interpolation" is such a neat-sounding word, isn't it? Many of us have a vague notion (within context) of what interpolation means, but you need to understand *precisely* what it means when the action is performed on your work.

*Interpolation,* in computer graphics is an application's *interpretation* of what something should look like, especially when the software does not have sufficient data to carry our your request. Interpolation is always an *averaging* process of some kind. Say, for example, that you have a color image that is 4 pixels wide and 4 pixels high, and you want the image to be four times this size: 8 pixels by 8 pixels.

There isn't a program on earth that can create the new image with the sensitivity and talent of an artist. The reason is obvious: computers have neither talent nor intuition—these are human qualities. This is why you run the computer, and not the other way around!

When you want to resize an image up or down, Photoshop searches for data to help support the application's decision about what the resized image will look like. It is you who determines how extensively Photoshop uses interpretation—how much Photoshop searches to come up with new data for the image.

## Bicubic Interpolation

*Bicubic interpolation* is the most sophisticated and elegant of Photoshop's resizing methods. It also requires the most processing power. In the year 2001, however, you probably would not notice even the slightest lag while Photoshop interpolates because our computers are so powerful. The image shown in Figure 7.1 is 4 pixels high and 4 pixels wide (outstanding art it's not), with two horizontal and two vertical pixels that contain a color. I've drawn imaginary grids on the right side of Figures 7.1 and 7.2 to help you visualize what's going on here.

The images at the bottom of Figure 7.1 show what you can expect from Photoshop when you command it to use bicubic interpolation (the default interpolation method) to make this artwork 8 pixels wide by 8 pixels high.

By looking at Figure 7.1 you can draw two conclusions about bicubic interpolation:

- The resizing of the art makes the component pixels in the new image show the visual content as being a tad fuzzy.

- Photoshop makes a smooth transition between background color and foreground color in this example. This effect is particularly important when you work with images whose *pixel count* (the number of pixels in the image) is far greater than the pathetic 16-pixel total we are looking at here.

Okay, so how did Photoshop come up with the intermediate pixels and pixel colors to fill in the gap caused by resizing the neighboring pixels? The term *bicubic* here means that Photoshop looked in all directions—horizontal, vertical, and diagonal— beginning with each pixel and then scouting outward. The new pixels are an *average* of the original pixel color, and the original pixel's *neighboring* pixel color. Photoshop performs a weighted average of the pixel and its neighbors along three directions and fits the new pixel between the original pixel and its neighbor.

Artistically speaking, you probably want to use bicubic interpolation all the time, whether you're increasing or decreasing an entire image or just a selection. When an image is resized so that it's smaller—for display on a Web page, perhaps—bicubic interpolation also makes the new image somewhat fuzzy. This happens because you're commanding Photoshop to toss away pixels from the original artwork, and Photoshop must reassign the remaining pixels an average of the original colors at any given point. And this ain't easy because, again, machines and applications are poor at guessing. They do the next best thing, which is called *averaging* <g>!

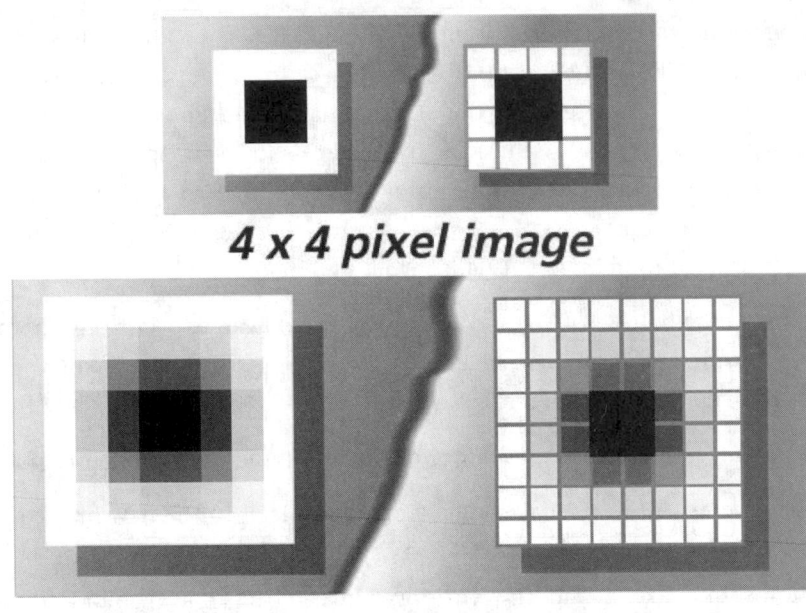

**4 x 4 pixel image**

**bicubic interpolation to 8 x 8**

**Figure 7.1**  By default, Photoshop uses bicubic interpolation to resize an image or an image area.

## Bilinear Interpolation

*Bilinear interpolation*, in contrast to bicubic, only scouts across the horizontal and the vertical grid of a pixel painting to arrive at new colors, and although bilinear interpolation performs averaging, it is not what math-type folks call *weighted* averaging, and the results (or lack of results) are visible.

Bilinear interpolation can be conducted on Photoshop images that you want to make larger or smaller. I would not recommend this process, however, unless you own a Mac Centra or a 386-class PC running on 16MB of RAM! Seriously, bilinear interpolation is less processor-intensive than bicubic because it does less examination of all the pixels in an image before it creates or deletes pixels as a result of averaging calculations.

The result of bilinear averaging (as shown in Figure 7.2—peek ahead) might not be obvious with very small images, as my famous 8-by-8-pixel artwork demonstrates. The new pixels and/or new pixel colors in an image on which you've used bilinear interpolation will not be as faithful to the original image as if the bicubic method was used, however, because you commanded Photoshop to perform a decent but not thorough investigation to come up with data to be averaged.

Qualitatively, you have no reason to change this interpolation preference in the General Preferences dialog box. Many applications do not even offer the option of bicubic interpolation.

**Note**

**Use Sharpening to Correct Any Fuzziness** You should make it standard operating procedure (SOP) that whenever you make a dramatic change in the number of pixels in an image, a trip to Photoshop's Sharpen filters is the smartest course of action. You can use a Sharpen command not only to fake restoring the focus of a large image made smaller through interpolation, but also to repair some of the focus to a small image that has been made much larger.

I recommend the Unsharp Mask filter at all times, except when you're creating a button or an icon for a Web page—when a 400 by 400–pixel image, for example, is reduced to 32 by 32 pixels. In this case, the Filter, Sharpen, Sharpen command produces an image that's a little exaggerated around the edges but that effectively communicates your artwork at a very small size.

## Nearest Neighbor Interpolation

*Nearest Neighbor interpolation* is the crudest, quickest way to shrink or enlarge an image. When you apply this method to an image, it rightfully earns the name *"no* interpolation" because the visual results are so wildly inaccurate. Nearest Neighbor interpolation might only be of some use when you are increasing the size of an image by an exact, whole amount, such as 4 times or 16 times an original's size. Because pixels are square, when you increase the height of an image by 2, you are also increasing the width by 2, and therefore twice the resolution of an image file means 4 times its original size.

Can you see now that the Nearest Neighbor method performs no calculations or averaging, but merely repeats the pixel color at the edge of the original? This can lead to really ugly and inaccurate work, especially if you are increasing the size of an image by a fractional amount or an amount that lies between two whole integers. In Figure 7.2, I increased the size of my famous 16-pixel artwork from 4 by 4 pixels to 6 by 6. As you can see, the deck was stacked: There is a 100% chance that Nearest Neighbor resampling will return an image area that is incorrect in size when a number such as 150% the original size is applied to the image. The "magic numbers" to use with Nearest Neighbor resampling are 4x, 16x, and multiples thereof.

I've spent a good deal of time running down the types of interpolation Photoshop offers, not because I want you to change your preferences, but because I want you to understand the visual results of interpolation. Photoshop is not the only thing on earth that uses interpolation—imagesetting devices (printers) and film recorders use averaging processes, too, and your hard copy of an image can be nicely or ineptly rendered. Now that you understand the difference between methods, you have an important question to ask a service bureau (or tech support) that you did *not* have when you began this chapter.

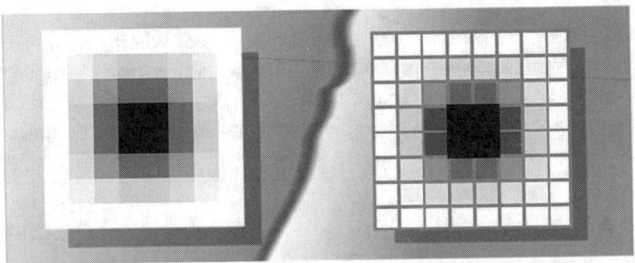

*bilinear interpolation to 8 x 8*

*Nearest Neighbor: 4x4 to 6x6 to 8x8*

**Figure 7.2**   Nearest Neighbor evaluation of an image to be shrunk or enlarged will usually create uneven, inaccurate image areas.

# Going from Continuous Tones to Halftones

Contrary to what the name might suggest, a halftone is *not* 50% of a tone! Halftones are the life blood of commercial printers, and are the only way you can get a continuous tone representation on paper. Continuous tones versus halftones merit a brief explanation, and then this section will get into the types of halftones that are at the designer's disposal.

## What's the Difference Between Continuous Tones and Halftones?

When you look at the world, and there's a sunset with a rock in the vicinity, you'll see a subtle, *continuous*, falloff of light on the rock. There's no sudden, jarring area of tone missing, as the light gradually changes on the rock's surface. This is a continuous tone image, because Nature has every color with which to display images as the sun emits a spectrum and as your eyes are equipped to receive the parts of the spectrum that depict the rock's tones.

On the other hand, a *halftone* consists of precisely *two* colors—not exactly our sunset scene! A halftone consists of an arrangement of dots (the foreground color, usually made up of black toner), against the paper (background) color. So how do you capture photographic qualities when your output is to a laser printer? You *simulate* continuous tones, which is done by the software instructing the printer to place dots of toner at different spatial intervals on the paper.

In Figure 7.3 I've created an exaggerated example so you can see what a halftone sample looks like compared to a continuous tone that traverses the page from black to white.

The pattern you see in the halftone in Figure 7.3 is an exaggeration of what anyone would expect from a laser printer. I think the resolution of the halftone is something like 15 lines per inch—a resolution so coarse you could drive your new car through there and not touch the paint.

We'll get into the mystical term "resolution" shortly, and demystify it. Next, though, let's take a look at how digital halftone cells help the accuracy with which a halftone image represents reality.

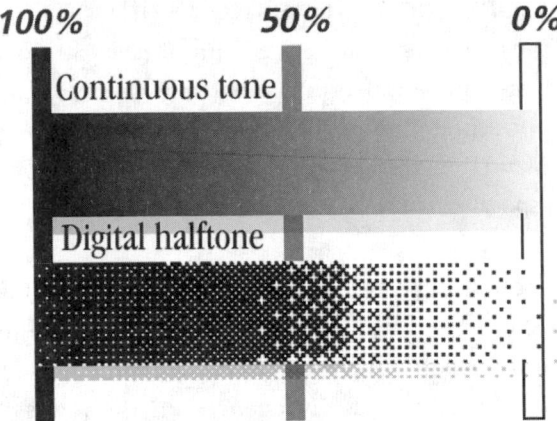

**Figure 7.3**  A continuous tone image makes seamless transitions between light and dark. Halftone images must rely on the density of toner dots at any given area to simulate a continuous tone.

## The Digital Halftone Cell

When you learn about halftoning, it is helpful to imagine a grid placed above your original, continuous tone work. This imaginary grid helps define every inch of the image in terms of density. Suppose, for example, that you have a photo of an ice-cream cone against a white background. Slip a screen from a window or a door on top of the photo, and you will see something interesting happen. Pick a cell in the screen; pick anyone. Then take a look at the tone of the photo that is framed by the cell in the screen window.

If the tone is 50% black, what Photoshop and your printer would do is fill half an invisible, corresponding, digital screen on top of the printed page with toner that occupies 50% of the cell.

Now here's where it gets weird for a moment. In traditional printing, commercial printers have historically put a physical film screen over a photograph to make a halftoned copy. The halftones are round (usually) and each halftone dot is confined to a predetermined cell in a line of halftone dots. In Figure 7.4 you can see a digital halftone cell compared to a traditional halftone. Digital halftone cells contain square (or rectangular) dots of toner, but in this figure you can see, in principle, how digital halftone cells closely mimic traditional coverage on a piece of paper or film. At the bottom of this figure you can see the specific coverage amounts.

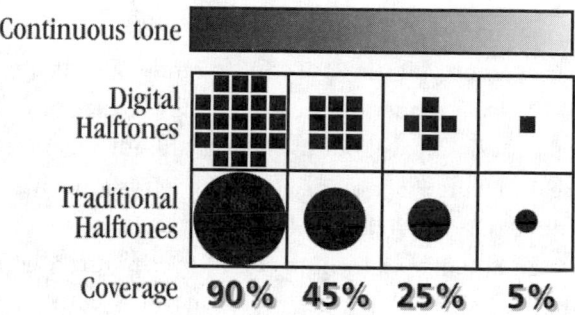

**Figure 7.4** Digital halftone cells are filled with a given number of dots that, viewed together (from a distance!), represent a specific tone.

In the following section, we'll get into PostScript technology and how it affects printing. The reason for the excursion into the PostScript world is that, among other things:

- PostScript technology is the only real method of organizing toner dots (or emulsion on film) so that they truly mimic traditional, physical halftone screens.

- Because PostScript technology extends beyond merely organizing dots and into pre-press, there are math formulas that you really should know about (I'll do the pencil work for you in this chapter) and refer to if you ever want to make your own camera-ready art from a personal printer for commercial, ink-on-paper printing.

## PostScript and Image Resolution

It's almost impossible to talk about PostScript rendering of images without talking about image resolution. Many readers have written to me in past years asking me what the input should be for a particular image, and I always have to respond with a question: What is your intended *output* for the file? It makes very little sense to choose an input resolution without first knowing whether the image is going to press, going up on the fridge, or going across the World Wide Web. Let's take a brief look at PostScript technology, and then get involved with *resolution*—both its meaning and how to calculate it.

## PostScript as a Halftone Dot Shaper

What you can expect when you use PostScript to render a continuous tone image is the most faithful halftone renderings possible today. Other printing technologies put different-sized dots on a page, but those dots are not organized in screen lines that pressmen use. In Figure 7.5, the image on the left is a (nearly <g>) continuous tone image of a duck. On the right is a PostScript halftone rendering of the same image. I've only used 30 dots per inch on the PostScript duck, which is a foolishly low resolution, but it helps display the individual dots better. Can you see how every tone on the duck on the left has a corresponding-size dot, and that, together, these dots represent the continuous tones?

**Figure 7.5**  A continuous tone image compared to a PostScript rendition of the same image.

It was not long after the invention of the traditional, physical halftone screen that the publishing world yearned for a little more flexibility in *how* a halftone is rendered. Does a single halftone always have to be circular? When a screen is applied to a continuous tone image at an angle other than right angles, what do you wind up with?

To answer these questions, take a look at Figure 7.6. Elliptical dots are being used to fill the digital halftone cells, and the screen created by Photoshop is at a 45° angle.

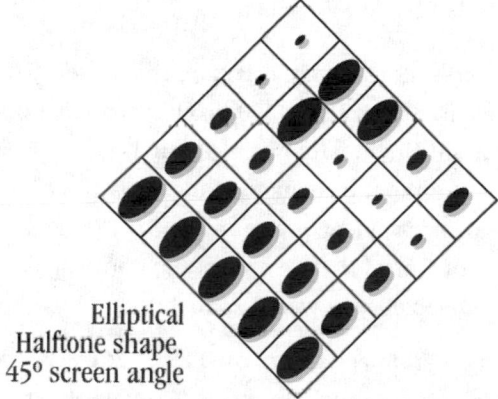

Elliptical
Halftone shape,
45° screen angle

**Figure 7.6**  Photoshop offers six different shaped halftone dots, one of which is elliptical, plus a custom function, plus any angle for the screen you choose.

It would help to squint at Figure 7.6 to get a better idea of how stylized a halftone print can be when you use halftone dots that are not circular. We'll be getting into Photoshop's print options later in this chapter. There are many interrelated factors that determine the best halftone print of your work. I'll try to cover them all in the least confusing way.

The first factor in image rendering is called *resolution*. Resolution determines how much detail is visible in your print, and also can tell you how many samples per inch you should set your scanner for.

## Image Resolution Is a Fraction

Several accurate analogies can help you understand the term "resolution" as it applies to computer graphics. I've chosen speed, specifically the speed of a car, as an analogy.

When you measure the speed of a car, it is conveyed in one set of units over a *different* set of units, such as 55 miles (a unit of distance) per hour (a unit of time). Image resolution is expressed similarly: Resolution can be defined as units of data over units of distance. When someone tells you that an image is 2" by 2" at 150 pixels/inch, they are expressing the number of pixels in an inch; this is the resolution of the image.

On the other hand, and unfortunately this happens all too frequently, if someone tells you that an image is 200 pixels by 200 pixels, they have not told you the resolution of the image at all! How many pixels per inch is this 200-pixel by 200-pixel artwork? A *pixel* (short for picture element) is merely a placeholder, an entity of no fixed size that holds a color value. For example, Red: 128, Green: 214, and Blue: 78 is the best description of a pixel that anyone could come up with. Resolution is the expression of how *many* pixels you want per inch.

If someone tells you that an image is supposed to be 2" by 2", you need to ask them what the resolution is, to create such an image. Conversely, if you are told that the resolution of an image is 300 ppi, you'd best ask this person for the physical dimensions of the image, as expressed in inches, picas, centimeters, and so on.

Let's take a stroll through the interface of a scanner and put all these nuggets of advice in order!

**Note**

**An Image Expressed Only in the Number of Pixels It Contains Is an Absolute Amount**   You learned in the preceding Note that resolution is somewhat flexible— you can decrease dimensions, increase resolution, and the number of pixels will remain the same. A good way to measure images destined for the Web or other screen presentations is by the number of pixels in the image. For example, a 640×480 screen capture will always contain 307,200 pixels, regardless of which monitor it is displayed on.

## Scanning to the Right Size

I have a fictitious assignment here that involves scanning a piece of wood to 8½" by 11" with ¼" trim around each side (so I need 9" by 11½" scanned). As I mentioned in the previous section, a pixel is a placeholder that only takes up space after you have entered it as the numerator of the resolution fraction.

I'll explain the highlighted numbers in Figure 7.7 shortly. What you're looking at is the TWAIN interface (a "corridor" between scanning hardware and imaging software—Photoshop) with a piece of wood imaged in the figure as a preview of what I'm going to scan.

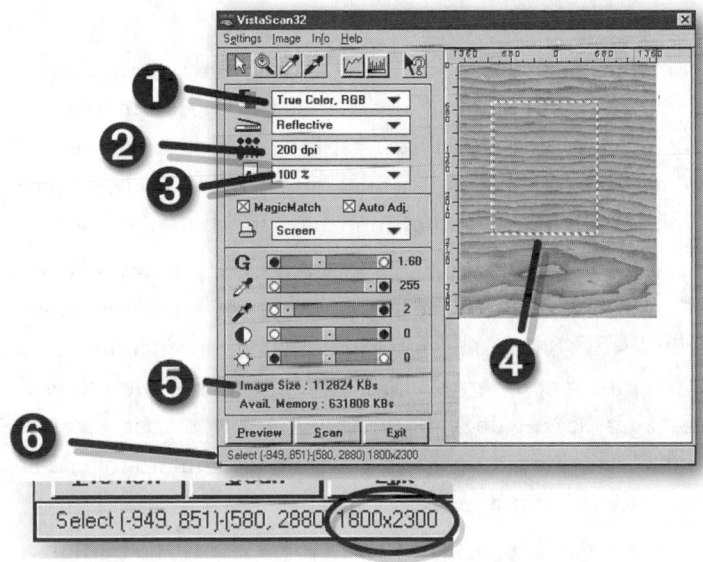

**Figure 7.7**  Your scanner's interface might not look like this one, but you will find the same options on most models.

Let's begin examining this scanner interface based on my need for a 9" by 11½" scan of some wood. First question, right? "At what resolution do you need the scan?"

I need the scan to be at 200 pixels per inch because my inkjet printer's resolution is 600 dots of ink per inch, and the guy at Epson told me that I should scan at one-third the final output resolution. This number is not carved in stone, but typically, for non-PostScript inkjet printers that use error diffusion as a rendering technique (which is impossible to quantify because the dots of ink are not arranged in rows), one-third the output should be your scanning input.

Now for those explanations of the callouts in Figure 7.7:

1. Color mode. This should seem familiar; you see a Mode drop-down list every time you press Ctrl(⌘)+N in Photoshop. I've chosen RGB color here; however, there will be times when you want to scan in Grayscale, and most scanners offer this option.

2. Resolution. I want to get into a quarrel with scanner manufacturers, because they label the resolution in *dpi* (dots per inch). And scanners are actually scanning *samples* per inch (or *pixels* per inch). A dot is *not* a pixel. I've set the resolution to 200 because my final output to my ancient inkjet printer is 600 dpi. Many modern printers now have much higher resolutions.

3. Scale. Most scanners will allow you to zoom in on whatever is on the scanner's platen. Because I have a large sample of wood here, I want the scan to be only 1 to 1 (100%). But if, for example, you wanted to scan a postage stamp and print it at 8½" by 11", you'd use the scale option to really zoom into the stamp. Scaling does affect resolution. If you scale a scan at 200%, for example, you are scanning four times the information you'd be scanning at 100% (twice the width, twice the height).

4. The cropping area. Scanners enable you to pick only the portion of the sampled object you want. My scanner (this is not shown in the figure) will tell me in pixels or in inches how large my crop box is. Generally, you choose the interface's cropping tool, and then drag to select the part of the image you want scanned. Most scanners also come with rulers in the preview window, so guesswork is not necessary.

5. Image Size. This feature tells you how much RAM will be required to hold and acquire the image, and is also a good indicator of the saved file size. You'll note in this figure that the image size is about 11MB. This means that to scan from within Photoshop, I must have at least this amount (ideally about three times the amount) of RAM available and an equal amount of

scratch disk space. Do not start a scanning session if your system resources are low—both Macintosh and Windows have resource meters that keep you posted on such matters. Scanning is so processor-intensive, it makes downloading files look like a picnic.

6. Absolute measurement. As described earlier, the height and width of an image as measured in pixels is an incomplete description. I've got 1,800 pixels in width by 2,300 pixels in height marqueed in the preview window. What makes these numbers meaningful is that I'm scanning at 200 samples/inch: 1,800/200 = 9 (inches), and 2,300/200 = 11.5 (inches).

**Note**

**Grayscale Mode Images Are 1/3 the Saved File Size of RGB Images**  The reason for this is that RGB images have three channels of image information, whereas grayscale images only have one channel (brightness).

End of story! You hit the scan button, and in moments you can save the image, which is perfectly proportioned, to hard disk and then print it later.

There are a few scanning issues I've overlooked in this section, such as interface options for contrast gamma control, saturation, and so on. My belief is to always "get it right in the camera" so your Photoshop correction work is not prolonged, but I've honestly never seen a scanner preview that was good enough to evaluate corrections you might make, using the interface controls. If an image looks halfway decent in preview, I scan, and then use Photoshop's features to make the image perfect.

We need to put the world of resolution and the world of PostScript together now, so you have some sort of guide to refer to when your scanner isn't my scanner, and your output device is not mine, either!

## The Input/Output Chart

I've put together in Figure 7.8 a table that includes a short list of scanning resolutions, the resolution of the printed work, and the expected file size of an acquired image. All these values presume that you are using PostScript technology—non-PostScript rendering technology is very difficult to measure, because non-PostScript printing does not follow any of the rules of traditional screening.

## Various Output and Input Resolutions

For a 4" by 6" image at 1:1 sampling versus printing resolution

| Resolution of Printed Work | Lines per Inch Output Device Uses | Recommended Scanning Resolution | File Size |
|---|---|---|---|
| 300 dpi | 45 lpi | 90 to100 samples/inch | 570 KB |
| 600 dpi | 85 lpi | 170 samples/inch | 1.99 MB |
| 1200 dpi | 125 lpi | 225 samples/inch | 3.48 MB |
| 2450 dpi | 133 lpi | 266 samples/inch | 4.86 MB |

**Figure 7.8**   Choose the printer resolution that most closely matches your printer, and you can see how large you should scan, and what the line screen frequency is.

When rules in science are followed, the results are totally predictable. The same is true of PostScript technology—there are rules, and the next section presents you with the math you need to create the best camera-ready prints.

## A Whole Bunch of Printing Math

Before you even consider making your own camera-ready prints, you should pay a call to the fellows who are going to make the printing plates, and ask the following questions:

- What is the line screen frequency and angle?

- What are the topmost and bottommost tones your presses can hold?

In Figure 7.9 you can see the "times 2" rule. Commercial press houses do not measure the resolution of a halftoned image in dots. Images are measured in *lines* of dots, and the expression *lpi* (lines per inch) is relevant to your work.

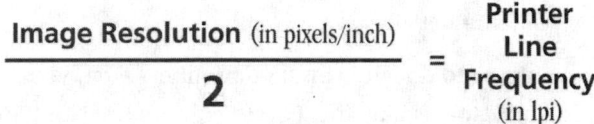

$$\frac{\text{Image Resolution (in pixels/inch)}}{2} = \text{Printer Line Frequency (in lpi)}$$

**Figure 7.9**   Your image's resolution has to be twice the print house's line screen frequency.

If a press house tells you that its line screen frequency is 100 lpi, then according to the formula in Figure 7.9, you need to scan an image (or modify the resolution, using Photoshop's Image, Image Size command) at 200 samples (pixels) per inch. When you do this, your halftoned image will be optimal.

Now, toner dots from a laser printer are fused to the paper; the page is instantly dry. Such is not the case with offset printing, where *ink* is rolled onto paper. Ink bleeds, and very few press houses can hold a screen that contains 100% black. The area on the printed page would be a puddle of ink. On the bright side, there is a screen limit to the lowest density of the screen (the white point). Because 100% white has to meet the next darker value, the closer you keep the white point to your second brightest tone, the more even the print will look, which leads us to Figure 7.10.

## How do you calculate lightest and darkest halftone areas?

**256 - [Halftone Density (in percent) x 2.56] =**

Brightness value

**Figure 7.10**   Print presses are wet, and laser prints are dry. Somehow, you need to change the tonal scheme of a print so that the print house's presses don't lay a puddle of ink on your work.

When you've got your image balanced to your liking, make a copy of it, and perform some tone reduction so the press house can make plates from your work. Let's say that the pressman tells you that the presses can hold 10% (90% black) and 97% (3% white) on the top end of the tonal range.

Let's plug these values into the equation in Figure 7.10:

$$256 - [90 \times 2.56] = 230.4 = \mathbf{25.6}$$

Great. What are you going to do with this 25.6 number? First, you're going to press Ctrl(⌘)+L in Photoshop to display the Levels command. Now, do you see the Output Levels area at the bottom? You type **25.6** in the left field.

Similarly:

$$256 - [3 \times 2.56] = 7.68 = \mathbf{248.32}$$

This is the number you type in the right Output Levels field. Click OK, save the image, print a copy, and cart it off to the print house.

Now, there is a trade-off between the number of shades of gray that a laser printer can simulate and the line frequency of the print. This equation might not be of value in your work with a commercial printer, but it does serve as an introduction for personal printing—how to optimize that image you're going to send.

## Lines per Inch Versus Shades of Black

This section header sounds like a weird football game, doesn't it? Actually, you can do some fun stuff, and bring certain images up to print house specs if you understand the relationship between line screen frequency and the number of tones a printer can simulate, using digital halftone cells.

In Figure 7.11 you can see the equation for determining shades of black at a given line screen frequency. We'll plug some numbers into the equation shortly.

Sometimes, you might want a special effect to enhance the visual content of a print. If you reduce the lines per inch the printer produces, you not only can get this effect, but also increase the number of shades the printer is capable of producing. You're not changing the resolution of the printer; you're simply playing with the input.

**How many shades of gray can your printer simulate?**

$$\frac{\text{Printer Resolution (in dpi)}}{\text{Printer Line Frequency (in lpi)}} = n^2 = \text{shades of gray}$$

**Figure 7.11**   You can change the number of grayscale values if you are willing to sacrifice image resolution.

Let's say your printer is capable of 600 dpi; a PostScript printer will output about 85 lines per inch. So let's plug these numbers into the equation:

600 (dpi)/85 (lpi) = 7.06 (squared) = 49 unique shades

Now, 49 unique shades of black will probably not get you where you're going. Most grayscale images have almost 200 unique tones. Let's try lowering the line screen to 45 lpi (not a very high lpi resolution, but it's generally acceptable):

600 (dpi)/45 (lpi) = 13.33 (squared) = 196

Whoa! Not bad! There will be practically no banding when you represent a continuous tone image at 45 lines per inch.

Hey, how else can you make personal "tack'em on the corkboard" prints look super-special with limited resolution and money?

## PCL Printing and Error Diffusion

Although the demands of PostScript printing are higher than those of non-PostScript printing, it would be nuts to ignore the alternatives to PostScript printing.

Hewlett-Packard has a very decent Resolution Enhancement Technology that belongs to the PCL (Printer Command Language) family of rendering methods. Every printer manufacturer has a different technology, but HP seems to hold the lead on high-fidelity, non-PostScript rendering.

In Figure 7.12, the duck on the left was done using HP printing technology at 30 dpi, just to make the rendering technique visible to the eye. The results of the technology are not as elegant as PostScript printing, but the duck definitely has halftone shades across its body. The halftones are not really good enough to make a press screen from, but again, these prints are for you and your family and not for the world.

On the right of Figure 7.12 is a duck rendered by using error-diffusion printing. Error-diffusion printing can be done from several applications other than Photoshop, or you can turn an image into an error-diffusion print by using Photoshop's Image, Mode, Bitmap—and then printing it as a normal image. Error-diffusion printing makes a soft, pleasing image using non-PostScript technology, but you absolutely *cannot* take one of these prints to a print house without getting laughed out the door! Error-diffusion prints are not rendered in lines, and they have no regard for digital halftone cells.

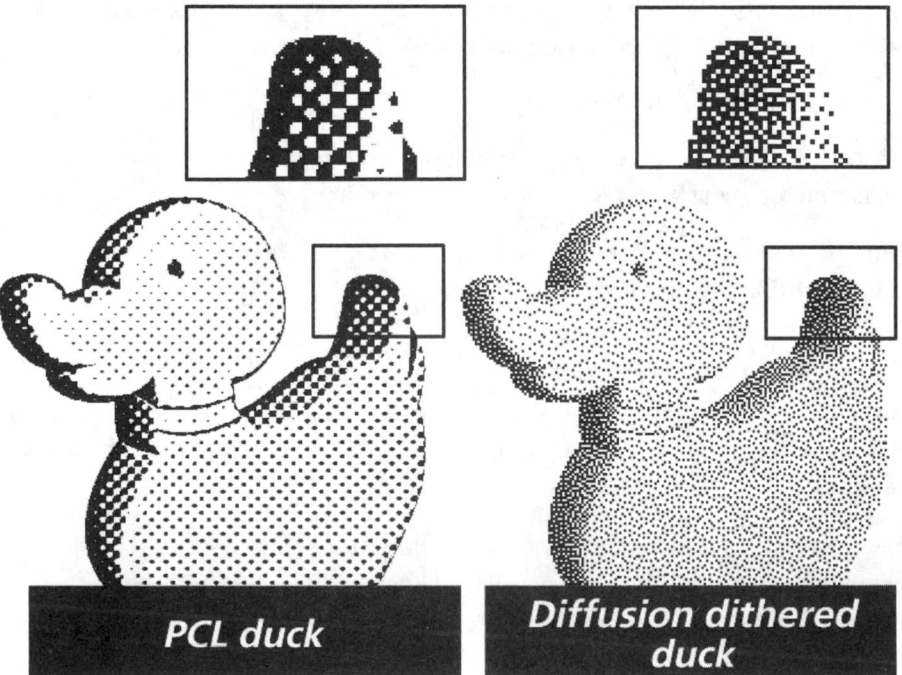

**Figure 7.12**    Printer Command Language and error-diffusion printing are only two of the non-PostScript methods for making an interesting personal print.

## Mezzotints

A line of digital halftone cells is not the only way to represent continuous tones. Mezzotinting is not as refined a printing process as PostScript, and a mezzotint image is usually highly stylized—your attention can be torn between the visual content of the image and the way the print is executed, using lines, dots, and "worms" (more on this in a moment).

There's one newspaper in the United States that refuses to use halftoned photographs of anyone—pictures of financial moguls are done by using a mezzotint screen. Figure 7.13 is a cold-hearted parody of the newspaper, using a line-type mezzotint. As you can see, the screening process is quite visible, but you can make out the face of the gentleman, and the combination of the mezzotint and the visual content is quite aesthetically pleasing.

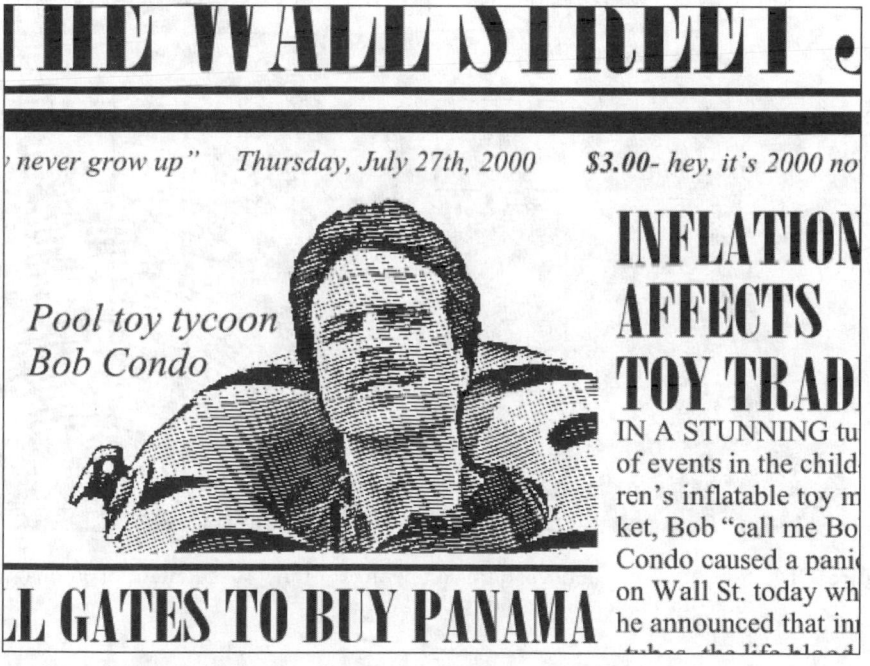

**Figure 7.13**  Inflation actually has a positive effect on most pool toys.

*Stochastic* (random) screening produces tiny shapes that look like worms, and the patterns are actually measured in worms per inch. Figure 7.14 shows a stochastic print. Stochastic printing is all computer-generated—print houses cannot duplicate a pattern that shifts according to the input brightness of an image at any given point. To the right of the stochastic duck is a line screen mezzotint that shows highlights going at one cut angle, with the deeper shades having a different line direction.

After this glowing review of other screening types, particularly mezzotints, I've got some good news and some bad news. The bad news is that Photoshop's Mezzotint filter (found under Filter, Pixelate) is miles from the quality effects and options Adobe's products are known for. You could not use Photoshop's Mezzotint filter to create the mezzotint effects shown in Figures 7.13 and 7.14.

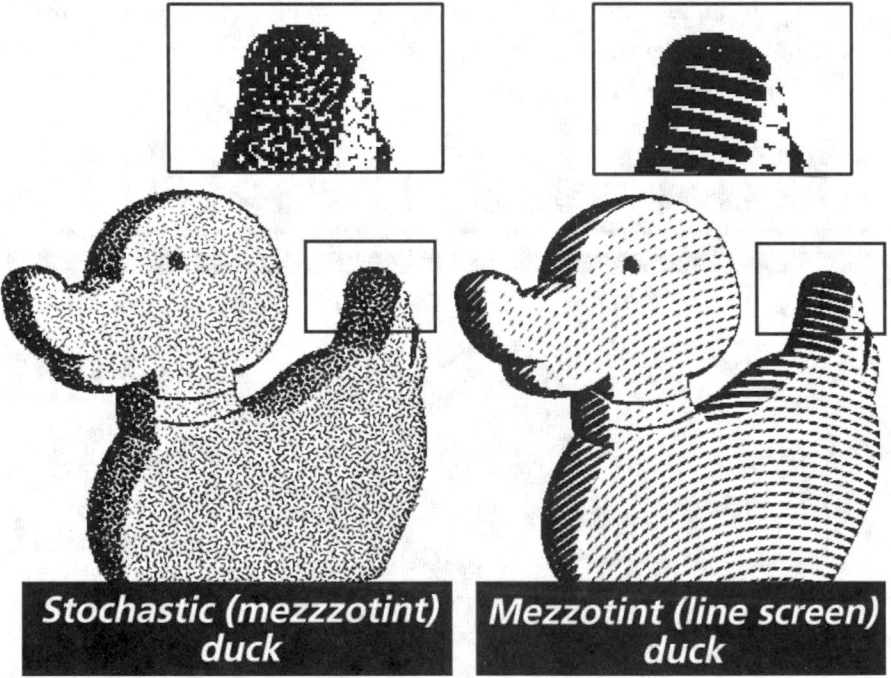

**Stochastic (mezzzotint) duck**

**Mezzotint (line screen) duck**

**Figure 7.14**  If you do not mind a pattern competing for the visual content of an image, mezzotinting could be your ticket.

The good news is that Andromeda Software offers a comprehensive assortment of mezzotint screens, over which you have complete control with respect to line frequency, angle, and so on. They are available online for download at http://www.andromeda.com—all you need is a credit card and a fast Internet connection.

So far, we've spent a good amount of time on the fine points of printing, without much explanation of how to print from Photoshop. Allow me to correct this oversight…

## Printing Options in Photoshop

There are two categories of output I'd like to cover—business output and commercial art—both of them under Photoshop's roof. First, printing from Photoshop is not as effortless as, say, printing from Microsoft Word. But then again, you're printing *art* from Photoshop, whereas you're printing formatted text from Microsoft Word—there's a chasm of sophistication you'd need to ford to bring the two applications' printing engines even remotely closer together.

Let's first look at the way Photoshop lets you know when the resolution of a file you want to print needs tuning.

### The Image Size Command: A Career-Saver

Remember the "image dimensions decrease as resolution increases" line a few pages back? Well, Photoshop is a strict enforcer of correct image dimensions; it's a waste of paper to allow an image to be printed with clipping, all because the dimensions were not set up correctly.

In Figure 7.15 you can see an image I want to print. Before printing it, however, I clicked on the Document Sizes area in the workspace, and a frame popped up to tell me that this image is going to print off the edges of my paper.

In Figure 7.16, I pressed Ctrl(⌘)+P—and to my surprise, I got my wrist slapped! Photoshop pops up a warning every time you try to print something that will run off the page.

Now, there's a very easy solution to making this dolphin picture print, without your changing a pixel of the visual content. Photoshop is capable of resizing an image, but this means that you change the number of pixels, interpolation takes place, and you print a fuzzy image.

The solution lies in the first math formula in this chapter: If you increase the resolution of the image, you decrease the physical dimensions. Choose Image, Image Size to access the options for changing the resolution of the image.

**Figure 7.15**    Before printing, try to make it a practice to check the image frame. The large "x" shows the extent of the image, when printed at the current dimensions and resolution.

**Figure 7.16**    Choose to cancel printing if you get this warning.

What happens when you pour a quart of water into a 12-ounce glass? You get a spill, and this is sort of what happens when you decrease the dimensions of the image to the extent that the resolution is now far higher than your printer can print.

This is *okay,* though—the excess printing information is simply discarded during printing time, and you lose perhaps 15 seconds on a print job by doing this. But I feel it's better to waste a little print spooling time than to change the visual content of the image forever. Check out Figure 7.17. Notice that I've decreased the dimensions so that the image will print to an 8½" by 11" page. And do *not* check the Resample Image box in the Image Size command.

**Do not *resample image***

**smaller inches=larger resolution**

**Figure 7.17**   Increase the resolution so that the physical dimensions of the artwork will fit on a page.

If you're printing to a PostScript device, you will want to choose File, Page Setup before you start printing. This is only a 1000+ page book, and therefore I can't go into every printing option—but how about the two most important ones?

In Figure 7.18, you can see the Page Setup dialog box. You probably want to click on Screens after all of this chapter's talk about screening. It is from Screen that you get to pick the line frequency and angle, as well as the shape of the dots on the page. Also, you might want to enable Corner Crop Marks, because your art might not take up the whole page, and you might want to frame your work (so that it is centered in the frame).

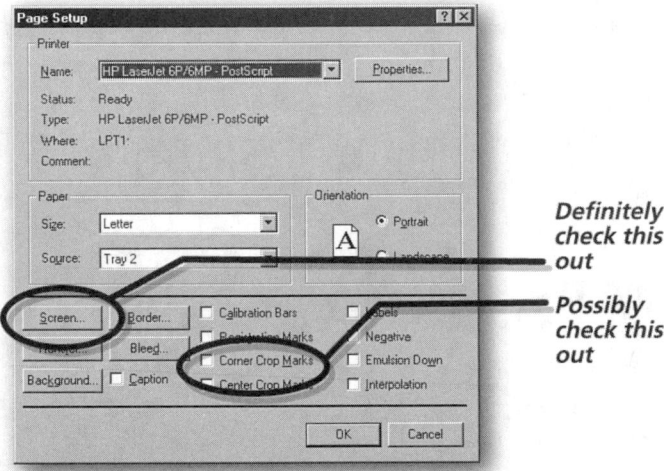

**Figure 7.18**    You really might want to set only two options, unless you're an experienced imaging-type person.

Let's take a look at what you'll see when you click on the Screen button. In Figure 7.19, I make my recommendations for a 600 dpi PostScript printer. Eighty-five (85) lpi is correct for a 600 dpi printer, and the use of diagonal screens (such as 45°) has been a long-standing tradition among physical plate-making experts. It seems that when you run a diagonal screen, folks notice the individual dots of ink less. Try running a 90° screen on a print, and you'll see what I mean.

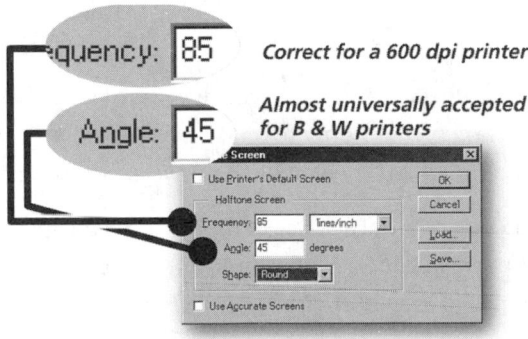

**Figure 7.19**    The recommended settings for a 600 dpi printer.

Ah, at last we arrive at my favorite part of Photoshop imaging. It's called *film recording,* and might or might not even involve Photoshop, unless the service bureau you use owns Photoshop. Film recording is sort of the opposite process to scanning. With film recording, you're turning a digital image into a 35mm slide (or other film format). The results are breathtaking, and the steps you'll need to know are just around the corner.

# Film Recording

Film recording from digital media is not a new process. If you hear a lot about it these days, that's simply because the price of film recorders has come down so much that if you've got two grand in your pocket, you could own a decent film recorder. Film recording has been fed by PowerPoint users for the past decade, but increasingly, fine artists have taken to putting images on a slide—the medium is eminently portable, and the colors are usually to die for!

## Steps to Film Recording

Pick up the telephone book and find a *slide service bureau.* Regular service bureaus do imagesetting work, set type, and do layouts, but  the slide service bureau owns the expensive machinery that will turn your Photoshop work into a pocket-sized wonder. You can expect to pay around $8 per slide, and if you've got a lot of work, you might negotiate a discount. These service bureaus are also happy to take film negatives and write the info to film.

The first step to film recording your work is to make certain that the image has the correct *aspect ratio.* Fine; what's an aspect ratio? It's a proportion expressed by the relationship of one dimension of something compared to the other dimension—Width:Height is an aspect ratio. Your image is going from data on a disk to a 35mm slide, let's say. Chances are pretty good that your image does not have the 3:2 aspect ratio that belongs to a 35mm slide. And a service bureau is not responsible for adding a background or creatively cropping your image. You don't want anybody but you cropping your work, the service bureau doesn't exactly welcome a request for clairvoyance, and it's really very simple to whip your image into the proper aspect ratio.

To give you an example of the best way to discover how far off you are with the image, press Alt(Opt)+click on the Document Sizes area of the workspace, as shown in figure 10.20. My wind-up toy picture isn't even close to having a 3:2 aspect ratio.

In my opinion, the easiest way to get an image properly formatted is to add a background to both the horizontal and vertical aspects of the image. In Figure 7.21, you can see the fail-safe method for picking out a background color that will not clash with the image. You press Alt(Opt) and click with the Eyedropper tool to pick up a background color that already exists in the image. Can you get more harmonious?

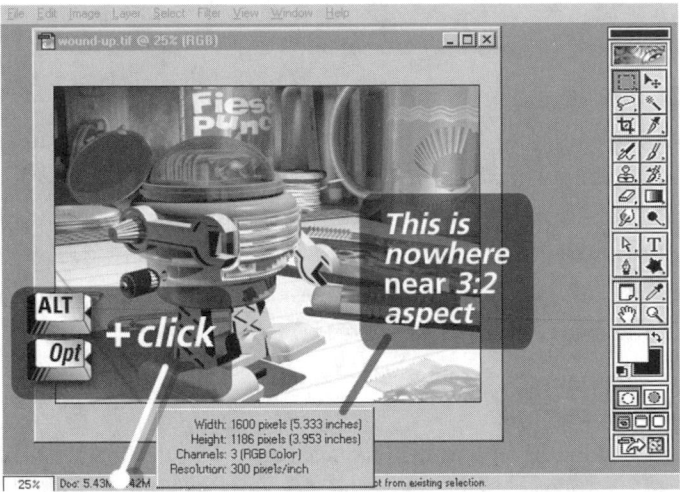

**Figure 7.20**   It's your call as to how your image is turned into film. Try to make it easy on the service bureau by investing some time in getting the proportion the same as that on 35mm film.

**Figure 7.21**   Alt(Opt)+click over a neutral area of the image to set the background you'll soon create.

Let's pay another trip to the Image Size dialog box. This time, we are deliberately going to change the dimensions with absolutely no regard to the resulting resolution of the file. Why? Because film recorders don't care about image resolution—all that matters is image size, as measured in MB.

In Figure 7.22, the Resample image box is unchecked, I've typed 1.7 (inches) in the Height field, and the Width field has changed to 2.2 (inches). This is good—it means that we can stop by the Canvas Size command and add to both the vertical and horizontal measurements of the image.

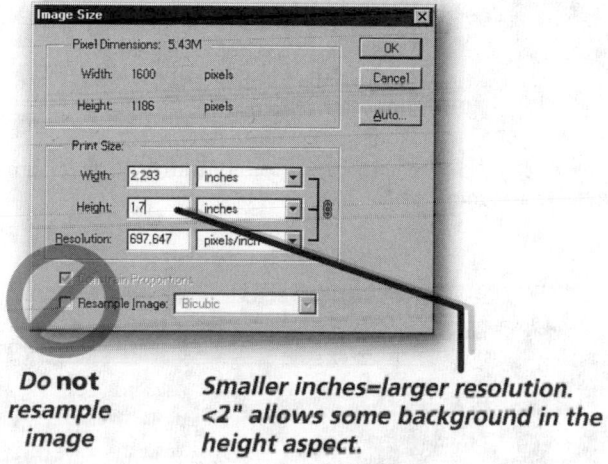

**Do not resample image**

**Smaller inches=larger resolution. <2" allows some background in the height aspect.**

**Figure 7.22**   Keep the Width under 3 and the Height under 2, and then you can add background color to both aspects of the image.

Now, choose Image, Canvas Size, and type **3** in the Width field and **2** in the Height field (see Figure 7.23). You've got a 3:2 image now! Click OK.

In Figure 7.24, you can see that I've add a little texture to the background areas of the image. You can do this, too, by filling the background area with a texture (you click with the Magic Wand tool, set to a Tolerance of 1 with no anti-aliasing, and then fill the area with a pattern.

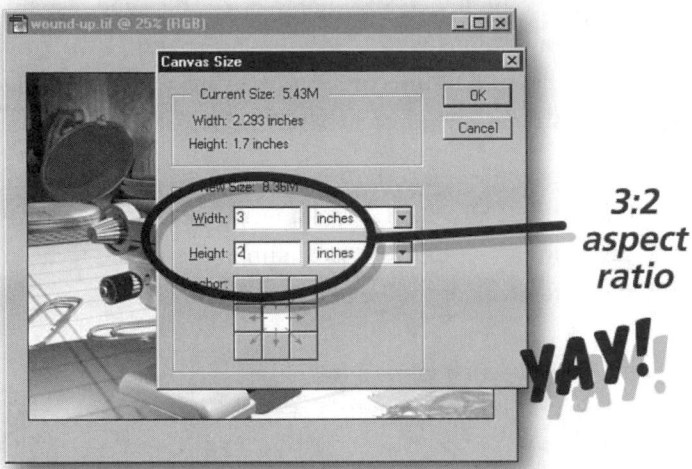

**Figure 7.23**  The aspect of the image is now ideal for film recording, simply because you added background to the image.

**Figure 7.24**  Get the image onto a Zip disk and truck it on over to your slide service bureau.

I never really mentioned what size is a good image size for film recording. I've had 900KB images written to slides, and the subject matter was simple enough that you never noticed the lack of image information. After experimenting for around a year with my slide service bureau, I've found that a 4.5MB image renders pretty well to film.

Here's a secret: Most RIPs (raster image processors—the software that enables a film recorder to render to film) will *interpolate* an image that is smaller than 18MB or so. This means that unless your image is 18MB, do *not* perform any interpolation yourself with Photoshop. Interpolation once is bad enough, but if it happens twice to your image before it's recorded, you might notice a resulting fuzzy 35mm slide.

**Note**

**Aspect Ratio Order**   Aspect ratio follows an order: The first number is the width of the image, and the second Is Its height.

Perhaps I've been a little brisk with my explanations in this chapter about a few concrete measurements and proportions. Clearly, a 2:3 aspect ratio is not the same as a 3:2 ratio. And most service bureaus prefer that you give them a wider-than-tall image because the film recorder that's writing the film, line by line, has fewer transverses to make if the image is wide.

## Summary

Hopefully, you now know why I didn't call this chapter "Printing Essentials." There are more ways to get your data onto hard copy than you can shake a stick at. This chapter covered three methods: camera-ready for commercial printing, personal printing, and film recording. I'm sure that by the time this book comes out there will be a score of other output devices that'll make your work take its rightful place as art in the many fields that require graphics.

# Chapter 8

# Enhancing Productivity: Automation and Other Cool Tools

The ability of Photoshop 6 to automate

steps that one would usually have to

repeat over and over (and over) has given

back to the graphic designer the single most precious commodity: time. Any feature that allows the creative process to *flow* instead of periodically coming to a screeching halt is invaluable to production artists, professionals who process images, and Web designers. Regardless of your area of interest (or level of expertise) in digital design, Photoshop 6 enables you to perform frequently used functions or a series of commands with the click of a button. In this chapter, we will discuss some of Photoshop's powerful automation features. You might be familiar with automation features, such as the Actions palette, from previous versions of Photoshop. This chapter also covers the updates to these features.

The designers of Photoshop 6 gave a lot of thought to the people who will use their product. Here is a list and brief description of Photoshop 6 automations:

- **Actions.** A series of commands recorded in Photoshop and saved for re-application later. We should get it straight right now that an *action* is a batch set of commands a user creates. The actions are accessed from the Actions palette. So when we talk about actions in this chapter, we are referring to the command sets themselves.

- **Droplets.** Small executable files composed (in Photoshop) of a saved action and (in ImageReady) as a set of optimization settings.

- **Batch Processing.** Applying one or more commands to images in a folder you specify as the target folder.

- **Picture Package.** This feature is a gem of an innovation carried over from version 5.5. If you have one photo, one sheet of inkjet paper, and the energy for clicking about three times in Photoshop <g>, you'll get multiple returns—a page of different-sized images.

- **Contact Sheet II.** This simple automation procedure can crank out pages of thumbnail images, with titles, from any folder on your hard disk (as long as the folder has image files, and not Excel spreadsheets or anything else). Good for onscreen previewing or printing, contact sheets are a welcome feature.

- **Web Site Creation.** This feature, which is covered extensively in Chapter 24, is not covered here. But it deserves mention here because it is a Photoshop automation feature.

- **External Automation.** Automation of Photoshop commands from an external program or script, such as OLE or AppleScript.

- **Presets Manager**. This feature is not an automation mechanism, but it is a timesaving device we take a nod at in this chapter.

Let's get familiar with this stuff! Spend some time here, and save a *lot* of time later...

## Introducing Actions

Leading question: What do you observe when you watch a group of young children on a playground? Typically you have yourself a noisy conglomerate of little people clamoring to be the center of attention. And attention they typically get, in one of two flavors: encouragement by their peers—or scolding by their peers.

But usually you'll see one child who is more reserved than the rest. He or she tends to play quietly, never really getting the attention of the more boisterous children. Yet this quiet child might very well one day grow up and cure the common cold or invent thermal underwear. Still waters run deep, as the saying goes, and we hear similar stories time and again.

So it is with actions. In past versions of Photoshop, actions remained somewhere up in the main menu on a palette somewhere. Actions never got the recognition they deserve—they were the quiet child, without much online documentation to get you playing with them. Well, it's the next millennium now, Photoshop 6 is more an environment than an application, and actions *are* worth your attention. Actions can turn tedious tasks such as resizing multiple images into fast, efficient processes. This author actually *detests* performing the same editing moves more than twice, and for me, actions are an out-and-out blessing. This powerful tool enables the user to record commands to generate what adds up to a complicated effect, repeat often-used steps, or create shortcuts that can be played back when needed.

You can use actions to generate images, starting with a blank canvas. You can find many popular text effects actions on the Web—strictly speaking, an action is a batch script that Photoshoppists write graphically through onscreen keyboard and cursor motions. You can even use an action to save the file in the format you want after the action has run its course.

Most Photoshop tools and commands can be used in creating actions. For those occasions in which the action requires user input or application of a tool (such as paint), you can insert a stop within the action, complete with user instructions. This is an extremely helpful feature, especially for actions created by a third party.

What's the deal with third-party actions? They are actions recorded by other people and distributed online, in Photoshop add-on packages, and so on. Some excellent Web sites deal solely with action creation, and some even allow their visitors to upload actions to give to others. A few of these resources are mentioned at the end of this chapter.

### Displaying the Actions Palette

To access this jack-of-all-trades feature, you can choose Window, Show Actions to access the Actions palette, or (and this is a good shortcut to remember) press F9. The Actions palette has two operational modes: Button and Edit (or List). We'll just call it List mode for the remainder of the chapter. In Figure 8.1, you can see the default mode—List—for the Actions palette.

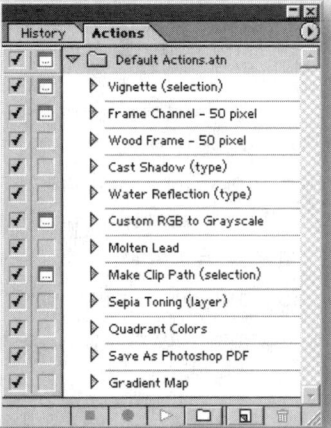

*Actions palette—Edit (List) mode*

**Figure 8.1**    This is the Actions palette in List mode, the mode in which you'll see it in this chapter. In this mode you can edit and create new actions.

Figure 8.2 shows the Actions palette in Button mode. To toggle between the two modes, you have to open the Actions palette menu. To do so, click the right arrow in the circle at the upper-right corner of the palette. Click Button Mode. If Photoshop was in List mode, it switches to Button mode. If Photoshop was in Button mode, it switches to List mode. Simple! To decide which mode to use when, you need to know what each mode offers and what you are trying to accomplish with the action. Let's take a closer look at these modes.

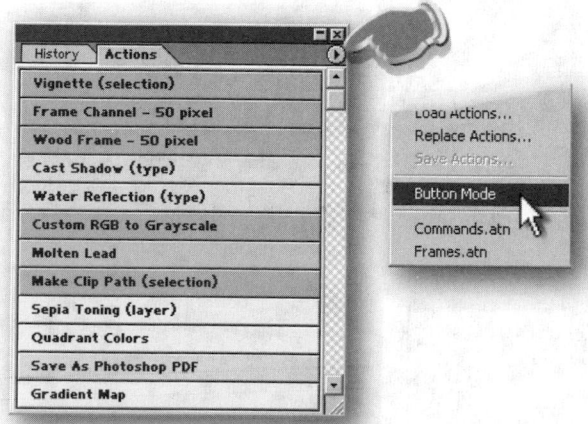

## Actions palette—Button mode

**Figure 8.2**   The Action palette in Button mode. As you'll see, it's pretty Spartan in appearance, and there are times when you cannot access certain features for the price of a button display of actions.

Because you can get more out of the Actions palette in List mode than in Button mode, we'll start with the List mode layout.

### List Mode

The List mode of the Actions palette is the more complicated of the two palette modes, and it's also the more functional. As the name implies, you can use this mode to alter action sets, change settings, correct messages, and so on. When you initially open Photoshop, you'll find that actions are displayed in List mode by default. Figure 8.3 shows the List mode on the palette, with callouts that are explained soon.

**Tip**

**Use the List Mode as a Photoshop Tutor**   Setting the Actions palette to List mode is an excellent way to teach yourself Photoshop and many of its nuances! Say you appreciate an effect someone created with an action, but have no idea how it was accomplished. In List mode, you can examine every step in the effect and see which settings were used for each command, and in what order. You can also edit the action to suit your own tastes (we suggest that you click on the palette flyout and choose Duplicate if you want to "action hack").

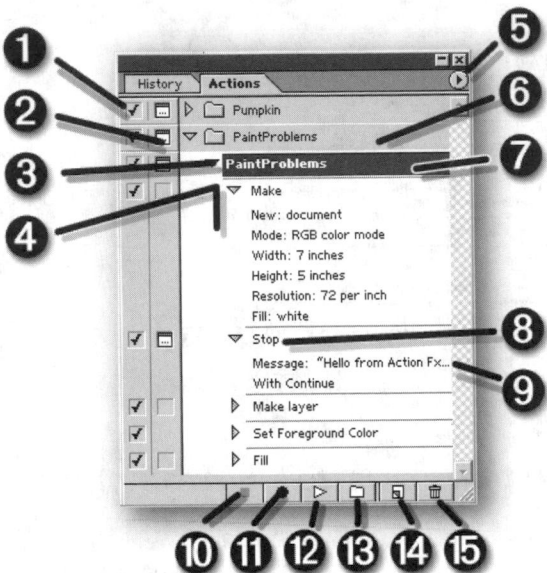

**Figure 8.3**    Feature-packed is an understatement. The Actions palette's List mode is a virtual all-you-can-eat buffet for those who want to build sophisticated custom action sets.

Table 8.1 identifies the elements in the Actions palette's List mode. In this chapter, you work with many of these settings.

**Table 8.1    The Elements of the Actions Palette in List Mode**

| Element | Function | Benefit |
|---|---|---|
| 1 | Toggles actions or commands on/off. | Shows what an action will produce with some settings turned off. |
| 2 | Modal Control that toggles the command settings for the command. When deactivated, actions proceed automatically with default settings. | When activated, you can view default settings or input your own settings for that command. |
| 3 | Expand or contract action command listing. | Shows command list for action (arrow points down) or hides command list (arrow points horizontally). |
| 4 | Expands settings for this command. | In the case of a stop, shows part of the stop message. |
| 5 | Opens Actions menu. | Use to create new actions or sets, edit and save actions, load actions and change Actions palette mode from Button to List. |
| 6 | Name of set containing one or a group of actions. | Change name of set by double-clicking set name. |

| Element | Function | Benefit |
| --- | --- | --- |
| 7 | Name of an action within a given set. | Change name by double-clicking the action within the palette. |
| 8 | Inserted stop. | Use to give directions, add copyright notices, annotate your action, or direct people to your Web site. |
| 9 | Stop message. | Double-click this section or the stop command to edit your message. |
| 10 | Stops the action in progress or stops recording of an action. | Allows you to try out different settings before including them in the action. When you work with a text action, you should stop recording the action before you enter the text and then resume after it's in place; otherwise, the action will enter the same text every time you run it. |
| 11 | Begins recording an action. | *Once activated, it's recording every move.* |
| 12 | Plays an action, or resumes an action that was stopped. | In List mode, you can select any command in the action, press Play, and the action will process that action from the command selection. |
| 13 | Creates new set in which to place your action or series of actions. | Remember—actions can only be saved in sets! |
| 14 | Starts new action recording within active set. | You may also drag an action from one set into a new set, later. |
| 15 | Delete any set, action, or step command within an action by dragging and dropping the selection here. | If you accidentally delete a step, you can undo (correct) the deletion in the Histories palette. |

## Button Mode

In Button mode, actions are, surprisingly enough, displayed as, um...buttons. This mode is a great one for beginners or for simple tasks because it enables you to do one thing: to launch actions you see on the palette with the simple click of a button. Unfortunately, that's *all* you can do in Button mode. No editing, no pausing, nada— empty enchilada.

## Selecting Actions

To select an action, click on its name in the palette. If you would like to run more than one action on the image, just press Shift and click to select a group of sequential actions, or Shift+click to pick and choose actions as desired. The only limitation we can mention here is that multiple actions can only be run if they are in the same folder. Once you click Play at the bottom of the palette, all the selected actions will perform their tasks on the image. This option is not available in Button mode. Yep—yet another reason *not* to use Button mode in your work. Its versatility is hampered in that you're at the mercy of the individual who created the action.

## Exploring the Action Palette Menu

The Actions palette menu shown in Figure 8.4 serves as the control board for creating, editing, loading, and saving actions. The Actions palette menu can be a powerful tool when mastered. Let's take a peek at this often overlooked but incredibly useful feature.

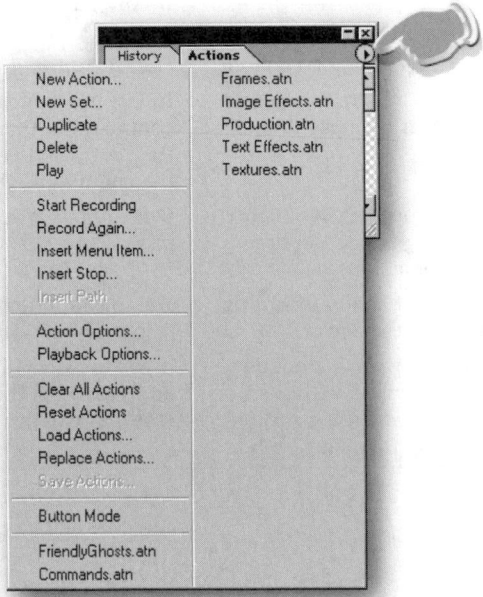

**Figure 8.4**    Use the Actions palette's menu to make it even easier to create and use actions.

As you can see, the menu is divided into six sections—on both operating systems there is a line drawn between groups on the menu. Most of them are self-explanatory—their name implies and defines their function. Also, the record, play, stop, new action, and delete functions are available here and serve the same purpose as the icons on the bottom of the Actions palette when it's in List mode. Photoshop 6 offers a new feature by allowing us to view our most recently loaded actions in the bottom area of the menu. A few commands in this menu might not be self-explanatory; they are explained in the next five sections.

### Insert Menu Item

Some items in Photoshop 6 can't be recorded as components of actions, which is why we have the "Insert Menu Item" command. By using this command, you can insert commands found on the Photoshop menus (such as View or Window) or manually add Painting/Toning and Tool options. The Insert Menu Item dialog box acts like a wizard, telling you how to accomplish your goal. And, of course, the palette must be in List mode.

Photoshop is very flexible with the Insert Menu Item command. You can insert menu items at *any time*—while you're recording an action or even when you no longer are recording it. Not only that, but you can insert an Insert Menu Item command *anywhere* within an action. To add the command to the end of the action, you must select the action's name in the palette. To insert the command at any point within the action, you select the command within the action *after* which you want the new command to occur. The Insert Menu Item will then appear *after* the selected command. When a menu item in an action requires a response in a dialog box, the action pauses until you click OK.

### Insert Path

You can use the Insert Path command to insert paths made with the Pen tool or with any of the Shapes tool's shapes, as long as they are added to an image in Work Path mode (see Chapter 12 for more information about Shapes). The way this command works is that you must have a path (named or Work Path; it makes no difference) in an image; then you choose the Insert Path command wherever in your action script you want the Actions palette to render a path. You no longer need the path in the image after you have essentially recorded the path into the action. If you open an action step (by clicking the triangle so it's in the downward position), you will be stunned by the elaborate (and long) description of the path you saved to the action (see Figure 8.5). This author only added a rounded rectangle to the action "recipe!"

As wonderful as this command is, though, be careful with it. First, this command is memory-intensive, so you may want to test the waters by including a very simple path in an action before trying to render an Adobe Illustrator masterpiece into the action!

Another thing to watch out for is that inserting more than one path into an action causes the previous path/paths to be overwritten. It is wise to save each path in the Paths palette while you *record* your action. This way, no data or complicated paths will be lost, and you still have your inserted path in the action of your dreams.

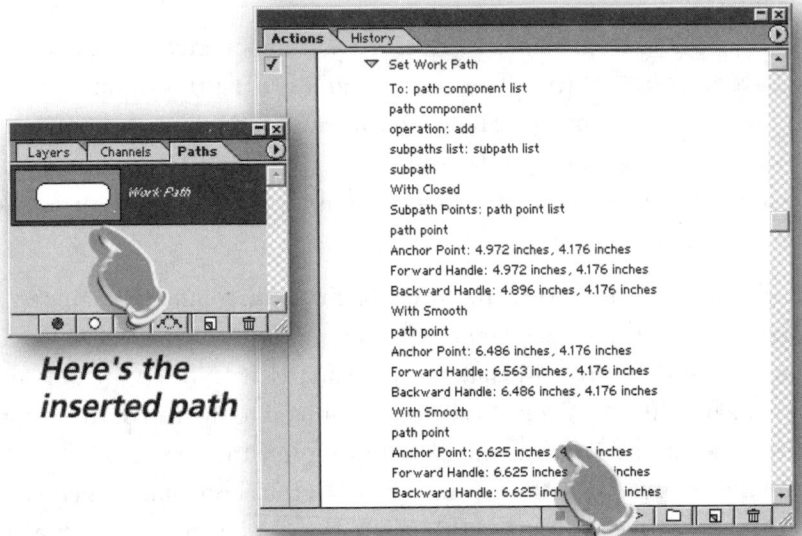

**Figure 8.5**    This figure shows only half the description of a rounded rectangle path inserted into an action. K.I.S.S. might be a good catch phrase when you're designing actions that insert paths!

### Set/Action Options

What is displayed here depends on whether a set, or an action *within* a set, is selected. These commands enable you to rename the set or action, let you assign your action to a function key (60 are available), color code your action for organization in Button mode, and assign your action to a set. Essentially, this is a variation on Options boxes for other Photoshop features.

### Playback Options

Choosing Playback Options from the Actions palette menu enables you to set the speed at which the actions will play (see Figure 8.6). You can set a delay within the action or choose Step by Step mode, which is an excellent training tool! If you're pressed for time or have had a few cups of Folger's high-test, click Accelerated and watch Photoshop whiz through the action like a kid with a cable modem on the Web!

Playback options also operate as a "Mr. Fixit." When an action is running in Accelerated mode, it is difficult to pick out where an error is occurring. When you step down the speed and watch the palette progress through the commands in the action, you can catch where the error occurs, and later perform any tweaking necessary to make the action run correctly.

Photoshop 6 enables you to insert audio annotations into a document, and Playback options are what you use to accomplish this. When selected, the action will stop processing until the audio annotation has finished playing. "Good Morning, Dave. Would you like to play a game of chess?" <g>

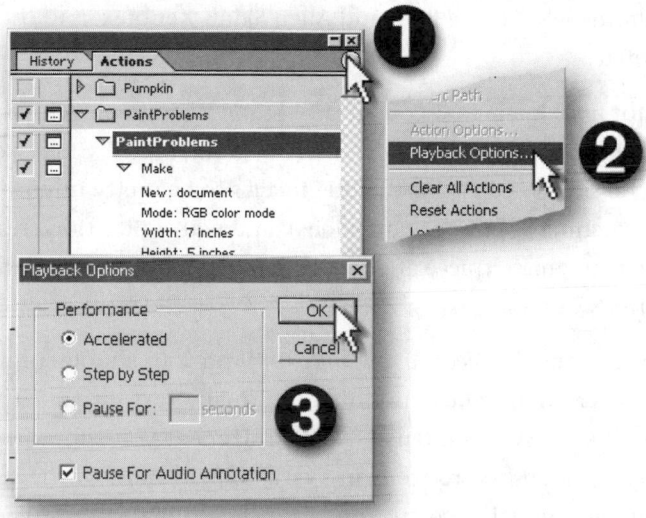

**Figure 8.6** Playback options control the speed at which an action is executed. This feature can also be run in a step-by-step way to clean up any errors that you've made as you built the action.

## Clear Actions and Reset Actions

Clear Actions does just what it sounds like—it's a digital Mr. Clean! This function clears the Actions palette of *everything* residing there. Not to worry; you can always reload the palette sets that came with Photoshop, and sets you have saved. So why would you want to clear the palette? Usually, when you're creating new actions it helps to have a clear palette, just to avoid visual clutter.

Maybe you don't want to dump the palette but have rearranged things to the point of confusion. In this case you can choose Reset Actions, which loads the default actions back into the palette. Before using either of these options, be sure to save any action sets you have created or they will be gone forever!

## Creating Actions

The primary use for the Actions palette is to enable the user to reduce the number of steps used to achieve an effect. This can be done by creating shortcut keys, by simple batch processing of images, and even by high-end interface designing. Actions can be applied to images, text, shapes, and Photoshop menus and tools, and can include most of commands and settings available. A very special property of actions is that you can include a third-party filter in the action script. We've tried it with Andromeda's Cutline filter and Alien Skin's Xenofex, and the action ran like a congressman.

Imagine for a moment that you are a big-time Web site developer, and you need a dozen page titles that are louder than a jackhammer when your visitors click through the site. So you want the title images to be pretty intense (as in "intricate" and "eye-catching"—but not obnoxious), and you realize that creating each image, one painstaking masterpiece after another, is going to take you until the next passing of Haley's Comet.

We've been saving the *pièce de résistance* until now. In a moment, we will guide you through the creation of an action that'll turn any text into a 3D piece of cut glass. How's that for classy *and* intense? Now, realize that you will learn many principals in this example, and there are many variations to most of the steps, so take your time to understand why we ask you to do certain maneuvers. Then, later, you can create dozens of variations on the cut-glass text.

Now, please understand that once you start recording an action, to stop for no good reason is a little like stepping out of a moving car. Examples in this book usually don't exceed 10–12 steps, but to create a knockout action more steps are necessary. So we've broken the action-creation technique into a two-parter, as follows—so you *and* the author can get up and get a cold drink!

Here's how to create the action that will generate the text effect needed for the Web site.

### Example 8.1    Creating an Elegant Action, Part I

1. Press F9 if the Actions palette isn't already onscreen. Save any actions you might have created, and then choose Clear All Actions from the palette menu. You have a clean palette now (sort of like eating a cracker before tasting the house wine <g>).

> **Warning!** If an error message appears when you open the CD files, press Ctrl(⌘)+Shift+K and then choose Adobe RGB (1998) from the Working Spaces, RGB drop-down list. See Chapter 3 for more information.

2. Click the New set icon. Let's name the new set **My Text Effects**. Now, click the New action icon, and name it **Title Text**.

3. Click Record.

4. You want this action to make a new image each time you use the action, so press Ctrl(⌘)+N. In the New dialog box, specify an image with a white background, 8 inches in width by 5 inches in height at 72 dpi. Use RGB Color Mode and press Enter (Return).

   You want to preserve the background so this fancy text you're creating can be added to different images as a layer. Um, the easiest way to do that is to create a new layer.

5. On the Layers palette (F7 if it's not onscreen), click the Create a new layer icon.

   It's time to enter the text. Because you don't want the same text every time, you want to stop the action at this point.

6. Click the Stop icon at the bottom of the Actions palette.

   Let's pop up a dialog box at this point to remind you of what the settings are for the text.

7. From the Actions palette menu, click Insert Stop. When the Record Stop dialog box opens, type a message that reminds you that, at this point, you will be entering text into your image. The note should say: "**Read this and then click Stop. Choose the Type Mask tool, and a bold font at 180 points in size. Once you've clicked Stop and your text is in the image, press the Play button on the Actions palette to resume.**" Check the Allow Continue option, and click OK.

   At this stage, your screen should look a lot like Figure 8.7.

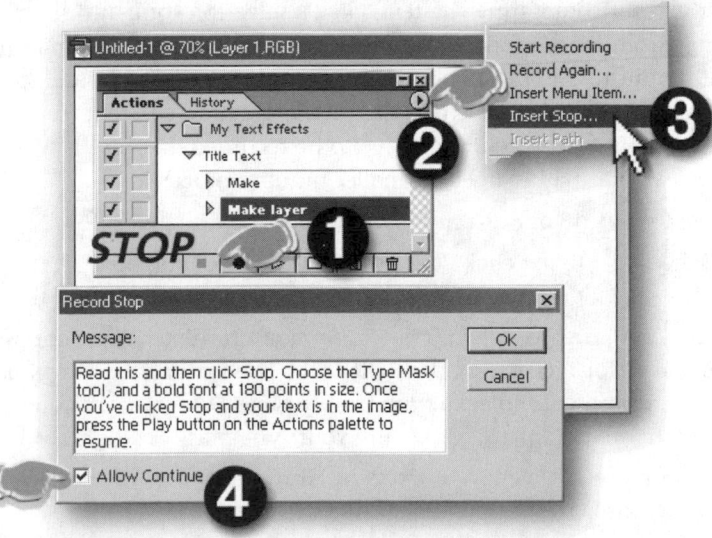

**Figure 8.7**  Leave yourself, or any other user, directions for manually intervening with the actions script to make custom text.

8. Follow your own directions—pick a nice, legible, bold font such as Lithos or Stop, as shown in Figure 8.8.

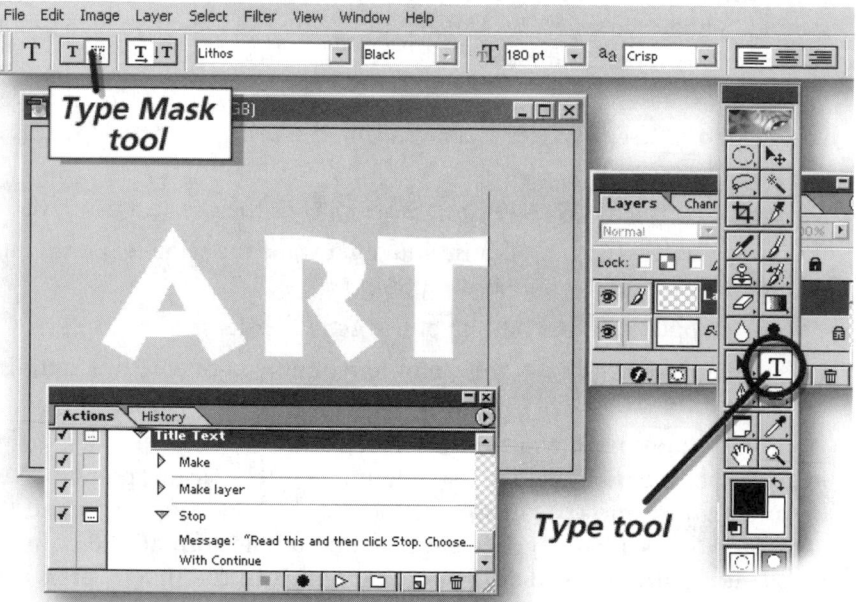

**Figure 8.8**    The text is going to be exquisitely detailed, so choose a bold font to allow room inside each character to show off the detail.

9. After you finish entering the text, click a selection tool, and the text will change from Mask mode to Standard (editable) mode with a marquee selection of your text apparent. With a selection tool (such as the Rectangular Marquee tool), drag inside the marquee and center the text (see Figure 8.9). You do not want this editing move to be recorded, because it will foul up other text that has a larger or smaller number of letters.

   You've followed your directions from the dialog box.

10. Click Record. Do *not* click Play, as it said in the dialog box! That's for *users*; you're a *programmer* for a while.

11. Click on the foreground color selection box on the toolbox, choose black from the Color Picker, and then click OK. The actions script will *not* make the foreground color black if you simply press D for default colors—you have to hand pick black. Make sure your type mask is still active!

12. Fill the marquee selection by pressing Alt(Opt)+Delete (Backspace), and then Press Ctrl(⌘)+D to deselect the marquee.

13. On the Layers palette, click the Add a Layer Style icon (the *f* icon), and then choose Bevel and Emboss from the flyout menu.

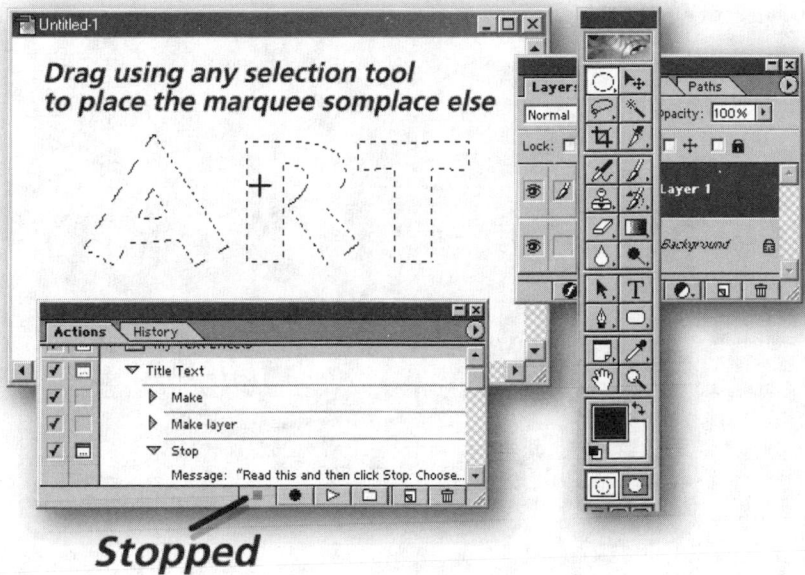

**Figure 8.9**   Center the text marquee, but do not record this action.

> **Note**
>
> **What's a Layer Style?**   It's a bunch of layers grouped into a single parcel, each layer having a different property. For those of you familiar with Photoshop 5 or 5.5, a Layer Style is simply a fancy new term for Layers Effects. That's why the Layer Style button on the Layers palette still has an *f* on it (for *effects*).

14. In the Layer Style box, choose Inner Bevel, Chisel Soft, and type **13** in the Size entry field (it's almost impossible to do this using the Size slider). These controls are marked 1, 2, and 3 in Figure 8.10. You can sort of see a preview rendered to a square in the Layer Style dialog box. Item 4 in Figure 8.10 is to click the down arrow next to Gloss Contour, and then click on the circled contour on the contour pop-up (the pop-up help calls this the Ring-Double Gloss contour). Press Enter (Return) to close the pop-up. Don't worry; pressing Enter (Return) on this occasion does not close the dialog box.

    The Layer Style palette is the size of a small elephant, and you probably can't see the effect applied to your type.

15. Drag the Layer Style title bar down and to the right until you can see what you're going to create. In Figure 8.11, the author's pretty happy with the nice detail of the "base coat" of type, so let's pretend you're happy, too—click OK.

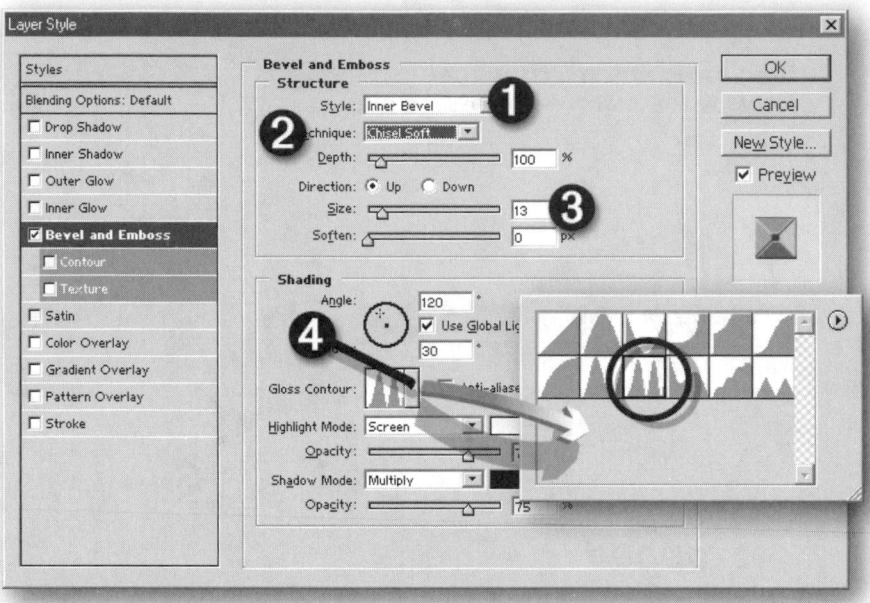

**Figure 8.10**    Follow step 14 to create custom embossed type on Layer 1.

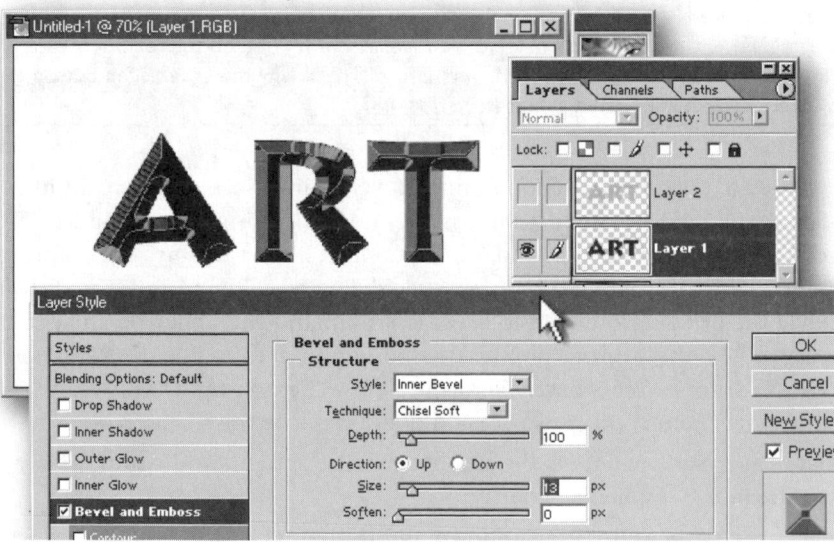

**Figure 8.11**    Take a look at the image window to see that the Layer 1 text is what you want for the base of the fancy text.

**16.** Click the Stop button on the Actions palette. We're going to take a break now. If you do not know how to take a break, follow the short tutorial in the following section. Do *not* close the Untitled image file or Photoshop—you do not need to keep the file you're using for programming the action, so you'll eventually delete it. But not right now.

Because books are not accessed in real time—you can close a book at any time, and even skip sections—it will seem like just a few moments until you get back to programming the script for the fancy text action.

## Taking a Break

Breaks are important—you wouldn't want to drive a car without them. So we are going to take a break now—you can take a break in your car if you like, or follow these steps:

### Example 8.2    Putting On the Break

**1.** Get up.

**2.** Read and take to heart this message.

**3.** Go outside, take a deep breath, hold it, and then slowly exhale. Los Angeles readers: Stay in an air-conditioned room, take a deep breath, and then slowly exhale.

**4.** Plant a tree.

**5.** Say "Hi" to someone you don't know.

**6.** Flash the peace sign at a police officer.

**7.** Do something beautiful.

**8.** Okay, break is over, and we need to finish the fancy text action.

## Continuing to Create the Elegant Text Action

Okay, we're refreshed now, so let's get straight to the Actions palette and the untitled, layered image:

### Example 8.3    Creating an Elegant Action, Part II

1. Click Record on the Actions palette. Right-click (Macintosh: hold Ctrl and click) on Layer 1, and then from the context menu, choose Duplicate layer. In the Layer dialog box, name this new layer **Layer 2** to avoid future confusion. Click OK.

2. Ctrl(⌘)+click on the Layer 2 title to load the opaque pixels as a marquee selection, and then click on the foreground color selection box on the toolbox. In the Color Picker, choose a nice gold, such as R:241, G:204, and B:0. Click OK to exit the Color Picker.

3. Press Alt(Opt)+Delete (Backspace) to fill the selection on Layer 2 with gold. Now, we don't want the Emboss effect on Layer 2 (we're going to do something even more special to the gold text), so drag the Effects title below the Layer 2 title on the Layers palette into the Trash (see Figure 8.12).

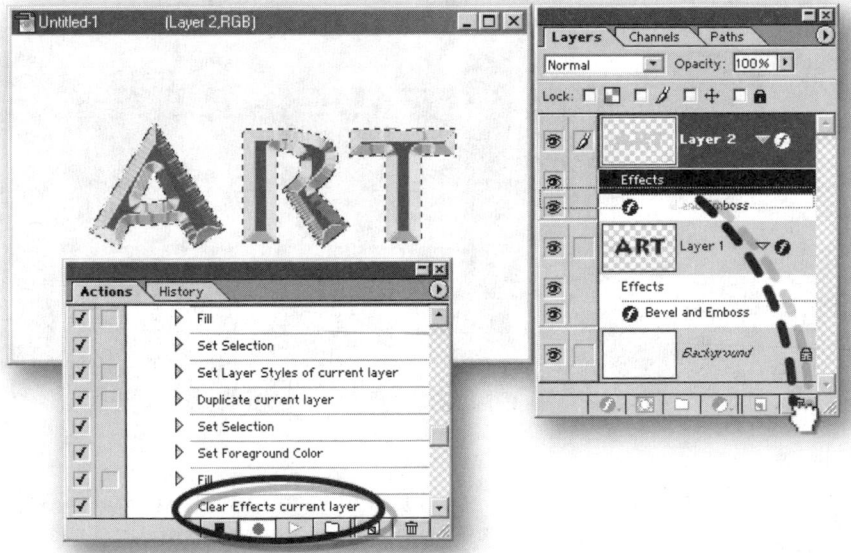

**Figure 8.12**    Trash the effects attached to Layer 2.

4. Press Ctrl(⌘)+D to deselect the marquee.

5. Press F6, click the Styles tab, and then (although you can choose any style you like), click the menu flyout button and choose Buttons.asl. A dialog box appears asking you if you want to Cancel, Append, or simply replace the current Styles set (OK). Click OK, and you can get the previous set back on the palette at any time using the same moves here.

6. Click on the Flat Rounded normal icon on the Styles palette to apply it to the gold text, as shown in Figure 8.13. Now, we want the Layer 1 chiseled effect to show through, and we can plainly see that this style is covering the Layer 1 text.

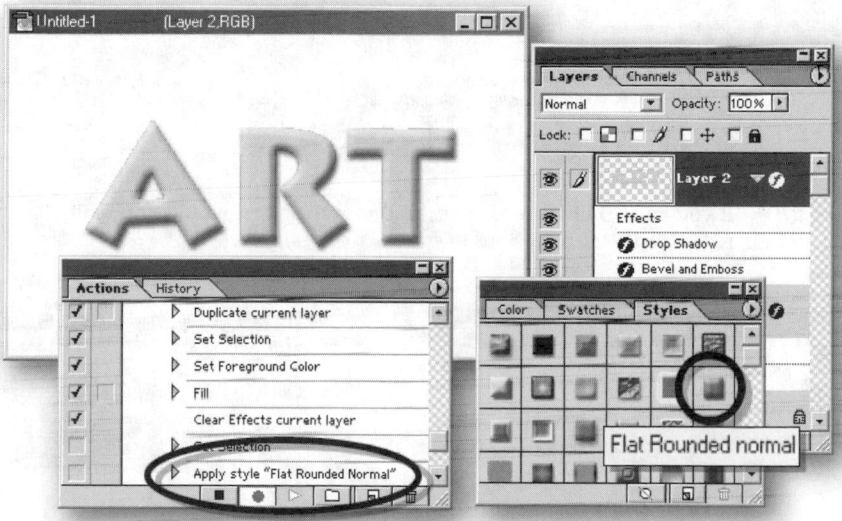

**Figure 8.13**   Apply a style to Layer 2. You can then change the amount of Layer 1's visibility by modifying the contents of Layer 2.

7. Click the Add a Layer Style button, and then click on Blending Options.

8. In the General blending field of the Layer Style dialog box, choose Overlay from the Blend mode drop-down. Then click OK, and you've got yourself a masterpiece onscreen, as shown in Figure 8.14.

9. Click Stop on the Actions palette. Now, scroll up to the Title Text title for the action on the Actions palette, click on it to highlight it, and then click Play. This time, type **Music** as the text when the dialog box pops up. As you can see in Figure 8.15, the effect is the same—only the name has changed.

10. You can close any image window you like now. Your Title Text action can generate more fancy text at any time in the future.

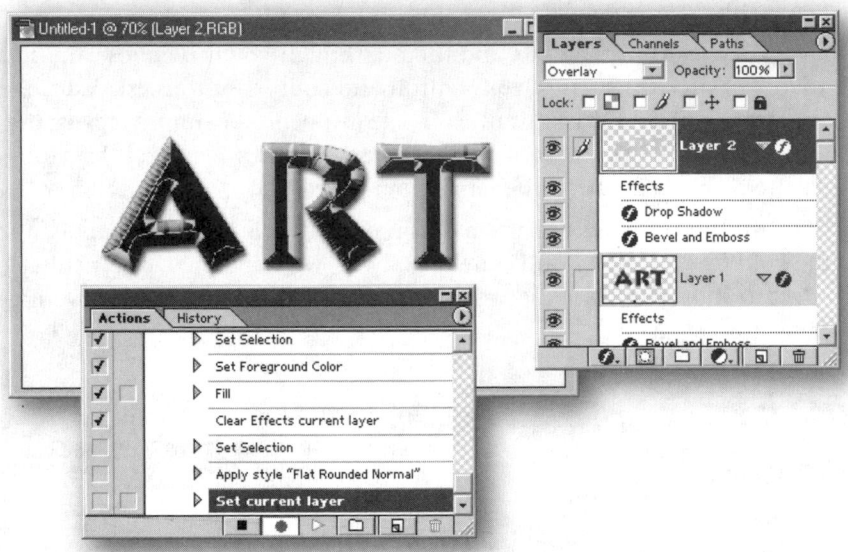

**Figure 8.14**  If you had 20 of these elegant headlines to create, would you really like to repeat more than 15 steps over and over again?

**Figure 8.15**  The action you programmed can now be used to dress up any text you choose.

An action script wouldn't be as attractive as it is to folks who want to avoid repetitive, potentially tendon-shredding computer work if you couldn't post-edit an action. In the following sections, we discuss how to edit an action after you've created it and how to play only part of an action.

## Playing Portions of Actions and Undoing Action Commands

When you play an action, the series of commands within the action are executed in the sequence in which the action was recorded. Though the technique needed to play a whole action is pretty much self-explanatory (press the Play icon), you can also choose *individual* settings within the action to play, or groups of settings by using the Shift+click selection maneuver. If you need to use the Undo option—Ctrl(⌘)+Z—only the last command executed will be undone. You can, however, delete several commands by deleting items from the History palette. It is wise to take a snapshot of the History palette (see Figure 8.16) before making any changes, so that an accidentally deleted step may be recovered. Photoshop 6 has a default of 20 histories; they may be changed manually in Preferences. To return to the original image, you simply click on the image at the top of the History palette.

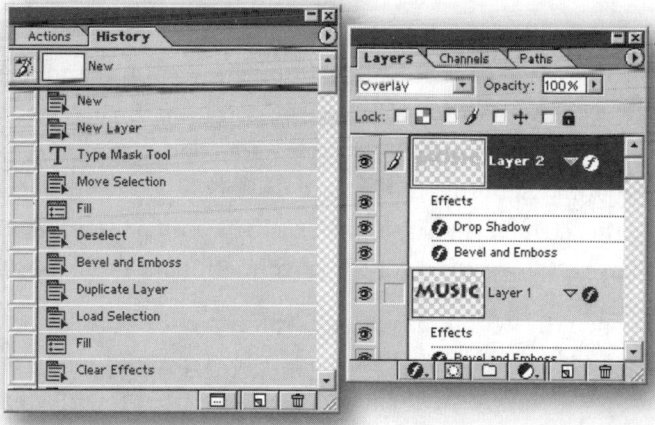

**Figure 8.16**    The History palette can be used to edit mistakes or unwanted commands in an action.

## Editing Actions

The versatility of the Actions palette allows for existing actions to be updated or edited, and some discussion on the subject is warranted at this point. An understanding of the way commands work together to achieve an end is helpful; once you have that understanding, editing steps becomes intuitive. Some of the ways actions can be edited follow:

- By recording/including additional commands.

- By rearranging or deleting existing commands.

- By duplicating commands. You can do this in a number of ways. You can choose the command or action and choose Duplicate from the Actions menu. You can Alt(Opt)+drag the command to a new location in the action, thereby creating a *duplicate* of that step when the mouse button is released. Simply selecting the command or action and dragging it to the New Action icon will reproduce it also. *Note:* Sets also can be duplicated in this manner!

- By changing action location, or categorizing actions in sets with similar actions. Selecting the action and dragging it to a new set will relocate the action. This is great if you have a series of steel effects you would like in a set called "Steel," or image processing actions that should be in a single category. It is entirely up to you! Find the file system that works for you, and stick with it. You are *not* locked into anyone else's idea of organization.

## Managing Actions

Those of us who create or collect actions from the Web may soon find our hard drives cluttered with nondescript .ATN files with no idea of what the end effect will be. For this reason it is important to properly name and categorize your actions or action sets, or you may soon run out of hard disk space, patience, hair, and organization! Later in this chapter we have some excellent online resources for actions, so it will help to have a filing system for those wonderful but numerous tiny files.

When you first open the Actions palette, you will notice a set called Default Actions. These are pretty basic (wood frame, cast shadow for type, and so on) but the beginner to Photoshop will appreciate them and can learn from them by expanding the action to show individual steps.

These are not all the actions that shipped with the full version, however! If you go to the Adobe Actions folder (Adobe, Photoshop 6.0, Presets, Photoshop Actions) you will find six sets of actions in these categories: Commands, Frames, Image Effects, Production, Text Effects, and Textures. These actions are fantastic, and the developers have put a lot of time into the possible needs of their customers.

There are 118 additional actions in these categories, not including the default actions (12 actions), for a total of 130! Each group is already color coded, and many have been assigned hotkeys as shortcuts for ease of use. If a person is interested in learning actions, we strongly recommend spending some time with these pre-defined additions to Photoshop. Figure 8.17 shows an expanded palette with all the shipped actions loaded.

**Tip**

You can return to the Actions palette's original action by clicking the palette flyout button, and choosing Reset Actions. BUT (and this is a big "but") you need to save any Action set you've created before you Reset Actions, or your scripts will be lost forever!

| Actions | | | | |
|---|---|---|---|---|
| Crop (selection) | Flatten ...  Shft+F2 | Purge All  Shft+F3 | Select ...   Shft+F4 | Grow (s... Shft+F5 |
| Flip Hori... Shft+F6 | Flip Ver... Shft+F7 | Rotate ...   Shft+F8 | Rotate ...   Shft+F9 | Rotate ... Shft+F10 |
| New Sn... Shft+F11 | New S...  Shft+F12 | Spatter Frame | Strokes Frame | Waves Frame |
| Ripple Frame | Drop Shadow Fra... | Photo Corners | Cut Out (selectio... | Recessed Frame ... |
| Vignette (selecti... | Frame Channel – ... | Wood Frame – 5... | Brushed Aluminu... | Foreground Color... |
| Wild Frame – 50 ... | Aged Photo | Blizzard | Light Rain | Lizard Skin |
| Neon Nights | Oil Pastel | Quadrant Colors | Sepia Toning (gr... | Sepia Toning (lay... |
| Soft Edge Glow | Soft Flat Color | Soft Focus | Neon Edges | Soft Posterize |
| Colorful Center (... | Horizontal Color ... | Vertical Color Fa... | Gradient Map | Flourescent Chalk |
| Letter Canvas 150 | Letter R Canvas ... | Tabloid Canvas 150 | Tabloid R Canvas... | Legal Canvas 150 |
| Legal R Canvas 1... | 640 x 480 | Save As GIF89a ... | Conditional Mode ... | Batch Processing |
| Reduced Color Pa... | Fit Image | Custom RGB to G... | Custom CMYK to ... | Make Clip Path (s... |
| Save As JPEG Me... | Save As Photosh... | Make Button | Thin Outline (typ... | Medium Outline (... |
| Bold Outline (type) | Brushed Metal (t... | Cast Shadow (ty... | Chrome (photo &... | Clear Emboss (ty... |
| Die Cut (type) | Frosted Glass (p... | Sprayed Stencil (... | Text Panel (sele... | Water Reflection... |
| Wavy (type) | Wood Paneling (t... | Warp Squeeze (t... | Confetti (type) | Running Water |
| Parchment Paper | Recycled Paper | Sandpaper | Wood – Pine | Wood – Oak |
| Wood – Rosewoo... | Wood – Rosewoo... | Split Wood | Asphalt | Bricks |
| Black Granite | Cold Lava | Gold Sprinkles | Green Slime | Ink Blots |
| Marble | Molten Lead | Neon Rubber Bands | Obsidian | Pastel Glass Tiles |
| Psychedelic Strin... | Rippled Oil | Rusted Metal | Stained Glass | Stucco |
| PostScript Patte... | Sunset | Marbled Glass | | |

**Figure 8.17**   If you ever wondered where the action is, clearly it's in Photoshop.

It is easy to tell, when each section has been color-coded, what aspect, or type of action one will be working with. Like the overall purpose of the Actions palette—to save you time—the color-coding serves to save even more hassle in the long run.

Once you have a large collection in a certain category, you may also want to transfer them to disk. The file size for .ATN files is generally small (7KB–20KB) so many can be stored on a 1.44MB floppy disk and retrieved when needed. Simply click on the set, go to Save Actions in the Action menu and select where you want them stored—it's *that* simple.

When you begin to use actions and see their usefulness, you may want to add other effects to your repertoire. At the end of this chapter is a list of actions sources online. There are some excellent third-party resources on the Internet devoted to Photoshop Actions, and these Web sites are great for filling up your toolbox! Whether you are interested in Photo Effects or creating Metal Fonts, or even if you want to share your own actions with the online community, these sites are fantastic to browse and download from.

## Using Droplets

Photoshop 6 has included a new feature that can be used to work along with actions. The Droplet feature is found in both Photoshop and ImageReady; to see how to create a droplet in ImageReady, check out Chapter 23.

*Droplets* are actually small executable files. These little programs can be placed in a convenient location, such as your desktop. Files may then be dragged and dropped onto the Droplet icon and are processed instantly. Photoshop does not have to be running prior to executing the droplet, as the droplet will open Photoshop for you, process the file with the corresponding action, save and close the files in its new form. Take this scenario:

A client calls and says she needs to have 1,500 images converted to sepiatone ASAP! Now, you have a sepia action that ships with Photoshop, but applying this action to 1,500 images will consume a lot of time. You could batch convert them (that's covered shortly)…but another quick, easy, and relatively painless way to do it ASAP is to use a droplet.

Droplets are a fantastic addition to the already loaded Photoshop 6 toolbox, and deserve to have a bit of time devoted to them. More automation is always good automation!

### Creating an Action to Become a Droplet

Unfortunately, droplets in Photoshop (unlike ImageReady) must be created from actions, and the Title Text doesn't really cut it as an action that'll show you batch processing as the droplet and batch features in Photoshop do. So before you create the droplet, let's create a very simple action—reducing the width of a bunch of files to 250 pixels (let's say because you want to put them in an HTML table). Then you need to sharpen the image (resizing always causes blurring), and then colorize it so it's a steeltone image, very similar to the sepiatone-type image, except that the resulting image has tones of steel blue.

If you've read and done the preceding text example, this action is going to be a comparative breeze to create.

### Example 8.4   Creating an Action for a Droplet

1. On your desktop, create a folder called **MyImages**. Close any open images you might have in Photoshop's workspace right now.

2. In Photoshop, on the Actions palette, choose New Set from the flyout menu, name the set **WebWork** in the dialog box, and then press Enter (Return).

3. On the Actions palette, choose New Action. In the New Action dialog box, type **Steeltone JPEG Gallery**, an evocative name you will certainly remember later. Click the Record button in the dialog box.

4. Open an image from the Examples/Chap08 file. It doesn't matter which TIFF image you choose; it's simply the target for the transformations the action will produce. We chose fishbone.tif.

5. Choose Image, Image Size. Make sure the Constrain Proportions and the Resample Image options are checked. Type **250** in the Width field, as shown in Figure 8.18, and then click OK.

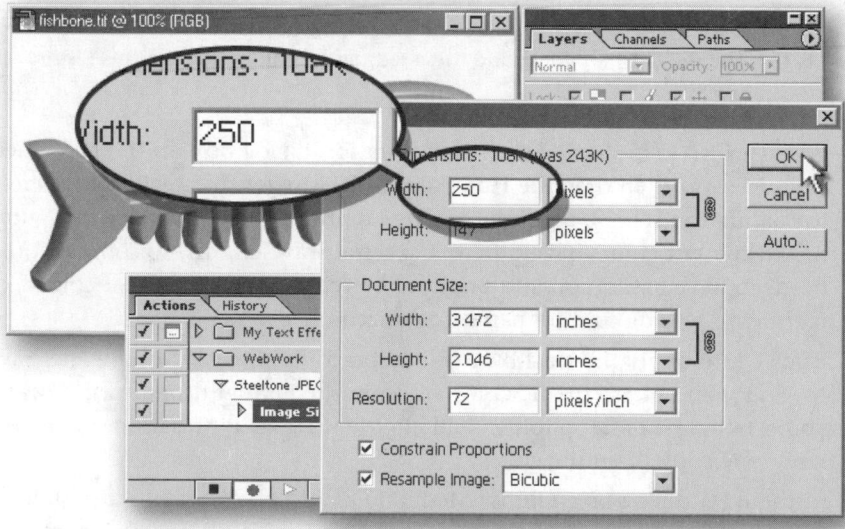

**Figure 8.18**   Specify that all images to be processed will be 250 pixels in width.

The height of an image when you run a droplet will default to the proportional scaling of the width; it'll change according to the proportions of the image, but all images will be 250 pixels in width.

6. Choose Filter, Sharpen, and then Unsharp Mask. See Figure 8.19 for the settings you should use—through trial and error, the author has found that these are good, omnibus settings for gentle sharpening. Click OK to apply the filter.

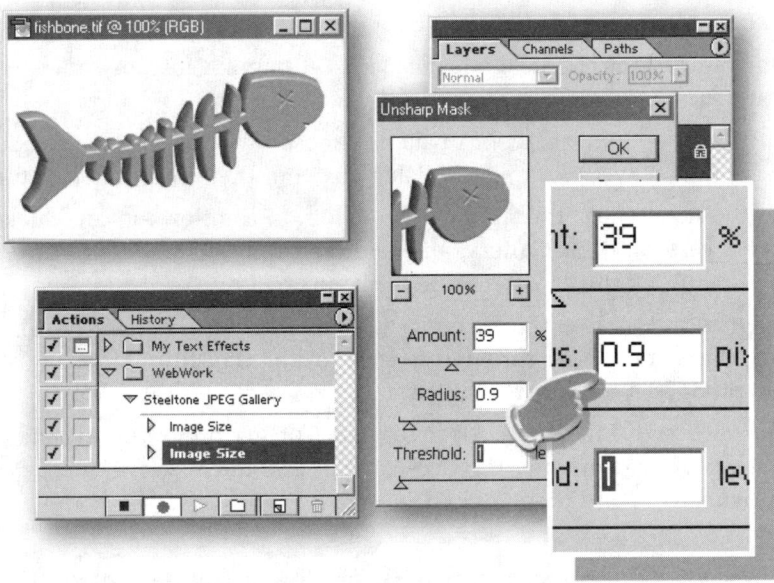

**Figure 8.19**   Use the Unsharp Mask and these settings to mildly sharpen this resized image.

7. Press Ctrl(⌘)+U to display the Hue/Saturation dialog box. In the box, check Colorize, and then drag the Hue slider to 203 to get the steel tone, decrease the Saturation to –28, and increase the Lightness to 5, as shown in Figure 8.20. Different colors have different spectral wavelengths, so some colorizing needs to have Saturation and Brightness tweaked, whereas other colors require no fussing to get a perfect colorized image.

8. Click OK to apply the steel-blue coloration to the image. Choose File, Save As, and then choose the JPEG format from the Format drop-down. Locate your MyImages desktop folder, and choose it as the destination for the JPEG steel tone copy of an image.

9. In the JPEG dialog box, choose Medium Quality of about 6 on the slider, and check the Baseline Optimized Format option. We'll not go for the Progressive JPEG, because all browsers and applications do not support the

streaming, progressively increasing resolution of this JPEG type when it is downloaded. See Figure 8.21 for a view of the JPEG settings, and then click OK to save the image as a JPEG with the same name as the TIFF image.

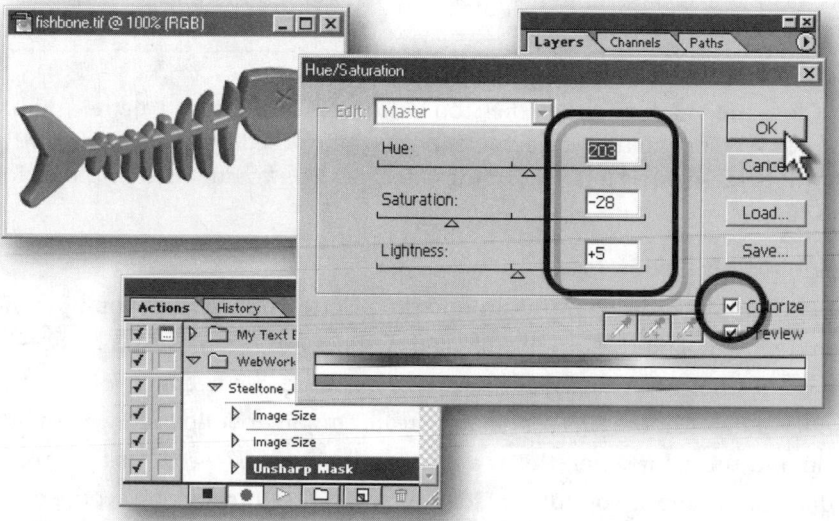

**Figure 8.20**   Use the Colorize command in the Hue/Saturation dialog box to make a green fish blue fish (one fish...sorry, wrong book).

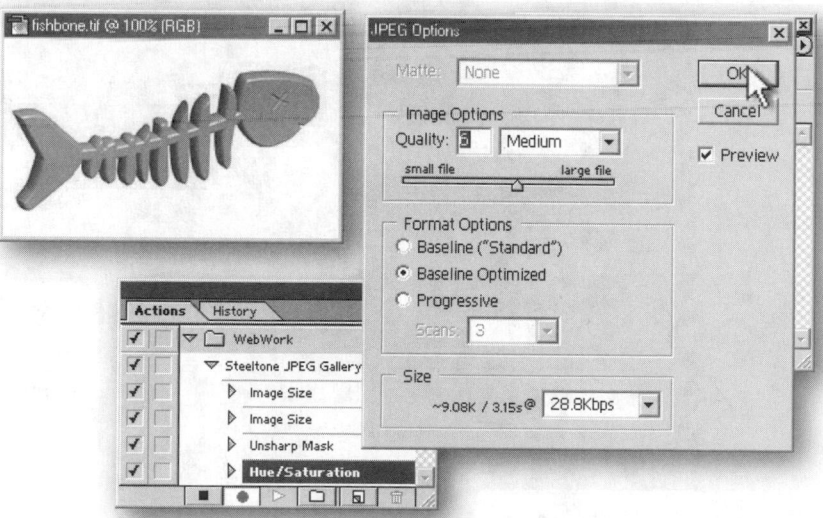

**Figure 8.21**   Choose moderate compression (decent quality) for the action that transforms TIFF images to the JPEG file format.

> **Note**
>
> **Check Out the Speed**    Notice that at the bottom of the JPEG Options dialog box, it tells you that the image will travel across the Internet to someone's browser, assuming they are using a 28.8K modem (which is not really fast in the age of cable modems), in a little more than three seconds. This is good. You're presenting a nice, large picture that appears quickly on a visitor's screen.

10. Close the image and click the Stop button on the Actions palette. You have a nice Web-oriented action now. And we can proceed to create a droplet that will batch-process images according to the steps you defined in the action.

## Working with Droplets

It always helps to know your way around the palettes, menus, and pop-ups you will be working with, and the Droplet dialog box shown in Figure 8.22 is no exception. Although it's not exceedingly difficult to understand, we need to point out just a few of its quirks. Choose File, Automate, Create Droplet to follow along with our discussion and this figure. Um, this is a working discussion—we cover the options in this dialog box, and if you follow along with the Steeltone action, you will find a droplet that you created on your desktop.

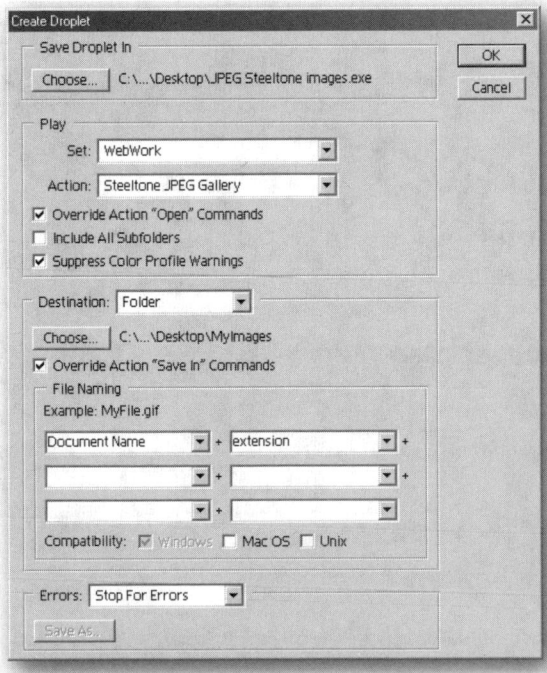

**Figure 8.22**    The Create Droplet dialog box in Photoshop will create an encapsulation of the currently chosen action on the Actions palette.

Before you do anything more, copy the contents of the Examples/Chap08 folder to the MyImages folder you created on the desktop.

### Example 8.5    Creating a Droplet

1. Choose File, Automate, Create Droplet. The dialog box should look similar to that shown in Figure 8.22.

2. Click Choose at the top of the box to decide where you want the droplet saved when all is done. In Figure 8.22, you can see that we chose the desktop. In this step, you will also be prompted to name the droplet. *Hint:* Make it easy on yourself and be a tad explicit about what the droplet does.

3. Read through the next few bulleted items and take the suggested actions or adapt them to your own needs:

   - The Override Action "Open" Commands is an option we *have* to discuss. Selecting this item forces the droplet to ignore any command in the action that begins with File, Open. Now, the Steeltone action started with File, Open, and then you chose an image from the Companion CD. In this instance you want to override the Open command in the action when you're programming the droplet, so check this option.

   - The Include All Subfolders option enables all folders *within* a folder dropped onto the droplet to be processed with the action. If you don't check this option, only images in the *root folder* get processed. And because we want to process only the images in the MyImages folder, and MyImages is a root folder, leave the Include All Subfolders option unchecked.

   - Check the Suppress Color Profile Warnings option. The images in your folder have been color corrected and tonally balanced by the author. If you're using a profile other than Adobe RGB (1998), you probably don't want a nag box popping up and alerting you, whenever an image is opened, that it doesn't match your current color space profile in Photoshop. When you have color-critical work that someone else handed you and is paying you $$$ to process, enable this feature and perform the necessary color space conversions. See Chapter 3 for the big picture on color profiles.

   - Another biggie is the Override Action "Save In" Commands option in the Destination field. If the action was created with a specific destination, or save-to, folder attached to it, the droplet will bypass this command when this option is selected. Say the author forgot where he saved the target image when programming the action. He'd check the Override "Save In" Commands option, choose Destination:Folder, and then in the directory box, he'd choose the Desktop, and the MyImages folder. You can see this in Figure 8.22.

- The File Naming section of the Create Droplet dialog box looks as though it could be confusing. Not to worry. Here's how it works: It enables us to format the file-naming *sequence*. Some of the options you'll find in this field are extension, serial numbers, date, and so on. When you are naming your file, you can select items to be inserted into the default names for the files, such as document name, serial number in numeric or alphabetical format, date the file was created, as well as file extension. Basically, any information you want to include can be dropped in. In this example, we don't do anything to the File naming field because we want to preserve the filename and change the extension to JPEG. Document Name and extension are the defaults for this feature.

- Choose an option for processing errors. Stop for Errors will halt the process until you confirm the error message. Log Errors to File records each error to file without stopping the droplet. When processing is complete a dialog box will appear noting errors. You may view the errors or save them to a file for later viewing. The Stop for Errors selection enables you to see firsthand where the problem is occurring, so you can edit the action and not waste time, and it's the option we recommend.

4. Click OK, and Photoshop writes an executable file to your desktop. All you need to do now is minimize Photoshop, and then drag the MyImages folder on top of the droplet, as shown in Figure 8.23. In Figure 8.24, the author attempted to screen-capture the droplet in action. Trust me, the process goes pretty fast on new machines!

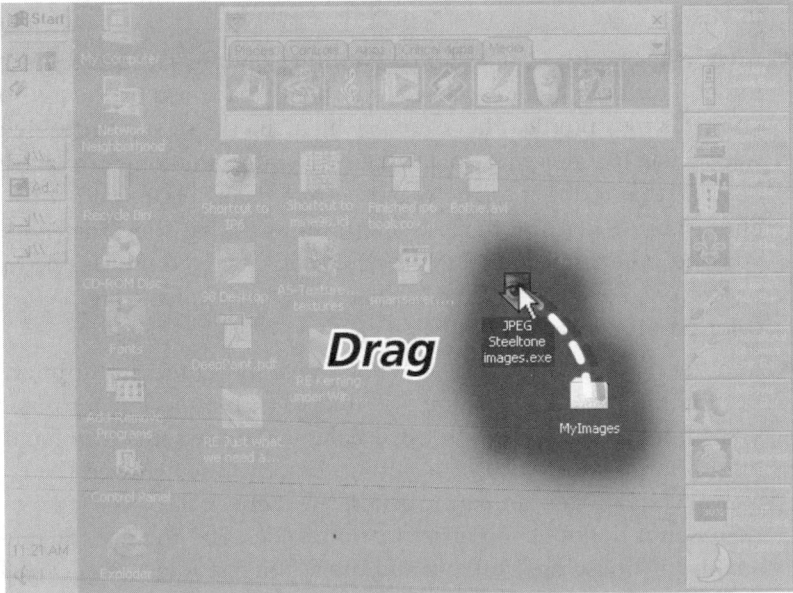

**Figure 8.23**    Drag the folder on top of the droplet for blindingly fast batch processing.

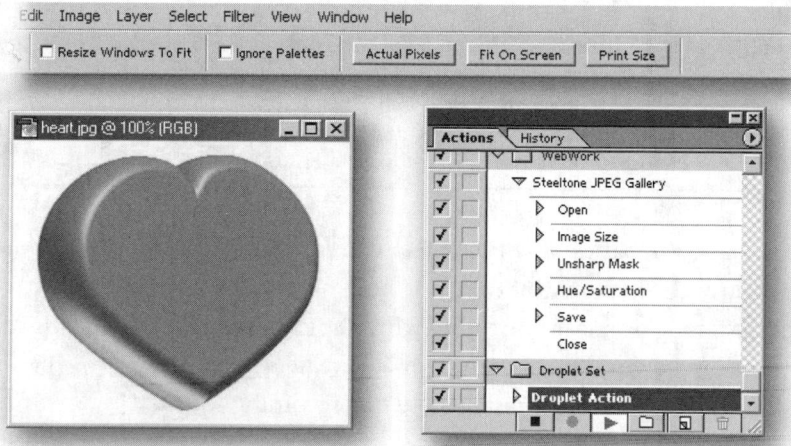

**Figure 8.24**   If you watch the batch droplet process verrrry closely, you might see something like this. Hey, automation is supposed to save time, right?

Once the processing festival has concluded, you'll see that Photoshop does not automatically close, and the workspace is fallow—no images! Where are they? Well, the originals are still in the MyImages desktop folder, as are all 10 processed Steeltone JPEG images. So get to writing up a fictitious bill for our fictitious client!

Before long, droplets will probably have their own following online. Soon droplets, like actions, will be featured on Web sites. Sharing scripting is one of the great freedoms that Web-content creators have.

## Handling Droplet Compatibility

Although droplets give you the option of choosing which systems they will be compatible with, you still need to be concerned with a couple items in regards to ensuring cross platform compatibility. When you're creating droplets for use on both Windows and Macintosh OS, the following should be noted:

- For a droplet created on a PC and loaded onto a Macintosh OS, drag the droplet onto the Photoshop icon. This will cause Photoshop to launch and update the droplet for use on the Macintosh.

- For conversion from a Macintosh droplet to Windows, simply change the file extension on the droplet to .EXE. The droplet will now be compatible on both systems.

**Warning**

**A Droplet Must Be Able to Find the Correct Folder**    Keep in mind that in order for the droplet to perform correctly on a new system, Save To folders and the like that were included in the action recording or droplet creation need to exist on the new system as well. A droplet created with a target destination of MyImages can't really save to that folder if it doesn't exist on the new host machine.

Once you have the basics down and feel comfortable working with actions and droplets, you will be amazed not only at how functional they are in nearly every aspect of designing or image correcting with Photoshop, but also with the amount of time that can be saved by learning how to create your own scripts, when necessary. Imitate, learn, and then master these two recording features!

## Using the Photoshop Batch Command

Although it's not as user friendly as a droplet (there's no cool desktop icon to play with), you do have the option of using the Batch command to process folders of images and their subfolders. Batch processing can also be used with a scanner with a document feeder or digital camera (a plug-in for these may require a plug-in module; check out www.Adobe.com for more information). Another thing to consider is that the plug-in may not be set up for batch processing, so you may want to check out the plug-in creator's Web site or contact them with any questions on this matter.

The Batch dialog box, shown in Figure 8.25, is nearly identical to the Create Droplet dialog box. The procedure for using it is basically the same.

Like droplets, you can save the processed images to a new folder, leave them open, or save and close to the original location. Batch processing operates in nearly the same way as droplets do, the main difference being the lack of a handy icon onto which you can drop images or folders to be batch processed. There is no executable file—the processing occurs within Photoshop itself. Whereas droplets will launch Photoshop for you, Photoshop needs to be open for you to use the Batch command.

Here's a quick walk-through of batch processing. If you read the droplets section, this might seem familiar—the process is nearly identical. You can use the Steeltone action if you like; and if you do, you already know how to fill out many of the fields in the Batch dialog box.

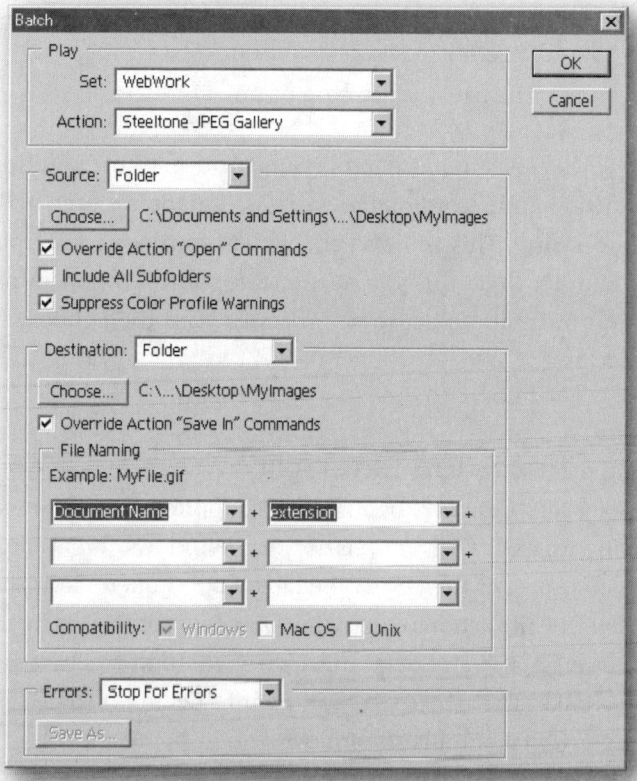

**Figure 8.25**  With the Batch dialog box you can set up the processing of an image or a folder of images.

### Example 8.6  Batch Processing Files in Photoshop

1. Choose File, Automate, Batch.

2. Select your Set and Action from the pop-ups.

3. Select a source folder to contain the images you want to process with the action.

4. You may override any Open commands in the action if you need to. If the action does not include an Open command, you may deselect this option. You may select all subfolders to be processed, as well; import to process digital camera images or scanned images; or choose to process only open files.

5. Decide where you want to save the enhanced images. (Choose None to leave the files open, choose Save and Close to overwrite the original images and save to the same folder, or pick Folder to save to a new location on your hard drive.) Check the Override Action "Save In" Commands checkbox.

6. Select a File Naming convention (see the preceding droplets section).

7. Select an option for error processing.

8. Click OK and let the batch processing begin.

Another point when you are batch processing: You may use multiple actions by creating a new action and recording the Batch command for each action you want to use during processing. This will also enable you to process multiple folders in a single session. In order to do this you must create shortcuts (Macintosh: aliases) of the folders within the main folder to be processed, and then choose to include All Subfolders.

## Automating Photoshop Externally

Thanks to the excellent designers behind Photoshop 6, automation can be accomplished externally as well. OLE automation for Windows, or AppleScript for the Macintosh (which is part of the OS), will enable you to open Photoshop and begin processing files or execute actions externally. QuicKeys for the Macintosh (you have to buy this program) is also a popular third-party addition to Photoshop for speeding up repetitive tasks. Though we will not go into detail on these resources, some benefits to using external automation follow:

- It allows for an image capture program (attached to a cam, perhaps) to snap the images, process them through Photoshop, and automatically upload them to a Web site.

- It's great for after-hours Photoshop work. An external script can shut down your system after Photoshop has completed its tasks—hours after you have left the office!

If you have other questions about OLE, contact Microsoft Corporation or visit their Web site at www.microsoft.com. For questions about AppleScript, see your Macintosh OS documentation, consult their Web site at www.apple.com/applescript/, or contact Apple Computers.

Up to this point, we've concentrated on the most hands-on automation features in Photoshop, as oxymoronic as that might sound. Droplets, the Batch feature, and actions can be fine-tuned or built from the ground up to exactly suit your tastes and needs.

But there are other automation features in Photoshop that deserve a brief nod here. Sometimes you need only a little help from Photoshop, because your need is modest but your time, like everyone's, is a most valuable commodity.

# Exploring Other Automation Features

Automation in Photoshop doesn't stop at Batch files. You'll want to explore two other easy-to-use and fun-to-have features: Contact Sheets and Picture Package. Both of these little jewels are located in the File, Automate menu.

## Working with a Contact Sheet

The Contact Sheet feature in version 5.5 was so popular that Adobe released the sequel: Contact Sheet II. Hopefully, you're familiar with the taxi driver's tour of the photography trade, the contact sheet. All the negatives on a roll of film are exposed directly to a sheet of photographic paper (the images are a tiny 35 millimeters, most often). So you have a quick reference for images from that roll that you want to enlarge. And conversely, you might want to put a big X through the duds on the roll.

Photoshop goes one step further. With the digital Contact Sheet, you can pick a folder of images that can come from any source, as long as they're in digital format. JPEGs can happily co-exist with TIFFs and PSDs, images from 50 years ago can go next to images taken yesterday with your digital camera—you get the drift.

In the following tutorial, you can use the images in the MyImages folder (you might want to delete the JPEG images to prevent repeat images on the contact sheet).

Here goes. This is a simple example of a specific need for automation:

### Example 8.7   Creating a Contact Sheet

1. Choose File, Automate, and then choose Contact Sheet II. A huge dialog box appears.

2. At the top of the dialog box, click the Choose button, and then choose the MyImages folder on the desktop. It is not necessary to check the Include All Subdirectories option in this instance.

3. The Document field should probably be left alone, unless you want a high-resolution contact sheet from which to print to your inkjet printer. If this is the case (and you're not building a screen show), change the resolution to about 200 ppi. Do not change the dimensions—inkjets do not print edge to edge on an 8½" by 11" page.

4. Here's where you really have to think deeply. Not! In the Thumbnails field, choose the number of columns and rows you want on the sheet. This depends entirely on how many images you have for the Contact Sheet. If you go with the 10 winners in the MyImages folder, your Contact Sheet II dialog box will look like Figure 8.26. Um, it should go without saying that when you increase the total number of images on a sheet, Photoshop automatically shrinks the images. Photoshop is very poor at stretching a physical sheet of inkjet paper <g>. In fact, I left two blank spaces on the sheet in Figure 8.26 to enable Photoshop to maximize the dimensions of the 10 images, while leaving room for me to write some notes on the page.

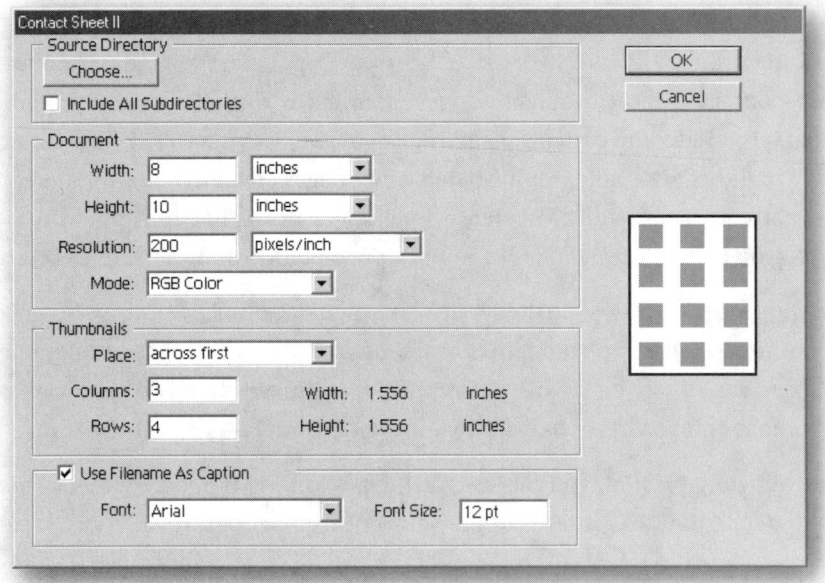

**Figure 8.26**    The Photoshop Contact Sheet II is great for previewing the entire contents of a folder in one fell swoop, or for showing off a printed copy.

5. Thumbnails aren't of much use without a title, so choose your font and the font size as your last step before you click OK. Photoshop writes the filenames beneath each image for easy identification. *Hint:* If you're under 50 years old you can probably use a 10 point font instead of 12 point. Ten point looks like magazine text, whereas 12 point looks like newspaper text, to accommodate people with vision problems and because newsprint tends to soak up ink and blot in text.

6. Click OK, and in a moment you'll see an image something like that shown in Figure 8.27. That's it! Oh. Yes—images are placed on a layer, so you might want to flatten the resulting contact sheet so you can share it with people who don't use Photoshop.

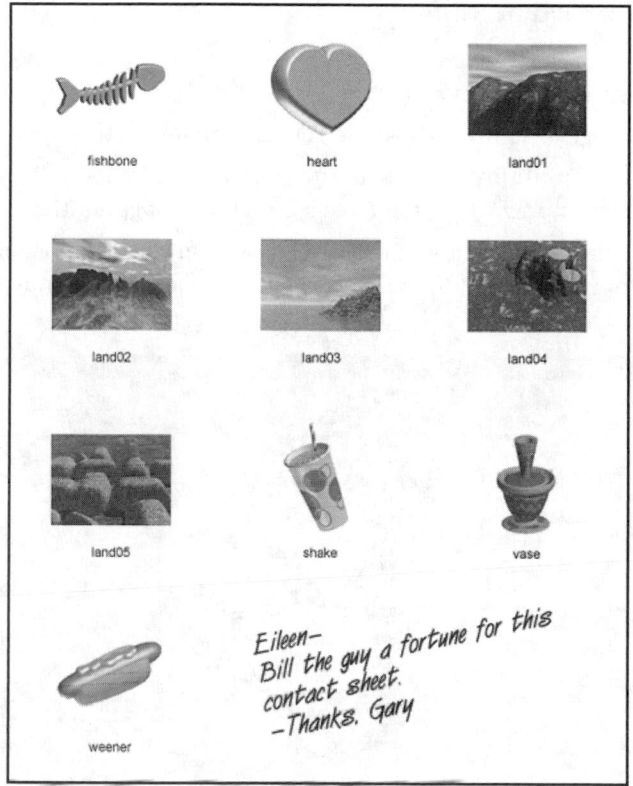

**Figure 8.27**   The finished contact sheet can be a reference for folders or a sample sheet for clients.

Our automation tour stops now at the Picture Package. We call it the "school picture package," and you'll soon see why.

## Digging into the Picture Package

Remember in school when the local photographer who low-balled all the other photographers came to the auditorium, snapped a picture, blinded you for several moments with the flash, and in a few days, your folks bought various sizes of the same unflattering picture? One for the grandparents (the big copy), several wallet sizes for your aunts and uncles, and you got to keep the really small ones for all your school sweethearts.

Well, Photoshop doesn't come with an auditorium (it's getting big enough for one, though!), but you can now produce multiple pictures that'll fit on a single sheet of inkjet paper. Get a photo of someone right now and open it in Photoshop. (Oh. It has to be a *digitized* picture.)

Now, let's produce a Picture Package.

### Example 8.8    Packaging Pictures on a Page

1. Open an image of someone. Choose File, Automate, Picture Package.

2. Click the Use Frontmost Document option. This is to choose the current active image window when you have a bunch of images in the workspace.

3. In the Document field, choose the Layout. As you can see in Figure 8.28, the author's going for the traditional "cheaper by the carton" layout.

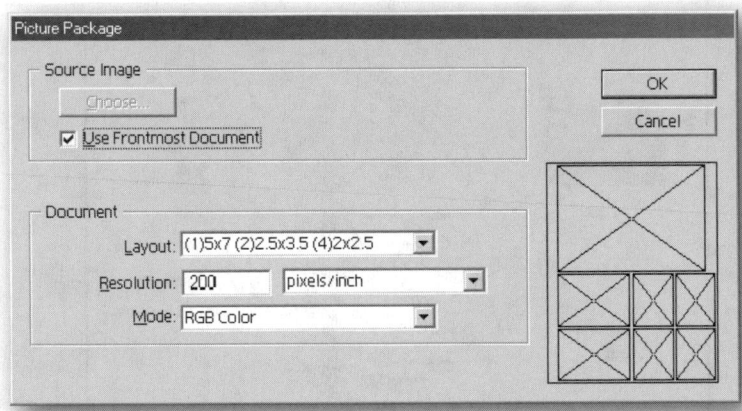

**Figure 8.28**    What a blast from the past! Picture Package files can be printed to an inkjet, and then it's up to you to find a metal ruler and an X-Acto™ blade.

4. Decide on image resolution. The default of 72 pixels/inch doesn't do it for an inkjet printer. You need something like 200 pixels/inch for decent inkjet prints. Click OK, and you'll get a layout something like Figure 8.29. Say "hi" to cousin Brent, everyone. Surprise, Brent! You didn't think I had the guts to run with your picture, did you <g>?

5. Pass out the images to your family. Don't forget to tell them how expensive and complicated they were to produce.

We think we've dug straight to the bottom of the automation bag in Photoshop, but if you think about it, what more could you ask for? You have a completely pro-grammable scripting engine, a way to parcel a complex script into an icon that exe-cutes the script, and a couple of ways to organize and distribute your images. Not bad for one submenu item off the File list!

**Figure 8.29**    Picture Packages are sort of like multiple returns on a single investment.

## Another Cool Tool: The Preset Manager

The Preset Manager does not automate tasks, but it's better than aspirin when some-one has messed with any of your seven palettes in Photoshop. Let's take a look at this hidden Treasure.

### Accessing the Preset Manager

Unfortunately, the Preset Manager does not have a hotkey—you need to make it display onscreen by choosing Edit, Preset Manager (toward the bottom of the menu). You have complete control over what palettes will load the next time you launch Photoshop using the Preset Manager. You can save a custom palette, load one you've already created, and even delete a palette, all from a central location. In Figure 8.30, you can see the drop-down list being dropped down—choose one palette at a time, and specify which one you want to load. If you check your Photoshop installation directory, the installation CD, or some sites on the Web dedicated to creating custom palettes, you will find an ample supply of brushes, styles, and so on from which to choose.

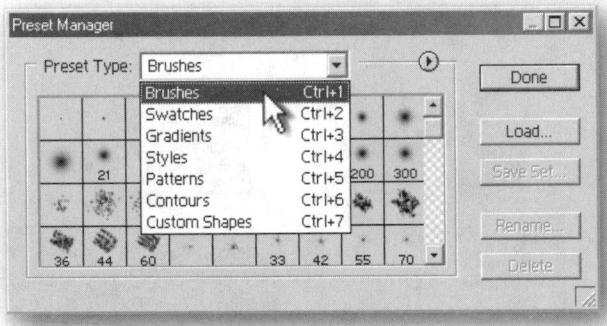

**Figure 8.30**    The Preset Manager enables you to pick all seven of Photoshop's palettes and load a set you need into the palettes.

"Simplify," "automate," "help." Although none of these terms is a *tool* in Photoshop, they are all requirements for the creative soul who wants to build a masterpiece with little or no unnecessary moves. You can go through *enough* unnecessary moves in the *real* world! Does anyone need more cleaning rags and turpentine <g>?

## Summary

The capability of Photoshop to repeat procedures is definitely beneficial to all areas of use. Of course there is still some legwork on the part of the designer—where is the fun in creating if the software does it *all* for you? By now you can see the benefit to using these tools and are already thinking of ways to apply them to your work. Photoshop is a resource that can change your outlook on the captured image. It can change the way you work, and ultimately, it could change your career.

## Resources

http://actionfx.com

**Action Fx Photoshop Actions Resource**

Free and membership.

http://www.photoshopuser.com

**The National Association of Photoshop Professionals official Web site**

Membership site, but well worth the price! Also, members receive a year subscription to *Photoshop User Magazine,* which alone is worth the membership fee.

http://www.actionxchange.com

**The Action Xchange**

Thousands of free actions by Photoshop users all over the globe. New updates daily!

# Part II

# Digging Deeper Into the Treasure Chest

# Chapter 9

# Selecting in Photoshop: Ah, the Many Ways to Select Stuff

Quite often you might find that you

need to select a portion of a photograph,

or graphic image before you can work

with it. Or you might need to isolate a

section of an image before you apply a special effect. It's times like these when Photoshop truly shines. In fact, Photoshop offers more than a dozen ways to make a selection—something for every situation you can imagine.

## Using the Selection Tools

The upper portion of the toolbox houses a variety of straightforward selection tools. In this chapter, we briefly discuss these tools and some useful modifier keys. You might want to have a document open in Photoshop to practice using some of those tools and modifier keys mentioned later (any size document is peachy, such as 400 pixels wide by 300 pixels high...you choose. Just make it big enough to have room to experiment).

### The Marquee Selection Tools

Figure 9.1 displays the tools list menu of the available marquee selection tools at the top-left corner of the toolbox. They are as follows:

- Rectangular Marquee tool
- Elliptical Marquee tool
- Single Row Marquee tool
- Single Column Marquee tool

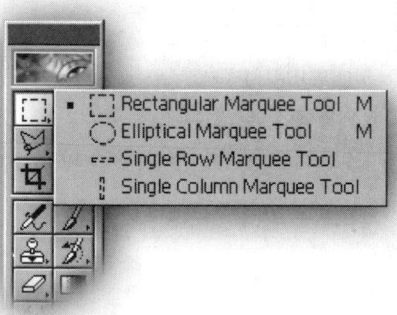

**Figure 9.1**    Click and hold your mouse over the upper-right Marquee tool on the toolbox.

Using these powerful tools is easy, but making them even more powerful is just as easy—combine them with *modifier keys*. Photoshop 6 provides some of these modifier options as icons on the Options bar when a selection tool is active. So you can click on the Options bar, or learn some modifiers that will speed up your work.

The Rectangular and Elliptical Marquee tools draw rectangular and elliptical selections—who would've guessed, right? <g>. Holding down the Shift key while dragging a selection with the Rectanglar or Elliptical Marquee tool constrains the selection to a perfect square or a perfect circle, respectively. Holding down the Alt(Opt) key when dragging a selection with either tool drags a selection starting at the center point. So what happens when you press Shift+Alt(Opt) when dragging with these tools? You guessed it—a perfect square or circle that starts from the center point. Because Adobe is not anxious for you to accidentally move the visual contents within a selection, clicking inside and dragging a selection marquee (rectangular, elliptical, lopsided, whichever) moves only the marquee, and not a piece of the underlying image. Only moving selections with the Move tool moves the marquee's contents. And for those of us who go way back with Photoshop, this selection moving convention was not always so—we need to relearn a little.

The Single Row and Single Column tools allow you to click in a document and create a 1-pixel-wide row or column the width or length of the entire document. You can position this row or column selection by clicking and then dragging to the desired location (or position the pointer inside the marquee selection and drag to a new location). This is a particularly useful duo of tools when an image has a line of corruption running through it. You pick a row or column next to the corruption, duplicate it, and put it over the flaw. Most of the time, the viewing audience will not detect that there's two identical rows of pixels in your image.

## The Lasso Tools

Figure 9.2 shows the Lasso tools list. These tools include the following:

- Lasso tool
- Polygonal Lasso tool
- Magnetic Lasso tool

Click and drag with the Lasso tool to draw freehand selections. The Polygonal Lasso tool draws straight edge selections. No dragging is needed with this tool. Just click the corner points of the selection.

**Note**

**Completing Your Selection**    If you are using any of the Lasso tools and release the cursor before you complete the selection, Photoshop will complete the selection for you by drawing a line segment connecting the first and last points. If you don't want Photoshop to close your selection with a straight line, click once on the first point of the selection to close it yourself.

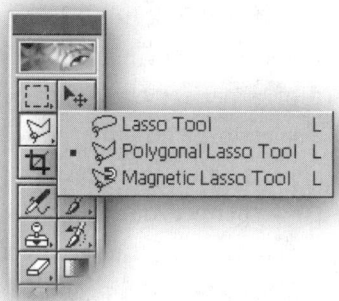

**Figure 9.2**    The Lasso tools list is located below the Marquee tools on the Toolbox.

The Magnetic Lasso tool works best in areas of high contrast. Click once along the edge of an image area you want to select, release the mouse button, then drag around the object edge. If the color contrast between image area edges is strong enough, the Magnetic Lasso tool will do a very good job of snapping to the edge of the area you want to select.

**Tip**

**Toggling Between the Lasso and the Polygonal Lasso Tools**    Toggling between the Lasso and Polygonal Lasso tools can be accomplished by holding down the Alt(Opt) key. Try testing this in the practice document: choose the Lasso tool, hold down the Alt(Opt) key, and start dragging a free-form selection. Before completing the selection, continue to hold down the Alt(Opt) key and release the mouse button, thus toggling to the Polygonal Lasso tool. Click points to create straight lines with the Polygonal Lasso tool. To toggle back to the Lasso tool, hold down the mouse button once more and drag instead of clicking.

**Note**

**Accidental Loss**    This would not be a comprehensive book if we didn't make recommendations every now and then. For beginners, and especially experienced users, the Polygonal Lasso tool can be a mixed blessing. It's darned easy to lose a selection if you accidentally click after closing a selection marquee, and to add insult to injury, you've started a new polygon selection after losing the one you want.

Suggestions? Remember to press the spacebar to toggle to the Hand tool and then select a "quieter" tool (such as the Rectangular Marquee tool) directly after making a polygonal selection. Pressing Ctrl, similarly, will toggle the tool to the Move tool, and then you have a chance of choosing a different tool without beginning another selection in the image.

Our best suggestion, if you are having problems mastering the Polygonal Lasso tool, is to always use the (normal) Lasso tool, and then press Alt(Opt) when you need to click straight line segments of a selection marquee.

## The Crop Tool

Located just below the Lasso tools is the Crop tool. When using the Crop tool, drag a selection around the area of the image you want to keep. When you release the mouse button, a bounding box will display with handles at the corners and sides that you use to resize or reposition the crop area. Placing the cursor inside the box and dragging to the desired location repositions the crop area. When you finish the Crop tool's bounding box adjustments, double-click inside the box or press the Enter (Return) key to apply the crop. If you change your mind and don't want to crop the image, press Esc to cancel the operation, or right-click (Macintosh: hold Ctrl and click), and choose Cancel from the pop-up menu.

**Tip**

**Moving the Contents of a Selection Area**    As mentioned earlier, the Move tool is the only tool that can move image content when a marquee selection is active. Holding down the Ctrl(⌘) key quickly toggles to the Move tool from almost any tool. Holding down the Ctrl(⌘)+Alt(Opt) *floats* a copy of the content within a selection and allows it to be moved elsewhere in the image (in other words, creates a duplicate of the selected area).

## The Magic Wand Tool

The Magic Wand tool, located on the toolbox just to the right of the Lasso tools, selects areas of similar color in an image. For example, if you have a large area you want to select that consists of mostly red-colored pixels, clicking once somewhere in the red area will select all the surrounding pixels of the same color. By default, the *contiguous* option on the Options bar is checked for the Magic Wand tool. In plain English, this means when the contiguous option is checked, pixels of similar color *need to be touching one another* to be selected by clicking the Magic Wand tool. When this option is unchecked, clicking on the same red area will select *all* similar red areas in the document.

# Extending the Possibilities

You can make complex selections with the help of modifier keys, or by using the selection option icons on the Options bar, which enable you to add, subtract, or intersect selections with a combination of any of the selection tools. Figure 9.3 shows the selection modifier icons that are on the Options bar when a selection tool is chosen. These icons will be referred to frequently in the following set of steps. You can use the icons in the following ways:

- Clicking the Subtract from Selection icon—or holding down the Alt(Opt) key—makes your next selection subtract from a current selection. This is indicated with a minus sign, which appears next to the cursor.

- Clicking the Add to Selection icon—or holding down the Shift key—adds to the current selection. A plus sign appears next to the cursor when this option is active.

- Clicking the Restrict Selection icon (or holding down the Alt(Opt) and Shift keys together) enables you to create an intersection of two or more selections. This selection modifier mode displays an x next to the cursor when using the marquee tools, but a minus sign will be displayed when using the Lasso tools.

- If you have extremely good dexterity and can hold down the spacebar while dragging the mouse to make a selection, you can reposition the selection as it is being made.

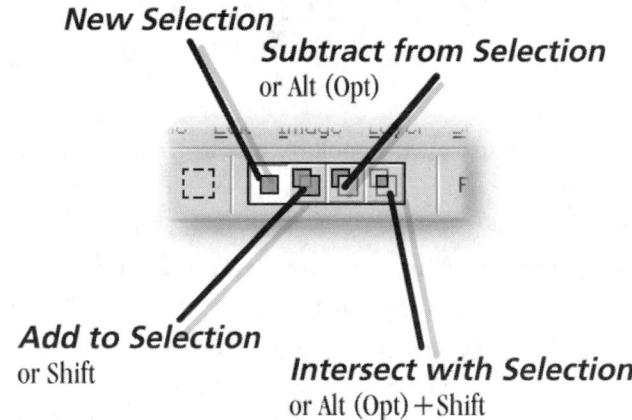

*New Selection*

*Subtract from Selection*
or Alt (Opt)

*Add to Selection*
or Shift

*Intersect with Selection*
or Alt (Opt)+Shift

**Figure 9.3**    Use the selection option icons on the Options bar (or the keyboard shortcuts) to add, subtract, or intersect selections using a combination of any of the selection tools.

**Tip**

**Using a Modifier Key to Perform More than One Function**    A modifier key can be used to do more than one thing at a time. For example, you might want to use the Shift key to add a selection to an existing selection and also use it to constrain the Elliptical Marquee tool to a perfect circle. To accomplish both tasks, as in this example, hold down the Shift key to add to the selection, but as you drag with the mouse, lift your finger off the Shift key and then press down on the Shift key again to constrain the selection to a perfect circle. This enables the Shift key to perform both modifier functions at the same time.

If all these choices and possibilities aren't enough to keep you busy, Photoshop *also* provides an option on the Select menu to transform selections (similar to the Transform tool on the Edit menu, which is used to alter layer information). Ctrl(⌘)+T is the shortcut to adding the Transform bounding box to an active selection. The Transform Selection box has control handles for resizing and also allows rotation when the cursor is placed near an outside corner of the box. Right-click (Macintosh: hold Ctrl and click) inside the box to see a context menu with a range of choices such as Distort, Skew, Flip Horizontally, and so on. Double-click inside the box or press Enter (Return) to apply the changes and exit the bounding box. The Esc key is used to exit the box without applying any of the changes.

## Combining Basic Selections to Define an Image

All these concepts will make more sense if we put them into practice rather than simply read about them. Let's apply some of these options and features and design an illustration of a tool, which seems appropriate here. You will use the Marquee and Lasso tools to define a wrench shape selection, making use of the modifier icons—to become more familiar with them. Once the shape is completed you will add color and dimension to the image.

### Example 9.1    Adding and Subtracting Selections

1. Press Ctrl(⌘)+N to open a new document. Make the new document **400** (pixels) width and **400** (pixels) length, RGB mode, **72** (pixels/inch) for Resolution, and White for Contents. Press Enter (Return).

> **Warning!**   If an error message appears when you open the CD files, press Ctrl(⌘)+Shift+K and then choose Adobe RGB (1998) from the Working Spaces, RGB drop-down list. See Chapter 3 for more information.

2. Choose the Elliptical Marquee tool on the toolbox. On the Options bar next to Style, click the arrow to access the drop-down menu and choose Fixed Size. Type **90** (pixels) for Width and Height, as shown in Figure 9.4.

**Figure 9.4**   Choose Fixed Size from Options bar and type **90** (pixels) for Width and Height.

The Fixed Size option enables you to just click to create an ellipse or rectangle if you know the size you need in advance (the default option of Normal enables you to determine the size as you drag).

**3.** Click and drag to position the circular selection near the top middle of the document. Another circle is needed near the bottom. Click the Add to Selection icon on the Options bar (a plus sign should appear next to the cursor). Click and drag the second circle into a position directly below the first circle as seen in Figure 9.5.

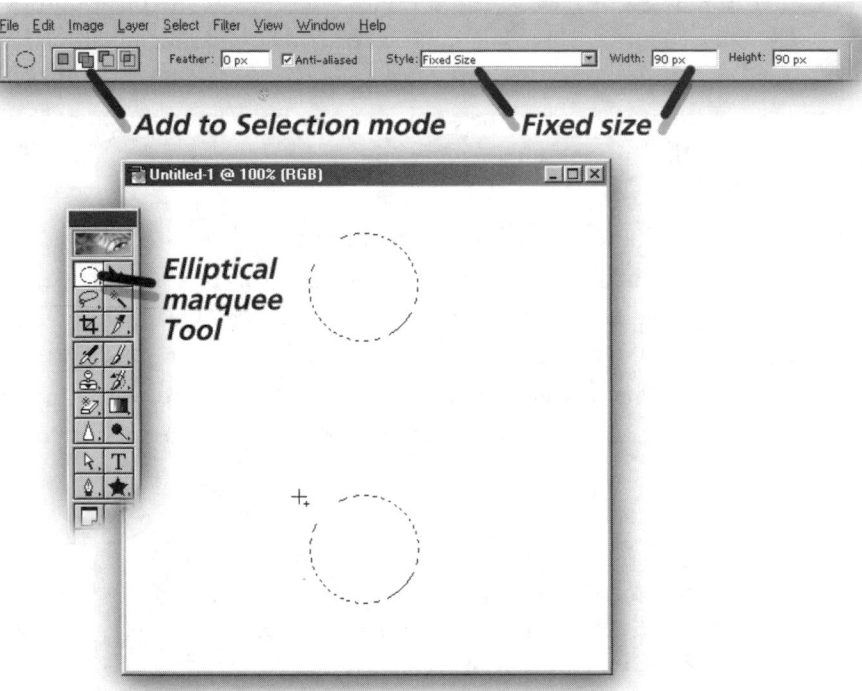

**Figure 9.5**   Click the Add to Selection icon on the Options bar and add a second circle of the same size under the first circle created.

**4.** Click the Marquee tools list on the toolbox and choose the Rectangular Marquee tool (or press Shift+M until the Rectangular Marquee is the selected tool). On the Options bar, choose Normal for the style. Click the Subtract from Selection icon, a minus sign appears near the cursor. Drag a rectangle as shown in Figure 9.6 near the top circle to create a shape like the business end of a wrench. While dragging the rectangle, hold down the spacebar to position the rectangle in the desired spot.

While the top circle is starting to look wrench-like, you need to add and subtract a few more selections to make the bottom circle look like a handle.

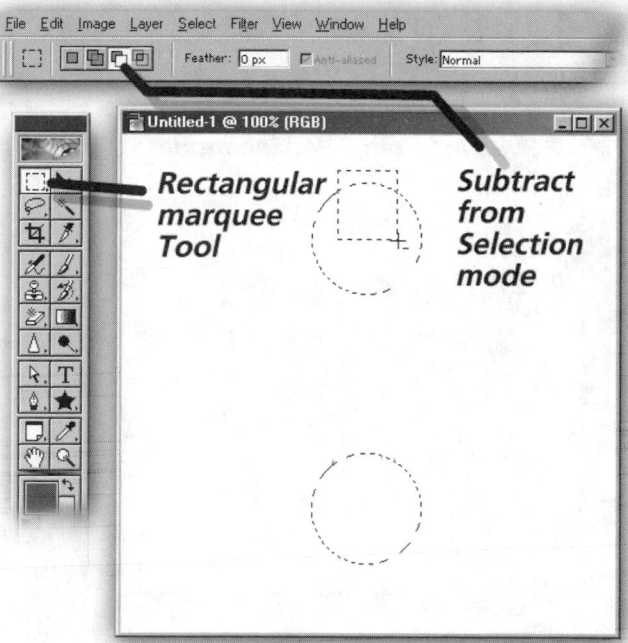

**Figure 9.6**   Click the Subtract from Selection icon on the Options bar and choose Normal Style to subtract a rectangle from the upper circle selection.

5. Choose the Elliptical Marquee tool from the toolbox, or press Shift+M to switch to it. On the Options bar, choose Fixed Size and type **60** (pixels) in both the Width and Height fields. Click the Subtract from Selection icon if it is not already chosen. In the document, click and drag to position the circle inside the lower circle, as shown in Figure 9.7.

   In the next step, make a straight edge near the bottom of the inside circle you just created. Because the inside circle on the handle was a product of subtraction, you will need to *add* to the circle to change the bottom edge of the interior circle to a straight edge.

6. On the toolbox, click the Polygonal Lasso tool (or press Shift+L until the Polygonal Lasso tool is chosen). Click the Add to Selection icon from the Options bar. Click the first point starting on the left side between the two lower circles (at the halfway point of the inner circle). Hold down the Shift key to constrain the movement horizontally, and then click a second point on the right side between the two circle selections. Release the Shift key and continue clicking between the two circles around the lower half until you reach the beginning point to close the selection, as shown in Figure 9.8.

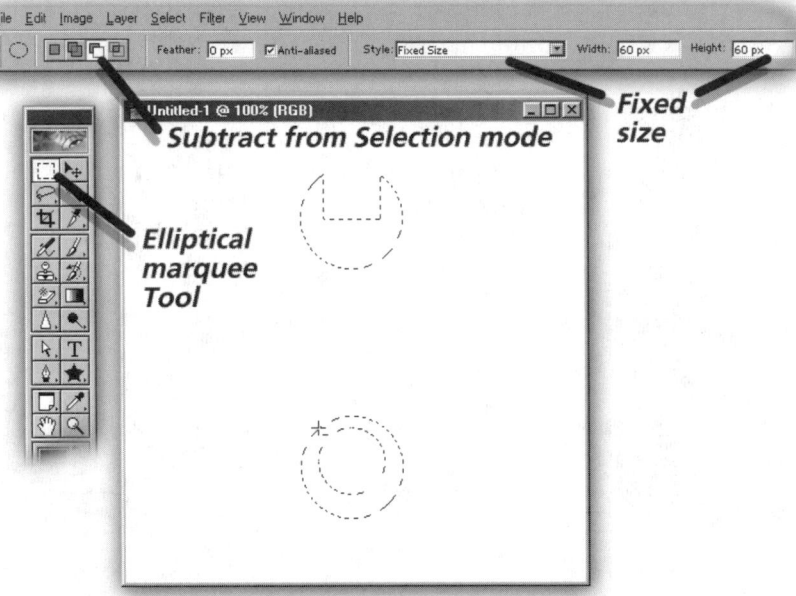

**Figure 9.7**   Subtract a Fixed Size 60 (pixels) circular selection from the lower circle to help create a handle.

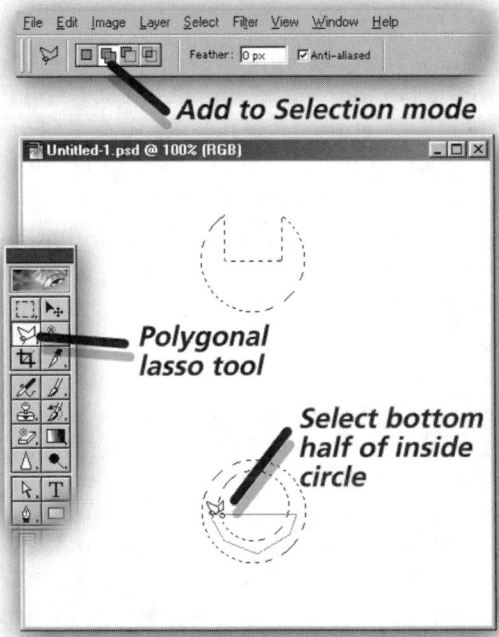

**Figure 9.8**   Click the Add to Selection icon on the Options bar and use the Polygonal Lasso tool to add the next selection to the inside circle on the bottom.

The wrench needs a handle between the two ends or it won't work, and certainly wouldn't sell well at Sears.

7. Switch to the Rectangular Marquee tool (or press Shift+M until the Rectangular marquee is chosen). On the Options bar, choose Normal for Style and click the Add to Selection icon if it is not already chosen. Drag to add a rectangular shape between the two wrench ends. Hold down the spacebar as you drag to reposition the selection to the desired location as shown in Figure 9.9. Leave the document open for the next part of the assignment.

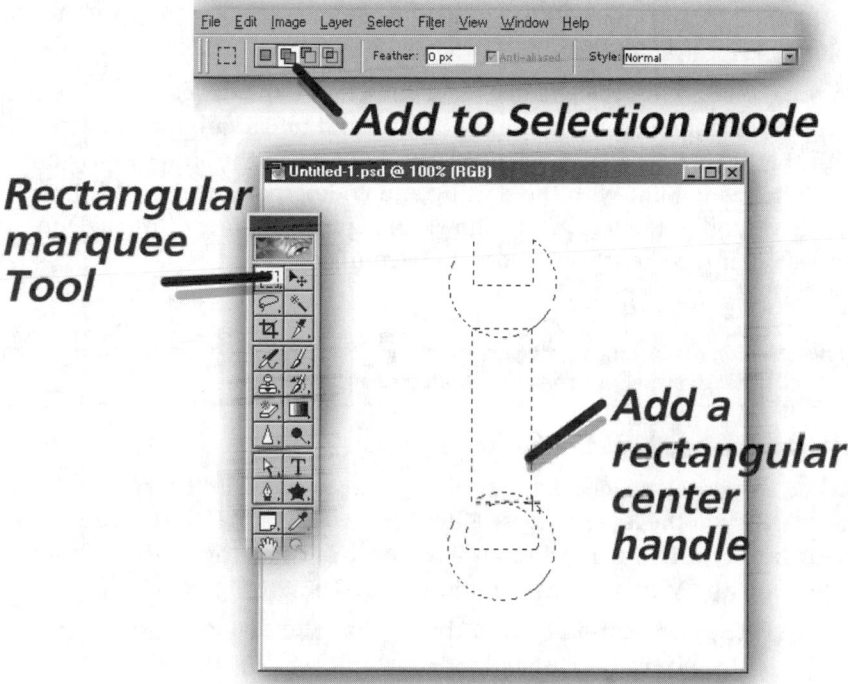

**Figure 9.9**   Click the Add to Selection icon on the Options bar and choose Normal Style to add a rectangular handle to give the selection its final wrench form.

## Adding Color to the Selection

You should have a good idea by now how modifier icons and keys can be used in combination with selection tools to produce a desired selection shape. With the wrench selected, let's have some fun by making use of the Gradient tool—and filters—to give a metallic look to the wrench.

Example 9.2    Coloring the Selection with a Metallic Look

1. While the wrench selection is still active, Alt(Opt)+click the Create new layer icon near the bottom right of the Layers palette. Holding Alt opens a dialog box where you can name this layer. In general, it's a good habit to name layers, especially if your composition consists of three or more layers.

2. In the Name field, type **Wrench**. Click OK.

3. To apply a gradient fill to the wrench selection, click the foreground color selection box on the toolbox and choose a light gray; R:204, G:204, B:204. Click OK to exit the Color Picker. Click the background color selection box on the toolbox and choose a darker gray (such as R:129, G:129, B:129) in the Color Picker. Click OK to return to the workspace.

4. On the toolbox, click the Gradient tool and choose the Reflected Gradient icon on the Options bar. Choose the Foreground to Background gradient. With the Wrench layer as the active layer, hold down the Shift key as you drag a horizontal line with the starting and ending point within the inside handle section of the wrench, as shown in Figure 9.10. Press Ctrl(⌘)+D to deselect after the wrench selection has been filled.

**Tip**

**Use Shift to Constrain Lines**    Holding down the Shift key when dragging constrains the line to a precise vertical, horizontal, or 45-degree angle.

Let's give the gradient a brushed metal look.

5. On the Layers palette, check the first box next to the word Lock, to lock the transparency of the layer. Choose Filter, Noise, Add Noise. In the Add Noise dialog box, type in **4** for the Amount, choose Gaussian for the Distribution and choose the Monochromatic option. Click OK. See Figure 9.11.

6. Choose Filter, Blur, Motion Blur. In the Motion Blur dialog box, type **45°** for the Angle, **15** (pixels) for Distance, as shown in Figure 9.12. Click OK. Uncheck the Lock Editing Layer Transparency option on the Layers palette. Press Ctrl(⌘)+Shift+S to access the Save As dialog box. Name the file **Wrench.psd**, and find a convenient location for it on your hard disk. Click Save.

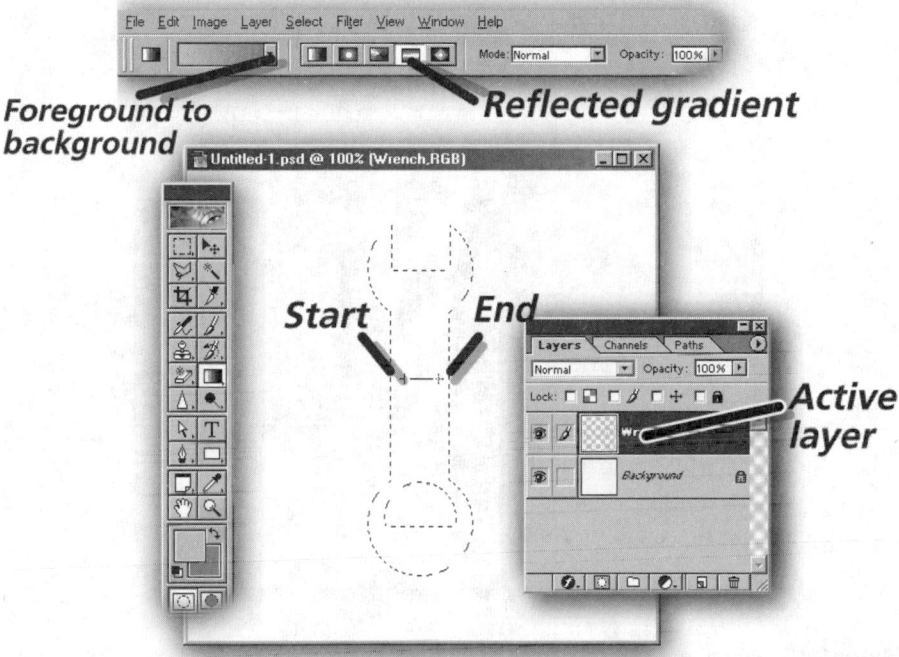

**Figure 9.10**   Choose the Reflected Gradient icon on the Options bar and with the Background to Foreground Gradient, drag a horizontal line within the handle selection to add color and form.

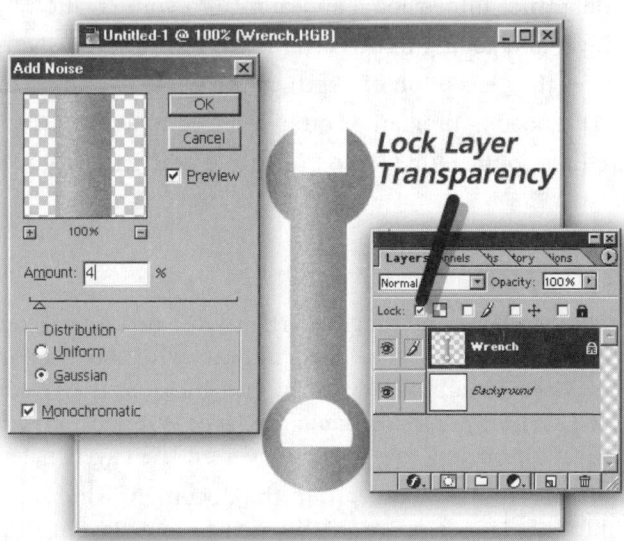

**Figure 9.11**   Lock the layer transparency on the Layers palette to apply the Add Noise filter to only the color information on the layer and to preserve its shape.

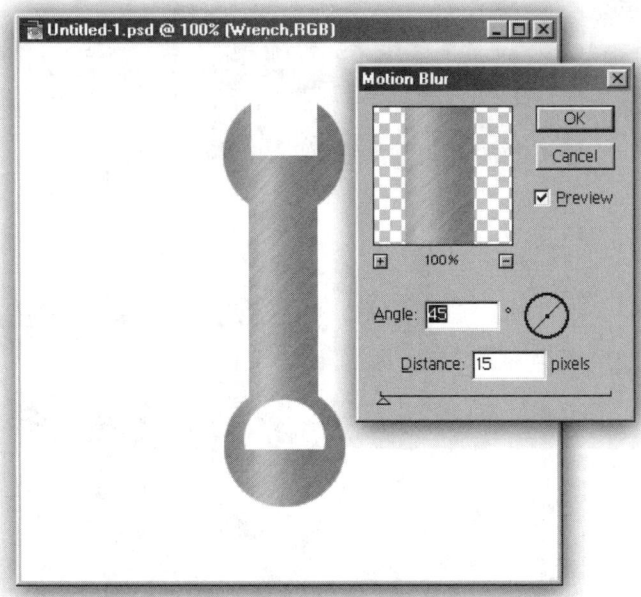

**Figure 9.12**    Apply the Motion Blur filter with an Angle of 45° and a Distance of 15 for a brushed metal look.

## Giving Dimension to the Selection

You will now add a three-dimensional appearance to your creation by using a copy of the Wrench layer and adding to this layer (with tools previously used) to make a selection that gives the perception of depth to the wrench. Extending the depth of an object in a 3D modeling program is often referred to as *extruding*. We are trying to *simulate* extruding, so the term "Wrench Extrude" will make a good name for this layer.

### Example 9.3    Adding Dimension

1. Click the Wrench layer and drag it to the Create new layer icon near the bottom of the Layers palette. A new layer appears with the title Wrench copy. Right-click (Macintosh: hold down Ctrl and click) on the Wrench copy layer and choose Layer Properties. Rename the layer **Wrench Extrude** and click OK. Drag this layer below the Wrench layer on the Layers palette.

2. Press V to switch to the Move tool. In the document window, drag slightly down and to the right to move the Wrench Extrude layer to a position that appears to add depth to the original Wrench layer, as shown in Figure 9.13.

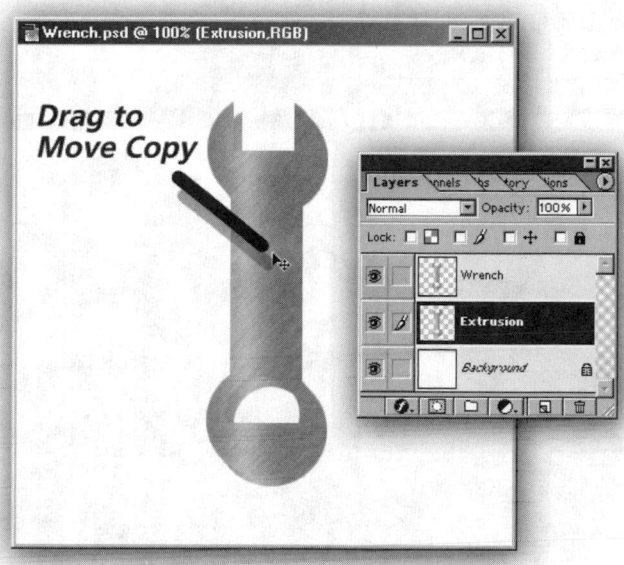

**Figure 9.13**    Drag the Wrench Extrude layer slightly down and to the right. This copy of the wrench will be used to give the appearance of depth to the image.

3. Hold down Ctrl(⌘) and the spacebar to toggle to the Zoom (in) tool and drag a square around the top-left edge of the wrench, to zoom into this area. Hold down the Ctrl(⌘) key while you click the Wrench Extrude layer to load the layer nontransparent areas as a selection marquee.

4. On the toolbox, click the Polygonal Lasso tool (or press Shift+L until you have the Polygonal Lasso tool chosen). Click the Add to Selection icon on the Options bar. Click points (as shown in Figure 9.14), connecting the corner of the Wrench end to the corner of the Wrench Extrude end. Continue to click points inside the wrench area, and then close the path at the beginning click point.

   The selection is visible on the Wrench layer, but the active layer is the Wrench Extrude layer (below the Wrench layer). *This* is where changes will actually be made. Because the Wrench layer is on top, the changes made will not be seen within the Wrench layer area.

5. Click on the foreground color selection box on the toolbox and choose a dark gray; R:90, G:90, B:90. Press Alt(Opt)+Delete (Backspace) to fill the selection with the dark gray.

   It will help to have the Brush Size option active while painting so that you can easily see where color will be applied. The next step will show how to choose this preference if it is not already active.

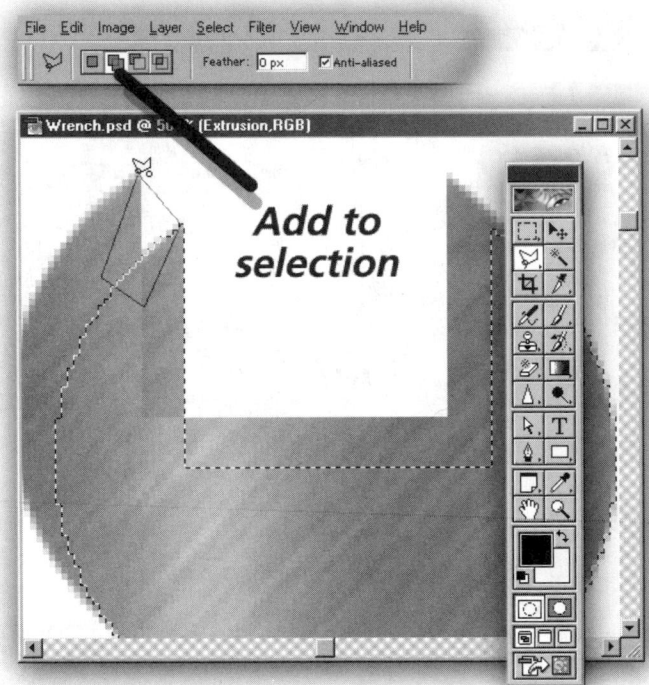

**Figure 9.14**    Click the Add to Selection icon on the Options bar and use the Polygonal Lasso tool to add the missing corner, giving the appearance of depth.

6. Press Ctrl(⌘)+K to access the Preference dialog box, then press Ctrl(⌘)+3 to access Display and Cursors preferences. Change the option under Painting Cursors to Brush Size and click OK.

7. Press Ctrl(⌘)+H to hide the selection. Click the Airbrush tool. On the Options bar, set the pressure to **20%** and click the arrow next to the brush type to access the Brush palette. Choose a large, soft-edge brush on the Brush palette (the 35-pixel brush works well).

8. Press D (default colors) and with black as the foreground color, stroke along the edges where the Wrench and Wrench Extrude objects meet to help give more definition to the image. Keep the Brush Size cursor only slightly within the Wrench Extrude area and most of the Brush Size cursor on top of the Wrench layer, as shown in Figure 9.15. Darken the remaining edges in the same manner to suggest depth (press the spacebar to toggle to the Hand tool and drag within the document to view the remaining wrench areas as you paint). Press Ctrl(⌘)+the minus key to zoom out for a more complete overall view if needed. When you are satisfied, press Ctrl(⌘)+D to deselect the marquee.

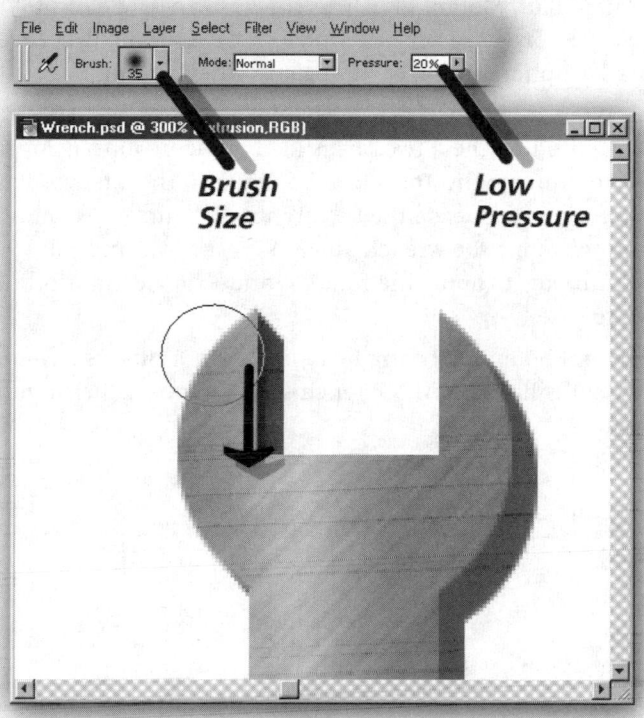

**Figure 9.15**   Keep the Brush Size cursor close to the edge as shown and paint a slight amount of black color to the edge areas to help add depth.

It is important to note that even though the marquee selection was hidden, it was still active. If you choose to hide a selection, don't forget to deselect it when done.

**Note**

Photoshop 6 has so many nonprinting elements you can tap into, you might find yourself wanting to hide one element, but not another. Ctrl(⌘)+H hides everything: the grid, guides, selection marquees, and so on. If you run into a situation where you want to hide a selection but keep guides you created onscreen, choose View, Show, and then click Show Options. In this box, you can check items that you always want shown (Ctrl(⌘)+H will not hide them—you have to choose View, Show, and then manually turn off an element).

**9.** Make sure the Wrench Extrude layer is still the current editing layer on the Layers palette. Check the first box next to the word Lock to Lock Editing Layer Transparency. Choose Filter, Noise, Add Noise and then apply an Amount of **4**, choose Gaussian for Distribution and check the Monochromatic option. Click OK.

10. Choose Filter, Blur, Motion Blur. This time use an Angle of **–45°** and keep Distance at **15** (pixels). Click OK. Uncheck the Lock Editing Layer Transparency option on the Layers palette when finished.

11. Click the Wrench layer and then click on the box to the left of the Wrench Extrude layer to link these two layers (a chain icon appears in the box). Press Ctrl(⌘)+T to bring up the Transform box around the wrench. Position the cursor near a corner outside the box. When the cursor becomes a bent two-headed arrow, rotate the wrench about 45° as shown in Figure 9.16. Press the Enter (Return) key to apply the rotation and exit the Transform box. Press Ctrl(⌘)+S to save.

The Transform bounding box may appear only around the wrench object, but because it is linked to the Wrench Extrude layer, all changes apply to *both* layers.

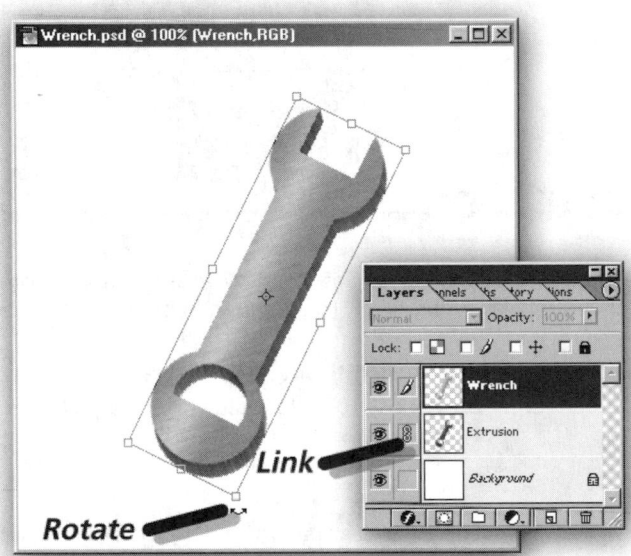

**Figure 9.16**    Link the Wrench and Wrench Extrude layers on the Layers palette. Press Ctrl(⌘)+T to rotate the wrench 45°. Press Enter (Return) when finished.

### Giving a Shadow to the Wrench

A drop shadow is needed just about now. I'm pretty sure that somewhere in Design 101 class they teach you that all design work must have a drop shadow. Photoshop has a Layer Style feature that makes drop shadows a snap. Or a click.

You will make a shadow using the Layer Style option later in the chapter. Because this chapter covers selections, it'll be a better learning experience for you to make the first shadow the "old-fashioned way." This method not only is good to know if you need to control a specific aspect of the shadow, but also demonstrates how the layer information can be used to make an active selection marquee. Modifier keys work much the same way with Layer selections as they do with the selection tools.

### Example 9.4    Creating a Drop Shadow

1. Click the Background layer to make it the active layer. Hold down the Alt(Opt) key and click the Create new layer icon near bottom right of the Layers palette. Title the layer **Wrench Shadow** in the Name field of the New Layer dialog box. Click OK.

   Why make the Background layer active? When you create a new layer, Photoshop places it *above* the current active layer. Because the new shadow layer needs to be below the Wrench Extrude layer, you had to make the Background layer the active layer.

2. Hold down the Ctrl(⌘) key and click the Wrench layer to load the wrench as a selection. Hold down the Ctrl(⌘)+Shift key and click the Wrench Extrude layer to add this layer information to the selection (notice a plus sign appears near the cursor when you click the additional layer as in Figure 9.17).

**Figure 9.17**    Add to the Wrench selection by holding down the Ctrl(⌘)+Shift keys while clicking on the Wrench Extrude layer.

3. Press D (default colors)—black is the current foreground color. With the Wrench Shadow layer still selected as the active layer, press Alt(Opt)+Delete (Backspace) to fill the selection with black. Press Ctrl(⌘)+D to deselect.

4. Press V to switch to the Move tool and drag the shadow down and slightly to the right as shown in Figure 9.18. The same Design 101 lesson that states a drop shadow is required *also* states that it be down and slightly to the right!

**Figure 9.18**   Moving the Wrench Shadow layer down and slightly to the right is the first step to making this layer appear like a shadow.

Shadows are not typically solid black with well-defined edges, so let's apply a filter and a few layer settings to soften this one.

5. On the Layers palette, lower the Opacity to **70%** and change the Layer mode from Normal to Multiply for this shadow layer. Choose Filter, Blur, Gaussian Blur. When the Gaussian Blur dialog box appears, pick a number for the Radius that gives a nice blur edge (**4** or **5** works well) as seen in Figure 9.19. Click OK. Press Ctrl(⌘)+S to save.

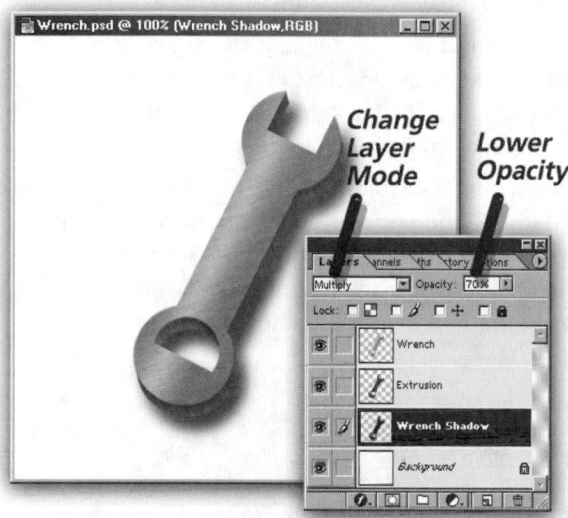

**Figure 9.19**    Before applying the Gaussian Blur filter to the Wrench Shadow layer, change the opacity on the Layers palette to 70% and the Layer mode from Normal to Multiply for the finishing touches.

## Using Channels to Create Selections

The plain white background needs some improvement. Because the wrench is a metallic object, let's keep with the look by creating a metallic grid background. We will make use of the Channels palette to create a channel, which allows grayscale information to be saved and used in a variety of ways. Filters can be applied to a channel and, as with layers, channel information can be loaded as a selection.

### Note

**How the Color Halftone Filter Works**    The Color Halftone filter simulates the effect of a halftone screen. The radius determines the size of circles in pixels (from 4 to 127). The screen angles for each channel determine the angle at which the circles will appear (0 would be perfectly horizontal). For a Grayscale image (or when working with channels such as the Alpha channel that use grayscale information only), a screen angle value is needed only for Channel 1. When applying the filter to an image from the Layers palette, use Channels 1, 2, and 3, for RGB images (which correspond to the red, green, and blue channels).

Similarly, for CMYK images, all four channels are used to correspond to the cyan, magenta, yellow, and black channels. If, for example, you wanted to create the same dot image from this assignment on a New Layer in the Layers palette of our RGB image (rather than on a New Channel), an angle value of 45 would be needed for Channels 1, 2, and 3. The main advantage to applying the filter to a channel rather than a layer is the ease in which a channel enables you to use grayscale information as a selection. Step 5 in Example 9.5 demonstrates this.

### Example 9.5   Creating a New Background

1. Click the Background layer to make it the active layer. Click the foreground color selection box on the toolbox and choose a light gray; R:215, G:215, B:215. Click OK. Click the background color selection box on the toolbox and choose a darker gray; R:99, G:99, B:99. Click OK.

2. Press G to switch to the Gradient tool. On the Options bar, click the Reflected Gradient and choose the Foreground to Background as the gradient in the drop-down list (first gradient choice on the top left row). Drag a diagonal line perpendicular to the wrench handle with starting and ending points outside the handle area, as shown in Figure 9.20.

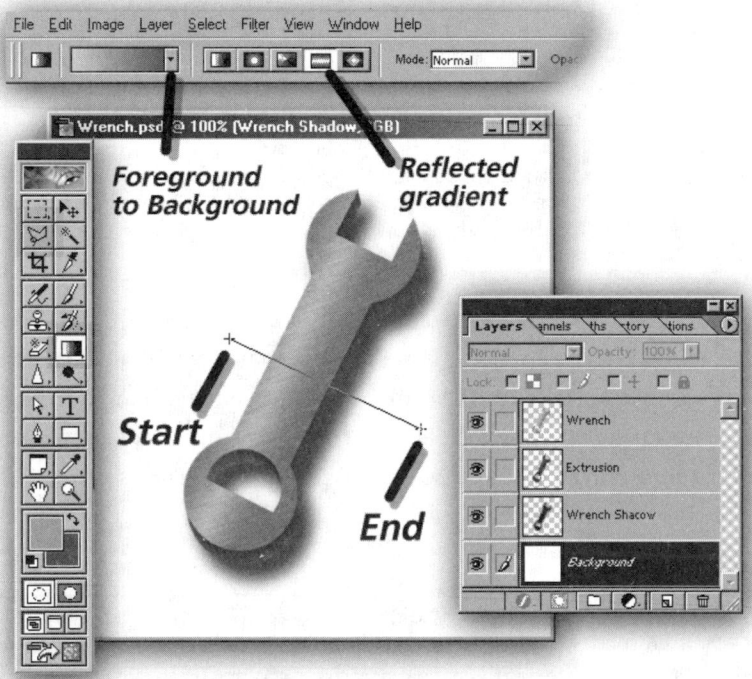

**Figure 9.20**   With the Background layer active, drag a gradient within the document that is perpendicular to the wrench handle to create a background that makes use of the Reflected Gradient using foreground and background colors.

3. Click the Channels tab to display the Channels palette (or choose Window, Show Channels if you detached Channels from the Layers palette). Click the Create New Channel icon near the lower-right corner of the palette. A new channel titled Alpha 1 appears. Click on the foreground color selection box on the toolbox and pick a gray color around 50% (R:134, G:134, B:134). Click OK. Press Alt(Opt)+Delete (Backspace) to fill the Alpha 1 channel with the gray color.

4. Choose Filter, Pixelate, Color Halftone. In the Color Halftone dialog box, choose a Max. Radius of **40**. This creates circles with a radius of 40 pixels. Choose an Angle of **45** in Channel 1 (don't worry about the other channel angles because the Alpha 1 channel is grayscale information only). Click OK.

5. Hold down the Ctrl(⌘) key and click the Alpha 1 channel. If the selection appears around the circles only, press Ctrl(⌘)+Shift+I to create an inverse selection so that the marquee is around the outside edges of the document as well.

   For users who've used previous versions of Photoshop, Shift+F7 still works to create the inverse of a selection in Photoshop, but ImageReady requires the three-finger Ctrl(⌘)+Shift+I.

6. Click the Layers tab to return to the Layers palette and click the Background layer to make it the active layer. Hold down the Alt(Opt) key and click the Create new layer icon. In the New Layer dialog box, name the new layer **Grid**. Click OK.

7. Click the foreground color selection box on the toolbox and change the foreground color to the light gray previously used; R:215, G:215, B:215. Click OK. The background color should still have the darker gray specified; R:99, G:99, B:99.

8. Click the Gradient tool. The Reflected Gradient should still be the current gradient choice along with Foreground to Background on the Options bar. Starting at the outside lower-right side of the wrench handle, drag a diagonal line ending near the upper-left side of the wrench handle as shown in Figure 9.21.

9. **Optional**: If you would like to add more highlights to the metal Grid layer, click the Airbrush tool and on the Options bar set the Pressure to **20%** (mode at Normal) and choose a large brush from the drop-down menu. A 100-pixel brush works well. Then, stroke the light gray in an area where you want to add some highlights (in the same diagonal angle as the gradient) or press X to switch to the dark gray and add darker gray to an area that might need darker tones.

   If you don't like what you see, you can press Ctrl(⌘)+Z to undo the last step (or use the History palette to undo more than one step) and retry the shading and highlighting until the desired look is achieved.

10. Press Ctrl(⌘)+D to deselect. Photoshop's Layer Styles are perfect for bringing the Grid layer to life. Choose Layer, Layer Style, Bevel and Emboss. In the Bevel and Emboss dialog box, choose Inner Bevel for Style. Choose **140** for Depth and **4** (pixels) for Size (see Figure 9.22). Before closing the dialog box, add a drop shadow. On the menu list to the left of the dialog box, click the Drop Shadow option and highlight it to display the dialog box options on the right side of the dialog box. Change the Opacity to **65**, leave the Angle at 120, change Distance to **9**, and Size to **8** (see Figure 9.23). Click OK.

**Figure 9.21** Apply a Reflected Gradient to the Grid layer by dragging the Gradient tool in a perpendicular line to the Wrench.

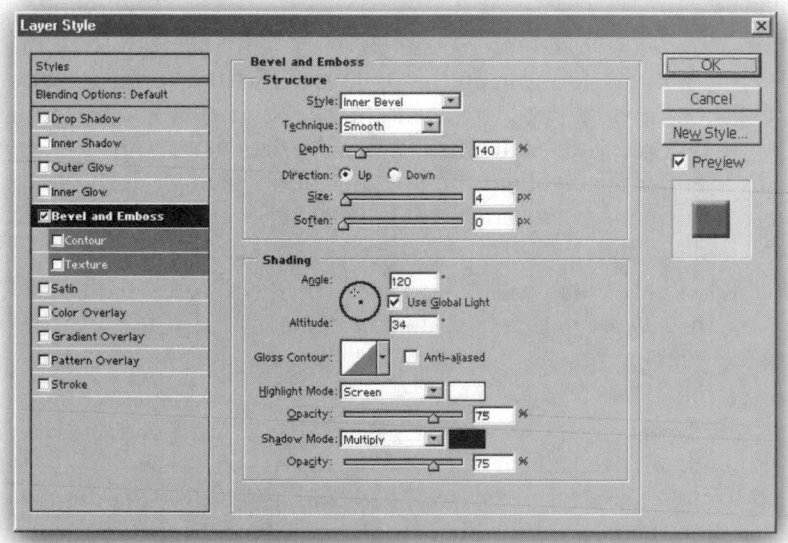

**Figure 9.22** Apply the settings shown here to the Grid layer for an Inner Bevel Style.

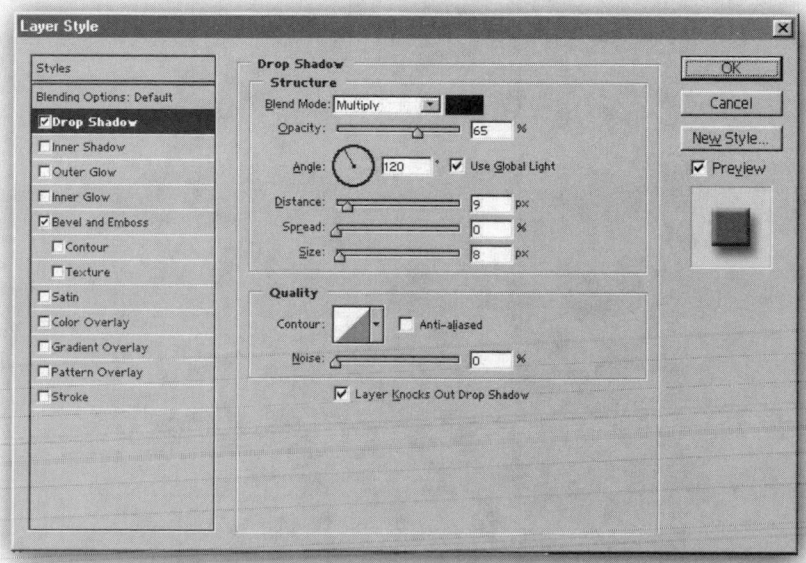

**Figure 9.23**   Add a drop shadow to the Grid layer before exiting the dialog box.

When you chose the Bevel and Emboss Style, Photoshop also applied the effect to the outside edges of the image document. Yikes! That wasn't what you wanted! Here's how to correct the problem.

11. Right-click (Macintosh: hold Ctrl and click) on the *f* mark on the Grid layer and choose Create Layers (or choose Layer, Layer Style, Create Layers). When the Warning dialog box appears, click OK. This puts each effect on a separate layer and groups these layers to the Grid layer.

**Tip**

**When You See an *f* In a Layer**   When you apply Layer Styles, an *f* appears on the layer where the styles were applied. Double-click on the *f* for instant access to the dialog box. Changes to the style can be made at any time. In addition, there are a variety of options available with a right-click (Macintosh: hold down Ctrl and click) on the *f*. For example, right-click (Macintosh: hold down Ctrl and click) on the *f* and choose Copy Style, then right-click (Macintosh: hold down Ctrl and click) on another layer and choose Paste Style to instantly paste the same style settings to other layers.

12. Switch to the Crop tool. Drag a rectangle close to the inside of the beveled edges of the document. You can use the handles to adjust the edges until the selection looks like the one shown in Figure 9.24. Press the Enter (Return) key to apply the cropping.

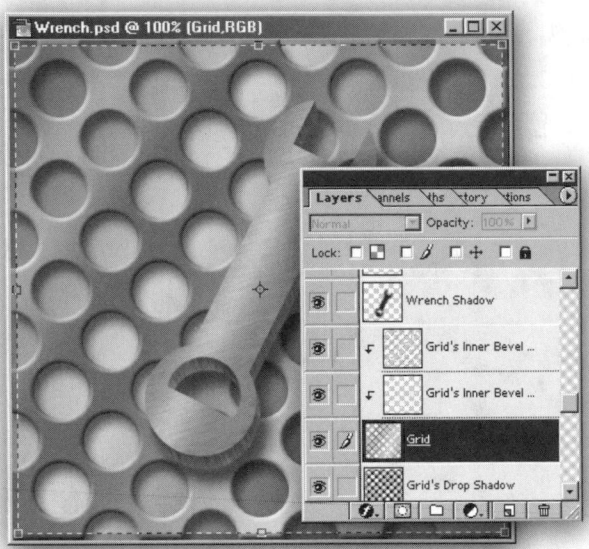

**Figure 9.24**  Use the Crop tool to eliminate the beveled edges near the outside edges of the document. Press the Enter (Return) key to apply the crop.

If the Crop tool doesn't let you get a selection close to the edges of the document, it might be because the Snap options are enabled. Choose View and make sure the Snap option is unchecked. Choose View again and choose Snap To, None. Alternatively, you can hold down the Ctrl key when dragging the Crop handles to temporarily disable the Snap option.

Let's add a little color to the Grid layer to bring out some warmth.

13. Click the Grid's Inner Bevel layer to make this the active layer. Hold down the Alt(Opt) key and click the Create New Layer icon. Name this new layer **Color**. Click OK in the New Layer dialog box.

14. Click the foreground color selection box on the toolbox and choose a warm brown; R:91, G:55, B:20. Click OK. Press Alt(Opt)+Delete (Backspace) to fill the Color layer with brown. Lower the Opacity on the Layers palette to **20%**. Press Ctrl(⌘)+S to save your work. Leave the document open for the next steps.

**Warning**

**When Ctrl(⌘)+S Doesn't Work**   When entering a value in a palette (for example, entering an opacity change in the Layers palette), Photoshop will keep the palette active until you click outside of the palette. Therefore, the Ctrl(⌘)+S command might not respond unless you click the title bar of the document to make the document active.

## Making Magic Wand Tool Selections

So far we have made use of the Rectangular and Elliptical selection tools, as well as the Polygonal Lasso tool. We have also made use of Layer information and Channel information to make selections. One of the many useful tools not yet mentioned is the Magic Wand tool. This selection tool works best in an area where color is consistent.

To demonstrate how easy it is to separate or select a part of the image with the Magic Wand tool, you will add text to the wrench image. In the steps to follow, you will open a text image created in a program called Xara3D 4. This is a great little program for doing some quick and fun three-dimensional looks. If you would like to find out more information on this product, Web site information is provided at the end of this chapter.

The image you will use has three-dimensional text on a white background. In trying to isolate the text from the background, the initial instinct might be to select the text with various tools or to apply several different methods to accomplish the task. It's important to assess the image to determine the best and *easiest* method for selecting and isolating a part of the image. Because the background is one color (white), it is easier in this example to select what you *don't* want, and then choose the inverse of the selection to capture what you need. There might be many situations when this technique can be applied.

### Example 9.6   Adding Three-Dimensional Text

1. Press Ctrl(⌘)+O to open a document. Alternatively, Windows users can double-click on an empty space of the Photoshop background (the gray area) to quickly access the Open dialog box. The Macintosh version of Photoshop does not support an application background. Open the WrenchTitle.tif image from the Examples/Chap09 folder on the Companion CD.

2. Click the Magic Wand tool on the toolbox. On the Options bar, set the Tolerance to **32**. To control which white areas will be selected, leave the Contiguous box checked. As mentioned earlier, "contiguous" means to limit the extent of a selection to pixels that *neighbor* similarly colored pixels. If the Contiguous box was unchecked, and an area of the white background is clicked on, all white areas will be selected. That would include some white areas in the text itself, which would be wrong.

   A range of numbers would actually work well for the Magic Wand Tolerance option because you are selecting an area of one color with a well-defined edge where the color ends.

3. With the Magic Wand tool, click anywhere on the white background area of the WrenchTitle.tif. A selection marquee appears around the outside areas of the 3D letters. Click the Add to Selection icon on the Options bar (or hold down the Shift key) and click the white area inside the letter "R" that was not selected in the original selection, as shown in Figure 9.25.

**Figure 9.25**    Use the Add to Selection icon on the Options bar and click inside the white area of the letter "R" with the Magic Wand tool to add this area to the selection.

4. Position the two documents so that you have a view of both documents on your screen. Click the title bar of the WrenchTitle.tif to make it the active document. Press Ctrl(⌘)+Shift+I to create the inverse of the selection.

Press V to switch to the Move tool and drag the selected text from the WrenchTitle.tif image into the wrench.psd document. Close the WrenchTitle.tif document without saving changes.

Notice that the letters appear to have a small edge of white surrounding each letter (see Figure 9.26). This edge of white that remains from the background is referred to as *fringing*. Fringing happens when a foreground image element has anti-aliasing pixels around the edge meeting the image background. Anti-aliasing is generally a good thing (as you'll see throughout this book), but the Wrench type is selected from a white background, and the edge pixels that keep the lettering smooth become painfully visible when the Wrench 3D lettering is dropped against a dark background. The good news is that fringing of this type is easily corrected with Photoshop's Defringing feature.

5. Position the Wrench letters near the top center of your wrench.psd document. Choose Layers, Matting, Defringe. In the Defringe dialog box, enter **1** (pixel) for Width. Click OK and watch the fringe disappear.

6. Right-click (Macintosh: hold down Ctrl and click) on the Layer 1 and choose Layer Properties. Rename the layer **Wrench Text**. Click OK.

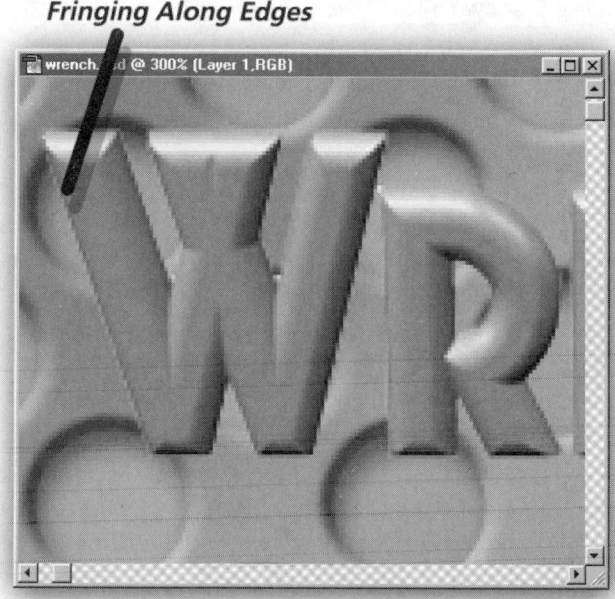

**Figure 9.26**   A small amount of fringing remains around the edges of the letters.

7. **Optional:** To move or reposition the wrench, click the Wrench layer to make it the active layer and then click the square to the left of the Wrench Shadow layer to link it. (The Wrench Extrude layer should already be linked. If it isn't, click the square to the left of this layer to link it, also.) Press V to switch to the Move tool if it is not already selected, and reposition the wrench. Press Ctrl(⌘)+S to save the document.

## Final Touches

Of course, the Drop Shadow Law applies to the 3D wrench letters as well as the rest of the image. You will once again use the time-honored, manual steps to create a drop shadow and you can then apply a *gradient* to the shadow. Why? Read on!

If you examine the text carefully, you will notice that the text is at an angle at which the top of the letters appears to be closer to the viewer. A shadow behind these letters then needs to be richer and darker at the base of the letters and trail off to a lighter color as the top of the letters tilt closer to the viewer (but farther away from the background shadow). This is why we'll use a gradient for the shadow layer. Here's what needs to be done.

### Example 9.7   Adding Shadow to Text

1. On the Layers palette, click the Color layer to make it the active layer. Hold down the Alt(Opt) key and click the Create new layer icon at bottom-right corner. Name the new layer **Text Shadow**. Click OK to add the layer to the composition.

2. Hold down the Ctrl(⌘) key and click the Wrench Text layer to load the text outline as a selection marquee. Click the eye (Visibility off) to the left of the Wrench Text layer (the eye icon disappears) to temporarily hide this layer so the changes made to the Text Shadow layer are easily viewed.

3. Click on the foreground color selection box on the toolbox and select a gray color; R:125, G:125, B:125. Click OK. Click on the background color selection box and choose black; R:0, G:0, B:0. Click OK to return to your work from the Color Picker.

4. Press G to switch to the Gradient tool. On the Options bar, click the Linear gradient icon and be sure the Gradient box on the Options bar is showing the Foreground to Background color styles. In the document, click the starting point outside the top of the "W" (on the Wrench selection outline), hold down the Shift key (to constrain the movement vertically) and drag downward to the inside bottom of the "W" as shown in Figure 9.27. Press Ctrl(⌘)+D to deselect.

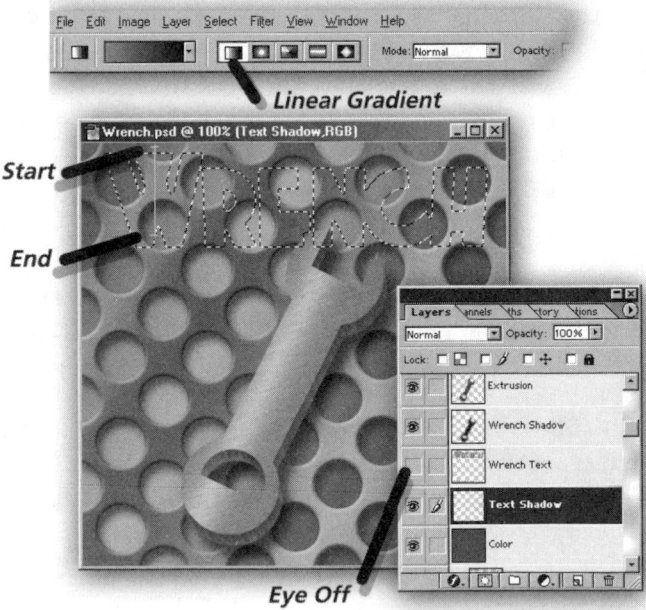

**Figure 9.27**   With the Text Shadow layer as the active layer, drag a Linear Gradient from top to bottom to give the Text Shadow a more dimensional look. Uncheck the Eye to the left of the Wrench Text layer for a better view of the selection.

5. Click the box to the far left of the Wrench Text layer to view this layer again (the eye icon will reappear). Press V to switch to the Move tool, and with the Text Shadow layer still active, move the shadow down and slightly to the right.

6. On the Layers palette, lower the Opacity for the Text Shadow layer to **75%** and change the Layer Mode from Normal to Multiply. Choose Filter, Blur, Gaussian Blur. In the Gaussian Blur dialog box, type **3** for Radius (see Figure 9.28). Click OK. Press Ctrl(⌘)+S to save your work.

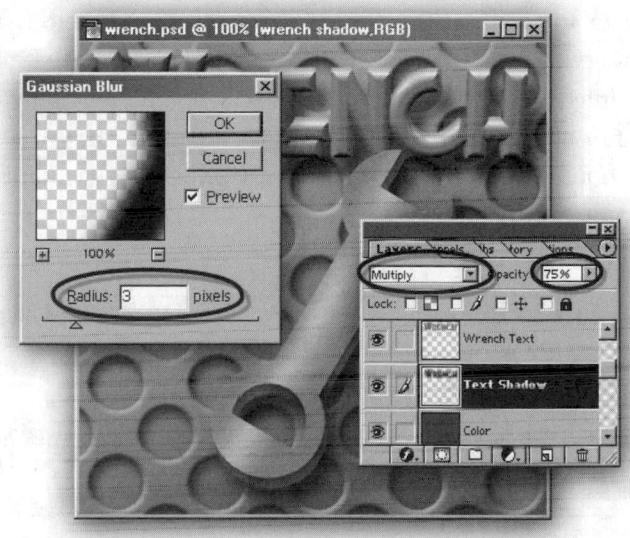

**Figure 9.28**   Adjust the Opacity and Layer Mode on the Layers palette for the Text Shadow layer. Apply a Gaussian Blur with a radius of 3.

## Making Crop and Quick Mask Selections

Hopefully, the selection workouts so far have provided many of the selection basics needed to accomplish most of your own tasks. The beauty of Photoshop is that it provides you with dozens of ways to do the same thing. There is no right or wrong way of doing a particular task, just choices.

There are a few selection tools that weren't discussed in the wrench exercise. We'll use a different project to help demonstrate some other selection techniques that will come in handy in the future.

We all have photographs lying around that have great subject matter, but the background is lacking in appeal. The photograph used in the next project is an example of this. The photo is of a cute little girl (excuse my prejudice showing—she's related <g>), all dressed and ready to go trick-or-treating for Halloween. The walls of our home just don't seem to provide an exciting backdrop for this little girl in her costume. You will separate the Halloween girl from the background of this image so we can use this cowgirl in another image later in the book.

To select the girl in this image, you will use Photoshop's Quick Mask mode. Quick Mask is another way to make selections. It puts Photoshop in a temporary mode where you can make use of painting tools, selection tools, and just about anything you have access to, to paint and fine-tune the area you want to select. Although our needs for this project are very simple, it will interest you to know that filters can also be applied to painted Quick Masks while in this selection mode. Applying filters can produce some fun effects when the Quick Mask areas are converted to marquee selections, which makes Quick Mask mode a very powerful selection tool. Let's get started on the project at hand.

**Tip**

**A Quick Access to the Brush Palette**    The Brush palette can always be accessed quickly by holding down the Shift key while you right-click (Macintosh: hold down Ctrl and click). The palette will display near the cursor position, so choose a spot in the document window where the palette will not intrude on your view of the image. Click outside the document window to close the palette. (Clicking *inside* the document window will cause you to paint when this might not be your intention!) Pressing the Enter (Return) key is a safe way to close the palette without unexpected painting.

### Example 9.8    Separating a Subject from the Background

1. Press Ctrl(⌘)+O to open the cowgirl.tif from the Examples/Chap09 folder on the Companion CD.

   First, crop out a large section of the unnecessary image information.

2. Press C to switch to the Crop tool and drag a rectangle around the cowgirl cropping away most of the background image. When you release the mouse button, there will be square handles on the bounding box that surrounds the girl. If adjustments are needed, click and drag these handles until the bounding box is at a desired size and position, as shown in Figure 9.29. Press the Enter (Return) key to apply the Crop tool.

3. Select the Polygonal Lasso tool from the Lasso tools list (or press Shift+L until the Polygonal Lasso tool is selected). Click around the inside edges of the cowgirl's costume (it doesn't have to be exact, just get as close to the edge as possible) as seen in Figure 9.30. Press Ctrl(⌘)++ to zoom in if needed. Press the spacebar to toggle to the Hand tool and drag the document to move your view along as you work.

**Figure 9.29** Use the Crop tool to eliminate a lot of unnecessary background. Drag a selection around the cowgirl and press Enter (Return) when ready to apply the crop.

**Figure 9.30** Use the Polygonal Lasso tool to select most of the cowgirl. Click close to the edges, but precision is not necessary at this point.

4. Press D (default colors of black and white). Alt(Opt)+click on the Quick Mask icon on the toolbox until the button looks like a shaded circle with an unfilled rectangle surrounding it, as shown in Figure 9.31. This method of operation for the Quick Mask tool makes everything you tint a future selected area, and areas with no Quick Mask tint will not be selected, once you move the image back into Standard Editing mode.

By clicking on the icon, you are now working in Quick Mask mode.

Choose
Selected
Areas

Double-Click
for Quick Mask Options

**Figure 9.31**    Double-click the button that looks like a shaded circle with an unfilled rectangle around it to see the Quick Mask options.

A red tint appears over the cowgirl where the selection marquee used to be. Don't worry—there isn't really red paint or anything on the image. The red color is just an indicator of where the selection will or will not be when you exit Quick Mask mode. You will fix the selection to make it more precise while in Quick Mask mode. The colors on the toolbox should be the default colors of black and white. Black applies Quick Mask tint—and when a mistake is made, white removes Quick Mask.

5. Press B to switch to the Paintbrush tool and be sure the Opacity on the Options bar is at **100%**. Click the arrow next to the current Brush tip on the Options bar to access the Brush palette. Choose the third brush from the left on the top row.

6.  Hold down Ctrl(⌘) and the spacebar to toggle to the Zoom tool and drag a marquee around the left edge of the cowgirl near the face. Press Ctrl(⌘)+ + if you need to zoom in closer. With black as the foreground color, paint in areas that are missing near the edge of the cowgirl. If you make a mistake, press X to switch to white and paint with white to remove the areas of red mask that are not wanted.

    While in Quick Mask mode, nothing is permanent. The color painted is just to indicate where a selection will be made when you exit Quick Mask mode. Toggle between white and black paint colors to remove mask color or to add mask color, respectively.

7.  Hold down the spacebar to toggle to the Hand tool, drag to maneuver the view around the edges in a clockwise direction to paint and fine-tune the edge selection. Paint with black to add the red color where needed. Also switch to smaller or larger brush sizes as needed. At the top of the head and to the right side of the cowgirl is a strip of shadow area that parallels the edge of the costume. This shadow area should not be part of the selection. Press X to switch to white for the foreground color and paint away any mask (red color) that is over the unwanted shadow area. Press X to switch black to the foreground and paint with black to get the selection to the edge of the head and side of the costume.

8.  When you arrive at the left shoe, switch the brush size to the first row, first brush on the left. Lower the opacity on the Options bar to **40%**. With black as the foreground color, paint the shoelace that dangles off the left shoe (see Figure 9.32).

    The lower opacity makes the selection slightly transparent, so the shoelace selection will take on some color from the new background (when placed in a different image) giving it a more natural look.

9.  Return the Opacity to **100%** and the brush size to the third from the left on the top row. Continue to work around the remaining edges painting with black to add mask color where needed, and painting with white to remove mask color in spots where you don't want Quick Mask. When you have arrived back at the beginning point and all desired areas are painted, press Q to exit Quick Mask mode (or click the Edit in Standard Mode icon as shown in Figure 9.33). A selection marquee replaces the area where there was Quick Mask.

    If you want to make more changes to the selection now, press Q to toggle back to Quick Mask mode, paint or erase the adjustments, and press Q to exit Quick Mask mode again.

10. Press Ctrl(⌘)+J to place the selected cowgirl onto a separate, new layer.

**Figure 9.32**   Use a smaller brush size at 40% opacity to paint in the shoelace dangling off the left shoe. The lower opacity will help to make the selection look more natural.

**Figure 9.33**   Click the Edit in Standard Mode icon on the toolbox to exit the Quick Mask mode (or press the letter Q to exit). The red tinted area that was visible in the Quick Mask mode is now replaced with a selection.

**11.** Drag the Background layer into the Trash at the bottom-right corner of the Layers palette. Press Ctrl(⌘)+Shift+S to save the document as **cowgirl.psd** (the native Photoshop file format). Save this file to your hard drive; the image will be used again in a later chapter.

## Summary

Not only can you combine selection tools to make complex selections, but you can also make use of selection tools *within* a selection mode such as Quick Mask.

Before closing this chapter, there are a few more ideas that might improve how you work on selections. Photoshop's Select menu offers a wealth of options regarding selections. You are probably familiar with the Select All, Deselect, and Inverse selection options by now, but there is also a Reselect option that will reload the last selection used in the image.

The Select, Color Range command works much like the Magic Wand tool in Contiguous mode, but there are far more options in the Color Range's dialog box than with the Magic Wand tool and the Options bar. You'll want to use this command, its Fuzziness slider, and its Eyedropper plus tool when you want to pick a broad range of color, or choose colors that are not alike all at once.

Photoshop also offers a Modify option, which among other things, allows you to specify a pixel increment to expand or contract the selection. Another very useful feature is the Transform Selection, which gives you the same Transform options available for image transformations. This option allows everything from resizing and rotating a selection to distortion and perspective, just to name a few.

There's something for every situation, and, in most cases, there are a number of ways to achieve the same goal. The goal of this chapter was to provide a deeper understanding for the most commonly used selection tools and the many ways to modify these selections to give them extra power. This is only the tip of what can be achieved.

## Resources

http://www.i-us.com/products/xara3d4/xara3D4.htm
A link to the i-us Xara3D 4 site that offers product information and download information (demo and purchasing) for the Xara3D 4 product.

# *Chapter 10*

## Building Images Layer by Layer

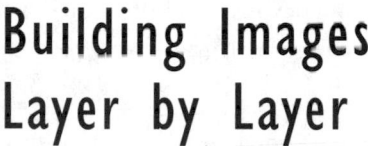

When you import or scan an image into

Photoshop, Photoshop generally treats

that image as one layer, a background

layer, like the one sheet of paper you can

hold in your hand when looking at a photograph print or a finished piece of artwork. If you're opening a new document, it's analogous to setting up a fresh canvas.

Photoshop enables you to build images, using the feature of Photoshop layers as you work. New image layers are easily created on the Layers palette. Additional layers are similar to the *cels*—sheets of acetate—that traditional cartoonists use in animation. Layers are stacked, and this is the way elements of a scene come together. Each layer might have something different drawn on it, and each one can be moved around independently without affecting the placement of the other objects or transparencies surrounding it. When there is no image drawn on a transparency (or layer) you can easily see through to the layers below.

Where Photoshop differs from the sheets of acetate analogy is that Photoshop's layers enable you to do so much more with stacked layers. With the Layers palette, layers can be changed in a variety of ways.

*Layer Mode* is one example. The default Layer Mode is Normal, but Photoshop provides a number of other mode options that change the way a layer interacts with the layers beneath it. The Layers palette also gives you the ability to change opacity, which affects the transparency level of opaque areas on the layer.

*Layer Effects* can be applied to achieve certain specialized effects such as a drop shadow, beveling, and inner and outer glows, to name a few.

*Adjustment Layers* is another powerful option available on the Layers palette. Photoshop offers a variety of ways to improve an image through changing brightness/contrast, hue/saturation, color balance, and so on. You apply these changes directly to the layer (through the Layer menu) or you can use an Adjustment Layer (from the Layers palette) to make these changes. Adjustments are performed by adding different values of black to the layer, or white to remove edits. It's like painting an image in areas where you used to have to marquee select the layer, and then apply local changes. Feedback is immediate with Adjustment Layers; you see changes as you paint. One of the main advantages to using an Adjustment Layer is the ability to come back to this layer at a later date and make changes to the adjustment settings.

## Becoming Familiar with Layer Basics

When you're creating a multilayered document or image, changes made to the image are applied to the active layer. When you view the Layers palette, the active layer is highlighted and a paintbrush icon appears next to the layer, indicating that it is the current editing layer and can be modified. You cannot paint on more than one layer at a time.

On the Layers palette there are two columns along the left side of the layers. The far-left column indicates layer visibility. Clicking the boxes in this column toggles the layer on and off (an eye icon appears when the layer is on). The boxes in the next column (to the left of a layer thumbnail) are used to link layers to an active layer. The active layer has a Paintbrush icon in this column to indicate that the layer can be edited. When boxes in this column are clicked, a chain icon appears, indicating that the layer is linked to the active layer. You can link many layers and perform stuff on more than one layer at a time. For example, you can move more than one layer at a time when layers are linked, and you can use the Transform feature on multiple layers that contain nontransparent image areas when the layers are linked. This means you can rotate and resize more than one layer's contents when you apply a link between them.

Until you decide to combine or merge layers, each layer remains independent of the neighboring layers. You can edit or reposition a layer without disturbing the others. The Layers palette lists all the layers, with the top layer being the image item that is in the forefront. Dragging a layer to a new position in the layer list on the palette changes the layer order.

In the following sets of steps, you will work toward building a digital collage. In the process, the goal is to acquaint you with basic layer properties, linking layers, and layer masks. Because physical scrapbooking is a fun pastime, it seems to be equally fun (or even more fun!) to duplicate a scrapbook look—*digitally*. Using three photographs, you will create a layered collage with a scrapbook's characteristics.

## Building Layers

The first steps lay the groundwork for the image. Many scrapbook ideas include a layered series of different textured papers to serve as a matting or frame for the pictures. You will create some neutral paper looks to help provide a nice frame for the images.

The scanned photographs used in this collage have a resolution of 150 pixels/inch. Therefore, your new document will be created with the same resolution. The pixel width and height for the collage is equivalent to about 7 inches. These settings fit comfortably on a sheet of paper and provide sufficient resolution so that you can print the final image if you choose.

After completing this collage image, you might want to try a similar project with your own family images. Keep these ideas in mind when you're determining the dimensions for a new document. Decide what resolution to scan the family photographs and maintain a consistent resolution for the collage document.

RAM costs less than chewing gum today, and as a Photoshop owner (who also read Chapter 4), you're well aware that you can never have enough RAM. The standard today is 256MB; it will reach ½ a GB to 1GB within the year. So, chances are good that you can write your collage to a printer with no processing or spooling problems. But if you're broke like the authors, you might have only enough system RAM to squeak by certain processes, printing being one of them.

It is here that you must strike a balance. Rule One in imaging is knowing what your target output resolution and device is before you create a piece. If you have 64MB to 128MB of RAM onboard, you are *not* going to go printing your piece if the piece is 25MB in file size. Keep RAM in mind, look frequently at the document sizes area in Photoshop to see how much RAM and hard drive space you are using in the creation of the piece, and settle for a nice 600 dpi print instead of a 1200 dpi print until you buy more RAM. BTW, printers take RAM, too. One of our inkjets has 24MB of RAM onboard, so it can handle the *spooling* (a process of queuing up the image and interpreting the data for print, one chunk at a time) of large images. Let's get to work building some new layers.

### Example 10.1   Building New Layers

1. Press Ctrl(⌘)+N. In the New document dialog box, type **1050** (pixels) for Width and **1050** (pixels) for Height. Type **150** (pixels/inch) for Resolution and set Mode at RGB color. Choose White for Contents. Click OK.

> **Warning!**   If an error message appears when you open the CD files, press Ctrl(⌘)+Shift+K and then choose Adobe RGB (1998) from the Working Spaces, RGB drop-down list. See Chapter 3 for more information.

2. Hold the Alt(Opt) key and click the Create new layer icon at the bottom of the Layers palette. In the Layers Properties dialog box, type **Paper1** for the Name. Click OK to return to the workspace.

3. Press Shift+M until the Rectangular Marquee tool is chosen. On the Options bar, choose Fixed Size from the Style drop-down list. Type **950 px** for Width and **950 px** for Height. (See the note about Mixed Fields.)

   Dragging the Rectangular Marquee tool to an approximate size can create a square selection in Normal Style mode. But because the dimensions of the document are known to be 1050 pixels, it is easy to calculate a precise square size and create a square selection that allows for a 50-pixel border.

4. Place the cursor near the upper-left corner. Click and drag to center the square selection within the document window, as shown in Figure 10.1.

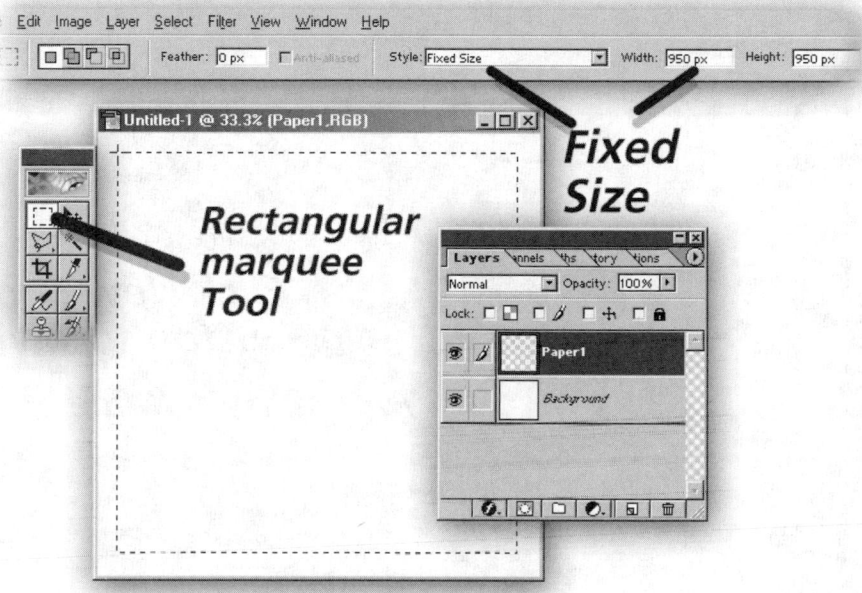

**Figure 10.1**   Select the Fixed Size Style option from the Options bar, with a 950 (pixel) width and height. Click and drag to center the square selection in the document window.

Nudge the selection, if necessary, using the arrow keys to center the selection within the document window.

5. Click the foreground color selection box on the toolbox and choose a pale brown color; R:138, G:121, B:106 is cool. Click OK to exit the Color Picker.

6. Press Alt(Opt)+Delete (Backspace) to fill the selection with color. Press Ctrl(⌘)+D to deselect the marquee.

   The paper would look nice with a subtle drop shadow. You will create a drop shadow and save it as a Style to use for the remaining paper layers.

7. Double-click the Paper1 layer. In the Layer Style dialog box (it's huge; you can't miss it), click the Drop Shadow option listed on the left side of the box. This option should now be highlighted with a view of the drop shadow options on the right side of the box. Change the Opacity to **75%**, **143°** for Angle, **5** (px) for Distance (of the shadow away from the thing casting the shadow), **5%** for Spread (the clarity of the shadow's edges), and **13** (px) for Size (how blurry the shadow is).

8. Click the New Style button. In the New Style dialog box, type **Paper Shadow** (see Figure 10.2). Click OK to exit the New Style dialog box. Click OK to exit the Layer Style dialog box.

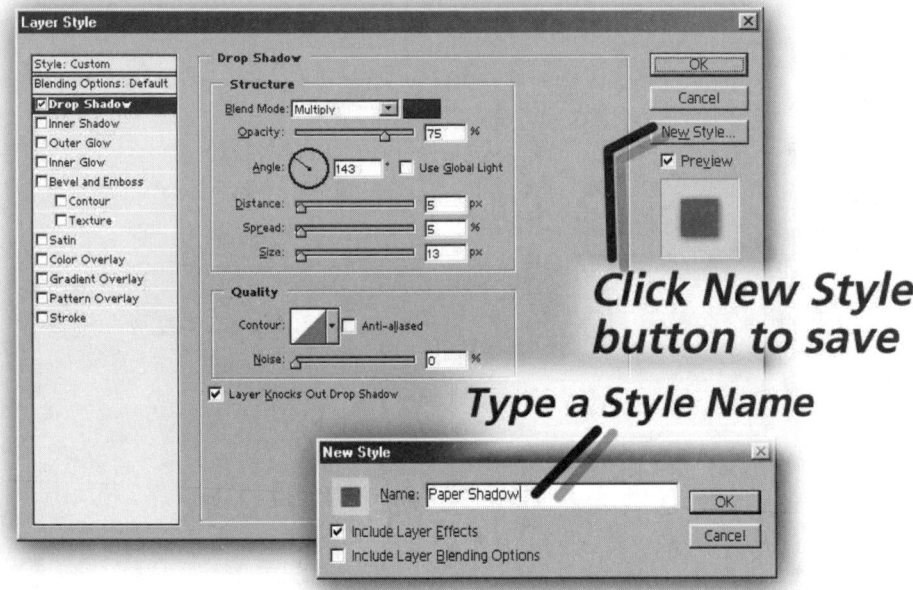

**Figure 10.2**   Choose the Drop Shadow options shown here. Click the New Style button to save these options as a Style.

9. On the Layers palette, the Layer Style information can become distracting. Click the arrow next to the *f* mark for the Paper1 layer to close this information, and to make the Layers palette appear less cluttered. Now let's add a grainy paper effect.

10. On the Filter menu, choose Noise, Add Noise. In the Add Noise dialog box, type **5%** for Amount, choose Gaussian for Distribution, and click the Monochromatic option (see Figure 10.3). Click OK.

   Gaussian noise is crunchier in appearance than the granular default type of noise in this filter box, and Monochromatic means that only one color will be used for the noise particles—one color, and a possible 256 different brightness values for the noise.

11. Alt(Opt)+click the Create new layer icon at the bottom of the Layers palette. In the Layer Properties dialog box, type **Paper2** for the Name. Click OK.

12. Make certain that the Rectangular Marquee tool is still active and that Fixed Size is the Style. Type **920** (pixels) for Width and Height.

13. Click near the upper-right corner of the document, and drag to center the square selection over the previously created paper square (see Figure 10.4).

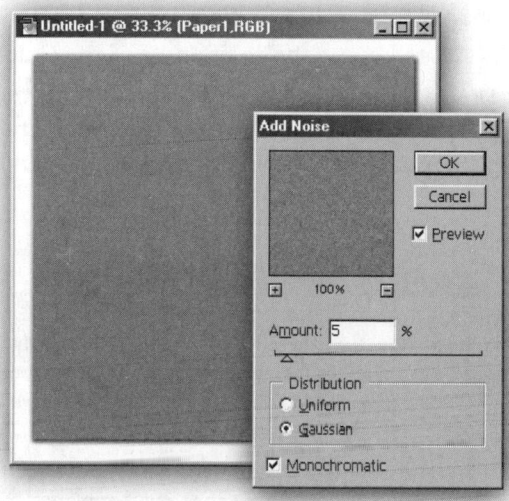

**Figure 10.3**   In the Add Noise dialog box, choose the Gaussian and Monochromatic options and type 5 for Amount. Click OK.

**Figure 10.4**   Set the Rectangular Marquee tool options for Fixed Size (for Style) and 920 (pixels) Width and Height. Click and drag to center a square selection in the document window.

14. Click the foreground color on the toolbox and choose a light beige color; R:247, G:247, B:240 would be wonderful and looks like the default color for computers. Click OK to choose the color and exit the Color Picker.

15. Press Alt(Opt)+Delete (Backspace) to fill the square with the beige color. Press Ctrl(⌘)+Shift+S to choose the Save As command. Name the document **Scrapbook.psd**. Click Save, and leave the document open for the steps to come.

**Note**

**Mixed Fields for Units**   New to Photoshop 6 is the *mixed field*. A number entry box can take alphabetical information. And there's a good reason for this. In the previous set of steps, we asked that you type values for the Rectangular marquee tool and then type **px** after the number. We asked you to do this because you might have changed units before you read this book.

By default, the unit measurement in these Height and Width boxes (and other areas in Photoshop) is pixels, expressed as *px* after a number. But—and here's the big *but*—you can easily change a field's pixel unit to inches by typing **in** after a number. If you see no unit after a number in a number box, assume it's pixels. Similarly, in the Character or Paragraph palette, assume that fonts are measured in points, so you'd see something like 35pt in the Type field. And in keeping with this new style of entry box, you can make text 5 inches tall if you type 5in in the text field on the palette.

## Adding Patterns to Layers

To add a unique look, a pattern will be made and added to this paper in the next group of steps. A path for the pattern has already been provided for you in a separate file on the Companion CD. The next steps will show you how to access the file and make a pattern from the path we've provided.

### Example 10.2   Creating a Pattern in Layers

1. Open Floral.psd in the Examples/Chap10 folder of the Companion CD.

2. Click the Path tab to view the Paths palette (or go to the Window menu and choose Show Paths). Ctrl(⌘)+click the Floral title to load the path as a selection.

3. Click the foreground color selection box on the toolbox and choose a slightly darker beige; R:207, G:204, B:188. Click OK to exit the Color Picker. Press Alt(Opt)+Delete (Backspace) to fill the selection with color. Press Ctrl(⌘)+D to deselect the marquee.

4. Click the Layers tab on the grouped palette to view the Layers palette. Drag the Layer 1 layer onto the Create new layer icon to duplicate this layer (see Figure 10.5).

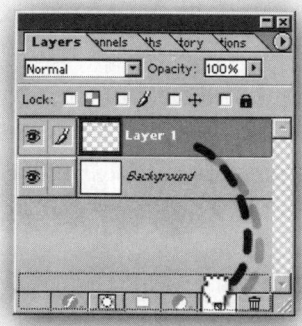

**Figure 10.5**   Drag the Layer 1 layer to the Create new layer icon to duplicate the layer.

5. Press Ctrl(⌘)+T to bring up the Transform command. A bounding box will appear around the Floral pattern. Place the cursor inside the bounding box and drag the floral copy to the lower-left corner of the document.

6. Right-click (Macintosh: hold Ctrl and click) inside the bounding box and choose Flip Horizontal.

7. Right-click (Macintosh: hold Ctrl and click) inside the bounding box again, and choose Flip Vertical as shown in Figure 10.6. Press Enter (Return) to exit the Transform command and apply the changes.

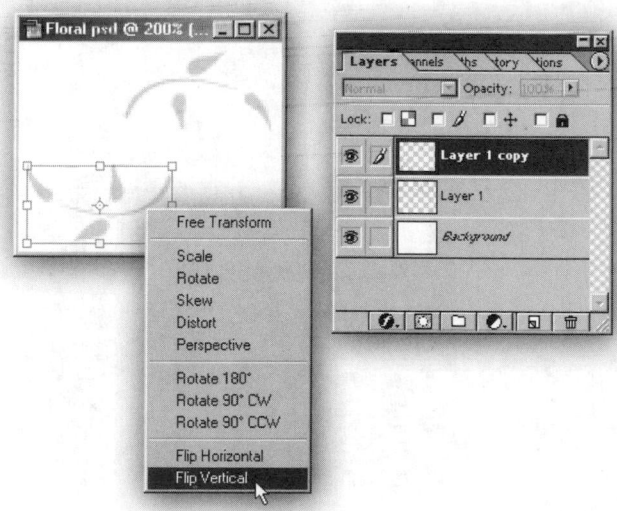

**Figure 10.6**   Press Ctrl(⌘)+T and right-click (Macintosh: hold Ctrl and click) inside the Transform box to Flip Horizontal, and then right-click (Macintosh: hold Ctrl and click) and this time, choose Flip Vertical. Move the Transform box to the lower-left corner of the document window.

**8.** Press Ctrl(⌘)+E to merge the layer with the layer below. Click Save and leave the document open for the steps to follow.

You will make use of a filter to ensure that the pattern will tile correctly when used. By *correctly*, we mean that the tile will repeat across any size background while all edges align perfectly with the previous and next tile. Here's how to use the document's dimension size to help tile the image using the Offset filter.

### Example 10.3    Using the Offset Filter to Make a Seamless Pattern

**1.** Right-click (Macintosh: hold Ctrl and click) on the document title bar and choose Image, Image Size. Note that the Width is 100 pixels and the Height is 80 pixels. Click Cancel.

You're measuring things in pixels quite often in this chapter. If the Image size dialog box doesn't default to pixels as units, cancel out of the box, press F8 to display the Info palette, and then click the XY crosshairs at the bottom left of the palette, and choose pixels from the palette menu. Then continue with these steps.

**2.** Go to the Filter menu and choose Other, Offset. In the Offset dialog box, type **50** (pixels right) for Horizontal (half the Width measurement of the document). Type **40** (pixels down) for Vertical (half the Height measurement of the document). Choose Wrap Around for Undefined Areas, as shown in Figure 10.7. Essentially, you've turned the pattern inside out. Click OK.

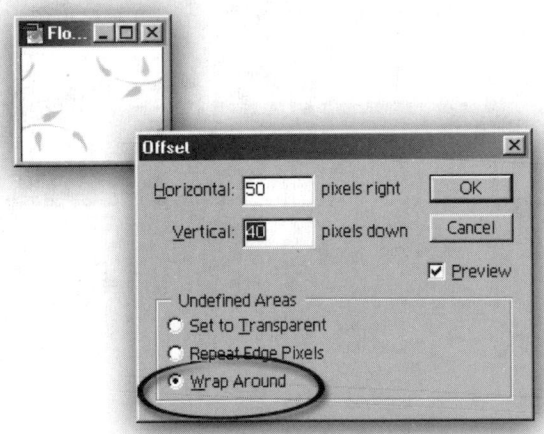

**Figure 10.7**    Use the Offset filter to ensure that the pattern will tile without flaws.

The pattern shows no flaws after the Offset filter is used. No additional work is needed. The pattern is ready to tile on the Paper2 layer of the collage document.

**Note**

**Seamless Edges**    You will not always be this lucky with the Offset command. Occasionally, when you turn a pattern inside out, there will be hard edges in the center of the picture ending at the image window edge, like a cross. What you do in this instance is use the Clone Stamp tool to sample a small area, use a very soft tip brush, and paint away the edges. *Then* you have your seamless tile!

3. Drag the Background layer to the Trash at the bottom of the Layers palette. Press Ctrl($\mathcal{H}$)+A to select All.

4. Choose Edit, Define Pattern. When the dialog box appears for naming the pattern, click OK to accept the default name. Close the Floral.psd document. If you want to save this pattern for future use, choose Yes to save the file to your hard drive; otherwise, choose No to close without saving changes.

5. On the Edit menu, choose Fill. In the Fill dialog box, under Contents, click on the drop-down list for Use and choose Pattern. Click on the Custom Pattern drop-down list and make sure the Floral.psd is picked (see Figure 10.8). Click OK to apply the pattern to the selected area (the whole image).

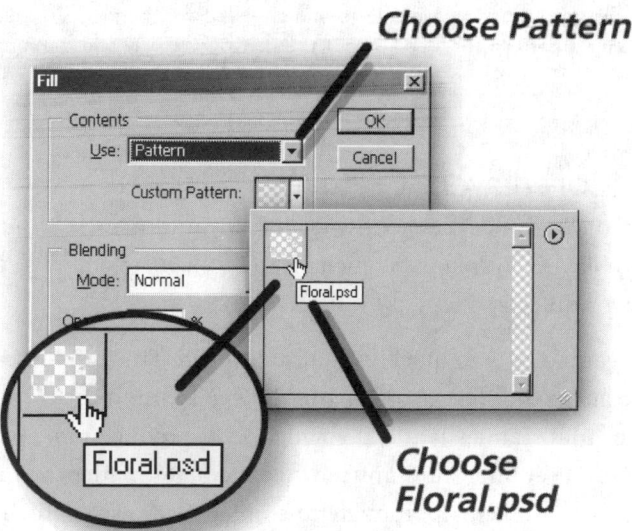

**Figure 10.8**    Choose Edit, Fill to access the Fill dialog box. Choose Pattern, and use the Floral.psd pattern to fill the Paper selection.

6. Go to the Filter menu and choose Noise, Add Noise. In the Add Noise dialog box, type **2** for Amount, choose Gaussian for Distribution, and click the Monochromatic option. Click OK. Press Ctrl(⌘)+D to deselect.

7. Click the Styles tab to view the Styles palette (or go to the Windows menu and choose Show Styles). Click the Paper Shadow style, created earlier, to apply the same shadow to the Paper2 layer.

8. Press Ctrl(⌘)+S to save your work. Leave the document open for the next exercise.

**Tip**

**Saving Your Patterns**    As with Brushes and Styles, you can save a collection of patterns in Photoshop 6, which is a new and welcome feature. When's the last time you lost the source file for a pattern, right?

By default, all new patterns you choose to save are appended to the default patterns collection. If you choose to load a new palette (this is done through the Edit, Presets Manager command) and then come back to the default without saving first, all your new appended patterns are gone.

*Suggestion:* Before building a large collection of patterns, choose Edit, Presets Manager, choose Patterns as the Preset type, choose Save Set, and then type a unique name for the pattern set. Then, all future saved patterns will be added to this palette, and when you choose Fill (and pick Pattern), you can click the Custom pattern button, click the round flyout button on the Pattern palette, and choose Save Patterns. So there really are two ways to save a pattern (or a collection), the convoluted way and the long way<g>.

## Exploring More Layers Features

We have only touched the surface of what layers can do. So far, you have created new layers to achieve a layered-paper look for the collage, making use of Layer Styles along the way for quick and easy drop shadows.

You have also learned how to quickly duplicate a layer. This produced a copy of the floral design to aid in the creation of a pattern. Keep in mind the technique used for making patterns that seamlessly tile, if you decide to produce some patterns of your own. Should the Offset filter show any flaws in the pattern after the filter is applied, just use whatever tools seem appropriate to correct the flaws in the image, and the pattern should work wonderfully. (*Hint:* Use the Clone Stamp tool to reconcile edges apparent in an offset image, as we mentioned in an earlier Note.)

## Taking Advantage of the Layer Mask Feature

The square papers in our collage look a little too perfect. Often scrapbook designs might include interesting edge treatments for the border papers used for matting. Let's alter the edges of the second paper to duplicate this design idea. We will make use of layer masks to make a torn-edge effect for the Paper2 layer. A third paper layer will be made and the same masking technique applied to this layer as well.

When you wear a mask (at Cinderella's ball, for example), you think of something that hides your face. Your mask has areas that aren't masking your face. Around your eyes, for example, the mask lets your eyes show through—unless it's part of your shtick to bump into walls all night. A layer mask works on the same premise. The difference is that when you hide part of a layer, the layer(s) below show through wherever the mask is applied.

Just like putting on a party mask, the changes are not permanent. Your face still exists behind the mask, and so does the layer image that you apply a mask to. When working on a layer mask, painting with black color will mask (hide) layer information. If you make a mistake or change your mind about an area, painting with white will undo (unhide, if there's such a word) the masked area and let the layer images areas show through again. If this concept sounds familiar, it's because it is very much like Quick Mask Mode.

If you decide you like the changes made with a mask, and would like to make those changes permanent, you can *apply* the mask, and the areas on the layer (that are hidden by the mask) will then permanently disappear—a flaw in the party mask analogy, since you can't make your face look like your mask permanently unless you're Jim Carrey.

It's always easier to understand these ideas by doing, so let's get started with some masking.

### Example 10.4   Masking the Edges

1. Press Ctrl(⌘)+spacebar to toggle to the Zoom. Drag a rectangle area near the edge of the second paper to zoom in on the edge area. Press Ctrl(⌘)++ if a closer zoom is needed.

2. Press the spacebar to toggle to the Hand tool, and drag the document until there is a good view of the paper edge.

3. With the Paper2 layer still the active layer, click the Add a mask icon at the bottom of the Layers palette, as shown in Figure 10.9.

**Figure 10.9**   Increase the zoom level to have a comfortable view of the paper edges. Click
the Add a mask icon to add a mask to the Paper2 layer.

When you're painting on a layer mask, a circle appears in the second column square to the left of the layer title on the Layers palette. This indicates that color is being applied to a layer mask.

4. Press D for default colors. Press B to switch to the Paintbrush tool.

5. Press Shift and right-click (Macintosh: hold Ctrl and click) to access the Brush size palette. Choose a large hard-edge brush on the top row, second from the right (Hard Round 13 pixels, as shown in Figure 10.10). Press Enter (Return) to close the Brush palette.

6. With black as the foreground color, start painting in a crude, irregular fashion along the edge of the second paper. Click (instead of dragging) along the edges. Occasionally add a dragging motion to create a rough edge. Another tip is to periodically press X to switch to white as the foreground color, and click some of the edge areas back in. Press X to switch back to black as the foreground color, and continue clicking around the edges in the same manner.

The lack of steadiness of your brush strokes can be enhanced by holding the mouse button with one hand, and holding an electric hedge trimmer with the other. Just kidding, but you get the idea? Or use small circular motions as you push the cursor around the edge.

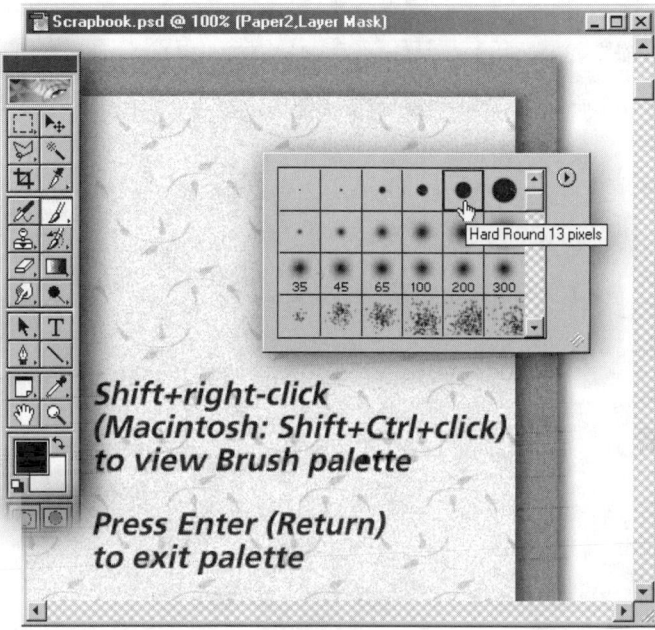

**Figure 10.10**   Press Shift and right-click (Macintosh: hold Ctrl and click) to view the Brush size choices. Press Enter (Return) after choosing the large hard-edge brush in the upper row.

7. Press the spacebar to move your view as you work around in a clockwise direction to paint away the edge area, as illustrated in Figure 10.11.

**Tip**

**Creating Old Edges**   If you're out to imitate what is called a *deckled edge*—very popular on expensive books—use the technique described in step 7. An alternative way to age the edges of an illustration of paper is to mask the layer, draw a path that is exactly on top of the piece of paper, set the Paintbrush tool to about 50%, Dissolve mode, and then stroke the path by clicking the Strokes path icon on the Paths palette. Then apply a small amount of Gaussian blur to the layer.

**Tip**

**Paint Out Mistakes**   If a mistake is made, press X to switch to white as the foreground color, and paint over the mistake area. When you are ready to resume masking away more of the image, press X to switch to black as the foreground color, and continue to paint on the layer mask.

**Figure 10.11**    With a Layer Mask active on the Paper2 layer, paint away a jagged edge area of this paper layer. If a mistake is made, press X to switch to white. Paint away the mistake, press X to switch to black, and resume painting.

8. When you're finished, press Ctrl(⌘)+– to zoom out and view the results. If you're satisfied, right-click (Macintosh: hold Ctrl and click) on the Layer mask and choose Apply Layer Mask, as shown in Figure 10.12. Naturally, if you are *not* satisfied, take your time (this book will not run away!) and finesse the edges until they look rough and naturally aged.

**Note**

**Saving a Mask for Later**    A Layer mask can be saved with the file and not discarded or applied. You might want to come back and make changes to the mask later.

Keep in mind, however, that everything you keep in a file adds to the file size and resources needed to work on the file. If your computer has an ample supply of memory, and this isn't a concern, we recommend that you keep the Layer mask on any image you're not 100% happy with.

9. Press Alt(Opt) and click the Create a new layer icon at the bottom of the Layers palette. In the Layers Properties dialog box, type **Paper3** for the Name. Click OK.

10. Switch to the Rectangular Marquee tool (press M). Change the Style on the Options bar to Normal. Drag a rectangular marquee selection that overlaps the previous paper layer, while leaving a slight border, as shown in Figure 10.13.

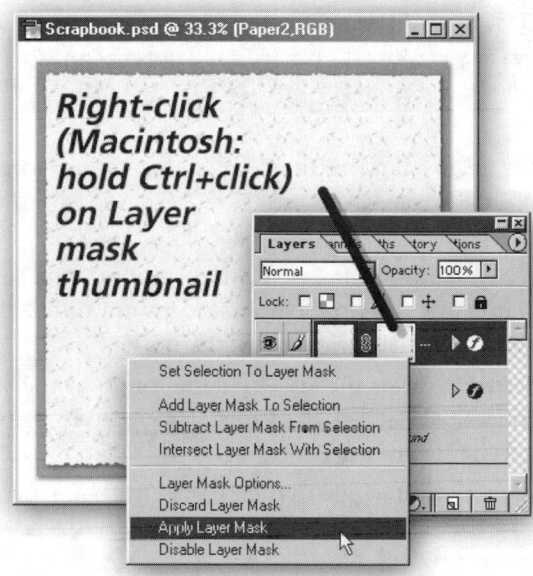

**Figure 10.12**    Right-click (Macintosh: hold Ctrl and click) the Layer mask thumbnail on the layer title and choose Apply Layer Mask when you are satisfied with your masking results.

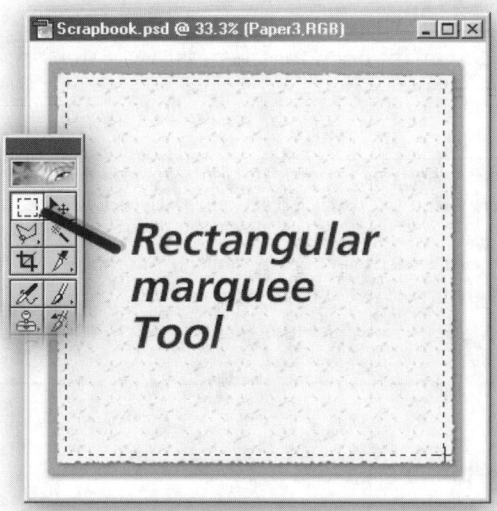

**Figure 10.13**    Drag to make a third rectangle selection in preparation for a third paper layer.

**Tip**

**Use the Spacebar to Reposition the Marquee**    If you would like to reposition the Rectangular marquee as you create it, hold down the spacebar *while you drag* to move the selection.

11. Using the same beige color (for the floral design) as the foreground color (R:207, G:204, B:188), press Alt(Opt)+Delete (Backspace) to fill the selection with color.

12. Choose Filter, Noise, Add Noise, type 5 for Amount, choose Gaussian for Distribution, and click the Monochromatic option. Click OK. Press Ctrl(⌘)+D to deselect the marquee after you apply the noise.

13. Click the Styles tab to view the Styles palette (or go to the Window menu and choose Show Styles). Click the Paper Shadow style you created earlier to apply the same shadow to the Paper3 layer.

14. Press Ctrl(⌘)+spacebar to toggle to the Zoom (in) tool. Drag a rectangle area near the edge of the third paper to zoom in on the edge area. Press Ctrl(⌘)++ if a closer zoom is needed.

15. Press the spacebar to toggle to the Hand tool, and drag the document until there is a good view of the paper edge.

16. With the Paper3 layer still the active layer, click the Add a mask icon at the bottom of the Layers palette.

17. Repeat steps 4–7. Have fun with the edge masking. Try a combination of clicking and stroking with the Paintbrush. Press Ctrl(⌘)+S to save your work, and keep the document open for the next set of steps.

**Tip**

**Getting Rough**    Another way (whew!) to create rough edges on paper is to use the Lasso tool just pixels inside the paper object on the layer. Draw the edge as though you're a car out of control. Then press Shift+F7 (or the more recent Adobe shortcut for creating the inverse of a selection—Ctrl(⌘)+Shift+I)—and fill everything but the paper with masking color. Then, deselect and apply the mask.

The point here is that you can paint with a painting tool *or* fill a selection with color to work on a Layer mask.

## Hooking Up with Linking Layers

The groundwork preparation is complete for the collage. The matting and border papers are screaming to frame an interesting subject. Time to pour some family photographs into this collage.

You will be adding two photographs to the collage in the steps that follow. In a pretty impressive example showing the power of linking layers, the steps will walk you through a digital special effect that is frequently seen in magazines. It's an effect with which the photograph is made to look like a typical old-time photograph (with the white border surrounding it). The photo always looks as though it is curled slightly, while it is lying on the table or on a stack of other photographs.

This effect is not only fun and easy to create, but it works very well in our scrapbook collage look. The effect adds dimension as well as that less-than-perfect human touch to the arrangement of family photos on the scrapbook page.

To achieve part of the antique photograph effect, you will use the Shear filter. When you use this filter, it is best to limit the area around the image to which you need apply the filter. For this reason, you will open the photo files and create most of the photo effects and preparation in the original file. Then you'll transfer the completed layered effect to the collage file. This is where a particular advantage to linking layers will become evident.

**Note**

**The Shear Filter in a Small Area**    If there is ever a need to apply the Shear filter on a small area contained in a larger document area, just drag a rectangular marquee selection around the smaller area to which the filter will be applied. Be sure to make the rectangular selection include a little room around the borders of the area, to leave room for the Shear filter to work when it moves around some of the pixel values.

You will need to expand the canvas of the photo files so that you have working room to apply a border and the filter effects. You also need to convert the Background layer to a normal Photoshop layer so that you can apply filters.

### Example 10.5    Creating a Curled Photo Using Linked Layers

1. Open Photo.tif in the Examples/Chap10 folder on the Companion CD.

2. Double-click on the Background Layer. Click OK to accept the default title in the Layers Properties dialog box. Right-click (Macintosh: hold Ctrl and click) the title bar of the Photo document, and choose Canvas Size. In the Canvas Size dialog box type **600** (pixels) for Width and **475** (pixels) for Height. Naturally, you change the units in the drop-down boxes in this dialog only if they display something *other* than pixels (inches, gallons, and fortnights are a no go). Click OK to apply the Canvas size change.

3. Press Alt(Opt) and click on the Create a new layer icon at the bottom of the Layers palette. In the Layers Properties dialog box, type **Photo1** for the Name. Click OK.

4. Drag the Photo1 layer below Layer 0 on the Layers palette. Drag a corner of the image window away from the image, making sure to view a sufficient background area around the photo. At 100% viewing resolution, from your thumb tip to the first knuckle is a good distance to expose the transparency grid at the bottom of the image. Press M to switch to the Rectangular Marquee tool. Drag a rectangular marquee selection around the photo, giving enough border edge to resemble the border seen on older photographs, as shown in Figure 10.14.

**Figure 10.14**    Drag a rectangular marquee selection around the photo, giving enough border edge to resemble the border seen on older photographs.

 **Tip**

**Checkerboard Guide**    The checkerboard transparency indicator that Photoshop uses is a helpful guide in determining an even border around the photo.

5. Press D for default colors. Press X to swap white to the foreground color. With Photo1 as the active layer, press Alt(Opt)+Delete (Backspace) to fill the marquee area with white. Press Ctrl(⌘)+D to deselect the marquee. Press Ctrl(⌘)+Shift+E to merge the two visible layers.

6. Drag the Photo1 layer to the Create a new layer icon to duplicate this layer. Drag the Photo1 copy layer below the original Photo1 layer. Right-click (Macintosh: hold Ctrl and click) on the Photo 1 copy layer, and choose Layer Properties. In the Layer Properties dialog box, type **Photo1 Shadow** for the Name. Click OK to return to the action.

7. Press X to swap black to the foreground color. Press Alt(Opt)+Shift+Delete (Backspace) to fill this copy with color. Press V to switch to the Move tool. Drag in the document window to move the shadow slightly down and to the right.

**Note**

**Filling with a Shortcut** Alt(Opt)+Delete (Backspace) is the keyboard shortcut to fill a selection or layer with color. Adding *Shift* to this keyboard shortcut is the same as turning on the Preserve Transparency option, filling the image on the layer with color, and then turning the Preserve Transparency option off again.

The Preserve Transparency option protects the transparent area of a layer. Therefore, only the image area on a layer is filled with color when you use the Alt(Opt)+Shift+ Delete (Backspace) keyboard shortcut.

If the Alt(Opt) key is replaced by the Ctrl(⌘) key in either of these keyboard shortcuts, the results are the same except that the *background color* is used as the fill color.

8. Choose Filter, Distort, Shear. Make sure Wrap Around is the Undefined Areas choice. In the upper-left corner of the Shear dialog box is a grid with a straight line down the middle. Click the center point of this line and drag it slightly to the left. A subtle effect is necessary, so be careful not to drag too far, as shown in Figure 10.15. Click OK to apply the effect and return to the image.

**Figure 10.15** In the Shear dialog box, click to make a point of the center line, and drag a small distance to the left.

9. On the Layers palette, lower the Opacity to 65% and change the Layer mode to Multiply.

10. Choose Filter, Blur, Gaussian Blur. In the Gaussian Blur dialog box, type 5 (pixels), as shown in Figure 10.16. Click OK to apply the blur.

**Figure 10.16** Change the Layer Opacity to 65% and the Layer mode to Multiply. Type 5 in the pixels field in the Gaussian Blur dialog box.

11. Click the Photo1 layer title on the Layers palette to make this the active layer. Choose Filter, Distort, Shear, and click the Defaults button in the dialog box to reset the Shear default settings. It is necessary to create a point in the middle of the line first. This keeps the middle of the image in a stationary position when you drag the top and bottom end points. So, click in the middle first. In the grid (at the upper-left corner), click the center of the line to create a point. Click and drag the top and bottom ends of the line slightly to the left. Again, aim for a subtle effect and move the ends a small distance, as shown in Figure 10.17. Click OK to apply the effect.

A few minor adjustments are needed on the two layers to make the curling photo better. First, the Shear filter along with the Gaussian Blur filter will cause some of the shadow layer to show along the left edge of the photo. This is the wrong place for the shadow to be showing, given the current angle of the photo. The Photo1 layer might also need to be nudged into a better position.

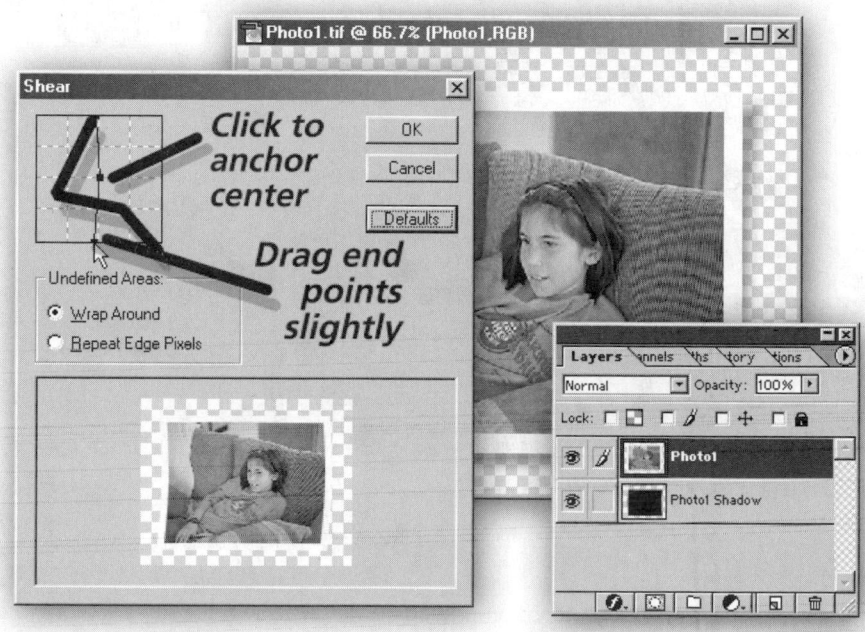

**Figure 10.17**   In the Shear dialog box, click the center point to anchor the center. Click and drag the top and bottom end points slightly to the left, as shown.

12. Click on the Photo1 Shadow layer to make this the active layer. Press Shift+L until the Polygon Lasso tool is the active tool. Make a selection to encompass an area on the left side of the photo that will represent an area where shadows should *not* appear, as shown in Figure 10.18. Press the Delete (Backspace) key. Press Ctrl(⌘)+D to deselect the marquee.

13. Press V to make the Move tool the active tool. Click the Photo1 layer title on the Layers palette to make it the active layer. Drag the Photo1 layer or use the arrow keys to nudge it into a position where the middle section of the right side of the photo is close to the edge of the shadow (also shown in Figure 10.18).

14. Click on the second column to the left of the Photo1 Shadow layer to link this layer to the Photo1 layer. A tiny link icon should appear. Position the Scrapbook.psd document and the Photo.tif document so that you have a clear view of both images. Press Ctrl(⌘)+– to zoom out of both documents, if necessary.

15. Click the title bar of Photo.tif to make this the active document. Click and drag the Photo1 layer image into the Scrapbook.psd document, as shown in Figure 10.19.

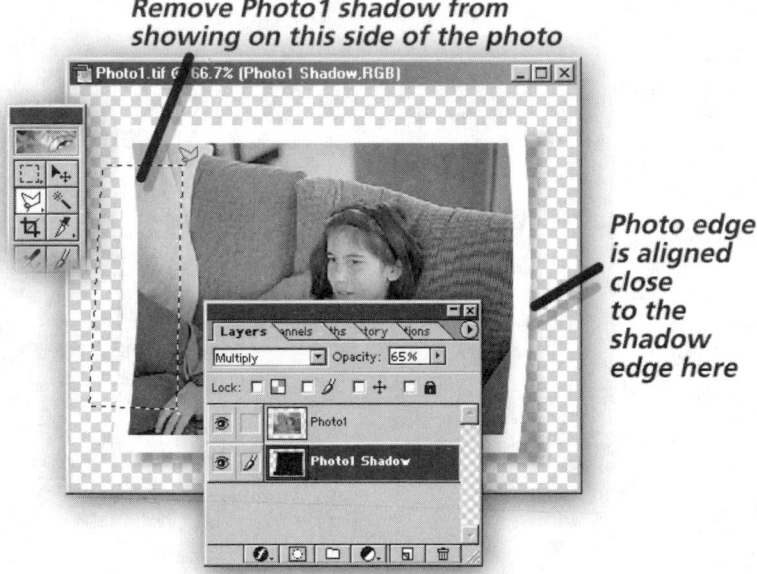

**Figure 10.18**   Make a selection to encompass an unwanted area of the shadow along the left side of the image. With the Photo1 Shadow layer as the active layer, press Delete (Backspace) to clear this shadow area.

**Figure 10.19**   Position both documents so that there is a clear view of both. With Photo.tif as the active document, click and drag the linked images into the Scrapbook.psd document.

Because the Photo1 and Photo1 Shadow layers are linked, both layers will appear in the Scrapbook.psd document when the image is dragged into the document window.

**16.** Close the Photo.tif image without saving changes. Position the Photo1 photograph near the upper-right corner (in relation to Paper3) in the Scrapbook.psd document window.

The Photo1 and Photo1 Shadow layers will move together because a link is still active between these layers.

**17.** Press Ctrl(⌘)+T to activate the Transform command. On the Options bar, type 6 for the Angle (see Figure 10.20). Press Enter (Return) to apply the rotation. Double-click inside the Transform box or press Enter (Return) to apply the Transform effect and exit the Transform command. Press Ctrl(⌘)+S to save your work.

Because the Photo1 and Photo1 Shadow layers are still linked, the Transform tool applied the rotation to both layers.

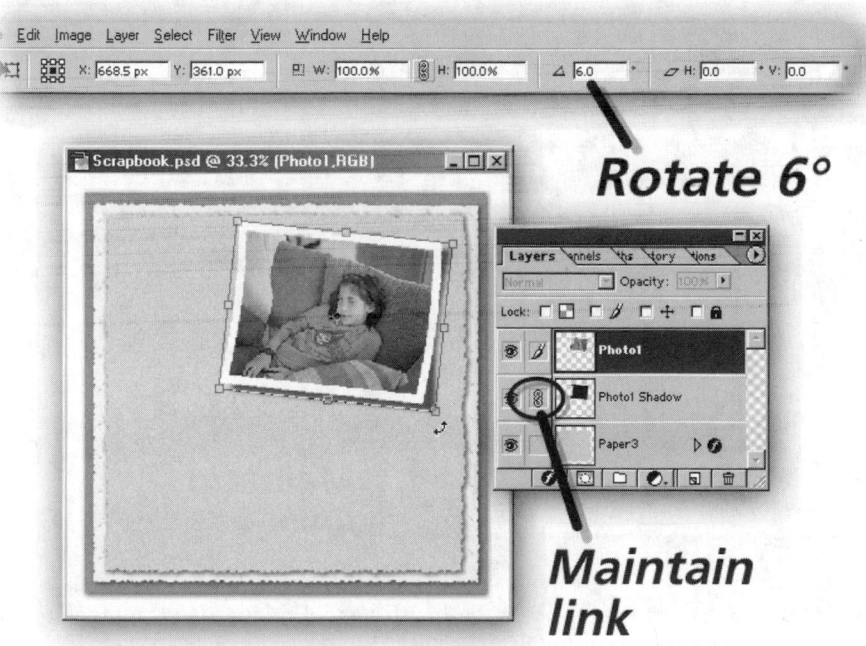

**Figure 10.20**    Press Ctrl(⌘)+T to access the Transform tool, and type 6° Angle on the Options bar to rotate the linked images slightly clockwise.

18. Open Photo2.tif from the Examples/Chap10 folder on the Companion CD. Repeat steps 1–16, making the following changes to the steps:

Replace any references to Photo1 with Photo2.

Change Canvas Size to **425** (pixels) Width and **420** (pixels) Height.

When opening the Shear dialog box, click the Defaults button each time to reset the dialog box to the default settings before you make changes.

19. Instead of completing step 17 with Photo2, press Ctrl(⌘)+T to activate the Transform command. On the Options bar, type **–11** for the Angle. Click inside the Transform box, and drag Photo2 to the position shown in Figure 10.21. Double-click inside the Transform box or press Enter (Return) to exit the Transform command and apply the changes. Press Ctrl(⌘)+S to save your work.

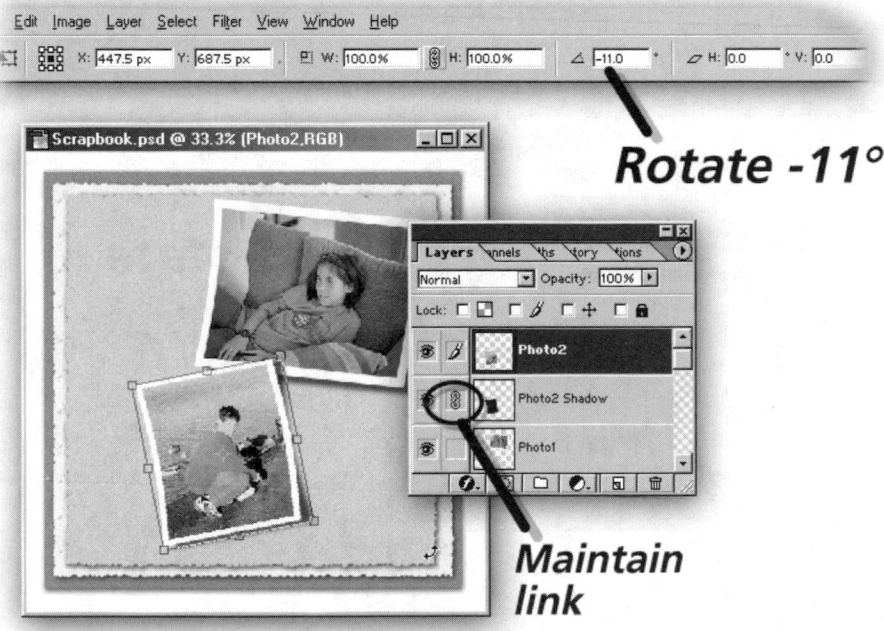

**Figure 10.21**    Press Ctrl(⌘)+T to access the Transform tool, and type –11° for the Angle on the Options bar to rotate the image slightly counterclockwise.

## Creating Effects within Layers

Hopefully you've seen some of the power of layers now, and can understand how linking layers are helpful in moving and transforming image information simultaneously on more than one layer.

Many scrapbooks make use of photo corners to attach a photo to the page. Our collage wouldn't be complete without a similar effect. In the next exercise, the first few steps will prepare Photo3 with a white border, similar to the ones in Photo1 and Photo2. Instead of a curl effect, however, photo corners will be placed on the photograph. We've provided a file on the Companion CD that contains the paths for the corners. The following steps will show you how to use the file.

### Example 10.6   Adding Photo Corners

1. Open Photo3.tif from the Examples/Chap10 folder on the Companion CD.

2. Double-click on the Background layer. Click OK to accept the default title in the New Layer dialog box. Right-click (Macintosh: hold Ctrl and click) the title bar of the Photo3 document, and choose Canvas Size. In the Canvas Size dialog box, type **350** (pixels) for Width and **375** (pixels) for Height. Click OK.

3. Press Alt(Opt) and click the Create a new layer icon at the bottom of the Layers palette. In the New Layer dialog box, type **Photo3** for the Name. Click OK to apply the name.

4. Drag the Photo3 layer below Layer 0 on the Layers palette. Drag a corner of the image window away from the center of the image to make sure there's at least one screen inch of window background surrounding the image. Press M to switch to the Rectangular Marquee tool. Drag a rectangular marquee selection around the photo, giving enough border edge to resemble the border on old-time photos, as shown in Figure 10.22.

**Figure 10.22**   As in the procedure used on the previous photos, make a rectangular marquee selection around Photo3, leaving border room around all the sides.

5. Press D for default colors. Press X to switch white to the foreground color. With Photo3 as the active layer, press Alt(Opt)+Delete (Backspace) to fill with color. Press Ctrl(⌘)+D to deselect the selection marquee. Press Ctrl(⌘)+Shift+E to merge the two visible layers.

6. Press V to switch to the Move tool. Position the Photo3.tif and Scrapbook.psd documents so that both can be viewed easily. Click the title bar of the Photo3.tif to make this the active document. Drag the Photo3 image into the Scrapbook.psd document, as shown in Figure 10.23.

**Figure 10.23**    Position to view both documents, and drag the Photo3 image into the Scrapbook.psd document window.

7. Press Ctrl(⌘)+T to activate the Transform command. Type –3.5 in the Options bar field for the Angle to slightly rotate the image counterclockwise. Click in the Transform box, and drag Photo3 to a position in the upper-left corner of the image, as shown in Figure 10.24. Press Enter (Return) to apply the changes and exit the Transform command.

8. Click the Add a layer style icon at the bottom of the Layers palette and choose Drop Shadow. In the Drop Shadow dialog box, leave the Opacity at 75%, make sure the Use Global Light option is not checked, and type **135** for Angle, **4** for Distance, **0** for Spread, and **4** for Size (see Figure 10.25). Click OK.

**Figure 10.24**   Press Ctrl(⌘)+T to activate the Transform tool and enter –3.5 for Angle to rotate slightly.

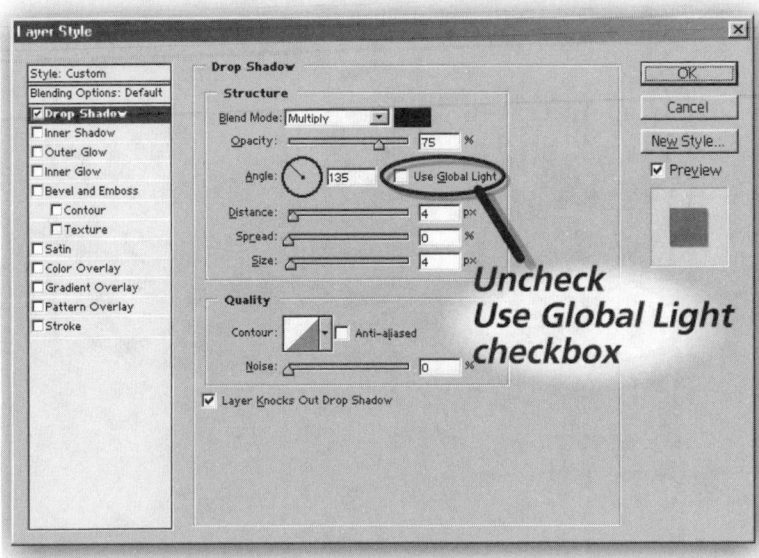

**Figure 10.25**   In the Drop Shadow dialog box, be sure the Use Global Light option is not checked, and apply the settings as shown.

The Use Global Light option causes any changes to the Angle amount to be applied to all layers to which a Layer Style has been applied. Because the shadow for Photo3 needs to appear different than the shadows for the paper matting, the Use Global Light option must not be checked, so that the Angle settings for the Photo3 will not affect the Angle settings for the paper matting shadows.

9. Open FrameCorners.tif in the Examples/Chap10 folder on the Companion CD.

   The paths for the frame corners are already drawn, and located on the Paths palette. The next steps will show you how to transfer the path to the Scrapbook.psd file and use the paths to make the frame corners for Photo3.

10. Click the Paths tab to view the Paths palette for the. Press A (or Shift+A) to switch to the Path Component Selection tool (solid arrow).

11. Position FrameCorners.tif so that there is room in the workspace to see both the Scrapbook.psd file and FrameCorners.tif. Click on the Frame Corner path title on the Paths palette and drag it into the Scrapbook.psd document window as shown in Figure 10.26. Close FrameCorners.tif without saving changes.

12. Press Ctrl(⌘)++ to increase your view of the Scrapbook document, if necessary. Press the spacebar to toggle to the Hand tool, and drag the document so you can view the corner paths.

**Figure 10.26**   Drag the Frame Corner path title from the FrameCorners.tif file into the Scrapbook.psd document window to transfer the .paths.

13. With the Path Component Selection tool, drag a marquee selection around one of the corner paths to select one of the photo corners, as shown in Figure 10.27. Press Ctrl(⌘)+T to access the Path Transform command. Click inside the bounding box and drag the photo frame corner to the corresponding corner location of Photo3.

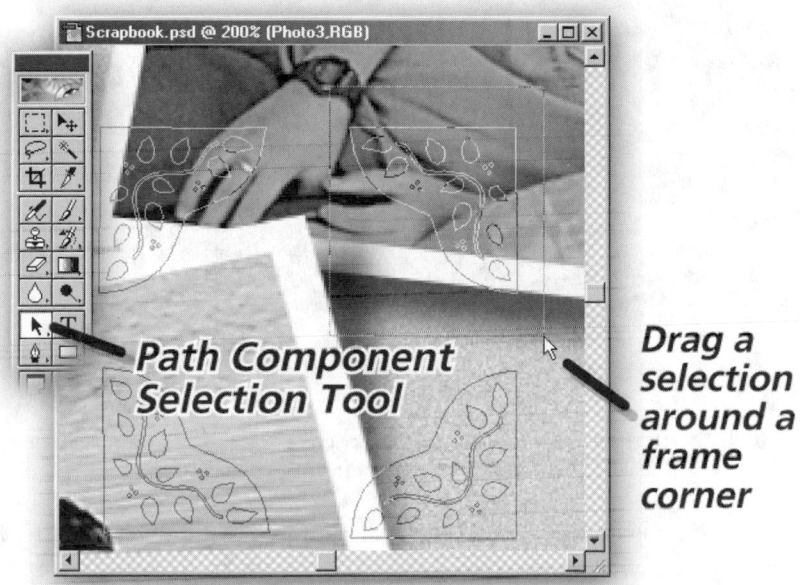

**Figure 10.27**  With the Path Component Selection tool, drag a selection around one of the corner paths to select the path.

14. Place the cursor outside the corner of the bounding box. When the cursor changes to a curved two-headed arrow, rotate the path so that it looks like it's at the same angle as the photo. If necessary, click inside the bounding box and then nudge it in the appropriate direction to have the outside edges of the corner path line up with the edges of Photo3, as shown in Figure 10.28. When you get the path in position, press Enter (Return) to exit the Transform command. Then, click outside the path area to deselect the path.

15. Repeat steps 13 and 14 for the remaining three corner paths. Press the spacebar, when necessary, to move your view into the document window.

16. Click the foreground color selection box on the toolbox and choose a pale beige color; R:223, G:223, B:213. Click OK.

17. With the last corner path still selected, click outside the path area to deselect the path. Press Ctrl(⌘)+Enter (Return) to create a single (*discontinuous*—the paths are not connected) selection marquee based on the geometry of the paths.

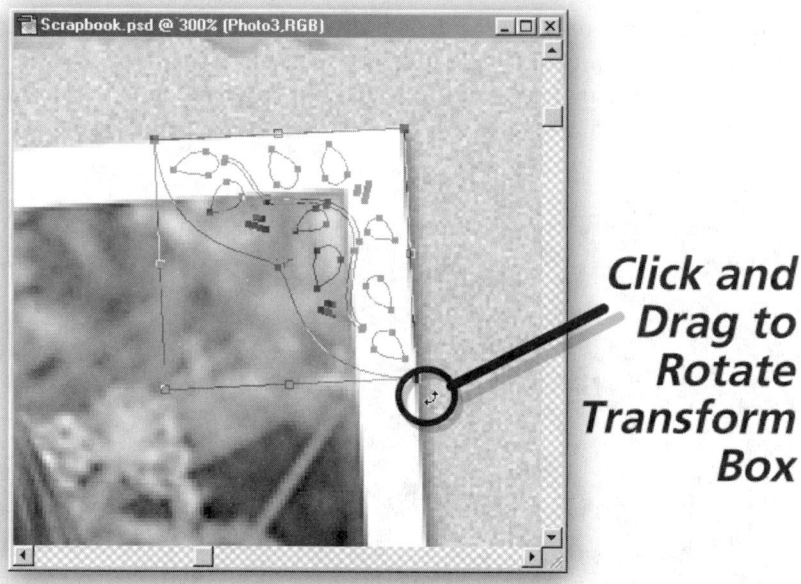

**Figure 10.28**   With the Transform bounding box active, drag to position the frame corner at the correct location. Rotate and position the path as necessary.

**18.** Click the Layers tab of the grouped palette to view the Layers palette. Press Alt(Opt) and click on the Create a new layer icon at the bottom corner of the Layers palette. In the New Layer dialog box, type **Photo Corners** for the Name. Click OK.

**19.** Press Alt(Opt)+Delete (Backspace) to fill the marquee selection with the foreground color. Press Ctrl(⌘)+D to deselect the selection.

Now you will add some dimension to the corners.

**20.** Click the Add a layer style icon at the bottom of the Layers palette and choose Drop Shadow from the drop-down list. In the Layer Style dialog box, make sure the Use Global Light option is not checked. Keep the default settings for Opacity (75%), Angle (120°), and Spread (0). Type **3** for Distance and **3** for Size.

**21.** Click the Bevel and Emboss option listed on the left side of the Layer Style box to move to this dialog box option. Choose Inner Bevel from the drop-down list for Style and choose Smooth for Technique. Type **50%** for Depth, **2** for Size, and **0** for Soften. Under Shading, make sure the Use Global Light option is not checked. Type **120°** for Angle, **50%** (Screen) for Highlight Mode. Altitude can remain at 30°, and Shadow Mode at 75% (Multiply). See Figure 10.29.

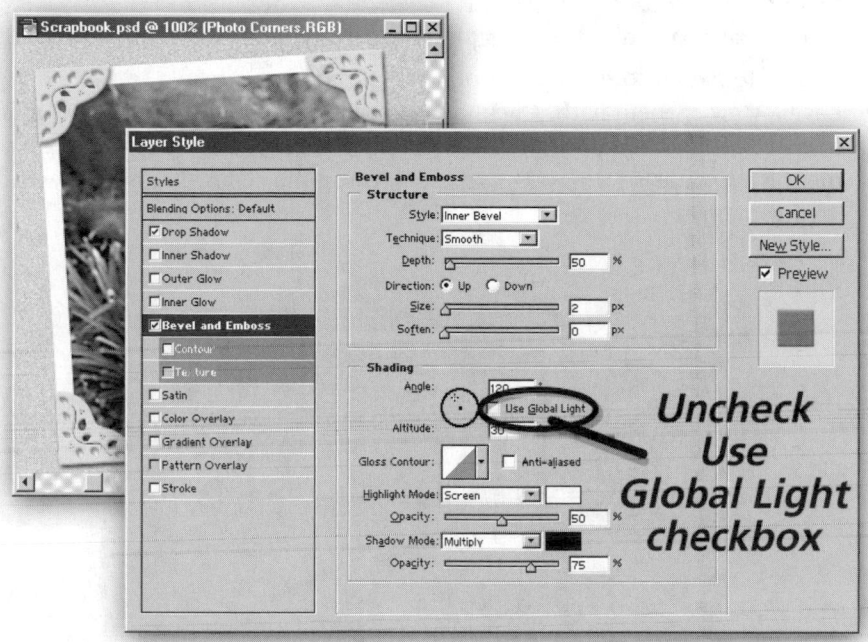

**Figure 10.29**   Use the settings shown in the Bevel and Emboss dialog box to add dimension to the Photo Corners.

**22.** Press Ctrl(⌘)+S to save your work. Keep the document open for the steps to come.

## Adding Type to Layers

The collage is almost complete. It seems to be missing something, though. There is too much empty space in the lower-right corner of the image. Because scrapbook pages usually have a date—documenting the photographs on a page—this would be a good spot for just that.

Adding a script font is the final touch needed for the page. We included the text as a bitmap in a separate file on the Companion CD, so you do not need to own the exact font we used. The next steps show how to use this file to add the text to the collage. When you're creating a collage on your own, use the Type tool to type the desired text, and experiment with the font.

### Example 10.7   Adding Text as a Graphic

1. Open ScrapText.psd in the Examples/Chap10 folder on the Companion CD.

2. Press V to switch to the Move tool. Position both documents so that you have a view of them both. Click the title bar of the ScrapText.psd document to make it the active document. Drag the text into the Scrapbook.psd document window, as shown in Figure 10.30. Close the ScrapText.psd file without saving changes.

**Figure 10.30**   Position both documents near each other. With the Move tool as the active tool, drag the text from the ScrapText.psd file into the Scrapbook.psd file.

3. With the text layer as the active layer, click the Add a layer style icon at the bottom of the Layers palette, and choose Drop Shadow.

4. In the Drop Shadow dialog box, make sure the Use Global Light option is not checked, and leave the Opacity at 75%, Angle at 120°. Type **3** for Distance, and **3** for Size, as shown in Figure 10.31.

5. Click on the Bevel and Emboss option on the left side of the dialog box. In the Bevel and Emboss area of the Layer Style dialog box, choose Emboss from the drop-down list for Style and leave Smooth for Technique. Type **200%** for Depth, **1** for Size, and **0** for Soften.

6. In the Shading section of the dialog box, be sure that the Use Global Light option is not checked. Type **120°** for Angle, **34°** for Altitude. Highlight Mode should remain at Screen (75%), and Shadow Mode at Multiply (75%). See Figure 10.32.

7. Press Ctrl(⌘)+S to save your work.

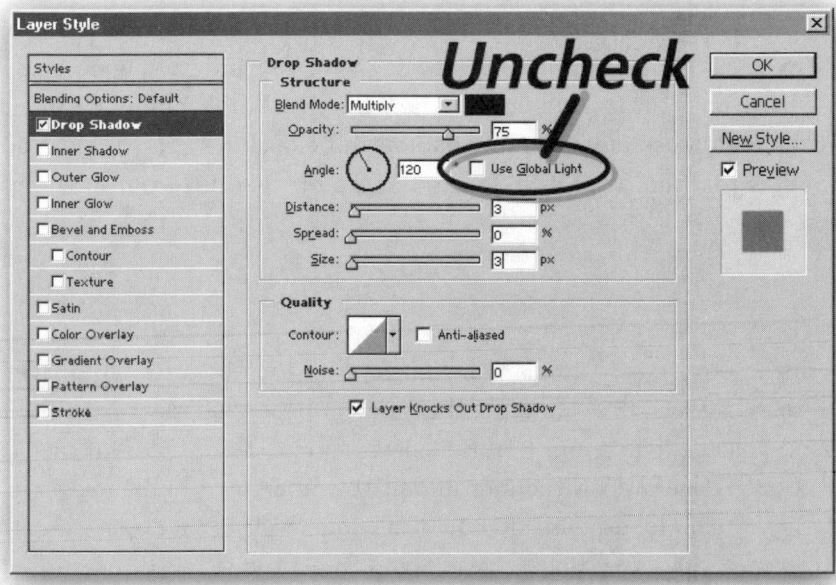

**Figure 10.31**    Add a drop shadow to the text layer with the settings shown.

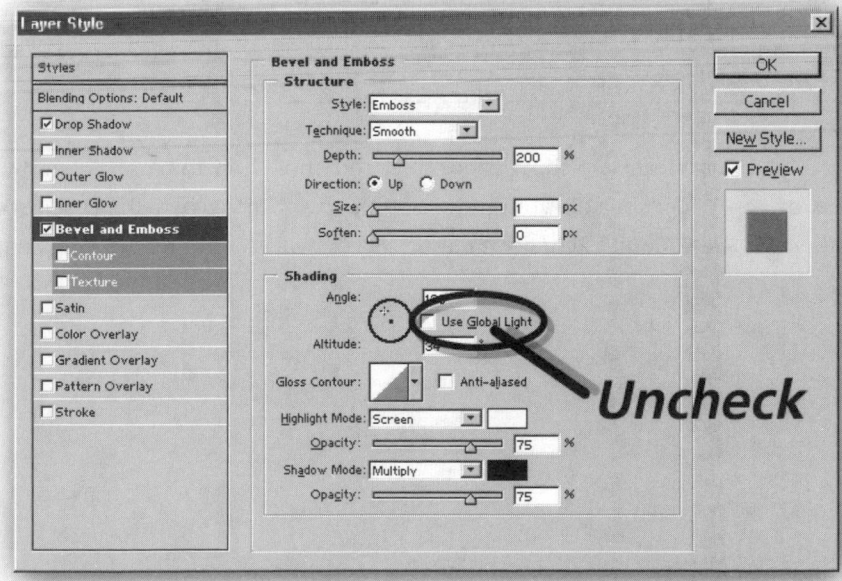

**Figure 10.32**    Add a Bevel and Emboss effect to the text layer with the settings shown here.

There was a time when the phrase, "Making something out of nothing" meant that a person was a hypochondriac. But with Photoshop 6, as you've seen in this chapter, layers can be an indispensable tool for starting with very little and ending up with art that fairly cries out for a frame. You now have several techniques at hand for adding dimension, texture, and other photorealistic qualities to a collage. And the best thing is that you don't have to pry the cap off that dried out tube of paste anymore!

## Summary

Layers are a powerful way to maintain control over each object in an image. You used separate layers in this collage for the different papers, photos, text, and photo corners. If you decide to return to this file later, to replace the color for the Paper2 layer, it can be done easily without disturbing the other items in the image. In this respect, layers allow for experimentation on a grand level. And it doesn't stop there. Experimenting with Layer Modes, Layer Styles, and Layer Masks can contribute to the fun.

**Tip**

**Duplicate Any Layer that You May Need to Use Again**    Create a duplicate of the layer you want to make changes to and turn off the original layer. Then experiment to your heart's delight. If you don't like the changes, you can always delete the layer and still have the original layer intact.

In Photoshop, practically anything is possible. You know how to paint a shadow and a piece of paper now, but do you know how to paint using paths and selections? Sounds weird, huh? But it's actually *fantastic,* as you will see in the following chapter.

# *Chapter 11*

## Painting with Pen and Path Selection Tools

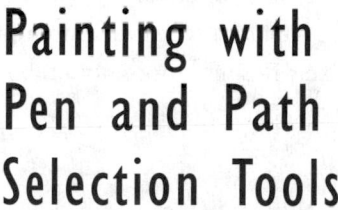

There are two categories of digital graph-

ics; bitmap and vector. Bitmap graphics,

also called pixel-based or raster graphics,

are created using rows and rows of rec-

tangular pixels of different colors. A pixel

is simply a placeholder for a value (a color). Viewing a scene through a wire mesh screen door is a fair visual example of the nature of bitmap graphics. Photoshop is primarily an image editing program that is bitmap-based. If you have ever painted a diagonal line that appears jagged, this is bitmapping at its worse. Photoshop uses *anti-aliasing* to help minimize the jagged-edge effect. Anti-aliasing is the placement of transitional colors between neighboring pixels of different colors.

Open a document in Photoshop. With the Line tool, draw a diagonal black line on a white background. The line appears smooth at the 100% zoom level (normal view). Now magnify a section of the line to 700% or more, as shown in Figure 11.1. You'll notice that the transition between the black line and the white background is made up of black pixels at different brightness values. A major disadvantage in having an image that relies on pixel information becomes apparent when you attempt to modify the size or resolution of the image. The pixels become more noticeable, resulting in a loss of focus and poor display of image detail.

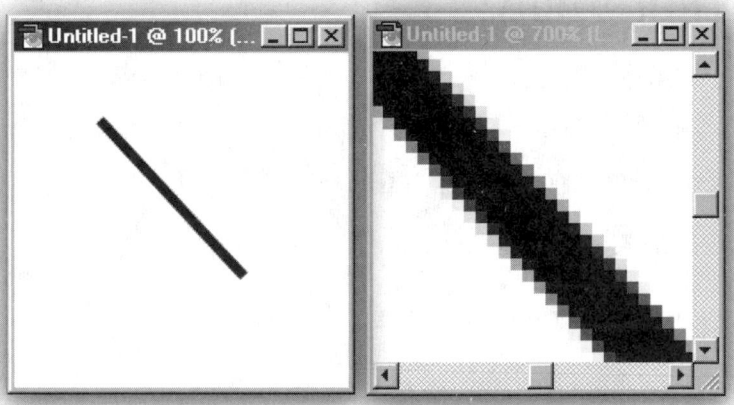

**Figure 11.1**    Bitmap programs use anti-aliasing to keep edges looking smooth (at normal view on the left). When magnified (view on the right), the transition of pixels that contributes to this smooth appearance becomes more apparent.

Vector-based graphics are the other side of this computer graphics coin. Any line drawn in a vector program such as Illustrator, CorelDRAW, or Xara, is defined for the computer in mathematical terms. Because the computer has a mathematical interpretation for a line, this allows resizing in any direction and to any magnitude without the loss of resolution or clarity. All the computer is doing is multiplying or dividing math equations that constitute the line. Fortunately for you and me, the mathematical equations generated by drawing a line are transparent to the user. We never have to get into the math, and for most of us (including the author), this is a good thing. We only need to concern ourselves with what we are drawing onscreen—hey, we're artists and not mathematicians, right? Okay, some of us actually *are* mathematicians...

When drawing vector-based lines, there are rules that the user should be aware of. Once these rules are understood, creating lines and curves will become easy with practice.

Photoshop has two Vector tools: the Pen tool and the Path Selection tools. The Pen tool gives you the power to create vector-based lines within Photoshop. Lines drawn with the Pen tool are referred to as *paths*. These paths are stored on the Paths palette. When using the Paths palette, the paths themselves are not printable, but the paths can be made into *selections* for use in the image document. Furthermore, the paths can be permanently saved for reuse. Paths can also be filled, and saved in a format such as Acrobat (PDF) so that when printed, the vector outlines and fills print as crisp and clean as is physically possible. They're as clean as vector (type 1 and TrueType) fonts. Paths can even be transferred and used in other Photoshop files or between other programs such as Illustrator.

**Note**

**You Must Name a Work Path If You Want to Save It**    When you draw a path in Photoshop, it is stored in the Paths palette as a Work Path. This Work Path is only temporary. If you deselect the path and later draw a different path, the new path will replace the old path on the Work Path title.

If you want to permanently save the path for future use, it is necessary to name the Work Path. Naming is easily accomplished; just double-click the Work Path title (or click the arrow in the upper-right corner of the Paths palette and choose Save Path from the palette menu). In the Save Path dialog box, type a new name for the path or accept the default path name, and click OK.

Figure 11.2 shows the flyout menus for the Pen tool and Path Selection tools. Adobe has made it easy to access most of these tools with modifier keys, instead of clicking on the flyout menus to switch tools. When the Pen tool is active, pressing the Alt(Opt) key toggles to the Convert Point tool, and pressing the Ctrl(⌘) key toggles to the Direct Selection tool. Additionally, if the Auto Add/Delete checkbox is checked on the Options bar, the Add Anchor Point tool will automatically toggle on when the Pen cursor is over a path. Similarly, the Delete Anchor Point tool will automatically toggle on when the Pen cursor is over a point on the path.

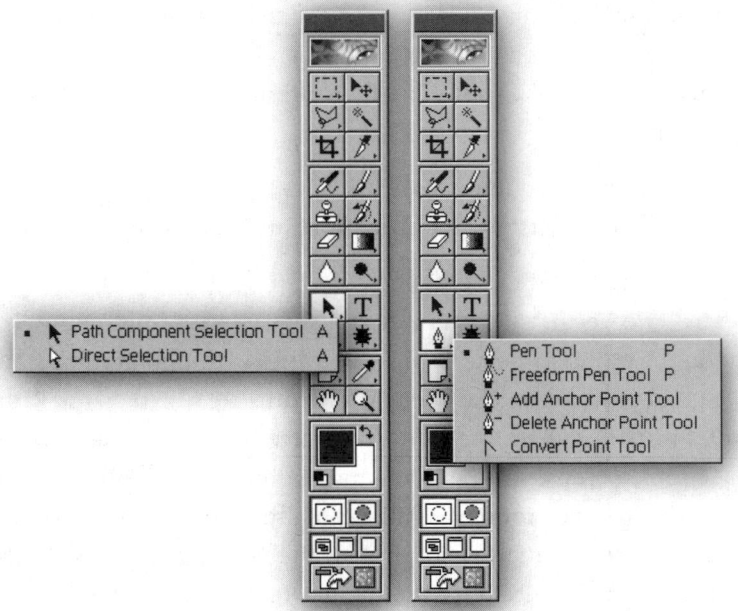

**Figure 11.2**    The tools lists for the Pen tool and Path selection tools.

## Understanding the Pen Tool Rule—Think of Points

In order to understand the Pen tool, think back to early math lessons in grade school. You might remember a time when your teacher tried to convey the concept that, "at least two points are required to define a line or line segment." Never will that be truer than when using the Pen tool.

The Pen tool creates points, which define the way a line segment looks. Adobe calls these anchor points, and so shall we. In a sense, you don't actually draw a line with the Pen tool, you define the points that make up the line. There are three *main* anchor point types:

- Corner
- Smooth
- Sharp

## Using the Corner Anchor Point

The corner point is the easiest to draw. With the Pen tool selected, click a spot and click again in another spot (remember, two points to make a line). The line segment created between the two anchor points is a straight line. When several connected lines make up a shape, we call the shape a *path* and the lines are called *path segments*. Again, this is Adobe lingo, so we are using it to match Adobe documentation.

In the following set of steps, you will practice the creation of useful corner points by drawing a simple triangle. Hopefully, a few concepts will become clearer along the path. Sorry <g>.

**Note**

**The Rubber Band Option**   Want to preview path segments as you draw them? The Options bar has a Rubber Band option when the Pen tool is active that enables you to see the path segments as you move your cursor in the image. The segments are not permanent until you click the next point.

Example 11.1   Using Corner Point

> **Warning!**   If an error message appears when you open the CD files, press Ctrl(⌘)+Shift+K and then choose Adobe RGB (1998) from the Working Spaces, RGB drop-down list. See Chapter 3 for more information.

1. Open Practice.psd in the Examples/Chap11 folder on the Companion CD.

   The file has an active layer, titled Practice, and a few hidden layers. Leave them hidden for now (we'll get to those later).

2. Press P to switch to the Pen tool. Click once in the document near the bottom-left side to make the first of three anchor points for a triangle.

3. Hold down the Shift key (to constrain the movement to vertical) and click near the bottom-right side of the document.

   There should now be a straight horizontal line near the bottom of the document. So far the line created is considered an open path segment.

4. Click a third point at the top-middle of the document, forming another straight-path segment.

5. Close the path by clicking the last point at the same location as the first point created.

   A circle appears next to the Pen cursor indicating that the path is about to be closed (see Figure 11.3).

   The wonderful thing about paths is they can be modified at any given moment in time. If you are not satisfied with the location of any of the three points that make up the triangle, making changes are easy.

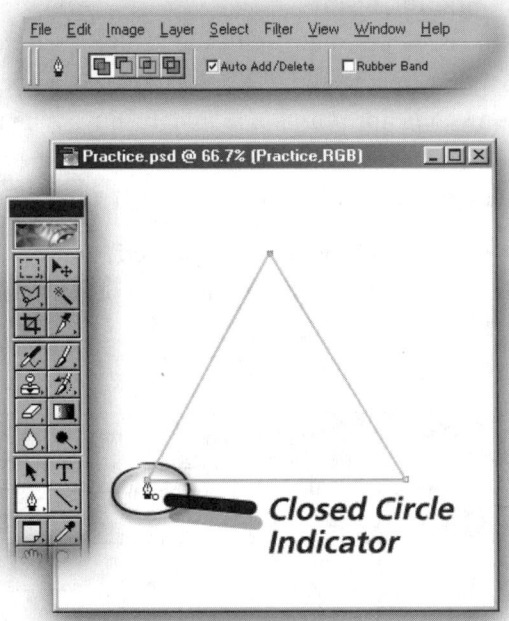

**Figure 11.3**   Use the circle indicator on the Pen cursor to help determine when to click and close the path.

6. Hold down the Ctrl(⌘) key to toggle to the Direct Selection tool (the cursor changes to a hollow arrow), click and drag a point to move it to a different location.

   Notice how the path segments associated with the point move to reflect the changes being made. The anchor point that is *selected* is solid, while the *unselected* points are hollow.

7. Hold down the Ctrl(⌘) key and nudge the selected point with the arrow keys on your keyboard.

   The anchor point moves by one screen pixel nudging with the arrow keys— the farther your viewing resolution, the greater a distance one keyboard nudge will do. A whole new world of control and precision should start to become apparent. Let's try one more experiment.

8. Hold down the Ctrl(⌘) key to continue accessing the Direct Selection tool, and then click *and drag* a path segment instead of an anchor point.

   You can either change the position of the segments that make up a path, or the individual anchor points.

9. Click the Path tab on the Layers/Channels/Paths/Yada Yada palette to view the Paths palette (or choose Window, Show Paths). Double-click on the Work

Path title and in the Save Path dialog box type **Triangle**. Click OK. Hide the path by clicking on an empty area on the outside of the path title on the Paths palette. Click the Layers tab to return to the Layers palette. Press Ctrl(⌘)+S to save your work. Keep the document open for the next adventure.

## Creating Curves with Smooth Anchor Point

A smooth anchor point is called smooth because a path segment that passes through it doesn't change direction at all. Therefore, the area of path segment surrounding the smooth anchor point is, well…*smooth*! Smooth anchor points are made with a click and drag motion. The click creates the initial point and the dragging motion creates the direction lines that extend from the point. These direction lines are used to control the curve of the path segment.

Again, we will use a practice exercise to make a simple shape. This set of steps uses smooth anchor points to create a circular shape.

### Example 11.2   Using Smooth Points to Create Curves

1. Open Practice.psd in the Examples/Chap11 folder on the Companion CD if it is not already open in Photoshop's workspace.

2. Click the square (eye icon) to the left of the Circle Template layer on the Layers palette to view this layer. The template guides you along in this example.

3. Press P to select the Pen tool from the toolbox, click the green dot next to the number 1, and then drag upward until you reach the end of the red template handle (see Figure 11.4).

   Notice as you drag that a direction line is made in the opposite direction (indicated by blue handles on the template).

4. Click and drag the number 2 green template dot until reaching the end of the second red direction line.

5. Continue the same technique on dots 3 and 4 dragging in the direction of the red direction lines. To close and finish the circle, move the Pen cursor over the first green dot, and when you see a circle appear next to the cursor icon, click once (see Figure 11.4). This closes the path. No dragging is required when closing the path, as shown in Figure 11.4.

   You should now see a circle path that is the same shape as the template.

6. Click the eye to the left of the Circle Template layer to turn off the layer. Click the Paths tab to view the Path palette. Double-click the Work Path and in the Save Path dialog box type **Circle**. Click OK. Press Ctrl(⌘)+S to save your work.

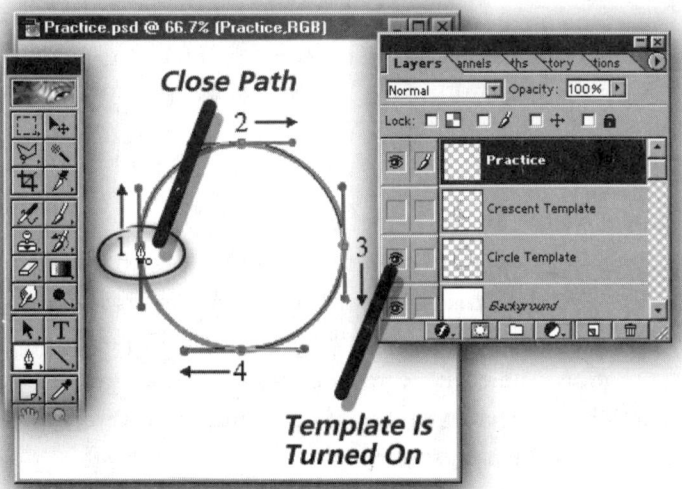

**Figure 11.4**   A circle can be described by four path segments, each of whose anchor points have a smooth property.

We will experiment with the points on the circle path. Worried about ruining that perfect circle? Don't worry. Because you saved your work, experiment to your heart's content in the following steps. There is a File, Revert command as the last step that puts the path back to the condition it was when you last saved the path.

**7.** Press Shift+A until the Direct Selection tool is active (the hollow arrow tool). Click anywhere on the circle path to display the points. Click on any curved path segment of the circle and drag.

Notice how the curved path segment responds to the dragging, and the direction lines associated with the curved path segment adjust according to the curve you modify by dragging.

**8.** Click on a point to see both direction lines associated with that point (the anchor point will have a solid fill). Click on the end of one of the direction lines and drag in any direction on the *direction point*.

Notice that you can also change or control the shape of the curve this way as well. If you drag up and down on the end of the control handle, the opposite handle responds like a seesaw.

**9.** Click on the point and drag the point to a different spot. Nudge the point with the arrow keys on the keyboard.

The points, direction lines, and path segments can all be changed using similar techniques.

**10.** If you saved the work as instructed in step 6 of this experiment, return to the circle shape by choosing File, Revert. Or get in some additional practice by turning the Circle Template layer back on and adjusting the direction points and lines to return to the circle shape of the template. Leave the document open for the next steps.

The File, Revert option will return the document to the point at which it was last saved.

## Working with the Sharp Anchor Point—The Point with Two Independent Handles

The sharp anchor point is a point with two independent direction lines. As you noticed in the previous steps, the direction handles on a smooth point respond with a seesaw effect. With a sharp point, the direction lines respond independently. This type of point is most commonly used when you have a sharp peak connected to curved lines when creating a path. Using the Convert Point tool on the direction points on direction lines to redirect the direction line creates a sharp anchor point.

In the following steps, the emphasis will be on sharp anchor points, the Convert Point tool, and the Direct Selection tool. You will make changes to the circle-shaped path to create a crescent-shaped path. You can select the Convert Point tool or the Direct Selection tool from the tools list. However, in most situations, it is more efficient to keep the Pen tool selected and toggle to the Convert Point and Direct Selection tools using modifier keys. You will use these modifier keys in the creation of the crescent shape from the circle.

### Example 11.3   Using the Convert Point Tool and Sharp Points to Change a Path Shape

**1.** If the Circle Template layer is showing, click the eye icon to the left of the Circle Template layer on the Layers palette to hide this layer. Click the square (eye icon) to the far left of Crescent Template layer title to turn on this layer.

**2.** Click the Paths tab to display the Paths palette and click on the Circle path to make this path visible. On the Paths palette, click the triangle at the upper-right corner of the palette and choose Duplicate Path from the flyout menu. When the Duplicate Path dialog box appears, rename the path **Crescent** and click OK.

**3.** Press P to switch to the Pen tool. Hold down the Ctrl(⌘) key to toggle to the Direct Selection tool and click anywhere on the path to make the anchor points visible. Continue to hold down the Ctrl(⌘) key and click the anchor point near the number 2 green dot, and then drag the anchor point to reposition it onto the number 2 green dot location (see Figure 11.5).

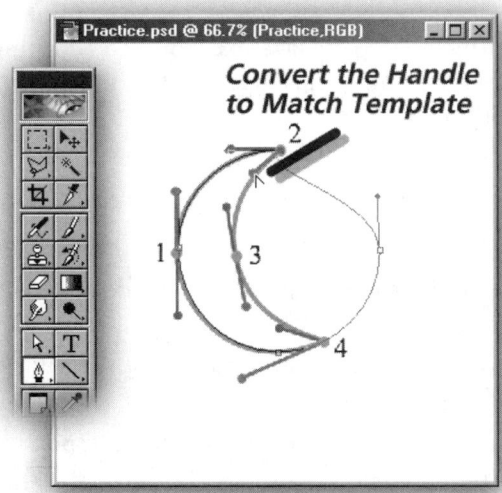

**Figure 11.5**   Toggle to the Convert Point tool with the Alt(Opt) key then click the direction point and drag to match the position of the direction line on the template.

4. Hold down the Alt(Opt) key to toggle to the Convert Point tool, and click on the end of the right handle (opposite the blue template line) and drag this direction line into position over the red line on the template as seen in Figure 11.5.

   You just created your first sharp point (two curved lines that meet at a sharp anchor point).

5. Hold down the Ctrl(⌘) key to toggle to the Direct Selection tool and drag the anchor point on the right side of the circle to the location of the number 3 green dot (on the template). Continue to hold down the Ctrl(⌘) key and drag the direction point (at the end of the direction line) (from point 3) to match the angle of the template lines as shown in Figure 11.6.

   Note: Because this is still a smooth point, dragging on one handle end will make the opposite handle follow in a seesaw fashion.

   To complete the crescent shape, you need to alter the anchor point near point 4 on the template.

6. Hold down the Ctrl(⌘) key, click the circle point near point 4 of the template and drag to relocate it over point 4 on the template. Continue to hold down the Ctrl(⌘) key and drag the left handle end to match the angle and length of the red template handle of point 4. Hold down the Alt(Opt) key to toggle to the Convert Point tool, click and drag the right direction point so the direction line matches the location and length of the blue template line of point 4, as shown in Figure 11.7.

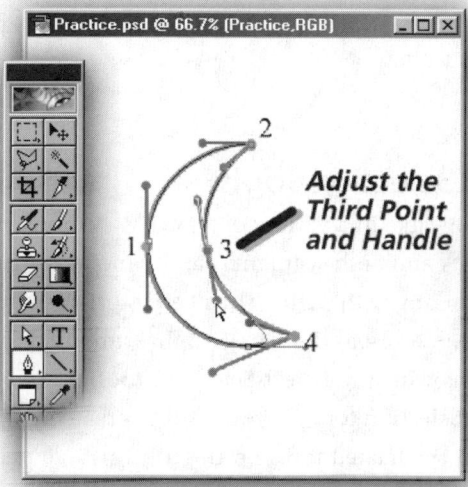

**Figure 11.6**   Hold the Ctrl(⌘) key to toggle to the Direct Selection tool and drag the right circle point and direction lines (by their direction points) to match point 3 on the template.

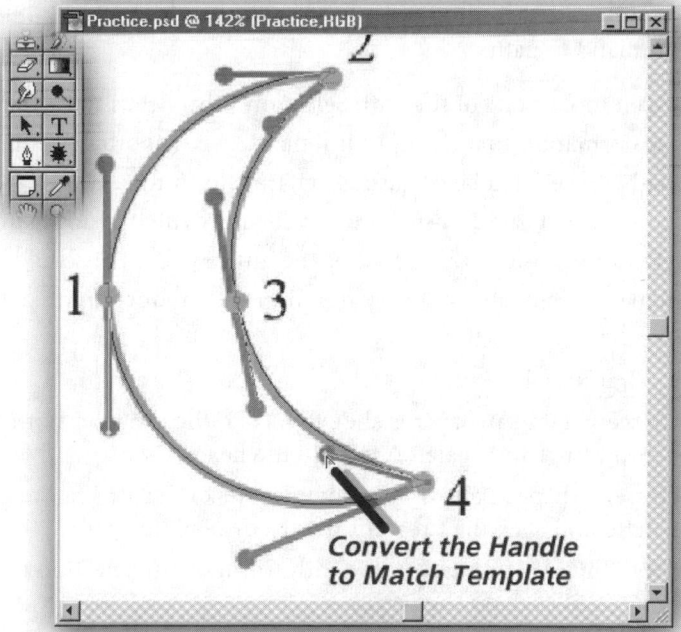

**Figure 11.7**   Hold the Ctrl(⌘) key to move point 4 onto the template and the Alt(Opt) key to move the direction lines (by dragging their direction points) to match the template.

**7.** As a final touch, hold down the Ctrl(⌘) key and adjust the point and lines at point 1 if needed. Press Ctrl(⌘)+S to save your work. Keep the document open for the next phase.

## Using the Path Selection Tools

Paths are forever changeable in a variety of ways. As demonstrated in this chapter's routines, anchor points and path segments can be moved and reshaped. Keep your goal in mind when working with paths. The need to often switch tools is quite common. The Path Selection tools, as the name implies, are used for selecting a point or portion of the path (as with the Direct Selection tool), or the entire path (as with the Path Component Selection tool). If you need to create or alter a part of the path, then the Pen tool and the related tools on the tools list are needed.

In order to prepare the crescent-shaped path for some fun later in the chapter, we'll now demonstrate how Photoshop's Free Transform option can also be used to reshape and modify paths.

In the same way that you can use the Free Transform command to alter image information (resize, rotate, flip horizontally, distort, and so on), you can apply the Free Transform command to paths.

However, the Pen tool or one of the Path Selection tools needs to be the active tool to apply a transformation to a path. Additionally, it is important to make sure all points on a path are selected before using the Transform tool. If only one point or a few points are selected, the Transform tool will apply the transformations to only the selected portions of the path instead of the entire path. This could produce an interesting shape, but probably not very useful in the production of art.

### Example 11.4   Transforming Paths

**1.** If the Crescent Template layer is showing, click the eye icon to the left of this layer (on the Layers palette) to hide the layer.

**2.** If the crescent-shaped path is not showing, click the Paths tab to display the Paths palette and click the Crescent title to display this path.

**3.** Press A (or Shift+A) to switch to the Path Component Selection tool (the solid arrow) and click on the path.

You will now see solid squares at each point on the path indicating that all points are selected.

4. Press Ctrl(⌘)+T to activate the Transform tool. On the Options bar, click the Constrain Proportions icon and type **140%** for Width. Press Enter (Return). Type **–30** for the Angle (see Figure 11.8). Press Enter (Return).

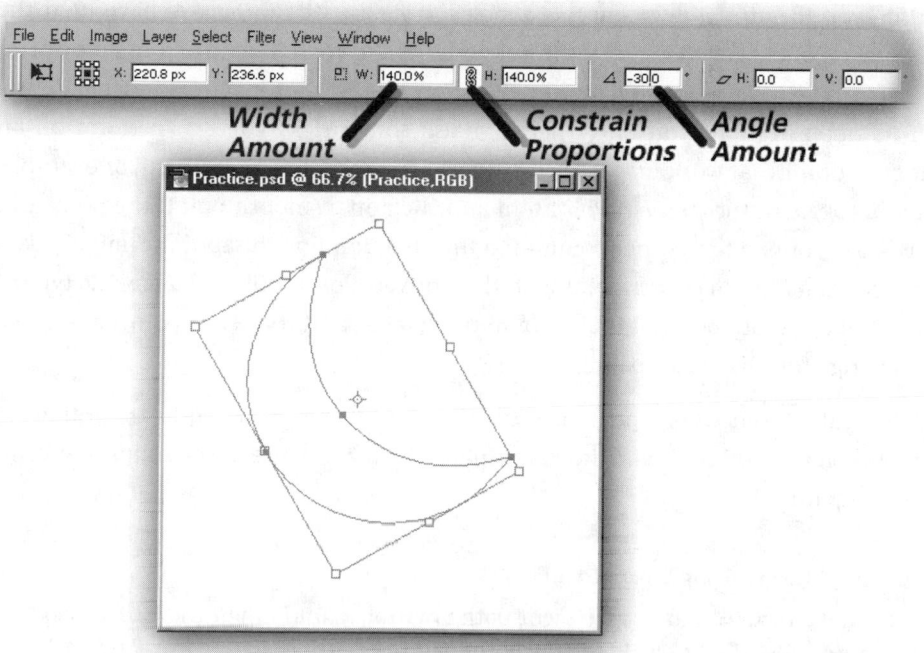

**Figure 11.8** On the Options bar, click the Constrain Proportions link icon and type **140%** for Width and **–30** for Angle.

5. Press the Enter (Return) key to exit the Transform command and apply the changes. Press Ctrl(⌘)+S to save your work. Keep the document open for the next steps.

## Using Paths to Help Paint an Image

Unlike Custom Shapes, which can be added to an image as bitmap fills (depending on your choice on the Options bar), paths are nonprinting vector objects. Paths are not made up of pixels. Paths remain separate from the bitmap image. Once a path has been created, it can be saved and later used in a variety of ways, including converting the path to a selection; filling the path with color; or stroking the path (adding color to the border of a path). Unlike Custom Shapes and text, a filled path will not display a crisp outline when exported to such formats as PDF. So the concept here is that paths are useful tools to arrive at various painting and editing goals with a specific piece.

Also keep in mind a few concepts about *altering* a path. So far, we have used the Convert Point tool to change the property of an anchor point from smooth to sharp, and in the process changed a direction line so that it moves independently of its opposing direction line. There are also some tricks you can perform on an anchor point that work independently of the anchor's direction lines. For example, if you toggle to the Convert Point tool and click on a smooth point, the point will instantly convert to a corner point—and the direction lines disappear. Similarly, you can click and drag a corner point with the Convert Point tool to change this type of point to a smooth point. It is also common to add points or delete points as needed to change the shape of a path.

Using path geometry as the basis for a selection is demonstrated in the following steps. You will add color and life to this image by making use of the simple crescent-shaped path.

### Example 11.5    Adding Color to a Path

1. Make certain that the Crescent path is visible. Hold down the Ctrl(⌘) key and press the Enter (Return) key to load the path as a selection. The path disappears.

2. Click the Layers tab to view the Layers palette. Click on the Practice layer to make this the active layer. Click on the foreground color selection box on the toolbox and choose a soft muted green color; R:136, G:181, B:176. Click OK. Press Alt(Opt)+Delete to fill the crescent shape with this color.

3. Press J to switch to the Airbrush tool. Press D for the default colors of black and white. Press X to switch white to the foreground color. On the Options bar, type **20%** for Pressure. Click the Brushes tab to show the Brushes palette and choose a large soft brush such as the 100-pixel tip. Keep a small portion of the Brush tip touching the inside of the crescent-shaped marquee (a large portion of the Brush should remain outside of the crescent selection). Brush a stroke of white along the inside curve as seen in Figure 11.9. If necessary, stroke a couple of times to give the highlight more emphasis, but try for a subtle look. Press Ctrl(⌘)+D to deselect the marquee selection.

   If you do not like the first stroke and want to try again, press Ctrl(⌘)+Z to undo the last stroke, or use the History palette to go back as many strokes as needed. Deselect the marquee when you are satisfied with the results.

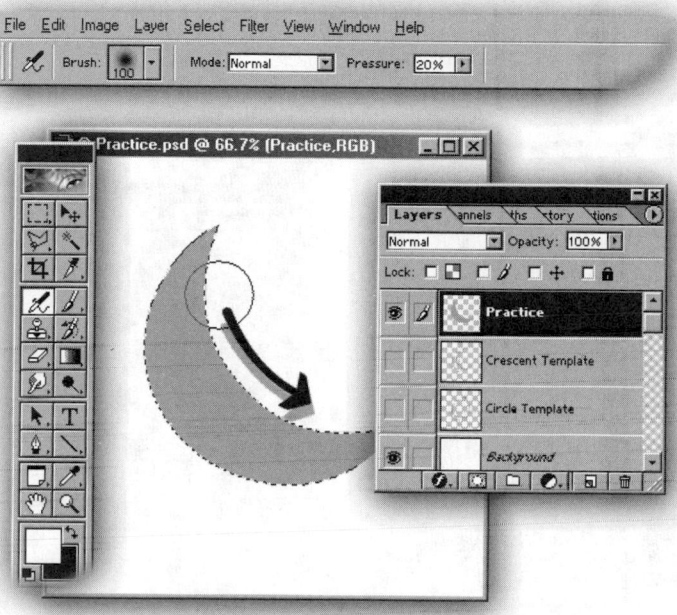

**Figure 11.9**   Use a large, soft brush at 20% pressure to stroke a soft, white highlight on the inside crescent arc.

4. Click on the Background layer to make this the active layer on the Layers palette. Click on the foreground color selection box on the toolbox and select a nighttime green color; R:0, G:105, B:104. Click OK. Click on the background color selection box on the toolbox and choose a dark navy color; R:25, G:4, B:57. Click OK.

5. Click the Gradient tool and choose the Linear Gradient tool on the Options bar. Choose Foreground to Background from the Gradient drop-down list. Click near the top of the image while holding down the Shift key to constrain the gradient to vertical and drag to the bottom of the image as shown in Figure 11.10.

   Let's add some stars. We will use a filter to make the star effect, but the target layer must have a black fill to make this trick work. By changing to Screen mode, the black on this layer will be hidden and the color will show through.

6. Hold down the Alt(Opt) key and click the Create new layer icon near the bottom-right corner of the Layers palette. When the New Layer dialog box appears, type **Stars** for the name and change the mode to Screen. Click OK.

7. Press D for the default colors of black and white. With black as the foreground color, press Alt(Opt)+Delete to fill the Star layer with black.

   The layer fills with black on the Layers palette but not in the image.

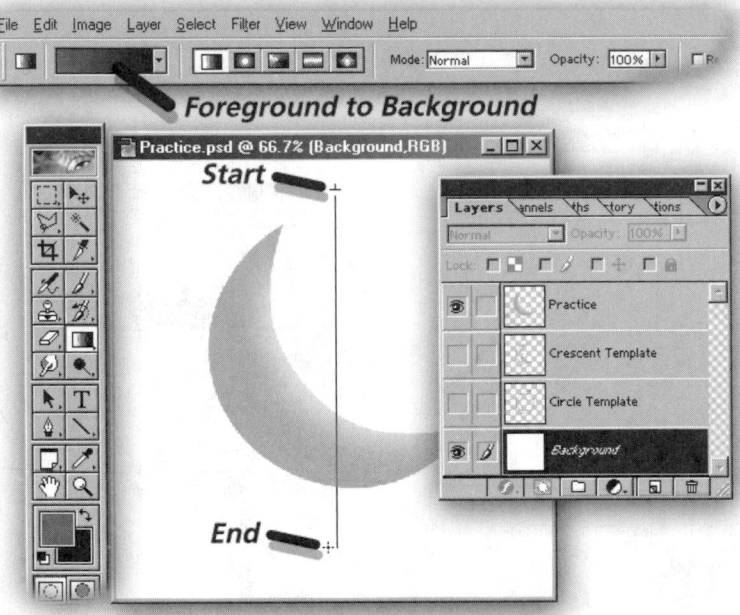

**Figure 11.10**   Hold down the Shift key while dragging a vertical gradient starting near the top and ending near the bottom of the image.

8. Press Shift+M until the Elliptical Marquee tool is the active tool. Drag anywhere in the image to create a circular selection the size of a star. (Optional: Hold down the Shift key if you want to constrain the selection to a *perfect* circle.)

9. Choose Filter, Artistic, Plastic Wrap. A star effect should be visible in the preview window of the Plastic Wrap dialog box, as shown in Figure 11.11. Adjust the sliders to your liking and click OK. Press Ctrl(⌘)+D to deselect.

10. To repeat the process and create more stars, make another circular selection in the image and press Ctrl(⌘)+F to apply and repeat the last filter settings used. Press Ctrl(⌘)+D to deselect. Repeat this process until you are satisfied with the number of stars in the image.

    Don't forget to make some very small circle selections. A variety of sizes is a nice effect. Also avoid cluttering the scene with too many stars. Simplicity is always a good design goal—a dozen stars of different sizes should add to the piece without making it look like *Star Wars* or something.

11. Press Ctrl(⌘)+S to save your work.

**Figure 11.11**   Choose Filter, Artistic, Plastic Wrap to create a star effect within a circular selection on the Star layer.

## Mixing Images with a Path

All this image needs now is a cow jumping over the crescent shape and you would have a nice illustration for a children's nursery rhyme book. Hey, forget astronauts. We don't have a jumping cow available, but we *do* have a sitting cow ready to be placed on the moon. Actually it's a standing cow you worked with in Chapter 9, but with a few adjustments, we can make this cowgirl appear to be sitting.

### Example 11.6   Placing an Image on a Path

1. On the Layers palette, click on the Practice layer to make this the active layer. Press Ctrl(⌘)+O to open a document. Open cowgirl.psd, found in the Examples/Chap11 folder on the Companion CD or use the Cowgirl.psd image you created in Chapter 9.

2. Position the Practice.psd and Cowgirl.psd documents onscreen so that both documents can be seen. Click on the title bar of cowgirl.psd to make it the active document. Press V to switch to the Move tool and drag the cowgirl into the Practice.psd image window as seen in Figure 11.12.

**Figure 11.12**   Position the documents so they can both be viewed. With the Move tool, drag the cowgirl into the Practice.psd document.

3. Close the cowgirl.psd file without saving changes. On the Layers palette, hold down the Alt(Opt) key and double-click on the Layer 1 title. In the Layer Properties dialog box, type **Cowgirl** for the name. Click OK.

4. With the Move tool still active, position the Cowgirl in the document window so that she is at a good spot for sitting on the right side of the moon. In other words, if her legs bent toward our view, she'd appear to be perched on the bottom scoop of the moon. There might be a fringe area surrounding the Cowgirl that needs eliminating.

5. Choose Layers, Matting, Defringe. In the Defringe dialog box, enter **2** for the pixel width and click OK.

   We will apply the Shear filter to bend the cowgirl's legs into a sitting position. An area should first be defined before applying the filter because we want to limit the area of change to the legs.

6. Choose the Rectangular Marquee tool and drag a rectangle marquee selection around the leg and shoe area of the cowgirl making sure to include some area outside her body on both sides, as shown in Figure 11.13.

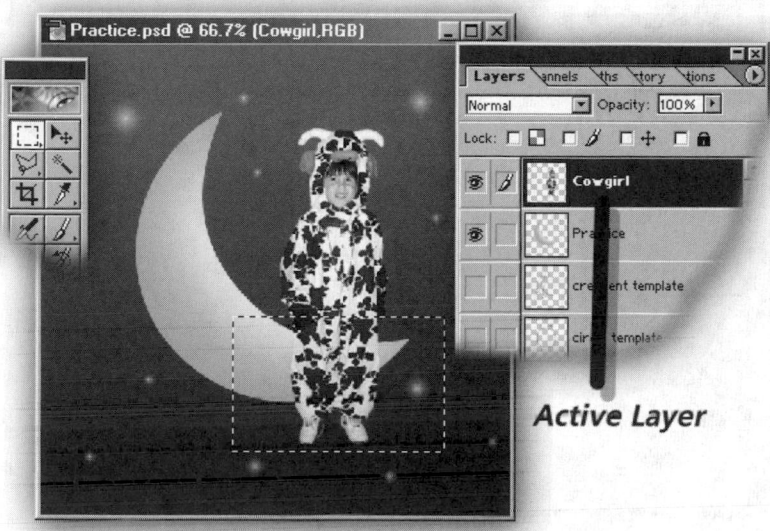

**Active Layer**

**Figure 11.13**   Drag a rectangle marquee around the leg area of the cowgirl. Leave room on the sides to apply the distortion.

7. Choose Filter, Distort, Shear. In the Shear dialog box, choose Wrap Around. In the upper-left corner of the dialog box is a grid. Click to make a point on the first line under the top edge and drag the point over slightly to the right. Drag the bottom point over to the right slightly until the curve looks something like Figure 11.14. Click OK.

   The Shear filter blurs the pixels, so you need to apply an Unsharp Mask to compensate for this.

8. Choose Filter, Sharpen, Unsharp Mask. In the dialog box type **60%** for Amount, **1.7** (pixels) for Radius, and **5** for Threshold levels. Click OK. Press Ctrl(⌘)+D to deselect the legs.

9. Press Ctrl(⌘)+F to apply the previous filter settings (Unsharp Mask filter) once more to the entire cowgirl layer to add sharper definition to the face and remaining areas.

**Note**

**The Professional's Choice**   You will frequently see a reference to using the Unsharp Mask filter to add visual snap to a picture. Although there are several other Sharpen filters, the Unsharp Mask is the choice of professionals due to its subtlety and many controls for optimizing the filter. It's the choice of professionals, and that is why we don't drag out this book enumerating filters that don't quite make the grade.

Of course, the only thing missing now are some...you guessed it—*drop shadows!*

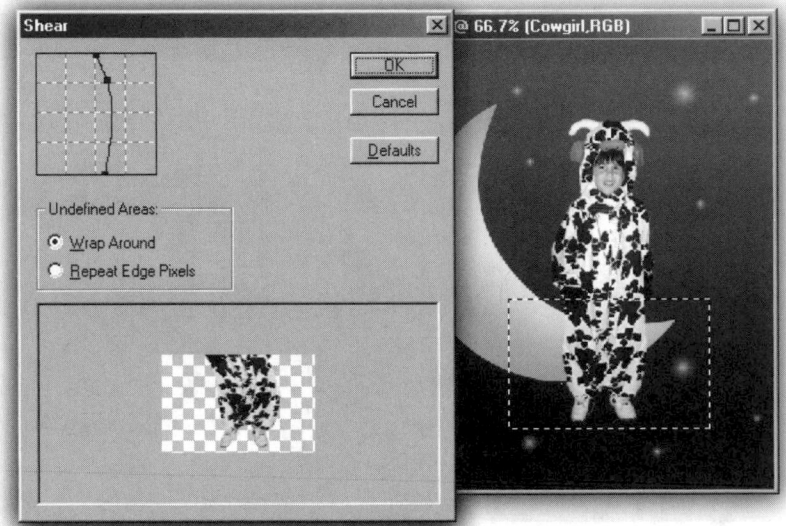

**Figure 11.14**   In the Shear dialog box, drag the bottom point slightly to the right. Click to create a new point on the first line down from the top and drag to move this point over slightly to the right, as shown.

10.  Choose Layer, Layer Style, Drop Shadow. In the Drop Shadow dialog box, type **65** for Opacity, **131** for Angle, **10** for Distance, **0** for Spread, and **8** for Size. Click OK.

11.  On the Layers palette, right+click (Macintosh: hold Ctrl and click) on the *f* mark on the Cowgirl layer and choose Copy Layer Style. Right+click (Macintosh: hold Ctrl and click) on the Practice layer and choose Paste Layer Style to apply the shadow to the crescent-moon shape as shown in Figure 11.15.

There should probably be a slight shadow appearing on the moon under the left side of the cowgirl's legs. Here's how to quickly apply such a shadow.

12.  Right+click (Macintosh: hold Ctrl and click) on the *f* mark of the Cowgirl layer and choose Create Layer. Click OK in the warning dialog box that pops up.

13.  Right+click (Macintosh: hold Ctrl and click) again on the Cowgirl layer and choose Paste Layer Style.

There is now a duplicate shadow of the cowgirl. One is a Layer Style effect, and one as a separate shadow layer. We will group the separate shadow layer with the moon (Practice) layer to have this shadow only appear where the moon appears.

14.  On the Layers palette, click the Cowgirl's Drop Shadow layer to make this the active layer. Press Ctrl(⌘)+G to group this layer with the Practice layer below it.

**15.** Press V to switch to the Move tool and move this shadow so that a slight amount appears behind the left leg and moon, as shown in Figure 11.16. Press Ctrl(⌘)+S to save your work.

**Figure 11.15**   Right+click (Macintosh: hold Ctrl and click) on the layers to Copy Layer Styles and Paste Layer Styles.

**Figure 11.16**   Move the Cowgirl's Drop Shadow slightly to the left of the legs. The Layers palette indicates the Cowgirl's Drop Shadow layer is grouped with the layer below it by indenting the image icon and displaying an arrow pointing to the layer below.

## Using Paths in Other Programs

Hopefully the Practice.psd lessons in this chapter have helped you to understand the Pen tool. If you have never used programs such as Illustrator but would like to start, all this Photoshop Pen tool stuff applies to Illustrator as well as many other vector-based drawing programs.

Another important thought to keep in mind is that paths created in Photoshop can be copied and pasted into Illustrator and similarly, paths created in Illustrator can be pasted into Photoshop. When you select and copy a path in Illustrator and open a document in Photoshop to paste this path, a dialog box will appear and Photoshop will ask if you want to paste as pixels or paste as a path. The "paste as pixels" option will immediately create a bitmap version of the path resulting in a pixel representation of the path, at the size at which is exists in Illustrator. The "paste as path" option will not only paste the path information into the document, but will also have the path located on a Work Path title in the Paths palette. Renaming the path title enables you to permanently store the path information for future use.

## Tracing with the Pen Tool

The next example, an image of flowers, will give you more practice with the Pen tool. I sketched out a quick idea for the flowers on paper. I find it helpful to sketch the idea first. Scan the sketch, and then use the scanned sketch as a template to draw the paths. Once the hard work of drawing paths for the sketch is completed, the painting fun begins. You will see firsthand how to take a rough sketch and transform it from its raw form to something that is polished upon completion.

A project like this requires a lot of repetitive and redundant steps. In the interest of saving time and my wrists from carpal tunnel syndrome while documenting the steps, I went through the trouble of creating most of the path work with the exception of a leaf near the bottom-left of the sketch. We will finish the paths associated with this leaf in the steps. Afterward, gradient fills and the Airbrush tool will be used to paint the remaining image (some of the work has already been done for you, too). This part of the example demonstrates how to use path information to provide selections for painting an image.

As you draw the paths for Example 11.7, you will find it easier to draw if you keep one hand on the mouse and the other near the Ctrl(⌘) and Alt(Opt) keys to access the modifier keys. This enables you to quickly toggle to the Direct Selection or Convert Point tools respectively, as the need for these tools arise.

It is helpful to toggle to the Convert Point tool while creating a smooth point to move one of the control handles slightly. This instantly changes the attributes of the smooth anchor point to a sharp point, which allows the handles to be adjusting independently (giving greater control of the path curves). This technique will be used consistently in Example 11.7.

### Example 11.7   Completing the Path Work

1. Press Ctrl(⌘)+O to Open a document. Look in the Examples/Chap11 folder on the Companion CD and open the FlowerSketch.psd image.

2. Press Ctrl(⌘)+spacebar to toggle to the Zoom tool and drag a marquee selection around the leaf near the bottom-left corner to magnify the area for better viewing. If you need to zoom in closer, press Ctrl(⌘)+ the plus key to increase the magnification. Press the spacebar to toggle to the Hand tool and scroll until the bottom leaf area of the document is in view.

**Tip**

**Set Up Keyboard Zoom to Automatically Resize Windows**   Ctrl(⌘)++ and Ctrl(⌘)+− increases or decreases the zoom level of your image. When adding Alt(Opt) to these keyboard shortcuts (for example, Ctrl+Alt+ + [⌘+Option+ +]) the image window will resize to accommodate the new zoom level.

You can make it the default response to have the window resize by toggling a preference for it in the Preference dialog box. Press Ctrl(⌘)+K to open the General Preference dialog box and click on the Keyboard Zoom Resizes Windows checkbox. Click OK to exit the dialog box. Now Ctrl(⌘)++ will resize the window *and* increase zoom simultaneously. Adding the Alt(Opt) key now has the reverse function of increasing or decreasing the zoom level *without* resizing the window.

3. Choose the Pen tool from the toolbox. On the lower-left corner area of the leaf, click and drag a short distance to create the control handles for the first point. Before releasing the mouse button, press the Alt(Opt) key and drag the top handle slightly to convert it to an independent handle as shown in Figure 11.17.

4. Working in a clockwise direction, click and drag a second point a short distance from the first. Press Alt(Opt) to toggle to the Convert Point tool and adjust the upper handle slightly toward the direction of the curve.

5. Click and drag a third point on the leaf halfway up the left side. Again, press the Alt(Opt) before completing the drag and move the control handle slightly to conform to the curve, as shown in Figure 11.18.

   Don't worry if the curves of the path do not match the leaf sketch precisely. You will adjust the direction lines and fine-tune the path after completing it.

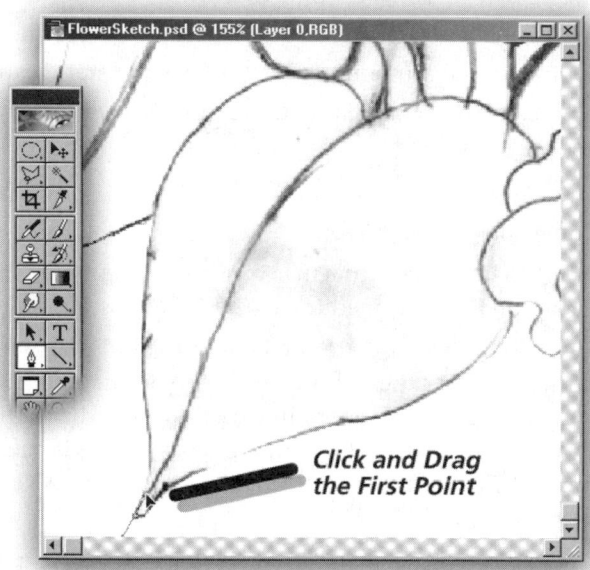

**Figure 11.17**   Click and drag to create the first point near the bottom corner of leaf. Press the Alt(Opt) key and move the top handle toward the direction of the next curve.

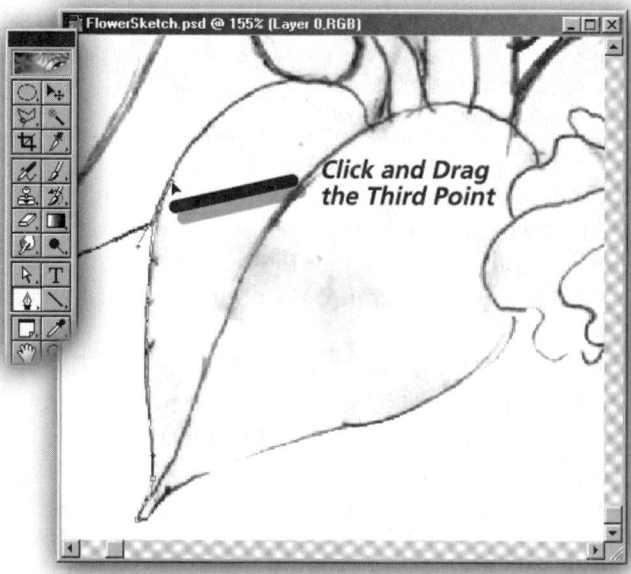

**Figure 11.18**   Click and drag to create the third point around the halfway point of the left side on the leaf. Press the Alt(Opt) key and move the top direction point toward the direction of the curve.

6.  Click and drag a fourth point near the top edge of the leaf, hold down the Alt(Opt) key before completing the drag to move the direction point at the end of the direction line in the direction of the sketch.

7.  Press the spacebar to toggle to the Hand tool and adjust the view of the image if needed. Click and drag a fifth point downward at the V-shaped area of the leaf. Before completing the drag, hold down the Alt(Opt) key and drag the direction point upward to prepare the curve for the other side of the V-shape (as shown in Figure 11.19).

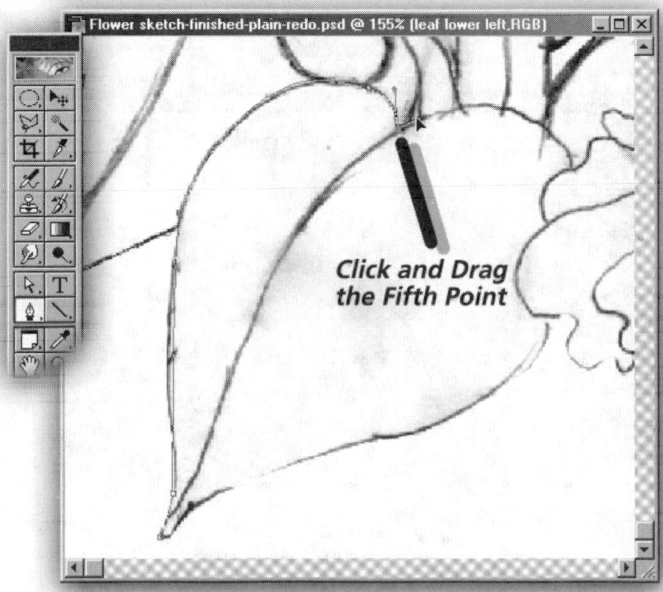

**Figure 11.19**    Click and drag to create the fifth point at the top of the V-shaped area of the leaf. Press the Alt(Opt) key and move the bottom direction point in a V-shaped direction to prepare for the direction of the next curve.

8.  Continue to click and drag points around the lower-right side of the leaf, each time using the Alt(Opt) key before completing the drag to move the direction point (and line) slightly in the direction of the sketch. Press the spacebar as needed to move the view of the document. When you reach the starting point, place the cursor over the first point created, and when a circle appears next to the pen cursor, click to close the path (see Figure 11.20 for point placements).

9.  Press Shift+A until the Direct Selection tool is the active tool (the hollow arrow). Again, work in a clockwise direction. Click on a point to view the direction lines for that point. Drag the direction point on the direction line

to adjust the direction line (and path) to match the curves of the sketch. If needed, drag and reposition the points. Continue to adjust the direction lines until the curves for the path match closely to the curves intended for the leaf.

Because the scanned sketch is a *rough* sketch, do not worry about exactness in your path creation efforts. Just aim for a close representation of the leaf with nice curve transitions for the path. The path can also overlap the flower to the right because you will color each path on a separate layer. Keep in mind that layers will be used later in order to hide areas you want to hide. Profound Truth #1,342,701: Don't bother with artistic details the audience will never see.

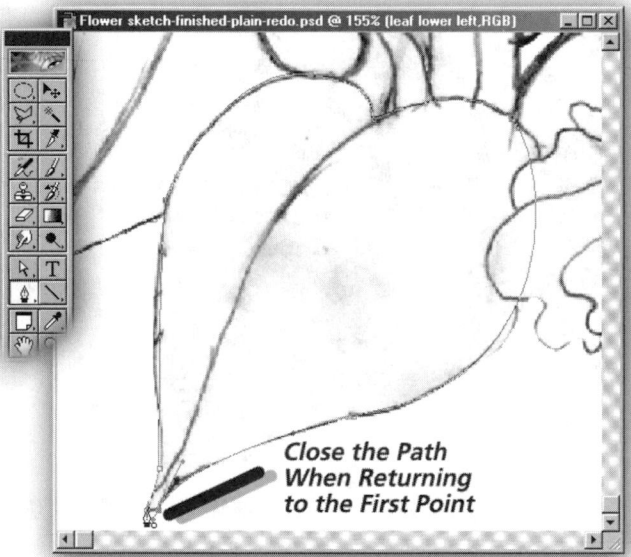

**Figure 11.20**    Continue to click and drag around the right side of the leaf. Press the Alt(Opt) key and move the direction points and lines in the direction of the curves. When a circle appears next to the cursor at the first point, click to close the path.

**10.** Click with the Direct Selection tool somewhere in the document—away from the path—to deselect the current path.

You'll need to start a new path to represent the center curve that runs down the middle of the leaf. We will show you later how the path will be useful for a nice coloring effect of the leaf. Only the curvature of the centerline is important for our next path; the remaining path can be anywhere outside of the leaf to close the path. Don't worry about the placement of points outside of the leaf. We will show you how to make ingenious use of this path later.

**11.** Press P to switch to the Pen tool. On the Options bar, click the Add to selection icon if it is not already chosen. Click and drag the first point outside the lower-left corner of the leaf's center. Hold down the Alt(Opt) key before completing the drag to alter the direction line slightly (see Figure 11.21).

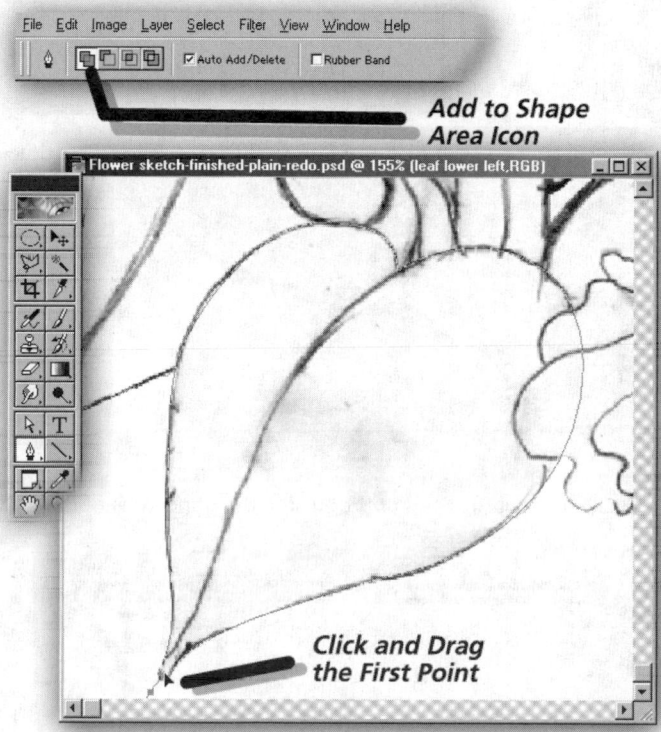

**Figure 11.21**   Click and drag the first point of the new path outside the lower corner of the old path. Press the Alt(Opt) key and drag the upper direction point (on the direction line) in the direction of the leaf's centerline curve.

**12.** Click and drag your second point near the middle of the leaf's centerline curve. Hold down the Alt(Opt) key before completing the drag to move the direction line slightly.

**13.** Click and drag your third point outside the leaf area near the top V-shape of the leaf. Again, hold the Alt(Opt) key to move the direction line slightly (see Figure 11.22).

**14.** Click points (without dragging) along the outside of the lower leaf area until you reach the first point created. Click on the first point to close the path as shown in Figure 11.23.

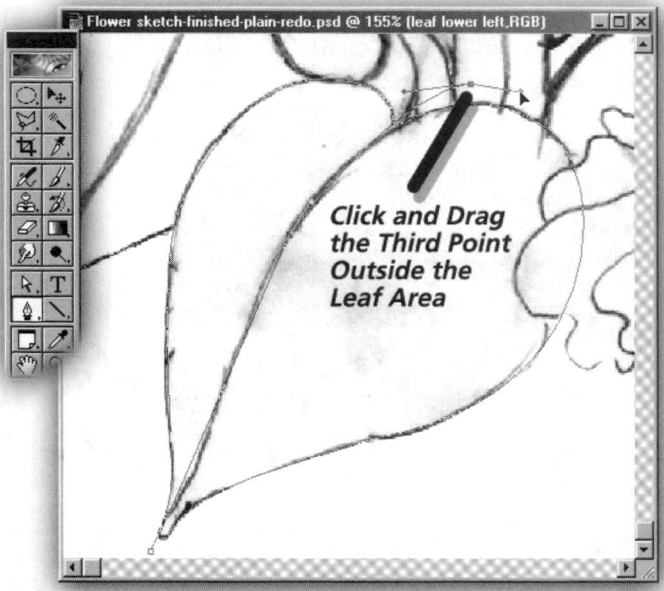

**Figure 11.22**    Click and drag the third point outside the upper area of the leaf.

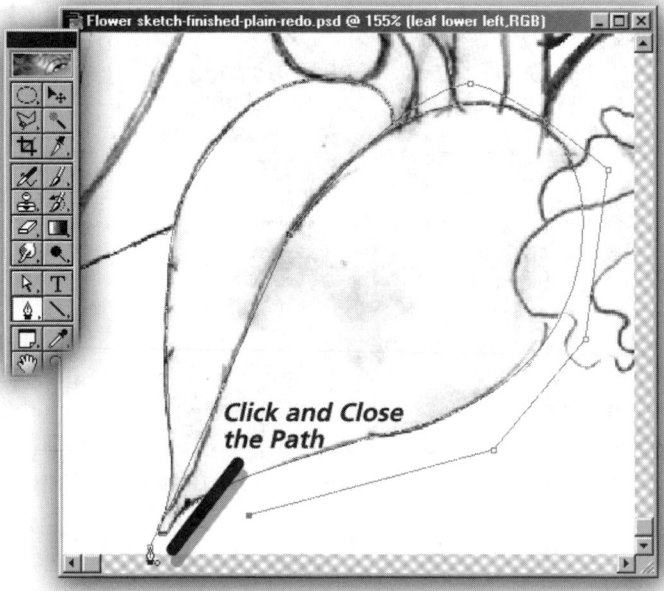

**Figure 11.23**    Click points along the right outside leaf area. Click to close the path when back at the first point created (a circle appears next to the cursor to indicate this).

**15.** Hold down the Ctrl(⌘) key while you adjust the points and associated lines along the centerline to match the curvature of the sketched line. The path should look similar to the one shown in Figure 11.24.

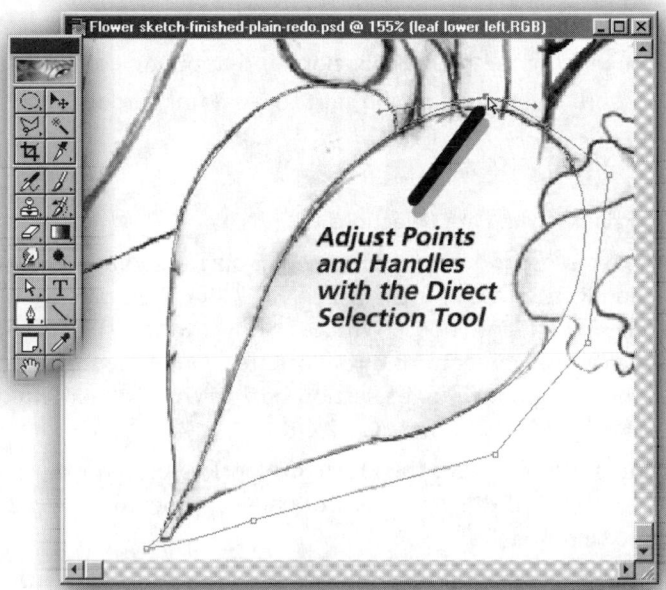

**Figure 11.24**   While holding down the Ctrl(⌘) key to toggle to the Direct Selection tool, adjust the direction lines by moving their direction points and make the curve inside the leaf match the centerline curve of the sketch.

## Reinforcing Your Understanding of Path Selection Techniques

Creating paths for a large project can be a tedious task. With patience, however, the task can be accomplished easily, and the results will be well worth the effort because paths provide a smoother and more precise selection than pixel strokes.

Keep in mind how you plan to use a path (for future projects). As demonstrated with the leaf path that you created, you will use the curvature information of the centerline paths, but the remaining part of that path is of no importance. Similarly, if you observe the paths that make up the flowers, the curves that are a part of the flower edges are necessary information. The remaining parts of the path—the part of the flower petals that is behind other petals—will not be visible. This might become clearer when you start turning on the layers to the parts of the image that have been painted already. Many of these parts will look incomplete, but after finishing and adding the parts in the example, the incomplete areas will not show through.

Again, some of the layers have been created for you. There is no dazzling filter work involved in the upcoming steps. The main ingredients involve the repetition of choosing a path, making the path a selection, and applying color to the selection. Gradually, your work will pay off as you start to see a final product. Let's get started on polishing off this piece.

### Example 11.8    Painting with Path Selections

1.  Click on the foreground color selection box on the toolbox and choose a yellow color; R:225, G:225, B:112. Click OK. Click the Swatches tab to view the Swatches palette (or choose Window, Show Swatches). Alt(Opt)+click on an empty area near the bottom of the palette to save the foreground color. Click on the background color selection box on the toolbox and choose an orange color; R:255, G:76, B:41. Click OK.

    It will be important to have the Brush Size option chosen from the Preference settings. If this option is not chosen, proceed to step 2, otherwise move on to step 3.

2.  Press Ctrl(⌘)+K to bring up the Preferences dialog box. Press Ctrl(⌘)+3 to access Display & Cursors. Under Painting Cursors, choose Brush Size. Click OK.

3.  On the Layers palette, click the eye icon square to the left of the Purple Flower Layer Set. Click the arrow to the left of the folder icon on the layer title to open up the set, as shown in Figure 11.25.

    Sets are created by choosing New Layer Set from the flyout menu on the Layers palette, and then layers can be dragged into the folder (representing the new set) for easy organization of compositions. Remember what a pain it was in Photoshop to scroll the Layers palette from here to Minneapolis with 25 layers on the palette?

4.  Click the Petal 5 layer to make this the active layer. Press the Alt(Opt) key and click the Create new layer icon near the bottom-right corner of the Layers palette. In the Layers Properties dialog box, type **Stem 1** for the Name. Click OK.

5.  Click the Paths tab to view the Paths palette. Click the Flower2 title. Hold down the Ctrl(⌘) key and click the stem path at the center of the purple flower. Click the Loads path as a selection icon near the bottom of the palette, as shown in Figure 11.26. Click on an empty space below the path titles to deselect the remaining paths.

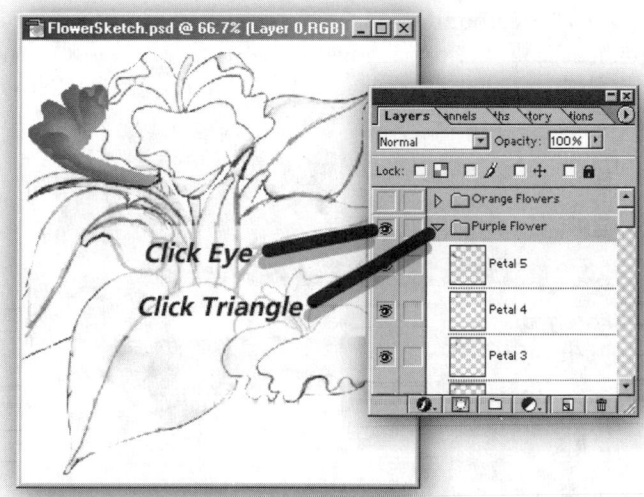

**Figure 11.25** Click the eye icon to turn on the Purple Flower Layer Set. Click the triangle next to the folder to open the set and view the layers.

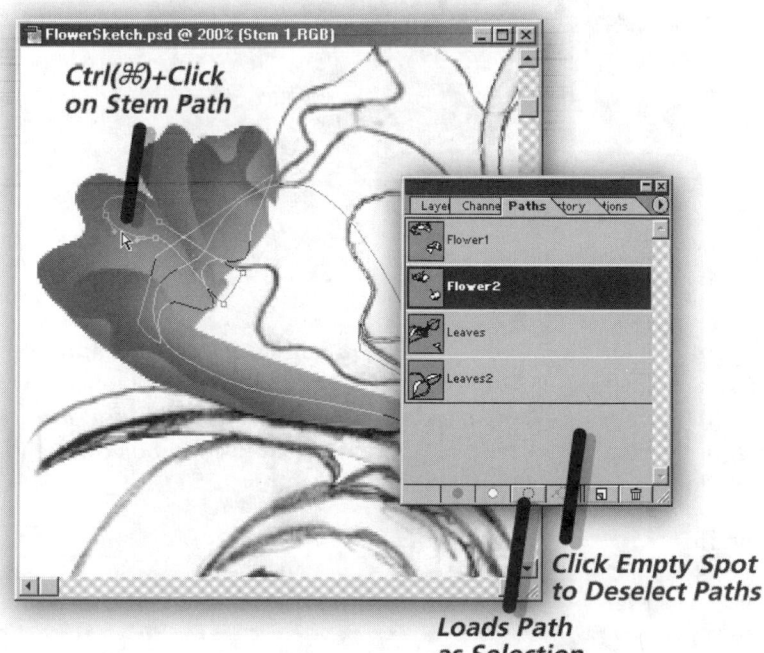

**Figure 11.26** Hold down the Ctrl(⌘) key and select the flower stem path. Click the Loads path as a selection icon to make the path a selection. Click on an empty space on the palette to deselect the paths.

**6.** Click the Gradient tool. On the Options bar, click the Linear gradient icon and choose the Foreground to Background gradient on the drop-down list. Drag a gradient from the upper edge of the selection to just outside the lower edge of the selection (see Figure 11.27). Press Ctrl(⌘)+D to deselect.

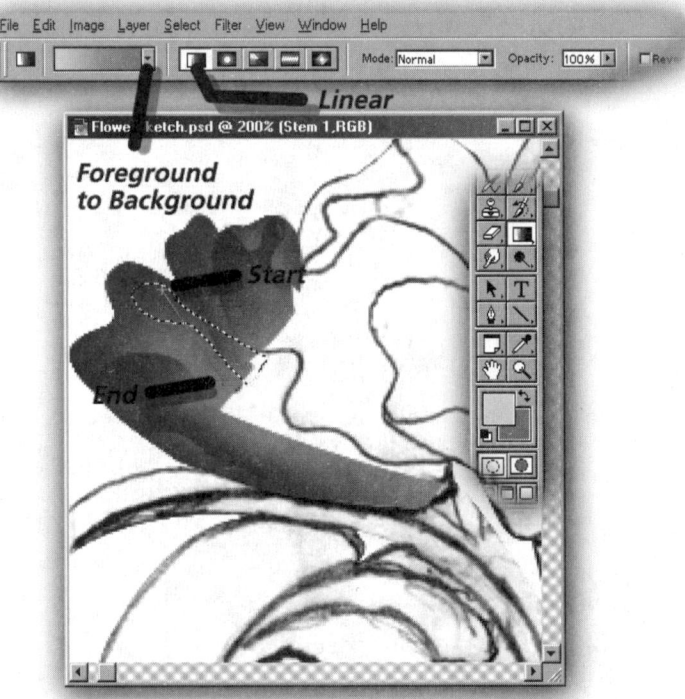

**Figure 11.27**   Drag a diagonal gradient from the upper edge of the selection to just outside the lower edge.

**7.** Click on the foreground color selection box on the toolbox and select a lilac color; R:146, G:153, B:220. Click OK. Click the Swatches tab to view the Swatches palette. Alt(Opt)+click an empty area at the bottom of the palette to save the color. Click the background color selection box on the toolbox and choose a purple color; R:152, G:46, B:144. Click OK.

### Warning

**Saving a Swatch Collection**   Colors you add to the Swatches palette are not permanent additions. Yes, new colors or deleted colors will remain this way from session to session. *But...*all you have to do is load a new palette, such as the Web-legal palette and then switch back to the default palette, and the colors you saved are gone. You must save the swatches (click on the palette flyout menu and choose Save Swatches, and give the swatches collection a unique name) in order to preserve a swatches collection to which you've made custom additions or subtractions.

**8.** Click the Layers tab to view the Layers palette. Press the Alt(Opt) key and click the Create new layer icon near the bottom-right corner of the Layers palette. In the Layers Properties dialog box, type **Petal 6** for the name. Click OK to return to your work.

**9.** Click the Paths tab and click the Flower2 path title to make it visible in the image window. Hold down the Ctrl(⌘) key and click the large flower petal toward the front of the flower (see Figure 11.28) in the image window. Doing this toggles the current tool to the Direct Selection tool and anchor points are revealed. Click the Loads path as a selection icon near the bottom of the Paths palette. Click on an empty space below the paths titles to deselect the remaining paths.

**Figure 11.28**  Ctrl(⌘)+click the large front petal path from the Flower2 path title.

**10.** Drag a gradient from the middle-right side of the selection to the upper-middle left side of the selection, as shown in Figure 11.29.

**11.** Press J to switch to the Airbrush tool. On the Options bar, set the Pressure to 20%. Choose a large, soft brush (65-pixel). Press X to switch the dark purple color to the foreground. Alt(Opt)+click on an empty space on the Swatches palette to save this color. Keep a small portion of the brush in the selection area, stroke additional dark purple tones along the top and left edge of the petal selection.

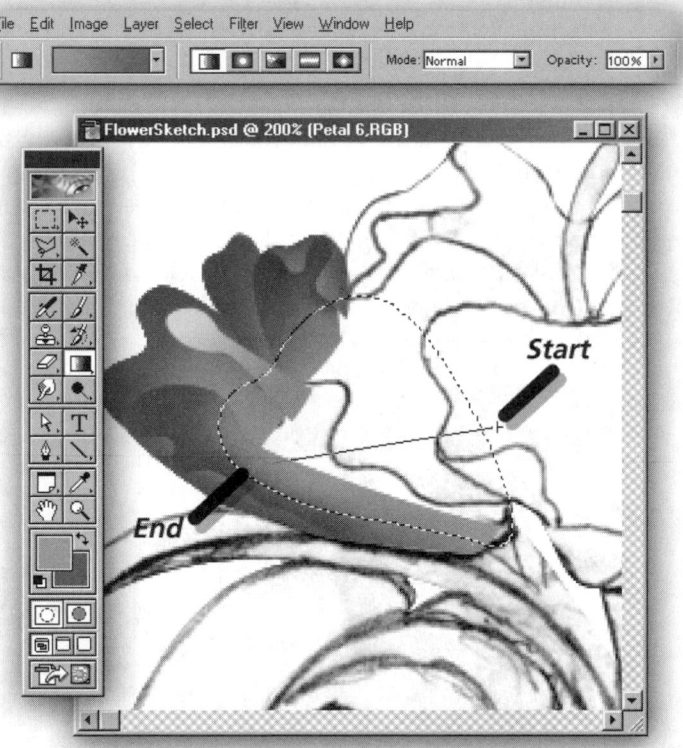

**Figure 11.29**   Drag the gradient up just a bit and to the left of the selection.

Use your own artistic judgment whenever asked to stroke color in these steps. Stroke more than once if it seems to be needed. The low pressure setting on the Airbrush tool allows for color to be added in a subtle fashion, layer upon layer, in a manner of speaking.

12. Press X to switch colors again. Click on the foreground color selection box on the toolbox and choose a darker purple color; R:105, G:26, B:99. Click OK. Alt(Opt)+click on an empty space on the Swatches palette to save this color. Stroke along the same top and left edge of the selection with only a fraction of the brush portion inside the selection area (to add additional form and color). When satisfied with the results, press Ctrl(⌘)+D to deselect.

13. Click the Flower2 path title on the Paths palette. Hold down the Ctrl(⌘) key to toggle to the Direct selection tool, and select the curl edge path at the top of the front petal, as shown in Figure 11.30. Click the Loads path as a selection icon on the palette and click on an empty space below the titles to deselect the paths.

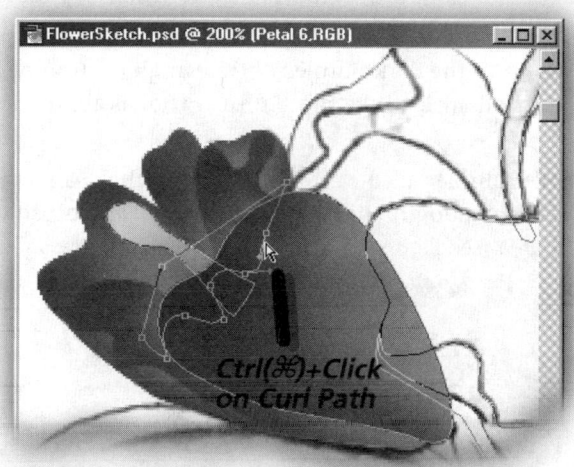

**Figure 11.30**  Ctrl(⌘)+ click the curl path to select this path from the Flower2 path title.

14. Return to the Layers palette and Alt(Opt)+click the Create new layer icon at the bottom of the palette. In the Layer Properties dialog box, type **Petal 7** for the Name. Click OK.

15. Press the Ctrl+Alt+Shift (⌘+Option+Shift) keys and click the Petal 6 layer on the Layers palette to remove the selection outside the petal area of Layer 6 (the intersection of the two selections, as shown in Figure 11.31).

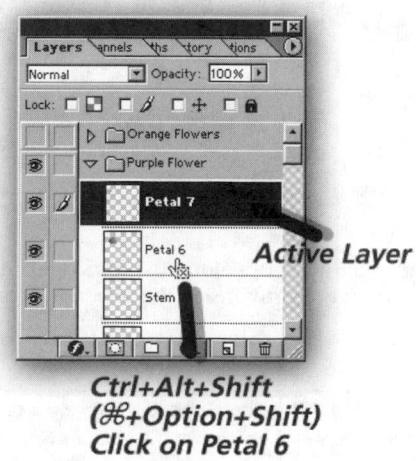

**Figure 11.31**  Press Ctrl+Alt+Shift (⌘+Option+Shift) and click the Petal 6 layer to intersect both selections. An x appears next to the cursor to indicate saving only the *intersection* of selections.

**16.** Click the lilac color from the Swatches palette (the color that was saved earlier). Press Alt(Opt)+Delete to fill the marquee selection.

**17.** Press X to switch to the dark purple. With a small portion of the brush inside the selection area, stroke the Airbrush tool along the top edges of the selection.

**18.** Click the darker purple saved earlier on the Swatches palette (R:105, G:26, B:99). Stroke again along the top edge with less of the brush cursor inside the selection area (see Figure 11.32). Press Ctrl(⌘)+D. Press Ctrl(⌘)+S to save your work.

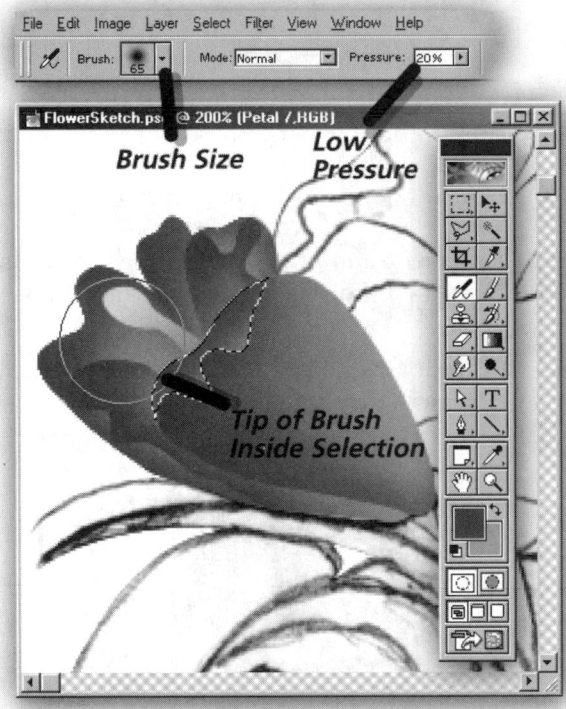

**Figure 11.32**    Stroke darker purple colors along the top edge of the selection, keeping the Brush cursor edge slightly inside the selection area.

 **Note**

**Direct vs. Path Component**    It is the author's preference to use the Direct Selection tool to select a path, and then convert it into a marquee selection. The Path Component Selection tool can also be used to select an "inert" path in an image and reveal its anchor points. However, in general, the Direct Selection tool is more versatile (you can move anchor points when the need arises, and the Path Component Selection tool doesn't do that). So the art lesson that follows uses the Direct Selection tool…and I guess if yours is broken, you could use the Path Component Selection tool <g>.

## Selecting Paths That Exclude Transparent Areas

In the next of the assignment groups, you will paint in the remaining leaves. There will be a variety of green tones suggested and it might help to save them on the Swatches palette for easy access because a number of the same colors will be used repeatedly.

Because a lot of the painting techniques are similar to the previous flower techniques, there will be some assumptions made in the steps to follow. When switching to the Gradient tool, the Options bar will continue to have the settings for the gradient at Foreground to Background and the Linear Gradient icon chosen. For the Airbrush tool, the pressure on the Options bar will be 20%.

### Example 11.9   Mixing Path Selections and Layer Information

1. Click the arrow next to the Purple Flower Layer set on the Layers palette to close this folder. Click the eye icon to the left of the Leaves folder to turn on these layers. Click the arrow next to the Leaves folder to open this layer set.

2. Click the Back Stems layer to make it the active layer on the Layers palette. Alt(Opt)+click the Create new layer icon at the bottom of the palette. In the Layer Properties dialog box, type **Right Leaf** for the name. Click OK to return to the piece.

3. Click on the foreground color selection box and change it to a yellow-green color; R:184, G:204, B:59 in the color Picker. Click OK to return to the workspace. Click on the background color selection box and choose a dark green color; R:5, G:77, B:42. Click OK. Click the Paths tab to switch to the Paths palette. Click the Leaves2 title. Hold down the Ctrl(⌘) key and click the large leaf path on the right side to select this path (see Figure 11.33).

**Note**

**Save Your Colors**   It helps to save these colors on the Swatches palette because they will be used again. Alt(Opt) click on an empty space of the Swatches palette to save the color. If you click without pressing the Alt(Opt) key, a dialog box opens in which you can name the color.

4. Click the Loads path as a selection icon at the bottom of the Paths palette. Click on an empty space below the paths titles to deselect the remaining paths.

5. Press G to switch to the Gradient tool. Options on the bar should still be set to Linear, and Foreground to Background. Drag a gradient from the top-left side to the bottom at a slight angle toward the right as seen in Figure 11.34. Press Ctrl(⌘)+D to deselect.

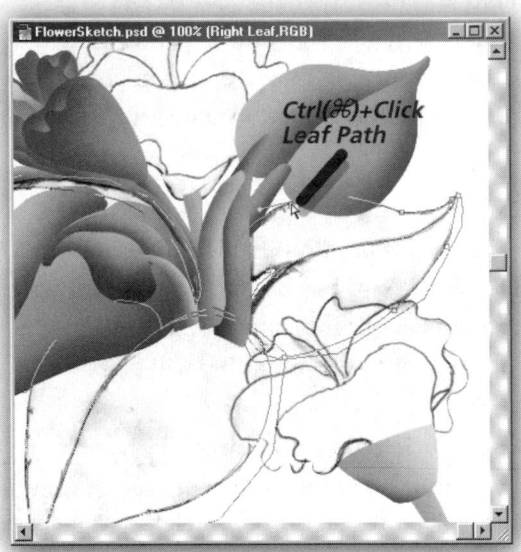

**Figure 11.33**    Hold Ctrl(⌘) and click the leaf path on the right from the Leaves2 path title to choose this leaf path.

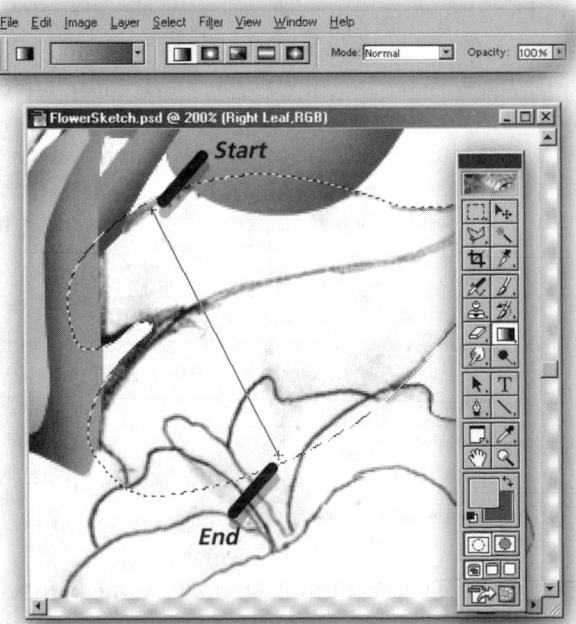

**Figure 11.34**    Drag a gradient from the top-left side to the bottom at a slight angle toward the right.

6. On the Paths palette, click the Leaves2 title. Hold down the Ctrl(⌘) key to toggle to the Direct Selection tool and click the centerline path next to the leaf path just chosen in the image window (see Figure 11.35). Click the Loads path as a selection icon near the bottom of the Paths palette. Click on an empty space below the paths titles to deselect the remaining paths.

7. Click the Layers tab to return to the Layers palette. With Right Leaf as the active layer, choose the Lock Editing Layer Transparency option near the top of the Layers palette (see Figure 11.36).

**Note**

**Masking Transparent Pixels** The Lock Transparent Pixels option on the Layers palette (as the title implies) keeps transparent areas on a layer transparent. You might think of this feature as a paint repellant or an automatic way to mask transparent pixels. This option is only available on layers that contain transparent pixels. When more than one layer in an image contains transparent pixels, each layer can have its own setting, i.e. two layers could use the Lock transparent pixels feature while others don't. In the image we're working on now, the transparent area in the image is the area around the leaf. With the option enabled for this layer, the leaf area is now the only area to which color can be applied, because that is the only part of the layer that has nontransparent pixels.

The advantage of preserving transparent areas is soon apparent because the centerline selection extends outside the leaf area. Keep in mind that it is all right to have a portion of the brush outside the leaf area when painting. With the transparent areas protected, no paint will be applied outside the leaf.

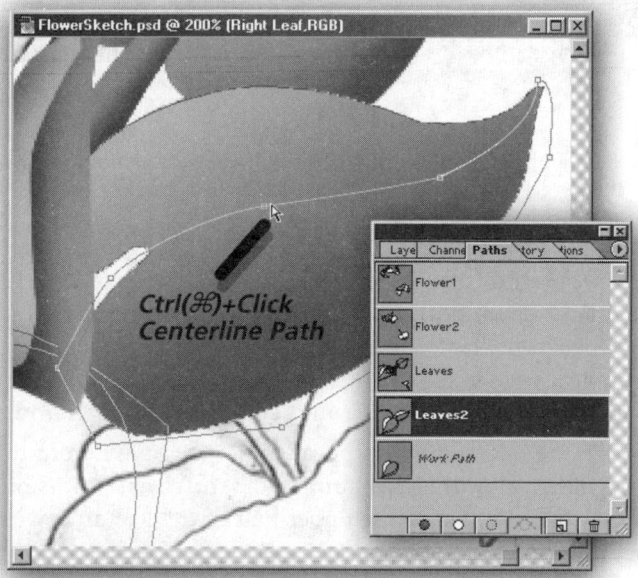

**Figure 11.35** Hold Ctrl(⌘) and click the right leaf centerline path from the Leaves2 path title to select the centerline leaf path.

**8.** Click the Airbrush tool and choose the 100-pixel brush from the Options bar. Brush an additional amount of the yellow-green foreground color along the centerline (keep most of the brush outside the selected area, as shown in Figure 11.36).

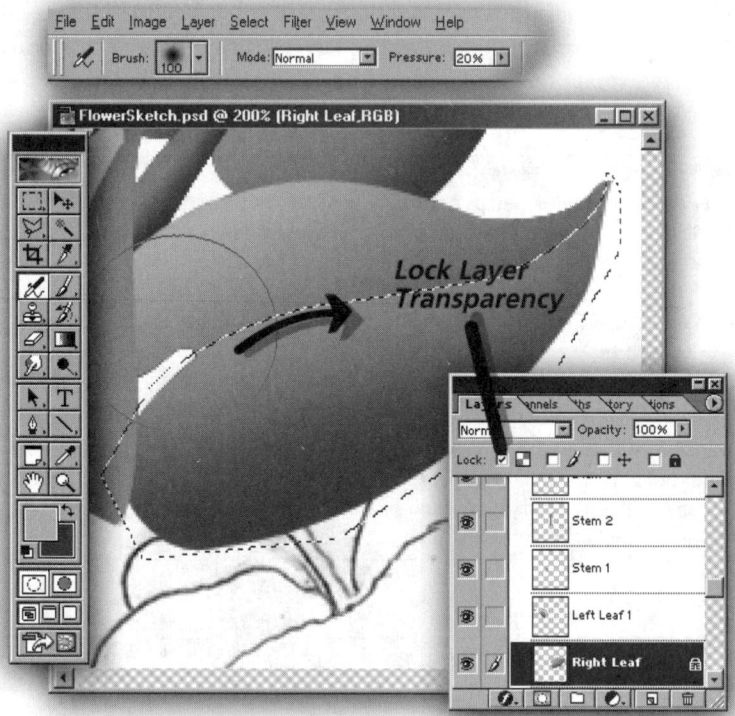

**Figure 11.36**    Paint along the centerline (with the Lock Transparency option checked on the Layers palette), keeping most of the brush cursor outside the selected area.

**9.** Click the foreground color selection box on the toolbox and choose a darker green; R:4, G:32, B:18. With a small amount of the brush cursor touching the lower edge of the leaf, stroke a small amount of the darker green along the bottom leaf edge. Press Ctrl(⌘)+Shift+I to make the inverse of the selection. Press X to switch the background color to the foreground.

Even though the selection may appear to be the same if your document is at a high-magnified view, the selection is now the inverse of its original shape. Color is now being added to the upper-half of the leaf area, with dark greens near the centerline.

**10.** Brush a small amount of dark green along the centerline on the upper-half of the leaf (keeping a large portion of the brush on the bottom-half of the leaf, as shown in Figure 11.37).

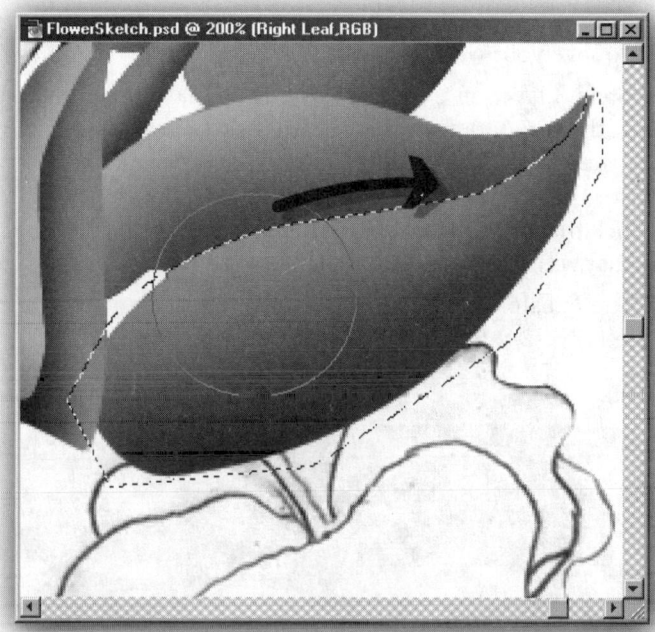

**Figure 11.37** Paint along the centerline while keeping most of the brush cursor outside the selected area (on the lower-half of the leaf).

11. Press X to switch colors again and repeat a small stroke of the darker green along the same centerline. Press Ctrl(⌘)+D to deselect when you are pleased with the results. Uncheck the Preserve Transparency option on the Layers palette.

12. Click the Paths tab to switch to the Paths palette. Click the Leaves2 title. Hold down the Ctrl(⌘) key to toggle to the Direct Selection tool, and click the stem path on the upper-left side. Click the Loads path as a selection icon near the bottom of the Paths palette. Click on an empty space below the paths titles to deselect the remaining paths.

13. Click the yellow-green color if it was saved on the Swatches palette (or click the foreground color selection box and return it to the yellow-green color; R:184, G:204, B:59). Click OK. Press Alt(Opt)+Delete to fill the marquee selection with the foreground color.

14. Press X to switch the background to the foreground. Click the Airbrush tool (and the 35-pixel size brush). Press Ctrl(⌘)++ to get a closer view of the area. With only a small portion of the brush inside the selection area, stroke the darker green along the bottom edge of the stem.

**15.** Click the foreground color selection box and switch to the deeper green; R:4, G:32, B:18, and stroke again along the bottom edge. Press Ctrl(⌘)+D. Press Ctrl(⌘)+S to save your work.

**16.** Click the Stem 3 layer on the Layers palette to make this the active layer. Hold down the Alt(Opt) key and click the Create new layer icon near the bottom of the Layers palette. In the Layer Properties dialog box type **Lower Left Leaf** for the Name. Click OK. Click the Paths tab to switch to the Paths palette. Click the Work Path title. Hold down the Ctrl(⌘) key and click the leaf path that was created in an earlier step (see Figure 11.38).

If you did not create the path in the earlier step, these paths are provided for you on the Leaves2 title (the leaf path to the lower-left side).

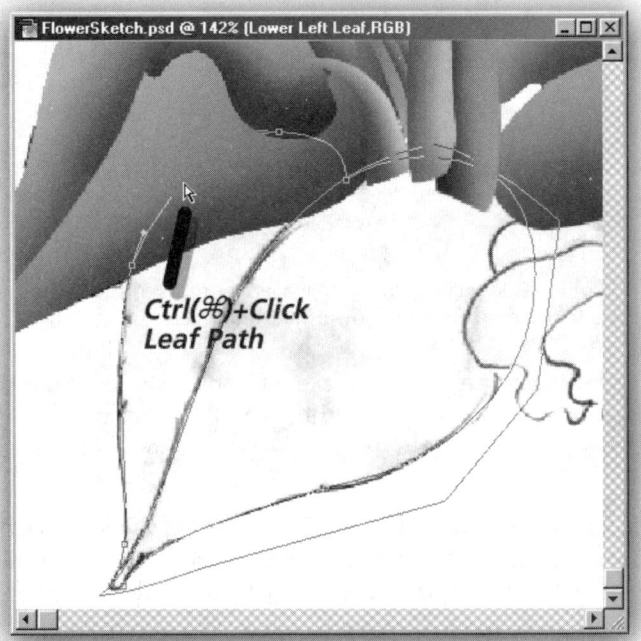

**Figure 11.38**    Hold down Ctrl(⌘) and click the leaf path to choose this path from the Work Path title.

**17.** Click the Loads path as a selection icon near the bottom of the Paths palette. Click on an empty space below the paths titles to deselect the remaining paths. Click the foreground color selection box and choose the yellow color; R:222, G:227, B:49. Click OK. Click the background color selection box and choose the dark blue-green color; R:26, G:94, B:86.

**18.** Press G to switch to Gradient tool (Linear and Background to Foreground options on the Options bar). Drag a gradient from the top-left corner to the lower-right side of the leaf as in Figure 11.39. Press Ctrl(⌘)+D to deselect the selection.

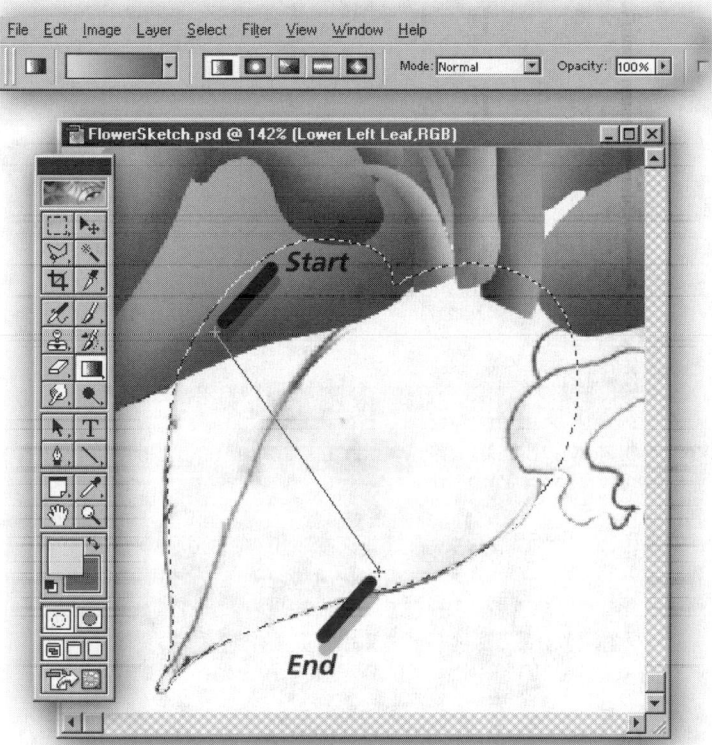

**Figure 11.39**  Drag a linear gradient from the top-left corner to the lower-right side of the leaf selection.

**19.** Click the Work Path title on the Paths palette. Hold down the Ctrl(⌘) key to toggle to the Direct selection tool and click the centerline path for the leaf in the image window, as shown in Figure 11.40. Click the Loads path as a selection icon near the bottom-right corner of the Paths palette. Click on an empty space below the paths titles to deselect the remaining paths.

**20.** Click the Layers tab to return to the Layers palette. Choose the Lock transparency layer option near the top of the Layers palette. Click the Airbrush tool and choose the 200-pixel size brush. Drag along the centerline area with the yellow foreground color as needed (see Figure 11.41).

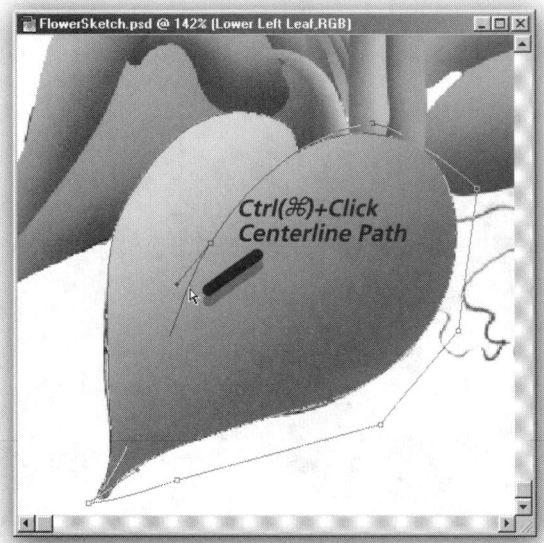

**Figure 11.40**   Hold down the Ctrl(⌘) key and click the centerline path to select this path from the Work Path title.

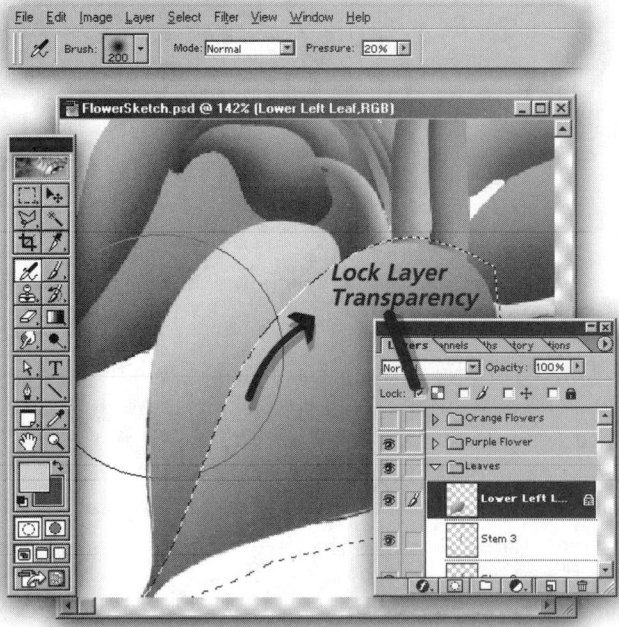

**Figure 11.41**   Choose the Lock transparency layer option on the Layers palette and paint using the Airbrush with a large, soft tip along the centerline.

Paint with a small portion of the brush inside the selection area near the lower tip. Gradually allow more of the brush inside the selection area as you move toward the top of the centerline leaf area.

21. Press X to switch the background color to the foreground. If needed, stroke along the bottom right edge of the leaf. Press Ctrl(⌘)+Shift+I to create an inverse of the selection. With the blue-green color as the foreground, stroke a small amount of color along the centerline on the upper half of the leaf (keep a large portion of the brush outside the selection area on the lower portion of the leaf, as shown in Figure 11.42).

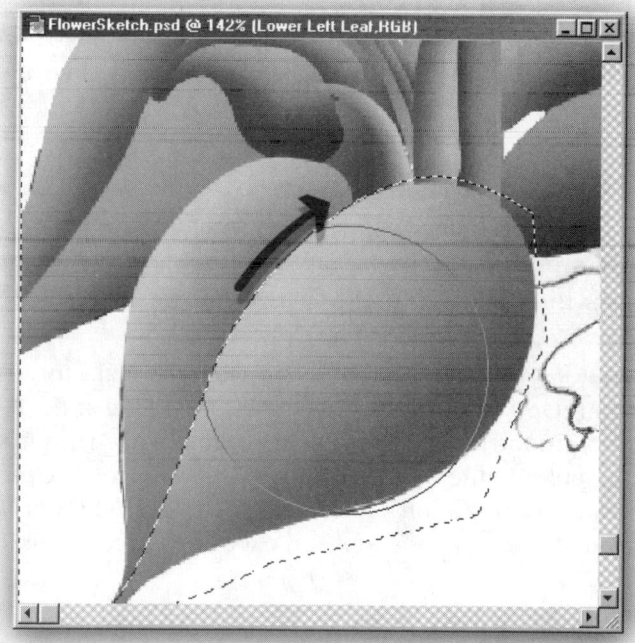

**Figure 11.42**   Create an inverse of the selection and paint along the centerline with the blue-green color with most of the brush near the lower leaf portion outside the selection area.

22. **Optional:** Click the foreground color selection box on the toolbox and choose a softer blue-green color; R:108, G:162, B:156. Click to add small amounts of this color to the centerline (with only a small portion of the brush tip inside the selection area). Press Ctrl(⌘)+Shift+I to create an inverse of the selection and click to add small amounts of the color to the lower area of the bottom half of the leaf. Press Ctrl(⌘)+D to deselect the marquee. Uncheck the Lock transparency layer option on the Layers palette. Press Ctrl(⌘)+S to save your work.

## Honing In on Path Selection Techniques

Whew! You put in enough painting to totally deface the World Trade Center! But there should be some *awesome* leaves to show for it. We just need to add the color for the remaining flowers, and give the image a background gradient for the finishing touch.

Although the colors will change, the technique will remain similar to what you have done so far. You will build both remaining flowers at the same time, working with layers to make the petals that are closer to the back and working your way toward the foreground petals.

Continue to make use of the brush size cursor for the Airbrush. Keep a small portion of the Brush within a selection area when adding subtle color transitions. Let's get started with the ending.

### Example 11.10     Practicing More Path Selections

1. On the Layers palette, click the arrow next to the Leaves folder to close this layer set. Click the eye icon to the left of the Orange Flowers Layer to view this set. Click the arrow next to the Orange Flowers folder to open up this layer set.

2. Click the Flower3 layer title on the Layers palette to make this the active layer. Press Alt(Opt) and click the Create new layer icon at the bottom of the Layers palette. In the Layer Properties dialog box, type **Stems** for the Name. Click OK to return to the work. Click the foreground color selection box on the toolbox and choose a soft yellow; R:255, G:255, B:112. Click OK. Click the background color selection box and choose a soft red color; R:255, G:76, B:41. Click OK.

3. Click the Paths tab to view the Paths palette. Click the Flower2 title. Hold down the Ctrl(⌘) key to toggle to the Direct Selection tool and click the stem path in the center of the top orange flower. Press the Ctrl(⌘)+Shift and click the stem path in the center of the bottom orange flower as seen in Figure 11.43, to add this path to the current paths.

4. Click the Loads path as a selection icon near the bottom of the Paths palette. Click an empty space below the paths titles to deselect the remaining paths. Press Alt(Opt)+Delete (Backspace) to fill the selection with the yellow color. Press J to switch to the Airbrush tool and choose a 35-pixel brush size from the Options bar. Press Ctrl(⌘)++ to increase to magnification. Hold down the spacebar and drag with the Hand tool in the document until you have a clear view of the top selected stem.

**Figure 11.43**   Hold down Ctrl(⌘) and select the first stem path. Press the Ctrl(⌘)+Shift to add the second Stem path.

5. Press X to switch the soft red color to the foreground. Click along the left edge and bottom of the stem to add small amounts of the red color (keep a small portion of the brush inside the selection area when painting, as shown in Figure 11.44).

6. Press the spacebar and scroll the document with the Hand tool until the lower stem is in view. Repeat step 5. Press Ctrl(⌘)+D to deselect the marquee when you're satisfied with the results.

7. Click the foreground color selection box on the toolbox and choose an orange color; R:255, G:156, B:0. Click OK. Click the background color selection box and choose a red color; R:232, G:33, B:0. Click OK. On the Paths palette, click the Flower2 title to make the path visible in the document. Hold down the Ctrl(⌘) key to toggle to the Direct selection tool, and click to select the large flower petal path on the lower-right orange flower (see Figure 11.45).

**Figure 11.44**    Keep a small portion of the brush inside the selection area when adding the soft red color to the bottom and left edges.

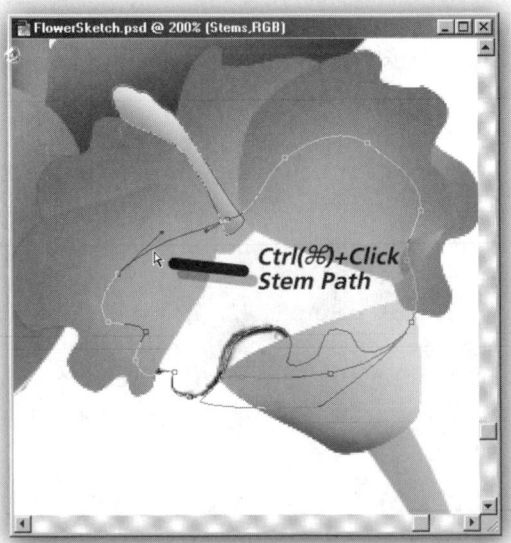

**Figure 11.45**    Select the large petal path from the Flower2 path title.

8. Click the Loads path as a selection icon near the bottom of the Paths palette. Click on an empty space below the paths titles to deselect the remaining paths. Click the Layers tab to view the Layers palette. Press the Alt(Opt) key and click the Create new layer icon at the bottom of the palette. In the Layer Properties dialog box, type **Flower4** for the Name. Click OK to return to the action.

9. Press G to switch to the Gradient tool (Options bar set on Linear and Background to Foreground). Hold down the Shift key and drag a vertical gradient from the bottom middle to just below the top of the selection as shown in Figure 11.46. Press J to switch to the Airbrush tool and choose a 100-pixel size brush. Click to place addition orange in the center lower-middle area.

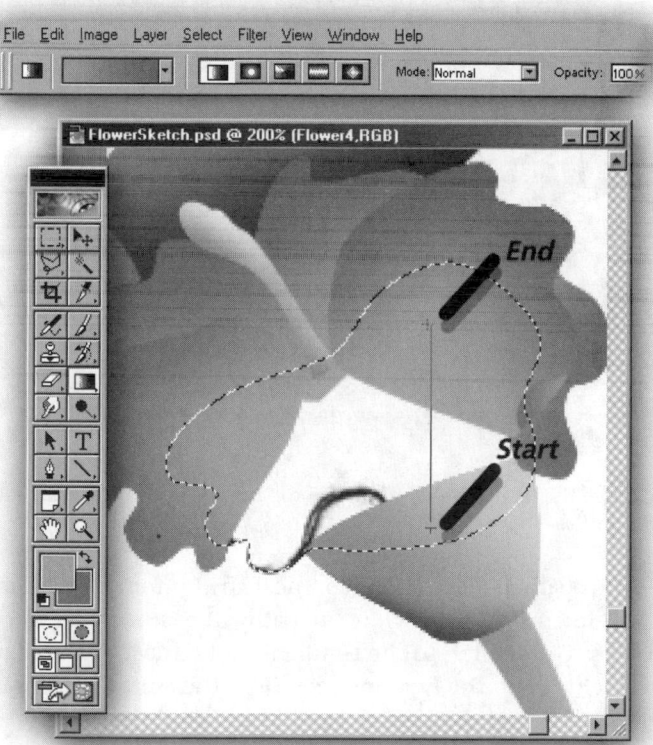

**Figure 11.46**   Click at the bottom middle of the selection and drag a vertical gradient to just below the top of the selection area.

10. Press X to switch red to the foreground color and click to add more red along the upper and left edges of the image. Keep only a small portion of the brush inside the selection area. Press Ctrl(⌘)+D to deselect the marquee when you are happy with the results.

**11.** Press the spacebar and drag to scroll the document until the upper orange flower is in view. Press X to switch the orange color to the foreground. Click the Paths tab to view the Paths palette. Click the Flower2 title. Hold down the Ctrl(⌘) key to toggle to the Direct selection tool and click the large flower petal path below the stem of this flower, as shown in Figure 11.47.

**Figure 11.47**    Choose the large petal path on the top orange flower from the Flower2 path title.

**12.** Click the Loads path as a selection icon near the bottom of the Paths palette. Click an empty space below the paths titles to deselect the remaining paths. Press G to switch to the Gradient tool (Linear and Foreground to Background settings on the Options bar). Hold the Shift key to drag a vertical gradient starting at the bottom middle and ending at the top middle of the selection, as seen in Figure 11.48.

**13.** Press J to switch to the Airbrush tool (and the 100-pixel size brush). Click in the lower-middle area of the selection to add more orange to that area. Press X to switch to red and click along the top and outside edges to add more red if needed. Keep only a small amount of the brush inside the selection area. Press Ctrl(⌘)+D to deselect the selection marquee.

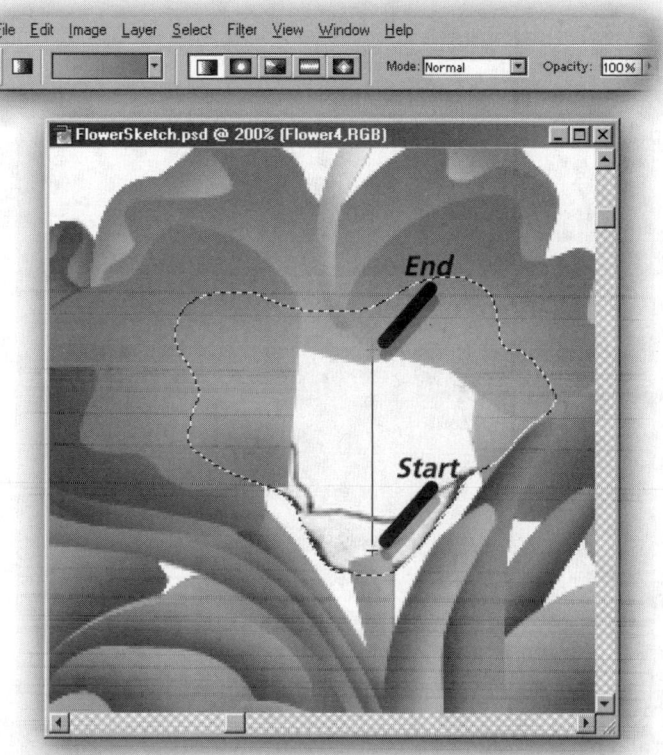

**Figure 11.48**  Drag a vertical gradient starting at the middle bottom of the selection area to the middle top.

14. On the Paths palette, click the Flower2 title. Press Ctrl(⌘)+ – to reduce the magnification so that both orange flowers are in view. Hold down the Ctrl(⌘) key to toggle to the Direct selection tool and click the petal lower curl path at the bottom of the petal just painted. Press Ctrl(⌘)+Shift and click to add the lower curl path on the bottom orange flower to the selected paths as shown in Figure 11.49.

15. Click the Loads path as a selection icon near the bottom of the Paths palette. Click an empty space below the paths titles to deselect the remaining paths. Click the Layers tab to return to the Layers palette. Hold down the Ctrl+Alt+Shift(⌘+Option+Shift) keys and click the Flower4 layer title, to intersect the selection with the selected areas of this layer.

16. Press Alt(Opt) and click the Create new layer icon at the bottom of the Layer Palette. In the Layer Properties dialog box, type **Flower5** for the Name. Click OK to return to your work. Press X to switch the Orange color to the foreground. Press Alt(Opt)+Delete (Backspace) to fill the selection with the foreground color.

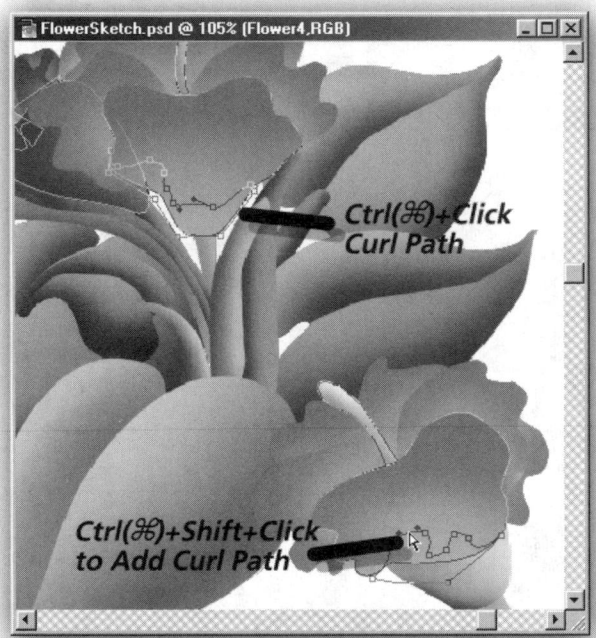

**Figure 11.49**    Select the curl path to the top orange flower. Press the Ctrl(⌘)+Shift key to add the curl path of the bottom flower to the path selections.

**17.** Press J to switch to the Airbrush tool. Choose the 45-pixel brush tip. Press Ctrl(⌘)++ to increase the zoom view. Press the spacebar and drag the document until the top orange flower is in view. Press X to switch the red color to the foreground. Stroke a small portion of color along the upper edges of the curl selection to add red.

**18.** Press the spacebar to toggle to the Hand tool and drag the document until the lower orange flower is in view. Repeat step 17 by stroking along the upper edges of the selection area in the same manner as shown in Figure 11.50. Press Ctrl(⌘)+D to deselect the marquee.

**19.** Click Layer 0 to make this the active layer. Click the foreground color selection box on the toolbox and select a nighttime green color; R:0, G:105, B:104. Click OK. Click the background color selection box on the toolbox and choose a dark navy color; R:25, G:4, B:57. Click OK.

**20.** Press G to switch to the Gradient tool (with Linear and Foreground to Background options chosen on the Options bar). Press the Shift key to drag a vertical gradient starting near the top of the image and ending near the bottom of the image as shown in Figure 11.51. Press Ctrl(⌘)+S to save your work.

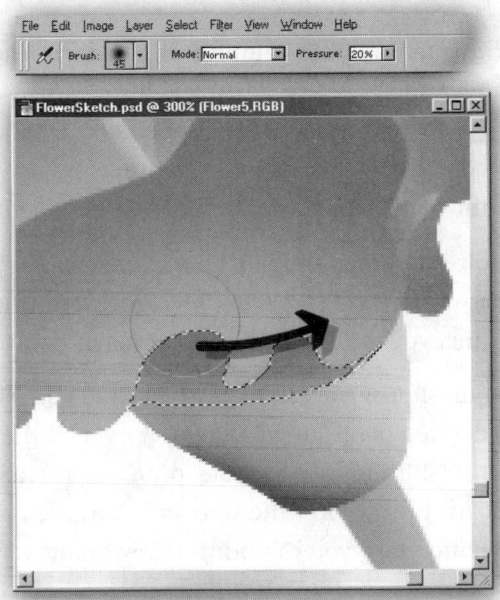

**Figure 11.50**   Use a 45-pixel Airbrush tip to stroke a small amount of red color along the top edges of the curl selections.

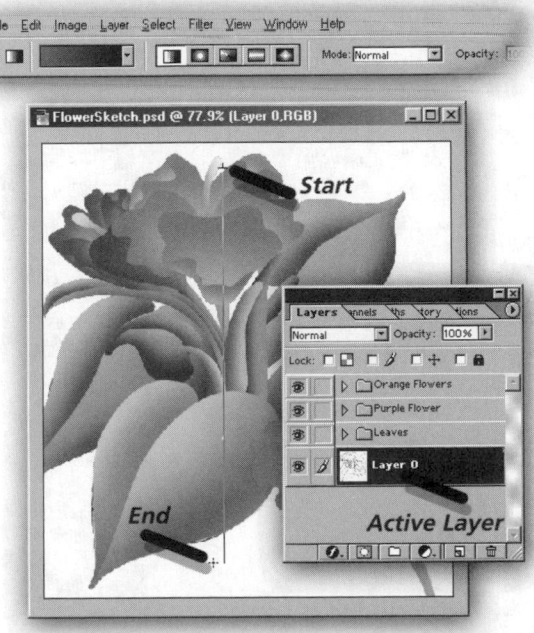

**Figure 11.51**   With Layer 0 as the active layer, drag a vertical gradient from the top to the bottom.

## Summary

The majority of this chapter involved painting and, though it might have seemed to focus on the Gradient and Airbrush tools, you also learned another important lesson: How to make paths become useful selection tools. Hopefully, the flower-creation marathon accomplished this task by demonstrating how to create paths, as well as how to make the paths work to accomplish a desired look for the image.

The quality of art is directly proportional to the earnest amount of work you put into it. The flower was not a "here's how to draw an ellipse" tutorial, but through effort and understanding, you arrived at something magnificent.

Yet another facet of Photoshop 6 is about to be revealed to you. Photoshop can honestly be considered a desktop publishing program. It's got all the controls you need for text kerning, baseline shifting, and a whole lot of other fancy terms we haven't defined yet. But trust us. Just beyond the next page are the makings of a professional, two-sided, invitation card you can print to any home inkjet printer. C'mon!

# Chapter 12

## Introducing Shapes: Someplace Between Paths and Selections

At some time in your life (probably from à disgruntled Social Studies teacher) you've undoubtedly heard the line:

*A camel is a horse that was designed by a committee.*

Well, a camel and a Photoshop Shape are similar—the Shape was probably designed by a bunch of talented programmers. However, to *define* a Shape is a challenge, because it is neither fish nor fowl. In this chapter, the most striking thing you will learn about Shapes is that they can exist in one of three states, and can be converted from one state to another. A Shape can be any of the following:

- A simple predefined painting whose region is filled with the current foreground color.

- A Work Path, which can be edited, stroked, filled, and turned into a marquee selection, if you feel like it.

- A Shape Layer, where a new layer is created in the image, and wherever you drag the cursor to create a premade shape, the interior of the shape is filled with the current foreground color. You can apply a Style to a shape, and you can edit it with the Direct Selection tool and the Convert Point tools. You can convert the shape to a simple filled shape on a layer, you can move the Shape with either the Path Component Selection tool or the Move tool, and this chapter shows you all sorts of cool things you can do with Shapes. Best of all (not that this removes any confusion), a Shape can be vector or bitmap in nature, depending on how you specify which type of Shape you want to create.

Despite their refusal to be precisely defined, Shapes are a lot of fun (they're time-savers, too). In this chapter, you will learn the ins and outs of Shapes, and we'll even show you how to create a Shape to add to a palette.

## Exploring the Shape Tools

There are six different shapes on the Shape tools list on the toolbox. Five of them are fairly intuitive to work with, and one—the Custom Shape tool—could be called a *freeform* tool, because you can load anything that can be expressed as a path as a member of the Custom Shape group. The rest of the tools are straightforward: Rectangle, for example, produces rectangles, and so on. In the sections to follow, you'll look at options for modifying the basic shapes. And you will use Filled Region mode for Shape creation, so it will seem as though you are filling a marquee selection—something that feels closer to home.

In Figure 12.1, you can see the tools list with all the Shape tools. Interestingly, Adobe has made the Line tool a Shape tool, but working with it is much the same as in previous versions of Photoshop.

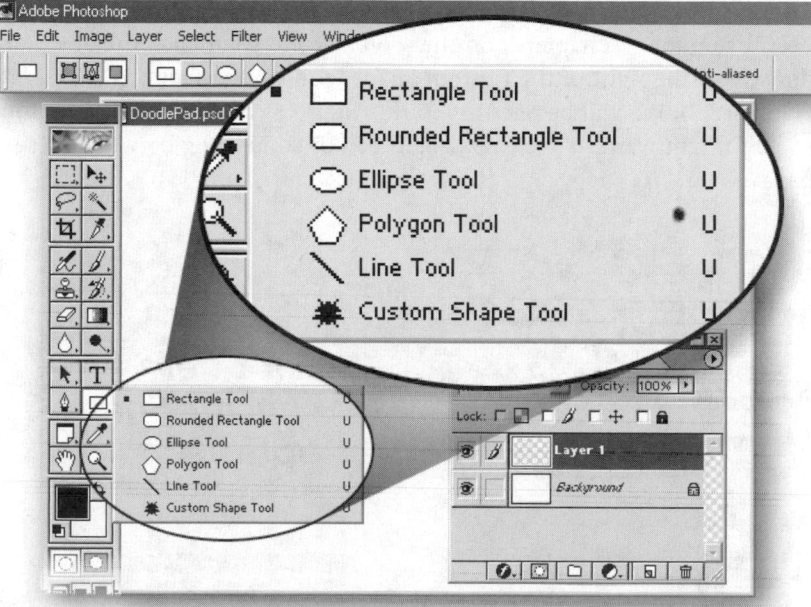

**Figure 12.1**   The Shape tools list is where you choose the shape of the Shape you want to create. I know, I know…

Let's start at the top of the list, with the Rectangle tool.

## Refining the Shape of a Rectangle Shape

A sub-palette of options sprouts off the Options bar when a Shape tool has been chosen. This probably happens because all the options simply won't fit on the Options bar—and most assuredly not in languages that have longer names for their U.S. English equivalents.

There are no grades and no points for the following steps. In fact, there is no artistic point at all to these steps—you're simply going to get a feel for what is possible with a Shape tool.

Let's try out the Rectangle tool:

**Example 12.1   Checking Out the Rectangle Shape Tool**

1. Start a new document—press Ctrl(⌘)+N. Make the document 7 inches wide and 5 inches tall, 72 pixels per inch, RGB color Mode, and Contents: White. Press Enter (Return) to add the empty image window to the workspace.

> **Warning!**   If an error message appears when you open the CD files, press Ctrl(⌘)+Shift+K and then choose Adobe RGB (1998) from the Working Spaces, RGB drop-down list. See Chapter 3 for more information.

**2.** Click the Rectangle Shape tool (*not* the Rectangular Marquee tool you've been using for 11 chapters!) on the toolbox, and then click the down arrow directly to the right of the Custom Shape icon on the Options bar (see Figure 12.2). We will be referring to this figure as the discussion continues, so you might want to stick a baseball card or something between these pages.

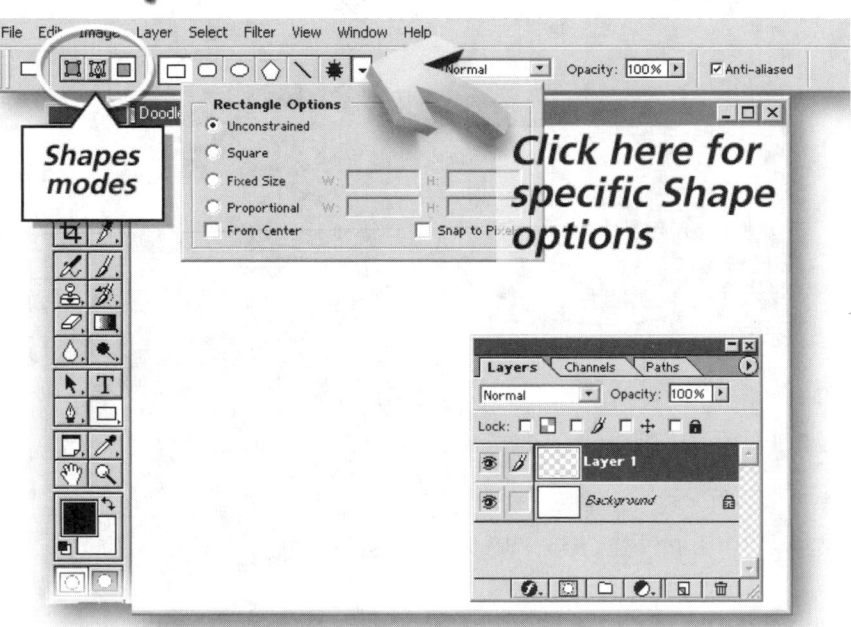

**Figure 12.2**    The Rectangle Shape tool, with all options extended in the workspace.

**3.** Click on the foreground color selection box on the Color Picker, and then choose a color you know you won't get sick of for a while. You'll be filling lots of shapes with this color in the sections to come. Pick an office color or something.

**4.** Click the Create new layer icon on the Layers palette (press F7 if the palette isn't onscreen). By default, this is the current editing layer; its default name is Layer 1.

**5.** Chances are that by this time in the book, you've played with the Opacity and Blending mode drop-down boxes on the Options bar. If you have not, click on the rightmost of the set of three buttons (the Shapes mode buttons) to the left of the Shapes on the Options bar (it's called the Create filled region button), and then drag a rectangle in the image window. Then, play with the modes and opacity settings to get a feel for the way these options can help integrate something you create with a background.

In fact, ModernTimes.psd in the Examples/Chap 12 folder on the CD was created so that you could experiment with settings on a layer on which you created a shape. By creating shapes against a background, you will truly get a feel for blending modes. Multiply, Color Overlay, and Screen are our favorites—they produce the most striking changes to layers underneath the layer with the shapes.

**6.** Now that the blending modes and Opacity have been thoroughly investigated, try clicking the drop-down button directly to the right of the shapes, called out by the huge arrow in Figure 12.2. Take a look at Figure 12.2 closely. You will find that:

- Use of the default, Unconstrained mode enables you to draw a filled rectangular shape of any proportion or dimension within the image window.

- If you click the Square option, you will always draw filled rectangles whose height and width are identical.

- The Fixed Size option enables you to define the absolute height and width of a rectangle you draw. It's going to feel as though the rectangle is drawing itself! We recommend adding the suffix *px* after you type the number—for example, Width: **25 px**—so you're defining the rectangle in pixels. Especially when you're doing Web work, using pixels to define dimensions is much easier than using inches (particularly when you have a fractional value, such as $3\frac{11}{16}$").

- The Proportional option is much handier than you'd think. Suppose you type **4** in the Width field, and **3** in the Height field. This is the aspect of a monitor—4:3. You can make sure your rectangle will fill the screen, edge to edge, when a user zooms in on the rectangle to sufficient resolution, such as 800×600 pixels (which has the lowest common denominator of 4 by 3, get it?). By choosing Proportional and then typing 4 and 3 you ensure that the rectangle you're creating will fill the screen, provided that whoever is looking at the screen zooms in to a resolution of 800×600 pixels (or other multiples of 4 and 3).

- The From Center option is handy when you already have a center point defined for other shapes on different layers. It might not be award-winning art, but using this option would enable you to add a square (click Square), perfectly centered on top of a centered circle, and so on. The From Center is simply a different way of doing things, based on your specific artistic needs.

- If you found the documentation for Snap to Pixels to be a little lean in Adobe's documentation...so did we. The name is inappropriate. Here's what this option does: Photoshop is all about *anti-aliasing*—the placement of background color pixels mixed with the foreground object in an image. Because pixels are rectangular, and diagonal lines and curves are not, you need anti-aliasing to create smooth-looking curves and diagonal lines.

With Snap to Pixels enabled, no sides of the rectangle are anti-aliased, which is good because the sides are either perfectly horizontal or vertical. This Snap to Pixels option becomes more important as we look at *other* shapes. With the feature turned off, you will get about a 1 pixel anti-aliasing—a blend of the foreground color and the image background—around the four sides of the rectangle. The result looks like some sort of mistake with Snap to Pixels turned off, and we recommend that you keep Snap to Pixels turned on most of the time. By the way, when it comes to rendering curves and such, the Snap to Pixels option is ineffective for all Shapes. There will be anti-aliasing on curves and diagonal lines regardless of how hard you plead.

7. Drawing rectangles is not exactly a world of fun, so after you've checked out the Options bar's Rectangle Options, press Ctrl(⌘)+A to Select All, press Delete (Backspace), And then hit Ctrl(⌘)+D to deselect the marquee. You have a clean slate, as it were, on Layer 1 now.

**Note**

> **Hit or Miss**    Gail doesn't like us to use the word "hit" when it comes to keyboard commands, but we thought that just once we could squeak by with it in step 7. An author educated in grammar uses the word *press*. We guess the secret's out now. <g>

## Examining the Rounded Rectangle Shape Tool

If you check out Figure 12.3, you will see that the Rounded Rectangle tool has all the suboption features of the Rectangle Shape tool. It's the Options bar that shows a tiny difference: a Radius field. The number you type in this field determines the roundness of the corners. A small number will produce a shape that looks like Scandinavian furniture, whereas a large number in this field enables you to produce shapes that look like those plastic outdoor jungle gyms.

### Example 12.2    Mixing Shapes with Filled Selections

1. You might as well name and save the image in the workspace ('cause there's more fun to come!). Call it **DoodlePad.psd**, and save it to hard disk in Photoshop's native file format. Keep the image open.

2. With the Rounded Rectangle tool, and with the Radius set to 10 px, drag a rectangle about one quarter the size of the image window, toward the upper-left corner of the screen.

3. Choose the Lasso tool, hold Alt(Opt), and then click a triangle at the bottom of the rectangle, as shown in Figure 12.4, and fill it with foreground color. You have a wonderful template now for a speech balloon. Press Ctrl(⌘)+D to deselect the marquee.

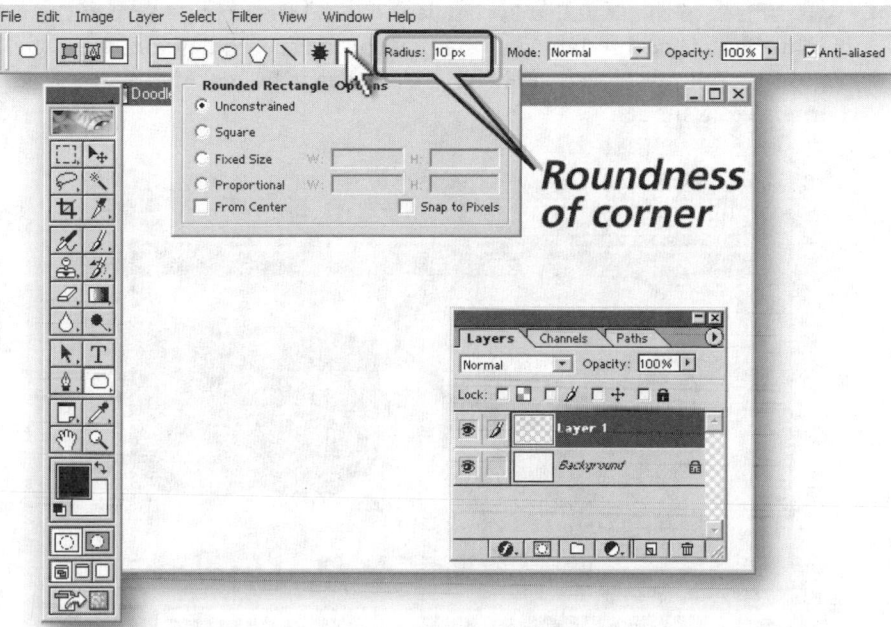

**Figure 12.3**    The Rounded Rectangle options are the same as those for the Rectangle shape, but Radius (corner roundness) is an option on the Options bar.

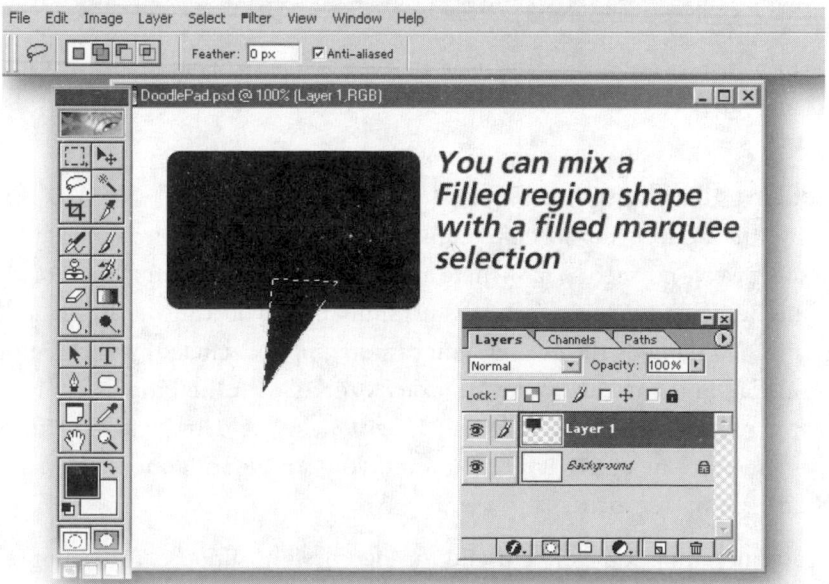

**Figure 12.4**    You can mix painting and filling selections with Shape tools that are in Filled region mode. There is *no* difference with respect to the type of pixels you are adding to the image.

4. Switch back to the Rounded Rectangle tool, and then type **40 px** in the Radius field. Drag a rectangle to the right of the speech balloon. See (in Figure 12.5) how you can approach a circle shape by making the rounded corners large enough?

**Figure 12.5**    The shape produced by the Rounded Rectangle tool can be dramatically changed by the degree of roundness you assign the corners.

## Introducing the Ellipse Shape Tool

Naturally, the options for an ellipse are going to be different from those for the Shape tools we've covered so far—there are no straight lines in an ellipse (or at least there shouldn't be)—but the options are similar. As you can see in Figure 12.6, Unconstrained mode is the default, you can drag perfect circles by clicking on the Circle option, and you can specify an exact size. As with the Proportional option, you enter numbers in the Width and Height fields, and by default, Photoshop assumes the units are pixels. But if you want, you can type a number, leave a space, and then type **in** (for inches).

The Proportional option can be useful for logo design. Suppose, for example, that you had work from the Ford Motor Company. In the logo, an ellipse whose proportions were decided upon years ago surrounds the name Ford in script. When you learn what the proportions are (bring a ruler over to our garage sometime), you can faithfully reproduce part of the logo to any size.

Finally, the From Center option, when chosen, enables you to drag an ellipse, starting from the center. As mentioned earlier, if you're into Photoshop grids and guides, you can use the From Center option to exactly center different shapes as you draw them—no Move tool and repositioning required.

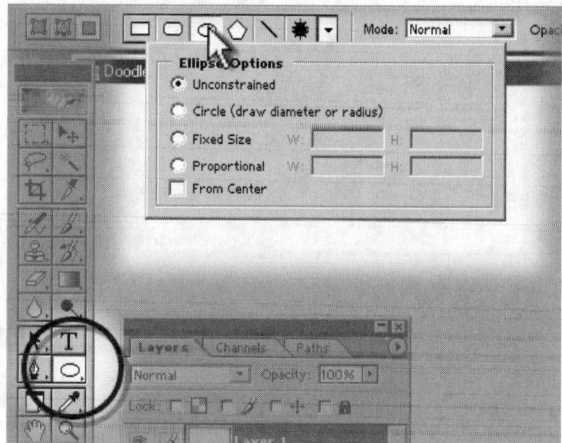

**Figure 12.6**   The options for the Ellipse Shape tool provide you with everything you need to make a shape that is completely curved.

## Exploring the Polygon Shape Tool

The Polygon Shape tool is the second most interesting shape-generating feature of all the shapes tools. It produces a terrific variety of shapes, as long as you know what the options mean. By default, when the tool is chosen, the polygon on the Options bar has five sides (all are straight lines) that meet at five vertices. This setting is very useful for drawing tiny Pentagons—unfortunately, there is no Capitol Building or Washington Monument tool.

If you click the down button on the Options bar, you will see a palette like the one shown in Figure 12.7. If you increase the number of sides on the Options bar, you will soon be drawing something that looks more like a circle than a polygon, and we have yet to discover any interesting shapes by merely increasing the number of sides. However, if you click the Indent Sides By option (#1), and then type a value from 35 to 50, you will have a star shape, a 12-pointer, as shown in Figure 12.7 (#2).

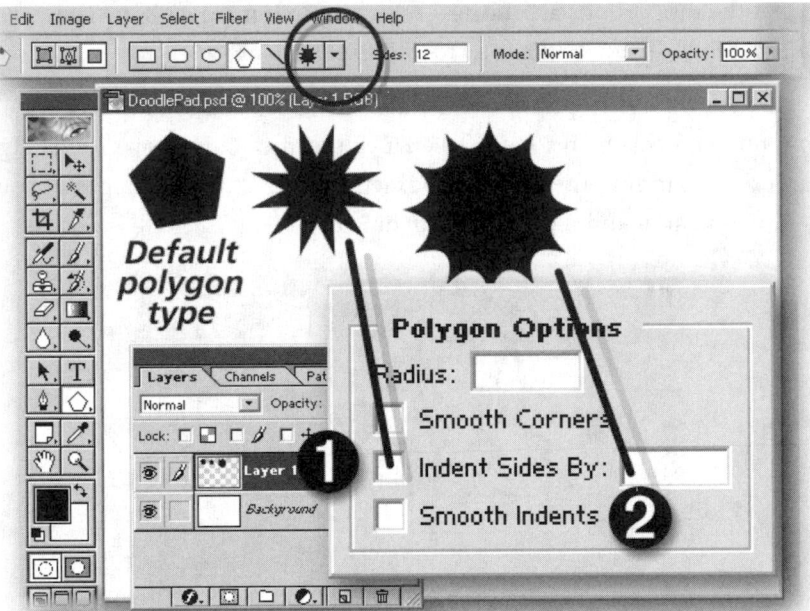

**Figure 12.7**   The Polygon tool comes with oodles of variations that dramatically change the shape of the Shape.

If you want to draw a sort of child's star, without the sharp edges that make the shape look like a martial arts weapon, click the Smooth Corners option. The Radius option determines the size of the polygon, and the Smooth Indents option helps to create shapes that look like bursts. This option can be *verrrrry* useful if you're into package design—how about placing "New!" inside a polygon that has smooth indents?

## Checking Out the Line Shape Tool

This is sort of an odd Shape tool because it can contain no fill—all the other shapes are made up of fills, and you can add a stroke to the outside of them. Nope, the Line tool makes lines, and lines with arrowheads—useful for callouts in documentations. Users of previous versions of Photoshop will be happy to know that the Line tool has not changed at all—Adobe simply put the options in different places.

On the Options bar, the really important options for the Line tool are Weight—expressed in any unit you like—and whether you want anti-aliasing. Most of the time, you'll want anti-aliasing turned on so the edge of a line has the same general feel as other shape edges in a composition. But if you need a precise line drawn horizontally or vertically—with no transitional edge pixels—the Options bar is where you turn off anti-aliasing.

Figure 12.8 shows a 12-point line drawn with anti-aliasing turned on. Now there's another option that you can access only from the keyboard. If you want to constrain the direction of a line by 45°, hold Shift as you drag.

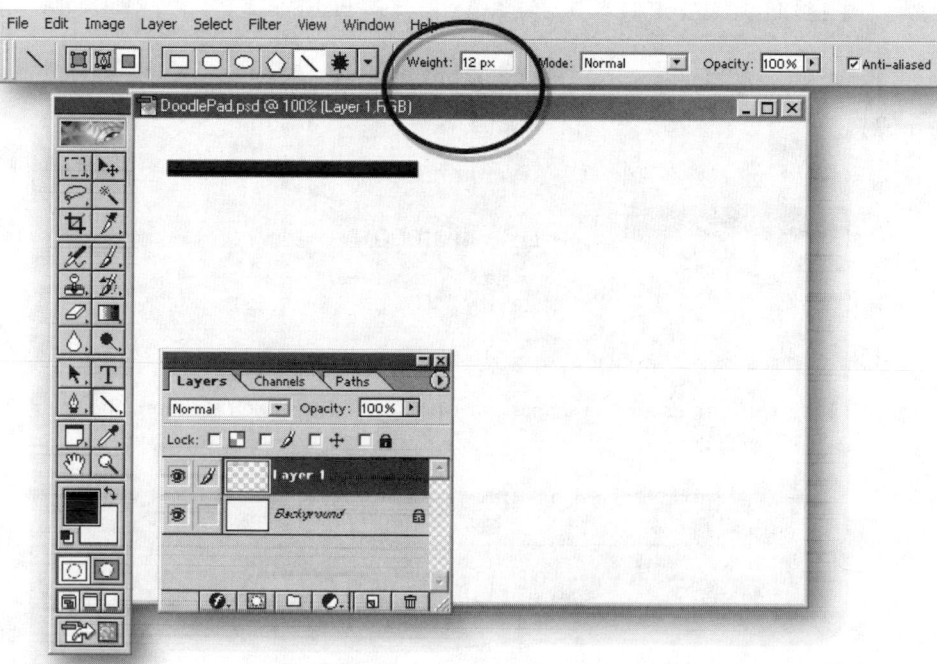

**Figure 12.8**   The Line tool has become one of the Shape tools in version 6 of Photoshop.

When you click the Shape down arrow on the Options bar, you will see a box like the one shown in Figure 12.9. As you can see, you have the option of adding arrow-heads to the start of a line, to the end of a line, or to both, in case someone doesn't know whether they're coming or going.

The arrowhead Width and Length are relative to the width of the line, and the Concavity refers to how severely the butt of the arrowhead is bent inward, as shown in Figure 12.10.

**Tip**

**Arrowheads on Tap**   If you want a more exotic shape for an arrow, you aren't limited to the Line tool's option. By the end of this chapter, you will learn how to make your own Shapes palette. You can then convert all the Zapf Dingbat fonts to a Shapes palette—it has lots of interesting arrowheads. Just don't try to go selling or sharing it—the font characters are protected by law in the same way the purchase of a commercial typeface is.

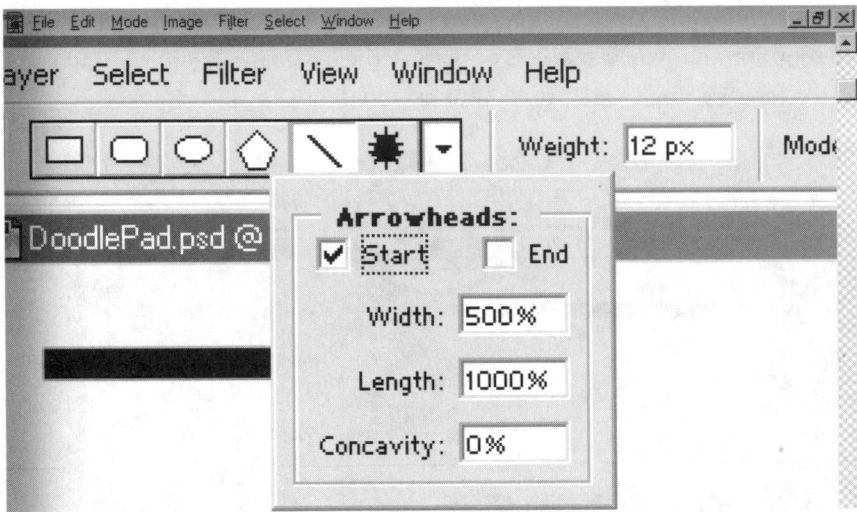

**Figure 12.9**   The options for line shapes consist of arrowheads, their location, and their shape.

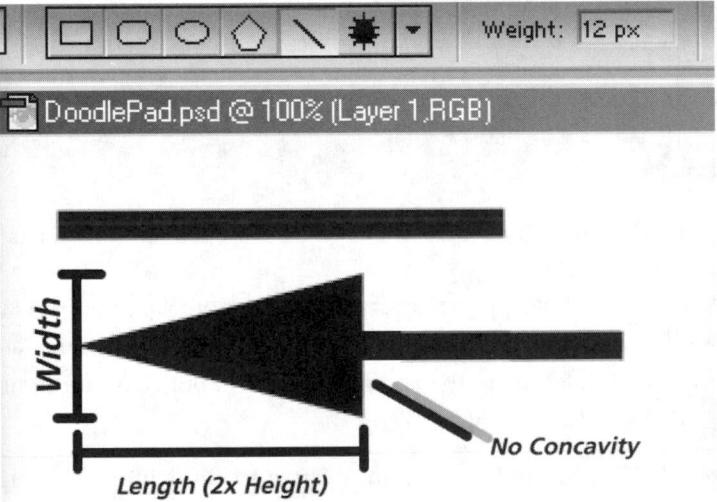

**Figure 12.10**   Width, Length, and Concavity are the options for letting Photoshop draw an arrowhead for you.

Next and final stop for Shapes is the Custom Shape tool. This feature in Photoshop brings the bitmap artist and photographer closer by far to understanding the way Adobe Illustrator works.

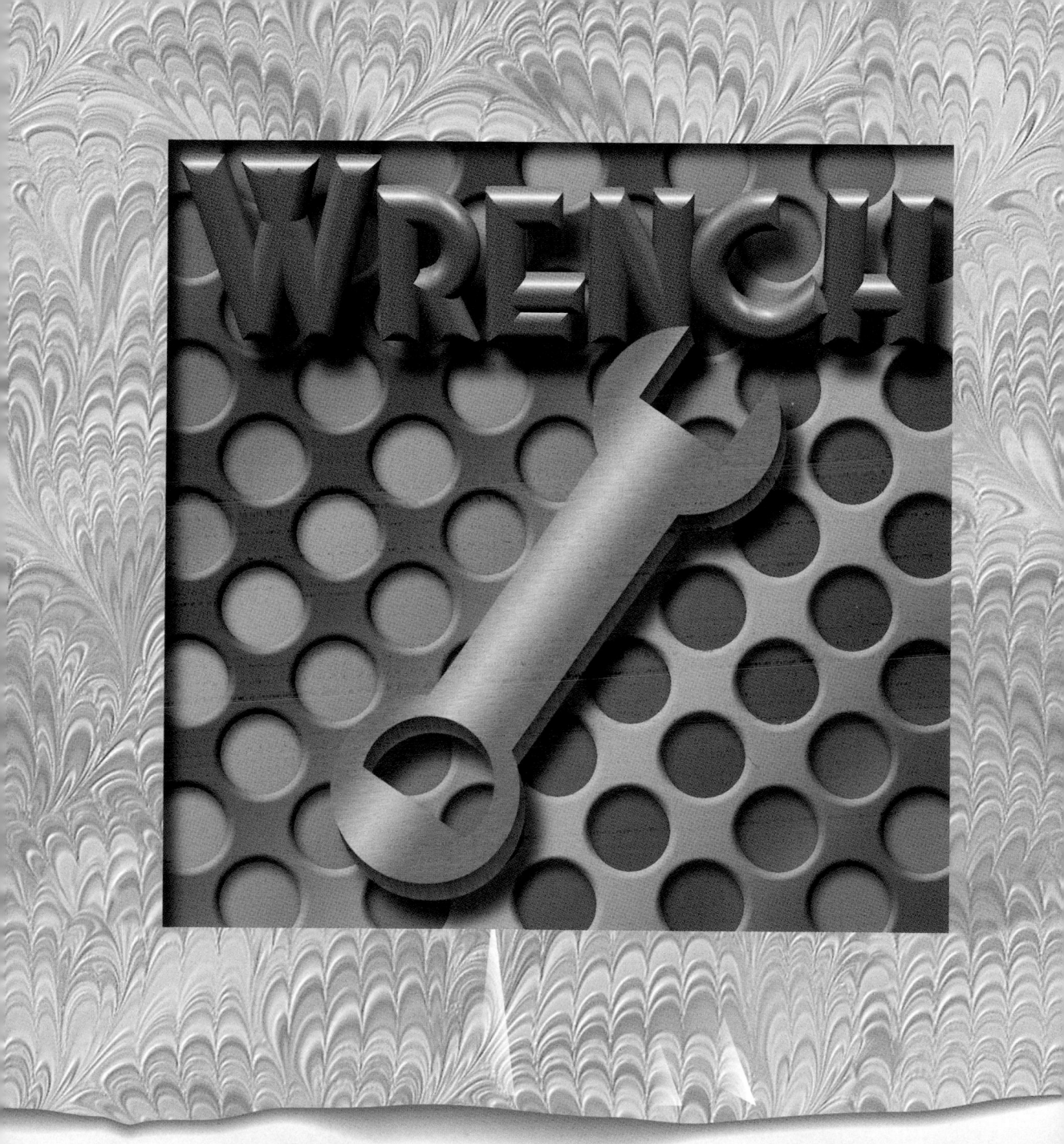

**"Wrench"** In Chapter 9, you learn how to create this illustration, using little more than Photoshop's selection tools! It's an incredible assignment that's easy to follow and produces professional results.

*Artist: Mara Nathanson.*

**"The Slice Tool"** Both Photoshop and ImageReady can slice an image into smaller parts and reassemble them by generating an HTML table. This is one way to dramatically reduce the total size of an image—you limit the color palette in slices that do not have many colors. Check out Chapter 24!

*Artist: Gary David Bouton.*

**"Getting Your Feet Wet"** In Chapter 2, you get to experiment with this image before you've read anything important in the remainder of the book. We'll guide you and visually demonstrate Photoshop 6's new features because we know that nobody likes to have to learn to swim in order to wade!

*Artists: Everyone, we think.*

**"We Come in Peace"**    This image has absolutely nothing to do with the book, except that Lars (opposite page) hunts these guys, and the Alien Skin Software staff goes to work in attire you *wish* you could wear to the office.

*Photo: Courtesy Jeff Butterworth.*

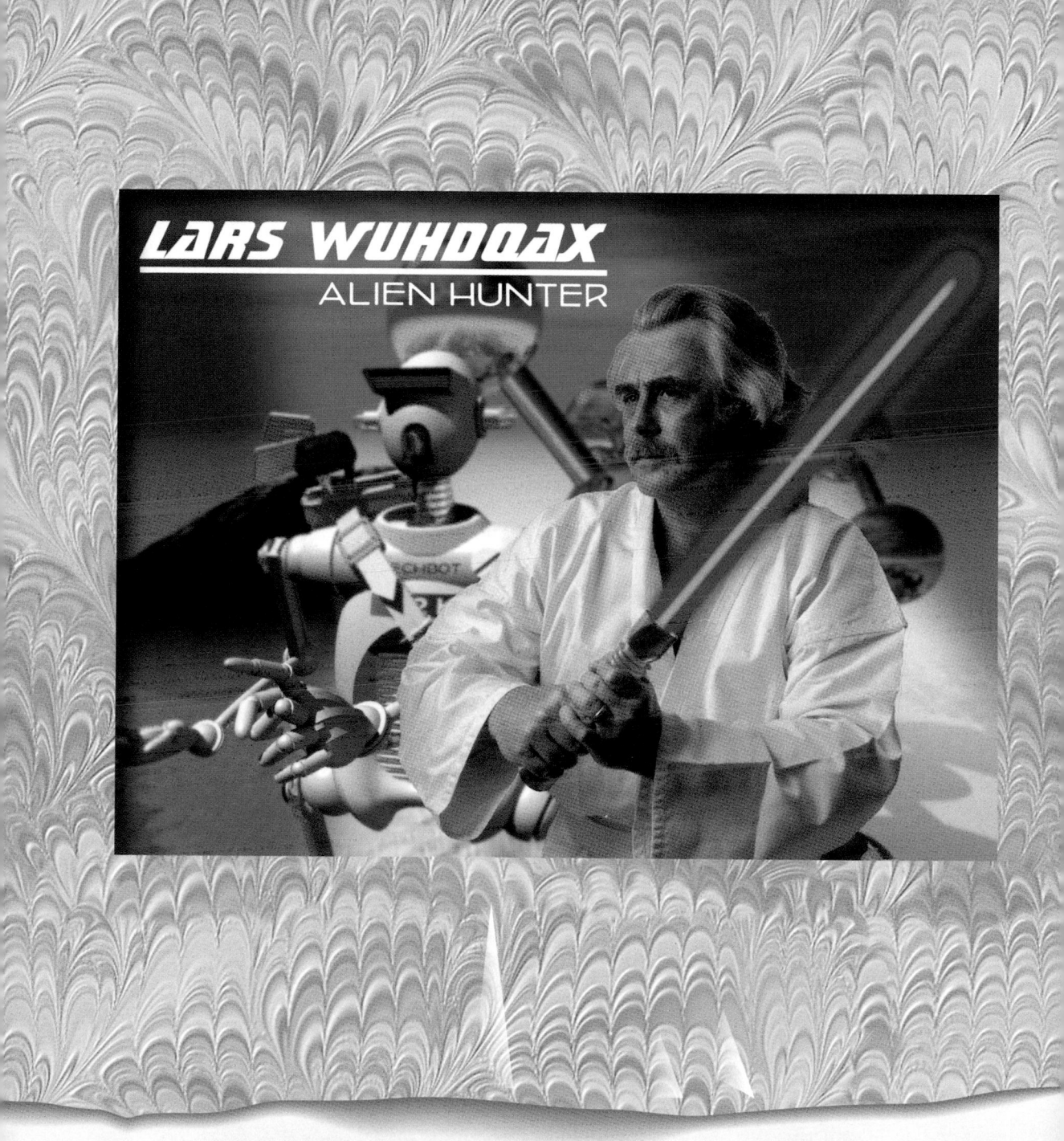

**"Lars Wuhdqax"** It's sci-fi time in Chapter 20. Don't have the budget for a Hollywood epic? No problem. This chapter takes you through the considerations for integrating rendered 3D objects with photographs of people.

*Photographer: Ed Guarente.*

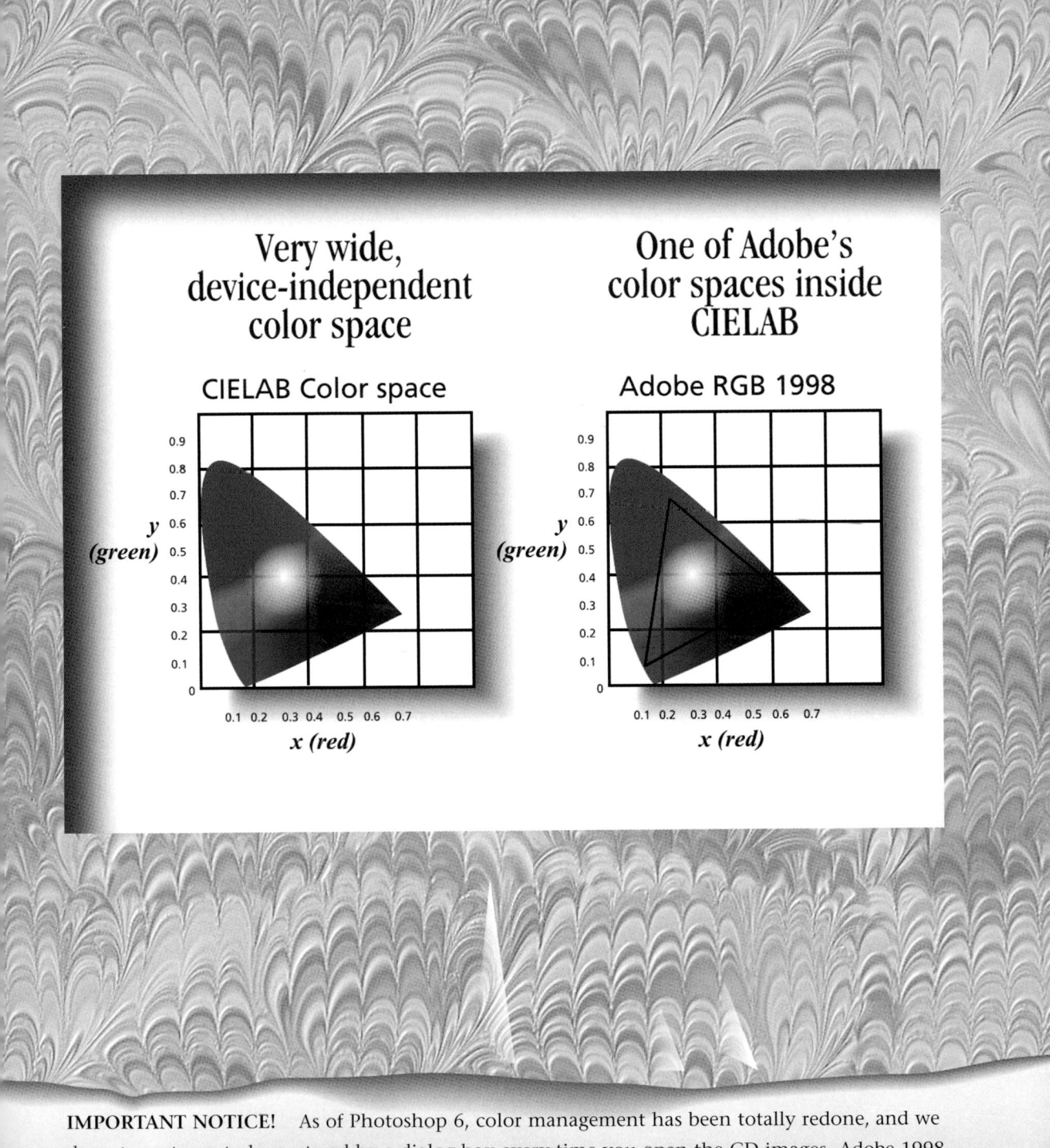

**IMPORTANT NOTICE!** As of Photoshop 6, color management has been totally redone, and we do not want you to be pestered by a dialog box every time you open the CD images. Adobe 1998 RGB color space is the preferred color space for our lessons in this book, and as you can see, it's a smaller space than CIELAB, which is the host for exchanging color spaces. Read Chapter 3 first, and get your color profiles correct in Photoshop. *Forget* the default of sRGB. Then all the other chapter examples will work flawlessly (as will your own work).

The LAB color is shown here in 3D space, as opposed to 2D space on the facing page. As you can see, there are three channels: Luminance, channel A, and channel B, which are chromacity channels. The LAB color mode can help you remove color from a picture to make a grayscale image by simply discarding the chromacity channels.

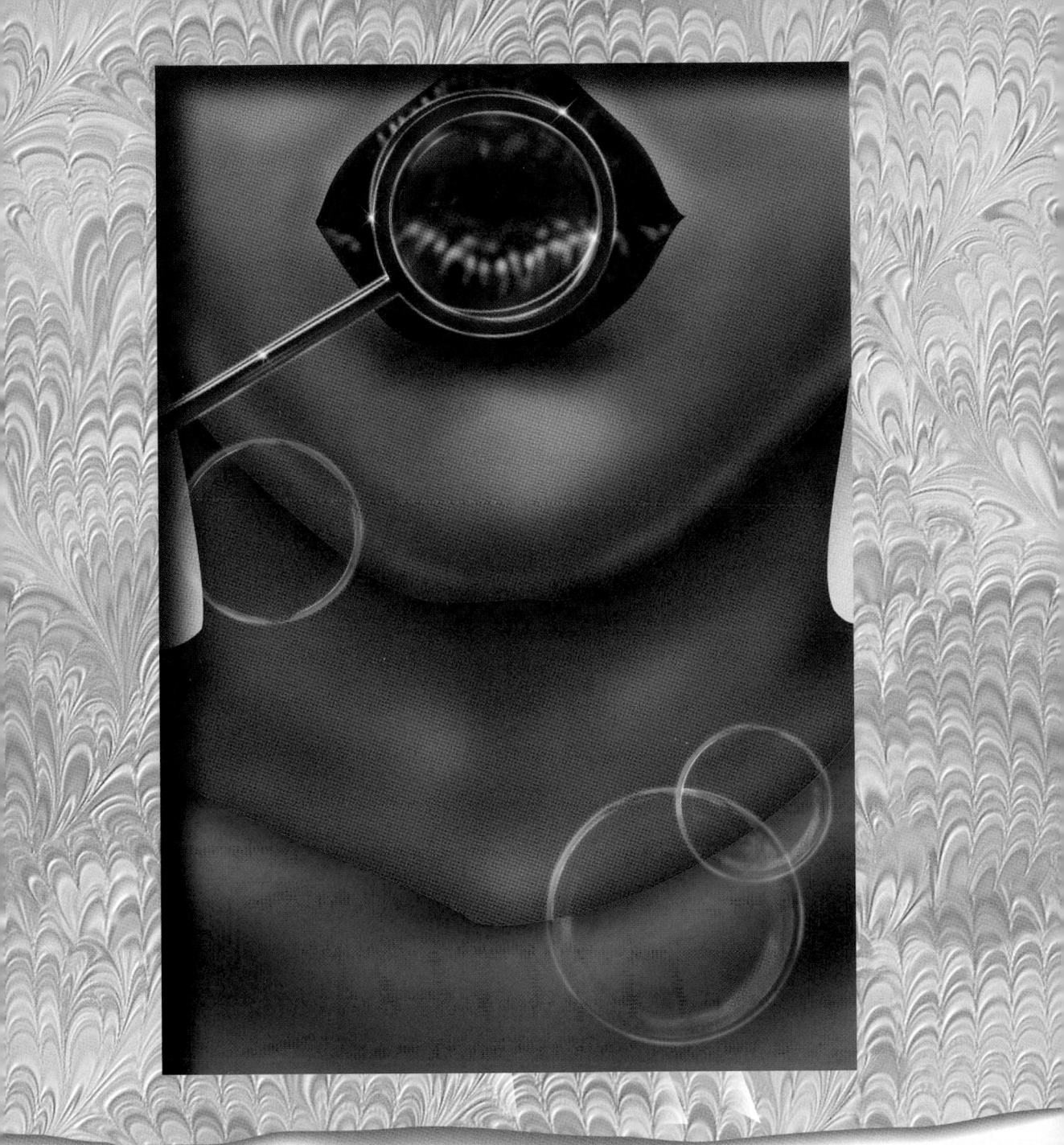

**"Blowing Bubbles"**  In Chapter 21 you'll get hands-on experience pushing Photoshop's special effects filters to the max. Learn how to create the pearlescent bubbles in this picture in less time than you can say, "Hey, where's the bubble wand?"

*Artist: Mara Nathanson.*

**"Flower"** In Chapter 10, you'll learn how to manipulate paths and selections to overlay color fields and come up with some pretty beautiful foliage.

*Artist: Mara Nathanson.*

**"David"** When you optimize an image for the Web, you need to examine the visual content carefully, and see which method will make the smallest, most beautiful reproduction. As you can see, this image is primarily made up of golds. So should you save it in PNG, JPEG, or GIF format? Read Chapter 23 and discover for yourself!

*Artist: Gary David Bouton.*

**"Ariana and Renee"** Sometimes a perfect picture cannot be taken. But with Photoshop you can graft together two flawed pictures to make a natural, perfect photograph. Chapter 16 is your guide to quality photographic retouching.

*Photographer: Gary Kubicek.*

"**Liquify!**"  In Chapter 17, it's not just about making your boss's picture look funny. We get into the Extrude command and spend some serious time getting you proficient with perhaps the most powerful of Photoshop's tools: the Clone Stamp tool.

*Gary Kubicek.*

**"Meat Surprise"** If you've read our other books, this assignment isn't really a surprise; it's *typical*. Chapter 13 takes you through the creation of this attractive label, and you'll see how to create embossed, extruded, warped text, and more.

*Artist: Mara Nathanson.*

**"Terri"**    One of the most popular sections in our *Inside* series is the restoration of heirloom images. Come see how it's done in Chapter 15.

*Retouching: Gary Kubicek.*

# Pizza Perfect

It's pretty hard to mess up a pizza—the basic ingredients can fill a shopping bag for less than ten dollars, and if your guests or family are hungry enough, they'll make it disappear! However, making the *perfect* pizza requires a little more time and planning, and we have some recommendations for making the ultimate crowd-pleaser:

**Tomatoes** —Your best choice are the round ones; square tomatoes are hard to find, and they usually cost too much. Slice them about 3/8 of an inch thick, and try to put them on the pizza *after* you've put the cheese and sauce on it. Generally, folks don't like the green sort of tomato, as these are easily confused with peppers. Put about one tomato slice per slice of pizza that you are planning on serving on the pie. Also, if you are scanning the pie instead of baking it, make sure you get all the seeds off the scanner's platen before scanning other stuff.

**Mushrooms** —these are sometimes optional for the perfect pizza. Some people simply don't like fungus on their meals. However, they're an inexpensive addition to the recipe, the color contrasts nicely with all the other toppings, and you can always choose to put mushrooms on half of the pizza, to allow guests their choice. Mushrooms for pizzas should be sliced height-wise, like the mushrooms you find on those $7 a plate salads in hotel restaurants, and the supermarket is perhaps the best place to find them.

**Pepperoni** — pepperoni is one of those "pizza staples", without which you have no pizza! Generally, pizza parlors, even those that advertise "extra pepperoni" go a tad skimpy on these wonderful, round morsels of meat. It is usually best to buy pre-sliced pepperoni. It's a little more expensive than buying a stick, but it you whine a little in front of the butcher, you can get a bargain on slicing. Add at least one hundred pieces to a medium pizza, and two to three hundred for larger pies.

**"Pizza Perfect"**    This layout could have cost a magazine thousands of dollars to create. But it cost us about $3 and some time with a scanner. In Chapter 19, learn how to accurately place and run body text in Photoshop, and see how a scanner can save the day when photography is impossible.

*Scanning Supervisor: Gary Bouton.*

**"The Boat"**   A boat on a highway with a water truck in front of it? Yep, that's surrealism, and you'll learn to make the impossible look plausible in Chapter 18. Hey, if the guy in the boat speeds, does he get a ticket from a sheriff or the Coast Guard?

*Photographer: Gary Kubicek.*

## Exposing Custom Shapes

Photoshop ships with some very nice predefined shapes for the Custom Shape palette(s), but what you can do with them is perhaps more important than the fact that the feature exists. What you have in the Custom Shape tool is the capability for someone with absolutely no art skills to get right to work in Photoshop as a designer. As you can see in Figure 12.11, the Filled region mode is still active (from the Line and arrow work). To create this figure, I clicked the down arrow to the right of the Custom Shape icon, picked a heart shape, pressed Enter (Return) to confirm the choice, and then simply dragged diagonally in the workspace. Notice that because I didn't choose the Constrain option, I could make the heart shape a little wider than the default shape.

**Figure 12.11**   Pick a symbol from the Custom Shapes palette, and drag to any proportion or dimension in an image window to render the shape.

At the time of this writing, only CorelDRAW has a Symbols palette resembling Photoshop's Custom Shapes palette, and as you will see, a palette of preset drawings is a powerful tool. It took a good three seconds to place a filled heart in an image window, to my preferred proportions. One simply *cannot* design such a heart free-hand as quickly. This is part of the power of Custom Shapes.

Wanna know more?

## Making Shapes That Are Work Paths

We've dished up a healthy serving of information on the Pen tool and paths in this book, and here (you'll like this <g>) is a second serving. Briefly, any shape you create can be created as a path instead of a filled region in a window. At the beginning of the chapter, we mentioned that a Shape can be a Work Path. This is the second of the three states of Shapes.

If you think about it, a vector premade shape is the best of both vector and pixel worlds. You are not confined to the flat color of a filled region—you can fill a selection based on a path with a gradient color or even with a photograph. You can modify the shape of the Shape by using the direction Selection and other Pen tools, and you can use the Transform command to skew, rotate, or change the dimensions of a Shape as it exists as a path.

Here—let's perform a short set of steps to show how flexible a shape as a Work Path can be.

### Example 12.3   Custom Shapes as Work Paths

1. If you have not yet chosen a shape from the Shape palette, click the down arrow to the right of the Custom Shape option on the Options bar, click on the heart shape (or another shape, if you prefer), and then press Enter (Return).

2. On the Options bar, click the Creates Work Path option, the middle button of the three buttons you can see in Figure 12.12. Drag the cursor in a diagonal direction in the image window until you have a heart-shaped path. Now, to reveal part of the power of the Custom Shape tool, choose the Direct Selection tool from the toolbox and make the heart a little cartoonish by dragging on its anchors and direction points, as shown in Figure 12.12.

   If you glossed over Chapter 11, you might not be aware of what can be done with a path. The following steps are not a recap of Chapter 11, but instead show you what some of the basic path features are good for. A Work Path Shape has exactly the same properties as a work path that you create using the Pen tool.

3. On the toolbox, choose a medium-shade color for the foreground color. Press F7 if the Layers palette is not in the workspace, click on the Paths tab, and then click the Fills path with foreground color icon, as shown in Figure 12.13.

   We have undocked the Paths palette to show you that we are working on a layer, and that a Work Path has indeed been registered on the Paths palette list. You now have a filled heart.

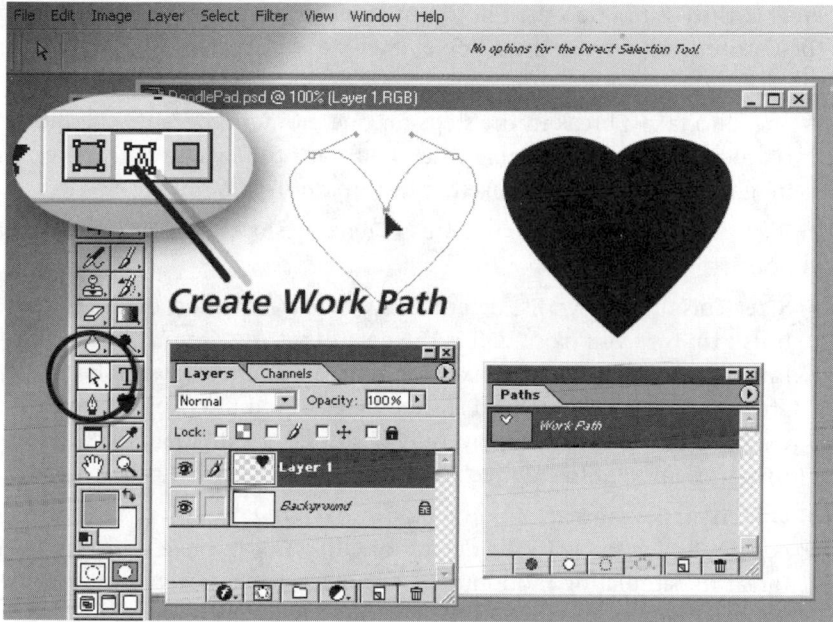

**Figure 12.12**   So what if you can't paint a heart shape? Use the Custom Shapes palette and then edit the work path shape to suit your particular artistic needs!

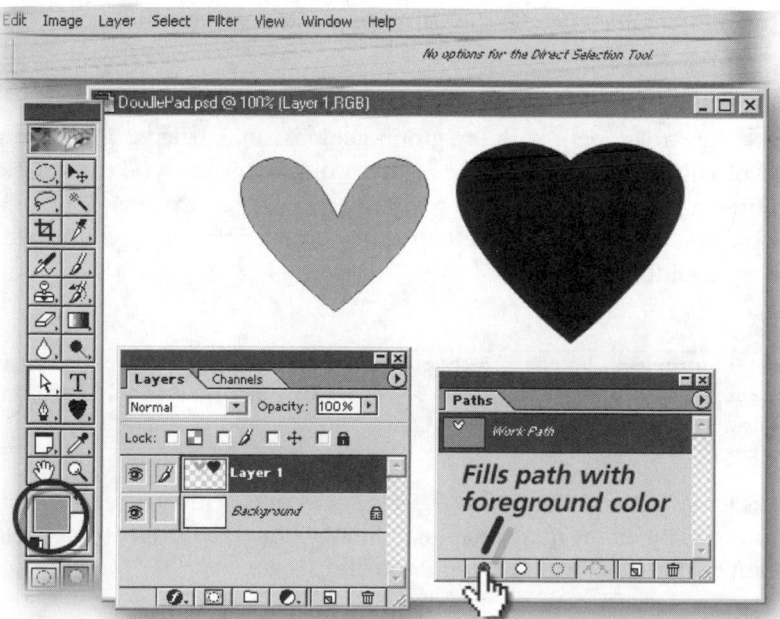

**Figure 12.13**   The Paths palette is your key to filling and stroking paths, and also for making selections based on a path shape.

**4.** Press Ctrl(⌘)+Z to undo the fill. Choose the Paintbrush tool, and then from the Options bar, choose the 17-pixel diameter tip, and press Enter (Return) to confirm your choice.

We need to take a break in the steps for one moment, because the Brush Dynamics options are available when you want to make brush strokes, and we're going to ask you to stroke the heart path in a moment.

In Figure 12.14, you can see the Brush Dynamics options (#1). These are the options:

- **Size.** This drop-down list determines where a reduction of size in the brush tip is as you paint. Off is the default setting. If you choose On—the brush tip will fade to zero pixels in however many steps you type into the Steps box. Stylus is the third feature here, which offers pressure control over the size of the brush, but only if you have a digitizing tablet installed, and Photoshop recognizes the stylus software driver.

- **Opacity.** Like the Size option, you can have the opacity of your stroke constant by going with the default of Off, you can have a stroke fade out (great for simulating motion blur) in however many steps you specify, or you can control opacity with a digitizing tablet and stylus.

- **Color.** This one is fun. By default, color is Off, but if you choose On from the list and then specify steps, you will be stroking with the foreground color, gradually changing to the background color. The Stylus option produces the same effect as the On setting, but you have more control when you use a stylus.

Back to the experiments…

**5.** Click the Strokes path with foreground color icon, labeled 2 in Figure 12.14. Bravo! This is one way to create a glow around objects—you use a dark background, a light foreground color, and then specify in the blending modes drop-down on the Layers palette that the layer upon which you stroke is in Screen blending mode.

**Warning**

**Use the Paintbrush**    You *have* to choose the Paintbrush tool before you stroke a path. If you do not, the path stroking will be done with the Pencil tool at its default size, and you will *not* be happy with the results.

**6.** Press Ctrl(⌘)+A and then press Delete (Backspace). This freshens the layer so you can learn about more Shapes and paths. Press Ctrl(⌘)+D to deselect the marquee. Keep the window and Photoshop open.

**Figure 12.14**   You have brush dynamics to play with as you stroke a path.

There was a time when you had to remember all the fancy key modifiers to add to a selection, subtract from one, and so on. But with Photoshop 6, these *Boolean operations* (add, subtract, intersection, and so on) are only a click or two away. C'mon into the following section, and you'll see how to blend the shapes of paths.

## Getting Creative with Shape Intersections

It's funny; this author accidentally re-created the logo of a local grocery store—Sweetheart Market—by filling the non-overlapping areas of two hearts. The following steps are not meant to get you into copyright infringement, so use any shape you like from the Custom Shapes palette. Let's face it; you've been staring at a heart in these figures long enough. Now, what you will do next is learn how to apply fills using overlapping shapes as the outlines.

### Example 12.4   Filling Overlapping Shapes

1. Drag a shape on the image window. Immediately, four buttons appear on the far left of the Options bar. From left to right, they are Add, Subtract, Intersect, and Exclude Overlapping areas. Click the far right button *before* you make any shapes. Doing this sets the mode of creation in the image window.

2. Draw a second shape, about the same size as the first. The idea is to get the shapes to overlap. If they do not, choose the Select Path Component tool from the toolbox, and then click and drag the second shape so that it overlaps the first. Simply as a point of interest, a check button (called *Dismiss Target Path*) whose function is to hide a path appears on the Options palette (see Figure 12.15). We advise against using this button, because after you've hidden a path you have to visit the Paths palette and click the Work Path title to make the path visible again. So, because you have to go there anyway, you might as well use the Paths palette to hide and reveal the path.

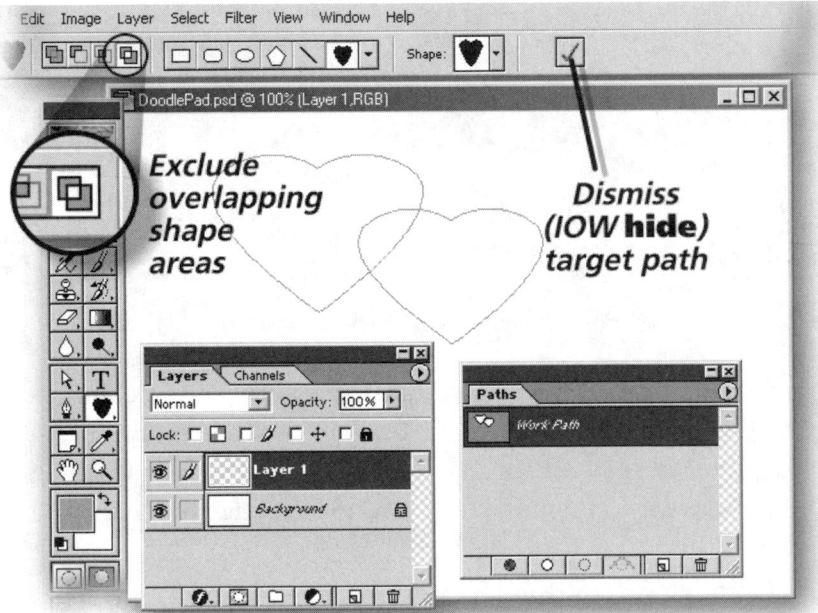

**Figure 12.15**    Choose the Exclude overlapping shape areas, and then create two shapes that overlap in the image window.

Don't be surprised if the paths themselves don't change. The Exclude overlapping shapes areas button applies only to selections and filling regions—the paths do not change in any way.

**Warning**

**Quick Duplication of Paths**    Do not hold down Alt(Opt) while you reposition a shape or you will leave behind a copy of the shape. This is a neat way to make multiple paths very quickly, but only when you *want* this feature, you know?

3. There are two ways to fill the non-overlapping areas now. One is to click on the Fills path with foreground color—and then you click the check button on the Options bar to *dismiss* the paths (hide the paths from view). The other way, which might intrigue you, is to Ctrl(⌘)+click on the Work Path title on the Paths palette (which simultaneously loads the paths as a selection and hides them). In Figure 12.16, the author didn't get too artsy on you. He simply filled the selection with foreground color. *But—you* can create a gradient within the selection, or even paste a Clipboard image into the selection. So the selection method of converting overlapping paths does have its advantages.

4. Clean off the layer so you can do more fun things in the next section. Keep the image window and Photoshop open.

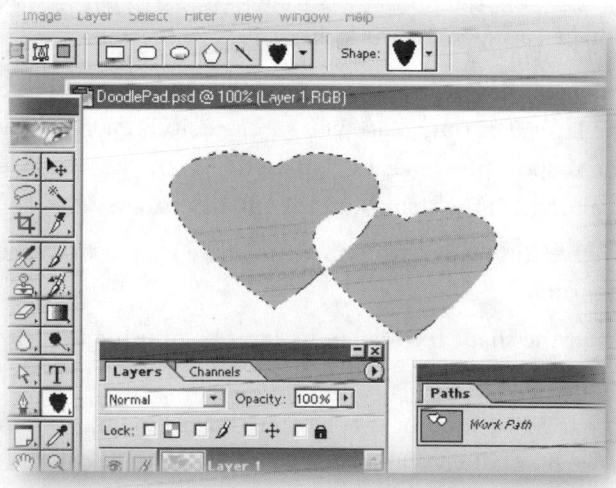

**Figure 12.16**   When shapes are placed in the image window while any of the Overlapping Shapes options buttons are pressed, you can create selections that can be filled, and *exclude* or *include* parts of the paths.

In the following section, you will work more extensively with fills for shapes, and we also have a gift for you. We designed a palette of extremely exotic shapes, and you'll work with them and also learn how to make a shape palette of your own.

## Using Someone Else's Custom Shapes

Photoshop was designed to be extensible from the ground up, so there is a provision in Photoshop for users to create their own palettes of shapes—or at least add to an existing collection of Photoshape shops.

We can see an immediate appeal for designers and ad agency people, not to mention Web people. Imagine capturing a company logo, being able to fill it with Photoshop Styles, and then reproduce the logo to almost any size you can imagine (more than four or five pixels, okay?).

Let's use the following section to get oriented and set up the grounds for some fireworks.

## Loading a Custom Palette and New Mode for Shapes

Admittedly, setting up the workspace is not as exciting as using a customized workspace, but bear with us for a step or two here.

We have not yet touched upon the third mode of the Shapes tool. This mode is called Create Shape Layer, and it works like this:

- When a shape is dragged, a new layer is created in the image, and a solid fill covers the layer. The only place you *see* the color, however, is where you've drawn the shape. This is like a Clipping Group in Photoshop, except that you're dealing with the shape and the fill as separate items.

- You can move the shape with either the Move tool or the Select Path Component tool.

- You can edit the shape to show more layer color using the Direct Selection tool.

- You can change the interior shape color at any time by flooding the layer with a new color. All you do is pick a new foreground color from the toolbox, and press Alt(Opt)+Delete (Backspace).

- You can use all the Add, Subtract, and so on buttons on the Options bar, and immediately see the results as you create overlapping shapes.

- You can turn this special layer into an ordinary layer, without paths, by choosing Layer, Rasterize Layer.

- You can add Styles to a shape on a clipping path layer.

Now do you understand that some serious graphics pyrotechnics are in store for us? Follow these steps:

### Example 12.5  Creating a New Palette and a New Shapes Mode

**1.** Carefully check out Figure 12.17, so you fully appreciate the differences between (#1) the Clipping Path layer shape tool, (#2) the Work Path mode for shapes, and (#3) the Filled Region mode for shapes. Click the button marked (1). Then click the down arrow next to the current Shape on the Options bar, click the flyout menu button, and choose Replace Shapes. In the dialog box, direct a path to the Examples/Chap12 folder on the Companion CD, and choose Icons.csh. As you can see in Figure 12.17, you have some seriously commercial shapes now.

Do not worry that you are actually overwriting the current shapes by choosing Replace Shapes. Adobe's choice of words here is misleading. Adobe-created shapes are hard-wired in Photoshop's code, so you cannot accidentally delete a palette from within Photoshop. What Replace Shapes *really* means is that you want a clean slate, and then you want your choice of palettes to appear.

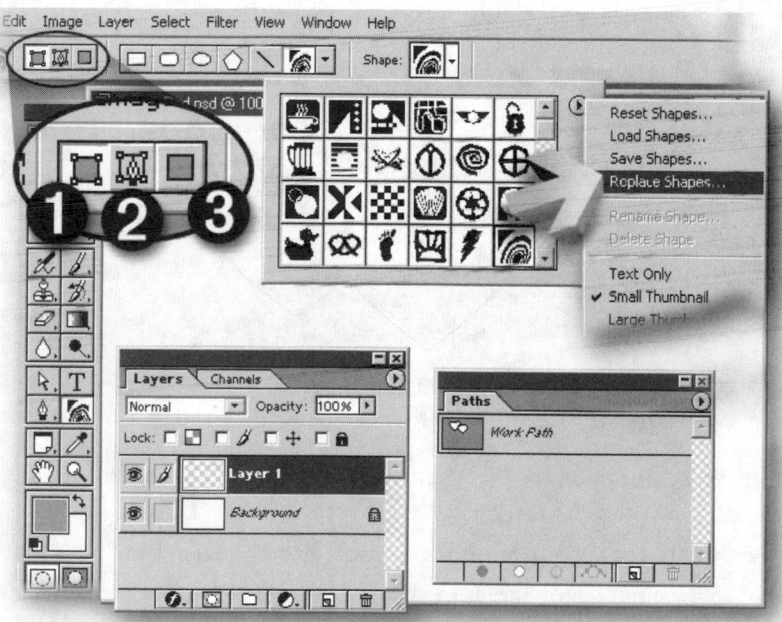

**Figure 12.17**  Icons.csh is a palette designed by the author, with an eye toward helping designers make up logos for clients. We give the use of this palette freely to our readers.

**2.** Look ahead to Figure 12.18, and see which Shape the author chose for the next few steps. It looks like a technology company logo, don't you think? Hold Shift to constrain proportions, and then drag the cursor until the Shape is about two screen-inches big.

There are two modes to the Options bar when the Shapes tool is chosen. You can toggle between them by clicking the clipping path thumbnail on the Layers palette (see Figure 12.18). In one mode, you have the addition and subtraction buttons for overlapping shapes you might add to the clipping path layer, and in the other mode, you have type of shape (Filled Region, Work Path, blah, blah) and the Styles drop-down list (see Figure 12.19). Don't worry here; we'll guide the exploration.

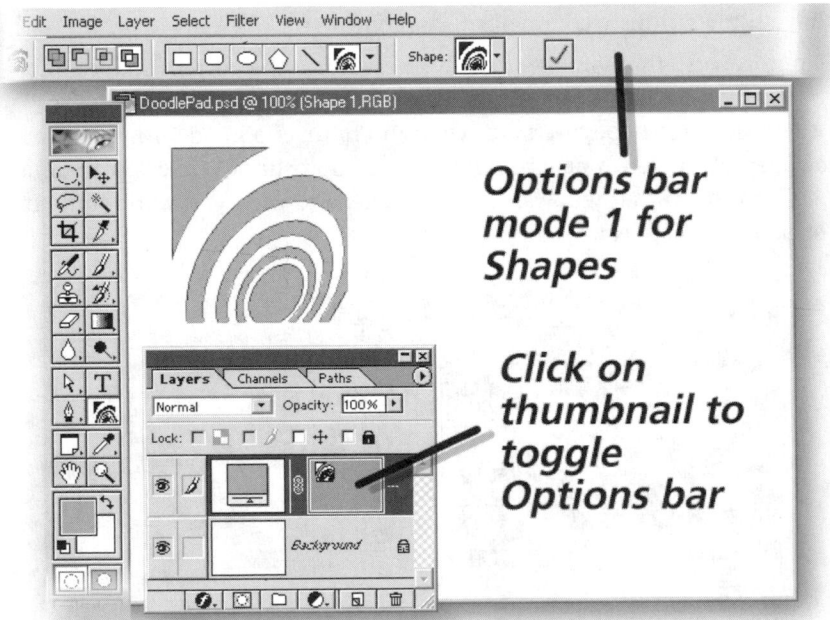

**Figure 12.18**    Clicking the thumbnail will toggle the Options bar from one useful set of options to another.

**3.** Click the thumbnail icon so that the Styles option appears on the Options bar, as shown in Figure 12.19.

**4.** Click the Layer Style icon on the Options bar to reveal the Styles palette.

The style called Color Target from the Buttons.asl palette was available, and we'll presume that this style made it to the shipping version of Photoshop 6. Click the flyout arrow on the Styles palette, choose Buttons.asl from the list, and then click OK to confirm the replacement. Drag the thumbnail of the style from the palette and drop it on the shape, as shown in Figure 12.20. As you can see, this looks like one impressive logo—easily worth thousands of dollars in your dreams <g>.

**Figure 12.19**   This is the alternate configuration for the Options bar.

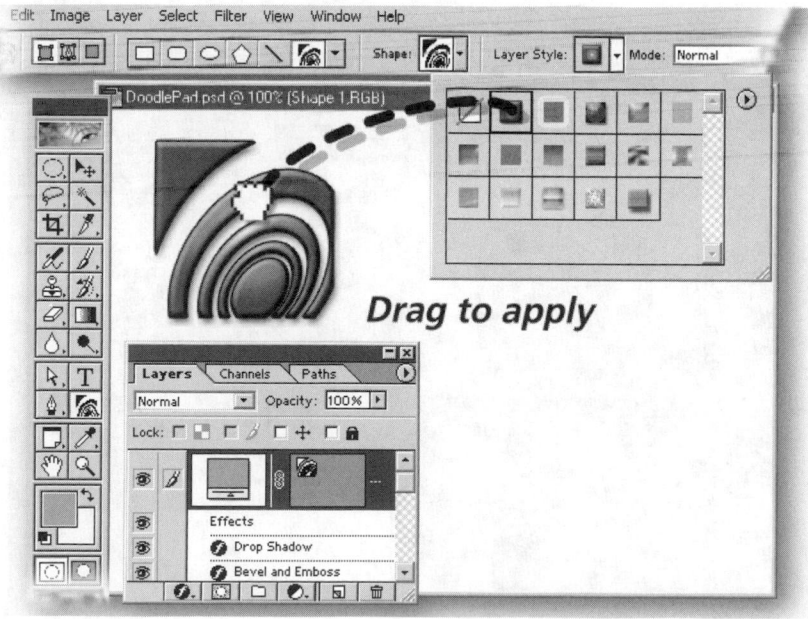

**Figure 12.20**   Add a Style to a Clipping Path layer, and you've got instant, embellished artwork.

By the way, although it might seem, logically, that the style would be applied to the entire layer, it is not. A style is applied to the center of a clipping path, so a clipping path layer can have many different shapes of the same style, all of which look the same, but each of which has had the style applied to it separately.

**Tip**

**Customizing a Style**   If you like most—but not all—aspects of a style, don't despair. By clicking the triangle next to the layer name on the Layers palette, you reveal all the layer effects that went into the Style. Then you can double-click the particular effect that annoys you, and alter it in the Layer Style dialog box.

5. Get out your best condensed, sans serif font (we're going to use Impact because Microsoft gave it away free with Explorer) and type **General Doodads, Inc.** to the right of the logo, stacked, as shown in Figure 12.21. Look carefully at the settings on the Character palette in Figure 12.21 for an idea of what the optimal settings might be for this assignment.

Also, keep in mind that during the split-second you clicked the Type tool, a new layer was created for text. So you are no longer working on the logo clipping path layer—the current active layer is the Type layer, marked by a capital T on the Layers palette.

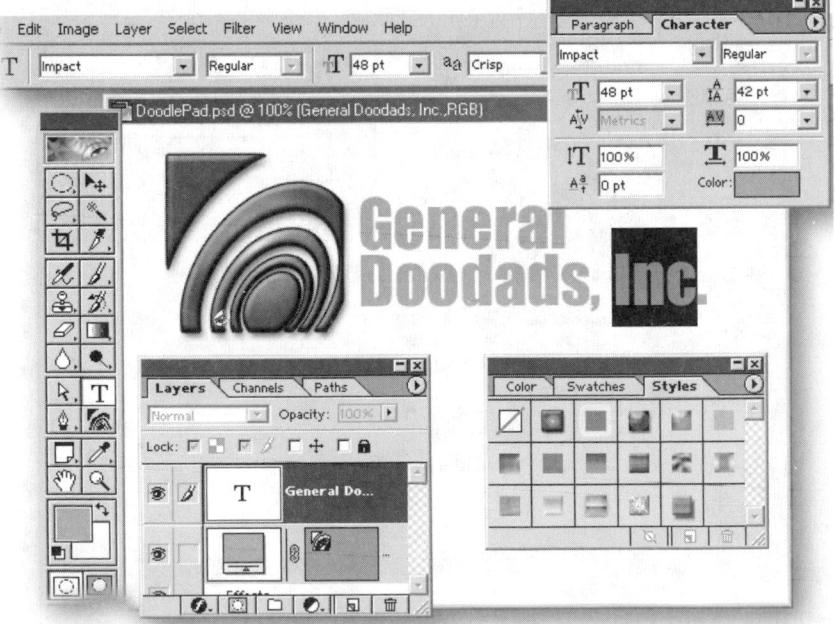

**Figure 12.21**   Add text to the logo to give it a strong, modern look.

6. Press F6, click the Styles palette tab, and then choose Text Effects.asl from the palette menu. Choose Chiseled Sky from the palette, and apply it to the text by clicking once on the thumbnail.

7. Most of this step is written into Figure 12.22, but here goes anyway. The Chiseled Sky is not right for the text because the text is against white. What you want to do is remove the Gradient Overlay component of the Chiseled Sky style; then the text will turn a solid blue, deeper than the blue in those popular acrylic leisure suits.

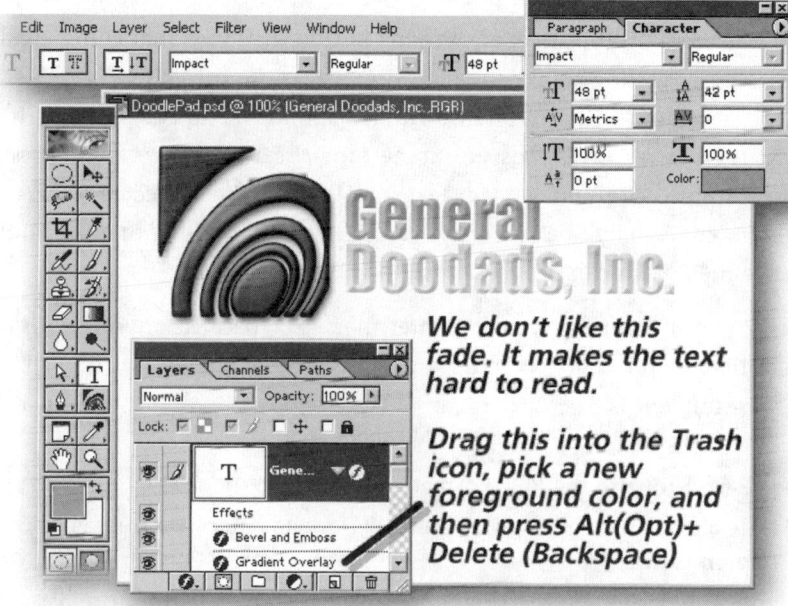

**Figure 12.22**  Trash the Color Overlay in this Chiseled Sky style and the text will be much easier to read.

8. Save your work as **GeneralDoodads, Inc.** to your hard disk, and keep it open in Photoshop. We have to talk about vectors and stuff before we export the design.

The best format for exporting this work is the Acrobat PDF style, and we'll tell you why in the following section.

## Exporting to the PDF Format: Agile with Bitmaps, Accurate with Vectors

The Adobe Acrobat format—commonly known as a Portable Document Format (PDF)—has been around for years. It wasn't until recently, however, that Adobe licensed applications from other vendors for a limited edition of the code that writes a PDF file. Adobe is trying to make PDF a standard, and they seem to be succeeding in the graphics and desktop publishing communities.

The next step toward universal appeal is to allow Photoshop 6 to write a PDF file, but not simply any type of PDF file. You see, a PDF file can contain text, vector graphics, and bitmap graphics. Now, with Photoshop 6, you can embed vector typefaces (99% of all digital fonts are vectors). So this means that you can send a Photoshop piece in PDF format to a commercial printer and the printed result will be smooth graphics and super-crisp text.

Actually, the word on the street at the time of this writing is that commercial press houses are really getting to like the PDF format because the code in the files is sort of like PostScript, but without the historic errors; that the houses prefer RGB images and make their own conversions; and something *else* important. Now, a press house with Photoshop 6 can edit any mistakes—colors can be corrected, layers can be made a different opacity, spelling errors can be fixed. Everything that the Photoshop PSD native file format can do, a Photoshop PDF file can do.

In a way, the PDF format is actually better than PSD, because anyone with Acrobat Reader (a free viewer) can see your work simply by exporting to the PDF format. Here's how simple it is.

### Example 12.6    Saving to the PDF Format

1. Create a piece of artwork. The General Doodads piece we were guiding you along on is fine.

2. Choose File, Save As, and then choose Photoshop PDF from the list of file formats.

   You'll now see a dialog box (see Figure 12.23).

3. The authors aren't big on the JPEG format when ZIP compression is available, so we recommend you choose the ZIP encoding option

4. Check Image Interpolation. This option ensures that the bitmaps in the PDF file will remain smooth in appearance when you zoom in and out of the document.

5. The Include Vector data setting should be checked if you have a Work Path, a clipping path layer—any design element that has anchors and path segments.

6. Check Embed Fonts. Now the font you use will not only be shown correctly in the document, but you will also be able to reopen the file in Photoshop 6 at any time in the future and change the font.

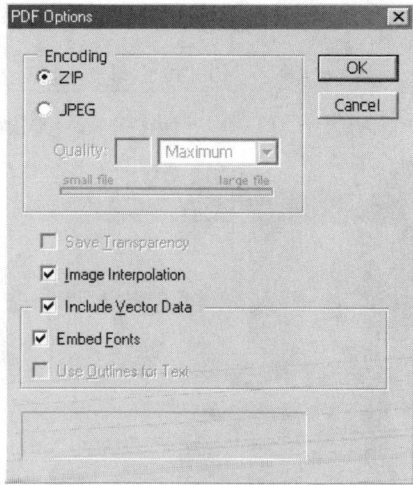

**Figure 12.23**   The choices are pretty clear, and the checklist is short for saving your work in Photoshop's PDF file format.

**7.** Click OK. Close the piece and then reopen it to see that the layers and text are still intact. Then, open the file in Acrobat Reader and see what you think of your presentation.

**Note**

**How to Avoid Pixelation**   We were working with an extremely small file compared to the files you might send to a commercial press. If you zoom into the General Doodads.PDF file, you'll start to notice the pixels that make up the bitmap part of the design.

The way to avoid the unwanted detection of pixels in the image is to create an image in Photoshop that is high resolution—at least 2MB–3MB in file size.

This will also make the saved file larger, naturally.

**Tip**

**There's PDF...and there's PDF**   We tried to open a Photoshop 6 PDF file in Illustrator 9, and were actually somewhat successful. There were layers, the typeface was wrong (we don't know which application failed us on that), and there were indeed anchors and path segments we could edit.

Perhaps by Illustrator 10, the two programs will work seamlessly together on the PDF file format. It seems only logical because the PDF format is a special version of PostScript, and Illustrator is 100% PostScript.

Let's take a quick look at the General Doodads piece in Acrobat Reader using 400% zoom. You'd expect to see pixels all over the place, right? Check out Figure 12.24.

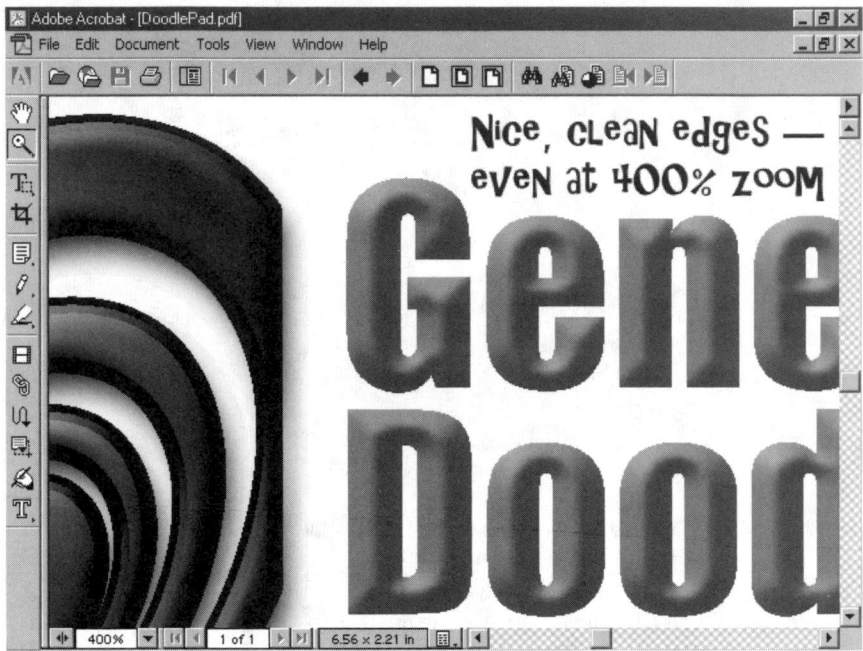

**Figure 12.24**   When a vector outline "traps" its fill, you see only clean edges in Acrobat Reader.

Then again, suppose you didn't read the previous section, exported to PDF, and did not check the Include Vector Data or the Embed Fonts options. At 400% viewing resolution, this PDF file would look like Figure 12.25—which looks like the best graphic you could produce on a personal computer in 1989.

Now let's take a brief look at a feature that can help you design your own logos.

## Using the Combine Feature

As mentioned earlier, you cannot use the Boolean buttons (Add, Subtract, and so on) to change the physical nature of overlapping paths; they affect only the way the overlapping paths are filled. Well, that's true enough, but Photoshop *does* have a special option that enables you to perform a path-changing operation on two or more vector paths when they overlap. It's called the Combine button.

This option is more useful now that we've made it sound (it's the same as Illustrator's Pathfinder functions and Xara's Combine Shapes options), so it's best if we walk through this one, step by step:

**Figure 12.25**  Severe pixellation is the result when you export a design to PDF format, and do not include vector or font information.

## Example 12.7   Creating a Logo Using Combined Shapes

1. Open a new image; it can be as small as 400 by 300 pixels, Color Mode, 72 pixels per inch. Make sure that Icons.csh is the Custom Shape palette in Photoshop. This file is in the Examples/Chap12 folder on the Companion CD.

2. Make sure that the Work Path icon button is clicked on the Options bar rather than on the clipping path layer. Choose the lightning bolt shape from the Icons.csh palette, and then press Enter (Return) to confirm your choice.

3. Hold Shift to constrain proportions, and then drag the lightning bolt shape until it is about three-quarters the height of the image window.

4. Click the Custom Shapes icon on the Options bar once more, choose the circle with a cross inside it, and then press Enter (Return).

5. Hold Shift and drag a shape that is about as large as a (US) quarter.

6. Choose the Path Component Selection tool, and then drag the circle shape to the top center of the lightning bolt so it overlaps the top of the lightning bolt. Next, with the circle at the top center of the lightning bolt marquee select both shapes, and then click the Add (shapes) button on the Options bar (see Figure 12.26).

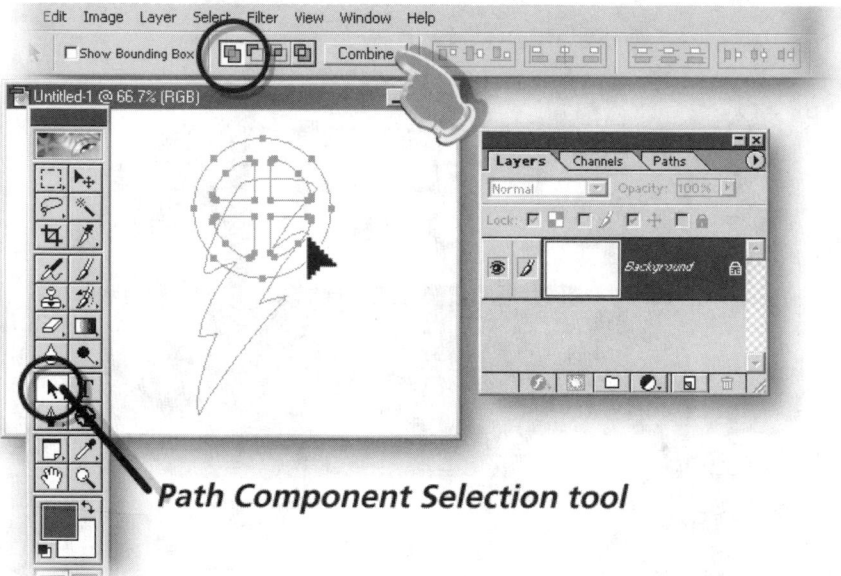

**Path Component Selection tool**

**Figure 12.26** Marquee select overlapping shapes with the Path Component Selection tool, choose a combination mode, and then click Combine.

7. Click Combine on the Options bar, as shown in Figure 12.26. This figure doesn't show the result of this step, which is the combined shape.

8. Now, if you'd like to be known as a Jiffy Graphics House, it's not hard to put a coat of paint on the combined paths. Press F6, click the Styles tab, and then click the Styles menu button. Choose Styles.asl from the list of styles.

9. Click the Create new layer icon at the bottom of the Layers palette (F7), pick a nice light purple on the toolbox for the foreground color, and then, on the Paths palette, click the Fills path with foreground color icon at the bottom left of the palette.

10. Now, click the Floating Plastic Style (on the Styles.asl palette), or drag the icon and drop it on the design, as shown in Figure 12.27. By the way, and this is not obvious, any style that is shown as a gray icon will not add a color to the shape you drop it onto. The foreground color of the shape will remain the same color.

11. You can close the image without saving at any time. Point made. Keep Photoshop running.

Okay, you've played with the authors' Shapes, and you've used Photoshop's Shapes. Now it's time to learn how to create your own Custom Shapes.

**Figure 12.27**   Instant art! All you need is to combine two or more interesting shapes and then fill them with an interesting Style.

## Creating Your Own Preset Shapes

The process of creating your own Custom shapes palette is not difficult. Probably the hardest thing is deciding what you want on the palette. Is there a theme? Do you decide based on the frequency of shapes you'll use? Is the palette solely for keeping your clients' logos?

These questions you'll have to answer for yourself, but as for the mechanics of making your own Shapes palette, it isn't hard. This one sentence sums up the process:

*A Custom Shapes palette begins with a single design.*

Regardless of whether you own Illustrator, it is an excellent idea to become proficient with the Pen tools. We've devoted some quality space to the operation of the tools in this book, and you should practice when time allows. The Pen tool isn't just for making templates for selections or fills—it's what you use to design Shapes.

Candidly, the author feels more at home working on vector designs in Illustrator than in Photoshop. You don't *have* to use Illustrator to make custom shapes, but it doesn't hurt. A good alternative is to use whatever means you prefer—scanning, painting, whatever—to bring a design into Photoshop, and then carefully trace around the design using the Pen tools.

Unfortunately, the only gateway between Illustrator and Photoshop at the moment is the Clipboard. No other drawing program can put PostScript on the Clipboard, and an Illustrator-generated PDF file is read into Photoshop as a pixel-based document—no vector information.

So there is our short history on PDF files and Photoshop vector information. Now let's begin a new Custom Shapes palette.

### Example 12.8   Creating Your Own Custom Shapes

1. Begin by designing something. Why not use Photoshop and the Pen tools? Then, having created a design, sit tight while we explain what to do in Illustrator. Shortly, we'll show you how to transport designs from Illustrator to Photoshop.

2. If you designed something in Illustrator, take notes on how large the design is, press Ctrl(⌘)+A to Select All, and then press Ctrl(⌘)+C to copy the design to the Clipboard, as shown in Figure 12.28.

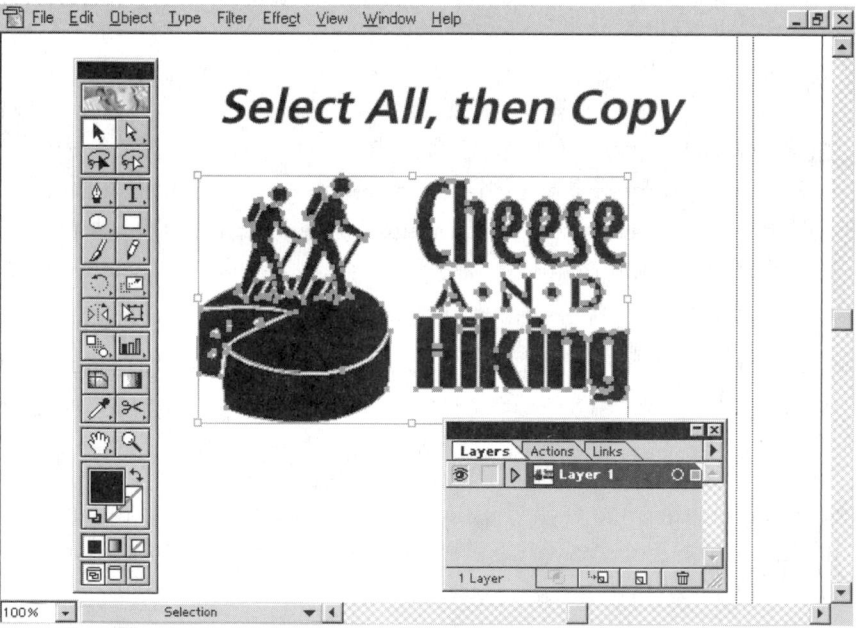

**Figure 12.28**   Choosing a black fill will help you visualize your Illustrator design, but Photoshop shapes consist of vector outlines only.

3. If you're an Illustrator user, you can close Illustrator now, open Photoshop, and press Ctrl(⌘)+V. The Paste dialog box appears, as shown in Figure 12.29. Choose the Paste As: Path option, and then click OK.

4. Okay, Illustrator users and folks who've designed something in Photoshop are on equal ground now. Choose Edit, Preset Manager; choose Custom Shapes, choose Load, and then load the Blank.csh file from the Examples/Chap12 folder on the Companion CD. This is an empty Shapes palette with one starter shape you can delete at any time.

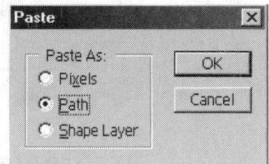

**Figure 12.29**
Photoshop understands what's on the Clipboard. If it's vector PostScript, Photoshop offers three different choices as to how the data is imported.

5. Make sure that the image window contains only paths that you want because this step will add everything that's a vector from the window onto a slot in the Blank.csh Custom Shapes palette. Choose Edit, Define Custom Shape, as shown in Figure 12.30.

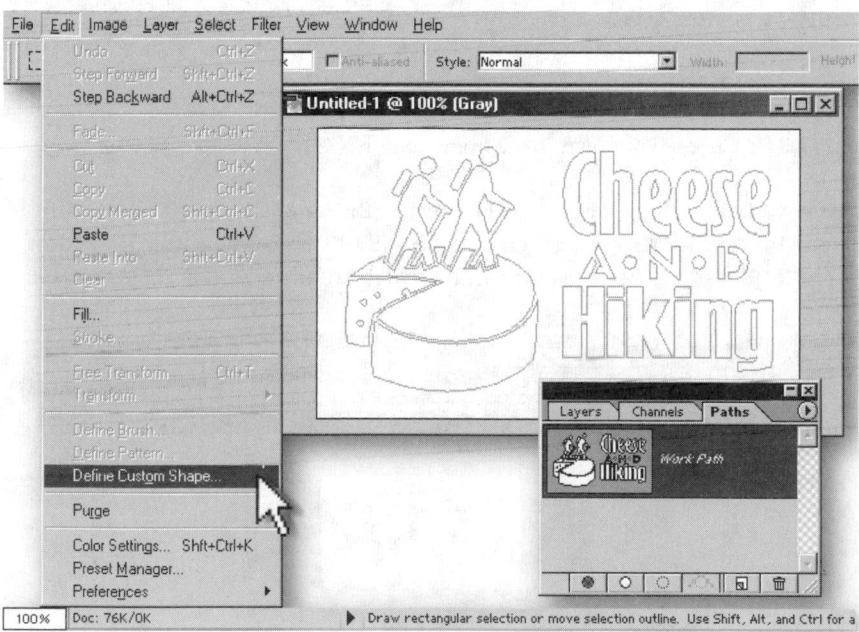

**Figure 12.30**   Make sure only those vectors you want are on the image window, and that everything is the way you want it, before you define a Custom Shape.

6. In the Shape Name dialog box, type the name of the shape you're saving to the Blank.csh palette (you can rename this palette at any time, from within Photoshop or from a directory window).

7. Finally, check out the Custom Shape you made. Choose the Custom Shape tool, click the Create a new shape layer button on the Options palette, and choose your design from the palette on the Options bar's flyout, as shown in Figure 12.31.

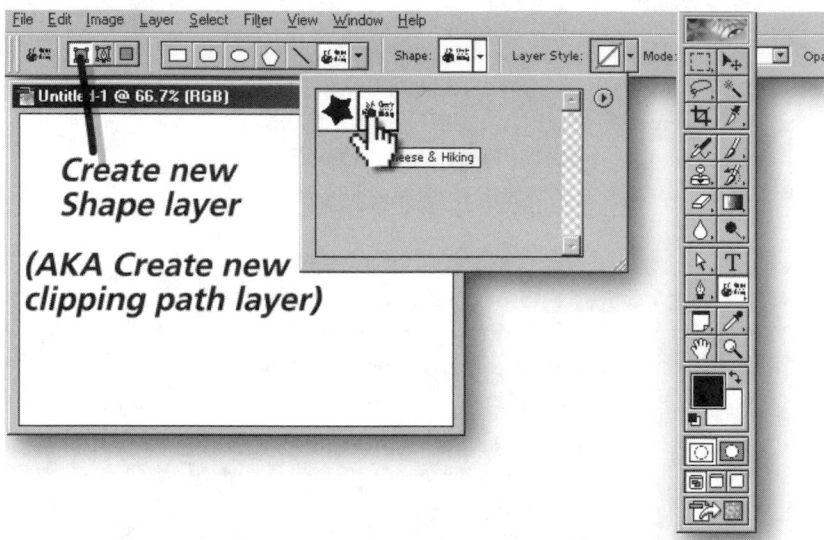

**Figure 12.31**   Choose your own shape from your own Custom Shapes palette.

8. Have a ball! As you can see in Figure 12.32, the author held down Shift to constrain proportions, and created his client's logo in an image window. These shapes are vectors and can be scaled to any size you need.

**Figure 12.32**   Get yourself a better client than ours, and make your client's logo part of your own Custom Shapes palette.

Let's not forget *physical* shape in our quest for knowledge about Photoshop's shapes! After writing this, the author has a strange craving to mow the backyard and flex and sprain a muscle or two! It's good to take regular breaks from your hunched-over Power User position, you know!

## Summary

Shapes come in three types: Filled region, plain Work Path vectors, and clipping path layers (again, a vector type of graphic). You have editing control of a shape you lay down on an image window, you can recolor a shape's interior, and do much more. But the point you should take away from this chapter is that Photoshop Shapes are there to reduce the amount of manual labor you would otherwise have to perform if you needed the same shape at different sizes.

Oh, yes. The PDF file format is the perfect home for designs that feature shapes because a PDF file will retain the vector information from Shapes.

In Chapter 13, you'll get more experience with Photoshop's advanced type controls, and you'll see how to use Photoshop as a desktop publishing program.

# Chapter 13

# Creating Special Effects with Type

When it comes to working with text, regardless of what program you are using, there are two major distinctions that I can't stress enough:

- **Text as a graphic.** This occurs when the text is rasterized or converted to a pixel representation of text. In other words, you see the image as text, and I see the image as text, but as far as your computer is concerned, it's just another graphic and that's how the computer treats it. The text editing capabilities are no longer available—so make sure there are no spelling errors before you make the choice to convert text into a graphic.

- **Text as (editable) text.** This kind of text is—well, editable. Photoshop now offers vector text capabilities. This gives you the option to scale text smoothly to any size without losing clarity. Other options available are kerning and leading, to name a few, similar to programs such as InDesign and PageMaker.

There will be certain times when you will need to convert text from editable text into graphic or rasterized text. You may be asking yourself, "Why would I ever want text as a graphic when I lose the ability to edit it?" Unfortunately, there are many situations where you will have to make that trade-off. For example, Photoshop will not allow filters to be applied to text until it has become rasterized. You will find a few examples in this chapter where the text on the layer is a graphic. The ability to edit the text is no longer an option.

**Tip**

**Before You Rasterize Text**   It helps to keep the original text layer. There may be many reasons for having this layer available; therefore, make a copy of your text layer by dragging it to the Create a new layer icon on the Layers palette. Turn off the visibility icon for the original Text layer, and then click on the Text copy layer, and choose Layer, Rasterize, Type. If you need to return to the file months later to see which font was used for a specific project, you still have access to this information (through the original Text layer).

## Examining Type Modes

When the Text tool is active, Photoshop gives you two ways to enter text:

- **Create a Text Layer.** With this option selected, text entered in a document is stored on a new type layer. The new layer is automatically generated for you when text is entered in the document window. You can edit the text at any time, using the Text tool and this layer.

- **Create a Mask or Selection.** Sometimes referred to as a *type mask*. This option will create a selection border in the shape of text. The type selection will appear on the active layer (not a separate type layer) and can be copied, moved, filled, or stroked just like any other selection created in Photoshop.

With either of the two type modes there is the option to enter (or orient) the text horizontally or vertically (see Figure 13.1).

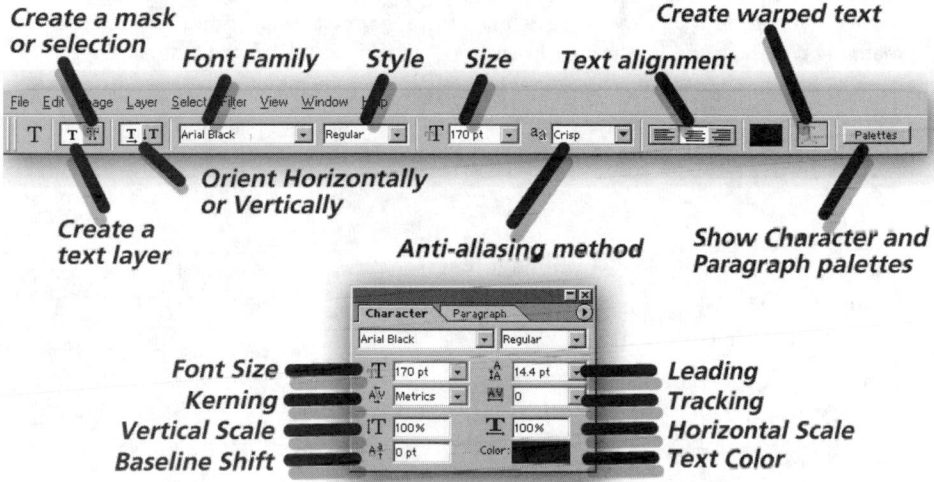

**Figure 13.1**   Overview of the Text tool options available on the Options bar and the Character palette.

# Text Effects

There are a few goals I would like to focus on in the sections to follow. One goal is to help familiarize you with Photoshop's new text features. The other goal is to help you think of text graphically. This is not to be confused with the previous discussion that distinguishes "editable text" from "text as a graphic"(although this is important too)—but rather to think about how text can enhance a design. The fonts, along with colors and effects that we choose are all a part of using text on an artistic level to help enhance a design. Text is not only used to communicate a message, but also can help set a mood and compliment the overall look and appeal of your work.

## Metal Text Effect

One of my favorite text tricks is to give text a metallic look. Not just any metallic look, but one that reflects the color of the image into which the text is placed. I like

to think of Photoshop tricks that achieve certain effects as recipes. This first example shows you one of my favorite recipes.

> **Note**
>
> **Font Substitution for Examples**   The fonts used in this chapter's examples are
> mentioned by name. If you do not have these fonts installed on your computer, you may
> substitute a similar font. When you substitute a font, however, be aware that an adjust-
> ment may be necessary to the suggested point size, tracking, or any other font options
> mentioned in the example. The adjustments needed will depend on the font chosen.
>
> If you prefer to use the same text as that shown in the examples, you may skip any steps
> that refer to the Text tool and use the files that are provided for you on the Companion
> CD. The file to use will also be mentioned in the examples.

### Example 13.1    Creating Reflective Metal Text

> **Warning!**   If an error message appears when you open the CD files, press Ctrl(⌘)+Shift+K and then choose Adobe RGB (1998) from the Working Spaces, RGB drop-down list. See Chapter 3 for more information.

1. Open BkgrdColor.tif in the Examples/Chap13 folder on the Companion CD.

2. On the Layers palette, make a copy of the Background layer by dragging the layer to the Create a new layer icon at the bottom of the palette (see Figure 13.2).

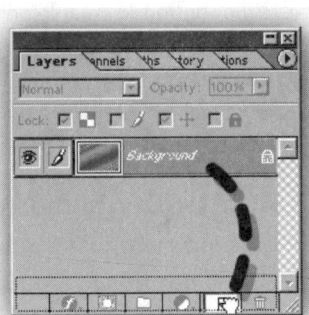

**Figure 13.2**   Make a copy of the Background layer.

The Brush Script font is used for the next step. Similar fonts include Gallante, Kaufman Bold, Brody (from CorelDRAW), or Brushwood. If you would prefer to skip step 3 and use the font provided on the Companion CD, then open the Greetings.psd file from the Examples/Chap13 folder. Drag the Greetings layer into the BkgrdColor.tif document window (holding down the Shift key as you drag to center the text in the document).

3. Press T to switch to the Text tool. On the Options bar, click the Color tab and choose a purple color; R:152, G:46, B:144. Click OK. Click the Left align text icon, and then click the Palettes button. In the Character palette, the

Brush Script font was chosen with a point size of **48** and tracking set to **25**. Click near the left edge of the document, and type **Greetings**. If this font is not available and you would like to substitute a similar font, the point size and tracking may need to be adjusted to meet the needs of the font chosen. Highlight the word you just typed and adjust the numbers. When you're satisfied with the results, click the Commit any current edits button at the right of the Options bar (see Figure 13.3).

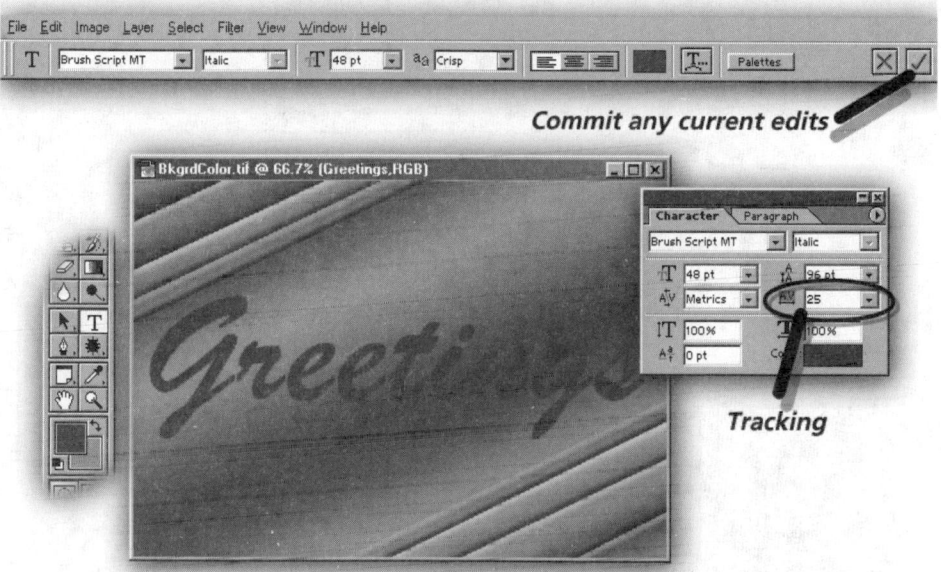

**Figure 13.3**    Set the text and font options using the Options bar and palettes. The checkmark button at the right of the Options bar will commit any current edits.

4. Press Ctrl(⌘)+T to access the Transform tool. On the Options bar, click in the Rotate box and type **–26.7**. Click inside the Transform box and drag to center the text, if necessary (see Figure 13.4). Then click the Commit transform button at the right of the Options bar.

5. Ctrl(⌘)+click on the Greetings layer to load the text as a selection. Click the Channels tab (or choose Window, Show Channels) to view the Channels palette. Click the Save selection as channel icon at the bottom of the palette (see Figure 13.5). Press Ctrl(⌘)+D to deselect the text.

6. Click on the newly created Alpha 1 channel to make it active, and then choose Filter, Blur, Gaussian Blur. In the Gaussian Blur dialog box type **1** (pixels) for the Radius. Click OK.

   The blur that you apply to the Alpha 1 channel will determine the bevel effect for the next steps. A higher Radius number can be used, but typically a Radius of 1 will produce a nice effect.

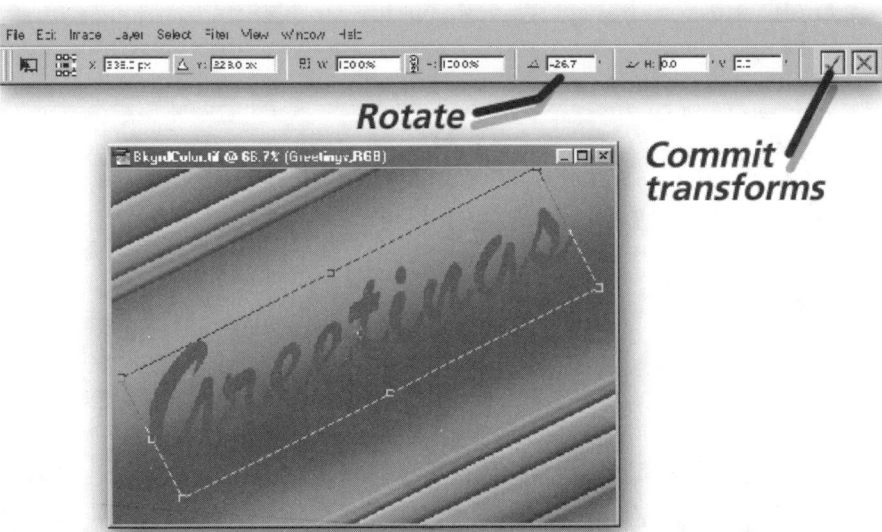

**Figure 13.4**    Use the Transform options to rotate text and center it within the design.

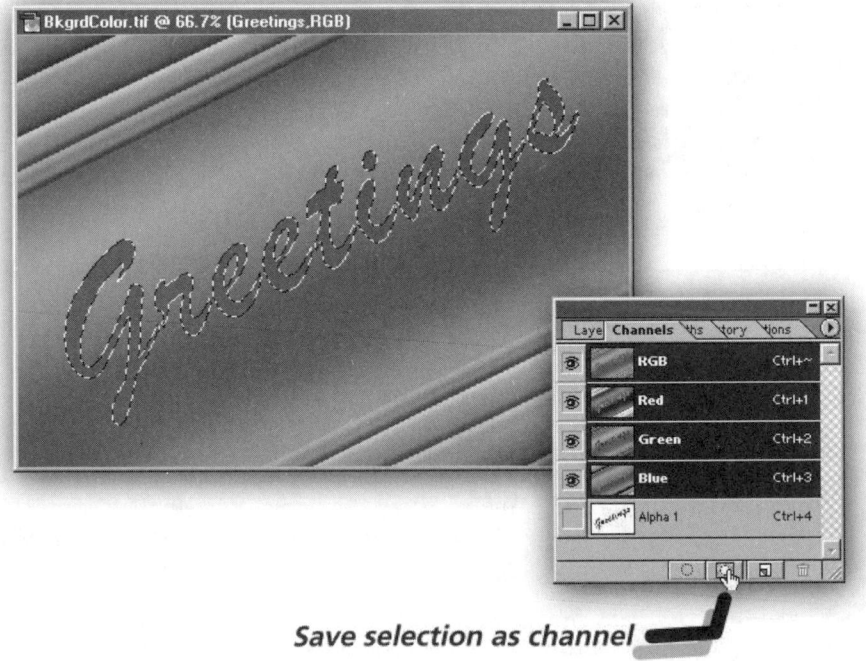

**Figure 13.5**    Load the text as a selection and save the selection as a channel.

7. Click the Layers tab to return to the Layers palette. Click on the Background copy layer to make this the active layer. Click the eye (visibility) icon to the left of the Greetings layer to turn this layer off.

8. Choose Filter, Render, Lighting Effects. In the Lighting Effects dialog box, choose Alpha 1 from the Texture Channel drop-down list. Click on the Spotlight points in the preview window and drag the lighting direction and side points until the lighting effects for the Greeting text appear satisfactory (see Figure 13.6). Click OK.

The default Spotlight in the Lighting Effects dialog box opens with the light source at the bottom-right corner of the preview window. My first instinct is to drag this light direction to the upper-right side, because this direction is consistent with my other instinct to move drop shadows down and to the right.

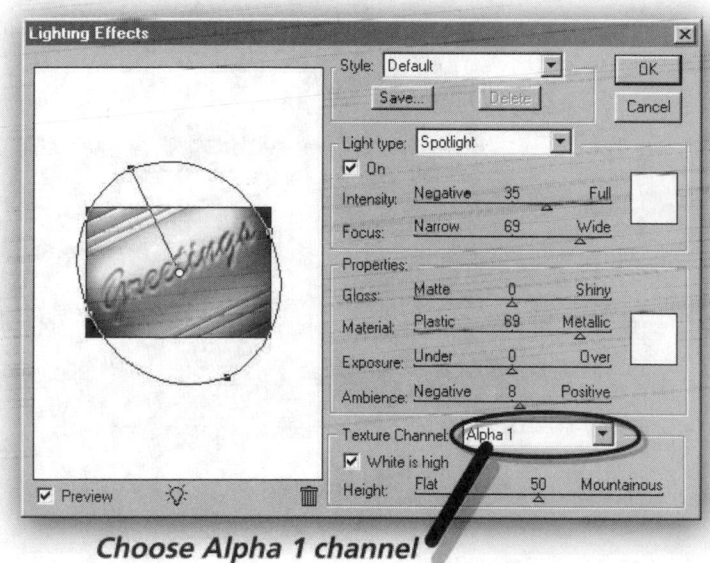

**Choose Alpha 1 channel**

**Figure 13.6**    With Alpha 1 chosen as the Texture Channel, adjust the lighting in the preview window of the dialog box.

The next step involves the Curves dialog box and can be tricky. If you have trouble getting the desired results the first time, you can press the Alt(Opt) key to change the Cancel button in the dialog box to a Reset button. Therefore, if you need to start from scratch, Alt(Opt)+click the Reset button.

9. Press Ctrl(⌘)+M to open the Curves dialog box. The dialog box opens with a diagonal line on the main grid. Starting on the first vertical grid line near the left side, click on the diagonal line to create a point. Drag and move this point up. Click a second point on the curve line, slightly to the right of the

first point created. Drag this point down. Click again to create a third point on the curve line (slightly to the right of the second point). Drag this third point up. Make a fourth point (to the right of the third point you made) and drag the point down. The curved line should look like the one in Figure 13.7. The goal is to watch the text in the document window and adjust the curve points created until the text shows a pleasant array of colors, in addition to a shiny metal texture.

Whoa! The colors on the background look pretty funky, too. Don't let this worry you. Just concentrate on the way the colors appear on the text. The next steps show how to eliminate the funky background.

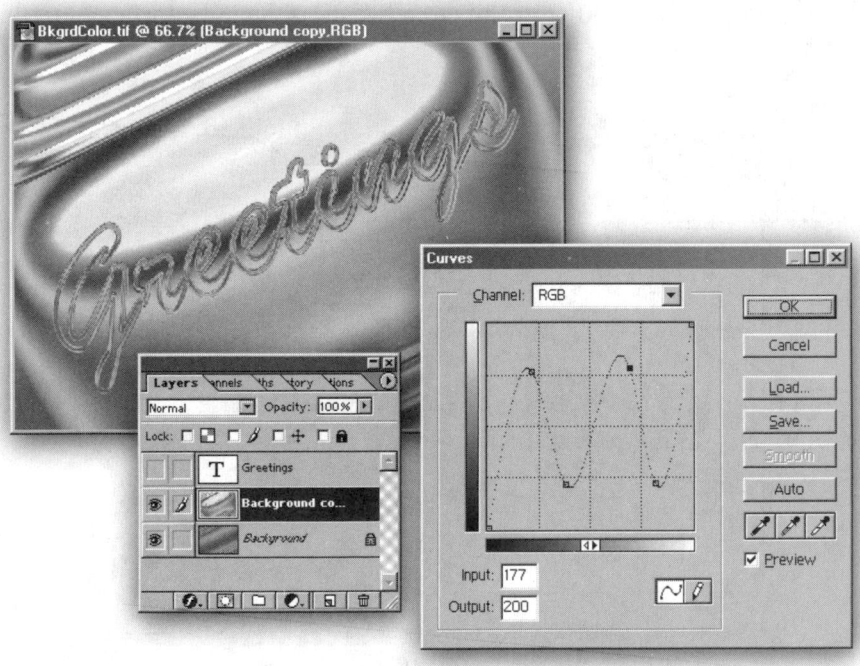

**Figure 13.7**   Adjust the diagonal line in the Curves dialog box to make it resemble the curved lines shown in this figure. Watch the text in the document to get a desired effect.

We will need to select the text on the Background copy layer. We will use the Greetings layer to make a text selection. The filters, however, have increased the size of the text. The selection is too small. Here's how to fix the text selection so it's the necessary size.

**10.** Ctrl(⌘)+click on the Greetings layer to load the text as a selection. Choose Select, Modify, Expand. In the Expand Selection dialog box, type **3** (pixels) as the amount to Expand By (see Figure 13.8). Click OK.

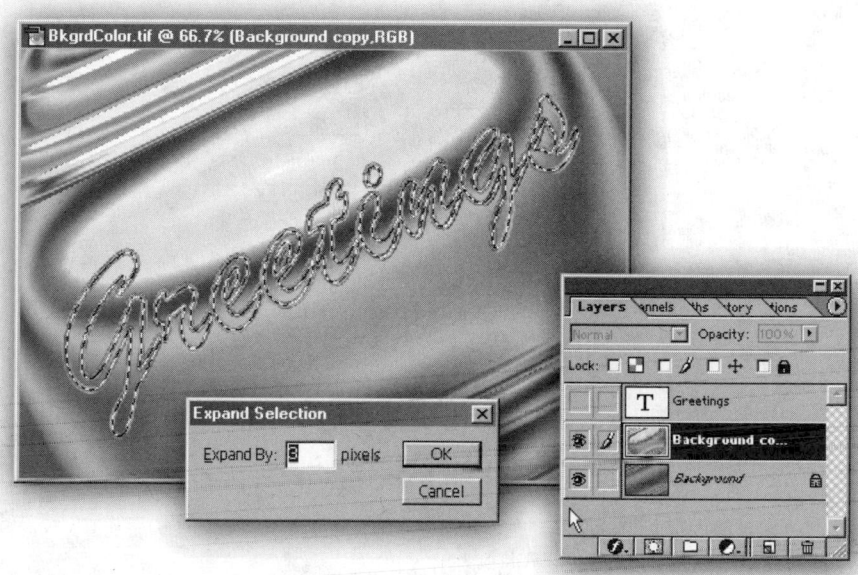

**Figure 13.8**  Expand the selection by three pixels.

When you're applying these steps to a project of your own, it may be necessary to play with the Expand By number to fit your needs. You will not be able to see if the Expand By number is correct until you click OK and apply the Expand Selection. If you expand the selection and the pixel amount is not correct, press Ctrl(⌘)+Z to undo the last command, and then try again with a different pixel amount.

11. Press Ctrl(⌘)+Shift+I to invert the selection. With the Background copy layer still active, press the Delete (Backspace) key to clear the selection. Press Ctrl(⌘)+D to deselect.

    The text, of course, is missing a drop shadow.

12. Click the Add a layer style icon at the bottom of the Layers palette, and choose Drop Shadow. In the Layer Style (Drop Shadow) dialog box type **65%** for Opacity, **123** for Angle, **10** for Distance, and **12** for Size (see Figure 13.9). Click OK.

    The previous filters we applied gave the text a slight blurry appearance. The Unsharp Mask is a perfect filter to fix this. Again, the settings chosen are not written in stone. They were determined by experimenting, which as you may have guessed by now, is always encouraged.

13. Choose Filter, Sharpen, Unsharp Mask. In the Unsharp Mask dialog box, type **87%** for Amount, **1.7** for Radius, and **4** for Threshold (see Figure 13.10). Click OK.

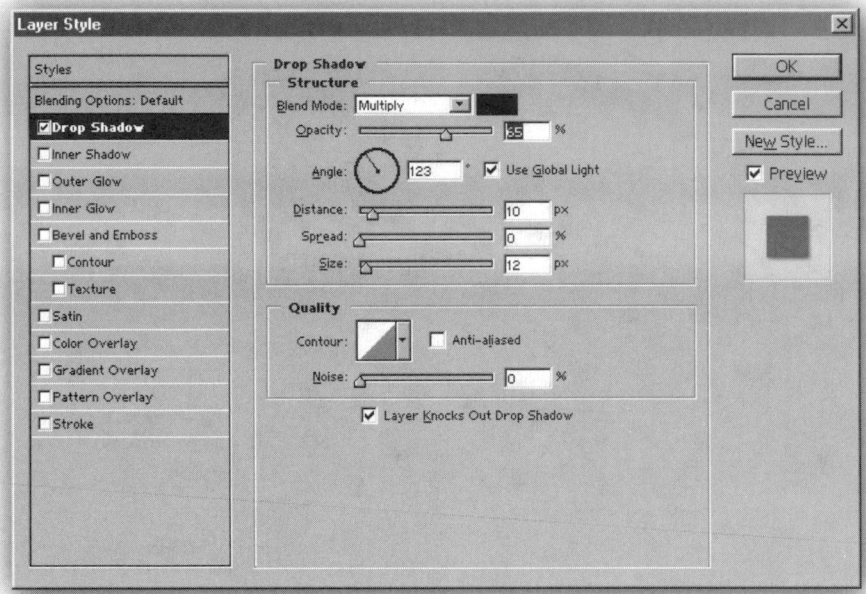

**Figure 13.9**    Add a drop shadow to the text using the settings shown in the figure.

**Figure 13.10**    Add clarity to the text by using the settings shown in the figure for the Unsharp Mask.

At the beginning of this example, were you wondering why a purple color was chosen for the Greetings text layer? When you're working with this effect, you can use the color of the original text layer to add different tones to the shiny look. All that's needed is an interesting color combined with the right layer mode and opacity. Experimenting with the text color along with the layer modes and opacity can add to the fun of a project like this.

14. Click on the Greetings layer to make it the active layer (and to turn on the visibility). On the Layers palette, change the Opacity to 50%. Experiment with different layer modes to see which one you like best. For this example, I have chosen Color Dodge, as shown in Figure 13.11. (Other choices that seem to work well are Screen and Hue.)

**Figure 13.11**    Change the Opacity and Layer Mode of the Greetings layer to add extra pizzazz to the text.

The following steps are optional; they are included here to show how you can easily add a few sparkles of reflective light to the text, if you want to. Photoshop ships with additional brushes. We will use one of the brushes from the Assorted brush file.

15. Alt(Opt)+click the Create a new layer icon at the bottom of the Layers palette. In the New Layer dialog box, type **Sparkles** for the Name. Click OK.

16. Press J to switch to the Airbrush tool. On the Options bar, set Pressure to 60%. Click the drop-down arrow to view the Brush palette. Click the arrow

in the upper-right corner of the palette for the drop-down list of palette options, and choose Load Brushes. In the Load dialog box, navigate to the Brushes folder and double-click on the Assorted Brushes.abr file to load it. Scroll down to view the brushes, and choose the Crosshatch 4 brush shown in Figure 13.12.

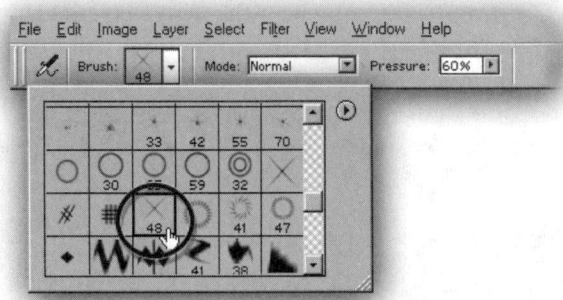

**Figure 13.12**    Choose the Crosshatch 4 brush and set Pressure to 60%.

17. Press D for the default colors. Press X to switch white to the foreground. With the Sparkle layer still active, click once at spots where the light seems to hit the text. The goal is to make a sparkle where it seems natural for light to reflect one.

18. Change the Pressure on the Options bar to **40%**. Click on the Brush drop-down menu, and choose the Soft Round 27-pixel brush. Position the brush over the previous (Crosshatch) brush strokes, and click once near the center of each crosshatch (see Figure 13.13). Press Ctrl(⌘)+Shift+S to save the file.

This example used a Background layer with lots of color. The color on this layer provided an interesting reflective quality when the Lighting Effects filter and the Curves dialog box were applied to it. However, this recipe also works really well with a solid white background layer. A white background will provide a silvery metal effect. Again, combine this silvery effect with a color version of your object on a separate layer (a navy-blue color, for example). Then, lower the opacity for that layer and try out different layer modes. The result can be quite stunning and realistic.

As mentioned in previous chapters, these steps do not need to be limited to text only. This effect can also be applied to clip art images, logo shapes, or anything else you might imagine.

**Figure 13.13**   Add hints of sparkles to the text easily by using the right brushes.

## Grouping an Image with Text

This next example is a text trick that is frequently used in advertisements. By grouping an image with the text, you see the image in the text itself. This trick also gives you the advantage of moving the text around to locate the perfect spot for the text and image to reside together—in other words, the spot that lets you see just the right portion of the image in the text.

### Example 13.2   Using Text Layers to Group an Image with Text

1. Open Sunset.tif in the Examples/Chap13 folder on the Companion CD. Press D for the default colors.

   The next step uses the Gill Sans Ultra Bold Condensed font. Any thick font—Arial Black and Impact are two examples—will work. If you prefer to skip step 2 and use the font provided on the Companion CD, then open the SunsetText.psd file from the Examples/Chap13 folder. Drag the SUNSET layer into the Sunset.tif document window (holding down the Shift key while dragging, to center the text in the document).

2. Press T to switch to the Text tool. Click the Left align text icon on the Options bar. Click the Palettes button. In the Character palette, choose the font Gill Sans Ultra Bold Condensed with a point size of **60** and tracking set to **25** (see Figure 13.14). Click near the left edge of the document window and type (all capital letters) **SUNSET**. If this font is not available and you want to substitute a similar font, the point size and tracking may need to be adjusted to suit the font you choose. Highlight the word you just typed, and adjust the numbers. When you're satisfied with the results, click the Commit any current edits button on the right of the Options bar.

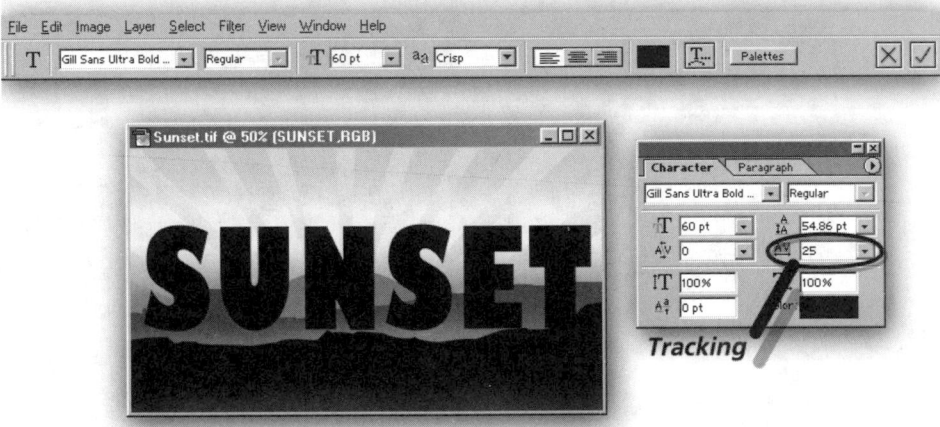

**Figure 13.14**    Use the Options bar and palettes to adjust text size and tracking. Click the Commit any current edits button when finished making changes.

Let's add a bevel and drop shadow to the text.

3. Click the Add a layer style icon at the bottom of the Layers palette, and choose Bevel and Emboss. In the Layer Style dialog box, choose Inner Bevel as the Style. Make sure the Use Global Light option is not checked. Set Depth at **100%**, Size at **8** (px), Angle **120°**, Altitude **22°**, Highlight Mode Opacity at **100%**, and Shadow Mode Opacity at **100%** (see Figure 13.15).

4. Click the Drop Shadow option on the left side of the Layer Style dialog box to add a drop shadow. Make sure that the Use Global Light option is not checked, and set Opacity at **75%**, Angle **120°**, Distance **9** (px), and Size **12** (px) (see Figure 13.16). Click OK.

5. On the Layers palette, drag the Background layer to the Create a new layer icon at the bottom of the palette to make a copy of this layer. Drag the Background copy layer above the SUNSET text layer. Press Ctrl(⌘)+G to group the Background copy layer with the text layer below (see Figure 13.17).

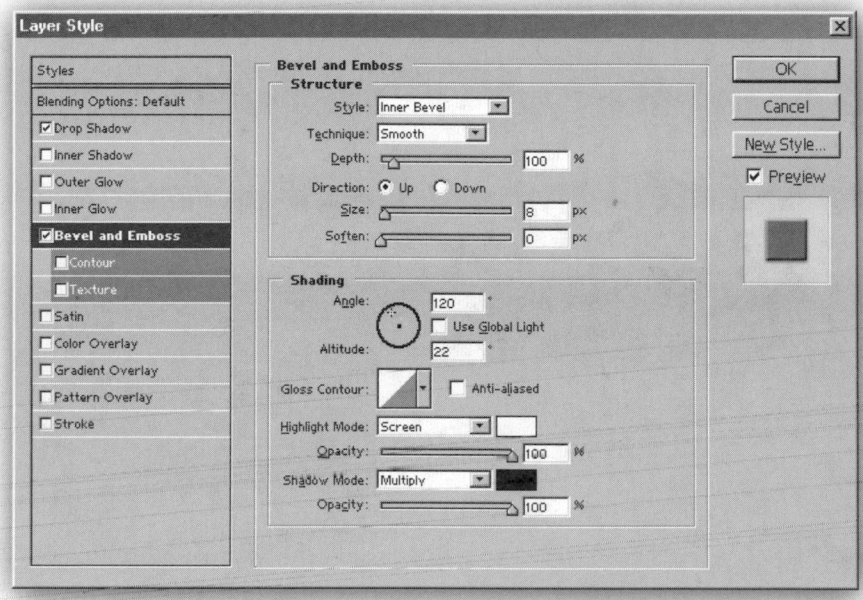

**Figure 13.15**    Use the settings shown in the figure to apply a bevel effect to the SUNSET text layer.

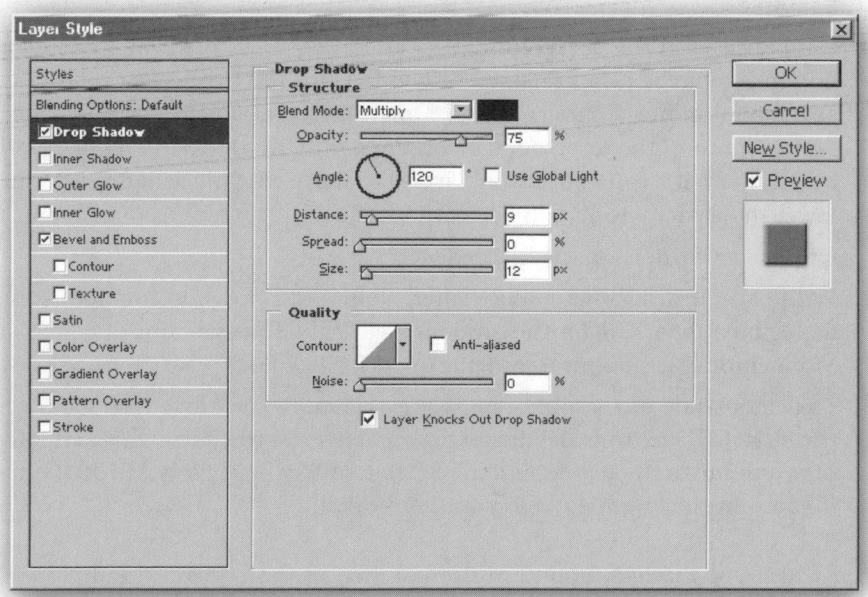

**Figure 13.16**    Use the settings shown in the figure to add a drop shadow to the SUNSET text layer.

**Figure 13.17**    Group the Background copy layer with the SUNSET text.

Now that the image is grouped, there are tons of possibilities for other effects. What are they? Let's play with the original Background layer to give a sample.

6. Double-click on the Background layer and click OK in the New Layer dialog box to accept the default name of Layer 0. Click the Create a new layer icon at the bottom of the Layers palette. Drag this layer below Layer 0. Press X to switch white to the foreground color. Press Alt(Opt)+Delete (Backspace) to fill Layer 1 with white. Click on Layer 0 to make this the active layer, and lower the Opacity to **75%** (see Figure 13.18).

Or play with filters to add extra effects.

7. With Layer 0 still active, choose Filter, Noise, Add Noise. In the Add Noise dialog box, type **12%** for the Amount. Select the Gaussian and Monochromatic options (see Figure 13.19). Click OK.

8. To demonstrate one last idea, press V to switch to the Move tool. Click on the SUNSET layer to make the text layer active. In the document window, drag and move the text around to a different location. Press Ctrl(⌘)+Shift+S if you want to save the file to your hard drive.

When you move the text around in the last step of the previous example, notice that the text always maintains the original background opacity and texture because it is grouped to a copy of the original Background layer.

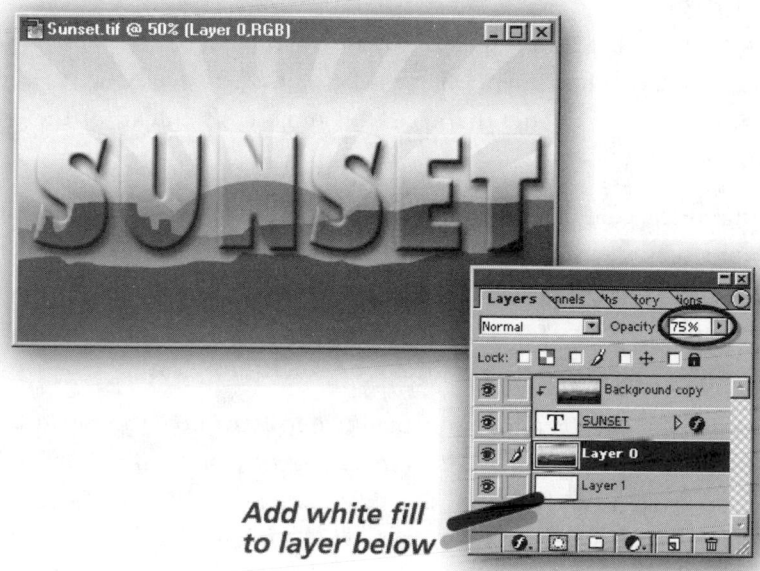

**Add white fill
to layer below**

**Figure 13.18**    Give the Background layer a lighter appearance by lowering the opacity and preparing a white layer beneath it.

**Figure 13.19**    Use the settings shown in the figure for the Add Noise filter.

## Text on a Path

Text is essential to the design of an advertisement. In the next few examples we will be working with a fictitious client (Mama Zebest) and her equally fictitious product (Meat Surprise). The first battle that faces this project is the text for the company name—Mama Zebest.

The advertisement contains an oval-shaped cameo image that will appear on all company products. The trend or initial instinct in this situation is to wrap the text around the shape of the image. Who am I to argue with instincts? The best way to accomplish this is to place text on a path. You can place text on a path by using a vector drawing program, such as Illustrator or CorelDRAW.

If you have a copy of Illustrator and would like to learn how to prepare text on a path for this project, then follow along in the next example. If you do not own a copy of Illustrator or would prefer to skip this example, an EPS file (the result of this example) has been provided on the Companion CD.

What is an EPS file? I like to describe an EPS (Encapsulated PostScript) file as a generic file format that contains vector information. An EPS file can be opened and edited in any vector drawing application such as Illustrator or CorelDRAW.

The goal for the next example is to create a path for the text with an arch that's similar to the oval-shaped logo in the product advertisement. The logo is provided as a separate file (MamaLogo.tif) on the Companion CD, to use as a template in Illustrator.

### Example 13.3   Working with Illustrator to Place Type on a Path

1. Open Illustrator. Choose File, New, and then press Enter (Return) to accept the default settings in the New Document dialog box.

2. Choose File, Place. In the Place dialog box, double-click on the MamaLogo.tif file in the Examples/Chap13 folder on the Companion CD to place the file in the document. Press Ctrl(⌘)+spacebar to toggle to the Zoom tool, and drag a marquee around the image to zoom in. Press Ctrl(⌘)++ if you need to zoom in closer. Press the spacebar to toggle to the Hand tool, and center the image in the window for a better view.

3. Press F7 to view the Layers palette (if it is not already in view). On the Layers palette, click the column to the left of the thumbnail to lock the layer (see Figure 13.20). Click the Create new layer icon at the bottom of the palette.

**Figure 13.20**   The image is being used as a template. Locking the layer prevents unintentional movement of the image while you work.

4. Choose the Pen tool from the toolbox. At the bottom of the toolbox, click on the Fill color and choose None. Click on the Stroke color and choose Black. Click and drag up to make the first anchor point at the middle of the image's left edge (see Figure 13.21).

   The stroke color for the path is temporary. It helps you to see your path while you work. When text is placed on the path, the stroke color will change to None.

5. Click and drag at the top edge of the image to make the second anchor point. Then click and drag down to the middle of the right edge to create the third anchor point (see Figure 13.22).

   Don't worry about the shape of the curve at this point. We will fix that later.

6. Press A to switch to the Direct Selection tool (the hollow arrow tool). Click each anchor point and drag on the direction lines that extend from the point to shape the path to match the edge of the template image (see Figure 13.23).

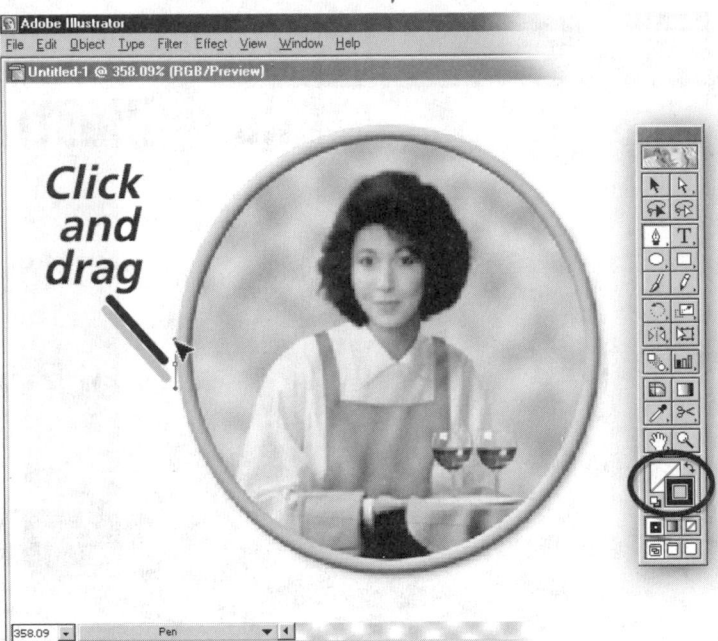

**Figure 13.21**    Select the Pen tool and set the Stroke and Fill colors on the toolbox: Make the first anchor point for the path.

**Figure 13.22**    Make the second and third anchor points at the positions shown in the figure.

**Figure 13.23**    Drag on the direction lines until the direction lines and the path resemble the arch shape shown in the figure.

7. Press V to switch to the Selection tool (solid arrow tool). Click on the path to select the entire path. If the Transform palette is not visible, choose Window, Show Transform. On the Transform palette, highlight the entry in the H: (Height) box and type **64 pt**. Press Ctrl(⌘)+Enter (Return) to proportionally resize the path (see Figure 13.24).

   You can let Illustrator do the math for you by also pressing the Ctrl(⌘) key when you press Enter (Return) to change height or width in the Transform box. This keyboard shortcut will enable proportionate resizing without knowing the measurements for both dimensions.

   The path is ready to have text placed on it. I chose a font called TimeScrDMed. If you do not have this font, experiment with other fonts. Remember to adjust point size and tracking when you use a different font.

8. Press Ctrl(⌘)+T to view the Character palette. Choose TimeScrDMed as the font, and type **21 pt** for size. Choose the Type tool from the toolbox, click on the path near the left side of the oval, and type **Mama Zebest** (see Figure 13.25).

   Don't worry if the text is off center. This will be adjusted in a later step.

**Figure 13.24**   Resize the path proportionally using the Transform palette.

**Figure 13.25**   Click on the path and type the text.

9. With the Text tool still active, click in front of the letter *Z*. Type **260** in the kerning field of the Character palette to increase the space between the two words (see Figure 13.26).

**Figure 13.26**   Use the Character palette to adjust kerning between the words.

Now let's make sure the text is centered properly.

10. Choose the Direct Selection tool from the toolbox. Click in front of the word *Mama*. An I-beam will appear in front of the text. Click and drag the I-beam to move the text along the path. Use your artistic judgment to center the text (see Figure 13.27).

Be careful where you drag. Your text could end up in a mirror image position along the path. Why? The I-beam can be dragged across the path to flip text direction along the path. If this happens to you, drag the I-beam across the path to flip it back to the other side of the path.

11. Drag Layer 1 to the Trash (the template is no longer needed). Choose File, Save As, and type **MamaZebest** for the filename. In the Save as type drop-down list, choose Illustrator EPS, and then click Save. Click OK to accept the default settings in the EPS Format Options dialog box. Close Illustrator.

**Figure 13.27**   Adjust the location of the I-beam to change the starting point of the text along the path.

Now, having created the type on a path in an Illustrator document, our goal is to transfer this text into our Photoshop project. Since this is a vector file, Photoshop will need to *rasterize* (convert to pixels) the graphic information in the file.

## Placing Text

How do we rasterize EPS file information? There are several options. One option is to select the graphic item in Illustrator and choose Edit, Copy. Then paste the graphic in a Photoshop image with the Edit, Paste option. A dialog box appears with the option to "paste as pixels."

Another option is to choose File, Open in Photoshop. Photoshop will greet you with a Rasterized Generic EPS Format dialog box. What does this mean? Photoshop is asking you to make a decision in advance for the size and resolution of the image. Once the new size information has been entered in the dialog box, the math is performed to resize the image, and the file is converted to pixels and opened.

The third option, which is the one we will use for this example, is the File, Place option. Similar to the Copy and Paste option, placing a file enables you to make the decision about size while you're viewing the image. When you use the Place method, the image will appear with a bounding box that has an X through it. This box responds in much the same way as the transform bounding box. Once all the changes are made, press Enter (Return) to apply the changes; the math is performed while Photoshop converts to pixels.

Our text on a path was created with a portion of the actual image as a template, so the size is correct and will not need adjusting. We will need to move the image into the correct position in the document. Using the Options bar to help adjust the location will help to familiarize you with the Place command and its Options bar.

### Example 13.4 Using the Placing Command to Place an EPS File

1. Open Mama.tif in the Examples/Chap13 folder on the Companion CD. Choose File, Place, and navigate to the MamaZebest.eps file in the Examples/Chap13 folder on the Companion CD (or use the file that you created in the previous example). Click Place.

   If you are using the EPS file that you created in the previous example, the X and Y coordinate values in the next step might vary slightly, especially if a different font was used. Click in the bounding box and nudge in any direction, using the arrow keys to help center and position the text over the logo.

2. On the Options bar, type **443.5** (px) for X and **70.0** (px) for Y. Click the Commit Place button on the right side of the Options bar (see Figure 13.28).

   Let's give the text a new color and layer effect.

3. Click the foreground color on the toolbox and choose a golden yellow color; R:255, G:156, B:0. Click OK. With the MamaZebest.eps layer still the active layer, press Alt(Opt)+Shift+Delete (Backspace) to fill just the letters with the color.

4. Click the Add a layer style icon at the bottom of the Layers palette, and choose Bevel and Emboss. In the Layer Style dialog box, make sure the Use Global Light option is not checked. Type **225** for Depth, **3** for Size, **120°** for Angle, and **39** for Altitude. Leave the remaining options at their default settings (see Figure 13.29). Click OK.

5. Choose File, Save As and save the file in the PSD format. Keep the file open for the next example.

That was easy enough. However, the advertisement still lacks the product title and slogan.

**Figure 13.28**    Use the Options bar's X and Y coordinates to help position the placed EPS file. Click the Commit Place button to the right when finished.

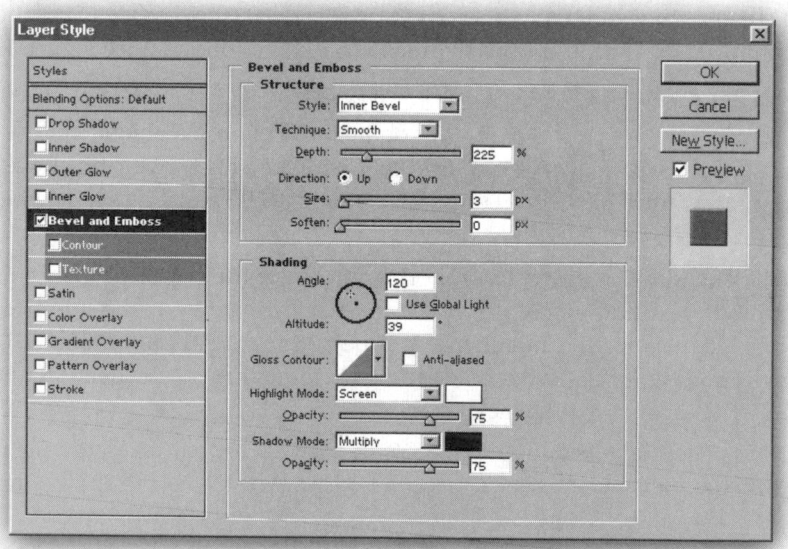

**Figure 13.29**    Use the settings shown in this figure to add a bevel and emboss effect to the text.

## Adding a Stroke Effect to Text

We definitely need some text to identify the slop on the plate. Good thing Mama Zebest has decided to call this dish "Meat Surprise." Finding a more specific title might be tough. The product slogan is equally appropriate, as you will find out later in the example.

The next major decision facing this project is which fonts to choose, along with styles and effects (if any). The product slogan seemed to be screaming for a script font. Not everyone may have the script font I chose, so I provided the rasterized text in a file on the Companion CD (if you want to use this font).

Many script fonts will look equally good, however. If you choose to experiment with the ones available to you, just remember to adjust the point size and tracking. These settings often are dictated by what is visually appealing to you. The numerical values in the steps of the next few examples were obtained by highlighting the text in question and experimenting with the numbers. In other words, I'm not so perfect and knowledgeable that I instinctively pull these numbers from my brain (although I often like to give the impression that this is the case). Truth be told, I often agonize over the numbers until I find the visual appeal that I'm seeking. I'm encouraging you to do the same.

The font chosen for the remaining text in this project is Arial and its variations. I love this font because it has such a simple look. Never underestimate the power of simplicity. Another reason I love this font is that just about everyone has it installed on their system (or a close look alike font, such as Helvetica). With this in mind, let's begin adding text.

### Example 13.5   Applying Text Effects

1. Press D for the default colors. Press X to switch white to the foreground. Press T to switch to the Text tool. On the Options bar, choose Arial Black for the font, type **45 pt** for size, and then press Enter (Return).

   Why Arial Black? It's a nice, thick, simple font. If you do not have Arial Black, there are many other fonts you can substitute in this example. Helvetica (Bold), Swiss, or Impact may be good choices. Remember to adjust the point size and tracking.

2. Click near the lower-left side of the image, and type **Meat Surprise** (see Figure 13.30). Click the Commit Any Current Edits button on the right of the Options bar. If you need to reposition the text, press V to switch to the Move tool, and move the text where you want it.

**Figure 13.30**    Click and type the text in the document window. Click the Commit Any Current Edits button when finished.

If you need to move the text while you are still editing, hold down the Ctrl(⌘) key to toggle to the Move tool and reposition the text.

3. Click the Add a layer style icon at the bottom of the Layers palette, and choose Drop Shadow. In the Layer Style dialog box, make sure the Use Global Light option is not checked. Type **50%** for Opacity, **120°** for Angle, **4** for Distance, **0** for Spread, and **6** for Size (see Figure 13.31).

Now, let's add a center fill to the text to simulate a stroke effect, with an additional effect of an inner shadow.

4. Alt(Opt)+click the Create a new layer icon at the bottom of the Layers palette. In the New Layer dialog box, type **Yellow Fill** for the name. Click OK.

5. Click on the foreground color on the toolbox and choose the golden yellow color; R:255, G:156, B:0. Ctrl(⌘)+click on the Meat Surprise layer to load the text selection. Choose Select, Modify, Contract. In the Contract Selection dialog box type **3** pixels (see Figure 13.32). Click OK.

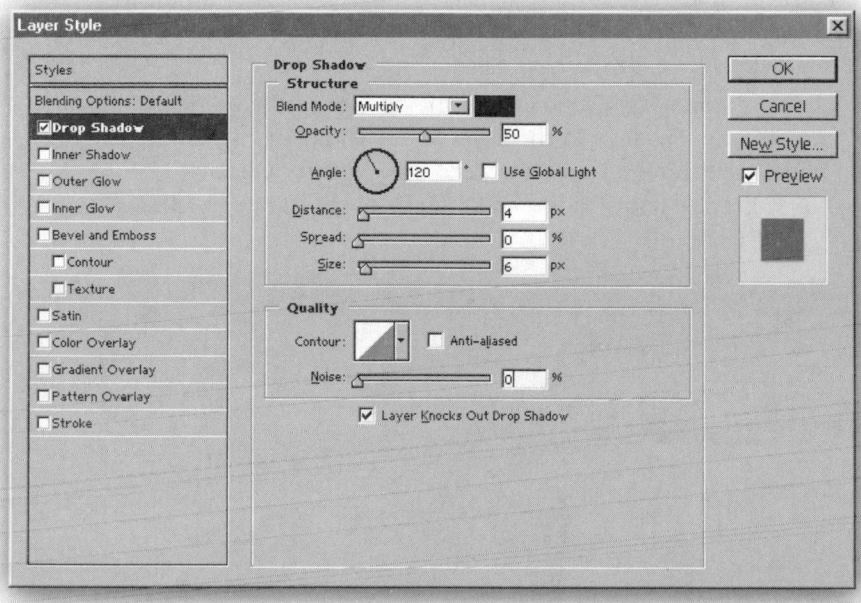

**Figure 13.31** Use the settings shown in the figure to add a soft drop shadow to the text.

**Figure 13.32** Contract the text selection by 3 pixels.

6. With the Yellow Fill layer as the active layer, press Alt(Opt)+Delete (Backspace) to fill the selection with the golden yellow color. Press Ctrl(⌘)+D to deselect.

7. Click the Add a layer style icon at the bottom of the Layers palette, and choose Inner Shadow. In the Layer Style dialog box, make sure the Use Global Light option is not checked. Type **50%** for Opacity, **120°** for Angle, **4** for Distance, **0** for Choke, and **5** for Size (see Figure 13.33).

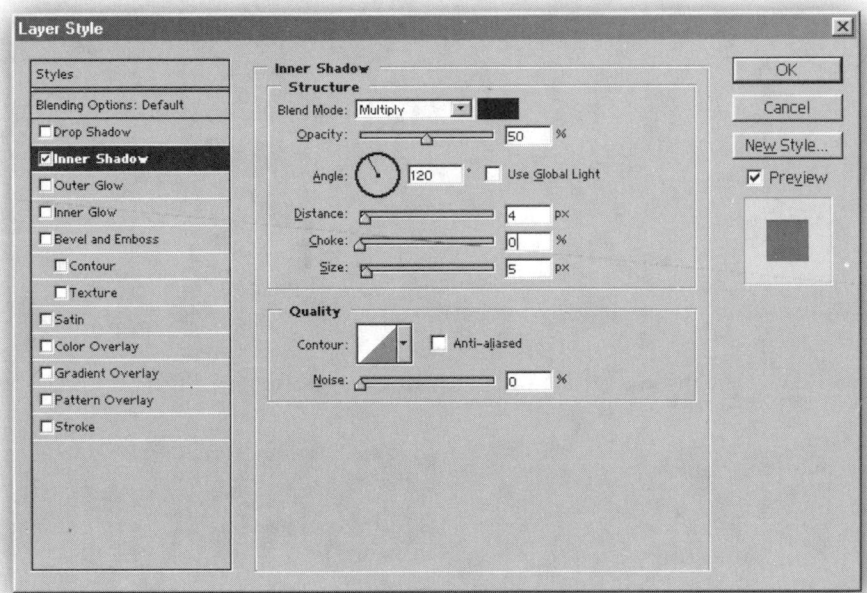

**Figure 13.33**   Use the settings shown in the figure to add an inner shadow to the text.

We will now add and center the slogan text under the product name. I chose a script font called Rage Italic. Other script fonts that also work well are Artisan, Vladimir Script, Gallante, or Pageant. Remember to adjust point size and tracking with different fonts. A Slogan.psd file has been provided in the Examples/Chap13 folder on the Companion CD if you prefer to use the text provided from this file in lieu of step 8.

8. Press D for the default colors. Press T to switch to the Text tool. Choose Rage Italic for font. Click the Palettes button on the Options bar to view the Character palette. Type **20 pt** for the font size and **12** for Tracking (see Figure 13.34). Click under the "Meat Surprise" text in the document window and type **If you can find meat, we'll be surprised!** Click the Commit Any Current Edits button to the right of the Options bar.

**Figure 13.34**   Use the Character palette to adjust tracking, and type the text as shown. Click the Commit Any Current Edits button when finished.

**9.** Press Ctrl(⌘)+S to save your work. Keep the document open for the next example.

Most of the advertisement design work is complete. But our client would like to add one more selling point to the image. Again, the text in the next example seemed to scream for Photoshop's new warped text feature.

## Warped Text

The text that will be added in the next example gives you the perfect opportunity to get acquainted with this new warped text feature. I thought it might be nice to make a frame shape to place the text on—to help call attention to this added selling point for the product. To save time, a path shape has been provided for you. The first few steps will show you how to access this path and create the framework on which the text will be placed.

After the text has been typed and adjusted, we will apply a warped style to the text. A variety of styles is available. When you're applying a warped text style, the text remains editable. You can change the content of the text at any time without changing the warped shape of the text. So let's get started and find out how this feature works.

### Example 13.6    Creating Warped Text

1. Open the Mama.tif file and click the Paths tab to view the Paths palette. Ctrl(⌘)+click Path 1 to load the path as a selection. Click the Layers tab to return to the Layers palette, and then click the Create a new layer icon at the bottom of the Layers palette three times to create three new layers.

2. Click on the foreground color on the toolbox and choose a muted pink color; R:222, G:124, B:149. Click OK. Then, with Layer 3 as the active layer, press Alt(Opt)+Delete (Backspace) to fill the selection with the pink color (see Figure 13.35).

**Figure 13.35**    Fill the selection on Layer 3 with a muted pink color.

3. Press D to return to the default colors. Click on Layer 2 to make this layer active. Press Alt(Opt)+Delete (Backspace) to fill the selection with black. Press X to switch to white. Click on Layer 1 to make this layer active. Press Alt(Opt)+Delete (Backspace) to fill the selection with white. Press Ctrl(⌘)+D to deselect.

4. Press V to switch to the Move tool. Press the left-arrow key once, and then press the up-arrow key once. Click on Layer 2 to make it the active layer. Press the right-arrow key once, and then press the down-arrow key once (see Figure 13.36).

**Figure 13.36**   Move the black and white fills, using the arrow keys, to get an embossed look.

Arial is the font to use for the next step. Again, if Arial is not available, Helvetica, and Swiss might make good substitutes. Remember to experiment with point settings to achieve a similar look when you substitute different fonts.

5. Click on Layer 3 to make this the active layer again. Press T to return to the Text tool. On the Options bar, click the Center text icon. Click the Palettes button to view the Character palette. Choose Arial (Regular) for the font, type **15 pt** for size, and **13 pt** for leading (peek ahead at Figure 13.37). White should still be the foreground color (and therefore the default text color). Click in the document window (near the newly created pink shape) and type **With Real**, then press Enter (Return) and type **Meat Smell** (see Figure 13.37).

Before applying a warp feature to the text, let's tighten up the tracking and kerning in a few spots.

**Figure 13.37**   Choose text settings on the Options bar and Character palette, and then type the text.

6. Click in front of the word *Real*. Hold down the Alt(Opt) key and press the left-arrow key twice until the kerning reads –40 on the Character palette. Click and drag to highlight the words *Meat Smell*. In the tracking field on the Character palette choose **–75** (see Figure 13.38).

7. Click the Create Warped Text icon on the Options bar. In the Warp Text dialog box, choose Arc Upper as the Style option. Type **+50** for Bend (see Figure 13.39). Click OK. Click the Commit Any Current Edits button to the right of the Options bar.

   The angle of the text now needs to be adjusted to fit into the pink shape created earlier. If you have used a font substitute, you may need to adjust the numbers in step 8 to center the text within the pink frame you created earlier.

8. Press Ctrl(⌘)+T to access the Free Transform option. On the Options bar, type **–16.5** for Rotate, **132.9** for X, and **284.0** for Y. Click the Commit Transform button to the right of the Options bar (see Figure 13.40).

**Figure 13.38**   Tighten the tracking on the "Meat Smell" text to keep an equal distance with the text above it.

**Figure 13.39**   Use the Warp Text settings in the figure to change the shape of the text. Click the Commit Any Current Edits button when finished warping the text.

**Figure 13.40**    Use the Options bar settings shown in the figure to center the text within the pink frame. Click the Commit Transform button when finished.

There's just one more detail needed to add a little contrast to the warped text.

9. Drag the With Real Meat Smell layer to the Create a new layer icon to make a copy of this layer. Click on the original layer below the copy to make it the active layer. Press V to switch to the Move tool. Press X to switch black to the foreground, and then press Alt(Opt)+Shift+Delete (Backspace) to fill the text on this layer with black. Press the down-arrow key once, and press the right-arrow key once (see Figure 13.41).

10. Press Ctrl(⌘)+S to save your work.

Now, if this image doesn't make your mouth water for some Meat Surprise, I don't know what will!

**Figure 13.41**   Add a black shadow text layer to complement the look of the pink frame.

## Summary

The early part of this chapter differentiates between editable text and text as a graphic. Even the editable text, however, is similar to the concept of graphics, in the sense that text is often an integral part of design work (whether the text is editable or rasterized).

Keeping text editable while you try to achieve a certain effect has significant advantages. However, this may not always be possible to achieve more complex effects.

When I tried to decide which effects to teach in this chapter, I was overwhelmed with the possibilities. The variety is infinite. And consider the added variable of one effect having a dramatically different look when it is applied to a different font. My goal for this chapter was to focus on examples that would help provide the mental tools for experimentation.

# Part III

## Exploring the
## Cool Stuff

# Chapter 14

## Color Correcting and Exposure: Basic Image Improvement

"Color correcting" is sort of an odd term,

isn't it? For example, what is an *incorrect*

color? Plaid?

You need to accept the phrase within a given context: How faithful is an image's colors to the source's colors? *Color correcting* means "to make acceptable or accurate." Part of the success of manipulating images in Photoshop is inextricably linked to the practice of color correction. Correcting colors is a *must*—it's a cold, hard fact. Chances are that you will win the lottery before you scan a photograph or negative into Photoshop and find that the colors are perfect. Color correction ranks as the third inevitability in digital life, right after system halts and a monthly AOL CD in your mailbox. This chapter takes you from the most basic method of color correcting to the professional level.

Photoshop has many commands to adjust the colors in a photograph. Do not be overwhelmed by the power of these commands—they all work using the same principles. On the other hand, do not be tempted to push the pedal-to-the-metal and overuse this power. *Realistic* color rendition is the name of the game for this chapter. Not obscenely garish colors that will never print, not fleshtones that look like a manila folder—*realistic* color.

## Defining the Goal of Color Correcting

The goal of the following set of steps is to bring a photo into an acceptable color and tonal range for viewing on onscreen. The term "acceptable" needs qualifying from two realistic aspects:

- First, we don't always know or remember the actual colors in the scene. Let's say for example, I shot a picture of a spectacular sunset with my white yacht in the foreground and you offer to color correct the scan of the image. You know that the boat is white, therefore you make it white, but I disagree with the red in the sky—it's not the hue of red that I saw. Because you have no way of knowing the true colors in the scene, you correct for the known color(s) and move the rest into an *acceptable* range.

- Second, an image looks complete if there is a full range of tones from black to white. Without a black point and white point, the photo will look *flat*...lacking contrast. This is the philosophy we'll adopt when correcting the photos in this chapter:

  - Correct for the known colors

  - Adjust the remaining colors to fit into an acceptable range

  - Create a full range of tones

But before we explore the commands of color correcting, a few truisms need to be pointed out that have an impact on this chapter's contents:

- All the example images are in RGB mode and *color corrected for computer monitor viewing*. The RGB color space is big enough for all-purpose work and is ideal for digital images. If you plan to output your images (film, print, and so on), you might find the need to develop a different approach to correcting color than what is suggested here.

  The Adobe 1998 profile, as we recommended in Chapter 2, is the preferred default color space for all-around, general purpose imaging work. When working with the files in the Examples/Chap14 folder, and you get a message box that says Mismatching Profile, press Ctrl(⌘)+Shift+K, and change the RGB Working Space to Adobe RGB 1998. Then in the Color Management Policies section, make sure Preserve Embedded Profiles is the choice in all drop-down boxes, and be sure all the checkboxes are checked.

- Photoshop's Adjustment Layers is the preferred method for making corrections. An adjustment layer works like a filter on a camera lens, and the corrections are placed *into* this layer, leaving the original pixels unchanged. Each change you make to the original pixels degrades the quality. Adjustment Layers also allow you to modify your settings indefinitely, without harming innocent pixels.

**Warning**

**Accurate Histograms**   We strongly recommended that you uncheck the Use Cache for Histograms option in the Memory & Image Cache section of Photoshop's Preferences. When cache is used to calculate histograms (used in commands such as Variations, Levels, Curves) a quick, but much less precise method is used. In other words, unchecking this preference setting makes histograms more accurate!

- Perception of color can be very subjective, so you might not agree with some of the color settings given in the exercises. You might see a particular yellow that you would describe as a traffic-light yellow, whereas someone else might see it as a lemon yellow. You might prefer the colors in a photograph to have a pastel quality, whereas the guy next to you might prefer bold, fully saturated colors. We will address this issue in more detail later.

- All the example photographs are supplied as real-world examples—no changes were made to mess up the colors to make the following more impressive assignment. The images are either from PhotoCD or digitized using a film scanner.

# Touring Photoshop's Color Correcting Commands

Think of this chapter as a journey. If you are new to adjusting an image's colors, you'll want to start at the beginning of the trip. The first stop is Photoshop's most basic color adjusting tool: the Image, Adjust, Variations command. You'll find Variations easy to use and educational. The intermediate places of interest along our trip are Color Balance and Levels. Learn these commands and you'll have a greater understanding of manipulating color. You may want to pick up our journey at one of these locations if you already know, for example, that if you subtract cyan from an image, the color red increases.

Finally, the last stop is around the bend—Curves. (No pun intended. Well, maybe.) Curves is the imaging professional's tool of choice. People who are color production experts live and breathe in the Curves dialog box because it's the most powerful place to bring your images for correcting color.

Now that you have the color correction road map, all aboard! Next stop, Variations!

## Introducing Variations

The title of the color space used for the images in this chapter, RGB, refers to red, green, and blue. It's good to know those three colors, but what color do you remove if your photo has a greenish cast? Hint: it's not red or blue!

This is one way that Variations is helpful—if you are not familiar with the color wheel, you can see it in the lower-left section of the Variations dialog box (see Figure 14.1). The colors that face each other from opposite sides of the circle are the opposite of each other. In other words, if you add yellow, you subtract blue. If you subtract cyan, you add red. And if you add magenta you subtract green. Simple enough.

Another useful feature in Variations is that you can see thumbnails of your image with each of the correcting colors already added. This method is used in those self-serve picture copy machines now seen in some stores. The idea is that anyone can color correct his or her photo simply by picking the thumbnail that looks best.

Variations also enables you to lighten or darken your photo and limit the changes to one of three tonal ranges. You can also use Variations to increase or decrease the saturation of all the colors, and set the intensity of any correction. Variations works best on images that have a wide range of brightness values, not mostly light or mostly dark images. These are called by photographers *average-key* images, and they don't require precise color adjustments.

Okay, enough discussion. Let's try out the Variations command.

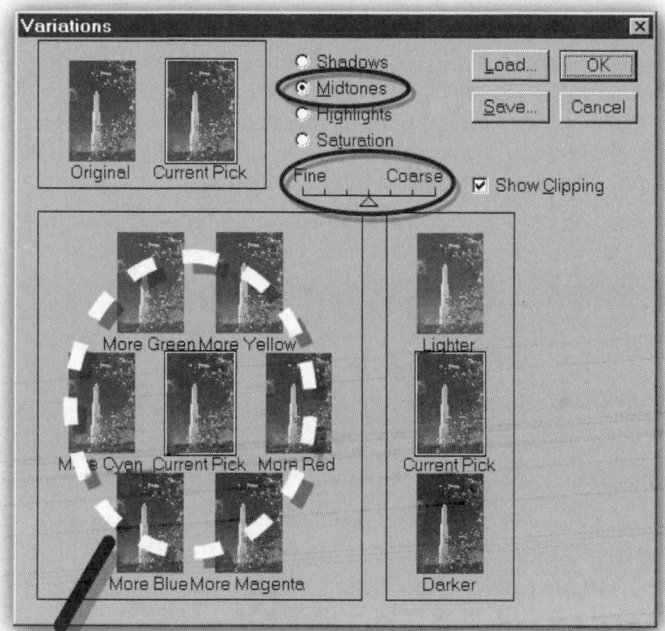

**Color wheel group**

**Figure 14.1**   Notice the color wheel in the bottom-left thumbnail group of the Variations dialog box.

### Example 14.1    Using the Variations Command

1. Open the Monument.psd image from the Examples/Chap14 folder on the Companion CD. Right-click (Macintosh: hold Ctrl and click) on the image title bar and choose Duplicate. Change the default name to **Monument Corrected** in the Duplicate dialog box and click OK.

> **Warning!**   If an error message appears when you open the CD files, press Ctrl(⌘)+Shift+K and then choose Adobe RGB (1998) from the Working Spaces, RGB drop-down list. See Chapter 3 for more information.

2. Identify any problems with the photo.

   This photo has three: the contrast is weak, the image has a slight yellow-green cast throughout, and the shadow-side of the branches is mostly green.

3. Choose Image, Adjust, Variations from the main menu. Select the Midtones and set the Fine/Coarse slider at the middle tick mark—the default setting. See the circled areas in Figure 14.1.

   Each tick mark on the Fine/Coarse slider doubles the amount of adjustment when moving to the right.

**Note**

**You Must Purge the Settings in Variations**    Of all Photoshop's color correction commands, only Variations has this quirk. For each trip to the Variations dialog box during the same Photoshop session, all the previous corrections are actually added to the settings. So when you open Variations for the third time, for example, the thumbnails that appear are affected by the corrections you entered during your first and second visit, even if you performed an Undo on the correction.

The workaround for this and a good habit to develop is to hold down the Alt(Opt) key and click the Cancel button (which turns into the Reset button). This procedure purges all previous settings.

4. Move the Fine/Coarse slider all the way to the right.

   Yikes, that's way too much correction, but hey…now you know what the slider does!

5. Move the Fine/Coarse slider one mark to the left of center.

   Remember, yellow is one of the problem colors and blue is the color opposite of yellow. At this position, the More Blue thumbnail shows that blue is neither overpowering nor too weak to eliminate the yellow.

6. Click once on the More Blue thumbnail.

   Immediately, all the thumbnails update with the amount of blue you just added (see Figure 14.2). You can keep visual track of all your changes by watching the Original and Current Pick thumbnails located in the upper left.

7. Let's tackle the green in the shadow areas of the branches. Choose Shadows to limit corrections to the darker tones of the image. Notice all the selectable thumbnails have updated to show the changes in the shadow areas. Move the slider one notch to the right, the center position, and click once on the More Magenta thumbnail.

   You may have noticed one limitation of Variations by now—the thumbnails do not allow you to zoom in and see the adjustments in detail. This makes precision correcting a guessing game. Yes, the settings in this example were developed from many trips in and out of Variations! Now that the color cast has been eliminated, it's time to add some contrast to this flat image.

8. Leaving the slider in the center position and Shadows still selected, click once on the Darker thumbnail.

   To increase contrast in the Monument Corrected image, the tonal range needs to be expanded. In other words, the darkest areas need to be made darker and the lightest areas lighter.

9. Select Highlights and click once on the Lighter thumbnail. Click OK to apply the corrections.

## Before & After Thumbnails

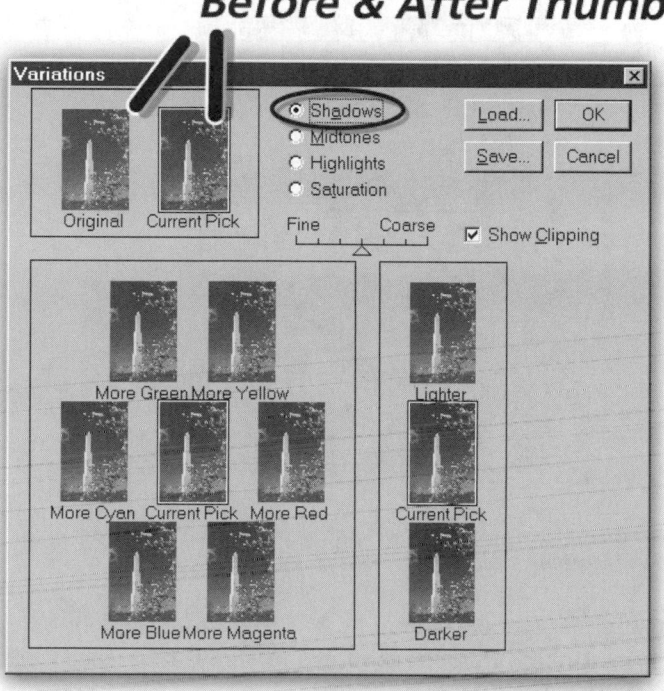

**Figure 14.2**   Keep glancing at the Original and Current Pick thumbnail group to compare the uncorrected image with live updates of the corrections you've entered.

There is one more step before we can show off our Variations masterpiece: sharpening the image using the Unsharp Mask filter.

**10.** Choose Filters, Sharpen, Unsharp Mask. Place your mouse cursor in the preview window, click and drag until you see some of the cherry blossoms. Set the Amount to **80**, the Radius to **1.0**, and Threshold to **0** (see Figure 14.3). Tip: Click and hold inside the preview window to see the area before the filter's settings are applied. Release the cursor and the preview window shows the proposed change once more.

**Tip**

**Correct Colors Before Using Unsharp Mask**   All scanned images need sharpening, including images digitized from a flatbed scanner, film scanner, drum scanner, PhotoCD, well, you get the idea.

We have observed that images tend to actually look sharper after color correcting; therefore, the Unsharp Mask should *not* be used *before* the corrections. Otherwise, oversharpening can occur, and ruin the image.

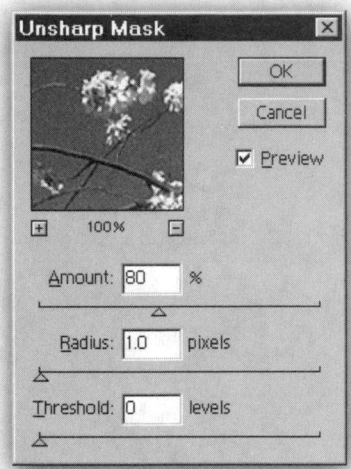

**Figure 14.3**  Move the image in the preview window to an area rich in detail, like the cherry blossoms, then adjust the settings.

11. From the main menu, choose Window, Tile to look at a side-by-side comparison from your trip to Variations as shown in Figure 14.4. Nice work! Close both images without saving them.

**Figure 14.4**  Using the Variations command can correct a color cast and improve contrast.

It's easy to figure out how Variations got its name—from the fact that you can see a variety of options before making a correction. The layout of the Variations box is helpful in learning to adjust colors, but as you progress on your color correction journey, you'll soon see that Variations is good for at least one thing—learning the color wheel. Color Balance is our next color correcting command to visit.

## Working with the Color Balance Command

When Gary Kubicek first learned Photoshop, he used only Color Balance to correct his photographs. After all, with his background in photography, color balance is a term he was very familiar with. Plus, digital and traditional darkroom color balancing operates under the same principle: adjusting the overall mixture of colors.

Color Balance is similar to Variations in that you are presented with the colors of a color wheel, but instead of using thumbnails to input your settings, you have sliders and a live preview in the target image window. Plus, Color Balance has these benefits over the Variations command: more precise tuning of adjustments (100 settings per color), dynamic updates in the image window (extremely useful), and the option of enlisting the help of another feature in Photoshop, the Eyedropper tool.

The Eyedropper is definitely a tool that you should use when color correcting photos. The Eyedropper can be used at the same time that the Color Balance dialog box is open, which enables you to sample color as you refine your color balancing work. The Eyedropper tool also can be used while working in the Levels and Curves dialog boxes. Let's take a quick look-see at what it can do for your imaging.

### *Introducing the Eyedropper Tool: The Perfect Color Judge*

Although your eyes can deceive you when evaluating color, the Eyedropper tool reads a color perfectly every time. A couple lines from a song written back in the '60s sums it up quite well: "Believe none of what you hear and half of what you see."

There are four factors worth mentioning here to help you understand why you can't always trust your eyes. First, as mentioned before, the perception of color varies from person to person. You might describe a particular yellow as banana yellow and the guy on the corner might describe it as lemon yellow.

Second, and quite inescapably, our eyes change (read *worsen*) as we age. There is an industry standard color perception test called the Munsell test. If you take this test today and then again 20 years from now, your score *will* be lower.

Third, our eyes are subject to a phenomenon referred to as *chromatic adaptation*, which occurs when our eyes adapt to a particular color problem and make it "better" the longer we stare at it. You can easily prove the concept by opening any example file on the Companion CD from this chapter and stare at it for a few minutes. The image will look better and better, almost to the point where you'll think, "The colors look fine."

Whoa! Let's think again! After you color correct the file and compare the before and after images, you'll fully appreciate and become a little leery of what you think you see because of chromatic adaptation.

Finally, our perception of a color is influenced by the *surrounding* colors. To illustrate this, open the image LightGreenDarkGreen.psd from the Examples/Chap14 folder on the Companion CD. The left circle appears lighter than the circle on the right. But how can you know for sure? You can't cover one circle, remember that shade of green, then look only at the other circle to determine if there is a difference. In this situation, you need the Eyedropper tool and its companion the Info palette, to determine the two shades of green (or is it one shade?).

**Tip**

**Don't Forget F8**   F8 is the hot key to display the Info palette, and it's well worth remembering when you have a lot of color correcting to do.

Let's work through a brief set of steps to familiarize you with the Eyedropper tool and the Info palette.

### Example 14.2   Using the Eyedropper and Info Palette

1. Open the image LightGreenDarkGreen.psd from the Examples/Chap14 folder on the Companion CD if it's not open already.

2. Press I for the Eyedropper (intuitive letter designation, isn't it?) and on the Options bar, choose 3×3 from the Point Size drop-down menu.

   For most color sampling, 3×3 pixels averaged to a single color, is ideal. The Point Sample option can give a misleading value, and 5×5 pixels can average too large an area down to a single color value.

3. Press F8 to display the Info palette.

   By default, the upper-left quadrant in the Info palette displays colors in RGB values, and this is the area of the Info palette where you want to focus your attention for the next two steps.

4. Place the cursor over the left circle. In the Info palette, notice the reading: 120, 219, 0 as shown in Figure 14.5.

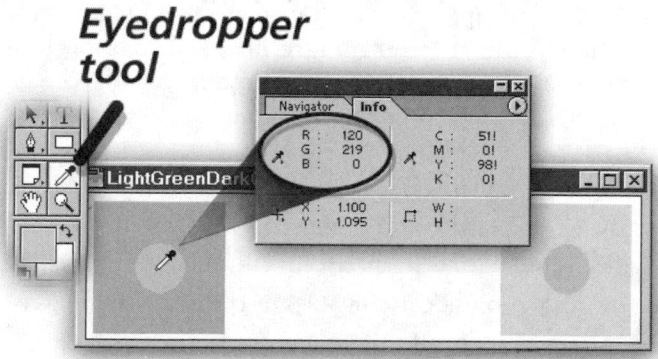

**Figure 14.5**   Use the Eyedropper tool to determine precise color values.

**5.** Move the cursor over to the right circle.

Same numbers, right? But your eyes tell you differently.

**6.** Press Shift+I to choose the next tool tucked under the Eyedropper tool, the Color Sampler tool. Now click once on the left circle and then again on the right circle.

The Info palette extends vertically with the placement of a Color Sampler in the image. Notice each Color Sampler is numbered and has a corresponding readout in the palette (see Figure 14.6.) and that the RGB values are identical.

The Color Sampler tool is especially helpful when color correcting a photograph. In the LightGreenDarkGreen image, a Sampler can help if you're like me and too lazy to write down the numbers. More importantly, the Info palette can help to teach you about the Color Samplers!

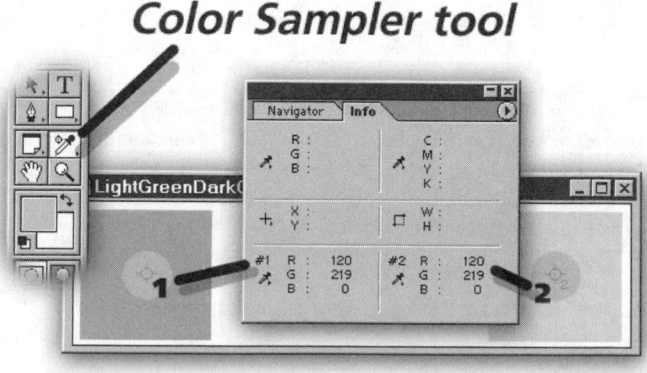

**Figure 14.6**   The two Color Samplers indicate that the two green circles are identical in color values.

7. Remove the Color Samplers by holding down the Alt(Opt) key, hover your mouse cursor over the #1 Sampler in the image (the cursor turns into a pair of scissors), and then click. Repeat this procedure for the #2 Sampler. Close the LightGreenDarkGreen.psd image without saving

You've learned how the primary additive red, green, and blue colors that make up a computer image can be equalized and changed by the introduction of the secondary colors cyan, green, and yellow (respectively) through the Variations command. You've also learned how to use the valuable-for-color-correcting Eyedropper/Color Sampler tool. It's time to apply all this knowledge to the Color Balance command.

### Correcting with Color Balance and the Color Sampler

Some things just naturally go together: apple pie and ice cream, Donald Trump and money, Bill Gates and *lots* of money, and, of course, color correcting and the Color Sampler. In the following steps, you'll learn how to determine the known colors in an image, adjust those colors, and watch the rest of the colors fall into their proper values.

### Example 14.3    Adjusting Color By the Numbers

1. Open TwoWomen.psd from the Examples/Chap14 on the Companion CD.

   What was your first impression of the overall color? Did it look okay to you, or did you notice a slight reddish-yellow colorcast? Remember, the longer you look at the photo, the more your color perception "corrects" the image.

   What are the known colors in the photo? It's safe to assume that the curtains are white and that the dark area in the lower right of the image is a shadow with no important detail.

**Tip**

**RGB Percentages in Some Skins**   "Correct" fleshtones are something on which we often have predetermined opinions. But in fact, fleshtones can vary widely due to lightness and darkness of the skin as well as the ambient lighting in the photo. Generally, red and yellow are the prominent colors in light-colored skin. Or in terms of percentages, green is about 60–75 percent of red, and blue is 45–60 percent of red.

2. Click and hold on the Eyedropper tool and choose the Color Sampler from the flyout list on the toolbox. Be sure the Sample Size on the Options bar is set to 3×3 Average.

3. Press Ctrl(⌘)+spacebar to toggle to the Zoom tool and click two or three times just above the head of the woman on the right. Click a Color Sampler in the light vertical fold in the curtains, as shown in Figure 14.7.

The curtains are not a solid white, but that's okay. We're just looking to neutralize the existing color.

4. Press the End key to move the view of the image to the far, bottom-right area. Click in the darkest area you can find.

Scout for an area where the Info palette reads near 24, 7, 4, give or take a few points. Click. You now have two Sampler readings in the Info palette.

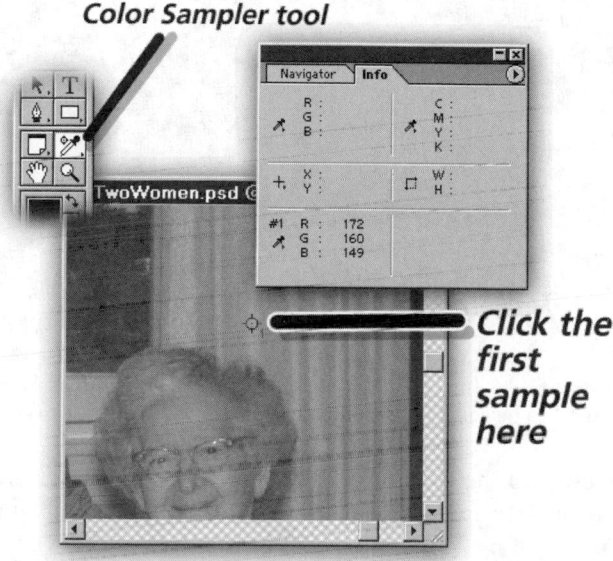

**Figure 14.7** Place the first Color Sampler in the even, bright white fold of the curtains as shown.

5. Press Ctrl(⌘)+0 to fit the screen image. Click the Create New Fill or Adjustment Layer icon at the bottom of the Layers palette (third from right) and choose Color Balance from the drop-down menu.

In the Color Balance dialog box that appears, the #1 readout in the Info palette now shows two numbers for each of the RGB colors. The first number is the original value, and the second number is the adjusted value. Pay attention to the *second* number as you make adjustments.

6. Click Highlights in the Tone Balance field (the tonal range where the #1 Sampler is). On the Info palette, the color with the middle value should be green. Adjust the remaining colors to move their values closer to those of green, as shown in Figure 14.8.

Notice that you are not looking at the image—you are correcting by the numbers!

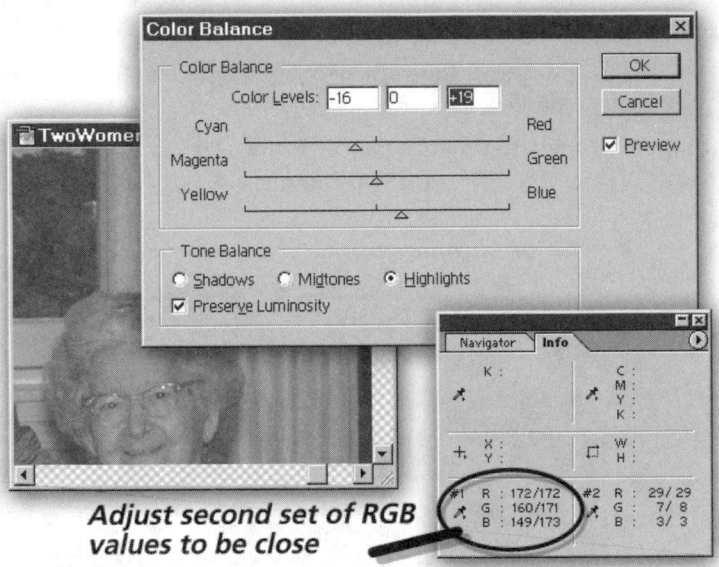

**Adjust second set of RGB values to be close**

**Figure 14.8**   To neutralize the color of the white curtains, adjust the second set of RGB values to be equal or near equal.

7. Click Shadows in the Tone Balance field. The red for the #2 Sampler (the shadow area in the image) is much higher than green and blue. Here, too, you are trying to make the three colors more neutral. Move the Cyan/Red slider to the left. Just how far to move the slider depends on where the Color Sampler is placed. Basically you want to bring the red down to within about 8 of the next highest number, then bring up the lowest number, blue, very slightly. See Figure 14.9 for an example of the Shadow settings.

8. Click Midtones. So far, you've been using the numbers to determine corrections. Because the midtone area doesn't have a Color Sampler, you'll need to view the image as you make your adjustments. My eyes told me to drag the sliders so the Color Levels readout showed 0, +9, +5. Enter these values or set your own depending on which results look better to you. Click OK to apply the settings.

While you were adjusting the shadows and midtones, you may have noticed values in all the Color Samplers changing. Not to worry—the change should not significantly affect the image.

Color Balance does not have a feature to lighten or darken the image. If you use Color Balance in your own imaging, don't stop at using only this command. You might need to enlist another command such as Brightness/Contrast.

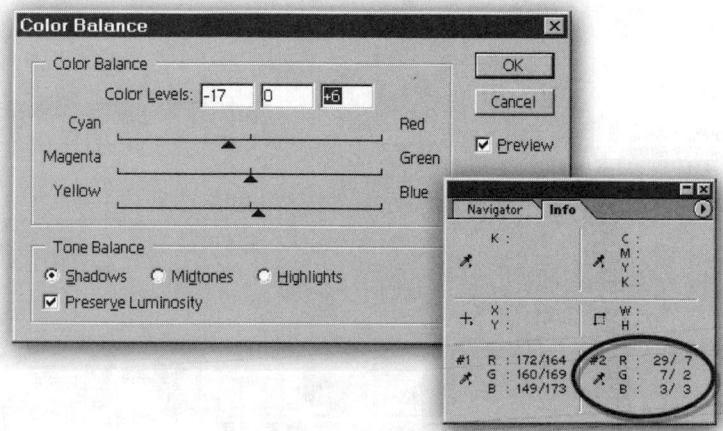

**Figure 14.9**  Adjust the shadows so the adjusted values of the #2 Sampler are numerically closer.

9. Click the Create New Fill or Adjustment Layer icon at the bottom of the Layers palette and choose Brightness/Contrast.

   Though the colors have been corrected, the image is still dark and flat, lacking contrast.

10. Move the Brightness slider to the right to about +28, and then move the Contrast slider to about +20 as shown in Figure 14.10. Click OK.

11. Click off, then on each of the two adjustment layer's visibility icons to see the before and after difference made by your adjustments. Close the image anytime without saving it.

You've learned a lot about color perception, using the Eyedropper tool and Info palette, and adjusting colors. Though you should consider Variations and Color Balance as basic color adjusting tools, all this information has but laid the foundation for the rest of the chapter.

Levels is the next stop, and a place where many experienced Photoshop users go to adjust their images.

You think if some of our politicians went there, they could adjust their images?

**Figure 14.10**   Using only Color Balance may work for some photographs but not all. Adjusting brightness and contrast is often needed as well.

## Using Levels to Adjust Images

You could in theory stop reading this chapter after this section and have enough skills to adequately tackle the majority of color problems you'll encounter in the future. But why wimp out at the status of "Most Adequate Color Manipulator?" Especially when we have more stops to make on our trek? The Levels command is, well, a *high-level color adjusting tool*. Why settle for less?

The Levels dialog box can seem intimidating to the new user, but knowing how to use Levels is a top-drawer addition to your Photoshop skills. Like Variations, you can lighten or darken the image. Like Color Balance, you can adjust colors with up to 100 settings. But Levels *also* gives you a lot more: a histogram (a visual graph of tonal values) for each channel, an option to save or load settings, and an Auto correction feature, just to name a few special feats.

The authors have seen numerous techniques applied to the Levels command, and three are worth mentioning. The first two techniques, the Auto feature and, what can be called "Quick and Dirty," are covered in the following steps.

### Example 14.4    Working with Two Simple Levels Techniques

1.  Open the 2Girls.psd image from the Examples/Chap14 folder on the
    Companion CD.

    Notice that the image lacks contrast and has a reddish tint.

2.  Right-click (Macintosh: hold Ctrl and click) on the image title bar and
    choose Duplicate. Type **Auto** in the As field and click OK.

    Creating a duplicate image allows a side-by-side comparison of the two tech-
    niques in this example.

3.  Click the Create New Fill or Adjustment Layer icon at the bottom of the
    Layers palette and then press Ctrl(⌘)+L. This is another key combo you want
    to memorize.

    The histogram in the Levels dialog box indicates that the tonal range is
    very limited, and bunched up in the lower midtone range, as shown in
    Figure 14.11.

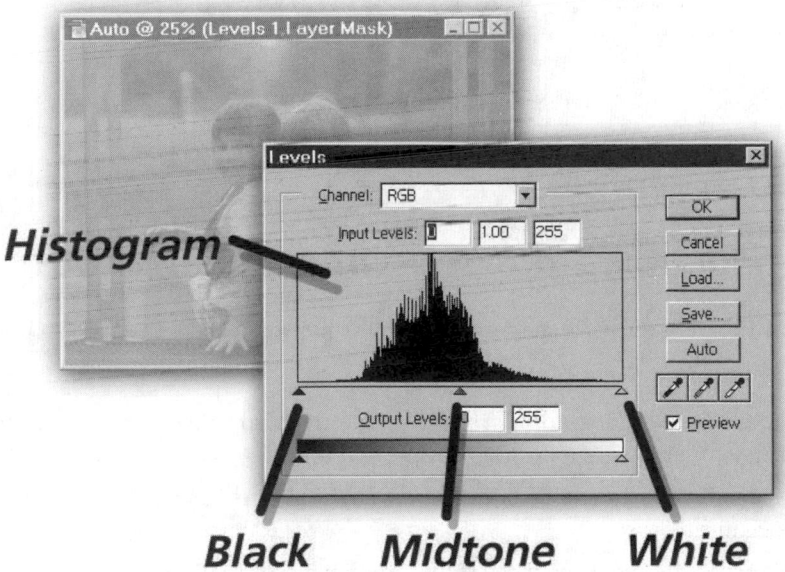

**Figure 14.11**    This histogram shows that no pixels with highlight and shadow values exist
in the image, typical of a low-contrast photograph.

4.  Click the Auto button. The histogram immediately shows that the pixels
    are remapped to extend to white and black, creating contrast in the image.
    Click OK.

5.  Make the other image, 2Girls.psd, active in the workspace by pressing
    Ctrl(⌘)+Tab. Click the Create New Fill or Adjustment Layer icon at the
    bottom of the Layers palette and choose Levels from the menu.

6. Click on the Channel drop-down at the top of the dialog box, and choose Red to view the Red channel.

You will toggle through each of the RGB channels. You can use the Channel drop-down at the top of the dialog box to remind you which channel you are working in.

7. Drag the black slider right to the point where the histogram shows the beginning of the darkest tonal values. Now, drag the white slider left where values are first indicated as shown in Figure 14.12.

I will refer to this area of a histogram with a nontechnical term: the "toe" of the graph—the point at each end of the readout where pixels first appear.

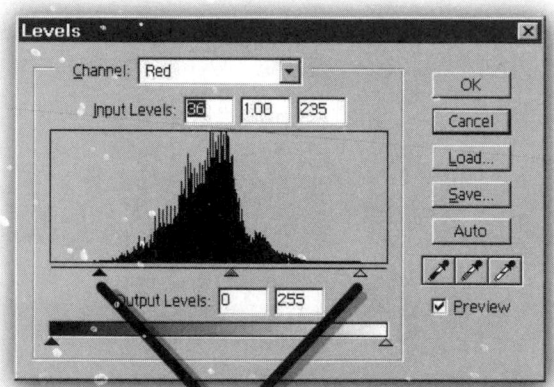

## Slide toward first point of tonal values

**Figure 14.12**   Drag the black slider and the white slider to the point where tonal values first appear in the histogram.

8. Choose the Green channel from the Channels drop-down and move the black and white sliders to their respective toes.

9. Choose Blue from the Channels drop-down and repeat the to-the-toe procedure.

10. Following the previous three steps, you have essentially removed any color cast and set normal contrast within each of the color channels.

11. Press Ctrl(⌘)+~(tilde) for the RGB channel.

Overall contrast and midtone adjustments are made in this channel.

12. Drag the black slider past the toe to the point where the tonal values start to increase. Move the white slider left to where the tonal values start to increase. Now, move the midtone slider a little to the left to lighten the midtone range. Suggested settings are seen in Figure 14.13. Click OK.

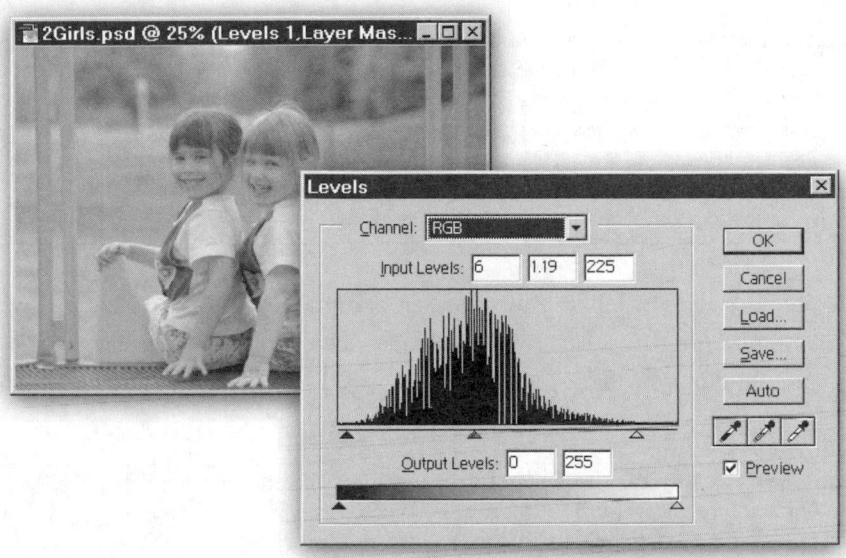

**Figure 14.13**   Add overall contrast and lighten the image in the RGB channel.

13. Press the Tab key to hide the toolbox and palettes. From the main menu, choose Window, Tile to arrange the images side-by-side.

    Which correction do you prefer? Even the black and white image in Figure 14.14 shows that the Auto feature didn't work as well as the manual method.

14. Close both images without saving them.

**Figure 14.14**   Compare the results of using two Levels techniques: Auto and a formulated manual adjustment.

**Tip**

**Customize the Auto Feature in the Levels Command**   The Auto command clips the white and black points. The default values of 0.5% created too much contrast in the Auto image. You can customize the clip range from 0 to 9.99 by holding down the Alt(Opt) key, click the Options button, and enter the new values for Black and/or White (the higher the number, the more contrast). But unless you have a multitude of images that would benefit greatly from a specific clip point setting and the Auto feature, we advise against customizing the Auto setting just because you can.

There *are* photographs where Auto does an acceptable job of tone balancing, but you may rarely run across such images. So just keep what you've learned about the Auto command in your back pocket.

**Tip**

**The Shortcut Key Way to Apply Level Settings**   If you don't like the results of the Auto feature but want to apply the same Levels settings to a number of images, and you don't want to take the time to create an Action (yes, you *can* create an action using any Levels setting), you can bring up the Levels dialog with the settings you previously applied—just press Ctrl(⌘)+Alt(Opt) whenever you choose Levels.

This procedure works no matter how you select Levels: Main menu+Alt(Opt), Ctrl(⌘)+Alt(Opt)+ L, or the Adjustment Layer icon on the Layers palette while holding Alt(Opt).

Another method is to use the Save feature and then Load those saved settings at another time.

I know Photoshop users that rely on only the manual technique used in the previous exercise and are happy with the results. After all, isn't that what Photoshop is about? Being happy with your results? Of course!

But the two essential elements of a photograph you are color correcting, the subject matter and the histogram, are almost like fingerprints, snowflakes, and the opposite sex—no two are identical. So, relying on a formula to hit a moving target isn't always the best approach.

In the next set of steps, you will take what you learned about the Color Sampler and Levels, and incorporate a couple more techniques to refine your color adjusting skills.

**Tip**

**Ignore Light Sources**   When selecting the area to use as a white point, ignore light sources (light bulbs, for example) and specular highlights (glare, reflections of the sun off chrome bumpers, etc.). There is no detail in these areas. In other words, allow these areas to simply blow out in brightness when applying your adjustments.

### Example 14.5   Using Levels and the Info Palette

1. Open the SanctaMariaGardenSchool.psd image from the Examples/Chap14 folder on the Companion CD.

   What are your first impressions of the color problems in this image? You should see reddish, dark, and flat qualities. Are there any known colors? Are there any colors we can safely assume? Is there an area we can adjust to pure white?

2. Press I and Shift+I, if needed, to choose the Color Sampler tool. It's safe to assume that the building is white, so place a Color Sampler (remember, Sample Size is 3×3 Average) on the sunny side of the building in a block that's between the rain pipe and the lamppost. Place a second Color Sampler on the shaded side of the building, inside another block. Just below the "AN" in "SANCTA" is a good area.

3. From the main menu, choose Image, Adjust, Threshold.

   The Threshold command displays a histogram of luminance values and converts images into high-contrast black and white images. The tones left of the slider drop to black, tones right of the slider become white. Moving the slider helps you find the darkest and lightest areas of the image.

4. Drag the slider to the right to the beginning of the highlight toe, about 166 in the Threshold Level readout as shown in Figure 14.15.

   You should see a few areas of white—ignore the dots and very small clumps of white.

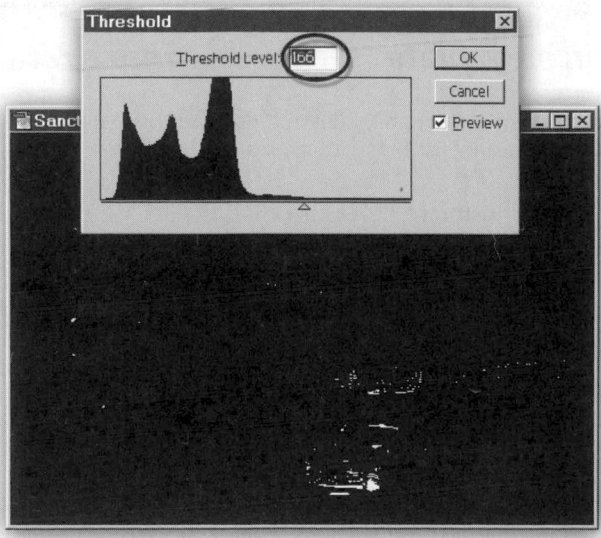

**Figure 14.15**   Use Threshold to find the lightest (or darkest) part of an image.

5. Toggle Preview off and on to see exactly where in the image the white areas are located. The lightest and largest areas of the image are the car's bumper and top part of the license plate. You can use the keyboard shortcuts (Ctrl(⌘)+spacebar) to access the Zoom tool and move your view closer to the car, as shown in Figure 14.16. Because the bumper is reflecting light, set the license plate as white. When you've visually located the top part of the plate, click Cancel.

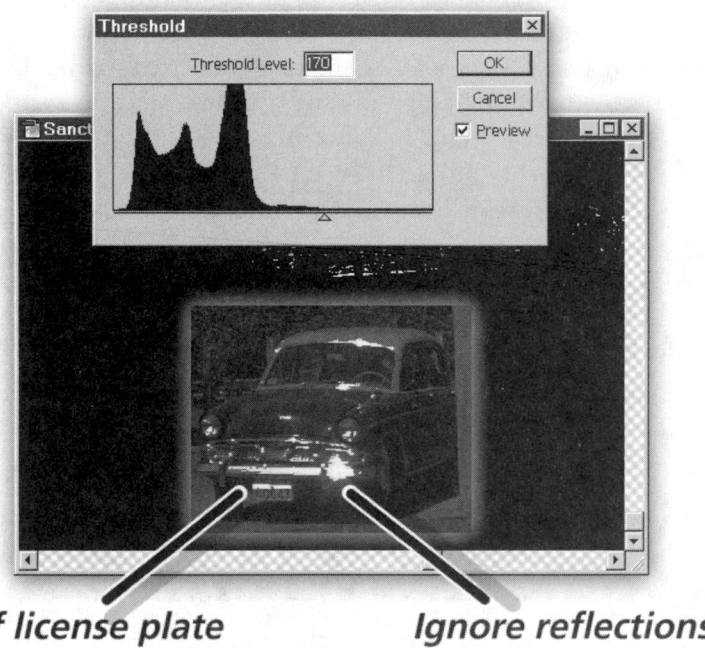

**Top of license plate          Ignore reflections**

**Figure 14.16**    Don't worry if your image doesn't look like this! This screen capture was edited to clarify the best white point area.

6. Create a Levels Adjustment Layer and click the Set White Point eyedropper (far right eyedropper under the Auto button). Press Ctrl(⌘)+spacebar and marquee zoom to the license plate. Click the top, white section we discovered in the previous step.

7. Press Ctrl(⌘)+Alt(Opt)+spacebar to toggle to the Zoom (out) tool and click enough times to return the image view to full view.

   The #1 Sampler readout in the Info palette shows that the sunny side of the building is slightly high in red, and low in blue.

8. Choose the Red channel from the Channels drop-down and drag the white slider slightly to the right until the red value is within 3 or 4 points of green.

9. Choose the Blue channel from the Channels drop-down and drag the white slider slightly to the left until the blue is within 3 or 4 points of green as shown in Figure 14.17.

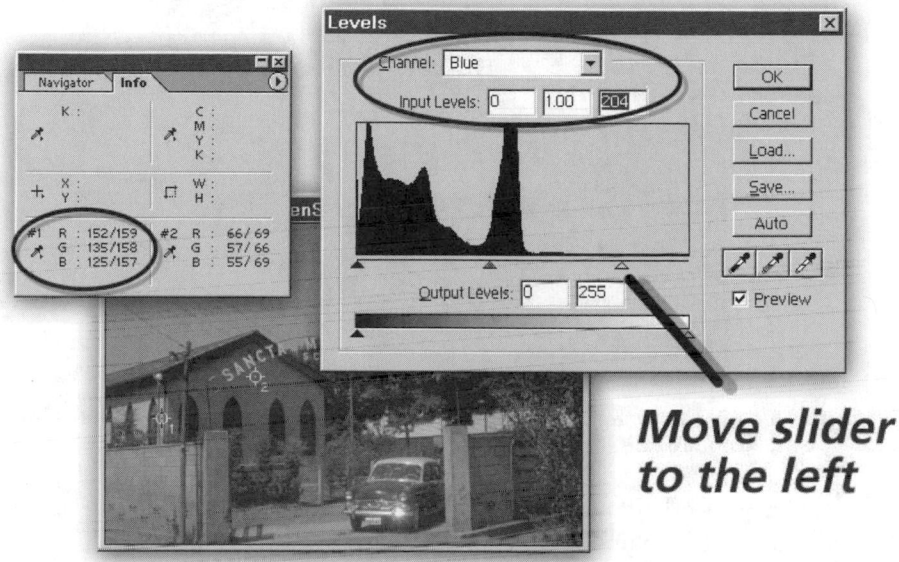

**Move slider to the left**

**Figure 14.17**   Adjust the white slider for the Red and Blue channels so that their values are closer to green.

That takes care of the lighter areas of the image. Let's turn our attention to the darker areas.

10. Look at #2 Sampler.

    Hey, what do ya' know? The numbers are *already* within an acceptable range just from our previous adjustments. (Yes, because we proof these exercises, I could have left out the #2 Sampler, but this is real life stuff, ain't it?) One last channel to adjust—the Composite channel.

11. Press Ctrl(⌘)+~(tilde) for the RGB channel. Remember, the adjustments in the Composite channel affect the *overall* contrast and brightness of the image. So take a moment to determine what kind of corrections would improve the image. Hint: Increase the contrast and brighten the midtones.

12. Drag the white slider left until about 239 or so (see the readout in the Input Levels field). Now drag the black slider to about 14. This adjustment drops out a lot of the detail in the windows, detail that was pixilated "junk"— results of an old slide and a bad PhotoCD scan. Finally, move the midtone slider left to about 1.13, as shown in Figure 14.18.

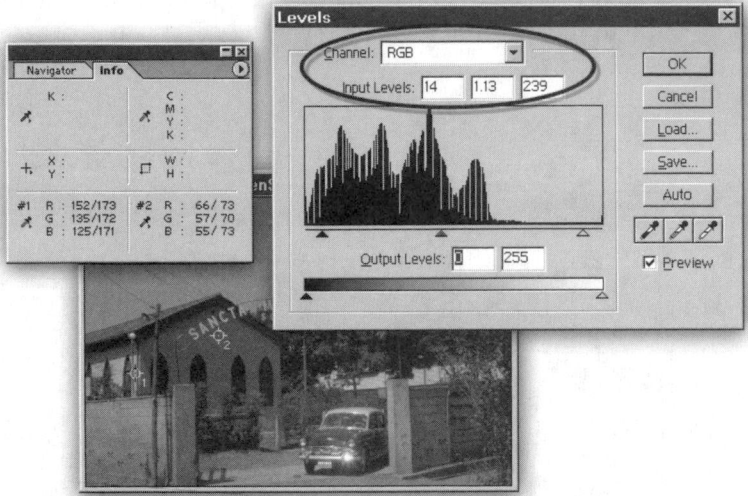

**Figure 14.18**   After adjusting the individual colors, make final corrections to the overall contrast and brightness of the image in the RGB channel.

The image is brighter and the added contrast gives a more dimensional appearance to the photo.

13. View the before and after images by toggling off and on the visibility of the Levels Adjustment Layer, as shown in Figure 14.19. Nice work! Keep this image on hard disk as a testament to your ever-increasing color correcting skills in this chapter, or close the image without saving it.

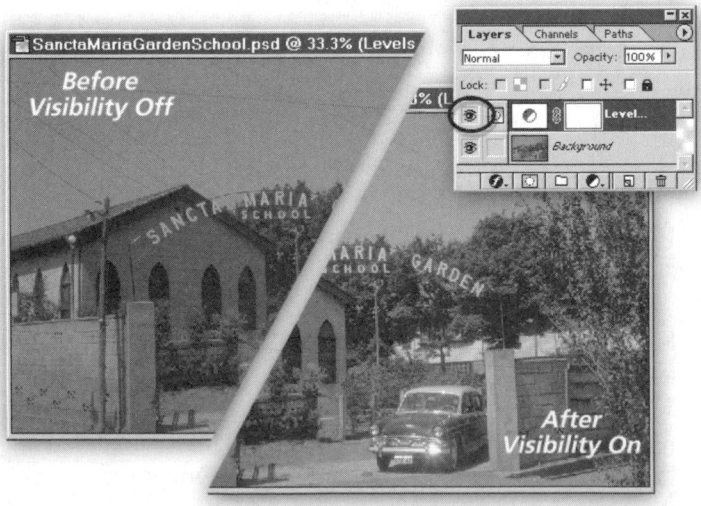

**Figure 14.19**   The difference between the before (with Visibility off) and after (with Visibility on) color corrections will be more apparent onscreen than in this figure.

Whew! You've covered a lot of ground in your color-correcting expedition. Let's pause for a moment and summarize:

- The Variations command is good for, well, learning how colors interact with their opposites.

- Color Balance taught you how to mix colors, but it doesn't include a way to adjust contrast or brightness.

- Levels has just about everything you'd want and need. I say "just about everything" because its drawback is you have only three sliders (areas) to adjust an entire tonal range.

On the other hand (if you have four hands), Curves, our last stop, has everything Levels has, and yet gives you up to 16 points to adjust the tonal range. You can think of Curves as Levels with 16 sliders, or Levels as Curves with only three points to make adjustments. Either way, you have an idea of the difference between the two color correcting commands. So, without further ado, let's move on to Curves.

## Handling Curves

There are people that live and work for a living in the Curves dialog box. They are called color production experts, and it's their job to prepare photographs for publication (the cover of *Life* magazine, for example). They would compare Curves to a scalpel and the other features we've discussed to a butter knife. We say this only to give you an idea of the power and potential of Curves. As a matter of fact, *books* have been written about Curves—only a few features in Photoshop can make that claim!

My own first few ventures into Curves was unproductive, to say the least. If you are new to Curves, a basic understanding of drawing curves is the first thing you need to learn. A short workthrough on Curves basics is highly recommended and what you'll do next.

The following steps will familiarize you with the Curves dialog box.

### Example 14.6   Cruisin' Into Curves

1. Open 3Kids3Bikes.psd from the Examples/Chap14 folder on the Companion CD.
2. Create a Curves Adjustment Layer by clicking the Create New Fill or Adjustment Layer icon located at the bottom of the Layers palette and choosing Curves from the menu.

The line on the graph represents the tonal values of the RGB channel. The bottom-left point is currently black and the top-right point is currently white. The center vertical gridline represents the midtone area as shown in Figure 14.20.

**Figure 14.20**   The graph in the Curves dialog box shows the three major tonal areas.

3. Move the cursor to inside the Curves graph, hold down Alt(Opt) and click inside the graph.

   You've changed the default four horizontal and vertical divisions to ten (seen in Figure 14.21). This is the preferred environment for the precision work that Curves can give you. By default, the shadows are to the left and highlights are to the right as indicated by the black to white horizontal gradient bar located under the graph. We will use this setting for this chapter.

4. Click and drag the white point, located in the upper-right corner, straight down by two gridlines. Now click and drag the black point, located in the opposite corner, straight up two gridlines as shown in Figure 14.21.

   Your image should now lack contrast and no longer have a pure white or black area. Lesson: The more horizontal the curve, the lower the contrast.

5. Hold down the Alt(Opt) key and click Reset. Click and drag the white point to the left by two gridlines, then click and drag the black point to the right by two gridlines, as seen in Figure 14.22.

   Your image should have a lot more black and white area, and have considerable contrast. Lesson: The opposite of step 4—the more vertical the curve, the more contrast.

**Figure 14.21** The more horizontal the curve, the lower the contrast.

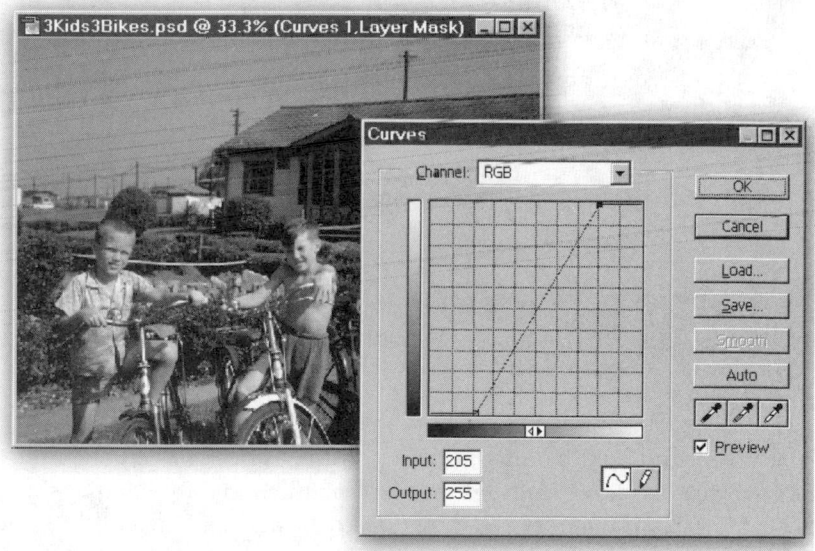

**Figure 14.22** The more vertical the curve, the higher the contrast.

6. Hold down the Alt(Opt) key and click Reset. Move the cursor to the center of the graph (the Input and Output should both read about 128) and click. This places a marker on the center of the curve (you can remove control points by dragging them completely off the graph line, at the high or low end of the graph line). Now drag the marker about one grid square toward the upper-left corner (see Figure 14.23).

Profound observation: Upward movement of the curve lightens tonal values.

7. Drag the marker down toward the lower-right corner about 2 grid squares (1 square past center) as shown in the graph at the right in Figure 14.23.

Lesson: Downward movement of the curve darkens tonal values.

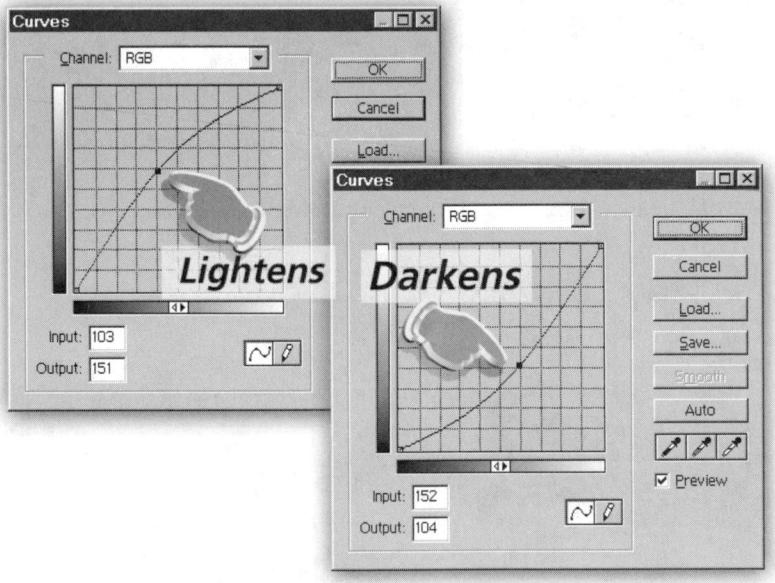

**Figure 14.23**   Upward curve movement raises tonal values and downward movement lowers tonal values.

8. Reset the curve by holding Alt(Opt) and pressing Cancel. Place the cursor on the curve, three gridlines up from the black point (Input and Output should each read 76), click a marker and drag directly downward one-half of a grid. Now place the cursor at the curve three gridlines down from the white point (Input and Output each 179), and click and drag down one-half of a grid.

The shape of this curve is a slight "S" and causes a higher contrast in the midtones. This is a very popular professional photography trick to improve image quality and add snap to a photo.

9. Click Cancel and close the image without saving.

Notice that the adjustments made to the curve were in the RGB channel. Each of the individual colors has a curve that usually needs adjusting. The first step to correcting the color in an image is to go to one of the RGB channels—that's where the problems are, not in the composite channel.

Collect all that you've learned about the Info palette, the Color Sampler tool, the Threshold command, RGB colors, Curves, and let's finish up this chapter with one more grand tutorial.

### Example 14.7   Correcting Color with Curves

1. Open 2CoolKids.psd from the Examples/Chap14 folder on the Companion CD.

   What was your first impression of the color? Flat? Yellow? What are the known colors? Is there an area of pure white? (Yes, that's a *serious* question.) Are there any neutral shadow areas?

   We can safely assume that the car is white (this photo was taken in the '60s, back when the only choices in car colors were white, black, red, and blue) and that the undisturbed snow at the right contains some blue and cyan from the sky. And, of course, there are fleshtones!

2. Press I, then Shift+I if needed, to choose the Color Sampler tool. Place the first Color Sampler in the smooth snow just to the right of the girl's head. The second Color Sampler goes in the center of the boy's chin. Place the third Color Sampler on the lighter area of the car's back-end, and the fourth tucks in the shadow area between the car's bumper and body. Refer to Figure 14.24 for these locations.

   Reminder: Sample Size in the Options bar should be set to 3×3 Average!

3. From the main menu, choose Image, Adjust, Threshold. Drag the slider to the right to approximately 239. Look for a large white area and toggle Preview off and on to view that location in the image (there are several clumps of white at the left of the image to choose from). Once you've settled on an area, click Cancel to return to the image and move any palettes that might be covering the area you determined from Threshold.

4. Arrange the workspace so no palettes are blocking your view of the Color Sampler and leave some room for the Curves dialog box. You can choose Window, Hide Options and/or Window, Hide Status Bar to create more screen real estate. Create a Curves Adjustment Layer. Double-click on the Curves icon on the Curves layer title to go to the Curve dialog box. Click the Set White Point eyedropper and click in the area found in the previous step.

5. Select the Red channel from the Channels drop-down in the curves box. Hover the cursor directly over the #1 Sampler, press Ctrl(⌘)+Shift and click.

**Figure 14.24**   Place a Color Sampler in the locations shown.

You just placed a point on the curve that corresponds with the tonal value under the #1 Sampler. Important note: Because you held down the Shift key, a marker was placed in the green and blue curves channels also!

6. Repeat step 5 for the remaining Color Samplers in the image, #2, #3, and #4 until you have 4 points on the red curve, as shown in Figure 14.25.

7. Click on the #4 Sampler and hold the mouse button down. Notice that there is a circle around one of the control points on the curve that indicates the point corresponding to the #4 Sampler. Click that point once to select it.

The #4 Sampler is reading a shadow, and shadows are usually neutral in color. Lower the red corrected value by pressing the down arrow twice and the right arrow twice. Many of the adjustments in this image are small and the arrow keys are ideal for making minor adjustments.

8. Find the colors that need correcting by reading the Info palette, and then use the technique in the previous step to adjust those colors. See Figure 14.26 for the shape of the curves for each of the colors.

Because the numbers in your Info palette might vary from ours, we cannot give you the exact numbers to aim for, but these are your goals:

- Increase the red and green for #1 Sampler to make the snow slightly more neutral.
- Increase the blue in #2 to remove the excess yellow in the skin tones.
- Bring the color values closer together for #3 because the car is white.
- Bring the red and green values closer to blue.

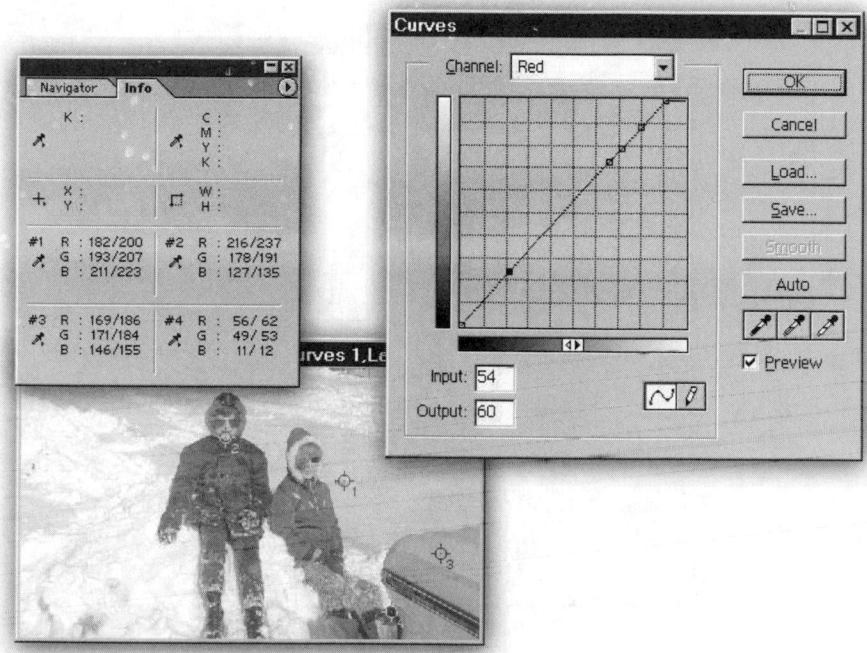

**Figure 14.25**   Press Ctrl(⌘)+Shift when clicking on the Color Samplers to plot the tonal values on the curve in all three color channels.

After fixing the colors, the last step is adjusting the overall tones.

9. Press Ctrl(⌘)+~(tilde) to select the RGB Composite channel. Click a control point at the center of the curve (the very center of the graph). Click and drag the point about one-half of a grid diagonally downward to the right, lowering the midtones enough to create some much-needed contrast. Click OK.

10. Toggle off and on the Curves Adjustment Layer's visibility to appreciate the changes you've made, then you can close this experimental file.

Yay! Bravo! Ya' made it! This color-correcting journey has come to an end and hopefully you've learned enough to start your *own* journey into perfecting your skills and your images. Don't get discouraged if correcting doesn't come easy to you. Like all worthwhile pursuits, it takes three things to succeed: practice, practice, and practice. Or one thing: determination <g>.

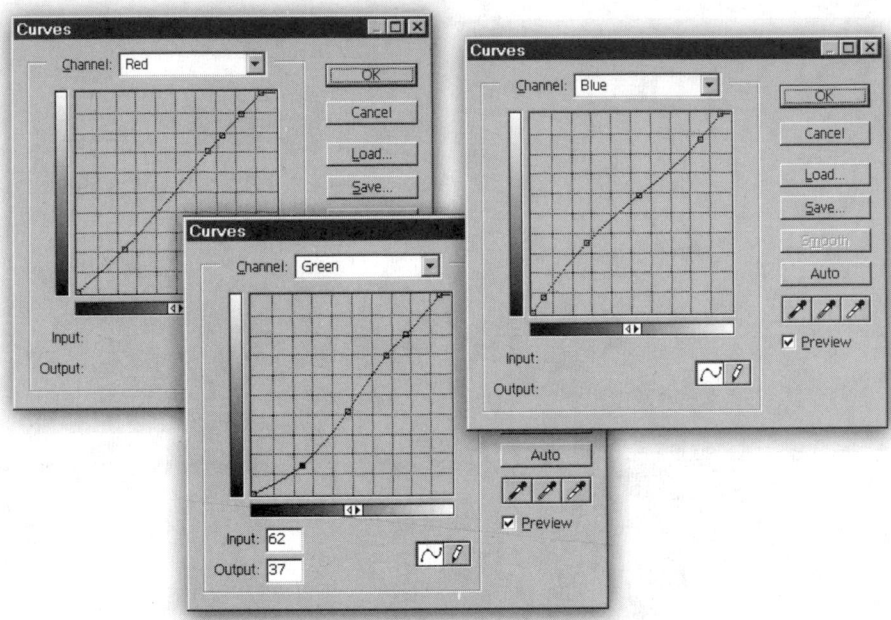

**Figure 14.26**    Aim for these shapes for each of the red, blue, and green curves.

## Summary

Photoshop gives you unmatched power to adjust your images. Find the command you are most comfortable and familiar with and master it, and then move on to a more powerful color correcting tool.

If working with photographs with Photoshop is your game plan for the future, color correcting is just *one* of the many operations you can perform on your images. You may even run across a photo that has more than color problems, like those precious old photos that have suffered the damages of time and physical deterioration. Read on, for Chapter 15 gives you the tips and tricks to repair an heirloom photo.

# *Chapter 15*

## Repairing an Heirloom Photo

It was time to move from the apartment into the house they just bought. While gathering the boxes that were stored in the basement, she peeked into one box and found her one and only baby picture and immediately started weeping. As she pulled the framed photo out for a closer inspection, her heart broke over the extensive damage to the photo. It had been in a very damp environment for only a year, yet much of the photo became glued to the glass, and mold stains were visible throughout the image.

This event happened about five years before Photoshop 1.0 was released and, at that time, it looked like all hope was futile for restoring the photograph to its original condition. Today though, we have a different mind-set and realize that through computer imaging, practically anything is possible.

In this chapter, you will restore a thirty-six year old photo that lost a lot of emulsion (the layer of a photograph that actually contains the image) in a tug-of-war between the pulling of the photo and the glass to which it had adhered. There are also stains from mold to remove. (Yes, there is a "strong possibility" that this is the photo discussed in the first paragraph!) The criteria for choosing a damaged photograph for this chapter is to use one that has many problems common to the average photo in need of a restoration. There are many other problems you may encounter that are not present in this chapter's image, so let's first take a look at common defects and concerns in working with the damaged heirloom photograph.

## Recognizing Issues Unique to Old Photographs

Unlike today's photos that have a smooth and flat surface and a full tonal range, every decades-old photograph has faded and many have a textured or hand-painted surface. Each photo can have a unique flaw with which you need to deal. Foreknowledge and preplanning are of great value when you set out on your restoration adventures.

### Digitizing a Warped Photo

A once popular way to display a photo was to glue it to a hard backing. Unfortunately, this backing material warped and became brittle over time, which made the photograph difficult to scan.

If the photo does not lie flat against the scanner's glass, the result can be an inferior scan (with parts of the image being out of focus, for example). Inexpensive scanners can leave a bluish cast where the material doesn't touch the glass and can also distort the image. Depending on the condition of the photograph's mounting material, you might be able to gently apply enough pressure to flatten the photo. Be careful, though! Breaking the heirloom photo in half is not the goal here!

A safer approach to bringing the warped photo into your computer is to have a quality photo lab create a copy negative of it, and then you or the lab can scan the negative, or have a film-processing place put the image onto a PhotoCD. I recommend the film scan over the PhotoCD—it's much sharper. Transparency scanners are cheaper than ever: The average price for an excellent scanner is around $750.

## Scanning a Wrinkled Photo

A wrinkled photo is much easier to scan than a warped photograph. A decent scanner will have no problem yielding good tonal values in and near the small creases. Often, though, you will need to place some weight on the scanner's lid to help flatten the image consistently across its surface. (This *Inside Adobe Photoshop 6* book is good for more than just reference.)

If the wrinkles are significant and the photographic paper is limp, there's a chance that elements in the photo won't line up to each other correctly. For example, a scan of a portrait with a severe wrinkle could show a mouth or nose that is not aligned on either side of the wrinkle. You must place the picture carefully on the scanner's *platen* (scanning surface), and then gradually apply pressure before scanning; otherwise, the scan will wind up with a distorted image.

## Scanning a Black and White Photo in Color

Most old black and white photographs develop a colorcast, usually sepia or a yellowish tint. No matter how subtle the cast is, detail will be lost if the image is scanned in B&W mode. Your best bet is to scan in RGB mode and then decide what to do with the color—keep the tint, or convert it to grayscale (this is strictly a personal choice). Some people prefer to keep that "aged" look, as it retains the charm of the photo. Sepia tints are especially popular.

On the other hand, some photos develop a less-appealing colorcast, such as green or magenta. If this is the case, you might want to consider converting the scan to grayscale or remove the tint with the Curves command, as covered in Chapter 14.

# Knowing the Characteristics of Your Output

Scan an old photograph and send it to a color printer, a color laser copier, a film recorder, a dye sublimation printer (a high-quality photographic printer), and any other output you might have access to (see Chapter 7 for details on outputting your image). Then compare each copy to the original under good lighting (the sun, for example), and notice, or better yet, write down the differences.

## Does the Resolution Match the Output?

You can arrive at the right resolution for scanning by trial and error. One obvious sign that you need to cram more pixels into your images is the size of the pixels in the output. If you can see the pixels with the naked eye, you haven't sampled enough of the image with your scanner. You can see a considerable difference in quality between a photo scanned at only 36 ppi (pixels per inch) and the same photo scanned at 200 ppi.

Detail is lost when a photo is under-scanned. On the other hand, if your machine is chugging away with every edit you apply to the image, there are too many pixels in the image. For example, if you output to a dye-sublimation printer for a 5×7 print, a 5MB file is adequate. There is no need to work on and then wait for a 40MB file to print. Larger-than-necessary image files only slow down the printer spooling process, while the printer ignores image information that'll never be printed.

**Note**

**Scanning for the Future**   Along with these guidelines, keep the future in mind. What I mean is, five years ago, a new computer came with 16MB of RAM, a 10MB file was huge, and a decent color printer cost in the five-figure range. Today, the standard computer is outfitted with 128MB of RAM, a 50MB file is not considered large, and a high-end desktop color printer is less than 500 bucks.

Projecting just five years into the future with these trends, you might kick yourself for spending hours (or days!) restoring an image at such a "low" resolution! (I chuckle at my so-called high-resolution images from the mid-'90s!) So, the point here is you might want to scan your photographs at a higher resolution than your current equipment needs, just to be ready for tomorrow's toys!

## Does the Color Match?

Something you want to look for when comparing the original print to the copy is *color saturation* (the intensity of the color). Does color saturation need to be reduced or increased? Does the colorcast need to be shifted (perhaps by adding a little magenta to eliminate the green)? Does a color shift need to occur throughout the entire image, or do you simply need to correct a particular color?

After performing all the color and tonal corrections you can think of, the photo might still have a color problem. Adding to this dilemma is the fact that old photos are more sensitive than new ones to any color changes you apply. You will find that a little change goes a long way. The same color correction applied to a photo taken yesterday and to a decades-old photo would have a much greater effect on the older photo. This inconsistency is due the loss of color and contrast in the older photo.

## How Are Details Reproduced?

Look closely at the details of your original photograph. A detail such as grain, for example, might not appear at all in the reproduced image or, on the other hand, the grain might be amplified. Texture can look greatly exaggerated and almost ruin a reproduction when a scanned, retouched image is printed. Notice areas in the finished print where you have used the Clone Stamp tool in your retouching. Do the edges of the brush show as smudges, or are they too sharp? Sometimes what you don't see on your monitor shows up in the output.

Now that you have a better understanding of some of the issues involved in acquiring and printing old photographs, it's time to move on to your first project.

# Restoring a Damaged Photograph

Here's an insider tip: All the examples in this book were written only after numerous and sometimes exhaustive trial and error to perfect the techniques. This chapter's image is no exception.

The photograph for this chapter is called Terri.psd (shown in Figure 15.1) and though it has numerous problems, it's not wise to simply go charging in, armed with all of Photoshop's power, and attempt to breathe life back into the photo. Take the time to inspect the "patient" and find out exactly what the problems are, and then decide the best method and order of administering the tools to restore the image.

## Taking that First Step: Inspect

I witnessed a "professional" photo restorer working on an image of a group of people. Most of one man's legs were missing due to a hole in the photo. The operator proceeded to use the Clone Stamp and sample from the small remaining areas in an effort to build the legs. The result was two highly patterned vertical bars that looked like anything but legs. If the "artist" had taken the time to inspect the photo, he would have noticed a pair of legs at the other side of the photo that would have worked very nicely to clone from. A little time using an analytical eye can not only save you time, but also save the image!

Open the Terri.psd image from the Examples/Chap15 folder on the Companion CD (see Figure 15.1). Let's start with the most obvious problem: all four sides are missing a large amount of image information. Fortunately, the stuff that's missing is not part of the subject, in other words, it's a lot easier to restore areas of plain background or fuzzy blanket than restore body parts.

**Figure 15.1**   Step one in restoring a damaged photograph is to find out exactly what is wrong with it.

Another problem to solve is the slight colorcast and lack of contrast. If you were restoring this photo for a client, ask the client if he prefers to keep the original color or have the color corrected. This is a legitimate issue. Many people actually want to retain any and all color problems—they feel it adds "charm" to the photo. For this exercise though, you will restore a small amount of the color and contrast.

Scattered throughout the photo is another challenge: The photo has many white and dark spots and a few stains. Notice though, where these blemishes are, or rather, where they are not. The spots and stains do not destroy hard-to-replace areas like eyes or a mouth. You will see that meeting this challenge is almost effortless.

Lastly, there is a very serious problem with the emulsion that you can clearly see when zoomed in to around 200% and is also shown in Figure 15.2. Extreme temperatures combined with high humidity can cause the emulsion to lose its smoothness (called *reticulation*).

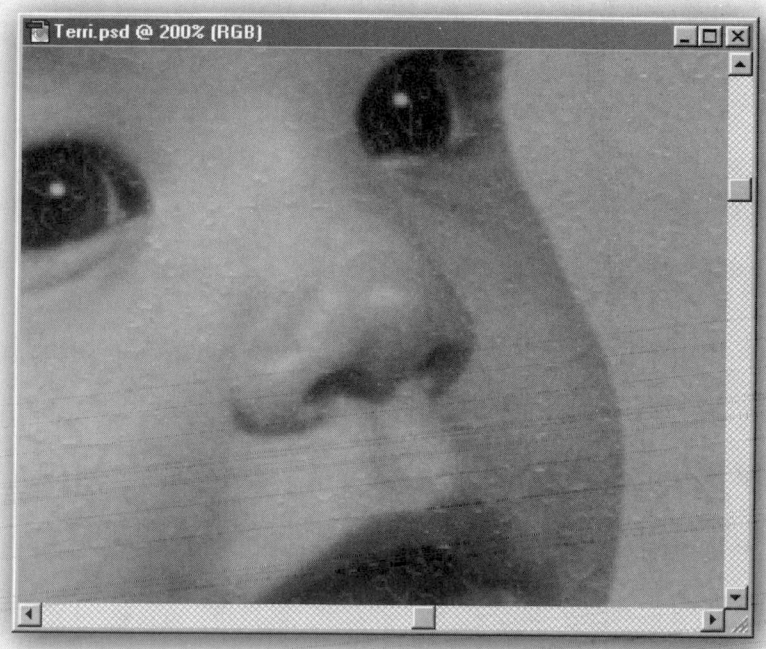

**Figure 15.2**   Damaged emulsion scans as well as photos with a textured surface—terribly!

Unfortunately, reticulated emulsion scans horribly, as do photos that are designed to have a texture on the surface of the emulsion. Many scanners have the option to scan with or without using the Unsharp filter. You can see the difference between Unsharp on and Unsharp off in Figure 15.3, but to see the figure's image in all its detail, open the file UnsharpOffAndOn.psd from the Examples/Chap15 folder on the Companion CD. (Note: These images were scanned at 300 ppi to increase the detail for illustration purposes.) Zoom in to at least 100% and the reticulation is even more obvious. The best bet, and what I did, is to scan the photo with Unsharp off. The image is not as sharp as it could be, but that's okay because an old photo can be excused from looking like it was shot yesterday.

Now that you are well-acquainted with the problems in this image, it's time to roll up your sleeves, collect your tools, and begin the restoration!

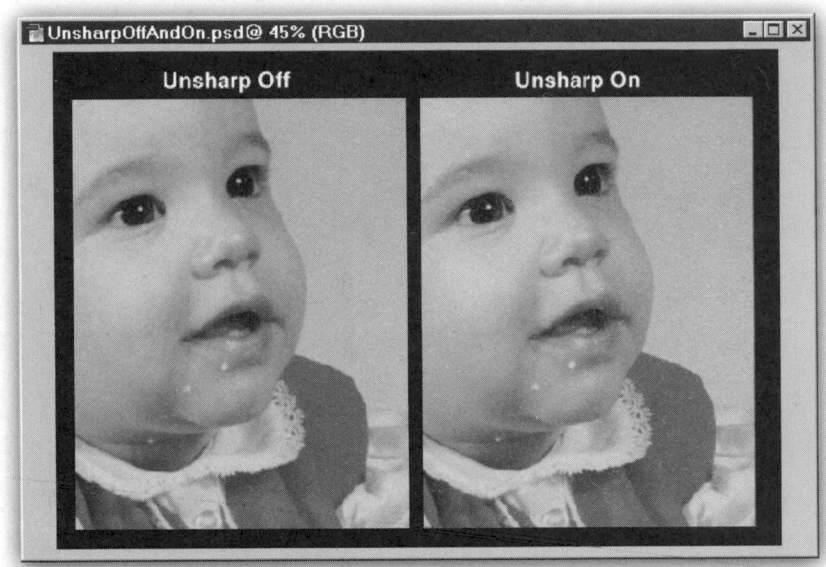

**Figure 15.3**    You can barely see the difference between scanning with Unsharp on and Unsharp off in this figure. For a better view, check out UnsharpOffAndOn.psd on the Companion CD.

## Cropping to the Important Stuff

You only need to do this once: spend three hours restoring an area of a photo only to decide afterward that you don't want that area in the final image anyway. From that kind of experience, the wise Photoshop artist learns to decide at the first edit to crop any unwanted or unnecessary areas in the photograph. It's sort of like ordering a large pizza when all you can eat is a medium. Well, after all, leftover pizza doesn't float my boat!

In the following example, you will crop out nonessential areas and create a white border.

### Example 15.1    Cropping and Creating a White Border

1. Open the Terri.psd image from the Examples/Chap15 folder on the Companion CD if it's not open already.
2. Press C for the Crop tool.

> **Warning!**    If an error message appears when you open the CD files, press Ctrl(⌘)+Shift+K and then choose Adobe RGB (1998) from the Working Spaces, RGB drop-down list. See Chapter 3 for more information.

The original photo is an 8×10 and you want to maintain that aspect ratio when cropping. Unfortunately, the Crop tool does not have a Constrain Aspect Ratio feature like the Marquee tool does. So, we need to do some math to work around this missing goodie.

3. Calculate the width and height in pixels for the cropped area. This is relatively easy, even without a calculator! The image is 200 ppi, so you multiply each dimension (8×10) by 200. (1600 for the width and 2000 for the height). Enter these values in the Options bar as shown in Figure 15.4.

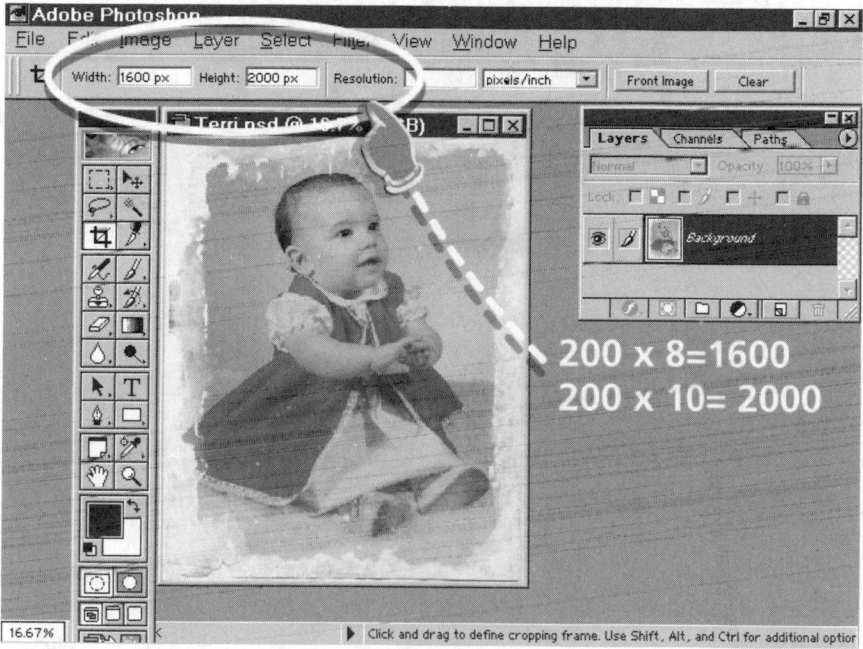

**Figure 15.4**   Calculate and enter the width and height for cropping to constrain the aspect ratio to 8×10.

Decision time—what goes and what stays? The damaged part of the red dress (at the left) is not worth keeping and restoring. You also should save some "breathing room" around her head and her left foot. Otherwise, everything else can go.

4. Keeping all this in mind, click near the top-left corner of the photo, directly above the point where the red dress starts to deteriorate and slightly above her head. Then, drag toward the bottom-right corner and just past the shoe. See Figure 15.5 for where your crop should be.

Unlike the Marquee tool, the Crop tool does not allow repositioning by using the arrow keys. To move the box, click and drag inside it. You can also resize the box by dragging on a corner anchor.

**Figure 15.5**   It's a lot easier to duplicate the furry rug and the background than it is to re-create lace, fabric, and folds in the fabric.

5. Double-click inside the Crop box to apply the crop.

6. Double-click the Background layer title in the Layers palette and click OK.

   This changes the Background layer into a regular layer with the name Layer 0.

   Notice that almost all the image areas near the edges of the photo require restoration and that there's a very good chance that this photo had a white border.

7. Right-click (Macintosh: hold Ctrl and click) on the title bar and choose Canvas Size from the context sensitive menu. Enter **8.5** for the width and **10.5** for the height as shown in Figure 15.6. Click OK.

8. Alt(Opt)+click on the Create a new layer icon located at the bottom of the Layers palette. In the Name field of the New Layer dialog box, type the word **Border** and click OK.

9. Press D for default foreground and background colors, and then press X to switch the colors so that white is the current foreground color.

10. Press Alt(Opt)+Delete (Backspace) to fill the Border layer with white. Now, Ctrl(⌘)+click the Layer 0 title in the Layers palette to load the contents as a selection, and then press the Delete key. The result is shown in Figure 15.7.

11. Press Ctrl(⌘)+D to deselect. Save the image as Terri.psd on your hard disk and leave the image open.

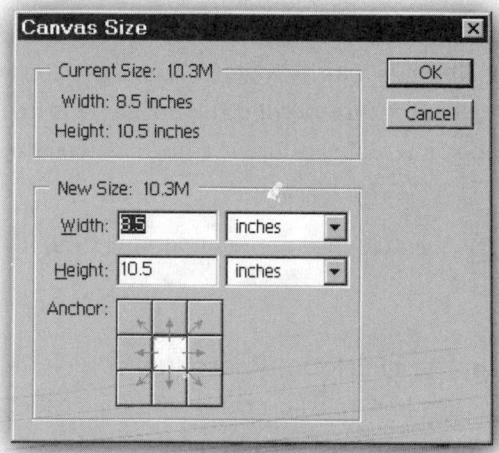

**Figure 15.6**   Add canvas to the image by using the values shown here.

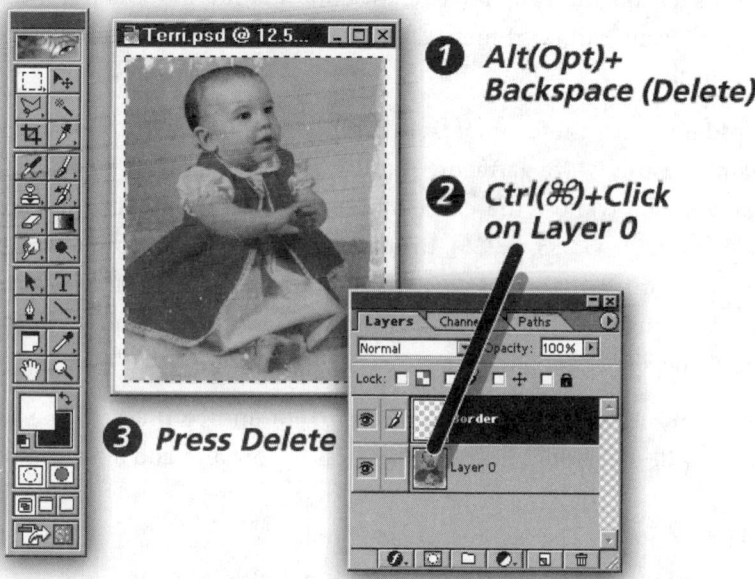

**Figure 15.7**   Create a white border on a separate layer using these three steps.

You might wonder why the border was placed onto a different layer and if you are conservative—in terms of RAM, that is—you might also wonder why you created the border now instead of at the end of the restoration.

Here's the scoop. Rebuilding the damaged areas near the edges of the photo is a lot easier when you don't need to take precautions against encroaching onto the border. Also, using the Clone Stamp at the edges of an image can cause problems if the Clone Stamp's sampling point runs beyond the image. This image needs extensive work at the edges and you're doing yourself a favor by creating the extra maneuvering room.

Now that the image has been cropped to the important stuff, it's time to correct the color.

## Correcting Color in the Heirloom Photograph

In Chapter 14, you learned how to adjust color with the goal of restoring the original colors. This is not always the goal with aged photos. Many years of deterioration that occurs naturally to all photographs destroys contrast and color saturation. With some of this information lost, if you apply a correction that creates a full range of tones (from black to white) and increase the color's saturation, the result could be a high-contrast, overly saturated mess. So, be careful and gentle when color correcting old photos!

The Terri.psd image for this chapter is no exception. The known colors in the photo are the skin and the white garment. You can safely assume the outfit is red and white, but you don't know the exact hue of the red. If you set the garment to become white (R:255, G:255, B:255), the contrast increases too dramatically for this photo and a lot of the flesh tones get wiped out. The artistic call here is to adjust the color just enough to remove the cast and to add a small amount of contrast to reduce the flatness of the tonal values.

Curves is the most precise tool for correcting color and contrast. In the following example, you will make the Terri.psd image less yellow and add a little contrast.

### Example 15.2    Applying Curves to an Aged Photo

1. Open Terri.psd from your hard disk if it's not already open.
2. Click and hold the Eyedropper in the toolbox, and choose the Color Sampler from the drop-down list. In the Options bar, click the down arrow for Sample Size and choose 3×3 Average.
3. Peek ahead to Figure 15.8 to see the location of the Color Sampler on the dress and click on that location in your image. Position the Info palette in the upper-left area of your screen to make room for the massive Curves dialog box coming up in the next step.

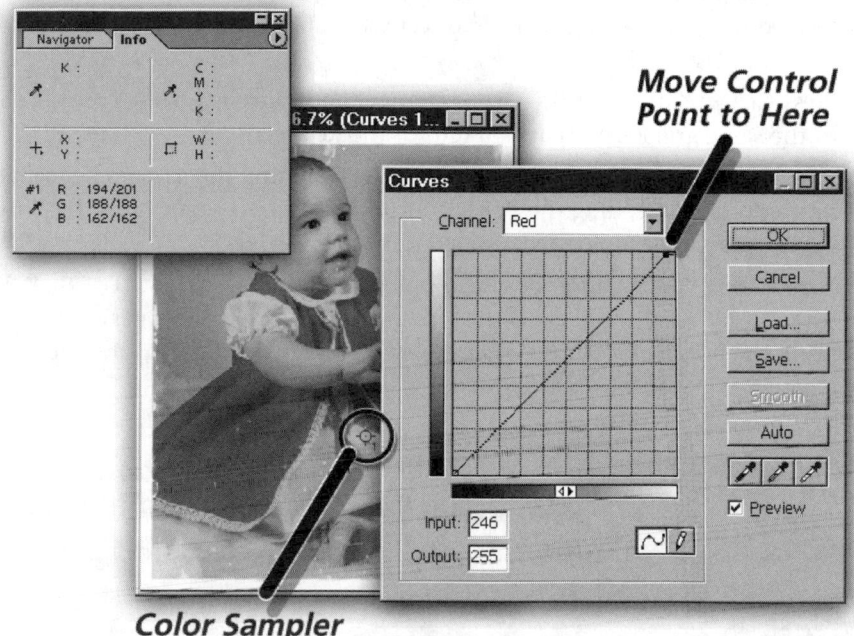

**Move Control Point to Here**

**Color Sampler**

**Figure 15.8**   Move the white control point in the Red channel directly left about one-half of a grid.

This places a Color Sampler in the image and brings up the Info palette. You can see the RGB values for Sampler 1 in the bottom-left area of the Info palette. Notice that the Color Sampler area in the photo should be a neutral color (the original color was white) and that the Info palette shows Red and Green are relatively close, but that the Blue is too low.

4. Click on Layer 0 to select it, then click on the Creates new fill or adjustment layer icon located at the bottom of the Layers palette (the circle that is half white and half black) and choose Curves from the menu.

By selecting Layer 0 first, the Adjustment Layer is placed just above the photo. You want the Curves Adjustment Layer to affect only the layer that contains the photo—not the Border layer.

**Tip**

**Apply Adjustment Layer Before Restoring**   I strongly advise Photoshop users to avoid applying any adjustment layers whenever possible. That way, you can change the settings indefinitely and not alter the original pixels.

But, damaged photos can require the use of localized color adjustments, or painting tools, which requires you to work around the adjustment layer. It has been my experience that applying the adjustment layer before restoring the image, rather than saving it, makes the process quicker and is less complicated.

5.  Press Ctrl(⌘)+1 to select the Red channel. Drag the control point that is located in the upper-right corner directly left about one-half of a grid as shown in Figure 15.8.

6.  Press Ctrl(⌘)+2 to select the Green channel and move the same control point to the same grid location as you did for the Red channel.

7.  Press Ctrl(⌘)+3 for the Blue channel. While watching the #1 Sampler reading in the Info palette, drag the white control point directly left until the Blue value is about five points below the next lowest value.

For example, the reading for where I placed the Sampler shows Green at 195 (the second set of numbers is the reading of the corrected values), so I'll bring the blue to about 190. Figure 15.9 shows the settings in the Info palette.

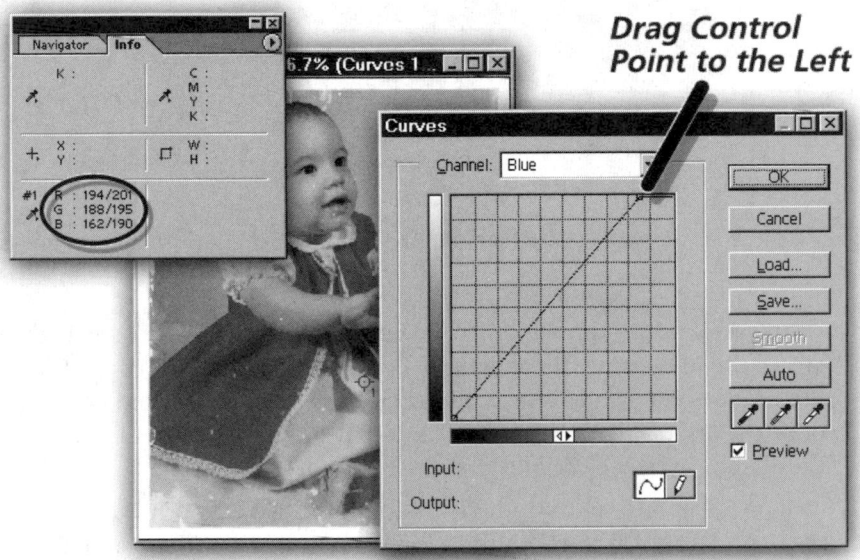

**Figure 15.9**   Drag the white control point in the Blue channel directly left until the adjusted Blue value is about five points lower than the Green value.

Performing steps 5, 6, and 7 raises the contrast in the areas closest to white in the image. You dragged the blue control point further than the other colors because yellow (the opposite color of blue) was too intense. But now, the skin tones contain too much blue and you'll correct for that in the next step.

8.  Click two points on the Blue curve (actually it's still a straight line), with each point being approximately one third the distance from each of the two end control points. The goal is to have three equal-sized segments on the curve. See Figure 15.10 for an idea of your click locations.

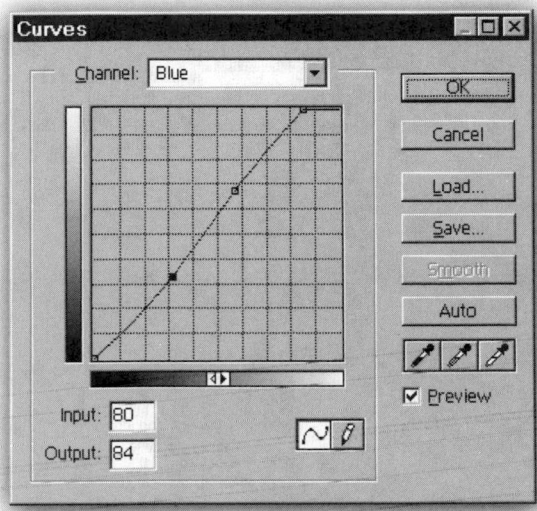

**Figure 15.10**    Add just enough yellow in the lower tonal range to remove the blue in the skin. Note: Your Input and Output values might be different depending on where you placed the control point.

9.  Click the lower point of the two control points you just created to select it, if it's already not selected. (It will become a black dot rather than a circle with a black outline when it is selected.) Nudge the point downward by pressing the down-arrow key three times, then nudge the point right by pressing the right arrow keys three times (see Figure 15.10).

    You now have a very slight S-curve in the Blue channel. This adds contrast and the needed yellow to the skin tones.

10.  Press Ctrl(⌘)+~ (tilde) to return to the composite channel (RGB). Click one control point on the curve in the center of the graph where the midtones are located.

11.  Nudge the point downward and to the right by pressing the down arrow twice, then pressing the right arrow twice. See Figure 15.11 for where your point should be.

**Note**

**Always Tread Lightly**    Notice how relatively small the adjustments were for the Blue and RGB channels. Those adjustments were so small in fact, that you used the arrow keys instead of the mouse.

As stated earlier, old and faded photographs lose tonal and color information that cannot be restored to its original condition. So, with this information missing, corrections have more impact on the image. Be gentle!

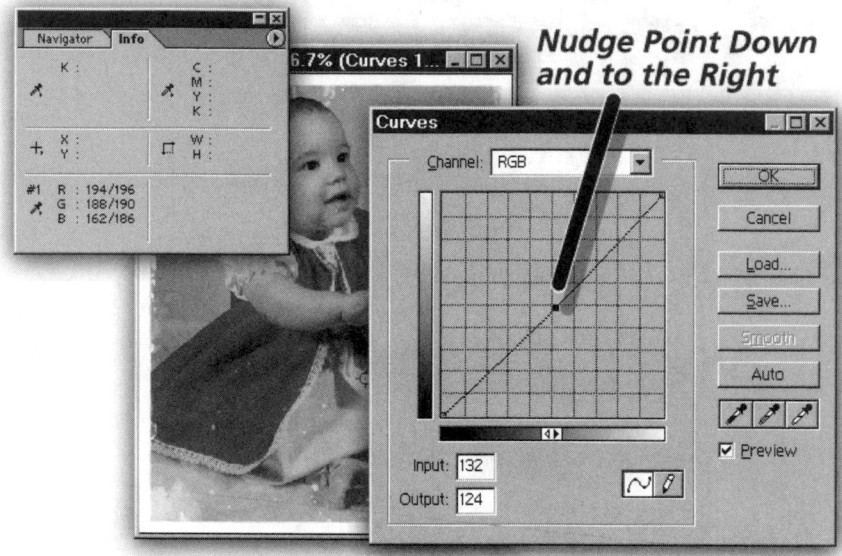

**Figure 15.11**    Slightly nudge the point down and to the right to darken the midtones.

**12.** With the Color Sampler tool still active, hold down the Alt(Opt) key, place your mouse cursor over the #1 Sampler in the image, and when the cursor changes to a pair of scissors, click to delete the Sampler. You can click the Close icon (the X) in the upper-right corner of the Info palette to close it— you won't be using that palette anymore in this chapter.

**13.** Press Ctrl(⌘)+E to merge the Curves Adjustment Layer down with the layer that contains the photograph, Layer 0.

**14.** Press Ctrl(⌘)+S to save your edits. Leave the image open.

I'll take my opinion about Adjustment Layers one step further. It is my practice when working on an image to frequently do a Save As and choose Save As a Copy in the Options field. That way, I'll have copies of the final image in different stages of completion. So, just before step 12 of the previous exercise in your own restoration, you might consider doing a Save As a Copy. You will then have a copy of the image before the Adjustment Layer was applied.

So far, you have cropped the image, created a border, and corrected the color. Now it's time to perform some more Photoshop magic to repair all the physically damaged areas to complete the restoration. Let's start by using the Paintbrush.

## Using the Paintbrush to Remove Stains

Coincidentally, I just painted my house for the first time in 10 years. The marks and stains my kids left on the walls were everywhere. After a couple coats of paint, my house looked like a model home. Okay, so where's the tie-in to this section of the chapter?

With a real paintbrush, you apply a coat of paint. But with your virtual paintbrush in Photoshop, you can specify how the paint reacts to the underlying image area. This feature, called Blending Modes, allows you to choose *how* the Paintbrush affects the pixels in the image. There are 18 Blending Modes from which to choose. The Color blending mode, for example, will change an existing color and still retain the detail and texture of the original image area. The Color blending mode is ideal for repairing the stained areas in our example image.

In the following example, you will use the Paintbrush in the Color mode and paint over the stained areas in the photo's background.

### Example 15.3   Removing Stains with the Paintbrush in Color Mode

1. Open Terri.psd from your hard disk if it's not already open.

2. Press B for the Paintbrush tool. Click the Mode down arrow in the Options bar and choose Color from the menu, click the Brush down arrow and choose the 200-pixel brush (see Figure 15.12).

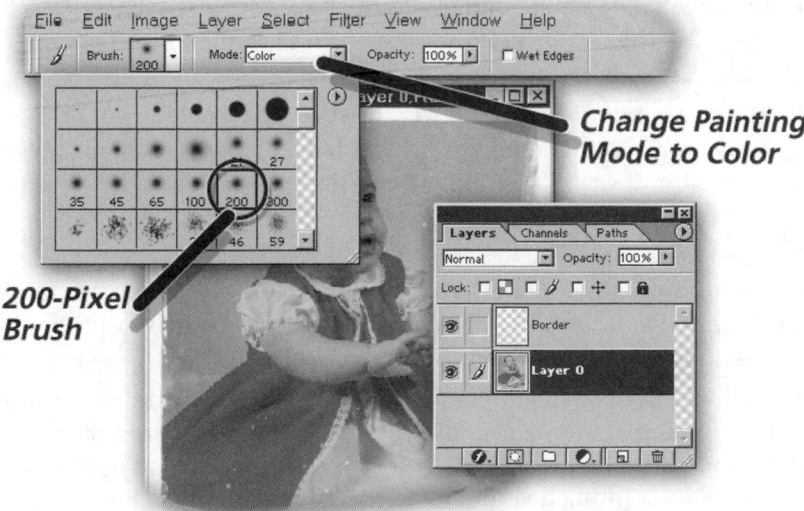

**Figure 15.12**   From the Options bar, choose the Color Blending mode and the 200-pixel brush from the Brush size palette.

**Note**

**Default Sample Point Size**    Your Sample Point size should still be set to 3×3 Average from the previous example. You can check this setting by pressing I for the Eyedropper, then looking at the Options bar for the Sample Size setting. (Be sure to press B afterward to return to the Paintbrush!)

The 3×3 Average Sample Point size is ideal for practically all your sampling needs. This setting should be your "default" setting!

3. Press Tab to hide all palettes, and then press F once to move to the Full Screen Mode With Menu Bar.

**Tip**

**Too Much Is Not Enough**    Regardless of where you set your screen resolution, you can always use more screen real estate. It's sort of like RAM and hard disk space—you can never have too much! To increase your workspace in Photoshop, get in the habit of pressing Tab and F once (or twice). This quick keyboard activity can double or even triple your workspace!

Hiding all palettes and moving your view to full-screen mode is ideal when you use tools that you access through keyboard shortcuts. You can zoom in and out (Ctrl(⌘)+spacebar+click or Alt(Opt)+spacebar+click respectively), and move the view of the image (spacebar+drag) to navigate around your artwork.

4. Press Ctrl(⌘)+spacebar to toggle to the Zoom tool and click twice in the top half of the image to zoom in.

5. Hold down the Alt(Opt) key to toggle to the Eyedropper tool and click once in the photo's background and once just above the furry blanket located at the right. See Figure 15.13 for this location. Be careful not to Alt+click on the stain that is to the right.

6. Position the Paintbrush directly over the stain (shown in Figure 15.13), click and drag slightly left and right until the stain completely loses its brownish color. This brush stroke takes only about two seconds—you don't need to overdo it.

   The stain has not disappeared, only the color has changed. But the new color makes using the Clone Stamp (a later exercise) much easier! Also, there is no need to paint over the white areas and pink areas at the edges of the photo—these areas will be completely replaced.

7. In the upper-right corner of the photo is a rectangular area that is discolored, and two areas that are stained. Alt+click below this area as shown in Figure 15.14, then, with one click+drag, paint over the entire discolored area. If the color you are painting does not closely match the surrounding area (it's okay if it's slightly darker), press Ctrl(⌘)+Z to undo and sample again in a close, but different area.

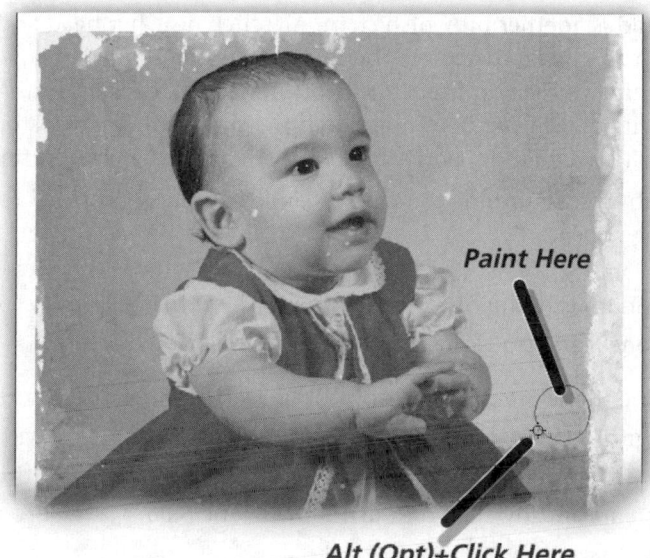

**Figure 15.13**   Because there are many shades in the background, sample the color near the stain, and then paint over the stain.

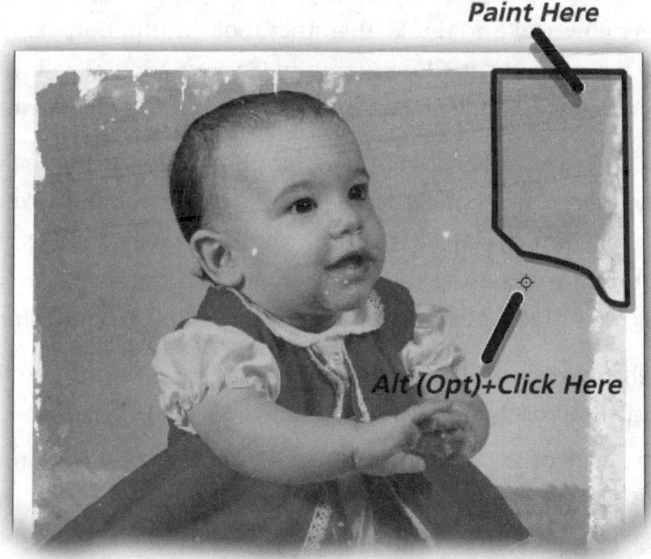

**Figure 15.14**   Sample a nearby color, then paint over the two stains and the discoloration in the upper-right corner.

8. There's one more area that you need to paint over. To the left of the little girl's head is another brownish stain. Alt+click near her head and just below the stain to sample the color. Then paint over the stained area, as well any other stains you see on the left side of the photo's background. Again, if the color you are painting does not match the surrounding area, stop painting, do a Ctrl(⌘)+Z to undo, and sample in a slightly different location.

9. Press Tab once to unhide the palettes and then press Ctrl(⌘)+S to save. Leave the image open.

Nice work! And it's certainly much easier to use the Paintbrush in Color Mode than to use the Clone Stamp to clone out those large, discolored areas.

Speaking of the Clone Stamp, this tool will be used to finish the restoration of the Terri.psd image. If you are not familiar with the Clone Stamp, you will not only get acquainted with it, but you will become very familiar with it by the end of this chapter. If you are already skilled in using the Clone Stamp, I'm sure you'll learn a few new techniques.

## Using the Clone Stamp to Clone Farm Animals, er, Pixels

The Clone Stamp is a tool that you will use frequently when restoring photographs. This tool is very powerful and unlike the other tools in the toolbox. Although you will learn a lot more about the Clone Stamp in Chapter 16, you will learn three key characteristics about the Clone Stamp: brush size, brush edge, and sampling area.

In the illustration I used earlier about the Photoshop "artist" using the Clone Stamp to rebuild a man's legs, not only was the process incorrect, but one of the smallest brushes was used, which added vertical cloning stripes to this Frankenstein creation—all three keys to using the Clone Stamp in a restoration were neglected. Each time the Clone Stamp is used consideration must be given to the following:

- Choose the correct brush size for the area you are cloning—too big and you'll easily encroach onto a surrounding area.

- Match the edge of the brush with the characteristics of the surrounding pixels. If the cloning area is an out-of-focus sky, a soft edge works fine. But, if the image is of a sharply focused brick wall, only a hard-edged brush will do.

- The correct sampling area is critical. A perfect example is the background area of this chapter's restoration image. The gradation of the lighter and darker areas needs to be repeated wherever necessary.

In the following example, you will remove the small spots that are located throughout the entire image while keeping in mind "The Three Keys."

### Example 15.4   Removing Spots Like a Pro

1. Open Terri.psd from your hard disk if it's not already open. Be sure you have the Full Screen Mode with Menu Bar view active (press the F key until you have this view) and that the toolbox and Options bar are not hidden.

2. Hold down the Ctrl(⌘)+spacebar to toggle to the Zoom tool and click on the girl's face until her chin and top part of her head are out of the viewing window (this zoom magnification is seen in Figure 15.15). If necessary, hold down the spacebar to toggle to the Hand tool and drag inside the image area to move the view.

> **Tip**
>
> **Seeing Your Brush Size Is Best**   When using the Clone Stamp or any other tool that allows various brush sizes, seeing the actual size of the brush while editing is essential for accurate strokes.
>
> To choose this view of your brushes, press Ctrl(⌘)+K for Preferences, choose Display & Cursors from the drop-down menu and select Brush Size and Precise (located in the bottom half of the dialog box).

3. Press S for the Clone Stamp and choose the 21-pixel brush from the Options bar. Be sure that the Mode is set to Normal, Opacity is 100%, Aligned is selected, and Use All Layers is not selected.

4. Place your mouse cursor just above and to the left of the white spot that is located to the right of the girl's ear. Hold down the Alt(Opt) key and click to set this point as the sampling area. Now place your cursor over the white spot and click+drag over the spot. Look at Figure 15.15 to see this step half completed.

5. Press the left bracket key ([) once and notice in the Options bar that the brush size is reduced to 20 pixels. Press the left bracket key once more to choose the 10-pixel brush (the brush is not labeled as "10"). Press Tab to hide all palettes—you won't need them for the rest of this example.

> **Tip**
>
> **Double Your Speed**   There are two keyboard shortcuts that you should use to speed up your editing work. The first shortcut is the bracket keys—the left bracket ([) reduces the brush size and the right bracket (]) increases the brush size. The second shortcut is to hold down the Shift key when pressing either of the two bracket keys. Shift+[ will soften the brush tip in 25% increments, and Shift+] will harden the tip in 25% increments.
>
> Using these keyboard shortcuts with one hand and your mouse (or pen) with the other hand, allows you to effectively double your editing speed. Besides, the Adobe software engineers tirelessly labored to provide this wonderful convenience for you!

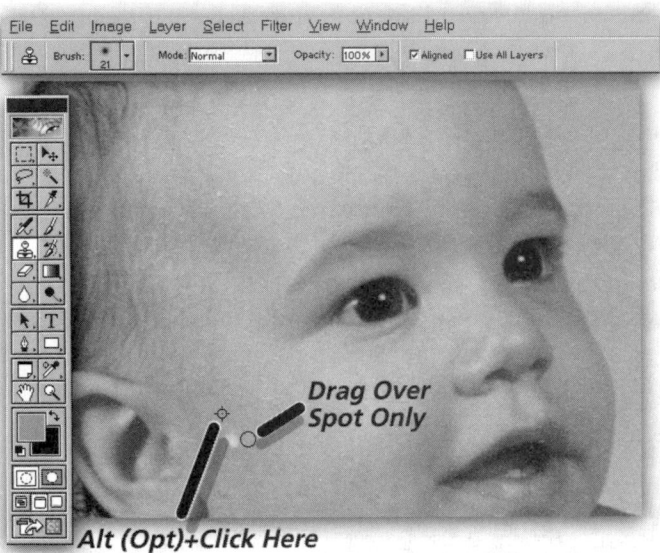

**Figure 15.15**   Click the sample area close to the white spot and use a brush size that is neither too big nor too small.

6. Above and to the left of the eye at the left is a yellowish spot. Alt(Opt)+click next to the spot and then paint over it.

7. Hold down the spacebar and click+drag downward in the image until the top of her head is in view. Press the right bracket key once to select the 20-pixel brush tip and remove the spots in the hair and forehead.

   From steps 4–6, you should have a good idea of how to best use the Clone Stamp on the spots in this image. For this step, be sure to continue any strands of hair and for the spots that are on the skin and the background, repair the skin areas and just outside the skin area. See Figure 15.16 for what your image look like after completing step 7.

8. Hold down the spacebar to toggle to the Hand tool and drag upward in the image until you can see her chin and neck. Use the Clone Stamp to remove the three spots. Be careful to repeat any lines or shading that should go over the area of the spot. For the area just under the lip, press the [ (left bracket) key once to reduce the tip size and use two or three different sample areas.

9. Hold down the spacebar and drag upward again to view the dress area. Find and clone over all spots on the dress and rug area. You will need to use the bracket keys to increase or decrease the brush size. Remove only the spots that are not part of the very large damaged areas at the edges of the image— we'll get to those areas in the next example.

10. Remove the four white spots that are located to the right of her face in the background of the photograph.

**11.** Press Ctrl(⌘)+0 to fit the entire image on your screen. Your image should look like Figure 15.17.

**12.** Press Ctrl(⌘)+S to save all your Clone Stamp work. Leave the image open.

**Figure 15.16**   Use the Clone Stamp to carefully remove the spots in the face and hair areas.

**Figure 15.17**   At this point of the restoration, your image should not have any small spots on or near the girl.

You've brought a lot of life back to this heavily damaged photo and only one more exercise completes this restoration!

You may have heard the sayings, "Start small, then work your way upward." and "Be faithful in the small things and you'll become a ruler over the greater things." Well, you've been using the Clone Stamp on the smaller defects, now it's time to repair the larger defects. You learned the importance of brush sizes, sample areas, and brush edges and removed the small spots that were scattered throughout the image.

Now is the time to introduce another important concept: The larger the brush, the more care must be used for each brush stroke. Large brushes help you work faster and in certain situations, like the edges of Terri.psd, large brushes are the only way to remove unwanted areas. But, the larger the brush, the larger and more obvious the mistake if the edits are not applied correctly. When using the Clone Stamp, I've developed the habit of pressing the Alt(Opt) key with my left thumb (to toggle to the Eyedropper), while keeping my pinky finger over the Ctrl(⌘) key and my middle finger over the Z key—always ready to do the Undo keystroke.

The following example will get you started on repairing the edges and provide some specific tips to help you complete the restoration.

### Example 15.5   Repairing Large Damaged Areas

1. Open Terri.psd from your hard disk if it's not already open. If you are following this example directly from the previous example, press F until Photoshop is in the Standard Screen Mode.

2. Hold down Ctrl(⌘)+spacebar to toggle to the Zoom tool and click three times over the area where the furry rug and the background meet at the right of the photo.

3. Press S for the Clone Stamp tool and choose the 45-pixel brush from the Options bar. Click once on the 45-pixel brush and the preset menu for this brush tip drops down. Drag the Hardness slider all the way to the left for 0% hardness and deselect Spacing as shown in Figure 15.18.

   Be sure Aligned is selected and Use All Layers is not selected in the Options bar. These settings cause the sampling area to follow your new brush stroke area and prevent the white border from being copied into the photo.

4. Alt(Opt)+click just above the small, dark smudges that are located to the left of the damaged edge, then click+drag over the dark smudges.

   You will need to sample from the areas closest to the damaged edges, so cleaning up those sample areas first is necessary.

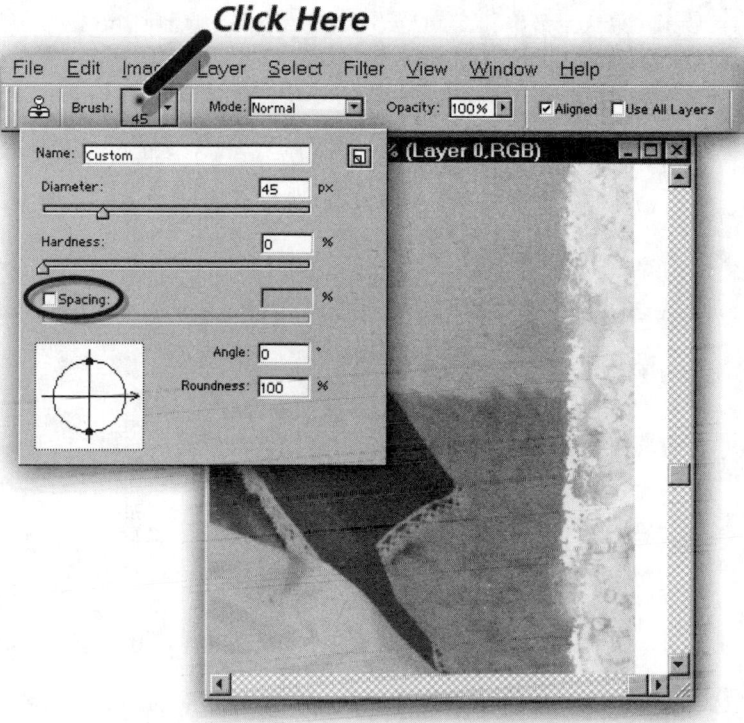

**Figure 15.18**   Each brush tip has a menu that allows you to customize the properties of the tip.

5. From the Options bar, choose the 100-pixel brush tip, then click on the tip to show the drop-down menu. Move the Hardness slider to 0% and deselect Spacing.

6. Alt(Opt)+click on the piece of fur shown in Figure 15.19, then place the brush so that it is half into the damaged area and half in the undamaged area, then click+drag directly right.

7. Alt(Opt)+click to set the sample area and drag straight down in the locations shown into Figure 15.20.

8. Use the same technique in step 7 and restore the fur area to the edge of the photo as shown in Figure 15.21.

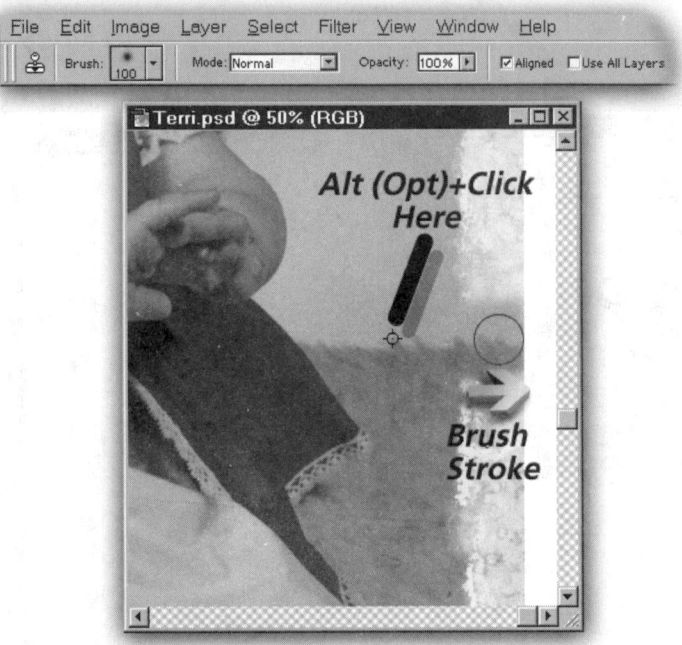

**Figure 15.19**    Repeat the line of the rug's edge to the right of the photo.

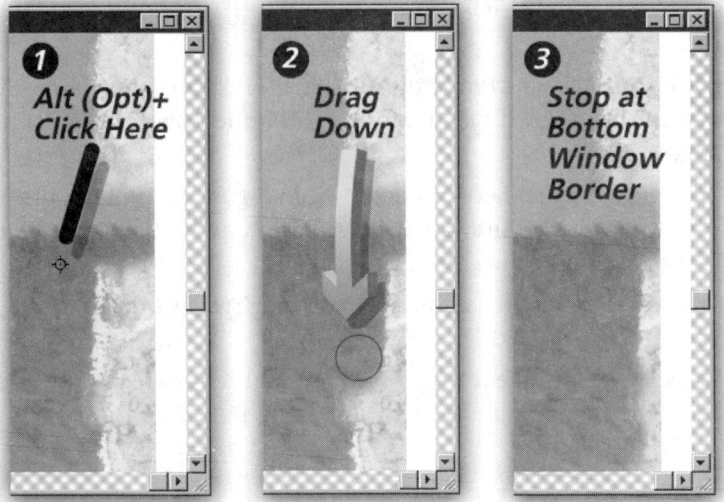

**Figure 15.20**    Restore the damaged area in the fur as shown here.

**Figure 15.21**    Complete the fur restoration in this area by cloning the fur to the edge of the photo.

9. Notice the patterns in the fur that developed from your brush strokes. Unless you are working with wallpaper, brick walls, and the like, you want to avoid leaving Clone Stamp patterns. You can sufficiently disrupt the patterns with only two motions of the Clone Stamp. Because these motions are too difficult to describe by using words, refer to Figure 15.22.

10. Complete the edge restoration, using the concepts and techniques in steps 3–9. Additionally, you will need to reduce the brush size for the smaller areas, especially around the head area. Don't forget to navigate around the image by holding down the spacebar to toggle to the Hand tool and drag inside the image window.

11. When you have finished restoring the edges of the photo, press the Home key to move the image view to the upper-left corner. Check for any areas that you may have overlooked that need to be removed by the Clone Stamp.

12. Press Page Down to move the image view down, and again, look for and repair any areas that you might have overlooked. Continue this systematic inspection using the Hand tool (press the spacebar) and Page Up key when necessary until you reach the bottom-right corner of the image.

13. From the main menu, choose Layer, Flatten Image. Press Ctrl(⌘)+S to save your changes. Pat yourself on the back if your image looks similar to Figure 15.23.

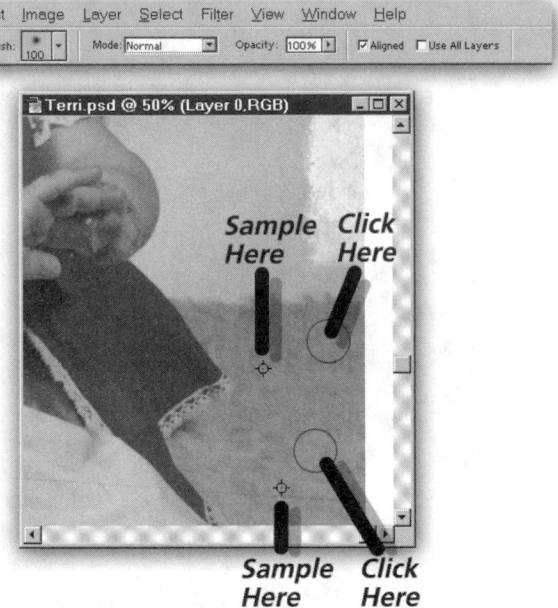

**Figure 15.22** Make your sampling area and brush area in a diagonal alignment to remove the pattern created by the vertical brush strokes.

**Figure 15.23** The completed restoration!

Completing this restoration using only the five examples in this chapter is excellent work! Come to think of it, if you enjoy this arena of using Photoshop, ask your friends and relatives if they have damaged photos that you could scan to practice with. Then, once your skills are sharpened, seriously consider starting a part- (or full-) time business in photo restoration!

## Summary

I remember a raging fire that decimated a neighborhood with very expensive homes near Los Angeles in the early 1990s. Several residents were interviewed by the news media as they stood in the ashes of what was once their homes. Each person had a similar reaction: "My insurance will replace everything except the photographs of my friends and family. Those photographs are gone forever."

This sentiment shows how precious and irreplaceable photographs are, and when they are damaged, we lose a part of the memories associated with them. But fortunately for us, there is Photoshop. And fortunately for everyone, there are people like us that can restore those damaged heirlooms!

Now that you've warmed up to the Clone Stamp, keep it at your side. Chapter 16 shows you how to fix a photograph that, for one reason or another, contains flaws. You can be sure the Clone Stamp will be used!

# Chapter 16

# Finding (and Fixing) Mistakes in Pictures

Have you ever taken a picture that you thought was perfect—only to get the photo back from the lab and notice, for example, that Aunt Nancy has a telephone pole coming out of her head?

Or maybe you were the *only* photographer at a family reunion, and in the group photo everyone was saying, "Cheese," but not everyone's eyes were open. Then you think, "Gee, I wish I had taken a few more photographs!"

If you snapped one photograph of your subject and that photo turned out to be flawless, that's success. If you have *consistently* taken flawless photographs—that's either pure genius, fantasy, or a lie. Almost everyone takes pictures, and *all* of us take flawed pictures.

*National Geographic,* a magazine known for its exquisite photography, employs some of the world's finest photographers. Yet, on average, for every 800 36-exposure rolls of film (a total of 28,800 frames), only 6–8 photos are chosen for the magazine. Granted, their standards are much higher than the average photographer's is, but their artistic resources are more polished. Across the entire spectrum of talent, *everyone* shoots imperfect photos. Fortunately, we no longer have to live with our mistakes—we have Photoshop and our expertise to fix our blunders.

## Assessing and Correcting the Compositional Errors

In Chapter 14, you learned about a phenomenon called *chromatic adaptation*—the longer you look at a photo that contains a color problem, the better the colors look. Well, in this chapter, you will learn about an opposite effect that we affectionately call Murphy's Law of Composition. This law states: The longer you look at a photograph, the *worse* it looks.

This is how Murphy's Law of Composition works: Instead of glancing at a photo and being satisfied, you discover that a more thorough examination always reveals a host of unwanted elements, or that the alignment of two objects is painful to look at (Aunt Telephone-Pole-Head Nancy), and so on.

The photo you have to work with in this chapter is a fine example of the good photo gone bad. In Figure 16.1, you can see our two subjects, Renee, and her two-year-old daughter, Ariana, in a relaxed pose on a picnic table. Although Ariana's grandmother would think it's perfect, we know better. Let's study the photo and find the mistakes in this picture:

- The most obvious problems are the uneven white border (caused by scanning the entire film area in the scanner) and the tilt of the photo, as evidenced by the picnic table, which apparently is leaning to the right.

- A grilling stand appears to grow out of Ariana's back. While this might be convenient and highly portable, it is a mistake nonetheless.

- The vehicles in the background and the picnic table at the right are distracting elements.

- And we can't forget the gratuitous tree-behind-the-head compositional no-no behind Renee.

- The grass needs some touching up in the patchy areas near the foreground and at the tire tracks at the left of the photo.

**Figure 16.1**   Here's a photo that only Ariana's grandmother would think is flawless.

There is one more item to address. The photographer had the foresight to shoot more than one photo (36, in fact). When you're working with people, especially children, it's not wise to leave anything to chance. Even so, only 2 of the 36 photos actually work for this chapter's assignments. In the other photo you'll use in this chapter, ArianaSmiling.psd, Ariana is—you guessed it—smiling. The completed image for this chapter looks much better with both girls smiling, so along with repairing the flaws previously listed, you will insert Ariana's smiling face into the ReneeSmiling image.

Okay, now that we are all smiling, let's start editing this imperfect photo.

## Cropping and Rotating the Image

As mentioned earlier, the white border-like area and the right-leaning table are the most obvious problems. It's worth mentioning that cropping to the subject(s) and leveling the image are two of the most frequently needed edits to improve the average snapshot.

In the following example, you will crop out the white border and rotate the photo.

### Example 16.1   Using the Transform Command and the Crop Tool

> **Warning!**   If an error message appears when you open the CD files, press Ctrl(⌘)+Shift+K and then choose Adobe RGB (1998) from the Working Spaces, RGB drop-down list. See Chapter 3 for more information.

1. Open the ReneeSmiling.psd image from the Examples/Chap16 folder on the Companion CD. From the main menu, choose File, Save As. In the Save As dialog box, make sure As a Copy in the Save Options field is not selected. Rename the file as Renee and Ariana.psd, and save it to your hard disk.

2. On the Layers palette (press F7 to display it), double-click the Background title and click OK. This step changes the Background layer, now named Layer 0, into a regular layer so that it can be rotated without introducing a new background color at the window corners.

   Usually, it's wise to give layers custom names to indicate the layer's contents. Though you will be creating several layers throughout this chapter, the new layers will be merged within the set of steps in which they are created. So adding the extra step to rename the layers is not a value-added procedure in this chapter.

3. From the main menu, choose View, Show, Grid. Press Ctrl(⌘)+K to display the Preferences dialog box. Click on the main drop-down menu, located at the top left, and choose Guides & Grid. For Gridline Every: enter .2 inches and for Subdivisions: enter 1. Now, click the color swatch in the Grid field and choose black in the Color Picker, as shown in Figure 16.2. Click OK for the Color Picker and also for the Preferences dialog box.

4. Press the Tab key once to hide all palettes, and then press the F key once to change the view of your workspace to Full Screen Mode with Menu Bar. Then, press Ctrl(⌘)+0 (zero) to zoom the image to Fit on Screen.

5. Press Ctrl(⌘)+T for the Transform command. There is now a box with six anchors wrapped around the image. Move your cursor just above the top center anchor (any anchor will work, but it's easier to write these steps if we are doing everything exactly the same). When the cursor turns into a bent double-headed arrow, click and very slightly drag in a counterclockwise direction until the picnic bench is as level to the gridlines as possible, as shown in Figure 16.3. (You're trying to align warped wood, so don't expect a perfect alignment.) Double-click inside the Transform box to apply the rotation (or press Enter [Return]).

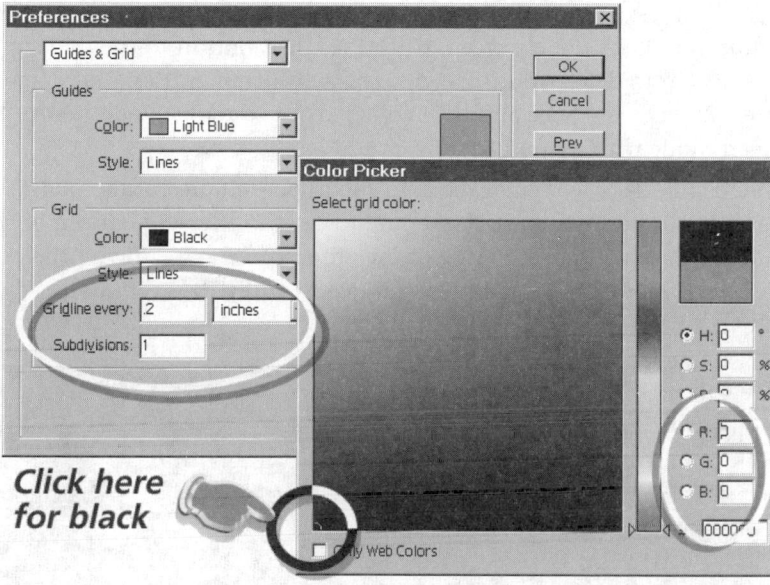

**Figure 16.2**    The default settings for the Guides & Grid do not work well for all images and should be changed to suit your needs.

**Figure 16.3**    Rotate the image just enough to make most of the picnic table line up with the horizontal grid lines.

6. Press C for the Crop tool and press the Enter (Return) key to show the Options bar if it's not onscreen. Click the Clear button to the right on the Options bar to delete width, height, and resolution entries. Then press the Enter (Return) key once and the Tab key twice to return your view to Full Screen Mode with Menu Bar.

7. Using Figure 16.4 as a guide, click in the upper-left area of the image, and then drag to the bottom right. Be sure to drag to the very bottom of the image. You can adjust each side of the crop box by dragging on the center anchors. Double-click inside the marquee to apply the crop.

**Figure 16.4**    Using the Crop tool, select the area shown here.

8. Press Ctrl(⌘)+H to hide the grid, and then press F twice to return to Standard Screen Mode. Press Ctrl(⌘)+S to save your changes. Keep the image open.

Correcting the most obvious flaw in a photo undeniably creates the most dramatic improvement. I don't know about you, but *I* feel a *lot* better knowing that the girls won't slide off the picnic table and into the white border.

One of the most popular digital imaging effects among the "gee-whiz crowd" is to place one person's head onto another person's body. Well, since we are sophisticated Photoshop users, we wouldn't *dream* of creating such an amateurish, cheap-trick kind of image. Instead, we will place someone's head (from one photo) onto *her own* body in another photograph.

## Compositing Two Photos Using Layers

Editing parts of a person's body, especially the face, requires more precise and artfully applied edits than almost anything else you can bring into Photoshop. After all, of the zillions of objects that we see, we are most familiar with the human body.

Your most important goal in the following set of steps is to correctly size Ariana's face from a different photo with her face in the image you are working on. Let's do some digital surgery.

### Example 16.2   Artfully Blending One Face onto Another Face

1. Open the Renee and Ariana.psd image from your hard disk if it's not open already. Press the Tab key to show the toolbox and palettes in the interface.

2. Open the ArianaSmiling.psd image from the Examples/Chap16 folder on the Companion CD. Press M for the Marquee tool (you want the Rectangular marquee tool) and loosely select around Ariana's head, as shown in Figure 16.5.

3. Press Ctrl(⌘)+C to copy the selected area to the Clipboard, and then close the ArianaSmiling.psd image without saving it.

**Figure 16.5**   Create a loose-fitting rectangular marquee around Ariana's face.

4. Press Ctrl(⌘)+V to paste the Clipboard's contents into the Renee and Ariana image. You now have a new layer, called Layer 1, which contains Ariana's smiling face.

5. Press V for the Move tool, and position the smiling face over the face that is not smiling. Precision placement is not necessary in this step.

6. Hold down Ctrl(⌘)+spacebar to toggle to the Zoom tool, and click three times on Ariana's face.

7. Press 5 to change the opacity of the new layer to 50%, and then press Ctrl(⌘)+T for the Transform command.

8. Position the box so that you can see both pairs of eyes and nostrils, and then rotate the box so that the eyes and nostrils are parallel to those on the other layer, as shown in Figure 16.6.

   If you want to do this the easy way, you can type –6.2 in the Set Rotation box in the Options bar. This is the amount we calculated when designing the assignment.

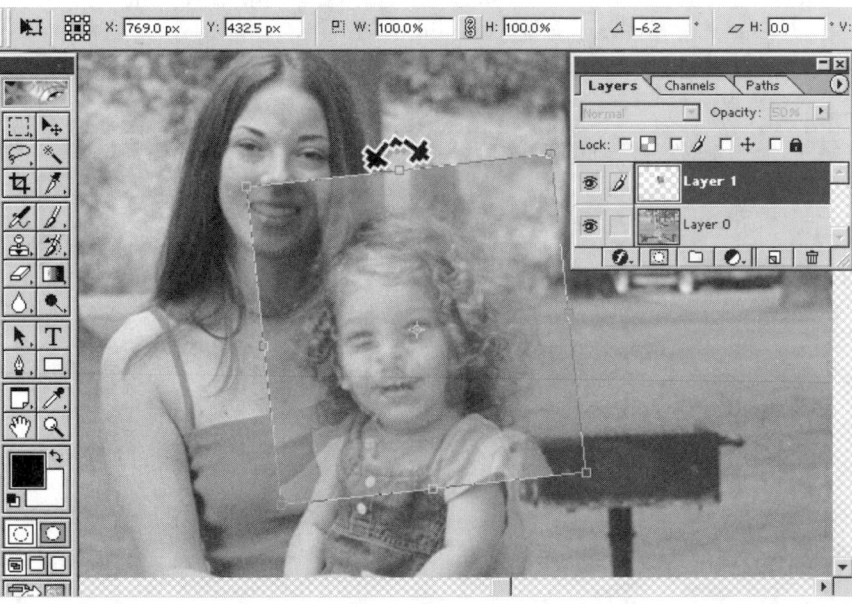

**Figure 16.6**    Rotate Layer 1 to align with the head tilt on Layer 0.

9. Hold down the Shift key and slightly drag one of the four corner anchors in toward the center of the box until the hairline, eyes, and nose align in size with those on Layer 0. You may need to use the arrow keys to nudge Layer 1 after scaling, to align the position of the facial elements. Figure 16.7 shows what your image should look like at this point.

**Figure 16.7** Scale and nudge Ariana's face to match her other face on Layer 0.

If you'd like to do this the easy way, type **83.1** in the W: and H: boxes in the Options bar. See, don't we go that extra mile for you?

10. Double-click inside the Transform box to apply the rotation and scaling. While the Move tool is still chosen, press 0 (zero) to return Layer 1's opacity to 100%.

    Actually, *all* selection tools, when chosen, enable you to type the Opacity value into the Layers palette without inserting your cursor into the field— you just type merrily away. But because we're using the Move tool, it seems like an ergonomic choice of tools to enable this Opacity shortcut.

11. Click the Layer Mask icon at the bottom of the Layers palette. Press D for default colors so that black is your foreground color. Press B for the Paint-brush, and choose the 35-pixel brush from the Options bar's Brush flyout.

**Tip**

**Use the Keyboard to Adjust the Hardness of Brush Tips** The hardness of any brush tip can now be adjusted by using the keyboard. Hold down the Shift key and press [ (left square bracket) to soften the tip, or press ] (right square bracket) to harden the tip. Each time you press either bracket key, the hardness is adjusted in increments of 25 percent. If you are not using an English language version of Photoshop, check the doc-umentation to find *all* the keyboard shortcuts for the language you are using. We're documenting the U.S. English edition of Photoshop in this book.

**12.** Starting at the top, center of Ariana's forehead and at the hairline, *carefully* paint along the outside outline of Ariana's face. Your brush will pass over her hair, neck, and ears. You may need to move the brush slightly into her face area to remove any double face edges. Figure 16.8 shows what your image should look like after this step.

If you accidentally paint too far into her face, press the X key to swap the foreground and background colors so that white is the current foreground color, and then paint over your mistake to remove the mask. Press X again to return black as your foreground color.

**Figure 16.8**    Paint layer mask along the outside of Ariana's face to show her hair, neck, and shirt on the bottom layer.

**13.** Paint layer mask over the remaining areas, *not* including her face, on Layer 1. The areas to paint are Ariana's hair, clothing, Renee, and the background. See Figure 16.9 for what your image should look like at this point.

If you'd like to check how well you positioned and masked Layer 1, repeatedly click off and on Layer 1's visibility icon (the eye icon) to see the alternating smiling and nonsmiling face.

**14.** Click, and then drag the Layer Mask thumbnail into the trash and choose Apply in the attention box. Press Ctrl(⌘)+E to merge Layer 1 into Layer 0, and then press Ctrl(⌘)+S to save your changes. Leave the image open.

**Figure 16.9** After painting layer mask over the remaining nonfacial areas, your image should look like this.

Congratulations, Doctor, er, Photoshop Artist—your operation was a success! Notice how much easier it is to blend only the face onto the existing face, rather than select, copy, paste, and blend the face *plus* the hair! Hair is one of the most difficult elements to select and edit—actually, it's a time-consuming, frustrating nightmare! So, place this trick of blending only the face, not the hair, in your Photoshop goodie bag.

Now, you will switch hats from surgeon to carpenter and use your tools to fill in the missing bench area in the lower right of the image.

## Creating Digital Lumber

Master carpenters are amazing to watch as they measure and cut wood into perfect-fitting pieces. What's more amazing is that their tools do not have buttons labeled "Ctrl(⌘)+Z" (Undo)!

In the following set of steps, you will create a wood area in the transparent area of the image, using layers, layer mask, the Clone Stamp, and Ctrl(⌘)+Z (if necessary).

Example 16.3    Filling in the Bench Area

1. Press Ctrl(⌘)+0 (zero) to move the image view to fit your screen. Then drag the image window from either of the bottom corners outward to make the window slightly larger than the image. Macintosh users: drag the Size box to show the background of the image window.

2. Press M for the Rectangular Marquee tool.

3. Place your cursor just outside the bottom-left corner of the image, and then click and drag up and to the right until you have selected the bench to the point where the transparent area begins (see Figure 16.10).

**Figure 16.10**    Use the Rectangular Marquee tool to select the area of the bench shown here.

4. Press Ctrl(⌘)+J to copy the selected area to a new layer. Press V for the Move tool, and make sure that the Auto Select Layer option is not selected on the Options bar.

5. Press Ctrl(⌘)+[ (left bracket) to send the new layer, Layer 1, backward to below Layer 0. Hold down the Shift key and click over the area of the bench where you created the marquee, and drag to the right until the bench area on Layer 1 meets the right edge of the image, as shown in Figure 16.11. Holding down the Shift key constrains this move to horizontal.

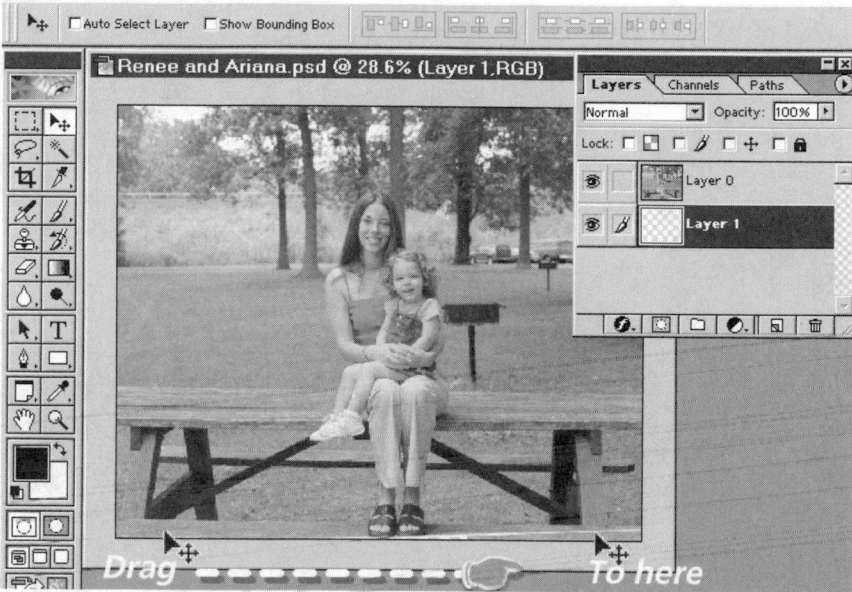

**Figure 16.11**   Move the copied bench area to the far-right bottom corner of the image.

6. If you have a keen eye, you'll notice a remaining transparent area. Click and drag Layer 1 down to the Create a new layer icon to make a copy of Layer 1. Intuitively, this new layer is named Layer 1 copy.

7. Again, hold down the Shift key, but this time click and drag to the left until the bench area on Layer 1 copy completely covers the transparent area, as shown in Figure 16.12.

8. Click on the Layer 0 title in the Layers palette to make it active for editing, and then click the Add a mask icon at the bottom of the Layers palette. Press B for the Paintbrush and choose the Soft Round 13-pixel brush from the fly-out Brush palette.

   Hover your cursor around the middle of the second row, and a pop-up tool tip will tell you which brush is the 13-pixel one.

9. Press D for default colors so that black is the foreground color. Press Ctrl(⌘)+spacebar to toggle to the Zoom (In) tool, and click three times over the bottom-right corner of the image. Starting at the right edge of the image, paint over the white line on the bench.

10. Once you've removed the white line to the left edge of the image window, hold down the spacebar to toggle to the Hand tool, and click and drag to the right until you see the remaining part of the white line. Paint layer mask over the remaining white area (see Figure 16.13).

**Figure 16.12**    Move the bench area on Layer 1 copy to the left until the transparent area is filled.

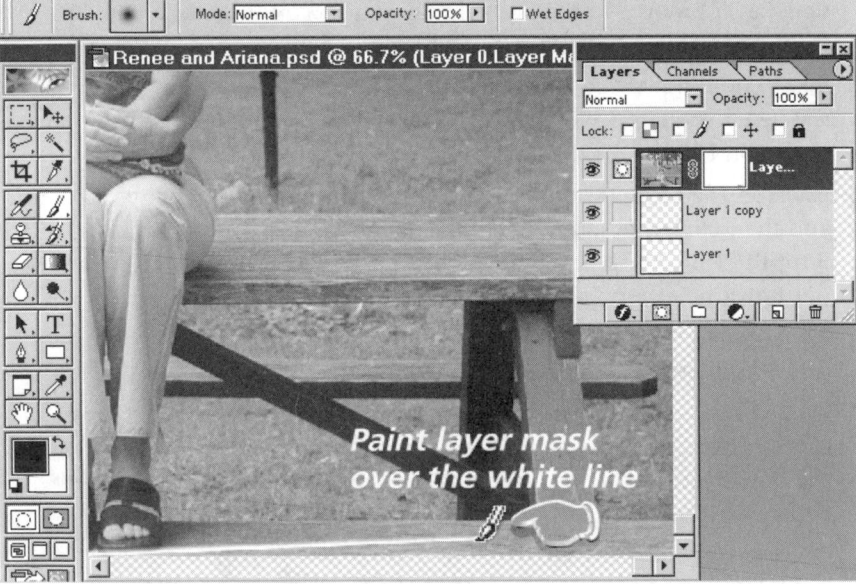

**Figure 16.13**    Paint the white line with layer mask to show the bench areas that you copied in steps 5 and 6.

If you go too far to the left and transparency begins to show, press X to exchange the foreground and background colors and paint that area with white to remove layer mask.

11. Press Ctrl(⌘)+Shift+E to merge all visible layers.

    Merge all visible layers is a powerful command. Notice that the layers merged into one layer and that the layer mask was applied without the alert message. Use this command when you are *certain* you want the results—and side effects—it produces!

12. Press Ctrl(⌘)+spacebar for the Zoom tool, and click twice over Renee's feet. The front area of her sandals needs to be reconstructed.

13. Press S for the Clone stamp tool and choose the Soft Round 9-pixel brush from the Brush flyout palette on the Options bar. Position the cursor over the upper-right area of Renee's right sandal (see Figure 16.14), and then press Alt(Opt) and click to set that point as the start of the sampling area. Beginning at the right side, where the sandal is missing, paint toward the left to create the missing sole areas. When the sampling area runs into the grass, Alt(Opt)+click at the original point again and resume painting.

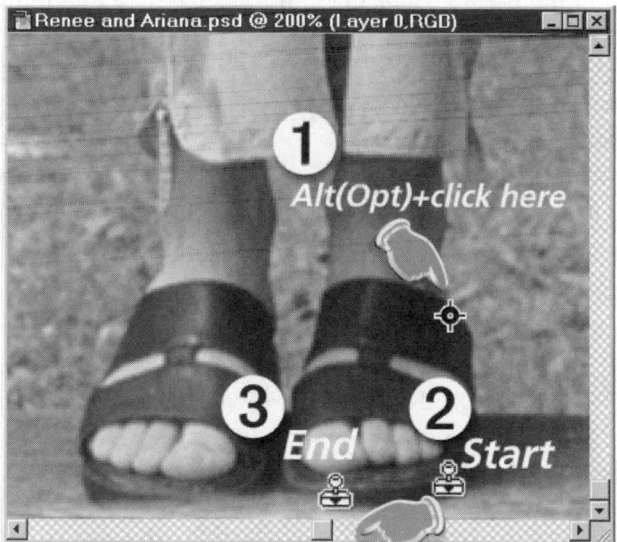

**Figure 16.14**   Set the start of the sampling area in the upper-right part of the sandal, and then paint the missing area of the sole.

14. Repeat the previous step for the left sandal, sampling from the upper-left sandal area. When you are happy with your shoe repair work, press Ctrl(⌘)+S to save your edits. Leave the image open.

Working on the digital wood bench is much quieter than banging away with a hammer on a real wooden bench. Your neighbors are grateful, especially if you go through the steps at night!

Let's take off the carpenter's hat, put on a park designer's hat, and use the Clone stamp to remove the grill stand.

## Retouching with the Clone Stamp

Unless you are extremely quick and observant when you take photographs, it is hard to notice when you juxtapose the main subject with a clearly defined object in the background. After all, you are there at the scene and you know what the various objects are and where they are placed. Then, once the photos are developed and that particular scene is now in two dimensions, you notice a grill appearing to grow out of one of your subjects, as in this chapter's photo.

But this problem doesn't throw you because you know that the metallic backpack Ariana appears to be toting can be detached using Photoshop. Be careful, though, to protect the part of the person where you'll use the Clone stamp tool.

In the following steps, you will create a selection that borders Ariana and Renee's arms, and then clone grass over the grill.

### Example 16.4   Removing the Grill Stand

1. Open the Renee and Ariana.psd image from your hard disk, if it's not open already. Press F once to move your view to Full Screen Mode with Menu Bar.

2. Hold down Ctrl(⌘)+spacebar to toggle to the Zoom tool, and click on the area where the grill stand touches Ariana until you see only the upper half of the stand. The number of mouse clicks will vary, depending on your initial zoom percentage and your screen's resolution.

3. Press L for the Lasso tool. In the Options bar, type **1** for Feather, and click Anti-aliased. Click and drag along the line of Ariana's shirt and Renee's arm where the grill makes contact with these areas, and then drag into Ariana's arm and back to the beginning of the selection. The area you should select is shown in Figure 16.15.

   The Feather value of 1 was determined by trial and error in an effort to match the edge fuzziness between contrasting pixels in the surrounding area.

4. Press Ctrl(⌘)+Shift+I to create an inverse of the selection, and then press Ctrl(⌘)+H to hide the marquee.

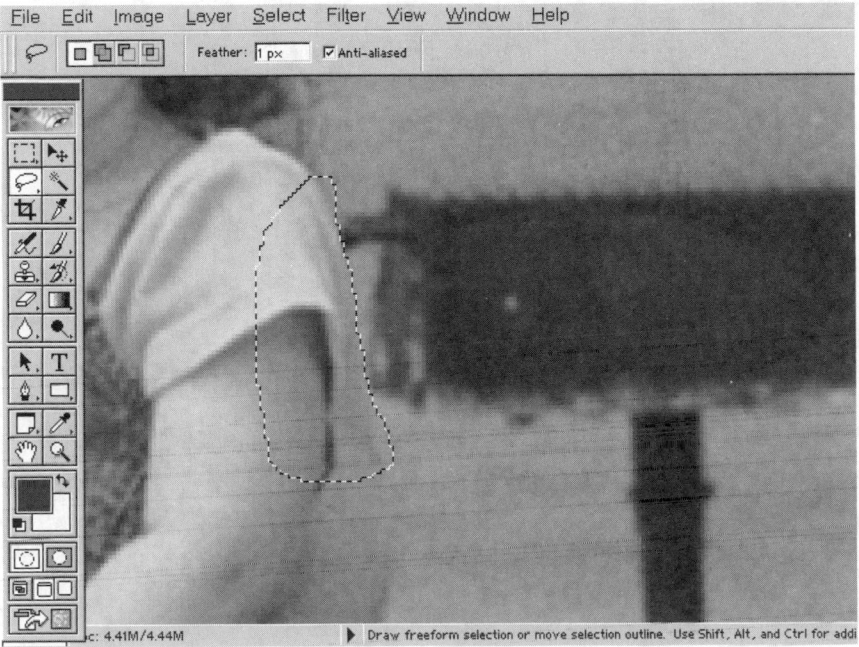

**Figure 16.15**   Use the Lasso tool to select along the edges of both arms.

**Tip**

**Want to See What's Going On?**   When you are editing up to the edges of a selected area, you need to see what's going on at the edges, and the marquee of a selection covers the edges of that selection. The command to hide the marquee (Ctrl(⌘)+H) is extremely useful because it enables you to see your edits as they are happening. You can also toggle back to view the marquee by pressing Ctrl(⌘)+H again.

In this version of Photoshop, you have complete control over the "persistence" of such nonprinting screen helpers as the grid, guides, selection marquees, and so on. If you want to toggle a selection to invisibility, but want to keep a guide onscreen, choose View, Show, Show Options, and then check the items that shall be persistent for a particular assignment. To hide persistent onscreen items, you need to go back to the Show Options box and change your preference, or else go to View, Show, and uncheck the item(s) you want hidden in the image.

5. Press S for the Clone Stamp tool, and choose the 21-pixel brush from the Options bar.

6. Using Figure 16.16 as a guide, click the initial sampling point—Alt(Opt)+click—just above and to the right of where the handle of the grill touches Ariana's arm area. Place the cursor over the grill handle, and then click and drag the cursor in a small circular motion.

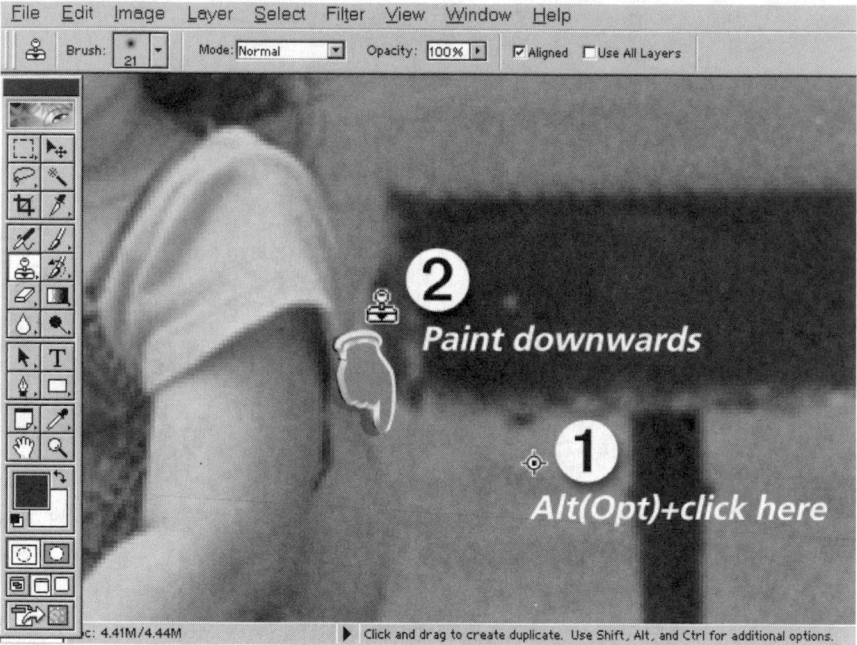

**Figure 16.16**    Use these two motions of the Clone Stamp tool to paint the grass area over the grill's handle.

7. Click another initial sampling point in the grass area just below the grill and about halfway between the arm and the pole. Starting at the top of the area of the grill that makes contact with the arm, click and drag downward to create grass over this part of the grill, as shown in Figure 16.17.

8. Press Ctrl(⌘)+Alt(Opt)+spacebar to toggle to the Zoom (out) tool, and click twice over the grill.

9. From the Brush flyout on the Options bar, choose the Soft Round 35-pixel brush. Press the Tab key to hide all palettes.

10. Clone grass areas over the remaining grill stand areas. Pay close attention to maintaining consistency in the different shading within the grass area. Also, to avoid creating an obvious pattern of repeated areas, try sampling in different grass areas.

11. When your image resembles Figure 16.18, press Ctrl(⌘)+D to deselect the (hidden) selection. Save the image and leave it open.

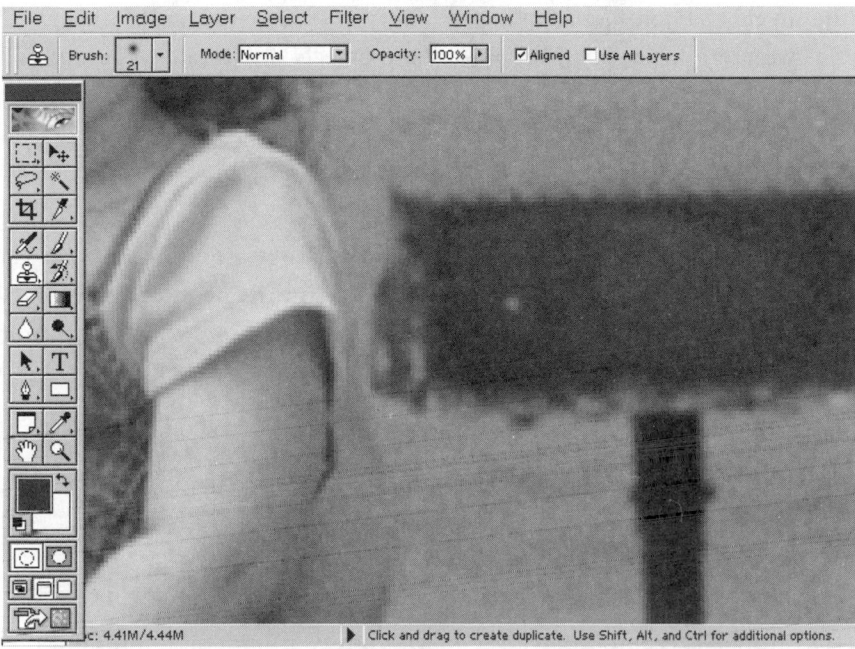

**Figure 16.17**   To keep consistency in the shading of the grass, sample below the grill, and then clone the grass area over the remaining grill area that contacts the arm.

**Figure 16.18**   After removing the grill stand, your image should look like this figure.

Ah, the magic of Photoshop! Having the tools to remove unwanted elements in a photo is wonderful. Neighboring subjects and objects that create some sort of odd-looking creation give you one reason to remove an element. Another reason to remove something is that it draws attention away from the main subject.

## Using Layers to Cover Distracting Areas

You've probably heard this statement many times, "They tore down all those beautiful trees to build a parking lot." Especially if you're sitting next to Joni Mitchell on a bus. Well, if that kind of urban development doesn't suit your fancy, here's a chance to do the opposite: remove the parking lot!

The two attractive gals in this chapter's image do not need to compete for attention with those vehicles in the background at the right.

It's time to be a traffic cop and move some cars.

### Example 16.5   Replacing the Vehicles with Foliage

1. Open the Renee and Ariana.psd image from your hard disk, if it's not open already. Press Ctrl(⌘)+0 to fit the image on your screen.

2. Drag either of the bottom corners of the image window away from the image. Press M for the Rectangular Marquee tool. Mac users, use the Size box to separate the image from the image background.

3. Starting just outside the left side of the image, where the road and guardrail meet the edge of the photo, click and drag down and to the right until you reach Renee's shoulder, as shown in Figure 16.19.

**Figure 16.19**   Using the Rectangular Marquee tool, make a selection around the area shown here.

4. Press Ctrl(⌘)+J to copy the selected area to a new layer. From the main menu, choose Edit, Transform, Flip Horizontal.

5. Press V for the Move tool. Click and drag directly to the right until the contents of this new layer touch the right edge of the image. Using the arrow keys, nudge Layer 1 up or down until the walkways near Ariana's head on both layers are aligned vertically.

6. Press Ctrl(⌘)+spacebar for the Zoom tool, and click twice over the contents of Layer 1 (the grass and trees). Click on the Add a mask icon at the bottom of the Layers palette.

7. Press B for the Paintbrush and choose the Soft Round 13-pixel brush (third from the left on the second row) from the Brush flyout palette. Press D for default colors so that black is the foreground color.

8. Press the Tab key to hide all palettes and make your workspace less cluttered.

9. Time for the magic. See the large tree trunk on Layer 0 that is the farthest to the right and visible just above the Layer 1 contents? Position your brush over that tree trunk and paint straight down to the bottom of the grass area on Layer 1. Repeat this procedure until you can see all of the trunk and part of the cars that are visible on both sides of the trunk, as shown in Figure 16.20.

**Figure 16.20**   Paint layer mask until the tree trunk and a small amount of the surrounding area are visible.

10. Press X to swap the foreground and background colors so that white is the current foreground color, and paint carefully along the sides of the trunk to remove layer mask (you might want to zoom in for this editing). The goal at this point is to show only the tree trunk. Toggle the foreground and background colors (press X) as necessary to accomplish your editing.

11. Two other trees on Layer 0, to the left of the tree you just worked on, need to be visible. Using the same techniques, paint layer mask so that these trees also show. The trunk above and near the horizontal middle of the Layer 1 contents is easy to see. The other trunk is somewhat hidden but is close to the far-left edge of the Layer 1 contents.

12. Press ] (right square bracket) twice to change the brush tip size to 30-pixels. Paint layer mask along the walk path enough to reveal the original walk path on Layer 0, and then paint into all the grass area below the walk path on Layer 1 (see Figure 16.21).

**Figure 16.21**     Apply layer mask to show the three tree trunks, the walk path, and the grass area.

13. Starting at the top of the Layer 1 contents, paint a horizontal row, move down one brush width, and paint another row. Continue this process until you reach the tops of the cars. If necessary, press X and paint to remove the layer mask over the cars to conceal them with the foliage. Your image should look like Figure 16.22, with part of a vehicle and the black pole showing.

**Figure 16.22**   After using as much of Layer 1 as possible to cover the vehicles, only two remaining elements need editing.

**14.** Press Ctrl(⌘)+E to merge the two layers. By now you should be proficient enough with the Clone Stamp tool that you do not need step-by-step directions to paint foliage over the vehicle and the pole. So go ahead and remove those two elements, and then press Ctrl(⌘)+S to save your edits. Leave the image open.

You have probably noticed by now that you frequently copy from existing areas in the image. Certainly you could have used the Clone Stamp tool and painted foliage over each of the vehicles and the parking lot. But that's like draining a swimming pool with a spoon! Isn't it easier to copy a suitable large area, and then work it into the area you don't want?

Okay, you're doing great. How about changing hats one more time? This time you'll put on a landscaper's hat to finish up the image.

## Adding the Final Touches

To finish up the Renee and Ariana image, you will use tools and techniques that you've already used in this chapter. The next tutorial covers a lot of ground (pun intended) and the directions in the steps are less specific, enabling you to work more on your own. Hey, if you've come this far, you'll do great!

Let's finish up this chapter with digital landscaping.

### Example 16.6    Creating Instant Grass, and Removing a Tree Without a Saw

1. Open the Renee and Ariana.psd image from your hard disk, if it's not open already.

2. Zoom in to the faces until both faces fill a little more than half your screen's height (100%–200%) and create a rectangular marquee over the left side of Renee's head, as shown in Figure 16.23.

**Figure 16.23**    Selecting the hairline is usually too difficult, so we will use a copy of the hair from the other side of Renee's head.

3. Copy the selection to a new layer (Ctrl(⌘)+J) and flip the layer horizontally (Edit, Transform, Flip Horizontal). Press 5 to change the Opacity to 50%, and then press Ctrl(⌘)+T.

4. Move the selection to the other side of Renee's head, and then rotate and move the area so that the hairlines are aligned. Apply the Transform (double-click inside the bounding box), and press 0 for 100% Opacity. On the Layers palette, create a layer mask (click the Add a mask icon).

5. Use the Paintbrush and the 27-pixel brush tip to paint layer mask in Renee's hair over to, but not including, the hairline. Paint also over Ariana's face and hair if necessary. When your image looks like Figure 16.24, press Ctrl(⌘)+E to merge the two layers.

6. Press the Page Up key once or twice (depending on your current zoom percentage) until you see the top of the image. Use the Clone Stamp to artfully clone leaves over the remaining tree trunk area above Renee's head.

**Figure 16.24**   Apply mask everywhere except at the hairline and the foliage to the right of the hair.

Place your sample points near the area you are cloning and avoid creating a cloning pattern in the leaves.

7. Use the Clone Stamp and the Soft Round 21-pixel brush tip to remove the tire tracks at the left side of the image.

8. Create a selection with the Polygonal Lasso tool (L) that runs along the upper-right edge of the table top and encompasses the areas of grass shown in Figure 16.25. Hide the marquee (Ctrl(⌘)+H), and clone grass over the areas where the soil is visible.

9. Deselect (Ctrl(⌘)+D) the marquee, and create another selection with the Polygonal Lasso tool in the grassy area just below the table top and to the right of Renee's legs. Hide the selection (Ctrl(⌘)+ H and clone from the grass area directly to the left of Renee's legs, as shown in Figure 16.26.

   Because the area at the left, from which you are sampling, is smaller than the area where you are painting, you need to set new sampling points frequently so that you don't copy parts of the picnic table into the grass area.

10. Deselect (Ctrl(⌘)+D) the marquee and save the image (Ctrl(⌘)+S. Figure 16.27 shows what your image should look like.

**Figure 16.25**    Use the Polygonal Lasso to select from the table top edge and around the areas in the grass where the soil is visible.

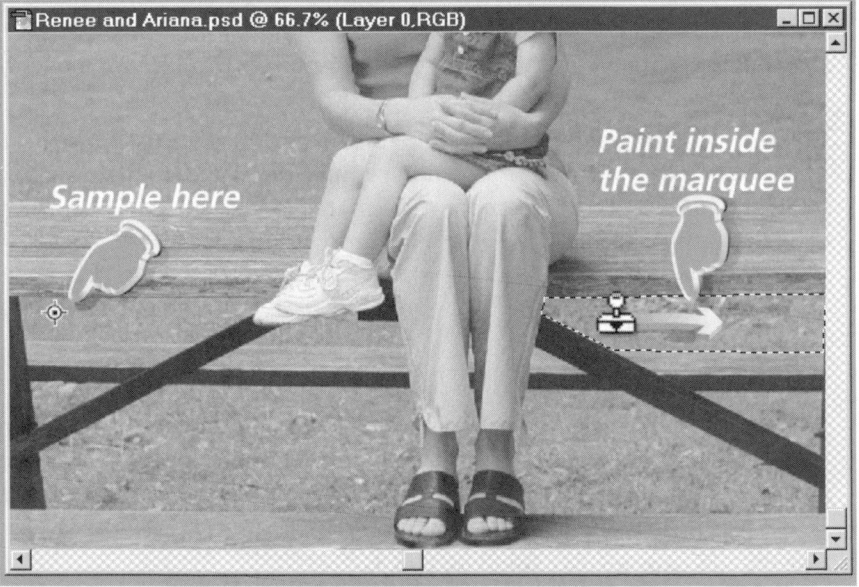

**Figure 16.26**    Select the grassy area to the right and under the table top, and clone from the grassy area directly to the left.

**Figure 16.27**   The final image with the flaws removed.

11. Before closing the image, open the original image, ReneeSmiling.psd, from the Examples/Chap16 folder on the Companion CD. Set the two open images side-by-side to admire your outstanding editing of the flawed photograph.

Replacing faces and cleaning up an image to make the subject the main focus of attention are only a couple of solutions to the problems found in flawed photographs. In your own photo collection, you'll probably find a multitude of other mistakes and imperfections to edit or remove, such as a group of power lines cluttering the background, a chip on your house's wood siding, or a friend you no longer speak to.

## Summary

Fixing the flawed photo does not use visually stunning techniques, special effects, and cool stuff like 3D modeling. It's sort of the plain vanilla aspect of digital imaging. Basically, you are using just a few tools and copying areas that you already have in the photo. But, wow! What a *significant* difference you can bring to your photographs!

You already put some serious mileage on your Clone Stamp tool, but there are many more avenues you can explore to further your skills with this essential tool. The next chapter investigates more aspects of the Clone Stamp and its nested buddy, the Pattern stamp tool. But wait—there's *more*. If you've ever labored with the selection tools in the effort to separate one element from the rest of the image, the Extract command might be just what you need. Additionally, if you'd like to add an effect that part of your image looks like it had melted, Liquify creates some intriguing results. Read on!

# Chapter 17

## Using the Clone Stamp Tool, Image Selection, and Distortion

Welcome to a chapter that has four stars:

the Clone Stamp, the Pattern Stamp, the

Extract command, and Liquify.

The tool called Rubber Stamp in earlier versions of Photoshop is now called the Clone Stamp tool. Only the name is new—everything else about the Clone Stamp is identical to the Rubber Stamp. The Clone Stamp, perhaps the most popular tool among image editors, is one of only three tools that paint image data.

The Pattern Stamp tool paints—you guessed it—patterns. Photoshop provides a few patterns, but you can create your own patterns (highly recommended!) and store them on your hard disk for use during a later Photoshop session.

The Extract command is similar to a combination of the Magnetic Lasso, the Background Eraser, and steroids. For example, in just a few, fairly effortless steps, you can select a tree and its intricate outline and remove the entire background from the image.

Liquify is, well, quite possibly Photoshop's most humorous command to play with. Liquify is an accurate name to describe the effect of this feature (and your creativity) on an image. You can push, pull, swell, or shrink—to name just a few effects—specific areas of the image.

The first star of this chapter is the Clone Stamp, a powerful tool that's well worth getting to know.

## Skillfully Using the Clone Stamp

If you're new to Photoshop, you might be vaguely familiar with the stamp tools. If you're a Photoshop veteran, surely you know the value and power of the stamp tools—especially the Clone Stamp.

Artists who restore and retouch photographs put more mileage on the Clone Stamp than any of the other tools on the toolbox. But even the average Photoshop user needs to use the Clone Stamp on scanned images to remove the white specks caused by dust on the surface of the print.

Skillful use of the Clone Stamp is not a matter of choosing any brush and a "good enough" *sampling point* (the area you Alt(Opt)+click on to specify where to start cloning from). There are three factors to consider when perfection is your goal: the brush size, the brush hardness, and the sample location. Brush size and hardness can be specified on the Options bar when the Clone Stamp tool is the current painting tool. See Figure 17.2 for the brush Hardness and Size locations.

## Choosing the Brush Size

The brush size can be as small as 1 pixel, as large as 999 pixels, and can be any design that you can imagine and create. You can access the Brush flyout palette (see Figure 17.1) by clicking the down arrow at the Brush field on the Options bar. The optimum size of the brush is best determined by trial and error—you'd be hard-pressed to find anyone who can consistently choose the correct brush size on the first try! As a general rule, you don't want to use a brush so large that you paint areas you don't intend to paint. Conversely, you do not want to use a brush size so small that the stroke itself is highly visible. Choose a brush you think might work well, make a stroke in the area you are editing, and then decide whether a larger or smaller brush tip would give you a better result. You'd be *amazed* at how much more quickly work moves along if you simply take a moment and fine-tune the brush size!

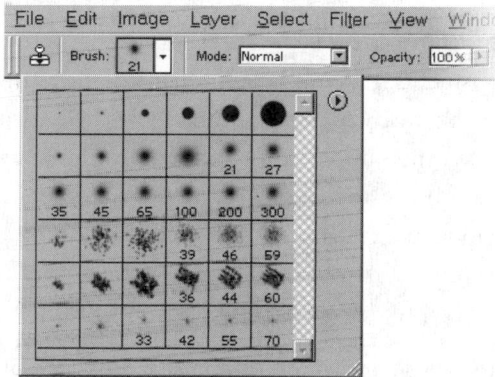

**Figure 17.1**   The Brush flyout palette is accessible on the Options bar by clicking the down arrow next to the brush icon.

## Setting Brush Hardness

Next on the list of three ingredients for perfecting your Clone Stamp brush stroke is the brush hardness. You can adjust the hardness of a brush tip in one of two ways: By clicking the brush tip icon to show the Brush Options palette (see Figure 17.2) and then dragging the Hardness slider, or by holding down the Ctrl(⌘) key and pressing a square bracket key ([ or ]) to decrease or increase the hardness setting in 25% increments. How do you know where to set the brush hardness? This, too, is trial and error. Again, paint a stroke, inspect the edges of the stroke, and if the edges are fuzzy, use a higher hardness setting. If the edges of the stroke are too obvious, use a lower hardness setting. You will see examples of various hardness settings in the first set of steps in this chapter.

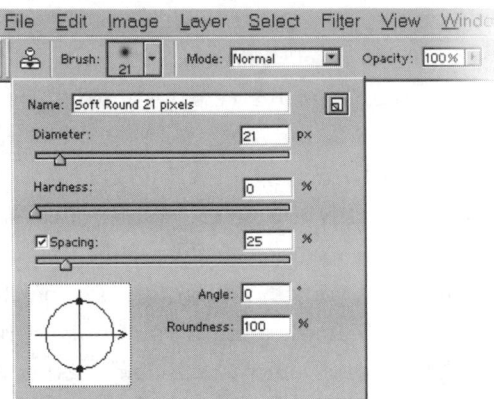

**Figure 17.2**    Brush tips can be customized in the Brush Options palette.

## Selecting a Sample Point

The third factor to consider is the sample point. For situations in which the area you are cloning from and the area you are painting show little variation in shading (a blank wall, for example), the sample point area might not be too important. But if the areas where you are using the Clone Stamp vary in shading (a long dress, for example), you must clone in a fashion that does not break up the pattern created by the shading. In the second tutorial in this chapter, you will work on an image where the sample point must be precise, to just one pixel, for the cloning to be successful.

Now that you've gotten the lowdown on how to use the Clone Stamp like a pro, let's get stamping. In the following set of steps, you will clone the numbers in an incorrect mathematical equation to create a correct equation. Sample points, brush sizes, and brush hardness will be explored along the way.

### Example 17.1    Clone Stamp Basics

> **Warning!**    If an error message appears when you open the CD files, press Ctrl(⌘)+Shift+K and then choose Adobe RGB (1998) from the Working Spaces, RGB drop-down list. See Chapter 3 for more information.

1. Open the AdditionProblem.psd image from the Examples/Chap17 folder on the Companion CD.

2. The width of the image window should be about three-quarters the width of your screen. If the image window is too small, hold down Ctrl(⌘) and press the + key once or twice, as necessary. Click and drag the bottom-right corner diagonally away from the image to create a little space between the image and the edges of the window.

3. Press Ctrl(⌘)+R to show the rulers. Press V for the Move tool. Click on the horizontal ruler (at the top of the image window) and drag down into the

image to the center of the horizontal line in the plus sign, and then release the mouse button. Next, click on the vertical ruler (at the left of the image window) and drag a guide to the center of the vertical line in the plus sign. Drag four more vertical guides into the image, placing one at the center of the 12, another at the center of the 9, then at the equal sign, and finally at the center of the 3. Your guides should be placed at the ruler locations of the guides shown in Figure 17.3.

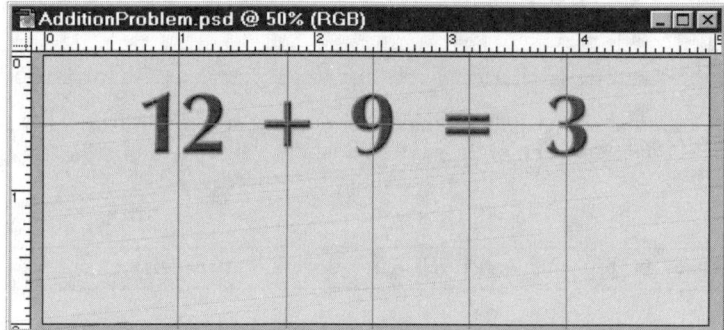

**Figure 17.3**   Place the vertical and horizontal guides at the center of each of the characters.

Any tool can be used to drag a guide into the image window, but only the Move tool can reposition or remove a guide.

4. Drag one more horizontal guide onto the image and place the guide at the 1½-inch mark on the vertical ruler. If your ruler does not display the units in inches, double-click the ruler to display the Units & Rulers Preferences box, and choose inches in the Rulers field.

5. Press S for the Clone Stamp tool. On the Options bar, choose the Soft Round 35-pixel brush. Hold down the Alt(Opt) key and place your cursor at the center of the + sign, where the horizontal and vertical guides intersect. When the dot in the center of the cursor is directly on top of the guide intersection, click to set this point as the initial sampling area. Release the Alt(Opt) key.

6. Place the cursor over the intersection of the guides directly below the + sign, hold down the Alt(Opt) key to change the cursor to the sampling cursor, and position the dot at the center of the cursor directly over the intersection of the guides. Don't click! Release the Alt(Opt) key and *do not* move the mouse. You have just perfectly aligned the sampling area and the area of the first brush stroke to the intersection of the guides. Now, press the mouse button and paint the + sign (*only* the + sign). As you paint, notice that the edges of the brush are soft, as shown in Figure 17.4.

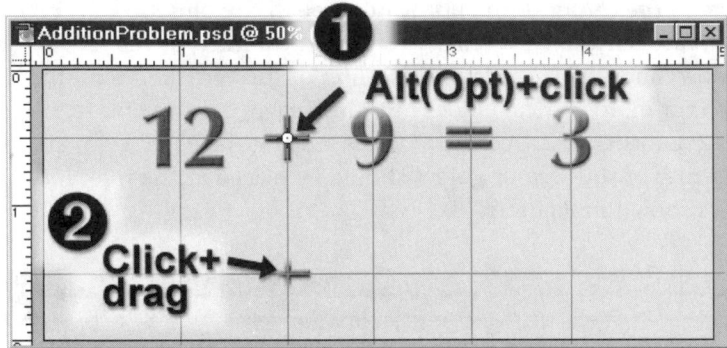

**Figure 17.4**    Place the sample point at the center of the + sign, and the initial brush stroke at the intersection of the guides below the + sign.

 **Tip**

The softness of this brush tip works well in image areas that are fuzzy or out of focus.

7. Click the 35-pixel brush tip on the Options palette to show the Brush Options palette. Drag the Hardness slider all the way to the right for 100% hardness, as shown in Figure 17.5. Press Enter (Return) to close the Brush Options palette with the new setting.

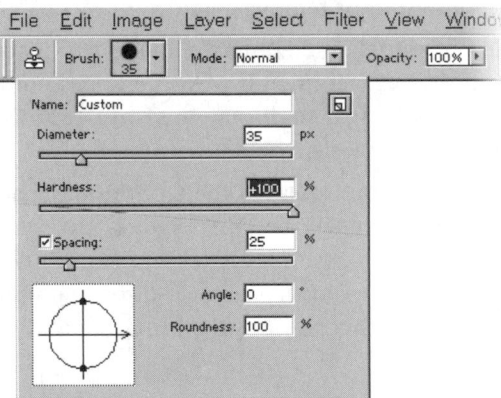

**Figure 17.5**    The Brush Options palette enables you to create custom settings for each brush tip.

8. Repeat the procedure in step 6 for setting the sampling point and the initial brush stroke, and clone the equal sign at the intersection of the guides directly below the equal sign. Notice that the hardness of this brush tip paints with 100% opacity at the edges of the tip.

*Opacity* is the amount of visibility that applied paint or a Photoshop layer's contents have. A brick wall, for example, is 100% opaque. A drinking glass, on the other hand, has a very low opacity because you have a fairly unobstructed view of objects behind it. The edge opacity of this brush tip resembles paint applied with a real world sponge instead of a cotton ball.

The 100% hardness setting is ideal when you are cloning image objects that have hard edges, such as graphics, for example.

9. On the Brush flyout palette, choose the (soft) 100-pixel brush. Use the procedure in step 6 to clone the 9 character at the intersection of guides below the 12, as shown in Figure 17.6.

   Notice that the 100-pixel brush is closer in size to the characters and therefore paints the 9 character faster than the 35-pixel brush tip you used earlier.

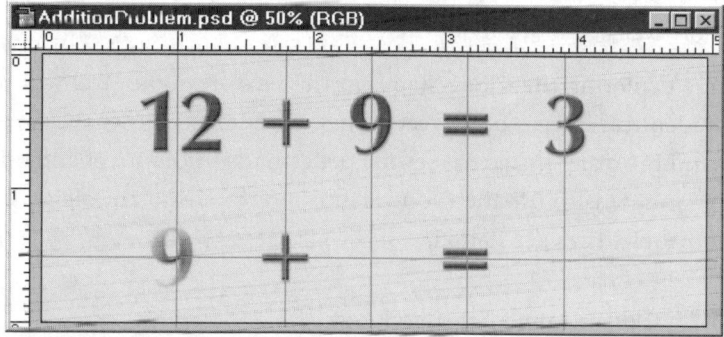

**Figure 17.6**   The click of the mouse button, without moving the mouse, clones most of the 9.

10. On the Brush flyout palette, choose the (soft)200-pixel brush and press Enter (Return). Click on the 200-pixel brush icon to show the Brush Options palette, set the Hardness to 100%, and drag the Diameter slider to 180 px.

11. Repeat the procedure for setting the sampling point and the initial brush stroke, and clone the 12 at the intersection of the guides directly below the 3. Notice that when you click the mouse button to begin cloning, the entire character appears; you do not need to move the brush because the brush's diameter is larger than the character.

12. Using the same brush tip, clone the 3 at the intersection of the guides directly below the 9 in the original equation (see Figure 17.7). Again, notice that you do not need to move the mouse.

13. From the main menu, choose View, Clear Guides. Then press Ctrl(⌘)+R to hide the rulers. You can either save the image to your hard disk or close the image at any time without saving.

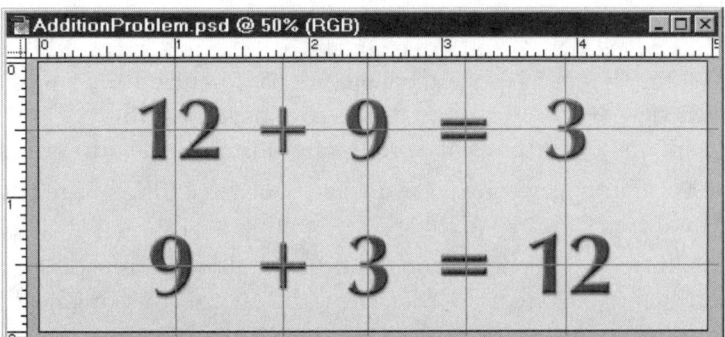

**Figure 17.7**    Clone the 3 under the original 9 using just one click with the 180 px brush.

Now that you have warmed up with the Clone Stamp tool and brushed up on your math, it's time to learn more about the tool.

You continue exploring the Clone Stamp in the next example. You will work with two almost identical images of a street corner. One image shows the front of a car at the left, and the other image has several pedestrians in the street and on the sidewalk. The goal here is to use the Clone Stamp tool to create an image that has no cars and no people. Let's get started.

### Example 17.2    Cloning from a Separate Image

1. Open the GeneseeStreet1.psd image and the GeneseeStreet2.psd image from the Examples/Chap17 folder on the Companion CD. (Windows users can hold down the Ctrl key and select both files to avoid a second trip to the Open dialog box.)

2. From the main menu, choose Window, Tile. Hold down the Ctrl(⌘)+spacebar keys to toggle to the Zoom tool, and click once or twice on the lower-left area of each image. The number of clicks depends on your screen's resolution setting. You want to see the very bottom of the image and at least up to the top of the Community Bank sign (peek ahead to Figure 17.8 to see the setup).

3. Press S for the Clone Stamp tool. From the Options bar, choose the 100-pixel brush on the Brush flyout palette, and then press Enter (Return). Click the 100-pixel brush icon, and change the Hardness setting to 100%. Press Enter (Return) to close the Brush Options palette, and then press the Tab key to hide all palettes.

4. Make sure that the GeneseeStreet1 image is the active image (click on the title bar if it is grayed out). Now, at this point, you're going to be doing some precision clicking, so you might want to press the CapsLock key on

your keyboard to toggle the cursor to crosshairs. Hold down the Alt(Opt) key and center your cursor inside the red circle on the left door of the bank (see Figure 17.8); then click to set this area as the initial sampling area.

**Figure 17.8**   Precisely center the sampling cursor inside the red circle on the left door of the bank's entrance.

5. Click on the GeneseeStreet2 image title bar. Hold down the Alt(Opt) key to toggle the cursor to the sampling cursor, and center the cursor inside the same red circle on the left door. *Do not click and do not move the mouse!* As in the previous set of steps, you are just positioning the cursor. Release the Alt(Opt) key—again without moving the mouse.

6. Now, click and release the mouse button. Did the lamppost area of your cloning align perfectly with the lamppost in the image? It should, because the lamppost is right next to the red circle on the door and you're using this giant-sized brush tip that eclipses almost everything in an area! If the lamppost in the target image at right doesn't appear to change at all, great! If the lamppost now looks as though someone dented it, press Ctrl(⌘)+Z for undo and try the sampling and cloning steps again. When your cloning lines up with the lamppost, move on to step 7.

7. Click and drag over the people you can see in the current view of the image (see Figure 17.9). You can release the mouse button and start painting again

in a different location because you've already set the sampling area perfectly. Notice that when you clone over the woman at the far left, you start to clone the white car also—that's okay, just don't clone too much.

**Figure 17.9**    This figure shows the cloning procedure in progress, with the image elements of the cloned areas perfectly aligned with the image.

8. Hold down the Ctrl(⌘)+spacebar to toggle to the Zoom (in) tool, and then click and drag to the left in the image (GeneseeStreet2) to move the view so that you can see the two ladies who are walking near the benches. Click and drag over the ladies. Again, there was no need to create another sample area—is that cool, or *what*?

9. Windows users, double-click on the image's title bar to open the image window to fit your screen. Macintosh users, maximize the image window so you can see the window background. Press Ctrl(⌘)+spacebar to toggle to the Zoom tool, and click once or twice on the white car and what's left of the human foot. You want to zoom in but still see the bottom of both lampposts.

10. Press Y for the History Brush tool, press the Tab key to show all palettes, and then press Shift+right-click (Macintosh: hold Ctrl and click), and choose the 21-pixel brush from the Brush flyout palette. Press Enter to finalize your choice and to ditch the Brush palette.

**11.** Paint over any areas of the white car that you might have cloned into this image. The History Brush is painting image information from the Snapshot in the History palette (Window, Show History). Whether you have the History palette open or not, the History Brush's default behavior is to restore image areas to their original state when the image was opened.

**12.** Press S (Clone Stamp) and choose the same 21-pixel brush from the Brush flyout palette by Shift+right-clicking (Macintosh: hold Ctrl and click). Press Enter to close the palette. Clone over the remaining leg, foot, and car areas. Here are some tips: For the areas in the sidewalk, sample to the right and be careful to keep the areas without shadow aligned. For the curb, sample to the left of the leg. And for the shadow of the leg, sample in the street area below the shadow (see Figure 17.10).

**Figure 17.10**   The three best sampling and initial brush stroke areas are shown in this figure.

**Warning**

**There's a Limit to the Usefulness of a Clone Sample Point**   The Clone Stamp tool is designed to help you avoid creating *clone patterns*—areas that are repeated by cloning over the already cloned areas. The Adobe engineers programmed the Clone Stamp tool to sample from the original image rather than from the painted area. In other words, if you clone too far in one direction, you will see the stuff you want to get rid of. In this case, you need to create a new sample area.

**13.** Press Ctrl(⌘)+0 to view the entire image (see Figure 17.11). Right now, you can do one of two things: Close both images or zoom in to the bench closest to the street signs. Practice what you've learned about the Clone Stamp tool and clone over the aluminum can and the Styrofoam cup to clean up after a litterbug.

**Figure 17.11**    The finished GeneseeStreet image after cloning over the people and the car.

To summarize what you've learned so far: Brush size, brush hardness, and the initial sample point are all important factors to a perfect stroke of the Clone Stamp tool. You also learned that you can clone from one image and paint in another image.

Tucked under the Clone Stamp in the toolbox is the Pattern Stamp tool—our next topic!

## Using the Pattern Stamp Tool

Quick, what do the following have in common: wallpaper, clothing, quilts, oriental rugs, and newborns? Answer: patterns—babies have a pattern of waking you up several times a night. Okay, so that was an easy question, given that the answer is in the title of this section. The point is that patterns can be found almost anywhere.

The Pattern Stamp tool is similar to the Clone Stamp tool, except that the Pattern Stamp tool samples from a pattern you have selected rather than from an area of the image. In other words, you do not Alt(Opt)+click to specify a sampling area. You simply choose a pattern and begin painting.

As mentioned earlier, patterns can be seen almost everywhere. In the following example, you will replace the name BUGS BUNNY on a Hollywood Walk of Fame star with your name. The star contains all the patterns you need to make your edits photorealistic.

Enough talking—let's move on and make you a star!

### Example 17.3   Covering Bugs Bunny with a Pattern

1. Open the WalkofFameStar.psd image from the Examples/Chap17 folder on the Companion CD.

2. Press the F key once for Full-screen mode with menu bar. Then press Ctrl(⌘)+spacebar to toggle to the Zoom tool, and click over the name BUGS BUNNY. Continue clicking until the text is about half the width of your screen.

3. From the toolbox, choose the Rectangular Marquee tool, and select a large area of the star's pattern just above the text. Figure 17.12 shows the area you should select. The image area outside the selection (the area you *don't* want) has been lightened for illustrative purposes. *Note:* On the Options bar, Feather must be 0 for the Define Pattern command to function.

4. From the main menu, choose Edit, Define Pattern. Type **Walk of Fame Star** in the Name field, and then press Enter (Return).

**Note**

**Saving a Pattern**   When you save a pattern, Photoshop will write the pattern to your hard disk so that you can use the pattern again in the future. But one condition must be met for your pattern to be saved: Photoshop must close down properly. If Photoshop does not close down correctly (if your computer crashes, for example), the pattern will not be saved.

5. Click the Create a new layer icon at the bottom of the Layers palette. On the toolbox, click and hold on the face of the Clone Stamp tool until the flyout menu appears, and then click the Pattern Stamp tool to choose it. On the Options bar, pick the Soft Round 35-pixel brush tip.

6. On the Options bar, click the down arrow next to the Pattern thumbnail to show the Pattern palette. Choose the Walk of Fame Star pattern you just created.

**7.** Position the cursor to the left of the letter B (in BUGS) and next to the lower half of the letter (see Figure 17.13); then click and drag directly right to clone the pattern over the bottom half of all the letters.

**Figure 17.12**   Select a large rectangular area from which to define the pattern.

**Figure 17.13**   Paint the pattern over the lower half of the text.

8.  Inspect the results of your brush stroke. Notice the fuzzy line at the top and bottom of your brush stroke. This fuzziness is caused by the brush tip's Hardness setting of 0%—the softest possible brush tip. You are a Photoshop artist and as such, you don't settle for anything less than the best in your imaging. Press Ctrl(⌘)+Z to undo this unacceptable brush stroke.

9.  On the Options bar, click the down arrow next to the brush tip preview to extend the Brush palette. Choose the fourth brush on the second row, Soft Round 17-pixel. Press Enter (Return) to close the palette, and then click the brush tip icon on the Options palette to display the Brush Options palette. Drag the Hardness slider all the way to the right to make the 17-pixel brush tip have 100% hardness.

**Note**

**Aligned Versus Unaligned Pattern Creation**    Very shortly, you are going to use the Pattern Stamp tool to erase Mr. Bunny's name, character by character. One of the options we've not covered yet with the Pattern Stamp tool is whether you choose to paint in aligned mode or not aligned. This checkbox is on the Options bar.

So what's the diff' between the two patterning modes? In aligned mode, the strokes you make with the tool begin *relative to* the position on the sample (you cannot see) as held in memory. If you've created a seamless tiling pattern, this is a splendid mode for pattern painting. This mode works for the following step because you are patterning over the lettering character by character, so relatively speaking, the cursor will be loaded with the pattern sample in different relative positions as you work. By the way, when you come to the end of a sample, it simply repeats, starting at the left edge of the pattern.

The unaligned option (the aligned checkbox is not checked) always starts your pattern painting from the dead *center* of the pattern sample. This is not wanted in the following step because every character on the star that you pattern over would have the same pattern sample in the center of each character—a giveaway that something phony's going on.

10.  Click and drag over the lines that make up the letter B, and then release the mouse button (see Figure 17.14). Now, click and drag over the lines that make up the letter U, and then release the mouse button. Repeat this procedure for the remaining letters.

11.  Press Ctrl(⌘)+S and save the image to your hard disk with the same filename. Leave the image open.

You might have wondered why you painted the pattern onto a new layer rather than on the Background layer. This method of placing new image content onto a new layer is beneficial because correcting mistakes is much easier when the mistake is on its own layer, rather than part of the rest of the image.

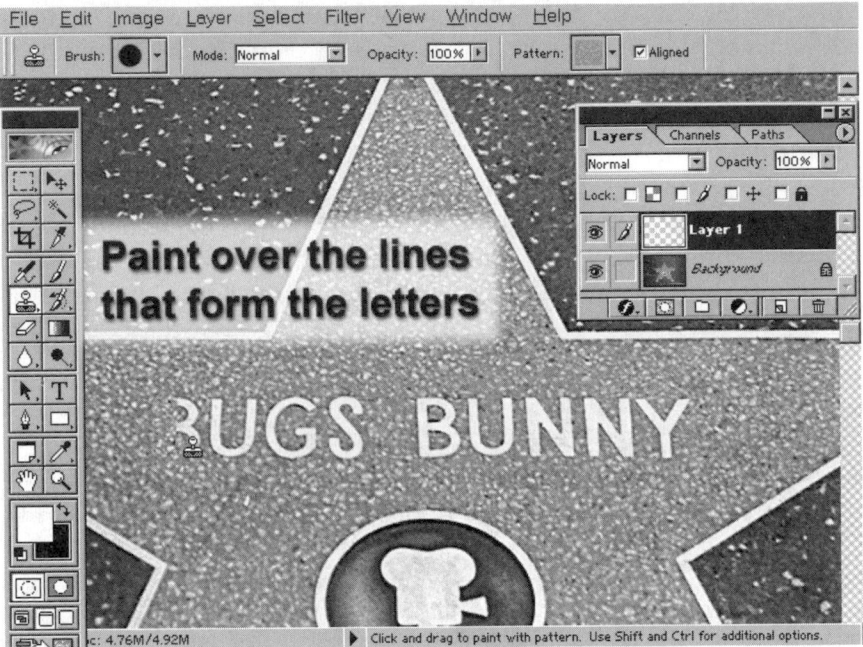

**Figure 17.14**    Leave no telltale signs of cloning—carefully clone over each letter.

Right now, you have a star on the Hollywood Walk of Fame just waiting for your name. In the following set of steps, you will create a new name for the Walk of Fame star, and then apply a pattern to your text, a pattern similar to the one in the BUGS BUNNY text.

### Example 17.4    Applying Your Name to Fame

1. Open the WalkofFameStar.psd image from your hard disk, if it's not already open. Press F to put the image in Full-screen mode with menu bar and be sure that you're zoomed in on the image to the extent that the upper half of the star fills the screen.

2. On the Layers palette, make sure Layer 1's Indicates layer visibility icon (the eye) is turned off so that your wonderful pattern cloning from the previous set of steps is hidden.

3. Press I for the Eyedropper tool. Be sure Sample Size on the Options bar is set to 3 by 3 Average. Click anywhere on the BUGS BUNNY text to sample the color.

4. Press T for the Type tool, and click just below the B in BUGS. You need a typeface that is similar or identical to that in the BUGS BUNNY text. On the Options bar, choose Arial Narrow (or a similar font), Bold, 20 pt, and Smooth (the settings shown in Figure 17.15).

**Figure 17.15**  Type the name you have chosen below the BUGS BUNNY text.

5. Type your first name or the first name of the person you want to impress in all caps (CURLY HOWARD is used in the figures). Before typing the last name, notice the spacing between the first and last name in the text you are emulating—the equivalent of two spaces, rather than the traditional one space. Press the spacebar twice, and then type the last name. Hold down the Ctrl(⌘) key and press Enter (Return) to commit the text to the type layer (see Figure 17.15).

   *Note:* If the name you've chosen is too long and runs outside the star's borders, choose a shorter name.

6. Press V for the Move tool. Click and drag on your text so that the letters overlap the BUGS BUNNY letters. Press 7 on the keyboard to change the opacity of the type layer to 70%. On the Layers palette, right-click (Macintosh: hold Ctrl and click) on the type layer title (your name), and choose Rasterize Layer.

   The camera was at an angle to the star when the photo was taken. There is a slight perspective to the BUGS BUNNY text that you need to simulate on the text you just created. Only after you rasterize a type layer are you able to apply any of the Transform commands.

7. Press Ctrl(⌘)+T (Transform) and right-click (Macintosh: hold Ctrl and click) inside the bounding box; then choose Perspective. Click the top-right anchor

and drag to the left until the vertical lines that make up your text near the left and right sides are parallel with the vertical lines in the BUGS BUNNY text, as shown in Figure 17.16.

**Figure 17.16**   Give your text a slight amount of perspective.

8. Double-click inside the transform box to apply the effect. Press 0 (zero) to return the layer's opacity to 100%, and then move the layer below the BUGS BUNNY text. Be sure not to cover the camera symbol inside the circle.

9. Click on the Background layer in the Layers palette, press M (Rectangular Marquee tool, the last-used marquee tool), and select as much of the inside area of the camera as possible (see Figure 17.17).

10. From the main menu, choose Edit, Define Pattern, and name the pattern **Gold Texture**. Click OK, and press Ctrl(⌘)+D to deselect. On the Layers palette, click on the layer that contains your name to make it the active layer for editing; then select the Lock transparent pixels option. This option is the first box after Lock (above the layer stack). You can see it checked in Figure 17.17.

11. Press S for the Pattern Stamp tool, and deselect Aligned on the Options bar. Using the same brush you used in the previous set of steps (17-pixel at 100% Hardness) and the texture in the BUGS BUNNY letters as a guide, paint the Gold Texture onto your text with short brush strokes, starting at different places within each character of your name (or Mr. Howard's). For example,

the B in BUGS contains a lot of dark texture, whereas the Y in BUNNY is lighter and has very little texture (see Figure 17.18). Although the texture isn't evident in the figures, it's clearly visible onscreen. To emulate this visually, your unaligned starting point for applying the pattern needs to start at different locations on each character.

**Figure 17.17** The pattern of light and dark gold color inside the camera symbol provides an excellent area from which to create a pattern.

**Figure 17.18** Use the texture in the original letters as a guide for where to paint the gold pattern onto your letters.

You might want to vary the intensity of your brush stroke. To reduce the intensity, press 7, for example, to change the brush's opacity to 70%. Press 0 to return the brush's opacity to 100%.

12. Press V for the Move tool, click and drag up your letters so that they are on top of the original letters. On the Layers palette, make Layer 1 visible (click on Layer 1's far-left column).

13. Press Ctrl(⌘)+0 to fit the image on your screen (see Figure 17.19) and see your name on the Hollywood Walk of Fame! Save, and then close, the image.

**Figure 17.19**   It's ironic that when you become a star, folks in Hollywood walk all over you.

In Chapter 23 you'll see how to optimize your Walk of Fame image—or *any* image for that matter—for your Web site or as an email attachment to send to your friends!

Having covered the topic of the Pattern Stamp tool, it's time to move on to another subject. But if you want to complete the image without a tutorial, here's how:

Notice that everywhere the gold color borders the pattern inside the star, there is a purplish line. This purplish line should also go around the borders of your letters. This is basically what you need to do: Create a copy of the text layer and deselect the Lock transparent pixels option. Load the layer contents as a selection, and then Expand (Selection, Modify) the selection by 1 pixel. Feather—press Ctrl(⌘)+ Alt(Opt)+D—the selection by 1 pixel, and fill the selection with the purplish color (sample the border with the Eyedropper tool). Deselect the selection. For the final touch, apply the Add Noise filter with an Amount of about 14%, Gaussian, and Monochromatic.

Now that I'm writing to a star, let's move on to the next topic: the Extract command.

## Extracting a Foreground Object

Sooner or later in your digital imaging adventures you will need to select an area of an image where the selection tools in Photoshop's toolbox just wimp out on you. For example, try selecting along the edge of a person's hair with the Lasso tool, and keeping that line perfectly natural looking—it's impossible. Fortunately, Photoshop's Extract feature does a powerful job of selecting (and extracting) wispy, intricate edges.

Here's the situation: A client presents you with two photos—one of his house with a cloudy sky, and one of a pile of dirt under a cloudless sky. He is going to sell his house and wants you to create an ad for him. Because of the climate he lives in, taking a photo of his house on a cloudless day is a once-a-month possibility and he doesn't have time to wait. So, it's your job to replace the sky in the photo of his house with the other photo's cloudless sky.

The first thing you notice are the trees in the yard, and you immediately realize that selecting around all the leaves and branches requires something more sophisticated than the selection tools in the toolbox. So, you wisely turn to the Extract command to select those difficult edges, add some cool Photoshop tricks, and have this client in awe of your talent.

In the following example, you will use the Extract feature to define the edges of the treetops and the housetops. Then, after deleting the cloudy sky, you will add a bright, sunny sky.

### Example 17.5   Removing and Replacing a Cloudy Sky

1. Open the House4Sale.psd image from the Examples/Chap17 folder on the Companion CD. Make sure that the History palette (Window, Show History) shows a snapshot of the image (you should see a thumbnail of the image and the title House4Sale.psd). If you do not have a snapshot of the image, click the Create new snapshot icon located at the bottom of the History palette.

2. On the Layers palette (Window, Show Layers), click and drag the House layer to the Create a new layer icon at the bottom of the palette. From the main menu, choose Image, Adjust, Brightness/Contrast, and drag the Contrast slider to about +30. Click OK.

By increasing the contrast of the image you help the Extract command find the edges of the image elements.

3. From the main menu, choose Image, Extract. In the Tool Options field, type 40 in the Brush Size field.

4. Press Ctrl(⌘)+spacebar to toggle to the Zoom (in) tool, and click twice on the trees at the left of the image. (If you do not see the tops of the trees after zooming in, hold down the spacebar to toggle to the Hand tool, and then drag the image to move the view so that the tops of the trees are visible.) With one brush stroke, use the Edge Highlighter to paint along the tops of the trees from the left edge of the image to the roof of the house (see Figure 17.20). If you make a mistake, you can use the Eraser tool to erase unwanted highlighting.

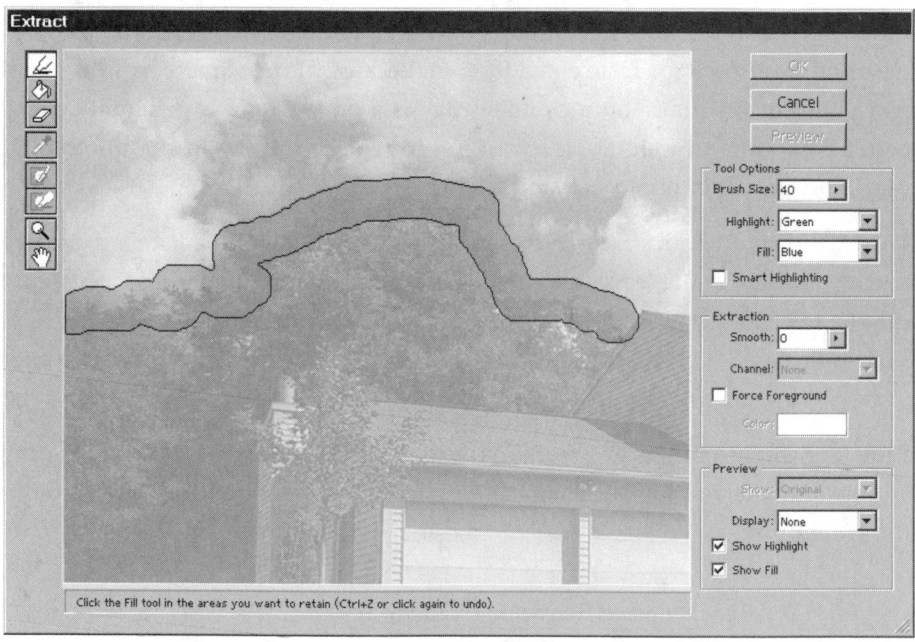

**Figure 17.20**    Paint the Edge Highlighter so that the tree tops and the sky are covered by the brush stroke (the preview image has been edited for illustrative purposes).

5. Hold down the spacebar to toggle to the Hand tool, and drag the view of the image so that you can see the entire roof of the house. In the Tool

Options field, select Smart Highlighting, and then type **20** in the Brush Size field. Paint highlighter along the edge of the roof and the right side of the house, as shown in Figure 17.21. Paint slowly and be careful to keep the edge of the roof inside the brush cursor.

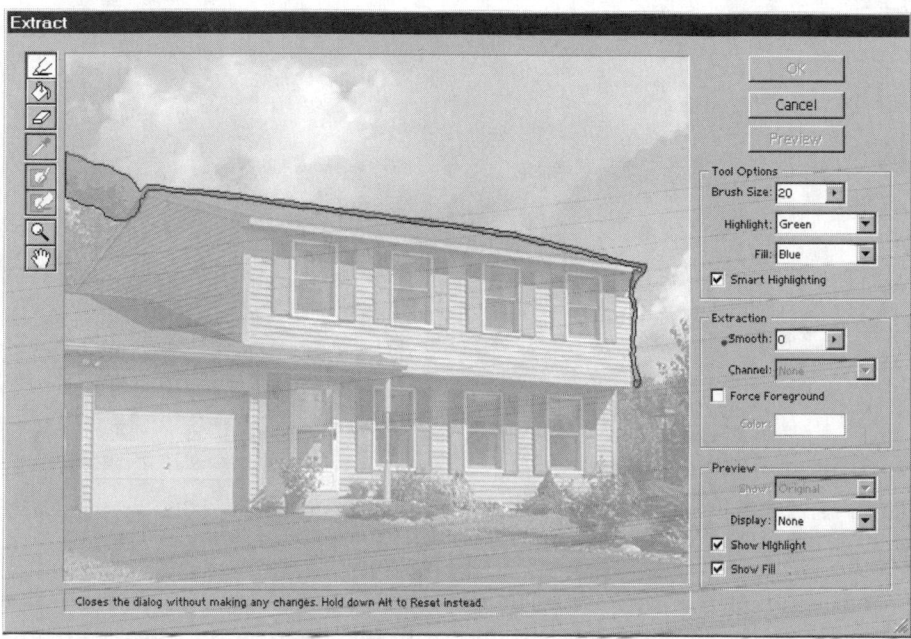

**Figure 17.21**   Use Smart Highlighting when you're painting Edge Highlighter on well-defined edges (the image in the preview window was lightened for illustrative purposes).

If you run out of mouse pad during this long brush stroke, you can stop painting, reposition your mouse on the pad, and resume painting—just be sure to paint one continuous line that contains no breaks.

6. Toggle to the Hand tool (hold down the spacebar) and drag to the left in the preview window so that you can see the tree in the front yard and the house next door. Paint along the roof line of the house on the right. Then, to finish the highlighting, deselect Smart Highlighting, increase the Brush Size to 40, and paint along the tree line of the tree in the front yard and along the tree line in the background (see Figure 17.22).

7. Hold down the Ctrl(⌘)+Alt(Opt)+spacebar to toggle to the Zoom out tool, and click twice in the preview window so that you can see the entire image. Click the Fill tool (second tool from the top), and then click anywhere in the image below the highlight. The Fill tool applies a mask over the area you want to keep. Click OK, and go get your favorite beverage while the Extract command processes your settings.

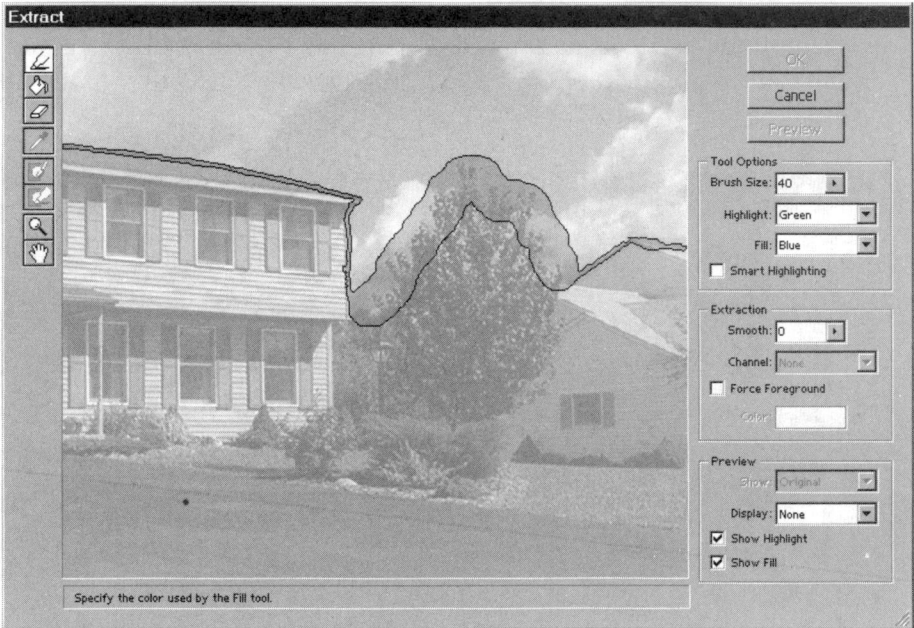

**Figure 17.22**    Paint edge highlight along the roof line of the house on the right and along the tree line of the tree in the front yard.

As mentioned in step 7, the Fill tool applies a mask over the area you want to keep. If your entire image is filled with the mask, press Ctrl(⌘)+Z (undo). Inspect the highlight, locate the break(s) in the line, and paint highlight on the gaps to close the line completely.

8. Welcome back. Don't be alarmed that the image appears the same as before you used Extract—you're seeing the original image's sky area from the House layer. On the Layers palette, turn off the House layer's visibility (click the eye icon). Most likely, the Extract command removed some areas of both houses along the edge where you painted. No problem. Press Y for the History Brush, and choose the third brush on the top row of the Brush palette on the Options bar (you click the down arrow to the right of the brush tip image).

9. Press F for Full screen mode with menu bar, and zoom in (Ctrl(⌘)+ spacebar+click) to the roof of the house. Click one end of the missing roof line, and then hold down the Shift key and click the opposite end of the missing area (see Figure 17.23).

Holding down the Shift key connects your first click and your second click with a straight (and fast!) brush stroke.

**Figure 17.23**   Restore the missing areas by painting in a straight line with the History brush.

The History Brush restores the deleted areas with image information from the snapshot that was created when you opened the House4Sale image. The layer you are painting on is the layer in which you adjusted the contrast in step 2.

10. Use the Hand tool (hold down the spacebar) to move the image view to another missing area at the roof line, and use the same paint stroke technique you used in step 9 to restore the image area. Continue this restoration procedure for all the remaining missing areas on the roof and on the side of the house, including the house on the right. When you've restored all the missing areas, press Ctrl(⌘)+0 to fit the image on your screen.

   If you inadvertently paint into the sky area, press Ctrl(⌘)+Z to undo the paint stroke.

11. Ctrl(⌘)+click on the House copy layer title on the Layers palette to load the contents as a selection. Drag the layer, House copy, to the Trash, and then click the visibility icon for the House layer. Press Ctrl(⌘)+Shift+I to create an inverse of the original selection, and then press the Delete (Backspace) key.

12. Press Ctrl(⌘)+D to deselect. Open the CloudlessSky.psd image from the Examples/Chap17 folder on the Companion CD. On the Layers palette, drag the Background layer into the House4Sale image. Click on the CloudlessSky title bar, and close the image.

13. On the Layers palette, drag Layer 1 down below the House layer. Press V (Move tool), click and drag the image to position the sky to cover the transparent area (as shown in Figure 17.24).

**Figure 17.24**   Got a cloudy day? Create a sunny day with a little help from the Extract command.

14. From the main menu, choose Layer, Flatten Image. Press S (Clone Stamp), zoom in (Ctrl(⌘)+spacebar+click) to the trees, and touch up the areas that still show the cloudy sky. The 21-pixel brush on the Brush palette is ideal for these areas.

15. Press Ctrl(⌘)+S and save the image to your hard drive. If you do not want to save your work, close the image after you finish reading the rest of this section on the Extract command.

It's always good business sense to do something extra for your client. Because his house is for sale and you did all that work to create a cloudless sky, why not create a sign for the front yard? Well, the sign has already been created for you, and it's called 4SaleSign.psd. You can open the image from the Examples/Chap17 folder on the Companion CD. On the Layers palette, simply drag the layer (House for Sale Sign) into the House4Sale image, and then use the Move tool (V) to position the sign as shown in Figure 17.25.

Time to move on to the chapter's final topic: the Liquify command. If you enjoy doing silly things to your images, you'll want to hang out with Liquify on a regular basis—this command is guaranteed to bring a smile, if not a good chuckle, from you and your audience.

**Figure 17.25**   For a finishing touch, add the sign that says, "HOUSE FOR SALE—Sunny Sky Included!"

## Using the Liquify Command

In almost all amusement parks, you will find at least one caricature artist's booth. This is the place where you actually pay someone to draw a goofy, exaggerated likeness of yourself. The artist exaggerates your features—a big nose is rendered extra large in the sketch, and a thin neck is drawn to the width of a pencil, for example.

If you enjoy this style of art, you'll love Photoshop's Liquify feature. Liquify enables you to enlarge or shrink specific areas of your image with just a brush stroke. You can also push an area of the image, creating an effect similar to pushing your finger through a painting before the paint has dried. As a matter of fact, Liquify is one of Photoshop's most customizable commands, and this section is designed so that you only get your feet wet. You can explore many more features of the Liquify command in your own imaging. But for now, let's take the concept of the caricature and play with a rubber ducky. No, not in the bathtub—in *Photoshop*.

In the following tutorial, you will use several brushes in the Liquify dialog box to accentuate many of the features of a rubber ducky.

### Example 17.6    Distorting a Duck

1. Open Ducky.tif from the Photoshop 6.0 Samples folder on your hard disk. If you do not have the Samples folder on your hard disk (placed there during the process of installing Photoshop), ask a friend or co-worker for the image, or reinstall Photoshop, this time only choosing to install the images, and unchecking the program's installation when you get to this point in the application setup.

   You might be presented with the Embedded Profile Mismatch alert. If so, choose Convert document's colors to the working space, and click OK.

2. Press D for the default colors to make white the background color. From the main menu, choose Layer, Flatten Image.

3. Right-click (Macintosh: hold Ctrl and click) on the image's title bar, and choose Canvas Size from the Context menu. Type **9** in the Height field, and choose the bottom-center chiclet (see Figure 17.26). Click OK.

   The new canvas extends the height of the image at the top of the image, and the color of the new canvas is the background color, white.

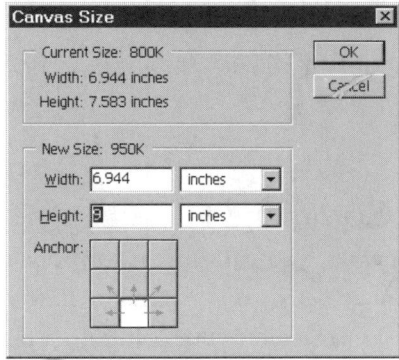

**Figure 17.26**    Click the bottom-center chiclet to add canvas at the top of the image.

### Warning

**Getting Out of the Box**    Like many of the dialog boxes, the Color Picker and such in Photoshop, there are two ways to exit the box: You can press Enter (Return) or click OK.

It's particularly important *not* to press Enter (Return) while in the Liquify dialog box because your edits will be applied, and you'll find that the Liquify dialog box is gone. So do not, for example, press Enter (Return) after filling out a number field in the Liquify dialog box. Instead, press Tab to commit to the values you've typed and to move on to other boxes, and save that Enter (Return) keystroke for when you're finished in this fun-house mirror place called the Liquify command.

4. Right-click (Macintosh: hold Ctrl and click) on the image's title bar, choose Duplicate, and click OK. Drag the image's title bars to arrange the images on your screen so they are side-by-side. Then click on the Ducky copy.tif title bar to make it the active image for editing.

**Note**

**Stepping Back**   Photoshop's new menu item, Step Backward, is not available while you work in the Liquify dialog box. But the Ctrl(⌘)+Z key combination will undo your last brush stroke. Your best bet is to apply only one brush stroke and then decide whether you want to keep or undo that stroke before using your brush again.

5. From the main menu, choose Image, Liquify.

6. Change the Brush Pressure option (in the upper-right area of the dialog box) to 100, and then click the Twirl Clockwise tool (second tool from the top on the left side of the dialog box). Place the cursor over the top of the duck's head, and press the left bracket ([) or right bracket (]) key to change the brush size so that most of the duck's forehead is inside the brush tip. Peek ahead to Figure 17.27 to see the area that your brush should cover.

Brush size in the Liquify dialog is not consistent across various screen resolutions. For example, 60 is a good brush size for a screen resolution of 800×600, whereas 100 works well for a 1280×1024 screen resolution. Additionally, using the bracket keys give you a more interactive, quicker way to determine the most suitable brush size.

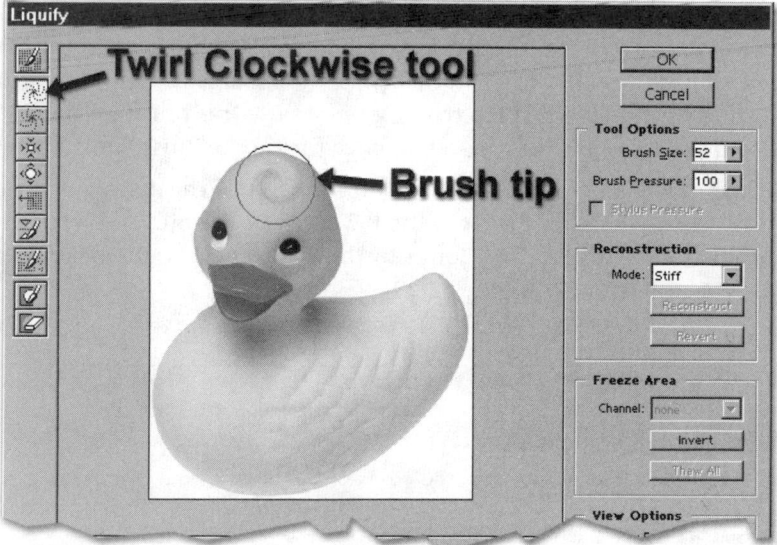

**Figure 17.27**   Give the ducky a hair-do by using the Twirl Clockwise tool.

7. Click and hold down the mouse button for about six seconds to twirl the feathers on the top of the duck's head, as shown in Figure 17.27.

8. Click the Bloat tool (fifth from the top). Place the cursor over the duck's right eye, and use the left bracket ([) key to reduce the brush size until the tip is slightly larger than the eye, as shown in Figure 17.28.

**Figure 17.28**    Reduce the brush tip until it is slightly larger than the eye.

9. Click and hold down the mouse button for about three seconds. The effect of the Bloat tool happens quickly because the brush pressure is set at 100. Repeat this step with the left eye.

10. Choose the Pucker tool (fourth from the top). Place the cursor over the duck's bill and use the right bracket (]) key to enlarge the tip so that the bill fits snugly inside the tip. You're not going to use this brush on the duck's bill—the bill was used only as a reference to size the brush for the next step.

11. Click and drag along the front and bottom edges of the duck. Start your brush stroke at the front edge to the lower left of the bill, and work the brush back to the tail. About four slow brush strokes should make the duck look slim and trim (see Figure 17.29).

**Tip**

**Liquify Brushes Aren't Confined to Foreground Matter**    Applying the Liquify brushes at the edges of the duck also affects the background, but because the background is a solid color, you don't notice any changes.

If you need to apply a Liquify effect at the edges of an object in your own imaging, copy or paste that object onto a separate layer, and then use the Liquify command. That way, the surrounding image areas will not be edited.

**12.** Choose the Bloat again. Place the cursor over the duck's bill and use the left bracket ([) key to decrease the size of the brush so that the brush covers only the open area of the bill. Click and hold down the mouse button for about four seconds (see Figure 17.30).

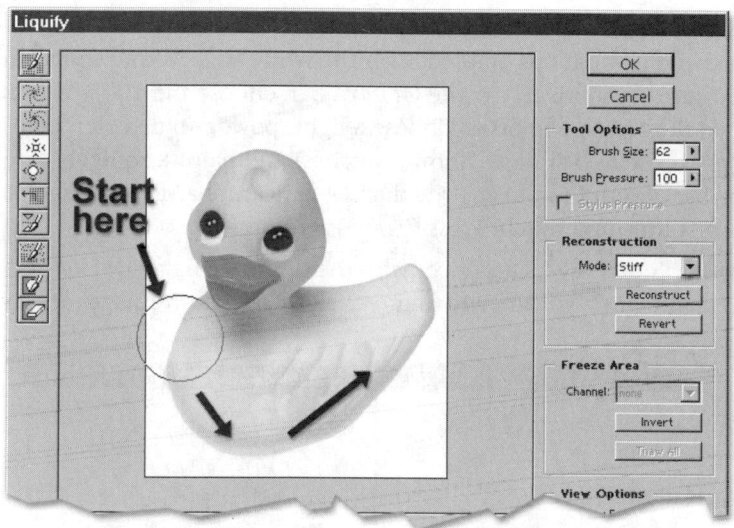

**Figure 17.29**   Move the Pucker brush slowly along the front and bottom edges of the duck for an instant weight-loss effect.

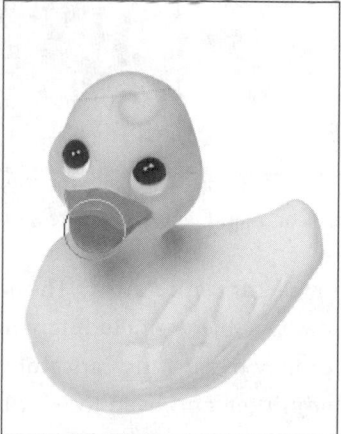

**Figure 17.30**   The Bloat tool moves pixels away from the center of the brush area.

13. Select the Warp tool (the top tool). Place the cursor over the tip of the duck's tail, and click and drag upward ever so slightly. You only want the duck's tail to point upward, you're not trying to warp the tail into something like an antenna. Click OK to finish liquifying and to return to the altered image in Photoshop's workspace.

14. Press W (Magic Wand). On the Options bar, set Tolerance to 100, select Anti-aliased and Contiguous, and click on the white background in the image. Press J for the Airbrush. On the Options bar, choose the 100-pixel brush tip and set the Pressure to 50%. Choose a light, powder blue color from the Swatches palette (Window, Show Swatches) and paint a squiggly line in the white background to outline the duck. A caricature artist sketches similar lines as a finishing touch. Press Ctrl(⌘)+D to deselect.

15. Compare your image, Ducky copy, to the original image, Ducky (see Figure 17.31), and enjoy your newly found talent. Close both images at any time.

**Figure 17.31**   With the Liquify command, you can create a caricature in just minutes.

Congratulations, you are now a caricature artist! The techniques you learned in these steps can be applied to any subject—including, and especially, people. So, if you've ever wanted to earn money by creating caricatures, pack up your computer, a digital camera, a good color printer, and head to your local amusement park!

## Summary

We've covered four features that Photoshop offers: the Clone Stamp tool, the Pattern Stamp tool, Extract, and Liquify. You've learned the importance of customizing the brush tip when you're using the Stamp tools. You've learned how to select intricate borders (a tree line), and how to create liquid effects in an image. Certainly your creative juices started flowing while you were reading this chapter.

And if you cannot get enough of a good thing, hang onto your hat (hats have been known to protect your creativity from strong breezes) because the next chapter is going to sweep you and your talents from the fanciful and the real to the *sur*real.

# Chapter 18

# Making the Impossible Look Plausible: Surrealistic Photoshop

Most people can recognize a particular

piece of art as representing the surrealis-

tic genre. But when they're asked, "What

does the word surreal *mean*?", most likely

the answer will be given in terms of examples—"flying cows" and "melting watches"—not as a definition. Webster's dictionary defines surreal in just eight words: "Having the intense irrational reality of a dream."

So, guess what? We all dream; therefore, we all create surreal images every day, or rather, every night! Think of it; you don't dream in Cubist, Baroque, neoclassical, or any other artistic style, you dream in surrealism. Now that you realize you have more in common with this chapter's subject than you first thought, read on and let's get irrational!

## Developing a Surrealistic Concept

In my part of the country, there are numerous lakes. Even though the summers are short and the winters are long and brutal (try 160" of snow per year!), the people here love to go boating. There are always boats in the water and boats on the highway being towed to or from the water. There is such a passion for boating that if it were possible, people would probably drive their boats on the highway too.

Now there's an idea—create a surrealistic image of someone driving a boat *in* the highway. And to make the image more interesting, place a couple cars in the adjacent lanes to add dynamic tension between "this is real, but this is not real." Additionally, add some water to the image to strengthen the boat element.

Now that the idea has been developed, take a look at Figure 18.1 to see this chapter's completed image. A boat is in the highway, following a truck carrying water. And check out the sky. At first glance, the sky appears partly cloudy. The sky is actually a crashing wave at a beach. So, there you have it—a boat riding in the highway, following a water truck, and a crashing wave for the sky. Okay, now it's time to open Photoshop, raise the anchor, and go for a surrealistic ride.

### Inserting and Transforming Layers

Quite possibly the Photoshop feature most used in this book (and by the majority of users) is Layers. Any imaging program that does not have layers is not worth its space on your hard disk—yes, layers are that cool! If you are not familiar with layers, you should take particular interest in Chapter 10.

For now though, the following set of steps take you through a couple basic uses of layers.

**Figure 18.1** A boat is supposed to be in water, not in the *highway!*

<u>Example 18.1 Placing the Boat in the Highway</u>

1. Open the Rt690.psd image from the Examples/Chap18 folder on the Companion CD.

2. Hold down the Ctrl(⌘) key and press the – (minus) key once to zoom out.

> **Warning!** If an error message appears when you open the CD files, press Ctrl(⌘)+Shift+K and then choose Adobe RGB (1998) from the Working Spaces, RGB drop-down list. See Chapter 3 for more information.

**Note**

> **Zooming to Resize** If you have Keyboard Zoom Resizes Window selected in Preferences (Ctrl(⌘)+K), you're all set (we highly recommend you use this setting). If you do *not* have this preference selected, go change your setting now—this method of zooming in is used throughout this chapter.

3. Open the TheBoat.psd image from the Examples/Chap18 folder on the Companion CD. Hold down the Ctrl(⌘) key and press the + key once to zoom in. Click on the bottom-right corner of the image window and drag approximately 1 screen inch downward and to the right. You will need to see the bottom edge of the image for the next step.

4. Press M for the Rectangular Marquee tool. Position your cursor below and to the right of the boat, but outside the image and in the image window. Click and drag up and to the left to select the boat and the wake on both sides of the boat. See Figure 18.2 for what you should select.

**Figure 18.2**    Select the boat and the wake on both sides of the boat.

5. Press Ctrl(⌘)+J to copy the selected image area to a new layer. The new layer, Layer 1, appears in your Layers palette (choose Window, Show Layers).

6. Hold down the Ctrl(⌘) key and press the – key once to zoom out. Click the image title bar and drag the image downward and to the right so that the Rt690.psd image is unobstructed by TheBoat.psd image.

7. On the Layers palette, click and drag Layer 1 into the Rt690.psd image, as shown in Figure 18.3.

8. Return to the TheBoat.psd image, click the close button, and choose No in the alert box.

9. Hold down the Ctrl(⌘) key and press + twice to zoom in. Drag the image window from the bottom-right corner away from the image approximately one inch.

10. Press V for the Move tool. Click on the boat and drag downward until the water area first touches the bottom of the image.

11. Press 6 to change the opacity to 60%, and then press Ctrl(⌘)+T for the Transform command.

    In the next step, you will size and position the boat; being able to see through Layer 1 will make that step much easier.

12. Hold down the Shift key and click and drag the top-right corner anchor downward and toward the left until the very front of the boat has just a little breathing room behind the truck. Keep holding down the Shift key and move the transform box left or right to position the boat directly under the truck (see Figure 18.4).

**Figure 18.3**  Drag the layer containing the copy of the boat, Layer 1, into the Rt690 image.

**Figure 18.4**  Scale and position the boat, using the Transform command.

Holding the Shift key constrains the change of scale to maintain the proportions of the boat and water layer contents. Holding the Shift key when you're moving the transform box left or right constrains the movement to 0°.

13. Double-click inside the Transform box to apply the command. Press 0 (zero) to return Layer 1's opacity to 100%. Press Ctrl(⌘)+S and save the image to your hard disk. Leave the image open.

If you don't know how much time and effort would go into completing the previous steps *without* using layers, I can't tell you because there aren't enough pages in this book!

When working with layers, you might have a situation in which you need to select part of that layer's contents and place it on a new layer. Hmm, that situation just happens to be the next topic.

## Separating Two Image Areas on the Same Layer

Let's say you have a layer that contains one red square and one blue square and you need to select the blue square and move it to a new layer. One click of the Magic Wand, with a tolerance setting of 1, will quickly select the blue square.

But in real life—digital life, that is—creating a selection and moving the selected area to a new layer is not always that simple. But that's okay; Photoshop has some cool tools to make this process easier, as you will see in the following example.

### Example 18.2    Taking the Boat Out of the Water

1. Open the Rt690.psd image from your hard disk, if it's not already open.

2. Hold down the Ctrl(⌘) key and press the + key enough times so that the boat vertically fills most of your workspace. You might need to toggle to the Hand tool (spacebar) to move the image view to the boat. Be sure the image window extends from the top to the bottom of your workspace (you can peek ahead to Figure 18.5 to see this setup).

3. Position the cursor on the Lasso tool and hold down the mouse button until the tools list appears. Then click the Magnetic Lasso tool. In the Options bar (press the Enter key to show the Options bar if it's not visible), enter the following settings: Feather 0, Width 8, Edge Contrast 50, Frequency 22, and Anti-aliased should be selected (these settings are shown in Figure 18.5). Now, pick any point at the boat's edge and click and drag along the entire circumference of the boat, as shown in Figure 18.5. For a more accurate selection, try to keep the crosshair of the Magnetic Lasso cursor on the edge of the boat.

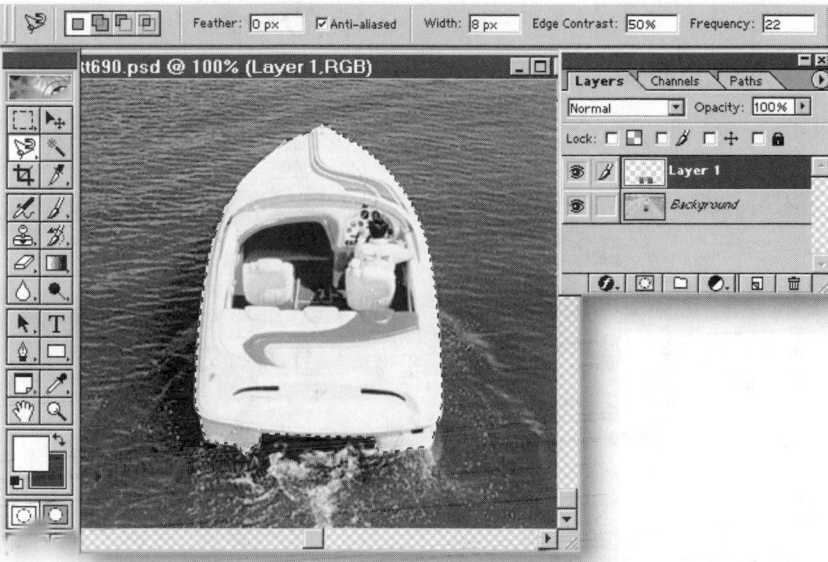

**Figure 18.5**    Let the Magnetic Lasso tool do the hard work of selecting the contrasting edges between the boat and the water.

4. Your selection probably needs a couple minor adjustments (mine did!), so press Q for Quick Mask mode, press B for the Paintbrush, and choose the first brush on the second row on the Brush palette. Paint quick mask (foreground color black) in the water area where it does not contain mask—you want quick mask everywhere except in the boat area. When you are happy with your quick mask area, press Q to exit Quick Mask mode.

   If you carefully followed step 3, there should be only two or three small areas that require editing. If you have quick mask in the boat area, make the foreground color white (X) and paint to remove the mask.

5. Press Ctrl(⌘)+Shift+J to cut the boat area to a new layer, titled Layer 2 by default. Now is a good time to give the layers more descriptive names. Hold down the Alt(Opt) key and double-click the Layer 2 title in the Layers palette. Type **Boat** in the Name field and press Enter. Next, hold down the Alt(Opt) key again and double-click the Layer 1 title. Type **Water** in the Name field and press Enter.

6. Click on the Boat layer to select it, hold down the Alt(Opt) key, and click the Indicates layer visibility icon (the eye) located to the left of the layer thumbnail. This key and mouse click combination hides all layers except the layer on which you click. With all other layers hidden, you can clearly see the colors of the pixels at the boat's edges—and some of those colors shouldn't be there (see Figure 18.6).

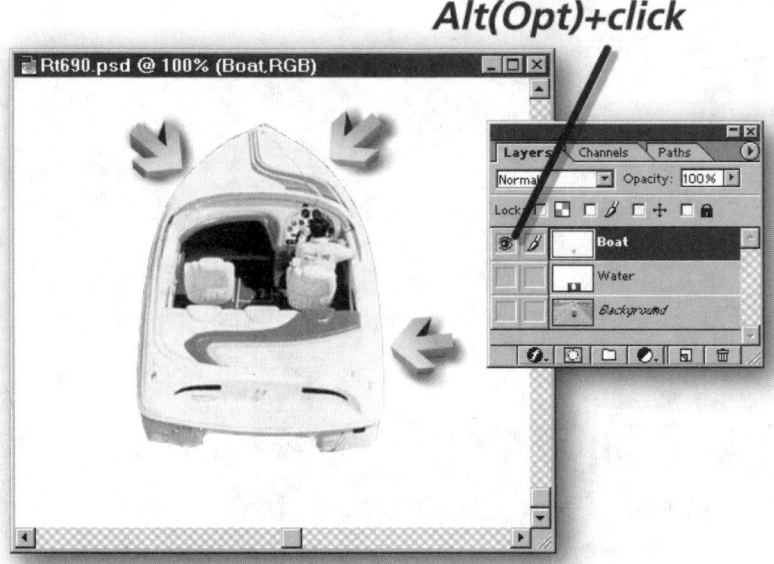

**Figure 18.6**   Hide all layers except the Boat layer to see the edges of the boat (the default checkerboard transparency was changed to white for this figure).

7. From the main menu, choose Layer, Matting, Defringe. Type **1** in the Width field and click OK. The Defringe command replaces the color of any pixels at the edges of the layer contents with the color of nearby pixels.

8. Hold down the Alt(Opt) key and click the Indicates layer visibility icon (the eye) again to show all hidden layers.

9. Notice that the edges of the boat are a tad sharper than the edges at contrasting areas in the boat, like the edges of the red stripe, for example. To make something look believable, details such as edge sharpness must be consistent. Press R for the Blur tool, and choose the second brush from the left on the second row in the Brush palette.

10. Press 4 to change the brush pressure to 40%. You want to drag the cursor along the circumference of the boat with a constant speed for each stroke.

**Tip**

**Push or Pull?**   Use whichever direction you find more accurate for moving the mouse—pushing it away from you or pulling it toward you—for the vertical drag to blur the sides of the boat. I don't know about you, but it's a lot easier for me to paint accurately when I'm pulling the mouse toward myself.

**Note**

**Too Much Blur?**   Along with the pressure of the brush, the effect of the Blur tool is determined by how long you apply it at any location. For example, if you click and hold down the mouse button and do not move the cursor, the blur effect increases. The point here is to use the pressure of the brush *and* the time you place the cursor on an area to get the amount of blur you want.

**11.** After you have blurred the sides and back areas of the boat, Alt(Opt)+click on the Boat layer visibility icon to show all hidden layers. Press Ctrl(⌘)+0 (zero) to zoom the image to fit your screen. Yeah, I know, the image doesn't look any different than when you started these steps, but all your hard work shows in the Layers palette and will pay off in the next section of this chapter.

**12.** Press Ctrl(⌘)+S to save your changes. Leave the image open.

You can select just about any image element to move to a different layer by using one selection tool, or a combination of tools. But always take a close look at the edges of the element you've cut out—most often you'll need to finesse the edges to make them blend in with the surrounding image elements.

Once you have an image area on its own layer, you can apply any edit you want and not affect the other areas of the image. Now that the water area in this chapter's image is on a separate layer, we can make the water look less like water and more like the road.

## Using Curves and Layer Blending Modes

The most important statement in this chapter is this: Experiment with and study *everything* that Photoshop has to offer you. And Photoshop has a lot to offer! Take Layers, for example; you have opacity, transparency, effects, layer sets, transform, adjustment layers, type layers, masks, and blending modes. And that is not a complete list of all the commands associated with layers!

Back to the Rt690 image. Currently, the water looks out of place (yeah, I know, the boat is out of place, too). So, let's use some of our expertise to combine two commands and make the water blend in with the road:

### Example 18.3    Creating Liquid Concrete

**1.** Open the Rt690.psd image from your hard disk, if it's not already open.

**2.** Click on the Water title in the Layers palette to make it the active layer for editing.

3. Hold down the Ctrl(⌘) key and press the + key two or three times until the boat is approximately half the height of your workspace. Press the spacebar to toggle to the Hand tool, and then click and drag in the image to move the image view so that you can see both the entire boat and water areas.

4. In the Layers palette, click on the Mode drop-down arrow and choose Luminosity from the flyout menu, as shown in Figure 18.7.

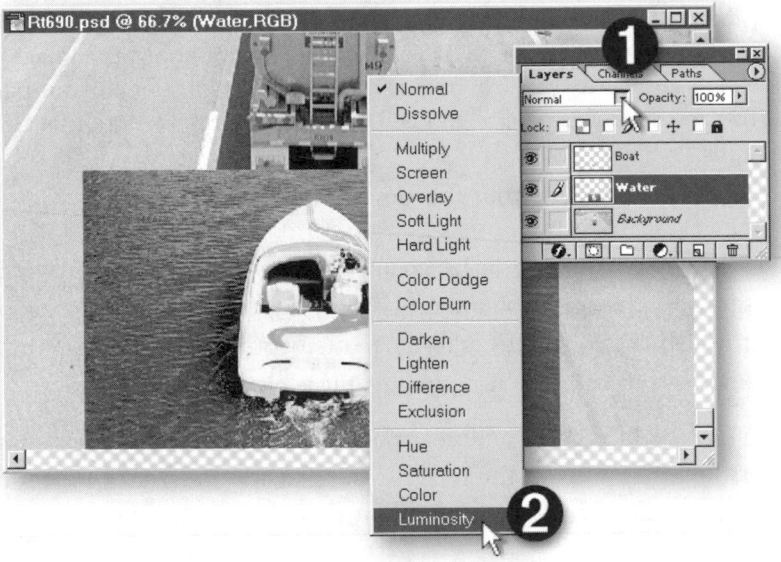

**Figure 18.7**   In the Layers palette, choose Luminosity from the Mode Flyout menu.

5. Click the Create new fill or adjustment layer icon (half-black, half-white circle) and choose Curves from the drop-down menu. If your Curves graph is divided into four rows and four columns, Alt(Opt)+click inside the graph to increase the divisions to 10×10.

6. Click the control point in the bottom-left corner of the Curves graph, and drag the point straight up by five and a half grid lines. Then, click a point midway between the left control point you just moved and the control point in the upper-right corner. Move this new point diagonally upward to the left about one grid height (see Figure 18.8). Click OK.

7. Right now, all the layers below the adjustment layer are effected by the Curves settings—not a good thing! Let's correct this. Hold down the Alt(Opt) key and place your cursor at the border of the Curves 1 (adjustment) layer and the Water layer. When the cursor changes into two overlapping circles with an arrow pointing to the left (see Figure 18.9), click the mouse to create a clipping group. This clipping group restricts the Curves adjustment to the layer immediately below.

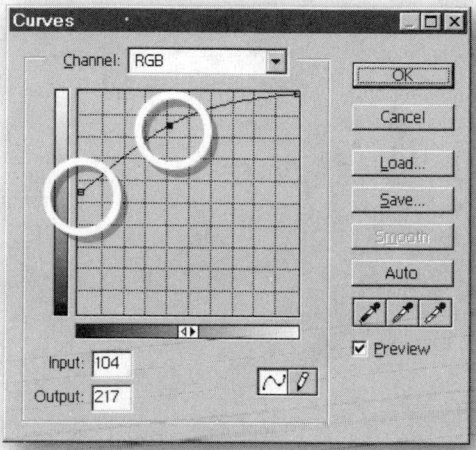

**Figure 18.8** Raise the black point and midtone values to make the water match the road surface's lightness.

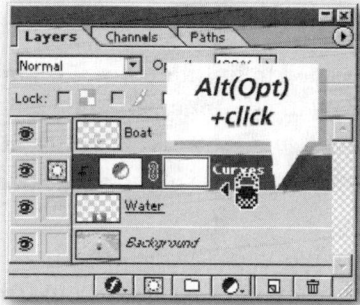

**Figure 18.9** Hold down the Alt(Opt) key and align your cursor at the border of the Curves and Water layers, then click.

8. Click on the Water layer to make it active for editing. Click the Add a mask icon (second from the left at the bottom of the Layers palette). Press B for the Paintbrush, and choose the 100-pixel brush from the Brush palette on the Options bar.

9. Press D for default colors to make black the current foreground color.

10. Notice the beginning of the boat's wake in the water that begins near the passenger area. This line of waves, extending back to the rear of the boat, are the areas of water you want to keep. So, use the Paintbrush to apply layer mask in the other areas of the water. See Figure 18.10 for what your image should look like.

**Figure 18.10**    Paint layer mask to remove all the water areas except where the boat creates the wake.

11. Two more edits are needed to finish up this illusion. First, press 4 to reduce the Paintbrush's opacity to 40%, and paint one quick stroke over the edge of the left water area. Paint another stroke over the right edge of the water area.

    These two brush strokes reduce the abrupt transition between the road and the water.

12. Next, in the Layers palette, click the Opacity arrow and drag the slider to about 80%. This applies a slight transparency to the water layer to blend the water and road a little more.

13. Press Ctrl(⌘)+0 to zoom the image to fit your screen. Press Ctrl(⌘)+S to save your liquid concrete illusion. Leave the image open.

There ya' go, water in the concrete—or is it concrete in the water? Either way, you performed the illusion without getting your hands wet.

Now that you are a pro at working with layers, you'll find the next section a breeze.

## Adding and Aligning Layers

Let's take a look at the Rt690 image that we've edited so far: The boat is in the high-way and behind a truck. Adding a car at either side of the boat would increase the dynamic tension between the real and the surreal. After all, here's a boat in the highway, yet the surrounding vehicles are moving along as though nothing is out of the ordinary.

In the following set of steps, you are going to add two cars to the Rt690 image, using techniques on layers you've already used.

### Example 18.4   Adding Cars to the Highway

1. Open the Rt690.psd image from your hard disk, if it's not already open. Click on the top layer, Boat, to select it.

2. Open the CarAtLeft.psd image from the Examples/Chap18 folder on the Companion CD. Click on the image title bar and drag the image so that you can see most of the Rt690.psd image.

3. Hold down the Shift key, click on the Background layer in the Layers palette, and drag the layer into the Rt690 image.

   Holding down the Shift key forces the layer to be centered in the Rt690 image.

4. Click the close icon in the CarAtLeft image. Press M for the Rectangular Marquee tool, and drag a selection around the red car, as shown in Figure 18.11.

**Figure 18.11**   Create a selection around the red car with the Rectangular Marquee tool.

5. Click the Add a mask icon located at the bottom of the Layers palette. Voilá! You've added another car in just a few steps. Well, almost—you need to blend the edges of this layer to the Background layer.

6. Hold down the Ctrl(⌘) key and press the + key two or three times to zoom in so that the car is approximately half the screen's height. If necessary, hold down the spacebar to toggle to the Hand tool, and move the image view to place the car in the center of the window.

7. Press B for the Paintbrush tool, then press 0 (zero) for 100% brush opacity. Choose the 65-pixel brush tip from the Brush palette on the Options bar, and press D (for default colors) so that black is the foreground color.

8. Paint layer mask in the road area around the car. You do not need to paint up to the edges of the car but you want to paint close to the car. Figure 18.12 shows a marquee around the area to which you want to apply layer mask. (Note: your image will *not* show a marquee—this is for illustrative purposes.)

**Figure 18.12**   The area within the marquee is where you want to apply layer mask.

9. Click on the active Layer mask thumbnail, drag it to the Trash, and choose Apply in the alert box.

10. Open the CarAtRight.psd image from the Examples/Chap18 folder on the Companion CD. Drag the Background layer in the Layers palette into the Rt690 image. Click the Close icon in the CarAtRight.psd image.

    Notice that you did not use the Shift key to center the layer in the Rt690 image. Here's the reason: the camera was on a tripod when the Rt690 and CarAtLeft photos were shot, so the images are perfectly aligned. But the camera was moved before the CarAtRight photo was shot, so you'll need to perform the alignment.

**11.** Press V for the Move tool, and then press 6 to change the Opacity to 60%. Click and drag this new layer, Layer 2, to align the car to the Background layer. Use the arrow keys to nudge the layer into alignment, if necessary. Key areas to align are the white lines and the brown litter next to the solid white line above the car, as shown in Figure 18.13. When you are happy with the alignment, press 0 to return to 100% opacity.

**Figure 18.13**   Use image elements like the white lines, the pole, and the litter to help you align the layers.

**12.** Drag a marquee (M) selection around the car, and click the Add a mask icon at the bottom of the Layers palette. Blend the car to the Background, using the techniques in steps 7–9.

**13.** Press Ctrl(⌘)+E to merge Layer 2 down with Layer 1. Alt(Opt)+double-click on the Layer 1 title, type **Cars** in the Name field, and click OK. Press Ctrl(⌘)+S to save the two cars, um, your changes. Press Ctrl(⌘)+0 and see Figure 18.14 for what your image should look like. Leave the image open.

The technique of holding down the Shift key while dragging a layer into another image is worth remembering when you need that layer to be centered in the image. This technique would definitely come in handy, for example, if you were paid big bucks to photograph a large group of kindergarten graduates. Undoubtedly, one photo won't be enough. So, you set your camera on a tripod and take about 10 pictures. In each photo someone is not smiling or has closed eyes. No problem. You Shift+drag the photos into one image and then apply layer mask wherever it's needed to show everyone smiling with their eyes open—every photo in perfect registration.

**Figure 18.14**    The Rt690 image after the two cars were added.

Pop quiz: Take a look at your Rt690 image and find a big continuity error. Here's a clue: The sun is shining on the boat as well as on the cars and truck. Good work! That's right, the boat is missing a shadow.

## A Shadow Is a Shadow Is a Shadow—Not!

Yes, we are departing from reality in this chapter's image, but we need continuity in the characteristics that say "this is real" (qualities such as lighting and shadows). Now, the boat was photographed with the sun at the same angle as the highway, so lighting is not an issue here. But a shadow needs to be created for the boat, and this shadow must have the same characteristics as the shadows already in the image (from the truck and the car at the right). These characteristics include: a bluish tint, a grainy appearance, and an almost sharp edge.

To create drop shadows for graphics, you can simply use Layer Effects, but to create shadows for use in a photograph, you need to use more than one Photoshop command. Let's examine the existing shadows and create a similar shadow for the boat.

### Example 18.5   Creating a Credible Shadow

1. Open the Rt690.psd image from your hard disk, if it's not already open. Zoom in to the boat by holding down the Ctrl(⌘) key and pressing + until the boat is approximately half as tall as your workspace.

2. Alt(Opt)+click the Create a new layer icon at the bottom of the Layers palette, type **Shadow** in the Name field, and press Enter (Return). Click on the Shadow layer title and drag the layer down just below the Boat layer (between the Boat layer and the Curves 1 adjustment layer).

3. Ctrl(⌘)+click on the Boat layer to load the layer contents as a selection. Press Ctrl(⌘)+Alt(Opt)+D for Feather Selection, type **.5**, and then click OK.

   The selection you created is the outline of the shadow for the boat. The feather value of .5 was determined by experimentation with the goal of matching the edge sharpness of the truck's shadow. A feather setting of 0 created an edge that was too sharp, and a setting of 1 created an edge that was too soft. Continuity in image elements such as shadows is paramount in making a composite convey reality.

4. Press D for default colors so that black is the foreground color, and press Alt(Opt)+Delete (Backspace) to fill the selection. Press Ctrl(⌘)+D to deselect.

5. Press V for the Move tool. Hold down the Shift key and press the left-arrow key once to move the shadow area 10 pixels to the left, then press the down-arrow key once. Release the Shift key and press the left-arrow key three more times to move the contents 3 more pixels to the left.

   The distance and direction the shadow extends away from the boat should be about the same as the shadow that is cast from the car at the right, because the car, not the truck, is closer in size and height to the boat.

6. While we're discussing the continuity of the shadow's length, notice that the boat's shadow is black whereas the truck and blue car's shadow is blue-cyan and has a grainy quality. Let's fix this discrepancy. On the Layers palette, select Lock transparent pixels. Press I for the Eyedropper tool and select 5 by 5 Average for the Sample Size on the Options bar. Click inside the truck's shadow area, as shown in Figure 18.15.

7. Press Alt(Opt)+Delete (Backspace) to fill the boat's shadow area with the new foreground color. From the main menu, choose Filter, Noise, Add Noise. Adjust the slider to about 6.86 and select Uniform, as shown in Figure 18.16.

8. Hold down the Ctrl(⌘) key and press the + key once to zoom in to the boat—you'll need a closer view of the boat for the next several steps. Click the Add a mask icon at the bottom of the Layers palette. Press B (Paintbrush tool), choose the 27-pixel tip from the Brush palette on the Options bar, and with black as the current foreground color, paint layer mask on the shadow that extends beyond the back of the boat (peek ahead to Figure 18.17 to see this area where the shadow is removed).

**Figure 18.15**   Click the Eyedropper tool inside the truck's shadow to sample the blue-cyan color.

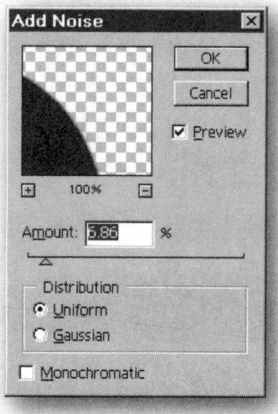

**Figure 18.16**   The settings shown here add just enough noise to duplicate the grain pattern in the truck's shadow.

9. From the Brush palette on the Options bar, choose the second brush from the left on the second row. After you press Enter (Return) to hide the Brush palette, click the brush tip to show the Brush Tip Options palette. Drag the Hardness slider to 50%, and then press Enter (Return).

10. Paint a free-form squiggle along the shadow's edge in the water area. The idea is to imitate the bending of the line of a shadow's edge caused by the turbulence at the water's surface, as shown in Figure 18.17.

**Figure 18.17**  Create a wave-like effect at the shadow's edge.

**11.** Choose the 65-pixel brush tip from the Brush palette on the Options bar, and press 4 to change the paintbrush's opacity to 40%. With one stroke, click+drag over the wave-like shadow area. On a sunny day, a shadow cast on a road surface is dark and well defined. Conversely, a shadow cast on water is not very dark, and the water distorts the shape.

**12.** Press Ctrl(⌘)+S to save your changes. Leave the image open.

If you were able to follow the preceding steps, you are now able to replicate the characteristics of any shadow you might have in your photographs. When you analyze existing shadows, remember to look at their color, edge sharpness, graininess, length, and the direction in which they're cast.

All the major elements are in place now: the boat, the cars, and the boat's shadow. It's time to spruce up that bland sky.

## Using Curves and Layer Blending Modes (Again)

If you've ever walked in a desert for days without water, you've probably seen a mirage (the optical illusion of a large body of water near the horizon). Okay, you don't have to go to that extreme to see a mirage. Actually, you can create a mirage right there at your computer after you complete this section of the chapter.

In the following set of steps, you will insert a breaking wave from a beach scene into the sky of the Rt690 image. Then, you will manipulate the water to resemble a partly cloudy sky. Grab your boards—surf's up!

### Example 18.6    Making a Splash in the Sky

1. Open the Rt690.psd image from your hard disk, if it's not already open. Double-click on the Background layer, type **Rt690** in the Name field, and click OK.

2. Press F for Full screen mode with menu bar, and then hold down the Ctrl(⌘) key and press the + key once or twice so that the width of the image is almost the width of your screen.

3. Press W for the Magic Wand tool. On the Options bar, type **44** for the Tolerance, and select Anti-aliased and Contiguous. Click in the sky area, as shown in Figure 18.18.

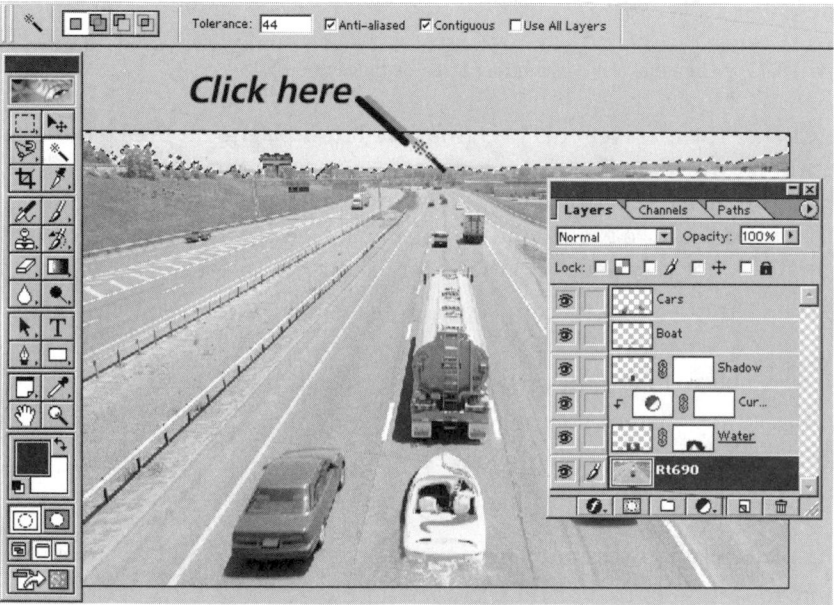

**Figure 18.18**    Use the Magic Wand tool and a tolerance of 44 to select the sky area.

4. Press Ctrl(⌘)+Shift+I to invert the selection. Now that everything except the sky area is selected, click the Add a mask icon at the bottom of the Layers palette. The area *not* selected, the sky, is automatically masked (as indicated by the checkerboard pattern) and the selection is deselected—sort of like the idea behind the saying, "...two birds with one stone."

5. Open the Curl.psd image from the Examples/Chap18 folder on the Companion CD. Press M for the Rectangular Marquee tool, and select the right two-thirds of the wave (see Figure 18.19).

**Figure 18.19**   Select the area of the curl shown here.

**Tip**

**Be Careful What You Toss!**   If you plan to shoot photographs for your Photoshop imaging, don't toss the "bad" photos into the wastebasket. Look at the photographs for the potential they all have: Small areas of a photo, even the seemingly insignificant areas, could be valuable to an image you create a few years from now.

For example, the Curl.psd image is one photo from an overexposed roll shot at a beach three years ago. I wanted to trash the entire roll because it wasn't up to my standards—I'm glad I didn't!

6. Press Ctrl(⌘)+C to copy the selected area, and then click the Close button at the upper-right corner of the image window. Press Ctrl(⌘)+V to paste the curl area onto a new layer, Layer 1. From the main menu, choose Edit, Purge, Clipboard. There's no need to eat up valuable RAM to hold an image you don't need to paste again.

7. Alt(Opt)+double-click on the Layer 1 title, type **Curl** in the Name field, and then click OK. Click on the Curl title and drag the layer below the Rt690 layer so that the Curl layer is at the bottom of the stack.

8. Press V for the Move tool, and make sure Auto Select Layer in the Options bar is not selected. Click and drag in the image to move the Curl layer contents up so that the part of the crashing area of the curl is near the horizontal center of the image (see Figure 18.20).

**Figure 18.20**   Position the Curl layer so that the crashing area of the curl is near the center of the image.

9.  If the selection you made in the Curl.psd image was close to the width of the selection shown in Figure 18.19, there is at least one transparent area (at the right) visible in the image. Press Ctrl(⌘)+T for the Transform command, and click+drag the middle anchor on the right side of the Transform box to the right edge of the image. Drag the left middle anchor to the edge of the image, if necessary (see Figure 18.21). Double-click inside the Transform box to apply the command.

10. Let's make the Curl layer look a little more like the sky. Click the Create new fill or adjustment layer icon at the bottom of the Layers palette, and choose Curves from the menu.

11. Drag the lower-left control point straight up to the third from the top gridline. (Note: if your Curves graph does not show the 10 divisions we set previously in this chapter, Alt(Opt)+Click inside the graph.) Drag the upper-right control point to the left by two gridlines. Click the Channel drop-down and choose Red. Click a control point on the curve in the middle of the graph and drag diagonally downward to the right about ¼ of a grid. Click the Channel drop-down again and choose Blue. Click a control point in the middle of the graph and drag diagonally upward to the left about ¼ of a grid (see Figure 18.22). Click OK.

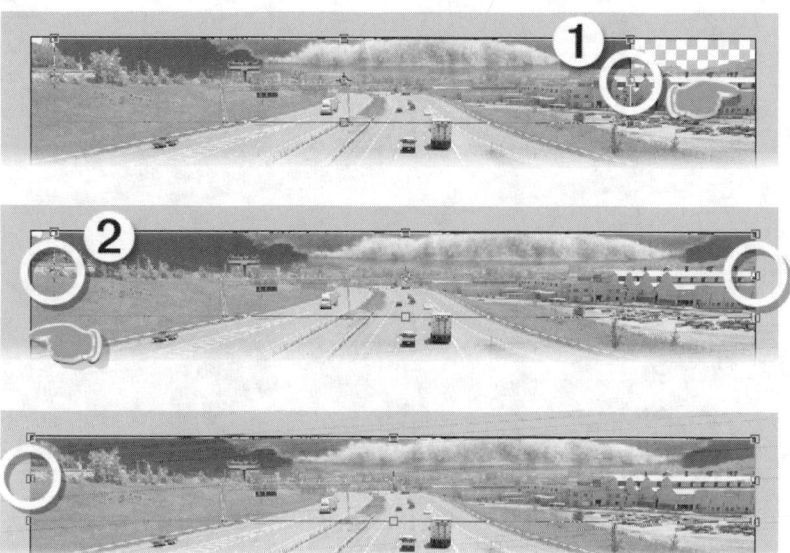

**Figure 18.21**  Use the Transform command to stretch the Curl layer to the width of the image.

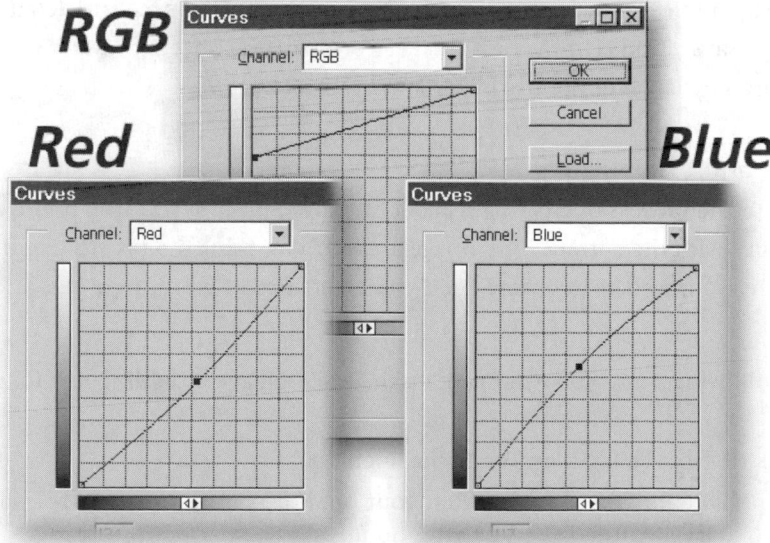

**Figure 18.22**  Move the curves in the RGB, Red, and Blue channels to raise the black point and remove the red and yellow from the new "sky."

12. Press Ctrl(⌘)+0 to fit the image view to your screen (see Figure 18.23). Press Ctrl(⌘)+S to save your edits. Leave the image open.

**Figure 18.23**    Time for a status check: Your Rt690 image and Layers palette should look like those shown here.

For most people who see your Rt690 image at this stage of development, the image could be complete—not many people take the time to examine the details. But as the quote says, "God is in the details." Let's bolster this concept of water everywhere for boating by labeling the truck's tank "WATER."

## Adding and Manipulating Text

Similar to the process of creating realistic shadows, placing text in a photo requires continuity with the surrounding image areas. If you want the text to blend in convincingly, you need to replicate such characteristics as grain, lighting, angle, and size.

In the following steps, you will finish up the Rt690 image by adding text to the tank.

### Example 18.7    False Labeling: The Digital Method

1. Open the Rt690.psd image from your hard disk, if it's not already open. The Rt690 layer in the Layers palette should still be selected for editing.

2. Press F, if necessary, to select Full screen mode. Hold down Ctrl(⌘)+spacebar to toggle to the Zoom tool, and click+drag a tight-fitting rectangle around the back end of the tank to zoom in (this technique is called a *marquee zoom*). The back end of the tank should now fill most of your screen.

3. Press L for the Polygonal Lasso tool. Here's the plan: Select the sign located behind the ladder without selecting the ladder. Here's the method: Select a generous portion of the tank around and including the sign that extends to the left of the ladder. Then, choose the Add to selection option on the Options bar and continue selecting the sign. See Figure 18.24 for what your selections should look like.

**Figure 18.24**   Use the Polygonal Lasso tool to create the four selections shown in this figure.

4. Press S for the Clone tool, and choose the second brush from the left in the second row on the Brush palette on the Options bar. Clone the tank area over the sign. Figure 18.25 shows where to sample and where to begin the brush stroke for each of the four selections.

5. Show the Channels palette (Window, Show Channels) and click the Save selection as a channel icon (the second icon from the left) at the bottom of the palette. Press Ctrl(⌘)+D to deselect.

6. Press I for the Eyedropper tool, and then select Point Sample from the Sample Size menu in the Options bar. Click on the diamond-shaped sign at the left and just above the light fixture.

7. Press T for the Type tool. On the Options bar, choose a thick, sans-serif font such as Arial Black, and type **1.7** for the font size. Click in the image to the left of the ladder and about the third rung down from the top. Type **WATER** (all caps). Press Ctrl(⌘)+Enter (Return) to enter the text.

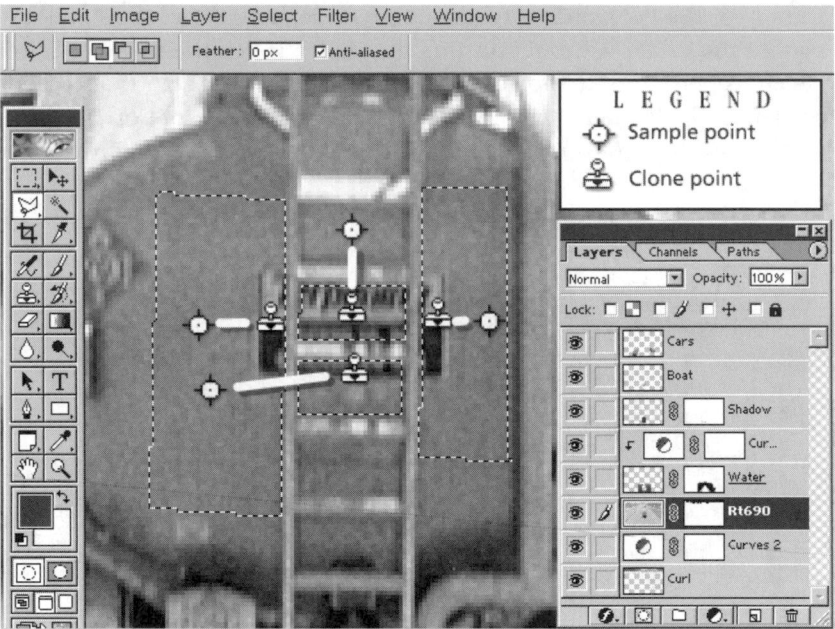

**Figure 18.25**    Alt(Opt)+click on the "Sample" area, and then begin the Clone Stamp tool brush stroke on the "Paint" area.

8. Press D for Default colors so that black is the foreground color. Choose the Line tool from the toolbox and make sure that the Create new shape layer option is selected in the Options palette. Place the cursor in the center of the light fixture at the left of the tank, click+drag to the center of the red light fixture at the right side (Figure 18.26 shows where you should draw this line).

**Note**

**Lines Can Make Shapes**    The Line tool in Photoshop 6 is part of the new Shapes tool set. Shapes can be reshaped. You can create a shape as a vector, as a path, or as a rasterized shape. You can also create custom shape libraries to use later.

9. Click on the WATER layer in the Layers palette, and then press Ctrl(⌘)+T for the Transform command. Click the center anchor on the top and drag upward about one-half the current height of the text. Next, place your cursor just outside the transform box, and then click and rotate the box so that its bottom is parallel with the black line (see Figure 18.26). You can click inside the transform box and drag it closer to the line to help you align the angle of the box. Press Enter (Return) when you are happy with the transform.

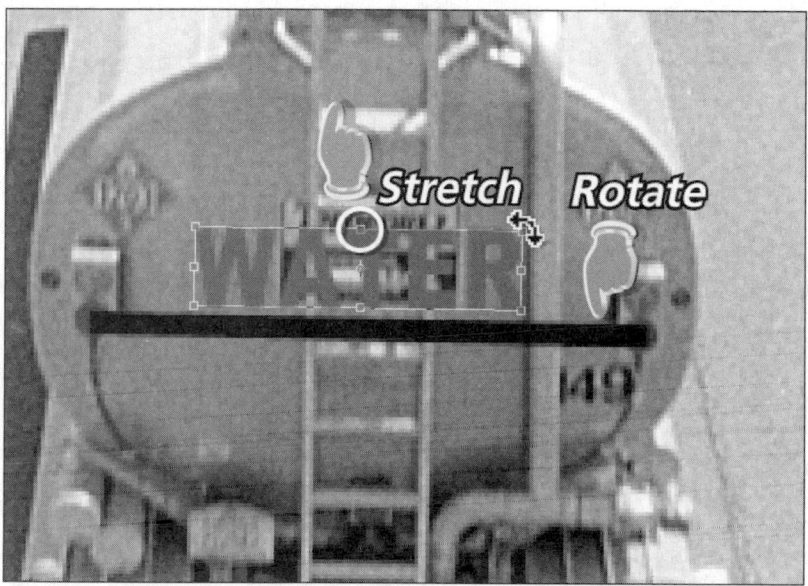

**Figure 18.26**    Vertically stretch the text, and then slightly rotate the transform box to match the angle of the line.

10. Click+drag the Shape 1 layer to the Trash. Press V for the Move tool, and use the arrow keys to nudge the text so that the letter *T* is horizontally centered inside the ladder. Right-click (Macintosh: hold Ctrl and click) on the WATER layer title, and choose Rasterize Layer from the menu.

    When text is not rasterized, you can change the text, the font, and the color. After the text is rasterized, you cannot edit the text by using the Text tool, but you can apply filters and other commands that you would use with a normal layer.

11. The WATER text needs to be "grunged" somewhat to reflect the fuzziness and graininess of the other elements at the back of the tank. Here's how: From the main menu, choose Filter, Noise, Add Noise, type **4** as the Amount, and select Gaussian for the Distribution. Click OK. Now choose Filter, Blur, Gaussian Blur, type **.3** for the Radius, and click OK.

12. Remember those selections you saved as a Channel back in step 5? This is why you saved those selections: Display the Channels palette if it's not visible, and then Ctrl(⌘)+click on the Alpha 1 channel to load it as a selection. Press Ctrl(⌘)+Shift+I to invert the selection, and then press the Delete key. Cool? Instant behind-the-ladder text!

13. Drag the Alpha 1 channel to the Trash. From the main menu, choose Layer, Flatten Image, and then press Ctrl(⌘)+0 and admire your surrealistic master-piece (see Figure 18.27). Save your changes and close the image—the end of this chapter is near.

**Figure 18.27**    Yes, this is the same image as the first figure in this chapter, but hey, it's good enough to look at again!

Although the end of the chapter is indeed near, hopefully this is the beginning of your adventures in surrealistic imaging.

Before you continue those adventures, you should surf over to some of the Web sites listed in the Resources section at the end of this chapter. You'll find wonderful surrealistic artwork from masters of this genre who create either on the traditional canvas or the digital canvas. You're bound to be inspired!

## Summary

You've learned how to manipulate layers, use layer modes, adjust curves, and apply layer mask, just to name a few skills. Remember to experiment with all of Photoshop's features—there are times in the creation of an image that you might need a particular effect that's tucked way down in a submenu. If you invest the effort to learn what Photoshop has to offer you, the pay-off is highly rewarding.

If you use your scanner only for digitizing photographs or documents, you're in for a surprise—you can scan food! Yes, even tomatoes! So, before you take another bite of your sandwich, check out the next chapter and add more spice to your images.

## Resources

http://www.magritte.com

The official René Magritte Web site. Just the first image on the home page, "The Dominion of Light," will make you want to see all the images in this Web site!

http://daligallery.com/

http://www.salvadordalimuseum.org/

Almost everyone has seen Salvador Dali's famous painting that shows melting pocket watches, "Persistence of Memory." Combined, these two Web sites cover nearly all you need to know about Dali—one of the grand masters of surrealism.

http://artchive.com/ftp_site.htm

A huge site that contains hundreds of artists who represent different styles, mostly of painting. Scroll down in the left frame and click on Surrealism to see a list of artists and links to thousands of images.

http://www.surrealism.org/

Perhaps the best resource on the Web containing information, artists, events, and links pertaining to surrealism.

http://www.cyberium.net/imagine/

Wonderfully simple, like Magritte, and strangely fascinating, like Dali, Italian digital artist, Guido Poggi, shows his captivating and unique perspective on reality.

http://www.worldzone.net/arts/surrealities/

Almost 100 artists who work with paint or pixels are given lots of Web space to show their surrealistic creations.

http://www.uelsmann.com/

This is Jerry Uelsmann's Web site. Uelsmann is one of the masters in surrealistic photography; he is also *the* master at photo compositing in the darkroom.

http://www.oknet1.net/~alterart/index2.html

An alternative artwork gallery specializing in surrealism.

# Chapter 19

## Saving the Day with Photoshop and a Scanner

"Bouton, that story on pizza has been bumped up to this issue."

"When's the layout due?"

"Yesterday. You might need to work late tonight."

"Where do I get a photographer at this hour?"

"Don't confuse the issue with questions, Bouton. Finished art and layout, my desk, 9 a.m. sharp, tomorrow. And lose that calendar—it's in bad taste."

"But it's of the Smurfs…" (door slams).

Wait, the story gets *much* better. So much so, that it's become this chapter!

When someone hears the word "Photoshop," the most common mental image is that of a *photograph* that has been manipulated to enhance or otherwise change the reality of the original scene. As shown throughout this book, however, a camera is only one of the ways in which an image can be acquired. If you have an assignment whose image content needs to be digitized almost immediately, a flatbed scanner can be an invaluable tool. The electronics in scanners that cost thousands of dollars only a few years ago can be found today in scanners with a street price of as little as $300. This chapter shows how to use a few common household items, a flatbed scanner, and Photoshop in the same way a photographer uses a studio to produce professional-quality imaging work.

# Connecting Your Scanner to Photoshop

Before getting creative, it is important to know how the objects you place on a scanner go through installed hardware and software to appear in Photoshop.

## The TWAIN Interface and the Scanning Pipeline

Photoshop uses an import filter—similar in some ways to one of the Filter menu filters—to import data from scanning hardware. The most popular standard for *handshaking*—the process by which the operating system realizes and accepts an input device such as a scanner—is accomplished by TWAIN. TWAIN is an open-architecture protocol supported on both Windows and Macintosh platforms.

**Warning**

**If You Can't Take the Twain, Get a Driver**   We're making the assumption here that your scanner is a fairly recent one—if it is not, and it doesn't support TWAIN, its drivers *must* be a Photoshop plug-in module. Check the manufacturer's Web site for the latest drivers.

**Note**

**The Reader's Digest Version of TWAIN's History**   "TWAIN" is an acronym for Toolkit Without An Interesting Name, a somewhat flippant term used by the creators of this standard—a consortium of hardware and software manufacturers including Eastman Kodak, Hewlett Packard, and Logitech.

Logitech has offered a clearer meaning for TWAIN in recent years. There is computer hardware and there are data acquisition peripherals such as scanners and digital cameras. The method by which the two different technologies communicate is a protocol—it is where the "twain meet."

## Software and Hardware Requirements

Before getting down to business in this section, make sure that all your scanner's hardware and software components are installed correctly. Otherwise, your scanner will not be able to "talk" to Photoshop. The following list begins with what you need for your scanner and includes what you need for Photoshop:

- **A flatbed, color scanner.** Other scanning devices are available—drum scanners are capable of high-resolution sampling of both transparent (slide) and reflective (physical) art, and hand-held scanners are fun—but you need a flatbed scanner to sample real-world objects. Flatbed scanners look and behave a lot like traditional photocopiers, and indeed are very useful in businesses for digitizing documents into electronic fax format. The UMax Vista 12 flatbed scanner used in this chapter is a single-element scanner, and about three years old. Although the sample images you work with in this chapter are good, a scanner purchased more recently is bound to give you similar or superior results.

- **An interface card.** Typically, the cards that enable the scanner to hook into the computer's bus are SCSI (Small Computer Serial Interface). If you already have a SCSI card installed, it is possible to plug the scanner right into the SCSI chain of devices presently installed on your system. If you do so, make certain that the scanner's SCSI ID is set so that it does not conflict with other devices in the chain, and that the last device in the SCSI chain is *terminated* (this is a switch on most SCSI hardware today). Most scanners sold today are Plug and Play; the operating system will find an address for the device that does not conflict with other input/output hardware.

  If your scanner comes with a proprietary, non-SCSI interface card, you must use that card.

- **A TWAIN driver.** This is a software component of the scanning pipeline to Photoshop. Photoshop 6 ships with TWAIN drivers for the most popular brands of scanning hardware. Additionally, many scanning manufacturers provide their own drivers. The author uses the UMax 32-bit TWAIN driver for Windows, and as you'll see in the figures in this chapter, the TWAIN interface provides several options. All TWAIN drivers display different interfaces, according to the manufacturer's specifications. Although the TWAIN interface for your own scanner might not look the same as the one in this chapter's figures, basic support is usually offered for scanning resolution and color mode, and occasionally offered for brightness, gamma, and contrast tuning.

## Directing Photoshop to Locate the TWAIN Source

If you're scanning for the first time, you must install the TWAIN driver(s) so Photoshop can find them when you restart your computer. The following steps show you how to accomplish this:

1. First, install the TWAIN software drivers. Many manufacturers offer wizards to lead you through the process. Trust us, this does not require a degree in plumbing.

   Turn on the scanner and put something on top of the scanning element (called the *platen*).

2. Restart your computer.

3. Open Photoshop and choose File, Import, and then choose from the TWAIN devices listed in the menu. In ImageReady, you must choose TWAIN Select, and then choose the scanner. You see, digital cameras and film scanners are TWAIN-compliant, too; and you might also own one or more of these devices.

After a scanner driver has been selected, all you need to do in subsequent scanning sessions is choose File, Import, and then click on the device you want to use.

**Tip**

**Scanning Fragments System RAM**    If you have an evening of scanning ahead of you, it's a good idea to restart your operating system after acquiring, say, five or six large images. Several scans of 5MB or more can fragment your computer's memory. That is why a wise thing to do is to flush the data held in RAM by booting up again before you work with the images in Photoshop.

# Composing for the Magazine Article

Rule #1 in imaging (I know, we've said this a thousand times in this book!): Before doing *anything* creative, know what your output medium and resolution are. And as the quality of the printed image increases, so must the size of the file you acquire. This isn't really a chapter on resolution. Several devices are used in the assignments, so we are going to provide you with target resolutions for your scanner and you can follow along using the same precision that professionals demand.

## General Input/Output Guidelines

Most magazines and books today are prepared electronically; the camera-ready artwork and text is rendered to film from an *imagesetter*—a PostScript device that can simulate line screens and angles used in traditional halftone screening. Typically, a color magazine is printed at a resolution of about 2,540 dots per inch (dpi), but the resolution of the original files that make up a page are *not* measured according to printed dots. *Line frequency* is the unit of measurement; the number of lines of dots that make up a printed page is what you need to find out before you scan.

For line frequency, you can determine what the scanning resolution should be by using this simple formula, called the "Times 2" rule:

> The final print (expressed in lines per inch) requires that the object be
> scanned at twice the lines per inch value of the line screen.

Although the number of lines per inch might be unique, depending on which specific printing press you use, a common line screen is 133 lines per inch (lpi). Using the "Times 2" rule, you can see that if the pressman tells you that the line screen is 133 lpi for a publication, you should scan at 266 samples (pixels) per inch.

Now, the correlation between lines per inch and dots per inch on a page is not an exact because, for example, you can lower the line frequency to increase the number of unique brightness values in a black-and-white print. This is confusing, and this is reality. Table 19.1, a Plug and Play chart we've prepared, can be used with a number of printing devices without you having to perform a ton of math. It shows the output device and then the resolution required for optimal printing at 100% of the size of the image.

### Table 19.1   Scanning Resolutions for Output

| Device | Resolution of Image |
| --- | --- |
| 300 dpi PostScript laser printer | 45–60 pixels/inch |
| 600 dpi PostScript laser printer | 85–106 pixels/inch |
| 1200 dpi PostScript laser printer | 212 pixels/inch |
| 2540 dpi imagesetting machine | 266 pixels/inch |
| 600 dpi PostScript color laser printer | 85–106 pixels/inch |
| 720 dpi inkjet printer (720 by 360 dots/inch) | 120 pixels/inch |
| True 720 by 720 color inkjet | 240 pixels/inch |
| 1440 by 720 dpi color inkjet | 240 pixels/inch |

As you can see in Table 19.1, you might be overscanning material for printed results. Profound Truth #6,207: A pixel is *not* a dot! We have heard too many sad tales of a designer who was told that the final output was to be 300 dpi, so they scanned the image at 300 *pixels*/inch. *No way!* As you can see in the table, for 300 dpi output an image must be scanned at no greater resolution (at 1:1 printing size) than 60 pixels per inch, maximum.

To reproduce such an image, if you normally scan at high-resolution settings, you'd have to use Photoshop's Image, Image Size command to reduce the resolution so that it's compatible with your printer; as a result, the physical dimensions of the image would increase. But because your scanner has an interface in which you can work, a little preplanning will make your direct sampling adventures rewarding and accurate.

Now you understand that scanning frequency has an impact on the printed results (in other words, don't overscan or underscan—know your output before you begin). It feels like time to do a little calculating—let's order a pizza from the shop around the corner so you can scan the pizza elements and get to "photographing" the stars of this pizza article.

### Always Work from a Layout. Always Measure.

In the pizza assignment you will work from a page layout created in Illustrator, measure the space allowed for graphics, and then scan to the same dimensions. You will be working with files that, individually, are not overly large. But with additional layers, applying effects, and working between several image windows, you might want to restart your system before continuing. In this way you ensure that system memory is unfragmented, and you can, therefore, move about efficiently and quickly with the design work.

A little math here shows that a typical 8½"×11" magazine page featuring a full-page graphic at 266 samples per inch adds up to an image file 2261 pixels wide by 2926 pixels high—an 18.9MB file when saved in RGB color mode, and 25.2MB when saved in CMYK color mode. This size image is unreasonably large to work with except in production environments whose computers have 512MB or more of RAM installed—and no, this section does *not* ask you to work with such an image!

One creative workaround to making magazine-quality work begins at the design phase. Instead of featuring one large image, several smaller images can effectively illustrate an article. In Figure 19.1, you can see the layout (in Illustrator) for a fictitious article on the perfect pizza. The grays areas on the layout are called *greeking*—you're reserving space for the actual article text by placing greeking in the layout. Notice that there is the page and then the printable area, called the *live area*—the area within which all elements must lie (or the magazine trimming operation will truncate some design work). Notice that there is an unequal amount of border around the live space. This is a left-facing page, so almost an inch is given to the right border, and the bottom of the page takes a magazine footer (ex: *Non-Gourmet Gazette, page 22*). The top and left margins are ½". The area allotted to the images is small compared to the white field containing text.

**Figure 19.1**   Carefully measure the size of the objects you need to scan for a layout, to ensure accurate sizing and placement when the page is assembled.

The PizzaLayout.ai file is in the Examples/Chap19 folder, if you would like to check out the design in a vector drawing program that can read Illustrator or EPS files.

In the Illustrator file, the Rectangle tool was used to draw a tight box around a drawing of a tomato, one of the three images that make up the page. The Info palette tells you that the box is 2.29" wide by 2.4" high, so this is the size as measured in inches that a tomato slice must be scanned, at 266 samples per inch.

## Other Preliminary Considerations

In addition to line-screen frequency, other questions you might put to a client about an assignment are what the *trim size, bleed size,* and *live area* of the layout should be. Here are brief explanations of those three terms

- The *trim size* of a document is the physical size of a page after it has been trimmed from a press run. The 8½"×11" page you hold in your hands in a magazine almost never starts out at this size, but is slightly larger, so that the mechanism that passes paper through high-speed presses can hold onto the page (which tends to leave dents, registration marks, and occasionally, grease on the outside areas). If you are laying out the page yourself, it is imperative to know the trim size so that you know what size to compose the document to—the PizzaLayout.ai file, for example, is composed correctly.

- The *bleed size* is the excess amount surrounding the trim size that allows an image on a page to be trimmed flush with the edge of the page as viewed in the bound magazine. For example, if you want coffee beans pouring into the page beginning at the page's edge, you must compose an image larger than the trim size. A bleed size for a document might be 9½"×12", allowing an additional ½" around the final, trimmed page. If you do not account for bleed size when you design a page whose content extends to the page's edge, some paper white will most certainly be visible at the edge.

- The *live area* of a page is usually the area within which you have to compose the page. The live area excludes the margins and the header or footer of the publication. The only time a designer gets to ignore the live area on the page is when the page bleeds, due to one or more graphical elements that are designed to "fall off the page."

Figure 19.1 does not show the colors used in the layout in which pizza toppings are placed against a white background. This was a deliberate design decision to conserve Photoshop memory requirements to complete a design that will print at high resolution. The white of the page will carry the small amount of white background in the pizza topping images.

Before Famous Elmer's Country Style Pizza delivers your scanner objects and you plug in your scanner, read the following section, which describes some precautionary measures for protecting the scanning surface of your expensive hardware. You *do not* place chewing gum, a sloppy tomato, or anything that might be dusty or flaky on a scanner's imaging surface without first protecting that surface.

**Warning**

**Scan Sloppy Stuff at Your Own Risk!**   Neither the authors nor New Riders will be responsible for damaged equipment. Please read the following section before proceeding!

## Protecting a Scanner's Platen and Electronics

Take a close look at both the scanner's imaging surface and the thing that holds it in place above the scanning elements (the electronics). Typically, the glass is held in place by a gasket made of plastic or rubber. This gasket is *not* airtight—lint and dust can most certainly be introduced into the electronics. This is why the lid to the scanner should be closed when the machine is not in use, and why the scanner should be covered with a sheet of plastic or a custom dustcover when it isn't used for long periods of time. The gasket is there merely to hold the glass in place and to provide some buffering for the glass plate when the scanning element is in motion and the scanner's housing buzzes a little.

Directly sampling objects is wonderful, but flowers, leaves, a tomato slice, and other real-world objects can spread moisture and fine particles of lint, dust, or pollen across the scanning platen, and this debris can pass through the gasket and into the electronics. To prevent this from happening, you can use one or two items that do not interfere with the opacity of the scanning platen but do ensure that stuff shaken loose from the scanned object remains outside the scanner's electronics

- Get some acetate from a commercial art supply store. Do not get "prepared acetate"; this type has been finely sanded so you can paint on it, but the sanded surface also scatters light and ruins your scan. Similarly, do not get tinted acetate; smoked acetate looks wonderful for presentations, but will make your scanned images look dull and smoky. Try to find the thinnest acetate possible; the thinner the acetate, the more easily the scanner can sample what's behind the acetate.

- Use plastic wrap from the supermarket. Plastic wrap is harder to work with than acetate because it tends to cling to itself instead of to the scanner's platen. It's much cheaper than acetate, however, and is much thinner. The images in the Examples/Chap19 folder on the Companion CD were scanned with plastic wrap protecting the scanner platen.

In Figure 19.2, you can see how plastic wrap should be affixed over the scanner. You begin with a sheet of plastic at least two inches wider and longer than the gasket on the scanner. Using strong adhesive tape, begin by securing alternate corners of the plastic, and then add tape at various places *outside* the platen to make certain that there are no creases in the plastic wrap. Creases *will* show as highlights in a scanned image.

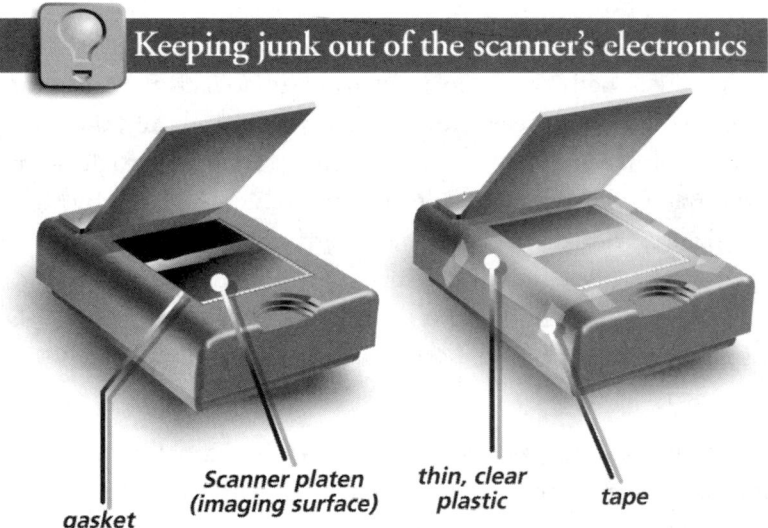

**Figure 19.2**   Protect the platen and gasket of your flatbed scanner with acetate or plastic wrap when you scan messy or dusty objects.

Okay, if you're game for some hands-on image acquisition, you don't need to order a whole pizza as Bouton did to get the ingredients. Get a tomato, a mushroom, and some pepperoni slices from the fridge or the store. Slice the tomato, but do not slice the mushroom yet (mushrooms brown very quickly unless they are dipped in lemon juice and then dried). In the following section, you will scan the first element of the magazine article.

## Scan First, Edit Later

You might want to ask for the assistance of spouse, friend, or co-worker when you're working with food. Your hands tend to get a little greasy or wet, which makes it difficult to move the mouse and type to acquire the images. In the following steps, you will scan the tomato, then the mushroom, and finally the pepperoni. You will save them to a file on your hard drive, and *then* edit the images—it makes no sense to alternate scanning with editing!

Table 19.2 shows the items' dimensions that you will need to define in the scanner's TWAIN interface. These are the dimensions used for the PizzaLayout.ai layout:

### Table 19.2  Pizza Topping Dimensions

| Item | Width | Height |
| --- | --- | --- |
| Tomato | 2.28" | 2.40" |
| Mushroom | 1.75" | 1.74" |
| Pepperoni | 2.12" | 1.44" |

There is plenty of editing to perform with scans of food. If you don't want to hassle with scanning, you can use the toppings provided in Photoshop's PSD format in the Examples/Chap19 folder. As Fate would have it, they are called Pepperoni.psd, Mushroom.psd, and Tomato.psd <g>.

If you do want to get your hands dirty, however, keep these two things in mind while you work:

- The measurements do not have to be precise to two decimal places when you define the crop box in the TWAIN interface. Layouts are *approximations* of the finished design—if you come close to the desired dimensions, a good production department can work the text around any inconsistency in the elements. If you'd like, Photoshop 6 is so capable at text handling, we've included a text file, Pizza.txt, for you to use at the end of the layout assignment to finish the design.

- When you get to laying out the pepperoni, remember that everything scanned is the mirror image of what you see with your own eyes. Therefore, if you want the pepperoni slice to the right to be on top of the two other slices, it will appear to your eyes to be the bottom piece when you place it on the scanner's platen (you're reversing your view to accommodate the scanner's view).

All set? Follow these steps to scan the pizza toppings.

### Example 19.1    Scanning Pizza Toppings

**Warning!**    If an error message appears when you open the CD files, press Ctrl(⌘)+Shift+K and then choose Adobe RGB (1998) from the Working Spaces, RGB drop-down list. See Chapter 3 for more information.

1.  In Photoshop, choose File, Import, and then choose your scanner model from those listed on the Import menu. The TWAIN interface for the scanner appears within Photoshop.

2.  Specify **266** samples per inch as the Resolution. This is occasionally called *dpi* (dots per inch) by some scanner interface manufacturers.

3.  Specify **Inches** as the unit of measurement in the TWAIN interface. The controls for the units of measurement can be located practically anywhere on the interface, as there is no standard for TWAIN displays. The UMax TWAIN interface features the units options on a drop-down to the right of the Input × Scaling fields.

4.  Go slice a tomato that is about two or three inches in diameter. You might want to slice it a little thicker than you would for sandwich making because the thicker the slice, the less likely the seeds are to fall out on the way to the scanner.

5.  Place the tomato slice on the plastic, cover the tomato with a sheet of white paper, and then gently lower the scanner's lid. Do *not* exert pressure—for obvious reasons.

6.  In the TWAIN interface, drag its crop box so that you have a very tight selection around the tomato slice. Adjust the scaling of the sampling so that the height and width are approximately the same as those listed in Table 19.2. As you can see in Figure 19.3, the tomato slice is physically larger than is required for the magazine article, so the crop box is scaled to 73%. When the sample measurements are correct, click Scan.

7.  Some TWAIN interfaces will not permit you to return to Photoshop until you have closed the TWAIN interface. If this is the case with your scanning software, close the interface, and then save the image in Photoshop's workspace as Tomato.psd in Photoshop's native file format. Close the image, choose File, Import, and then choose your scanner once more.

8.  Carve a mushroom lengthwise into several slices. Although you need only one image, you might want to experiment with different angles for the mushroom as it will appear in the article. Bosses sometimes appreciate innovative additions to their concept from their "photographers."

9.  Place the mushroom slices on an area of the plastic where the tomato *wasn't*. The tomato most likely left moisture on the plastic and you do not want to clean this because you might move the plastic or create a crease in it. Alternatively, you can take a moment now to replace the plastic.

10. With many scanners, you must prescan when you have changed the image on the scanning surface. Click Preview, if necessary, and then drag the crop box around one of the mushrooms (see Figure 19.4). Click Scan when you

think you have the ideal mushroom image. Then, before closing the TWAIN interface, increase the size of the crop box to include all the mushrooms—an image you might want to use in the future, with a minimal additional investment of time. Let's face it: How often are you going to scan mushrooms?

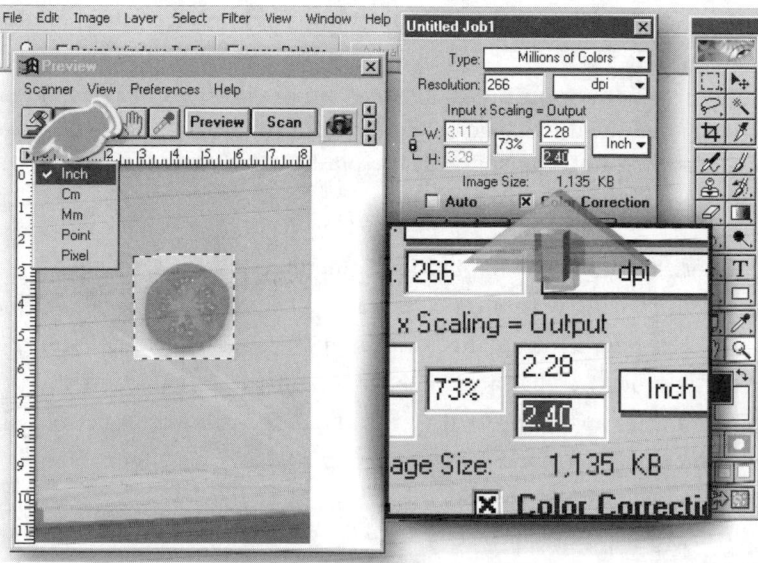

**Figure 19.3** Scanner interfaces usually offer a scaling feature. Use it to make the resolution and dimensions of the scan the same size as the tomato featured in the layout.

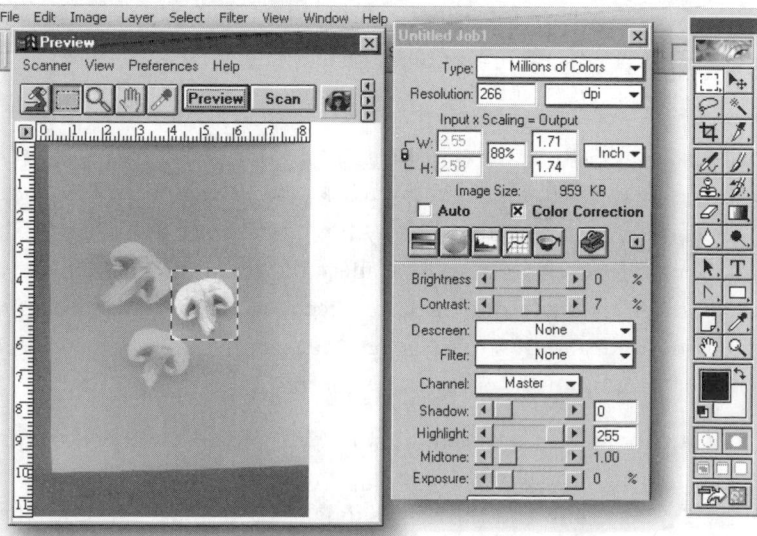

**Figure 19.4** Seize the moment; when you have to scan something unusual, take several images, posed at different angles, at different resolutions!

11. Perform the same scanning steps with the pepperoni. After you have acquired all three images (and perhaps some bonus images for personal use), take a look at them in Photoshop. If they need minor color correction, this is okay—press Ctrl(⌘)+B and use Photoshop's Color Balance controls to make the corrections—and your scanning adventures with pizza toppings are over. Close the image windows, close Photoshop, and restart your operating system to refresh system RAM.

12. While the system boots up again, clean up the mess you have created. Carefully remove the plastic or acetate from the scanner (arc the plastic upward so that nothing spills off the plastic), toss away the plastic, and then remove the tape from the scanner.

As in traditional food photography, it's sometimes difficult to get food to look attractive and appetizing without the assistance of a professional, called a *food stylist* in the advertising trade. You might notice that although the scans (and the images provided for you on the CD) accurately represent the tomato and the other toppings, they're not as appealing as they could be. The following sections show you how to become your own food stylist by using Photoshop's effects filters.

## Preparing Food for Filtering

If this pizza article were a real assignment, your boss might insist on unretouched images. The best way to convince your superior(s) that it might be better to *stylize* the elements, would be to show him or her the unretouched, raw scans. Let's assume that your boss agrees with you (fictitious as this might sound), and accepts your call to filter the scans to make more appealing images.

For an assignment such as this, or practically any assignment in which food is involved, a "painterly" look conveys the shape, color, and texture of the object while removing unappetizing elements such as the grease on the pepperoni (the scanning element will indeed heat up anything placed on the platen). The game plan is this: You will use Photoshop 6's Gallery Effects filters to slightly stylize the scans, add soft drop shadows using the layer effects, and make a most effective, compelling, and handsome addition to the magazine layout. Many of the Gallery Effects filters work best with bright colors and low contrast.

Have we thought about the background of these images yet, and how to separate the foreground elements? Nope. But we shall, right now. After trying several techniques, including the Extract command (it takes as long as other tools, and the edgework is not always refined), we decided upon the Magnetic Lasso tool to drag a path around the tomato. You'll see that precision and speed come to you almost effortlessly.

**Note**

**I Don't See a Menu Listing for "Gallery Effects." What Gives?**   We're using the term "Gallery Effects" to distinguish between artistic filters and filters that simply modify image areas, such as the Gaussian Blur tool. When Adobe purchased Aldus Corporation several years ago, three versions of Gallery Effects were inherited and incorporated into several Adobe products.

There is no special place where you find Gallery Effects filters on the Filter menu—they are more or less sorted according to the effect they produce.

In the following steps, you will use the Magnetic Lasso tool, select the tomato and put it on its own image layer, and then experiment with the Hue/Saturation command to make the tomato image an ideal candidate for the Gallery Effects filters.

### Example 19.2    Peeling a Tomato (From Its Background)

1. Load the Tomato.psd image you saved earlier to hard disk, or load the Tomato.psd image from the Examples/Chap19 folder on the Companion CD. Zoom in to a 200% viewing resolution of the image.

   The Magnetic Lasso tool has been around since Photoshop 4, but if you've never used it, it operates a little differently than other tools. You make an initial click on the color edge of something in an image, and then you *hover*—you guide—the cursor, but *without* holding the mouse button.

2. With the Magnetic Lasso tool, dragging but *not* clicking, carefully trace around the edge of the tomato. Click to lay down an anchor only where you see that the Magnetic Lasso tool is not tracing accurately. Most of the time, anchors will appear automatically. Use the default settings on the Options bar for the Magnetic Lasso tool; this tool was designed for separating image areas that display a lot of contrast, and the tomato against off-white qualifies.

   It is actually better for the finished image if you create many anchor points (see Figure 19.5), making the outline a little rough, uneven, and natural-looking (tomatoes are almost never perfectly spherical, as depicted in the Illustrator layout). When you reach the edge of the window, hold down the spacebar to toggle to the Hand tool, and then drag your view of the window to areas that are undefined by the Magnetic Lasso tool. *Important:* Do *not* release the spacebar until your cursor is back to the last anchor along the path. If you release the spacebar before that last anchor, you will resume guiding the tool someplace off in outer space.

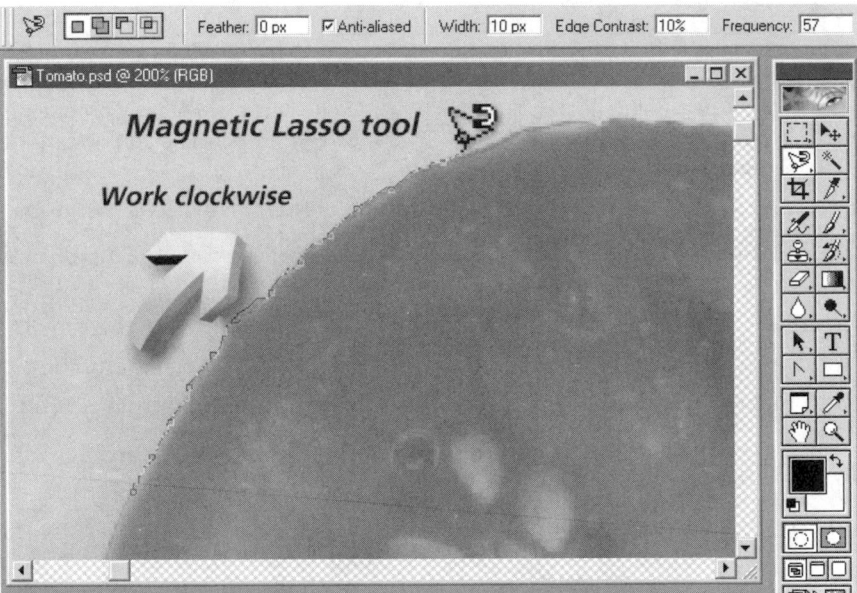

**Figure 19.5**    Hover around the edge of the tomato to allow the Magnetic Lasso tool to auto-select the edge of the tomato. If the tool is messing up in a specific area, click to manually place an anchor, and then continue hovering the cursor.

**Note**

**Correcting Errors You Made with the Magnetic Lasso Tool**    To backtrack after you have misplaced an anchor, hold down the Delete (Backspace) key and click the previous anchor point. Then release the Delete (Backspace) key and continue guiding the cursor around the edge of the object in the image.

3.  Work clockwise around the tomato's edge, and when you arrive at the beginning point, release the mouse button and a selection will appear.

    Users of the Tomato.psd image on the Companion CD have the path created and saved within the image. Click the Paths tab on the grouped palette, and then press Ctrl(⌘)+click on the path title to load it as a selection. Alternatively, you can click the Loads path as selection icon on the Paths palette.

4.  Right-click (Macintosh: hold Ctrl and click) within the selection marquee with any selection tool currently chosen, and then choose Layer Via Cut from the context menu (see Figure 19.6).

**Figure 19.6** Isolate the tomato from the background by loading the path as a selection, and then cut the tomato to a new layer.

5. Use your own artistic eye on this step. The tomato has to be unrealistically colorful and a little bright for the Dry Brush Filter to bring out more appetizing visual qualities. Press Ctrl(⌘)+U to display the Hue/Saturation dialog box. The tomato needs to be more saturated, and a little lighter—the amount of change depends on your own scan (see Figure 19.7). The Tomato.psd image is right on target with respect to lightness and color.

If the tomato looks wrong, first check Edit, Color Settings, and make sure that Adobe RGB 1998 is the default working space. Then check to see whether View, Proof Setup is on your operating system's RGB color choice. If these are correct and the tomato still appears in need of color correction, open the Hue/Saturation dialog box to add saturation and lightness. It all sort of depends on the way your scan came out.

6. Choose File, Save As, and then save your work as Tomato.psd to your hard disk; keep the image open.

It's useful to experiment with different images and different settings with filters in Photoshop 6. You never know when you'll have to hide—or embellish—something.

 **Tip**

**Making an Image Ready for Gallery Effects Filtering** It's been my experience that almost without exception, a low-contrast, light, colorful image works best with the artistic (Gallery Effects) filters.

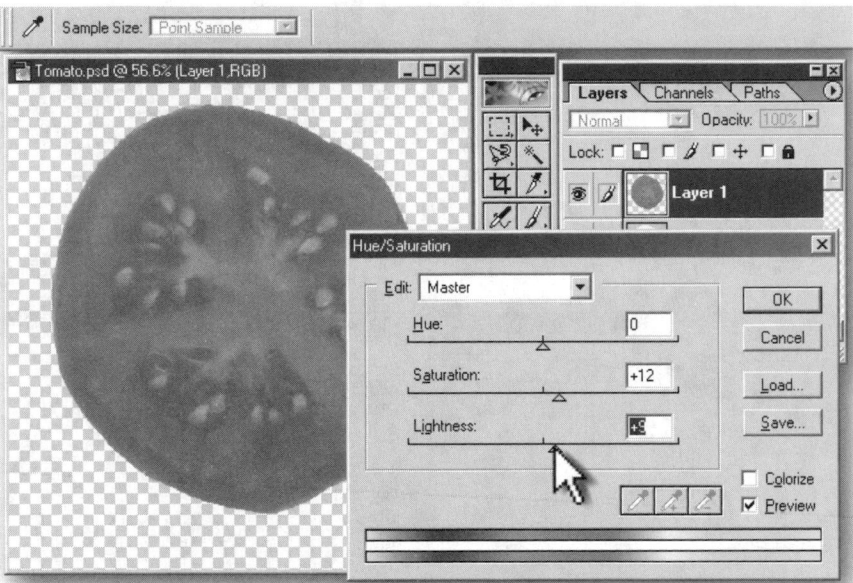

**Figure 19.7** Do not think of realistic color correction when you're adjusting the image. *Anticipate* which colors and brightness will look best when the image is filtered.

## Defringing the Tomato

With the background still present in the Tomato.psd image, it's hard to tell where the tomato ends and the background begins. It's important for this layout that the tomato edge contains no background pixels, because if you apply a Gaussian blur as a drop shadow to the tomato, any fringing will separate tomato from shadow.

Here's what you do to ensure that the tomato is precisely cut:

### Example 19.3 Perfecting a Tomato's Edges

1. On the Layers palette, uncheck the visibility icon for the Background layer. The checkered transparency grid is now visible, but not all that useful. Why? Because the grid contains white, and white is the color we are trying to elim-inate around the edge of the tomato. Make sure you are at 100% viewing res-olution of Tomato.psd. If you're zoomed out below 100%, you will not accurately see the edges of the tomato because Photoshop uses *interpolation* (displays an approximation) on zoom percentages less than 100%.

2. Press Ctrl(⌘)+K to display the Preferences dialog box, and then choose Transparency & Gamut from the top drop-down list.

3. The factory setting for the transparency grid is Medium size and Light colors. Click on the Grid Colors drop-down list, choose Dark, and then press Enter (Return).

4. *Now* you can see what's going on with the tomato edge. If there's a thin white line at the edge of the tomato, choose Layer, Matting, and then choose Defringe. Make the Defringe amount **1** pixel in the dialog box, and then click OK. If there's no fringe, don't do a thing in this step. In either event, your tomato slice should look like the one in Figure 19.8.

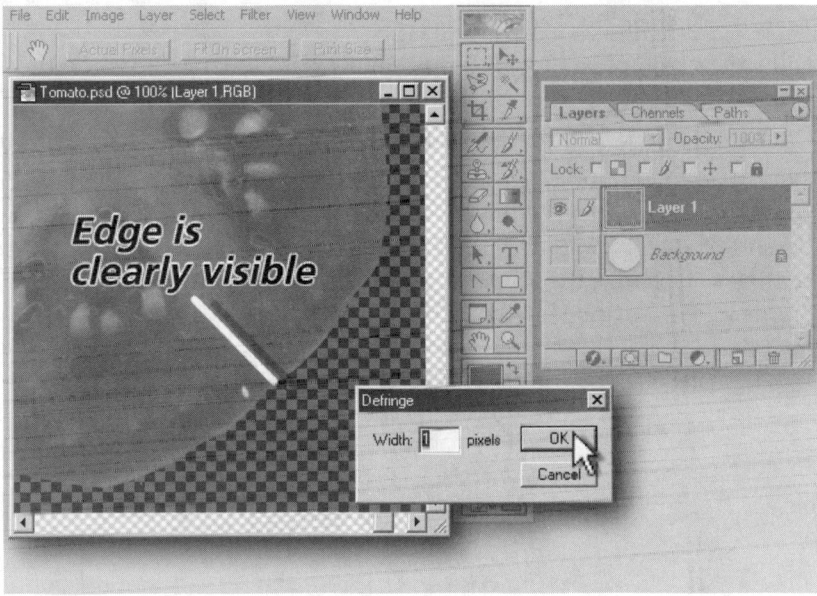

**Figure 19.8**   Change the transparency color to get a good look at the tomato edge.

5. Press Ctrl(⌘)+S, and then go back to Transparency & Gamut Preferences and change the transparency grid back to its more general-purpose Light Grid color.

**Tip**

**Setting the Transparency Grid Based on Your Image**   You might not believe it, but once in a while you might come across a picture that has gray checks in it—a sock, a blouse, whatever. In this situation, changing the Grid color to dark in the Transparency & Gamut Preferences box will do nada for you. You need to click on the color swatches beneath the drop-down boxes, and pick some really awful color such as chartreuse for both the check colors.

Then, any flaws in the edgework, and any other transparent areas in the image will instantly become visible.

## Applying Multiple Filters

Through trial and error, we've discovered that the best way to stylize a tomato slice is to apply several different filters. The Dry Brush effect helps sharpen the contrast between the meat and the seeds of the tomato, and the Watercolor effect then emphasizes the color differences in the tomato through the use of subtle outlines around areas of color contrast. In the following steps, you create a tomato image that is both realistic *and* idealistic!

### Example 19.4    Stylizing the Tomato Using Artistic Filters

1. Click the visibility box to the left of the Background layer to make the layer visible.

2. Click on the Layer 1 title, choose Filter, Artistic, and then choose Dry Brush.

3. Click the minus button below the image to zoom out the preview window so that you can better see the effect. Drag the Brush Size slider to 3, drag the Brush Detail to 10, and drag the Texture slider to 1 (see Figure 19.9). These settings will change the tomato image, but not dramatically. This step is a "primer coat" for the Watercolor filter. Click OK to apply the effect.

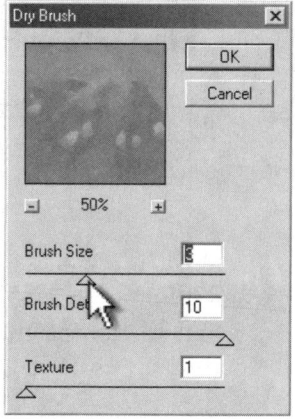

**Figure 19.9**   Apply a subtle amount of Dry Brush filtering to the tomato image.

4. Choose Filter, Artistic, and then choose Watercolor.

5. In the Watercolor dialog box (see Figure 19.10), drag the Brush Detail slider to 9, drag the Shadow Intensity to 0, and leave the Texture slider at its default of 1. Click OK to apply the effect.

6. The Watercolor filter makes even the brightest colors a little dull, because part of its filtering process is to add neutral shading to the image. There's

nothing wrong with the effect; it's the *tones* that need more contrast in the image. Press Ctrl(⌘)+L.

7. In the Levels dialog box, drag the White Point slider to about 190, and then drag the Midpoint slider to about .80. Look at the image in the workspace. If it needs a little higher white point, or more contrast (accomplished by dragging the Midpoint slider to the right), make those changes now, and then click OK to apply the tonal changes.

8. Press Ctrl(⌘)+S; keep the file open.

Shadows cast by photorealistic objects usually are sharp around their outlines. But because the pizza toppings are stylized, you can get away with using the Gaussian Blur dropshadow technique to "lift" the topping elements off the final magazine layout, giving the layout more visual interest.

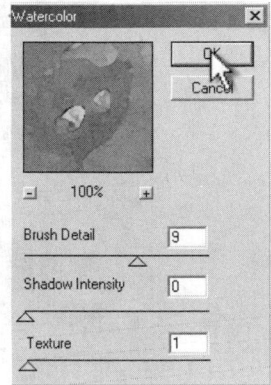

**Figure 19.10**
A high amount of brush detail and no shading effect produces a soft yet distinct wash of colors in the image.

## Adding Drop Shadows to the Pizza Toppings Images

The next step is to add a Gaussian Blur drop shadow to the tomato image. The procedure has been covered in several chapters, but there's more than one way to design a drop shadow. In this chapter, you'll see a "quick-and-dirty way" to achieve the effect.

Briefly, you copy a layer's contents by dragging the layer title into the Create a new layer icon at the bottom of the Layers palette. With black as the foreground color, you click on the Layer 1 title, press Alt(Opt)+Shift+Delete (Backspace) to fill only the nontransparent areas of Layer 1; the Layer 1 copy is the top layer and the one we use for the tomato image. The Layer 1 layer should be the current layer now.

You then apply the Gaussian Blur filter to spread the contents of the layer into a soft-edged shape. In the Gaussian Blur dialog box (see Figure 19.11), type **17** in the pixels field, and then click OK. Next, with the Move tool, move the black contents of the layer so that the Gaussian Blur effect can be seen to the bottom-right of the tomato on the top layer in the image.

Set Opacity to about 60% (see Figure 19.12), and set the layer mode to Multiply. Consistency across images is important. Remember the percentage of opacity you use here for future work on the other images.

**Figure 19.11**   You produce shadows with softer edges by using high Gaussian Blur settings.

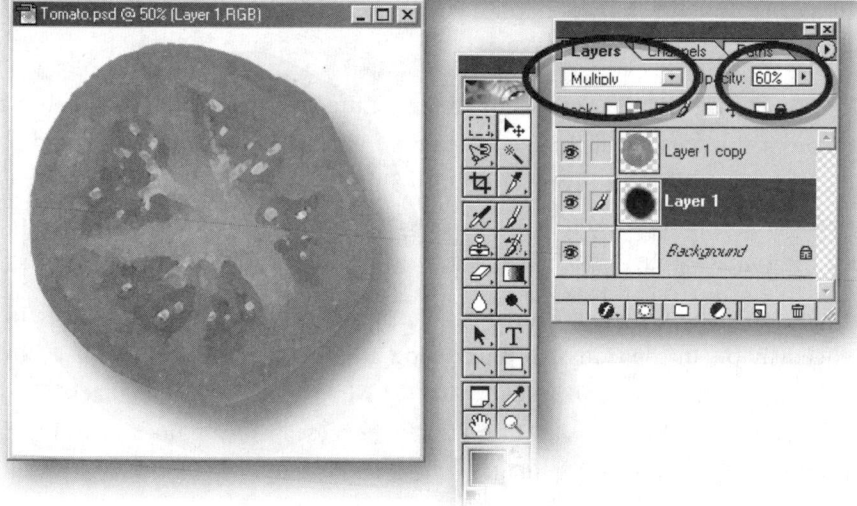

**Figure 19.12**   Reduce the opacity of the shadow to create a softer effect.

Drag the Background layer title into the Trash on the Layers palette, and then choose Merge Visible from the Layers palette's flyout menu. You're finished with this image. Press Ctrl(⌘)+S, close the image, and close Photoshop for the moment.

To prepare the pepperoni and mushroom for the magazine article, use the same steps as those described in the previous sections. If you would like to see how the integration process—that of aligning the images relative to their position on the layout—happens, Pepperoni.psd and Mushroom.psd on the Companion CD have been retouched so that you can get hands-on experience with another Photoshop tool we haven't covered yet. It's called the Magic Eraser tool. All you need to do is click on the background of the Pepperoni and the Mushroom images and the white disappears, leaving transparency around the toppings. Click and hold on the Eraser tool on the toolbox, choose the Magic Eraser tool, and click on the background, as shown in Figure 19.13.

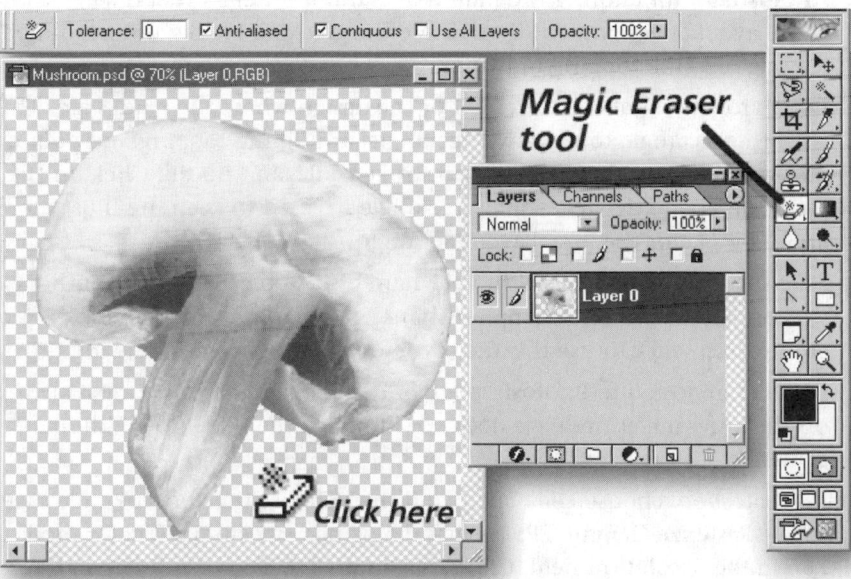

**Figure 19.13**   Depending on the task, the Magic Eraser tool can take care of several steps in one swoop (or click).

Next, filter the images and create drop shadows. Because the mushroom image is highly textured, you do not need to use the Dry Brush Effect before you apply the Watercolor filter. The pepperoni image will look its best if you follow the same steps as those used to filter the tomato.

## Using Crop Marks and a Template

It seems eons ago that designers had to manually trace a layout area onto vellum, place the vellum over a photostatic copy of an image, and then use a pocket calculator to decide upon the scaling of the images to complete a layout. Today, to accomplish your part of this magazine layout, all you need is the area of the Illustrator file that contains the illustrations of the toppings. You then place the toppings you have retouched on top of the template, merge the layers, and you're home free.

The next example shows how to crop the image area on the Illustrator layout, import the cropped area to Photoshop, and meld the separate toppings into one high-resolution image.

### Example 19.5    Integrating the Design Work

1. In Illustrator (or another program that can import EPS files), open the PizzaLayout.ai design, and then delete the greeking blocks and headline text, leaving only the topping drawings.

2. Draw crop marks at the lower left of the design where the guides are. Then, with the Rectangle tool, draw a rectangle around the topping and your crop marks, and assign the rectangle no stroke width and no fill. Click on the page border and delete a similar rectangle we used to keep the Illustrator file at 8½" by 11" for the PizzaLayout.ai design.

3. Save the files as Toppings.ai to your hard disk. Toppings.ai—the authors' version, located in the Examples/Chap19 folder—contains the drawings and crop marks; you can use this file if you don't own a vector drawing program.

   EPS files imported to Photoshop are only as large as the outermost element on the page; the entire page does not import if there are no additional elements.

4. In Photoshop, choose File, Open, and then choose the Toppings.ai image. In the Rasterize Generic EPS Format dialog box, specify RGB color mode and 266 in the Resolution field. Click OK to start the conversion from vector art and bitmap format.

5. When the Toppings drawing appears, open Tomato.psd from your hard disk and then, with the Move tool, drag the image into the Toppings.ai image window (see Figure 19.14).

6. With the Move tool, position the tomato as close to the center of the template illustration of the tomato as you can. Notice that the scan is very, very close in resolution and shape to this element in the Illustrator layout.

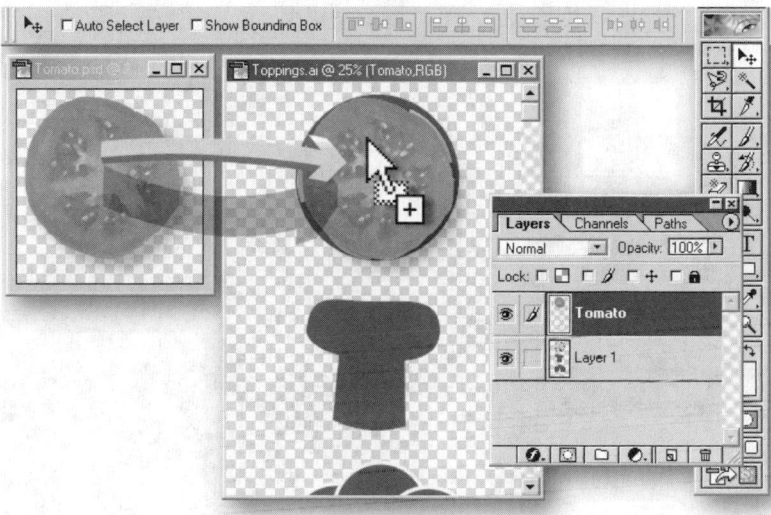

**Figure 19.14** Understanding resolution pays off! The tomato image fits almost perfectly into the Perfect Pizza design.

It's usually a good idea to take a moment and label the layers in a multilayer composition. So, in Toppings.ai, label the layer title from the tomato you dragged over. You do this by right-clicking (Macintosh: hold Ctrl and click), choosing Layer Properties, and then typing **Tomato** in the Name field.

Save the Toppings.ai image as Toppings.psd, in the Photoshop file format, to your hard disk.

7. Open the Mushroom.psd image, and drag the image into the Toppings.psd image window. Then position the mushroom to match the drawing on the template.

8. Perform step 7 with the Pepperoni.psd image (see Figure 19.15). When the pepperoni is positioned correctly, hide the Layer 1 template by clicking the eye icon on the Layers palette, and then press Ctrl(⌘)+Shift+E (Layer, Merge Visible) from the Layers palette's flyout menu. This reduces the saved file size (and also you would not want to work with a composed design with layers in which objects could accidentally be bumped around). Press Ctrl(⌘)+S. Keep the image open, and close the others without saving.

Originally, we were going to conclude the story by having Mr. Bouton turn over Toppings.psd to his boss, muttering a few things as he prepares to go home. But that would be too simple! Photoshop has everything you need to add *typesetting* and a catchy 3D headline to the layout, so there's only one reason we're pausing here.

**Figure 19.15**   After the elements are in the proper position, merging layers helps reduce the saved file size.

And that's to explain why we've offered *low* resolution images of this article's components on the Companion CD.

## Creating a Low-Resolution Finished Design

An 8½" by 11" layout (with a background; we forgot the handsome butcher block wood background) at magazine quality (266 pixels/inch) plus ½" all the way around because this will be a bleed page now (and the grippers on a press need extra area to hold the paper) and would be about 28MB.

This book is about teaching, and not about torturing your system. You would need at least 112MB, *in addition* to what Photoshop and your system are using, to create the design at magazine resolution. However, if we compose to 125 pixels/inch, the layout will require only about 20 extra MB with which to work, and this is sufficient resolution for you to print a copy of the finished design on an inkjet in low mode.

Here's how to set up the page and add a smaller copy of the toppings image:

### Example 19.6   Creating a Small Final Design

1. Create a path segment for each of the two crop marks at the bottom right of Toppings.psd. Then, with the paths visible and both paths selected (use the

Path Component Selection tool to marquee select the paths), choose Edit, Stroke, and type **3 px** in the Width field. When you shrink the toppings image, the crop marks would vanish if they remained 1 pixel wide.

2. Press Ctrl(⌘)+E to merge down the two layers into one. Choose Image, Image Size. Make sure the Resample Image option is checked. Type **125** in the Resolution field, and then click OK. Choose File, Save As, and then save this small image as Toppings125.psd to your hard disk. By doing this, you can prepare the full-sized layout any time in the future.

3. Click on the top layer title on the Layers palette—the layer with the toppings. Choose Filter, Sharpen, Unsharp mask. Amount should be 39%. Type **.9** in the Radius field, and type **1** in the bottom Threshold field. Press Enter (Return). Minor sharpening of the toppings is necessary; you just lopped 15MB off the original file!

4. Choose File, New, and then type **9.5** in the Width (inches) field, and **12** in the Height (inches) field. Type **125** in the Resolution field, choose RGB color, Contents: White, and then press Enter (Return). Save this image to hard disk as PizzaArticle.psd. Keep it open.

5. Press Ctrl(⌘)+R to show the rulers, and then drag a vertical guide out of the vertical ruler and place it at 1½" bleed, and another ½" to bring the guide to the live area on the page. Drag a horizontal guide out of the horizontal ruler and place it at 1".

6. Scroll to the bottom left of the page and place a horizontal guide at 10¼". Don't worry; we did the math for you to allow for a magazine footer at the bottom of the page.

7. Scroll to the bottom right of the page, and plant a vertical guide at 8". Again, we did the math for you to take into account that this is a left-facing page, and there needs to be some room for the glue on the right margin.

8. Press Ctrl(⌘)+R to hide the rulers, double-click the Hand tool to fit the page in Photoshop's window, and then click on the title bar of the Toppings125 image. On the Layers palette, link the layers. With the Move tool, drag the image(s) into the PizzaArticle.psd image window, and then position the crop marks at the lower-left corner of the window, where the guides meet (see Figure 19.16). We left the crop marks a little in view in this figure to show you where their final position should be.

    By the way, if you note any resistance when you try to move the linked images, choose View, and then uncheck Snap.

9. Unlink the crop mark layer from the toppings layer, and then drag the crop mark layer into the Trash. Press Ctrl(⌘)+S, and keep the PizzaArticle window open. You can shut the toppings window.

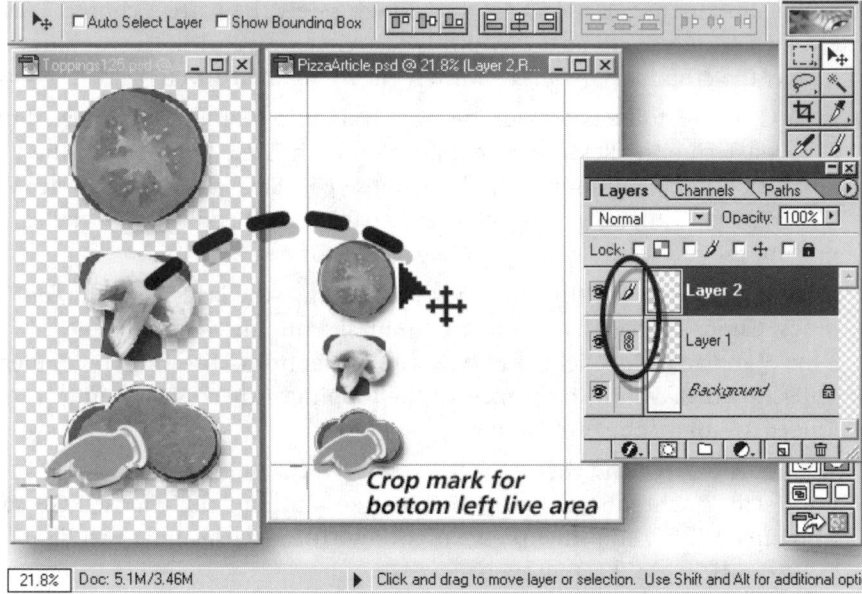

**Figure 19.16**   Drag the linked layers into the page design, and then align the live crop marks with the live guides.

 **Note**

> **When Can You Violate Live Space in a Layout?**   Yes, the drop shadow for the pepperoni does violate the live space in the layout. You can ignore this, because in reality, space outside the live space has been allotted for a magazine footer, and it's okay—even creative—to violate the footer on a page. Alternatively, you can scoot the layer up until the drop shadow clears the live guide.

Although Photoshop doesn't let you import text (but probably will in version 7), you can indeed place text on the Clipboard, click an insertion point with the Type tool, and then paste. With paragraphs of text, this runs a single line of type off the image edge. But no problem; it's easy enough to add hard breaks, "reel in" the text that runs off the window edge during the process, and then justify the text by using the Paragraph palette controls.

Yes, all this setup means is that you are going to add text to the PizzaArticle layout, and put a few production people out of business <g>. You'll also learn a secret for creating wraparound text.

## Adding the Article to the Page

Take a look at Figure 19.17 for a moment. This is the finished article, trimmed to fit the magazine. You'll notice that text wraps around the ingredients on the page, and that the paragraphs are flush right. This is the look we are going for in the article.

**Figure 19.17** The finished article. Note the way the left edge of each paragraph wraps around the images.

We used Garamond Condensed as the font, and strongly urge you to use it, too. If you cannot find Garamond Condensed, try Clearface, Galliard Condensed, or some other condensed font. A condensed font greatly improves your chances of having the paragraph lines break in the same places ours did.

Here's how to add text to the article.

### Example 19.7 Adding Text from the Clipboard

1. In a plain text editor, open the Pizza.txt article from the Examples/Chap19 folder of the Companion CD.

2. Just for practice, highlight and copy only the paragraph about the tomato to the Clipboard.

You'll notice many periods in the text. This is the secret to wrapping Photoshop text. You push a line in by adding periods, and then paste over the periods with a copy of the background layer.

3. Click the Palettes option on the Options bar. On the Character palette, specify 12-point Garamond Condensed (or whatever font you came up with), Auto Leading, and black Color.

4. In Photoshop, click the Type tool, and then press Ctrl(⌘)+V to paste the text, as shown in Figure 19.18.

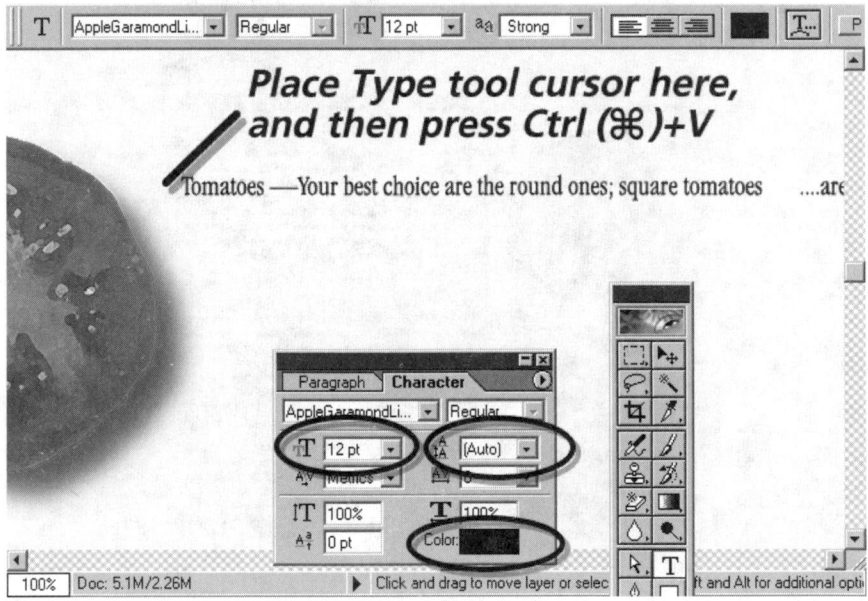

**Figure 19.18**    The pasted text will run outside the window, but that's okay. Photoshop holds items that fall outside the window, and you'll have plenty of time to place hard breaks in the paragraph.

5. This is a little tedious, but worth the extra moments for the effect you'll create. Place the Type tool cursor at the first period in a string of periods, and then press Enter (Return). In Figure 19.19, you can see a few completed lines. If you can visually erase the periods, do you see how the left edge of the paragraph is forming an indent to accommodate the round shape of the right side of the tomato?

6. Highlight the first word: Tomatoes. On the Character palette, choose 18 from the point size flyout. Highlight the whole paragraph, and then on the Paragraph palette choose right justified. Finally, use the Move tool to move the periods, but not the text, into the tomato image so that your article looks like Figure 19.20.

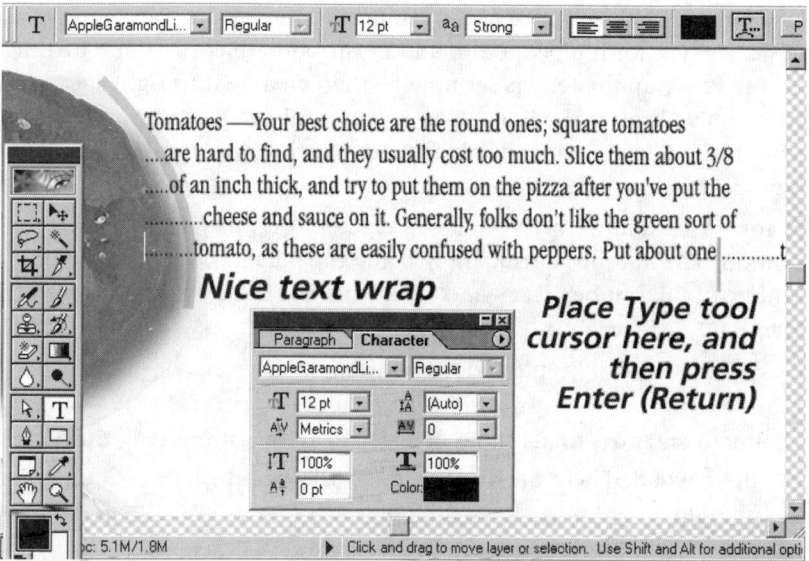

**Figure 19.19**    Create your own text wrap by inserting characters that eventually will take on the background color.

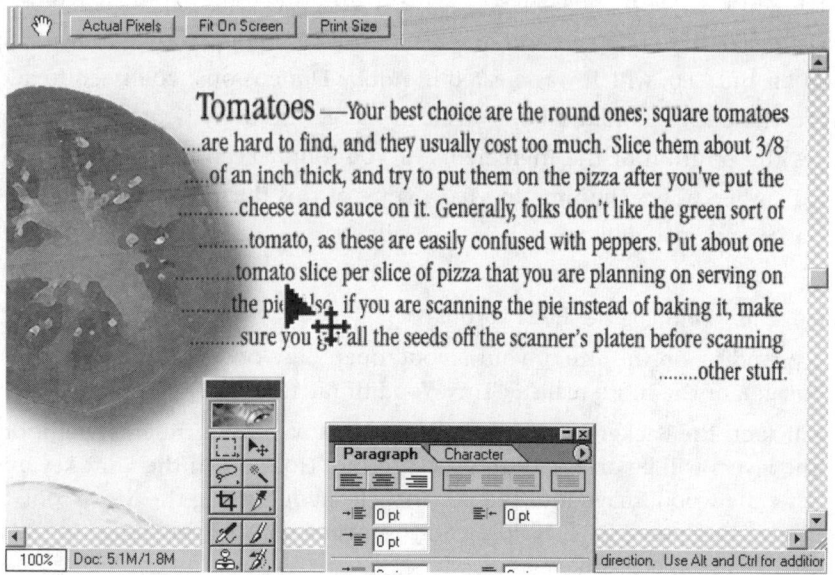

**Figure 19.20**    The text itself is right justified with text wrapping on the left side. All that's needed is to paste over (eliminate) the periods used to force the individual lines over.

7. You can add the pepperoni and the mushroom copy on your own. When you paste the text for the pepperoni and mushroom, make sure the justification on the Paragraph palette is set to left—then change it to right justification after you've broken the lines. Your layout might require extra periods or a word kicked down a line, depending on which font you use. Play with the type.

    As for the headline copy you saw in Figure 19.17, use center paragraph justification. The author painstakingly made the paragraph fully justified, but a centered look can be great—and takes only the time it takes to break the lines.

8. Press Ctrl(⌘)+S and keep the document open.

We are going to enter the final phases of page layout by introducing the background image of light wood. There are two scales to the wood on the Companion CD: BigWood.tif, which is for those hearty Photoshoppists who want to do a 266 pixels/inch layout; and TinyWood.tif, a sheet of wood scaled for a layout at 125 pixels/inch.

## Finalizing the Layout

Three things need to happen next: You need to add a snappy 3D headline (provided for you on the CD), which was created in Adobe Dimensions; you need to add the wood to the background; and you need to merge the ingredients against it. This finalizes the position of the ingredients. If you didn't keep a spare file as recommended earlier, now's the time to save a copy of this document under a different name, an *alias* if you will. Sorry....

### Example 19.8    Finishing the Pizza Layout

1. Depending on the size of your layout, open BigWood.tif (the 266 ppi image), or the more realistic TinyWood.tif (at 125 ppi).

2. Click on the Background layer on the Layers palette so the next addition to the layers will be on top of the background. Hold down the Shift key and drag the wood image into the PizzaArticle layout, using the Move tool, as shown in Figure 19.21. Holding Shift moves a copy of the image to the center of the target window.

3. Uncheck the Visibility (the eye) icon on all text layers leaving only the ingredients, the white background, and the slab of wood. Choose Merge Visible from the Layers palette's flyout menu, as shown in Figure 19.22.

**Figure 19.21**   Add a light wood texture to the article, so the text is still legible but the ingredients' colors have something to play off of.

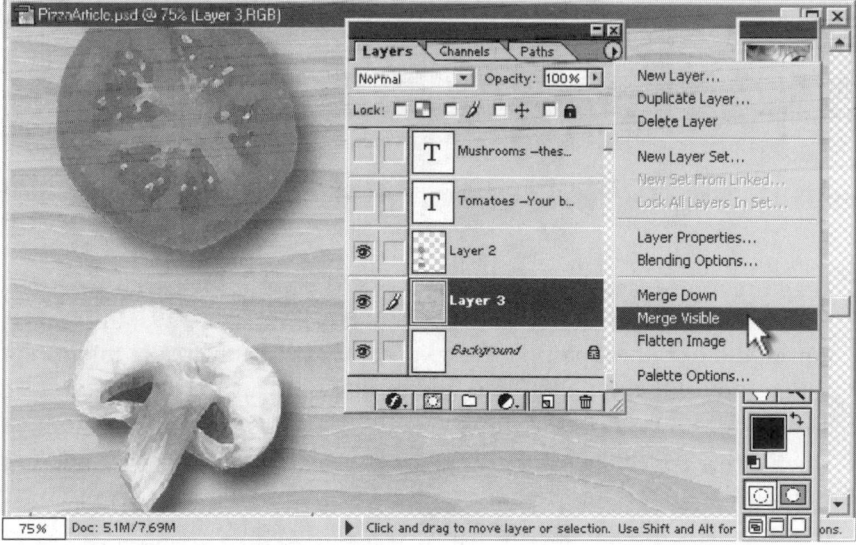

**Figure 19.22**   Merge the toppings with the wood layer.

4. You'll need to do this several times, but we only need to show it to you once. Restore the visibility of all the text. With the Lasso tool, hold Alt (to toggle to the Polygonal Lasso tool), and then with the background as the current editing layer, click around the periods to encompass them in a selection, as shown in Figure 19.23. Then right-click (Macintosh: hold Ctrl and click), and choose Layer Via Copy.

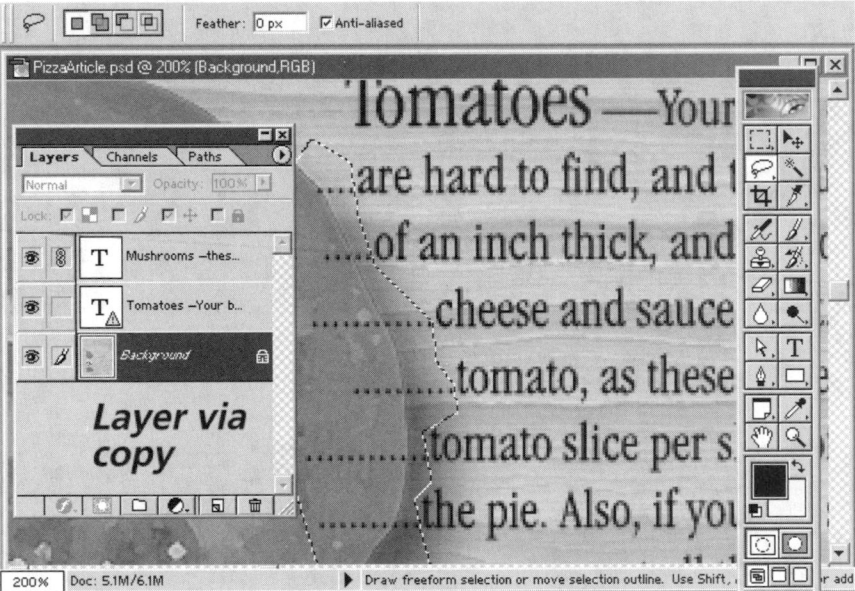

**Figure 19.23**    Copy an area of the background that will perfectly hide the periods on the text layers.

5. Drag the copied layer portion to the top of the list in the Layers palette. By the way, the reason you see only two text layers in Figure 19.24 is that the author did not finish pasting the text. But that's not the really interesting thing—notice that for all intents and purposes, the periods were never there. The copied hunk of the background is the perfect replacement part!

6. Open either PerfectBig.psd (266 ppi) or PerfectTiny.psd (125 ppi), and (using the Move tool) drag the contents of the file into the PizzaArticle.psd image, positioning it at the upper right of the layout to add symmetry to the layout, as shown in Figure 19.25.

7. That's it! The layout is complete, and if you wanted to send this to a print shop that's hip to Acrobat format, you could save this file to the PDF format, embed the fonts, and the text would print as clean as if you'd typed it in Quark or InDesign. By the way, you can add a page footer if you want, but you don't need our help to do that. There's no need to collapse the type layers, so a quick Ctrl(⌘)+S and then closing the file gets us outa here.

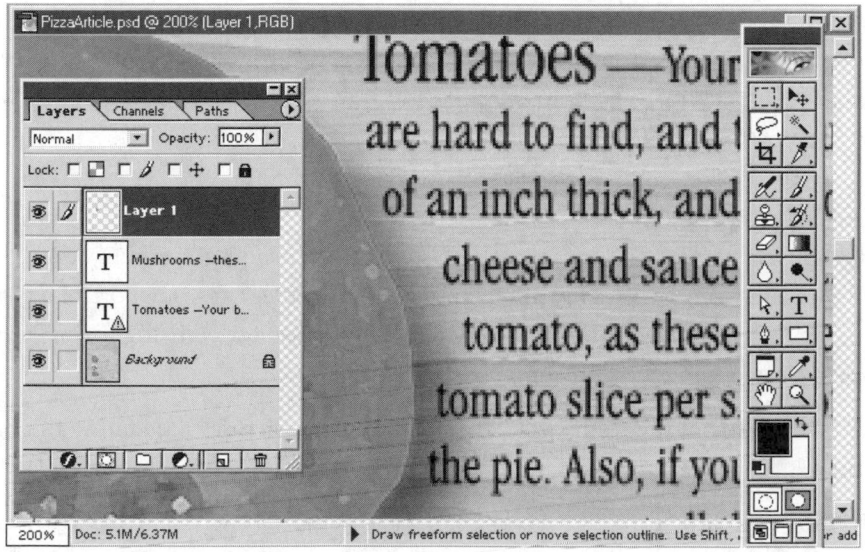

**Figure 19.24**  Drag the background copied area to the top of the list in the Layers palette.

**Figure 19.25**  Add the headline—a tasty finishing touch to a greasy article!

C'mon now, tell the truth. Wasn't it fun designing a page layout that looks as good as anything in a magazine? You learned about measuring, filtering food to make it look more appetizing, what a live area is, and how to align type any way you like. That's why we have an...

## After School Special

Now that you have your hands on lots of powerful techniques, it would be a shame not to try them out on a totally different magazine article. These are portfolio pieces in a way, okay? You will need to show any production, advertising, or magazine house that you know how to compose on a computer.

Here's an outline of the things you'll need to do, with pictures illustrating the finer points:

1. This is an article about everyone's recent fascination with coffee. As you can see in the finished ad in Figure 19.26, scans of coffee beans and a mug are required. The author cheated with the mug—it's a model, not a scan. It was very easy to create, using trueSpace, because the two components—the mug and the handle—are geometrically simple. But with the right texture, lighting, and a handmade drop shadow (Hint: Copy the mug, fill it with black, add a Gaussian blur, and then use the Skew transform function to move the shadow to the left), the mug looks photographic. These objects are in the Examples/Chap19 folder on the Companion CD. We have a tiny mug and a large mug in the Chap19 folder for doing magazine resolution or economy resolution layouts. Or you can acquire the mug yourself.

2. Obviously, we'd not have a finished design if there were no layout from which to work. Coffee.ai is in the Examples/Chap19 folder on the Companion CD, and it can be brought into Photoshop at any resolution (you might want to stick with the undemanding 125 ppi). In Figure 19.27, you can see the layout in Illustrator. Notice that this article bleeds off the top of the page, so more room (and beans) are needed.

The author used different weights of Lubalin Graph for the text in this article, and began it with a *drop cap* (a large initial letter). You can use any font you own that you feel helps make this a clean, legible article.

**Figure 19.26**   If it's a simple object and you left your camera in your other pants, create and render a model, or ask a friend to.

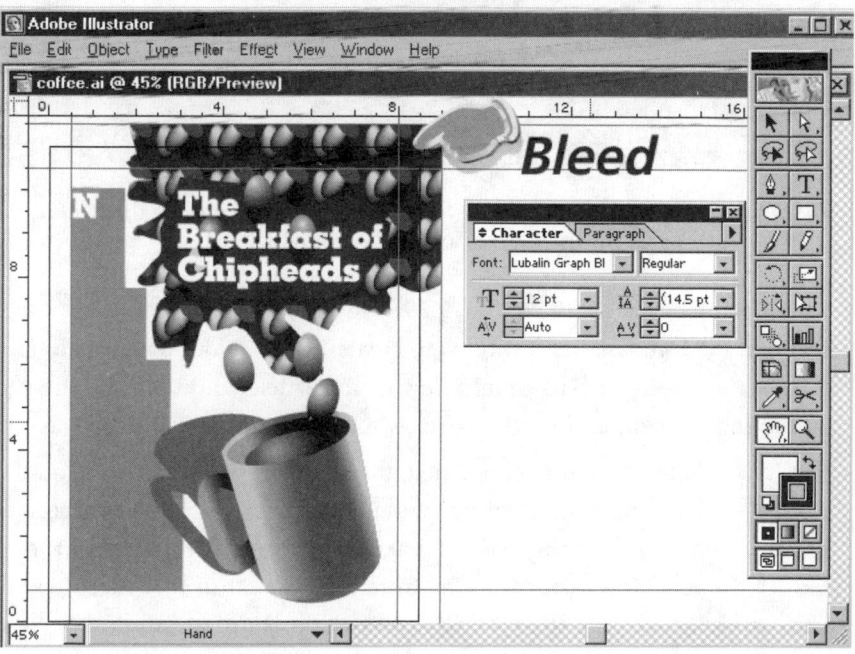

**Figure 19.27**   Work the layout to perfection and it will then be easier to scale the text and the objects on the page.

This is not a step. Figure 19.28 is simply a screen capture to show you how the coffee cup was done. Again, it's not that hard to model such a cup in Dimensions or some other program. It's a hollowed out cylinder, and an oval that was swept using a smaller oval to make the handle. The application makes all those lines—your own contribution is quite modest compared to the interpolation and stuff that a modeling program does for you to define surfaces.

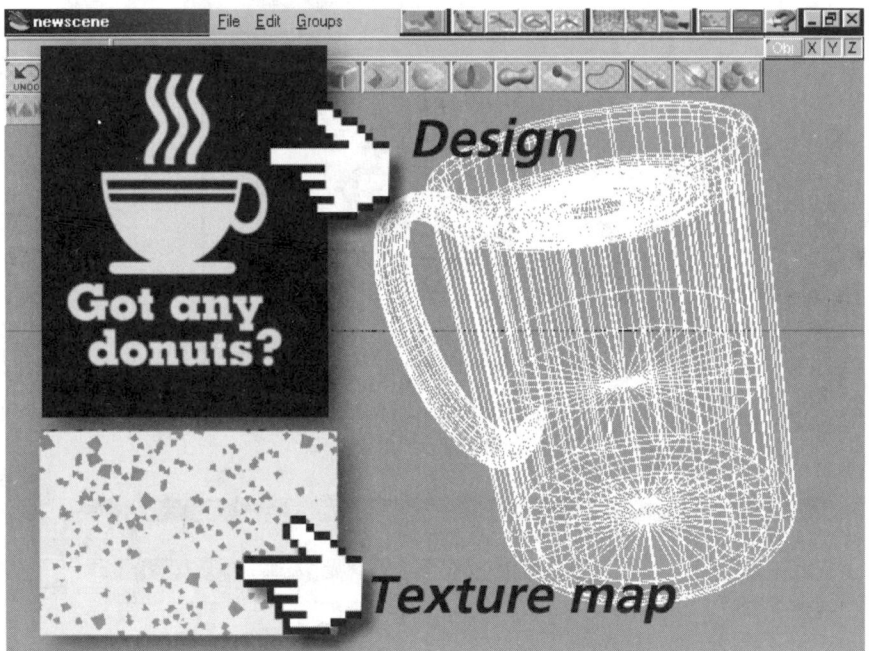

**Figure 19.28**    No camera? No time? Model a simple object. Chances are that within the context of a magazine article, no one will notice that it's fake.

3. As far as the beans go, in Figure 19.29, you can see an ample supply was scanned for you. Our suggestion is to create in the layout a marquee selection of the way the beans should flow in the article, and then use the Clone Stamp tool to sample from the Beans.tif picture and paint into the layout.

4. Finally, as far as the text is concerned, it's flush left in this article. You do not need to use the periods and copying layers trick with this text because common sense tells you where to break a line to follow the flow of the space left for the text. You're not working from right to left in this ad, so text wrap is more easily accomplished. The file, Coffee.txt is in the Examples/Chap19 folder on the Companion CD.

Finito!

You can do a lot more with a scanner than acquire coffee beans and vegetables. Think of the bright color of autumn leaves, the remarkable textures created by uncooked pasta—anything that is basically flat should be on your reminder list the next time your boss drops in with another ridiculous deadline.

**Figure 19.29** You should have smelled the scanner when we scanned the beans. The scanning element heated them up and the whole room smelled like Starbucks <g>.

## Summary

We hope you got a lot out of this chapter, and more importantly, that you learned how Photoshop's integrated environment enables you to stay with the application from beginning to end. You gain real Photoshop power once you are comfortable working with a tool, using the shortcut to get to another tool, and problem-solving to come up with innovative uses for Photoshop's tools. The rules are your own, because you are the designer—never forget that.

We're glad that modeling played a minor role in this chapter. In the next chapter, you will be immersed in models as props and backgrounds, and see how the pros do it in Hollywood. You'll learn how to make photographic and synthetic objects come together into a fantastic scene!

# Chapter 20

# Mixing 3D Graphics with Photographs

Jar-Jar Binks, Stuart Little, a velociraptor, the Terminator. What do all these have in common? Answer: They all get together on Thursday nights for canasta.

Seriously, they are all digital creations that interact seamlessly with human actors in the motion pictures. How is it done? In a word, *tediously*—frame by digital frame, the synthetic actors have to be composited with digitized footage of real surroundings, and then the composite has to be rendered to film. It took an estimated 80 SGI workstations processing around the clock to crank out the dinosaurs in *Jurassic Park*. Fortunately, this chapter limits our scope of ambition to turning out but a single frame in which digital creations and photographs coexist.

This author spent a good three years with a decent modeling and rendering program, turning out fantastic creations and homages to traditional art (renderings of cameras and bowls of fruit, to name but a few). Then he got gutsy one day and decided to try inserting a digital fire hydrant into a photographic scene. Was it a success? Yes and no. It encouraged the author to start fooling around, blending digital creations into digitized photography, but first he had to learn a few ground rules.

## Understanding Modeling

We take it for granted, watching pet food commercials, that animals can talk. We never noticed that about seven years ago that the Pillsbury Doughboy, once the product of stop-motion animation, is now a model. It seems as though even television has embraced digital technology to do both the plausible and the impossible.

So, what's a model?

A *model* (usually—the technology is ever-changing) is a three-dimensional wireframe representation of a real world object. There are three parts to creating ("drawing") a model:

- The modeling phase, where the user bends and sweeps path segments and anchors to represent surfaces,

- The surfaces are calculated by the application as a collection of polygons, and

- Finally, the rendering engine smoothes and writes to screen or file the finished scene.

Lots of things go into the scene, even if you want only one object. Lighting, camera angle, surface properties (shiny, textured, and so on), shadows and reflections (and more) have to be calculated by the rendering engine. And that's why smart modeling folk do their scene composition during the day, and let the computer calculate and render all night!

Figure 20.1 is of a wireframe model that was created by telling the modeling program, "Spin a half-circle 360°, and plot, as a surface, all the areas in which this spinning travels through space." What you wind up with is the surface or Mr. X's head—a sphere. Similarly, the arms and legs are paths that were rotated 360° in space, and the surface was plotted by areas the spinning path crossed. Finally, the body is a simple *extrusion*—a surface formed by pushing an outline through space, and plotting as a surface all the points it hits.

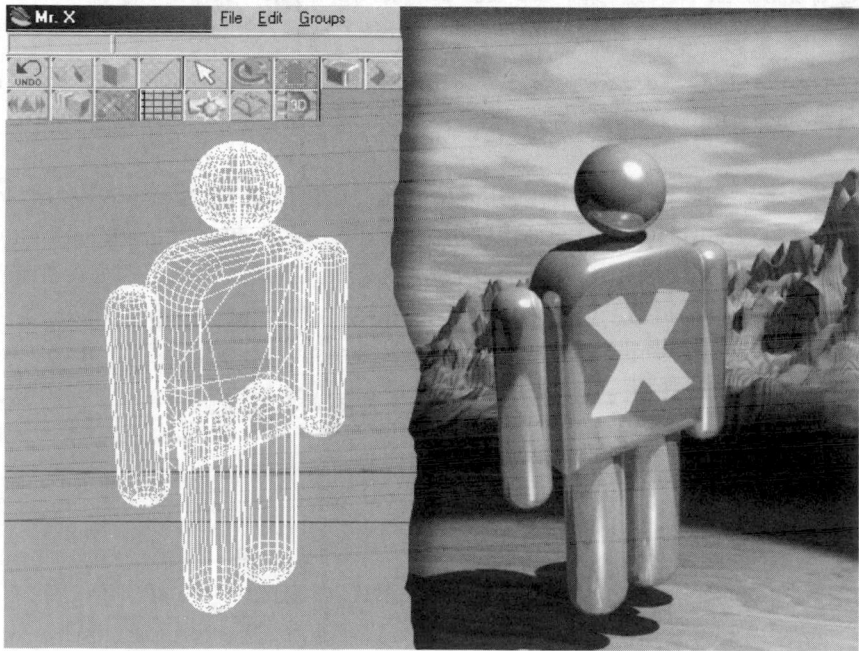

**Figure 20.1**   Left: Mr. X as a wireframe model. Right: Mr. X as a finished, rendered pixel image.

Is this an ambitious or even a realistic rendered model? It depends on the context into which you place the rendered model. If you were to place the finished model image in a toy store window, no one would probably notice. Stick Mr. X next to a photo of a person, however, and the model will serve only to evoke laughter from an audience.

So you need to take into account a laundry list of considerations to pose, surface, and render a digital creation. But that doesn't mean you cannot use digital creations in your work, even if you have no modeling program or experience. This chapter is meant to teach you how to *incorporate* models with photos of people—to show you how it's done, and more important, to get you to realize that the *integration talent* is as important as modeling skills.

> **Tip**
>
> **Watch Your Lighting and Camera Angle**    If you take away only one thing from this chapter, it should be this:
>
> *Be very careful in your lighting and camera angle of the real objects, and then matching the lighting and camera in the model objects will be a snap.*
>
> For example, the photographer who took the photo of Lars, shown in Figure 20.2, used soft lighting coming into the scene from the left, and was at about the same height as Lars was standing. Therefore, the background spaceship should have *no* fancy chrome specular highlights, and the robot is not going to blind you with reflections from lights either. As you work through the chapter with these images, keep these things in mind.

It's entirely possible to take a rendering from Adobe Dimensions (a good entry-level modeling program), and with the right highlights and shading, make it look natural in a photographic scene. This chapter addresses the characteristics of a real photograph—camera angle, lighting, surface texture, reflectance, depth of field—not oddly, these terms also are used in modeling. It's not the modeling talent part we're trying to teach here—it's the concept work, and the techniques for putting the pieces together.

And with that...

# Isolating the Foreground Hero: Introducing Lars Wuhdqax

Any guy who romps around outer space in a karate outfit waving a glowing sword is bound to attract attention, especially the attention of Mr. George Lucas. So the following example is *nothing* like any movie you've seen, okay?

We're going to build a composition starring Lars Wuhdqax, Alien Hunter, along with his molecular spaceship and his trusty mechanical assistant, TechBot Y2K.

Let's begin at the beginning, with a photo from long, long ago.

## Masking the Hero from the Background

In Figure 20.2, you can see a makeshift prop—one of the first considerations in photographing the real part of the composition. A flashlight and a plant stake were held by Lars Wuhdqax so that a laser light coming out of a model of a more serious-looking handle could be added to the scene later. In acting, this would be called your "mark." The author did not have the budget to create a prop laser sword, nor to buy a seamless background for Lars, so masking him out of the breakfast nook will be a tad of a challenge, but this book is all *about* practicing.

This primary image of the composition needs to be turned into a layered image. To do this, you open the Lars.tif image from the Examples/Chap20 folder of the Companion CD, and double-click on the Background title. The New Layer dialog box appears in which you can name the layer. I suggest you name it **Lars Wuhdqax** because there will be several layers to this image.

**Figure 20.2**    Convert this ordinary image into a layer image so you can get rid of the breakfast nook in the background.

Instead of tutorial steps on how to separate Lars from the breakfast nook, the following steps are intended as hints on what to do, and which tool to use around the various parts of Lars' silhouette. You probably have already read *very* thorough chapters about selecting stuff (Chapter 9 comes to mind), so you don't need that information here!

## Tips for Isolating the Hero in the Image

1. Click the Add a mask icon at the bottom of the Layers palette. Press D (default colors) so you're working with black paint, which hides areas on a layer.

2. Zoom in to about a 200% viewing resolution at the bottom right of Lars' karate outfit, choose the Paintbrush tool, click the Brush icon on the Options palette, choose the upper-right tip on the palette, press Enter (Return), and start working carefully on the outside edge of Lars' karate outfit, as shown in Figure 20.3.

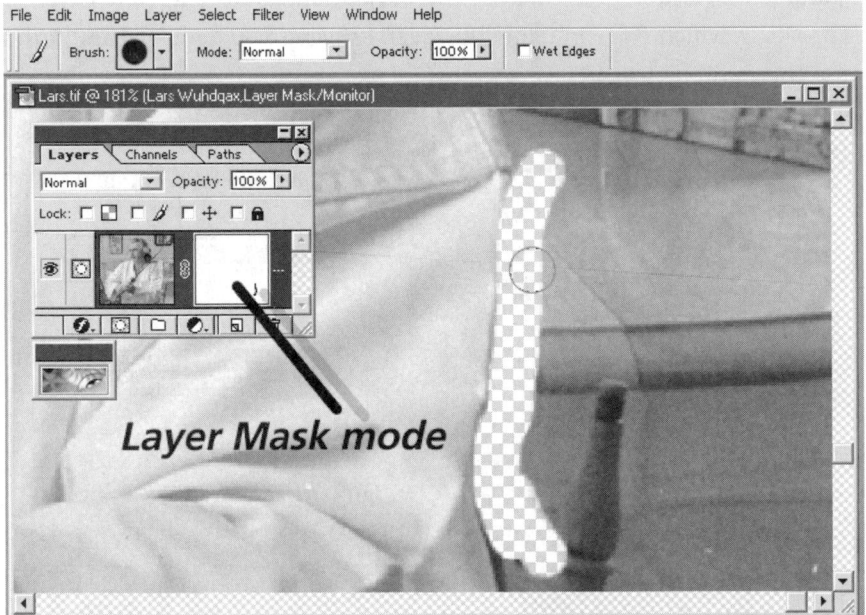

**Figure 20.3**  The easiest way to create a character on an empty layer is to hide everything except the character.

3. Work your way up the right side (stage right) of the karate outfit until you hit the plant stake that is sticking out of the flashlight, as shown in Figure 20.4.

4. At this point, it might be good to remove large areas from the image. You've created a path between the karate outfit and the background, and you can run the Lasso tool along this "gutter" (the Layer Mask path), and close the selection to the *outside* of Lars. Then press Alt(Opt)+Delete (Backspace), and then Ctrl(⌘)+D to hide large areas.

5. When you reach the hair, use a small tip (the third from the left, top row on the Options bar flyout palette), making precise strokes beginning at the hair, and getting looser in precision as you complete a stroke. Doing this will enable you to use the Lasso tool more easily around the outside of the hair areas.

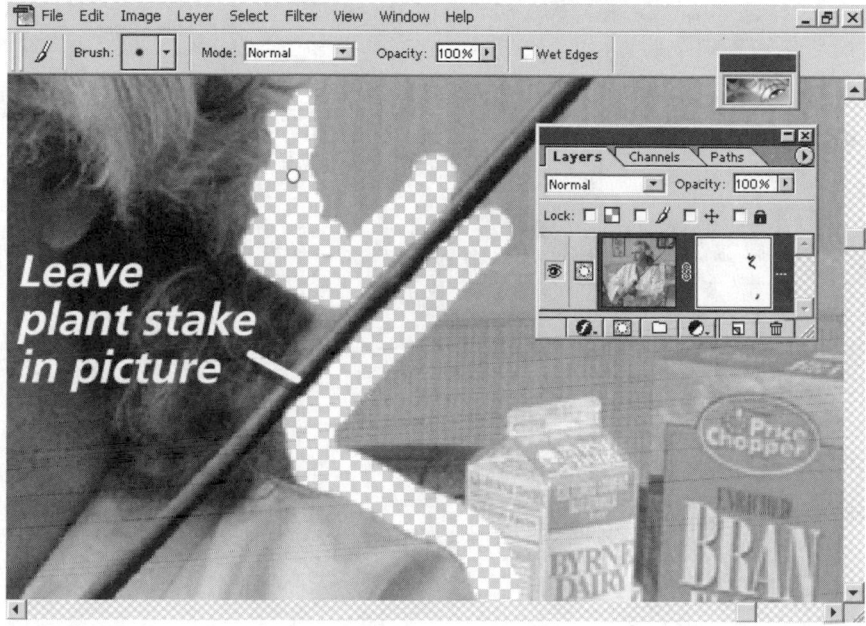

**Figure 20.4**    Leave the plant stake in the selection; you'll paint over it to create a laser effect later.

6. Over on the left side of Lars (stage left), you can switch back to a hard, large brush tip to finish separating the karate outfit from the background.

7. Finally, use the Lasso tool on large areas, fill the selections with foreground color to hide them, and then deselect the marquee.

8. Drag the Layer Mask thumbnail into the Trash, and click Apply in the query box. Keep the image open and save it to your hard disk as Lars.psd, in Photoshop's native file format.

It is this author's belief that this book should give you a workout of sorts—that strange new things on your computer screen will become second nature to manipulate. But we don't believe that failing on one part of this book's tutorials should bring your need to work and learn to a screeching halt.

For this reason, an alpha channel has been created in the Lars picture that we didn't tell you about until now because we really want you to practice your skills. If, on the other hand, your selection skills aren't terrific, you can still work through this epic assignment by Ctrl(⌘)+clicking the alpha channel icon on the Channels palette, and then right-clicking (Macintosh: hold Ctrl and click) and choosing Layer Via Copy from the context menu, as shown in Figure 20.5.

**Figure 20.5**   If your selection skills aren't quite ready for prime-time, Ctrl(⌘)+click on the alpha channel (#1), and then choose Layer Via Copy from the context menu (#2).

If you choose the short route here, make sure you've named the layer "Lars Wuhdqax," and that you've dragged the Background layer into the Trash. So, users with some experience and those with none are now in the same place in the assignment.

## Making Room for the Other Elements

The Lars image was cropped to cut down on file size while you work—the complete image simply contains the rest of the breakfast nook. But you need more room than is currently in the image to add a molecule starship, a robot buddy, and perhaps a little text later.

In the steps to follow, you'll enlarge the canvas, and actually learn a new trick with background composition. You see, the background we rendered for the scene is a little too small (the author misplaced his calculator)—it won't fill an image of the size you will create. The background was created in Bryce 4, as shown in Figure 20.6, from a few geometric shapes. But the rendering time was *lonnnng*, and without taking the time to render it again, this time to size, we adopt the adage, "Desperation is the Mother of invention." <g>

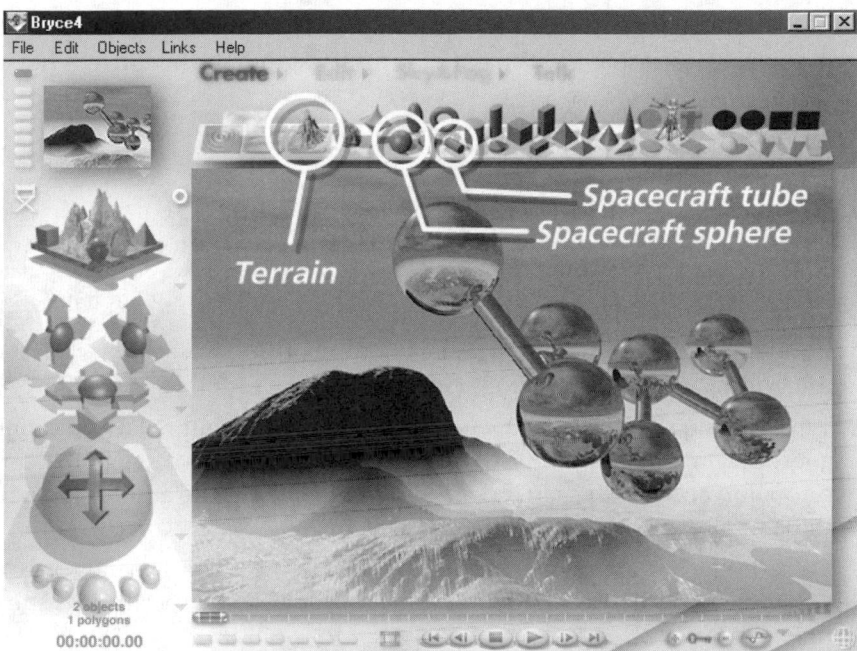

**Figure 20.6**   Bryce4 is an application that makes child's play out of rendering structures and terrains. Now, if only there were a program to remind the author of the *final rendering size…*

**TIp**

**Don't Overwork a Piece, for Time's Sake**   Although the world is a visually complex place:

- Most of the detail in the world comes from texture and not shape.
- The camera isolates a part of the world and makes the resulting image much less complex.

Add to these wisdoms that the piece you are doing is sort of an advertisement—it's staged, so the audience expects visual choreography. IOW, Uncle Fred isn't wandering around just behind the main elements.

This is why there is only a spaceship, a piece of rock, lots of overcast sky, and snow in the Bryce rendering (Tundra.tif). Add Lars and a robot, and there's plenty of detail in the scene. Any more and the scene would look overworked in the same way a drawing can be overworked.

Know when to stop.

Instead of re-rendering, we'll *enlarge* the image (thus seriously hurting the focus and adding pixelation to the background), but then you'll use the Gaussian Blur filter.

This not only helps make the hero of the composition stand out more, but also it's photographically correct to have an out of focus background when there's not a lot of light pouring into the image.

Here goes:

**Example 20.1    Enlarging the Composition
                  for Other Elements**

1. Choose Image, Canvas size.

2. Choose pixels as the unit of measurement in both the Width and the Height drop-down boxes.

> **Warning!**   If an error message appears when you open the CD files, press Ctrl(⌘)+Shift+K and then choose Adobe RGB (1998) from the Working Spaces, RGB drop-down list. See Chapter 3 for more information.

3. Type **1296** in the Width field, and type **981** in the Height field. You cannot guess these numbers by yourself because you haven't run through the entire tutorial to arrive at the correct size for the canvas. But the authors did and these numbers work best for this piece.

4. Click on the bottom-right chiclet in the Anchor area. This expands the canvas horizontally and vertically from the anchor area you specified, as shown in Figure 20.7.

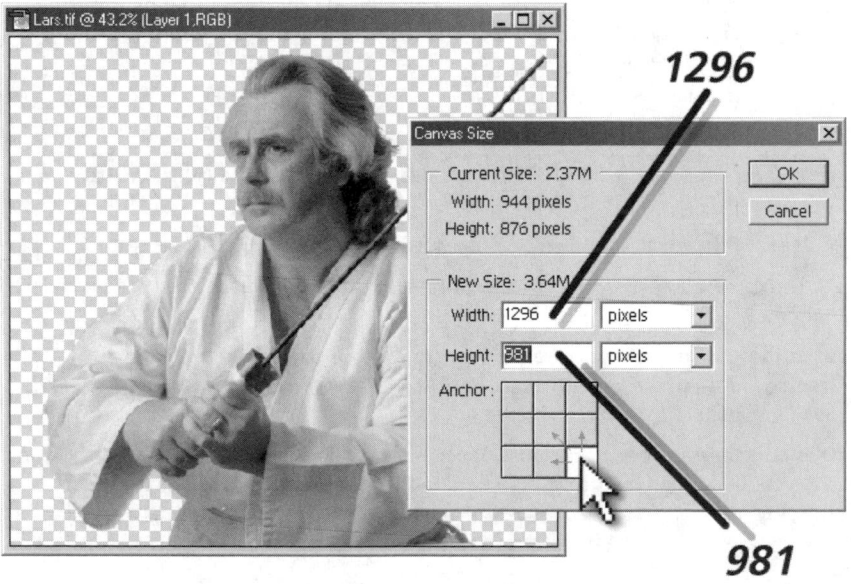

**Figure 20.7**   Add canvas area to the left and top of the existing image.

5. Open the Tundra.tif image from the Examples/Chap20 folder on the Companion CD. Position it in the workspace so you have a clear view of both the Lars image and the tundra. With the Move tool, drag the tundra

image into the Lars image, and then press Ctrl(⌘)+Left bracket ([). This command sends the current layer one layer backward, so the tundra is now behind our hero, as shown in Figure 20.8. Name the layer "Tundra" when you get a chance, to avoid future confusion. You can close the Tundra.tif image at any time now.

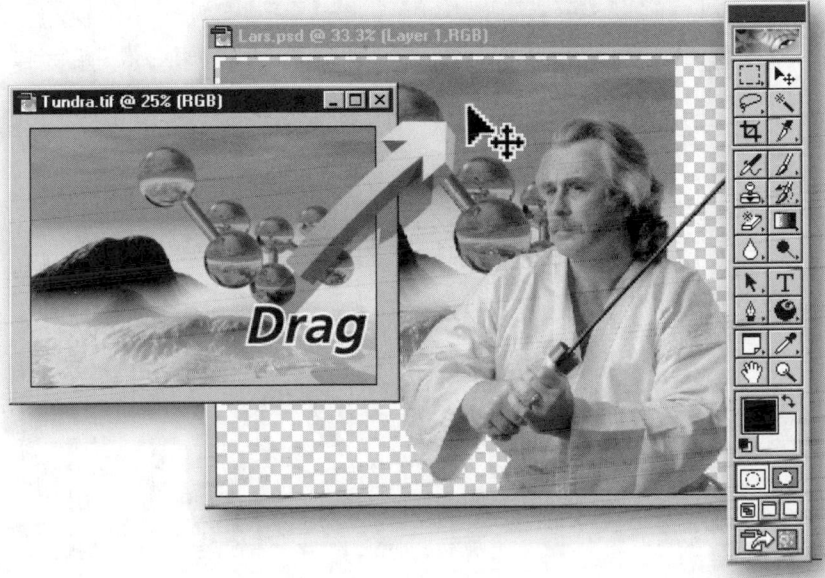

**Figure 20.8** Copy the image to a different image window, using the Move tool, and then send it behind the Lars layer.

6. Widen the image window so you can see lots of image window background. Windows users can use the Maximize/Restore button to make the window take up the entire workspace in Photoshop.

7. With the Move tool, position the image on the Tundra layer in the upper right of the image window and then press Ctrl(⌘)+T to put the Free Transform bounding box around the image.

8. Right-click (Macintosh: hold Ctrl and click) on the image, and then choose Scale from the context menu. Then, hold Shift and drag the bottom-left bounding box handle to just slightly outside the image area, as shown in Figure 20.9. The Shift key modifier constrains the proportions of the Transform box, but as you can see in Figure 20.9, you can also click on the horizontal and vertical link button on the Options bar to achieve the same result (Hint: The keyboard shortcut is faster).

9. Press Enter (Return), or double-click inside the bounding box to finalize the transformation (the scaling). The image of the tundra looks pretty crummy, right? This sort of thing happens when you dramatically change the size of

a bitmap image, whose pixels are finite, and Photoshop is left to "guess" what the new, additional pixel colors should be. But you're not quite done yet.

10. Choose Filter, Blur, Gaussian Blur. Type **4.5** pixels in the Gaussian Blur dialog box, as shown in Figure 20.10, and then click OK.

**Figure 20.9**    Holding Shift keeps the image you're scaling equal in proportion to the original dimensions.

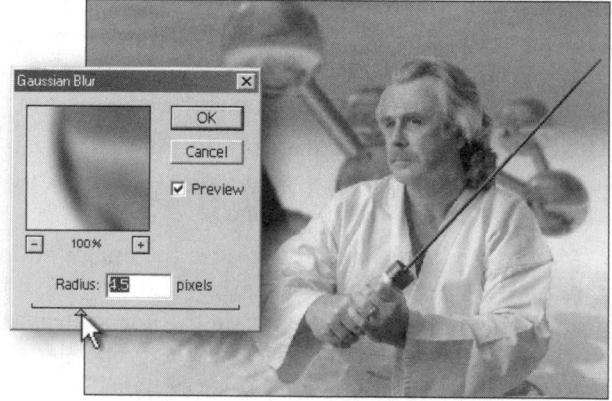

Fuzzing the tundra will hide pixelation

**Figure 20.10**    If you scale an image up too much, you will see harsh edges in the image. But this is okay if the goal is to have a background such as this one, which is out of focus in the finished composition.

**11.** Press Ctrl(⌘)+S; keep the file open.

In the next section, you'll add a spotlight in front of the tundra and behind Lars to highlight the hero in white against a background of white.

## Adding a Touch of Spotlight

Okay, Lars is the hero of the image and the imaginary film, so we could justify putting a spotlight on him for that reason alone. But have you noticed also that there is really not much visual business going on in the background? There's only the molecule ship. From a compositional point of view, you can make the top of the image a little darker and let the lightness open up the image toward the bottom, where Lars and the molecule ship are located. Then, if you decide to add text later, the top of the image will hold reversed (white on black) text. And compositionally, you have not overcomplicated the scene.

Here's how to add subtle shading to the scene:

### Example 20.2   Highlighting a Hero

1. Hold Alt(Opt) and click the Create new layer icon. Doing this displays the New layer dialog box, so you can name the layer and create it in one fell swoop. Name the layer **Spotlight**, and click OK. You now have a spotlight layer on top of the previously used layer, the Tundra layer.

2. Zoom out of the image and drag the window edges away from the image so you can see the background. With the Polygonal Lasso tool, create a polygon around Lars, suggesting a spotlight that broadens at the bottom. Press Ctrl(⌘)+Shift+I to pick the inverse of the selection, press Alt(Opt)+Delete (Backspace) to fill the selection, as shown in Figure 20.11. Press Ctrl(⌘)+D to deselect the selection marquee.

3. Press Ctrl(⌘)+Alt(Opt)+F to display the last-used filter's dialog box without actually applying the filter. Drag the slider to about 23 pixels, click OK, and wait a moment, even if you have a fast machine.

4. Choose Multiply from the Layers drop-down list for the Spotlight layer, and then drag the Opacity slider down to about 53%. If you don't have a lot of RAM and hard disk space, you can press Ctrl(⌘)+E to merge the Spotlight layer down into the background layer to conserve resources. If you've got a fast, powerful machine, you may want to keep the Spotlight layer separate from the background.

5. Press Ctrl(⌘)+S; keep the file open.

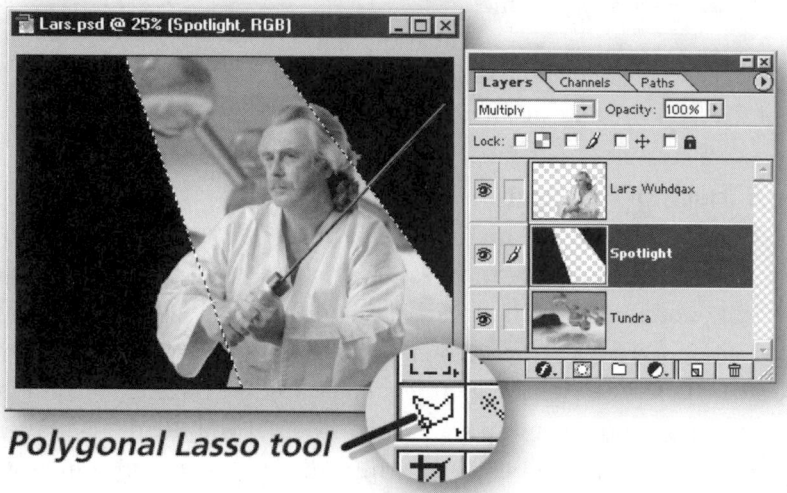

Polygonal Lasso tool

**Figure 20.11**    Create a spotlight by inverting the shape of a spotlight, and then fill the selection with black.

Next on the agenda is adding TechBot Y2K at Lars' side. In the next section, you'll not only place Y2K in the scene, but selectively blur him/it so he/it is also truly in the scene and not on top of it.

## Adding a Robot to the Composition

One of the wonderful things about computer graphics (*CG*, the term popularly used in Hollywood), is that the scale of a digital creation placed next to a photograph of someone is transparent; you have little or no way of knowing whether you're looking at a full-scale model of something, or a computer graphic.

 **Tip**

**Avoid Creating a Perfect Image**    What you're going to do shortly is selectively blur the robot to suggest that the aperture of the camera was small and that the robot is standing behind Lars. Other "false clues" you can add to a computer graphic is the addition of noise to simulate film grain, and imperfect cropping, so the photography doesn't look stiff and staged.

This scene was preplanned so that Y2K's legs would never show in the finished image. This author only rendered Y2K's hips and a little of the legs, mostly to save time. So the bottom of the Y2K image must be placed at the bottom of the Lars.psd image. Figure 20.12 shows the beginning of the construction of the robot. On the left are a few geometric shapes that, when put together creatively, make a complex-looking figure. On the right are the paths used to extrude, sweep, and lathe around a direction in space to define the surfaces of the robot. See? It really shouldn't feel intimidating to get into modeling—a lot of complex models are made up of cylinders, spheres, and the like.

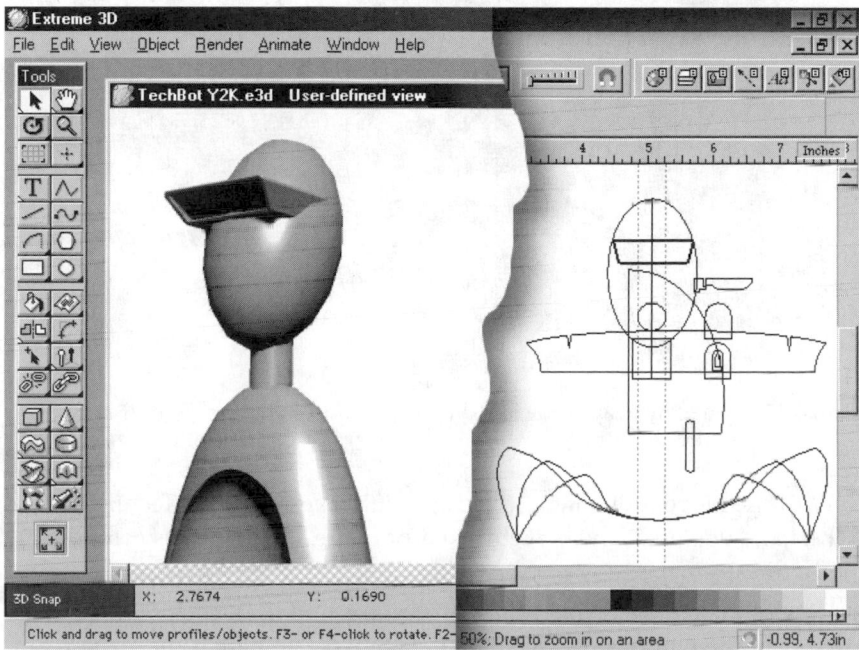

**Figure 20.12**   The computer graphic of the robot might look complex, but it's actually the textures and lighting that make it look realistic.

Now, Y2K is so rich in detail, that to try to pack more attention into the scene would be overdoing it. Lars is going to get his laser sword soon, and it's actually a fun tease to your audience to hide some of the detail of the robot. It adds realism to the scene—we're *used to* seeing inept cropping <g>!

Here's how to place and blur a robot in the Lars composition:

### Example 20.3   Adding Y2K to the Scene

1. Open the TechBot.psd image from the Examples/Chap20 folder on the Companion CD. The robot is on its own layer.
2. Drag the TechBot Y2K title on the Layers palette into the Lars.psd image window, as shown in Figure 20.13. You can close the TechBot image at any time now.

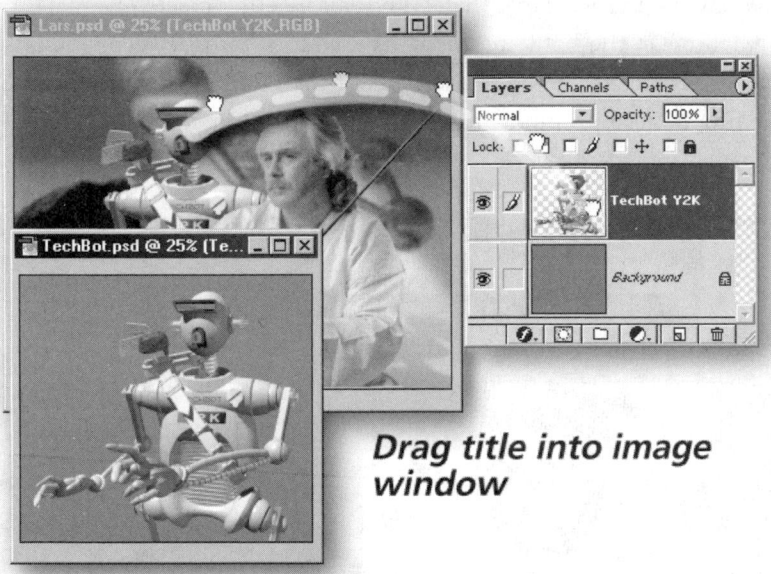

**Drag title into image window**

**Figure 20.13**   Dragging a layer title into an image window puts a copy of that layer on top of the current layer, which is what you want to do in this example.

3. With the Move tool, drag the TechBot Y2K layer until the TechBot is behind Lars and its right hand is slightly out of frame. Again, clumsy cropping adds photorealism.

4. Choose the Gradient tool from the toolbox, and then click on the Radial type on the Options bar. What you're going to do here is mask the robot so its hands (which are closest to you) are in focus. The focus gradually decreases as you come to view the edges of the TechBot.

5. Press D and then press X to make white the current foreground color. Click the down arrow to the right of the gradient sample on the Options palette, and hover your cursor over the swatch on the palette. Make sure the gradient type is Foreground to Background.

6. Alt(Opt)+click (if necessary) the Quick Mask icon, so that color indicates selected areas in the image and your image is now in Quick Mask mode. You can tell that the Quick Mask is set up as Color Indicates: Selected Areas when the Quick Mask icon is a black circle inside of a white rectangle.

> **Note**
>
> **The Gradient Thumbnail Reverses**   Don't freak out, but when you reverse what the Quick Mask tint overlay represents, the gradient thumbnail on the Options bar will reverse direction.
>
> All is well, and when you click the Standard Editing mode button, the gradient will reverse again to foreground from background on the Options bar.

7. With the Radial Gradient tool, click between the TechBot's hands, and then drag as far away as possible with the tool as shown in Figure 20.14.

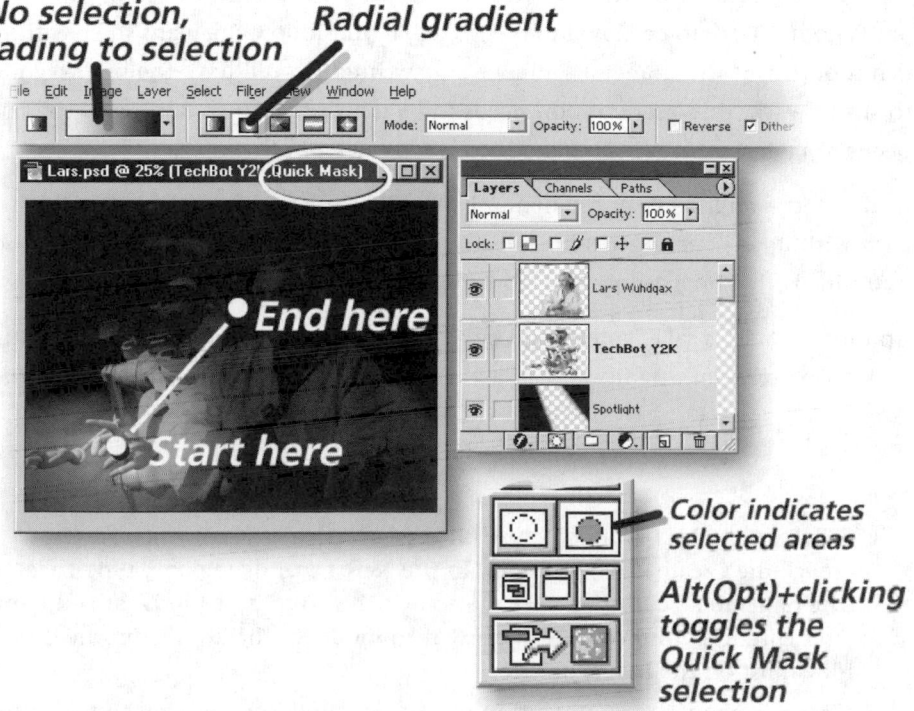

**Figure 20.14** The Quick Mask starts at 0% strength at the hands of the TechBot and increases to 100% at the edges of the TechBot.

8. Click the Standard Editing mode icon to the left of the Quick Mask button, and you now have a selection marquee in the image. If you like, press Ctrl(⌘)+H to hide the marquee lines, so you can better see the transformation that is about to take place. The selection's still active; it's the dotted line "marching ants" on the screen that's hidden.

9. Press Ctrl(⌘)+Alt(Opt)+F to display the last-used filter's dialog box.

10. In the dialog box, decrease the blurring strength to about 2 pixels, about half of what you used to blur the tundra.

11. Press Ctrl(⌘)+D, and then press Ctrl(⌘)+S; keep the file open.

Avast! I have no idea what that means, but pirates in movies seem to say it a lot. Are you ready to get involved in some high-tech swordplay?

## Creating Lars' Laser Light

In the Shapes chapter (Chapter 12), you saw how to create a glow effect by stroking a path. Lars' laser sword will be created the same way, with a twist or two. First, paths do not have to be closed to be stroked. If you follow the plant stake with the Pen tool (this is the strangest sentence ever written), you'll have the path segment to stroke. Also, this laser creation needs to be done on its own layer, and the layer needs to be in Screen blending mode to stand out from the image.

In the steps you'll perform momentarily, you'll create and stroke an open Pen tool path with a fat, semitransparent foreground color, and then stroke the path a second time with a brighter, more opaque color to represent the core of the laser light.

And for accuracy's sake, you should be aware that laser hits in the motion pictures look absolutely nothing like a real laser in action! Here's how to make a *theatrical* laser:

### Example 20.4  Leaping Lasers!

1. Click on the Lars Wuhdqax title on the Layers palette, and then Alt(Opt) +click the Create new layer icon. In the New Layer dialog box, type **Laser** in the name field, and then click OK to exit the box. The Laser layer is the top and current editing layer. Choose Screen mode for the layer from the drop-down list on the Layers palette.

2. Zoom to about a 50% resolution of Lars.psd, hold the spacebar to toggle to the Hand tool, and then drag the image until the plant stake in Lars' hand is in the center of the window.

3. Choose the Pen tool from the toolbox, and then click an anchor at the bottom part of the plant stake, and another at the top of the stake.

4. Click on the foreground color selection box on the toolbox, and choose a brilliant green in the Color Picker. Click OK to return to the scene.

5. Choose the Paintbrush tool and then on the Options bar, click the down arrow next to the brush tip, and choose the 100-pixel tip from the flyout palette. On the Options bar, lower the Opacity for the Paintbrush tool to about 65%.

6. Click the Strokes path with foreground color icon on the Paths palette, as shown in Figure 20.15. Pretty cool, huh?

7. Choose the 35-pixel Brush palette tip from the Options bar, click on the foreground color selection box, and pick a lighter green color (more white in the color) than you currently have selected. Click OK to get back to the action.

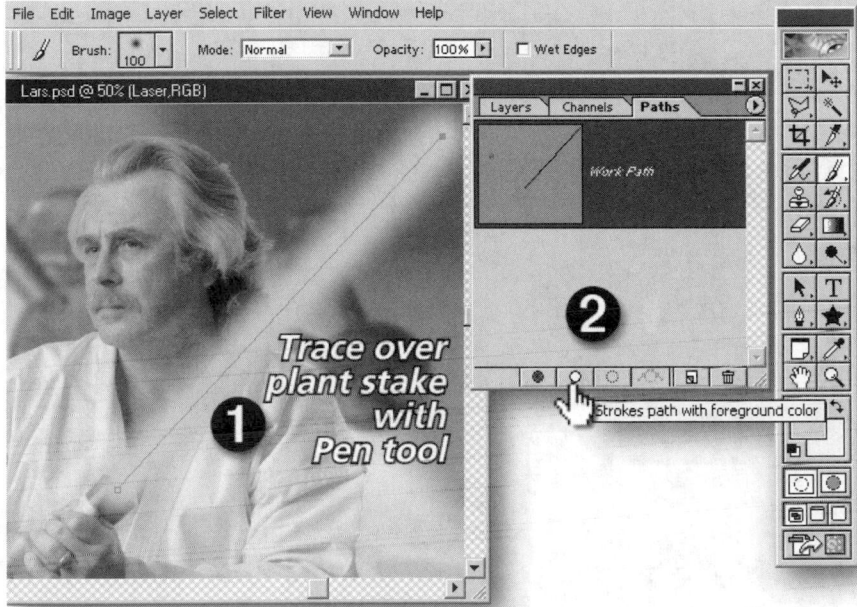

**Figure 20.15**   Create a path (#1) and then stroke it (#2) with a wide, diffuse color while a layer is in Screen mode does indeed produce a light- or laser-type effect.

8. Click the Strokes path with foreground color icon on the Paths palette. You can drag the Work Path icon into the palette's Trash at any time now.

9. You need to clean up the bottom of the laser light so it appears to be coming from a source and not lying on top of a source. Choose the Eraser tool, choose Airbrush from the Mode drop-down on the Options bar, and drop the Pressure down to about 25%. Choose the 65-pixel tip from the Brush palette (by clicking the down arrow next to the brush, and then pressing Enter (Return) to prove your intentions are sincere), and then press D (default colors).

10. Make a curving stroke or two at the bottom of the laser light, as shown in Figure 20.16. Press Ctrl(⌘)+S; keep the file open.

The Airbrush tool, even when it's used only as an Eraser tip, is a powerful retouching tool. Even at partial strength, it gives you a great deal of control over the amount of erasure or paint you're applying. And unlike other tools, the Airbrush tool leaves no edges. Your work is always undetectable if you practice with this tool/setting.

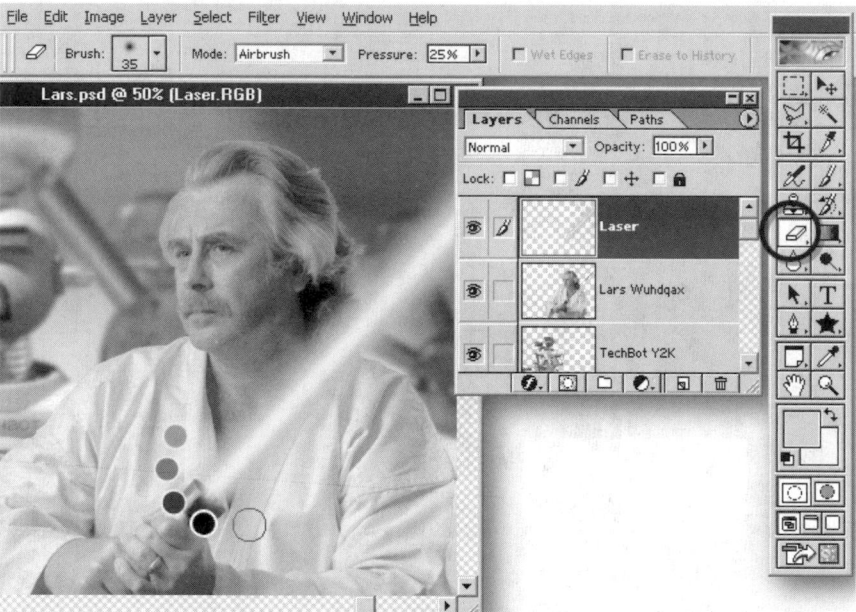

**Figure 20.16**    Remove some of the light from the bottom tip of the stroke by using the Eraser tool in Airbrush mode.

## Adding a Suitable Handle to the Sword

Okay, we're sure you were waiting to see what I was going to do with the stupid-looking plastic flashlight that Lars is brandishing. If you were doing this scene, you might want to paint a lathed table leg a metallic color or something. What we did requires a little more retouching to work, but hey, almost *anything* can be rendered *on-the-fly* with the right software. A metallic handle was built in Caligari's trueSpace (a 3D graphics program), sizing and making the angle of rotation the same as the plant stake.

So you're basically in business by copying the handle to the Lars.psd composition, and then masking away areas around the handle where Lars' fingers should be.

### Example 20.5   Adding a Handle to the Sword

1. Open the handle.psd image from the Examples/Chap20 folder on the Companion CD.
2. Click on the Lars Wuhdqax title on the Layers palette, and then with the Move tool, drag the handle image into the Lars.psd window, as shown in Figure 20.17. Close the Handle.psd image without saving.

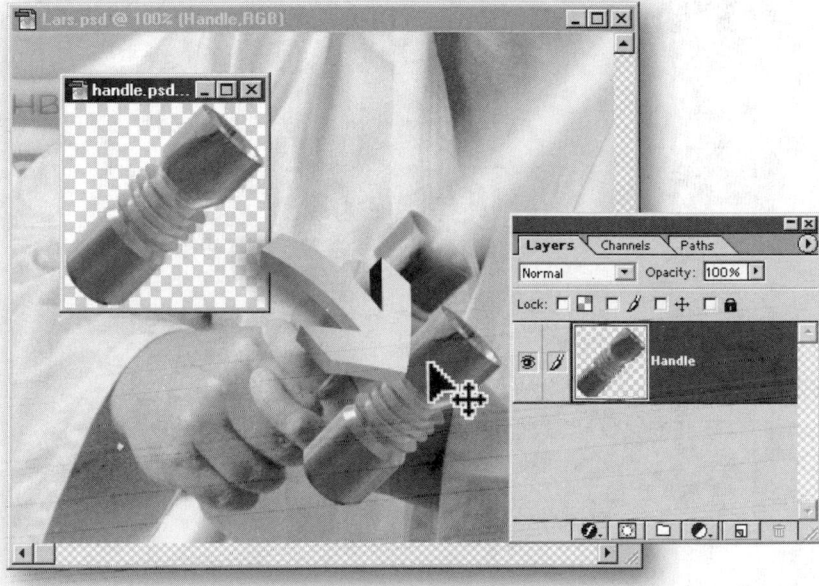

**Figure 20.17**   Pick the layer on which you want the new layer to land, and then use the Move tool to drag it there.

3. Zoom to 200% on the image. Position the handle so that its outside edge is behind the end of the laser light. Basically, you're placing the modeled handle over the flashlight. Click the Add a mask icon at the bottom of the Layers palette.

4. Choose the Paintbrush tool, and press 0 on the keypad to make the Paintbrush 100% opaque. On the Options bar, click the down button to the right of the brush icon, and then choose a hard-edge (top row) Brush palette tip. Choose the third tip from the left and see how you feel about it. Carefully stroke around the edges of Lars' fingers to hide the unwanted part of the handle, as shown in Figure 20.18.

5. If you stray into Lars' fingers, press X (swap foreground/background color selection boxes) and then paint to restore the parts of the fingers. Then press X again, and conclude your retouching work. Then, drag the Layer Mask thumbnail into the Trash, and when the query box comes up, click Apply.

6. Press Ctrl(⌘)+S; keep the file open.

One last element in the composition needs refining. As you can see, the handle is not wide enough to cover the plastic flashlight top in the image. This is easy enough to fix if you read Chapter 17. If you didn't, we're *still* going to walk you through the procedure <g>.

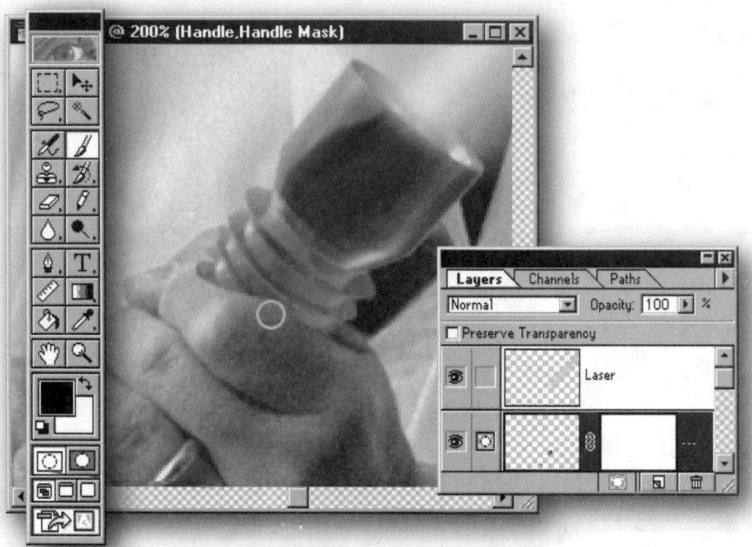

**Figure 20.18** In Layer Mask mode, foreground black hides image areas and white restores hidden areas.

## Adding Texture to the Outfit Using the Clone Stamp Tool

The flashlight top is so close to a monochrome karate outfit that you can easily paint karate outfit texture over the flashlight head. Here's how to finish our episode with Lars Wuhdqax, Alien Hunter:

### Example 20.6   Cloning Over the Flashlight

1. Click on the Lars Wuhdqax layer title on the Layers palette to make this the active editing layer. Choose the Clone Stamp tool, and make sure Use All Layers is *not* checked on the Options bar.

2. Shift+right-click (Macintosh: hold Ctrl and click) to reveal the Brush palette next to your cursor (Aha! A quicker way of doing something! Make a note!) On the Brushes palette, choose the second-from-last tip in the second row, and then press Enter (Return) to close the palette.

3. Alt(Opt)+click a sampling point near, but not too close to, the flashlight head in the image. Then make some strokes over the flashlight head to replace it with karate outfit texture, as shown in Figure 20.19.

4. Repeat step 3 as many times as necessary (two or three applications of the Clone Stamp tool should do it).

5. Press Ctrl(⌘)+S. Keep the file open.

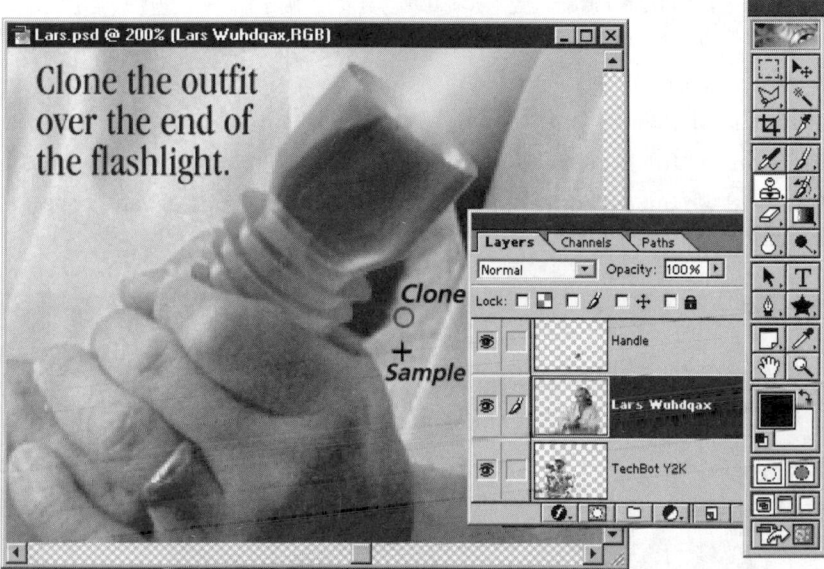

**Figure 20.19**   Keep resampling in different clothing areas, and keep painting over the edge of the flashlight until you can no longer see it.

What we'd recommend at this point is that you do one or more of the following with the composition and Photoshop:

- Choose Edit, Purge, and then choose All. This releases resources held on the Clipboard and in RAM for multiple undos in Photoshop. Your system will stop creaking and swearing at you now. As held in memory, this layered image is 11MB, a fairly large image if your system has less than 100MB of RAM (Photoshop and ImageReady want 96MB).

- Press Ctrl(⌘)+Shift+S. This is the shortcut for Save As, and it's a good shortcut to add to your list. In the Save As dialog box, name the file, pick a location for the file, check the As A Copy checkbox in the Save Options field, choose the TIFF file format for the saved copy, and uncheck the Layers checkbox so the TIFF file can be read by programs other than Photoshop. Then close your working copy, Lars.psd.

- Choose Flatten Image from the Layers palette's flyout menu. Now, you can save the image in almost any format, but you can no longer access the power of editing the individual layers.

If you now want to put icing on the cake (or simply embellish this image a little more…that was supposed to be funny), follow these steps to add a title to the piece:

### Example 20.7    Adding a Title

1. Open the Title.psd file from the Examples/Chap20 folder on the Companion CD.

2. With the Move tool, drag the layer into the Lars image.

3. Position the title so it's in a location similar to that seen in Figure 20.20.

4. That's it! Go out for some popcorn and those tiny drops of candy that instantly remove fillings.

**Figure 20.20**    Science fiction is simply another avenue that leads to all sorts of other photo-fiction when you have experience with Photoshop.

Okay, this is the end of the tutorial, and if you feel tired and inspired simultaneously, this is not a bad thing. You've had quite a workout in what you might have thought was a "simple" image composition assignment. But if you think about it, did we ever do anything that wasn't covered in earlier chapters? It's how you *integrated* different techniques that led to the successful completion of some pretty handsome stuff.

Who needs to dwell 49 times on the same technique? You learn the foundation items, and then work your way up from there. That's why this chapter's so close to the end of the Photoshop chapters.

If any of you are curious about what *type* of aliens Lars Wuhdqax hunts, we really can't show you a picture—he's already hunted them. Alien hunting isn't typically for the faint of heart or young eyes, and we really don't need to get into that. But fortunately for the computer graphics community, Lars spares the lives of *friendly* aliens—as you can see in Figure 20.21.

**Figure 20.21** Hey, we've done cheaper plugs in past books…

## Summary

There is a definite direction in your tutelage from this book. The direction is *up*; you're becoming more experienced because you already know a wide-base platform of tricks and steps that lead to results in Photoshop. Learning Photoshop the right way—the authors believe—is the house metaphor. You build a decent foundation, and the rest will come quickly with the assurance of stability. Hopefully, this is what you've discovered in this book. And you can apply this learning technique to other books.

With luck, a few of them will be Bouton books.

In Chapter 21, you'll be treated to the unofficial Festival of Filters, held in every version of Photoshop. The exploration of filters is sort of a hammock between the last chapter on Photoshop and the first chapter on ImageReady—so we're going out with a bang. The same filters you'll learn about in Chapter 21 are also in ImageReady—get your hands on some in one program, and they'll come naturally and instinctively to you in the other. So, with over 100 filters in Photoshop (no, we are not going to cover *all* of them—just the ones that have the most creative potential)—let's get hiking!

# Chapter 21

## Using a Boatload of Native Photoshop Filters

I remember once watching my mother

putting on makeup when I was young.

She commented to me that the key to

putting on makeup was not to cover up or create an unnatural look, but to enhance what is already there.

The same might apply to Photoshop filters. When you're making an image in Photoshop, whether you are creating it from scratch or making changes to an existing image, your goal is to have a finished product that has a certain "Wow" factor. It might be wise to avoid certain filter effects that have become cliché, because your goal is not to display your final product and have people recognize and list the exact filter effects you used.

Instead, the "Wow" factor should be subtler. Maybe something looks realistic, and no one figured out that you created the object instead of importing a picture. Maybe the filter added a texture or a lighting effect that enhanced the image without becoming the main focus of the image.

## Using Filter Effects

Photoshop ships with a myriad of filters and effects, all of which can have very useful results. Learning what these filters do may be half the battle. The other half is to know when to use them.

To make this matter even more complex, there might be many instances where one filter alone doesn't do the trick. A combination of filters may be needed to make a certain effect happen correctly.

### Combining Filters for Realistic Effects

This first example shows you how to create and add to an existing image a few extra details, with the help of filters—in fact, a combination of filters.

Many filters on the market are famous for making spheres or orb-like objects. Instead of shooting for the obvious sphere effect, we will start with an image and add some spheres in the form of bubbles—the kind of bubbles you used to blow when you were a kid. Hopefully, if it's done correctly, your friends will be amazed at the realism of these bubbles—and won't be able to tell how they were made.

Example 21.1   Combining Filters for Realism

1. Open BlowingBubbles.tif in the Examples/Chap21 folder on the Companion CD.

2. Alt(Opt)+click the Create a new layer icon at the bottom of the Layers palette. In the New Layer dialog box, type **Bubble** for the name. Click OK.

**Warning!**   If an error message appears when you open the CD files, press Ctrl(⌘)+Shift+K and then choose Adobe RGB (1998) from the Working Spaces, RGB drop-down list. See Chapter 3 for more information.

3. Choose the Elliptical Marquee tool from the toolbox. On the Options bar, choose Normal from the Style drop-down list. Hold down the Shift key and drag a circular selection near the lower-right side of the image (see Figure 21.1).

4. Press G to switch to the Gradient tool. Click the Radial Gradient icon on the Options bar. Click the gradient on the Options bar to open the Gradient Editor dialog box (see Figure 21.1).

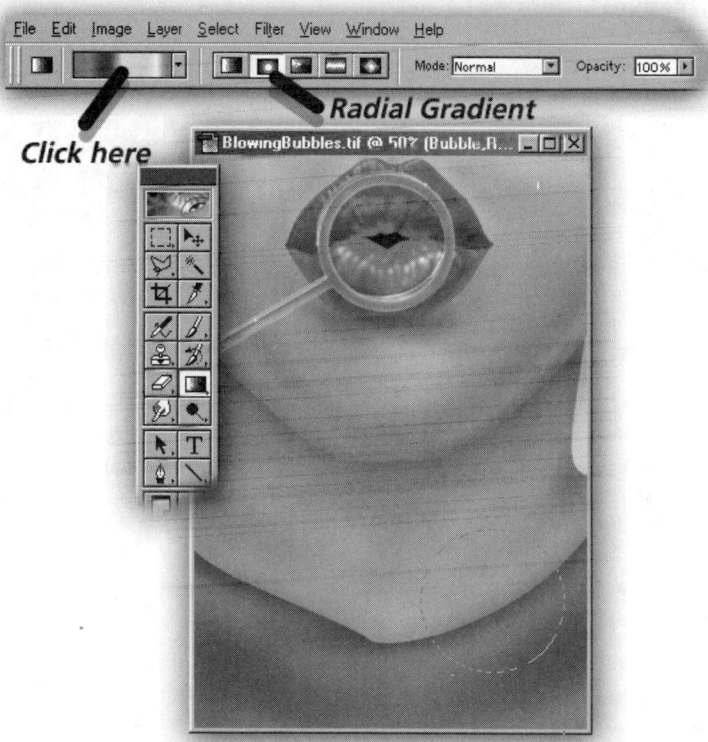

**Figure 21.1**    Choose the Radial Gradient icon from the Options bar. Click the gradient to edit the gradient.

5. In the Gradient Editor dialog box, click on the Spectrum gradient as a starting point. Drag the light blue color stop (in the center) down and away from the bar to delete this color from the gradient. Click the red color stop at the far right and type **40** in the Location box. Click the following color sliders and type the numbers listed for each Location: yellow = **50**, green = **60**, blue = **70**, and purple = **100**. Type **Bubble** in the Name box. Click on an empty space in the Preset area to add the gradient to your preset choices. The Gradient Editor dialog box should look like Figure 21.2. Click OK.

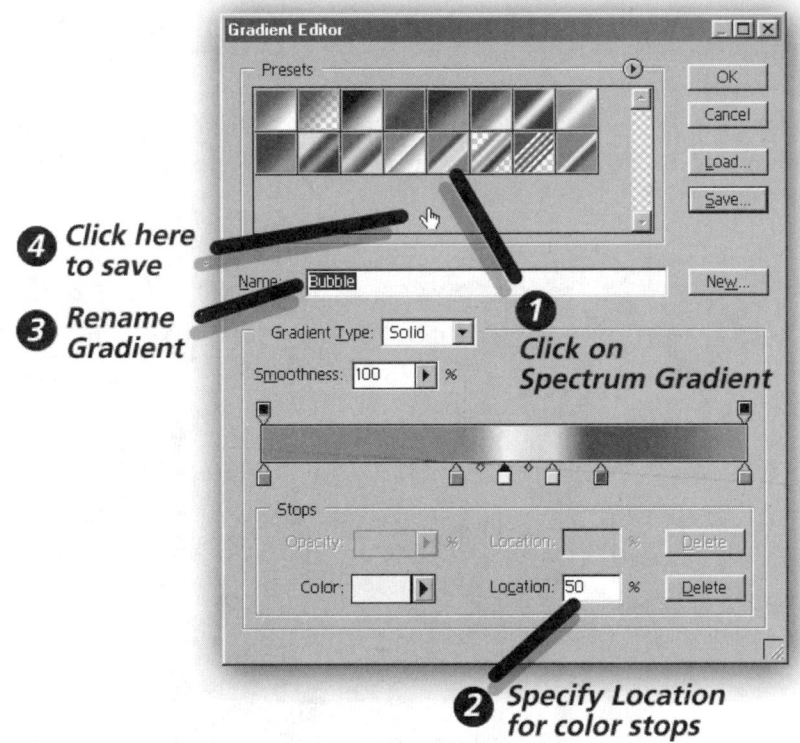

**Figure 21.2**   The Spectrum gradient was used as a starting point for a rainbow gradient.

6. Drag a radial gradient from the center of the circle selection to the outer
   edge of the selection, as shown in Figure 21.3.

7. Choose Filter, Distort, Spherize. In the Spherize dialog box, type 100% for
   Amount (see Figure 21.4). Click OK. Press Ctrl(⌘)+F to apply the same filter
   again.

   The Spherize filter pushes the center of the selection towards the outside,
   thereby creating a spherical effect with our rainbow colors. The default setting of 100% is ideal for preparing the contents of our selection for a round
   look. Applying the filter a second time further emphasizes the round quality
   produced by the Spherize filter.

8. Press D for default colors. Click the Add a mask icon at the bottom of the
   Layers palette. Hold Alt(Opt)+click on the layer mask thumbnail to display
   the mask in the document window, as shown in Figure 21.5. Ctrl(⌘)+click on
   the image thumbnail on the Bubble layer to load the selection.

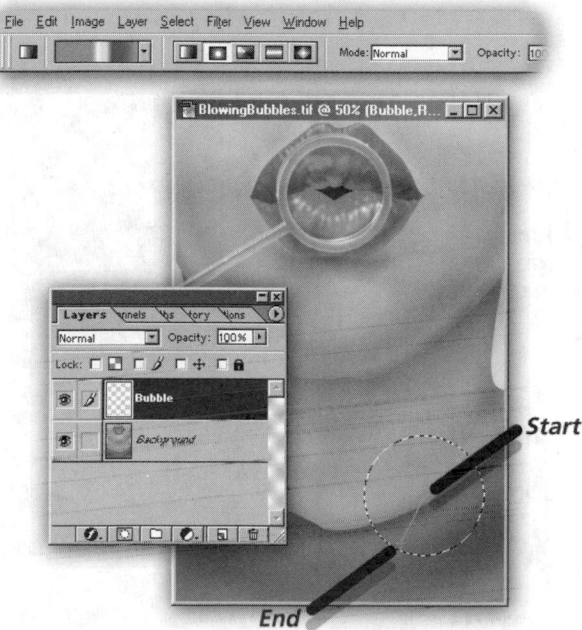

**Figure 21.3**   Start the gradient drag at the center point and end near the outer edge of the circle.

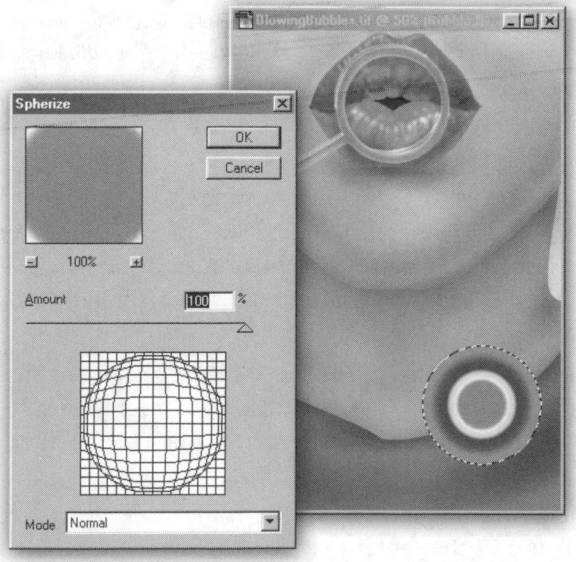

**Figure 21.4**   Apply a setting of 100% for the amount in the Spherize dialog box.

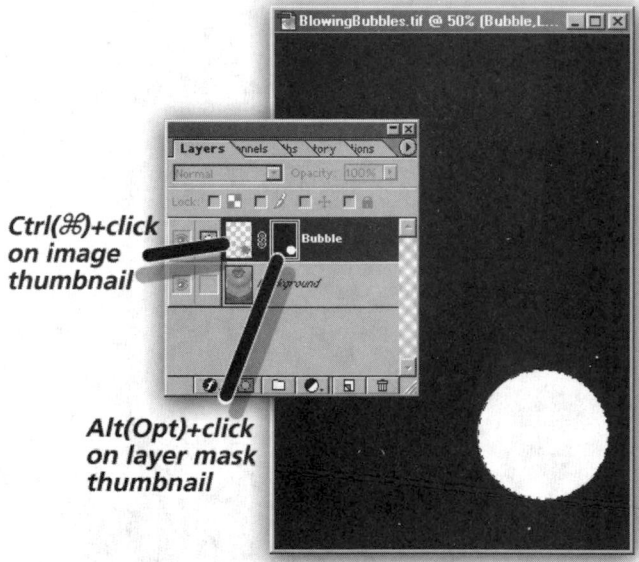

**Figure 21.5**   To prepare for the next filter that will be applied, it helps to see a larger view of the mask thumbnail.

**Note**

**Adding a Layer Mask and Viewing**   When you're adding a layer mask, an active selection will result in a black mask surrounding the selection. When there is no active selection, the mask layer will be white, which means the layer is still completely visible.

By clicking the layer mask thumbnail, you can edit the mask while the image remains visible in the document window. Alt(Opt)+click on the layer mask thumbnail to view the mask in the document window.

9. Choose Filter, Render, Different Clouds. The filter generates a random effect. If the result is not a nice marble effect like the one shown in Figure 21.6, then press Ctrl(⌘)+F repeatedly until the result is similar (it may take a dozen or more times).

10. Choose Filter, Distort, Spherize. In the Spherize dialog box, use the setting of **100%** for Amount. Click OK. Press Ctrl(⌘)+F to apply the Spherize filter a second time to help emphasize the rounded quality this filter produces.

11. Press J to switch to the Airbrush tool. On the Options bar choose **20%** for Opacity. Choose the 35-pixel brush size. With black as the foreground color, paint a small area in the center and two quadrants (top-right and bottom-left, for example, as shown in Figure 21.7).

Choose the quadrants that are best for the marble effect you are working with. The goal is to have a balance between light and dark marbling.

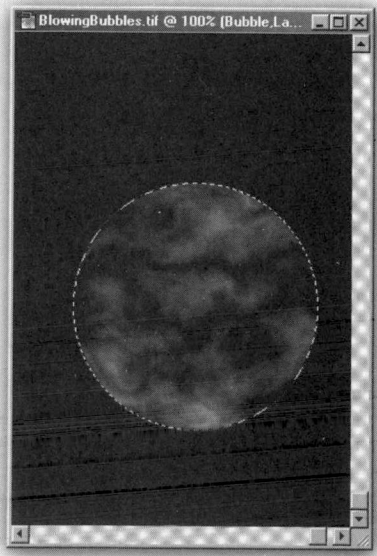

**Figure 21.6**   Apply the Different Clouds filter to the selection and repeat as necessary until the effect is a nice marble fill.

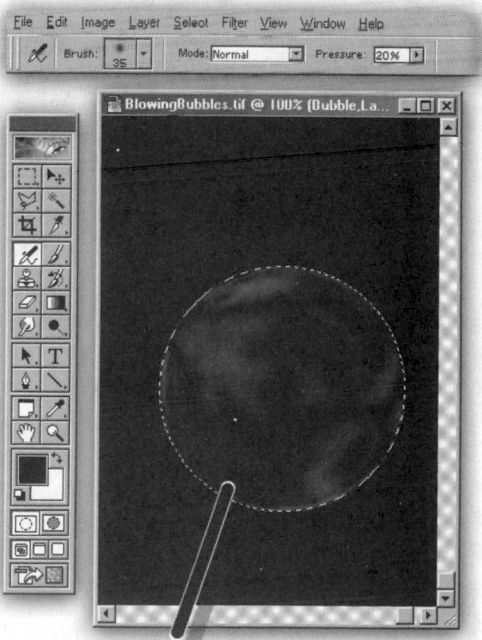

*Airbrush additional black paint*

**Figure 21.7**   Add some black paint with the Airbrush to make the mask denser and more transparent in areas of the selection.

**12.** Click the image thumbnail to view the image in the document window. On the Layers palette, change the layer mode to Hue.

**13.** Drag the Bubble layer to the Create a new layer icon to duplicate it. Change the layer mode of the copy to Color Dodge and the Opacity to **70%** (see Figure 21.8).

Color Dodge mode will progressively brighten the base color of the underlying layers to reflect the blending colors.

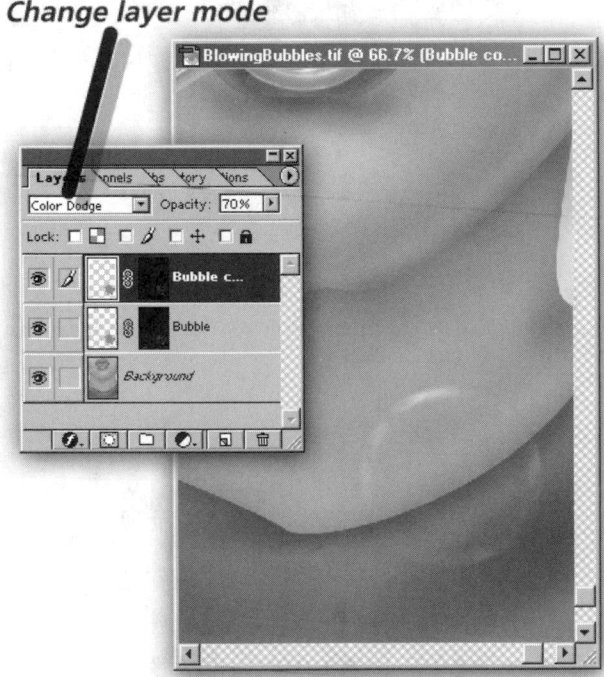

**Figure 21.8**   Changing the layer mode helps to achieve the bubble effect.

**14.** Drag the Bubble copy layer to the Create a new layer icon to duplicate this layer.

Duplicating this layer clarifies the color in the bubble and the definition of the swirls. You may want to duplicate the layer again until you have bubble definition you are satisfied with. The next few steps will create a glow around the bubble edge.

**15.** With the top layer selected in the Layers palette, Alt(Opt)+click the Create a new layer icon and type **Glow** for the Name in the New Layer dialog box. Click OK.

**16.** Choose Select, Modify, Border. In the Border Selection dialog box, type **3** (pixels) for Width (see Figure 21.9). Click OK. Choose Select, Feather, and type **2** (pixels) for Feather Radius. Click OK.

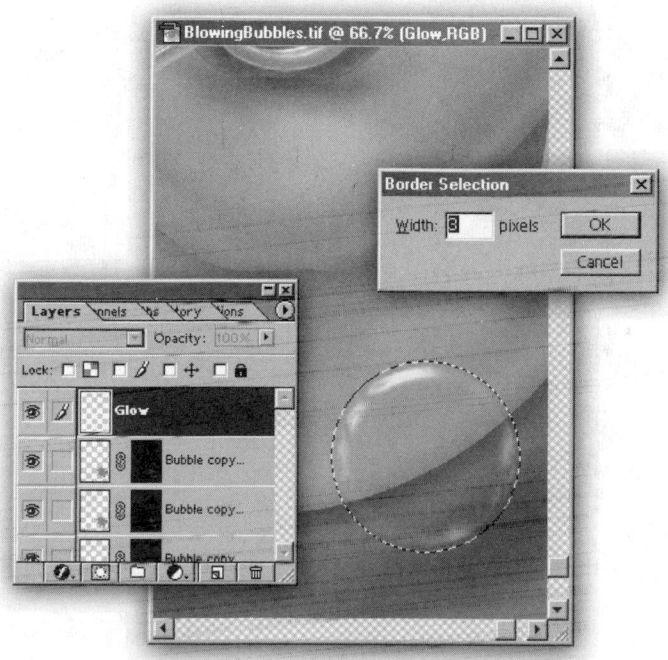

**Figure 21.9**   Give the border selection a width of 3 pixels.

**17.** Press X to switch to white as the foreground color. Press Alt(Opt)+Delete (Backspace) to fill the border selection with white. Press Ctrl(⌘)+D to deselect.

**18.** Click the Add a mask icon at the bottom of the Layers palette. Press J to switch to the Airbrush tool (the opacity setting for the Airbrush should still be set at 20%). If black is not the foreground color, press X to switch black to the foreground. Paint sections of the border to soften the glow effect in some of the areas (use your own artistic judgment here). On the Layers palette, change the layer mode to Color Dodge and lower the Opacity to 50%, as shown in Figure 21.10 (the opacity amount is also a matter of personal taste).

**19.** Click in the columns to the left of each layer thumbnail to link the bubble layers. A chain icon will be visible to indicate the layers are linked (see Figure 21.11). With the layers linked you can move the bubble around as a unit. Press Ctrl(⌘)+Shift+S, title the file **Bubbles.psd**, and save the file to your hard drive.

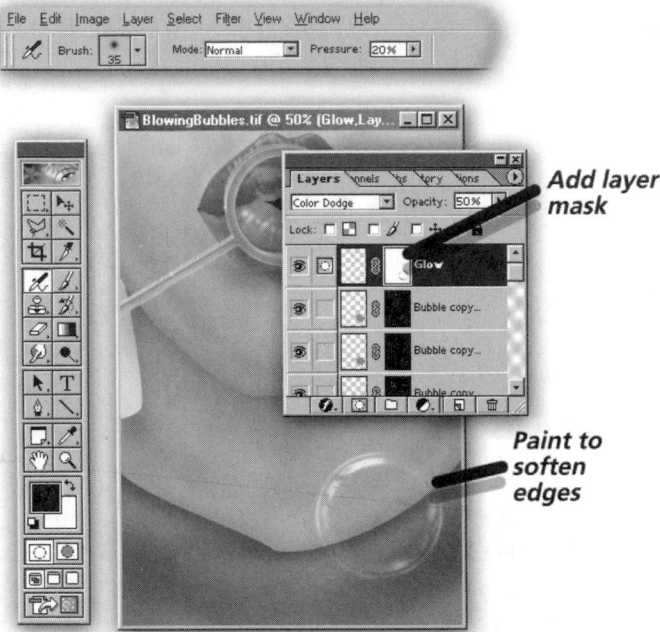

**Figure 21.10**    Use the Color Dodge layer mode and opacity to create a glow effect. Paint on a mask to soften the glow.

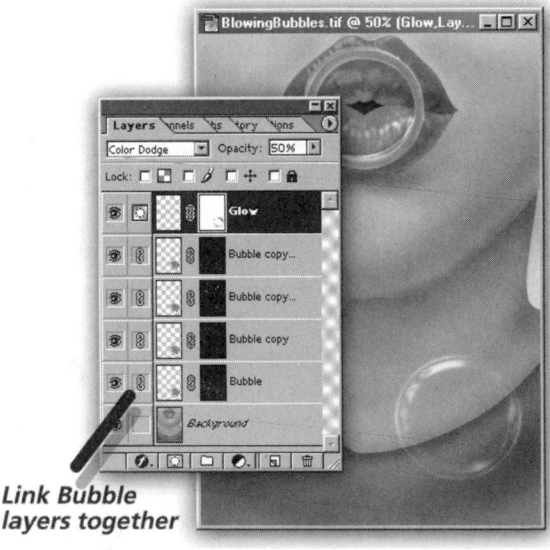

**Figure 21.11**    Link the bubble layers so they behave as a single object.

This example was just an introduction to the many fun things you can do with filters. Try the example on an actual photograph, such as a stock photo of clouds. You'll be amazed at how real these bubbles can look.

## Combining Filters for Artistic Effects

Want to know some other tricks with real photos? The next example separates the person in the foreground of a photo from the background. A variety of filters are then applied to the background to give it an artistic quality. The result can be striking, with the foreground object still in focus and a contrasting artistic background. Remember that I've just experimented to obtain the finished result for this example. It helps to make a copy of the layer and then experiment. If the results aren't pleasing, you still have the original layer on which to try a different combination of filters.

In the interest of time, the person in the photograph has already been separated for you using a product called Corel KnockOut. This program does a wonderful job of masking difficult areas such as thin strands of hair. It even handles transparent objects well—a glass of water, for example. The program exports a file that includes an alpha channel of the separated item. The next example shows how to use the alpha channel and then apply the filters. To find out more about Corel KnockOut, see the "Resources" section at the end of this chapter, which includes the URL for its Web site.

### Example 21.2    Artistic Filter Combinations

1. Open MakeUpParty.tif in the Examples/Chap21 folder on the Companion CD.

2. Choose Select, Load Selection. In the Load Selection dialog box, make sure Alpha 1 is chosen as the Channel (see Figure 21.12). Click OK. Press Ctrl(⌘)+J to put the selection on its own layer.

    If you would like to view the Alpha 1 channel, it can be found on the Channels palette. Another way to make the channel into a selection is to Ctrl(⌘)+click on the Alpha 1 channel in the Channels palette.

3. On the Layers palette, drag the Background layer to the Create a new layer icon at the bottom of the palette to create a duplicate layer on which to experiment.

    First, you'll apply the Pointillize filter, which yields different colors based on the active background color in the toolbox. Want to have fun with this? Let's separate a small section and apply the filter with a different active background color from the rest of the image.

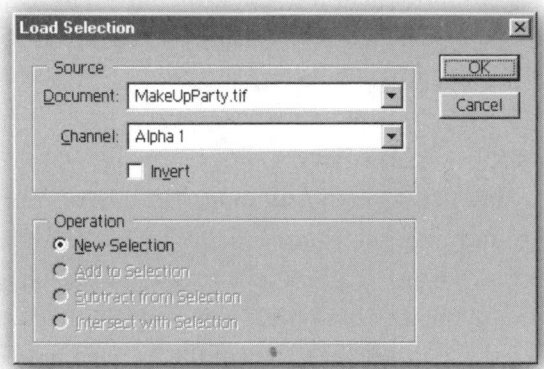

**Figure 21.12**   Load the Alpha 1 channel provided in the file as a selection.

4. Choose the Polygonal Lasso tool from the toolbox. Drag the corner of the document window away from the image to extend the border area surrounding the image window. An area of wall on the left side of the image has a lighter color than the rest of the wall area. Start at the upper-left area, slightly in from the corner, and click with the Polygonal Lasso tool. Click again at the lower edge (following the color transition of the wall). Click at the remaining corners outside the image, as shown in Figure 21.13, to section off this area.

**Figure 21.13**   Select the left portion of the wall with the Polygonal Lasso tool.

5. Click on the background color. Choose a soft, muted green color; R:136, G:181, B:176. Click OK. Choose Filter, Pixelate, Pointillize. In the Pointillize dialog box, choose **5** for Cell Size (see Figure 21.14). Click OK.

**Figure 21.14** A Cell Size of 5 gives a nice artistic effect.

6. Press Ctrl(⌘)+Shift+I to invert the selection. Click on the background color and choose a beige color; R:207, G:204, B:188. Click OK. Press Ctrl(⌘)+F to apply the same filter (Pixelate, Pointillize) previously used. Press Ctrl(⌘)+D to deselect.

7. Choose Filter, Artistic, Watercolor. In the Watercolor dialog box, type **7** for Brush Detail, **1** for Shadow Intensity, and **1** for Texture (see Figure 21.15). Click OK.

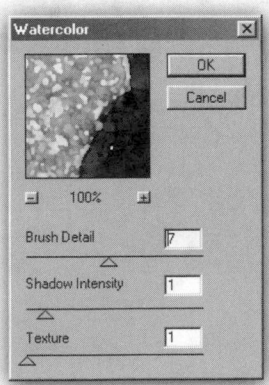

**Figure 21.15** Using these settings in the Watercolor dialog box help to accentuate the artistic flavor of this example.

**8.** Choose Filter, Brush Strokes, Angled Strokes. In the Angled Strokes dialog box, type **50** for Direction Balance, **15** for Stroke Length, and **3** for Sharpness (see Figure 21.16). Click OK.

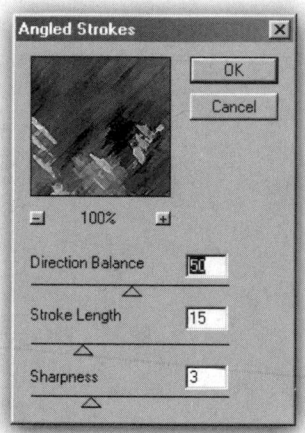

**Figure 21.16**    The settings for the Angled Strokes filter were chosen to keep the strokes balanced (not too small, not too large).

**9.** Choose Filter, Artistic, Poster Edges. In the Poster Edges dialog box, type **2** for Edge Thickness, **1** for Edge Intensity, and **2** for Posterization (see Figure 21.17). Click OK. Press Ctrl(⌘)+S to save your work.

**Figure 21.17**    Using these settings for the Poster Edges filter help to keep consistent color tones that are harmonious with the rest of the image.

The filters in this previous example were chosen for two reasons. First, these filters build upon each other to add a painterly impressionistic style to the image. Second, they also provided a subtle distortion of the background information to help draw attention to the main subject matter.

Let's review: So far, we've used one combination of filters to help build our bubbles, and another combination to add an artistic background to a photograph. What else can filters do? They can also be used to add texture.

## Texturizing with Filters

The next example covers two methods you can use to add texture to art or photographs. Always remember that these methods can be applied to any image. As you go through the steps, think of ways to apply these methods to images you might have lying around.

The image used in this example is an illustration of a flower design. But what if you have a photograph of real flowers from your garden, for example, and you want to add texture to just a few of the flowers in the photograph? Easy—you make a selection of the flowers to which you want to apply texture, and then, using one of the methods in the example, experiment with textures.

The first method shows how to use the image information displayed in the Channels palette as a source of texturing. The second method shows how to use a separate pattern file as a source of texture. You can create patterns of your own and use them to add texture, or use patterns that ship with Photoshop.

For this example, the Floral.psd file created in Chapter 10 makes a wonderful pattern file for adding texture to the Background layer. The floral theme of this pattern file compliments the flower image used for the next example. If you would like to refer to Chapter 10 and prepare the Floral.psd file yourself for this example, keep in mind two minor changes to the examples that show you how to do this: Pattern files used with the Texturizer filter need to be grayscale, so the Floral.psd file needs to be prepared with a black color (instead of the beige color used in Chapter 10). Also, the finished file was rotated clockwise 90° because this pattern direction seemed to flow better with the image. The altered version of the Floral.psd file (for the next example) is provided for you in the Examples/Chap21 folder of the Companion CD if you do not want to prepare the file yourself.

### Example 21.3  Texture with Filters

1. Open Flowers.psd in the Examples/Chap21 folder on the Companion CD.

2. Click the Channels tab to view the Channels palette (or choose Window, Show Channels). The Red channel seems to have lighter shades of gray information (which will result in nice subtle effects). Drag the Red channel to the Create new channel icon at the bottom of the palette (see Figure 21.18) to duplicate this channel.

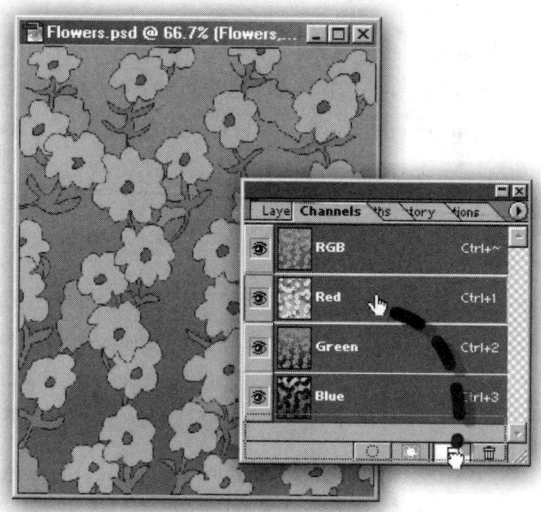

**Figure 21.18**    Make a copy of the Red channel.

3. Click the Layers tab to return to the Layers palette. Click on the Flowers layer to make it the active layer.

4. Choose Filter, Render, Lighting Effects. In the Lighting Effects dialog box, choose Directional from the Light type drop-down list. Click the end of the directional line and drag it to the 12 o'clock point. Drag to a position (peek ahead at Figure 21.19) where the colors of the flowers in the preview box are similar to the flower colors of the original image. Drag the Gloss slider to 25. Choose Red copy from the Texture Channel drop-down list, and move the Height slider to 19. Click OK.

   The Height slider affects the depth of the texture. The higher the number, the more pronounced the effect. We chose a setting of 19 because it yields an attractive subtle effect; if you want a more obvious effect, however, feel free to experiment with this slider on your own.

5. Click on the Background layer in the Layers palette to make this the active layer. Choose Filter, Texture, Texturizer. In the Texturizer dialog box, choose

Load Texture from the list of Texture options, and then navigate to the Floral.psd file provided for you in the Examples/Chap21 folder on the Companion CD, and open it. Type **75%** for Scaling, **8** for Relief, and choose Top from the list of Light Direction options (see Figure 21.20). Click OK.

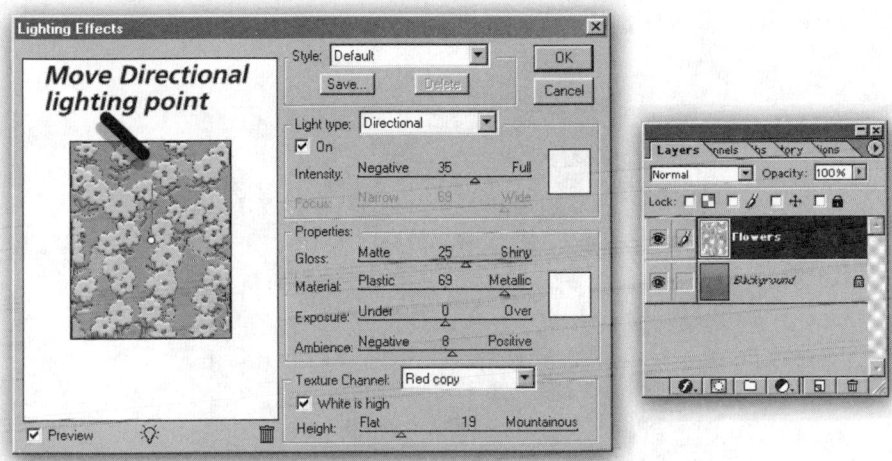

**Figure 21.19** Adjust the Directional lighting point to match the color in the preview box with the original color in the document window.

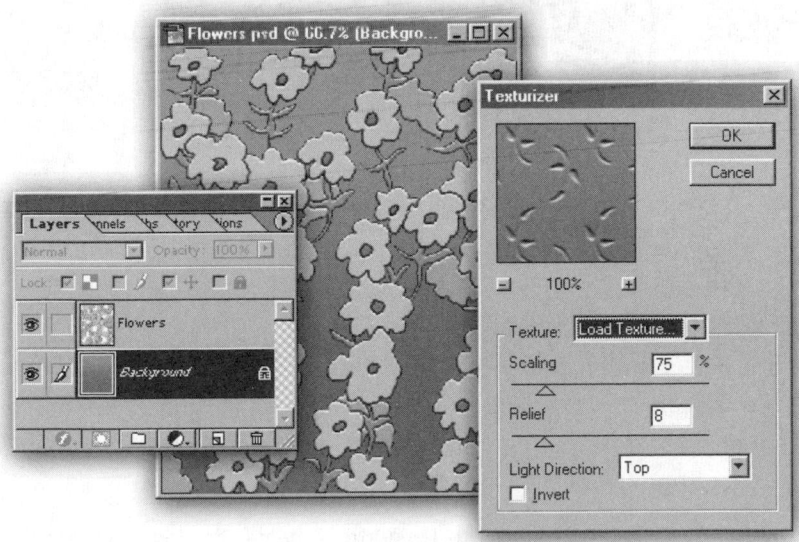

**Figure 21.20** The Scaling and Relief settings in the Texturizer dialog box add just the right texture to the Background layer.

**6.** Choose File, Save As and save the file to your hard drive if you want keep the file for future reference.

Adding texture to an image isn't hard at all—is it? The texture added in the previous example provided a charming element to a very simple design (the final image can be seen in Figure 21.21).

**Figure 21.21**   Your final image should look similar to this after the texture has been added.

## Using Filters for a Quick Background Change

The Lighting Effects filter, which you used to help create a texture for the flower design, is extremely versatile. It has a number of preset lighting styles that serve as a good foundation for various lighting effects. One of my favorite tricks is to change a photo's background with the help of the Lighting Effects filter.

Friends frequently give me photos to fix. Often, their only complaint is the background. Maybe it is too cluttered, or simply not interesting enough, which detracts from the main subject in the photo. Of course, the most time-consuming part of such a project is to get a good selection of the subject you want to keep in the photo. So again, in the interest of time, I used the KnockOut program (mentioned earlier in the chapter) to make an Alpha channel selection for the next project.

After the subject has been selected and separated onto a different layer, any background changes can be made effortlessly. You can substitute stock images of exotic vacation spots or design your own artwork.

For this example, I show a few quick fixes to obtain a nice uncluttered background. This example shows two concepts. The first acquaints you with the wonderful possibilities the Lighting Effects filter can provide. The second makes you aware of how easily the look of an entire image can be changed on the simplest level with just a gradient fill and the help of a few filters.

### Example 21.4    Background Lighting Effects

1. Open OldPhoto.tif in the Examples/Chap21 folder on the Companion CD.

2. Choose Select, Load Selection. In the Load Selection dialog box, be sure that Alpha 1 is chosen as the Channel option. Click OK. Press Ctrl(⌘)+J to place the selection on its own layer.

3. Click on the Background layer to make it the active layer. Alt(Opt)+click on the Create a new layer icon at the bottom of the Layers palette. In the New Layer dialog box, type **Gradient** for the Name. Click OK.

   A simple Foreground to Background gradient will be used. What colors do you choose when you're deciding on a new background? I find it helpful to look at the image and decide whether I want to keep or emphasize any colors from the original. For this image, I picked colors that complimented the dress. Remember, however, to experiment with colors on your own when you do a project like this. Whatever seems to work—the colors can range from soft neutral shades to wild and crazy ones, or even be colors sampled directly from the original image.

4. Click the foreground color and choose a soft, muted pink; R:190, G:126, B:130. Click OK. Click the background color and choose a soft, muted green; R:136, G:181, B:176. Click OK.

5. Press G to switch to the Gradient tool. Make sure that the Radial Gradient icon is selected on the Options bar and the Gradient type is Foreground to Background. Press the Shift key and drag a horizontal gradient, starting at the center of the document and ending outside the right edge, as shown in Figure 21.22.

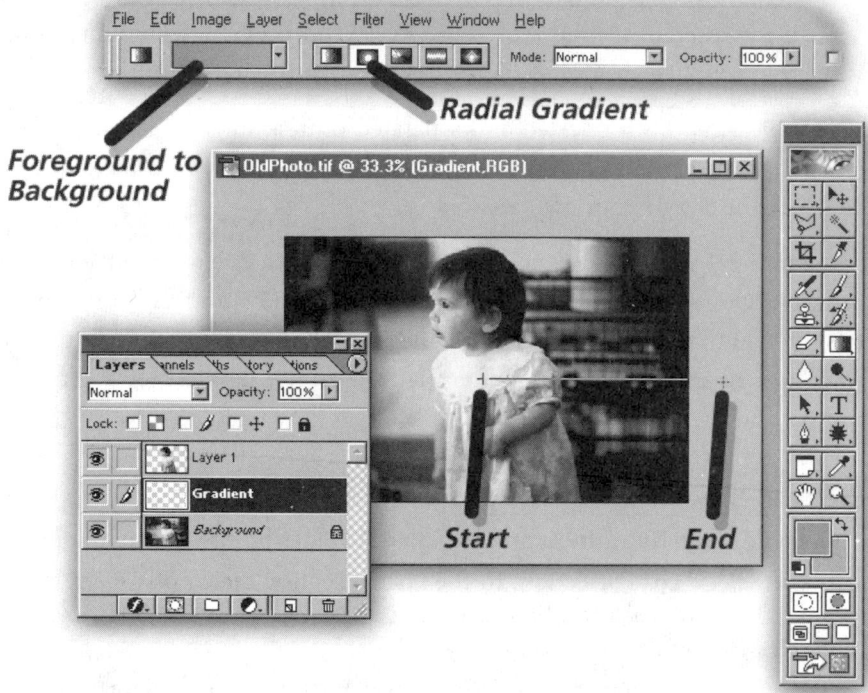

**Figure 21.22**    Drag a horizontal gradient, starting at the center and ending outside the right edge of the document window.

Photoshop provides a variety of preset styles for lighting effects, a feature of the Lighting Effects filter that the average Photoshop user may overlook. This example uses one of the preset styles without changing any of the settings, but here too, you can use these styles as a starting point and alter them in any way that appeals to you.

6. With the Gradient layer as the active layer, choose Filter, Render, Lighting Effects. In the Lighting Effects dialog box, choose Crossing Down from the list of Style options (see Figure 21.23). Click OK.

The original photo has a grainy quality, but the Gradient layer you've created has smooth color transitions. We need to add grain to the Gradient layer to give it a similar feel to the rest of the image. How do we do this? Filters, of course!

7. Choose Filter, Noise, Add Noise. In the Add Noise dialog box, type 2 for Amount, choose the Gaussian option for Distribution, and check the Monochromatic option (see Figure 21.24). Click OK.

8. Choose File, Save As and name the file **PhotoRedo.psd**. Keep the file open for the next example.

**Click here**

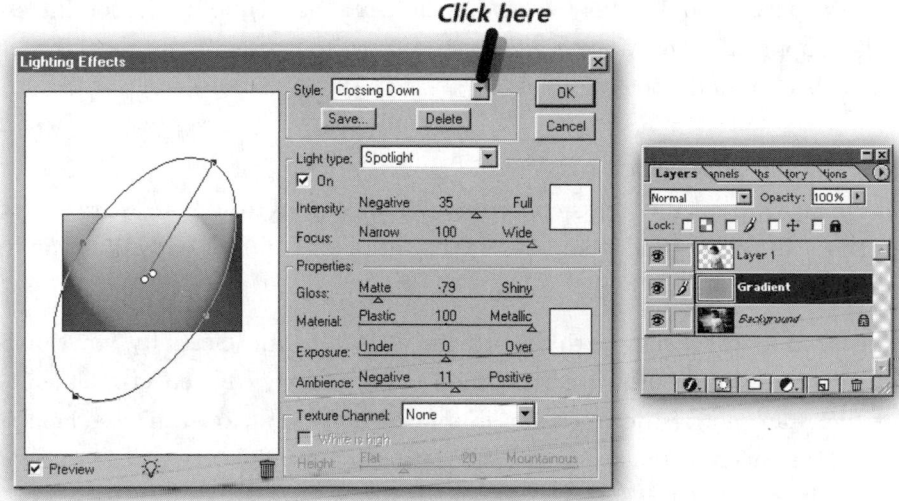

**Figure 21.23** The Crossing Down Style from the preset list adds a double spotlight effect to the background gradient. These spotlights cross each other in opposite directions, which helps to explain the name of this style.

**Figure 21.24** The Add Noise filter is used to add a grainy quality to the Gradient layer to match the grain of the original photo.

The new background definitely seems less cluttered. As mentioned earlier, this is a quick-fix approach. Any range of ideas can be used to create interesting and exciting new backgrounds for a photo.

## Using Filters with Quick Mask

Want to take the quick fix one step further? A popular trick to add pizzazz to a photo or image is to give it a funky border edge. There are tons of third-party filters on the market that do just that.

Can't afford to invest in more third-party filters? With a little creativity, you can use the native filters that ship with Photoshop to create jazzy edge effects. Remember that filters are not restricted to image information only. You can use them on channel information, and also with masks. We will use a filter in Quick Mask mode to get the next effect.

Because the main subject in the current document extends down to the bottom edge of the document window (and her head almost reaches the top edge), we will need to expand the canvas height to get some working room for the next example. Why is this important? We will be cropping away some of the image. Expanding the height allows us to keep all of the little girl (the main focus of this photo) without risking losing part of her head (and we all know how painful that can be). By expanding the height in both directions, we also get to keep most of her pretty dress near the bottom edge of the document.

When expanding the Canvas Size of a document there is something else to consider. Photoshop uses the active background color to fill in the added space of the Background layer. Most often, white is the desired color for the background. Therefore, we will reset the colors in the toolbox to the default colors (this will make white the background color) before going to the Canvas Size dialog box.

### Example 21.5    Using Filters with Quick Mask

1. The PhotoRedo.psd file should still be open. Press D for the default colors (white should be the background color). Right-click (Macintosh: hold Ctrl and click) on the title bar of the document window, and choose Canvas Size. Type **700** (pixels) for Height (see Figure 21.25). Keep the default center anchor active to expand the canvas size equally in both directions. Click OK.

2. Click on the Background layer to make this the active layer. Press X to switch white to the foreground. Press Alt(Opt)+Delete (Backspace) to fill the Background layer with white.

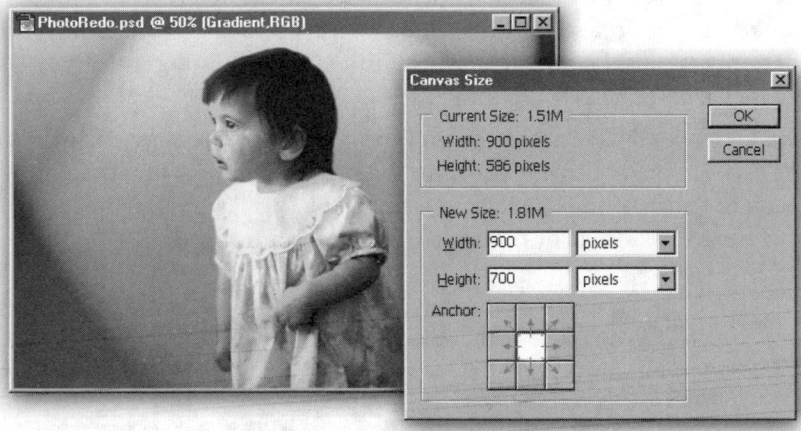

**Figure 21.25**   The height of a document can be changed using the Canvas Size dialog box.

3. Click on Layer 1 to make it the active layer. Press Ctrl(⌘)+E to merge this layer with the Gradient layer. With the Gradient layer as the active layer, choose the Rectangular Marquee tool from the toolbox. Starting near the upper-right area of the image, drag a rectangle selection around the subject, as shown in Figure 21.26.

Remember to hold down the spacebar, if necessary, to reposition the rectangle as you drag. The goal here is to keep the image information inside the rectangle selection, and also keep some of the image area as a border outside the rectangular selection.

**Figure 21.26**   Drag a rectangular selection that surrounds the main subject.

4. Press Q to enter Quick Mask mode. Choose Filter, Brush Strokes, Sprayed Strokes. In the Sprayed Strokes dialog box, type **12** for Stroke Length, and **15** for Spray Radius. Leave Stroke Direction at the default Right Diagonal (see Figure 21.27). Click OK.

The Quick Mask is black in the preview window of the Sprayed Strokes dialog box. If you place your cursor in the preview window and drag until you reach the edge of the Quick Mask selection (as in Figure 21.27), you will be able to see the results of the filter settings you are applying.

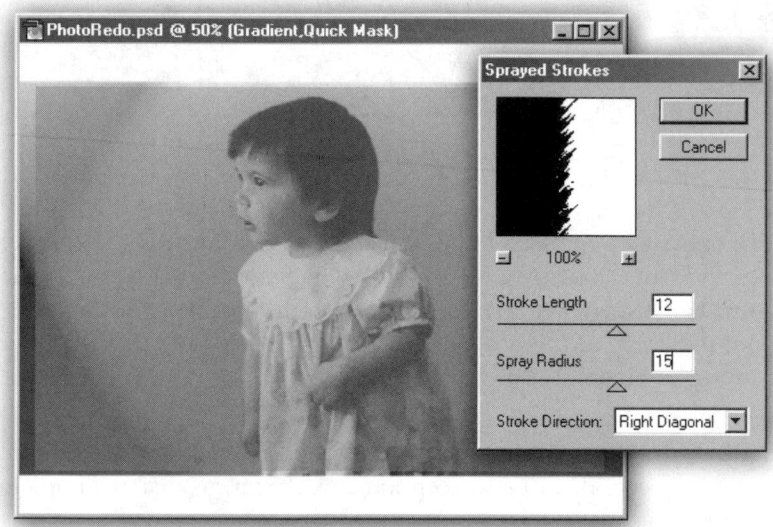

**Figure 21.27**    The Sprayed Strokes settings can be used to give an artistic edge to the Quick Mask selection.

When we exit the Quick Mask mode, the mask selection will cover the area we want to keep. We need to delete the areas outside the selection. How do we fix this? It will be necessary to invert the selection in the next step.

5. Press Q to exit Quick Mask mode and make the resulting mask into a selection. Press Ctrl(⌘)+Shift+I to Invert the selection. Press Delete (Backspace) to clear the contents of the selection (see Figure 21.28). Press Ctrl(⌘)+D to deselect.

6. For a final touch, click the Add a layer style icon at the bottom of the Layers palette and choose Drop Shadow. In the Layer Style dialog box, type **85%** for Opacity, **74°** for Angle, **7** for Distance, **0** for Spread, and **35** for Size (see Figure 21.29). Click OK. Press Ctrl(⌘)+S to save your work.

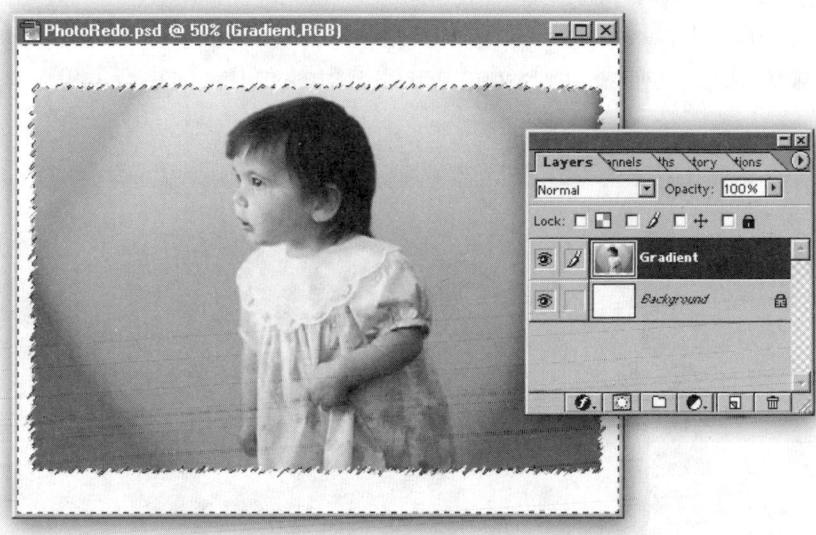

**Figure 21.28**   Invert the selection and press Delete (Backspace) to clear the border area around the image.

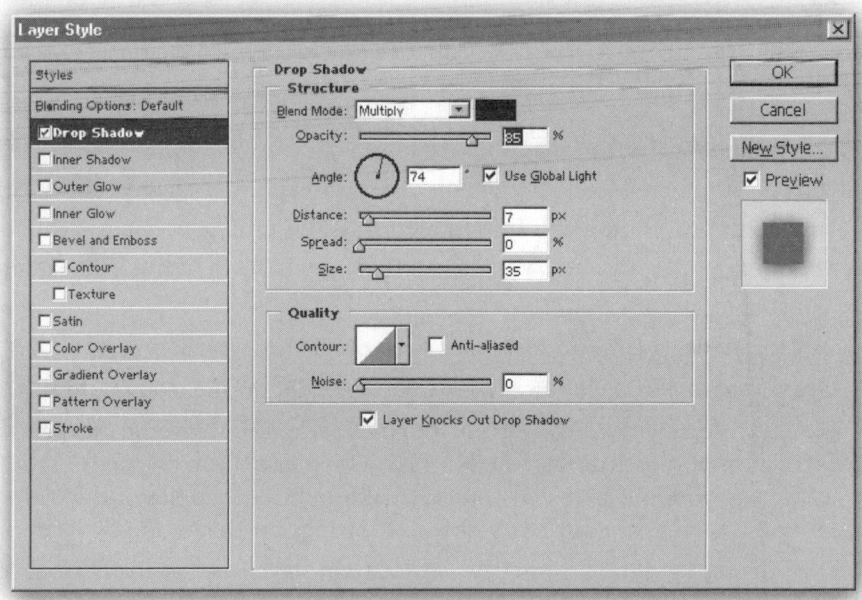

**Figure 21.29**   Add a soft Drop Shadow to the Gradient layer for an extra effect.

Congratulations! With just a few easy changes, you have managed to take an average, everyday photograph and make it appear as if a professional backdrop and lighting were available when the photograph was taken (see Figure 21.30).

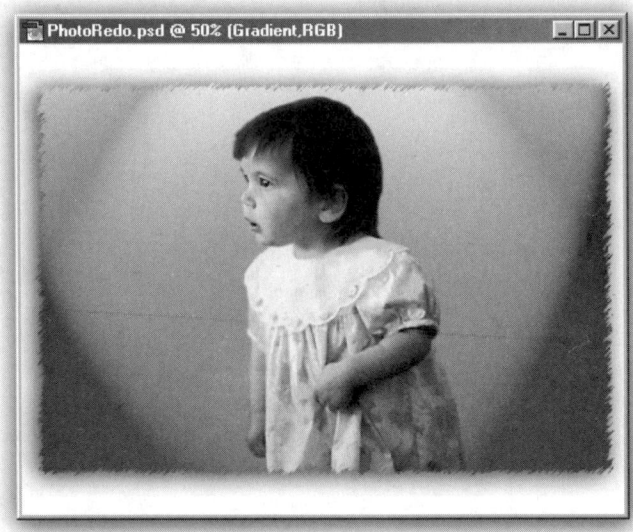

**Figure 21.30**    The final image has a nice artistic edge border and a professional backdrop.

## Producing Line Art with Filters

Have you ever wanted to use a photograph as a starting point for a drawing? Wished you could convert a photograph into line art in just a few simple steps? One particular Photoshop filter can help you do just that, as you'll see in the next example.

### Example 21.6    Using a Filter to Make Line Art from a Photograph

1. Open NapTime.tif in the Examples/Chap21 folder on the Companion CD.

   The next step creates a copy of the original Background layer (for experimentation purposes only). You don't have to create this copy, but the advantage of doing so is that you can make additional copies of the background layer if you want to try different settings for this example.

2. Drag the Background layer to the Create a new layer icon at the bottom of the Layers palette to make a working copy of the layer.

3. With the Background copy layer still active, choose Filter, Blur, Smart Blur. In the Smart Blur dialog box, type **4** for Radius, and **45** for Threshold. Choose High Quality, and choose Edge Only Mode (see Figure 21.31). Click OK.

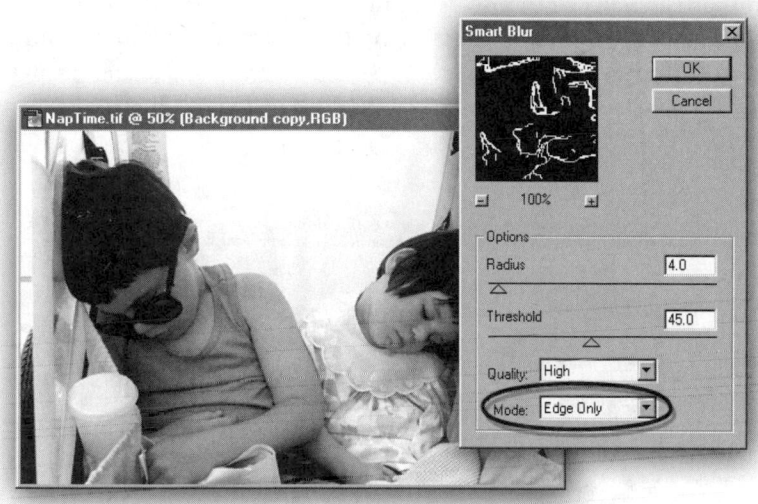

**Figure 21.31**    Use the Smart Blur settings to create quick-and-easy line art from a photograph.

Adjusting the Radius and Threshold settings will vary the amount of detail for the final line art results.

The filter gives a result that looks like a negative, with white lines on a black background. The next step fixes this and reverses the colors.

4. Press Ctrl(⌘)+I to invert the line art (see Figure 21.32). Choose File, Save As to save your work.

**Figure 21.32**    Using the Edge Only mode from the Smart Blur settings and inverting the results can produce line art from a photograph.

A beautiful, artistic effect can also be achieved by changing the mode from Edge Only to Overlay Edge. This Mode setting produces a striking colorized line-art version of your photograph (see Figure 21.33). The NapTime.psd file located in the Examples/Chap21/Gallery folder of the Companion CD has separate layers to show the results for both modes.

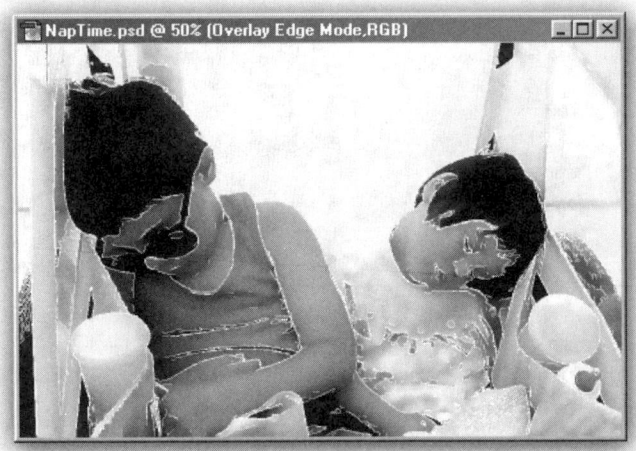

**Figure 21.33**    Changing the mode of the Smart Blur filter to Overlay Edge will give you a beautiful, artistic result.

Instant line art. That's all there is to it! Lower settings for the Radius (around 15 or under) may work well with Threshold values in the 40–60 ranges. A Radius in the higher ranges of 50–60 might require a higher Threshold (around 90–100). Changing the mode to low quality will also affect the detail that this filter produces.

One more concept might be helpful to remember: The filter can be used to create a more detailed line drawing of the photograph. Then you can use the Eraser tool to eliminate the details you don't want.

## Summary

Filters provide an unlimited source for experimentation. They can be combined with other filters to achieve a powerful effect, or used one filter at a time for a specific task. There are too many possibilities for just one chapter, but I hope this has provided a wide range of ideas that can serve as a good starting point for your own projects.

When you review the ideas in this chapter, try not to limit yourself to the specific situations used here. For example, the frame edge effect used in Example 21.5 does not need to be restricted to a photo only. This effect can be applied to shapes and rendered text, or used to change the edge of a clip art design. The same idea can be used with other filters to achieve different edge effects. The most important idea is to explore. Try different settings. See what appeals to you. Have fun!

## Resources

http://www.corel.com/corelknockout/ver1_5/index.htm
Corel's site for information on the Corel KnockOut version 1.5 product.

# Chapter 22

# Working with Type

"New and Improved!" is an ad slogan we have all seen for, well, as long as we can remember. Frankly, this burst that appears on everything from toothpaste to cars begs the obvious question, "If it's new, how can it be improved?" And the authors have lost confidence is such a selling point ages ago.

However, let's regain our faith for a moment in product claims. When Adobe states that the Type tool in Photoshop 6 is "New and Improved," you'd better *believe* it! Photoshop finally has a Type tool that is equivalent in power to the Type tool in an illustration program (such as Adobe Illustrator). Gone is the big, clunky, obstructive, Type tool dialog box, New is a method of entering text *directly* into your image, as you would using a DTP program or a word processor. We also have at our fingertaps the features of a text bounding box, auto-hyphenation, and paragraph control, to name a few others.

Working with type, though, is not simply a matter of knowing how to use the Type tool. Anyone can add type to his or her image, but understanding and using good *design* is what sets the professional apart from the amateur. With design in mind, this chapter is divided into two sections. The first section explores typefaces and some basics of good design when using type. The second section takes you through a project, using Photoshop's Type tool to create an ad for a 27-year high school reunion.

## Understanding Typefaces and Type Design Principles

First, notice the last word in the heading: "Basics." It is impossible to explain everything about typefaces and design in one chapter, much less *half* a chapter! The study, creation, design, and application of type is a profession, and many books have been written on the subject. (As of this writing, if you enter "typography" in Amazon.com's search engine, 712 book titles are listed!) If you find working with text fascinating, we highly recommend that you buy a few good books on the subject.

If you're as old as we are—and collectively, the authors age is slightly lower than the national deficit—you remember the good old days of the manual typewriter. Choosing a typeface (font) was simple—you used the (only) typeface that came with the typewriter! Things started getting complicated when IBM introduced the Selectric typewriter where the font element (that metal ball with all the characters on it in the center of the typewriter well) and you could swap the type balls to use exotic fonts such as Script, Delegate, and Orator (this is thinly veiled sarcasm, okay? <g>) However, the variety of monospaced fonts was meager, the daisy-wheel element eventually replaced the (expensive!) IBM type balls, and as a personal publisher, the level of quality you could attain was a step above the cave paintings in Altamira.

Then came the personal computer and the curse of having hundreds, or thousands of typefaces to choose from. For the novice, having this massive selection of fonts was like being in a candy store with someone else willing to pay the bill. Newsletters, brochures, letters, and anything else that required text suddenly looked like an all-you-can-eat buffet—a different typeface for each paragraph or article. Additionally, the layout of the text lacked the basic design principles that books and newspapers have used for decades—fonts best for headlines were used in paragraph text and made reading very difficult, for example.

The problem was the worst on the Windows platform, where CorelDRAW users were treated to over 1,000 fonts, some of high quality, while others would barf a PostScript device. And every Corellian felt compelled to use as many fonts as possible, without realizing that entries for the fonts were being made in win.ini and if win.ini got over 64K, your machine would not run properly. The Macintosh has a built-in limitation of 250 fonts loaded at the same time, and you know, professionally, that's about all you ever need on a daily basis. Wild fonts such as Renee Mackintosh (after the Scottish furniture designer) Arnold Boecklin, Shelley Allegro, and others really need to be loaded about once every year—you only use this stuff for weddings and holidays.

Okay, enough complaining. Let's take a look at five basic classifications of typefaces.

## Classifying and Choosing Typefaces

During the decision process of buying a new car, you have an idea of your needs and you've created a list, or classification, of the vehicles that best meets those needs. Then you decide which vehicle to buy. Why should choosing a font be any different?

The following classifications should help you get started with identifying and knowing where to use (and *not* use!) certain categories of fonts.

### Serif

*Serif* is a Latin word that means *feet*—the "your socks go over them" type, and not the measurement. The identifying characteristics of a serif font are the small extensions (the feet) at the ends of the lines that make up the letter. Figure 22.1 shows examples of two serif fonts and identifies the feet areas.

**Figure 22.1**    Serif typefaces have a finishing stroke on most letters.

The serifs help guide your eye along the line of text and make identifying letters and words easier and quicker. For these reasons, serif fonts are ideal for *body text* (paragraph text). Most likely, this book you are reading has the body text set in a serif font.

### Sans Serif

The *sans serif* typeface is without (sans) feet (see Figure 22.2). The strokes, or lines, that make up each letter are simple and straightforward in design.

**Figure 22.2**    The less ornate sans serif font is strong for quick recognition of short lines of text.

The most frequently seen use of a sans serif font is in the headlines of a newspaper. San serif fonts also work well in subheads, captions, callouts—situations in which only one or two lines of text are used and the text must command attention.

> **Note**
>
> **Choosing a Family** Within families of typefaces, there are subclasses. There aren't many you need to know to become proficient at type selection. In fact, we're only going to highlight two here: the Roman and the Gothic classes. Roman fonts have thick and thin lines making up the stems (the strokes) that make a letterform. You can have Roman Serif (#1 in Figure 22.3; the font is called Garamond), and Roman Sans Serif, marked #2 in Figure 22.3—this font is called Optima.
>
> On the other side of the family, you have your Gothic fonts. Gothic fonts are easy to detect because the strokes that make up the character are uniform in weight. Although you don't come across a lot of Gothic serif fonts, Lubalin Graph, (named after Herb Lubalin, a designer and font creator in the 1960s–1970s) #3 in Figure 22.3, is a Gothic serif font, and number 4 here, is VAG Rounded, a Gothic sans serif face.

**❶ Roman Serif**

**❷ Roman Sans Serif**

**❸ Gothic Serif**

**❹ Gothic Sans Serif**

**Figure 22.3** Fonts can come in Roman or Gothic versions.

## Script

Script typefaces are easily identified as having the characteristics of elegant handwriting. Script fonts are often very beautiful and can even evoke emotions. Set, for example, the words, "I love you" in Arial or Helvetica (a stoic sans serif font available on most computers). Then rewrite those words in a script font, like Deanna Script or Vivaldi, and notice which of the two typefaces best conveys the intended emotions (see Figure 22.4).

**Figure 22.4**    Script typefaces convey a personal and warm touch, whereas the sans serif font is cold and inflexible.

Although the script typeface seems more personal than most other fonts, avoid using a script font for body text or long lines of text. Similar in application to the sans serif font, the script font looks best in short lines of text, as in logos or invitations.

### Decorative

The decorative font is designed for basically one reason: to attract attention. These fonts come in the widest range of designs (see Figure 22.5) and are sometimes referred to as Display faces.

The decorative font is not designed for readability in long lines of text; rather, it is good for dramatic emphasis. The decorative font works well, for example, in advertisement headlines, restaurant menus, logos, and posters.

### The Pi Font

The Pi font, short for Picture, is not made up of an alphabet at all, but instead is made up of tiny symbols, cartoons, fingers pointing, and so on. Zapf Dingbats is perhaps the best known Pi font, but there are many others, sometimes called *ornaments* or *extras*. Adobe Minion, for example, a Roman serif font, has an accompanying font called Minion Ornaments. These Pi fonts are used by designers to embellish a headline, such as putting a "plum" (that's what the design is called in typography) on either side of ornate text, as shown in Figure 22.6.

**Figure 22.5** You find the widest range of designs in the decorative style typeface.

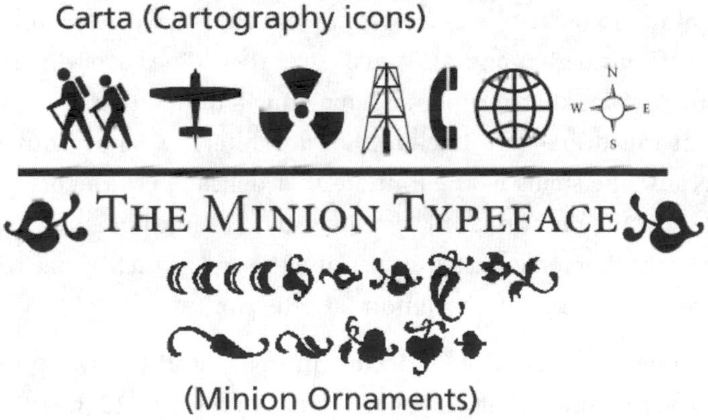

Carta (Cartography icons)

THE MINION TYPEFACE

(Minion Ornaments)

**Figure 22.6** Pi fonts are particularly useful for people who design or use photography, but are not skilled with a drawing program.

Your use of Pi fonts should be limited. Pi fonts can perk up a menu or a flyer; however, the overuse of them makes your layout look like a letter that was postmarked several times from Mars. Pi fonts are possible because typefaces are actually tiny programs that contain vector information and are decoded by a display system such as Adobe Type Manager. Technically, there is no difference between the information in a picture font and a Roman font, for example. Pi fonts are usually best worked with in Illustrator, Xara, other drawing programs, or Photoshop, because you usually need to scale the pictures on-the-fly. And DTP and word processors don't scale fonts with as much ease as an art program.

These are just a few of the many classifications of typefaces. To complicate, or organize matters (depending on your point of view), most classifications can be divided into many subclassifications.

Now that you are able to classify typefaces, what are some general rules that can help you use fonts with good design sense? Read on!

## Type Design Principles

We have three principles of design to share with you. These principles can get you started in the right direction when you're using type in your designs.

### *Consider the Technical Constraints*

"What technical constraints? If the font is on my computer, I can use it, right?" Well, not without compromising good design. There are two limitations worth mentioning: the characteristics of the font and your intended output.

The thickness of the lines that make up the letters can determine what point size to use and what not to use. For example, some serif fonts have very thin lines that are part of each letter's design and at a small size, these lines can virtually disappear, leaving your text looking terrible and making it difficult to read. For example, there's a font called Premiere Liteline that absolutely will not print to a 300 dpi printer—because the stems in the font are that delicate. On the other hand, some fonts don't show their beauty until they are seen at a large point size. Opus is a good example of a font that looks best large because the end of each stroke that comprises each character is convex—unlike almost all other fonts.

The other limitation concerns your document's output. If you will print your document, be aware that some fonts look good only at a high dpi (dot per inch), whereas other fonts look quite good at any dpi. For example, a font named Bergamo looks best above 300 dpi, whereas a different font named Futura looks good at both low and high resolution. What should you look for when determining the lowest acceptable dpi for a particular font? Look for loss of detail in the finer areas of the characters. The characters in some typefaces have very thin lines in the design. If these thin lines are no longer visible at your working dpi, choose a different font.

**Tip**

**You Get What You Pay For**    *Hinting* is a property of a typeface. Again, typefaces are actually a collection of vectors inside a tiny runtime program. Hinting is not always added to a font; it is a process by which the font (program) describes itself as having bolder characeristics at small point sizes.

Shareware fonts typically do not have hinting because typeface design programs are either $4,000 or $29 next to the *Better Homes & Gardens* at the checkout stand.

Often, investing in a quality family of typeface pays off in the long run. Adobe, URW, and MonoType all have the reputation for selling quality fonts.

Paper is another consideration. Thinner, more detailed fonts tend to look lousy on standard copy paper but print very nicely on high grade, glossy stock. Heavier fonts, like Franklin Gothic, hold up well on most any paper.

On the other hand, if you do not intend to print your document, but plan to keep the text in electronic format (PDF, the Web, for example), sans serif fonts are much easier to read on the computer screen than serif fonts are. You can test this concept for yourself the next time you are working in your word processing program. Here's how: Type two identical sentences, each on a separate line. Make one sentence a serif font (such as, Times New Roman) and the other sentence a sans serif font (such as, Arial or Helvetica). Determine which sentence is easier to read. Next, zoom out until one of the sentences is almost too difficult to read, but the other sentence is quite legible. Guess which font wins?—the sans serif font. If you have a Web site, it would be a good idea to change any text to a sans serif font during your next update.

**Tip**

**Surprise Fonts**    Microsoft, long known for "silent upgrades"—which is a polite way of saying some MS programs sneak stuff onto your hard disk to make system conflicts or errors vanish, has helped Web designers become more creative with typeface layouts.

If you've purchased a Microsoft program lately, or upgraded MS-Explorer, you will find some new TrueType fonts on your system, such as Georgia, WebDings, and Trebuchet MS. Why are we being gifted with fonts? Microsoft is seeding the Web—eventually everyone will own these fonts, which are more legible and fancier looking than the default of Times New Roman in browsers—and even today, right now, sites are being designed with these fonts included.

Check out your installed fonts. You might be pleasantly surprised!

### Know the Typefaces

If you will be working with type, you should know which fonts you have and you should know your most-used or favorite fonts like the top of your mouse.

Here are some questions you can answer when you're getting to know a font:

- Does this font look good at any point size? Does it lose its detail as it gets smaller?

- How readable is this font in paragraph text?

- Does this font use more (or less) horizontal space than other fonts at the same point size?

- Does the font look darker or lighter at small sizes?

### Support Your Message

Type should help communicate and support your message, not overwhelm it. The reader's attention should be drawn to what you are communicating, and not to the font you think looks really cool.

For example, if you are creating an image, such as an advertisement for an upcoming accountants' meeting, your font choice should be somewhat conservative in design. Whereas, if you were designing an ad for a rock concert, you could easily use a decorative font to help convey your message.

The standard wedding invitation is good example of the font supporting the message. Elegant or script typefaces are used almost exclusively for wedding invitations because of their warm, personal design (the Gothic sans serif font Bernhard Fashion is creeping into invitations). An example of the contrast between supportive and nonsupportive fonts for a wedding invitation is shown in Figure 22.7.

Now that the foundation of good type design has been laid, it's time to move on to the second part of this chapter: Designing a reunion advertisement.

## Using Photoshop's Type Tool

As previously mentioned, Photoshop's Type tool has finally grown up and can play in the big league. If you're familiar with previous versions of Photoshop, you'll love this enhanced typography set. If you are new to Photoshop, well, you've jumped on board at a good location in Photoshop's voyage to Designer's Utopia.

Without further ado, let's pop in an 8-track, start up the Type tool, and take a spin on the pixel highway.

**Figure 22.7**   Which font supports the message for this wedding invitation? You're kidding, right <g>?

## Creating a '70s-Style Advertisement

Here's the project: Create a hip, '70s-poster–style ad for a 27-year high school reunion. The specifications are 8×10 at 150 ppi for printing on a desktop printer and snail mailing (*Hint:* Do *not* use this term at the Post Office; they *really* hate it and might decide to cancel you).

Research was required to find out what colors were predominantly used for posters, the common typefaces, and the overall design style of that era. Performing a Web engine search on "1970s posters" provided Web addresses that contained hundreds of posters. The common characteristics included: low-tech design (no gradient fills, no drop shadows, no reflective surfaces, no 3D effects, etc.); an assortment of colors that seem gaudy by today's tastes; wavy, free flowing text; and a flat, two-dimensional appearance. Cutting edge for the '70s is rather boring for the new millennium, which makes it easier for us to concentrate on learning how to use the Type tool <g>!

In the following set of steps, you will warm up the Type tool and create the headline for the ad.

Example 22.1    Creating a '70s-Style Headline

1. Open the Reunion.psd image from the Examples/Chap22 folder on the Companion CD.

2. Press T (Type tool). If the Character/Paragraph palette group is not showing, click the Palettes button on the Options bar.

> **Warning!**   If an error message appears when you open the CD files, press Ctrl(⌘)+Shift+K and then choose Adobe RGB (1998) from the Working Spaces, RGB drop-down list. See Chapter 3 for more information.

3. Click the Color swatch at the bottom right on the Character palette to show the Color Picker. Type **0042b1** in the # field, and click OK (see Figure 22.8).

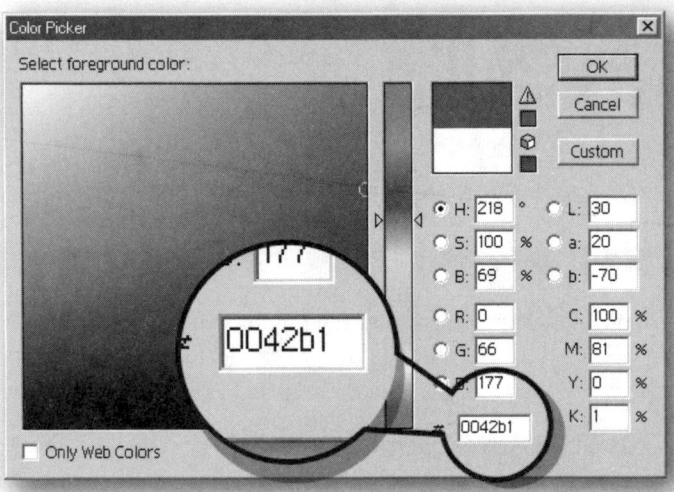

**Figure 22.8**    Every color has an alphanumeric designation, which makes selecting specific colors much easier than entering values in all the other 13 fields!

**Note**

**Why the Alphanumeric Value?**    The *reason* why every color has an alphanumeric designation on the Color Picker is that background and other colors are specified in Web (HTML) documents as an alphanumeric value, and Photoshop's the top tool for creating Web media.

4. From the Character palette, choose a sans serif font that has thick characters, like Franklin Gothic Heavy, Hobo, or Gill Sans Ultra. (Hobo is used in the figures.) Set the font size to 48, the Tracking to –25, and the Vertical Scale to 200%. Click in the image to the right of the hippie wearing a hat, and type the words **REUNION  TIME!** with two spaces between the words (see Figure 22.9). Then, press the Enter key on the numeric keypad to commit the changes to this new type layer (titled REUNION TIME!).

**Makes the font appear to be a condensed member of the font family**

**Figure 22.9**   Use a thick, sans serif font with the settings shown here in the Character palette.

> **Note**
>
> **Moving Your Text**   If you need to move text *before* committing your changes, place the mouse cursor outside the text area—the cursor changes to the Move tool. There are four ways to commit changes to a type layer:
>
> - Click the checkmark on the Options bar.
> - Press the Enter key on the numeric keypad.
> - Press Ctrl(⌘)+Enter (Return).
> - Click to select any tool on the toolbox.

5. From the main menu, choose Image, Liquify. You are immediately greeted with Photoshop's alert stating that the type layer needs to be rasterized first and that the text will no longer be editable. Click OK.

   We could have rasterized the Type layer first and by-passed the alert, but step 5 showed you that a Type layer is limited in the kind of edits that can be applied.

   It's time to give your text that groovy, '70s free-flowing style.

6. Choose the Bloat tool (the fifth tool from the top at the upper-left corner) and in the Tool Options field, set the Brush Pressure to 50. Now, position the top of the cursor over the top of the letter R and press either the left bracket ([) or the right bracket (]) to size the cursor so that the cursor is about ½ the height of the letter.

7. Center your cursor over the top half of the letter (the R), click and hold down the mouse button for about seven seconds, while very slightly pushing the expansion of the letter upward. Repeat this technique for the bottom half of the letter, and push the expansion downward; then bloat the letter T and the ! (see Figure 22.10).

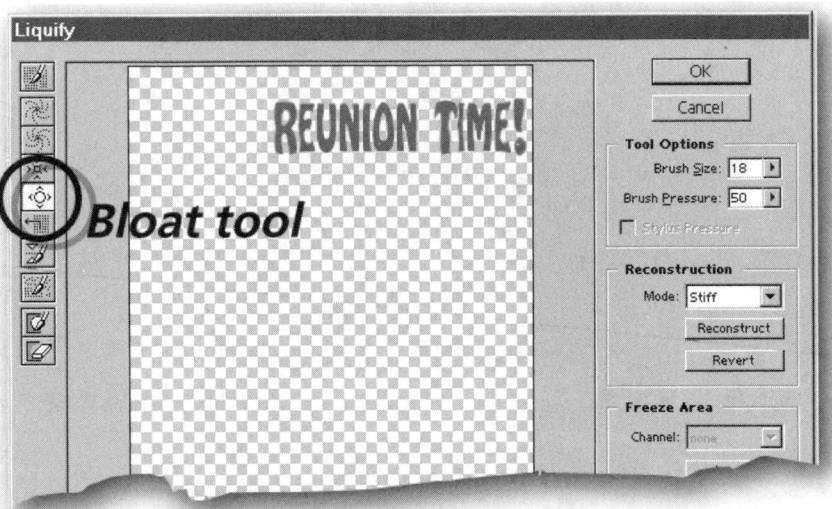

**Figure 22.10**    Bloat the top half and the bottom half of the characters R, T, and ! to create free-flowing shapes.

8. Choose the Pucker tool (the tool immediately above the Bloat tool). Randomly, and for only about two seconds, apply the tool to most of the other letters.

   The objective of step 8 is to create curves in the otherwise straight lines that make up the characters.

9. Choose the Bloat tool again, but increase the size of the brush (use the ] key) so that the brush is slightly larger than the tallest letter. Click and hold for only about two seconds on two or three different areas of the text. When your text looks sufficiently groovy (or wavy), click OK (see Figure 22.11).

   Outlining text was a common design technique to help attract attention, and whereas it may have taken the artist hours to create, you will apply an outline in just three steps.

10. On the Layers palette, Ctrl(⌘)+click on the REUNION TIME! layer title to load the layer contents as a selection.

11. Click on the Foreground color swatch on the toolbox to display the Color Picker. Type **FF1873** in the # box for a fluorescent-looking pink ( I believe

"dayglo" was the term when I was younger). Click OK. From the main menu, choose Edit, Stroke. Type **8** for the Width, and **Outside** for the Location (see Figure 22.12). Click OK.

**Figure 22.11**  This zoomed-in view shows that the Bloat and Pucker tools in the Liquify command are ideal for creating some far-out–looking text.

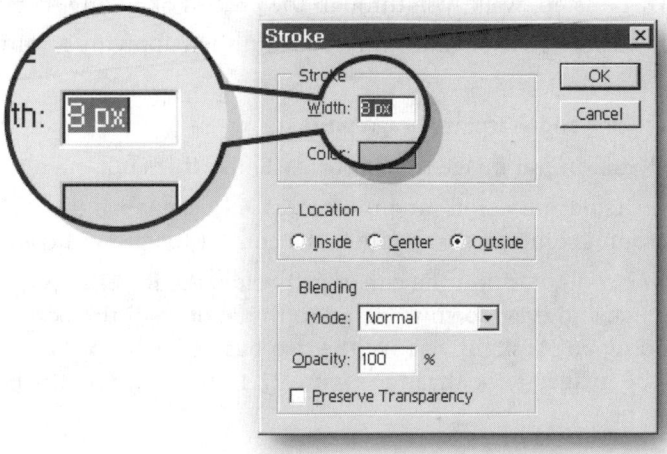

**Figure 22.12**  Stroke an outline of the text with a pinkish-red color.

**12.** Press Ctrl(⌘)+D to deselect. From the main menu, choose File, Save As, and save the image to your hard disk. Leave the image open and crank up your Led Zeppelin 8-track.

Hey, you just created some far-out text, man!

One line of text is, well, just one line. What if you have a paragraph's worth of text? Controls specific to paragraphs are some new toys Adobe has developed and included in this upgrade.

If you work with text in an illustration or desktop publishing program, you are already familiar with terms like *hyphenation, Roman hanging justification,* and *first line indentation.* If you are not familiar with those terms, you *will* be by the time you finish this chapter! You'll also understand why we used to put vinyl flowers on the back of our VW.

One more toy included in this version of Photoshop is the feature to warp text. The Warp command enables you to distort text into a variety of shapes and gives you control over the orientation and perspective of the warp effect. The best part of this feature is that you can return to the warp text layer at any time and either choose a different warp or remove the warp entirely. You can keep on editing the warp effect until you render the warp text layer, at which point the editable text becomes plain pixels.

Oddly, the next set of steps walks you through the process of adding several lines of text, using some of the new paragraph controls, and then applying a warp effect.

### Example 22.2    Adding and Warping Paragraph Text

**1.** Open the Reunion.psd image from your hard disk if it's not open already.

**2.** Press D for the default colors, and then press X to exchange the foreground and background colors so that white is the current foreground color.

**3.** Press T (Type tool). Position the cursor just below the R in REUNION  TIME!, and then click and drag downward and to the right until the bottom of the type bounding box is slightly above the two businessmen in the lower-right corner of the image. (Peek ahead to Figure 22.13 to see where the bounding box should be.)

**Figure 22.13**   Use a type bounding box when you're inserting more than one line of text.

**Note**

**More Power Over Your Text**   The type bounding box is another new feature to Photoshop. Until you render the text, the box is always available and enables you to resize, reshape, and reposition the group of text by dragging on the anchors. To access a previously created bounding box, double-click the type layer's thumbnail, located on the Layer's palette.

4. On the Character palette (click the Palettes button on the Options bar if the Character palette is not visible), choose Arial Rounded MT Bold (or a similar thick, rounded font). Enter **20** for the font size and **–25** for the *tracking* (the space between two or more characters). Type the following with a hard return (Windows: press Enter; Macintosh: press Return) after each sentence (see Figure 22.14). If you like, you can open Reunion.txt from the Examples/Chap22 folder in a text editor, copy it to the Clipboard and then paste it to the Type tool (you can do this sort of stuff!):

Remember the days when hip-
hugging bell-bottoms were cool?
Now that they are back in style,
are you saying, "Been there,
done that."?

Well, come to the 27th Wakefield
High School Reunion and tell us
what you've been doing!

Can you say, "Haircut?"

**Note**

**That Makes Sense**   Chances are that you will not get through your career without working with a copywriter. Nor will you survive without hearing the term "breaks," as in "This line is breaking well." Notice that the areas where we've told you to break lines makes "reading sense." For example, "Been there," is broken before the next line, "done that." Readers will mentally insert a pause at the end of each line, so always try to break a thought within a paragraph so that it reads well.

And if you are not using Arial Rounded, bold, chances are that your lines will not break as we've outlined them for you here. When this happens, tighten the tracking on the font to gain paragraph width, or manually condense the font by about 5% (readers will not notice this trick).

You might have noticed that we did not superscript the "th" in 27th (as today's word processing programs are programmed to do automatically). The main reason we did not superscript that text is that the superscript format was rarely used in the '70s. The other reason is that the warp effect used in step 10 will make that text extremely difficult to read.

**5.** Press the Enter key on the numeric keypad to commit your text to the type layer.

As mentioned earlier, you might not be using Arial Rounded, Bold, and therefore not getting the line breaks that you want. Smooshing the font is only one solution. You might have one line that contains only a closing (right) quotation mark and a question mark. This is not good! This is a situation in which having paragraph control is truly valuable! If your text is breaking uncomfortably:

**6.** On the Layers palette, double-click the layer thumbnail of this text layer. The bounding box reappears and all the text is highlighted.

**7.** Show the Paragraph palette. Click the Justify last left button at the top center of the palette and enter **22** for Add space after paragraph. Twenty-point type, with 22-point paragraph spacing provides a good, clean read—and you need legibility to the point of being heavy-handed. Why? Because you'll warp this text shortly and other spacings and ornamental fonts would turn too gook.

**Note**

**Use Justify Last Left to Avoid Extra Spacing in Last Line**   Although Add space after paragraph is self-explanatory, Justify last left might need clarification: Every line of text in the paragraph is adjusted to extend from the left to the right borders of the bounding box, except the last line. Otherwise, the space between the letters on the last line could be so w i d e that the words might be very difficult to read.

**Figure 22.14** Just a couple of adjustments in the Paragraph palette organize the text into a more readable design.

8. On the Paragraph palette, click the flyout menu icon (black triangle at the upper-right corner) and choose Roman Hanging Punctuation.

If your text had a punctuation mark at the beginning or end of a line, that mark is now outside the bounding box and all the letters line up vertically along the left and right edges of the box. Whether to use this feature is generally a designer's call—there are no hard-set rules stating when and when not to use hanging punctuation, but it *will* show a prospective employer that you know how to use this typographic element. By the way, as a common example, bulleted lists are supposed to have hanging indents.

9. Press the Enter key on the numeric keypad to commit the changes to the type layer.

10. From the main menu, choose Layer, Type, Warp Text. Click on the Style flyout menu and choose Wave. With Horizontal selected, enter **12** for Bend, **4** for Horizontal Distortion, and **5** for Vertical Distortion (see Figure 22.15). Click OK and wait—this command requires a lot of time!

11. Press Ctrl(⌘)+S to save your edits. Leave the image open and flip on your favorite AM rock radio station.

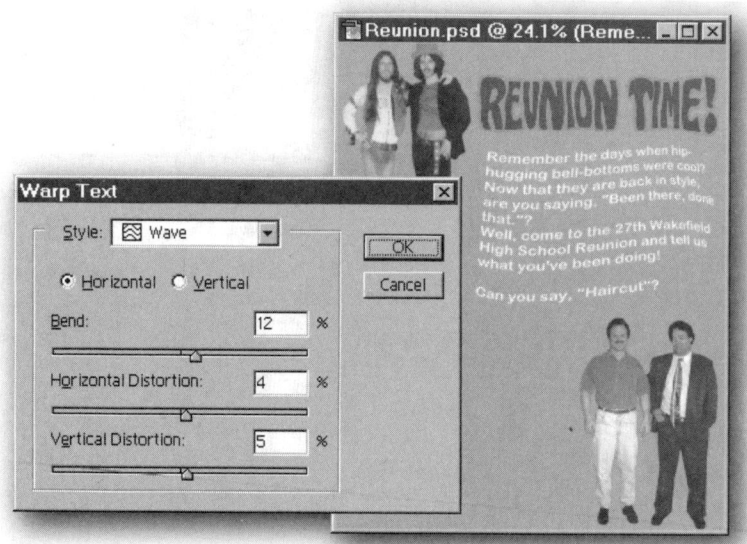

**Figure 22.15**   Add a Wave Warp with the settings shown in this figure.

So far, you've added one line of text and applied the Liquify command. Then, you added several lines of text using the type bounding box.

Let's finish this image by adding the important information—you know, stuff like where and when the reunion is held!

### Example 22.3   Using Paragraph and Character Controls

1. Open the Reunion.psd image from your hard disk if it's not open already.
2. Press T, and click and drag a bounding box that encompasses most of the blank area in the lower-left quadrant of the image. Hold down Ctrl(⌘)+ spacebar to toggle to the Zoom tool, and click over the box enough times to make the height of the box slightly less than the height of the Photoshop workspace.
3. On the Character palette, set the Leading to Auto and the Color to white. Then, on the Paragraph palette, set the Add space after paragraph (lower-right area of the palette) to 0.
4. Use the same font as in the previous set of steps (Arial Rounded, for example), and at 16 point size, type the following:

   **Information:**

   **Place:**

   **Wakefield High School**

**Arlington, Virginia**

**Date:**

**May 29, 2001**

**Time:**

**Noon–Midnight**

**Contact:**

**Vicki Barber**

**703.555.1234**

The upper portion of the image is in the hip '70s style. But because the two men in the lower half of the image look a tad conservative, let's reflect this style in the treatment of the text down here.

**5.** Drag your cursor over the top line of text to select the word Information.

**6.** On the Character palette, change the Size to **20** points and horizontally scale (immediately above the color swatch) the text to 200%. Then, click on the flyout menu and choose Small Caps (see Figure 22.16).

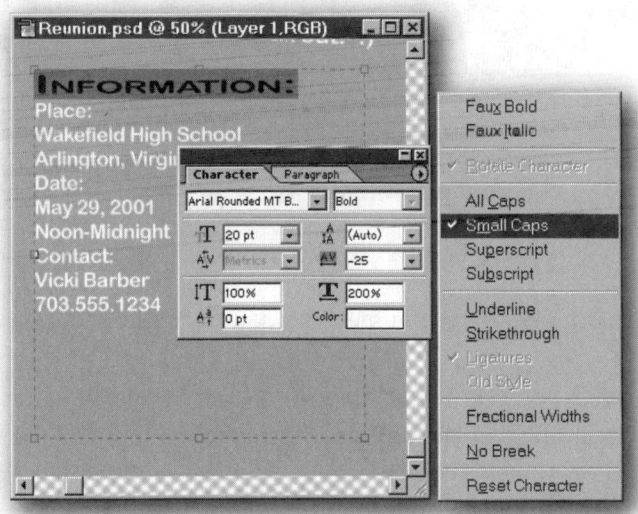

**Figure 22.16** Use the Character palette to give the word "Information" prominence within this group of text.

**7.** Press the right-arrow key once to deselect the word Information:, and place the cursor at the right end of the line. Show the Paragraph palette and enter **12** for the Add space after paragraph. All the text below the cursor has moved down by 12 points.

**8.** Show the Character palette. Select the word Place: and choose Small Caps from the flyout menu on the Character palette. Repeat this procedure for the words Date:, Time:, and Contact:.

These four words are similar to subheads and should be different than the text immediately below.

**9.** Click to insert the cursor after the word Virginia. On the Paragraph palette, enter **10** for Add space after paragraph. Repeat this spacing procedure after the lines that contain: May 29, 2001 and Noon–Midnight (see Figure 22.17).

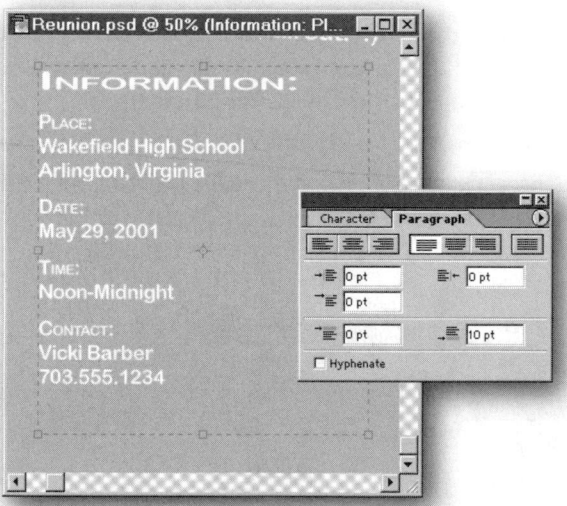

**Figure 22.17**    Add 10 points of space after each of the sections shown in this figure.

**10.** Press the Enter key on the numeric keypad to commit your changes to the text layer.

**11.** Press Ctrl(⌘)+0 (zero) to move the view of your image to fit the screen.

Even with all the text you created, the image still looks a little bare. Let's add a photo of the school, but create the effect as if the photo had been screened onto the paper (remember, the intended output of this assignment is hard copy).

**12.** Open the WakefieldHighSchool.psd image from the Examples/Chap22 folder on the Companion CD.

**13.** On the Layers palette, click and drag the layer into the Reunion image. Now, drag that new layer, Layer 1 (containing the school photo), to just above the Layer 0 that contains the image's background (green) color.

Next you create the effect as though the photo had been screened onto the green "paper."

**14.** Press Ctrl(⌘)+U (Hue/Saturation) and drag the Saturation slider all the way to the left. Click OK. From the main menu, choose Image, Adjust, Posterize. Enter **3** and click OK. On the Layers palette, change the mode to Multiply and the Opacity to 40% (see Figure 22.18).

**Figure 22.18**    After reducing the saturation and applying the Posterize command, change the layer mode to Multiply and adjust the Opacity to 40% to simulate a screened-on look to the photo of the school.

One last and important touch—improving the composition.

**15.** Press V (Move tool) and uncheck Auto Select Layer on the Options bar. (Auto Select Layer is a wonderful feature, but not when you're working with small elements like the text in this image.) On the Layers palette, click on the Information: layer to make it active for editing and then, in the image, move the layer so that the text is near the lower-left corner of the image.

**16.** Click on Layer 1 (containing the photo of the school) on the Layers palette, and drag in the image to place the lower-left corner of the driveway behind the word Information. Then, click on the layer titled 99 in the Layers palette and drag in the image to move the older, short-haired guys to the left, centering them between the right edge of the image and the text at the left, as shown in Figure 22.19. Press Ctrl(⌘)+S to save your changes, and go get a Slurpee at the 7-Eleven.

**Figure 22.19**    The completed reunion flyer.

You've successfully manipulated text in a free-flowing, '70s style as well as in a more conservation design. Photoshop makes entering text as easy as possible and leaves the hard part—creating good design—to you.

## Summary

We've taken a quick tour of typefaces and of basic design using type, and put some of that knowledge to practical use designing the reunion image.

Just as you use imaging to communicate ideas to your viewers, text is certainly another obvious way to communicate. You would do well to perfect your skills in effectively using type. And that means practice, observe, study, and read books on the topic. Besides, when you create a wonderful image that also needs text, you surely want to strengthen your image by using that text in a professional way.

In the next chapter we begin our adventure into Photoshop's companion, Image-Ready, and how to optimize images for the Web. And you know, only five years ago, the word *Internet* brought puzzled looks to most people's faces. Now you can hear retired folks in the grocery store talking about their grandchildren's Web sites!

## Resources

http://www.fontsite.com

Sean Cavanaugh, co-designer of this Web site, is the author of *Digital Type Design Guide*—this author's favorite book on type. On Sean's Web site you'll find lots of very useful information, fonts at 100% off the regular price, a bookstore, and links to some of the best type-oriented sites.

http://www.angelwerks.com/channelzero/format.htm

Channel Zero offers free, very distinctive, high-quality fonts online.

Another good book you should buy on the new age of electronic typesetting is *The Computer Is Not a Keyboard*, a thin (about $10) feature-packed book that gets you thinking about using text and typefaces instead of the left-justified, carriage return typewriter. It was written by Robin Williams (no, *she* is *not* the comedian), by Peachpit Press.

# Part IV

# Introducing ImageReady: Moving to the Web

# Chapter 23

# Optimizing Images for the Web

Although the beginning of the ImageReady chapters starts right here, there is massive overlapping of features between Photoshop and ImageReady.

It's possible, given the trend toward more Web features in Photoshop, that by the time version 7 is released there will be only Photoshop—and no ImageReady.

## Optimizing Means Making Smaller, Right? Not Entirely

When we think of the word *optimize,* we often envision the best possible outcome of something, regardless of any downside effects. For example, a guy might spend four hours searching for the right shirt to wear on a date, and although he looks good at her door, he's also an hour late.

Optimizing images follows the same pattern. You need to optimize images for the Web because the smaller the picture, the faster it will travel across the Web. And by *optimize,* we mean generally *losing* some original image information to meet the download speed requirements for the file. The loss of original image information is the downside to optimizing. The real trick to optimizing is to know *which parts of an image can be discarded without anyone being the wiser,* and which ImageReady tricks you can use to further disguise the reality that this tiny gem onscreen is a pale imitation of your original masterpiece.

This chapter will take you through some standard (and many exotic) ways of preserving a copy of your work at the smallest file size possible. We think the word *gems* is particularly appropriate for optimized images, because they are small *and* beautiful. In particular, you learn a great deal about two forms of compression: lossy and lossless.

## Saving Images for the Web

If Figure 23.1 looks overwhelming, not to worry. This is the Photoshop screen you see when you choose File, Save For Web.

This is actually an all-in-one dialog box for image format, compression, dithering options, presets, resizing, border color, and more (if that's possible). We are going to go through the process of optimizing an image in ImageReady so you can

- Deal more wisely with this Photoshop dialog box, or
- Not deal with Photoshop at all when an image needs to be optimized.

We like the clean, well-organized look of ImageReady, and before this chapter is through, so will you.

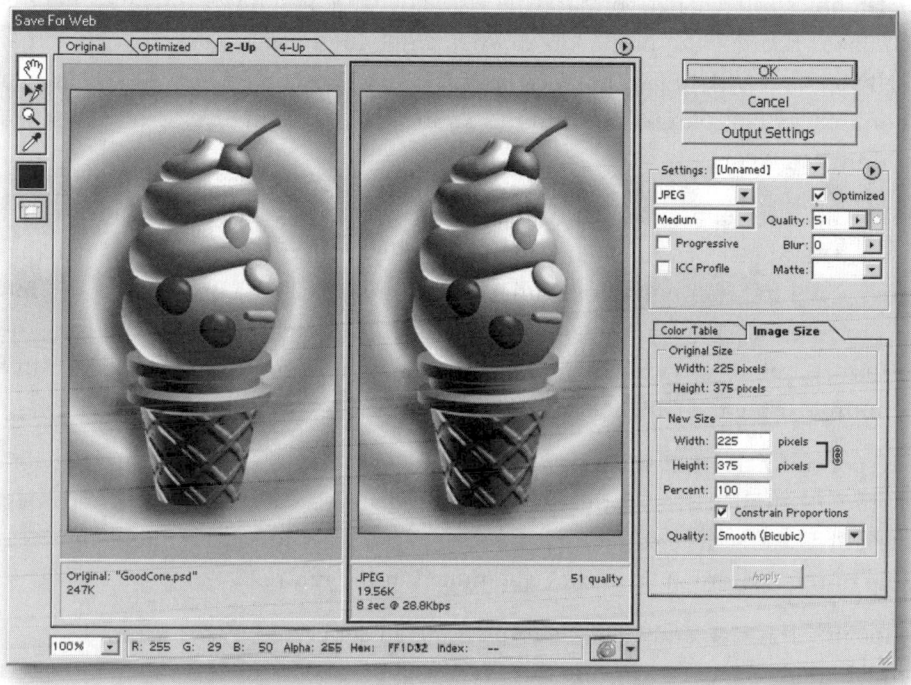

**Figure 23.1** Welcome to the Photoshop Web Center—kitchen sink, five AA cells, and bells and whistles included <g>!

## Introducing the Image File Formats for the Web

Three file formats—GIF, JPEG, and PNG—are supported by browsers today. However, Jim Clark, the former CEO of Netscape, didn't just pull these file formats out of his hat. We don't even *know* whether Jim wears a hat!

The JPEG file format was created by the Joint Photographers Experts Group, hence the acronym. And it took quite a while to perfect and even longer for Web browsers to accept this file format. JPEG works its magic by discarding tones in an image. The human eye is relatively insensitive to tonal differences in the higher ranges (brightest areas), and most family pictures and outdoor pictures have a lot of tones in the mid-to high-brightness ranges. JPEG does not touch the colors in an image because the human eye is more sensitive to color changes than to tone (brightness) changes.

It takes a while for the computing community to adopt and embrace anything new, especially file formats. Quite frankly, even as recently as a decade ago, the JPEG file format had not been widely accepted.

The Graphics Interchange Format (GIF) was widely used on BBSes (private and public bulletin boards—the precursors to Web sites). GIF images were tiny gems that usually broke copyright laws but looked terrific on a Mac or a PC because GIF images are limited to 256 colors or less and the color capability of many video subsystems was only 256 colors.

Today, GIF is an option for file formats when you save an optimized image, but UniSys, the holder of the patent on the GIF file format, has been rumbling that there's going to be an outrageous surcharge on images created by using its GIF format processes (*algorithms*). We've been mindful of the potential liability of using the GIF format, but we also suspect things will iron out in the future and we'll all be able to continue using the GIF file format.

In response to the GIF surcharge issue, along came PNG, the Portable Network Graphics file format. This format was designed to eventually replace GIF. The best part of PNG is that its creators *gave* the code to the graphics community—the ownership of the file format cannot be questioned in the future.

Although GIF, JPEG, and PNG file formats are all supported by browsers, it's up to your ISP to implement them. You can't very well prepare a site using all PNG images if your ISP's servers don't support this file format. We'll spend a good deal of time working with the GIF and the JPEG formats in this chapter, but we also cover the PNG format later in this chapter.

## Comparing JPEG to GIF

File formats are sort of like frames you'd buy to surround a physical painting. There's the right frame, and there's the wrong, inharmonious frame for a given picture. Just as no two pictures are alike, GIF and JPEG compression both have strong points that we'll discuss so you can save time choosing a compression option in the future.

And the best way to help the discussion is through a visual aid. So fire up ImageReady, and you'll play with an image on CD that shows off strong and weak points to file formats.

### Example 23.1    Looking at Optimization: A First Study in Compression

1. In ImageReady, open the Monochrome.psd image from the Examples/Chap23 folder of the Companion CD. See Figure 23.2.

   The filename is not real catchy, but it describes the picture very well. All you see in this image are shades of gold—no blues, not a hint of moss green—nada.

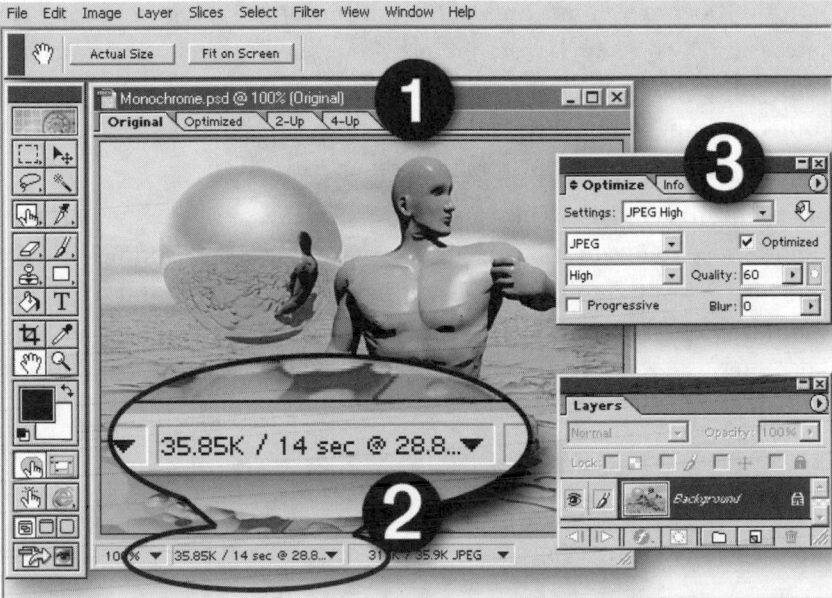

**Figure 23.2**    An image that has a certain characteristic, such as many shades of the same color, will determine which compression format to use to make the image Web-worthy.

2. Choose Optimized in Bytes size and transfer time, using a 28.8 modem, from the Document Sizes area at the bottom of the window.

3. Choose JPEG High compression from the Optimize palette's Settings pop-up.

As you can see in Figure 23.2, the picture looks wonderful, and it takes a *quarter of a minute* to download this image. Surely we can do better than 14 seconds to download—that's what this chapter is all about. We need to compare image formats, how much data can afford to be lost, and also compare the compressed image's visual content to that of the original.

Instinctively, when you see an image that appears photorealistic in content, you choose JPEG for compression. Why? Because JPEG's color capability is 16.7 million colors, whereas GIF's is limited to 256 colors.

Now, you should train your eye on the following three places when you're performing optimization on images:

- **On the image itself.** It helps to go to the 2-Up view, where you can see the original image on the left and the proposed optimized image on the right.

- **On the Document Sizes area at the bottom of the image window.** This area can tell you how fast an optimized image will travel using different modem speeds, it can tell you the original size versus the optimized size, and other relevant stuff. When you have an image open, click the Document Size area and choose a reading from the pop-up lists.

- **The Optimize palette.** This palette is to ImageReady as the Options bar is to Photoshop. You want it onscreen most of the time. The Optimize palette provides a wealth of necessary features, presets, and total control over the optimization of the image. In Figure 23.3, you can see two lists popped up, and a few callouts to areas on the Optimize palette we'll cover in this chapter.

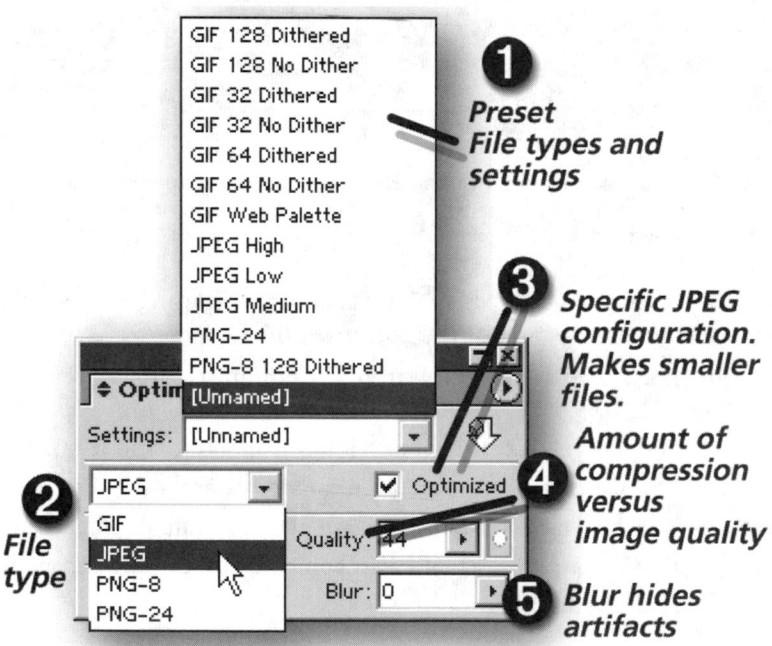

**Figure 23.3**   The Optimize palette is your key to making beautiful images as small as possible.

## Recognizing Optimize Palette Elements Common to JPEG and GIF

Let's take a look at some of the elements on this palette that are common to both JPEG and GIF file formats (the options change as you change the Optimize file format). The numbers in the following list refer to the callouts in Figure 23.3.

- **Preset File Types and Settings (#1).** As you can see in Figure 23.3, Adobe has provided you with a number of preset options. These options are meant as a base setting that you customize as you watch your image change in the preview window within the image window.

- **File Type (#2).** You can choose any file format from the Settings pop-up, but if you decide later to do a little compression comparative shopping, here's a drop-down that makes it quick and easy to change formats (and subsequently change the display of certain options on the palette).

- **Optimized is a JPEG-specific option (#3).** Checking Optimized creates smaller files (by a nominal amount, usually), but makes the file less than universally compatible with browsers and older imaging applications.

  For example, one of the authors uses Paint Shop Pro version 2 (PSP2) for quick looks at files. PSP2 was designed in 1993 and doesn't recognize optimized JPEG files. The point: Know your audience. Many underfunded institutions don't have the hardware to support newer operating systems and browsers. If you're catering to these institutions (and this sometimes means branches of the government), don't check the Optimized box.

- **Another JPEG-specific option is Quality (#4).** The Settings pop-up list contains three presets—JPEG High, JPEG Medium, and JPEG Low—but you will want finer control over the compression, so in the Quality field, type any value that makes the image look good in the Optimized pane of the window.

- **Blur does exactly what you think it does (#5).** Why would you want to use Blur? Because at high compression levels, JPEG images take on *screen trash,* more eloquently called *artifacts* by programmers. Whatever you choose to call it, highly compressed JPEG images display an ugly brand of noise at object edges, and blurring the image takes away some of the artifacts. Blurring also *blurs the image,* so be a good artistic judge, and use blurring only when an image could not look any *worse.*

## Comparing Lossy and Lossless Compressions

We need to digress for a moment and talk about two compression types: lossy and lossless. Why? Because compression types determine whether original image data is lost, or some other means of compressing with original image fidelity should be used.

### Lossy Compression

The practice of lossy compression might be compared to a carny magician who stuffs an elephant into a glass of water. Obviously, even the smallest of elephants (newborns weigh about 300 pounds) will not fit inside a Hess Traveler's coffee mug. But *part* of the elephant would—the trick (not to sound cruel) would be to decide which parts of the elephant have to be discarded.

Fortunately, we're not working with elephants here, so you can wear your good shoes in this section. We're working with pixels that create a weave that we see as an image. Lossy compression—in a nutshell—is the discarding of nonessential visual elements in a digital image to make the image a lot smaller in file size. Let's see what the *working* definition of lossy compression is.

These are the prime benefits of lossy compression:

- The compressed file opens up to the full picture size on-the-fly. No decompression utility, such as WinZip or StuffIt, is required.

- A JPEG file (with which lossy compression is usually associated) can contain 16.7 million colors because the compression routine does not affect color, it affects tones.

- A JPEG file, when it's created using the High Quality setting, *usually cannot be distinguished from the original*—and still gives you from 5–10 times compression over the original. Yup, a 1MB file can easily become a 100K file and look darned close to the original.

So, why don't we use JPEG images all the time? Because the structure of JPEG compression allows it to discard tones that the committee that designed the JPEG standard felt would go unnoticed. And as we know, there's a big difference between what *you* allow to go unnoticed, as an artist, and what the public allows to go unnoticed. JPEG is sort of a game. If you get lucky by using a picture that JPEG compression *likes*, then you've got a wonderful compressed image. On the other hand, if the JPEG algorithms don't understand all the image content, you wind up with an unacceptable image.

In Photoshop, the only file format that offers lossy compression is JPEG. JPEG is also an option when you're saving TIFF images—in this case, some of the original visual information is discarded when the file is saved, exactly as though you'd saved to JPEG format.

Besides loss of original image information, JPEG has another weakness: It cannot handle sudden changes in visual content in an image, such as you'd see, for example, in a photograph of someone tossing confetti at the camera lens. This sort of image is called a *high-frequency image* because there is a lot of change in values between pixel and neighboring pixel. You will notice *artifacts* (noise; pixels that aren't where they belong) if you use moderate compression on high-frequency images.

To summarize: JPEG is a good format for capturing lots of colors without having to do any dithering. It also can slightly blur the image at higher compression settings, and is usually inappropriate for images in which many different colors are randomly distributed around the image.

### Lossless Compression

Two kinds of images can be said to have *lossless compression*:

- A GIF or other type of indexed color image in which you remove pixel colors before you save the image. The image, therefore, looks the same every time you open it, but usually is not the same as the original.

- An image that uses a lossless algorithm (recipe), such as the Lempel-Zev Walsh (LZW) technique. This formula examines the entire image for redundant strings of code, and then shorthands the code. For example, which is quicker: to say the number "one," and then say "zero" one hundred times, or to say "one followed by one hundred zeros" (don't try this as an experiment unless you are totally bored with life). Photoshop offers you the option of compressing TIF images by using LZW compression, and these images open on-the-fly just as JPEG images do. We usually don't think of a file that's been through WinZip or StuffIt as a losslessly compressed file, but technically, it's been compressed with no loss of original data. Images of this type simply need a third-party program to decompress, and if you have a lot of images, it's less of a pain to use compression that expands on its own.

Now, when referring to Web images, we generally skip the LZW-type compression because it's not offered for GIF and PNG format images. We'll cover PNG files later in this chapter. GIF images are almost always a product of presaving color reduction, and will display the same way every time you open them (after some color values are knocked out of them). GIF's strength is that, unlike JPEG, is has no problem displaying high-frequency images. There are no artifacts around areas of sudden value change in a GIF image. GIF's weaknesses are that the GIF file format can only hold 256 unique colors, and you usually have to use dithering on the image to prevent *banding* (a hard edge in the image between colors that the GIF format was unable to reconcile).

To summarize: The GIF format is best for images that have many colors belonging to the same hue (a golden sunset, for example, would be excellent for GIF compression), but GIF, due to its limited color palette, is usually unacceptable for scenes of carnivals, birthday balloons, and other color-rich scenes.

Now that you understand the plusses and minuses that accompany GIF and JPEG compression, let's really work with some images to leverage out the best quality against the smallest file size.

## Choosing Between JPEG and GIF

The following should not be taken as a study in superiority—no two images are the same, and therefore your choice of compression for Web images is going to be made case by case. But this will be an interesting set of steps to thoroughly check out and weigh the pros and cons of file format choice with respect to a single image.

### The Showdown: First Example

Let's begin: you are tossed the Monochrome image, and reflexively you open ImageReady. Here's how to do the comparison shopping.

### Example 23.2    Testing the Compression Waters

1. With the Monochrome.psd image from the Examples/Chap23 folder of the Companion CD open on your screen, double-click on the Hand tool to bring the image to 100% viewing resolution if necessary, or alternatively, press Ctrl(⌘)++ until the title bar of Monochrome.psd says 100%.

2. Press F10 to display the Optimize palette. Get comfortable with this shortcut—you use the Optimize palette almost all the time in ImageReady.

3. Click the 2-Up tab on the image window. Resize the image window, hold the spacebar, and drag inside either window to scroll to the naked bronze guy.

4. Click in the left pane to make it the active pane. On the Optimize palette, choose GIF 32 Dithered from the Settings pop-up, choose Adaptive from the Color resampling drop-down, and then drag the Dither slider to 100%.

5. Click in the right pane, and then choose JPEG High from the Settings list.

    As you can see in Figure 23.4, the GIF image looks almost as good as the JPEG, but it will travel across the Net one second faster than the JPEG image.

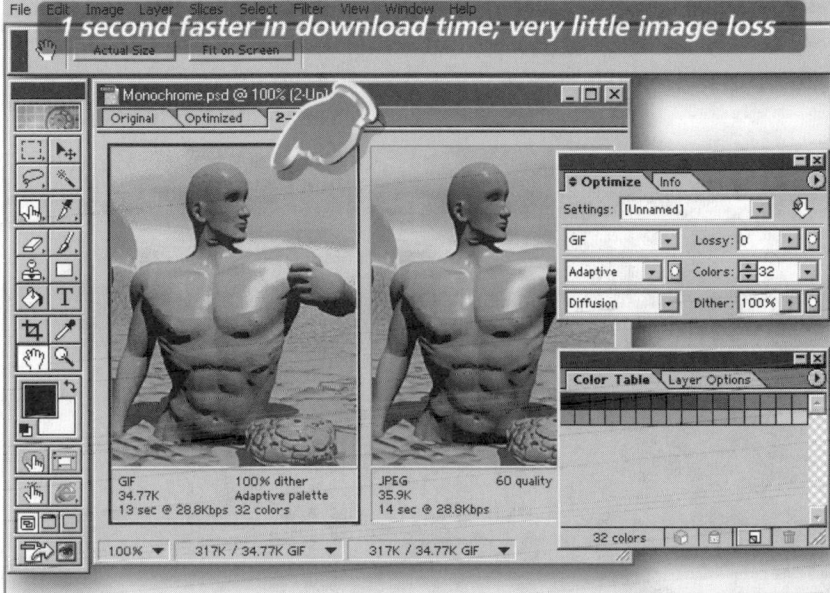

**Figure 23.4**   GIF compression works best when the image does not have lots of different colors.

Okay, one second doesn't sound like a lot, but what if you had 10 of these images to display on your site, hmmm?

The highest setting for JPEG compression doesn't really make this a fair fight. To exaggerate a little, let's see the foibles of making the JPEG image *reallllly* small.

6. Click in the left pane and choose Original from the Settings pop-up. Now click in the right pane and drag that Quality slider down to 14.

As you can see in Figure 23.5, we now have gross artifacts in the JPEG image—it looks like a lawn care truck backed over it a few times. The lesson here? Drag the quality setting for JPEG compression images down until the image looks gross, and then inch the quality back up again until the image looks acceptable. Adobe put a Quality slider on the Optimize palette for a reason!

7. Click back to the GIF settings on the Optimize palette. Choose File, Save Optimized As, and then save the image as a GIF image to your hard disk.

Macintosh users: A file extension is necessary for posting images on the Web. This is not a Microsoft thing. All Internet servers need to tell browsers what the MIME type of a file is. The convention used is a file extension, such as MyFile.gif for GIF format images and MyFile.jpg for JPEG format images.

8. You can close golden boy at any time now. Keep ImageReady open.

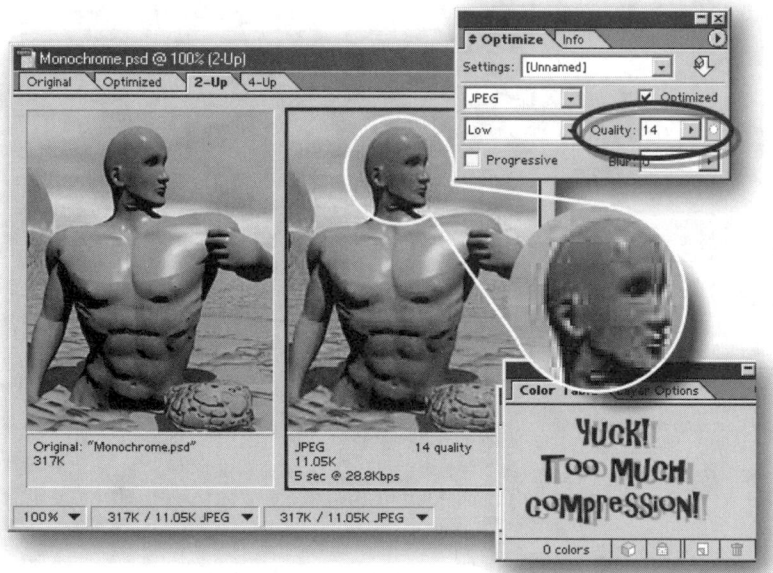

**Figure 23.5**   There is no reason to try to force a JPEG copy of the image that is smaller than its GIF counterpart when you lose image fidelity in the process.

It's JPEG's turn to shine now, so coming up next is an evaluation of a specially prepared image in both GIF and JPEG formats.

## The Showdown: Return of the JPEG

As mentioned earlier, JPEG really does nicely when an image has more than 256 colors. No dithering is produced in the compression process, but a little loss of focus is possible (and easily corrected).

Splatter.psd on the Companion CD was created using just about everything the author had to toss at it. Painter nozzles, paint tools from several paint and animation programs (including Photoshop, natch), and then we spilled some Italian dinner on it for good measure. This is one *colorful* image.

In the steps that follow, you will check out what GIF can do for this image, and then try JPEG compression on it. You sort of know the answer already to the compression choice, but play along here to experience the discovery for yourself.

### Example 23.3   Compression Doesn't Always Mean Color Reduction

1. Open the Splatter.psd image from the Examples/Chap23 folder on the Companion CD. Increase your viewing resolution to 100%.

2. Click the 2-Up tab on the image window, and then click in the left pane, choose GIF 32 Dithered from the Settings pop-up, choose Dither 100% on the Optimize palette, and choose Adaptive as the color reduction type.

3. Click in the right pane of the image window, and then choose JPEG High from the pop-up.

   As you can see in Figure 23.6, there is a significant difference in image quality (GIF is a royal loser here), and the JPEG image actually travels on a 28.8 connection a whopping (no kidding, this is a whopping figure on the Net) *three seconds* faster than the visually impoverished GIF version.

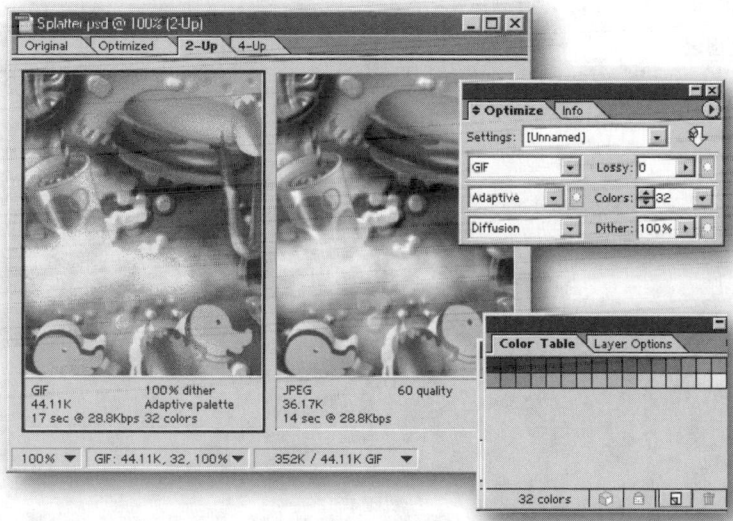

## Lots of colors and not that many tones

**Figure 23.6**   JPEG compression performs much better than GIF in situations where there are tons of colors in the image.

Now, we can add a couple touches to the proposed JPEG compression on a copy of the Splatter image—touches that will improve its looks and also speed up Web travel time even more. Ready?

4. You might as well click the Optimized tab of the image window so you can concentrate on the JPEG compression here. First, choose JPEG Medium from the Settings pop-up. Oops—we used a little too much compression and the visual content of the image is presently wrestling with artifacts and massive blurring. It's time to take control. Click the Quality slider and drag it up to about 44.

The image now looks nicer and will download at 10 seconds, using a 28.8 connection. Impressive, eh? We're not done yet.

**Note**

**Don't Pay Any Attention to the Preview Window in the Unsharp Mask Dialog Box** When you look at the Optimize pane in the image window and decide to sharpen the image, you are shown the *original* image and the proposed sharpening, *not* the Optimized image and the proposed sharpening. Therefore, sharpening an image that is displayed in the optimized window is trial and error—do *not* pay any attention to the preview window in the Unsharp Mask dialog box, and as a rule of thumb, sharpen the image by no more than 40 percent to bring out detail, and no more than 60 percent when an image is severely blurry. Higher values will force you to undo the operation and try again, because too much Unsharp Masking produces an image about as handsome as a photocopy.

5. Choose Filter, Sharpen, Unsharp Mask. Ignore the preview window (shown in Figure 23.7), and set the parameters in the box to **64%** Amount, **.9** pixels as the Radius (fractional amounts of a pixel are acceptable within certain Photoshop processes), and **1** level of Threshold.

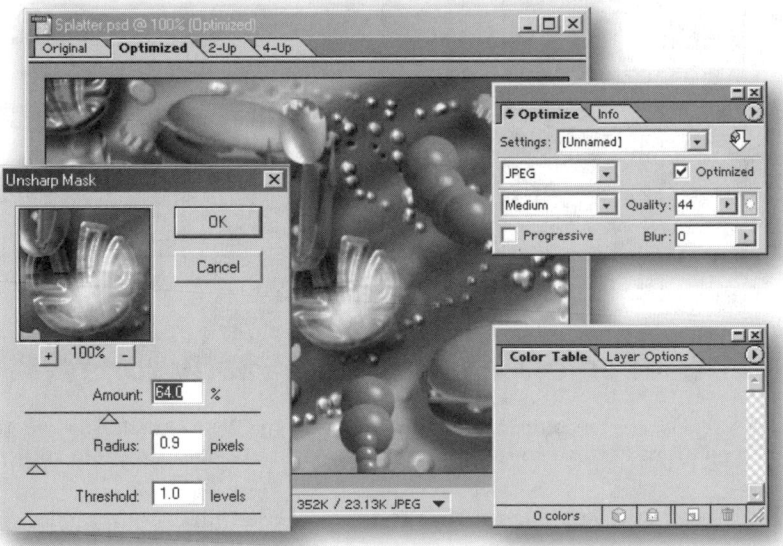

**Figure 23.7**    ImageReady has only one type of sharpening—Unsharp Mask—so learn how to use it effectively (and invisibly).

Although Adobe has documentation on the Unsharp Mask, review time would be good right here. The Amount of Unsharp Masking is the intensity of sharpening the edges in the image, from 1 to 500. So 40 is a pretty mild, yet pleasingly subtle, amount of sharpening. The Radius of the effect specifies the distance from a color edge pixel required for this area to be affected by the filter. The Radius set at .9 pixels tells Photoshop to go easy on the *neighbor sharpening*. Why? Because this is a small file. Use higher values for 25MB files and such. Finally, the Threshold setting determines the range of contrast required between edge pixel and neighboring pixel before the pixel's inclusion in the sharpening process (the addition of contrast). The lower the number here, the more pronounced effect, so our recommendation of 1 rounds out the other two parameters and usually produces sharpening that is almost undetectable by the viewer.

6. Choose File, Save Optimized As, and then save a copy of the image to JPEG file format. You can close the PSD image onscreen at any time. Keep ImageReady open.

**Note**

**Don't Save a JPEG That's Been Edited**   In case we missed explaining this elsewhere in the book, it's usually not a good idea to edit a JPEG image and then save it as a JPEG once more. Although most of the image quality has been knocked out of an image the first time you compress it using JPEG algorithms, we've experimented and learned that second and third savings of a JPEG file to the JPEG format cause further, minor, reduction in image quality.

Our recommendation (always) is to keep the original design in PSD, PDF, or TIFF format on your hard disk, and then optimize a copy to JPEG format. Then, if you discover a flaw in the JPEG image, you can go back to the original and perform compression again.

Examples are fine and fun (hopefully!), but we really need to cover some working definitions of options found on the Optimize palette when you're saving to GIF and JPEG. And the best way to do this is by presenting the options in list format.

Authors hate writing lists about as much as readers hate reading them. But they're an effective way to present information one cannot stick in a set of tutorial steps.

As long as we are giving you a thorough compression education, let's take apart what Adobe has to offer with both types of compression.

## Checking Out the GIF Optimize Palette Options

Take a gander at the left side of Figure 23.8 as we run through the callouts. These callouts are options we've not covered in the tutorials.

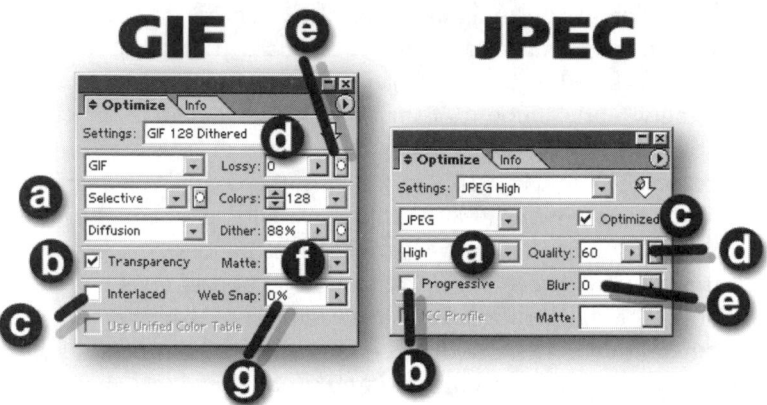

**Figure 23.8**    These are your options when you choose GIF or JPEG as the optimized file format.

### Color Reduction Options

Callout *a* on the GIF palette points to Color Reduction Options. GIF offers several types of *color reduction* (the removal of colors to make the file size smaller). Selective, Adaptive, Perceptual, and Web will suit 99% of your optimization work; the rest of the options in this drop-down are self-explanatory and not really used in mainstream Web work.

- *Selective* color reduction creates a palette for an image, giving preference to those areas of color in the image that are predominant. What? Alright—if you have a picture of a blue lake and a few pine trees, the Selective color process (creation of a color palette, or lookup table; also called *palletization*) will reserve many shades of blue in the color table for the lake, and fewer colors (shades of green and brown) for the pine trees. Additionally, any *Web-safe colors* in the original image tend to be preserved in the color-reduced file. See the following Note for an inspired description of Web-safe colors.

- *Adaptive* color reduction makes no attempt in the reduction process to move colors toward the Web-safe palette. Although that's bad news for visitors who can view only 256 colors onscreen, the Adaptive process dedicates more palette colors to closely match the colors in the original image. The Adaptive color palette is made up of many shades of the predominant colors in the original image. For example, a blue sky and green meadow image would have loads of green and blue colors in the palette, and few (if any) pinks, oranges, or purples.

**Note**

**What Are Web-Safe Colors?**    The phrase *Web-safe color* comes from Netscape's invention of a palette of 216 colors (plus one neutral background color) that caused no dithering when viewed by browsers on a computer that could display only 256 colors. *Dither* is a term we'll cover in a moment—it means to create color pixel arrangements that, when viewed from a distance, simulate a color that is not in a palette. By using the Web-safe palette in your work, you are assured that visitors to your site who have a video card with 512K or less on-board (hey, think of charities and older computers donated to schools) will see pure colors instead of ugly dithering. The spectrum of the Web-safe palette is *uniform*—it holds as many color variations of green as of blue, and of other colors.

Photoshop and ImageReady offer Web palettes with which you can paint, and also the facility to reduce colors to the nearest match in the Web palette. It's not called the Netscape color palette anymore because Microsoft adopted it for the Explorer browser, and Adobe has also made the Web-safe palette fit within the color capability of Windows and the Macintosh's system palette—both of which have a maximum of 256 colors.

- *Perceptual* color reduction can create very attractive, limited-color images, because it gives preference to those colors to which the human eye is most sensitive. For example, our eyes can discern many more shades of green than of gold. A Perceptual color reduction routine would reserve space for lots of greens if the original image featured green. Typically, a Perceptual color palette is smaller than the other types of palette processes.

Now that you know what each type of color reduction does, you can be a better judge of which to use, given the specific image you want to post on the Web. Also check to see what each type of color reduction does to the traveling size of the image (at 28.8, usually).

Books intrinsically give you the opportunity to skip ahead and to go back. So, we're going to use this wonderful feature to show you different types of dithering. Then you need to return to Figure 23.8, where the rest of the Optimize palette's options still need to be uncovered.

## Dithering Options

If you open the FlyingEgg.psd image from the Examples/Chap23 folder of the Companion CD, you can play along in this (over)dramatization of different dithering types. We say over-dramatization because to easily see what each dithering type does, we will reduce the color of the FlyingEgg image to three colors, and no one is obtuse enough to reduce an image down to three colors except Gary Bouton's college roommate.

To recap: Dithering is a method of concealing the reality that lots of colors were removed during the optimization process. As an example, suppose you were given a piece of white paper and a black crayon and had the patience to draw a checker-board made up of only black and white squares. Then suppose that, after you'd finished, some insensitive clod asked you to represent 50% black—in other words, gray. Now, you might not have a gray crayon, but you *could* move the drawing far enough away from the clod so that the black and white areas optically meld, with gray the result, at least for appearance's sake.

The same "present it far away from them" technique is used in color reduction, and it's called *dithering*. Suppose you needed to reduce a picture of flowers down to 256 colors, you use the Adaptive technique, and all the flowers are red except for one pink one. Adaptive color reduction will give you lots of shades of green and lots of shades of red, but probably won't offer you one lousy true pink pixel in the new color palette. Instead, it comes up with the closest match—red—unless you use a dithering technique. If you use any of the dithering processes covered here, that pink flower will probably be displayed as red and white pixels in a small area, and the audience's eye will merge the colors into pink. In Figure 23.9, you can see the flying egg image as the original (okay, the original's in color), and then as a three-color, color-reduced image, but with no dithering. Notice that incredible banding is going on in the copy, which has nothing but three flat areas of color. See why we need dithering?

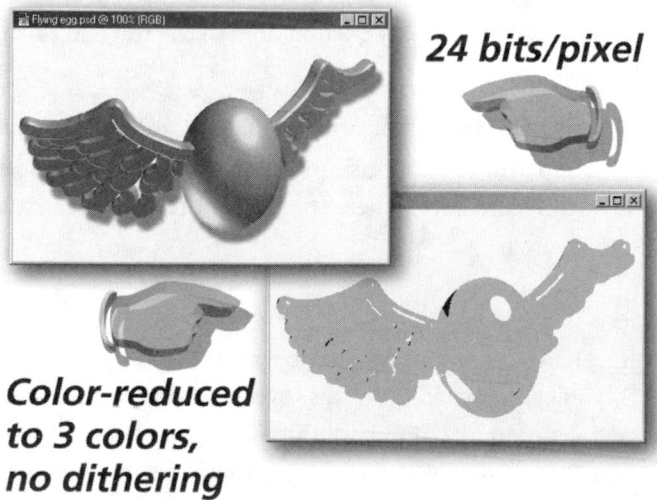

**Figure 23.9**   The choice to use no dithering is yours, but the image should be of an interface or something that does not have gradations in tones.

### Diffusion Dithering

In Figure 23.10, we're making progress. Diffusion dithering is the most common way to arrange color pixels to give the appearance of more colors than there really are. You will not see a pattern in diffusion dithering because the colors that together constitute a missing color are scattered in the image. The image has the look of one of those pebbled-glass shower doors. The authors feel that this is the best type of all-around dithering Photoshop provides.

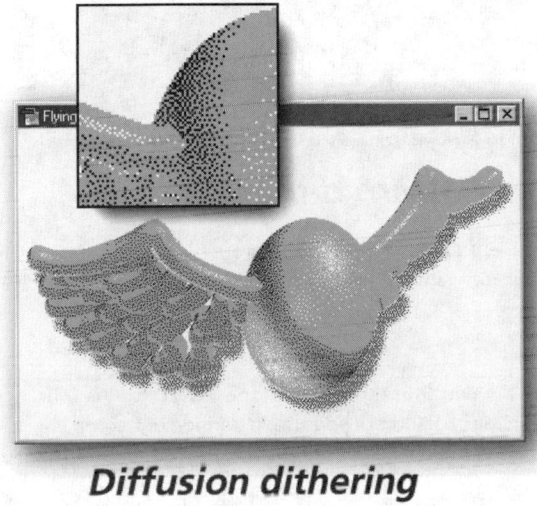

**Diffusion dithering**

**Figure 23.10**  Diffusion dithering is an eye-pleasing way to fake extra colors in a limited-color image.

### Pattern Dithering

In Figure 23.11 you can see an example of pattern dithering. This type of dithering is unacceptable for use with tiny images because the pattern overwhelms the visual content of the image. And you start having thoughts of wearing argyle socks and taking up knitting afghans. Seriously, you need a compelling reason for choosing pattern dithering, such as making the file a teensy bit smaller (this type of dithering has a minor impact on saved file size).

**Note**

**For Variety, Use DitherBox**  If you want to design with a limited palette of colors (like the Web palette), but want to break away from the distracting pattern dither type, check out Filter, Other, DitherBox. This utility enables you to determine the *weave* of a color fill, and use as many limited colors as you like to make up the palette. Using this filter, you can get inventive and actually make patterns that do *not* look like a Scotsman's kilt.

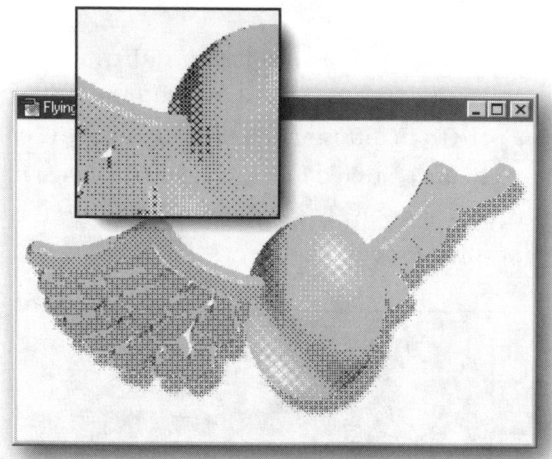

## Pattern dithering

**Figure 23.11**    Yuck! Blech! Phooey! What artist settled for pattern dithering? We've already said that diffusion is better!

**Tip**

**Consider File Size As You Make Up an Image Palette**   As long as we are discussing optimization, the fewer colors you use in an indexed color image, such as GIF, the smaller the palette in the header of the GIF file will be and the smaller the file will be.

So, if you want to create a GIF, and 128 colors is an option—but there are only 64 colors in the image—it would be wasteful and foolish to save the image with 128 colors defined.

### Noise Dithering

Finally, there's Noise dithering, which you see applied to the FlyingEgg image in Figure 23.12. Noise dithering was *not* created by Adobe for your run-of-the-mill images. Notice how lots of clumps of colors are deposited throughout the image? This dithering type is good for *sliced* images (covered later in this chapter). When you slice an image and then use different compression settings on the slices, there are bound to be telltale seams in the image, unless you apply the noise dithering disguise before you slice up the image. The noise takes the viewer's mind off the possibility that this might be a sliced image. Come to think of it, noise tends to take your mind off *everything,* doesn't it?

Congratulations! You are now an expert on the topic of dithering, and with this newfound knowledge you can butt into many more conversations at SIGGRAPH.

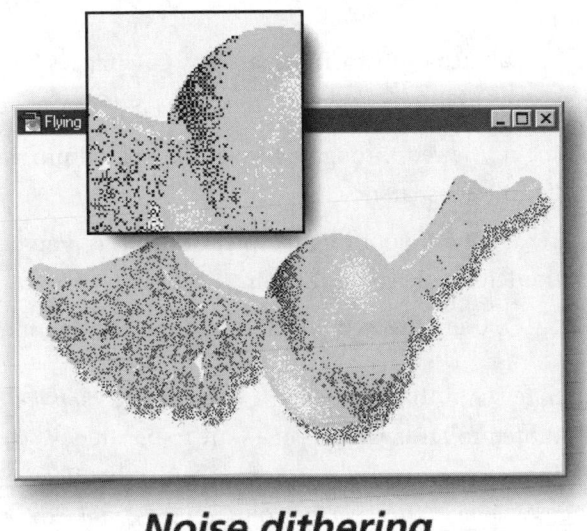

## Noise dithering

**Figure 23.12** Noise dithering is a special type of pixel rearrangement that not only helps simulate missing colors, but also helps mask the seams in a sliced image.

Now it's time to go back to the GIF and JPEG Optimize settings, so tear that page out of the book so you can refer to it, and keep on reading here. I'm *kidding*, okay? We've repeated the GIF part of Figure 23.13.

We left off at dithering types, so the next area to cover is the Transparency option.

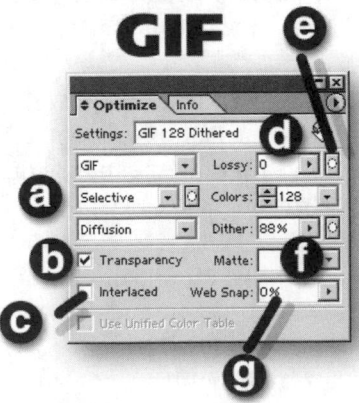

**Figure 23.13** Why, this looks very much like Figure 12.8! Let's check out the GIF options...

## Transparency and Thee

Callout *b* on the GIF palette points to Transparency. GIF images have a transparent property only if

- The image is being viewed through a browser or special program that knows how to handle GIF transparency.

- You left an area empty in your original picture. That is, you designed on an image layer and left a hole somewhere in the design.

- You have Show Options checked on the Optimize palette's menu.

It's important to understand that transparent GIFs have a *drop-out color*. That is, a color must be appointed to areas where you want transparency. The browser then reads the header of the image file and sees, for example, that deep blue is the transparency color. Then, wherever this specific color appears, you can see clear through that area to the background of the image.

Creating a transparent GIF is so simple it does not merit a full-fledged tutorial. All you have to do is follow these steps:

### Example 23.4    Making Part of a GIF Image Transparent in Browsers

1. Take any image you like, or use the HoleHead.psd image in the Examples/Chap23 folder of the Companion CD. What's important here is that the image is a layer. If you have an image you want to use, open it in ImageReady (press F7, Layers palette), double-click on the Background title on the Layers palette, and accept the default name. You now have a layer image.

2. Click the Add a mask icon at the bottom of the Layers palette, and then press D (Default colors). Choose the Paintbrush tool, and then from the Options bar, choose a hard-edge tip from the middle of the top row of the flyout Brush palette. Accuracy is not going to be stressed here; you're merely going to perform brain surgery.

3. In the Original pane of the image window, paint in the area of the guy's head where you can see bricks showing through. Then drag the Layer Mask icon into the Trash at the bottom of the Layers palette, click Yes in the query box, and you now have a guy with transparency sticking through his head.

4. On the Optimize palette, choose from the palettizing drop-down (callout *a*) and reduce the number of colors to make the image file small, but without too much dithering, as we've discussed. You should be watching the Optimized pane in the image window. Now, click on the Matte drop-down (callout *f* in Figure 23.13) and choose a color for the drop-out color.

5. Choose File, Save Optimized As, and save the image to your desktop in the GIF format. Then drag the image into Internet Explorer (or another browser that has survived Microsoft's initiative).

If you want to see the effect of a little HTML and a transparent GIF, drag the Clef.htm file into your browser from the Companion CD.

**Note**

**HTML or HTM?**    The proper extension to HTML documents is .html. So why is our gang here telling you to look on the CD for documents with an .htm extension? It's technology's fault—the hybrid CD cannot accept a four-letter extension and still be legible to both Macintosh and Windows users.

For the record, HTML files should have names such as mywebsite.html.

The importance to you of the Clef.htm page is that a transparent foreground item— the G-clef—is placed against a (brick) pattern, and not against a solid color. How was this done? The brick background was placed on a layer underneath the clef.psd image, and then the Eyedropper tool was used to sample a color of the brick (it's better to go darker than lighter). Then the Matte drop-down was clicked, and foreground color was chosen. The brick pattern was deleted and the image was exported with transparency.

Here's the subtle thing: there usually is fringing around the edges of transparent GIFs. When you use a solid background, the problem takes care of itself—you choose the same background color as the fringing. But when you have a patterned background, try to pick a matte color for the transparency, a color that's close to other colors in the background pattern.

### Interlaced

Callout *c* on the GIF palette points to the Interlaced option. Interlacing adds a little size to the saved file, but considering what it does, you might not care. *Interlacing* is a process by which the GIF image streams to the visitor's browser. In other words, the picture immediately begins to build on the visitor's browser. This is good, because it immediately tells the visitor that an image is coming in—and to please wait a moment or two.

### Lossy

Until Adobe invented it, there was no such thing as a lossy compression GIF. But now we have that capability (see callout *d* in Figure 23.13). This slider drops out colors, in addition to the colors you drop out during the conversion-to-GIF process.

Use the Lossy slider only if you desperately need to shave a second or two off the download time for an image. Used in large amounts, the Lossy option tends to really ruin an image.

### Weighted Gradient

Callout *e* indicates the Weighted Gradient button. This is a *super* feature! It enables you to mask off part of the image and then color-reduce and dither the areas that are not protected. An example of its use is coming up later in this chapter. The only proviso is that you must create an alpha channel in Photoshop that will be read as a mask. So bring the image into ImageReady with the alpha channel in place.

> **Note**
>
> **Creating a Channel for Weighted Optimization**    To create a channel to use as the basis for a weighted optimization in ImageReady, choose a selection tool, make a selection, and then choose Select, Save Selection. The weighted optimzation buttons then change from dimmed to active, and you can use the mask channel by clicking on the type of dithering, the Lossy box, or the Dither box on the Optimize palette to preserve the quality of the corresponding masked area in the image. You do not load the channel or anything—ImageReady knows when there's alpha channel masking information in a picture.

### Matte

Callout *f* on the GIF palette points to Matte. Not only does the Matte option determine the transparency color of images that have transparency, but if you decide to build an HTML document using an image in ImageReady, the Matte option specifies the background of that document. If an image has no transparent regions, the Matte option will still determine the background of the HTML document. To take advantage of this feature, pick a color from the Matte drop-down, choose File, Save Optimized As, and then choose a name and location, and check the Save HTML file option. The HTML code for this image is very simple. All it really contains is a reference to the GIF image and instructions that the background is a specific color you chose by using the Matte drop-down.

### Web Snap

Closely related to Web Crackle and Web Pop <g>. Okay, okay, this number field/slider (callout *g*) determines how much of the color information in the original image is pushed toward Web-safe colors when the colors are reduced to meet the limitations of the GIF 256-color file format. You may occasionally find that your color-reduced image looks great with Web colors included, whereas at other times you'll want to skip this option entirely.

Feeling a little more at home with the GIF Optimize palette? Hopefully you are also inspired and want to flex the power you now have at your fingertips.

Let's turn to the JPEG mode of the Optimize palette and see what sort of control we have over this sort of image.

## Checking Out the JPEG Optimize Palette Options

Naturally, because JPEG and GIF exist using different types of compression, you will find different options when you're operating in JPEG mode. Here's the run-down, beginning with callout *a* on the Optimize JPEG palette in Figure 23.14.

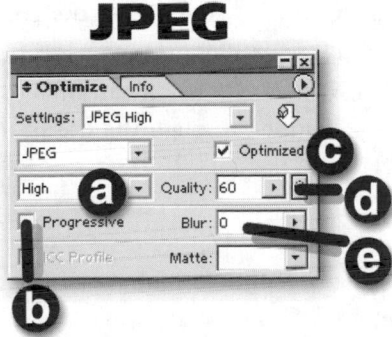

**Figure 23.14**   Where have you seen this handsome-looking figure with callouts before?

### Amount of Compression

Callout *a* is over the drop-down list that enables you to quickly determine a rough amount of lossy compression for the current image. On a scale of 1 to 100, High quality is at 60 (callout *d* shows where you can manually tune the compression), Medium is at 30, and JPEG Low is at 10. It has been the author's experience that if you want high compression and almost no image loss, a setting of around 80 does the trick; 30 is about as low as you want to go—artifacting begins at about 40 to 50. A quality of 10 provides excellent compression, but you'd only want to use this setting on a line drawing, or to send an image to someone you detest.

### Progressive

Callout *b* on the GIF palette points to Progressive. A JPEG image with the Progressive option is similar to a GIF image with the Interlaced option switched on. A progressive JPEG streams to the visitor's browser, showing a progressively more refined image until the last of the data is sent and the final image appears onscreen. Only recent browsers, such as Explorer 4 and later versions, support progressive JPEG images. Browsers created when dinosaurs ruled the earth cannot read a progressive JPEG.

### Optimized

JPEG was not always such an important file format, especially before the advent of the World Wide Web, so the graphics community put very little effort into improving it. Now you can optimize a JPEG image, and 90% of the graphics programs and browsers out there can read an Optimized JPEG (see callout *c* in Figure 23.14). The only difference you will notice between an optimized and a standard JPEG image is that the file size of the optimized image is slightly smaller.

### Quality

As mentioned earlier (in the discussion of settings for high, medium, and low image quality, the lower the image quality, the higher the compression), when you click on the flyout triangle, you'll see a slider that you can use to specify any figure for compression. Notice that JPEG compression can be restricted to areas indicated in an original image's alpha channel, through the use of the Masking Option button (callout *d* in Figure 23.13).

### Blur

Callout *e* on the JPEG palette points to Blur. Although the authors do not recommend using the Blur option, adding a blur to a JPEG image can help soften the rough edges left by the JPEG process. As mentioned earlier, JPEG compression leaves colors alone, but averages brightness values, which can leave artifacts (visual trash) and blocky-looking areas where there's a lot of detail.

As a final note, the JPEG version of the Optimize palette has a Matte field. Although there is no such thing as transparency in a JPEG image, you can surround the image with any color you like by choosing a matte color. Doing this generates a small HTML file that lists the file's name and the color for the background of what becomes a modest HTML document.

What with all the ink devoted to GIF and JPEG formats, we should now turn to the PNG file format, the newest format created for the Web. Let's see what it does.

## The Portable Network Graphic: PNG

If you really think about it, the GIF file format is more versatile than JPEG format. Not only is GIF a picture format, but you can also animate a series of GIF files (as shown in Chapter 25), and you can create transparent GIFs.

In the past five years, graphics programmers have been given a big push toward improving upon the GIF format. UniSys, the company that owns the patent on GIF technology, has been making intermittent noises that it wants to increase the fee for licensing the format (Adobe pays for the right to offer the GIF format in Photoshop and other programs), tax the end user for making GIF artwork, and has been making demands that we in the graphics community consider less than hospitable.

In response to further pushing by GIF's creators, along comes the Portable Network Graphics (PNG) file format, designed to eventually replace GIF. And the best part of PNG is that the creators of it *gave* the code to the graphics community—ownership of the file format cannot be questioned in the future.

Let's take a look at what PNG offers.

## PNG: Designed for the Future

If you run down the list of features that PNG supports, we don't think there's a weak point in it. In Figure 23.21, you can see the Optimize palette for the two types of PNG that Adobe supports: 8-bit and 24-bit. Let's run down the palettes, beginning with the 24-bit PNG.

## The 24-Bit PNG Graphic

To begin with, at the time of this writing, the 24-bit PNG file format offers compression if you save it in Photoshop, but offers no compression in ImageReady. A "PNG and Photoshop's Options" section is coming up soon. In Figure 23.15, you can see both modes of the Optimize palette when PNG is chosen.

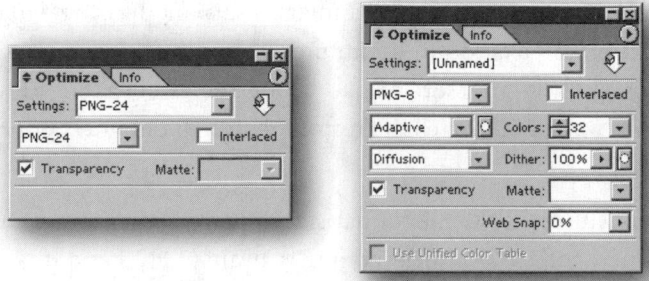

**Figure 23.15**   The Portable Network Graphic comes in two flavors: a 24-bit version that can take on the TIFF and PSD file format for the broad color space these types offer, and the 8-bit PNG, indexed mode format designed to usurp the GIF format one of these days.

A 24-bit PNG shrinks the overall file size of an original image by 33%. This makes the file format (without any of Photoshop's compression methods for PNG) not such a good choice for the Web, but it's *excellent* for archiving purposes on your hard disk. Why save images in other formats when PNG can shrink and save 'em using *lossless* compression, and save you 34% hard disk space? The PNG format does not discard tones, colors, or anything to work its compression, so we call it *lossless* compression.

A 24-bit PNG image can hold onto transparency information—up to 256 levels of brightness—through the use of an alpha channel. You can interlace a PNG image so that when you send it to a visitor, the visual information begins building itself immediately. And if you want a color to surround a PNG graphic on a Web page, use the Optimize palette's Matte color flyout. This is where you can determine the outside color on a Web page when this PNG graphic is shown through a browser.

### The 8-Bit PNG Graphic

Now, we're talking competition with GIF. We saved a number of graphics to both the GIF 256 Dithered format and the PNG 256 color (8-bit/pixel) format, and guess what? The saved file sizes are virtually the same—PNG dithers down to 8-bit as well as GIF does.

Additionally, when you choose PNG-8 from the Settings pop-up on the Optimize palette, you can choose a color reduction method, dithering, transparency (through a 1-bit/pixel alpha channel), choice of *size* of color palette, and other options you find with the GIF format.

Our advice is that if you want to display a still image that is currently a GIF image, you can replace the GIF image with a PNG image and avoid hearing about or being involved in any (UniSys) taxation in the future. Adding a charge for the use of the GIF format seems unlikely—it's sort of like taxing the atmosphere. However, the PNG format is one way of telling GIF's creators that Web designers do *not* sit back and watch.

The only problem with the PNG file format is that your ISP has to have the servers configured to display these files. Not everyone is aware of PNG and if your ISP isn't with the game, you cannot use PNG graphics anymore than you could present a VRML world on your site if your ISP doesn't speak VRML.

Lack of popular acceptance usually needs a compelling reason to change; in our opinion, PNG will catch on as soon as push comes to shove.

## PNG and Photoshop's Options

When you save an image to PNG format from Photoshop, you are presented (naturally) with a PNG Options box, in which you can choose to Interlace the image, or not. The PNG Options box, shown in Figure 23.16, is displayed when you choose File, Save As, and then choose the PNG file format. The Interlace option adds slightly to the saved file size, but the streaming algorithm enables you to send visual data and have it begin to build itself immediately after a visitor reaches your site.

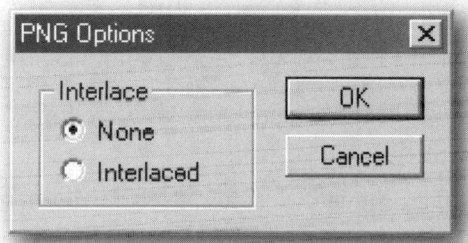

**Figure 23.16**   Photoshop only offers 24 bit PNG file saving, and you can choose from Interlaced or Non-Interlaced options.

To give you an idea of how competitive the PNG format can be compared with JPEG and GIF, the Games96.tif image was optimized to each of these formats. The envelope, please.

- **GIF.** 256 colors dithered 93.3K (download 34 seconds)
- **PNG.** 256 colors dithered, Adaptive compression 83.68K (download 31 seconds)
- **JPEG.** 70% Quality, Optimized and Progressive 63.71K (download 24 seconds @ 28.8K)

So the PNG format compressed better than the GIF file format. In a compression contest like this, JPEG will often be the winner because it discards original image data during the compression process.

Something we haven't tried yet is to selectively compress an image based on alpha channel information. That's our next step.

So far we've covered color reduction as a method of optimizing an image file. The word "optimize" means more than knocking image quality out of an image. Let's suppose you want to show a small, fast-loading preview of a piece of artwork. You'd create a thumbnail of the image, and post one or a dozen of them in something called a *table* in HTML code. The following section walks you through creating an optimal thumbnail image for a Web page.

## Creating an Optimized Thumbnail Image

We've heard two important things about thumbnail images on the Web

- Every pixel must count in an image that is so small you can almost count the number of pixels.

- Creating thumbnails, miniature masterpieces, is an art.

Therefore, the following set of steps is a little education in optimizing, but more important, a lesson in art.

### Example 23.5    Creating a Thumbnail

1. Open the Monochrome.psd image from the Examples/Chap23 folder of the Companion CD.

2. Choose Image, Image Size, and then in the Image Size box, type **150** in the New Size, Width field, as shown in Figure 23.17.

   Because the Constrain Proportions option is checked by default, if you place your cursor in the Height or Percent boxes after making the 150 entry, the values in these boxes will change accordingly. Bicubic Interpolation is the default method of changing the number of pixels in the image (it's the smoothest, best method), and you'll notice that the new size for the image— without any compression—is only 50K, down from over 300K.

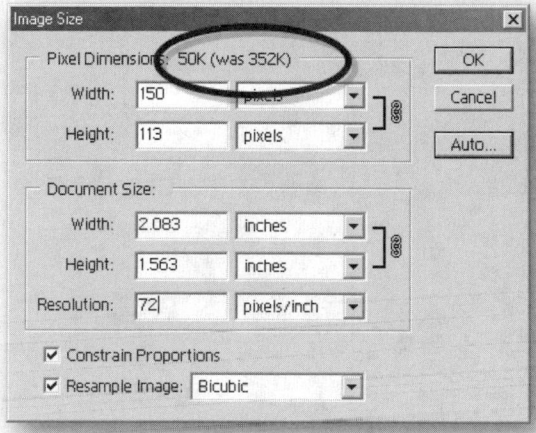

**Figure 23.17** Create a smaller version of the original image so visitors can quickly decide whether they want to see a larger version.

**Note**

**Why Use 150?** Why did we recommend 150 as the new width for the 400 pixel wide by 300 pixel high image? Because there's an old saying in theater, "play to the cheap seats." On the Internet, the cheap seats are those visitors who have a 15" monitor and can only show full color at 640×480 pixels.

And 150 times 4 is 600, a comfortable width in which to display four good-sized (IOW *visible*) thumbnail images.

3. Click OK, and then choose the 2-Up tab on the image window. You want to compare the original to the new image, so click in the left pane, and choose Original from the Optimize palette's Settings list. Then click in the right pane, choose GIF 32 Dithered from the Optimize palette's Settings list. Now choose Perceptual (because we tried this and it produces the highest acceptable amount of compression), and choose Diffusion as the Dither type if it's not already chosen.

4. Choose Size/Download time 28.8Kbps from the Document Sizes area at the bottom of the right pane window (click anywhere there is text at the bottom of the pane, or click the triangle). As you can see in Figure 23.18, the thumbnail image downloads at a mere 3 seconds. And that's with a 28.8 connection (which is giving way, even as we write, to cable modem service such as Road Runner and @home—which can be 100 times faster than a 56.6 connection).

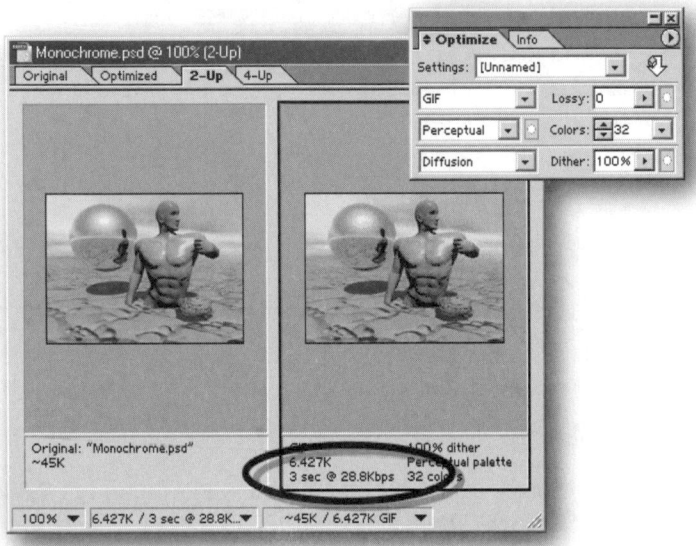

**Figure 23.18**    Just about anyone with any speed connection can quickly download a thumbnail that's only 6.4K in file size.

There's one last step: image sharpening. Choose Filter, Sharpen, Unsharp Mask.

5. Set the Amount to about 40 to 50, and keep the other settings you used. Get ready to press Ctrl(⌘)+Z if you don't get the right compression; as mentioned earlier, the preview window in the Unsharp Mask dialog box shows only the original sharpened, not the optimized image. (See Figure 23.19.)

**Note**

**Preview Windows Don't Show Previews**    At the time of this writing, the preview windows in all the filter dialog boxes do not show effects applied to optimized images, but only to the originals. But then again, we're writing this as the product is being developed. If, by chance, this is fixed in the retail version of Photoshop 6/ImageReady 3, forget the problem mentioned in step 5; we reported the limitation as a bug, and Adobe engineers will have performed yet another feat of magic in these two new applications.

6. Choose File, Save Optimized As, and then save the optimized thumbnail in GIF format to your hard disk. Close the original Monochrome.psd without saving. Keep ImageReady open.

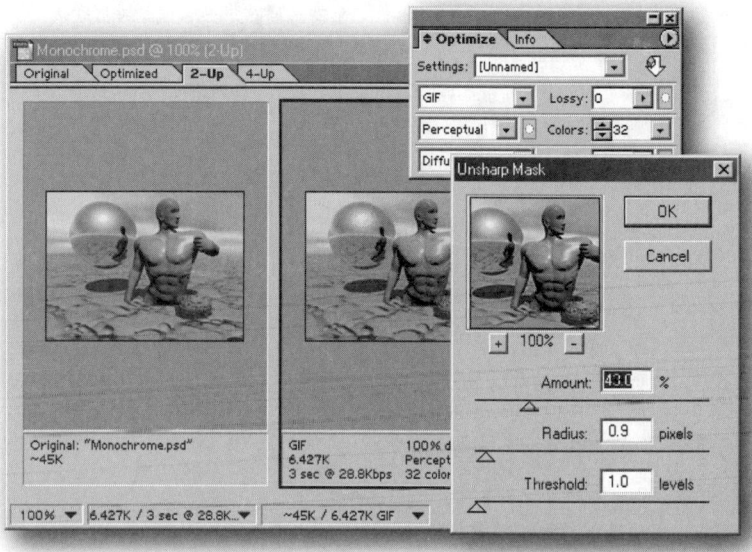

**Figure 23.19**   Although you have to go by trial and error, applying Unsharp Mask as a final optimization step helps bring out detail in really tiny images.

Optimizing, like most things in life, is at its best when the right portion has been doled out. We've seen many Web sites that take more than a minute to load because the Web author refused to compromise on the amount of pixels he or she was presenting. The other extreme is a bad thing, too. As an example, check out Figure 23.20. We deliberately added more than 50% compression to the GIF image in the right frame. Try this with an image for which you don't care much. Unwanted noise has been introduced, all for the sake of saving one second in download time. Part of the Zen of this whole optimizing jazz is to create the smallest, best-looking image for your Web site. *Forget* about the original image—it's a *copy* that you are trying to make as handsome as possible, and the copy will never (and probably *should* never) look exactly like the full-size original.

**Note**

**No Gallery Feature in ImageReady**   As long as we are talking about thumbnail images, there are contact sheets, Web photo galleries, and some templates that ship with Photoshop 6, but there is no HTML-driven thumbnail gallery feature in ImageReady. We'll cover automatic Web site construction in Chapter 24.

Are you ready to add Adobe's version of the word *droplet* to your graphics vocabulary?

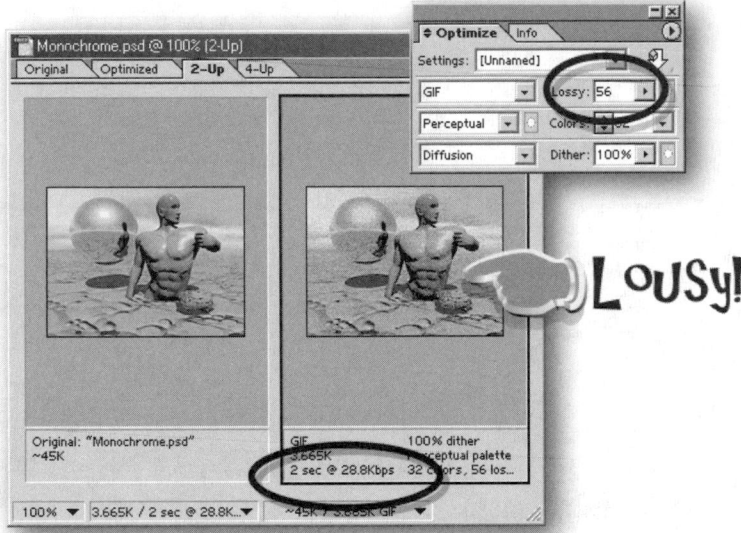

**Figure 23.20**    Don't sacrifice image quality to make a quick-downloading site. What does the visitor have to view once it's downloaded?

# Using Droplets to Optimize and Automate Processes

Although you can use the automation command in combination with the Actions palette to do a lot of cool batch-processing things, there's another utility Photoshop and ImageReady have that makes optimizing a bunch of images as simple as dropping one icon onto another icon—the droplet.

## Creating a Single Droplet That Can Handle Many Images

First, you'll see how easily a droplet is created and works, and then we'll get into the options you have for customizing a droplet.

### Example 23.6    It Begins with a Droplet

I. Open the Morning.tif image from the Examples/Chap23 folder on the Companion CD. Click the Optimized tab of the image window, and then create a specific group of settings for the image, so it looks nice, and the file size is small (check the document sizes area at the bottom of the window pane).

Don't fuss too much with the optimization settings—you can practice settings on your own—this tutorial is about droplets.

2. Click the droplet icon on the Optimize palette, as shown in Figure 23.21. Immediately, a filename is suggested for the droplet. The name is usually ponderously long because it is a list of what you've done to the image. Shorten the name if you like; you might regret this later—the default name does indeed tell you what the droplet does, but if you can shorthand the file name a little so the text under the droplet icon isn't the size of a playing card—that could go a long ways toward hard disk organization! Choose a location for the droplet (hint: pick your desktop, because we'll be using the desktop location in a moment), and choose Save.

**Figure 23.21**   A droplet is an executable file that carries commands (in sequence) that you've used on an image in ImageReady or Photoshop.

Your work is done in ImageReady. Now, let's say you have two other images (or 200—it doesn't matter to the droplet) to which you want exactly the same settings applied. (You might, for example, have a roll of film that has lots of pictures with the same lighting and colors). Minimize ImageReady and look at your desktop. Figure 23.22 shows a thumbnail TIFF file (Games96.tif) being dragged onto the droplet icon. The result? The settings you applied to Morning.tif for compression are applied to the Games96.tif image, and the resulting JPEG file lands exactly where the source file lies—in this case, on the desktop.

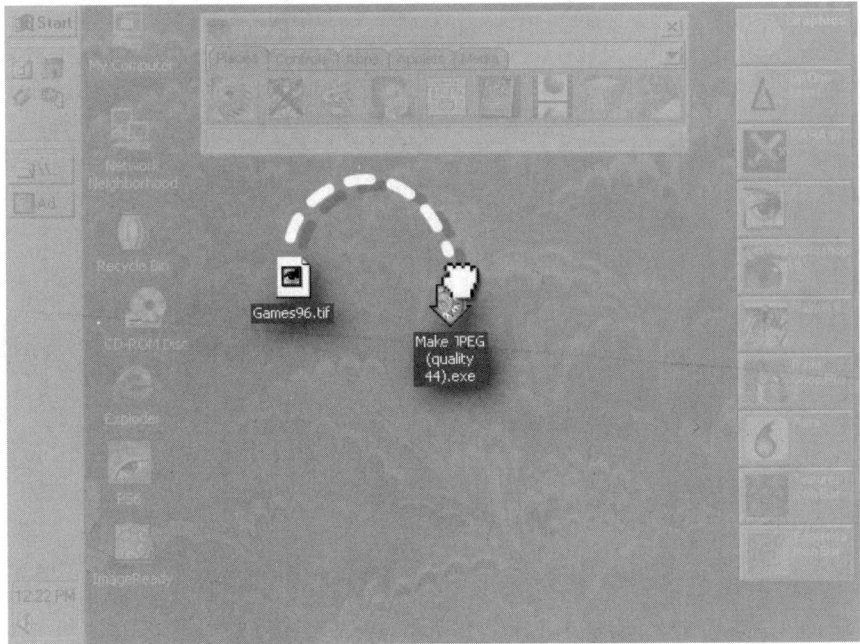

**Figure 23.22**    A droplet calls ImageReady, and then uses the program's features to perform a routine you've specified on any image you drop on the droplet.

3. Now drag Games96.tif from the Examples/Chap23 folder on the Companion CD to your desktop and perform this simple routine.

4. Drag the image edges on ImageReady so you can see both the droplet on the desktop and ImageReady's interface.

That's it! Class is out, and you now know how to save a specific set of procedures to file and run the procedure on any number of images in the future.

Droplets that you create interact with images and features in ImageReady in two very useful ways: You simply need to know where to drop and where you perform surgery on a droplet.

## Automating a Droplet: Hey, the Gang Is Dropping In

As mentioned earlier, a droplet not only saves ImageReady (and Photoshop routines), but it's an excellent automator of chores that would most surely drift your head off to the South Sea Islands. If it's straight batch processing of a few images on your desktop, marquee select them and then drag them on top of the droplet. A progress line will appear and then disappear after the processing has been done.

You can also customize batch processing; customizing is performed almost exactly as when you drag titles around, turn off actions, add new actions, or trash existing ones to customize an action on the Actions palette. What you do is drag the droplet icon into ImageReady's workspace, and then double-click the Batch Options title on this weird-looking palette that was an icon on the desktop. The Batch Options dialog box appears. This is where you can choose to drop optimized copies in a specific folder, add incremental extensions to the filename (*excellent* for animation stills), error trapping (Stop on error), and whether you want to see the images as they are processed. Wait. It gets cooler. In the next section, the History palette meets a droplet.

## Adding History Palette Commands to a Droplet

Once you've dragged a droplet into ImageReady's (or Photoshop's) workspace, you can remove a step by dragging it into the Trash on the palette. You can also make the droplet skip a step (and then you don't have to delete it) by unchecking the box in front of that step.

But perhaps the best feature, once a droplet had been created, is that History palette commands can be dragged onto the droplet list. Try this:

### Example 23.7 Tuning a Droplet

1. With a droplet open in list form in ImageReady, open any image and choose Window, Choose History.

2. On the Optimize palette, choose JPEG Low, and then type .5 in the Blur field.

3. On the History palette, drag the Change Optimize Settings over to beneath the Set Optimization to GIF89a title on the droplet list. Release the title once you see a thick line at the bottom of the last command on the list (the new command from the History palette will enter the list at the very end if you drop it on top of the entry with the thick line).

4. Click the list's title bar to make it the foreground element in the workspace. Press Ctrl(⌘)+S, and then close the droplet list. Congratulations! You've edited a droplet!

**Note**

**Use Droplets**    You can also build up an Actions list and then click on the flyout menu and make a droplet from the list. You could then edit the droplet or go back to the saved Action, and do some additions, subtractions, or editing.

## Compressing Only Part of an Image: Masking for Compression in Photoshop

As we explained earlier, that funny button on the Optimize palette is used to engage an Alpha channel in an image, and to protect a given area in an image from the loss of detail and quality that go hand in hand with compression. Our adventure has to begin in Photoshop, because you cannot add or edit channels in ImageReady.

To take the best advantage of this channel-masking feature when you're compressing an image, you need an image whose focal content is limited to a particular area. What we did with the Little Lee picture here is use the Radial type Motion Blur filter in Photoshop to throw everything except the little girl's face out of focus. Now, everything in the image, as shown in Figure 23.23, is quite unimportant—only the face needs to be preserved.

**Figure 23.23**    Whether you have an image or need to create an image whose prime focus is in a limited image area, defining the important area with a mask will help keep compression artifacts from distracting the viewer.

Let's try out this new Photoshop/ImageReady feature. If you have an image of your own, fine: Use it. If not, load the LittleLee.psd image into Photoshop from the Examples/Chap23 folder on the Companion CD.

### Example 23.8 Selectively Compressing an Image

1. Open the LittleLee.psd (or whatever) image in Photoshop. Choose the Elliptical Marquee tool on the toolbox and make a vertical oval around the little girl's face.

   Now, we do *not* want the compression in the image to simply come to a halt—we want the image to gradually take on compression artifacting from the little girl's face, moving outward to the unimportant background stuff.

2. Right-click (Macintosh: hold Ctrl and click), choose Feather from the Context menu, and then type **16** in the number field, as shown in Figure 23.24.

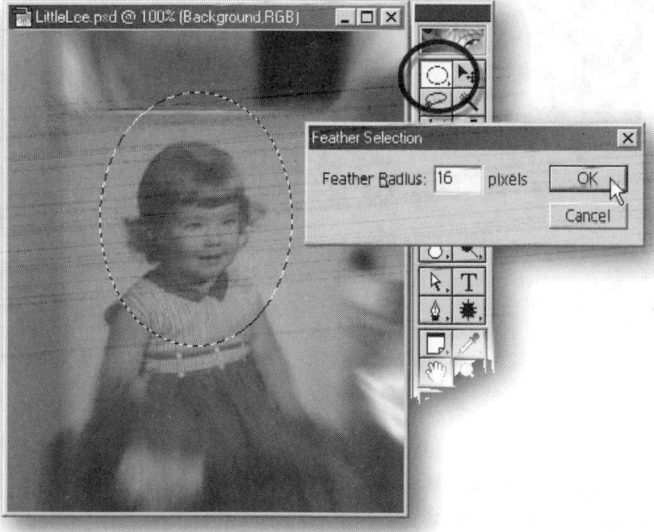

**Figure 23.24** Feather the selection around the girl's face, so that when the image is compressed, compression artifacts will gradually fade away as the eye moves toward the face.

A transitional distance of 16 pixels from selected to masked areas in an image is a lot, but we want the transition to be as smooth as possible when you compress the image.

**3.** Click OK; then, on the Channels palette (F7), click the Save selection as channel icon at the bottom of the Channels palette.

As you can see in Figure 23.25, the area that compression will not touch corresponds to the white area in the alpha channel. Conversely, black areas correspond to totally selected areas in the RGB view of the image.

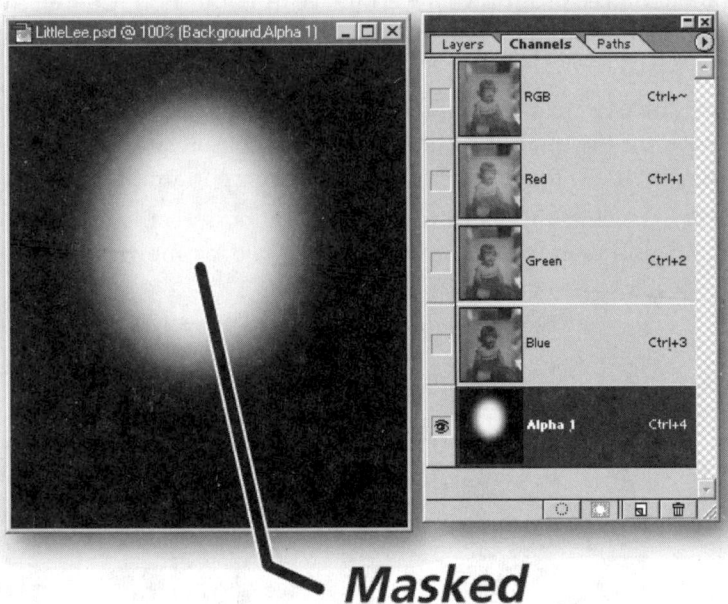

**Figure 23.25**    The girl's face will be protected (masked) when you perform compression on the image in ImageReady. And there will be no hard-edge ellipses in the image.

**4.** Save and close the image in Photoshop. Open the image in ImageReady; on the Optimize palette, choose JPEG compression, and then click the button to the right of the Quality box. The Modify Quality Settings box appears and you choose the Channel from the drop-down for the masking procedure. Then, really degrade the background of the image. As you can see in Figure 23.26, the selected areas (the blurry background) get a minimum of 0% and a maximum of 36% quality. ("Quality" becomes an interesting choice of words here!) Click OK to apply the compression to the selected parts of the image.

**Figure 23.26**   The white area in the alpha channel protects the little girl's face from compression.

5. Click the 2-Up tab on the Optimize palette. On the left pane, make this the original image by choosing Original from the Settings list on the Optimize palette. The right pane should be the little girl's picture after JPEG compression has been applied. Now, this is a vintage photo, and not in the best condition—so concentrate on the detail, and not on the flaws in the image.

   As you can see in Figure 23.27, the original image is 611K, and the optimized JPEG version is 7K. Wow! And can you honestly say that the original image's focal point has been even slightly compromised due to compression? (Hint: No!)

6. Choose File, Save Optimized As, and then save the JPEG image to your hard drive as LittleLee.jpg. You can close the image in the workspace (without saving) at any time.

We figured that soft-edged selections in channels would be a nice segue into the art of image slicing. Image slicing actually does carve a copy of an image into many different slices, but they are rearranged in a table, and each slice can have a different property. Read on!

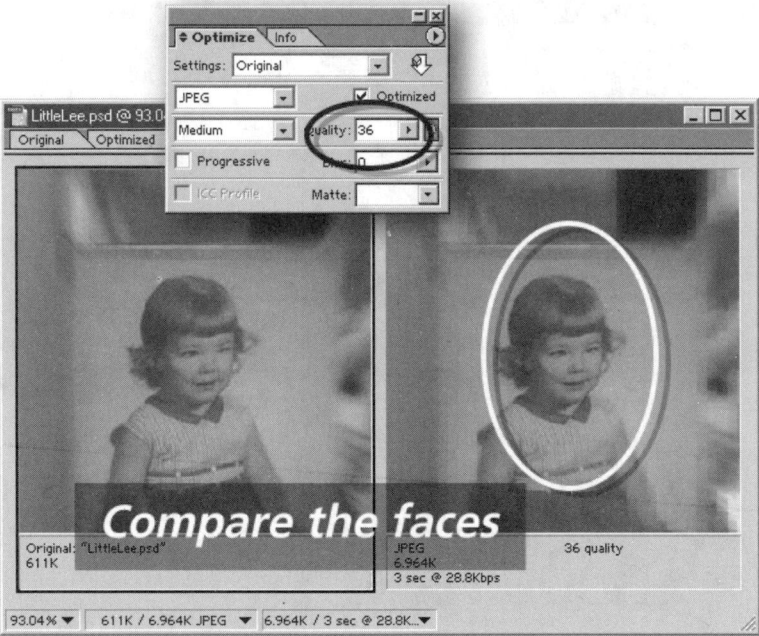

**Figure 23.27**    Selective compression can be your key to displaying lots of images on the Web at very small sizes without the traditional accompanying artifacts in the images' focal points.

## Slicing Images: Another Way to Optimize

The Image-slicing feature in ImageReady was not the first application to enable artists to play Benihana chef with an image. But ImageReady's Slice feature is very easy to use, and showing you how to optimize an image through slicing will also be easy.

Basically, you would want to slice an image for any of the following three reasons—and sometimes for more than one of them:

- To allow an image that is huge (100K or more) to load in a visitor's browser, one piece at a time. This action is equivalent to making image data into streaming data, but you control which image areas appear as the image assembles itself.

- You can tag an image slice with a link (to a different site or a different area of your own site), and you can provide an Alt tag that enables visitor's who have graphics turned off in their browsers to know what's onscreen. *This is a picture of a tree*, for example, would pop up onscreen when a visitor hovers over the right image slice. Adobe also enables you to put a message tag with the slice, so a visitor knows that the slice is a link, not a link, or whatever.

- Once an image has been sliced and put into a neat table by ImageReady, you can replace a piece of the sliced image with a GIF animation. In our *Inside Photoshop 5.5* book, we showed how to make a smiley face appear inside a sun within a sunset. It was an easy matter to make the sun a slice, and then use ImageReady's animation tools to create an animated GIF. You give it the same name as a slice, put it in the sliced image folder and you have an optimized image, only part of which moves. You'll see how to create animations in Chapter 25.

The first of the preceding reasons for image slicing is the one we'll start with. We'll use an image that, like the image of the little girl, is about 10% highlight and interesting, and 90% dull and worthless.

## Slicing a Clown

A simple child's clown was modeled against some wood tones, and the whole composition is spotlighted so that there is very little detail around the clown. Your first step is to isolate the clown image using the Slice tool. Then you'll decide how few colors you can get away with in the color-reduction process for the GIF file format.

### Example 23.9   Creating the Main Attraction in a Sliced Image

1. Open Franklin.psd from the Examples/Chap23 folder of the Companion CD. Then open the Optimize palette, and choose the Slice tool, as shown in Figure 23.28.

**Tip**

**Tips for Slicing**   You might not get exactly the right size slice going around the clown. To fix this, click and hold on the Slice tool, until the Slice Select tool is visible, and then click it. The Slice Select tool can be used to drag the borders of an existing slice in any direction.

Another necessary tip here is that your goal as a designer is to create as few slices as possible in an image. The more slices, the bigger the overall file size will be for the assembled image. Therefore, in this example, you want to create a slice only around the clown, because nothing else merits its own slice.

2. Create a tightly cropped slice around the clown, as shown in Figure 23.29. Then assign this slice GIF 128 compression with Perceptual dithering, and make it an Interlaced slice.

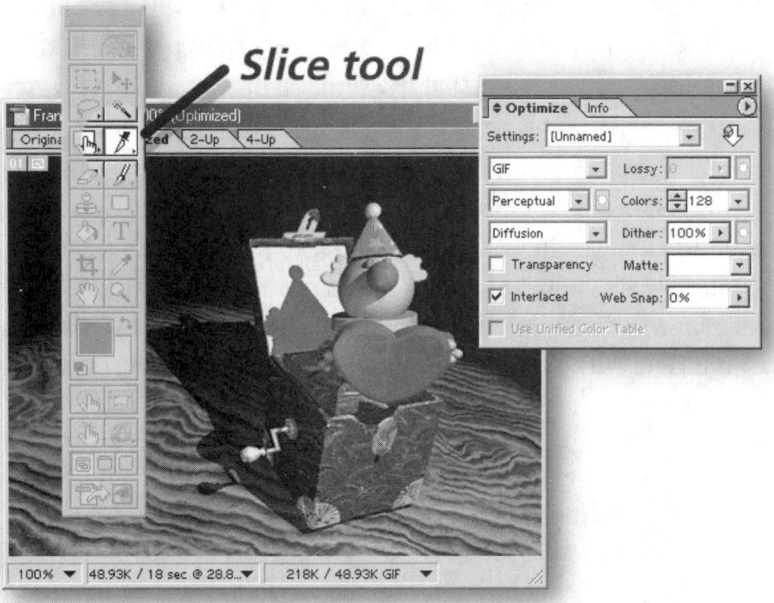

**Figure 23.28**   Choose the Slice tool for images whose foreground area of interest is very limited.

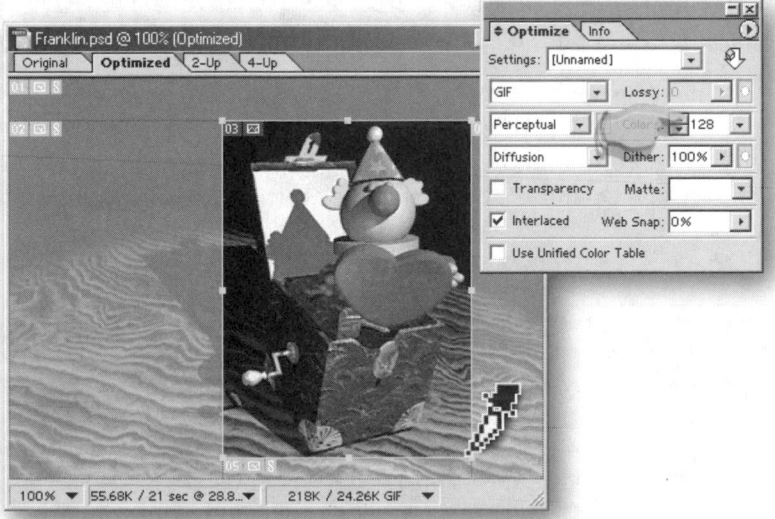

**Figure 23.29**   128 unique colors are enough to present a pretty nice picture of the clown, Franklin. None of the other slices needs that many colors to be pleasing to the eye, and that's where you pick up download savings.

Notice that as soon as you create a slice, the rest of the image takes on slice areas to surround the clown slice. Each slice has a number in its upper-left corner. You use these numbers to find a slice in the Images folder that ImageReady creates for you on your hard disk.

ImageReady is only an application, and it doesn't know that you want to assign different compression settings to other slices. So you need to spell it out for this image, as described next.

3. Right-click (Macintosh: hold Ctrl and click) over the area of wood directly to the left of the clown slice. From the context menu, choose Unlink Slice.

You see, by default, the compression settings you make for your first slice are used by all the other slices. As shown in Figure 23.30, we've knocked that wood back to 16 unique colors, with dithering. If you could see this image in color (on your screen, say), you'd notice immediately that the wood doesn't look much worse for the massive number of colors you've knocked out of it.

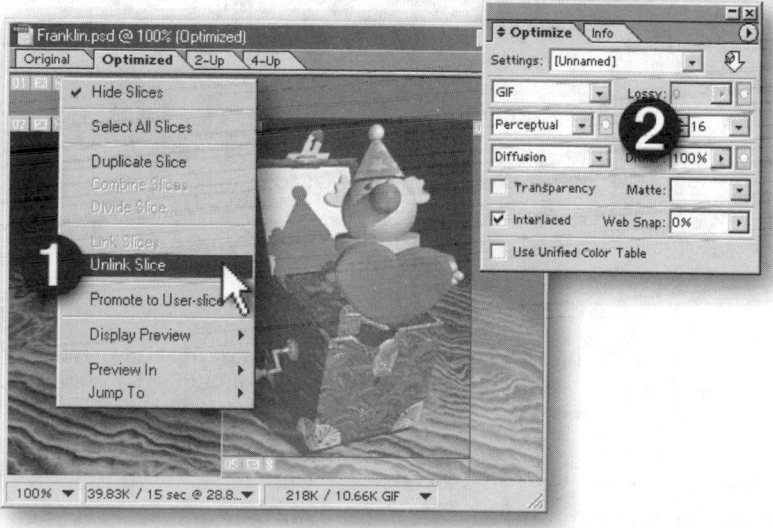

**Figure 23.30** After you unlink a slice, you can apply any compression settings you like within the file format of the optimized image (in this instance, the GIF format).

4. Go around the clown slice clockwise, clicking in a slice—one slice at a time to highlight it, use the context menu to unlink the slice, and then assign the slice the fewest colors possible so that it still looks like something (as opposed to a blobby mass of pixels).

Here's the fun part: assigning a link, a message, and an Alt tag to an image slice.

5. Click on the clown slice to make it the current slice, and then choose Window, Show Slice (or press F11).

6. Click the flyout button on the Slice palette, and then choose Show Options. The palette will extend down, and the Message and Alt fields will appear. In the URL field, type the location to which you want to whisk the visitor away, as shown in Figure 23.31. Now, in a browser, the visitor can activate the link by clicking anywhere in the clown slice.

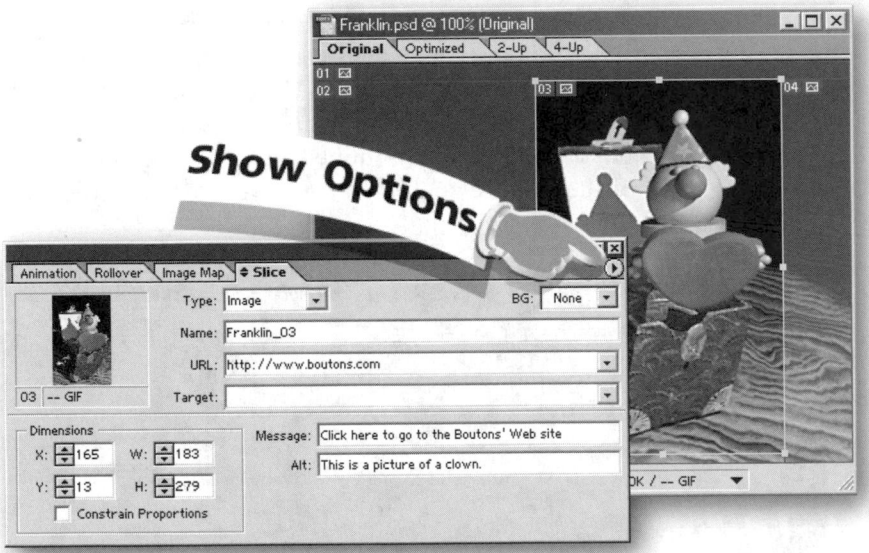

**Figure 23.31**    Assign the slice a link to a different site, provide a message in the visitor's browser concerning the image, and provide an Alt tag for those visitors whose browser doesn't support the display of the graphic.

7. Type a message in the Message field.

   This message appears at the bottom of the browser in the status line.

8. Type the message in the Alt tag.

   This message pops up only if the visitor's browser is incapable of showing the clown slice.

   We're not typing anything in the Target field because targets generally are used internally within a document: You can jump from one topic to a related topic by clicking on a highlighted phrase. Because this is not a multi-page document, because there's no text in the future Web page, and because this is not a book on HTML, we will leave the Target field blank.

9. Choose File, Save Optimized As, and then save the HTML document (don't worry about the image slices) as Franklin.htm on your own hard disk.

As you can see in Figure 23.32, a folder called Images will be written to your hard disk. The slices reside in the Images folder, the Franklin.htm document contains a carefully built table that houses the slices without showing any seams, and you have further reassurance that all is well at the bottom of this dialog box.

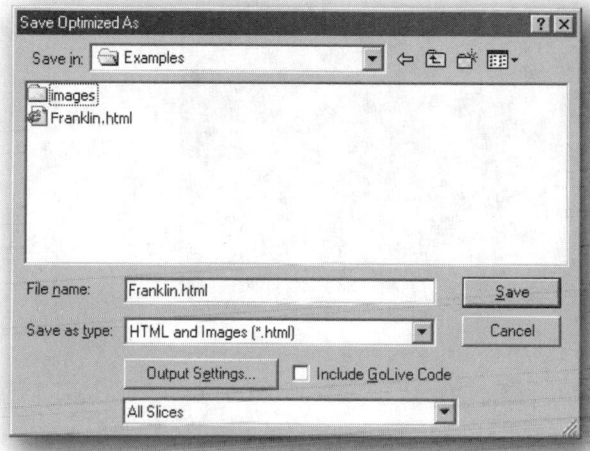

**Figure 23.32**   ImageReady handles the HTML code for the image slices. All you have to do is define areas in a sliced image and provide links if you want them.

**10.** Choose All Slices in the bottom drop-down box. Click on Save, and we're outta here.

Close the Franklin.psd image without saving and you can close ImageReady and Photoshop, as we are at the end of this chapter. But we have to do one last thing—drag the HTML file into the Web browser so you can see your handiwork.

In Figure 23.33, it sure looks like one whole image, doesn't it? But if you look at Figure 23.26, you can see that the image has gone from a 28.8 modem download time of 18 seconds to 15 seconds (trust us on the 15 second figure—ImageReady will not tell you the sum of the individual slices).

Besides optimizing an image (this chapter *is* about optimization!), you can have lots of creative fun with making links out of image slices, and posting messages that are triggered by hovering over a slice. Links are so much fun, in fact, that we devote a good part of Chapter 24 to the practice of making them.

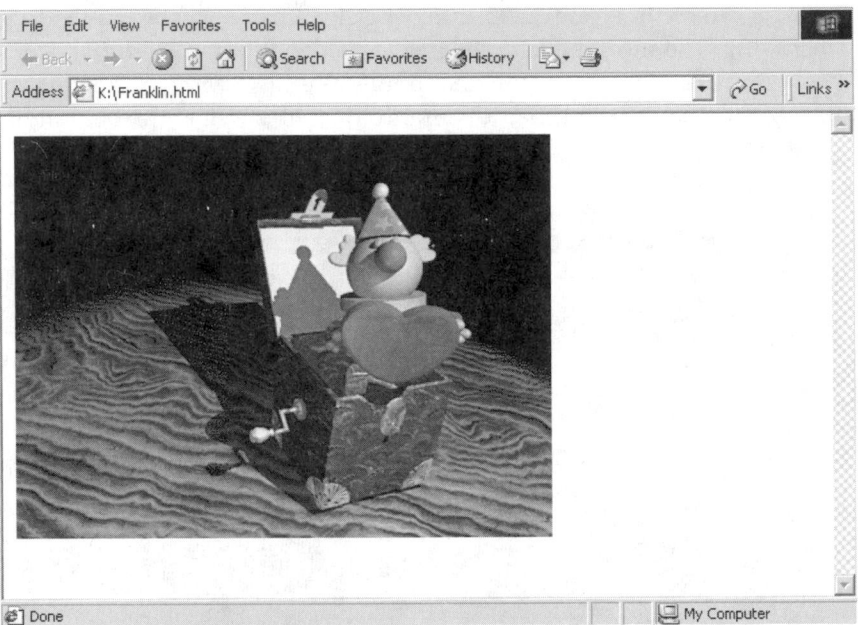

**Figure 23.33**   A sliced image can travel faster than a whole image because areas that are visually unimportant can be compressed more than the "star" of the image.

## Summary

We've taken you from working with nice, plump images to lean, fast-paced, well-tuned miniature masterpieces in this chapter. You have a better working definition of dithering than people who have read *Book X*, and you know why the smaller the palette, the faster the image travels. Add to this an understanding of the difference between images destined for the GIF format and images for JPEG, and you've amassed a pretty powerful number of practical facts you'll use every day in Web designing. And stay tuned for the emergence of PNG as the file format of choice. As with all new technology, it's simply a matter of time before something new draws attention.

Oh, yes, and remember to put the cap back on that Slice tool when you're done with it. Okay, we're kidding here.

In Chapter 24, you'll see how a single graphic can be assigned multiple locations as links on the Web. You provide the design for a control panel, and ImageReady provides the HTML code. We'll also take a brief look at how your optimized images (the ones you created after reading this chapter), can be neatly organized and linked to larger images in a tidy auto-gallery that Photoshop 6 provides. As a designer, the Web is at your doorstep. It's high time you invited it in!

# Chapter 24

## Creating Image Maps and Instant Web Galleries

It occurred to us that as we travel deeper

into Web graphics and the suitcase called

HTML, which makes sense of your graphics

and text, you deserve a break—specifically,

in this chapter.

So although this chapter will thoroughly familiarize you with the creative possibilities of image maps, we're also going to get your HTML socks wet with a small dip into a Photoshop feature that automates the Web site process. As with anything, the more automation you allow, the less control you have—but if you don't have your professional shingle hung out on the Web by now, you'll have the knowledge you need to do so by the end of this chapter.

## Exploring the Power of Image Maps

The largest misconception about image maps is: An image map contains the URL of a location, and when visitors click on a location's URL, they go to that location.

Wrong, wrong, wrong. For the record, there is absolutely *nothing* special about an image map: it's a collection of pixels. Period. What makes an image map work is a piece of HTML that ImageReady can write for you, and you don't have to touch the gooey scripting language. Image maps are made in ImageReady by using a tool to mark off a "hot" area of the image, and there are a few fields to fill out on the Image Map palette. Clean. Simple.

In Figure 24.1, you can see an illustration of the interface you will build in the following sections of this chapter, along with callouts for the button areas. As you can see, hot areas of an image are marked off with four coordinates, which are measured in pixels. They mark:

1. The near vertical edge
2. The far vertical edge
3. The far horizontal edge
4. The near horizontal edge

...in that order.

There are several instructions waiting for a browser to decode them in an HTML script, but the other piece you should be interested in from an image map standpoint is the *link*—the HTML reference, or HREF. You can see in Figure 24.1 that when you click a button—the top one, ART, for example—you're clicking on a hot spot in the image that links to a page called artpage.htm. The site you see is complete on the Companion CD (Examples/Chap24/ArtSite), and we'll get to clicking on it a little later.

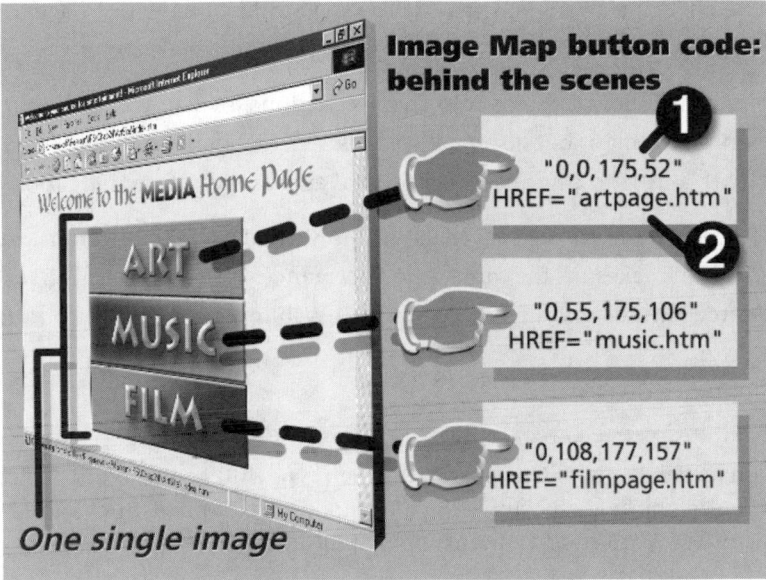

**Figure 24.1**   An image map is an image that has coordinates and a destination that travel with it in an HTML document.

### Warning

> **This Book Uses HTM, Not HTML**   In this book the extension for an HTML document is written as *htm*, as in mysite.htm. Um, this is not correct, but it works with most browsers. We don't want you to get off on the wrong foot here. The only reason we consistently tag an HTML document with the three-character htm extension is that the Companion CD is limited to displaying three-character extensions. This happens when you make a CD that works with more than one operating system.
>
> For all intents and purposes, Adobe ImageReady is correct when it writes, for example, mysite.html. And this is the way such a file should appear on the Web.
>
> The only problem with asking you to correct the extension in the tutorial steps to follow is that if you use the html extension one place and the htm extension in another place, the browser will not be able to find an image because the extension is incorrect.
>
> So for the Web, it's always "html." And for this book's assignments, it's always "htm."

It's time now to dive face forward into the fictitious Media Home Page site and its very real construction.

## Crafting the Image Maps for a Web Site

A *style* is a group of layer operations that results in a texture. Both ImageReady and Photoshop now come with several collections of styles located, oddly enough, on the Styles palette. This feature makes the creation of an image area that has rich detail a one-click operation. You can use the styles that came with ImageReady, but we're also going to show you how to *modify* an existing style.

We broke up the following steps into chapter sections, so you will not only be able to create an image map, but also make it look rich in detail, and you'll see how to edit an HTML a little to improve the graphical appearance of your creation.

Styles are applied one to each layer. Anything you add to a layer after a style has been applied to it takes on the same style appearance. Therefore, your first steps are to create three buttons on different layers for a Web interface, each button having a different style.

### Example 24.1    Creating Layers of Buttons in ImageReady

1. In ImageReady, press Ctrl(⌘)+N, and then type **400** in the Width field, **300** in the Height field, specify RGB color mode and 72 pixels/inch, and then specify Transparent as Contents of First Layer. Press Enter (Return) to return to the workspace.

2. Press Ctrl(⌘)++ or Ctrl(⌘)+–, if necessary, to make the image window display at 100%.

   Doing this gives you a perfect idea of how large the buttons should be—your audience will see the document at 100% resolution, too.

3. With the Rectangular Marquee tool, make an oversized button. Not much else will go into this Web page; we'll build smaller buttons later. We chose to enter values for the button dimensions the hard way, and used the Options bar, as shown in Figure 24.2 (basically to show off this feature).

4. Choose the Rectangular Marquee tool, choose Fixed Size from the Options bar's Style list, and then type the numbers the authors used for width (**177**) and height (**55**) (by default expressed in pixels).

5. Fill the rectangle, because a style will not transfer to transparent regions of an image. On the toolbox, choose any color you like for the foreground—99% of the styles you apply are only going to overwrite the existing color. Keep the marquee selected in the image.

**Note**

**You Determine the Units**    Units of measurement are left up to the designer some-times in Photoshop. In other words, number entry fields can sometimes take alphabet data, too. To make certain that you are playing with the units you want, you can tag a number with a space and then the letters *px* (for *pixels*).

Photoshop will pop up a dialog box if you try to put units or other alphabet data in a box that does not use this feature.

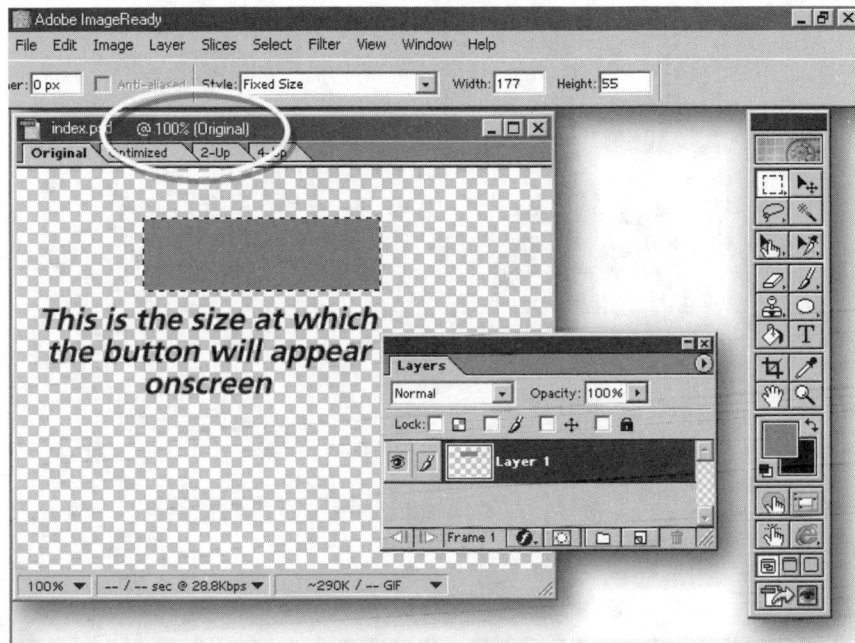

**Figure 24.2**   Create a rectangle that's larger than normal, but not the size of a supermarket, and then you will apply a style to the opaque regions of the layer.

6. Choose Window, Show Styles, and then from the default group (called Buttons), click the Button-Wood style and watch your rectangle in the image turn into a button (see Figure 24.3).

7. With the Rectangular Marquee tool, move the active selection marquee by pulling on it (with the cursor inside the marquee), until the selection marquee butts up against the bottom of the first button. On the Layers palette, click the Create a new layer icon at the bottom of the palette (see Figure 24.4).

8. Now that you are working on a new layer, you need to fill it. Pressing Alt(Opt) plus Delete (Backspace) fills a marquee selection, so why not do this?

9. Click a style button. We chose the faded purple one, but in your own work, you can choose any one you want, naturally.

10. Repeat steps 5–7 so that you have three buttons, arranged vertically. It is important that you choose the red button on the Styles palette—the one with the black outline called "Button-Shiney" if you hover the cursor over it—because we will show you how to *modify* it shortly.

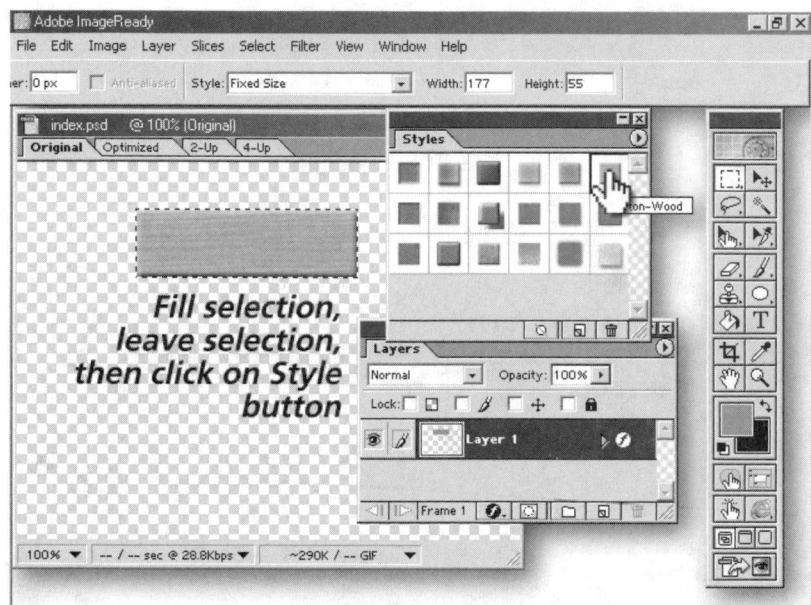

**Figure 24.3**   Once a style has been assigned to a layer, every selection you fill and every paint stroke you make takes on the style appearance.

**Figure 24.4**   Dragging a selection with a selection tool moves only the marquee selection, not the image content. Move the marquee down by dragging inside it until it is directly beneath the top button.

**11.** Press Ctrl(⌘)+D to deselect the marquee, return the Style on the Options bar to Normal (for the future), and then save the image as Index.psd in Photoshop's native file format to your hard drive. Keep the image open.

That red button doesn't really exist harmoniously with the other two muted buttons, so we'll edit the button's style.

## Editing a Style

A style, although very useful and a quick way to make buttons, is only a stack of layers, each of which contributes a different visual facet to the overall effect. In the steps to follow, you will change the red button into a deep green button that visually completes the button group.

Here's how to edit a style applied to a layer's contents:

### Example 24.2    Changing an Applied Style

**1.** You want to zoom in to 200% viewing resolution for a moment to better see the change you are going to make. Click on the far bottom-left area of the image window, the Zoom percentage field, and choose 200 from the list. Hold down the spacebar and drag in the image window until the red button is in plain view.

**2.** Chances are you're like the authors and didn't get fastidious and label each layer as you added it to the image. Therefore, on the Layers palette, choose the topmost layer (labeled Layer 3, most likely), and then click the triangle next to the icon with a letter $f$ in a circle (telling you that this layer is combined with effects). The triangle then turns downward, and a whole slew of layer effects titles drop down.

**3.** We are interested in the Color Overlay effects layer, circled in Figure 24.5. Click on that title and a Color Overlay palette will appear onscreen (labeled #3 in Figure 24.5).

**4.** Click the Color swatch on the Color Overlay palette to display the Color Picker. Choose a deep green (not so deep you can't tell it's green, however!), and then click OK. Now, if you like this button style and want to use it in the future, click the Style palette's menu button and choose New Style. Choose an evocative name and enter it in the Name field of the Style Options dialog box, and then press Enter (Return) to add the style to the current style collection. Keep Index.psd open.

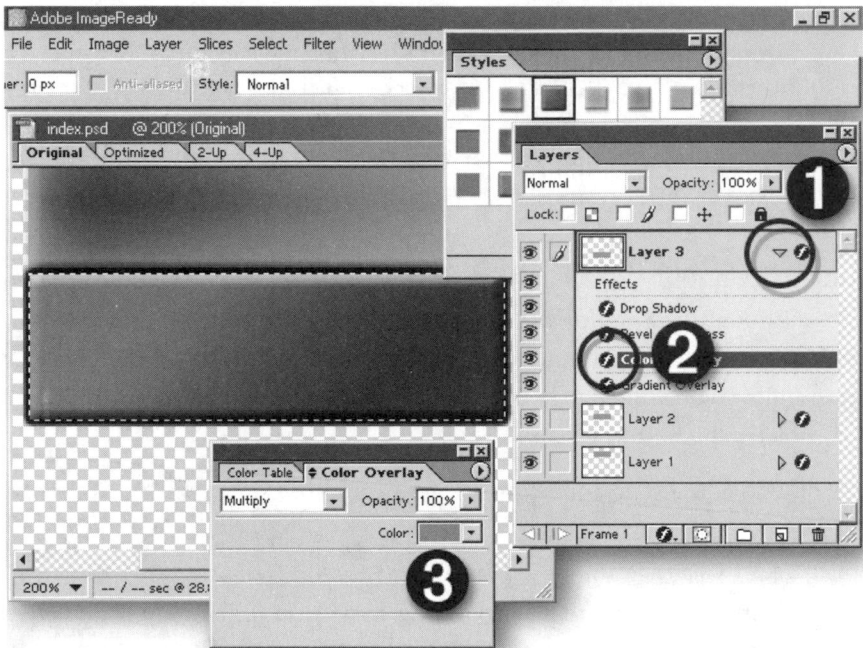

**Figure 24.5**   After you apply a style to a layer, a bundle of effects layers make up the style. You can open the bundle by clicking the Layer effects triangle (1), selecting the layer (2), and making modifications to the overall appearance of anything on this layer (3).

 **Tip**

**Being Web-Safe**   If you want to pick Web-safe colors (see Chapter 23), all you do is click the down arrow to the right of the Color swatch on the Color Overlay palette. You do this, and you will *not* display Photoshop's Color Picker, but you will be limited to Web-safe colors.

Here comes the hard part: adding text to the buttons. Fortunately, Adobe has made working with text simpler in this version of ImageReady than in any other version...and this book will walk you through the process.

## Working with Button Text

Here's a trick you can play on your friends: We'll tell you approximately how large the text needs to be on a button, without even typing the text. Text is generally measured at 72 points to an inch, and screen resolution is typically measured at 72 pixels per inch. Therefore, a point more or less equals a pixel. The height of each button is 55 pixels. Therefore, any text height less than 55 points will fit on the button. We recommend that you go with 40 points in type height (and use all caps so there are no typeface descenders as there are on a lowercase g or y) to make the text large enough to read, and small enough to fit nicely on the buttons.

Let's add text to the buttons:

### Example 24.3    Adding Type to the Buttons

1. Click the Layer 1 title on the Layers palette to make it the default editing layer.

2. Choose the Type tool from the toolbox, and immediately you'll see a Palettes button on the Options bar. Working from the Character palette is much easier than constantly stretching to reach the Options bar for type properties. Click the button, and the Character/Paragraph palette appears (we'll not be needing the Paragraph palette, but it's sort of a matched set). Double-click on the Zoom tool to bring the image window to 100% viewing resolution.

3. Click an insertion point on the top button in your image, and then type, in all caps, **ART**. Highlight the word with the Type tool cursor, and let's get down to work on the Character palette.

4. On the Character palette, choose Lithos from the font list (see the Note that follows this step), choose Black for the font, highlight the type size, and then type **40 px** (put a space after the zero) in the field, and click the Color swatch to display the Color Picker.

**Note**

**Substitutes for Lithos**    It would be nice if everyone owned the Lithos family of typeface, but then again it would be nice if we were all 10 years younger—except for 10-year-olds.

Acceptable substitutions for Lithos in this assignment are Futura, Helvetica, City Bold, and Compacta, to name but a few. You might need to reduce the size of the font, depending on which font you choose. Lithos is not a very wide font, and typefaces such as Helvetica take up more horizontal room than Lithos.

5. You'll add a style to the type on the buttons, so let's choose a light color, like a light purple. Why? Because one of the layer effects you'll add (it's nested in a style) will be Emboss, and Emboss tends to add heavy shadows to objects— so let's keep the font's base color light. Click the color swatch on the Character palette, choose the color in the Color Picker, click OK to return to the image, and the word ART is on a layer on top of the wood button.

6. With the Move tool, move the type so that it's centered on the wood button, as shown in Figure 24.6.

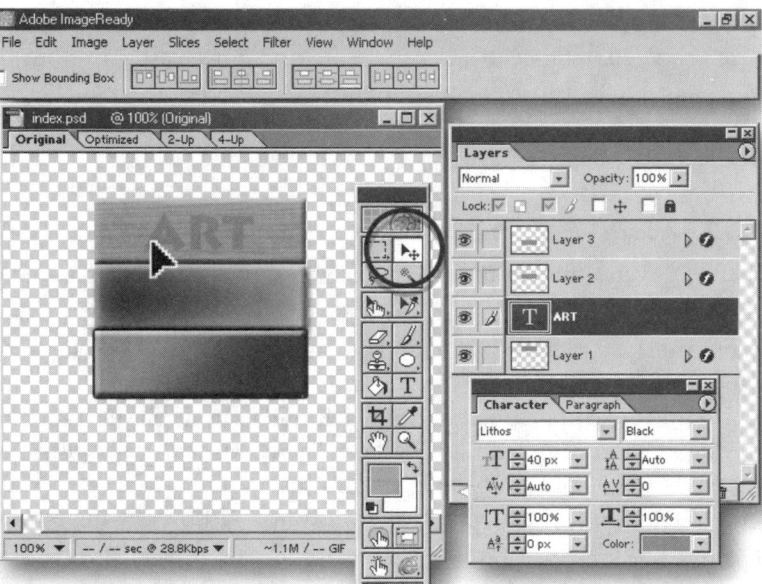

**Figure 24.6**    Use the Move tool to move type until it is centered on a button.

7. Now, to add an effect to the type, all you do is keep the layer as the current editing layer on the Layers palette (which means doing nothing), and then click a style on the Style palette. Click the style marked Floating Plastic (second row, third from the left at the time of this writing) to apply it. (Hint: All icons that have a dull gray on their face add *no color* to the area to which you apply them. This means that the light purple type is still light purple in color). As you can see in Figure 24.7, the word ART looks nice, but the drop shadow (part of the effect in the style) is way too far away from the lettering. Let's fix that.

 **Note**

**If You Don't Have a Style**    At the time of this writing, ImageReady opens with a default palette of Styles called Styles.asl. If you've played with the controls on the Styles palette to display, for example, the Buttons collection, Floating Plastic will not appear on the palette. So you know what? Choose a neutral (medium gray) style that contains a drop shadow on the current palette, apply it, and then we'll move on here to show you how to edit the style.

8. Click the triangle next to the *f* next to the word ART on the layer on the Layers palette. The layer effect is now shown in titles. Click the Drop Shadow title, type **12** as the Distance on the Drop Shadow palette, and then type **10** in the Size field on the Drop Shadow palette. The Size control determines the amount of diffusion to the drop shadow (you've just made it very

soft), and more important, the Distance amount determines how far the drop shadow is from the object (see Figure 24.8). You can close the Drop Shadow palette at any time now.

**Figure 24.7**    The amount of embossing is okay, but the style you applied has a drop shadow so distant from the type, it looks to have landed in Nantucket.

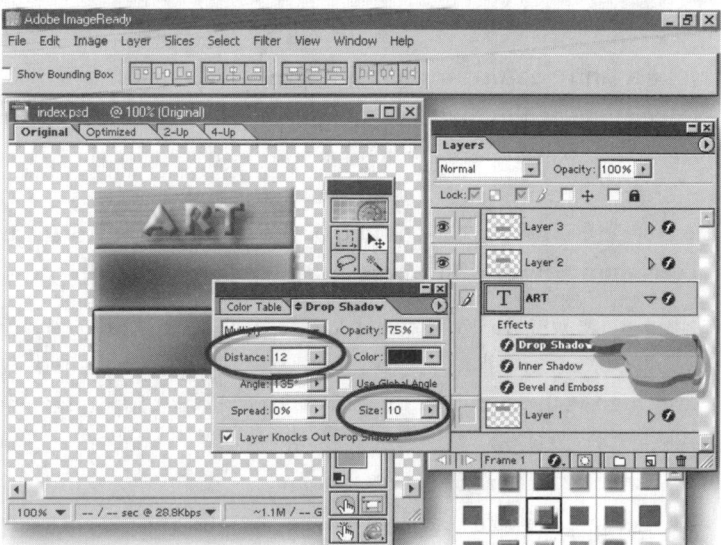

**Figure 24.8**    Pull the drop shadow in and increase its fuzziness by manipulating the options on the Drop Shadow palette.

Two approaches can be taken here to complete the type on all the buttons. Adobe is very big on layers, now they've been able to make the layers very small in saved file size and quick to work with. Therefore, we've recommended that you create different layers for the buttons, and then keep the layers separate—we did not tell you to merge them, did we? This enables you to work on each element of this composition at any time in the future, without messing up other elements.

9. You can merge the button layers now if you like, but we'd prefer it if you click the Layer 2 title now, and then click the Type tool in the image window, and follow steps 5–8 twice. Once for the word MUSIC on the middle button, and once for the word FILM on the bottom button. You can even save time by saving the drop-shadow–corrected floating plastic style to the Styles palette, and spare yourself the bother of step 8.

10. Keep the Index.psd image open. There's more fun yet to come!

We deliberately threw you a clunker in this assignment. The bottom button is one or two pixels wider than the other two because part of its styles effect is an outline that runs around the outside. This means that if you tightly crop the buttons composition without cropping any of the buttons, there will be some transparent space.

The transparent space is precisely the topic of the following section. What do you do with it? What does it want? Is it hungry? Follow along and we'll show you how to reconcile the reality that one button in a group of buttons is bigger than the others.

## Using a Background Feature for Web Pages

A very useful feature in this build of ImageReady is the Matte feature on the Optimize palette. It acts like mortar in a brick wall. No, actually the Matte feature is *better* than mortar: when an image has an HTML document driving it in a browser, or if nothing is specified for the background of the image, the Matte feature steps in and fills in everything between the image and the edges of the Web browser.

In the following steps, you will crop the layered image so there is as little unwanted space as possible outside the buttons (unused space equals unwanted extra download time), and then you will decide on a background color for the image map.

### Example 24.4    Creating an Image Map Background

1. With the Rectangular Marquee tool (make sure the Style is Normal on the Options bar, and not fixed size), drag from just outside the top left pixel in this image window to outside the bottom right pixel. You may want to

increase the viewing resolution of the image window to be very precise. It's important not to chop off part of the bottom button.

2. Choose Image, Crop.

3. On the Optimize palette, click on the menu flyout triangle in the circle at top right, and choose Show Options. Now, all options for optimizing an image are displayed. Click on the color field next to the word Matte. This displays the Color Picker.

   We've got some interesting ideas about extending this assignment and using the background color you choose for an additional element to this Web page.

4. In the Color Picker, choose a pale cream color, as shown in Figure 24.9, and *write down the RGB values for this color*. You *will* use them later.

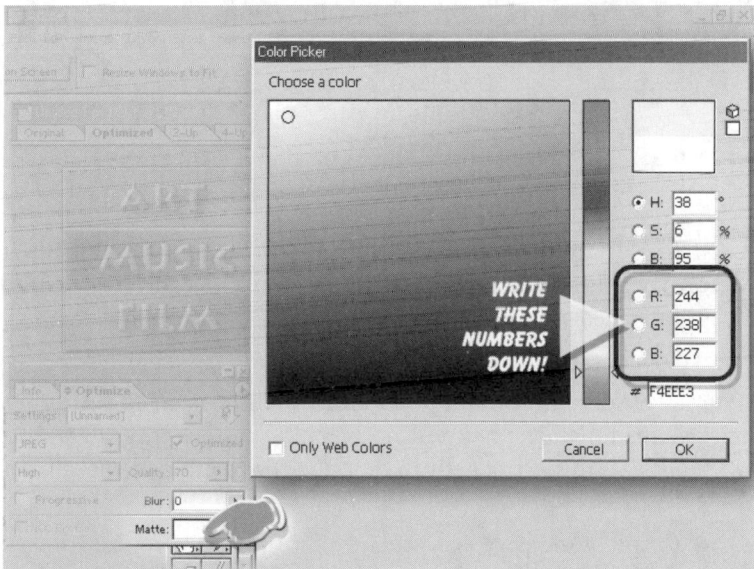

**Figure 24.9**   Choose a muted background for the image map. Also, remember what the RGB values are for future embellishment of this page.

5. It's time to let ImageReady write coordinates and page link names to file. With the Rectangular Image Map tool, draw a rectangle around the ART button. Then press F11, and click the Image Map tab on the palette. Here's where you start adding information to the mechanics of your Web page.

6. The default name of ImageMap_01 is in the name field (#1 in Figure 24.10). The shorter the name, the less HTML script a browser needs to cut through to bring you a page, so let's shorten this name to 01. To do so, highlight the ImageMap part, and then press Backspace.

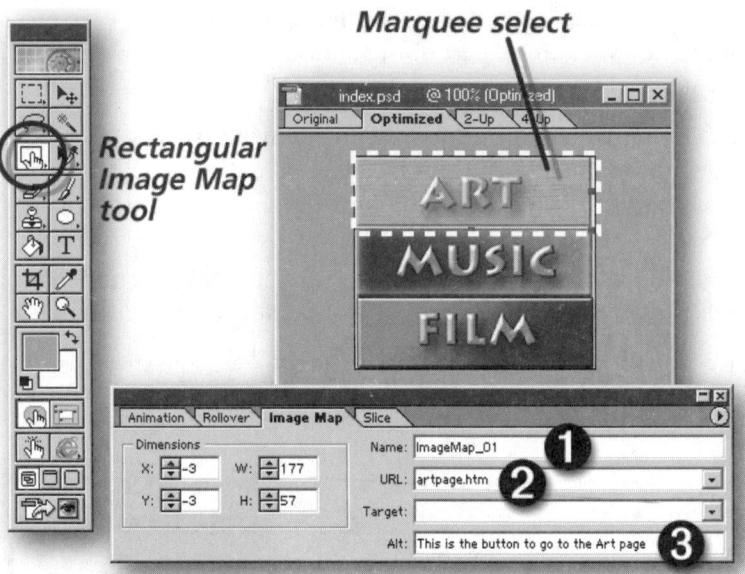

**Figure 24.10**   It is simple to fill in these fields as soon as you know what goes where, and ImageReady turns the fields into HTML scripting.

The URL for this link is called artpage.htm. We've prepared this file for you, and shortly we'll help you organize the elements of your Web site (admittedly, an intermediate to professional chore in and of itself).

7. Type **artpage.htm** in the URL field.

8. Sometimes surfers will turn graphics off in their browser to surf faster. The blind have reading machines, but no machine can describe a graphic. So it is courteous and to your benefit to describe the graphic in the Alt field (see Figure 24.10, #3).

   The URL to the Music page is music.htm, and the URL to the Film page is filmpage.htm.

9. Use the Rectangle Image Map tool to draw rectangles around the two remaining buttons, and then fill in the Name field (02 and 03, respectively, will do fine) and write a brief descriptor for each of the hot spots in the Alt field.

10. Click the Optimize tab on the image window, and then press F10, choose JPEG as the file format, and choose 70 for Quality settings. This creates a file that will download in only five seconds. Check the Optimize option on the Optimize palette, and then choose File, Save Optimized As, choose a new folder in the directory box (ArtSite is a good name for the folder); in the Name field, type **index.jpg**, and in the Save As Type field, drop the list down to choose HTML and images (*.html). Click Save.

**11.** Drop ImageReady down for a moment, and then open the ArtSite folder in the Examples/Chap24 folder of the Companion CD. From this folder, copy all the files (except index.jpg and index.htm) to the ArtSite folder you created in step 10. In your new folder, change the name of your html document from index.html to **index.htm**, so the links you've created can return you to the main page.

**12.** Double-click on the index.htm file in the folder on your system. Your Internet browser will be activated, and you will see a scene that looks something like Figure 24.11.

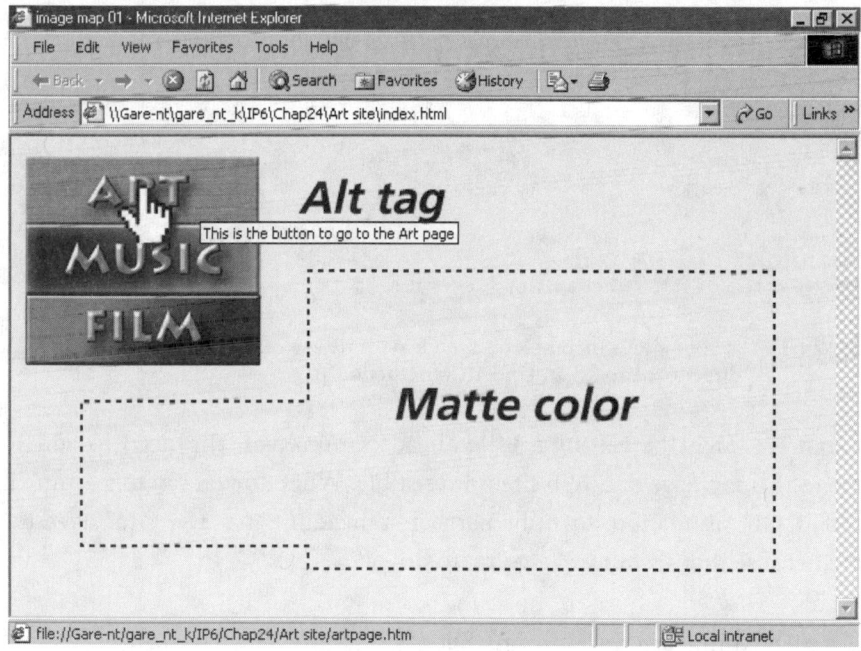

**Figure 24.11**   A Web site main page that contains an image map to visit other site areas.

**13.** Click any of the buttons.

When you copied the contents of the ArtPage on the Companion CD to your folder, you added the reference pages for the buttons—you know, the artpage.htm and so on—plus the graphics on the pages. And to be polite to your audience, the authors provided a Back button that returns the visitor to the top Web page…the one you designed. This is easy stuff; the home.jpg image is referenced in the artpage.htm to take the visitor to a page in the same directory (folder), called index.htm. In Figure 24.12, you can see that we were also gracious enough to provide a date as to when the art area would actually be up. (*Hint:* This is a good way to retain future visitors; they simply bookmark the location in their browser.)

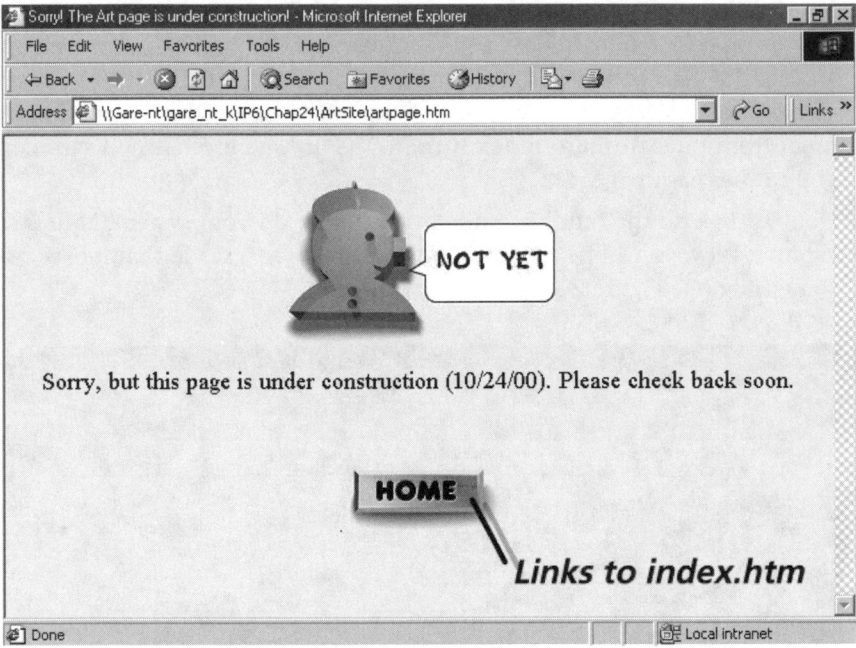

**Figure 24.12**   If your site is incomplete, *don't* leave a dead link on your top page. Instead, direct the link to an Under Construction page.

Although we might be getting a little ahead of ourselves, the need to add some finesse to this top page of a Web site is irresistible. What do you say to learning how to add a GIF animation to only part of a headline for the site? Please say, "Yes"...because that's what we're going to do <g>.

## Slicing and Replacing an Element Slice

As mentioned earlier, there's nothing special about images on the Web—all the power for an image to flash, disappear, link to other sites, and so on is written in HTML and references the image. Therefore, it makes it very easy to slip one image out of an HTML table, and slip one the same size and with the same filename into the table. With this method you can create a sizable graphic and have only a tiny part of it animate.

Now, we know that we've not arrived at the animation chapter (the chapter following this one). If you read books out of sequence, you might already know how to animate a GIF, but in any case, we've provided an animated GIF for you. So all you need to do is slice up a headline, replace file, and we'll show you how to add the headline to the Web page.

*Warning:* The following assignment does require a text editor so that you can mess around with ("hack" is a more impressive epithet) some of the HTML script.

**Note**

**The Role of Index**   We're trying to get you up and running as quickly as possible with all this Web stuff, and one thing we've not explained is why we insist on calling the graphic *index.gif* or *index.jpg.*

When you post a site on an ISP's server, in your site folder, the first thing a server looks for when dispensing a site to browsers is a file called index.html. Therefore, by naming the graphic "index," ImageReady is automatically naming your HTML document "index."

Just a small trick to make the construction of a Web site a little more fool-resistant (our lawyers said we could not use the term "fool proof").

We have a file called Welcome.tif in the Examples/Chap24 folder of the Companion CD. This is the headline for the Web site. We recommend that you use it because it has the right dimensions, but if you are adventurous, you can:

- Use your own headline, but create the word MEDIA in a bold font. This is the part of the headline that will animate.

- Remember that background color we told you to write down? Well, get it out and use it for the headline background. If you use a different color, it will clash with the matte color that surrounds the buttons.

Here's how to use a little ImageReady and a little HTML to create a headline for the Media Home Page:

### Example 24.5   Slicing and Replacing an Image Element

1. Open the Welcome.tif file from the Examples/Chap24 folder on the Companion CD.

2. Get out the Slice tool and draw a rectangle around the word MEDIA in the headline, as shown in Figure 24.13. Notice that the word MEDIA is slice #2 in the image. It's sort of important to know the name of the file you will replace.

   Also, on the optimization front, we've got a good tip for you. A solid color of text against a solid color of background generally produces no more than 12 total colors, usually 8. So save this sliced file, with the HTML document, to GIF format, 8 colors, no dithering, interlaced. Before you export anything, create a folder called Welcome on your hard disk. Why? Because we are going to create yet another file called index.htm, and you do not want to overwrite your button HTML file.

While in ImageReady, change the default names, such as Welcome_01.gif to the more succinct 01.gif, and so on. Take care to *keep the numbers the same* (see Figure 24.13)! The file references in the HTML document and the GIF filenames will be 01.gif, 02.gif, and 03.gif in the Images folder. Perfect!

**Figure 24.13**    Make MEDIA a slice. ImageReady will create the other slices, and then export both the optimized image(s) and the HTML script to a Welcome folder you've created on your hard disk.

You might not have exactly the same dimensions for the MEDIA slice, but here's what we did to animate the headline, and you can modify our instructions accordingly or use the media.gif image in the Examples/Chap24 folder from here on in; we did the work because the authors have already read Chapter 25.

3. Open media.gif in ImageReady, just to get an idea of how this animation is accomplished. In the source file, media.psd (also in the Examples/Chap24 folder for your inspection), four layers were created, and on each layer, the word MEDIA was tinted a deep color horizontally in different positions.

4. Click the Animation tab on the Slice palette and click the VCR-like play button. You'll see that the animation softly strobes the word. The best GIF animations whisper; they do not shout.

5. Okay, save the file you're looking at, the one we created as 02.gif, to your hard disk, overwriting the 02.gif image in the Images folder in the Welcome folder that ImageReady created a few steps ago. In Figure 24.14, you can see the individual images that make up the animated GIF. If you are creating your own animated word, make sure that the dimensions of the animation stills (assuming you read Chapter 25 or already know how to create animated GIFs with a utility) are exactly the same as 02.gif in that Images folder, and be sure to choose File, Save Optimized As when you save. Our GIF image that contained only the word MEDIA is 108 pixels wide by 38 pixels high, to give you a ballpark estimate from which to work.

**Figure 24.14**    An animation as a slice of a larger image will create an overall headline that is small, but (obviously) part of it *moves*.

6. Save your work, save the whales, and you can minimize or close ImageReady for the next set of steps. We're going to do some HTML editing to incorporate the headline with the animation into the buttons page you created earlier.

Now, you own the elements that will make up a sumptuous Web page like the one shown in Figure 24.15, but you need to work a little for it—specifically, working with a little HTML script. Not to worry—we'll guide you every step of the way.

**Figure 24.15**    Aligned and centered elements, a consistent background, and an animation on the Web page mark this work as that of a professional.

Here's how to combine the two index.htm documents and center the contents of the single page:

### Example 24.6    Combining Two ImageReady HTML Scripts

1. Let's begin by opening index.htm from the Welcome folder in a plain text editor. Both operating systems come with text editors. Do *not* use a word processor. A word processor puts hidden code fields in documents for italic, indents, and so on, and this will royally mess up your hacking work. BBEdit Lite and NotePad are two good text editors.

2. Find the line that says <!--ImageReady Slices (Welcome.tif)-- >, and *directly* after this line, type **<Center>** (directly before the <Table Width...> text). What you've done here is instruct a browser to center the Welcome text onscreen. Highlight everything you see in Figure 24.16 and copy it to the Clipboard. This HTML script portion is going into the buttons HTML document. Close this file, because you will shortly open another file named index.htm, and we do not want confusion.

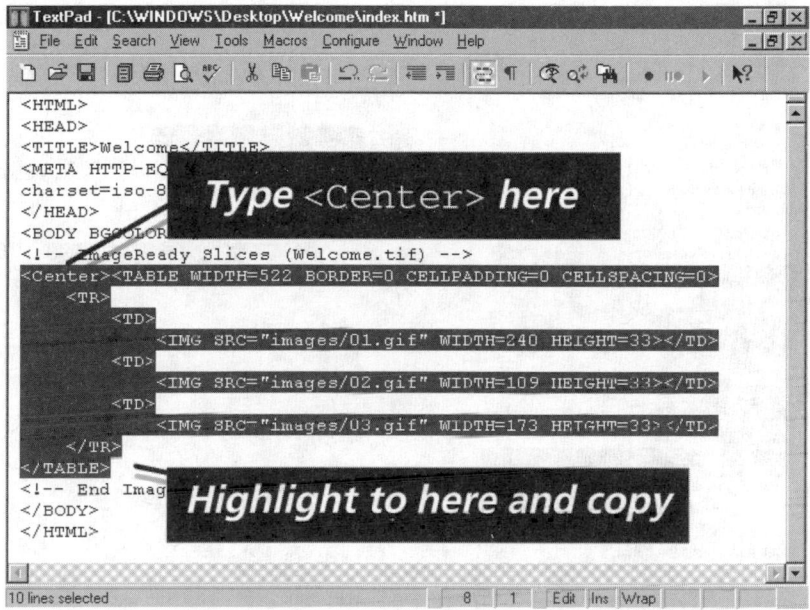

**Figure 24.16**   Add <Center> to the beginning of the table specifications in the index.htm script, and then copy the directions to the image sources and their dimensions down to the end of the table.

> **Tip**
>
> **The / Means Stop**   In HTML, a forward slash (/) in front of a word within greater than (<) and lesser than (>) signs means to terminate the initial command. So </Table> means "stop with the table. The table ends here." And </laughing> would mean, "Stop laughing." Every termination must have a corresponding initialization ahead of it. So as you can see in Figure 24.16, <Table..." begins right after your <Center> command. And yes, you will need to terminate the <Center> command after we fix up the buttons page.

3. Copy the Images folder from the Welcome folder to the ArtSite folder. Open the index.htm file from the ArtSite folder in a plain text editor. Paste the Clipboard contents, starting and ending at the points indicated in Figure 24.17. There's one last thing to do (to create "proper" HTML; in other words, pros won't laugh at you if they see your code).

4. Type </**Center**> to the point indicated in Figure 24.18. You're finished, and if you copied all the HTML files and images to the ArtSite folder from the CD's ArtSite folder (as we recommended a few pages ago), you are ready for some thrills now. Double-click the index.htm file and watch in your browser as the word MEDIA animates. If you click a button, the browser will take you to an "Under Construction" page, complete with a Home button (as shown in Figure 24.19).

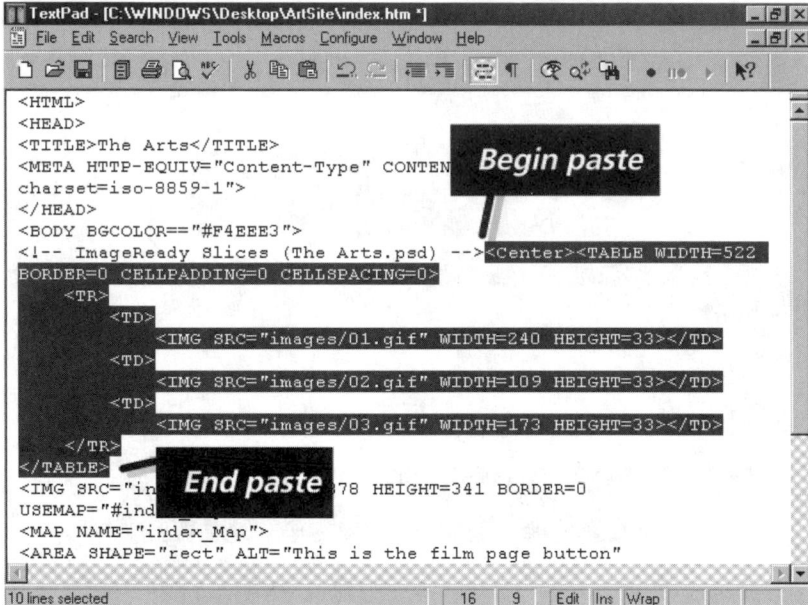

**Figure 24.17**    Add the Center attribute to the document, and add the animated headline to the index script for the top Web page you're creating—the one with all the buttons.

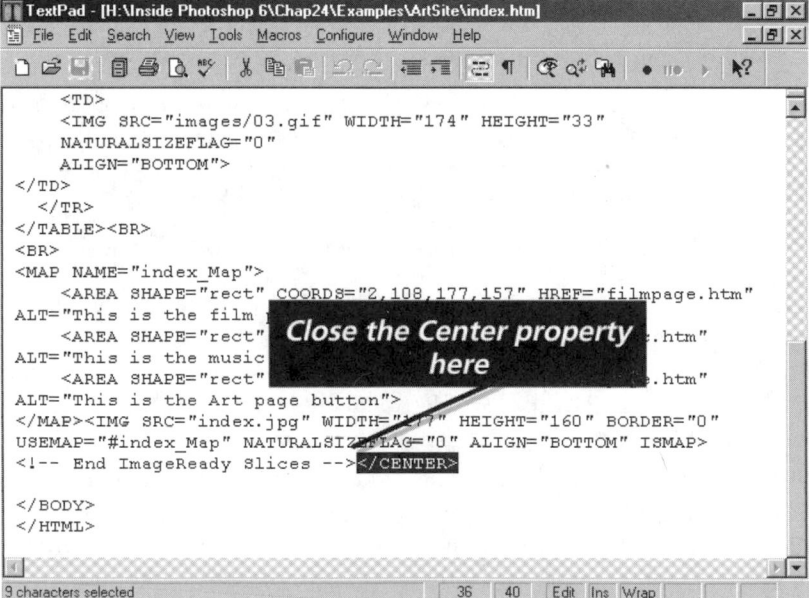

**Figure 24.18**    Place an end to the Center attribute as indicated here.

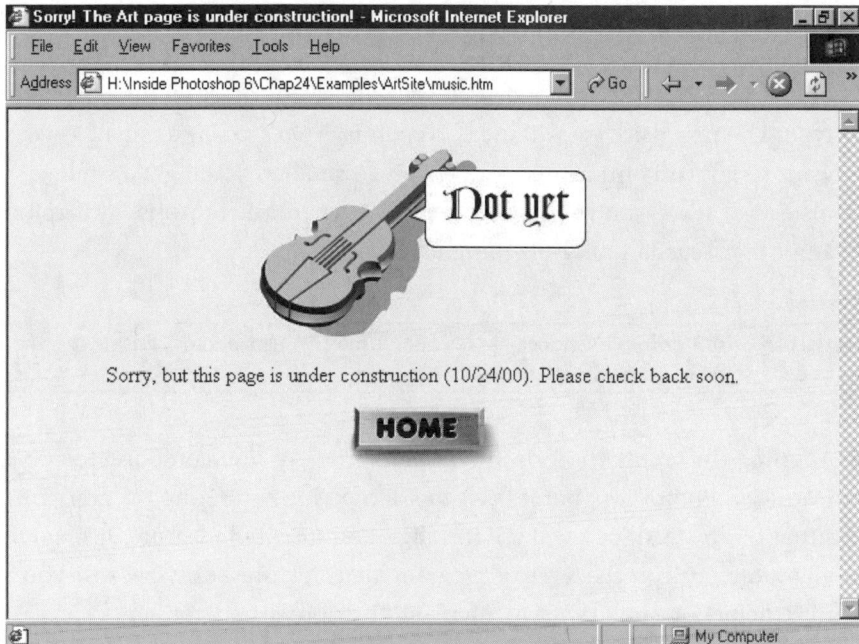

**Figure 24.19**    You have a fairly complicated Web site now, with Under Construction pages and a Home button that returns you to the page you designed!

Of course, if something doesn't work (HTML is very sensitive to spelling and spelling errors), you can always backtrack by using the ArtSite folder on the Companion CD. We assure you that it not only works, but we did the same steps we instructed you to do.

If you have an image map that is greater than three sites, you will definitely want to rethink how embellished the buttons will be. In fact, in the steps that follow we are going to build a matrix of nine URLs on an image map, and do absolutely nothing artsy about the appearance of the buttons. This is how you keep a site small in file size and quick to download. But the experience is far from boring or simple. You will learn how to use the Align and Distribute buttons in combination with layers of text.

## Working with Many URLs

Two relatively hard things (harder than peddling a bike, easier than using one of those ergonomic can openers) face you when you want to make a grid of URLs for your Web page:

- Deciding on the point size and type of font. We're going to show Futura Condensed in the screen figures that follow, because Futura is very clean (not ornamental) and a condensed style allows for more words per line of type. The point size we will use is 20 points. That's about as small as you want to go with anti-aliased text. If you go smaller, you'll get a smudge instead of text—you've probably seen sites where the buttons say Mrphxl and other Seussian, illegible things.

**Tip**

**Fonts for Small Points**    Choose Helvetica or Times Roman, no anti-aliasing, if your text needs to be less than 18–20 points.

- Aligning the text both horizontally and vertically. You could use the Grid feature in Photoshop, but it takes too darned long to set up for every unique situation. Instead, you will use the align and distribute feature. It's marginally more difficult than vector program align features, only because you need to remember to link layers to align and distribute their contents.

That said, why not dive right into the creation of the matrix? Neo? Morpheus? You guys ready?

### Example 24.7    Creating the Raw Elements for a Matrix of URLs

1. Create a new image that is 352 pixels wide and about 200 pixels high. Fill it with black.

2. Choose the Type tool, and then click the Palettes button on the Options bar. A lot of us find that working off the palette keeps you closer to the work, and therefore you save some time and keep your focus.

3. On the Character palette, choose white as the Color of the text, choose 20 px (pixels—a pixel is equivalent to a point). Type **People**, highlight the lettering with the Type tool cursor, and then choose Futura from the palette's top-left field, and Bold Condensed from the top-right field. Don't worry if you do not own this font. Pick something else that is sans serif and condensed, such as Univers, Helvetica, Olive Antique—ya *gotta* have one of these, and you can manually condense the font by using the Horizontally Scale controls above the Color box on the palette. See Figure 24.20 for the first entry into the matrix of URLs.

   Notice that a new layer appears on the Layers palette (F7), with a *verrrry* convenient auto-title.

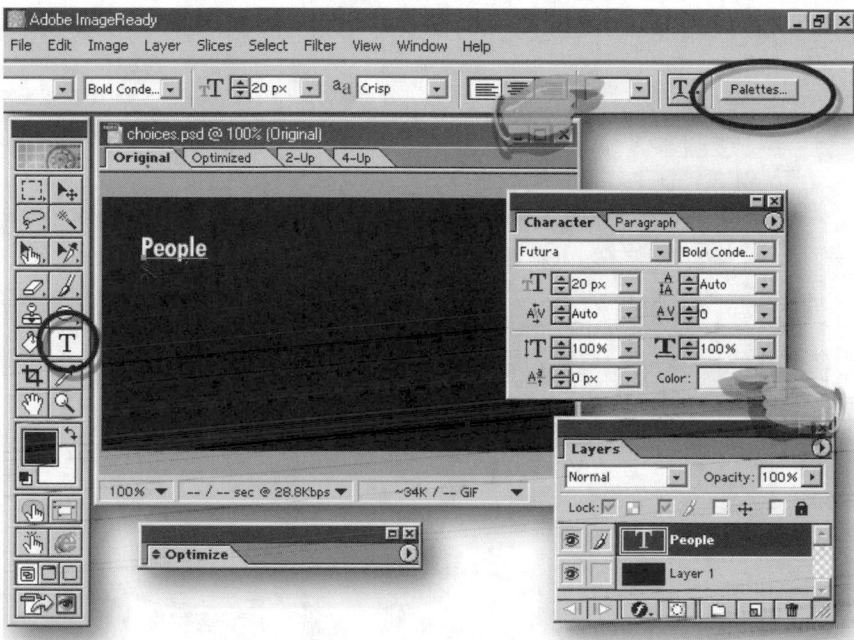

**Figure 24.20**   Use our recommendations for color, size, and font type so you can place your first matrix entry in the image window.

4. This doesn't have to look perfect because we're only going to align the layer type contents anyway, but from left to right, top to bottom, make the following entries in the image, and make sure each type entry is on its own layer. Ensure this by clicking the cursor somewhere away from the text to make that new entry (and later you can use the Move tool to position it better). Here's the list in table format. You can sneak a peek at Figure 24.21 to make certain you're doing okay.

| | | |
|---|---|---|
| People | Places | Things |
| Technology | Government | Recreation |
| Games | Work | Sleep |

5. Extend the Layers palette so you can easily see all the entries. Starting at the bottom, click the People layer, and then click the link icon to the Places and Things—IOW, the layers that correspond to the top row of entries in Figure 24.21.

6. Click the Align linked vertical layers icon, as shown on the Options bar in Figure 24.21. Wow! The top of the lettering forms such a straight line you could drag a guide to it and confirm this. Pretty neat feature, eh? Hide the link icons by clicking them now.

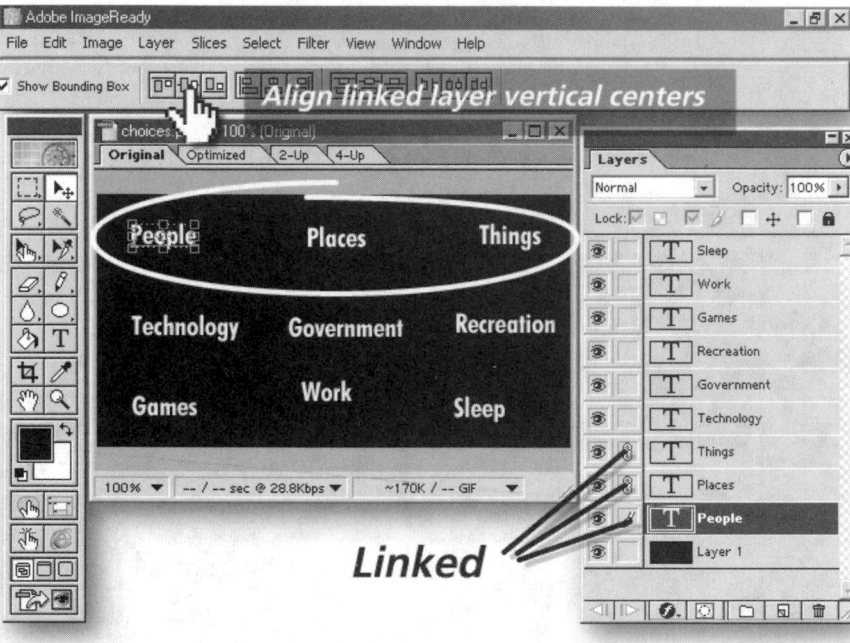

**Figure 24.21**    When you align vertical centers of areas on layers, the horizon becomes flat and consistent.

7. Click on the Technology layer (the layer doesn't make much difference in this technique), and then click a link on People and Games. Click the Align Linked layer horizontal centers button, as shown in Figure 24.22, to center the first column of text. Shortly, it will be time to use the distribution controls and really add a professional typesetter's touch to the composition.

8. You sort of get the idea by now. Choose three horizontal entries and align them by their vertical center. Then choose (link) three vertical entries and align them according to their horizontal center. When you finish, it's time to use the distribution tools.

9. Decide now on the extent of the text, the amount of space between entries, and the text's distance from the border. Using the Move tool, arrange the People, Technology, and Games entries to serve as a model for text distribution that the other entries will follow. Then, click the Distribute vertical centers button (the middle of the first distribution group of buttons on the Options bar). Unlink the layers and perform this step with the second and third columns of entries. Then work horizontally, so that all entries are equidistant from one another.

10. Save your work as Choices.psd to your hard drive, and keep the image open.

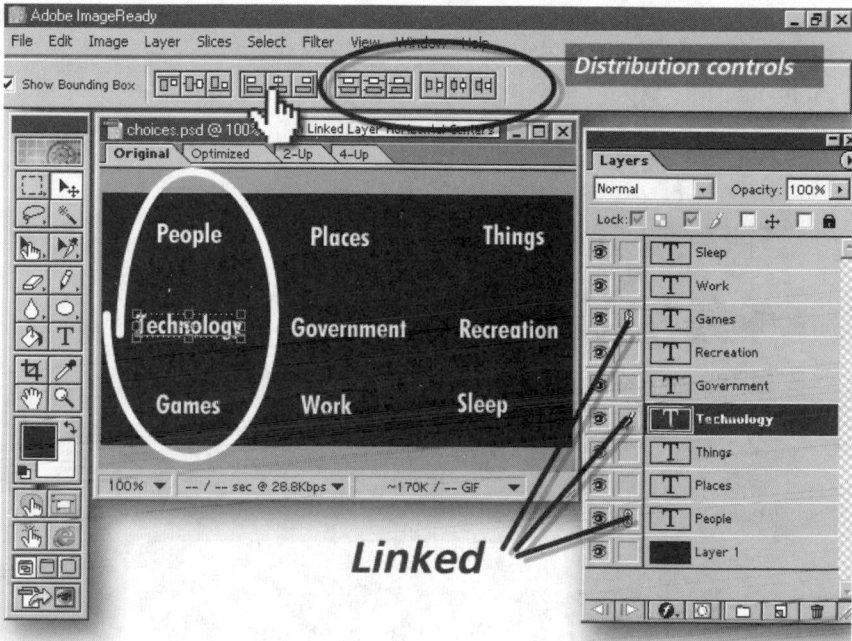

**Figure 24.22**   Align the linked layers vertically, according to their horizontal centers.

Let's see how low we can go in terms of colors in this image. The background is black, the text is white, and there's a smattering of anti-aliased pixels near the color edges. The smaller we can make the color palette, the more we save on download time.

## Optimizing the Grid of Names

This is really easy. Optimizing a grid of white names against a black background leaves room only for dithering options and the size of the color palette.

Here's an extremely short set of steps to get the grid optimized:

### Example 24.8   Optimizing a Picture That Has a Pittance of Colors

I. On the Optimize palette (F10), choose GIF as the file format, choose Custom as the Dither method, and choose No Dither from the Dither type drop-down list (which deactivates the dither amount slider). Type **12** in the Colors field (that ought to take care of the in-between colors at the edge of the anti-aliased text), choose Interlaced, and then click on the Matte color swatch, which will display the Color Picker. Type **A7A297** in the # field, click OK, and now you have a background color for the page. Check out Figure 24.23.

Choose the 2-Up view from the tabs on the image window. You'll notice no difference between the original and the proposed optimized image.

*Profound truth:* You do not need dithering if you can capture all the colors in an image with a custom color table.

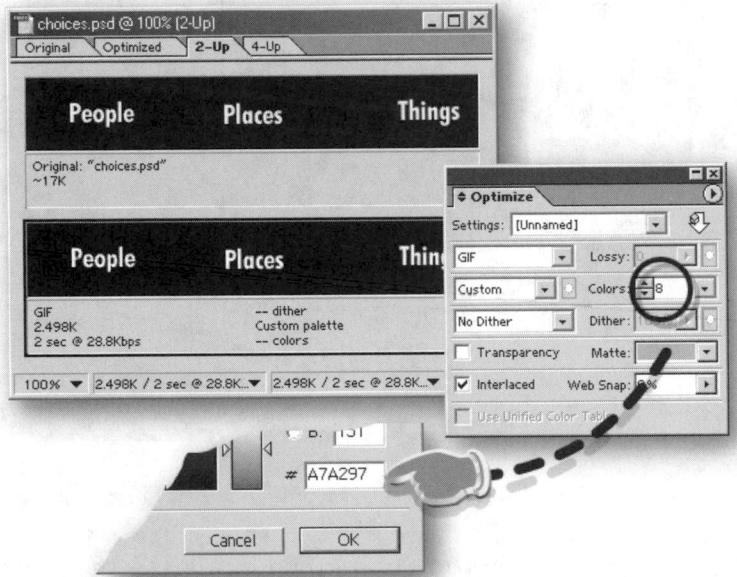

**Figure 24.23**    Although you'd usually want to apply dithering to GIF images, when the number of colors is very small in the original image, you do not need to make up extra colors through dithering.

2. Save the image and keep it open.

Now comes the easy part—you will assign names to areas you highlight by using an Image Map tool, assign URLs (they will all be the same; they'll lead to an Under Construction document), and provide an Alt tag for those visitors who cannot see the image map.

### Example 24.9    Applying Image Maps to the Image

1. Choose the Rectangle Image Map tool, and drag a rectangle around the word People in the Choices.psd image. It does not have to be a tight rectangle—it only needs to keep out of the way of the rectangles you've yet to draw around the other text.

2. In the Name field on the ImageMap palette (F11, then Tab over), shorten the name to **01**.

3. In the URL field, type **cons.htm**, the name of an Under Construction file we have prepared for you.

4. In the Alt field, type **People**, the name of the text around which you are putting the Image Map rectangle. Take a look at Figure 24.24 to see what the Image Map palette looks like right now.

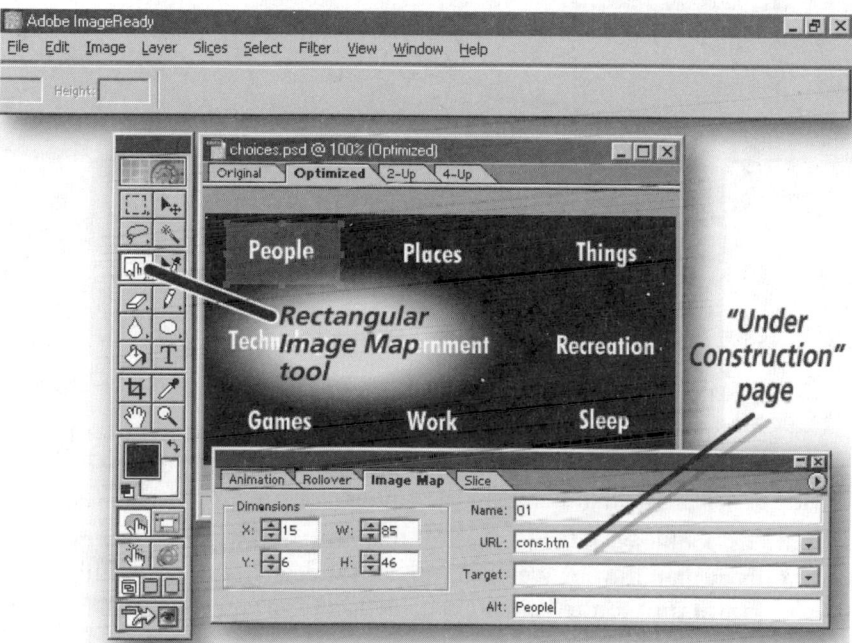

**Figure 24.24**   Use the Rectangle Image Map tool to encompass the different text in the image, and then assign it an Alt name, a reference Name (for ImageReady to link), and an URL.

5. Keep going! Follow steps 1–4 to create Image Maps for all the items you've typed. Keep the URL as cons.htm for all the items. This way, clicking an item will take the visitor to the Under Construction page, and this page has a Home button on it.

6. Create a new folder on your desktop. Call it **Answer**. Then, in Image-Ready, choose File, save Optimized As, type **index.htm** in the Name field, and choose HTML and Images from the Save As Type drop-down list, as shown in Figure 24.25. To be consistent with the rest of this chapter's suffixes, do not put an *l* at the end of index.htm.

7. Copy everything from the Answer folder in the Examples/Chap24 folder on the Companion CD to the Answer folder on your desktop *except* the Choices.gif file and the index.htm file.

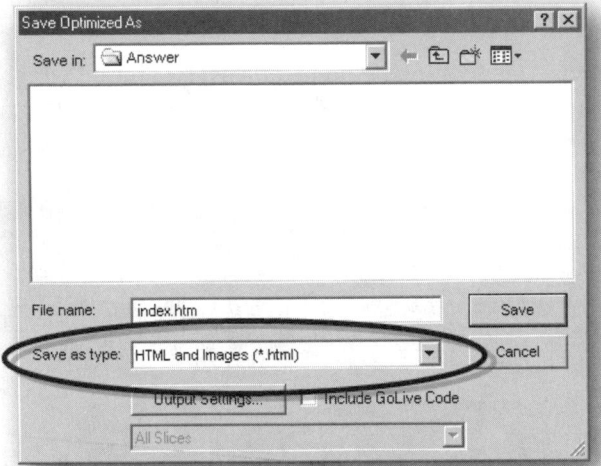

**Figure 24.25**   You are saving two files to the Answer folder: an HTML text file, and the image to which the HTML script has plotted hot spots.

You are copying two image files, AnsPage.gif and a.gif, which the authors used in a more complete version of this site on the Companion CD, along with the elements that make up the Under Construction page.

8. That's it! Double-click the index.htm filename. You will see your nine-hot spot image map in your Web browser, and if you click on any title, your browser will turn to the Under Construction page you copied to the folder.

Isn't it amazing how much HTML you can learn in a Photoshop book <g>? You just created a single top Web page whose elements take up a microscopic 4 kilobytes! Talk about optimization! A *housefly* can't land on 4 kilobytes!

## Let's Talk HTML Again

In the first example, the Media Web site, we showed you how to center the top page graphic by digging into the HTML script with a plain text editor. You also now know how to add a script to the beginning of another script to blend HTML and make a more sophisticated-looking presentation.

Please examine the index.htm file in the Examples/Chap24/Answer folder in a plain text editor, and compare it to your own index.htm file in the Answer folder on your desktop. You will see that we inserted the following lines

```
<IMG SRC="AnsPage.gif" WIDTH="361" HEIGHT="82"
ALIGN="BOTTOM"BORDER="0" NATURALSIZEFLAG="3">
```

into the top of the page. In English, this means the document is referencing an *Image Source*, followed by the image's name, size, and how it should be positioned. After that, we inserted

```
<IMG SRC="a.gif" WIDTH="107" HEIGHT="108"
ALIGN="BOTTOM" BORDER="0" NATURALSIZEFLAG="3">
```

which is basically the same string of scripting as the first graphic we put in the page. Then, there's a line of text, and then we close out and the ImageReady HTML script runs to the bottom of the document.

In Figure 24.26, you can see how it all comes together. If you'd like to play the authors' version of the Web site, go for it. The index.htm script is in the Examples/Chap24/Answer folder.

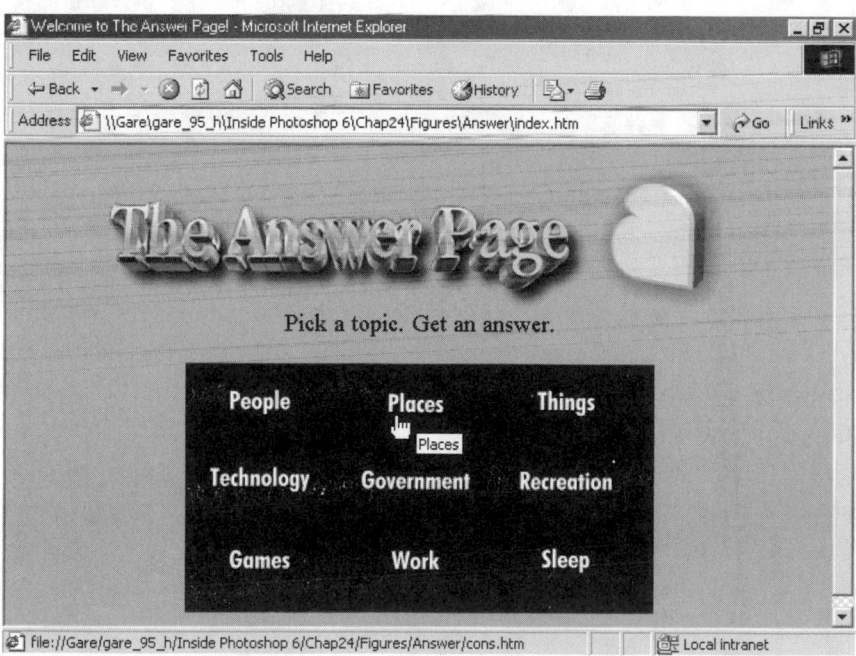

**Figure 24.26**   An inviting top page doesn't have to take up a lot of bandwidth. This page, now ornamented with a headline and animated logo, is only 29K.

In Figure 24.27, and in case you're reading this on a train or at the seaside with no computer in view, you can see what happens when a visitor clicks on any of the image map hot spots.

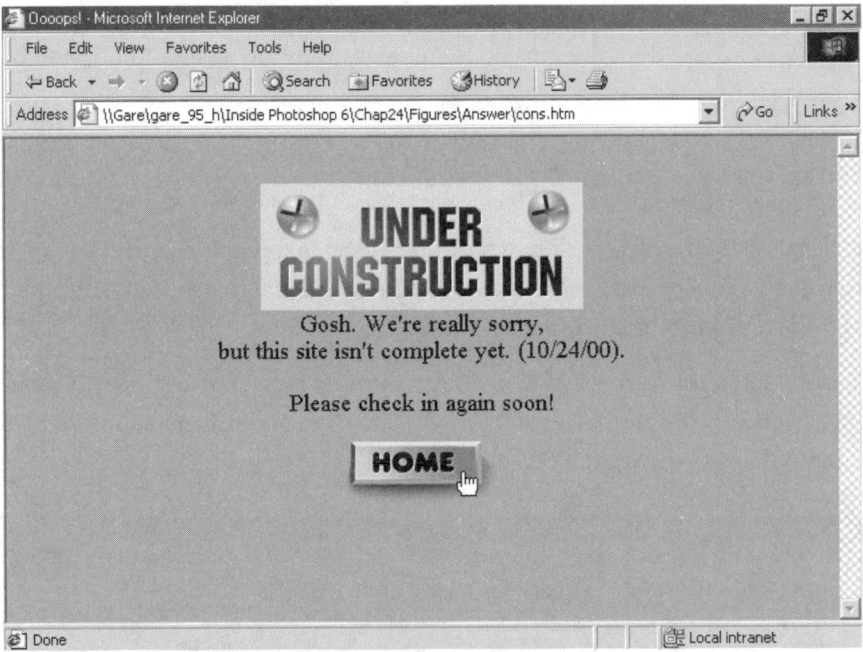

**Figure 24.27**    When you need to post a site, but aren't done with it, by all means, link to an Under Construction page. Never leave a dead link on your site. It's offensive, and you lose potential customers.

I've got this nagging feeling now that I've taught you all to make every link on a top Web page to an Under Construction page. No, no, no. We designed the Under Construction pages to save Web site creation time—it gave us the chance to show you how links work, without much regard to *what* the links link to. You're supposed to link the People image map hot spot to a document you create called people.htm, and so on. We simply didn't have the time to build six or seven complete, complex sites for you on the Companion CD. Besides, we need to teach a little ImageReady between building sites, you know <g>.

## Links Come in Shapes

To be up front about a personal opinion, this author (hi everyone—it's Gary Bouton once in a while in this book!) discourages ImageReady users from using the exotic style of image map shapes. ImageReady offers circular and polygonal (essentially, a freeform shape with all straight sides) tools, so that you can create form-fitting image maps. Unless you're really tight for space on a page (and if you are, rethinking the design would be a good first move), there's little reason to create an exotic bounding area for an image map hot spot. And there's a good reason *not* to do this: Some browsers have a difficult time reading the coordinates of an image map hot spot that is not rectangular.

But we're here to enlighten, not to get opinionated. Most of the time.

If you want to create a circular image map, we'd best start with an image area that is circular. In the following steps, you'll create the art for the image map and then apply the bounding shape that will be referenced in an HTML document.

### Example 24.10   Creating a Round Image Map

1. Press Ctrl(⌘)+N to create a new document. Make it 300 pixels high by 400 pixels wide, Contents of First Layer: White, and then press Enter (Return). On the Layers palette (F7), click on the Create a new layer icon on the bottom of the palette.

2. Click the face of the Rectangular Marquee tool on the toolbox, and choose the Elliptical Marquee tool. Unless, of course, the Elliptical Marquee tool is already showing on the toolbox.

3. Hold down Shift to constrain the shape of the ellipse to that of a circle. When the circle is about as large as the headlight knob in a car, release the cursor.

4. Press F7 to display the Layers palette, and then click the Create a new layer button.

5. Press Alt(Opt)+Delete (Backspace) to fill the marquee selection with fore-ground color. Color makes no difference—it's opacity on the layer we are after. You cannot apply an ImageReady style to a totally transparent area. Press Ctrl(⌘)+D to deselect the marquee.

6. Choose Window, Show Styles, and then click the palette menu button and choose Glass Buttons, as shown in Figure 24.28. Click any of the styles on the palette, and *boing*—anything nontransparent on a layer takes on the glass button shading, as shown in Figure 24.28.

7. Press F11 if the Image Map palette isn't onscreen, click the Image Map tab, and then on the toolbox. Hold on the face of the Image Map tools until the Circular image map tool flies out, and choose it.

   Unlike Photoshop, ImageReady has tear-off tools, which you'll see illustrated in the next figure. This feature is handy for the designer and essential for the author who wants to show lots of stuff onscreen at one time.

8. Begin at the upper left of the glass button rendering, and drag down to the bottom right, as shown in Figure 24.29. You can reposition the image map bounding box by using the Image Map Select tool (at the end of the tear-off

in Figure 24.29); you can even make numerical entries on the Image Map palette to refine the position of the hot spot. It's all interactive, so you can see how close you come to a perfect fit with this hot spot marker on the image.

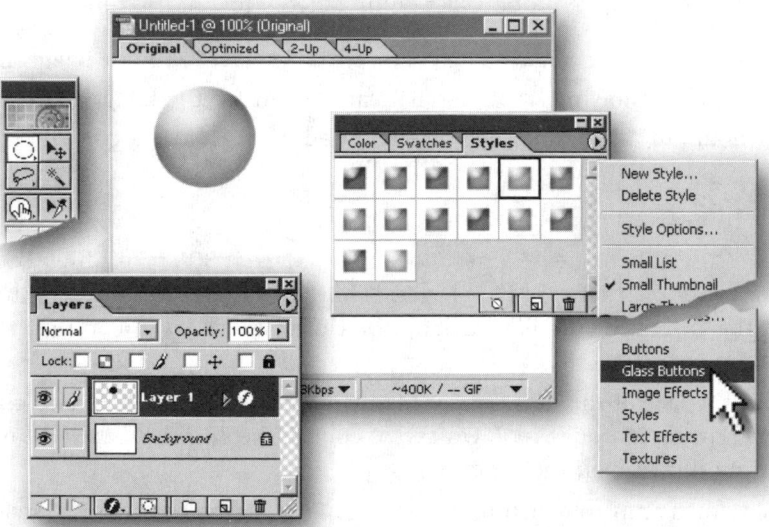

**Figure 24.28**   The Glass Buttons style fits the criteria for the shape of the image map button, and besides, it looks cool.

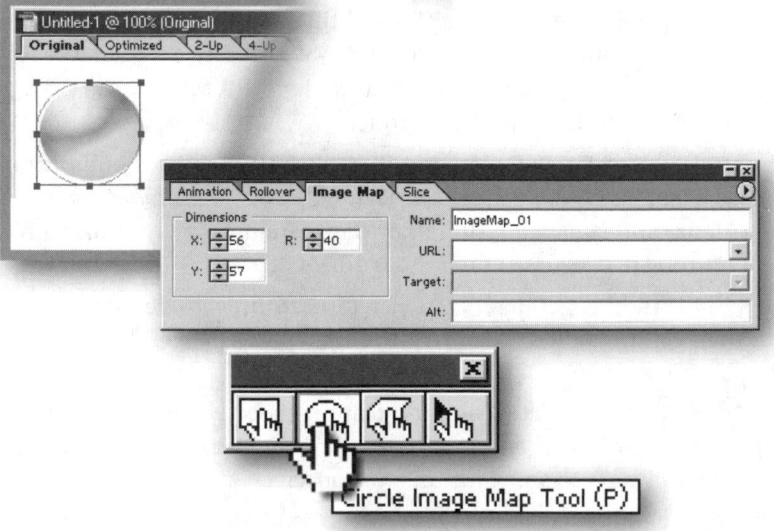

**Figure 24.29**   ImageReady enables you to make a custom fit of a hot spot whose image is circular.

9. From what you've learned so far in this chapter, you can embellish this image, or leave the experience as an education in nonrectangular image mapping. By the way, you can indeed mix different types of image maps in a single image. A circle here, a nonparallel trapezoid there, and so on.

   Keep ImageReady open. You can close the button image at any time without saving it.

Okay, okay, we've got a real-world assignment here where it only makes sense to use a nonrectangular image map. In the next section, you will add hot spots to planets revolving around the sun. This will also be your first experience in creating links that are nowhere near each other. So far, we've only done groups of buttons. Fun ahead—read on!

## Mapping the Universe Using Circular Hot Spots

As you can see, there are about 2.7 steps from conception to delivery of a Web page that has image maps links:

1. You have to optimize the image itself for downloads that proceed with alacrity (fast downloads, okay?).

2. You need to create hot spot areas that are obvious to the visitor by using the Image Map tools on the toolbox in combination with the Image Map palette.

2.7 You might need to hack the HTML script slightly if you don't own an HTML editor such as GoLive, FrontPage, or NavGold 3.

The assignment we have in store for you should be particularly interesting. From the image's concept, its fate was to have very few colors but to look sumptuous and spacey. Additionally, you'll see by the end of the assignment how to use an image as a background tile, instead of always using solid colors. This is the HTML part of the assignment.

So let's get cracking and design the My Solar System Web page.

### Example 24.11   A View of the Solar System. What a Site!

1. Open the SolarSystem.tif image from the Examples/Chapter 24 folder.

   As mentioned earlier in this book, JPEG versions of originals can look a little fuzzy because the JPEG process is casting away certain values and averaging others to produce a small image. The way to defeat this unwanted side effect is to sharpen the image *before* optimizing it to JPEG.

2. Choose Filter, Sharpen, Unsharp Mask. Set the Amount to **50%**, Radius of **1** pixel, and Threshold of **1** pixel. Click OK. The image will look a little as though it's been spending time with a photocopier. This is *okay;* we're not done yet.

3. Press F10 to display the Optimize palette, and then choose JPEG Medium from the Settings drop-down.

4. Check the Optimized option, and lower the Quality to 50. As you can see in Figure 24.30, the visual integrity of the picture couldn't be better, and the document sizes field at the bottom of the image window tell us that this image will download in 5 seconds using a 28.8 connection. Impressive!

   If your document sizes area doesn't show download times, click and hold on it, and then pick this option from the pop-up list.

**Figure 24.30**    The optimized version of this graphic will speed its way to your audience's browsers.

5. With the Circle Image Map tool, draw a circle around the upper-right planet in the system, as shown in Figure 24.31. Again, if the circle needs modifying or repositioning, you can do this right on the Image Map palette (press F11 to show/hide it) by entering different numbers in the fields.

   For the name of this map hot spot, replace the default name with **01**. The URL (as always) is cons.htm (an Under Construction page we designed for you), and the Alt tag which pops up to identify the link when you view the page in the browser is Welcome to (insert fictitious, favorite planet here)_____.

6. Repeat step 5 with the other two planets, each time adding 1 to the number in the name (as in 02, and 03). Keep cons.htm as the link URL, and make up some other weird planet names for the Alt tag. Hey, it's our solar system, and any planet that wants to can be a member.

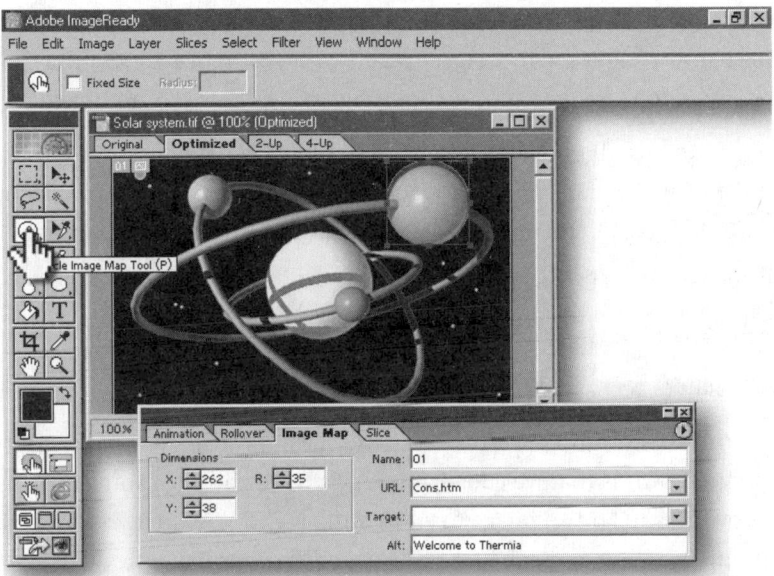

**Figure 24.31**   Circle image map hot spots act exactly like rectangular ones except that when a circle image map is highlighting a circle shape in the design, the circle image map is a form-fitting selection area. There's no chance of a visitor clicking on the wrong area.

7. On your desktop, create a folder named **system**. In ImageReady, choose File, Save Optimized As, choose to save both the HTML and the image, and save the HTML as index.htm.

8. Duck out of ImageReady, and let's see what we can do on the HTML optimization side of things.

First, you will want to copy cons.htm, droid.jpg, and home.jpg to your system desktop folder just to get the Under Construction page working. If you double-click index.htm right now, the image map you create will appear in the browser and clicking a planet will take you to the Under Construction site.

But we'll bet you want a little more out of this sci-fi site, no? Read on!

## Applying Scripting Language to Your HTML File

The following are suggestions, so they are not presented as a numbered list.

First, you want to center the image map. You already know how to do this; in a plain text editor, place a **<Center>** tag right after the <BODY BGCOLOR...> line toward the top of the text, and then place a **</Center>** tag to terminate the property before the </BODY> tag at the bottom of the document.

Here's what's going to get the oooohs and ahhhhhs from your audience. Instead of a plain background, add a GIF image. The browser will repeat across the breadth of the browser window any image that's specified as the background image.

Do this: Copy the bk.gif image to your System folder on your desktop. This is a puny 322-byte file of white stars against a black background. Now, remember where you put the <Center> tag? Look up in the text document to find the following line

`<BODY BGCOLOR="#ffffff">`

Change this line to

`<BODY BGCOLOR="#ffffff" BACKGROUND="bk.gif">.`

Now, the only basic difference between the authors' title Web page (see Figure 24.32) and your own is that we added a bitmap title to the page and a little text. You already know how to add an image to an existing HTML file, so if you want this "My Solar System" headline, copy the mss.gif image from our Examples/Chap24/system folder on the Companion CD to the System folder on your desktop.

The dramatic change in the page was simpler than you'd think, huh?

Hey, how would you like to experience room service for composing HTML pages? That is, how would you like to see how Photoshop can generate a really decent looking site, with real links (not construction links) and all—and to top it off, all you need to do is answer a few questions.

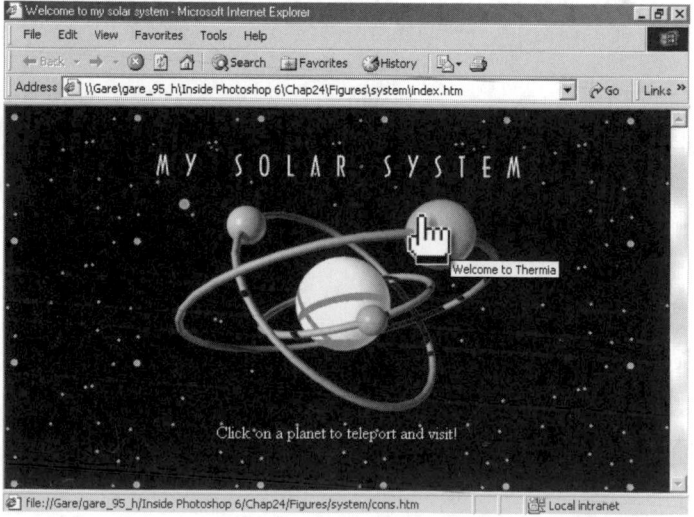

**Figure 24.32**   Add a starfield for the background by adding half a line of HTML to the script file.

# Photoshop's Web Photo Gallery

It's time to close ImageReady and open Photoshop because there's a positively brilliant set of macros at hand in the File menu, and we want you to work through them. Not to worry; it's not *real* work. The File, Automate, Web Photo Gallery is an automation tool that can take your photos or drawings and put thumbnails on the top page, make the thumbnails link to larger versions of the art, and return or cycle your view to see the rest of the site. We cannot think of a more pleasant way to spend five minutes (*artistically,* okay?) than to fill out the fields in the Web Photo Gallery, and let Photoshop resize and organize a complex HTML document for you.

## Operating the Web Photo Gallery

Before you begin this excursion, do two things:

1. Create an In and an Out folder on your desktop. The Out folder is necessary for Photoshop to write to, and the In folder will contain original images.

2. Either get from your stockpile, or copy from our Examples/Chap24/AutoArt folder on the Companion CD, *10* images you can use to make up a Web site. If you're using your own images, try to find ones that are about 500K in file size. By doing this, you limit the amount by which Photoshop has to resize the full size view of your work. Resizing always degrades image focus and quality somewhat.

If you're ready to do some simple keystroking, here's the magic formula to "instant" Web design...

### Example 24.12    Working with Photoshop's Web Photo Gallery

1. In Photoshop, choose File, Automate, Web Photo Gallery. An intimidating, huge dialog box appears with cryptic messages.

2. Refer to Figure 24.33 for the locations of what is about to be described. Choose Table from the Styles drop-down list. This type of look for the page includes a nice texture and bumpy borders. Your other choices do not. In the Options drop-down list, choose Banner. A banner is a headline, and these always look nice on a site. That's area #1 in Figure 24.33.

3. In the Site Name field, type the, um, site name. The #2 callout in Figure 24.33 shows that we chose Bouton's Web Gallery for the site name. Under Photographer, you can type anything you like. Gary Bouton wanted to show off illustrations instead of photographs, hence Bouton Illustrations is the entry here. In the Date field, type the date. This might sound stupid, but months from now, a visitor might want to know exactly how stale your site is. Or how fresh.

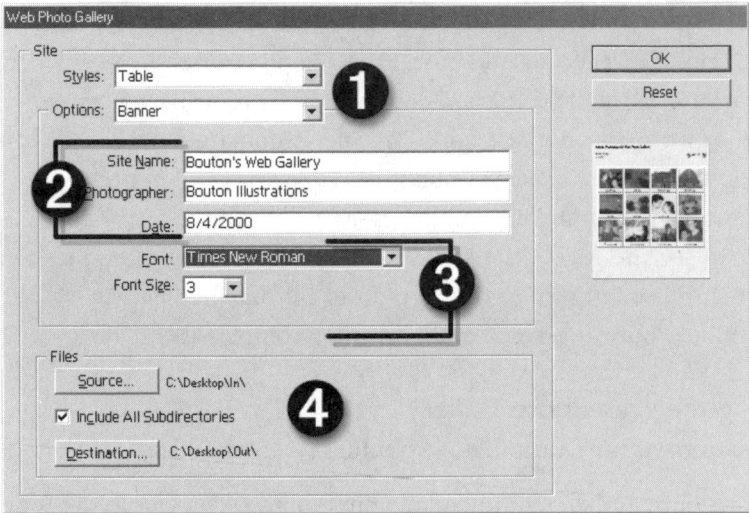

**Figure 24.33**    Follow along with the options you want, and Photoshop will create the Web
site for you, using as many pages as necessary.

4. In callout #3 in Figure 24.33, you have a choice of Font. You are limited to
   the fonts that browsers support natively. Why not go with Times New
   Roman? In the Font Size box, type **3**. This is a confusing box. What does 3
   mean? It means that all the info you typed will be displayed at *three levels
   above the standard type height* in HTML documents. Trust us. Three is plenty
   big enough to display your name and site contents.

5. In the Files field, click Source, which displays a directory box. In the direc-
   tory box, locate and choose the In folder you created on your desktop. Click
   OK to choose the In folder. Then, click the Destination folder, and choose
   Out from the list of file locations in the directory box. Don't close anything.
   This set of steps has only covered page one of the automation.

Okay, you've filled out page 1 of the Web Gallery automation. Let's tackle page 2.

### Example 24.13    Filling Out More Automation Data

1. Drop down the Options list and choose Gallery Images.

2. Let's resize the images for the full-size versions on the Web site. Check the
   Resize Images option, and type **350** in the pixels field, as shown in Figure
   24.34. Forget about the Medium drop-down box. That's for people who have
   no idea how large they want their gallery images.

3. Go with Medium JPEG Quality for the full-size gallery images. Either drag the slider until you see 5 in the Quality box, or type **5** if you've had enough of sliders for one day (see Figure 24.34).

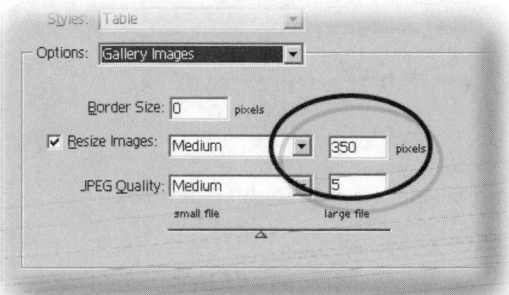

**Figure 24.34**   Decide on the size and JPEG quality of the Web gallery images.

4. This may be the end of the steps, but not the end of decisions you have to make. Keep everything open, and we'll start a new set of steps to make the Editors believe we understand New Riders' book styles.

### Example 24.14   Specifying Thumbnail Image Display and Size

1. Drop the Options box down once more and choose Gallery Thumbnails.

2. Check the Caption: Use Filename option. Now, every page with your full-size work will have the name of the file right there to identify it for your visitor. So visitors can call you and say, "Smithers, I'll pay $4,000 US for that 'Fishbuck' image on your site." Alternatively, you can take the trouble to fill out File, File Info for every image you want to post, *prior* to entering into this Web automation thing. In which case, you'd choose the Use File Info Caption option. It's your call. Given the template quality of this site, we felt it was like trying to gild a lily to embellish the image page with lots of text information.

3. In the Font and Font size fields, why not go with Arial and size 3 (the same as the top page text). A good reading-distance type size is +3 (plus three), as you'll seen in a site creation program such as PageMill.

4. Here's the moment of truth that will shape the design of the top Web page: how many rows and columns of images? Well, we have 10 images, so we guess five columns and two rows would make a neat arrangement (see Figure 24.35).

5. Finally (for this page), leave the Border size at 0 (zero). Keep this dialog box open; there's a little more to come.

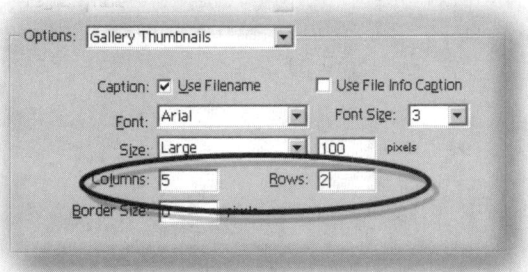

**Figure 24.35**   Set your rows and columns in this dialog box.

## Specifying Text and Background Colors

Link, background, text, and banner color need to be specified (see Figure 24.36). Basically, you are on your own here, but remember that if the background color is going to be dark, your text and banner need to be light colors. Otherwise, they will be difficult to read.

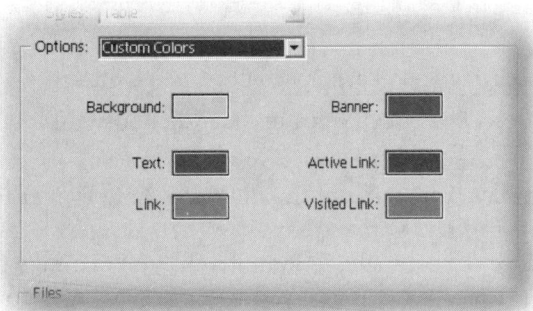

**Figure 24.36**   Remember to make your text and banner easy to read by choosing colors that contrast with the backgroud.

Here's how to complete the questionnaire, start the machinery, and generate a Web gallery site:

### Example 24.15   Adding Color to the Gallery

 1. Click the Background swatch, and choose a neutral, but warm, light color from the Color Picker. Although this Web gallery style has a texture for the background, occasionally there might be a server accident and the image won't load. Here's where you decide on the color of the background in the unlikely event of a server problem. Colored text will stand off nicely from this color. Try out #CBCAFB in the Color Picker for the background.

2. Click the Banner swatch and choose a rich blue, such as #404363. Naturally, the choice is yours, but remember that this style of Galley has a textured background, so text must be a little strong in color and large in size to dominate over the background texture.

3. Click the Text swatch, and in the Color Picker choose #404363—the same as the banner color. Why not?

   The following three decisions don't impact on the site, because this particular Gallery style features no text links. But if you were to experiment with an HTML editor and this document, we'd recommend:

   - The color of a link on this site can be anything you choose, but again, it's good to stick with dark text colors when the background is a light texture. We chose #A06565 in the Color Picker—a burnt brick color, pleasing to look at but definitely signifying something special in the text.

   - For the color of an active link, why not go with pure blue: #0000FF.

   - For the color of a link that the visitor has already accessed in the past, try out #6B6B53. It's a dull olive, and works well with the other colors except the active link color.

4. Ready? This is your big moment. You've finished making your choices and now need only to click the OK button in the upper right. Wait a few minutes, and when Photoshop has finished processing, you can close Photoshop, open the Out folder on your desktop, and double-click the index.html file. The extension *html* here is cool because:

   - It's the accurate suffix for an HTML file.

   - You didn't use any HTML script from the CD, so there's no possibility that the Web site will fail because the references have mixed suffixes (*.html versus *.htm).

In Figure 24.37 you can see the author's Web Gallery as displayed in Microsoft Explorer. It's a glorious site, thanks to Photoshop's new features. Here you see the visitor clicking the land06.jpg thumbnail, which will take the visitor to a larger version of the image.

In Figure 24.38, you can see the title, the full-size picture, and the navigation controls for going back by one page, going forward by one page, or going up (going to the top, introductory page).

**Note**

The authors would appreciate not actually finding the CD artwork up on a WWW site. We deliberately made it interesting, but not world-class art, to discourage its use outside the tutorial. In any event, it's more fun to use your own artwork and actually go into business on the Web than to post our picture of frankfurters flying through space!

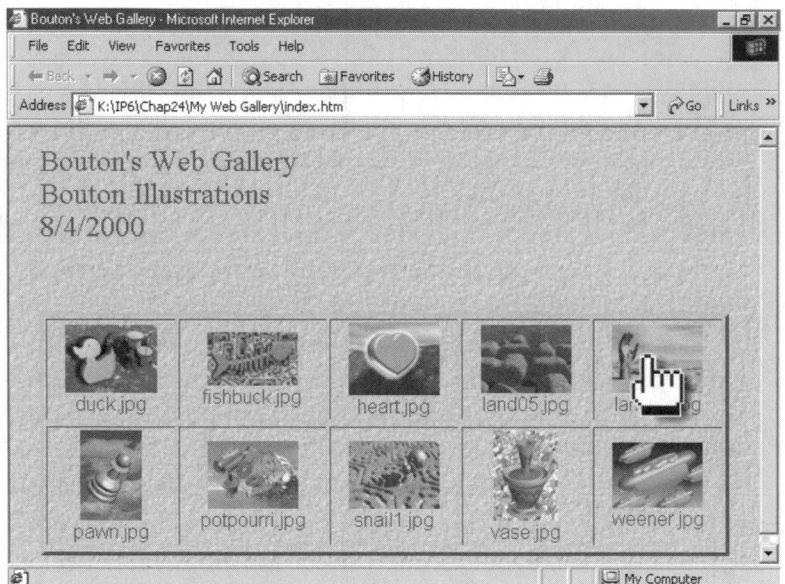

**Figure 24.37**    The top page of the Web Photo Gallery that Photoshop created.

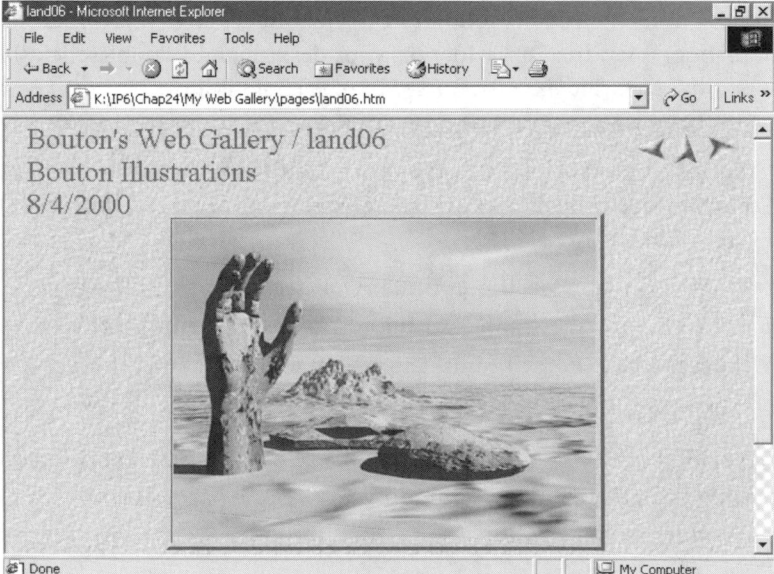

**Figure 24.38**    When you have several linking pages and more than one level on a site, it's called a *system*. Photoshop generates a simple system site, but, hey, it *works* and if you learn some HTML, you can make this site even more intricate.

HTML scripting and ImageReady and Photoshop's features appear to go inextricably hand in hand. Therefore, it was necessary to teach one to properly learn to use the other in this chapter. It's fun though, isn't it? Writing little tags and stuff in a text document and having it impact on the design of a Web page?

## Summary

You now know not only how to create an image map, but also how to change the shape of the hot spot, how to blend two HTML documents together to create a beautiful top page, how to apply styles, and most important, how to manipulate text in a text editor as you do an image in an image window. The combination of a little understanding of scripting language along with the power of ImageReady makes your computer a haven for striking, compelling Web page work. Wouldn't it be cool if your style of Web page construction started a trend on the WWW? Hey, stranger things have happened. For example, Jim Clarke bought heavily into Microsoft stock last week!

Chapter 25 takes you away from static graphics to a world where everything seems to move under its own power. Animated GIFs and buttons that respond to cursor coordinates might sound hard to create, but not when ImageReady has basically automated the process for you. Simply sit back and flex your creativity, and ImageReady will do the rest.

# Chapter 25

# Creating Rollovers and Animations

Although you use entirely different steps for creating a rollover than you do for a GIF animation, both pieces of Web media move—and motion spells excitement.

So if you thought image optimization was useful and image slicing was cool, hang onto your lunch pails, because the best, quite literally, is yet to come.

In this chapter, we'll show you how to make an *interesting* GIF animation (as opposed to a typical one) and how to make an impressive rollover group of buttons for your top Web page to intrigue the visitor.

## Understanding a Rollover and Scripting Language

A *rollover* belongs to the Web element class of JavaScripts. *Rollovers* are multiple images that appear at different times on a Web page, and the specific graphic is displayed by the visitor's hovering or clicking over the image area. In case you don't know what a JavaScript is, it has nothing to do with Java programming, and is most closely related to other scripting languages, such as AppleScript, or the batch file that executes commands depending on user input. Let's dig a little deeper before we do anything in ImageReady, okay?

To repeat, in case you haven't had your first coffee and croissant of the day: JavaScript has nothing to do with the Java programming language. It was originally called LiveScript by Netscape Communications, which later decided that LiveScript needed a sexier, yet very misleading new name.

We're all a little guilty of using terms loosely sometimes, especially when we talk to other people in the same line of work or with the same interests—and that can be misleading to newcomers. Right now, we want to help you understand what we mean by *scripting language*.

A scripting language is *not* code.

We often call HTML "a few lines of code," but it's really "a few lines of scripting language," like *lingo* is used to script Macromedia Director shows. *Engineers* write code; we artists can handle scripting—and you can do a lot with scripts.

A JavaScript is perhaps the most courteous way to display information that reacts to cursor movement while the visitor navigates your Web site. JavaScripts are never downloaded to a visitor's computer. Java *applets* (actual Java programming of small utilities) need to assemble parts of themselves on the host's machine and—I don't know—doesn't that make you a little nervous, as in, "assemble virus here?" Fortunately, Java*Scripts* cannot breach your machine.

Also, because JavaScripting is text commands, not code, you can read and copy anyone's script, and they in turn can read and copy yours. This isn't stealing, folks; in fact, many sites that feature rollover buttons and slide shows actually tell you to download the script. Now *that's* called sharing, and that's the spirit of the Web—learning through imitation.

Although there are many different types of JavaScripts, ImageReady offers a graphical interface for creating only one of them—the really cool one—the rollover. A *rollover* is what makes a button or illustration change when you click on it, hover the cursor over it, release the cursor, and so on. Rollover navigation buttons can add a lot of polish to your Web page, so let's get going!

## Creating the First State for the JavaScript Button

By default, when you enter a Web site, you aren't clicking on anything immediately, so the first *state*—the set of conditions by which the JavaScript knows which image to display—is called the *default state*. This state exists when you're not clicking on anything.

We think that "Knock here" is a slightly humorous message on a button in its default state, and the following steps show you how to create such a button.

### Example 25.1   Preparing the Default Button

1. Press Ctrl(⌘)+N, and in the New dialog box specify that an image should be created that's 75 pixels tall by 200 pixels wide; then click Contents of First Layer: Transparent. This is, for sure, a large size for the button, but not if it's the only thing on the HTML page!

2. Fill the layer with foreground color (press Alt(Opt)+Delete [Backspace]), and then press F6 if the Styles palette is not currently in the workspace.

3. On the Styles palette, choose Styles from the palette flyout (click the triangle in a circle at the top), and then drag the Button-Purple thumbnail into the image window (or click once on the thumbnail). You can identify this thumbnail by hovering over the top row, second-from-left thumbnail (see #1 in Figure 25.1).

4. Choose Window, Show Character (don't we *usually* show character?).

   The Character/Paragraph grouped palette is much easier to work with than the Options bar—for example, you can place it right next to the image window and cut down on your mouse mileage.

5. With the Eyedropper tool, click over the lightest part of the button, click on the foreground color selection box on the toolbox, and then lighten the purple a little more—values of R:204, G:186, and B:217 are splendid. Click OK to return to your work.

6. Choose the Type tool (See #2.). Click the Center Aligned icon on the Options bar. On the Character palette, click the tiny down-arrow to pop up the Web-safe color palette and other options. Click on the Foreground color choice. Now your text will be in that lighter shade of purple.

7. Click an insertion point in the middle of the button. Type **Knock Here**.

   We suggest that you choose on the Character palette a heavy font, such as Kabel at 30 points, for the type (see #3). The text is added to a new layer (see Figure 25.1).

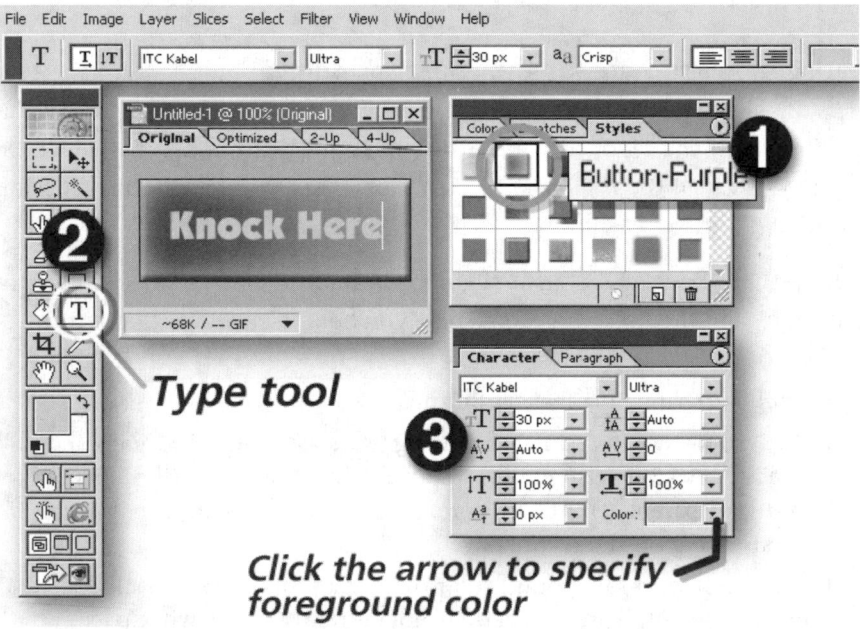

**Figure 25.1**    Apply a style to the layer, choose a color for the text on the Character palette, choose the font and size, and then use the Type tool to enter **Knock Here**.

**Tip**

**One-Stop Shopping for Type**    If you like to keep your workspace sparse in Photoshop and you're really adept at applying attributes from a menu, you can right-click (Macintosh: hold Ctrl and click) over a Type layer, and as you can see in Figure 25.2, you have everything except the color of the text at your disposal on the context menu.

You can pick up the color from the Options bar. This is one way to limit the number of palettes you have onscreen.

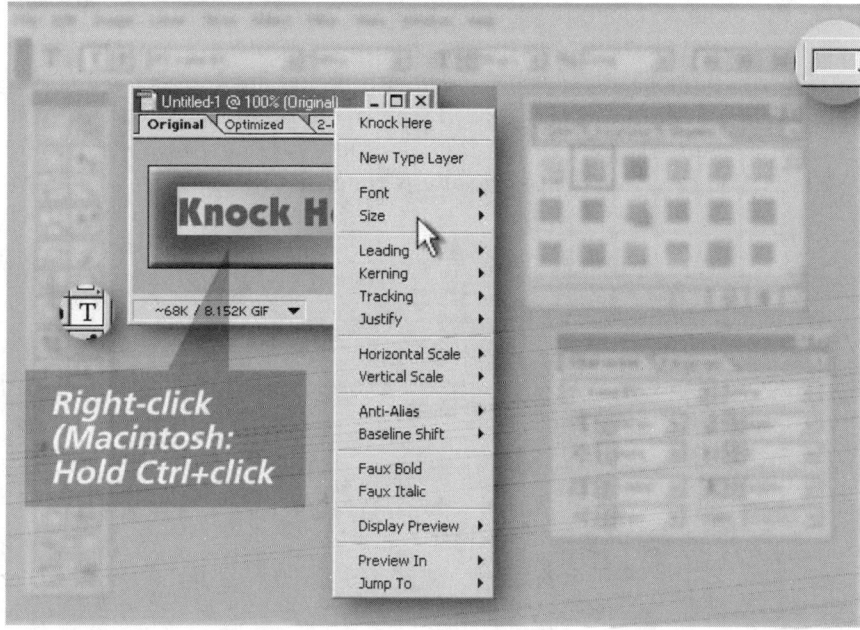

**Figure 25.2** Right-click (Macintosh: hold Ctrl and click) for most of the text attributes you're looking for.

8. Click the *f* icon at the bottom of the Layers palette, and choose Bevel and Emboss from the layer filters list, as shown in Figure 25.3.

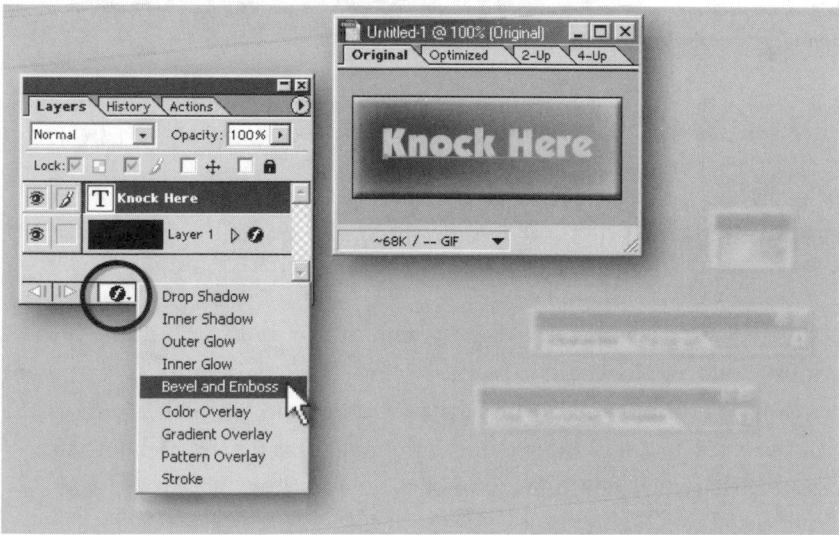

**Figure 25.3** Add some punch to the button text by adding an emboss effect.

9. On the Bevel and Emboss palette, choose Pillow Emboss from the top drop-down, and Chisel Soft from the lower drop-down list, as shown in Figure 25.4. You do not need to experiment with the other controls for this assignment, but do indeed experiment in your own work, especially with the Use Texture feature. There is no confirmation button or anything with Layer effects; you can close the palette at any time, and the changes you've made are applied.

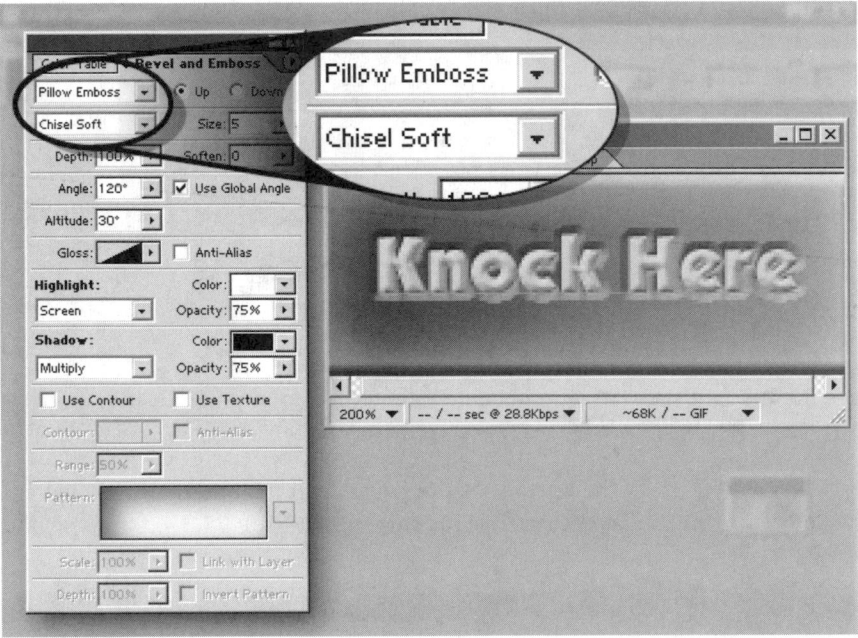

**Figure 25.4**    Add a dynamic look to the text by embossing it. You can also choose the light direction, type of emboss, and other parameters in this dialog box.

10. Choose Flatten Image from the Layers palette's menu flyout. You now only have a Knock Here layer on the Layers palette and in the image. Save the image to hard disk as Welcome.psd, in Photoshop's native format.

You've completed the design of the default state of this rollover button. Choose Window, Show Rollover Now, and keep the Rollover palette open from this point on. As you can see, a tiny copy of the button you designed is at the front of the palette with the word "Normal" above the thumbnail. This means "default" state—what the visitor will see without having to click on anything.

The second state for the rollover will be a Welcome! button that appears when the visitor's cursor hovers over the Knock Here button.

## Creating a "Hover Over" State for the Button

Let's get a little more adventurous with the second button for the JavaScript rollover. You'll keep the button basically the same overall color as the first button, but you'll add banding to the shading (by learning a new technique) and make the color lighter than that of the Knock Here button. The audience will see immediately that this is no mere image map button. Finally, you'll create new text so the button will seem to change its message.

Here's how to create a button that will appear when the *MouseOver* state is in effect (the visitor has the cursor over the button):

### Example 25.2    Creating Graphics for the MouseOver State

1. Create a second state for the graphic by clicking the Creates new rollover state icon at the bottom of the Rollover palette. By default, the second button is called the Over button, which is what we want. If you wanted a different state in your own work, you could click the down arrow, and choose from a list of other states.

2. Create a new layer in the graphic by clicking the Create new layer icon at the bottom of the Layers palette. Then press Ctrl(⌘)+Delete (Backspace) to fill the layer. Drag the deep purple–style thumbnail into the image window to apply the style.

3. Click the Effects triangle on the title directly beneath the Layer 1 title on the Layers palette.

   This causes all the effects that make up the layer to cascade down, and you can change any of the components.

4. Choose a medium gray foreground color from the Color Picker, and then press Alt(Opt)+Delete (Backspace). As you can see, a layer that has a style can sometimes be changed by changing the base color. Other styles will not change at all with a change in base color.

5. Double-click on the Color Overlay title on the Layers palette (see #1 on Figure 25.5). A Color Overlay palette will pop into the workspace. Click on the Color field on this palette to display the Color Picker (see #2). Choose a lighter shade of purple here, and then press Enter (Return) to return to the workspace.

   While we're at it, let's change the shading effect that is part of the style.

6. Double-click on the Gradient Overlay title; then, on the Gradient Overlay palette that appears, choose Yellow, Violet, Orange, Blue from the drop-down list of gradient presets, as shown in Figure 25.6.

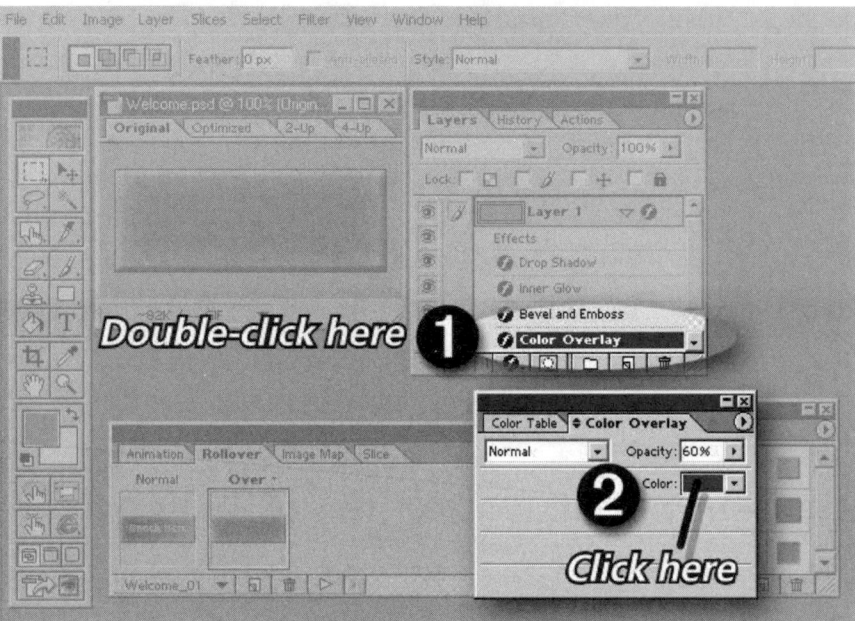

**Figure 25.5**    All the components of a style can be changed, deleted, and modified.

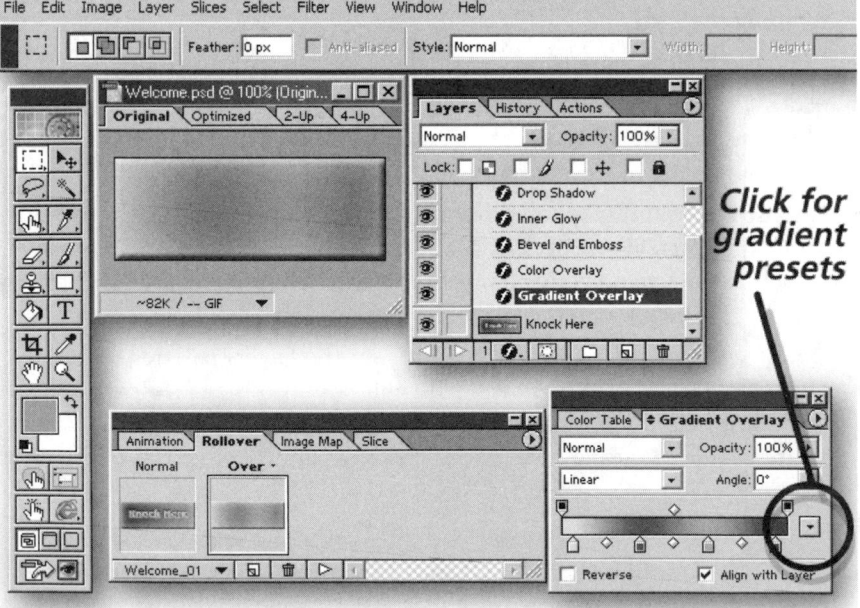

**Figure 25.6**    Change the shading on the button from a Linear Gradient to the preset multicolored scheme.

Does this change the button to the exact colors shown on the color strip on the Gradient Overlay palette? Not at all; what you've done is "influence" the sum total of the base layer, the Color Overlay, and the Gradient Overlay to display the banding—the tonal quality—on the button. It's still got a *little* purple in it.

**Tip**

**Change Opacity and Blending Mode to Emphasize a Color**   If you want more of one type of effect to be obvious in the color blend that makes up a button, try changing the opacity and blending mode (Normal, Multiply, and so on) when these options are available. For example, you can do something really strange to the Gradient Overlay right now if you choose Difference from the blending modes drop-down on the top left of the Layers palette.

7. With the Type tool, click the center of the button (remember, you left the alignment of the Type tool to centered), and then type **Welcome**, using the last-used font and font size. With the Move tool, click the type so it is selected. Now, the Type layer doesn't care at all about what the Color Overlay was for the underlying button, so you must either click the color swatch on the Character palette or click the swatch on the Options bar. Clicking either one displays the Color Picker, where you choose a nice deep purple, press Enter (Return), and viola, the text has changed color.

8. Add a pillow emboss effect by clicking the Effects icon to display the flyout on the Layers palette, and then choose Bevel and Emboss from the flyout.

9. Click the triangle next to the *f* on the Layers list (see #1 in Figure 25.7), and then double-click on the Bevel and Emboss title. A Bevel and Emboss palette appears in the workspace. To fine-tune the emboss, do the same thing you did with the default state text: Change the upper drop-down to Pillow Emboss, and then change the lower drop-down list to Chisel Soft (#2). The type layer and the button layer together are going to represent the MouseOver state on the Rollover palette, as shown in Figure 25.7.

   We don't know why merging down does not work with layers that have effects tagged to them, but you *cannot* use the Ctrl(⌘)+E command to make a single layer out of the type and the button.

10. Okay—hide the bottom, Knock Here layer, by clicking the eye icon to the left of its title. Then, press Ctrl(⌘)+Shift+E to merge visible layers, as is elegantly illustrated in Figure 25.8. Now, you have a first and second state image for the rollover button. Do this: Click on the first frame on the Rollover palette, hide the Welcome layer, and reveal the Knock Here layer using the Layers palette. Then, click on the second Rollover palette frame and make sure that the Welcome! frame is visible. Press Ctrl(⌘)+S; keep the file open.

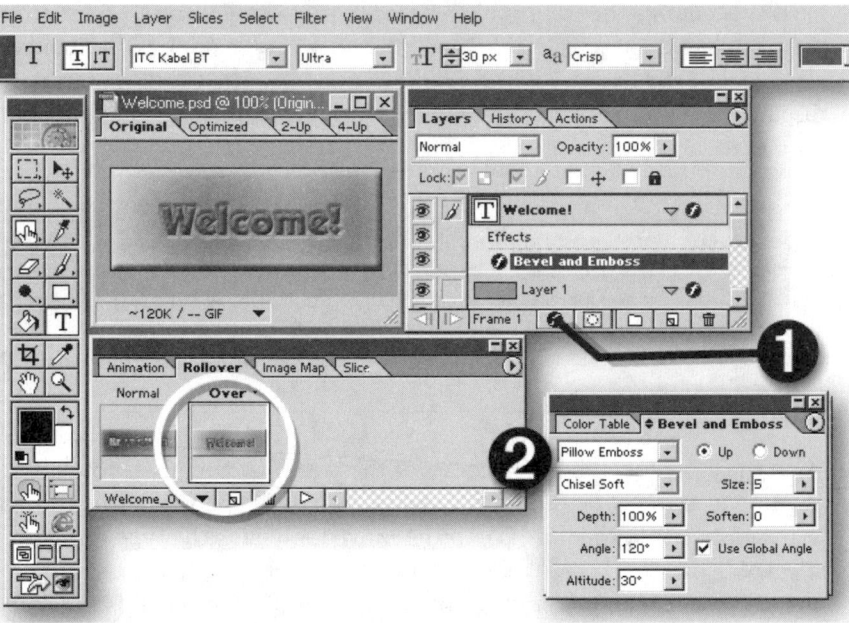

**Figure 25.7**  The second button exists on two layers right now, but we'll correct this.

**Figure 25.8**  Merge all the visible layers—this includes only the new type layer and its corresponding button.

**Tip**

**Use Patterns Overlay for Buttons**   The truth will come out, sometimes Tips pop up in this book when there's no other good place to put them! Seriously, did you notice that one of the effects shaders is the Pattern Overlay? Which patterns are available when you click the Pattern button on the palette?

In Figure 25.9, you can see that a new image window has been filled with the Bubbles pattern. You simply add a fill to a layer, and then click on the title of the pattern. You can use these patterns for anything you like; these patterns tile, but because they are so small, you can't use them on images larger than say, a button, before you begin to see the repeats in the tile.

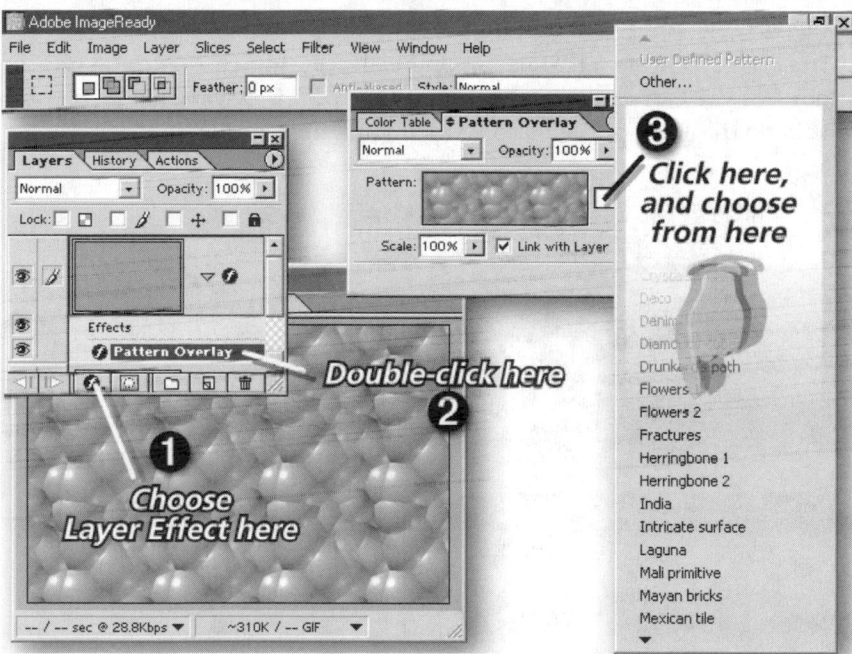

**Figure 25.9**   ImageReady ships with over a dozen interesting patterns that can be components of effects; or you can use them, undiluted, as an image background.

The next section should come as no surprise to you. You're going to create the MouseDown state for the button. This is what all visitors will see when they click the button, and you'll want to attach a URL to this button. Come see for yourself!

## Creating the Third State for the Button

A button that's really deep in color will make a splendid "entrance" when folks click on your rollover button. So let's make it a nearly black button with gleaming green text that says "Loading" (as in, "Now I'm going to load this page you asked for").

We'll play around with an undiscovered feature or two, but basically, to do the third state for this Web object, you do this:

### Example 25.3    Creating the MouseDown State for the Button

1. Click the Create new layer icon at the bottom of the Layers palette, and then fill the layer (see Figure 25.10). We suggest 4F4F4F, a deep shade of warm black, as the foreground color. You specify this by typing **4F4F4F** in the # field, and then press Tab to make the entry and move to a different field (that you don't use), and then click OK.

2. Click the Creates a new rollover state button on the Rollover palette. You can see that Down is the state assigned, by default, to the new entry.

3. Drag the fifth-from-left Style button—called Button-Up—into the image window. As you can see in Figure 25.10, the button is a deep color, but you can still see the edges of the button—the highlights and shading.

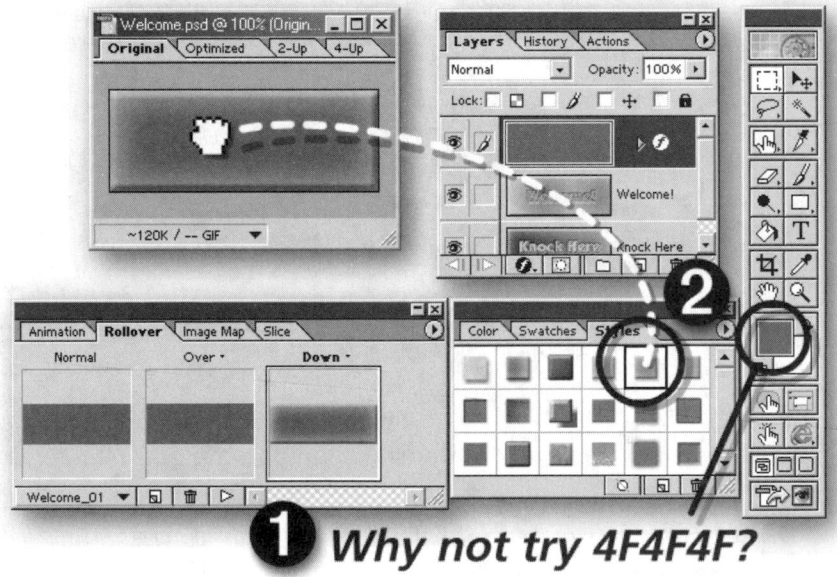

**Figure 25.10**    Some of the buttons on the Styles palette require that you already have a dark or light color filling the current layer. The one you're dragging is one of those Styles palette buttons.

4. Add the word **Loading** to a type layer on top of the button. Make it a bright green color.

5. Click the Layer Effects *f* icon at the bottom of the Layers palette and make the lettering Pillow Embossed with a Chisel Soft, as you've done with the other two buttons.

6. Now, click the right-facing triangle directly to the right of the Angle field on the Bevel and Emboss palette, and then drag the line in the circle down until the number in the field is about –57°.

You'll notice in Figure 25.11 that because the Use Global Angle option is checked, the type and the underlying button layer both change lighting direction. You *want* this to happen, because now the button looks indented (as though you had physically pushed it in with the cursor).

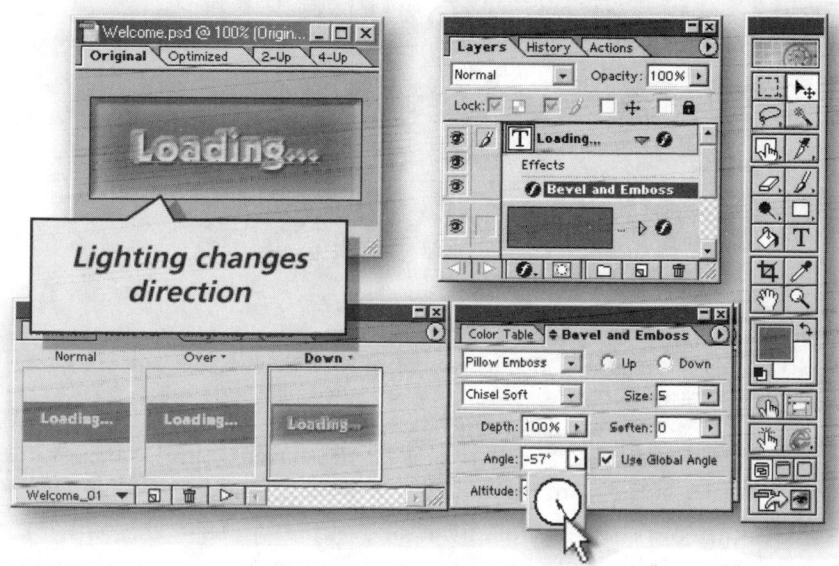

**Figure 25.11**   Change any underlying layer that has effects applied to it by keeping the Use Global Angle option checked.

7. Extend the palette by choosing Show Options on the palette's flyout menu. See #1 in Figure 25.12. You're going to make this text a little less hard on the eyes by softening the shadow areas. Click the Shadow Opacity, then specify about a 48% opacity by either typing **48** in the field or by dragging the feature's slider (#2). You can close this palette any time you like now.

8. Hide the Knock Here and Welcome layers, and then press Ctrl(⌘)+Shift+E to merge the Loading type with the button. Make every layer visible by clicking to make the eye icons visible in the eye column to the left of the titles. By using the Layers visibility icons and the thumbnails on the Rollover palette, be sure frame one is the Knock Here image (layers Welcome! and Loading are hidden on the Layers palette). Frame two on the Rollover palette features the Welcome! layer, so make Welcome! visible on the Layers palette, and click the visibility icon for Loading to make it invisible.

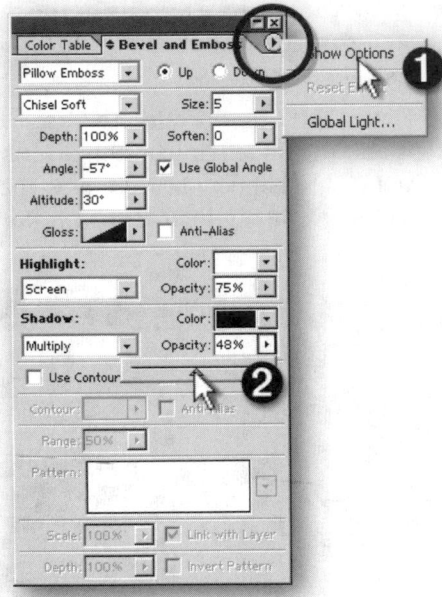

**Figure 25.12**   You can make the highlight and shadow any color you want, and even increase or decrease the percentage of their opacity.

9. Click on the Loading layer title to make it the current editing layer. In the Rollover palette, the third thumbnail (Loading) should be highlighted.

10. For kicks, try out the behavior of the rollover button. First, click either the triangle or the icon circled in Figure 25.13, and then hover and click and move the cursor away from the button in the image window. Cool, huh? Click the triangle a second time to *stop* all this behavior!

11. On the Optimize palette (press F10), choose JPEG High from the Settings field, and make sure the Progressive option is not checked. This rollover button is small (about 11K for all three images) and it is the only element on the Web page, so you can splurge a little with JPEG quality. Click the triangle in the circle, choose Show Options from the flyout menu, and then click on the Matte color field. In the Color Picker, choose a deep blue.

    When you eventually see the rollover in the Web browser window, it will be framed against a deep blue background.

12. Right-click (Macintosh: hold Ctrl and click) on the layer title to Loading… (*not* the thumbnail image!), and then choose the New Layer Based Image Map Area option, as shown in Figure 25.14. Doing this enables you to add a URL to any of the three images—which is what you'll do shortly.

    If you could watch the Image Map palette right now, you'd see it come alive from its totally dimmed state. Now, you can make an entry or two in the palette's fields.

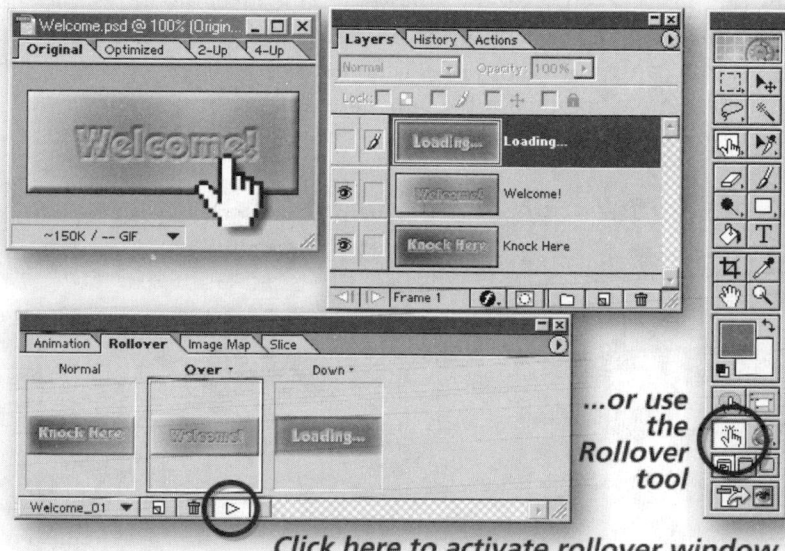

**Figure 25.13**   You can preview how your rollover will work by clicking either the triangle at the bottom of the Rollover palette, or the Rollover tool.

**Figure 25.14**   Make the MouseDown state trigger a link to a URL.

**13.** Click the Image Map tab on the Rollover grouped palette. In the URL field, type your favorite URL. We're using the Boutons' home page in this example, because…why not? The Alt field should be used to provide an audio description of the graphic for the blind, and for visitors who have Web graphics turned off in their browsers (to surf faster). See Figure 25.15.

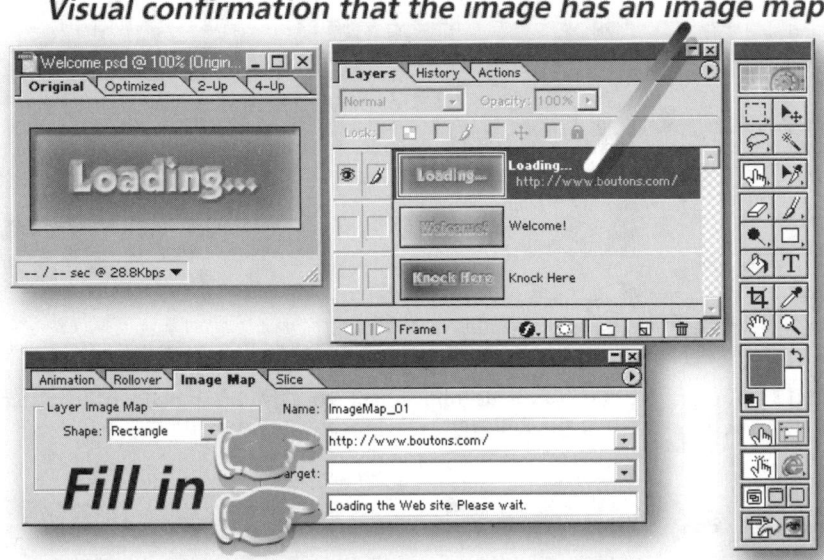

**Figure 25.15**    Fill in a URL on the Image Map palette, add a description of what's going on in the Alt field, and you're all set to export the HTML script and component images.

**14.** Basically, you're done! Choose File, Save Optimized As, and then type **index.htm** for the filename. Be sure the drop-down Save As Type list has HTML and images showing. Click Save. Now you can go to index.htm on your drive (wherever you saved it) and double-click it to see the rollover in action.

Two things we need to point out about the previous set of steps:

- You might want to be a neater designer than the author and actually use ImageReady guides when you're placing text. You can pull guides out of rulers, exactly as you do in Photoshop—all you do is press Ctrl(⌘)+R for the rulers. By aligning the text in a finicky, obsessive manner, the rollover looks more professional and is easier to read.

- It's a good practice to name the first file a visitor will encounter index.html (this book uses *.htm because the CD won't accept a four-character extension for biplatform disks). "Index" is the first page served up by a server when you go to a specific location. Although your Web page with the rollover button is only one page, it's still good practice to name the top page index.htm(l).

Okay, we probably can guess the answer, but have you tried out the Web page in your browser yet? The button is in the upper-left corner of the browser, and you wonder what you did wrong, as is painfully obvious in Figure 25.16.

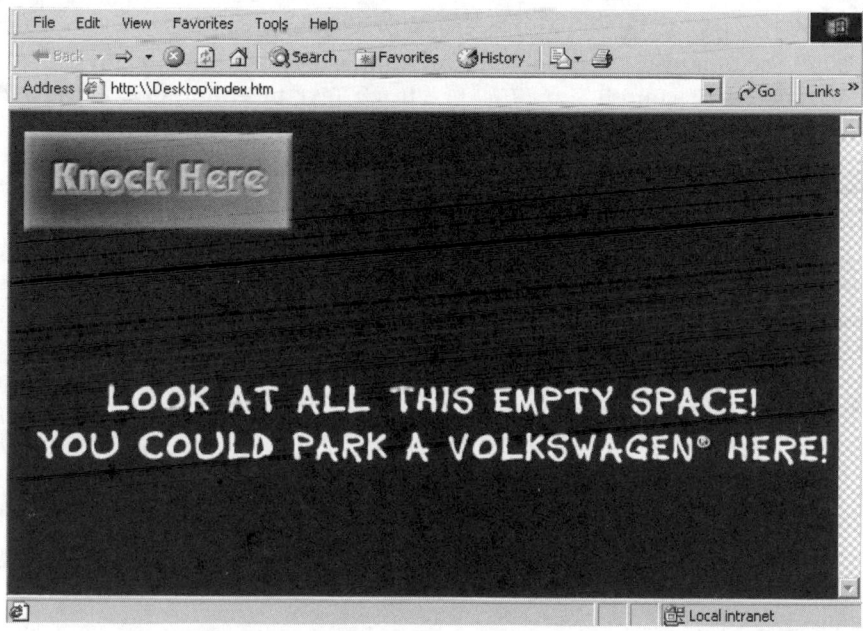

**Figure 25.16**   "Hey, I've got all the room in the world on this page, and the stinking rollover is stuck in a corner? What gives?!"

You did *nothing* wrong. ImageReady designs Web elements but doesn't know how to place them on a page as an HTML editor does (GoLive! is Adobe's current offering for an HTML editor). But you know something? HTML is only text, and we are going to show you how to mess with the HTML text (okay, call it "hacking" if you want—the authors prefer "messing") so that your button is centered on the page.

Come along!

## Messing with HTML Text

We know that HTML authoring shouldn't be part of a Photoshop book, but darn it!—we artists are into cosmetics and an upper-left corner rollover button onscreen looks as though the creator is inept, uneducated, and probably doesn't floss.

So just this once (yeah, right) we're going to break with convention and lead you through a tutorial that will center this and other buttons you put on Web pages. Get a text editor (not a word processor; word processors litter documents with hidden codes for indents, headings, and so on), and meet us right under this exercise header:

### Example 25.4   Typing HTML that Will Center Graphics

1. Find the index.htm file you just saved in ImageReady. Find a plain text editor such as Macintosh Simple Text or Teach Text, or Windows Notepad. Now, open the Index.htm file in the text editor. A lot of cryptic text is in this guy, huh?

2. Scroll down until you find the line

   ```
   <!-- ImageReady Slices (Welcome.psd) -->
   ```

   Directly above it, type the following:

   ```
   <Center>
   <P><CENTER> </CENTER></P>
   <P><CENTER> </CENTER></P>
   <P><CENTER> </CENTER></P>
   <P><CENTER> </CENTER></P>
   ```

   Now, we all make typing errors, so this important nugget of script you want to put into the index.htm file can be located in the Examples/Chap25 folder. It's called HackScript.txt. You can open the file in a plain text editor and cut and paste. In any event, the top of the document should look like the text in Figure 25.17.

3. Scroll down to the bottom of the document. Tags and attributes that are within greater and less than brackets (<like this>) have an opening and a closing; this is proper HTML—if you ignore it, bad things will happen. So, we've got an open <CENTER> attribute at the top of the page that needs closing. Type:

   ```
   </CENTER>
   ```

   at the line right after </MAP> and before

   ```
   <!--End ImageReady Slices-->
   ```

   as shown in Figure 25.18.

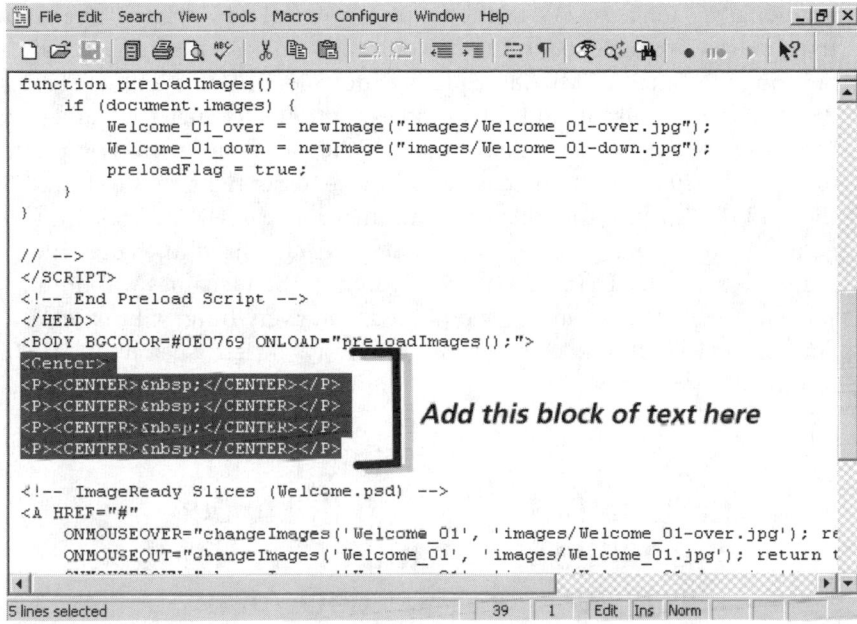

**Figure 25.17**   Add these five lines of text to the script to center the rollover.

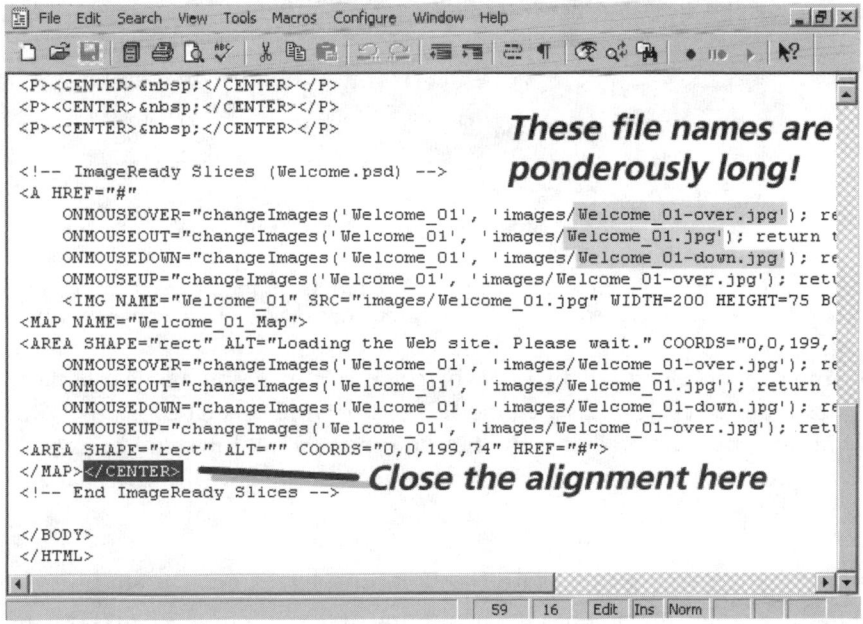

**Figure 25.18**   Close the work you opened at the top of the HTML file.

**4.** (Optional) As long as we're in the script, if you feel adventurous, the names that ImageReady assigned to the JPEG files that make up the rollover are a tad too long. Small HTML files equal fast download. Take a look at Figure 25.18. If you feel like it, and this is indeed optional, change the names of the files in the HTML document to match the names of the files on the right of Figure 25.19. ImageReady creates an Image folder right next to the HTML file, and that's where the rollover components are stored. Naturally, if you goof with the names in the HTML script, you are obliged to change the names as shown in Figure 25.19. If you do not, the filenames will not be the same in the HTML document you hacked, and everything will not work and you'll have wasted time. References must always be letter-perfect in HTML scripts.

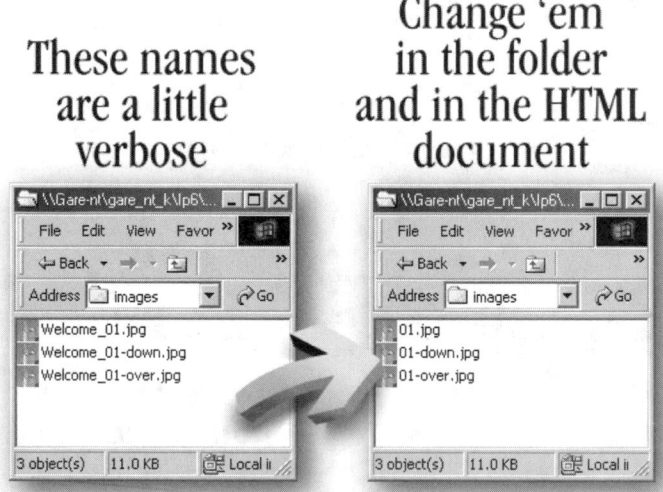

**Figure 25.19**    People who manually change HTML scripts without the benefit of an HTML editor are called experts, gurus, innovative, ingenious, and masochistic.

**5.** You're done. Don't tell anyone where you got the script changes, because it's not the best HTML style (and the author will get laughed at by HTML purists), but save and close the file, and then drop it into your browser. Surprise! That rollover button is in the center of the page now! What a relief!

We'll bet that between playing with HTML in Chapter 23, and the stuff we've covered in this chapter, it won't be long before you decide on one, perhaps both, of the following:

- You'll start getting creative as a post-production effort with many more of ImageReady's HTML exports.

- You are highly motivated to get an HTML editor so that you can move script snippets around as objects instead of facing the terror of real, live text<g>!

Well, we think we've dedicated the space necessary to document how ImageReady does rollovers. And we've saved the best for last in this book. GIF animations are next on the agenda, and they are so easy to create, we'll spend most of the rest of this chapter covering ideas and how to implement them. Looking at a screenplay is *always* more interesting than looking at a camera!

## Introducing ImageReady GIF Animations

A discovery that surprised everyone a few years ago was that the combination of Netscape Navigator 2.0 and a GIF file that contained multiple images would play an animation when loaded in the browser. Microsoft (which is no one's fool) quickly emulated the technology, and it wasn't long before GIF animation kits were being offered all over the Internet. After years of messing around on the Internet scene, the authors have come up with several principles. Here's the first one:

*The technology shouldn't be more sophisticated than your idea.*

One of the perks to owning ImageReady 3 as a sidekick to your Photoshop purchase is that Adobe makes it simple to create GIF animations. And at the same time, you have more control and options for the animated GIF than you probably will ever need. We'll point out all the features of ImageReady's Animation palette, but because much of the palette is self-explanatory, the primary emphasis will be on *concept*—the idea behind the animation. It's all too easy to use Adobe's wonderful technology to produce an uninspiring piece.

You'll create four different types of animations in this chapter, each with its own reason for being. To a certain extent, all animations on the Web, especially banners, have but one purpose—to catch your eye. But you need to follow through! Once you have the visitors' attention, what are you going to tell them? Now, that's the gateway to coming up with a concept.

As you're creating animations, remember this second principle:

*The animation should be short in time, small in dimensions, and contain a minimum of colors.*

There's nothing more depressing for the creator, and nothing quite as irritating for the viewer, as an animation that takes more than five seconds to load and animate. This is the Internet, and we're all surfing on Internet Time (where about one traditional year equals five Internet minutes). Speed is your friend because you're using immediate thrills to introduce visitors to your site. If you catch your audience by surprise (for example, by having a page that downloads in five seconds), they will come back because you're a good showman.

Our final principle for creating an animation is

> *The story line of a GIF animation has to be simple, and it should end where it begins.*

This is called looping, and you get more play out of your work when the animation repeats nonstop. By *simple*, I can think of three types of scenes that you can follow:

- **The camera or the object moves.** You are constrained to left, right, up, and down because you cannot rotate around a 2D object. (There are 3D animation packages, such as XARA 3D, that can animate in 3D.)

  An example of this type of scene is a logo that flies on and then off the screen, from left to right. We'll show you how to do an animated object in this chapter.

- **The object's outline changes shape.** You might morph one object into another (for example, changing a company's logo into the product the company makes), or the object might simply wiggle, changing the contour of its shape. In this chapter you will learn how to create a bouncing ball that changes shape as it hits the ground.

- **The object's texture changes.** A good example of this is what MTV used to do with their logo; the logo remained the same shape, but colors and textures changed within the logo. We have an example of texture-changing coming up that is eye-soothing (you're *supposed* to do this on the Web), and easy to create.

Surely, you can think right this minute of at least 50 examples of animations that fit into these categories. We'll start with the authors' examples, but they only exist to show you the features for animation in ImageReady, and what each option does.

## Using an Action and Your Own Art

The Actions palette in ImageReady more or less serves the same purpose as the one in Photoshop, except that ImageReady's presets can give you a leg up on animating stuff. There are Actions on the Actions palette that create zoom-ins and outs, and Actions that rotate your artwork.

In the steps to follow, you actually get your hands right on the controls. The authors will just sit in the back row here, and call out the instructions for creating an animation with the camera zoom supplied by a script provided on ImageReady's Actions palette, and any art you might care to use.

### Example 25.5   A Little Adobe and a Little of Your Own Inspiration

1.  Launch ImageReady. It would be a good idea to put ImageReady's icon on the desktop as a shortcut (alias) so that when you don't want to load Photoshop to get to ImageReady, you're all set.

2.  Open the Hi.psd image from the Examples/Chap25 folder of the Companion CD. An unnecessary layer was added to the background of this image because we wanted to check for anti-aliasing after the file was created. One of your first moves is to drag the Background title on the Layers palette (press F7, and you will be using the Layers palette that displays often in animations) into the Trash. Then, press F11 to display the Animation palette, (see Figure 25.20). You will also need the Optimize and Color Table palettes for animation, but these can be minimized by double-clicking on the title bar at the top of the palette, and then stowed in a corner of the workspace.

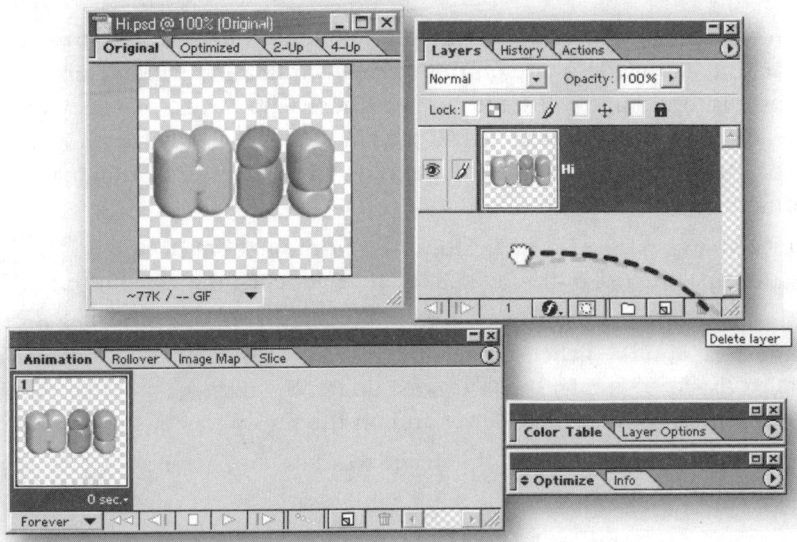

**Figure 25.20**   When you press F11, the keyboard shortcut to Window, Show Animation, the Animation palette displays.

3. Now, when you tell ImageReady to duplicate a frame, you are also duplicating the length of time the image is onscreen. By default, all new frames are created to display for zero seconds (we know, this is impossible—what Adobe means is that there is no delay in loading a frame). So the first thing you want to do is set a time of .1 seconds for the first frame. This is done by holding the cursor on the time area to the lower right of the thumbnail preview on the Animation palette to make a menu pop up, and then you choose .1 seconds (a good choice for the speed of the animation, considering that every class of machine on earth is plugged into the Web), as shown in Figure 25.21.

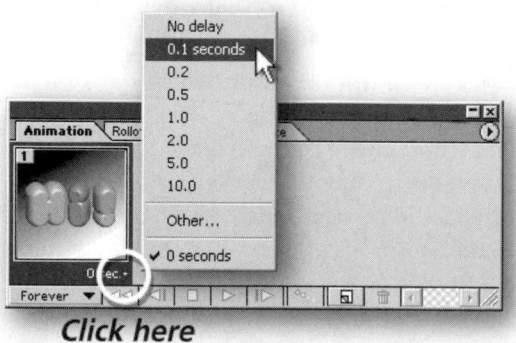

**Figure 25.21**    Set the time that the first frame will be onscreen to .1 seconds.

A tenth of a second might seem too fast when it's played back on your machine, but when it's up on the Web, the animation will probably please most visitors. Some will see it too fast (those who have a processor and RAM greater than yours) and some will see it a little too slowly (those who have a processor and RAM that's less than yours—like an Intel XT or a toaster or something).

4. Once you've set the time, click on the Spinning Zoom In title on the Actions palette (#1 in Figure 25.22), and then click the play button (#2).

5. On the Animation palette, scroll to the last frame (frame 12), click on the time area, and then choose 2 seconds, as shown in Figure 25.23. This is called *timing*. If you let the last frame linger, the message will make a more lasting impression on the viewer and on the phosphors of the monitor.

6. Click the Optimized tab on the image window, and extend the Color Table and Optimize palettes.

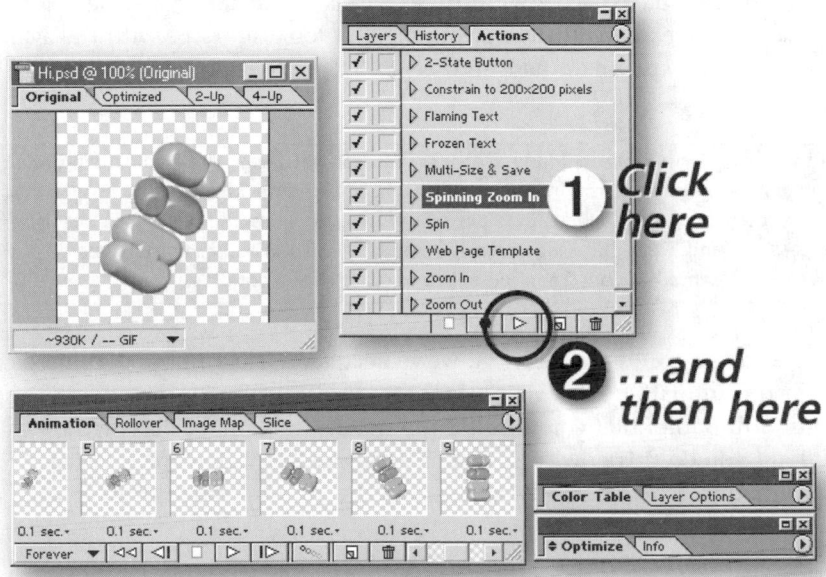

**Figure 25.22**   Set the length of each frame before you allow the Actions palette to automatically animate your image by copying and then editing the first frame.

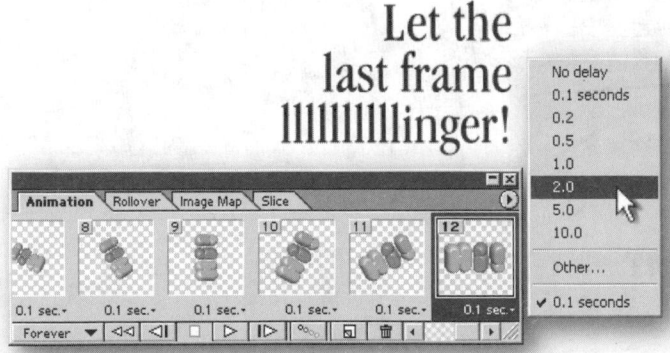

**Figure 25.23**   Once the object has ceased spinning, it would be nice to let the audience gaze at the message before the animation begins to repeat.

7. On the Optimize palette, choose GIF 32 Dithered. The next field is automatically set to GIF when you're creating an animation. The reason you want the Color Table extended is to see how different dithering types display a reduced set of colors that the original art had. Selective, Adaptive, Perceptual, and Web dithering types will change the color palette for this animation, and you want to see how closely you can get a color table that includes the most original image colors.

**8.** The authors have played with the scenarios for dithering and have found that Selective and Diffusion create the best-looking frame with the available colors. But experiment here and see if you can't outdo us.

> **Tip**
>
> **Animations Don't Need Many Colors**   You can get away with a minimum of colors in an animation because the frames are changing all the time. Unlike static images that are subject to scrutiny for indefinite periods of time, an animated GIF keeps changing its appearance. And if the dithering on each frame is a little excessive, who's going to notice it when the frame lasts onscreen for only a fraction of a second?

**9.** As you can see in Figure 25.24, we've decreased the number of unique colors for the animation to 25, lost a K or two for the animation by doing this, and the still frames that comprise the animation look pretty decent. So why don't you do this now? Also notice in Figure 25.24 that the saved size of the animation is a wonderfully small 15K. The gum on the bottom of your *shoe* is bigger than 15K!

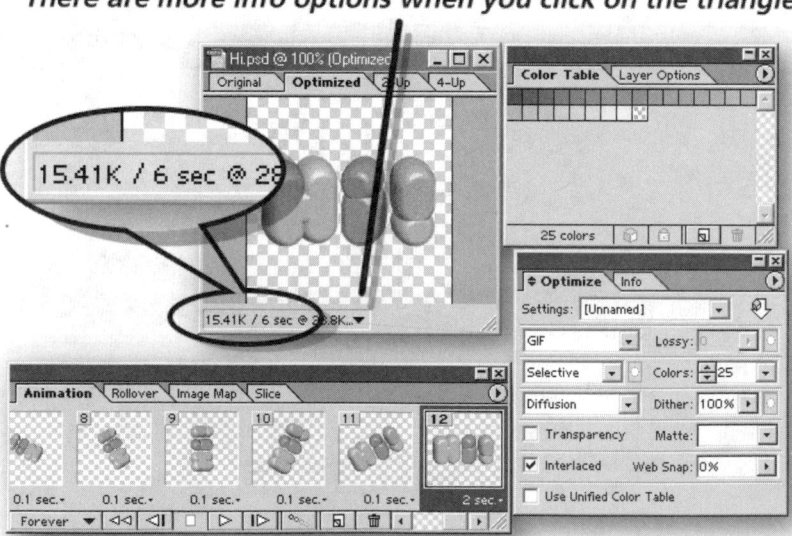

**Figure 25.24**   Experiment with a number of colors and type of diffusion, and then check out the saved file size of the animation.

**10.** You must choose a Matte color for the background of the animation because Client X is going to put the animation on a Web page, and there must not be a seam between the animation and the background color.

As you've seen in the preceding figures, the Transparency option on the Optimize palette is unchecked. The reason why is because with the Transparency box checked, the image will have to anti-alias against a background color the client has decided upon. It is much more goof-proof to create an animation whose background, edge to edge, matches the site's background color. Therefore, it would be a good idea, right now (if this were a paying assignment), to get on the Marconi and ask the guys who are designing the Web page what the background color is. Ask them to express it in both hexadecimal and in RGB color (in increments from 0 to 255, *not* in percentages). Pretend right now that you're talking to the guy designing the pages. He says, "Sir, the background color is CC33FF in hexadecimal." End of conversation.

**11.** Click the background color selection box on the toolbox. In the Color Picker, check the Only Web Colors option, and then type **CC33FF** in the # field, as shown in Figure 25.25. Press Tab to make the entry, and then click OK to exit the Color Picker.

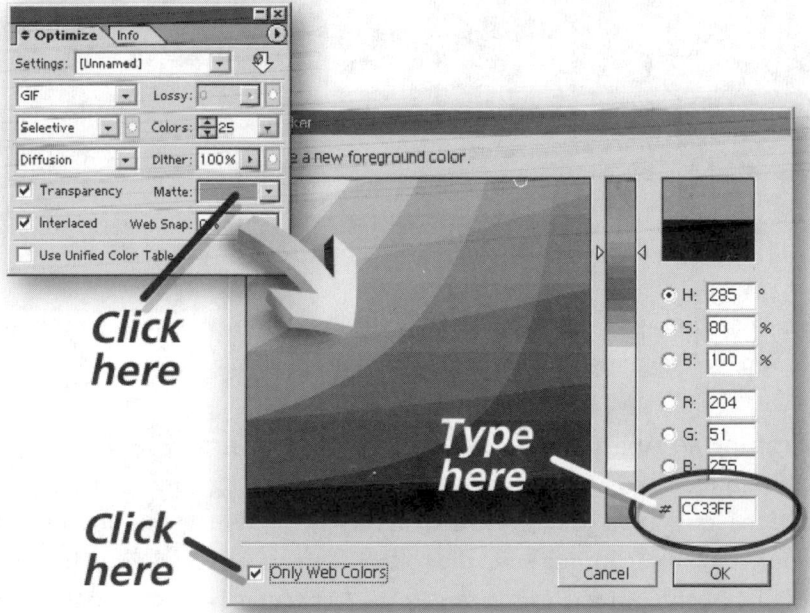

**Figure 25.25** Pick a color background against which the GIF animation can anti-alias.

**12.** Choose File, Save Optimized As, and then call the animation Hi.gif. You can preview the animation at any time by clicking the Animation palette's Play button. (You stop the animation with the Stop button—these buttons are just like VCR controls, except they never flash "12:00" after a power outage.)

**13.** Save the animation in the workspace as Hi.psd in Photoshop's native file format (your only option for layered images). You can close ImageReady to decrease the burden on system resources, and take a gander at your work on "the Big Screen"—Internet Explorer. You can drag and drop the GIF file from a folder onto the Explorer icon, or if you want to see this animation in context, look on the Companion CD in the Examples/Chap25 folder for a file called index.htm. Double-click it, and you'll see a whole composed page with the animation, as shown in Figure 25.26. Or you can twirl this book around to make this page look animated.

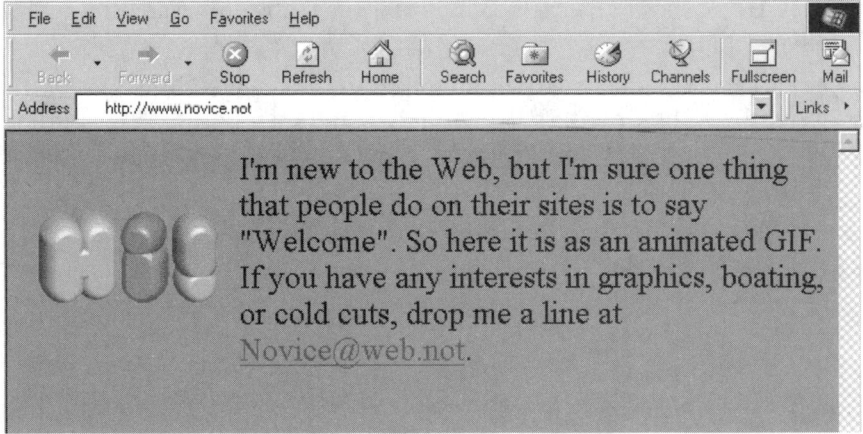

**Figure 25.26**    It adds a touch of class when your animation blends seamlessly with the background of the document.

In the next section, you will work without the animation assistance of the Actions palette. Yup, you're going to handcraft a short animation.

## Handcrafting an Animation: It's All Done with Layers

You'll find in the upcoming example that in animation by hand you use a combination of the Animation palette and the Layers palette. When you click on that tiny page icon on the Animation palette that creates a new frame, it does so by using the currently highlighted frame as the target, the last frame as the destination for the new frame, and it also copies all layers, intact, to the new frame position. What this means, in a nutshell, is that you have the same elements to play with at any given duplicate frame that you have with the original. Actually, nutshells aren't contingent upon anything here. You can add to the current frame—edit objects or create new layers—and all the work is reflected in a duplicate frame of your work.

The next assignment is, quite literally, *fun*. We've provided you with a PSD file on the Companion CD that has the word *fun* floating on a cartoonish background. Your assignment is to make the word bulge out at the visitor (the object's outline changes shape—example #2 in the list of animation possibilities earlier in the chapter), and eventually come full circle and assume its default shape. The only special-effects equipment you need is a single Filter, Distort, Pinch command. Here's how to get animating:

### Example 25.6   Animating by Hand

1. In ImageReady, open the Fun.psd file from the Examples/Chap25 folder on the Companion CD. Make sure you have the Layers palette out (press F7 if it's not).

2. On the Animation palette you will see one frame. Click on the time area and choose .1 seconds.

3. On the Layers palette, drag the Fun! title into the Create new layer icon, as shown in Figure 25.27. A new Layer, Fun! copy, appears; it is the current editing layer.

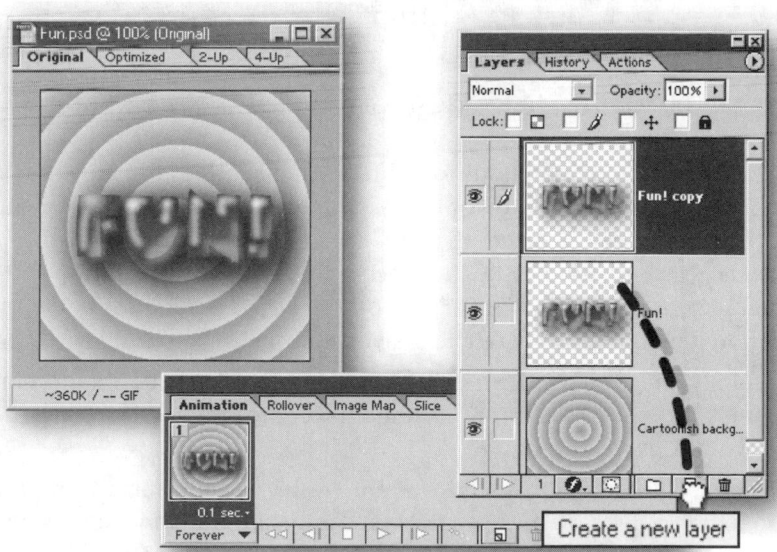

**Figure 25.27**   Double your fun by dragging the original layer title into the Create new layer icon.

4. On the Animation palette, click the Duplicates current frame button; you now have a frame 2 that contains all the layers in the original image, as you have specified.

**5.** Choose Filter, Distort, Pinch. Drag the slider to the left until it reads −38 or so. You're really punching, not pinching, the image, as you can see in Figure 25.28. Click OK to apply the change to the new layer.

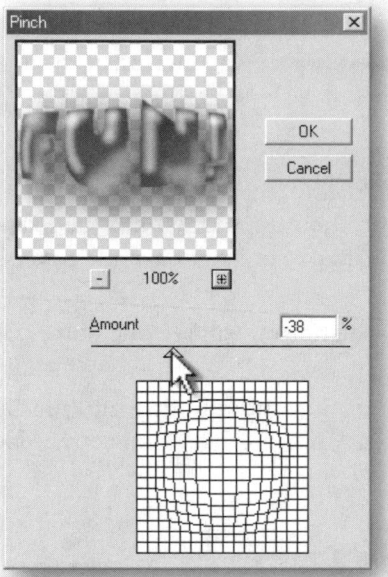

**Figure 25.28**    The Pinch filter can bow a selection either inward or outward.

**6.** Using the first, original, undistorted frame, repeat steps 3–5 so you have a Fun! copy 2 layer at the top of the stack, and then apply the Pinch filter, but at the amount of −55 rather than at −38, so the Fun! text looks really bloated. Now, methodically, click each frame on the Animation palette, and then hide or reveal the word "Fun!" on the Layers palette so that each animation frame holds only one text layer and the background layer.

Naturally, the order of the text is important; the last frame should have "Fun!" at its most bloated. You should have three frames at this point, as shown in Figure 12.29.

**7.** With frame 2 highlighted, click the Duplicates current frame icon on the Animation palette. Right now, frames 2 and 3 are the same, but we want frame 3 to be frame 4, so drag the new duplicate frame to the end of the palette.

The word inflates, and then deflates, as intimated in Figure 25.30.

**8.** Play your animation in ImageReady by clicking the play button on the Animation palette, and look at the image window. Fun, huh?

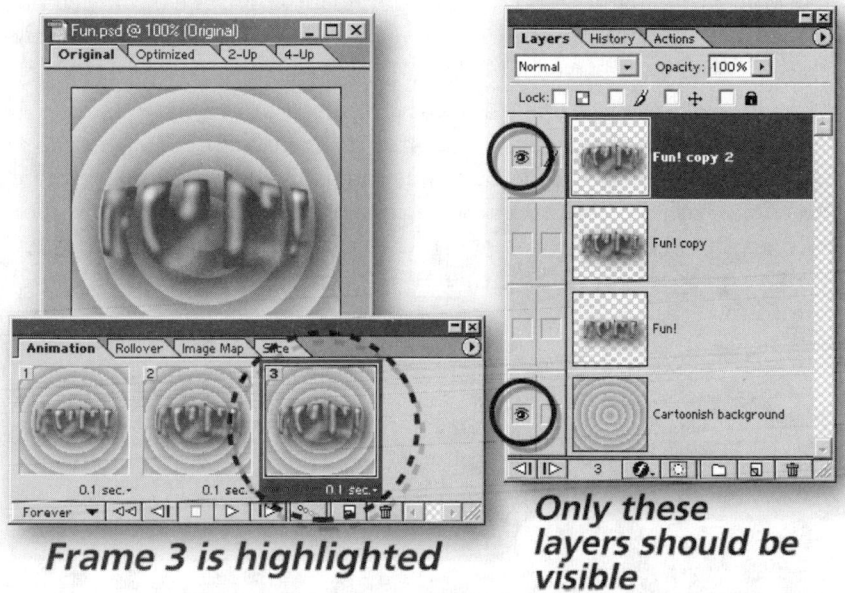

**Frame 3 is highlighted**

**Only these layers should be visible**

**Figure 25.29**   The layers that are visible at any given frame are the ones that will be written as part of the GIF animation.

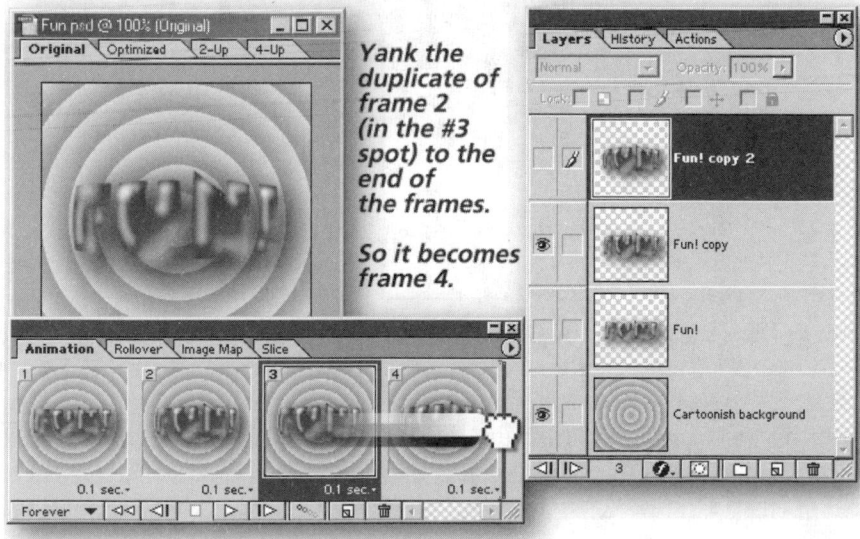

**Yank the duplicate of frame 2 (in the #3 spot) to the end of the frames.**

**So it becomes frame 4.**

**Figure 25.30**   Duplicate frame 2 and move it to frame position 4 so that in the animation, the Fun! lettering will appear to deflate to its original size back again at frame 1.

**9.** Use your own judgment as to how the animation must be optimized now. In Figure 25.31, you can see that Adaptive dithering, Pattern-type dithering, and 32 colors have been chosen.

The file is still a fairly large 39K, as you can see in the Document Sizes area, but there's a reason or two for this. First, there are lots of colors in the image—17 more than in the Hi! animation—there's a background where Hi! had none, and the dimensions of the image are huge as animations for the Web go. If you really want to post this Fun! sign on the Web, we suggest shrinking and sharpening the frames—60% of the original size will still bear some fun.

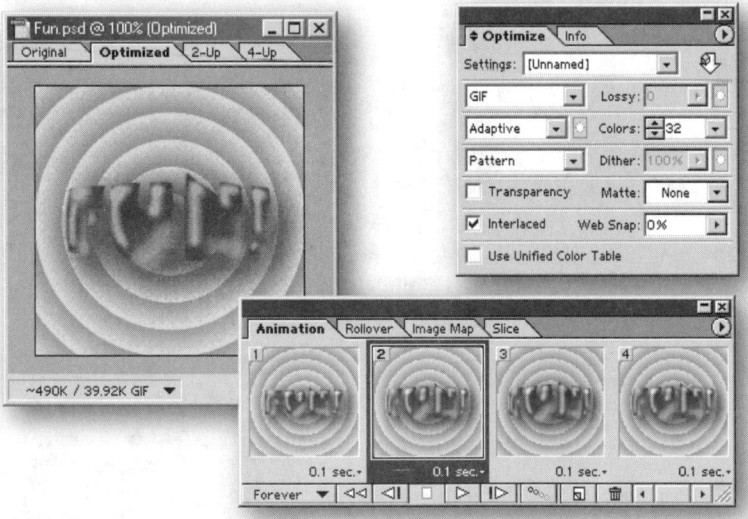

**Figure 25.31**    The file is a little large, but it's a lot of fun.

**10.** Choose File, Save Optimized As, and call the animation Fun.gif.

**11.** Save the animation in the workspace as Fun.psd, in Photoshop's native file format. You can close the file at any time now.

The finished animation is placed on an HTML page called Fun.htm, and it resides in the Gallery folder in the Chap25 folder on the Companion CD. Double-click the HTML filename, and see what was *added* to the page; it's a small animation, using The VALIS Group's Flo' and ImageReady. Actually, you can do the same thing using Photoshop's Liquify command (see Chapter 18).

We've covered all the options you need to make an animated GIF. But we'd like to leave you with an idea or two on which you can create a miasma (okay, not a miasma...a plethora) of variations.

## Blueprints for Future Animations

We're confident that your head is filling with ideas faster than the Boardwalk at high tide, but please allow us to kibitz for a moment. We've got two more animations you can try out, and they are *splendid,* for lack of a hipper phrase.

### The Bouncing Ball

This animation is only five frames, but you'll be surprised at how terrific it looks on a Web page at any size. Part of the reason it looks so, well...animated, is that one of the rules for animation set forth by Disney and carried on today by PIXAR's John Lasseter was observed. It's called *stretch and squish.* An object, specifically one that bounces up and down, must observe conservation of mass. So when the ball hits the ground, it not only flattens but also becomes wider. And when it bounces back up, to exaggerate the motion, you make the ball lean and tall. In the last frame, the ball pretty much resumes its first position and shape.

So two things are going on here: Change of placement in space, and change of shape. How can you lose? Notice the size of the shadow created for the ball in Figure 25.32, and simply design these frames in ImageReady, using the techniques you already know.

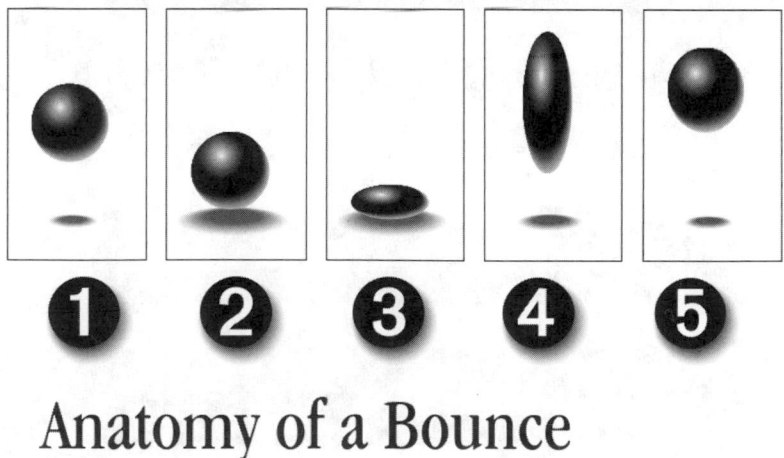

**Figure 25.32**   Here's the blueprint for a very jelly-like bouncing ball.

Check out the Bouncer.htm document in your browser. The file's in the Examples/Chap25/Gallery folder.

> **Note**
>
> **Use the Files on the CD for Animations**    As an extra bonus, you can open and use the PSD files in the Gallery folder to create animations in ImageReady. These are the files the author used to create the tutorials, and although I'd like you to build all these animations completely unassisted (okay, this book is, technically, "assistance"), I'm going to delete the files eventually. So it's better to loan than to throw out.

## The Subtle Elevator Effect

You can keep an image's shape and location stationary, and still add animation by changing the colors or textures inside the shape of the hero of the GIF animation. Although you can't see it too well, because the book's in black and white, an elevator effect is going on in Figure 25.33. A light green travels vertically down the lettering and is gradually replaced with black. Then the cycle starts again. If you want to see this in color, moving, check out Examples/Chap25/Gallery and load download.gif in your Web browser.

Here are the blueprints:

**Figure 25.33**    Follow these illustrations to make a four-frame color-shifting animation.

We've all seen all types of animated GIFs on the Web, and even seen deals such as "100,000 GIF animations for $12." But we feel it's much more personal to provide things you yourself have created for your Web site—and you wouldn't be reading this book if you didn't want to become a Content Creator.

## Summary

**Frame 1:** The author tells you about the three different types of animation, and how you can use ImageReady to create them.

**Frame 2:** You get your feet wet with a graphic the author provides, and an animation action from the Actions palette.

**Frame 3:** You slowly develop an interest in GIF animation, and you now create your own animation, using only the sketchiest of details from the author.

**Frame 4:** You realize that you don't need the author anymore. You create a two-hour GIF movie that's only 38K and makes Flash look sick. You head for Hollywood.

**Frame 5:** Fade to black; roll credits.

Hey, it's a little piece of the Web that's like Hollywood. Anything can happen.

Say, have you noticed that this book feels heavier on the left side than it does on the right? This is a sure indicator that you're almost finished reading it!

In Chapter 25½, we spend practically no time on Photoshop, no self-indulgent humor for once, and we spend all the time on *you*. That's right: You. What do *you* want from your future in computer graphics and Photoshop? Where do you go from here to learn more? What are the most important things for you to remember and take away from this book?

Oh, what a fortunate coincidence—the authors have already *been* down that mysterious and anxiety-provoking road, and in the next chapter, we give you—our most important student—the very best advice from our experience...

# Part V

# Closing Thoughts

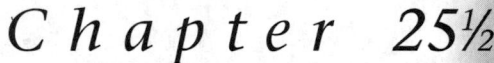

# Chapter 25½

## Here's Where the Path Divides

I'm not talking about using the subtract

operation or the Paths palette, or even

very much about Photoshop in this

chapter. We've been giving you directions and leading you on what we feel has been a directed path for several hundred pages now. And—oops!—it's the end of the book.

And now you wonder where you go from here, and you've got this impossible sign-post in front of you.

This book would be incomplete if we didn't go that extra pixel, or yard, or mile, and close with some help for artists, budding creative types, and people who have a love of art that Photoshop brings them closer to. It is here that I attempt to answer some larger questions than those that lie inside that beige box next to you. (It could be *any* color these days—the *teal* box, okay?)

Let's read that signpost and examine which of the many routes you'd like to explore long after you've closed the cover of this book. Remember that unlike normal people, you are a *creative soul*. You think outside the box, and you know that you can take more than one path—perhaps all of them are of interest to you...

## What's on the Companion CD?

The answer is, "Stuff that's so good you'll never want to lose or break it!" We really do put important files and applications on our Companion CD. So take care with it!

Aside from the Examples folders containing the tutorial files, the Boutons hand-crafted stock photography, we make available one-of-a-kind fonts in both Macintosh and Windows formats, seamless tiling textures, and clip art, and we scour the earth (that's why it's so clean) for demoware and shareware that really perks up a creative person's mood—and work. You will not find run-of-the-mill offerings on the CD, because our task is not to simply fill a CD. We're trying most of the time to fill your head! <g>

Check out the contents and we're certain you'll feel that our CD is a change of pace.

## Can I Make a Career Out of Photoshop?

Business models in America have been changing a lot ever since powerful personal computers hit the country. My spouse and I live in a suburban neighborhood that looks a little like *Leave It To Beaver* country, but in the year 2000, instead of folks dropping by to borrow a cup of sugar, they ask if we have a spare USB cable lying around. One neighbor even forwarded an email attachment to us and asked that we make him a high-resolution print of the sonogram that depicted his unborn grand-child. Take a step back—this is weird stuff, isn't it? I've found that a *lot* of our neigh-bors work at home, even when the company they work for has offices in town, and the only reason to do a face-to-face is for conferences and bonding with your supe-riors.

I'd say, "Yeah, go for it" if you have the skills and want to become a freelance Photoshoppist. The money is there, and chances are good that you can work right out of your home. Get a cable modem and an account with UPS, and think of a let-terhead for the invoice template you create in PageMaker!

How do you develop a reputation and get clients? Here are a few thoughts...

- Build a Web site that shows prospective clients what you can do. Use it as your online resumé. (*Hint:* Use what you've learned in the last part of the book on ImageReady as your jumping-off point.)

- Visit photofinishers (including the one-hour places) and offer your services as a freelance or part-time retoucher. Lots of folks ask their photofinisher to do restoration work.

- Visit commercial printers and offer to take their overflow design, layout, or prepress work.

- Enter design contests, submit your work for display in online galleries, share your Photoshop knowledge in online forums on i-us.com, on the Adobe forums, or on usenet. I was discovered by New Riders (and they'll never forget it) because I entered the CorelDRAW World Design Contest about a million years ago and my work was featured in a coffee table book that an editor saw. Contests are excellent discovery opportunities.

- Find clients on freelance and expert exchanges like ework.com or elance.com.

As I mentioned, business models are changing. There are companies called *learning companies* these days. They seek to learn from clients and employees, and they are open to change and willing to share knowledge with clients. Learning companies don't rest on convention. We have a power company in town here that sent about 50% of the work force home with their own laptops. Why? It was cheaper than the rent on 10 floors in a downtown building.

There are other companies that are inflexible, but you might still work for them as a contractor, and turn a decent buck.

Large advertising agencies can be opportunities in two different ways. First, the Information Technologist (the IT) is so overburdened with extending and maintaining a network, that s/he doesn't have the time to train employees in business and art applications. So, teaching these people after hours could be one career, but you could also get into an agency with what you know about Photoshop. Chances are good that you know more than the person who quit yesterday because work was too confusing.

I just rattled off a number of scenarios for gainful employment, all because you understand, and want to continue understanding, Photoshop better than the next guy or gal. There's more, for sure—whether you want to commute or work at home.

Can you make a career out of Photoshop?

Yes.

## Should I Quit Work and Go Study Computer Graphics?

This question has been put to me many, many times in email, and I'm putting the answer here due to the reality that the answer might have an impact on your career.

I know of several people who have been displaced by company downsizing. And many of them are happier and sometimes richer after taking some time to think, taking a night course or two, and going into business for themselves.

**Question:** Should I quit work?

**Answer:** Only if you hate your work enough.

**Question:** Should I go study computer graphics?

**Answer:** Absolutely not.

Art was here long before computer graphics and will be around a million years from now. Computer graphics are no different than any other type of graphics. For those of us old enough to remember, photography was not originally accepted as an art form. It wasn't until the 1950s that it carved a niche for itself as an expression of art. So if you're going to become a computer artist, you should study *art*. Taking a course in Illustrator, for example, will not make you a better artist. It will only make you more familiar with Illustrator. However, if you take a course in fashion design, basic design, watercolor, advertising design, or a host of other college courses, you will learn composition, balance, color, perspective, depth of field—essentially all the artistic components you can manipulate on paper, canvas, or in Photoshop's workspace.

You learn the rough stuff first, and then you work your way down to the fine details. It's true in art—you begin with a rough sketch that you embellish—and it's true in an education that'll better prepare you for computer graphics applications. Study art, and then you'll better understand *computer* art.

## Should I Learn Other Programs, in Addition to Photoshop?

Yes, even though I mentioned earlier that trying to learn too many applications can dilute your talent and keep you from really soaring with a single application. Photoshop is the great integrator of different media—photos, renderings of 3D models, text, special effects, drawings, you name it. But Photoshop all by itself cannot claim to be the best source for *originating* files that are expertly assembled in Photoshop.

For example, the cover of this book was created with the help of Photoshop, but a modeling program and a drawing program also were necessary to complete it. I could not have hand-painted the spheres to look as real if I'd painted them in Photoshop. And I needed paths from a vector program as the basis of the scene I modeled. When I had finished modeling, I brought the file into Photoshop, extracted the spheres to about eight different layers, and then filtered them.

My recommendation is to get familiar with a drawing program, an entry-level modeling program such as Adobe Dimensions, and a DTP program such as InDesign or PageMaker. Hey, that's only three more programs, in addition to Photoshop. If you wanted to play the "desert island" scenario, you could be a complete creative resource on the island with just these four programs. Of course, there are plug-ins and occasional *applets* (not quite applications) you might want, but if you focus on Photoshop as your artistic drafting table, and let other applications (and digitized photos) provide you with the raw artistic materials, you'll come out on top every time. Chapter 19 requires that you have a scanned image of pizza toppings, a piece of wood, and a 3D title (and the title doesn't even have to be 3D). So what's our creative laundry list here? Photoshop, a scanner, and Adobe Dimensions. Look at the color section of the book for the pizza article. The article looks fairly finished, doesn't it?

Rule of thumb: Use Photoshop for everything you can in a design, until you hit a brick wall. Then, think of what it will take, on the software side of things, to complete the design. Photoshop is highly compatible with applications you might already own, and I've said this in every book, so here it goes again:

> *There isn't an image on earth that wouldn't look a little better if you*
> *passed it through Photoshop.*

# What Stuff Didn't This Book Cover?

This book was a challenge to us because Photoshop 6 is about twice as big as version 5.5, and we had a limited number of pages in which to document the program. Something had to give! We cut back on tutorials to the extent that you'll work only with really *important* tutorials. But we also had to leave one or two things out of the book, and the decision as to what to keep and what to leave out was based on a feature's importance. Here's the list of features we left out...

### The Annotation Tool

The Annotation tool is a novel idea; you can write down and embed a message in PSD, PDF, and TIFF file formats. If you have sound on your machine (and a microphone), you can use the Annotation tool to record your voice and embed it in an image.

Although this appears to be a wonderful way to send instructions for a piece to your co-workers or a commercial press, let's think about this one for a moment. There are two downsides to the Annotation tool: First, by embedding media in your artwork you can make a TIFF or PSD file totally illegible to those who don't own Photoshop 6. Second...I don't know, but I guess I'm low-tech about some things. I've *paperclipped* a cover letter along with a proof of my artwork and sent it to commercial presses, and the people who work there didn't have any problem reading *my* "annotations."

The feature seems not nearly as important as other stuff we documented comprehensively in this book.

## The Slice Tools in Photoshop

I think it's a pretty fair prediction that Photoshop 7 or 8 will see the end of ImageReady. Already, many Photoshop 6 features, such as optimizing a GIF or JPEG export, and slicing an image, overlap ImageReady.

Although we did not cover the Slice tools in the Photoshop chapters, we did in the ImageReady chapters. The tools are the same in both programs.

## The Quick Edit Feature

Long live the Quick Edit feature! Adobe engineers kicked the Quick Edit feature out of Photoshop for a very legitimate reason: Quick Edit cannot handle layers, and it is now possible to create and save to the TIFF format with layers.

Um, *so what?*

Version 4 saw the end of Quick Edit, which is really a shame, because although Adobe engineers have done a magnificent job with memory handling, some designers still do not have enough RAM in their machines to handle big assignments. Many Windows and Macintosh machines are shipping with only 64MB of RAM, which is not enough to run Photoshop, let alone perform minor edits to a large file.

Let's say, for example, that a 10MB file is a large file. You need 50MB of RAM and hard drive space to work with it in Photoshop. You do not have 50MB to spare, and all you want to do is put your company name on a small part of the picture.

If, and only if, you own version 3 or 4 of Photoshop, you can take Quick Edit (it's called QuickEd.8BP in Windows) and put it in the Plug-Ins/Filters folder. And then—you know what? You will have the Quick Edit feature on the File/Import menu.

Figure 25½.1 shows how you mark an area you want to import (the chair, which is only 2MB), import the slice of the whole image, retouch it, and then use the File/Export/Quick Edit Save to seamlessly weld the edited area to the original image. Think of billboard designers and such who will benefit from this covert tidbit we share with you here! <g>

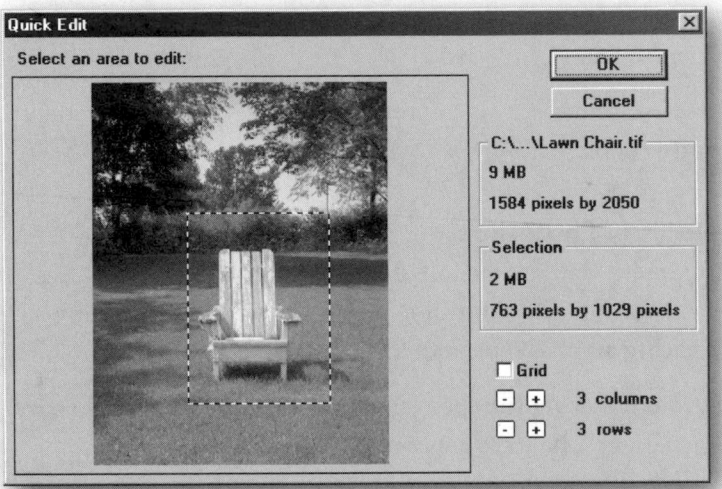

**Figure 25½.1**    Quick Edit doesn't ship with Photoshop 6, but if you own version 3 or 4 of Photoshop, you can successfully copy the plug-in to Photoshop 6's Filters folder...and it *will* work!

## Should I Read Other Books?

Sure, why not? Although the authors haven't read every competing book, and therefore cannot make specific recommendations—books belong to a publisher, but it would be naive to say that knowledge does, too—soak up as much good information as you can about your favorite application. Certainly, there will be other authors with different points of view, but the authors of *Inside Adobe Photoshop 6* provide the best recommendations we can, based on our personal experience. Clearly, one person's experience will not be the same as another's.

You might want to get your hands on some college texts (Addison-Wesley is a good resource) on computer graphics, light and color theory, and other topics that we touch on in this book. There's a world of information out there on digital images.

What do *you* think you would like to learn about in more detail?

# Where Do I Go From Here?

Ah, the bottom sign on the signpost, and also the hardest question for me to answer.

Almost unanimously, readers have expressed a desire for the direction from this point to be upward and onward. From almost eight years of mail—some physical, but mostly email today—I've concluded that there are several personal/intellectual qualities that can help to ensure success with computer graphics.

Please allow me to define *success*. It's *not* making the most money—it's being happy where you are in your career, and energetic enough to always want to pursue higher goals. And it's not about *achieving* the goals you set for yourself. As a folk saying goes, "It's not the destination, but the ride there that is the true experience." So plan to have fun, a rewarding ride, and when you get "there," wherever that might be in your creative pursuits, smell the air, take a break…refresh yourself.

I have had my nose stuck to my monitor for so long writing this book that I missed the summer! Now *that* is a shame.

Okay, the qualities:

- **Determination.** Almost all the successful creative people in the world have a healthy ego and do not let criticism cut their careers short. I'd say the formula for success is 90% determination and 10% talent.

- **Perspective.** If you sit at your workstation long enough, you will empty all your inspiration into pixel-based designs, and have nothing left to give. Get outdoors! At a party, engage in a discussion that has nothing to do with computers! Take up pottery!

  What I'm trying to say here is that an imbalance in your life is not only not healthy, but it also thwarts you from being a good designer. Take impressions from the outside world and distill them into personal creative expressions. There is not one piece of art I've done—that anyone likes—that does not have its roots in a feeling, an impression, an emotion, a slice of time and space in my past.

- **Humility.** "What are you, stupid?" I heard this line at a computer education center, coming from an instructor. It was a good learning center, I think, because the instructor was fired after class. What on earth was this guy trying to accomplish? Growing ego food on company time?

  I don't care what type of machine you use, or even whether you own Photoshop right now. If you look at nature, everything grows at its own speed. And you mustn't cop an attitude about where you are in life, at least not in front of other carbon-based life forms. Why not? Because besides looking like the hind-end of a horse to most people, the lack of humility is a blinding thing. It artificially puts you on the top of the mound, when in reality, you still have a long way to climb.

You will notice that the most successful people on earth are also the most generous ones, the most modest, and those who listen and don't offer advice unless they are asked.

I have a favorite saying, "Music travels twice as far when you let someone else blow your own trumpet."

My wish is that you are happy with what you do, that you have the personal drive to continue, prosper, and grow as a creative person. And I hope I'll see you again in the next book.

## Resources

http://www.elance.com
Visit this site for tons of listings for freelance, contract, and set-fee work.

http://www.ework.com
Post your resumé at this site, and while you're there take a look at their contract and freelance job listings.

http://www.i-us.com
Check out the graphic forums and freelance forums on i-us. Sometimes offering free help is the best way to find paying opportunities.

http://www.creativepro.com
Check out this site for graphic industry news, for databases containing information on advertising agencies, prepress services, products and supply directories, and graphics-oriented publications.

# *A p p e n d i x*

# The *Inside Adobe Photoshop 6* CD-ROM

So you're wondering what's on the CD-ROM and how to use it? Glad you asked! The short answer is, "Lots!"

The long answer is found in the following pages. Be sure to check out these three sections:

- Instructions on how to install Acrobat Reader 4
- Descriptions of the contents of the Companion CD-ROM
- What to do if you have problems with your Companion CD
- Information concerning special offers in the book

## Instructions for Installing Acrobat Reader 4

The Inside Adobe Photoshop 6 Companion CD contains a number of Adobe Acrobat PDF files. Of particular importance are the ClipArt2001.pdf and fonts2001.pdf file, which are your guides to the clip art and fonts in the Boutons folder, crammed onto the CD (okay, technically, Mr. Jay Payne stuffed the CD); and ipsgloss6.psd, the Online Glossary. Because PDF files are so important to the CD, we're beginning our discussion of the CD with an explanation of how to install the Reader program.

**Note**

**Not All Help Files Are Created Equal**   In the Boutons/Tilers folder are three image folders and three ReadMe folders, which correspond to each file by number. Inside the Read_Me_1, folder, for example, you'll find the index.htm file. Double-click this file to launch the HTML file in your browser. There, you will see all the Tilers seamless tiling textures in thumbnail format. It'll make it easier if you can pair up a texture you like with the file's name (which is in the HTML document).

If you already have Reader 4 or later installed on your machine, you can ignore this first section and move right on to the "What's on the CD?" section of this appendix! If you do not have Acrobat Reader 4 installed and you've chosen not to use the Companion CD's install program, it's really quite simple to install Acrobat Reader.

### For Macintosh Users

To install the PPC Macintosh version of Acrobat Reader, follow these steps:

1. Access the Software/AdobeReader4 Mac folder on the Companion CD, and then double-click the Reader Installer icon.

2. Click Continue on the splash screen, and then click Accept in the End User License Agreement screen.

You should be aware that you are accepting the terms and conditions of installing Reader 4.05. The "short version" of this agreement states that you can install and use the Reader utility on your machine (only Power Macintoshes can use the Reader; it's not designed and will not run on 68K machines). Additionally, you can share a copy of Reader 4.05 with friends, but you cannot distribute Reader 4.05 as part of a sales tool. You also cannot decompile the program or alter it in any way. These are pretty liberal terms by anyone's measurement, right?

3. When the Installer displays options for where you want the program installed, click Select Folder, select an installation folder (or choose to create a new one), and then click Select.

4. Click Install.

   If you have any applications running in the background, click Continue, and Acrobat will automatically close the application(s).

5. That's it. Restart your computer when prompted after installation is completed, and you now have a gateway to all the information on the Companion CD.

## For Windows Users

To install the Windows version of Acrobat Reader, follow these steps:

1. Double-click the ar405eng.exe file in the Software/AdobeReader4 Win folder on the Companion CD-ROM. Click Yes when prompted to continue the installation.

2. Click Next in the Welcome screen, and click Yes in the End User License Agreement screen.

   You should be aware that you are accepting the terms and conditions of installing Reader 4.05. The "short version" of this agreement states that you can install and use the Reader utility on your machine. Additionally, you can share a copy of Reader 4.05 with friends, but you cannot distribute Reader 4.05 as part of a sales tool. You also cannot decompile the program or alter it in any way. These are pretty liberal terms by anyone's measurement, right?

3. Click Browse in the following screen to specify a directory for Acrobat Reader, select a folder (or choose to create a new one), click OK, and then click Next.

4. After installation is complete, you'll see a screen that prompts you to read the ReadMe file that accompanies Reader. You can uncheck this option box, and click Finish.

5. Click OK in the dialog box that thanks you for choosing Adobe Acrobat. You do not have to restart your computer; you can check out the PDF files on the Companion CD right away.

# What's on the Companion CD?

We're really proud of the CD that accompanies this book. You won't believe all the goodies it contains!

## The Glossary Folder

In the root of the CD is the ipsgloss6.pdf file, an Acrobat document that is the book's Glossary. It's more than 300 pages in color, thoroughly indexed and with scores of cross-references. You need Acrobat Reader 3 or later to access this file.

## The Boutons Folder

In the Boutons folder, you'll find original clip art (over 70 pieces), The Clouds Catalog (volume 1), stupid videos the author created in animation programs, as well as one-of-a-kind typefaces in both TrueType and Adobe Type 1 formats. These are display and symbol fonts that can be used to spruce up a headline or add a simple piece of artwork to a layout in Photoshop, Illustrator, and any application that can read a typeface.

## The Examples Folder

The Examples folder has subfolders, marked Chap02, Chap20, and so on. (Please note that Chapters 1, 5, 7, and 25½ do not require files.) When you read the examples in the chapters, you'll be asked to access something such as BigFile.tif from the Examples\Chap20 folder. Locating the materials you need to work through this book is a snap. Double-click Examples, and then navigate to the folder listed in the text.

## The Software Folder

In this folder are several subfolders that contain working demos or totally functional programs that we feel work well with Photoshop. The following sections list the programs. We're pretty proud of our legwork.

### The Adobe Folder

As we've already told you, this folder contains the latest version of Adobe Acrobat Reader for Windows and the Macintosh. You will need Acrobat Reader to browse some important PDF files on the Companion CD.

### The AlienSkin Folder

In this folder, you'll find a collection of plug-ins by AlienSkin Software for Photoshop in both Macintosh and Windows versions: the wild Xenofex collection. The filters, such as Baked Earth and Constellation, are really fantastic. Check out these filters, and you'll undoubtedly want to purchase at least one set.

### The Andromeda Folder

Andromeda Software has allowed us to feature their Screens 3 and Cutline filters on the CD. You can only preview the effects, but if you check out the chapter on printing, you can see how powerful and crisp they can make any image...even an image of my Uncle Vernon.

### The Creoscitex Folder

There are two demo products in this folder, Powertone and Silvertone. Powertone is an Adobe Photoshop plug-in for Macintosh and Windows. This incredible plug-in generates dynamic and colorful images that can be printed with only two inks. Two-color printing will never be the same! Silvertone creates dynamic color separations that electrify the printed page with metallic ink. Print requirements for the fashion, cosmetics, automotive and soft drink industries will benefit from the incredible added value of Silvertone separations. Using Silvertone, users are able to print a car that has realistic metal hub-cabs, a windshield that reflects light, and shiny metallic red paint by using only one additional ink.

### The Play Folder

This folder contains the Macintosh and Windows versions of Amorphium, a modeling program that can generate GIF animation still frames. At *MacWorld* magazine's 15th annual Editors' Choice Awards, Play's Amorphium was honored with an Eddy award for the best 3D graphics software of 1999.

The program is a departure from working with 3D polygons in space. Instead, you moosh 3D solid objects around using the various tools and wind up with designs you couldn't do in any other program. It's truly like working with clay or putty onscreen. You instantly become talented with 3D graphics and animations, too! Amorphium is designed for all skill levels.

### The Xara Folder

This is a Windows-only drawing program. Wait a minute—to say it's only a drawing program is like saying the Statue of Liberty won't fit in a Size 7 dress. XaraX is a fully functional, 2-week time limited program that is highly compatible with Photoshop. It slips in and out between vectors and bitmaps with ease and precision. If you know CorelDRAW, you'll feel right at home with this state-of-the-art-drawing program. In fact, all the screen annotations and the color signature in this book were generated out of XaraX.

Happy hunting on the CD. We think you'll discover some real gems—especially the just-for-fun pineapples!

## What to Do If You Have Problems with the Companion CD

For more information about the use of this CD, please review the ReadMe.txt file in the root directory. This file includes important disclaimer information as well as information about installation, system requirements, troubleshooting, and technical support.

**Note**

**Technical Support Issues**   If you have any difficulties with this CD, you can access our tech support Web site at http://www.mcp.com/press/CSupport_form.cfm.

## Special Offers in the Back of the Book

Finally, the publisher and the authors are out to save you some bucks with firms we've known and trust as being outstanding in their respective fields. Graphic Masters can save you up to $250 on film recording work. And if you ever wanted a T-shirt with the Alien Skin alien on it, check out the fantastic deals on Alien Skin Xenofex and Eye Candy filters (you get the T-shirt when you pop for the product). In fact, many of our demo versions on the CD are accompanied with a discount ad in this book. How about that!

# *Index*

## S

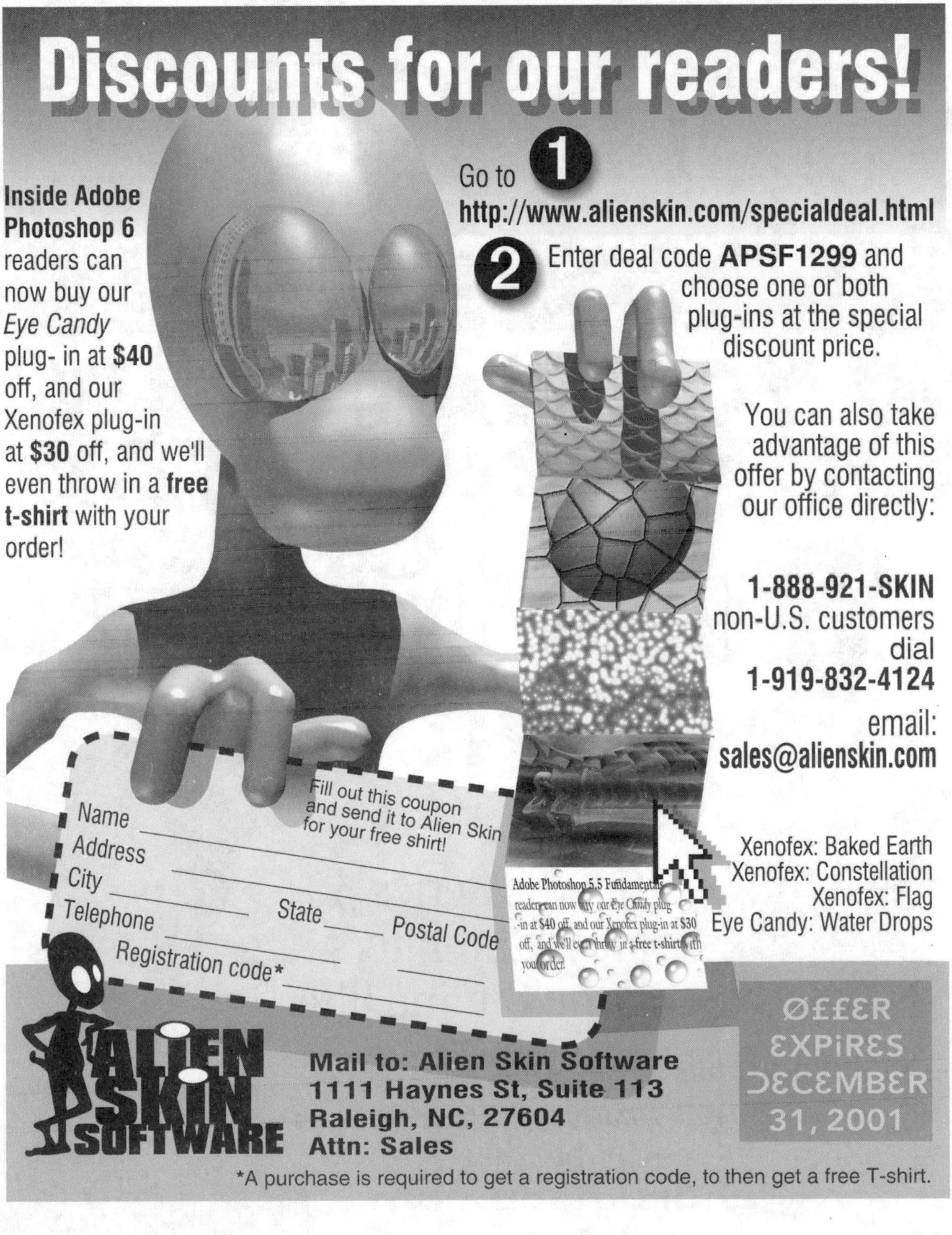

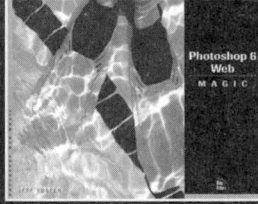

## The *Inside Adobe Photoshop 6* CD

The CD that accompanies this book contains valuable resources for anyone using Photoshop 6, not the least of which are the following:

- **Example files.** All the example files provided by the authors are here. The files help you with the step-by-step tutorials.
- **Bouton files.** The CD contains many fonts, texture maps, and other goodies created by the authors.
- **Photoshop 6-related third-party software.** This included several demos and plug-ins.

## Accessing the Example Files from the CD

To load the files from the CD, insert the disc into your CD-ROM drive. If Autoplay is enabled on your computer, the CD-ROM setup program starts automatically the first time you insert the disc. You should copy the files to your hard drive.

NOTE: This CD-ROM uses long and mixed-case filenames, requiring the use of a protected mode CD-ROM driver for computers using Windows.

**Technical Support Issues**

If you have any difficulties with the CD, you can access our tech support web site at http://www.mcp.com/press/CSupport_form.cfm.